THE MYSTICAL ELEMENT OF RELIGION

THE MYSTICAL ELEMENT OF RELIGION

As Studied in
Saint Catherine of Genoa
and Her Friends

FRIEDRICH VON HÜGEL

Introduction by
Michael Downey

A Herder & Herder Book
The Crossroad Publishing Company
New York

The Crossroad Publishing Company
370 Lexington Avenue, New York, N.Y. 10017

This is a reprint of the second edition originally published in 1923 in London by J. M. Dent & Sons and in New York by E. P. Dutton & Co.

Printed in the United States of America

Library of Congress Cataloging-in-Publication Data

Hügel, Friedrich, Freiherr von, 1852–1925.
The mystical element of religion : as studied in Saint Catherine of Genoa and her friends / Friedrich von Hügel ; introduction by Michael Downey.
p. cm.
Originally published: 2nd ed. London : J.M. Dent & Sons ; New York E.P. Dutton, 1923. With new introd.
"A Herder & Herder book."
Includes bibliographical references and index.
ISBN 0-8245-1790-3
1. Catherine, of Genoa, Saint, 1447–1510. 2. Religion—Philosophy. 3. Mysticism. I. Title.
BX4700.c36 H9 1999
248.2'2—dc21 99-33007
CIP

1 2 3 4 5 6 7 8 9 10 03 02 01 00 99

CONTENTS

CONTENTS OF THE FIRST VOLUME

Part I. Introduction

CONTENTS OF THE SECOND VOLUME

PART III. CRITICAL

INTRODUCTION TO THE 1999 EDITION

In 1997, the Crossroad Publishing Company launched a series entitled *Milestones in Catholic Theology*, with the aim of making available once again several significant theological works that had gone out of print. Volumes in that series include Karl Rahner's *The Trinity*, with an introduction by Catherine Mowry LaCugna, Romano Guardini's *The Spirit of the Liturgy*, with an introduction by Joanne M. Pierce, Johann Adam Möhler's *Symbolism*, with an introduction by Michael J. Himes, and Yves Congar's *I Believe in the Holy Spirit*. Also under its Herder & Herder imprint, Crossroad is now bringing back into print a number of important studies on mysticism and spirituality.

It is fitting that Friedrich von Hügel's *The Mystical Element of Religion as Studied in Saint Catherine of Genoa and Her Friends* should be the first volume to be published in the new series. The enduring value of *The Mystical Element of Religion* is attested to by the number of contemporary studies in mysticism and spirituality that draw upon von Hügel's seminal insights in this work. As but one example, von Hügel's understanding of the mystical element of religion plays a key role in Bernard McGinn's heuristic sketch of the nature of Christian mysticism in the general introduction to his multi-volume *The Presence of God: A History of Western Christian Mysticism*.[1]

The Mystical Element of Religion appears again at the turn of the third Christian millennium, a period that has seen the rise of a great interest in spirituality. Just what is meant by the overused word "spirituality" is not altogether clear in many instances. Certainly, interest in spirituality extends well beyond the contours of a specifically Catholic or Christian spirituality. Moreover, in common usage a sharp separation is drawn between spirituality and religion of any sort, Christian or other. All too often spirituality is juxtaposed to reli-

[1] See Bernard McGinn, *The Foundations of Mysticism* (New York: Crossroad, 1991), xvi; see also 65, 293–96.

gion, with an implicit judgment that spirituality and the sacred are essential, while religion, perhaps helpful to some, is unnecessary to living a deeply spiritual life. In such a view religion is incidental, and indeed may be an obstacle in walking a spiritual path. Today spirituality is often understood as a very individual, personal, indeed private matter, whereas religion entails participation in the life of a community, in its worship, adhering to its norms and values. Religion is often given short shrift, if not baldly denigrated.

At play in such a misconception of spirituality is a rather narrow understanding of religion according to which religion is virtually synonymous with "religious institution." One of the great achievements of Friedrich von Hügel, however, was the formulation of a cogent, compelling philosophy of religion in which religion is not equated with the religious institution. In the language of our own day, his was a more "holistic" approach in which the various elements of religion are held together in a noble tension. Indeed, he considered these elements to be mutually supportive. In this way, far from seeing the institutional dimension as the whole of religion itself, von Hügel showed that the ultimate purpose of a religious institution is to mediate, or communicate, the experience of the sacred, of God. Such mediation occurs, in part, through the religious body's sacred texts, communal worship, traditions, social arrangements of leadership, authority, governance. The religious institution is at the service of the various factors that come into play in the human quest for God, precisely because humans are social, communal beings.

Therefore, even though von Hügel developed his understanding of religion at the turn of the last century, when rigorous speculative inquiry was often suspect and when reasons for despairing of the "institutional" Catholic Church were not in short supply, his conception provides no support for those who would advocate simply leaving religious institutions and trying to "go it alone" in the spiritual life. In his view, there remains a need for texts, traditions, structures of community and authority which the religious institution safeguards and serves, albeit sometimes quite poorly. Again, von Hügel always strove to see religion in its entirety, as a complex phenomenon consisting of various elements that are distinctive and even in a certain tension with each other, but that cannot stand on their own.

Philosopher of religion, lay theologian, and biblical exegete, Baron Friedrich von Hügel was a married man and father of three daughters. Born in Florence (1852) of an Austrian father and a Scottish mother, Friedrich von Hügel, who suffered from a serious hearing impairment as a result of an early illness, was an autodidact and an independent scholar who lived most of his life in England, dying there in 1925. A contemporary of those who played key roles in the Modernist controversy, von Hügel was friend to several of them, most notably George Tyrrell. While sympathetic to many of the claims and convictions of those referred to as "the Modernists," von Hügel did not follow them when their convictions led them outside the Catholic Church. Though no doubt some found him a coward unwilling to accept the consequences of his intellectual convictions, far more of his contemporaries found in him a voice both balanced and moderate, all the while hospitable to a wide range of ideas and points of view. At the turn of this century, von Hügel is looked to with increasing frequency as an example of the creative but costly tension that lies at the heart of Catholic faith and practice in our time.

Friedrich von Hügel read and wrote widely. Though he is best known for his books, essays, and addresses on various religious, ecclesiological, and biblical topics, his writings also include a vast number of letters on a wide range of topics. Perhaps the most important of his letters are those in which he responded to requests to give spiritual counsel to people in different walks of life. These letters give every indication that von Hügel was not only a philosopher of religion, lay theologian, and biblical exegete, but also a deeply respected and trusted spiritual guide.

Of the many works in various genres that von Hügel left behind, the most important is *The Mystical Element of Religion as Studied in Catherine of Genoa and Her Friends*. After setting the framework of the three elements of religion and providing some background material, von Hügel introduces Caterina Fiesca Adorna. Born in Genoa in 1447, Catherine was a laywoman who left behind no writings. Von Hügel gleans the details of her life and spiritual doctrine from other sources. After several years in an unhappy marriage, Catherine underwent a profound conversion, an experience of the love of God that changed her life. For the rest of her years she was guided by the experience of the love of God. Her conversion also had an effect on her heretofore wayward husband. Together they moved into a small house near a hospital. There they devoted themselves to the care of the sick. Later they moved into two small rooms in the hospital itself. From 1490 to 1495 Catherine served as the matron of the hospital. Following the death of her husband, Catherine continued her care of the sick until 1496, when she was prevented from doing so by poor health. She died in 1510.

While the focus of this volume is a study of the life and legacy of Catherine of Genoa, its major achievement is von Hügel's understanding of the three elements of religion. Von Hügel understood the person to be intrinsically religious. The religious dimension in human existence inclines us to the sacred and binds us to it. Religion has various elements. Said another way, the religious dimension of the human person is expressed in various ways.

First, there is the institutional element. This is based on sense and memory and refers to that which is external, authoritative, historical, and institutional in religion. Through the institutional dimension our quest for the sacred, for God, is formalized, structured, made concrete, embodied, rendered visible. Here traditions, texts, persons, patterns of community, and authority embody our sense of the sacred, mediate it to us, and facilitate our communion with it. A common misunderstanding, in von Hügel's day as well as our own, is that the institutional element alone defines religion, so that religion is seen as synonymous with rules, regulations, laws, structures, and authority. For von Hügel, however, the institutional element, while indispensable, is only part of what defines religion.

The second element of religion, the intellectual, is based on the human capacity for reasoning, for argument and abstraction, and refers to the critical, speculative, and philosophical dimension of religion. Here the formulation of cogent systems of thought and the development of our capacity for critical reflection help clarify our understanding of God and communicate it to others. Such inquiry can also serve to critique and strengthen ourselves and our communities when the gift and presence of the sacred in our midst is betrayed. In von Hügel's day, this dimension of religion was sadly underdeveloped in the Catholic Church to which he belonged.

The third dimension is what von Hügel calls the mystical element of religion. Based on the exercise of will and action, this refers to the experiential, intuitive, emotional, and mystical element of religion, "where religion is rather felt than seen or reasoned about, is loved and lived rather than analyzed, is action and power, rather than either external fact or intellectual verification" (vol. I, p. 53). This is a way of speaking of the experience of the sacred, of God, or the experiential dimension of religion. While many in our day might be more prepared to ascribe this mystical element to spirituality than to religion, von Hügel showed that it properly belongs to religion—when religion is taken in the entirety of its dimensions.

For von Hügel all three elements have a place. There needs to be an interaction, a cross-pollination among the three. The institution must be attentive to the intellectual and mystical dimensions of the human quest for God. Nevertheless, it is also true for von Hügel that the quest for God must be related to a religious body in which texts, traditions, and communities mediate the presence of God. Further, the mystical quest must attend to the rigorous intellectual element as well. Indeed, while he saw the mystical element as the summit of religion, von Hügel insisted that all three are necessarily present at the same time, and that the key to the highest spiritual life is the attainment of the proper balance among the three.

From the perspective of the student of spirituality, *The Mystical Element of Religion* is truly, to use the words of Bernard McGinn, "one of the masterpieces of the modern study of mysticism."[2] This is so not only because of von Hügel's understanding of the three elements of religion, but for several other reasons as well. First, while today it has become widely recognized that studies of spirituality must be interdisciplinary, von Hügel's approach was well ahead of its time. Because Catherine of Genoa left no written corpus, von Hügel had to look to a wide range of other sources, and to draw upon a wide hermeneutical repertoire in an effort to understand and to articulate the spiritual legacy of his subject.

Second, the focus of the contemporary study of Christian spiritual-

[2] McGinn, *The Foundations of Mysticism*, 293.

ity is on Christian religious experience as such, on the experience of the Christian spiritual life as it is actually lived. As a discipline, the study of Christian spirituality is concerned with all that enters the Christian's experience of the spiritual life. Von Hügel does not turn first to written texts or documents in an effort to understand Catherine's religious experience, but looks instead to her *life*, to her actual practice of living the gospel. Moreover, it is from the experience of one woman, examined in historical context, that he articulates an understanding of mysticism and its crucial role in the mature religious personality.

Third, studies in Christian spirituality today recognize the need to look to those at the margins, to listen to the voices of those who have often been overlooked in earlier approaches to theology and spirituality. Von Hügel did not look to the mainstream for his subject of investigation. Rather, he looked to one of those people usually marginalized in prevailing understandings of Christian mysticism and the spiritual life: a lay, married woman whose way of life did not easily fit any of the inherited categories of Christian holiness.

Fourth, it is now more commonly recognized that all Christian spirituality is *ipso facto* trinitarian spirituality, that is, relational. Perhaps most important from the perspective of the student of Christian spirituality is that von Hügel does not examine the life of Catherine in isolation, as a discrete, individual text, as it were. His study is of Catherine of Genoa *and her friends*, indicative of von Hügel's recognition that all authentic Christian spirituality is trinitarian and thus includes that relational dimension. Christian religious experience, precisely as Christian, is a participation in the central Christian mystery of a communion of persons, divine and human, in loving, eternal relationship.

Friedrich von Hügel lived and wrote at a time of great upset, suspicion, and divisiveness in the Catholic Church. He was a lay Roman Catholic theologian of moderation and balance who saw the need for the three elements of religion, understood the nature of the relationship among them, and recognized the crucial importance of holding them together in a noble tension. In every age the mature, integrated religious personality seeks to do likewise. Von Hügel saw in Catherine Fiesca Adorna an ordinary woman of great holiness who managed to live such a life in circumstances quite different from his own. He made her spiritual doctrine available to his contemporaries. Through the publication of *The Mystical Element of Religion*, the first volume in the new series *Milestones in the Study of Mysticism and Spirituality*, the legacy of Catherine of Genoa, and of Friedrich von Hügel, is available once again to a new generation of scholars and students.

Michael Downey
Saint John's Seminary, Camarillo
Archdiocese of Los Angeles
Eastertide 1999

SELECT BIBLIOGRAPHY

The following bibliography chiefly includes books by Friedrich von Hügel. In addition, anthologies of his writings as well as a few books about his life and legacy are provided.

For more complete bibliographies see James J. Kelly, *Baron Friedrich von Hügel's Philosophy of Religion* (Leuven: University Press, 1983), 14–26, and Ellen M. Leonard, *Creative Tension: The Spiritual Legacy of Friedrich von Hügel* (Scranton, Pa.: University of Scranton Press, 1997), 209–23.

Friedrich von Hügel's Writings

Essays and Addresses on the Philosophy of Religion. London: Dent, 1921.

Essays and Addresses on the Philosophy of Religion. Second Series. Edited by Edmund Gardner. London: Dent, 1927.

Eternal Life: A Study of Its Implications and Applications. Edinburgh: T. & T. Clark, 1912.

The German Soul in Its Attitudes towards Ethics and Christianity. The State and War. London, Paris, Toronto: J. M. Dent & Sons, 1916.

Letters from Baron Friedrich von Hügel to a Niece. Edited with an introduction by Gwendolen Greene. London: Dent, 1928.

Letters of Baron Friedrich von Hügel and Professor Norman Kemp Smith. Edited by Lawrence F. Barmann. New York: Fordham University Press, 1981.

The Life of Prayer. London: Dent, 1927.

The Mystical Element of Religion as Studied in Saint Catherine of Genoa and Her Friends. 2 vols. London: Dent, 1908.

The Papal Commission and the Pentateuch. With Charles A. Briggs. London: Longmans, Green & Co., 1906.

The Reality of God and Religion and Agnosticism. Edited by Edmund Gardner. London: Dent, 1931.

Selected Letters, 1896–1924. Edited with a Memoir by Bernard Holland. London: Dent, 1927.

Some Letters of Baron von Hügel. Edited by F. R. Lillie. Chicago: Printed privately, 1925.

Anthologies of von Hügel's Writings

Baron von Hügel: Man of God. Compiled and introduced by P. Franklin Chambers. London: Collins, 1964; first published in 1945.

Readings from Friedrich von Hügel. Compiled and introduced by Algar Thorold. London: Dent, 1928.

Spiritual Counsels and Letters of Baron Friedrich von Hügel. Edited with an introduction by Douglas V. Steere. New York: Harper & Row, 1964.

Books about von Hügel

Barmann, Lawrence. *Baron Friedrich von Hügel and the Modernist Crisis in England.* Cambridge: University Press, 1972.

Bedoyère, Michael de la. *The Life of Baron von Hügel.* London: J. M. Dent & Sons, 1951.

Kelly, James J. *Baron von Hügel's Philosophy of Religion.* Leuven: University Press, 1983.

Leonard, Ellen M. *Creative Tension: The Spiritual Legacy of Friedrich von Hügel.* Scranton, Pa.: University of Scranton Press, 1997.

Nédoncelle, Maurice. *Baron Friedrich von Hügel: A Study of His Life and Thought.* London: Longmans, Green & Co., 1937.

Petre, Maude. *Von Hügel and Tyrrell: The Story of a Friendship.* London: Dent & Sons, 1937.

Whelan, Joseph P. *The Spirituality of Friedrich von Hügel.* London: Collins, 1971.

NOTE TO THE SECOND IMPRESSION

Four months have sufficed to require a Second Impression of this lengthy study of difficult and complex themes. And this evidently not because, but in spite of, certain peculiarities of style,—Germanisms strange on the part of the son of a pure Scotchwoman, resident in England for some thirty-six years and more.

I take this success to be due, predominantly, to the profound importance and abiding interest of the subject of the book, and to the general character of the method attempted here. May the very defects of the work help to bring home to the reader this inexhaustible richness of its subject-matter, and to indicate the pre-existence, the super-eminence, the independence of the august object of religion, as compared with those very aspirations and convictions which this object itself occasions and incites, and which our analyses so inadequately fathom. God, the Divine Spirit, is indeed before, within, and after all our truest dignity and deepest disquiet.

If some years hence a Second Edition is called for, I shall hope greatly to improve the book, largely by the aid of my various critics' strictures and requirements, which, so far, have, for the most part, been so kindly and so just.

F. v. H.
Kensington, W.
March 1909

"Grant unto men, O God, to perceive in little things the indications, common-seeming though they may be, of things both small and great."

St. Augustine, *Confessions*, Bk. XI, ch. xxiii, I.

PREFACE TO THE SECOND EDITION

THE following book has now been published fifteen years, and its vitality so far has greatly consoled the writer. It has apparently come to stay for some years yet; certainly there is still a considerable demand for it, although it has been out of print for six years. But such a lapse of time as are three lustres, especially in the life of a man no longer young, brings many a pang and desolation with it—many deaths, and changes even more distressing, amongst the men who so largely helped to give this book whatsoever of worth it may possess. Father Tyrrell has gone, who had been so generously helpful, especially as to the mystical states, as to Aquinas and as to the form of the whole book, for so many years, long before the storms beat upon him and his own vehemence overclouded, in part, the force and completeness of that born mystic. And above all, Abbé Huvelin has gone, the man whose name nowhere appears in this work, but who was for me then, and who is for me still, the greatest manifestation of the spirit of sheer holiness which I have been privileged to watch and to be moved by at close quarters, throughout these seventy years of life. Then amongst my German scholar friends, Heinrich Julius Holtzmann has gone, to whom I owe so much in New Testament, especially Pauline, questions, and who never ceased to do me kindnesses. And now I write under the immediate impression of the relatively early death (a death which, until ten days ago, never entered my head as possible so soon) of Professor Ernst Troeltsch, to whom, in the most fundamental questions of religious philosophy, this book owes very much.

Perhaps some further force, precision, interest and utility may be given to this work if I here attempt shortly to do three things. I will first adduce the chief objections to this or that content or peculiarity of the book—the various kinds of advice tendered for any republication of the work—and, in each case, I will add my admissions, distinctions or re-affirmations concerning the points in question. I will next give a list of the chief books, new in themselves or new to me, since Easter 1908, which, if I had rewritten the work, I would carefully have utilized for this edition. As good, or even better, books may exist; I only guarantee that the books thus put forward, each with a short but definite appraisement, have been found by myself to be directly instructive, or at least unintentionally suggestive. And I will end by the indication of the main changes in my own mind since I wrote my last preface, and an explanation concerning what has been attempted in this re-issue, and who are the kind friends who have seen it through.

It will, I think, suffice if I give only the substance of the several objections and recommendations, with the names of their principal spokesmen. I give them roughly in the order from the more general to the more particular.

Kindly and generous critics, such as Bishop Charles Gore, desired, not a re-issue of all the 850 pages of the whole work, but simply a separate publication of Chapter II—the thirty-two pages concerning the "Three Elements of Religion." But other judges, not less competent, wanted the republication of the entire work; and the fact that some readers cared more for this part and others for another part, and that no part was without those who specially desired its retention, decided me, if I did republish, to republish all. At bottom, the entire work is but one long, if largely only implicit, protest against the far more common booklet presentation of the Philosophy of Religion. Not as though the large majority of men, as truly dear to God as the minority I have in mind, would not require to the last, as we all require at the first, simple booklets on religion. I only mean that it is not of necessity a presumption to find oneself slowly, in later life, and with persistent surprise, solicited to write, and to do so, not for the readers of compilations, but for the writers of first-hand works. After all, there exist poets' poets, do there not? Why not then also writers' writers or thinkers' thinkers?

Then Dr. Gore wondered why I had chosen, as my example of the spiritual, and especially of the mystical life, a distinctly not central, not readily understandable, not immediately applicable life and character. Would not, *e. g.*, St. Teresa have been a more useful example for my purpose? Well, as a matter of fact, I did not first decide to write a useful book and then look about me for the most appropriate example. I happened first to learn to love, and to live in, the world of Caterinetta Fiesca Adorna, and was slowly brought, by such a love and life, to various questions made thus vivid for my own mind and practice. Only after many years did any thought of writing about her come to me, and only in the writing was I drawn on and on to formulate also these problems and to attempt to answer them. For my own mind, this is the only fruitful course. I should arrest the attraction of the subject which springs thus from a certain quite unforced affinity between itself and myself, were I to reverse the process and first settle upon a theme and then seek out the material best suited for its illustration. The nearer are our literary processes to the methods by which actual life, in its stress and poignancy, instructs us, the better I believe are the results of our scholarly endeavours. Besides, I was attracted at first, and I became more and more interested later on, in the saint of Genoa, not because of any immediately practicable suggestions furnished by her for my own life or that of others, but by certain rich and spiritual graces and deep and delicate doctrines hardly to be found elsewhere in as clear an articulation. Then, too, there was her outlook, almost no more quite Christian, because hardly still historical, which raised the whole great question as to the need and place of history and institutions in the spiritual life. And, finally, I here found rarely clear contrasts between genuine contemplative states and the more or less simply psycho-physical conditions which dogged them—conditions clearly perceived by the Saint, and by her alone, to be *maladif* and merely the price paid for the states which alone were of spiritual worth and significance. Nothing of all this, I felt, may be immediately necessary for the life of the average Christian, yet it can widen our outlook and deepen our awe, and can teach us certain central laws and facts of the spiritual life which will never grow stale for thoughtful minds. And, indeed, in variously lesser degrees and different ways, these same laws and facts operate within the minds and souls of men not specially remarkable, even though such minds are unable to analyze these lesser operations at work within themselves.

Bishop Gore added two general strictures which I am sure are entirely deserved: that the book was too largely made up of quotations or semi-quotations, and that the narrative portion was the least successful—that it lacked the charm and ease of the true story-teller's presentation. The latter point I so much felt myself from the first that I seriously thought of seeking, Dutch painter-like, a collaborator—this colleague to do the living figures and I to work out the general philosophical introduction and the later analysis together with the psychological and evidential questions. But such a fellow-worker was not forthcoming, and I now believe it to be, after all, a real advantage that the man who presents the examples and the man who introduces and who analyzes them should be the same person, since only thus a strict identity of standpoint is really possible. As to the excess of quotation, it has, alas, to remain here as it was; but I have striven my best to escape the defect in my later writings, I hope with some success.

Dr. Boyce Gibson, now Professor in far-away Melbourne University, kindly wrote me a very valuable letter after reading every word of the work. He very instructively described how he, sprung from and reared amongst the most severe of Protestant Puritans, had, nevertheless, not been jarred by one fact, one comment, up to the death of Ettore Vernazza—that he had spontaneously revered and keenly followed the grand heroisms of Caterinetta and her disciple Ettore; but that he had felt a sudden change and a distinct drop, from that orientation and those heights, when he came to Battista—that here indeed his Protestant prejudices were aroused, and the magic which environed that older group had somehow disappeared. "Would it not be well," he concluded, "in any later edition to stop the narrative with Ettore's death and to start the studies of the last Part with Caterinetta and Ettore only?" I wrote back that I myself had, all along, been strongly impressed by the same contrast, that I too felt a difference—I breathed quite easily only in the earlier air and with some difficulty in the later—that this coincided respectively with pre-Tridentine and post-Tridentine Catholicism and furnished one more illustration of how little true is the contention of most Protestants and not a few Catholics, that the Protestant Reformation had been a pure blessing, however disguised, at least to the Old Religion. But then, I was not out to write primarily a dramatic story which must finish with the end of its one harmonious interest, nor had I sought out only what helped me straight away. I had here been primarily busy with giving a reach of spiritual life, sufficiently long and sufficiently varied to include all the chief facts in the growth and the contraction of a saintly soul's influence and image across the generations up to the ultimate fixation of this image. It was not that glorious, buoyant, delightfully spontaneous life of those two older figures, when taken alone, which seemed to me to yield the full, many-sided instruction which I had sought and had found, in the first instance, for myself alone; but it was that earlier existence, that spiritual dawn and morning full of poetry and promise of the earlier generation, together with the afternoon and evening, more or less prosaic, of the later generation, mirrored in its relatively abstract, somewhat doctrinaire, and a little banalized presentation of those earlier figures, so recently alive, which I found to yield full instruction for myself and, as I hoped, for others. And, indeed, is there not a pathetic instruction in watching the insertion of the copper alloy into the pure gold?—a relative debasement which becomes necessary so soon as men require coin—that is, a metal sufficiently resistent to the clumsy handling of the multitude to be able to persist in the transmission of a value, and indeed a precise value, even though it be not the highest. There is surely a pathos here most thoroughly characteristic of the abiding limitations and homely needs of our poor humanity; and this later stage fits well into the frame of the book, since I intended the work to include everything up to the moment when the image of St. Catherine ceased to grow or to change.

Père Léonce de Grandmaison, the French Jesuit writer distinguished on precisely this class of subjects, in a long, most kind review of the book, gently bantered me for more or less assuming that the mystical sense, or anything at all really like it, was, if not universal, at least common amongst mankind—he evidently thought it a rare endowment, a very real exception, and not the rule at all. But Dr. Alfred Caldecott, Emeritus Professor and former Dean of King's College, London, in a charming paper, which I felt to be influenced by a very important truth, on "Some Unchartered Mystics" (*The Quest*, April 1920), asked leave to reverence the great mystics from afar, but to be actually helped and expanded by such gleams of intermittent mysticism as shine out from Carlyle and John Stuart Mill, from Charles Lamb and Oliver Wendell Holmes—gleams which are evidently apprehended by Dr. Caldecott as themselves in turn simply specimens of what is to be found, more or less, in human life at large. Thus Père de Grandmaison and Dr. Caldecott seem to contradict each other and yet to agree in contradicting me. For myself, I now feel that three points here require greater discrimination than can be found in the following work. Nothing could well be more true and important than Dr. Caldecott's protest against straining to find our help beyond where we succeed in finding help at all: I should have liked now to add a section in which I would have specially utilized Walter Bagehot's wonderful paper upon William Cowper (written out of the fullness of a most touchingly close personal knowledge) upon the danger, increasingly great in our more and more overwrought, nervously weak and psychically unstable times, of all straining and all strainedness. But such a wise moderation must, surely, never mean the unbroken relegation into the dim background of our lives of the great massive figures and an exclusive attention to the slighter ones, unless, indeed, Dante is to disappear before Tennyson, and Beethoven before Sir Arthur Sullivan. And then as to the cases cited by Dr. Caldecott, I do not doubt that Père de Grandmaison would answer with me, though much better than myself, that here we have not a mere difference of degree but a difference of kind; and that the mysticism he and I are out for is not simply a condition and experience (however dim, and however remotely caused by the actual presence of God within the world) of some kind of Reality not ourselves, but is an experience (more or less clear and vivid) of God as distinct, self-conscious, personal Spirit. And finally all this now raises in my mind not so much the question as to any awareness or experience which could properly be called mystical, and which we could nevertheless hold to be universally prevalent, but the question as to the implications of all our knowledge—of all such certainty as we possess, however little we may ourselves draw forth these implications into the full light of our own minds, and as to whether we do not all, as a matter of fact, act and think in ways fully explicable only as occasioned and determined, in some of their most striking features, by the actual influence of the actually present God. Uranus did not know itself to be deflected by Neptune; indeed even astronomers did not know, till some two generations ago, what produced this deflection; yet the deflection was real and Neptune was real, and the deflection was really produced by Neptune.

And, as the last criticism, Mr. Algar Thorold (to whom my cordial thanks for valuable services will be properly accorded presently) has submitted to me that readers could find their way about in the book more easily if all that concerns the Saint were to be finished up in the first volume, and if the second volume were exclusively to deal with the similar cases and questions as they are found to exist or to arise in the lives of other saints, or of ordinary mortals. I suspect now that this would indeed form a clearer ground-plan, yet I also feel that it would mean another book from that which I really intended to write. My method throughout was to take the several questions separately and completely, to start each one always with the Saint and her immediate circle, and then to widen out the ambit of the inquiry—to act somewhat like a stone which, when dropped into water, produces wider and wider circles to the last of its influence. The method may indeed be a wrong one, but it is part of the vitals of the book; and if there is really a better one, others will, in course of time, be able to succeed better by means of this their different method than I have succeeded with my own.

The new bibliography concerns the following places and points :—

Volume I, pp. 65–77. The Conflict between the Three Elements.

J. B. Pratt. *The Religious Consciousness*, 1921. A valuable book, especially the last five chapters.

Friedrich Heiler. *Das Gebet*, 1920. A rarely rich collection of facts considered through and through by a sensitively religious mind, although a fundamental contradiction runs through all as to the institutional element. This has now been somewhat mitigated in a supplement.

Dom Cuthbert Butler. *Western Mysticism*, 1922. Copious evidence as to three great mystical men-saints grouped under illuminating headings. Scholarly dating and appraisement of the sources; and an admirable sense of proportion and a balanced sanity throughout.

God and the Supernatural, 1920, contains a very thoughtful paper by E. I. Watkin on "The Church as the Mystical Body of Christ."

Evelyn Underhill. Interesting progress from *Mysticism*, 1911, full of breadth and charm, but lacking the institutional sense, after several excessively mystical works, to *The Life of the Spirit*, 1922, bravely insistent upon history and institutionalism, and furnishing a solidly valuable collection of papers.

Abbé Henri Brémond. *Histoire Littéraire du Sentiment Religieux en France*, especially Volumes I and II, 1916, and III, 1921. A truly great work, a storehouse of deeply significant materials presented and analyzed with all but unbroken mastery.

Volume II, pp. 90–101. The Areopagite.

New excellent translations of *The Divine Names* and *Mystical Theology*, by Holt, 1921.

Volume II, pp. 102–110. Jacopone da Todi.

Important new critical text by G. Ferri, Bari, 1915. And Evelyn Underhill, *Jacopone da Todi*, 1919, a careful and skilful utilization of all the extant, almost entirely internal, evidences for a study of the man and his spirit, and noble renderings of the finest *Lode* by Mrs. Theodore Beck.

Volume II, pp. 259–275. Morality and Mysticism, Philosophy and Religion.

Ernst Troeltsch. *Die Soziallehren der cristlichen Kirchen und Gruppen*, 1912. A work of astonishing range and sober novelty of penetration, which would yield much instruction here also, though for the most part only indirectly.

Volume II, pp. 275–290. Mysticism and Limits of Human Knowledge.

Oswald Külpe. *Die Realisierung*, Vol. I, 1912. The only part published by the author himself, a mind strangely little interested in religion, but which, in this relatively complete volume, admirably probes, and takes the clearest, most articulate stand against, all and every Monism. It develops a Critical Realism, tested in every possible way. I have been greatly braced by this eagerly virile yet thoroughly mature performance.

N. Kemp Smith. *Commentary on Kant's Critique of Pure Reason*, 1918. A masterly work, the first to extend Vaihinger's epoch-making analyses to the entire *Critique*, and which constitutes a new phase in the study in England of the facts and problems concerning knowledge as collected and probed by Kant. Kemp Smith draws out fully and clearly the rich constructive content of the relatively few and scattered parts which give us Kant's latest thinking in this *Critique*, a *Critique* now demonstrated to be a mosaic of documents markedly different from each other in doctrine and in abiding value.

W. E. Hocking. *The Meaning of God in Human Experience*, 1922. I have not yet mastered this work, but Part 4 I already find truly admirable.

Volume II, pp. 319–325. Relations between God and the Soul.

Clement J. C. Webb. *Problems in the Relations of God and Man*. Part 3 is especially valuable. And *God and Personality;* the first five lectures are particularly instructive. I only wish I did not, in other places of the latter book, come upon passages which I cannot understand except somewhat pantheistically.

Volume II, pp. 336–340. The Divine Immanence, Spiritual Personality.

Dr. A. S. Pringle Pattison's delightfully written *The Idea of God*, 1918, is excellent as against Agnosticism and indeed in its general programme, but unfortunately does not itself maintain throughout the "one-sided" Relation between God and Man so admirably pressed without a break by Professor A. E. Taylor in his noble "Theism" in Hasting's *Encyclopædia of Religion and Ethics*, 1921.

God and the Supernatural, 1920, contains a valuable paper on "The Idea of God," by the Rev. M. C. D'Arcy, S.J.

And finally, as to what I would change were I rewriting this book and as to how this new printing of it has been accomplished, the following is, I think, sufficiently full for the first point and complete as to the second.

I can only find one change in my mind—a change which is, I believe, no more than a full development into a quite conscious decision of what, in 1908, was already predominant but not yet persistently articulate and comfortably final. I have become increasingly clear as to how right was the man we now mourn, the late Professor Troeltsch, when, in reviewing so nobly tempered and often so beautiful a book as Dr. Edward Caird's *Evolution of Religion*, he pointed out how slender was the *religious* power and fruitfulness of all Hegelian interpretations of religion. This judgment of my friend dates from 1893 or so, when he was but twenty-eight years of age. I did not disagree, yet only some twenty years later did I myself come to see with final vividness and fullness how deep and how far that intuition leads him who accepts it as true. By now I perceive with entire clarity that, though religion cannot even be conceived as extant at all without a human subject humanly apprehending the Object of Religion, the reality of the Object (in itself the Subject of all subjects) and its presence independently of all our apprehension of it,—that its Givenness is the central characteristic of all religion worthy of the name. The Otherness, the Prevenience of God, the One-sided Relation between God and Man, these constitute the deepest measure and touchstone of all religion. And, if this be so, it follows that religion has no subtler, and yet also no deadlier, enemy in the region of the mind, than every and all Monism. The two Idealisms, the Real and Subjective, and indeed also Materialism, doubtless possess their element of truth for certain stages of inquiry or for certain ranges of abiding fact or permanent apprehension. But the central and final philosophic system and temper of mind which is alone genuinely appropriate to the subject-matter of religion is, I cannot doubt, some kind of Realism. And since much has been put forward with regard to these deepest matters since Descartes definitely started Modern Philosophy, and since these "modern" positions, so largely incomplete and so strangely full of Pantheism, have been re-tested with admirable sagacity and fruitfulness during even these last thirty years; the Realism we require will have to be, not a Naïve Realism (which would simply ignore all the mixture of truth and error since Descartes, and the criticism also of Kant's first *Critique* itself), but a Critical Realism constituted after, and in part through, the most careful sifting of these various Idealisms, Materialisms, even Scepticisms—theories which often bear along, in their muddy or perverse currents, fragments of truth demanding incorporation in a system truly congenial to them.

That early intimation of 1893 or '94 which I have noted as proceeding from Ernst Troeltsch was followed, up to his death, by a succession of most impressive studies and even great works from the same rich source, all full of the Autonomy of Religion—of religion as constituting a realm of facts and experiences which Philosophy indeed can and should study, which Philosophy can even help on to further fruitfulness by its clarification of them, but which do not derive their first or primary authority from it, any more than do the facts of plant and animal life, or the realities of the heavenly bodies and their movements, derive their claim to acceptance from Botany, Zoology or Astronomy.

Now the many-sided, ever-deepening apprehension of these great truths has more and more attached me to that current of Realism which finds its first and still largely unsurpassed exponent in Plato; and, in modern times, is represented by Thomas Reid, and then by those late and more or less intermittent, astonishingly vivid insights of Kant. This same Realism has, in recent years, been largely represented by Lotze, but especially now by the late Dr. Cook Wilson and Mr. Prichard, his disciple, and by Professor N. Kemp Smith, in the British Isles; by the noble Kant scholar, Dr. E. Adickes, by Oswald Külpe and others in Germany; and by Dr. Hocking and others in America. Of course, much more remains to do in this direction, and equally of course this school does not exhaust all the elements of truth to be attained. It will reach its zenith, and will thereupon grow hard and incapable of further acquisitions, and will finally, for a time, be supplanted by one or other of its rivals.

I purposely passed over in this list any Patristic or Mediæval thinkers, although St. Augustine and Aquinas especially are great also as thinkers and, as such, are very dear to me. I have done so simply because, though often admirable as thinkers, they are still greater as witnesses, not to how to analyze and theorize religion, but to the reality, the force, the necessity of religion itself and how to live it.

All this means that, much as I admire especially Thomas Hill Green, indeed also Richard Nettleship and Edward Caird among the English Hegelians; and again, much as I have learnt from Hegel's own *Phaenomenology of the Spirit* and from his *Philosophy of Law*, I find less and less of full and final adequacy in their treatment of religion. And, in some ways at the opposite pole, I do not succeed in deriving genuine satisfaction from Henri Bergson and his school. Though Bergson is indeed a perfect model as a writer and full of the best intentions as a man, I do not find that, as a thinker, he ever really gets beyond Naturalism and Monism. He never attains to a ground sufficiently broad and deep for that spiritualism which he so sincerely desires.

I am thus driven to find my main home in a tradition which, at present, possesses no writer comparable to the charm of those English Hegelians, or to the brilliancy of this Frenchman. But in spite of their relative clumsiness I find markedly more room for, and adequate apprehension of, religion in the British, German and American Realists described. And indeed I find amongst recent writers the deepest and most many-sided philosophical apprehension of what religion really is in Dr. Troeltsch's writings—writings largely lacking in all literary charm and not a moment to be compared, in this respect, with the two more or less immanentist groups I have referred to.

But all this I hope fully to consider in the new work on which I am engaged with so much delight.

My debt to France, as already indicated, is beyond all repaying in the matter of religion, that deepest of all experiences of the deepest of all facts. And then (like all of us but more than most of us) I owe abiding gratitude to France in all matters of historical method and of order, lucidity and style; would that I knew how to profit better than I have done in these last three important points! And in Philosophy itself I still look with deep admiration to the ethical and spiritual *flair* in the works of Professor Maurice Blondel, whom it is a high honour to claim as friend, and in such a gem as is the *Théorie de l'Éducation* of our common friend, the Abbé L. Laberthonnière.

In Italy I derived much help from Professor Bernardino Varisco; but not all the delicate scent for history of Benedetto Croce, nor the ethical strenuousness and formal lucidity of Professor Giovanni Gentile can hide from me the strange non-religiousness of Croce, nor the Monism of Gentile, who thus renders himself incapable of finding any logical place for so much that is true and genuinely eloquent in his writings.

This re-issue of the work of 1908 is a careful reprint of the text of that year, with the exception of the misprints (here, we trust, reduced to a minimum) and of some six passages which have been slightly modified in their form. There is also an important correction of a translation of mine from *Jacopone da Todi* in Volume II, page 103, line 2, which I owe to Mrs. Stuart Moore (Evelyn Underhill), who pointed out to me the reading *medecaroso* for *mendecaroso*, a reading now most firmly established by Dr. Ferri and approved by him also in her own book, *Jacopone da Todi*. All the quotations from the Bible and from Aquinas have been carefully verified.

It is to Mr. Algar Thorold, who has himself written with distinction upon an Italian mystical Saint, that I owe the final establishment of the Text of this new edition, and I hereby thank him warmly for all his careful and minute labour. He has been helped in the toil of the proofs by Mr. James Waglyn, of Stratton-on-the-Fosse, an expert in such matters, and by the same kind and skilful friend who did me the same tedious service for the first publication of this book. I alone am responsible for the revision of the Appendix.

I should have liked my new big book to be ready by now, so as at last to have something new and large to dedicate to the Senates of the Universities of St. Andrews and of Oxford which, respectively in 1913 and 1921, encouraged my labours by the honorary degrees they then conferred upon me. They very certainly did so in recognition of such care, toil and sympathy as may be traceable in the present work. Hence I want, in this place, at least simply to thank, with all due respect, these two very ancient and most distinguished bodies for thus aiding my attempts to do better in these greatest of subject-matters, which perennially attract, humble and satisfy, and then re-enkindle the mind of him who gives himself wholly to them.

FRIEDRICH VON HÜGEL.

Kensington,
Ash Wednesday, 1923.

PREFACE TO THE FIRST EDITION

THE following work embodies well-nigh all that the writer has been able to learn and to test, in the matter of religion, during now some thirty years of adult life; and even the actual composition of the book has occupied a large part of his time, for seven years and more.

The precise object of the book naturally grew in range, depth and clearness, under the stress of the labour of its production. This object will perhaps be best explained by means of a short description of the undertaking's origin and successive stages.

Born as I was in Italy, certain early impressions have never left me; a vivid consciousness has been with me, almost from the first, of the massively virile personalities, the spacious, trustful times of the early, as yet truly Christian, Renaissance there, from Dante on to the Florentine Platonists. And when, on growing up, I acquired strong and definite religious convictions, it was that ampler pre-Protestant, as yet neither Protestant nor anti-Protestant, but deeply positive and Catholic, world, with its already characteristically modern outlook and its hopeful and spontaneous application of religion to the pressing problems of life and thought, which helped to strengthen and sustain me, when depressed and hemmed in by the types of devotion prevalent since then in Western Christendom. For those early modern times presented me with men of the same general instincts and outlook as my own, but environed by the priceless boon and starting-point of a still undivided Western Christendom; Protestantism, as such, continued to be felt as ever more or less unjust and sectarian; and the specifically post-Tridentine type of Catholicism, with its regimental Seminarism, its predominantly controversial spirit, its suspiciousness and timidity, persisted, however inevitable some of it may be, in its failure to win my love. Hence I had to continue the seeking and the finding elsewhere, yet ever well within the great

Roman Church, things more intrinsically lovable. The wish some day to portray one of those large-souled pre-Protestant, post-Mediaeval Catholics, was thus early and has been long at work within me.

And then came John Henry Newman's influence with his *Dream of Gerontius*, and a deep attraction to St. Catherine of Genoa's doctrine of the soul's self-chosen, intrinsic purification; and much lingering about the scenes of Caterinetta's life and labours, during more than twenty stays in her terraced city that looks away so proudly to the sea. Such a delicately psychological, soaring, yet sober-minded Eschatology, with its striking penetration and unfolding of the soul's central life and alternatives as they are already here and now, seemed to demand an ampler study than it had yet received, and to require a vivid presentation of the noble, strikingly original personality from whom it sprang.

And later still came the discovery of the apparently hopeless complication of the records of Catherine's life and doctrine, and how these had never been seriously analyzed by any trained scholar, since their constitution into a book in 1552. Much critical work at Classical and Scriptural texts and documentary problems had, by now, whetted my appetite to try whether I could not at last bring stately order out of this bewildering chaos, by perhaps discovering the authors, dates and intentions of the various texts and glosses thus dovetailed and pieced together into a very Joseph's coat of many colours, and by showing the successive stages of this, most original and difficult, Saint's life and legend. All this labour would, in any case, help to train my own mind; and it would, if even moderately successful, offer one more detailed example of the laws that govern such growths, and of the critical method necessary for the tracing out of their operation.

But the strongest motive revealed itself, in its full force, later than all those other motives, and ended by permeating them all. The wish arose to utilize, as fully as possible, this long, close contact with a soul of most rare spiritual depth,—a soul that presents, with an extraordinary, provocative vividness, the greatness, helps, problems and dangers of the mystical spirit. I now wanted to try and get down to the driving forces of this kind of religion, and to discover in what way such a keen sense of, and absorption in, the Infinite can still find room for the Historical and Institutional elements of Religion, and, at the same time, for that noble concentration upon not directly religious contingent facts and happenings, and upon laws of causation or of growth, which constitutes the scientific temper of mind and its specific, irreplaceable duties and virtues. Thus, having begun to write a biography of St. Catherine, with some philosophical elucidations, I have finished by writing an essay on the philosophy of Mysticism, illustrated by the life of Caterinetta Fiesca Adorna and her friends.

The book's chief peculiarities seem to spring inevitably from its fundamental standpoint: hence their frank enumeration may help towards the more ready comprehension of the work.

The book has, throughout, a treble interest and spirit; historico-critical, philosophical, religious. The historico-critical constituent may attract critical specialists; but will such specialists care for the philosophy? The philosopher may be attracted by the psychological and speculative sections; but will the historical analysis interest him at all? And the soul that is seeking spiritual food and stimulation, will it not readily be wearied by the apparent pettiness of all that criticism, and by the seemingly cold aloofness of all that speculation?—And yet it is the most certain of facts that the human soul is so made as to be unable to part, completely and finally, with any one of these three great interests. Hence, I may surely hope that this trinity of levels of truth and of life, which has so much helped on the growth of my own mind and the constitution of my own character, may, in however different a manner and degree, be found to help others also. This alternation and interstimulation between those three forces and interests within the same soul, and within this soul's ever-deepening life, is, in any case, too fundamental a feature of this whole outlook for any attempt at its elimination here.

Then there is a look of repetition and of illogical anticipation about the very structure of the book. For the philosophical First Part says, in general, what the biographical Second Part says in detail; this detail is, in reality, based upon the critical conclusions arrived at in the Appendix, which follows the precise descriptions of the biography; and then the Third, once more a philosophical, Part returns, now fortified by the intervening close occupation with concrete contingent matters, to the renewed consideration, and deeper penetration and enforcement, of the general positions with which the whole work began.—Yet is not this circular method simply a frank application, to the problems in hand, of the process actually lived through by us all in real life, wherever such life is truly fruitful? For, in real life, we ever start with certain general intellectual-emotive schemes and critical principles, as so many draw-nets and receptacles for the capture and sorting out of reality and of our experience of it. We next are brought, by choice or by necessity, into close contact with a certain limited number of concrete facts and experiences. And we then use these facts and experiences to fill in, to confirm or to modify that, more or less tentative and predominantly inherited, indeed ever largely conventional, scheme with which we began our quest. In all these cases of actual life, this apparently long and roundabout, indeed back-before, process is, in reality, the short, because the only fully sincere and humble, specifically human way in which to proceed. The order so often followed in "learned" and "scientific" books is, in spite of its appearance of greater logic and conciseness, far longer; for the road thus covered has to be travelled all over again, according to the circular method just described, if we would gain, not wind and shadow, but substance and spiritual food.

Then again, there is everywhere a strong insistence upon History as a Science, yet as a Science possessing throughout a method, type and aim quite special to itself and deeply different from those of Physical Science; and an even greater stress upon the important, indeed irreplaceable function of both these kinds of Science, or their equivalents, in the fullest spiritual life. Here the insistence upon History, as a Science, is still unusual in England; and the stress upon the spiritually purifying power of these Sciences will still appear somewhat fantastic everywhere.—Yet that conception of two branches of ordered human apprehension, research and knowledge, each (in its delicate and clear contrastedness of method, test, end and result) legitimate and inevitable, so that either of them is ruined if forced into the categories of the other, has most certainly come to stay. And the attempt to discover the precise function and meaning of these several mental activities and of their ethical pre-requisites, within the full and spiritual life of the soul, and in view of this life's consolidation and growth, will, I believe, turn out to be of genuine religious utility. For I hope to show how only one particular manner of conceiving and of practising those scientific activities and this spiritual life and consolidation allows, indeed requires, the religious passion,—the noblest and deepest passion given to man,—to be itself enlisted on the side of that other noble, indestructible thing, severe scientific sincerity. This very sincerity would thus not empty or distract, but would, on the contrary, purify and deepen the soul's spirituality; and hence this spirituality would continuously turn to that sincerity for help in purifying and deepening the soul. And, surely, until we have somehow attained to some such interaction, the soul must perforce remain timid and weak; for without sincerity everywhere, we cannot possibly develop to their fullest the passion for truth and righteousness even in religion itself.

And then again a Catholic, one who would be a proudly devoted and grateful son of the Roman Church, speaks and thinks throughout the following pages. Yet it is his very Catholicism which makes him feel, with a spontaneous and continuous keenness, that only if there are fragments, earlier stages and glimpses of truth and goodness extant wheresoever some little sincerity exists, can the Catholic Church even conceivably be right. For though Christianity and Catholicism be the culmination and fullest norm of all religion, yet to be such they must find something thus to crown and measure: various degrees of, or preparations for, their truth have existed long before they came, and exist still, far and wide, now that they have come. Otherwise, Marcion would have been right, when he denied that the Old Testament proceeds from the same God as does the New; and three-fourths or more of the human race would not, to this very moment, be bereft, without fault of their own, of all knowledge of the Historic Christ and of every opportunity for definite incorporation into the Christian Church, since we dare not think that God has left this large majority of His children without any and every glimpse and opportunity of religious truth, moral goodness and eternal hope. Yet such a recognition of some light and love everywhere involves no trace of levelling down, or even of levelling up; it is, in itself, without a trace of Indifferentism. For if some kinds or degrees of light are thus found everywhere, yet this light is held to vary immensely in different times and places, from soul to soul, and from one religious stage, group or body to another; the measure and culmination of this light is found in the deepest Christian and Catholic light and holiness; and, over and above the involuntary, sincere differences in degree, stage and kind, there are held to exist, also more or less everywhere, the differences caused by cowardice and opposition to the light,—cowardices and oppositions which are as certainly at work within the Christian and Catholic Church as they are amongst the most barbarous of Polytheists. I may well have failed adequately to combine these twin truths; yet only in some such, though more adequate apprehension and combination resides the hope for the future of our poor storm-tossed human race,—in a deep fervour without fanaticism, and a generous sympathy without indifference.

And lastly, a lay lover of religion speaks throughout, a man to whom the very suspicion that such subjects should or could on that account, be foreign to him has ever been impossible. A deep interest in religion is evidently part of our very manhood, a thing previous to the Church, and which the Church now comes to develop and to save. Yet such an interest is, in the long run, impossible, if the heart and will alone are allowed to be active in a matter so supremely great and which claims the entire man. "Where my heart lies, let my brain lie also": man is not, however much we may try and behave as though he were, a mere sum-total of so many separable water-tight compartments; he can no more fruitfully delegate his brains and his interest in the intellectual analysis and synthesis of religion, than he can commission others to do his religious feeling and willing, his spiritual growth and combat, for him.—But this does not of itself imply an individualistic, hence one-sided, religion. For only in close union with the accumulated and accumulating experiences, analyses and syntheses of the human race in general, and with the supreme life and teaching of the Christian and Catholic Church in particular, will such growth in spiritual personality be possible on any large and fruitful scale: since nowhere, and nowhere less than in religion, does man achieve anything by himself alone, or for his own exclusive use and profit.

And such a layman's views, even when thus acquired and expressed with a constant endeavour to be, and ever increasingly to become, a unit and part and parcel of that larger, Christian and Catholic whole, will ever remain, in themselves and in his valuation of them, unofficial, and, at best, but so much material and stimulation for the kindly criticism and discriminating attention of his fellow-creatures and fellow-Christians and (should these views stand such informal, preliminary tests) for the eventual utilization of the official Church. To this officiality ever remains the exclusive right and duty to formulate successively, for the Church's successive periods, according as these become ripe for such formulations, the corporate, normative forms and expressions of the Church's deepest consciousness and mind. Yet this officiality cannot and does not operate *in vacuo*, or by a direct recourse to extra-human sources of information. It sorts out, eliminates what is false and pernicious, or sanctions and proclaims what is true and fruitful, and a development of her own life, teaching and commission, in the volunteer, tentative and preliminary work put forth by the Church's unofficial members.

And just because both these movements are within, and necessary to, one and the same complete Church, they can be and are different from each other. Hence the following book would condemn itself to pompous unreality were it to mimic official caution and emphasis, whilst ever unable to achieve official authority. It prefers to aim at a layman's special virtues and function: complete candour, courage, sensitiveness to the present and future, in their obscurer strivings towards the good and true, as these have been in their substance already tested in the past, and in so far as such strivings can be forecasted by sympathy and hope. And I thus trust that the book may turn out to be as truly Catholic in fact, as it has been Catholic in intention; I have striven hard to furnish so continuous and copious a stream of actions and teachings of Christian saints and sages as everywhere to give the reader means of correcting or completing my own inferences; and I sincerely submit these my own conclusions to the test and judgment of my fellow-Christians and of the Catholic Church.

My obligations to scholars, thinkers and large spiritual souls are far too numerous and great for any exhaustive recognition. Yet there are certain works and persons to whom I am especially indebted; and these shall here be mentioned with most grateful thanks.

In my Biographical and Critical Part Second, I have had, in Genoa itself, the help of various scholars and friends. Signor Dottore Ridolfo de Andreis first made me realize the importance of Vallebona's booklet. Padre Giovanni Semeria, the Barnabite, put me in touch with the right persons and documents. The Cavalliere L. A. Cervetto, of the Biblioteca Civica, referred me to many useful works. The Librarian of the Biblioteca della Missione Urbana copied out for me the inventory of St. Catherine's effects. And Signor Dottore Augusto Ferretto, of the Archivio di Stato, made admirably careful, explicitated copies for me, from the originals, so full of difficult abbreviations, of the long series of legal documents which are the rock-bed on which my biography is built.

The courteous help of the Head Librarian of the Genoese University Library extended beyond Genoa. For it was owing to his action, in conjunction with that of the Italian Ministry, of the English Embassy in Rome, and of the British Museum Authorities, that the three most important of the manuscripts of St. Catherine's life were most generously deposited for my use at the latter institution. I was thus enabled to study my chief sources at full leisure in London.

The Rev. Padre Calvino, Canon Regular of the Lateran, made many kind attempts to trace any possible compositions concerning St. Catherine among the Venerable Battista Vernazza's manuscripts, preserved by the spiritual descendants of Battista's Augustinian Canonesses in Genoa; it was not his fault that nothing could be found.

The Society of Bollandists lent me, for a liberal length of time, various rare books. I shall indeed be proud if my Appendix wins their approbation, since it deals with subject-matters and methods in which they are past masters. Father Sticker's pages on St. Catherine, in their *Acta Sanctorum* (1752), are certainly not satisfactory; they are, however, quite untypical of the Bollandists' best work, or even of their average performances.

My obligations in my Psychological and Philosophical Parts First and Third are still more numerous and far more difficult to trace. Indeed it is precisely where these obligations are the most far-reaching that I can least measure them, since the influence of the books and persons concerned has become part of the texture of my own mind.

But among the great religious spirits or stimulating thinkers of Classical and Patristic times, I am conscious of profound obligations to Plato generally; to Aristotle on two points; to St. Paul; to Plotinus; to Clement of Alexandria; and to St. Augustine. And the Areopagite Literature has necessarily been continuously in my mind. Among Mediaeval writers St. Thomas Aquinas has helped me greatly, in ways both direct and indirect; Eckhart has, with the help of Father H. S. Denifle's investigations, furnished much food for reflection by his most instructive doctrinal excesses; and the extraordinarily deep and daring spirituality of Jacopone da Todi's poetry has been studied with the greatest care.

The Renaissance times have given me Cardinal Nicolas of Coes, whose great Dialogue *De Idiota* has helped me in various ways. And in the early post-Reformation period I have carefully studied, and have been much influenced by, that many-sided, shrewdly wise book, St. Teresa's Autobiography. Yet it is St. John of the Cross, that massively virile Contemplative, who has most deeply influenced me throughout this work. St. Catherine is, I think, more like him, in her ultimate spirit, than any other Saint or spiritual writer known to me; she is certainly far more like him than is St. Teresa.

Later on, I have learnt much from Fénelon's Latin writings concerning Pure Love, of 1710 and 1712; together with Abbé Gosselin's admirably lucid *Analyse de la Controverse du Quiétisme*, 1820, and the Jesuit Father Deharbe's solid and sober *die vollkommene Liebe Gottes*, 1856.

Among modern philosophers I have been especially occupied with, and variously stimulated or warned by, Spinoza, with his deep religious intuition and aspiration, and his determinist system, so destructive because taken by him as ultimate; Leibniz, with his admirably continuous sense of the multiplicity in every living unity, of the organic character, the *inside* of everything that fully exists, and of the depth and range of our subconscious mental and emotional life; Kant, with his keen criticisms and searching analyses, his profound ethical instincts, and his curious want of the specifically religious sense and insight; Schopenhauer, with his remarkable recognition of the truth and greatness of the Ascetic element and ideal; Trendelenburg, with his continuous requirement of an operative knowledge of the chief stages which any principle or category has passed through in human history, if we would judge this principle with any fruit; Kierkegaard, that certainly one-sided, yet impressively tenacious re-discoverer and proclaimer of the poignant sense of the Transcendent essential to all deep religion, and especially to Christianity, religion's flower and crown; and Fechner, in his little-known book, so delightfully convincing in its rich simplicity, *die drei Motive und Gründe des Glaubens*, 1863.

Of quite recent or still living writers two have been used by me on a scale which would be unpardonable, had the matters treated by them been the direct subjects of my book. In Part First whole pages of mine are marked by me as little but a *précis* of passages in Dr. Eduard Zeller's standard *Philosophy of the Greeks*. I have myself much studied Heracleitus, Parmenides, Plato and Plotinus; and I have, also in the case of the other philosophers, always followed up and tested such passages of Zeller as I have here transcribed. But I did not, for by far the most part, think it worth while, on these largely quite general and practically uncontested matters, to construct fresh appreciations of my own, rather than to reproduce, with due consideration and acknowledgments, the conclusions of such an accepted authority. And already in Part First, but especially in Part Third, I have utilized as largely, although here with still more of personal knowledge and of careful re-examination, considerable sections of Professor H. J. Holtzmann's *Lehrbuch der Neutestamentlichen Theologie*, 1897—sections which happen to be, upon the whole, the deepest and most solid in that great but often daring work. The same Professor Holtzmann is, besides, a most suggestive religious philosopher; and his penetrating though very difficult book *Richard Rothe's Speculatives System*, 1899, has also been of considerable use.

Other recent or contemporary German writers to whom I owe much, are Erwin Rohde, in his exquisite great book, *Psyche*, 2nd ed., 1898; Professor Johannes Volkelt, in his penetratingly critical *Kant's Erkenntnisstheorie*, 1879; Professor Hugo Münsterberg, in his largely planned although too absolute *Grundzüge der Psychologie*, Vol. I., 1900; Professor Heinrich Rickert, in his admirably discriminating *Grenzen der naturwissenschaftlichen Begriffsbildung*, 1902; and also two friends whose keen care for religion never flags—Professors Rudolf Eucken of Jena and Ernst Troeltsch of Heidelberg. Eucken's *Lebensanschauungen der grossen Denker*, 1st ed., 1890; *der Kampf um einen geistigen Lebensinhalt*, 1896; and the earlier sections of *der Wahrheitsgehalt der Religion*, 1902, have greatly helped me. And Troeltsch's *Grundprobleme der Ethik*, 1902, has considerably influenced certain central conceptions of my book, notwithstanding the involuntary, rough injustice manifested by him, especially elsewhere, towards the Roman Church.

Among present-day French writers, my book owes most to

Professor Maurice Blondel's, partly obscure yet intensely alive and religiously deep, work *L'Action*, 1893; to Dr. Pierre Janet's carefully first-hand observations, as chronicled in his *Etat Mental des Hystériques*, 1894; to Monsieur Emile Boutroux's very suggestive paper *Psychologie du Mysticisme*, 1902; to various pregnant articles of the Abbé L. Laberthonnière in the *Annales de Philosophie Chrétienne*, 1898–1906; and to M. Henri Bergson's delicately penetrating *Essai sur les Données Immédiates de la Conscience*, 2nd ed., 1898.

And amongst living Englishmen, the work is most indebted to Professor A. S. Pringle-Pattison, especially to his eminently sane *Hegelianism and Personality*, 2nd ed., 1893; to Professor James Ward, in his strenuous *Naturalism and Agnosticism*, 1st ed., 1899; to the Reverend George Tyrrell's *Hard Sayings*, 1898, and *The Faith of the Millions*, 2 vols., 1901, so full of insight into Mysticism; and, very especially, to Dr. Edward Caird, in his admirably wide and balanced survey, *The Evolution of Theology in the Greek Philosophers*, 1904.

But further back than all the living writers and friends lies the stimulation and help of him who was later on to become Cardinal Newman. It was he who first taught me to glory in my appurtenance to the Catholic and Roman Church, and to conceive this my inheritance in a large and historical manner, as a slow growth across the centuries, with an innate affinity to, and eventual incorporation of, all the good and true to be found mixed up with error and with evil in this chequered, difficult but rich world and life in which this living organism moves and expands. Yet the use to which all these helps have here been put, has inevitably been my own doing; nowhere except in direct quotations have I simply copied, and nowhere are these helpers responsible for what here appears.

And then there have been great souls, whom I cannot well name here, but whom I would nevertheless refer to in reverent gratitude; souls that have taught me that deepest of facts and of lessons,—the persistence, across the centuries, within the wide range of the visible and indeed also of the invisible Church, of that vivid sense of the finite and the Infinite, of that spacious joy and expansive freedom in self-donation to God, the prevenient, all-encompassing Spirit, of that massively spontaneous, elemental religion, of which Catherine is so noble an example. Thus a world-renouncing, world-conquering, virile piety, humble and daring, humane, tender and creatively strong, is at no time simply dead, but it merely sleepeth; indeed it ever can be found, alive, open-eyed, irresistible, hidden away here and there, throughout our earthly space and time.

In matters directly connected with the publication of the work I have especially to thank Messrs. Sciutto of Genoa, the photographers to whom I owe the very successful photographs from which the plates that stand at the head of my volumes have been taken; Mr. Sidney E. Mayle, publisher, of Hampstead, for permission to use the photogravure of St. Catherine's portrait which appeared as an illustration to a paper of mine, in his scholarly *Hampstead Annual*, 1898; Miss Maude Petre, who helped me much towards achieving greater lucidity of style, by carefully reading and criticizing all my proofs; and my publisher, who has not shrunk from undertaking the publication of so long a work on so very serious, abstruse-seeming a subject. Even so, I have had to suppress the notes to my chapter on "Catherine's Teaching," which throughout showed the critical reasons that had determined my choice of the particular sayings, and the particular text of the sayings, adopted by me in the text; and have had to excise quite a third of my Appendix, which furnished the analysis of further, critically instructive texts of the *Vita e Dottrina*, the *Dicchiarazione* and the *Dialogo*. If a new edition is ever called for, this further material might be added, and would greatly increase the cogency of my argument.

The work that now at last I thus submit to the reader, is doubtless full of defects; and I shall welcome any thoughtful criticism of any of its parts as a true kindness. Yet I would point out that all these parts aim at being but so many constituents of a whole, within which alone they gain their true significance and worth. Hence only by one who has studied and pondered the book as a whole, will any of its parts be criticized with fairness to that part's intention. To gain even but a dozen of such readers would amply repay the labour of these many years.

I take it that the most original parts are Chapter Eight, with its analysis of Battista Vernazza's interesting Diary; the Appendix, with its attempts at fixing the successive authors and intentions that have built up the *Vita e Dottrina*; Chapter Nine, which attempts to assign to psycho-physical matters, as we now know them, their precise place and function within the vast life-system, and according to the practical tests, of the great Mystical Saints; and Chapter Fifteen, with its endeavour to picture that large Asceticism which alone can effect, within the same soul, a fruitful co-habitation of, and interaction between, Social Religion, the Scientific Habit of Mind, and the Mystical Element of Religion.

Kirkegaard used to claim that he ever wrote *existentially*, pricked on by the exigencies of actual life, to attempt their expression in terms of that life, and in view of its further spiritual development. More than ever the spiritual life appears now as supremely worth the having, and yet it seems to raise, or to find, the most formidable difficulties or even deadlocks. I can but hope that these pages may have so largely sprung from the exigencies of that life itself,—that they may have caught so much of the spirit of the chief livers of the spiritual life, especially of St. Catherine of Genoa and of St. John of the Cross, and, above all, of the One Master and Measure of Christianity and of the Church,—as to stimulate such life, its practice, love and study, in their readers, and may point them, spur them on, through and beyond all that here has been attempted, missed or obscured, to fuller religious insight, force and fruitfulness.

FRIEDRICH VON HÜGEL.

Kensington,
Easter, 1908.

"He is not far from every one of us; for in Him we live, and move, and have our being."—Acts xvii, 27, 28.

"Where the Spirit of the Lord is, there is liberty."
2 Corinthians iii, 17.

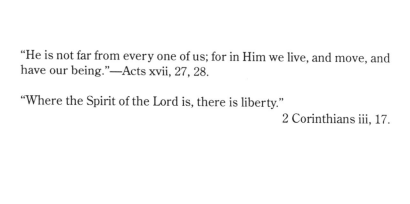

VOLUME FIRST

INTRODUCTION AND BIOGRAPHIES

PART I

INTRODUCTION

THE MYSTICAL ELEMENT OF RELIGION

CHAPTER I

THE THREE CHIEF FORCES OF WESTERN CIVILIZATION

INTRODUCTORY.

1. *An enigma of life: the Universal and Abiding does not move the will; and what does move it is Individual and Evanescent.*

Amongst the apparent enigmas of life, amongst the seemingly most radical and abiding of interior antinomies and conflicts experienced by the human race and by individuals, there is one which everything tends to make us feel and see with an ever-increasing keenness and clearness. More and more we want a strong and interior, a lasting yet voluntary bond of union between our own successive states of mind, and between what is abiding in ourselves and what is permanent within our fellow-men; and more and more we seem to see that mere Reasoning, Logic, Abstraction,—all that appears as the necessary instrument and expression of the Universal and Abiding,—does not move or win the will, either in ourselves or in others; and that what does thus move and win it, is Instinct, Intuition, Feeling, the Concrete and Contingent, all that seems to be of its very nature individual and evanescent. Reasoning appears but capable, at best, of co-ordinating, unifying, explaining the material furnished to it by experience of all kinds; at worst, of explaining it away; at best, of stimulating the purveyance of a fresh supply of such experience; at worst, of stopping such purveyance as much as may be. And yet the Reasoning would appear to be the transferable part in the process, but not to move us; and the experience alone to have the moving power, but not to be transmissible.

2. *Our personal experience as regards our own convictions.*

Experience indeed and its resultant feeling are always, in the first instance, coloured and conditioned by every kind of individual many-sided circumstances of time and place, of race and age and sex, of education and temperament, of antecedent and environment. And it is this very particular combination, just this one, so conditioned and combined, coming upon me just at this moment and on this spot, just at this stage of my reach or growth, at this turning of my way, that carries with it this particular power to touch or startle, to stimulate or convince. It is just precisely through the but imperfectly analyzable, indeed but dimly perceived, individual connotation of general terms; it is by the fringe of feeling, woven out of the past doings and impressions, workings and circumstances, physical, mental, moral, of my race and family and of my own individual life; it is by the apparently slight, apparently far away, accompaniment of a perfectly individual music to the spoken or sung text of the common speech of man, that I am, it would seem, really moved and won.

And this fringe of feeling, this impression, is, strictly speaking, not merely untransferable, but also unrepeatable; it is unique even for the same mind: it never was before, it never will be again. Heraclitus, if we understand that old Physicist in our own modern, deeply subjective, largely sentimental way, would appear to be exactly right: you cannot twice step into the same stream, since never for two moments do the waters remain identical; you yourself cannot twice step the same man into the same river, for you have meanwhile changed as truly as itself has done. *Πάντα ῥεῖ:* all things and states, outward and inward, appear indeed in flux: only each moment seems to bring, to each individual, for that one moment, his power to move and to convince.

3. *Our experience in our attempt to win others.*

And if we transmit this emotion or conviction to another mind, or if we seem to be able to trace such transmission when it has been actually effected in ourselves or in others, we shall find that, in proportion as one mind feeds, not forces, another, the particular bond and organization of the mental and emotional picture which cost us so much, moved us so much, has, in each case, been snapped and broken up; the whole has been again resolved into its constituent elements, and only some of these elements have been taken up into the already existing organization of the other mind, or have joined together in that mind, to form there a combination which is really new. Even a simple scent or sound or sight comes charged to each of us with many but most differing connotations, arousing or modifying or supplanting old or new ideas and impressions in the most subtle, complex, and individual manner. Insist upon another mind taking over the whole of this impression, and you will have rightly and necessarily aroused an immediate or remote hostility or revolt against the whole of what you bring. Hence here too we are again perplexed by the initial enigma : the apparently insurmountable individuality of all that affects us, and the equally insurmountable non-affectingness of all that is clearly and certainly transmissible from any one man to another.

4. *This mysterious law appears to obtain in precise proportion to the depth and importance of the truths and realities in view.*

And if we seem boxed up thus, each one away from our fellow, in all our really moving and determining inclinations and impressions, judgments and affections, with regard to matters on which we feel we can afford to differ deeply and to be much alone, we appear to be more and not less so, in exact proportion as the importance of the subject-matter increases. In moral and spiritual, in religious and fundamental matters, we thirst more, not less, for identity of conviction and of feeling; and we are, or seem to be, more, not less, profoundly and hopelessly at variance with each other than anywhere else.

And more than this : the apparent reason of this isolation seems but to aggravate the case, because here more than anywhere else imagination, feeling, intuition seem indeed to play a predominant, determining part; and yet here more than anywhere else we feel such a predominance to be fraught with every kind of danger. Thus here especially we feel as incapable of suppressing, indeed of doing without these forces, as of frankly accepting, studying, and cultivating them. Now and then we take alarm and are in a panic at any indication that these springs and concomitants of life are at work within us; yet we persist in doing little or nothing to find sufficient and appropriate food and scope and exercise for the right development, and hence the real purification of these elemental forces, forces which we can stunt but cannot kill. Nothing, we most rightly feel, can be in greater or more subtle and dangerous opposition to manly morality or enlightened religion than the seeking after or revelling in emotion; nothing, we most correctly surmise, can equal the power of strong feeling or heated imagination to give a hiding-place to superstition, sensuality, dreamy self-complacent indolence, arrogant revolt and fanaticism; nothing, even where such things seem innocent, appears less apt than do these fierce and fitful, these wayward and fleeting feelings, these sublimities and exquisitenesses, to help on that sober and stable, consistent and persistent, laborious upbuilding of moral and religious character, work, and evidence which alone are wanted more and more. Indeed, what would seem better calculated than such emotion to strain the nerves, to inflame the imagination, to blunt common-sense and that salt of the earth, the saving sense of the ridiculous, to deaden the springs of research and critical observation, to bring us, under the incalculably sapping influences of physical abnormalities, close up to where sanity shades off into madness, and ethical elevation breaks down into morbidness and depravity?

5. *The experience of the human race: the two series of personalities, movements, races.*

And the secular experience of the race would seem fully to bear out such suspicions. For have we not there a double series of personalities, events, and movements far too long and widespread not to be conclusive? On the one hand, there are those that seem to spring from dimly lit or dark feeling, to arise,—as it were, hydra-like, to sting and madden, or, mist-like, to benumb all life, and turn it into mere drift and dreaming,—from out of the obscure, undrained, swampy places of human ignorance and passion. On the other hand, there are those that are formed and fashioned by clear, transparent thought; and these flourish in the cultivated, well-drained plains of human science and strict demonstration.

Among the first series, you have the Pantheistic schools and personalities of the decaying Roman Empire, Plotinus the Ecstatic, and Jamblichus, and such other dreamers, straining up into the blue; the somewhat similar, largely subterranean, Jewish and Christian sects and tendencies of the Middle Ages; the Anabaptist and other like groups, individualistic, fantastic, in considerable part anomistic and revolutionary, of the Reformation period; and such phenomena as the Eternal-Gospel troubles and the Quietistic controversy in the Roman Church. And above all, in the East, we have, from time immemorial, whole races, (in the midst of a world crying aloud for help and re-fashioning, but which is left to stagnate and decay,) still dreaming away their lives in Buddhistic abstraction and indifference.

Among the second, the light, clear series, you have whole races, the luminous, plastic, immensely active Greek, the strong-willed, practical, organizing Roman, and the Anglo-Saxon determined " to stand no nonsense "; you have an Aristotle, sober, systematic; one side at least of the great Mediaeval Scholastic movement, culminating in St. Thomas, so orderly and transparent; above all, modern Physical Science, first subjecting all phenomena to rigorous quantitative and mathematical analysis and equation, and then reacting upon philosophy as well, and insisting, there and everywhere, upon clearness, direct comparableness, ready transferableness of ideas and their formulae, as the sole tests of truth. Descartes; Kepler, Galileo; Hobbes, Spinoza are, in increasing degrees, still perhaps the most perfect types of this clear and cool, this ultimately mathematical and Monistic tendency and position.

6. *The dark, intuitive personalities and schools, apparently a mere stop-gap, transition, or reaction against the clear, discursive ones.*

And further, the personalities and schools of the interiorly experimental, emotional kind seem to appear upon the scene but as stop-gaps or compensations for the other series, in periods of transition or reaction, of uncertainty or decay. So at the break-up of the Roman Empire (Neo-Platonism); so at the end of the Patristic period and just before the official acceptance of Scholasticism (St. Bernard); so during the foundering of the Mediaeval fabric of life and thought in the Renaissance of the fifteenth and sixteenth centuries (Pico, Paracelsus); so in the German Romanticism of sixty years ago, as a reaction against the survivals of the eighteenth-century Rationalism; so now again in our own day, more slightly, but not less really, in a revival of spiritual philosophy. It looks then as though the experimental-emotional strain could only thrive fitfully, on the momentary check or ruin of the clear and " scientific " school; as though it were a perhaps inevitable disease breaking in occasionally upon the normal health of the human mind. For the eventual result of the world's whole movement surely seems to be the reclamation of ever-increasing stretches of knowledge and theory from the dominion of vague, irresponsible, untestable feeling, and their incorporation in the domain of that unbroken, universal determinism, of those clear and simple, readily analyzable, verifiable, communicable, and applicable laws which, more and more, are found to rule phenomena wheresoever we may look.

7. *This seems especially to apply to the Intuitive-Emotional element of Religion.*

And if the prima facie trend of centuries of thought and conflict appears to rule out of court even such a fringe of individual experience and emotion as ever accompanies and stimulates all religion, the verdict of history, indeed of any survey of contemporary life, if only this be sufficiently large, would seem fatal to any type of religion in which this individual experience and emotion would form religion's core and centre, as in the case of the specifically experimental-emotional school generally, and of the Mystics in particular.

To take some such survey, let us look, to begin with, outside of where Catholic discipline and unity somewhat obscure, at first sight, even the legitimate and indeed the really existing diversities of school and tendency. In the Church's organism each divergence has ever been more largely tempered and supplemented by the others; and since the Reformation, indeed in part even more recently, owing to an entirely intelligible and in part inevitable, reaction, even most legitimate and persistent divergencies, which flourished in rich and enriching variety throughout the Middle Ages, have largely ceased to appear in any obvious and distinct embodiments. Let us look then first to where such diversities grow unchecked, and indeed generally tend to excess and caricature. Let us take contemporary English Protestantism, and then Foreign Protestantism in the large lines of its history. In both cases the experimental-emotional strain and group will seem to compare unfavourably with its competitors.

For if we look about us in England, we seem to have little difficulty in classing the tendencies within the Established Church under the headings of High, Broad, and Low; indeed we can readily extend this treble classification to all the various schools and bodies of English Protestantism. We can easily conceive of the greater portion of English Nonconformity as but a prolongation and accentuation of the Evangelical school in the Established Church: the readiness and ease with which the former at certain moments unite and coalesce with the latter, show quite conclusively how close is the affinity between them. We almost as readily think of the Unitarian and Theistic bodies as prolongations and further sublimations of the Anglican Broad Church view, though here, no doubt, the degrees and kinds of difference are more numerous and important. And if it would be hard to find an extension, still more an accentuation, of the Anglican High Church party amongst the English Nonconformists, a strain largely identical with the sacerdotal current elsewhere has always existed in the Presbyterian churches. Nor must we forget the powerful and constant, both repellent and attractive, influence exercised by Rome upon even those outside of her obedience. To be quite philosophical, the survey ought to include all types of English Christianity; and, in that case, the High Church position would rank rather as a dilution, as a variety, incomplete and inconsistent though it be, of the type represented most strikingly and emphatically by Rome, than as a variant of the types having their centres at Wittenberg and Geneva.

And if we next turn to German Protestantism, especially to the simultaneous variations of its short-lived, fluid, formative period, we shall there too find this treble tendency. The Evangelical strain will be represented here by the numerous Illuminist and Anabaptist personalities, groups and movements to which Luther himself had given occasion, which but emphasized or caricatured his own earlier Mysticism; but which, when they threatened, by their revolutionary, communistic fanaticism and violence, completely to discredit and ruin his own movement, he suppressed with such ruthless and illogical severity. And the Broad Church strain will here be found emphasized and caricatured in Socinianism, and in such milder forms of Rationalism as prepared the way for it or followed in its wake. And finally, the High Church strain is not so hard to discover in much of the doctrine and in some of the forms and externals of Orthodox, official Lutheranism. Indeed in foreign Protestantism generally,—in Zwinglianism, in Calvinism, and in its other bodies and sects, we can trace various forms of, and degrees of approximation to, one or other of these three types, the Historical, the Experimental, the Rational.

Now looking at the scene of battle, for the moment quite generally, it would seem as though, of these three types and tendencies, the Emotional and Experimental had proved itself decidedly the weakest for good, the strongest for evil of the three, and this both in the past and in the present, both in England and abroad. We have here in England, in the past, the Puritan excesses in Ireland, Scotland, and England itself; and later on and down to the present, the largely dreary and unlovely, narrow and unjust monotony of Evangelicalism. We have there abroad, in the past, the Peasants' War and the Anabaptist Saturnalia at Münster; and later on and down to the present, that Pietism which has so often barred the way to a just appreciation of Historical Christianity and to a candid acceptance of rational methods and results, and this without its being able to find any constructive or analytic working principle of its own. Both in England and in Germany, indeed throughout the cultivated West, only the Historical, Traditional school on the one hand, and the Rationalistic, Scientific school on the other hand, seem to count at all: it is they which alone seem to gain ground, or at least to hold it, at the Universities and amongst the thinking, ruling classes generally.

8. *Yet this adverse judgment will appear largely misleading, if we study the matter more fully.*

And yet this first aspect of things will, I think, turn out to be largely deceptive, to be but one side and one teaching of that noble inheritance, that great output of life and experience, past and present, which is ready to our hand for ever-renewed study and assimilation in human history and society, and which, taken as it really is,—as the indefinite prolongation of our own little individual direct experiences,—can alone help us to give to these latter experiences a full, life-regulating value. Let us take then the foregoing objections, and let us do so as but so many starting-points and openings into our great subject. This preliminary discussion will but prepare the ground and method for the following detailed study, and for the final positions of the whole book. Indeed even the book's opening question can be answered only by the whole book and at our labour's end.

I. The First of the Three Forces: Hellenism, the Thirst for Richness and Harmony.

We revert then to the apparent interior antinomy from which we started,—the particular concrete experience which alone moves us and helps to determine our will, but which, seemingly, is untransferable, indeed unrepeatable; and the general, abstract reasoning which *is* repeatable, indeed transferable, but which does not move us or help directly to determine the will. And we here begin by the study of the antinomy, as this has been explicated for us by Hellenism, the earliest and widest of the three main mental, indeed spiritual, forces that are operative within each of us Westerns, on and on.

1. *The antinomy in the pre-Socratics.*

Heraclitus appeared to us an impressive exponent of the former truth, of the apparent utter evanescence of these particular impressions and experiences, of the complete shiftingness of the very faculty within us and of the environment without us, by which and in which we apprehend them. An ever-changing self in the midst of an ever-changing world, basing its persuasiveness and persuadableness, indeed even its conscious identity with itself and its communion with others, upon the ever-changing resultants of all these changes: this would surely seem to be a house built not upon the sand but upon the quicksands.

Now we have to remember that Parmenides had, already in early Greek times, been equally emphatic, perhaps equally impressive, on the other side of this very question,—on the impossibility of Becoming, of Change; and on the certainty and knowableness of the utter Oneness and Permanence of all Being.[1] All that really *is*, he maintained, excludes all Becoming: the very notion of Being is incompatible with that of Becoming: the first is utterly without the second. All real Becoming would be equivalent to the real existence of Non-Being. Hence all Multiplicity and Becoming is necessarily but apparent, and masks an underlying absolute Unity and Permanence, which can be reached by the intellect alone. And this position of Parmenides was felt to be so strong, that all the subsequent Greek Physicists took their stand upon it: the four unchangeable elements of Empedocles, the Atoms of Leucippus and Democritus (atoms of eternally unchanging shape and size, and of one absolutely uniform and unchanging quality) are but modifications of the doctrine of Parmenides concerning the Oneness and Unchangeableness of Being.

[1] The remainder of this section is for the most part expressed in the words of Prof. Edouard Zeller's standard *Philosophie der Griechen.* I have used the German text.

But even Heraclitus himself is far removed from denying all Oneness, all Permanence. For, according to him, a permanent law of permutation runs through and expresses itself in the shiftingness of all things perceptible by sense; or rather one eternal physical substance, Fire, of ceaselessly active properties, is continually manifesting itself, in a regular succession of appearances, from fire to air, from air to water, from water to earth, and then backwards up again to fire.

And when once the Greeks begin to break away from all this Hylozoism,—these systems which uniformly, from Thales to Democritus, attempt to explain all things by some one living or moving Matter, without the intervention of Spirit or of Mind,—Spirit appears in Anaxagoras as the One, and as present, everywhere and in varying degrees, as the principle of the motion of that co-eternal matter which is here, on the contrary, conceived of as but apparently homogeneous anywhere, and as really composed of an indefinite number and combination of qualitatively differing constituents.

Thus in all its schools, even before Socrates and Plato, Greek philosophy clung to the One and the One's reality, however differently it conceived the nature of this Unity, and however much it may have varied as to the nature and reality of the Many, or as to the relation and the bond subsisting between that Unity and this Multiplicity. Only at the end of this first period do the Sophists introduce, during a short time marked by all the symptoms of transition, uncertainty, and revolution, the doctrine of the unknowableness, indeed of the unreality, of the One, and with it of the exclusive reality of mere Multiplicity, of evanescent Appearances.

2. *In Socrates.*

But Socrates opens out the second and greatest period of Greek philosophy, by reverting to, indeed by indefinitely deepening, the general conviction that Oneness underlies Multiplicity. And he does so through the virtual discovery of, and a ceaseless insistence upon, two great new subject-matters of philosophy: Dialectic and Ethics. It is true that in both these respects the Sophists had prepared the ground: they had, before him and all around him, discussed everything from every point of view then conceivable; and they had, at the same time, helped to withdraw man's attention from pure speculation about physical nature to practical occupation with himself. But the Sophistic Dialectic had ended in itself, in universal negation and scepticism; and the Sophistic Anthropology had, partly as cause, partly as effect of that scepticism, more and more completely narrowed and dragged down all human interest, capacity, and activity to a selfish, materialistic self-aggrandizement and a frank pleasure-seeking. Socrates indeed took over both these subjects; but he did so in a profoundly different spirit, and worked them into a thoroughly antagonistic view of knowledge and of life.

Socrates begins, like the Sophists, with the Multiplicity of impression and opinion, which we find occasioned by one and the same question or fact; and like them he refuses to take the Physicists' short cut of immediate and direct occupation with things and substances, say the elements. Slowly and laboriously he works his way, by the help of Dialectic, (for this has now become a means and not an end,) around and through and into the various apprehensions, and, at last, out of and beyond them, to a satisfactory concept of each thing. And the very means taken to arrive at this concept, and the very test which is applied to the concept, when finally arrived at, for gauging the degree of its finality, both these things help to deepen profoundly the sense of a certain Multiplicity in all Oneness and of a certain Oneness in all Multiplicity. For the means he takes are a careful and (as far as may be) exhaustive and impartial discussion and analysis of all the competing and conflicting notions and connotations occasioned by each matter in dispute; and the test he applies to the final concept, in view of gauging the degree of its finality, is how far this concept reconciles and resolves within its higher unity all such various and contrary aspects suggested by the thing, as have stood the brunt of the previous discussion and have thereby proved themselves true and objective.

Socrates again, like the Sophists, turns his attention away from Physics to Ethics; he drops speculation about external nature, and busies himself with the interior life and development of man. But the world in which Socrates' method necessarily conceives and places man, and the work and standard which he finds already latent in each man, for that man to do and to endorse in himself and in the world, are both entirely different from those of the Sophists, and occasion a still further, indeed the greatest of all possible deepenings of the apprehension of Oneness and of Multiplicity.

For the world of Socrates is a world in which Reality and Truth reign and are attainable by man; never does he even ask whether truth *is* or can be reached by us, but only what it is and where it lies and how it can be attained. And since Socrates instinctively shares the profoundly Greek conviction that Reality and Truth are necessarily not only one but unchanging, he assumes throughout that, since Truth and Reality do exist, Oneness and unchanging Being must exist also. And thus the Oneness of Reality and the Multiplicity of Appearance are re-established by him in Greek philosophy. And their apprehension is indefinitely deepened and extended, since, whatever *is* being knowable, and knowable only through Dialectic, and Dialectic having left us with concepts each in a sense a one and a many, Life itself, Reality and all Nature must, somehow and to some extent, be also a one and a many. And man according to Socrates is required, already as a simple consequence of such convictions, to discover and acknowledge and organize the One and the Many in his own interior life and faculties. For if his senses tell him of the Many, and his reason alone tells him of the One, and the Many are but appearances and the One alone is fully real,—then it will be in and through his reason that he is and will be truly man.

Thus immediately within himself does man have a continuous, uniquely vivid experience of the One and the Many, and of the necessity, difficulty, and fruitfulness of their proper organization; and from hence he will reflect them back upon the outer world, adding thus indefinitely, by means of Ethics, to the delicacy and depth of his apprehension of such Oneness and Multiplicity as, by means of Dialectic, he has already found there. But further, he now thus becomes conscious, for the first time at all adequately, of the difference between his own body and his own mind. And here he has no more a Oneness *and* a Multiplicity, he is directly conscious of a Oneness *in* Multiplicity, of a ruling and organizing power of the mind in and over the body; and the One here is unseen and spiritual, and the Many is here found to be an organism of forces and of functions designed, with profound wisdom, to correspond with and to subserve the soul. And this Microcosm is readily taken as a key and an analogy wherewith to group and explain the appearances of the world without. Much appears in that outer world as unreduced to system; but then similarly within us much is still in a state of chaos, of revolt. In that world no one ruler can be directly perceived; but then similarly within us, the one ruling mind is perceptible only in its effects. And this inner organization, ever required more than realized, is not a matter of abstract speculation, of subtle induction, adjournable at will; it is a clamorous consciousness, it is a fact that continually requires acts to back it or to break it. Strengthen it, and you have interior expansion and life; weaken it, and you bring on shrinkage and death. For the passions are there, active even if *we* refuse to be active, active against us and above us, if not under us and for us; and their submission to the reason, to effort, cannot fail, once our attention is fully turned that way, more than anything else to keep alive and to deepen our sense of the organization of all that lives, of the presence of the One *and* the Many, of the One *in* the Many, in all that truly lives at all.

3. *In Plato.*

Now this dialectical method and this ethical subject-matter get applied, investigated, and developed, with ever-increasing complexity and interaction, by Socrates, Plato, and Aristotle, the three spiritual generations of this, the greatest period of Greek Philosophy. And the more penetrating the method becomes, and the more deeply it probes the subject-matter, the more intense and extensive is found to be this Unity in Multiplicity both within man and without him.

In the teaching of Socrates both the method and the apprehension of Unity and Multiplicity are as yet, so to speak, in bud. Dialectic is here still chiefly a Method, and hardly as yet a Metaphysic as well. The soul here is as yet but simply one, and virtue is also simply one, and simply and directly identical with knowledge, and hence directly teachable: the very possibility that the will may not or indeed cannot follow, necessarily, automatically, the clear perception of what is really good for it, is one quite foreign to the mind of Socrates, indeed to all Greek thinkers up to the very end of the classical philosophy.

In Plato the methods and the results are both, as it were, in flower. Dialectic has here become both a systematic method, and a metaphysical system: not only are Ideas true, and the only means for reaching truth, but they alone are true, they alone fully *are*, and exist as separate self-subsisting realities. And as in the world within, Goodness is, in this profoundly ethical system, seen and willed and striven for as supreme, so also in the world without, is the Idea of Goodness considered as existing supreme from all eternity, and as somehow the Cause of all that truly *is*.

It is true that Plato nowhere succeeds in finding in his system a fitting place for a Personal God: for, among other reasons, the Platonic Ideas are all, from the lowest to the highest, but Hypostatized Concepts of Kinds, and are hence, quite consistently, considered to be perfect and supreme, in precise proportion as they are general. The highest Idea will thus of necessity be the most general, the most devoid of all determination, and hence the least personal of them all.

It is true also that in his Metaphysics generally he insists so much upon the complete severance and self-sufficingness of the Ideas as over against Appearances, that he prepares his own inevitable failure again to bridge over the gulf that he himself has thus dug too deep and broad. Especially misleading is his half-suggestion, that the transition to Phenomenal Multiplicity is but a further extension of the Multiplicity already observable in the world of Ideas. For these two Multiplicities are evidently entirely different in kind. Each Idea is conceived as necessarily eternal, unchanging, complete and perfect in its own way; whereas each appearance is conceived as necessarily temporal, changing, incomplete, and imperfect even in its own way.

It is true again, that, in Psychology, Plato breaks up the Soul into the three parts of the Reason, the Irascible Passions, and the Concupiscible Passions, and that he discriminates between them even as to their place of residence in the body. And correspondingly he distinguishes, in Ethics, the four Cardinal Virtues, Prudence, Fortitude, Temperance and Justice: he distributes the first three virtues among the three parts of the soul, allotting ever one of these virtues specially to one part, and makes Justice to be the general virtue that sees to each part carrying out its own special work and virtue, and respecting the work of the other two. And thus we seem to get away from the Oneness of the soul and the Oneness of virtue, as already taught by Socrates.

It is finally true that not only does Matter remain unexplained and treated as though in itself a mere nothing; but that it is considered, nevertheless, as somehow strong enough to hinder and hamper the Idea which really constitutes that Matter's sole reality. Hence also springs Plato's saddening aloofness from and contempt for all trades and handicrafts, for all the homely tastes, joys, and sorrows at all peculiar to the toiling majority. And herein he but considerably deepens and systematizes one of the weakest and most ruinous tradition of his class, age, and people, and falls far short of Socrates, with his deep childlike love of homely wisdom and of technical skill and productiveness. Indeed Matter is considered to be the one occasion of all sin, just as ignorance is considered to be the one true cause of sin. For although Plato throughout holds and proclaims free-will, in the definite sense of freedom of choice; and although he, in some passages, declares the ignorance which (according to him) is the necessary condition of a wrong choice, to be itself voluntary and culpable and to spring from an avoidable attachment to the world of sense : yet he clings, nevertheless, to the Socratic position that all ignorance and immorality are involuntary, that no man does or can act against what he sees to be for his own good.

All this would of itself suffice to show how and why the Platonic system has, as such, long ceased to live or to be capable of resuscitation. And yet even some of the apparent weaknesses just referred to are nearly or even entirely strong points in his scheme. So with his treble division of the Soul, if we but soften the distinction of actual parts into a difference of function or of object. For, already in Plato's own judgment, these parts admit of and require a regular hierarchy of subordination : the Irascible part is the natural ally, if properly tamed and broken in by the Reason, of this Reason against the Concupiscible part : it is the winged steed amongst the two horses of the chariot of the soul, and the charioteer, the Reason, has to see to it that this his winged steed flies not recklessly, but lends all its strength to keep its heavy, wingless, downwards-tending yoke-fellow from plunging them all into the deep and dark. Hence all this really makes for a true, because rich and laborious, Unity in Multiplicity. The same applies to the scheme of the four Cardinal Virtues; for here also there is a balancing and interaction of forces and of duties, which together are well fitted to deepen and fruitfully to unify the soul.

But above all, there are four main conceptions which, with varying degrees and kinds of clearness, consistency, and proof, run throughout the Dialogues, and which not all the ever-increasing perception of the complexity of their implications, nor all the never-ending costingness of their reproduction, have long kept mankind from accepting and working into their own inner life and into their outlook and labour upon the world without.

There is, first, the sense of the Universal nature of philosophy. Philosophy is here not a science alongside of other sciences, nor a sect existing with a view to the advantage of its members, nor a substitute for religion or science, art or action; but it stands for the totality of all mental activity, the nearest approach to an adequate realization of the reasonable nature of man. Hence philosophy has constant relations with all departments of human thought and action; or rather they all, with their several methods and ideals, come to enrich and stimulate philosophy, whilst philosophy, in return, reacts upon them all, by clarifying and harmonizing them each with itself and each with all the others.

There is, next, the constant conviction of the reality of moral accountableness on the one hand, and of the strength of the passions and of the allurements of sense on the other, of the costing ethical character of the search for light and truth, of the ceaseless necessity of a turning of the whole man, of conversion. "As the bodily eye cannot turn from darkness to light without the turning of the whole body, so too when the eye of the soul is turned round, the whole soul must be turned from the world of generation unto that of Being, and become able to endure the sight of Being, and of the brightest and best part of Being, that is to say of the Good."[1] Hence Philosophy is a Redemption, a Liberation, a Separation of the soul from the body, a Dying and seeking after death, a constant Purification and Recollection of the soul; and the four Cardinal Virtues are so many purifications;[2] and men who have once come to lay the blame of their own confusion and perplexity upon themselves, will hate themselves and escape from themselves into Philosophy, in order to become different and get rid of their former selves.[3]

There is, in the third place, the dominant consciousness of Multiplicity in Unity and of Unity in Multiplicity, and of the necessity of the soul's ever moving from one to the other—moving out of itself and into the world of Multiplicity, of sense and exterior work; and moving back into itself, into the world of Unity, of spirit and interior rest. Hence there is and ought to be a double movement of the soul. And this double action does not continue on the same plane, but the

[1] *Rep.* VII. 518*b*. [2] *Phaedo*, 67*c*, 64, 69*c*. [3] *Theaetetus*, 168*a*.

moving, oscillating soul is, according to the faithful thoroughness or cowardly slackness of these its movements, ever either mounting higher in truth and spirit, or falling lower away into the sensual and untruthful. For these its ascensions are "effortful," painful, gradual; they are never fully finished here below, and they nowhere attain to that absolute knowledge which is possessed by God alone.[1] "We ought," he tells us, "to strive and fly as swiftly as possible from hence thither. And to fly thither is to become like God"; but he adds, "as far as this is possible."[2]

And there is, lastly, an unfailing faith in an unexhausted, inexhaustible, transcendent world of Beauty, Truth, and Goodness, which gives of itself, but never gives itself wholly, to that phenomenal world which exists only by participation in it; and in a Supreme Goodness, felt and half conceived to be personal and self-communicative, as the cause of all that is anywhere beautiful and one and good.

These four characteristics of Universality, Conversion, Unification, Transcendence, we find them together in Greek philosophy once, and once only, namely in Plato. Twice again we have indeed a world-embracing, world-moving scheme placed before us, and in each case two of these four characteristics reappear in a deepened and developed form. For Aristotle works out, more fully and satisfactorily than Plato, the characters of Universality and of Unification; especially does the latter find a great improvement. And Plotinus insists, even more constantly and movingly than Plato, upon Conversion as a necessary means, and upon Transcendence as a necessary characteristic of all true philosophy. But Aristotle has lost the Conversion from out of his scheme, and also the Transcendence conceived as at the same time immanent in the world; and Plotinus has lost the Universality, and the Unification conceived as a Unity in Multiplicity.

4. *In Aristotle.*

As to Aristotle, the improvements upon Plato are marked and many. There is the doctrine of the non-existence of the General apart from the Particular; the doctrine of Matter as not simple Non-Being, but as Not-yet-Being, the Possible, the Not-yet-Actual, which is waiting the presence of the Form to give it the Actuality for which it is destined, since

[1] *Parmenides*, 134*c*. [2] *Theaetetus*, 176*a*.

Matter requires Form, and Form requires Matter; and the doctrine, here first fully developed, of Motion, the Moved and the Moving.

Since all Motion, Change, Natural Life spring from Form (and a particular Form), working in and with Matter (a particular and appropriate Matter), the ultimate First Moving Cause must Itself be all-moving and all-unmoved, that is, it must be Pure Form. We thus get the first at all adequate philosophical presentation of Theism: for this Pure Form is then shown to be eternal, unchanging, all thought, self-thinking, and absolutely distinct from the world which it moves. In all other real Beings the Form has, in various degrees, to contend with the manifold impediments of Matter; and in proportion to the Form's success, does the resultant Being stand high in the scale of Creation. The plant, with its vegetative and plastic soul, stands lowest in the scale of organic life; next comes the animal, with its sensitive and motive soul; and highest stands man, with his rational and volitional soul. And each higher Being takes over, as the lower part of his own nature, the functions and powers of the lower Being; and hence, since all Beings constitute so many several parts of the world's systematic whole, they are all deserving of the closest study. And Man, destined to be the highest constituent of this whole, can become so only by moving as much as may be out of his entanglement in the lower, the passive functions of his soul, and identifying himself with his true self, with that active power, that pure reason which, itself pure Form, finds its proper objects in the Forms of all things that are.

Thus we get a system of a certain grand consistency and an impressively constant re-application of certain fundamental ideas to every kind of subject-matter. But the Platonic Dualism, though everywhere vigorously attacked, is yet nowhere fully overcome.

For in Metaphysics, Plato's " One alongside of the Many " becomes with Aristotle the " One throughout the Many " : to the mind of the latter, the Separate General, Pure Form as existing without Matter, is a mere abstraction; Matter without Form is a simple potentiality; Matter and Form together, and they only, constitute the Particular, and (in and by it) all actual and full Reality. And only Reality, in the highest and primary sense, can, according to him, form the highest and primary object of Knowledge. Yet knowledge never refers to the Particular, but always to the General; and, in the Particular, only to the General manifested in it. And this is the case, not because, though the Particular is the fuller Reality, we can more easily reach the General within it; but, on the contrary, because, though we can more easily reach the Particular, the General alone is abiding and fully true and really knowable.

Again, for Aristotle the Particular, which alone really exists, is constituted a particular and really existing Being, in virtue of its participation in Matter; but it is constituted as abiding, true, and knowable, in virtue of its Form. The cause of its Reality is thus different from that of its Truth; the addition of the simple Potentiality of Matter has alone given Reality to the pure Actuality of Form.

Finally, for Aristotle all Movement, as comprehensive of every kind of change, being defined as the transition from Potentiality to Reality, as the determination of Matter by Form, can be called forth, in the last resort, only by a pure Form which, though the cause of all Motion, is itself unmoved, is pure Thought and Speculation, a thinking of thinking,—God eternally thinking God and Himself alone. Yet this God is, if thus safely distinguished from the world, yet hardly more Personal than Spirit was in Anaxagoras, or the Idea of Good was in Plato. For not only does Aristotle refuse Him a body and all psychic life, but with them he eliminates all Doing and all Producing, all Emotion and all Willing, indeed all Thinking except that of His own lonely Self-Contemplation. And yet the activity of the will is as essential to Personality as that of thinking; and thinking again we can conceive as personal only if conditioned by a diversity of objects and a variety of mental states. And this God's relations with the world are strangely few and still curiously materialistic. For He but sets the world in motion, and has no special care for it or detailed rule over it; and since, of the three or four kinds of motion, spatial motion is declared to be the primary one, and its most perfect form to be the circular, and since a circle moves quickest at its circumference, He is conceived as imparting to the world a spatial and a circular movement, and this, apparently, from a point in space, since He does so from outside. His transcendence is, so far, but a spatial one.

In Physics, Aristotle still constantly describes Nature as an harmonious, reasonable Being, an all-effecting force. There is here a mythical strain at work, and yet nowhere is a subject clearly defined to which these various qualities could be attributed.

In Anthropology, again, the active soul, the rational and free-willing, the immortal principle, is that which specially distinguishes and constitutes Humanity, and which indeed is the Form of the lower soul-powers and of the body as well. Yet it is these lower soul-powers, it is the passive, the vegetative and sensitive, the mortal soul-powers which, in and with the body, constitute this particular man, and only particular men are really existent. Where and how then is this living man's Personality, his indelible consciousness of the unity of his nature, to arise and to be found in all this medley?

And finally, in Ethics, Aristotle maintains and develops, it is true, the great Socratic tradition of conceiving all virtue as active, and demands with Plato that the whole man should, as much as may be, put himself into all his moral acts. Indeed Aristotle makes here the great advance of definitely denying the Socratic doctrine that virtue consists in knowledge, and of abolishing the Platonic distinction between ordinary and philosophic virtue. All moral qualities are, according to him, matters of the will; and arise, in the first instance, not through instruction, but through exercise and education. But in place of Plato's grandly organic, though still too abstract scheme of the Cardinal Virtues, each of the three partial ones pressing upwards and requiring and completing the others, and all three bound together by the general fourth, we get a more detailed and experimental, but only loosely co-ordinated enumeration and description of the virtuous habits, all of them so many means between two vicious extremes. The purificatory, recollective, self-fleeing, grandly organic, deeply religious tone and drift of Plato's philosophy, that priceless conviction that we must give all if we would gain all, has disappeared.

Everywhere then we get in Aristotle that noble Greek insistence, upon Action and Energy, upon Reason and Clearness, upon the General and Unification. But at all the chief turning-points we get a conflict between the General, which is alone supposed to be fully true, and the Particular, which is alone supposed to be fully real. And hence we are left with an insufficient apprehension of the inexhaustibleness of all Reality, of its indefinite apprehensibleness but ever inadequate apprehendedness. And above all, as both cause and effect of all this, we find here only a slight and intermittent hold upon the great fact and force of Personality in both God and man. In a word, if in Plato the abstracting process went in general still further than in Aristotle: in Aristotle the supply of experimental material of a spiritual kind which in Plato was ever enriching, supplementing and correcting the abstract reasoning and its results in matters of spirituality, is almost entirely in abeyance.

5. *In Plotinus and Proclus.*

In the third and last period of Greek Philosophy, we can pass by the Stoic and Epicurean, and also the Sceptical schools. For, great as was their practical importance and influence, these schools never aimed at embracing the totality of life; no one of them ever, as a matter of fact, cultivated more than one side of a purely individual self-education and peace-seeking. They reproduced and continued, on a larger scale, those interesting three minor Socratic schools which themselves had, even during the full times and universal systems of Plato and Aristotle, constituted as it were the backwaters away from the main stream of Greek speculation. The Stoic system carries on the Cynic school; the Epicurean, the Cyrenaic; and the Sceptical, the Megaric. Unity and Rest are monopolized by the Stoic, and Multiplicity and Movement by the Epicurean; whilst the Sceptic attempts to stand apart from and above both. What Socrates, Plato, and Aristotle, living in still many-sided and public-spirited times, had, in their lives and teaching, seen and practised together; now, in a period of spiritual poverty and self-seeking, is seen and practised by separate schools separately, each in external conflict with the other.

Only the system of that great mystical soul, Plotinus, has, for our present purposes, a claim on our close attention. Indeed this, the last great attempt at synthesis of the ancient Greek mind, will have to occupy us in such detail throughout a great part of this book, that here we can but briefly indicate its chief characteristics as regards the One and the Many.

It is then clear that Plotinus is an even more intensely and exclusively religious spirit than is Plato himself. Some of his descriptions of the soul's flight from the world of sense and of the soul's substantial touch of God in ecstasy, and again his penetrating apprehension of the timeless and spaceless characteristics of Spirit, have never ceased, at least indirectly, to leaven, and to lend much of their form to, the deepest recollective aspirations of religious souls in Europe and Western Asia, for some fourteen centuries at least.

Yet this religious sense is here so exclusive, and it thirsts so vehemently for perfect unity and for an infinite Superiority and utter Self-sufficingness of God, that it readily allies itself with, and reinforces by a massive enthusiasm and asceticism, the abstractive trend which, so strong at all times in Greek philosophy, was at this period already, for other reasons, growing more intensely abstractive than ever. Under this double influence Plotinus reduces the two great, deliberate, alternating movements of the soul,—its Outgoing to the Particular and Contingent, and its Incoming to the General and Infinite, as they are taught by Plato,—to one only, that of Recollection and Abstraction, a movement ever up and away, from all Multiplicity, to the One alone. And he denies to this One all Multiplicity whatsoever,—hence all such conscious, volitional action upon the world as is involved in Plato's magnificent, though never worked out, intuition that it is love, (some energizing analogous to our thinking, loving and willing the existence, the self-realization and the happiness of other self-conscious beings,) which moves the Good, as it were, to go out from Itself, and to communicate Itself to others. Here, in Plotinus's scheme, Man begins indeed with sense-impressions and imaginative picturings, with discursive reasoning and intuitive reason, with feelings, volitions, and energizings of every kind. But the more he moves up, the more of all this he leaves utterly behind; till, in ecstasy, all will, love, thought, consciousness, cease altogether. For man has thus been getting nearer and nearer, and more and more like, the One; and this One is just nothing besides sheer, pure Oneness,—it is neither Will, nor Love, nor Thought, nor Self-consciousness, in any degree or sense of these words.

Plotinus's scheme is thus indeed prompted by some of the deepest Mystical aspirations. But whilst in its one deliberate movement—that of man up to God—it starts from convictions and requirements that are deeply ethical, libertarian, spiritual, theistic: it will be shown, in its conception of the nature of the One and of this One's relations down into the world, to be curiously naturalistic and determinist, and subtly materialistic. Thus does Greek Philosophy end in an impressively all-devouring Abstraction, in an intense Realism destructive step by step, of precisely all that concrete, individual, personal Beauty, Truth, and Goodness, of all the spiritual, hence organic, interior, self-conscious reality, which had given occasion to this system. We have now but so many hypostatized abstractions, each more pale and empty than the other, each ever more simply a mere category of the human mind, indeed, but a category appropriate to Things and to Mathematico-Physical Laws, not to Spirit and to Ethico-Personal Organisms. The system, in its ultimate upshot and trend, is thus profoundly anti-Immanental, anti-Incarnational : a succession of increasingly exalted and increasingly empty Transcendences, each of which is, as it were, open upwards but closed downwards, takes the place of all deliberate operations and self-expressions of the Higher in and through the Lower, hence of all preveniences and condescensions of God.

And in Proclus, practically the last non-Christian Greek Philosopher, all these intensely abstractive, naturalistic features get finally and fully systematized, whilst but intermittent traces remain of Plato's richly manifold, organized activities and his at times strikingly incarnational conceptions; and only skeleton-schemes persist of those rapt recollective experiences of Plotinus which, derived in his case from direct experience, constitute him, among all Philosophers, as Dr. Edward Caird most aptly calls him, the "Mystic par excellence."

II. The Second of the Three Forces: Christianity, the Revelation of Personality and Depth.

Now the whole of this clear, conceptual, abstractive Greek method, in as far as it identified abstractions with realities, and names with things, and reasoning with doing, suffering, and experience; and sought for Unity outside of Multiplicity, for Rest outside of Energizing, for the Highest outside of Personality and Character as these are developed and manifested in the permeation and elevation of the lower; has in so far been succeeded and superseded by two other great world-moving experiences of the human race, experiences apparently even more antagonistic to each other than either appears to be to the Greek view: Christianity and Scientific Method.

1. *The unique fulness and closeness of unity in multiplicity of our Lord's life.*

As to Christianity, it is really impossible to compare it

directly with Hellenism, without at once under-stating its originality. For its originality consists not so much in its single doctrines, or even in its teaching as a whole, and in the particular place each doctrine occupies in this teaching, as in its revelation, through the person and example of its Founder, of the altogether unsuspected depth and inexhaustibleness of human Personality, and of this Personality's source and analogue in God, of the simplicity and yet difficulty and never-endingness of the access of man to God, and of the ever-preceding condescension of God to man. Hence if Christianity is thus throughout the Revelation of Personality; and if Personality is ever a One in Many, (and more deeply One and more richly Many, in proportion to the greatness of that spiritual reality): then we need not wonder at the difficulty we find in pointing out any one particular doctrine as constitutive of the unique originality of Christianity.

For a Person came, and lived and loved, and did and taught, and died and rose again, and lives on by His Power and His Spirit for ever within us and amongst us, so unspeakably rich and yet so simple, so sublime and yet so homely, so divinely above us precisely in being so divinely near,—that His character and teaching require, for an ever fuller yet never complete understanding, the varying study, and different experiments and applications, embodiments and unrollings of all the races and civilizations, of all the individual and corporate, the simultaneous and successive experiences of the human race to the end of time. If there is nothing shifting or fitful or simply changing about Him, there are everywhere energy and expansion, thought and emotion, effort and experience, joy and sorrow, loneliness and conflict, interior trial and triumph, exterior defeat and supplantation: particular affections, particular humiliations, homely labour, a homely heroism, greatness throughout in littleness. And in Him, for the first and last time, we find an insight so unique, a Personality so strong and supreme, as to teach us, once for all, the true attitude towards suffering.

Not one of the philosophers or systems before Him had effectually escaped falling either into Pessimism, seeing the end of life as trouble and weariness, and seeking to escape from it into some aloofness or some Nirvana; or into Optimism, ignoring or explaining away the suffering and trial which, as our first experience and as our last, surround us on every side. But with Him, and alone with Him and those who still learn and live from and by Him, there is the union of the clearest, keenest sense of all the mysterious depth and breadth and length and height of human sadness, suffering, and sin, *and*, in spite of this and through this and at the end of this, a note of conquest and of triumphant joy.

And here, as elsewhere in Christianity, this is achieved not by some artificial, facile juxtaposition: but the soul is allowed to sob itself out; and all this its pain gets fully faced and willed, gets taken up into the conscious life. Suffering thus becomes the highest form of action, a divinely potent means of satisfaction, recovery, and enlargement for the soul,—the soul with its mysteriously great consciousness of pettiness and sin, and its immense capacity for joy in self-donation.

And again, His moral and spiritual idealism, whilst indefinitely higher than that of any of the philosophers or prophets before Him, has nothing strained or restless, nothing rootless or quietistic, nothing querulous or disdainful, or of caste or sect about it: the humblest manual labour, the simplest of the human relations, the universal elemental faculties of man as man, are all entered into and developed, are all hallowed in smallest detail, and step by step.

And finally His teaching, His life, are all positive, all constructive, and come into conflict only with worldly indifference and bad faith. No teacher before Him or since, but requires, if we would not be led astray by him, that we should make some allowances, in his character and doctrine, for certain inevitable reactions, and consequent narrowness and contrarinesses. Especially is this true of religious teachers and reformers, and generally in exact proportion to the intensity of their fervour. But in Him there is no reaction, no negation, no fierceness, of a kind to deflect His teaching from its immanent, self-consistent trend. His very Apostles can ask Him to call down fire from heaven upon the unbelieving Samaritans; they can use the sword against one of those come out to apprehend Him; and they can attempt to keep the little ones from Him. But He rebukes them; He orders Peter to put back the sword in its scabbard; and He bids the little ones to come unto Him, since of such is the Kingdom of Heaven. Indeed St. Mark's Gospel tells us how the disciples begged Him to forbid a man who did not follow them from casting out devils in His name; and how He refused to do so, and laid down the great universal rule of all-embracing generosity: "He that is not against us, is for us."[1]

2. *This rich unity of life occasions three special presentations of it, the "Petrine," "Pauline," "Johannine."*

Now it is this very reality and depth, and hence the rich Unity, the growth, variety, and manifold fruitfulness of His life and teaching, which explain, as a necessity and an advantage, that we should have those successive pictures and conceptions of Him which already the New Testament presents. *Because* Socrates was so great and impressive, we have the two successive, remarkably divergent, portraits of him: the external, historical, by Xenophon; the internal, typical one, by Plato; and *that* is all. *Because* our Lord is so unspeakably greater, and continues, with inexhaustible freshness, to be the very life of the lives of Christians, we have three or four classical portraits of Him in the New Testament; and, in a certain true manner and degree, each successive age, in a measure each single soul, forms, and has to form, its own picture of Him.

We can roughly classify these pictures under the three successive types of the "Petrine," the "Pauline," and the "Johannine," provided we do not forget that the precise limits of the first of these divisions are difficult to draw, and that there are growths and diversities of aspect to be found within the Pauline type. For the Petrine type will here be sought in the Synoptic Gospels, and in particular in those accounts and sayings there which appear to give us the closest reproduction of our Lord's very acts and words and of the impressions produced by these upon the original witnesses. The Pauline type will embrace four main stages or developments: that of the four or five of the earlier Epistles—the two to the Thessalonians and those to the Galatians, Corinthians, and Romans; that of the Epistles of the Captivity, Colossians, Philippians, Ephesians; that of the Pastoral Epistles; and that of the Epistle to the Hebrews. And even in the least diversified, the Johannine type, there is the variation between the Gospel and Epistles on the one hand, and the Apocalypse on the other.

But taking these three types as each a unity, we shall hardly be guilty of an empty schematization, if the Petrine or Primitive-Apostolic group represents to us mainly the

[1] Luke ix, 44, 45; Matt. xxv, 51, 52; Mark x, 13–16; Luke ix, 50.

simplest statement of the external facts, and especially of the traditional, the Jewish side of our Lord's teaching; and if the Pauline and Johannine groups each mainly represent to us, in various degrees and combinations, the two manners in which the hidden significance of these facts, as intended for all men and for all time, can be penetrated, viz. by thought and speculation, and by feeling and operative experience.

Of course none of the three groups is without a large element common to it and to the other two : it is the same facts that are looked at and loved, by means of the same powers of the soul, and within the same great common principles and convictions. Only the precise antecedents, point of view, temper of mind; the selection, presentation, and degree of elaboration of the facts and of their spiritual meaning; the preponderance of this or that mental activity; the reasons and connections sought and seen, are often widely different in each, and produce a distinctiveness of impression which can be taken to correspond roughly to the three main powers of the soul : to the range of sense-perception and of memory; to that of reasoning; and to that of intuition, feeling, and will. If each group had *only* that element which can be taken as being its predominant one, then any single group would be of little value, and each group would imperatively require ever to be taken in conjunction with the other two. But, as a matter of fact, neither are the "Petrine" writings free from all reasoning and mystical affinities; nor are the "Pauline" free from the historic, positive spirit, or, still less, from the mystical habit; nor the "Johannine" free from the deepest teaching as to the necessity of external facts, or from some argument and appeals to reason. Hence each group, indeed each writing even singly, and still more all three groups if taken together, profoundly embody and proclaim, by the rich variety of their contents and spirit, the great principle and measure of all life and truth : unity in and through variety, and steadfastness in and through growth.

Specially easy is it to find in all three types the two chief among the three modalities of all advanced religion : the careful reverence for the external facts of nature (so far as these are known), and for social religious tradition and institutions; and the vivid consciousness of the necessity and reality of internal experience and actuation, as the single spirit's search, response and assimilation of the former.[1]

3. *The "Petrine" attestations: their special message.*

Thus the "Petrine" group gives us, as evidence for the observation and love of the external world: "Behold the birds of the heaven, how they sow not, neither do they gather into barns"; "Consider the lilies of the field how they grow; they toil not, neither do they spin: yet I say unto you, that even Solomon in all his glory was not arrayed like one of these"; "The seed springeth up and grows, the man knoweth not how; the earth beareth fruit of itself, first the blade, then the ear, then the full corn in the ear"; "When the fig-tree's branch is become tender and putteth forth its leaves, ye know that the summer is nigh"; and, "When it is evening, ye say: 'It will be fair weather: for the heaven is red.' And in the morning: 'It will be foul weather to-day: for the heaven is red and lowring.'"[2]

And as to reverence for tradition we get: "Think not that I came to destroy the law or the prophets; I came not to destroy but to fulfil." And this respect extends to existing religious practices: "Take heed," He says, "that ye do not your righteousness before men, to be seen of them," but then describes the spirit in which they are to practise their "*sedaka*," this "justice" which they are to do, with its three quite traditional divisions of alms-deeds, prayer, fasting, the three Eminent Good Works of Judaism. And again: "If thou offer thy gift upon the altar," the doing so is in nowise criticised.[3]

Indeed there is no shrinking from the manifestation, on the part of the crowd, of new and even rude forms of trust in the visible and external: "A woman which had an issue of blood twelve years, . . . came in the crowd behind, and touched His garment. For she said: 'If I touch but His garments, I shall be made whole.' And straightway the fountain of her blood was dried up"; and the crowds generally "laid the sick in the marketplaces, and besought Him that they might touch if it were but the border of His garment; and as many as touched Him were made whole"; and this

[1] I have been much helped throughout the remainder of this section by many of the groupings and discussions of texts in Prof. H. J. Holtzmann's *Lehrbuch der N. T. Theologie*, 2 vols., 1897. Inge's *Christian Mysticism*, 1899, has also, in its pp. 44–74, furnished me with some useful hints.

[2] Matt. vi, 26, 28; Mark iv, 27, 28; xiii, 28; Matt. xvi, 2, 3.

[3] Matt. v, 17; vi, 1, 2, 5, 16; v, 23.

"border" consisted doubtless in the blue tassels, the Zizith, worn by every religious Jew at the four corners of his cloak.[1]

And the twelve Apostles, whom He sends out with special instructions, "And they went out, and preached that men should repent. And they cast out many devils, and anointed with oil many that were sick, and healed them." Indeed there is, as the act preliminary to His public ministry, His baptism in the Jordan; and there is, as introductory to His Passion, the supremely solemn, visible, and audible act which crowns the Last Supper.[2]

But this same group of documents testifies also to a mystical, interior element in Our Lord's temper and teaching. "Blessed are the poor in spirit: for theirs is the kingdom of heaven," "Blessed are the pure in heart: for they shall see God," are Beatitudes which cannot be far from the *ipsissima verba* of Our Lord. "At that season Jesus answered and said, 'I thank Thee, O Father, Lord of Heaven and earth, that Thou didst hide these things from the wise and understanding, and didst reveal them unto babes: yea, Father, for so it was well-pleasing in Thy sight.' . . . 'Come unto Me, all ye that labour and are heavy laden, and I will give you rest. Take My yoke upon you, and learn of Me; for I am meek and lowly of heart: and ye shall find rest unto your souls. For My yoke is easy, and My burden is light.'" This deeply mystical passage doubtless expresses with a vivid exactitude the unique spiritual impression and renovation produced by Him within the souls of the first generations of His disciples. And the three Synoptists give us five times over the great fundamental mystical paradox: "If any man would come after Me, let him deny himself, and take up his cross, and follow Me. For whosoever would save his life shall lose it; and whosoever shall lose his life for My sake and the gospel's, shall save it." And the great law of interiority is recorded in St. Mark: "Hear Me all of you, and understand: there is nothing from without the man, that going into him can defile him: but the things which proceed out of the man are those that defile the man."[3]

And we get in Mark the fundamental interior virtue of

[1] Mark v, 25–29; vi, 56.

[2] Mark vi, 12, 13; i, 9, 10; Matt. iii, 13–19; Mark xiv, 22–25; Matt. xxvi, 26–29; Luke xxii, 15–19.

[3] Matt. v, 3, 8; xi, 25, 26, 28–30; Mark viii, 34, 35; Matt. x, 38, 39; xvi, 24, 25; Luke ix, 23, 24; xiv, 27; xvii, 33; Mark vii, 14, 15.

childlikeness, and the immanence of Christ in the childlike soul: "If any man would be first, he shall be last of all, and minister of all." "And he took a little child and set him in the midst of them: and taking him in His arms, He said unto them, 'Whosoever shall receive one of such little children in My name, receiveth Me: and whosoever receiveth Me, receiveth not Me, but Him that sent Me.'" "Suffer the little children to come unto Me; forbid them not: for of such is the kingdom of heaven." [1]

And the spirituality of the soul's life in heaven, and the eternal *Now* of God, as the Living and Vivifying Present, are given in all three Synoptists: "When they shall rise from the dead, they neither marry, nor are given in marriage; but are as angels in heaven. But as touching the dead, . . . have ye not read . . . how God spake unto him, saying, 'I am the God of Abraham, and the God of Isaac, and the God of Jacob'? He is not the God of the dead, but of the living." [2]

4. *The "Pauline" group of writings: its special teaching.* The Pauline group furnishes by far the greater amount of the explicit reasoning to be found in the New Testament; where, *e. g.*, does the New Testament furnish a parallel to the long and intricate argument of chapters third to eleventh of the Epistle to the Romans, with its constant "therefores" and "buts" and "nows"? Yet this same group of writings also emphasizes strongly, though more rarely, the external-act side of religion, and is deeply penetrated by the intuitive-emotional, the mystical spirit of Christianity.

The external, historical side is represented by the careful description and chronological arrangement observable in the account of six successive apparitions of the Risen Christ; and by the reference back to the acts and words used in the Eucharistic act at the Last Supper.[3]

Yet throughout the writings of St. Paul and of his school, it is the mystical, interior, experimental element that permeates the argumentative-speculative and the historical constituents. The chief manifestations of this mystical spirit and conviction, which really penetrates and knits together the whole of the Pauline teaching, can perhaps best be taken in a logical order.

First then it is St. Paul who, himself or through writers more or less dependent on him, gives us by far the most definite

[1] Mark ix, 35, 36; x, 14.
[2] Mark xii, 24–27; Matt. xxii, 29–33; Luke xx, 34–38.
[3] 1 Cor. xv, 3–8; xi, 23–26.

and detailed presentation of by far the most extraordinary experiences and events to be found in the New Testament outside of the Gospels themselves. For the author of the Acts of the Apostles gives us the lengthy description of the Pentecostal Visitation, and, three times over, the most vivid account of Our Lord's apparition to Saul on the way to Damascus. And St. Paul himself describes for us, at the closest first hand, the ecstatic states of the Christian communities in their earliest charismatic stage; he treats the apparition on the way to Damascus as truly objective and as on a complete par with the earlier apparitions accorded to the chosen Apostles in the first days after the Resurrection; and he gives us the solemn reference to his own experience of rapture to the third Heaven.[1] We should, however, note, in the next place, as the vital complement, indeed as the necessary pre-requisite, to this conviction and to the effectiveness of these facts,—facts conceived and recorded as external, as temporal and local,—St. Paul's profound belief that all external evidences, whether of human reasoning and philosophy or of visible miracle, fail to carry conviction without the presence of certain corresponding moral and spiritual dispositions in those to whom they are addressed. "The word of the Cross," the very same preaching, "is to them that are perishing foolishness; but unto us which are being saved it is the power of God." And the external, taken alone, can so little convince, that even the seeking after the external, without requisite dispositions, will but get us further away from its hidden function and meaning. "Jews ask for signs (miracles), and Greeks seek after wisdom (philosophy); but we preach Christ crucified, unto Jews a stumbling-block, and unto Gentiles foolishness; but unto them that are called, both Jews and Greeks, Christ the power of God and the wisdom of God. Because the foolishness of God is wiser than men; and the weakness of God is stronger than men." And the cause of this difference of interpretation is shown to lie in the various interior dispositions of the hearers: "The natural man receiveth not the things of the Spirit of God: for they are foolishness unto him; and he cannot know them, because they are spiritually judged; but he that is spiritual judgeth all things."[2]

And yet this mystery of religion has to be externally

[1] Acts ii, 1–13; ix, 1–9; xxii, 3–11; xxvi, 9–18; 1 Cor. xii; xiv; 2 Cor. xii, 1–9.

[2] 1 Cor. i, 18, 22–25; ii, 14, 15.

offered, to be preached to us, and is preached to all men; it is intended by God to be known by all, and hence it is He who stimulates men to external preaching and external hearing, as to one of the pre-requisites of its acceptance: "The mystery which hath been hid from all ages and generations: but now hath it been manifested"; he desires the Colossians to be strengthened in "the knowledge of the mystery of God and Christ"; and has to "speak the mystery of the Christ," to "make it manifest."[1]

And since this preaching, to be effective, absolutely requires, as we have seen, interior dispositions and interior illumination of the hearers, and since these things are different in different men, the degrees of initiation into this identical mystery are to be carefully adapted to the interior state of those addressed. "We speak wisdom among the perfect (τέλειοι)," the technical term in the heathen Greek Mysteries for those who had received the higher grades of initiation. "I, brethren, could not speak unto you as unto spiritual, but (only) as unto carnal, as unto babes in Christ. I fed you with milk, not with meat; for ye were not yet able."[2]

And since all good, hence also the external preaching, comes from God, still more must this all-important interior apprehension of it come from Him. In a certain real sense the Spirit is thus organ as well as object of this interior light. "But unto us God revealed" the wisdom of God "through the Spirit; for the Spirit searcheth all things, yea, the deep things of God. For who among men knoweth the things of a man, save the spirit of the man which is in him? even so the things of God none knoweth, save the Spirit of God."[3]

But further, the mystery revealed in a unique degree and form in Christ's life, is really a universal spiritual-human law; the law of suffering and sacrifice, as the one way to joy and possession, which has existed, though veiled till now, since the foundation of the world. "The mystery of Christ, which in other generations was not made known unto the sons of men, as it hath now been revealed to His holy apostles and prophets in the spirit." And this law, which is Christ's life, must reappear in the life of each one of us. "We have been buried together with Him through Baptism unto death, in order that, as Christ rose again from the dead through the glory of the Father, so we also may walk in the newness

[1] Col. i, 26; ii, 2; iv, 3, 4. [2] I Cor. ii, 6; iii, 1.
[3] I Cor. ii, 10, 11.

of life"; "We know that our old man was crucified with Him. . . . But if we have died with Christ, we believe that we shall also live with Him"; "If the Spirit of him that raised up Jesus from the dead dwelleth in you, He that raised Jesus from the dead shall quicken also your mortal bodies through His Spirit that dwelleth in you." [1]

Christ's life can be thus the very law of all life, because "He is the first-born of all creation, for in Him were all things created, in the heavens and upon the earth," "all things have been created through Him"; "and He is before all things, and in Him all things consist"; "all things are summed up in Christ"; "Christ is all in all." So that in the past, before His visible coming, the Jews in the desert "drank of a spiritual rock that followed them: and the rock was Christ." And as He Himself is the perfect image of God, so all things are, in varying degrees, created in the image of Christ: "(Christ) who is the image of the invisible God"; "in Him were all things created." And since man is, in his original and potential essence, in a very special sense "the image and glory of God," his perfecting will consist in a painful reconquest and development of this obscured and but potential essence, by becoming, as far as may be, another Christ, and living through the successive stages of Christ's earthly life. We are bidden "all attain . . . unto a full-grown man, unto the measure of the stature of the fulness of Christ," so that, in the end, we may be able to say with the Apostle himself: "I live; and yet no longer I, but Christ liveth in me"; a consummation which appears so possible to St. Paul's mind, that he eagerly, painfully longs for it: "My little children, of whom I am again in travail, until Christ be formed in you." And indeed "we all, with unveiled face reflecting as a mirror the glory of the Lord, are transformed into the same image from glory to glory, even as from the Lord the Spirit." [2]

We have then in St. Paul not only a deeply mystical element, but mysticism of the noblest, indeed the most daringly speculative, world-embracing type.

5. *The "Johannine" group: its characteristic truths.*

And finally the Johannine group furnishes us with an instance, as strong as it is conceivable within the wide pale of a healthy Christian spirit, of the predominance of an interior and intuitive, mystical, universalistic, spiritual and symbolic

[1] Eph. iii, 4; Rom. vi, 6, 8; viii, 11.
[2] Col. i, 15–17; Eph. i, 10; Col. iii, 11; 1 Cor. x, 4; Col. i, 15, 17; iii, 11; Eph. iv, 13; Gal. ii, 20; iv, 19; 2 Cor. iii, 18.

apprehension and interpretation both of external fact and of explicit reasoning.

The Visible and Historical is indeed emphasized, with a full consciousness of the contrasting Gnostic error, in the culminating sentence of the solemn Prologue of the Gospel, "And the Word became Flesh, and dwelt amongst us (and we beheld His glory)," and in the equally emphatic opening sentence of the First Epistle: "That which was from the beginning, that which we have heard, that which we have seen with our eyes, that which we beheld, and our hands handled, . . . we announce unto you." Hence too the Historical, Temporal Last Judgment, with its corporal resurrection, remains as certainly retained in this Gospel as in St. Matthew: "The hour cometh, in which all that are in the tombs shall hear His voice; shall come forth; they that have done good, unto the resurrection of life; and they that have done ill, unto the resurrection of judgment."[1]

And Reasoning of a peculiarly continuous, rhythmically recurrent pattern, is as present and influential everywhere, as it is difficult to describe or even to trace. For it is here but the instrument and reflex of certain Mystical conceptions and doctrines, of a tendency to see, in everything particular and temporal, the Universal and Eternal; to apprehend Unity, a changeless Here and Now, in all multiplicity and succession, and hence to suppress explicit reasoning and clear distinctions, movement, growth, and change, as much as may be, both in the method of presentation and in the facts presented. If the Synoptists give us the successive, and write, unconsciously but specially, under the category of Time: the Fourth Gospel consciously presents us with simultaneity, and works specially under the category of Space.

The Successive is here conceived as but the appearance of the Simultaneous, of the Eternal and Abiding. Hence the historical development in the earthly experiences, teachings, and successes of Christ is ignored: His Godhead, that which *is*, stands revealed from the first in the appearances of His earthly life. Hence too the various souls of other men are presented to us as far as possible under one eternal and changeless aspect; they are types of various abiding virtues and iniquities, rather than concrete, composite mortals.

[1] John i, 14; 1 John i, 1; John v, 28, 29.

God appears here specially as Light, as Love, and as Spirit. Yet these largely thing-like attributions co-exist with personal qualities, and with real, ethical relations between God and the world: "God so loved the world, that He gave His only begotten Son, that whosoever believeth on Him shall not perish, but have eternal life." The Father "draws" men, and "sends" His Son into the world.[1]

And this Son has eternally pre-existed with the Father; is the very instrument and principle of the world's creation; and "is the true Light that lighteth every man coming into the world." And this Word which, from the first, was already the Light of all men, became Flesh specially to manifest fully this its Life and Light. Indeed He is the only Light, and Way, and Truth, and Life; the only Door; the Living Bread; the true Vine.[2]

This Revelation and Salvation is indeed assimilated by individual souls and is received by them at a given moment, by a birth both new and from above, and is followed by a new knowledge. But this knowledge is not absolute nor unprogressive. Everywhere the Evangelist has indeed the verb γιγνώσκω, but nowhere the noun Gnosis; and the full meaning of the Revelation of the Father by the Son is to be only gradually revealed by the Holy Spirit. And this special new knowledge is not the cause but the effect of an ethical act on the part of the human soul,—an act of full trust in the persons of God and of His Christ, and in the intimations of the moral conscience as reflections of the divine will and nature. "If any man willeth to do His will, he shall know of the teaching, whether it be of God, or whether I speak from myself"; "He that doeth the truth, cometh to the light." [3]

And this trust, and the experimental knowledge which flows from it, lead to an interior conviction so strong as to make us practically independent of external evidences. Hence in the First Epistle, this "we *know*" is repeatedly emphasized: "We *know* that, if He shall be manifested, we shall be like Him"; "Ye *know* that He was manifested to take away sins." And this knowledge is communicated by the Spirit of God to man's soul; the spirit bearing witness, there within, to the truth of Christ's words, communicated

[1] I John i, 5; iv, 8; John iv, 24; iii, 16; vi, 44; xvii, 18.
[2] John xvii, 24; viii, 58; i, 3, 10; i, 9; I John i, 2; John i, 11; xiv, 6; x, 7–9; vi, 35; xv, 1.
[3] John iii, 3, 5; I John v, 10; John vii, 17; iii, 21.

from without. "It is the Spirit that beareth witness, because the Spirit is the Truth."[1]

External signs (miracles), and a certain un-ethical assent given to them and their implications, these things are, even at their best, but preliminary, and, of themselves, insufficient. Hence Our Lord can find "many who believed in His name, seeing His signs (miracles) which He did"; and yet could "not trust Himself to them." Nicodemus indeed can come to Our Lord, moved by the argument that "thou hast come a teacher from God, for no man can do the signs (miracles) that thou doest, unless God be with him." But then Our Lord's whole conversation with him renders clear how imperfect and ignorant Nicodemus is so far,—he had come by night, his soul was still in darkness. So also "many Samaritans believed in Him," because of His sign,—His miraculous knowledge of her past history, shown to the Woman at the Well; but more of them believed because of His own words to them: "We have (now) heard for ourselves, and *know* that this is indeed the Saviour of the world." Hence He can Himself bid the Apostles, in intimation of their full and final privilege and duty, "believe in Me" (that is, My words and the Spirit testifying within you to their Truth), "that I am in the Father, and the Father in Me"; and, only secondarily and failing that fulness, "but if not, then believe, because of the very works." And the whole Johannine doctrine as to the object and method of Faith is dramatically presented and summed up in the great culminating scene and saying of the Fourth Gospel: "Thomas" (the Apostle who would see a visible sign first, and would then build his Faith upon that sight) "saith to Him: 'My Lord and my God.' Jesus saith to him: 'Because thou hast seen Me, thou hast believed; blessed are they that have not seen, and yet have believed.'"[2]

And this Faith and Knowledge arising thus, in its fulness, at most only on occasion, and never because, of spatial and temporal signs, are conceived as a timeless, Eternal Life, and as one which is already, here and now, an actual present possession. "He that believeth on the Son hath eternal life"; "He that heareth My word, and believeth Him that sent Me, hath eternal life"; "We know that we have passed from death unto life"; "We know Him that is true, and we are in Him

[1] 1 John iii, 2, 5; v, 7.
[2] John ii, 23, 24; iii, 2; iv, 39, 42; xiv, 11; xx, 29.

that is true, even in His Son Jesus Christ. This is the true God and eternal life." [1] There is then a profound immanence of Christ in the believing soul, and of such a soul in Christ; and this mutual immanence bears some likeness to the Immanence of the Father in Christ, and of Christ in the Father. "In that day" (when "the Father shall give you the Spirit of Truth") "ye shall know that I am in My Father, and ye in Me, and I in you." [2]

III. Science: the Apprehension and Conception of Brute Fact and Iron Law.

But now, athwart both the Hellenic and the Christian factors of our lives, the first apparently so clear and complete and beautiful, the latter, if largely dark and fragmentary, so deep and operative, comes and cuts a third and last factor, that of Science, apparently more peremptory and irresistible than either of its predecessors.[3] For both the former factors would appear to melt into mid-air before this last one. *They* evidently cannot ignore *it; it* apparently can ignore *them.* If Metaphysics and Religion seem involved in a perpetual round of interminable questions, solved, at most and at best, for but this man and for that, and with an evidence for their truth which can be and is gainsaid by many, but cannot be demonstrated with a peremptory clearness to any one: Science, on the other hand, would appear to give us just this *terra firma* of an easy, immediate, undeniable, continually growing, patently fruitful body of evidence and of fact.

And not only can Metaphysics and Religion not ignore Science, in the sense of denying or even overlooking its existence; they cannot apparently, either of them, even begin or proceed or end without constant reference, here frank and open, there tacit but none the less potent, to the enterprises, the methods, the conclusions of the Sciences one and all, and this even in view of establishing their own contentions. And more and more of the territory formerly assigned to Metaphysics or Religion seems in process of being conquered by Science: in Metaphysics, by experimental psychology, and by

[1] John iii, 36; v, 24; 1 John iii, 14; v, 20.

[2] John xiv, 20, 21.

[3] I have been much helped in this section by Prof. R. Eucken's admirably discriminating, vivid book, *Die Lebensanschauungen der grossen Denker*, in its first and fourth editions, 1890, 1902.

the simple history of the various philosophical systems, ideas, and technical terms, and of the local and temporal, racial and cultural antecedents and environments which gave rise to them; in Religion, by an analogous observation and study of man in the past and present, of man studied from within and from without.

1. *Three characteristics of this scientific spirit.*

Now this scientific spirit has hitherto, since its birth at the Renaissance, ever tended to the ever-increasing development of three main characteristics, which are indeed but several aspects of one single aim and end. There was and is, for one thing, the passion for Clearness, which finds its expression in the application of Mathematics and of the Quantitative view and standard to all and every subject-matter, in so far as the latter is conceived as being truly knowable at all. There was and is, for another, the great concept of Law, of an iron Necessity running through and expressing itself in all things, one great Determinism, before which all emotion and volition, all concepts of Spontaneity and Liberty, of Personality and Spirit, either Human or Divine, melt away, as so many petty subjective wilfulnesses of selfish, childish, "provincial" man, bent on fantastically humanizing this great, cold thing, the Universe, into something responsive to his own profoundly unimportant and objectively uninteresting sensations and demands. There was and is, for a third thing, a vigorous Monism, both in the means and in the end of this view. Our sources of information are *but one*,—the reasoning, reckoning Intellect, backed up by readily repeatable, directly verifiable Experiment. The resultant information is *but one*,—the Universe within and without, a strict unbroken Mechanism.

If we look at the most characteristically modern elements of Descartes, and, above all, of Spinoza, we cannot fail to find throughout, as the reaction of this Scientific spirit upon Philosophy, the passion for those three things: for Clearness and ready Transferableness of ideas; for one universal, undeniable Common Element and Measure for all knowledge of every degree and kind; and for Law, omnipresent and inexorable. That is, we have here a passion for Thing as over against, as above, Person; for the elimination of all wilfulness, even at the cost of will itself, of all indetermination, obscurity and chance, even at the cost of starving and drying up whole regions of our complex nature, whole sources of information, and of violently simplifying and impoverishing the outlook on to reality both within us and without.

2. *Fundamental motive of entire quest, deeply legitimate, indeed religious : Spinoza, Leibniz, Kant.*

And yet how unjust would he be who failed to recognize, in the case of Spinoza especially, the noble, and at bottom deeply religious, motives and aspirations underlying such excesses; or the new problems and necessities, the permanent growth and gain, which this long process of human thought has brought to Religion itself, especially in indirect and unintentional ways!

For as to the motives, it ought not to be difficult to any one who knows human history and human nature to see how the all but complete estrangement from Nature and Physical Fact which (from Socrates onwards, with the but very partial exception of Aristotle) had, for well-nigh two thousand years, preceded this reaction; how the treatment of Matter and the Visible as more or less synonymous with Non-Being and Irrationality, as a veil or even a wall, as a mere accident or even a positive snare, lying everywhere between us and Reality, could not fail to require and produce a swing of the pendulum in the opposite direction. And the feeling and the perception of how superficial and unreal, how oppressively confined, how intolerably fixed and ultimate, how arrogant and cold and fruitless, such persistent neglect of the Data of Sense had somehow, at last, rendered philosophy, gave now polemical edge to men's zealous study and discovery of *this* world. This study was perceived, even by the shallower thinkers, to be fair and rational and fruitful in itself; and it was found, by some few deep spirits, to be a strangely potent means of purifying, enlarging, "deprovincializing" man himself. The severe discipline of a rigorous study of man's lowly, physical conditions and environment, things hitherto so despised by him, was now at last to purify him of his own childish immediacy of claim. The pettily selfish, shouting Individual was to pass through the broad, still, purgatorial waters of a temporary submergence under the conceptions, as vivid as though they were direct experiences, of ruthless Law, of Mechanism, of the Thing; so as to pass out, purified and enlarged, a Person, expressive of the Universal and Objective, of Order and of Law.

It is especially in Spinoza that this deeper, universally human and ethical, indeed we can say religious, implication and ideal of the rigorously scientific spirit is present in all its noble intuition and aspiration, and that at the same time, alas! this deep truth is forced into a ruinously inappropriate method and formulation. For the original end of the entire quest, an end which is still emotionally dominant and which furnishes the hidden dialectic of the whole,—Man, his nobility and interior purification and beatitude,—has here, intellectually, become but a means; Man, in the real logic of this system, is, hopelessly and finally, but a wheel in the huge mechanism of that *natura naturata* which Spinoza's own richness and nobility of character transcends with potent inconsistency. And this very system, which is so nobly human and Christian in its ethical tone and in its demand of a Conversion of the whole man, in its requiring man to lose and sacrifice his petty self that he may gain his true self and become a genuine constituent of the Universe and Thought of God, is also the very one which, by its ruthless Naturalism and Determinism of Doctrine and its universally Mathematical and Quantitative form and method, logically eliminates all such qualitative differentiation and conversion as impossible and futile.

The prima facie view of life as it presents itself to the clarifying, Scientific Intellect, namely the omnipresence of the determinist mechanism, has never been more impressively felt and pictured than by Spinoza; the dispositions and happiness of the purified, disinterested soul have rarely been experienced and described with more touching elevation and power. But there is no real transition, indeed no possibility of such, in his system, from that first aspect to this latter state; for that first aspect, that apparent determinism, is for his logic *not* merely apparent or secondary, but the very truth of truths, the very core and end of things.

And this bondage of mind to matter, this enslavement of the master to the servant, this narrow, doctrinaire intellectualism and determinism, is more hidden than cured in Leibniz, who, if he brings the immense improvement because enrichment of a keen sense and love of the Historical, loses, on the other hand, Spinoza's grandly Conversional tone and temper. A cheerful, easy, eminently sane but quite inadequate bustle of manifold interests; a ready, pleasant optimism; an endless laboriousness of the reasoning faculty; all this, even though carried out on a scale unique since the days of Aristotle, is necessarily unequal to face and bear "the burthen of all this unintelligible world."

And yet here, in him who may not unfitly be called the last of the Dogmatic Rationalists and Optimists, we have already those great perceptions which were destined more and more to burst the bonds of this cold, clear, complete, confining outlook. For one thing, as already stated, there is, alongside the love of the Material and Mathematical, an almost equal love of the Historical and Human. There is, for another thing, the deep consciousness of the Individuality and Interiority of all real existences,—all that *is* at all, has an inside to it. And, finally, in further enforcement of this latter doctrine, there is the fruitful conception of Sub-conscious States of feeling and of mind in all living things.

Yet it is only in Kant that,—with all his obscurities and numberless demonstrable inconsistencies, with all his saddening impoverishment of the outlook in many ways,—we get, little conscious as he himself is of such a service, the deep modern explanation of the ancient pre-scientific neglect and suspicion of natural research. Here we are led to see that the strictly Scientific view of Nature is necessarily quantitative, but that the strictly Ethical, Spiritual view of man is as necessarily qualitative; that the analysis of all natural phenomena but leads to judgments as to what *is*, whereas the requirements of human action lead to judgments of what *ought to be*. Here the weak point lies in the contrast, established by him and pushed to the degree of mutual exclusion, between Reason and Will. For the contrast which we find in actual life is really between the deeper reason, ever closely accompanied by deep emotion, this reason and emotion occasioning, and strengthened by, the action of the whole man,—and all this is not directly transferable; and the more superficial reasoning, having with it little or no emotion,—the action of but one human faculty,—and this action is readily transferable.

3. *Place and function of such science in the totality of man's life.*

The mistake in the past would thus lie, not in the doctrine that the Visible cannot suffice for man and is not his mind's true home; nor in the implication that the Visible cannot directly and of itself reveal to him the Spiritual world. The error would lie entirely in the double implication or doctrine, that there is really nothing to be known about Nature, or that what can be known of it can be attained by Metaphysical or Mystical methods; and again that strictly quantitative, severe scientific method and investigation can, even in the long run, be safely neglected by the human soul, as far as its own spiritual health is concerned.

We take it then that mankind has, after endless testings and experiences, reached the following conclusions. We encounter everywhere, both within us and without, both in the physical and mental world, in the first instance, a whole network of phenomena; and these phenomena are everywhere found to fall under certain laws, and to be penetrable by certain methods of research, these laws and methods varying indeed in character and definiteness according to the subject-matter to which they apply, but in each case affording to man simply indefinite scope for discovery without, and for self-discipline within.

And all this preliminary work and knowledge does not directly require religion nor does it directly lead to it; indeed we shall spoil both the knowledge itself, and its effect upon our souls and upon religion, if religion is here directly introduced. The phenomena of Astronomy and Geology, of Botany and Zoology, of human Physiology and Psychology, of Philology and History are, and ought to be, in the first instance, the same for all men, whether the said men do or do not eventually give them a *raison d'être* and formal rational interest by discovering the metaphysical and religious convictions and conclusions which underlie and alone give true unity to them and furnish a living link between the mind observing and the things observed. Various as are these phenomena, according to the department of human knowledge to which they severally belong, yet they each and all have to be, in the first instance, discovered and treated according to principles and methods immanent and special to that department.

And the more rigorously this is accomplished, both by carrying out these principles and methods to their fullest extent, and by conscientiously respecting their limits of applicability and their precise degree of truth and of range in the larger scheme of human activity and conviction, the more will such science achieve three deeply ethical, spiritually helpful results.

Such science will help to discipline, humble, purify the natural eagerness and wilfulness, the cruder forms of anthropomorphism, of the human mind and heart. This turning to the visible will thus largely take the place of that former turning away from it; for only since the Visible has been taken to represent laws, and, provisionally at least, rigorously mechanical laws characteristic of itself, can it be thus looked upon as a means of spiritual purification.

Such science again will help to stimulate those other, deeper activities of human nature, which have made possible, and have all along preceded and accompanied, these more superficial ones; and this, although such science will doubtless tend to do the very opposite, if the whole nature be allowed to become exclusively engrossed in this one phenomenal direction. Still it remains true that perhaps never has man turned to the living God more happily and humbly, than when coming straight away from such rigorous, disinterested phenomenal analysis, as long as such analysis is felt to be both other than, and preliminary and secondary to, the deepest depths of the soul's life and of all ultimate Reality.

And finally, such science will correspondingly help to give depth and mystery, drama and pathos, a rich spirituality, to the whole experience and conception of the soul and of life, of the world and of God. Instead of a more or less abstract picture, where all is much on the same plane, where all is either fixed and frozen, or all is in a state of feverish flux, we get an outlook, with foreground, middle distances, and background, each contrasting with, each partially obscuring, partially revealing, the other; but each doing so, with any freshness and fulness, only in and through the strongly willing, the fully active and gladly suffering, the praying, aspiring, and energizing spiritual Personality, which thus both gives and gets its own true self ever more entirely and more deeply.

4. *Science to be taken, throughout our life, in a double sense and way.*

In such a conception of the place of Science, we have permanently to take Science, throughout life, in a double sense and way. In the first instance, Science is self-sufficing, its own end and its own law. In the second instance, which alone is ever final, Science is but a part of a whole, but a function, a necessary yet preliminary function, of the whole of man; and it is but part, a necessary yet preliminary part, of his outlook. Crush out, or in any way mutilate or de-autonomize, this part, and all the rest will suffer. Sacrifice the rest to this part, either by starvation or attempted suppression, or by an impatient assimilation of this immense remainder to that smaller and more superficial part, and the whole man suffers again, and much more seriously.

And the danger, in both directions,—let us have the frankness to admit the fact,—is constant and profound : even to see it continuously is difficult ; to guard against it with effect, most difficult indeed. For to starve or to suspect, to cramp or to crush this phenomenal apprehension and investigation, in the supposed interest of the ulterior truths, must ever be a besetting temptation and weakness for the religious instinct, wherever this instinct is strong and fixed, and has not yet itself been put in the way of purification.

For Religion is ever, *qua* religion, authoritative and absolute. What constitutes religion is not simply to hold a view and to try to live a life, with respect to the Unseen and the Deity, as possibly or even certainly beautiful or true or good : but precisely that which is over and above this,—the holding this view and this life to proceed somehow from God Himself, so as to bind my innermost mind and conscience to unhesitating assent. Not simply that I think it, but that, in addition, I feel bound to think it, transforms a thought about God into a religious act.

Now this at once brings with it a double and most difficult problem. For Religion thus becomes, by its very genius and in exact proportion to its reality, something so entirely *sui generis*, so claimful and supreme, that it at once exacts a twofold submission, the one simultaneous, the other successive; the first as it were in space, the second in time. The first regards the relations of religion to things non-religious. It might be parodied by saying : " Since religion is true and supreme, religion is all we require : all things else must be bent or broken to her sway." She has at the very least the right to a primacy not of honour only, but of direct jurisdiction, over and within all activities and things. The second regards the form and concept of religion itself. Since religion always appears both in a particular form at a particular time and place, *and* as divine and hence authoritative and eternal ; and since the very strength and passion of religion depend upon the vigorous presence and close union of these two elements : religion will ever tend either really to oppose all change within itself, or else to explain away its existence. Religion would thus appear doomed to be either vague and inoperative, or obscurantist and insincere.

And it is equally clear that the other parts of man's nature and of his outlook cannot simply accept such a claim, nor could religion itself flourish at all if they could and did accept it. They cannot accept the claim of religion to be immediately and simply all, for they are fully aware of being themselves something also. They cannot accept her claim to dictate to them their own domestic laws, for they are fully aware that they each, to live truly at all, require their own laws and their own, at least relative, autonomy. However much man may be supremely and finally a religious animal, he is not *only* that; but he is a physical and sexual, a fighting and an artistic, a domestic and social, a political and philosophical animal as well.

Nor can man, even simply *qua* religious man, consent to a simple finality in the experience and explication, in the apprehension and application of religion, either in looking back into the past; or in believing and loving, suffering and acting in the present; or in forecasting the future, either of the race or of himself alone. For the *here and now*, the concrete "immediacy," the unique individuality of the religious experience for *me*, in this room, on this very day, its freshness, is as true and necessary a quality of living religion as any other whatsoever. And if all life sustains itself only by constant, costing renovation and adaptation of itself to its environment, the religious life, as the most intense and extensive of all lives, must somehow be richest in such newness in oldness, such renovative, adaptive, assimilative power.

5. *All this seen at work in man's actual history.*

Now it is deeply instructive to observe all this at work historically. For here we find every variety of attitude towards this very point. There are men of Religion who attempt to do without Science, and men of Science who attempt to do without Religion. Or again, men of Religion attempt to *level up*,—to assimilate the principles and results of the various sciences directly to religion, or at least to rule those scientific principles and results directly by religion. Or men of Science attempt to *level down*, to make religion into a mere philosophy or even a natural history. Yet we find also,—with so persistent a recurrence in all manner of places and times, as itself to suggest the inherent, essential, indestructible truth of the view,—another, a far more costing attitude. This attitude refuses all mutilation either of normal human nature or of its outlook, all oppression of one part by the other; for it discovers that these various levels of life have been actually practised in conjunction by many an individual in the past and in the present; and that, where they have been practised within a large organization of faith and love, they have ever led to a fuller reality and helpfulness both of the science and of the religion concerned. Hence the mind thus informed cannot doubt the truth of this solution, however difficult at all times may be its practice, and however little final at any time can be its detailed intellectual analysis.

IV. Summing up: Hellenism or Harmonization, Christianity or Spiritual Experience, and Science or Acceptance of a Preliminary Mechanism, all three necessary to Man.

To sum up all this first chapter, we have got so far as this. We have seen that humanity has, so far, found and worked out three forces and conceptions of life, forces which are still variously operative in each of us, but which find their harmonious interaction in but few men, their full theoretical systematization in none.[1]

There is the ancient, Greek contribution, chiefly intellectual and aesthetic, mostly cold and clear, quick and conclusive, with, upon the whole, but a slight apprehension of personality and freedom, of conscience and of sin, and little or no sense of the difference and antagonism between these realities and simply Mathematical, Mechanical laws and concepts. It is a view profoundly abstract, and, at bottom, determinist: the will follows the intellect necessarily, in exact proportion to the clearness of information of the former. And the strength of this view, which was possible even to that gifted race just because of the restrictedness of its knowledge concerning the length and breadth of nature and of history, and still more with regard to the depths of the human character and conscience, consists in its freshness, completeness, and unity. And this ideal of an ultimate harmonization of our entire life and of its theory we must never lose, more and more difficult though its even approximate realization has of necessity become.

There is next the middle, Christian contribution, directly moral and religious, deep and dim and tender, slow and far-reaching, immensely costly, infinitely strong; with its discovery and exemplification of the mysterious depth and range and complexity of human personality and freedom, of

[1] I have been much helped, towards what follows here, by pages 51 to 128 in M. Maurice Blondel's great book, *l'Action*, 1893.

conscience and of sin; a view profoundly concrete and at bottom libertarian. The goodwill here first precedes, and then outstrips, and determines the information supplied by the intellect: "Blessed are the clean of heart, for they shall see God." And the strength of this position consists in its being primarily not a view, but a life, a spiritual, religious life, requiring, implying, indeed proclaiming, definite doctrines concerning God and man, and their relations to each other, but never exhausted by these doctrines even in their collectivity, inexhaustible though these in their turn are by their union with the life of the spirit, their origin and end.

There is finally the modern, Scientific contribution, intensely impersonal and determinist, directly neither metaphysical nor religious, but more abstract even than the Greek view, in the mathematical constituent of its method, and more concrete in a sense than Christianity itself, in the other, the sensible-experiment constituent of its method. The most undeniable of abstractions, those of mathematics, (undeniable just because of their enunciation of nothing but certain simplest relations between objects, supposing those objects to exist,) are here applied to the most undeniable of concretions, the direct experiences of the senses. And this mysterious union which, on the surface, is so utterly heterogeneous, is itself at all explicable only on mental, metaphysical assumptions and on the admission of the reality and priority of Mind. It is a union that has turned out as unassailable in its own province, as it is incapable of suppressing or replacing the wider and deeper truths and lives discovered for us respectively by Hellenism and Christianity.

Only in the case that man could but reckon mathematically and observe with his senses, or in the case that man were indeed provided with other faculties, but that he found Reality outside him and within him to be properly apprehensible by the mathematico-experimental process alone, could there be any serious question of such a final suppression of by far the greater and deeper portion of himself. Instead of any such deadlock the facts of these last four centuries bear out the contention that neither can the religious life suppress or do without the philosophical and the scientific, nor can either of these other two lives suppress or permanently do without its fellow or without religion.

But all this and its detailed practical application will, I trust, become much clearer as we proceed.

CHAPTER II

THE THREE ELEMENTS OF RELIGION

INTRODUCTORY.

WE have found then that all life and all truth are, for all their unity, deeply complex, for us men at all events; indeed that they are both in exact proportion to their reality. In this, our second chapter, I should like to show the complexity special to the deepest kind of life, to Religion; and to attempt some description of the working harmonization of this complexity. If Religion turned out to be simple, in the sense of being a monotone, a mere oneness, a whole without parts, it could not be true; and yet if Religion be left too much a mere multiplicity, a mere congeries of parts without a whole, it cannot be persuasive and fully operative. And the several constituents are there, whether we harbour, recognize, and discipline them or not; but these constituents will but hinder or supplant each other, in proportion as they are not somehow each recognized in their proper place and rank, and are not each allowed and required to supplement and to stimulate the other. And though no amount of talk or theory can, otherwise than harmfully, take the place of life, yet observation and reflection can help us to see where and how life acts: what are the causes, or at least the concomitants, of its inhibition and of its stimulation and propagation, and can thus supply us with aids to action, which action will then, in its turn, help to give experimental fulness and precision to what otherwise remains a more or less vague and empty scheme.

I. THE THREE ELEMENTS, AS THEY SUCCESSIVELY APPEAR IN THE CHILD, THE YOUTH, AND THE ADULT MAN.

Now if we will but look back upon our own religious life, we shall find that, in degrees and in part in an order of succession varying indefinitely with each individual, three modalities, three modes of apprehension and forms of appeal and of outlook, have been and are at work within us and around.[1]

1. *Sense and Memory, the Child's means of apprehending Religion.*

In the doubtless overwhelming majority of cases, there came first, as far as we can reconstruct the history of our consciousness, the appeal to our infant senses of some external religious symbol or place, some picture or statue, some cross or book, some movement of some attendant's hands and eyes. And this appeal would generally have been externally interpreted to us by some particular men or women, a Mother, Nurse, Father, Teacher, Cleric, who themselves would generally have belonged to some more or less well-defined traditional, institutional religion. And their appeal would be through my senses to my imaginative faculty first, and then to my memory of that first appeal, and would represent the principle of authority in its simplest form.

All here as yet works quasi-automatically. The little child gets these impressions long before itself can choose between, or even is distinctly conscious of them; it believes whatever it sees and is told, equally, as so much fact, as something to build on. If you will, it believes these things to be true, but not in the sense of contrasting them with error; the very possibility of the latter has not yet come into sight. And at this stage the External, Authoritative, Historical, Traditional, Institutional side and function of Religion are everywhere evident. Cases like that of John Stuart Mill, of being left outside of all religious tradition, we may safely say, will ever remain exceptions to help prove the rule. The five senses then, perhaps that of touch first, and certainly that of sight most; the picturing and associative powers of the imagination; and the retentiveness of the memory, are the side of human nature specially called forth. And the external, sensible, readily picturable facts and the picturing functions of religion correspond to and feed this side, as readily as does the mother's milk correspond to and feed that same mother's infant. Religion is here, above all, a Fact and Thing.

2. *Question and Argument, the Youth's mode of approaching Religion.*

But soon there wakes up another activity and requirement

[1] I have found much help towards formulating the following experiences and convictions in Professor William James's striking paper, "Reflex Action and Theism," in *The Will to Believe*, pp. 111–114, 1897.

of human nature, and another side of religion comes forth to meet it. Direct experience, for one thing, brings home to the child that these sense-informations are not always trustworthy, or identical in its own case and in that of others. And, again, the very impressiveness of this external religion stimulates indeed the sense of awe and of wonder, but it awakens curiosity as well. The time of trustful questioning, but still of questioning, first others, then oneself, has come. The old impressions get now more and more consciously sought out, and selected from among other conflicting ones; the facts seem to clamour for reasons to back them, against the other hostile facts and appearances, or at least against those men in books, if not in life, who dare to question or reject them. Affirmation is beginning to be consciously exclusive of its contrary: I begin to feel that *I* hold *this*, and that *you* hold *that;* and that I cannot do both; and that I do the former, and exclude and refuse the latter.

Here it is the reasoning, argumentative, abstractive side of human nature that begins to come into play. Facts have now in my mind to be related, to be bound to other facts, and men to men; the facts themselves begin to stand for ideas or to have the latter in them or behind them. The measuring-rod seems to be over all things. And religion answers this demand by clear and systematic arguments and concatenations: this and this is now connected with that and that; this is true or this need not be false, because of that and that. Religion here becomes Thought, System, a Philosophy.

3. *Intuition, Feeling, and Volitional requirements and evidences, the Mature Man's special approaches to Faith.*

But yet a final activity of human nature has to come to its fullest, and to meet its response in a third side of Religion. For if in Physiology and Psychology all action whatsoever is found to begin with a sense-impression, to move through the central process of reflection, and to end in the final discharge of will and of action, the same final stage can be found in the religious life. Certain interior experiences, certain deep-seated spiritual pleasures and pains, weaknesses and powers, helps and hindrances, are increasingly known and felt in and through interior and exterior action, and interior suffering, effort, and growth. For man is necessarily a creature of action, even more than of sensation and of reflection; and in this action of part of himself against other parts, of himself with or against other men, with or against this or that external fact or condition, he grows and gradually comes to his real self, and gains certain experiences as to the existence and nature and growth of this his own deeper personality.

Man's emotional and volitional, his ethical and spiritual powers, are now in ever fuller motion, and they are met and fed by the third side of religion, the Experimental and Mystical. Here religion is rather felt than seen or reasoned about, is loved and lived rather than analyzed, is action and power, rather than either external fact or intellectual verification.

II. Each Element ever accompanied by some amount of the other two. Difficulty of the Transitions from one stage to the other.

Now these three sides of the human character, and corresponding three elements of Religion, are never, any one of them, without a trace or rudiment of the other two; and this joint presence of three such disparate elements ever involves tension, of a fruitful or dangerous kind.[1]

1. *Utility of this joint presence.*

In the living human being indeed there never exists a mere apprehension of something external and sensible, without any interior elaboration, any interpretation by the head and heart. We can hardly allow, we can certainly in nowise picture to ourselves, even an infant of a few hours old as working, and being worked upon, by nothing beyond these sense-perceptions alone. Already some mental, abstractive, emotional-volitional reaction and interpretation is presumably at work; and not many weeks or months pass before this is quite obviously the case. And although, on the other hand, the impressions of the senses, of the imagination and the memory are, normally, more numerous, fresh, and lasting in early than in later years, yet up to the end they continue to take in some new impressions, and keep up their most necessary functions of supplying materials, stimulants, and tests to the other powers of the soul.

[1] I have been much helped towards the general contents of the next four sections by that profoundly thoughtful little book, Fechner's *Die drei Motive und Gründe des Glaubens*, 1863, and by the large and rich conception elaborated by Cardinal Newman in his Preface to *The Via Media*, 1877, Vol. I, pp. xv–xciv.

Thus, too, Religion is at all times more or less both traditional and individual; both external and internal; both institutional, rational, and volitional. It always answers more or less to the needs of authority and society; of reason and proof; of interior sustenance and purification. I believe because I am told, because it is true, because it answers to my deepest interior experiences and needs. And, everything else being equal, my faith will be at its richest and deepest and strongest, in so far as all these three motives are most fully and characteristically operative within me, at one and the same time, and towards one and the same ultimate result and end.

2. *The two crises of the soul, when it adds Speculation to Institutionalism, and Mysticism to both.*

Now all this is no fancy scheme, no petty or pretty artificial arrangement: the danger and yet necessity of the presence of these three forces, the conflicts and crises within and between them all, in each human soul, and between various men and races that typify or espouse one or the other force to the more or less complete exclusion of the other, help to form the deepest history, the truest tragedy or triumph of the secret life of every one of us.

The transition from the child's religion, so simply naïve and unselfconscious, so tied to time and place and particular persons and things, so predominantly traditional and historical, institutional and external, to the right and normal type of a young man's religion, is as necessary as it is perilous. The transition is necessary. For all the rest of him is growing,—body and soul are growing in clamorous complexity in every direction: how then can the deepest part of his nature, his religion, not require to grow and develop also? And how can it permeate and purify all the rest, how can it remain and increasingly become " the secret source of all his seeing," of his productiveness and courage and unification, unless it continually equals and exceeds all other interests within the living man, by its own persistent vitality, its rich and infinite variety, its subtle, ever-fresh attraction and inexhaustible resourcefulness and power? But the crisis is perilous. For he will be greatly tempted either to cling exclusively to his existing, all but simply institutional, external position, and to fight or elude all approaches to its reasoned, intellectual apprehension and systematization; and in this case his religion will tend to contract and shrivel up, and to become a something simply alongside of other things in his life. Or he will feel strongly pressed to let the individually intellectual simply supplant the institutional, in which case his religion will grow hard and shallow, and will tend to disappear altogether. In the former case he will, at best, assimilate his religion to external law and order, to Economics and Politics; in the latter case he will, at best, assimilate it to Science and Philosophy. In the first case, he will tend to superstition; in the second, to rationalism and indifference.

But even if he passes well through this first crisis, and has thus achieved the collaboration of these two religious forces, the external and the intellectual, his religion will still be incomplete and semi-operative, because still not reaching to what is deepest and nearest to his will. A final transition, the addition of the third force, that of the emotional-experimental life, must yet be safely achieved. And this again is perilous: for the two other forces will, even if single, still more if combined, tend to resist this third force's full share of influence to the uttermost. To the external force this emotional power will tend to appear as akin to revolution; to the intellectual side it will readily seem mere subjectivity and sentimentality ever verging on delusion. And the emotional-experimental force will, in its turn, be tempted to sweep aside both the external, as so much oppressive ballast; and the intellectual, as so much hair-splitting or rationalism. And if it succeeds, a shifting subjectivity, and all but incurable tyranny of mood and fancy, will result,—fanaticism is in full sight.

III. Parallels to this Triad of Religious Elements.

If we would find, applied to other matters, the actual operation and co-operation, at the earliest stage of man's life, of the identical powers under discussion, we can find them, by a careful analysis of our means and processes of knowledge, or of the stages of all reflex action.

1. *The three constituents of Knowledge.*

Even the most elementary acquisition, indeed the very possibility, of any and all certitude and knowledge, is dependent for us upon the due collaboration of the three elements or forces of our nature, the sensational, the rational, the ethico-mystical.[1]

There is, first, in the order of our consciousness and in the degree of its undeniableness, the element of our actual impressions, the flux of our consciousness as it apprehends particular sights and sounds, smells and tastes and touches; particular sensations of rest and movement, pleasure and pain, memory, judgment, and volition, a flux, "changeless in its ceaseless change." We have so far found neither a true object for thought, nor a subject which can think. And yet this element, and this alone, is the simply, passively received, the absolutely undeniable part of our experience,—we cannot deny it if we would. And again, it is the absolutely necessary prerequisite for our exercise or acquisition, indeed for our very consciousness, of the other two means or elements, without which there can be no real knowledge.

For there is, next in the logical order of the analysis of our consciousness and in the degree of its undeniableness, the element of the various forms of necessary thought, in as much as these are experienced by us as necessary. We can, with Aristotle, simply call them the ten categories; or we can, with greater precision and extension, group them, so far with Kant, under the two main heads of the two pure "aesthetic" Perceptions of time and space, on the one hand; and of the various "analytic" Forms of judgment and of the Categories of Unity, Reality, Substance, Possibility, etc., on the other hand. Now it can be shown that it is only by means of this whole second element, only through the co-operation of these "perceptions" and forms of thought, that any kind even of dim feeling of ordered succession or of system, of unity or meaning, is found by our mind in that first element. Only these two elements, found and taken together, present us, in their interaction, with even the impression and possibility of something to reason *about*, and something *wherewith* to reason.

The second element then differs from the first in this, that whereas the first presents its contents simply as actual and undeniable, yet without so far any necessity or significance: the second presents its contents as both actual and necessary.

[1] See, for this point, the admirably clear analysis in J. Volkelt's *Kant's Erkenntnisstheorie*, 1879, pp. 160–234. This book is probably the most conclusive demonstration extant of the profound self-contradictions running through Kant's Epistemology.

By means of the first element I see a red rose, but without any feeling of more than the fact that a rose, or at least this one, *is* red; it might quite as well be yellow or blue. By means of the second element, I think of a body of any kind, not only as actually occupying some particular space and time, but as *necessarily* doing so: I feel that I *must* so think of it.

And yet there is a third and last element necessary to give real value to the two previous ones. For only on the condition that I am willing to trust these intimations of necessity, to believe that these necessities of my subjective thought are objective as well, and correspond to the necessities of Being, can I reach the trans-subjective, can I have any real knowledge and experience of anything whatsoever, either within me or without. The most elementary experience, the humblest something to be granted as really existing and as to be reasoned from, is thus invariably and inevitably composed for me of three elements, of which only the first two are directly experienced by me at all. And the third element, the ethico-mystical, has to be there, I have to trust and endorse the intimations of necessity furnished by the second element, if anything is to come of the whole movement.

Thus, here also, at the very source of all our certainty, of the worth attributable to the least or greatest of our thoughts and feelings and acts, we already find the three elements: indubitable sensation, clear thought, warm faith in and through action. And thus life here already consists of multiplicity in unity; and what in it is absolutely indubitable, is of value only because it constitutes the indispensable starting-point and stimulation for the apprehension and affirmation of realities not directly experienced, not absolutely undeniable, but which alone bear with them all the meaning, all the richness, all the reality and worth of life.

2. *The three links in the chain of Reflex Action.*

We can also find this same triad, perhaps more simply, if we look to Psychology, and that most assured and most far-reaching of all its results, the fact and analysis of Reflex Action. For we find here that all the activities of specifically human life begin with a sense-impression, as the first, the one simply *given* element; that they move into and through a central process of mental abstraction and reflection, as the second element, contributed by the mind itself; and that they end, as the third element, in the discharge of will and of action, in an act of free affirmation, expansion, and love.

In this endless chain composed of these groups of three links each, the first link and the last link are obscure and mysterious; the first, as coming from without us, and as still below our own thought; the third, as going out from us, and seen by us only in its external results, never in its actual operation, nor in its effect upon our own central selves. Only the middle link is clear to us. And yet the most mysterious part of the whole process, the effect of it all upon the central self, is also the most certain and the most important result of the whole movement, a movement which ever culminates in a modification of the personality and which prepares this personality for the next round of sense-perception, intellectual abstraction, ethical affirmation and volitional self-determination,—acts in which light and love, fixed and free, hard and cold and warm, are so mysteriously, so universally, and yet so variously linked.

IV. Distribution of the Three Elements amongst Mankind and throughout Human History.

Let us now watch and see where and how the three elements of Religion appear among the periods of man's life, the human professions, and the races of mankind; then how they succeed each other in history generally; and finally how they exist among the chief types and phases of the Oriental, Classical Graeco-Roman, and Judaeo-Christian religions.

1. *The Elements: their distribution among man's various ages, sexes, professions, and races.*

We have already noticed how children incline to the memory-side, to the external, social type; and it is well they should do so, and they should be wisely helped therein. Those passing through the storm-and-stress period insist more upon the reason, the internal, intellectual type; and mature souls lay stress upon the feelings and the will, the internal, ethical type. So again, women generally tend either to an excess of the external, to superstition; or of the emotional, to fanaticism. Men, on the contrary, appear generally to incline to an excess of the intellectual, to rationalism and indifference.

Professions, too, both by the temperaments which they presuppose, and the habits of mind which they foster, have various affinities. The fighting, administrative, legal and political sciences and services, readily incline to the external and institutional; the medical, mathematical, natural science studies, to the internal-intellectual; the poetical, artistic, humanitarian activities, to the internal-emotional.

And whole races have tended and will tend, upon the whole, to one or other of these three excesses: *e. g.* the Latin races, to Externalism and Superstition; the Teutonic races, to the two Interiorisms, Rationalism and Fanaticism.

2. *Co-existence and succession of the Three Elements in history generally.*

The human race at large has evidently been passing, upon the whole, from the exterior to the interior, but with a constant tendency to drop one function for another, instead of supplementing, stimulating, purifying each by means of the other two.

If we go back as far as any analyzable records will carry us, we find that, in proportion as religion emerges from pure fetichism, it has ever combined with the apprehension of a Power conceived, at last and at best, as of a Father in heaven, that of a Bond with its brethren upon earth. Never has the sacrifice, the so-to-speak vertical relation between the individual man and God, between the worshipper and the object of his worship, been without the sacrificial meal, the communion, the so-to-speak lateral, horizontal relations between man and his fellow-man, between the worshippers one and all. Never has religion been purely and entirely individual; always has it been, as truly and necessarily, social and institutional, traditional and historical. And this traditional element, not all the religious genius in the world can ever escape or replace: it was there, surrounding and moulding the very pre-natal existence of each one of us; it will be there, long after we have left the scene. We live and die its wise servants and stewards, or its blind slaves, or in futile, impoverishing revolt against it: we never, for good or for evil, really get beyond its reach.

And yet all this stream and environment of the traditional and social could make no impression upon me whatsoever, unless it were met by certain secret sympathies, by certain imperious wants and energies within myself. If the contribution of tradition is *quantitatively* by far the most important, and might be compared to the contribution furnished by the Vocabulary to the constitution of a definite, particular language,—the contribution of the individual is, *qualitatively* and for that individual, more important still, and might be compared to the contribution of the Grammar to the constitution of that same language: for it is the Grammar which, though incomparably less in amount than the Vocabulary, yet definitely constitutes any and every language.

And there is here no necessary conflict with the claim of Tradition. It is true that all real, actual Religion is ever an act of submission to some fact or truth conceived as not only true but as obligatory, as coming from God, and hence as beyond and above our purely subjective fancies, opinings, and wishes. But it is also true that, if I could not mentally hear or see, I should be incapable of hearing or seeing anything of this kind or of any other; and that without some already existing interior affinity with and mysterious capacity for discriminating between such intimations—as either corresponding to or as traversing my existing imperious needs and instincts—I could not apprehend the former as coming from God. Without, then, such non-fanciful, non-wilful, subjective capacities and dispositions, there is for us not even the apprehension of the existence of such objective realities: such capacities and dispositions are as necessary pre-requisites to every act of faith, as sight is the absolute pre-requisite for my discrimination between black and white. Hence as far back as we can go, the traditional and social, the institutional side of religion was accompanied, in varying, and at first small or less perceptible degrees and forms, by intellectual and experimental interpretation and response.

3. *The Three Elements in the great Religions.*

Even the Greek religion, so largely naturalistic up to the very end, appears, in the centuries of its relative interiorization, as a triad composed of a most ancient traditional cultus, a philosophy of religion, and an experimental-ethical life; the latter element being readily exemplified by the Demon of Socrates, and by the Eleusinian and Orphic Mysteries.

In India and Tibet, again, Brahminism and Buddhism may be said to have divided these three elements between them, the former representing as great an excess of the external as Buddhism does of abstruse reasoning and pessimistic emotion. Mahometanism, while combining, in very imperfect proportions, all three elements within itself, lays special stress upon the first, the external element; and though harbouring, for centuries now and more or less everywhere, the third, the mystical element, looks, in its strictly orthodox representatives, with suspicion upon this mysticism.

Judaism was slow in developing the second, the intellectual element; and the third, the mystical, is all but wholly absent till the Exilic period, and does not become a marked feature till still later on, and in writers under Hellenistic influence. It is in the Book of Wisdom, still more in Philo, that we find all three sides almost equally developed. And from the Hasmonean period onwards till the destruction of Jerusalem by Titus, we find a severe and ardent external, traditional, authoritative school in the Pharisees; an accommodating and rationalizing school in the Sadducees; and, apart from both, more a sect than a school, the experimental, ascetical, and mystical body of the Essenes.

But it is in Christianity, and throughout its various vicissitudes and schools, that we can most fully observe the presence, characteristics, and interaction of these three modalities. We have already seen how the New Testament writings can be grouped, with little or no violence, according to the predominance of one of these three moods, under the heads of the traditional, historic, external, the "Petrine" school; the reasoning, speculative-internal, the Pauline; and the experimental, mystical-internal, the Johannine school. And in the East, up to Clement of Alexandria, in the West up to St. Augustine, we find the prevalence of the first type. And next, in the East, in Clement and Origen, in St. Gregory of Nyssa, in the Alexandrian and the Antiochene school generally, and in the West, in St. Augustine, we find predominantly a combination of the second and third types. The Areopagitic writings of the end of the fifth century still further emphasize and systematize this Neo-Platonic form of mystical speculation, and become indeed the great treasure-house from which above all the Mystics, but also largely the Scholastics, throughout the Middle Ages, drew much of their literary material.

And those six or seven centuries of the Middle Ages are full of the contrasts and conflicts between varying forms of Institutionalism, Intellectualism, and Mysticism. Especially clearly marked is the parallelism, interaction, and apparent indestructibleness of the Scholastic and Mystical currents. Abelard and St. Bernard, St. Thomas of Aquin and the great Franciscan Doctors, above all the often largely latent, yet really ceaseless conflict between Realism and Nominalism, all can be rightly taken as caused by various combinations and degrees, insufficiencies or abnormalities in the action of the three great powers of the human soul, and of the three corresponding root-forms and functions of religion. And whereas, during the prevalence of Realism, affective, mystical religion is the concomitant and double of intellectual religion; during the later prevalence of Nominalism, Mysticism becomes the ever-increasing supplement, and at last, ever more largely, the substitute, for the methods of reasoning. "Do penance and believe in the Gospel" becomes now the favourite text, even in the mouth of Gerson (who died in 1429), the great Nominalist Doctor, the Chancellor of the then greatest intellectual centre upon earth, the University of Paris. A constant depreciation of all dialectics, indeed largely of human knowledge generally, appears even more markedly in the pages of the gentle and otherwise moderate Thomas of Kempen (who died in 1471).

Although the Humanist Renaissance was not long in carrying away many minds and hearts from all deeper consciousness and effort of a moral and religious sort, yet in so far as men retained and but further deepened and enriched their religious outlook and life, the three old forms and modalities reappear, during the earlier stages of the movement, in fresh forms and combinations. Perhaps the most truly comprehensive and Christian representative of the new at its best, is Cardinal Nicolas of Coes, the precursor of modern philosophy. For he combines the fullest adhesion to, and life-long labour for, External Institutional authority, with the keenest Intellectual, Speculative life, and with the constant temper and practice of experimental and Mystical piety. And a similar combination we find in Blessed Sir Thomas More in England, who lays down his life in defence of Institutional Religion and of the authority of the visible Church and its earthly head; who is a devoted lover of the New Learning, both Critical and Philosophical; and who continuously cultivates the Interior Life. A little later on, we find the same combination in Cardinal Ximenes in Spain.

But it is under the stress and strain of the Reformation and Counter-Reformation movements that the depth and vitality of the three currents get specially revealed. For in Germany, and in Continental Protestantism generally, we see (immediately after the very short first "fluid" stage of Luther's and Zwingli's attitude consequent upon their breach with Rome) the three currents in a largely separate condition, and hence with startling distinctness. Luther, Calvin, Zwingli, different as are their temperaments and both their earlier and their later Protestant attitudes and doctrines, all three soon fall back upon some form and fragmentary continuation, or even in its way intensification, of Institutional Religion,—driven to such conservatism by the iron necessity of real life and the irrepressible requirements of human nature. They thus formed that heavy untransparent thing, orthodox Continental Protestantism. Laelius and Faustus Socinus attempt the construction of a purely Rationalistic Religion, and capture and intensify the current of a clear, cold Deism, in which the critical mind is to be supreme. And the Anabaptist and other scattered sects and individuals (the latter represented at their best by Sebastian Frank) attempt, in their turn, to hold and develop a purely interior, experimental, emotional-intuitive, ecstatic Religion, which is warm, indeed feverish and impulsive, and distrusts both the visible and institutional, and the rational and critical.

In England the same phenomenon recurs in a modified form. For in Anglicanism, the most characteristic of its parties, the High Church school, represents predominantly the Historical, Institutional principle. The Latitudinarian school fights for the Rational, Critical, and Speculative element. The Evangelical school stands in close spiritual affinity to all but the Unitarian Nonconformists in England, and represents the Experimental, Mystical element. We readily think of Laud and Andrewes, Pusey and Keble as representatives of the first class; of Arnold, Stanley and Jowett as figures of the second class; of Thomas Scott, John Newton and Charles Simeon as types of the third class. *The Tracts for the Times*, *Essays and Reviews*, and (further back) Bunyan's Works, would roughly correspond to them in literature.

And this trinity of tendency can also be traced in Catholicism. Whole Religious Orders and Congregations can be seen or felt to tend, upon the whole, to one or the other type. The Jesuits can be taken as predominantly making for the first type, for fact, authority, submission, obedience; the Dominicans for the second type, for thought, a philosophico-speculative, intellectual religion; the Benedictines, in their noble Congregation of St. Maur, for a historico-critical intellectual type; the French Oratory, for a combination of both the speculative (Malebranche) and the critical (Simon,

Thomassin); and the Franciscans, for the third, for action and experimental, affective spirituality.

And yet none of these Orders but has had its individuals, and even whole secondary periods, schools, and traditions, markedly typical of some current other than that specially characteristic of the Order as a whole. There are the great Critics and Historians of the Jesuit Order: the Spanish Maldonatus, the New Testament Scholar, admirable for his time, and helpful and unexhausted still; the French Denys Petau, the great historian of Christian Doctrine and of its development; the Flemish Bollandists, with their unbroken tradition of thorough critical method and incorruptible accuracy and impartiality. There are the great Jesuit Mystics: the Spanish Venerable Balthazar Alvarez, declared by St. Teresa to be the holiest mystical soul she had ever known; and the Frenchmen, Louis Lallemant and Jean Joseph Surin. There are those most attractive figures, combining the Scholar and the Mystic: Blessed Edmund Campion, the Oxford Scholar and Elizabethan Martyr; and Jean Nicolas Grou, the French translator of Plato, who died in exile in England in 1800. The Dominicans have, from the first, been really representative of external authority as well as of the speculative rational bent; and the mystical side has never been wanting to them, so amongst the early German Dominicans, Tauler and Suso, and many a Dominican female Saint. The Benedictines from the first produced great rulers; such striking types of external authority as the Pope-Saints, Gregory the Great and Gregory VII (Hildebrand), and the great Benedictine Abbots and Bishops throughout the Middle Ages are rightly felt to represent one whole side of this great Order. And again such great mystical figures as St. Hildegard of Bingen and the two Saints Gertrude are fully at home in that hospitable Family. And the Franciscans have, in the Conventuals, developed representatives of the external authority type; and in such great philosopher-theologians as Duns Scotus and Occam, a combination which has more of the intellectual, both speculative and critical, than of the simply ascetical or even mystical type.

And if we look for individual contrasts, we can often find them in close temporal and local juxtaposition, as in France, in the time of Louis XIV, in the persons of Bossuet, Richard Simon, and Fénelon, so strikingly typical of the special strengths and limitations of the institutional, rational, experimental types respectively. And yet the most largely varied influence will necessarily proceed from characters which combine not only two of the types, as in our times Frederick Faber combined the external and experimental; but which hold them all three, as with John Henry Newman in England or Antonio Rosmini in Italy.

V. Causes operative in all Religion towards Minimizing or Suppressing one or other Element, or towards denying the need of any Multiplicity.

Let us end this chapter with some consideration of the causes and reasons that are ever tending to produce and to excuse the quiet elimination or forcible suppression of one or other of the elements that constitute the full organism of religion, and even to minimize or to deny altogether the necessity of any such multiplicity.

1. *The religious temper longs for simplification.*

To take the last point first. How obvious and irresistible seems always, to the specifically religious temper, the appeal to boundless simplification. "Can there be anything more sublimely, utterly simple than religion?" we all say and feel. In these regions, if anywhere, we long and thirst to see and feel all things in one, to become ourselves one, to find the One Thing necessary, the One God, and to be one with Him for ever. Where is there room here, we feel even angrily, for all these distinctions, all this balancing of divers faculties and parts? Is not all this but so much Aestheticism, some kind of subtle Naturalism, a presumptuous attempting to build up bit by bit in practice, and to analyze part from part in theory, what can only come straight from God Himself, and, coming from Him the One, cannot but bear the impress of His own indistinguishable Unity? And can there be anything more unforcedly, unanalyzably simple than all actual religion,—and this in exact proportion to its greatness? Look at St. Francis of Assisi, or St. John Baptist; look above all at the Christ, supremely, uniquely great, just because of His sublime simplicity! Look at, feel, the presence and character of those countless souls that bear, unknown even to themselves, some portion of this His impress within themselves, forming thus a kind of indefinitely rich extension of His reign, of the kingdom of His childlikeness. Away then with everything that at all threatens to break up a corresponding simplicity in ourselves! Poverty of spirit, emptiness of heart, a constant turning away from all distraction, from all multiplicity both of thought and of feeling, of action and of being; this, surely, is the one and only necessity for the soul, at least in proportion to the height of her spiritual call.

2. *Yet every truly living Unity is constituted in Multiplicity.* Now in all this there is a most subtle mixture of truth and of error. It is profoundly true that all that *is* at all, still more all personality, and hence above all God, the Spirit of spirits is, just in that proportion, profoundly mysteriously One, with a Unity which all our best thinking can only distantly and analogously represent. And all religion will ever, in proportion as it is vigorous and pure, thirst after an ever-increasing Unification, will long to be one and to give itself to the One,—to follow naked the naked Jesus. Yet all the history of human thought and all the actual experience of each one of us prove that this Unity can be apprehended and developed, by and within our poor human selves, only in proportion as we carefully persist in stopping at the point where it can most thoroughly organize and harmonize the largest possible multiplicity of various facts and forces.

No doubt the living soul is not a whole made up of separate parts; still less is God made up of parts. Yet we cannot apprehend this Unity of God except in multiplicity of some sort; nor can we ourselves become rightly one, except through being in a true sense many, and very many, as well. Indeed the Christian Faith insists that there is something most real actually corresponding to this our conception of multiplicity even and especially in God Himself. For it as emphatically bids us think of Him as in one sense a Trinity as in another a Unity. And it is one of the oldest and most universal of Christian approaches to this mystery, to conceive it under the analogy of the three powers of the soul. God the Father and Creator is conceived as corresponding to the sense-perception and Imagination, to Memory-power; God the Son and Redeemer, as the Logos, to our reason; and God the Holy Spirit, as corresponding to the effective-volitional force within us; and then we are bidden to remember that, as in ourselves these three powers are all united in One personality, so in God the Three Persons are united in One substance and nature. Even the supremely and ineffably simple Godhead is not, then, a mere, undifferentiated One.

And if we take the case of our Lord, even when He is apprehended in the most abstract of orthodox ways: we get either the duality of natures, God and Man; or a trinity of offices, the Kingly, the Prophetic, and the Priestly, —these latter again corresponding roughly to the External, the Intellectual, and the Mystical element of the human soul. And even if we restrict ourselves to His Humanity, and as pictured in any one Gospel, nay in the earliest, simplest, and shortest, St. Mark, we shall still come continually upon a rich multiplicity, variety, and play of different exterior and interior apprehensions and activities, emotions and sufferings, all profoundly permeated by one great end and aim, yet each differing from the other, and contributing a different share to the one great result. The astonishment at the disciples' slowness of comprehension, the flash of anger at Peter, the sad reproachfulness towards Judas, the love of the children, the sympathy with women, the pity towards the fallen, the indignation against the Pharisees, the rejoicing in the Father's revelation, the agony in the Garden, the desolation on the Cross, are all *different* emotions. The perception of the beauty of the flowers of the field, of the habits of plants and of birds, of the varieties of the day's early and late cloud and sunshine, of the effects of storm and rain; and again of the psychology of various classes of character, age, temperament, and avocation; and indeed of so much more, are all *different* observations. The lonely recollection in the desert, the nights spent in prayer upon the mountains, the preaching from boats and on the lake-side, the long foot-journeyings, the many flights, the reading and expounding in the Synagogues, the curing the sick and restoring them to their right mind, the driving the sellers from the Temple-court, and so much else, are all *different* activities.

And if we take what is or should be simplest in the spiritual life of the Christian, his intention and motive; and if we conceive this according to the evidence of the practice of such Saints as have themselves revealed to us the actual working of their souls, and of the long and most valuable series of controversies and ecclesiastical decisions in this delicate matter, we shall again find the greatest possible Multiplicity in the deepest possible Unity. For even in such a Saint as St. John of the Cross, whose own analysis and theory of the interior life would often seem all but directly and completely to exclude the element of multiplicity, it is necessary ever to interpret and supplement one part of his teaching by another, and to understand the whole in the light of his actual, deliberate, habitual practice. This latter will necessarily ever exceed his explicit teaching, both in its completeness and in its authority. Now if in his formal teaching he never wearies of insisting upon detachment from all things, and upon the utmost simplification of the intentions of the soul, yet he occasionally fully states what is ever completing this doctrine in his own mind,—that this applies only to the means and not to the end, and to false and not to true multiplicity. "The spiritual man," he writes in one place, "has greater joy and comfort in creatures, if he detaches himself from them; and he can have no joy in them, if he considers them as his own." "He," as distinct from the unspiritual man, "rejoices in their truth," "in their best conditions," "in their substantial worth." He "has joy in all things."[1] A real multiplicity then exists in things, and in our most purified apprehension of them; varied, rich joys related to this multiplicity are facts in the life of the Saints; and these varied joys may legitimately be dwelt on as incentives to holiness for oneself and others. "All that is wanting now," he writes to Donna Juana de Pedraça, his penitent, "is that I should forget you. But consider how that is to be forgotten which is ever present to the soul."[2] An affection then, as pure as it was particular, was ever in his heart, and fully accepted and willed and acknowledged to its immediate object, as entirely conformable to his own teaching. St. Teresa, on the other hand, is a character of much greater natural variety, and yet it is she who has left us that most instructive record of her temporary erroneous ideal of a false simplicity, in turning away, for a number of years, from the consideration of the Humanity of Christ. And a constant, keen interest in the actual larger happenings of her time, in the vicissitudes of the Church in her day, was stamped upon all her teaching, and remained with her up to the very end.

Perhaps the most classic expression of the true Unity is that implied by St. Ignatius of Loyola, when he tells us that "Peace is the simplicity of order." For order as necessarily implies a multiplicity of things ordered as the unity of the supreme ordering principle. Fénelon, doubtless, at times, especially in parts of his condemned *Explication des Maximes*

[1] *Works of St. John of the Cross*, translated by David Lewis, Vol. I, ed. 1889, p. 298.

[2] *Ibid.* Vol. II, ed. 1890, pp. 541, 542.

des Saints, too much excludes, or seems to exclude, the element of multiplicity in the soul's intention. Yet, both before and after this book, some of the clearest and completest statements in existence, as to the true unity and diversity to be found in the most perfect life, are to be found among his writings. In his Latin Epistle to Pope Clement XI he insists upon the irreducible element of multiplicity in the motives of the very highest sanctity.

For he maintains first that, though " in the specific act of Love, the chief of the theological virtues, it is possible to love the absolute perfection of God considered in Himself, without the addition of any motive of the promised beatitude," yet that " this specific act of love, of its own nature, never excludes, and indeed most frequently includes, this same motive of beatitude." He asserts next that though, " in the highest grade of perfection amongst souls here below, deliberate acts of simply natural love of ourselves, and even supernatural acts of hope which are not commanded by love mostly cease," yet that in this " habitual state of any and every most perfect soul upon earth, the promised beatitude is desired, and there is no diminution of the exercise of the virtue of hope, indeed day by day there is an increase in this desire, from the specific motive of hope of this great good, which God Himself bids us all, without exception, to hope for." And he declares finally that " there is no state of perfection in which souls enjoy an uninterrupted contemplation, or in which the powers of the soul are bound by an absolute incapacity for eliciting the discursive acts of Christian piety; nor is there a state in which they are exempted from following the laws of the Church, and executing all the orders of superiors." [1]

All the variety, then, of the interested and of the disinterested; of hope and fear and sorrow; of gratitude and adoration and love; of the Intuitive and Discursive; of Recollection and external Action, is to be found, in a deeper, richer, more multiple and varied and at the same time a more unified unity, in the most perfect life; and all this in proportion to its approach to its own ideal and normality.

Indeed the same multiplicity in unity is finely traced by St. Bernard, the great contemplative, in every human act that partakes of grace at all. " That which was begun by Grace,

[1] *Œuvres de Fénelon*, Paris, Lebel, Vol. IX, 1828, pp. 632, 652, 668.

gets accomplished alike by both Grace and Free Will, so that they operate mixedly not separately, simultaneously not successively, in each and all of their processes. The acts are not in part Grace, in part Free Will; but the whole of each act is effected by both in an undivided operation." [1]

VI. The Special Motives operating in each Element towards the Suppression of the other Elements.

Now the elements of Multiplicity and Friction and of Unity and Harmonization, absolutely essential to all life, everywhere and always cost us much to keep and gain. But there are also very special reasons why the three great constituents of religion should, each in its own way, tend continually to tempt the soul to retain only *it*, and hence to an impoverishing simplification. Let us try and see this tendency at work in the two chief constituents, as against each other, and in combination against the third.

1. *In the Historical and Institutional Element, as against all else.*

We have seen how all religiousness is ever called into life by some already existing religion. And this religion will consist in the continuous commemoration of some great religious facts of the past. It will teach and represent some divine revelation as having been made, in and through such and such a particular person, in such and such a particular place, at such and such a particular time; and such a revelation will claim acceptance and submission as divine and redemptive in and through the very form and manner in which it was originally made. The very peculiarity, which will render the teaching distinctively religious, will hence be a certain real, or at least an at first apparent, externality to the mind and life of the recipient, and a sense of even painful obligation answered by a willing endorsement. All higher religion ever is thus personal and revelational; and all such personal and revelational religion was necessarily first manifested in unique conditions of space and time; and yet claims, in as much as divine, to embrace all the endless conditions of other spaces and other times.

And this combination of a clearly contingent constituent

[1] *Tractatus de Gratia et Libero Arbitrio*, cap. xiv, § 47.

and of an imperiously absolute claim is not less, but more visible, as we rise in the scale of religions. The figure of our Lord is far more clear and definite and richly individual than are the figures of the Buddha or of Mahomet. And at the same time Christianity has ever claimed for Him far more than Buddhism or Mohammedanism have claimed for their respective, somewhat shadowy founders. For the Buddha was conceived as but one amongst a whole series of similar revealers that were to come; and Mahomet was but the final prophet of the one God. But Christ is offered to us as the unique Saviour, as the unique revelation of God Himself. You are thus to take Him or leave Him. To distinguish and interpret, analyze or theorize Him, to accept Him provisionally or on conditions,—nothing of all this is distinctively religious. For, here as everywhere else, the distinctive religious act is, as such, an unconditional surrender. Nowhere in life can we both give and keep at the same time; and least of all here, at life's deepest sources.

With this acceptance then, in exact proportion as it is religious, a double exclusiveness will apparently be set up. I have here found my true life :—I will turn away then from all else, and will either directly fight, or will at least starve and stunt, all other competing interests and activities—I will have here a (so to speak) *spatial*, a *simultaneous* exclusiveness. Religion will thus be conceived as a thing amongst other things, or as a force struggling amongst other forces; we have given our undivided heart to *it*,—hence the other things must go, as so many actual supernumeraries and possible supplanters. Science and Literature, Art and Politics must all be starved or cramped. Religion can safely reign, apparently, in a desert alone.

But again, Religion will be conceived, at the same time, as a thing fixed in itself, as given once for all, and to be defended against all change and interpretation, against all novelty and discrimination. We get thus a second, a (so to speak) *temporal, successive* exclusiveness. Religion will here be conceived as a thing to be kept literally and materially identical with itself, and hence as requiring to be defended against any kind of modification. Conceive it as a paste, and all yeast must be kept out; or as wine, and fermentation must be carefully excluded. And indeed Religion here would thus become a stone, even though a stone fallen from heaven, like one of those meteorites worshipped in Pagan antiquity. And the two exclusivenesses, joined together, would give us a religion reduced to such a stone worshipped in a desert.

Now the point to notice here is, that all this seems not to be an abuse, but to spring from the very essence of religion,—from two of its specific inalienable characteristics—those of externality and authority. And although the extreme just described has never been completely realized in history, yet we can see various approximations to it in Mohammedan Egypt, in Puritan Scotland, in Piagnone Florence, in Spain of the Inquisition. Religion would thus appear fated, by its very nature, to starve out all else, and its own self into the bargain.

What will be the answer to, the escape from, all this, provided by religion itself? The answer and escape will be provided by the intrinsic nature of the human soul, and of the religious appeal made to it. For if this appeal must be conceived by the soul, in exact proportion to the religiousness of both, as incomprehensible by it, as exceeding its present, and even its potential, powers of comprehension; if again this appeal must demand a sacrifice of various inclinations felt at the time to be wrong or inferior; if it must come home to the soul with a sense of constraining obligation, as an act of submission and of sacrifice which it ought to and must make: yet it will as necessarily be conceived, at the same time, and again in exact proportion to the religiousness both of the soul and of the appeal, as the expression of Mind, of Spirit, and the impression of another mind and spirit; as the manifestation of an infinite Personality, responded and assented to by a personality, finite indeed yet capable of indefinite growth. And hence the fixity of the revelation and of the soul's assent to it, will be as the fixity of a fountain-head, or as the fixity of river-banks; or again as the fixity of a plant's growth, or of the gradual leavening of bread, or as that of the successive evolution and identity of the human body. The fixity, in a word, will be conceived and found to be a fixity of orientation, a definiteness of affinities and of assimilative capacity.

Only full trust, only unconditional surrender suffice for religion. But then religion excites and commands this in a person towards a Person; a surrender to be achieved not in some thing, but in some one,—a some one who *is* at all, only in as much as he is living, loving, growing; and to be performed, not towards some thing, but towards Some One, Whose right, indeed Whose very power to claim me, consists precisely in that He is Himself absolutely, infinitely and actually, what I am but derivatively, finitely and potentially.

Thus the very same act and reasons which completely bind me, do so only to true growth and to indefinite expansion. I shall, it is true, ever go back and cling to the definite spatial and temporal manifestations of this infinite Spirit's personality, but I shall, by this same act, proclaim His eternal presentness and inexhaustible self-interpreting illumination. By the same act by which I believe in the revelation of the workshop of Nazareth, of the Lake of Galilee, of Gethsemane and Calvary, I believe that this revelation is inexhaustible, and that its gradual analysis and theory, and above all its successive practical application, experimentation, acceptance or rejection, and unfolding, confer and call forth poignant dramatic freshness and inexhaustible uniqueness upon and within every human life, unto the end of time.

All this takes place through the present, the *hic et nunc*, co-operation of the living God and the living soul. And this ever-to-be reconquered, ever-costing and chequered, ever-"deepenable" interpretation, is as truly fresh as if it were a fresh revelation. For all that comes from the living God, and is worked out by living souls, is ever living and enlivening: there is no such thing as mere repetition, or differentiation by mere number, place, and time, in this Kingdom of Life, either as to God's action or the soul's. Infinite Spirit Himself, He creates an indefinite number of, at first largely but potential, persons, no one of which is identical with any other, and provokes and supports an indefinite number of ever different successive acts on the part of each and all of them, that so, through the sum-total of such sources and streams of difference, the nearest creaturely approach may be achieved to the ocean of His own infinite richness.

2. *In the Emotional and Volitional Element, as against the Historical and Institutional Element.*

Now the tendency of a soul, when once awake to this necessary freshness and interiority of feeling with regard to God's and her own action, will again be towards an impoverishing oneness. It will now tend to shrink away from the External, Institutional altogether. For though it cannot but have experienced the fact that it was by contact with this External that, like unto Antaeus at his contact with Mother Earth, it gained its experience of the Internal, yet each such experience tends to obliterate the traces of its own occasion. Indeed the interior feeling thus achieved tends, in the long run, to make the return to the contact with the fact that occasioned, and to the act that produced it, a matter of effort and repugnance. It seems a case of " a man's returning to his mother's womb " ; and is indeed a new birth to a fuller life, and hence humiliating, obscure, concentrated, effortful, a matter of trust and labour and pain and faith and love,—a true death of and adieu to the self of this moment, however advanced this self may seem,—a fully willed purifying pang. Only through such dark and narrow Thermopylae passes can we issue on to the wide, sunlit plains. And both plain and sunshine can never last long at a time; and they will cease altogether, if they are not interrupted by this apparent shadow of the valley of death, this concrete action, which invariably modifies not only the soul's environment, but above all the soul itself.

Thus does a simply mental prayer readily feel, to the soul that possesses the habit of it, a complete substitute for all vocal prayer; and a generally prayerful habit of mind readily appears an improvement upon all conscious acts of prayer. Thus does a general, indeterminate consciousness of Christ's spirit and presence easily feel larger and wider, to him who has it, than the apparent contraction of mind and heart involved in devotion to Him pictured in the definite Gospel scenes or localized in His Eucharistic presence. Thus again does a general disposition of regret for sin and of determination to do better readily feel nobler, to him who has it, than the apparent materiality and peddling casuistry, the attempting the impossible, of fixing for oneself the kind and degree of one's actual sins, and of determining upon definite, detailed reforms.

Yet, in all these cases, this feeling will rapidly lead the soul on to become unconsciously weak or feverish, unless the soul manfully escapes from this feeling's tyranny, and nobly bends under the yoke and cramps itself within the narrow limits of the life-giving concrete act. The Church's insistence upon *some* vocal prayer, upon *some* definite, differentiated, specific acts of the various moral and theological virtues, upon Sacramental practice throughout all the states and stages of the Christian life, is but a living commentary upon the difficulty and importance of the point under discussion. And History, as we have seen, confirms all this.

3. *In the Emotional and Volitional, singly or in combination with the Historical and Institutional, as against the Analytic and Speculative Element.*

But just as the Institutional easily tends to a weakening both of the Intellectual and of the Emotional, so does the Emotional readily turn against not only the Institutional but against the Intellectual as well. This latter hostility will take two forms. Inasmuch as the feeling clings to historical facts and persons, it will instinctively elude or attempt to suppress all critical examination and analysis of these its supports. Inasmuch as it feeds upon its own emotion, which (as so much pure emotion) is, at any one of its stages, ever intensely one and intensely exclusive, it will instinctively fret under and oppose all that slow discrimination and mere approximation, that collection of a few certainties, many probabilities, and innumerable possibilities, all that pother over a very little, which seem to make up the sum of all human knowledge. Such Emotion will thus tend to be hostile to Historical Criticism, and to all the Critical, Analytic stages and forms of Philosophy. It turns away instinctively from the cold manifold of thinking; and it shrinks spontaneously from the hard opaque of action and of the external. All this will again be found to be borne out by history.

A combination of Institutionalism and Experimentalism against Intellectualism is another not infrequent abuse, and one which is not hard to explain. For if external, definite facts and acts are found to lead to certain internal, deep, all-embracing emotions and experiences, the soul can to a certain extent live and thrive in and by a constant moving backwards and forwards between the Institution and the Emotion alone, and can thus constitute an ever-tightening bond and dialogue, increasingly exclusive of all else. For although the Institution will, taken in itself, retain for the Emotion a certain dryness and hardness, yet the Emotion can and often will associate with this Institution whatever that contact with it has been found to bring and to produce. And if the Institution feels hard and obscure, it is not, like the Thinking, cold and transparent. Just because the Institution appears to the emotional nature as though further from its feeling, and yet is experienced as a mysterious cause or occasion of this feeling, the emotional nature is fairly, often passionately, ready to welcome what it can thus rest on and lean on, as something having a comfortable fixity both of relation and of resistance. But with regard to Thinking, all this is different. For thought is sufficiently near to Feeling, necessarily to produce friction and competition of some sort, and seems, with its keen edge and endless mobility, to be the born implacable foe of the dull, dead givenness of the Institutional, and of the equal givenness of any one Emotional mood. One of the spontaneous activities of the human soul, the Analytic and Speculative faculty, seems habitually, instinctively to labour at depersonalizing all it touches, and thus continually both to undermine and discrown the deeply personal work and world of the experimental forces of the soul. Indeed the thinking seems to be doing this necessarily, since by its very essence it begins and ends with laws, qualities, functions, and parts,—with abstractions, which, at best, can be but skeletons and empty forms of the real and actual, and which, of themselves, ever tend to represent all Reality as something static, not dynamic, as a thing, not as a person or Spirit.

Here again the true solution will be found in an ever fuller conception of Personality, and of its primary place in the religious life. For even the bare possibility of the truth of all religion, especially of any one of the characteristic doctrines of Christianity, involves a group of personalist convictions. Here the human person begins more as a possibility than a reality. Here the moral and spiritual character has to be built up slowly, painfully, laboriously, throughout all the various stages and circumstances of life, with their endless combinations of pleasure and pain, trouble and temptation, inner and outer help and hindrance, success and failure. Here the simply Individual is transformed into the truly Personal only by the successive sacrifice of the lower, of the merely animal and impoverishingly selfish self, with the help of God's constant prevenient, concomitant, and subsequent grace. And here this constantly renewed dropping and opposing of the various lower selves, in proportion as they appear and become lower, to the soul's deepest insight, in the growing light of its conscience and the increasing elevation of the moral personality, involves that constant death to self, that perpetual conversion, that unification and peace in and through a continuous inner self-estrangement and conflict, which is the very breath and joy of the religious life.

Only if all this be so, to a quite unpicturable extent, can even the most elementary Christianity be more than an amiable intruder, or a morbid surplusage in the world. And at the same time, if this be so, then all within us is in need of successive, never-ending purification and elaboration; and the God who has made man with a view to his gradually achieving, and conquering his real self, must have stored means and instruments, for the attainment of this man's true end, in constant readiness, within himself. Now our whole intellectual nature is a great storehouse of one special class of such instruments. For it is clear that the moral and spiritual side of our nature will, more than any other, constantly require three things: Rest, Expression, and Purification. And the intellectual activities will, if only they be kept sufficiently vigorous and independent, alone be in a position sufficiently to supply some forms of these three needs. For they can rest the moral-spiritual activities, since they, the intellectual ones, primarily neglect emotion, action, and persons, and are directly occupied with abstractions and with things. They can and should express the results of those moral, spiritual activities, because the religious facts and experiences require, like all other facts, to be constantly stated and restated by the intellect in terms fairly understandable by the civilization and culture of the successive ages of the world. Above all, they can help to purify those moral-spiritual activities, owing to their interposing, by their very nature, a zone of abstraction, of cool, clear thinking, of seemingly adequate and exhaustive, but actually impoverishing and artificial concepts, and of apparently ultimate, though really only phenomenal determinism, between the direct informations of the senses, to which the Individual clings, and the inspirations of the moral and spiritual nature, which constitute the Person. Thus this intellectual abstractive element is, if neither minimized in the life of the soul, nor allowed to be its sole element or its last, a sobering, purifying, mortifying, vivifying bath and fire.

VII. Three Final Objections to such a conception of Religion, and their Answers.

Now there are three obvious objections to such a conception: with their consideration, this Introduction shall conclude.

1. *This conception not excessively intellectual.*

Does not, in the first place, such a view of life appear

preposterously intellectual? What of the uneducated, of the toiling millions? What of most women and of all children? Are then all these, the overwhelming majority of mankind, the objects of Christ's predilection, the very types chosen by Himself of His spirit and of God's ideal for man, precluded from an essential element of religion? Or are we, at the least, to hold that an ethical and spiritual advantage is necessarily attached, and this too for but a small minority of mankind, to a simple intellectual function and activity? If there was a thing specially antagonistic to Christ and condemned by Him, it was the arrogance of the Schools of His day; if there is a thing apparently absent from Christ's own life it is all philosophizing: even to suggest its presence seems at once to disfigure and to lower Him. Is then Reasoning, the School, to be declared not only necessary for some and for mankind at large, but necessary, in a sense, for all men and for the religious life itself?

The answer to all this appears not far to seek. The element which we have named the intellectual is but one of the faculties of every living soul; and hence, in some degree and form, it is present and operative in every one of us. And there is probably no greater difference between these degrees and forms, with regard to this element, than there is between the degrees and forms found in the other two elements of religion. For this intellectual, determinist element would be truly represented by every however simple mental attention to *things* and their mechanism, their necessary laws and requirements. Hence, the Venerable Anna Maria Taigi, the Roman working-man's wife, attending to the requirements and rules of good washing and of darning of clothes; St. Jean Batiste de la Salle, the Breton gentleman, studying the psychology of school-children's minds, and adapting his school system to it; St. Jerome labouring at his minute textual criticism of manuscripts of all kinds; St. Anselm and St. Thomas toiling at the construction of their dialectic systems, —all these, amongst endless other cases, are but illustrations of the omnipresence and endless variety of this element, which is busy with the rules and processes that govern things.

And it is impossible to see why, simply because of their superior intellectual gifts and development, men like Clement of Alexandria and Origen, Cassian and Duns Scotus, Nicolas of Coes and Pascal, Rosmini and Newman, should count as necessarily less near to God and Christ than others with fewer of such gifts and opportunities. For it is not as though such gifts were considered as ever *of themselves* constituting any moral or spiritual worth. Nothing can be more certain than that great mental powers can be accompanied by emptiness or depravity of heart. The identical standard is to be applied to these as to all other gifts : they are not to be considered as substitutes, but only as additional material and means for the moral and spiritual life ; and it is only inasmuch as they are actually so used that they can effectively help on sanctity itself. It is only contended here that such gifts do furnish additional means and materials for the devoted will- and grace-moved soul, towards the richest and deepest spiritual life. For the intellectual virtues are no mere empty name : candour, moral courage, intellectual honesty, scrupulous accuracy, chivalrous fairness, endless docility to facts, disinterested collaboration, unconquerable hopefulness and perseverance, manly renunciation of popularity and easy honours, love of bracing labour and strengthening solitude : these and many other cognate qualities bear upon them the impress of God and of His Christ. And yet they all as surely find but a scanty field of development outside of the intellectual life, as they are not the only virtues or class of virtues, and as the other two elements each produce a quite unique group of virtues of their own and require other means and materials for their exercise.

2. *Such a conception not Pelagian.*

But, in the second place, is not such a view of life Pelagian at bottom? Have we not argued throughout, as if the religious life were to be begun, and carried on, and achieved simply by a constant succession of efforts of our own ; and as though it could be built up by us, like to some work of art, by a careful, conscious balancing of part against part? Is not all this pure Naturalism? Is not religion a life, and hence an indivisible whole? And is not this life simply the gift of God, capable of being received, but not produced by us ; of being dimly apprehended at present, but not of being clearly analyzed in its process of formation?

Here again there is a true answer, I think. Simply all and every one of our acts, our very physical existence and persistence, is dependent, at every moment and in every direction, upon the prevenient, accompanying and subsequent power and help of God ; and still more is every religious, every truly spiritual and supernatural act of the soul impossible without the constant action of God's grace. Yet not only does all this not prevent the soul from consciously acting on her own part, and according to the laws of her own being; but God's grace acts in and through the medium of her acts, inasmuch as these are good: so that the very same action which, seen as it were from without, is the effect of our own volition, is, seen as it were from within, the effect of God's grace. The more costly is our act of love or of sacrifice, the more ethical and spiritual, and the more truly it is our own deepest self-expression, so much the more, at the same time, is this action a thing received as well as given, and that we have it to give, and that we can and do give it, is itself a pure gift of God.

What then is wanted, if we would really cover the facts of the case, is evidently not a conception which would minimize the human action, and would represent the latter as shrinking, in proportion as God's action increases; but one which, on the contrary, fully faces, and keeps a firm hold of, the mysterious paradox which pervades all true life, and which shows us the human soul as self-active in proportion to God's action within it, according to St. Bernard's doctrine already quoted. Grace and the Will thus rise and fall, in their degree of action, together; and man will never be so fully active, so truly and intensely himself, as when he is most possessed by God.

And since man's action is thus in actual fact mysteriously double, it should ever be so considered by him; and he should, as St. Ignatius of Loyola says, "pray as if all depended on his prayer, and act as if all depended on his action." Hence all man's action, though really incapable of existing for an instant without the aid of God, and though never exclusively his own, can be studied throughout, preliminarily as though it were his exclusive production on its analyzable, human side. And man not only can, he ought to be as thoughtful and careful, as reasonably analytic and systematic about this study of his action as he was careful and consistent in its production,—in both cases, whilst praying and believing as though it were all from God, he can and should behave also as though this action were exclusively his own. As St. Thomas admirably says: "We attribute one and the same effect both to a natural cause and to a divine force, not in the sense of that effect proceeding in part from God, and in part from the human agent. But the effect proceeds entire from both, according to a different mode: just as, in music, the whole effect is attributed to the instrument, and the same entire effect is referred to man as the principal agent." [1]

3. *Such a conception not Epicurean.*

But, in the last place, is not such a view of life Epicurean? Where is the Cross and Self-Renunciation? Is it not Christ Himself Who has bidden us cut off our right hand and pluck out our right eye, if they offend; Who has declared that he who hateth not his own father and mother for His sake is not worthy of Him; Who has asked, "What doth it profit a man, if he gain the whole world, and suffer the loss of his own soul?" and Who has pronounced a special woe upon the rich, and a special blessing upon the poor in spirit? Does not our view, on the contrary, bid a man attend to his hands and eyes, rather than to their possible or even actual offending, euphemistically described here as "friction"; bid him love his father and mother, even though this introduce a conflict into his affections; bid him take care to gain, as far as may be, the whole of his own possible interior and exterior world, as though this would of itself be equivalent to his saving his soul; and thus bid him become rich and full and complex, an aesthete rather than a man of God? In a word, is not our position a masked Paganism, a new Renaissance rather than the nobly stern old Christianity?

Now here again a true answer is found in a clear intelligence of the actual implications of the position. For if the Intellectual action were here taken as capable of alone, or in any degree directly, forming the foundation of all our other life, so that on a mathematically clear and complete system, appealing to and requiring the abstractive powers alone, would, later on, be built, according to our own further determination, the Institutional and Experimental, or both or neither; then such a position, if possible and actualized, would indeed save us the simultaneous energizing of our whole complex nature, and would, so far, well deserve the accusation of unduly facilitating life; it might be taken as, at least, not beginning with the Cross. But here this is not so. For from the first the External and the Mystical elements are held to be at least as necessary and operative as the Intellectual element; and it is impossible to see how the elimination of this latter, and of the ever-expensive keeping

[1] *Summa c. Gentiles*, iii, c. 70, *in fine*.

it and its rivals each at their own work, could deepen the truly moral sufferings and sacrifices of the soul's life.

If again the Intellectual action were taken, as by Gnosticism of all sorts, as the eventual goal of the whole, so that the External and Mystical would end by being absorbed into the Intellectual, our Knowledge becoming coextensive with Reality itself, then we might again, and with still deeper truth, be accused of eliminating the element of effort and of sacrifice,—the Cross. But here, on the contrary, not only the Intellectual alone does not begin the soul's life or build up its conditions, but the Intellectual alone does not conclude and crown it. Eternally will different soul-functions conjoin in a common work, eternally will God and the souls of our fellows be for us realities in diverse degrees outside of and beyond our own apprehension of them, and eternally shall we apprehend them differently and to a different degree by our intelligence, by our affection, and by our volition. Hence, even in eternity itself we can, without exceeding the limits of sober thinking and of psychological probability, find a field for the exercise by our souls of something corresponding to the joy and greatness of noble self-sacrifice here below. The loving soul will there, in the very home of love, give itself wholly to and be fulfilled by God, and yet the soul will possess an indefinitely heightened apprehension of the immense excess of this its love and act above its knowledge, and of God Himself above both. And here again it is impossible to see how the elimination of the intellectual element, which becomes thus the very measure of the soul's own limitations, and of the exceeding greatness of its love and of its Lover, would make the conception more efficaciously humbling and Christian.

Both at the beginning, then, and throughout, and even at the end of the soul's life, the intellectual element is necessary, and this above all for the planting fully and finally, in the very depths of the personality, the Cross, the sole means to the soul's true Incoronation.

PART II

BIOGRAPHICAL

CHAPTER III

CATHERINE FIESCA ADORNA'S LIFE, UP TO HER CONVERSION; AND THE CHIEF PECULIARITIES PREDOMINANT THROUGHOUT HER CONVERT YEARS

INTRODUCTORY.

Each of the three Elements of Religion, again multiple. The two main functions of each.

We have so far considered religion as constituted, on its human side, by the interaction of three modalities,—the Historical, the Intellectual, the Experimental. But it is of course clear that each of these is again, just because it is a living force, a Multiplicity in Unity. The first distinction we can find in each would break each up into two parts.

The Historical modality readily gives us the function busy with the Historical Person and the function occupied with the Historical Thing. The former function will insist upon all the temporal and local sayings, doings, and happenings, that together make up the picture and memory of the Prophet or Founder; the latter will transmit certain rites and symbols instituted or occasioned by him. And either the suppression of these latter things, or the taking them apart from the person from whom they issued and to whom they ever should lead back, will turn out equally impoverishing: the very friction of this Thing, coming from a Person, and leading to a Person, and operating within our own personality, will be found to help to make the latter truly such.

The Intellectual modality will as readily split up into the Analytic and the Synthetic. The former will busy itself with distinguishing and weighing, and with reducing everything as far as possible to its constituent elements. The latter will attempt to reconstitute the living whole, as far as may be, in such terms of clear reason. The former will have more affinity with the discursive reason, the second with the contemplative; the former with religious History, and the approaches to religious Philosophy,—Physiology and

Experimental Psychology and the Theory of Knowledge; the latter with Religious Philosophy proper,—the Metaphysics of Religion.

The Experimental modality, finally, will as readily break up into Intuitions and Feelings of every mental and moral kind, and Willings, the determinations of which, close as they are to the feelings, are not identical with them, but often exist more or less without or even against them.

And this whole series of six movements exists only in Persons; it begins with an at least incipient Person and ends in the fullest self-expression of Personality, the determination of the will. And Things—both external (Institutions) and internal (analytic and synthetic Abstractions)—are but ever operative, necessary means towards the firm constitution and expansion of that rich life of the living soul within which the first apprehension and ordering of such thinkings and doings took their rise.

I. Proposed Study of the Mystical-Volitional Element in a Particular, Concrete Instance: St. Catherine of Genoa.

Now it is the fact of the Multiplicity in Unity, to be found in each of these modalities of religion, that makes it desirable to study each of them, as far as may be, separately. And of these the deepest and most near to our living selves, and hence also most far away from our clear analysis, is the Experimental. It is this Element then that I propose to study in a particular concrete instance: St. Catherine of Genoa.

1. *Disadvantages of such a method and of this particular instance.*

The disadvantage arising from such a method of procedure is obvious: no one life, even were it the richest and most completely knowable, can exhaust, can indeed do more than simply suggest, the true questions, let alone the adequate answers. But such a biographical study can hope to arouse attention and interest in the living facts of religion, in a manner in which no simple theory or generalization can do; and it can stand out, in the midst of any such attempt at explanation, as an emphatic reminder, to both writer and reader, of the inexhaustible richness and mystery, of the awe-inspiring and yet stimulating surplusage which is ever furnished by reality over and above all our best endeavours at commensurate presentation or analysis.

And quite special disadvantages attach to the study of this particular Saint. Her character, for one thing, is distinctly wanting in humour, in that shrewd mother-wit which is so marked a feature in some of the great Spanish Mystics, in St. Teresa especially, but which is not quite absent even in the less varied and very austere St. John of the Cross. There is, on the contrary, a certain monotony, a somewhat wearying vehemence, about our Genoese. Her experience, again, is without the dramatic vicissitudes of the reform of an Order or the foundation of Monasteries, as with St. Teresa; or of contact and even conflict with the temporal and spiritual officiality of her time, as with St. Catherine of Siena. Nor is her life lit up by the beautiful warmth of happy, requited domestic affection, nor is it varied and extended by the rich possession of children of her own. And again her life is obscured and complicated, at least for our comprehension of it, by a nervous ill-health which it is impossible for us to care about, in itself. And, finally, special difficulties attach to the understanding of her. Unlike St. Teresa, St. John of the Cross, and many other Saints, she did not herself write one line of her so-called "Writings"; and yet it is these, mostly very abstruse and at times all but insuperably difficult, "Writings," records which did not attain their present form and bulk till a good forty years after her death, that contain the most original part of her legacy to the Church.

2. *The drawbacks of the instance outweighed by its rare combination of characteristics.*

Yet all this is balanced if not exceeded by a rare and stimulating combination of characteristics. The very ordinariness of her external lot,—a simple wife and widow, at no time belonging to any Religious Order or Congregation; the apparently complete failure of her earthly life, which gives occasion to the birth within her of the heavenly one; the rich variety and contrasts of her princely birth and social position, and the lowly, homely activity and usefulness of her forty years of devotedness; the unusually perfect combination of a great external action and administrative capacity with a lofty contemplation; the apparent suddenness and whole-hearted swiftness of her Conversion, succeeded by the long years of interior conflict and painful growth, unhelped, practically unknown, by any one but God's inspiring Spirit, and these years again followed by a period of requiring and practising the ordinary mediate docilities; the strange nervous health of especially her later years, so carefully and truthfully recorded for us, a psychic condition interesting if but for her own lofty superiority to attaching any direct importance or necessarily miraculous meaning to it: all this, even if it were all, helps to give an extraordinary richness and instructiveness to her life.

But stimulating, transfiguring, embracing all this, appears her special spiritual apprehension and teaching, of a quite extraordinary depth, breadth and balance, distinction and refinement. The central oneness of the soul's nature and sufferings and joys here and hereafter, and the resultant psychological character and appeal, to be found in all true experience or forecasting of such things; the never-ceasing difference between Spirit and Matter; the incomprehensibility, but indefinite apprehensibleness, for the clean of heart, of God and spiritual realities; the pure disinterestedness of His love for us, and the corresponding disinterestedness of all true love for Him; the universality of His light and love, and the excess of His mercy above His justice; the innate affinity between every human soul and Him, and the immanence of Himself within us; the absence of all arbitrary or preternatural action in the forces and realities constitutive of the spiritual world and life; the constant union of right suffering with deep peace, and the final note of joy and of self-conquering triumph issuing from complete self-renunciation: all this and much more appears in her teaching with a spontaneity, breadth, and balance peculiarly its own.

3. *Men who have been devoted to her spirit. Its vitality.*

No wonder then that, from the contemporary circle of her devoted friends and disciples onwards, Catherine should have attracted, throughout the centuries and in many lands, a remarkable number of deep minds and saintly characters. The ardent young Spaniard, St. Aloysius Gonzaga, and the shrewd and solid Savoyard Bishop, St. François de Sales, love to quote and dwell upon her example and her doctrine. Mature theologians, such as Cardinal Bellarmine, the hard-headed controversialist; Cardinal Bona, the liturgical and devotional writer; and Cardinal de Berulle, the mystical-minded founder of the French Oratory; and again, such varied types of devotedness as Madame Acarie, the foundress of the French Reformed Carmelites; the Baron de Renty, that noble Christian soldier; Bossuet, the hard and sensible; and Fénelon, the elastic and exquisite,—all love her well. Such thoroughly representative ascetical writers again as the Spanish Jesuits Francisco Arias and Alfonzo Rodriguez; the French ones, Saint-Jure and Jean Joseph Surin; the Italian, Paolo Segneri; the Pole, Lancisius; and the German, Drexel, all drew food and flame from her character and doctrine. Then at the beginning of the nineteenth century, Friedrich von Schlegel, the penetrating, many-sided leader of the German Romantic school, translated her *Dialogue*. In our own time Father Isaac Hecker, that striking German-American, loved her as a combination of contemplation and external action; Father Faber strongly endorsed her conception of Purgatory; Cardinal Manning occasioned and prefaced an admirable translation of her *Treatise;* and Cardinal Newman has incorporated her Purgatorial teaching in the noblest of his poems, "The Dream of Gerontius." Indeed, General Charles Gordon also can not unfairly be claimed as her unconscious disciple, since her teaching, embodied in Cardinal Newman's poem, was, besides the Bible and "Imitations," his one written source of strength and consolation during that noble Christian captain's heroic death-watch at Khartoum. And among quite recent or still living writers, Mr. Aubrey de Vere has given us a refined poetic paraphrase of her *Treatise*, and Father George Tyrrell has developed its theme in one of his most striking Essays.[1]

I too have, in my own way, long cared for her example and teaching, and for the great questions and solutions suggested by both. A dozen times and more have I visited and lingered over the chief scenes of her activity; and the literary sources of all our knowledge of her life have been dwelt upon by me for twenty years and more.

I have but very few new details and combinations to offer, in so far as her external life is concerned. It is with regard to the growth of her historic image and the curious vicissitudes

[1] For the recent instances, see Walter Elliott's *Life of Father Hecker*, New York, 1894, p. 369; *The Treatise on Purgatory*, by St. Catherine of Genoa, with a Preface by Cardinal Manning, 1858, 1880; F. W. Faber's *All for Jesus*, ch. ix, sections iii–v; Aubrey de Vere's *Legends and Records of the Church and the Empire*, 1898, pp. 355, 356; George Tyrrell's *Hard Sayings*, 1898, pp. 111–130.

which I have been able to trace in the complication of her "Writings"; as to her spirit and teaching; and as to the place and function to be allotted in the religious life to such realities and phenomena as those presented by her, that I hope to be able to contribute something of value. For although the substance and the primary phenomena of religion are eternal, they appear in each soul with an individuality and freshness pathetically unique; and their attempted analysis and apprehension, and their relations to the other departments of human life, necessarily grow and vary. Indeed it would be truly sad, and would rightly tempt to disbelief in an overruling Providence and divine education of the human race, if the four centuries that intervene between our Saint and ourselves had taught us little or nothing of value, in such matters of borderland and interpretation as nervous health, the psychology of religion, and the distinguishing differences between Christian and Neo-Platonic Mysticism. Whole Sciences, indeed the Scientific, above all the Historic spirit itself, have arisen or have come to maturity since her day. Hence the realities of her life, as of every religious life, remain fresh indeed with the deathless vitality of love and grace, and but very partially explicable still; and yet the highest intellectual honour of each successive period should be found in an ever-renewed attempt at an ever less inadequate apprehension and utilization of these highest and deepest manifestations of Authority, Reason, and Experience, —of the Divine in our poor human life.

II. The Materials and Aids towards such a Study.

1. *The "Vita e Dottrina,"* 1551.

All the biographies of St. Catherine, and all the editions or translations of her "Works," are based upon the *Vita e Dottrina* published in Genoa, by Jacobo Genuti, in 1551. I work from the thirteenth Genoese edition, a reprint of that of 1847 (*Tipi dei Sordo-Muti*). All our knowledge of her mental and physical condition, and of her spiritual doctrine, is practically restricted to this book, and indeed, as we shall see, to its first two parts, the "Vita" and the "Trattato."

The *Vita* is, in its fundamental portions, the joint production of her devoted disciples, Cattaneo Marabotto, a Secular Priest, her Confessor; and Ettore Vernazza, a

Lawyer, her "spiritual son." Its fifty-two chapters (166 octavo pages) are only in small part narrative; quite thirty-five of them are filled with discourses and contemplations of the Saint, evidently, in the simpler of the many parallel versions accumulated here, taken down, at the time of the Saint's communication of them, with quite remarkable fidelity. But the whole suffers from the inclusion of much secondary, amplifying, repetitive matter; is badly arranged; is kept, almost throughout, above all definite indications of the precise successions, dates, and places; and is deficient in unity of view and literary organization. The result is, of necessity, largely insipid and monotonous.

The first of the "Works" is the *Treatise on Purgatory*—the seventeen chapters of which (17 pages) are again hard reading, owing to their evidently consisting of but a mosaic of detached, sometimes parallel sayings, spoken on various occasions and according to the experience and fulness of the moment, and without any reference to the previous one. I shall show reason for holding that this little collection of sayings was originally shorter still (consisting probably of but the matter which now makes up the first seven of its seventeen chapters); that the original chronicler and first redactor of these sayings was Vernazza; and that certain obvious and formal contradictions which appear in the present text must be theological glosses introduced some time between 1520 (or rather 1526) and say 1530 (at latest 1547).

The second of the "Works," the *Spiritual Dialogue between the Soul, the Body, Self-love, the Spirit, the Natural Man, and the Lord God*, is divided into three parts, and fills forty-five chapters (120 pages). I hope to show conclusively that this *Dialogue* was at first no longer than its present Part I; that even this did not exist before 1547; that the whole was written by one and the same person, some one who had never (at least intimately) known the Saint, and who had no other direct material than our present *Vita* and *Trattato*; that this person was the Augustinian canoness, Battista Vernazza, Ettore's eldest daughter; and that the whole has been written for the purpose of attempting some unification and systematization of what in the *Vita* appeared to the writer as wanting in unity and in correctness of wording or of feeling. In this case we get a fairly continuous restatement, in part a heightening, in part a minimizing of the historical facts of Catherine's life, which, just because we have thus a pragmatic, theological transfiguration of the older materials, caused by a penetrating admiration, and resulting in some true increase of insight into its subject-matter, forms a precious document for the psychology and the effect of such states of mind.

The Oratorian Giacinto Parpera's book: *B Caterina da Genova . . . Illustrata,* Genova, 1682, gives, in its three parts, respectively the opinions of Saints and theologians concerning the Saint; a systematic analysis of her doctrine; and an explanation of certain terms and declarations more or less peculiar to her. It is decidedly learned and in parts still useful, but pompously rhetorical and full of "anatomia," *i.e.* much wearisome numbering and indefinite sub-division. The Jesuit Padre Maineri's *Vita de S. Caterina di Genova,* Genova, 1737,—written on the occasion of her canonization,—contains nothing new.

2. *Later books on Catherine.*

A sensible discussion of difficult or obscure points connected with her life occurs in the Bollandists' Life of the Saint, written by Father Sticker in 1752 (*Acta Sanctorum,* September, Vol. V, ed. 1866, pp. 123–195). But the greater part of the discussion is vitiated by the assumption of the independent value, indeed of Catherine herself being the author, of the entirely secondary *Dialogo;* Sticker had not seen a single MS. life or document; and the most important part of her entire personality, her doctrine, had, according to the general plan of the work, to be passed over by him.

I have also had before me Alban Butler's accurate compilation; Monseigneur Paul Fliche's disappointing book, which, though he declares that he has consulted the MS. Lives, is but a rhetorical amplification of the Life of 1551, with here and there a useful date or other detail added by himself (Paris, 1881); and the Rev. Baring Gould's hasty and slipshod account, which completely ignores the "Works" (*Lives of the Saints,* Vol. X, ed. 1898).

But by far the most important printed matter which has hitherto appeared since 1551, indeed the only one which contains anything at all significant that is not already in the *Vita ed Opere,* is Sebastiano Vallebona's booklet, *La Perla dei Fieschi,* Genova, 2nd ed., 1887, 109 pp. It publishes many a painstaking recovery and identification of various dates and sites, relationships, family documents and contemporary events; and has helped me greatly in such matters.

3. *The Manuscripts.*

It is, however, to the careful analysis of the important still extant MS. material that I owe far more than to all the printed matter subsequent to 1551. And indeed I can say without exaggeration that this is the first serious attempt at a critical presentation of Catherine's Life and Teaching. A detailed account of my materials and method will be given in the Appendix to this volume.

III. Peculiarities of the Genoese Climate and Geographical Position; of the Ligurian Character; and of the Times into which Catherine was born. Her Family, Father and Mother.

Catherine Fiesca was born in Genoa, towards the end of the year 1447.[1] She thus belonged to a race and a time full indeed of violence and conflict, intrigue and cruelty, excessive in all things; but hence full too of courage and of daring, of boundlessly expansive energies, and of throbbing life

1. *The Genoese country and character.*

Lying at the foot of imposing mountain terraces, at the great central bend and chief natural harbour of the rocky, sun-baked, mountain-backed Riviera, Genoa formed, from early, pre-Roman days, the natural capital of this thin strip of territory which, eastward from Spezia and westward from Nice, looks all along towards the sea, and towards the broad blue sea alone. And the natural influences of the country seem ever to have been met and doubled by a fierce, explosive strain in the characters of the successive races that peopled this narrow, steep, hot sea-board. The ferocious, wild Ligurians gave the Romans trouble, right up to the end of their dominion; and the subsequent Lombard invasion and subjugation did little to change their character. The keen rivals of Venice, in her trade and power in the East, and the mortal foes of their competitor Pisa, so near to their own gates, the Genoese did much for trade and commerce, but little for science and art, and were feared and hated by the Tuscans, in their rich and fertile lands, and with their large

[1] I have done my best to recover the day, or at least the month, but in vain. The baptismal register of her Parish Church (the Duomo) is, as regards that time, destroyed or lost.

and liberal culture. Sailors, adventurers, free-booters; great merchants and carriers and ba ːers; conspirators and revolutionaries,—they have produ d great admirals, such as Andrea Doria; great administrative and warlike Popes, in the persons of the two masterful, irascible della Roveres, from the twenty miles distant Savona,—Sixtus IV, and Michael Angelo's friend and patron, Julius II; a great navigator, in Christopher Columbus; a fierce and fanatical, but lofty and utterly disinterested revolutionary, in Mazzini; and a brave, reckless condottiere in Garibaldi, born as far away as Nice, but whose mother came from the near Chiavari.

2. *The times into which Catherine was born.*

And our Saint was born in the midst of singularly active, changeful, far-outward-looking, swift-onward-moving times. Columbus had been born the year before; Fust and Gutenberg were printing the first printed books three years later; Constantinople was taken by the Turks when she was six years old.

The Mediaeval system was, at last, breaking up fast. That whole conception of life and polity of peoples had rendered services too great, indeed too unique, to civilization and religion; they had been for too long the faithful instrument, expression and result of a certain stage and aspect of human and Christian character and development, for this break-up not to have been slow, reluctant, and intermittent at first, notwithstanding the heavy blows levelled, often unconsciously, at the system from both within and without the Church. Pope Boniface's Bull, *Unam Sanctam,* which stretched and strained the Mediaeval conception to breaking-point (1302); the dreary blank and confusion of the seventy years of the Avignon exile of the Papacy (1309–1377); the thirty years' distraction of the great Papal Schism (1378–1409); the fierce revolts and tragic fates of Wycliffe and of Hus, in 1384 and 1415; the ineffectual Council of Constance (1414–1418),—all this had already taken place. And not even such saintly figures as Tauler and Blessed Henry Suso in Germany, and St. Catherine of Siena in Italy and France; or such nobly reforming characters as the French Chancellor Gerson, who had died eighteen years before our Saint's birth (1429); or the bold and spiritual German Philosopher-Cardinal Nicolas of Coes, who died when she was seventeen (1464),—could achieve more than to announce and prepare the transition to a great modification of Christendom, and to indicate the eternal and necessary source from which it must spring, and the new temporal, contingent form which it might take.

But the scandals, revolts, and repressions, on a scale and with results which turned Reform into Revolution, and broke up Western Europe into those two hostile camps, which towards the end of four centuries, we see, alas ! hostile still—these things were yet to come. Roderigo Borgia was to be Pope (1492–1503) only towards the end of her life. And only after she had been seven years dead, was Luther to nail his theses on the University-Church door at Wittenberg (1517), and more than a generation later were Mary Tudor in England and Philip II in Spain (1553–1598) to attempt, for the last time on so large a scale, the task of keeping and winning minds and souls, by ruthless physical repression.

Catherine lived thus within a period which, in its depths, was already modern, but not yet broken up into seemingly final, institutionalized internecine antagonisms. And hence we can get in her a most restful and bracing pure affirmativeness, an entire absence of religious controversy, such as, of necessity, cannot be found in even such predominantly interior souls as the great Post-Reformation Spanish Mystics. Her whole religion can grow and show itself as simply positive, and in rivalry and conflict with her own false self and with that alone.

3. *The Fieschi family.*

And the particular family from which she sprang, and the period of its history at which she appeared, each helped to bring right into her blood and immediate surroundings the more general conditions of her race and time.

The Fieschi had indeed a long past story, securely traceable through a good two centuries and a half before Catherine's birth. They sprang from the little seaside town of Lavagna, twenty English miles east of Genoa, where shipbuilding is still carried on. Here it was that Sinibaldo de' Fieschi, the first of the two Popes of the family, Innocent IV (1234–1254), was born, whose whole Pontificate was one long vehement struggle with his former friend, the masterful and sceptical Emperor Frederic II of Germany. His nephew was Pope, under the title of Hadrian V, for but a few months (1276). It was from Pope Innocent's brother Robert that St. Catherine was descended.

The Fieschi were the greatest of the great Guelph families of Genoa, such as the Grimaldi, Guarchi, and Montaldi. The great Doria family, with the Spinola, Fregosi, and Adorni, was as strongly Ghibelline. And the endless, fierce conflict between these two factions, in Genoa itself and along both Rivieras, led to the calling in, and to the temporary supremacy over Genoa, of the Dukes of Milan, the Counts of Montferrat, and of the Kings of Naples and of France. The Revolution of 1339, which put an end to the exclusive rule of the Nobles, and introduced elective Doges or Dukes as life-long heads of the Republic, really altered little or nothing of all this.

Indeed the Fieschi had, just now at Catherine's birth, reached the full height of their power and worldly splendour. For the two Popes of the family had already reigned two centuries before, and Cardinal Luca Fieschi lay buried in the Cathedral for over a hundred years; but the Fieschi now possessed numerous fiefs in Liguria, Piedmont, Lombardy, and even in the Kingdom of Naples; Nicolo Fieschi, a cousin of the Saint, was, in Catherine's time, a prominent member of the College of Cardinals; and her own father was Viceroy of Naples to King René of Anjou. There was indeed exactly a century yet to run, up to the beginning of the downward course of the family,—the disastrous conspiracy of the Fieschi against the Dorias (1547), which forms the subject of Schiller's well-known play.

Catherine's father had been Viceroy of Naples to that René Duc of Anjou, Count of Provence, Duke of Lorraine, and titular King of Naples, whose adventurous career and immensely popular character still stand out so vividly in history. The "roi débonnaire," the friend of the Troubadour and father of Margaret of Anjou, Consort to King Henry VI of England, figures life-like in Scott's *Anne of Geierstein*; and his strikingly *bourgeois* profile may still be seen, as part of the vivid portraiture of his kneeling figure which faces the corresponding one of his Queen, upon the great contemporary triptych picture, representing in its central division the Madonna and Child in the branches of a tree (in allusion to the Burning Bush and the Rod of Jesse), which hangs in the choir of the cathedral of Aix, King René's old wind-swept and now sleepy Provençal capital. Since Charles I of Anjou (1265–1285), the Angevine Kings had made Naples the capital of their Kingdom; Duke René was the last of the Angevines to hold or seriously to claim it. He lost it in 1442 to the Spaniards; but still in 1459 he attempted, by means of a Genoese fleet, to repossess himself of his old kingdom, so that

Catherine's father could, even up to the time of his death in 1462, retain the title of Viceroy of Naples. Her mother, Francesca di Negro, also belonged to an ancient and noble Genoese family.

IV. Catherine's Life, up to the Preliminaries of her Conversion: Autumn 1447–Mid-March 1474.

1. *The house where she was born; her brothers and sister.*

Catherine was born in one of the many palaces of the Fieschi, in the one which stood in the Vico Filo, close to the dark grey limestone façade of the Cathedral of San Lorenzo. The palace was hemmed in, on its two sides and at its back, by the houses of Urbano and Sebastiano di Negri, and was demolished when the then Piazza dei Fieschi was enlarged and became the present Piazza di San Lorenzo. The house now facing the Cathedral doorway occupies approximately the site of that old palace.

She was the youngest of five children. There were three sons: Giacomo, named after his father; and Lorenzo and Giovanni, no doubt named respectively after the great Roman deacon, the titular saint of the Cathedral, and who already appeared upon his gridiron, on the quaint Mediaeval relief over its portal; and after the Baptist, whose reputed relics lay there, in the great Chapel, rebuilt for them soon after this time (1451–1496). Last came the two daughters: Limbania, named after a beatified virgin and contemplative, a Genoese Augustinian Nun of the thirteenth century, and Caterinetta, christened and in all the legal documents always called by this diminutive, presumably after St. Catherine of Alexandria, who had an altar in the Cathedral. And the Cathedral was their Parish Church.

2. *Catherine's physical appearance; her qualities and habits of body and of mind.*

In this house, then, Catherine grew up and lived till she was sixteen. The beautiful, tall figure; the noble oval face with its lofty brow, finely formed nose, and powerful, indeed obstinate chin; the winning countenance with its delicate complexion and curling, sensitive, spiritual mouth-line; deep grey-blue spiritual eyes; the long, tapering fingers; the massive dark brown or black hair; still more the quickly and intensely impressionable, nervous and extremely tense and active physical and psychical organization; and then the very affectionate, ardent, aspiring, impatient and absolute qualities and habits of her mind and heart and will,—all these things we are not merely told, we can still see them and find them, in part, even in her remains, but more fully in her portrait, and above all, in her numerous authentic utterances.[1]

[1] Not a shadow of reasonable doubt is possible as to the authenticity of these relics. Buried as she was in the Church of the Hospital of Pammatone, which latter she had first simply served, and then directed and inhabited, during thirty-seven years, her resting-place remained a centre of unbroken devotion up to her Beatification and Canonization, when the relics were removed but a few yards upwards, and placed in their glass shrine above and behind the altar in the Chapel of the Tribune —the Deposito di S. Caterina—where they have rested ever since. The special character of the brow and of the hands is still plainly recognizable. Of the four or five portraits mentioned by Vallebona, not one can be traced back to her lifetime.

In the *Manuale Cartularii* of the Pammatone Hospital, under date of 10th July 1512 (p. 62), (I quote from an authentic copy which I found among various documents copied out by the protonotary P. Angelo Giovo, and prefixed to his MS. Latin life of the Saint preserved in the *Biblioteca della Missione Urbana*, Genoa, No. 30, 8, 140,) there is an entry of money (7 lire 10 soldi, equivalent to about £7 10*s.*) paid by the administrators of the Hospital to Don Cattaneo Marabotto, her Confessor and Executor: " Ratio sepulturae q(uondam) D(ominae) Catarinettae Adurnae pro diversis expensis factis p(er) D(ominum) Cattaneum Marabottum, videlicet *pro pictura* et apportari facere lapides ipsius sepulturae." The payment must have been either for expressly painting a picture, or for buying one already painted. We would, however, expect, in the former case, for the entry, in analogy with its final clause, to run: " pro pingi facere picturam." In the latter case, we are almost forced to think of the picture as painted by some friend or disciple of the Saint, not for herself or for her relations or friends (for in that case it would hardly have been sold, but would have been left or given to the Hospital), but for his own consolation, or in hopes of its being eventually bought for the Hospital (and this may well have been done during her lifetime). In any case, this entry attests that a portrait of the Saint was in existence at the Hospital not two years after her death, and which was approved of by one of her closest friends. I take it that that portrait was placed on her sepulchral monument erected to her in January 1512 in the Hospital Church. If still extant, at least in a copy, that original or copy is, presumably, at the Hospital still.

Now there are but three pictures at the Hospital which claim to be portraits of her and are not, avowedly, copies. (1) The large oil painting of her standing figure, in the room adjoining the closet now shown as the place where she died, is clearly a late, quite lifeless composition. (2) The portrait-head in the Superioress's room has been carefully examined for me by a trained portrait painter, who reports that the picture consists of a skilful ancient foundation now largely hidden under much clumsy repainting. (3) The picture reproduced at the head of this first

3. *The few certain details concerning her early years. Santa Maria delle Grazie.*

We have, as only too often in such older biographies, but very few precise and characteristic details concerning her early years. She had in her room a Pietà a representation of the Dead Christ in His Mother's arms, and we are told how deeply it affected her every time she entered this room, and raised her eyes up to it. The other points mentioned, her early bodily penances, silence, and gift of prayer (the latter said to have been communicated to her at twelve years of age), read

volume, now in the sacristy of the *Santissima Annunziata in Portorio* (the Hospital Church), is clearly the work of one hand alone. It is without the somewhat disagreeable look present in the previous portrait, a look doubtless introduced there by the unskilful restoration. If then the sacristy picture is a copy of the Superioress's picture, it will have been copied before the latter picture was thus repainted. This sacristy picture now hangs in an old-fashioned white-and-gold wooden frame with "Santa Catarina da Genova" in raised letters carved out upon it, a carving which is evidently contemporary with the frame's make. The frame thus cannot be older than 1737, the year of Catherine's canonization. But the portrait is without trace of a nimbus and carefully reproduces the very peculiar features of a particular face, head, and neck.

The original painting, thus still more or less before us in these two pictures, was evidently by no mean artist, and strikes a good connoisseur as of the school of Leonardo da Vinci (died 1519). There were several good painters of this school resident in Genoa about this time: Carlo da Milano, Luca da Novara, Vincenzo da Brescia, and Giovanni Mazone di Alessandria. In the very year of her death, and still more two years later, she was publicly and spontaneously venerated as Blessed, and this Cultus continued unbroken up to the Bull of Urban VIII, of 1625. Hence the further back we place one or both of these portraits, the more naturally can we explain the absence of the nimbus. Everything conspires, then, to prove that one of these portraits goes back, in some way, to the picture painted for or bought by Marabotto, and which adorned her monument from 1512 to 1593.

I have striven hard but in vain to find some scrap of Catherine's handwriting. The late Mr. Hartwell Grisell of Oxford, and the Cavaliere Azzolini dei Manfredi of Rome, both of them lifelong collectors of Saints' autographs, have kindly assured me that they have never come across a word even purporting to be in her handwriting. The fourteen wills and codicils made in her favour or by herself are all, according to the universal custom of the time and country, written throughout in a rapid, cursive hand by the lawyer himself alone, with certain slight signs (crosses or lines) for further identification of his authorship, but with no signature of any kind. There is no shadow of a true tradition as to any of her sayings or thinkings having ever been written down by herself. And the business books of the Hospital, kept, at least in part, by Catherine from 1490 to 1496, when she was its matron, have long ago been destroyed by fire.

suspiciously like simple assumptions made by her biographers, and in any case do not help to individualize her, in these years of uncertain, tentative, or as yet but little characteristic, forms of goodness.

But from thirteen, for three years onwards, the young girl is very certainly and deeply drawn to the Conventual life, as she sees it practised by her sister Limbania, who, true to the example of her own Genoese Augustinian Patron Saint, had become a member of the Augustinian Canonesses of our Lady of Graces, and now lived there happy and devoted in the midst of that very fervent and cultivated Community. Limbania was one of the nineteen Foundresses of this Convent, who, on August 5, 1451, received the habit of Canonesses Regular of the Lateran, from the hands of Padre Giovanni de' Gatti, at that time Superior of S. Teodoro outside the walls of Genoa, a house of the same Order. Among these Novices occur a Simonetta di Negro, no doubt a cousin of Catherine, and Nicola and Lucia da Nove, two sisters; these facts will have helped Catherine to hope for admission together with her own sister Limbania.[1]

The Convent and its Chapel, both secularized, are still in existence, at a quarter of an hour's walk from Catherine's palace-home. Moving from here, along the Vico Chiabrera, up the Via dei Maruffi (now San Bernardo), and across the latter, up one of the many steep, very narrow little alleys, to the Piazza dei Embriaci, and again up by the tall, slim, grey tower of the Crusader Guilielmo Embriaco, we arrive at last at a level, all but deserted, sun-baked piazza, called, after its Church, Sta Maria in Passione. Face this Church, and the long, tall house on your left hand, covered with dim, faded frescoes, is Limbania's Convent, so loved by Catherine. The right door leads into the Chapel, which Vallebona [2] found in 1887 in use as a wood-store, and which I saw in May 1900 turned into a music-hall: where the altar had stood, were a dingy stage, and tawdry wings. The pompous frescoes and stuccos on the walls and ceiling are evidently of the seventeenth century or even later. The adjoining Convent still retains a small figure of St. Augustine sculptured on a corbel on the vault of the first landing. The Byzantine, dark brown Madonna-and-Child picture, which Catherine so often prayed

[1] See *Opere Spirituale della Ven. B. Vernazza*, Genova, 1755, 6 vols., Vol. I, p. 3.

[2] *Op. cit.* p. 45.

before in the Chapel, can still be seen, on the left-hand wall of the Chapel of St. Thomas Aquinas, in the Church of S. Maria di Castello, which is close by, at a lower level than the Piazza of the Convent.

4. *Catherine's marriage. The Adorni family.*

The Convent Chaplain was Catherine's Confessor, and through him she attempted to gain the permission of the Nuns to enter their Community. But whilst they hesitated and put her off, on the very reasonable ground of her unusual youth, her father died (end of 1461); and a particular combination, from amongst the endless political rivalries and intrigues of Genoa, soon closed in upon the beautiful girl, member of the greatest of the Guelph families of that turbulent time. It was a bad and sorry business, and one likes to think that the father, had he lived, would not thus have sacrificed his daughter. For if in Shakespeare's Romeo and Juliet we have two youthful lovers joining hands and hearts, in spite of the secular enmity of their respective houses; here, alas! in real life, we have the contrary spectacle, the deep because dreary tragedy of two great rival factions making—rather, hoping to make—peace, by the enforced union of two mutually indifferent and profoundly unsuited young people.

Not but that socially the two were admirably matched. For Giuliano Adorno belonged to a family hardly inferior in antiquity and splendour to Catherine's own. Six different Adorni had been Doges of Genoa in 1363, 1385, 1413, 1443, 1447, 1461; and the one of 1413 had been Giuliano's own grandfather. They were Lords of the Greek Island of Chios (Scio), which they had helped to conquer for Genoa in 1349.

And now the last Doge of the family, Prospero Adorno, had just been driven from the Ducal throne by Paolo Campofregoso, the strong-willed representative of the great rival, though also Ghibelline, family of the Fregosi. Campofregoso was now both Duke and Archbishop of Genoa. By an alliance with the Fieschi, the most powerful of the Guelph families, the Adorni could hope, in their turn, to oust the Fregosi, and to reinstate themselves at the head of the great Republic. The ideals, antipathies or indifference of a girl of sixteen were not allowed to stand in the way; and so the contract was signed on January 13, 1463.

The marriage was celebrated soon afterwards in the Cathedral of San Lorenzo, in the Chapel of St. John the Baptist, since the Campanaro family, which had built it in 1299, and the

Adorni, who had married into and succeeded the Campanaro, were excepted from the rule prohibiting the access of women to this Chapel. Since Cardinal Giorgio Fieschi had recently died, Bishop Napoleone Fieschi, of Albenga, presided at the ceremony.

5. *Giuliano's character. Catherine's pre-conversion married life.*

Giuliano's father was dead; only his widowed mother, Tobia dei Franchi, remained. It was, however, with Catherine's mother, in the old Palazzo near the Cathedral, that the young couple were to live, and actually stayed, during the first two years.

Giuliano was young and rich; his two elder brothers occupied high naval posts; his first cousin, Agostino Adorno, was a man of noble character and great initiative; and a descendant of this cousin, also Agostino, was later on Beatified. But Giuliano himself did at first worse than nothing, and never did much throughout his life. A man of an undisciplined, wayward, impatient, and explosive temper; selfish and self-indulgent; a lover of obscure and useless, in one instance criminal, squandering of his time, money, health, and affections, he did not deserve the rare woman who had been sold to him; and would possibly indeed have managed to be a better man with a wife he had really loved, or with one of a temperament and outlook more ordinary and nearer to his own. As it was, he was hardly ever at home, and, according to his own later penitent admission and testamentary provisions, he was, some time during the first ten years of his marriage, gravely unfaithful to his wife.

Catherine, on her part, spent the first five of these dreary years in sad and mournful loneliness, at first in her mother's house, and afterwards, at least in the winter-time, in Giuliano's own palace, a building which stood exactly where now stands the Church of Saint Philip Neri, in the Via Lomellina (at that time, Via Sant' Agnese), and near the Piazza Annunziata. In the summer-time she would stay, mostly alone again, at Giuliano's country seat at Prà on the Western Riviera, just beyond Pegli, and six English miles from Genoa.

This latter property is still in existence, but was, some twenty years ago, on the extinction of the male line of the Adorni, sold to the Piccardo family. The present moderate-sized house, standing close to the high-road and sea-beach, although evidently rebuilt (probably on a considerably smaller scale) since Catherine's time, no doubt occupies part at least of the old site. But the Chapel which, in the Saint's days, adjoined the house, was described by Vallebona (in 1887) as turned into a stable; and in April 1902 an elderly serving-man of the Piccardo family showed me the precise spot, on a now level meadow expanse closely adjoining the house, where he himself, some fifteen years since, had helped to pull down this chapel-stable. He showed me the (probably seventeenth-century) picture representing the scene of the Saint's conversion, which had, at that time, been still in this building, and which is now hung up in a small Confraternity-Chapel near by in Prà.

As to money of her own, Catherine had, as we shall see later on, her dowry of £1,000, to which Giuliano had contributed £200. But we have no evidence of any good works performed by her in this decade, although, as we shall find, it must have been during these summers that she, at least occasionally, walked or rode over the wooded hill-path to the old Benedictine Pilgrimage Church and Monastery of San Nicolo in Boschetto, three or four English miles away. These buildings are now secularized and empty, but, even so, impressive still.[1]

It is but natural to suppose that she was as yet too little at one with her true self, to be able to surmount her lot, or even seriously to attempt such a task, by escaping from the false self and from all attempts at finding happiness within the four corners of the demands of her most sensitive and absolute disposition. To learn to do things well takes time, —and even if it be but the finding out that those things to do are *there*, ready and requiring to be done; or the seeing that we are doing them badly. Hence above all does the learning to suffer well, the turning pain into self-expansion and

Although the Church and Monastery belonged, as Catherine's Will of 1509 puts it, to " the Order of St. Benedict of the Congregation of Saint Justina in Padua "—a Congregation founded at Padua about 1430, which, later on embracing the principal monasteries of Italy, including Monte Cassino, came to be called the Cassinese Congregation—yet the community were evidently closely bound up with the Augustinian Canons Regular of the Lateran, or at all events with the foundation of the Convent of Augustinian Canonesses at Santa Maria delle Grazie. For the concession of Pope Nicolas V for the latter Convent is addressed to his " Beloved sons of Saint Theodore of Genoa " (Augustinian Canons) " and of Saint Nicolas in Boschetto." And this close connection with, and action for, a Church and Convent so dearly loved by Catherine, will have necessarily been one of the causes of her affection for the Benedictine country-side Church.

self-escape, as well as into fruitful action, require time, special graces, and unusual fidelity of soul. And even the noblest nature will usually begin by thinking of getting, rather than of giving; it will simply thirst to be loved, and to find its happiness in its own heart's perfect "comprehendedness."

Catherine tried to find relief, first in one attitude on her life's sad couch of mental suffering, and then in another; and neither brought her any alleviation. During the first five years she had hidden herself away, and had moped in solitude; the last five, she had given herself to worldly gaieties and feminine amusements, short, however, of all grave offence against the moral law. And at the end of these experiences and experiments she, noble, deep nature that she was, found herself, of course, sadder than ever, with apparently no escape of any kind from out of the dull oppression, the living death of her existence and of herself.

V. Her Conversion, with its immediate Preliminaries and Consequences, March 1473.

1. *Her prayer, March* 20, 1473. *Her conversion, March* 22.

From after Christmas-time in 1472, Catherine's affliction of mind had become peculiarly intense, and a profound aversion to all the things of this world made her fly anew from all human intercourse; and yet her own company had become insupportable to her, as nothing whatsoever attracted her will.

And at the end of three months, on the 20th of March 1473—it was the eve of the Feast of St. Benedict—she was praying in his little church still standing close to the sea, at the western end of Genoa, not far beyond Andrea Doria's Palace, built so soon after her death. And in her keen distress she prayed: "St. Benedict, pray to God that He make me stay three months sick in bed." [1]

[1] This evidently most authentic anecdote stands in the *Vita*, p. 3, in a doubly disconcerting context. Her prayers, always elsewhere recorded together with their effects, are here abruptly left, without any indication of their sequel; and the prayer for a *three months' illness* is followed by an attempted explanation of it—that she had gone through *three months* of mental *affliction*. I take it that some other continuation has been suppressed, or, at least, that the present explanation owes its "three months" to a quaint determination to find at least a retrospective correspondence between her prayer and the happenings of her life.

And two days later, when Catherine was visiting her sister at her Convent, Limbania proposed to her, since she declared herself indisposed to go to confession (although the Feast of the Annunciation was at hand), at least to go and recommend herself in the Chapel to the chaplain of the Convent, who was indeed a saintly Religious. And, at the moment that she was on her knees before him, her heart was pierced by so sudden and immense a love of God, accompanied by so penetrating a sight of her miseries and sins and of His goodness, that she was near falling to the ground. And in a transport of pure and all-purifying love, she was drawn away from the miseries of the world; and, as it were beside herself, she kept crying out within herself: "No more world; no more sins!" And at that moment she felt that, had she had in her possession a thousand worlds, she would have cast them all away.[1]

2. *Views and truths concerning this Experience.*

One of the various writers who have successively, and in great part differently, moralized upon the chief events of her life, dwells on this great moment as achieving in her soul all the usually lengthy and successive effects of the purgative, illuminative, and unitive progression, and as, in that one instant, bringing her soul to that highest state of transformation, in which the will is wholly united to God.[2] But having regard to the fact, patent on every page of her biography and "Works," that, for the remaining thirty-seven years of her life, her interior history represents one continuous widening and deepening and moving onwards of efforts, trials and pains, of achievements and ideals—a fact actually schematized by another writer (who, as I shall show, is the penultimate Redactor of the Life) not two pages lower down—it is clear that we must be careful to conceive this perfection as relative to her previous state or even to the final goodness of many saintly souls. We must, in a word, try to realize vividly, and constantly to recall, certain complex truths, without which the very greatness of the experience here considered will but help to check or deflect our apprehension of the spiritual life.

For one thing, the deeper and the more unique the soul's

[1] *Vita*, p. 4, first two paragraphs. I hope to show in the Appendix that we owe their getting on to paper to Ettore Vernazza, and that he derived their contents from Catherine herself, some time after 1495.

[2] *Ibid.* p. 4, § 3.

experience, and the richer such experience is, the more entirely does all that the soul is, and ever was, wake up and fuse itself in one indivisible act, in which much of the old is newly seen to be dross and is so far forth excluded; and in which the old that is retained reappears in a fresh context, a context which itself affects and is itself affected by all the other old and new ideas and feelings. It thus clearly bears the stamp upon it of the profound difference between Time, conceived as a succession of moments of identical quantity and quality, each in juxtaposition and exterior to the other, mathematical time, such as our clocks register on the dials, —a conception really derived from space-perception and exterior, measurable *things*—and Duration, with its variously rapid succession of heterogeneous qualities, each affecting and colouring, each affected and coloured by, all the others, and all producing together a living harmony and organic unity, all which constitutes the essentially unpicturable experience of the living *person*. Such a moment is thus incapable of adequate analysis, in exact proportion as it is fully expressive of the depths of the personality and of its experience: for each element here, whilst, in its living context, an energy and a quality which at each moment modifies and is modified by all the other elements, becomes, in an intellectual analysis, when each is separated from the others, a mere dead thing and a quantity.

And secondly, such an experience is throughout as truly a work of pure grace, a gift, as it is a work of pure energy, an act. And here again, the grace and the energy, the gift and the act are not juxtaposed, but throughout they stimulate and interpenetrate each other, with the most entirely unanalyzable, unpicturable completeness. It is indeed in exact proportion to the fulness of this inter-stimulation and penetration, to the organic oneness of the act, that such an act is this one particular soul's very own act and yet the living God's own fullest gift. Grace does not lie without, but within; it does not check or limit, but constitutes the will's autonomy.

And thirdly, it is an experience which leaves the soul different forever from what it was before; which purifies her perfectly, in and for that moment, from all her stains of actual sin committed up to that moment; and which materially strengthens her inclinations towards good and weakens her tendencies towards evil. But the soul herself lives on; and she lives but in and through successive acts of all kinds. Hence it is not an act,—there is none such, here below at least,—which takes or can take the place of fresh acts to be produced again and again throughout her life. The soul has not, in any sense or any degree, been approximated to that utterly paradoxical thing, a saintly automaton. She is not raised above the limitations and imperfections, the obscurities and conflicts, the failings and sins of humanity. She *could* fall away and commit grave sin; she actually *does* commit minor sins of frailty and surprise. Her interior efforts and experiences are now but on a larger, deeper scale, and on a higher plane, and take place from a new vantage-ground, a position which has, however, itself to be continually actively defended and reinforced. Temptation, trial, sorrow, pain; hope, fear, self-hatred, love and joy, with ever-renewed and increased aspiration and effort, all variously change and deepen their combinations and qualities, outlook and ideals. But they do not for one moment cease. All things but grow in depth and significance, in variety within unity, in interiority and interpenetration.

And finally, although conversions of the apparent suddenness and profound depth and perseverance of the one here studied, are rightly taken to be very special and rare graces of God, yet it would be but misinterpreting and depreciating their true significance to make their suddenness the direct proof and measure of their own supernaturalness or the standard by which to appraise the altitude of the goodness of other lives. God is as truly the source of gradual purification as of sudden conversion, and as truly the strength which guards and moves us straight on, as that which regains and calls us back. Hence such acts as Catherine's should not be entirely separated off from those acts of love, contrition and self-dedication which occur, as so many free graces of God in and with the free acts of man, more or less frequently in the secret lives of human beings throughout the world.

3. *The Second Experience, in the Palace.*

Catherine then was kneeling on, in these great moments of her true self's self-discovery and self-determination, with her true Life now at last felt so divinely near and yet still so divinely far: she was kneeling on, oblivious of time and space, incapable of speech—throughout a deep, rich age of growth, during but some minutes of poor clock-time—whilst the chaplain was called away by some little momentary matter. And when he returned, she was just able to utter: "Father, if you please, I should like to let this confession stand over to another time." And returning home, she was so on fire and wounded with the love which God had interiorly manifested to her, that, as if beside herself, she went into the most private chamber she could find, and there gave vent to her burning tears and sighs. And, all instructed as she had suddenly become in prayer, her lips could only utter: "O Love, can it be that Thou hast called me with so much love, and revealed to me, at one view, what no tongue can describe?" And her contrition for her offences against such infinite goodness was so great, that, if she had not been specially supported, her heart would have been broken, and she would have died.[1]

And yet, though her biographer, no doubt rightly, represents her feeling and dispositions as now at their uttermost,—they may well have actually been so, at that moment, for that moment,—they were nevertheless evidently capable of indefinite subsequent increase. Indeed it must have been on this same day, or on one of the next three days, that, in one of the rooms of the palace in the Via S. Agnese,—(the approximate spot is marked in the Church of St. Philip by a fine picture representing the scene, hung over the altar of one of the left-hand-side chapels,)—"Our Lord, desiring to enkindle still more profoundly His love in this soul, appeared to her in spirit with His Cross upon His shoulder dripping with blood, so that the whole house seemed to be all full of rivulets of that Blood, which she saw to have been all shed because of love alone." "And filled with disgust at herself, she exclaimed: 'O Love, if it be necessary, I am ready to confess my sins in public.'"[2]

4. *Two peculiarities of this Experience.*

Here two things are remarkable. This is, to begin with, her first and last vision (*visione*), which I can find, in the sense of a picture produced indeed "in the spirit," but yet

[1] *Vita*, p. 4, § 3; p. 5, § 1.

[2] *Ibid.* p. 5, §§ 2, 3. I have, together with the Bull of Canonization, deliberately omitted the first two sentences of § 3, which (with their representation of our Lord as appearing not alive with the Cross, but dead on it, and with their repetition here of the exclamation as to "no more sins" of her conversion-moment) form an interesting doublet, with a complex and eventful history attaching to it. See Appendix to this volume.

evidently apprehended with a sense of apparently complete passivity in the perceiving mind and of objectivity as to the perceived thing, and remembered as such throughout her life. For the frequent subsequent "sights" or picturings (*viste*) are avowedly only of the nature of profoundly vivid, purely mental, more or less consciously voluntary and subjective contemplations and intuitions; whilst her only other "visions," those seen during the last stage of her last illness, seem indeed to have been of an even more sensible kind than this *visione*, but they were entirely fitful and left no permanent impression behind them.

And again, this is the one only picture of any, even of a voluntary, meditational kind, concerning the Passion, to be found throughout her life; all her other contemplations and impressions of whatever kind are of other subjects.

5. *Her general confession.*

It was after these fundamental experiences that, once more in the Chapel of the Augustinianesses, apparently four days later, on the 24th of March, "she made her general confession, with such contrition and compunction as to pierce her soul." [1]

VI. The Two Conceptions concerning the Character and *Rationale* of her Penitential Period and of her whole Convert Life. The Position adopted here.

At this point of the Life two successive reporters or redactors introduce, respectively, a general reflection on the character and *rationale* of the period of penitence now immediately ensuing, and a scheme and forecast as to the stages in the ascensional movement of her entire convert life.

1. *The older conception.*

The first reporter,—evidently the same who, in connection with the Conversion scene, had described her soul as, there and then, at the culmination of holiness,—here says: "And although God, at the moment when," four days before, "He had given her that love and pain, had there and then

[1] *Vita*, p. 5*c*.

pardoned her all her sins, consuming them in the fire of His love; yet He, wishing her to satisfy the claims of justice, led her by the way of satisfaction, in such wise as to cause this special contrition, illumination, and conversion to last about fourteen months," and it is no doubt implied by him that frequent confession was practised throughout this time.[1]

Thus we get an impressive instance of the rich and complex experience on which the Catholic doctrine is built, as to how, on the one hand, pure and perfect love ever instantly obliterates all sin; how, on the other hand, such perfect love, in those who explicitly know and accept the Church's claims, involves a determination to confess all such grave sins as may have been committed; and how, finally, such subsequent confession is itself operative within the soul. For as between the soul and the body, so between the Mystical and Sacramental, there is a real and operative connection, though one which, however inadequately known by us, we know to be one not of simple identity or coextension.

And the experiences and doctrines here specially considered appear to require the conception of contrition and pardon as but the necessary expression and effect of true, operative love; and to demand the conclusion that purification participates in the essentially positive nature of love, its cause. The removal of bodily impurity is a negative act, and, as such, is limited and unrepeatable; but spiritual purification would thus, as something positive, be capable of indefinite increase and repetition. And hence the deep philosophical justification of repeated contrition and confession for the same sins, even though already pardoned. We shall find that such a view is also to be found in St. Catherine's own doctrine, though there is nothing to show that the thought of this paragraph is derived from Catherine herself. I take it to proceed from Cattaneo Marabotto.

2. *The later conception.*

The second writer, the penultimate Redactor of the book as we now have it, finds three successive levels in her whole life's constant growth and upward movement, and discovers a type of each in some love-impelled figure or scene of the Bible. And so the writer gets his periods symbolized respectively by the two New Testament scenes of Christ's feet, and the Penitent Magdalen drawn by Him to them, and of

[1] *Vita*, p. 5c.

Christ's breast, and the Beloved Disciple reposing peacefully upon it; and by the Old Testament poetic picture, and its allegorical interpretation, of Christ's (the true Solomon's) mouth, and the Bride's kiss. And some four years are assigned to the first period, " many " years to the second, and her last years to the last: 1478 and 1499 would be the approximate dates dividing off these periods. We shall find this scheme to proceed from Battista Vernazza.

Time-honoured though it be, this symbolism in no way fits Catherine's case. For, excepting during the short first period, her direct and formal occupation with the Sacred Humanity is, throughout her convert life, practically confined to the Eucharistic Presence; and again, her words and contemplations are (as indeed the unhappiness of her marriage experience would lead one to expect and as the whole temper of her mind and devotion require) quite remarkably free from all affinity to the Canticle of Canticles. And yet this, in so far inappropriate, framework helps to emphasize the all-important fact of the constant growth and deepening ever at work within her life.

Indeed, the short, general characterization of each of these successive periods which follows after each symbol here, is derived from passages of the *Vita* which are doubtless based upon direct communication by herself. Thus the detailed sight of her own particular sins and of God's particular graces towards herself, characteristic of the relatively short first period, is succeeded by the second, long and profoundly lonely, period of an apparent union of the divine and of the human personalities, in which all distinct perception of her own acts appears to have usually been lost,—a union which can lead her to the point of saying: " I have no longer either soul or heart of my own; but my soul and my heart are those of my Love." Yet in her third and last period, the consciousness of her own acts and of their differentiation is described as fully reappearing within her mind. For though we are presented here with a kind of immersion in the Divinity, in which she appears so to lose herself interiorly and exteriorly as to be able to say with St. Paul: " I live no longer, but Christ lives in me "; and though we are told that she was no longer able to discern between the good and evil of her acts, by means of any direct examination of them: yet her acts are now again perceived to be her own; to be some of them good and some of them faulty; and are seen, as several and as differing, by her own self, but "in God." [1] So did the Lady of Shallot, all turned away though she was from the world of sight, see in her mirror the different figures as, good and bad, they moved on their way, more truly and clearly than she had ever seen them formerly by any direct perception.

3. *Position adopted in this study concerning Catherine's spiritual growth.*

Now these periods of interior, experimental, mystical vicissitude and growth have also their corresponding variations of religious analysis and speculation, and of external actions and events; and these variations are not only the concomitants and expressions of the inner growth, but are also, in part, the subject-matter and occasion for the next stage of mystical experience. And since Catherine's special characteristic consists precisely in the richness and variety of her life at any one moment, and in the successive, ever-accelerated enrichment which it achieves almost up to the end, any obliteration of this successive growth, or any one-sided attention to any one aspect of her life during any one of its chief periods, will readily take all life-likeness out of her portrait.

Yet to achieve anything like this comprehension is most difficult, if only because it has to be attempted with the aid of materials which, where their registration is contemporary with the events chronicled, belong, all but the legal documents, to the last fifteen years of her life; and because, even within this last period, they are rarely furnished with any reference to their exact place within that period. There is throughout the book a most natural and instructive, indeed in its way most legitimate and even necessary, insistence upon the apparently complete independence and aloofness, the transcendence of her inner life. And this insistence goes so far that a self-sufficing Eternity, a completely unchanging Here and Now, floating outside and above even the necessary and normal affections, actions, and relations of human life and fellowship, seems, especially from after her conversion till up to the beginning of her physical incapacitation,[2] to have

[1] *Vita*, pp. 5*c*, 6,—as they appear in MS. "A." This matter of these periods has given me much trouble, since there are two rival traditions concerning them to be found, really unreconciled, within the oldest documents of the *Vita*. The point is fully discussed in the Appendix.

[2] *Ibid.* cc. ix–xli, pp. 21*c*—111*c*.

taken the place of the characteristically human struggle in and through time and space, with and through our fellow-creatures. As in Leibniz we get a divinely pre-established harmony between the dispositions and the acts of the body and those of the soul, which appear indeed as though indestructibly inter-related, but which, in reality, operate throughout without one instant's direct interaction: so here, the external is not indeed represented as neglected by her, nor as anything but in complete harmony with her inner life, and as indeed inspired by God, yet her own mind and soul are but reluctantly permitted to appear as expressing themselves in it, as requiring and affected by it. She appears as having got outside of, and away from, all the visible and purely human, rather than deeper into and behind it; to have achieved the ignoring of it rather than its conversion and transfiguration and its appointment to its own intrinsic place and function in the full economy of the soul's new life.

And yet all this is, even in the minds of the authors, but one aspect of this complex life, and one which, taken alone, would at once do injustice to its other aspect, the grand depth and range of its immanental quality. And even in as much as the transcendental aspect is really attributable to the predominant trend of Catherine's own character and teaching, it in no way invalidates the fact of the actual astonishing many-sidedness and balance of her life, especially before her last few years, but will be found to proceed essentially from her rare mode of achieving this many-sidedness and balance, or, more strictly still, from her own feeling as to this mode, and her analysis and theory of it. We have no direct concern with this her reflection at present: what she actually did and directly was, is all we would wish to try and sketch just now.

VII. Catherine and the Holy Eucharist.

1. *A daily Communicant from May 1474 onwards.*

On the following day, then, on the Feast of the Annunciation, 25th March, 1474, "her Lord gave her the desire of Holy Communion, a desire which never again failed her throughout the whole course of her remaining life. And He so disposed things that Communion was given her, without any care on her part; she was often summoned to receive it, without any asking, by priests inspired by God to give it to her." [1]

After trying every possible interpretation of this most annoyingly obscure text by the light of three or four other passages, I have come to think it to mean that, on this Lady-Day, she, for the first time since now ten years, received Holy Communion with a keen desire for its reception; and that this desire remained from this day forward unintermittently with her, till the end of her life: but that this desire, which at first may not have been set upon daily Communion, began to be satisfied by a daily reception only some time in May 1474. It is anyhow certain that from this latter date onwards she was a daily communicant up to September 13, 1510, the day before her death.[2] The exceptions were most rare,—I take it of an average of once or twice a year,—and were always owing to some insuperable obstacle, mostly of ill-health.

[1] *Vita*, p. 7*a*.

[2] I take the above to have been the actual course of events, for the following reasons. (1) The text just given talks of "the desire for Holy Communion" having been given to her on that day in 1474, and of this desire "never failing her throughout the remainder of her life"; but it does not say, that the desire for *daily* Communion was given to her then, or that such a desire was continuously satisfied from the first. (2) On page 18*b* we have: "For about two years she had this desire for death, and this desire continued within her, up to when she began to communicate daily." This passage, (which does not occur, here or with this Communion notation, in the MSS.,) originally without doubt referred to her later desire for death, carefully described by Vernazza (pp. 98*a*, *b*; 99*b*, *c*) as occurring in 1507—a description in the midst of which now occurs an account of certain death-like swoons which attacked her in 1509 (pp. 98*c*, and 133*b*; this latter experience is given in the MSS. as occurring in November 1509). Still this passage points to a tradition, or early inference, that the beginning of the daily communions did not synchronize with her conversion nor indeed with any other very marked date, but took place not many years after her return to fervour. (3) It is impossible to assume that she did not communicate at all during these first fourteen months, since there is no evidence that, even before her conversion, she had ever abstained from Holy Communion altogether, and since two Eastertides with their strict obligation recurred twice within this period. And if she did communicate repeatedly within this time, then this Lady-Day, three days after her conversion, would be a most natural occasion for one of these communions. And the desire and not its gratification would be mentioned, because the writer characteristically wants her conversion to be followed by something absolutely unintermittent, and such unintermittence attached, for the present, not to her communions themselves, but only to her desire for them.

2. *Her practice as regards the Holy Eucharist, throughout her Convert Life.*

Since Holy Communion was the great source and centre of her love and strength, and the one partially external experience and practice which was thus renewed day by day throughout her life, and in the spiritual apprehension and effect of which we cannot trace any distinct periods, I shall dwell here, once for all, upon the characteristics of this devotion of hers, which were at all special to herself.

For one thing, even her ardent love of Holy Communion did not suppress a bashful dislike of being noticed or distinguished in the matter: "At the beginning of her conversion she had at times a feeling as of envy towards Priests, because they communicated on as many days as they would, without any one wondering at it." "Once when, for a few days, the city was under an interdict, she went every morning a mile's distance outside of the city walls, so as to communicate; and she thought that she would not be seen by any one." [1]

Next, there is a most characteristic eagerness for interiorization, for turning the Holy Eucharist, perceived without, into the heart's food within; and a corresponding intensity of consciousness and tenderness at the moment of reception. "When she saw the Sacrament on the altar in the hands of the priests, she would say within herself: 'Now swiftly, swiftly convey it to the heart, since it is the heart's true food.'" And "one night she dreamt that she would be unable to communicate during the coming day, and waking up, she found that tears were dropping from her eyes, at which she wondered, since hers was a nature very slow to weep." And "when at Mass, she was often so occupied with her Lord interiorly, as not to hear one word of it; but when the time for Communion arrived, at that instant she would become conscious of exterior things." And she would say: "O Lord, it seems to me, that if I were dead, I should return to life to receive Thee; and that if an unconsecrated host were given to me, I should recognize it to be such by the mere taste alone, as one discerns water from wine." [2]

[1] *Vita*, pp. 8, 9. A MS. list of conclusions concerning various points of her life, which is contained in the volume *Documenti su S. Caterina da Genova*, in the University Library of Genoa, declares this interdict to have lasted ten days, and in the year 1489. This information is probably correct.

[2] *Ibid*. pp. 8, 9.

Again, her Communion practice bears upon it the stamp of a staunch virility; of a constant emulation between her own generous turning-away from its sensible consolations and the divine action, which seems to have maintained these consolations throughout her life; and of a determination to abstain even from such deeply consoling Communions, if such abstention were the more perfect practice for her. "One day, when she had communicated, there came to her so much odour and so much sweetness, that she felt as though in Paradise. But turning at once towards her Love she said: 'O Love, wouldest thou perchance draw me to Thee with these savours (*sapori*)? I desire them not, since I desire but Thee, and Thee whole and entire!'" And "one day a holy Friar,"—it was probably the Observant Franciscan, Father Angelo of Chiavasso (near Genoa), beatified later on,—"said to her: 'You communicate every day: what kind of satisfaction do you derive from it?' And she answered him simply, explaining to him all her desires and feelings. But he, to test the purity of her intention, said: 'There might possibly be some imperfection in such very frequent Communion,' and then left her. And Catherine having heard this, fearing such imperfection, at once suspended her Communions, but at the cost of great distress. And the Friar, hearing a few days later of how she cared more not to do wrong than to have all the consolation and satisfaction of Communion, sent her word by all means to return to her daily Communions; and she did so." [1]

And finally, her Communions produced effects direct and indirect, spiritual and psychical. The indirect, psycho-physical effects being variable, and related to the varying conditions of her health, will be noted as far as possible under the different periods of her life and, collectively, in the chapter on such psycho-physical questions. The spiritual effects no doubt grew, but this growth we have no sufficient materials for pursuing in detail. Yet they have throughout this peculiarity, that, central and all-permeating as this Eucharistic influence no doubt was, yet it nowhere takes the form of any specially Eucharistic devotion or directly Eucharistic meditation or doctrine, outside of Holy Communion itself and of the immediate occupation with *it*. Some deep indirect effects on her general tone, imagery, and teaching will be studied in our second volume.

[1] *Vita*, p. 7*b*.

VIII. Catherine and Confession and Direction.

1. *Catherine arouses criticism in the matter of Direction.*

Now if Catherine occasioned some criticism and testing of her spirit by the (for that period) very unusual frequency of her Communions,[1] it is equally on record that she aroused some surprise and apprehension, by the absence of all Direction, during the many years of the second period of her convert life. And if, in the matter of her daily Communions, she had readily entered into the suggestion that there might be imperfection in this her dearest habit, and yet had to continue along her unusual way, so too, in this matter of Direction, she evidently was from the first ever ready to proceed in the ordinary manner, and yet found herself compelled to follow a lonely course. "If she attempted to lean upon any one (*accostarsi ad alcuno*), Love instantly caused her mental suffering so great that she was obliged to desist, saying, 'O Love, I understand Thee.' And when she was told that it would be well, and more secure, if she were to put herself under obedience to another, and whilst she was in doubt as to what to do, her Lord answered her thus within her mind: 'Confide in Me, and doubt not!'"[2] Such suggestions will have been made and such scruples will have been suffered many a time, during the long years in which, in this matter, her way was an extraordinary one.

2. *The facts concerning Catherine's confessions. Catholic obligations.*

But in this matter of Direction and Confession, the *Vita*, if we were to take its present constituents as of uniform value, is astonishingly vague, ambiguous, and contradictory. Let us take the facts, in the order of their certainty, moving from the quite certain to the less and less certain ones; and let us then try and appraise the upshot of the whole examination.

We are then, first, absolutely certain that Catherine

[1] I have been unable to discover more than one case illustrative of the practice of that time and town. The Venerable Battista Vernazza, an Augustinian Canoness from 1510 to 1587, was not allowed daily Communion till the last years of her life. *Opere*, Genoa, 1755, Vol. I, p. 21.

[2] *Vita*, p. 116*c*. This passage opens a chapter full of the most authentic information, derived directly from Don Marabotto, her Confessor and close friend from 1499 onwards. I have, in her saying, read "Amore" for the "Signore" of the text of the *Vita*; my reasons will appear later on.

herself, not later than 1499,—this date shall be justified later on,—said to Don Marabotto, (and that he then and there, or shortly afterwards, wrote down,) the following words: "I have persevered for twenty-five years in the spiritual way, without the aid of any creature." And he, in this matter which concerns his own Confessing and Directing of her during the last eleven years of her life (1499–1510), twice over solemnly reaffirms and drives home the reality of the fact thus communicated to him by herself. "She was guided and taught interiorly by her tender Love alone, without the means of any [fellow-]creature, either Religious or Secular"; "she was instructed and governed thus by God, for about twenty-five years." [1] And conformably with this, we get the short dialogue between herself and Love, as just given, and such words as the following, which she declared that Love itself spoke to her mind,—evidently during, and probably at the beginning of, these many years: "Take from the remainder of Scripture this one word 'Love,' with which thou shalt ever walk straight . . . enlightened, without error, and (all this) without guide or means provided by any other creature." [2]

In the next place, it is equally certain that, with all her biographers down to this day (*e. g.* Monseigneur Fliche, pp. 350, 351), her words must be understood to exclude at least all Direction from those years. And it is, moreover, practically certain that at least the second Redactor (R. 2) of the *Vita* understood her words to apply to Confession also. For whereas, in the older tripartite scheme of R. 1, the four years of Penance of her first period were filled by her labours for "satisfying her conscience by means of contrition, confession, and satisfaction," R. 2 breaks up those four years into two periods,—the first, of "a little over a year"; and the second, of (no doubt) three years,—and does so with a view to thus making room for the "about twenty-five years" of Catherine's affirmation. Now whereas R. 2 in his first period talks thus of Confession; in his second one, he talks twice of Contrition, and twice of Sorrow, but nowhere of Confession; and again, whereas in his third (R. 1's second) period of "many" (no doubt twenty-one) years, there is still no reference to Confession, indeed here not even to Sin or Contrition in general; in the fourth (R. 1's third) period (of eleven years), when she was being regularly confessed and

[1] *Vita*, pp. 119*c*, 116*c*, 117*b*. [2] *Ibid.* p. 16*b*.

directed by Marabotto, she, it is true, "was incapable of recognizing, by direct examination, the nature of her acts, whether they were good or bad," but still she was able to see, and actually "saw all things," hence also these acts and their difference, "in God." [1]

Thirdly, it is certain that some reasonable doubt can be entertained as to whether Catherine's words, solemnly emphatic though they are, were not understood too literally by Marabotto and the second Redactor. Nothing is, indeed, more obvious and striking throughout all the authentic memorials of her, than the delightfully simple, grandly fearless veracity of her mind. She never speaks but according to the fulness of her conviction: like with all souls most near unto the child-like Master, Christ, it can be said of her that "one never knows what she is going to say next." And we shall find her insight into herself at any given moment, even with regard to such partly medical matters as her psycho-physical condition, to be quite astonishing in its depth and delicacy. Yet the fact remains, that she was as truly a person of intense and swiftly changing feelings, exaltations, and depressions, as she was one of a rich balanced doctrine and of a quite heroic objectivity and healthy spiritual utilization of all such intensities. This very heroism and objectivity of hers, so constant and watchful in all her practical decisions and general doctrinal statements, no doubt helped to make her feel both the need and the licitness of giving full and truthful utterance also to the intense and swiftly passing feelings of her heart.

One such utterance is specially to the point. She had already been for eleven years the much-helped penitent of that utterly devoted priest-friend Don Marabotto, when, in January 1510, he overheard her (the extant report of the scene is certainly his own and contemporary with the event) saying to God, shut up alone, as she thought, in one of her rooms: "There is no creature that understands me. I find myself alone, unknown, poor, naked, a stranger and different from all the world." Yet this does not prevent her finding comfort and, indirectly, even physical improvement, in and from Marabotto's sympathy and words, when these are offered to her not many hours later on.[2] The abnormally rapid and complete change of feeling depicted here, no doubt occurred

[1] *Vita*, p. 6. [2] *Ibid.* p. 140*b*, *c*.

during the last eight months of her life, long after her health had begun to break up permanently; and cannot directly illustrate her frame of mind during the years 1474–1499, when she was in health and relatively strong. Still, she was clearly ever of a high-strung, intense temperament; and her health was already seriously impaired when, in 1499, she spoke the words concerning the utter loneliness of that whole quarter of a century. And if the emphatic words, spoken to God Himself in 1510, were compatible with confession, and, indeed, a certain kind of continuous direction, at the very time and during eleven years before they were spoken: her words uttered in 1499 to Marabotto, will have been compatible with at least some confession during a period of years of which the first lay almost a whole generation behind her. And we shall find at least two other cases in which Marabotto appears, on Catherine's own authority, as having clearly misunderstood the nature of some phenomena connected with herself.[1]

Yet for all this, the account which we shall have to give later on of the characteristics of her confessions to Marabotto,—an account directly derived from himself,—makes it practically impossible to assume that even simple confession was practised, at all or otherwise than quite exceptionally, during those many years.

Now we have, as a fourth point, to remember that although the Fourth Council of the Lateran, in the year 1215, had decreed that "All the Faithful of either sex, after coming to years of discretion, are bound to confess all their sins at least once a year": [2] yet already St. Thomas Aquinas had, in his Commentary on the Sentences of Peter Lombard, composed in 1252–1257, taught that, since the divine institution and obligation extends, strictly speaking, only to the confession of mortal sins, "he that has not committed any mortal sins is not bound to confess venial sins, but it is sufficient for the fulfilling of the Church's precept, for him to present himself to the priest, and to declare himself free from the consciousness of mortal sin." [3] And nothing has changed, as to the nature and extent of this obligation, since Catherine's time. The Council of Trent, the decrees of which were confirmed by Pope Pius IV in 1564, more than half-a-century after her death, carefully explains that "*all* the sins" of the

[1] See here, ch. v, § ii, 2 and 5.
[2] Denzinger's *Enchiridion Definitionum*, ed. 1888, No. 363.
[3] *Summa Theologica*, III, supplem. quaest. 6, art. 3.

decree of 1215 means all "*mortal* sins"; and further declares that "the Church did not, by the Lateran Council, decree that the faithful should confess,—a thing she knew to be instituted and necessary by divine right," but had simply determined the circumstances and conditions under which this obligatory confession was to take place.[1] And Father Antonio Ballerini, S.J. (*d.* 1881), gives us the conclusions, identical with that of St. Thomas, of those great authorities Francis Suarez (*d.* 1617), Cardinal John de Lugo (*d.* 1660), and Herman Busenbaum (*d.* 1668),—all three Jesuits, like himself,—and himself endorses their decision. Suarez indeed declares this view to be the common opinion of Theologians.[2]

3. *Probable course of Catherine's confession-practice.*

With these four points before us, let us attempt to reconstruct some outline of what really happened in her own case, and try and show what constituted the specifically Catholic quality of this her practice, so unusual in the middle and later ages of the Church. We shall, then, do wisely, I think, by considering that the "twenty-five years," alleged by her own self, were, as a strict matter of fact, not more than twenty-one;[3] that during the first four convert years that preceded this middle period, just as during the last eleven which

[1] Denzinger, *op. cit.* No. 780; *Summa Theologica,* III, supplem. quaest. 6, art. 3.

[2] Antonii Ballerini, *Opus Theologicum Morale,* ed. Palmieri, S.J., Prato, 1892, Vol. V, pp. 576–597. The large variations in the earlier practice of Penitence and Confession are admirably described in Abbé Boudhinon's articles, "Sur l'Histoire de la Pénitence," in the *Revue d'Histoire et de Littérature Religieuses,* 1897, pp. 306–344, 496–524.

[3] The reason for this lies in the emphatic, repeated conviction of R. 1, based, no doubt, upon the authentic documents (probably Vernazza's memoranda) that he has incorporated, (a conviction which appears wherever his scheme was not tampered with by R. 2,) that her great penitential period lasted four years (so still on pp. 12*b*, 13*b* twice, 14*c*; and originally, no doubt, on p. 6*a*, and probably on p. 5*c*, where now we read "a little over a year," and "about forteen months" respectively). For not all the subsequent doctoring, that shall be traced later on as having been applied by R. 2 to some of the refractory passages, succeeds in making it likely that these penitential exercises outlasted the complete disappearance from her sight of her sins, which we have already quoted from the last likely passage. And it is equally improbable that formal and repeated Confession should not have formed part and parcel of the whole of this penitential time. On the other hand, "her Confessor," on p. 7*c*, and "the spiritual physician" on p. 8*a*, indeed all other mentions of a Confessor throughout the Life subsequent to her first convert Confession, will be shown in the Appendix to apply exclusively to Don Marabotto, and to the last eleven years of her life.

succeeded it, she had recourse to confession with the frequency considered normal in and for these times, in the case of a daily communicant living in the world; but that, during the intervening period, she was allowed to substitute that simple occasional, perhaps only annual, presentation of herself and declaration to the priest in the place of confession proper, which we have seen to be considered, in a case of such a purity of soul as hers, as sufficient for fulfilling the Church's precept, by a practical consensus of all the great casuist authorities. And thus we have here again a memorable, and this time a long-persisting, instance of how the intrinsic and operative connection between the Individual and the Social, the Mystical and the Institutional elements of Religion is not a simple identity or coextension,—a point which we already found exemplified during the first hours of her convert life.

And the Catholic spirit in this her present course will consist in her full observance of all to which the Church strictly obliges; in her readiness at all times to walk in the ordinary way, and in her repeated attempts, even during this second period, to do so; in her actually and fervently following the ordinary course whenever she could, *i. e.* in the first and last period; and finally in her ever faithfully obeying the prompting of God's Spirit which, by various converging spiritual peculiarities, circumstances and means, showed, with practical plainness, the kind and degree of extraordinary interior acts and habits which were to be, in large part, *her* form of the "Mind of the Church." For it is indeed certain that the special characteristic of the Catholic mind is not, necessarily, universally and finally, the conception and practice of sanctity under the precise form of the devotional spirit and habits special to the particular part or period of the Church in which that individual Catholic's lot may be cast. What *is* thus characteristic, is the continuous and sensitive conviction that there is something far-reaching and important beyond the Church's bare precepts, for every soul that aims at sanctity, to find out and to do; that this something (*sc.* the Church's mind) is, always and for all, *presumably*, the most fervent form and degree of the devotional temper and habits of the Church, as practised in that time and country; and that it is for God Himself, if He so pleases, to indicate to the soul that He now wants its fervour to consist in an observance of the Church's precepts and spirit under a form and with an application partially different from the most fervent practice of the ordinary devotions of that time and place, though this new observance will be no less costing or heroically self-renouncing than the other. And this He does usually by slow, often simply cumulative and indirect, but always solid, painful, and practically unmistakable, because unsought, means and experiences,—all these attained to well within the Church. For the Church's life and spirit, which is but the extension of the spirit of Christ Himself, is, like all that truly lives at all, not a sheer singleness, but has a mysterious unity in and by means of endless variety. Even at any one moment that spirit expresses itself in numerous variations, by means of various races, rites, orders, schools, and individuals. And yet not the sum-total of all these simultaneously present variations is ever as rich as is the sum-total of that spirit's successive manifestations in the past. Nor once more can this latter sum be taken as anticipating all the developments and adaptations which that ever-living spirit will first occasion and then sanction in His special organ, the Church. Catherine's particular, divinely impelled substitute for the ordinary devotional practice shall be described later on.

IX. Catherine and Indulgences.

A further peculiarity, somewhat analogous to the one just examined, seems to have characterized her devotional practice—in this case, throughout her convert life. It had therefore, perhaps, best be described in this place.

1. *The assertions of the "Vita."*

Three items of information are furnished by the *Vita*, on one and the same half-page.

(1) "She had such a hatred of self," says the *Vita*, "that she did not hesitate to pronounce this sentence: 'I would not have grace and mercy, but justice and vengeance shown to the malefactor. . . .'"

(2) "For this reason it seemed that she did not even care to gain the Plenary Indulgences. Not as though she did not hold them in great reverence and devotion, and did not consider them to be most useful and of great value. But she would have wished that her own self-seeking part (*la sua propria parte*) should rather be chastized and punished as it deserved, than to see it pardoned (*assoluta*), and, by means of such satisfaction, liberated in the sight of God."

(3) " She saw the Offended One to be supremely good, and the offender quite the opposite. And hence she could not bear to see any part of herself which was not subjected to the divine justice, with a view to its being thoroughly chastized. And hence, so as not to give this part any hope of being liberated from the pains due to it, she abstained from the Plenary Indulgences and also from recommending herself to the intercession of others, so as ever to be subject to every punishment and condemned as she deserved." [1]

2. *Three points to be noted here.*

Here I would note three things.

For one thing, there can be no serious doubt as to the authenticity of the saying that opens out this group of communications and as to the substantial accuracy of the two parallel, and (I think) mutually independent, reports as to her practice: since the saying belongs to the class of short declarations given in *oratio directa*, which we shall find to be remarkably reliable throughout the *Vita;* and the reports testify to something so unusual, so little sympathetic to the hagiographical mind, so much in keeping with the remainder of her doctrine and practice, that we cannot believe them misinformed. The author of the *Dialogo* evidently fully accepted these three passages, when, in about 1549, she paraphrases them thus: " She therefore made no account of her sins, with respect to their punishment, but only because she had acted against that Immense Goodness "; " She found herself to be her who alone had committed all the evil, and alone she wanted to make satisfaction, as far as ever she could, without the help of any other person." [2]

For another thing, we have absolutely final contemporary documentary evidence of the importance attached by herself both to Indulgences, and the gaining of them (at least by

[1] *Vita*, p. 56*b*, *c*. Her words as printed there are: " Io non vorrei grazia ne misericordia [nella presente vita] ma giustizia e vendetta del malfattore." But the words I have bracketed are certainly a gloss; for she is speaking here out of the fulness of her feeling, without the intrusion of reflection. And as regards temporal punishment in the other life, and the soul's attitude towards it there, she says in the *Trattato*, p. 180*b*: " Know for certain, that of the payment required from those souls (in Purgatory), there is not remitted even the least farthing, this having been thus established by the divine justice. . . . Those souls have no more any personal choice, and can no more will anything but what God wills."

[2] *Dialogo*, pp. 203*a*, 208*b*.

other people), and to Masses and prayers for the Dead, inclusive of herself when she should be gone. For as to Indulgences, we have entries in the Cartulary of the Hospital (under the dates of March 11, April 10, May 29, and August 23, 1510) of various considerable sums, amounting in all to over £300, paid by the Hospital, at the first date, for Catherine's nephew Francesco, at all the other dates for herself, for the withdrawal of a suspension of the Indulgences attached to the Hospital Church, and for the transference, in that year, of the day appointed for their acquisition. Both these matters were carried out in Rome by means of Catherine's second nephew, Cardinal Giovanni Fiesco. This, it is true, is evidence that only covers the last six months of her life.

But as to Masses and Prayers for her own soul after death, we have (1) her second Will, of May 19, 1498, where she leaves one share in the Bank of St. George (£100) to the Observant Franciscans of the Hospital Church, "who shall be bound to celebrate Masses and Divine Offices for the soul of Testatrix"; (2) her Codicil, of January 5, 1503, where she leaves (in addition) £3 apiece to two Monasteries "for the celebration of Masses for her own soul"; (3) her third Will, of May 18, 1506, which confirms all this; and (4) her last Will, of March 18, 1509, where she leaves £3 each to three Monasteries, which are each to "celebrate thirty Masses for her soul," £3 to a fourth Monastery for Prayers for her soul, and £25 to the Franciscans of the Hospital Church for the celebration of Masses to the same effect.[1]

The reader will at once perceive that these facts are fully compatible with the attitude so emphatically ascribed to her in the *Vita*, only if we take these latter statements as expressive of certain intense, emotional moods; or of some relatively short penitential period; or of what she did and felt with regard to herself alone and for whilst she was to live here below, not of what others should do for themselves at all times and for herself when she was gone.

And finally, we know exactly how and why the doctrine and practice described in those passages in the *Vita* were accepted by the Congregation of Rites, as forming no obstacle to her canonization. Pope Benedict XIV, in his

[1] From the authenticated copies of the entries in the Cartulary, prefixed to the MS. Life of the Saint in the *Biblioteca della Missione Urbana*, Genoa, Nos. 30, 8, 14; and from careful copies of the still extant original Wills made for me by Dott. Ferretto, of the Archivio di Stato, Genova.

great classical work on Beatification and Canonization, says, "After I had ceased to hold the office of Promoter of the Faith," (the date will have been between 1728 and 1733,) "I know that a controversy arose as to the doctrine of a certain *Beata*, with regard to the truth of which it was possible to have different opinions." And after giving this *Beata's* doctrine and practice as these are presented by Catherine's *Vita*, and citing the arguments used against their toleration, he proceeds: "But the Postulators answered (1) that this *Beata* had not omitted to gain Plenary Indulgences from any contempt for them, since her veneration for them was demonstrated by most unambiguous documents" (no doubt Cardinal Fiesco's action, in her name and at her expense, in Rome in 1510, is meant); "(2) that it is the doctrine of very many theologians, that those do not sin, who do not labour to gain Indulgences because they desire to make satisfaction in their own persons in this world or to suffer in the next; (3) that we should not confound safety with perfection: it appears indeed to be safer to atone for one's fault both by one's own good works *and* by Indulgences; but not more perfect, supposing that a man abstains from Indulgences because his love of God and his detestation of having offended Him are so great that he desires to make satisfaction to Him, by bearing the whole of the merited punishment; and (4) that examples are not wanting of perfect souls, that have, for a while, desired to bear, even for the sins of others, the pains of Hell itself, although without falling away from the friendship and grace of God. And hence the Congregation of Sacred Rites considered that this doctrine did not militate against the holiness of the said *Beata* or against the approbation of her virtues as heroic." [1]

X. Peculiarities concerning the Invocation of Saints and Intercessory Prayer.

And a third and last peculiarity is particularly instructive as showing how entirely an unusual, at first sight quietistic, practice is not restricted, in her case, to specifically Catholic habits.

[1] Benedicti XIV, *De servorum Dei Beatificatione et Beatorum Canonisatione*, ed. Padua, 1743, Vol. II, p. 239*a*.

1. *The facts.*

This peculiarity has already appeared in part in the second of the two accounts as to her attitude towards Indulgences. "She abstained from recommending herself to the intercession of others." And this is borne out, but (as we shall find) with certain unforeseeable restrictions, by the rest of the *Vita*. As regards even the Saints, one only invocation of any one of them is on record,—that of St. Benedict in 1474, already given.

And if she did not ask others for prayers for herself in her own lifetime, her own prayers for others were evidently rare, were apparently always concerned with their spiritual welfare, and were generally produced only under some special interior impulsion. Hence when asked, in 1496 or later, by Vernazza, in the name of several of her spiritual children, to pray that God might grant them "some little drops of His Love," she answers that "for these I cannot ask anything from this tender Love; I can but present them in His presence." This is, no doubt, because she sees them to be already full of the love of God. Whereas in 1495 the poor working man, Marco del Sale, is dying of a cancer in the face, and is in a state of wild impatience: so she prays most fervently for him. It is true that the *Vita* adds that she did so, "having had an interior movement to this effect. For she never could turn to pray for a particular object, unless she had first felt herself called interiorly by her Love." Still, this did not prevent her, in 1497, from praying most fervently for patience for her husband, (who was dying from a painful complaint,) simply "because she feared that he might lose his soul," and without any other more peculiar incentive than this.[1]

2. *The rich variety of her life.*

Evidently here again, as with the Confessions and Indulgences, her life and practice were indefinitely varied and spontaneous, and incomparably richer than the preconceptions and logic of at least some of her biographers will admit, or indeed than many of her own fervent sayings, so vividly expressive of certain moments or sides of her career or character, suggest or even seem to leave possible. But the underlying meaning and ultimate harmonization of these apparent inconsistencies between her doctrine and her practice, we can only gradually hope to find.

[1] *Vita*, pp. 56*c*; 3*c*; 95*c*; 124*c*, 125*b*; 122*b*.

CHAPTER IV

CATHERINE'S LIFE FROM 1473 TO 1506, AND ITS MAIN CHANGES AND GROWTH

LET us now attempt, as far as the often scanty and obscure evidence permits, to give, in the following two chapters, some general account of the changes and growth observable in her external surroundings, her human intercourse and social occupation, her physical health and psychical mood, and above all of those inner experiences and spiritual apprehensions of hers which dominated all the rest, during each of the three main periods of her convert life. This general account will, I trust, suggest the main points for our later investigations, and will show at once how largely artificial, though necessary, all such dividing into periods must be, in the case of so deeply unified and diversified an inner life as Catherine's.

I. FIRST PERIOD OF CATHERINE'S CONVERT LIFE: GIULIANO'S BANKRUPTCY AND CONVERSION; THEIR WORK AMONG THE POOR, MARCH 1473 TO MAY 1477.

1. *Giuliano's affairs. Catherine's attitude.*

The first six months of her first period (this latter we take to have extended from March 1473 to May 1477) were still spent in Giuliano's Palace of the Via Agnese and in his country mansion at Prà.[1] But all was now swiftly changing,

[1] I have followed here, for my *terminus a quo*, Vallebona rather than the Bollandists (who prefer 1474 for the date of her conversion), because the ten years required between her marriage in January 1463 and her conversion, have fully elapsed by March 1473, and because the earlier we place her conversion, the larger is the number of lonely convert years that we can find room for, and the more nearly accurate her own allegation of twenty-five years of such loneliness becomes. If we follow the chronology given in the text we get a thoroughly understandable sequence: Catherine's conversion, March 1473; Giuliano's bankruptcy, summer of that year; his conversion under the joint influence of her zeal and of his misfortune;

or already greatly changed, both around her and within. Anxiety, hope, grief, consolation—inasmuch as such feelings could still for her cluster around events external to her deepest spiritual life, and could make themselves at all separately felt during this period of profound absorption in her new large life of love and penance—must all have centred in her husband. For Giuliano had by now got his affairs into such disorder as to be unable to keep up his great social position; and by the autumn of 1473 he had sold his mansion at Prà, and had vacated and let his palace in Genoa itself.[1] He was also by now a very sincere convert, in his own manner and degree; and it was no doubt now that he told Catherine, although she can hardly have failed to know already, of the existence of a poor little girl whom, with an apparently ominous indication of weak indulgence on the part of his widowed mother, he had called Thobia.

We shall be able to prove Catherine's grand magnanimity and true, cordial forgiveness—directly, no doubt only for and at a later period; but the documents will show that she knew all the decisive circumstances long before, and there is no room for doubt that her dispositions had changed or grown as little as had her knowledge.

2. *Life in the little house outside the Hospital.*

Catherine and Giuliano had now, in the autumn of 1473, moved into a humble little house, in the midst of artisans, mostly dyers, and of the poor of various sorts, close to the Hospital of the Pammatone, even then already a vast Institution. This dwelling is probably identical, as to the site, with the house still standing at the junction of the Via S. Giuseppe with the Via Balilla, and which bears on its front a picture of Saints Catherine Adorna and Camillus of Lellis[2] at the feet of the Madonna. Since the income remaining to them still amounted, up to Giuliano's death in 1497, to the equivalent of some £1,200 a year,[3] this self-abnegation and the decision of the couple to settle in the midst of the poor and suffering, whom they were now determined to serve, and the execution of this decision, between Michaelmas and Christmas of the same year.

[1] Vallebona, p. 55.

[2] Lived 1550–1614, worked heroically amongst the poor and pestilential sick, founded the Order of the Fathers of a Good Death, and was himself at Genoa, already gravely ill, in 1613.

[3] Vallebona, pp. 55, 56, shows, from Giuliano's still extant will of 1497, how his income from his property in the island of Scios alone amounted to about 30,000 modern Italian lire. We shall study the instructive growth of legend in the matter of Catherine's "poverty" later on.

humble identification with the lives of the toiling, nameless poor, must have been an act of deliberate choice, and not one of any degree of necessity. It was never suspended or revoked by either of them.

They now agreed together to a life of perpetual continence; and Giuliano became a Tertiary of the Order of St. Francis,[1] amongst those attached to the Hospital-Church of the Santissima Annunciata in Portoria, itself served by Observant Franciscans. Their only little servant-maid, Benedetta Lombarda, was also a Franciscan Tertiary. But Catherine herself now shows, in this matter of the Religious State, an interesting clearing-up of her own special way and form of sanctity. We saw how much the fervent but inexperienced girl of sixteen had been moved and had longed to be an Augustinian nun; and now the sadly experienced wife of twenty-six, even in the midst of her first convert days, and though surrounded at home, in Church, and in the Hospital by Religious of the popular and expansive type presented by the Franciscans, (a type which her own deep sympathy with, indeed penetration by, the teaching of the great Franciscan Mystic, Jacopone da Todi, will show to have been closely akin to her own,) manifests no thought of becoming a Religious, even in the slight degree represented by the Third Order. And up to her death, thirty-seven years later, she never wavers on this point. A highly characteristic scene and declaration illustrative of this attitude of hers will be given further on.

The Hospital of Pammatone had been founded by Bartolommeo Bosco, one of those large-hearted merchant princes of whom Genoa has had not a few, in 1424, in the street of that name; and only quite recently, in 1472, the Friars of the adjoining Church of the Annunciata had agreed to the incorporation of their own infirmary for sick poor with Bosco's larger institution. Hence Catherine and Giuliano found 130 sick-beds always occupied by patients, and over 100 foundling girls, who were being trained as silk-workers, all ready to their hands and service.[2] Catherine was besides gradually introduced to the poor of the district, by the *Donne della Misericordia*—ladies devoted to such works of mercy—and betook herself to her tasks with characteristic directness and thoroughness.[3] She must first, and once for

[1] *Vita*, p. 122*b*.

[2] Vallebona, pp. 106, 108.

[3] An interesting legendary development in the *Dialogo* of this very straightforward account of the *Vita* will occupy us later on.

all, completely master all squeamishness in this her lowly work. So she betook herself to cleansing their houses from the most disgusting filth; and she would take home with her the garments of the poor, covered with dirt and vermin, and, having cleansed them thoroughly, would herself return them to their owners. And yet nothing unclean was ever found upon herself. She also tended the sick in the Hospital and in their homes, with the most fervent affection, speaking to them of spiritual things and ministering to their bodily wants, and never avoiding any form of disease, however terrible.[1]

II. Catherine and Tommasa Fiesca: their Difference of Character and *Attrait*. Peculiarity of Catherine's Penitence and Health during this time.

1. *Catherine's penances.*

And throughout this first period of four years, her penances were great. She wore a hair-shirt; she never touched either flesh-meat or fruit, whether fresh or dried; she lay at night on thorns. And by nature courteous and affable, she would do great violence to herself by conversing as little as possible with her relations when they visited her, and, as to anything further, paying heed neither to herself nor to them; and she acted thus for the purpose of self-conquest; and if any one was surprised at it, she took no notice.[2]

2. *Catherine and Tommasina.*

But one visitor must, even during this period, have been treated by her with much of her natural spontaneity and ardent expansiveness. She was a cousin of her own age, a Fiesca and a married woman like herself; like herself, too, in the wish, just now awakened, to belong entirely to God, and in her ultimate complete conversion and ardent love of God. We can attempt to describe her here, as throwing further light upon Catherine's idiosyncrasies, at this period in particular.

Tommasina was different from Catherine in the slow, tentative character of her first turning to God; and different, too, in the eventual form of her life; for, when later on a widow, she became first, in 1490, an Augustinian Canoness

[1] *Vita*, pp. 20, 21. [2] *Ibid.* p. 12.

at Santa Maria delle Grazie; and then, in 1497, a Dominican Nun at the Monastero Nuovo di San Domenico. This latter convent she had been given to reform and became its Prioress. In both houses she was known as Suor Tommasina (Fieschi).[1] She was different again in that she there spent some of her time in painting many a religious picture, chiefly of the Pietà, and a highly symbolical composition, illustrative of the moment of Consecration at Mass.[2] She executed also in exquisitely fine needlework a piece which represented, above, God the Father surrounded by many Angels, and, below, Christ with other figures of Saints. Finally she occupied herself in writing and produced in original composition a treatise on the Apocalypse, and another on Denys the Areopagite.

And the future Suor Tommasa showed now some of that precious gift of humour, denied to her otherwise greater cousin. For, no doubt with a bright twinkle in her eyes at the sight of Catherine's characteristic vehemence of onslaught, Tommasa would declare that Catherine was pushing her and giving her no quarter; and that it would be a great humiliation for herself if, after all said and done, she were to turn back. But any such feeling of even the possibility of such a relapse was amazing to Catherine, and she said: "If I were to turn back, I would wish that my eyes might be put out, and that I should be treated with every other kind of indignity."[3]

3. *Peculiarity of Catherine's penitence.*

But such intercourse as this must, during this first period, have been the exception. For her dominant, closely inter-related characteristics were now a continuous striving to do things contrary to her natural bias and an alert looking to do the will of others rather than her own. She moved about

[1] See an interesting article: "De Suor Tommasina Fieschi," by F. Alizeri, in *Atti della Societa Ligure di Storia Patria*, Genova, 1868, pp. 403–415.

[2] The choice of subjects may possibly betray the influence of Catherine—of the Pietà which Catherine had so much loved as a child, and of her special devotion to the Holy Eucharist. But the particular form of the latter is in Tommasina unlike Catherine: had Catherine painted that symbolical picture, it would have referred to the moment, not of Consecration, but of Communion.

[3] *Vita*, pp. 123, 124. Suor Tommasa did not die till 1534, over 86 years of age. I have been unable to discover her baptismal and her married names. We shall give some further details about Catherine's probable relations with her, as writer and as painter.

with her eyes bent upon the ground. Six hours a day were spent in prayer, and this although—perhaps just now in part because—the body greatly felt the strain: the strongly willing spirit had dominated the weak flesh. Indeed, during this time she was so full of interior feeling and so occupied within herself, that she was unable to speak, except in a tone so low as to be barely audible; she seemed dead to all exterior things.[1]

And these external circumstances and practices are all only the setting, material, occasion and expression of this her first period's actively penitential spirit, when she was persistently pursued by the detailed sight of her own particular inclinations, her own particular sins against God, and God's particular graces towards her own self. Her very acts of charity and of friendliness, her very prayers, get all restricted or prolonged, willed or suffered, as, at least in part, but so many occasions for a love-impelled, yet still reflective self-mastery and mortification. And it was no doubt during this time that, when present one day at a sermon in which the conversion of the Magdalen was recounted, her heart seemed to whisper to her: "Indeed I understand," so similar did her own conversion appear to her to that of the Magdalen.[2]

4. *Her physical health.*

As to her physical health, the fire which she felt in her heart seemed to dry up and burn her interiorly. And so great a physical hunger would possess her, that she appeared insatiable; and so quickly did she digest her food, that it looked as if she could have consumed iron. Yet she had no inclination to other than ordinary food, and did not fail to keep all the ordinary fasts and abstinences.[3]

III. Change in the Temper of Catherine's Penitence, from May 1474 onwards.

Time wears on, and Catherine is still in the same house, and with the same health, and with the same companions and occupations, penances and prayers. But the interior dispositions and emotional promptings, and the mental apprehension of them all, are gradually changing and are growing

[1] *Vita*, pp. 12, 13. [2] *Ibid.* pp. 5, 6, 14. [3] *Ibid.* p. 13.

wider and freer and less particularized. "She now began to experience a more affective way, so that she was often as though beside herself; and" though still "moved by a great interior thirst after self-hatred, and by a penetrating contrition, she would often lie prostrate on the ground"; she would do so, "hardly knowing what she was doing, yet somehow gaining thus some relief for her heart," overflowing as it was with a boundless, profound, but now more and more general, sorrow and tender love.[1] The note of a spontaneous, expansive, instinctive love is now growing in predominance in her prayer and human intercourse; and her very penances, though still performed, are now often practised from a general unreflective instinct of love-impelled self-hatred, without any conscious application to any particular inclinations or sins.

For as to her intercourse with others, she will probably already now have practised many an act of that beautiful and characteristic, impulsive, expansive tenderness, of which we shall have a good many examples from the end of her second period. And as to the character of her mortifications, we hear the following: "Whilst engaged on such great and numerous mortifications of all her senses, she was sometimes asked, 'Why are you doing this (particular) thing?' And she would answer, 'I do not know, except that I feel myself interiorly drawn to do so, without any opposition from within. And I think that this is the will of God; but it is not His will that I should propose to myself any (particular) object in so doing.'"[2] I take it that, with this growing intermittence in the sight of her particular sins, her Confessions, though still

[1] *Vita*, p. 6*a*.

[2] *Ibid.* 14*b*. I have introduced into my account a note of gradualness which is presented by no single (even authentic) document of the *Vita*, but which any attempt at harmonizing those documents imperatively requires. For there is, on the one hand, the repeated insistence upon her four years of particular penances for her own particular sins; and the vivid account of the final complete withdrawal of all sight of those sins and of all desire for those penances (*Ibid.* pp. 12*b*, 13*c*; 14*b*, 5*c*). And there is, on the other hand, the, apparently, equally authentic saying, as to her performing her penances, before the end of those years, without any particular object in view (*Ibid.* p. 14*b*). The only unforced harmonization is then to assume that a period, in which the sight of her particular sins had been at first all but unintermittent and then still predominant, had shaded off into another period, in which this sight occurred in ever fewer moments, until at last, at the end of four years, a day came on which it ceased altogether.

practised, will have become less frequent, and her Holy Communions more so.

IV. Catherine's Great Fasts.

1. *The assertions of the "Vita."*

And a little later on, again on the Feast of the Annunciation (March 25, 1476),[1] another change took place, a change primarily concerned with her health, but one which brought out also the deep spirituality of her religion. On this day she experienced one of those interior locutions, which are so well authenticated in the lives of so many interior souls; and "her Love said that He wanted her to keep the Forty Days, in His company in the Desert. And then she began to be unable to eat till Easter; on the three Easter Days she was able to eat; and after these she again did not eat, till she had fulfilled as many days as are to be found in Lent." [2] Similarly with regard to Advent. "Up to Martinmas" (November 12) "she would eat like all the world; and then her fast would begin, and would continue up to Christmas-Day." Her subsequent Lenten fasts are described as beginning with Quinquagesima Monday and ending on Easter Sunday morning.[3]

2. *Substantial accuracy of these accounts. Three facts to be remembered.*

I take it that there can be no reasonable doubt as to the substantial accuracy of this account. But the following three facts must be borne in mind as regards the physical aspect of the matter.

The fast, for one thing, is not an absolute one. The account itself declares that she now and then drank a tumblerful of water, vinegar, and pounded rock-salt.[4] And to this must be added both the daily reception of wine—I

[1] The only possible dates are 1475 or 1476. For the change referred to takes place "some appreciable time (*alquanto tempo*) after her conversion" (*Vita*, p. 10*a*); and yet it must be early enough to allow of twenty-three Lents and Advents between the beginning of the change up to its end. And this end came at latest in 1501 (p. 127*a*), but probably in 1499, the year in which Don Marabotto became her Confessor. The Lent of 1496 (what remained of it on Lady-Day of that year) seems to me the more likely of the two possible starting-points.

[2] *Vita*, p. 10*a*. [3] *Ibid.* p. 11*a*.

[4] *Ibid.* p. 10*b*.

suppose as much as a wineglassful—which was, according to a Genoese custom of that time, received by her, as a kind of ablution, immediately after her Communion; [1] and such slight amount of solid food as, when in company, she would force herself to take and would sometimes, though rarely, manage to retain.[2]

Again, the fast varies partly, in different years, in the date of its inception; and partly it does not synchronise with the beginning of the ecclesiastical fast. In the first year her Lenten fast begins on Lady-Day, in the following years on Quinquagesima Sunday; her Advent fast begins throughout on Martinmas, November 12.

And finally, the number of such fasts cannot be more than twenty-three Lents and twenty-two Advents. The MS. of 1547 has preserved the right tradition of a difference in the numbers of the Lenten and Advent fasts, but has raised the number of the former to a round, symmetrical one. It gives twenty-five Lents and twenty-two Advents. The printed *Vita* of 1551 levels the numbers respectively down and up to twenty-three Lents and as many Advents.[3] Some further minor physical points will be considered in a later chapter.

3. *Effect of these Fasts, and her attitude towards them.*

But two other matters are here of direct spiritual interest: the effect of these fasts on her spiritual efficiency, and her own two-fold attitude towards them. For we are told, again I think quite authentically, that during these fasts she was more active in good works, and felt more bright and strong in health, than usual; [4] answering thus to one of the tests put forward by Pope Benedict XIV, for discriminating supernatural, spiritually valuable fasts from simply natural ones. But with him we can find our surest tests in what is altogether

[1] *Vita*, p. 8*a*. [2] See below, next page.

[3] MS. "A," p. 24, title to chapter vii; *Vita*, p. 10*a*. Twenty-five Lents are too many, because: (1) it is impossible to interpret the "alquanto tempo dopo la sua conversione," when these fasts began (*Ibid.* p. 10*a*), as less than two years; and (2) it is impossible to bring her resignation of the Matronship of the Hospital lower down than the autumn of 1497, a resignation which the *Ibid.* (p. 96) tells us took place in consequence of her "great bodily weakness," which forced her to "take some food after Holy Communion to restore her bodily forces, even though it were a fast day." This allows for at most twenty-three Lents and twenty-two Advents.

[4] *Ibid.* p. 11*b*.

beyond the range of the physical and psychical: in her own moral estimate of all these matters. For one thing, there appears here again that noble shrinking from any singularity of this kind within herself, and from all notice on the part of others. "This inability to eat gave her many a scruple at first, ignorant as she was as to its cause, and ever suspecting some delusion; and she would force herself to eat, considering that nature required it. And though this invariably produced vomiting, yet she would make the attempt again and again." "She would go to table with the others, and would force herself to eat and drink a little, so as to escape notice and esteem as much as possible."[1] And again here, as in all matters visible and tangible, she shows an impressive loneliness in the midst of her more carnal-minded disciples. "She would say within herself, in astonishment" at their stopping to wonder at things so much on the surface: "If you but knew another thing, which I feel within myself!" And she would declare: "If we would rightly estimate the operations of God, we should wonder more at interior than at exterior things. This incapacity to eat is indeed an operation of God, but one in which my will has no part; hence I cannot glory in it. Nor is there cause for our wondering at it, since for God this is as though a mere nothing."[2]

4. *The fasts form no part of her penitence.*

These fasts, although beginning within her first period, are not characteristic of it; and her biographers rightly put them into a chapter distinct from her penances, properly speaking. These penances will have continued alongside of, and in between, these fasts for about a year after the beginning of the latter. And then at last, at the end of this first period of four years, "all thought of such (active) mortifications was, in an instant, taken from her mind in such guise that, even had she wished to carry out such mortifications, she would have been unable." For "the sight of her sins was now taken from her mind, so that she henceforth did not catch a glimpse of them,—as though they had all been cast into the depths of the sea."[3]

[1] *Vita*, p. 11*c*. I take the last section of this chapter (pp. 11, 12) to be a later, exaggerating doublet to this account.

[2] *Ibid*. p. 11*b*.

[3] *Ibid*. p. 14*b*, 5*c*.

V. Second, Central Period of Catherine's Convert Life, 1477–1499: its Special Spiritual Features.

We now come to the second, longest, and central period of her life, 1477–1499. But though at first sight Chapters VI to XLII and XLV of the *Vita* would seem exclusively to treat of these twenty-two years, examination proves this to be far from the case. If little or nothing from the first period is to be found there, very much from the third is embedded in those pages. And this scantiness of information springs from the simple fact that, during these twenty-two years, her inner life is led by herself alone, without any direct human aid or companionship; and her sufficient health, and the correspondingly large amount of external activity among the sick and poor, leave her but little or no time for those conferences and discourses amongst friends, of which her last period is full. This dearth of evidence is all the more to be regretted, since these central years represent the culmination of her balance and many-sided power.

1. *Interior change.*

For the first two years of this time she and Giuliano continued to live in their small house of the Portoria quarter, very busy, both of them, amongst the sick and poor, as well in the houses round about as in the Hospital. Indeed, externally, little or no change can have been apparent. It was the interior change, the moving away from the actively and directly penitential state into one of expansive love and joy, which alone, as yet, marked a new period.

2. *The Three Rules of Love. The Divine method of the soul's purification.*

Some time during these new beginnings it must have been that "her Love once said within her mind: 'Observe, little daughter, these three rules. Never say "I will," or "I will not." Never say "mine," but ever say "our." Never excuse thyself, but be ever ready to accuse thyself.'" And another time He said: "When thou sayest the 'Our Father,' take for thy foundation 'Thy Will be done.' In the Hail Mary, take 'Jesus.' In Holy Scripture take 'Love,' with which thou wilt ever go straightly, exactly, lightly, attentively, swiftly, enlightenedly, without error, without guide, and without the means of other creatures, since Love suffices unto itself to do all things without fear or weariness, so that martyrdom itself appears unto it a joy." [1]

But this her love, just because it is so real and from God, appears indeed to fill her at any given moment, yet it grows and shows her, at each fresh stage, both its own incompleteness and her own imperfection, in her and its former stages. "At any one moment the love of that moment seemed to me to have attained to its greatest possible perfection. But then, in the course of time, my spiritual sight having become clearer, I saw that it had had many imperfections." "Day by day I perceive that motes have been removed, which this Pure Love casts out and eliminates. This work is done by God, and man is not aware of it at the time, and cannot then see these imperfections; indeed God continuously allows man to see his (momentary) operation as though it were without imperfection, whilst all the time He, before Whom the heavens are not pure, is not ceasing from removing imperfections from his soul." [2]

As ever throughout her life, so now also, consolations are not the aim and end, but only the actual effects of her devotedness, and the ever fresh incentives to increased disinterestedness and self-surrender. And, with regard to these consolations, she again strove to escape all notice. "She would at times have her mind so full of divine love as to be all but incapable of speaking; and would be in so great a transport of feeling as to be obliged to hide herself so as not to be seen. She would lose the use of her senses and remain like one dead; and, to escape the occurrence of such things, she would force herself to remain in company as much as possible. And she would say to her Lord: 'I do not want that which proceedeth from Thee, but I want Thee alone, O tender Love.' But just because her love was so sincere and she fled from consolations, her Lord gave her of them all the more." [3]

3. *Her Ecstasies*

If on one of the many occasions when she had hidden herself away in some secret spot, she was ever discovered by any one, they would find her walking up and down, and seeming as though she would wish to do so without end; or they would come upon her with her face in her hands, prostrate on the ground, entranced, and with feelings beyond description or conception. "These ecstasies would almost always last

[1] *Vita*, p. 16*b*. [2] *Ibid.* pp. 23*a*, 49*a*.
[3] *Ibid.* p. 15*b*.

three or four hours; and if, on coming to herself, she spoke of the wonders she had seen, there was no one to understand her, and so she kept silence." "And if called during one of these trances, she would not hear, even though they did so loudly."[1]

This inattention would, however, occur only in case the call was simply one of curiosity. For on other occasions "she would remain as though dead for six hours; but on being called to the doing of any duty, however trifling it might seem, she would instantly arise and respond and go about the doing of this her obligation. And she would thus leave all, without any kind of trouble, according to her wont of flying from self-will as though it were the devil. And coming thus forth from her hiding-place she would have her face flushed, so as to look like a cherub, and to seem to have upon her lips the 'who then shall separate me from the love of Christ?' of the glorious Apostle." And "on thus arising from those trances, she seemed to feel stronger both in body and in soul,"[2] as in the case of the fasting.

Even in the midst of her work absorptions would occur like unto these in all but their length of duration: "At times her hands would sink, unable to go on, and weeping she would say, 'O my Love, I can no more'; and would thus sit for a while with her senses alienated, as though she had been dead. And this would occur oftener at one time than at another, according to the varying fulness of experience present in that purified mind."[3]

4. *Pure Love, independent of any particular state or form of life.*

And she was full of the conviction, and cared much for the formal acknowledgment on the part of others, that the possession and the increase of the most perfect love is independent of any particular state or form of life, and is directly dependent upon two things only, the grace of God and the generosity of the human will. "One day a Friar and Preacher,[4] perhaps to test her or because of

[1] *Vita*, pp. 15*c*, 97*a*, 15*c*. [2] *Ibid*. pp. 15*c*, 16*a*, 47*b*.
[3] *Ibid*. p. 17*b*.
[4] I translate *Frate predicatore* thus, because the generally well-informed Parpera (in his *Vita* of the Saint, 1681) identifies him with Padre Domenico de Ponzo, an Observant Franciscan and zealous preacher. Boll. p. 161 D. In other places, also, the *Vita* makes use of purely popular and misleading designations:—p. 117*b* "questo Religioso" is Don Marabotto, Secular Priest; pp. 94*c*, 95*a*, *c*, 98*c*, 99*b*, "Religioso" is Vernazza, layman; p. 123*b*, "Sorelle" is a Sister and Sisters-in-law. Even the final Redactor

some mistaken notion, told her that he himself was better fitted for loving than she, because he having entered Religion and renounced all things both within and without, and she being married to the world as he was to Religion, he found himself more free to love God, and more acted upon by Him. And the Friar went on, and alleged many other reasons. But when he had spoken much and long, an ardent flame of pure love seized upon Catherine, and she sprang to her feet with such fervour as to appear beside herself, and she said: 'If I thought that your habit had the power of gaining me one single additional spark of love, I should without fail take it from you by force, if I were not allowed to have it otherwise. That you should merit more than myself, is a matter that I concede and do not seek, I leave it in your hands; but that I cannot love Him as much as you, is a thing that you will never by any means be able to make me understand.' And she said this with such force and fervour, that all her hair came undone, and, falling down, was scattered upon her shoulders. And yet all the while this her vehement bearing was full of grace and dignity.—And when back at home, and alone with her Lord, she exclaimed: 'O Love, who shall impede me from loving Thee? Though I were, not only in the world as I am, but in a camp of soldiers, I could not be impeded from loving Thee.' "[1]

There is probably no scene recorded for us, so completely characteristic of Catherine at her deepest: the breadth and the fulness, the self-oblivion and the dignity, the claimlessness and the spiritual power—all are there.

VI. Catherine and Giuliano move into the Hospital in 1479, never again to quit it. She is Matron from 1490 to 1495.

The special character, both in form and content, of Catherine's spiritual life and doctrine will occupy us in

in the Preface, p. viii*c*, calls the Secular-Priest Marabotto and the Layman-Lawyer Vernazza, " divoti religiosi."

[1] *Vita*, pp. 51, 52. I take this episode to have occurred whilst the pair were still living out of the Hospital, because of the *giunta in casa*, which could hardly be applied to their two little rooms in the latter, whilst this sensitiveness to the opinion of others in this matter of love appears psychologically to be more likely during the early years of her convert life than from 1490 onwards, when, as Matron, she occupied a separate little house within the Hospital precincts (hence *sua casa* in *Vita*, p. 96*b*).

Chapter VI. Here we have as yet specially to busy ourselves with its external and social occasions and effects. And these effects were both large and constant; indeed they were on the increase up to 1497, two years before this second period comes to a close.

1. *Catherine and Giuliano occupy two small rooms in the Hospital.*

For in 1479 the couple shift their quarters from outside the Hospital to within that great building, and there, for eleven years, they together occupy two little rooms, living without pay and at their own expense, but entirely devoted to the care of the poor sick and dying and of the orphans collected there.[1] Indeed Catherine never again lived outside the walls of the Hospital during the thirty-one years that still remained to her on earth.

2. *Catherine's double life here*, 1479–1490.

And here in these rooms, and for eleven years, she worked among the sick, as but one of their many nurses. The spacious, high, white-washed, stone-flagged wards, with the great tall windows shedding floods of glaring light or cheering sunshine, according to the season without and to the mood of the poor sick within, stand still as they stood in Catherine's day. True, new wards have been added; the lay female Nurses of her time have been in part replaced by Nursing Sisters, and the Observant Friars by Capuchins; much, very much has been discovered since, both as to man's body and as to the facts and functions of his mind; all things, and man's interpretation of all things, seem as though irretrievably changed. And yet the mystery of devoted love, its necessity, difficulty, and actual operative presence, as an occasional pang and aspiration in us all, as a visible, dominant influence in some of us, remain with and in us still unchanged, with all the freshness of an elemental force, indestructible, inexhaustible. This devoted work of Catherine, this her serving of the sick "with the most fervent affection, and immense solicitude," [2] had also the remarkable circumstance about it that,

[1] I shall give reasons in due course for holding that the rooms still shown in the Hospital as Catherine's are different from any ever occupied by herself, and that the little house within the Hospital grounds, in which she died in 1510, and into which she (and Giuliano) probably moved in 1490, has long ceased to exist.

[2] *Vita*, p. 20*b*. This characteristic fact has been "explained away" in the *Dialogo*. See Appendix.

"notwithstanding all this her attentive," outward-looking "care, she never was without the consciousness of her tender Love; nor again did she, because of this consciousness, fail in any practical matter concerning the Hospital." [1]

3. *Matron of the Hospital*, 1490–1496.

And this double life continued thus, and grew in depth and breadth. And at the end of fourteen years of such humble service, she was, in 1490, appointed Matron (*Rettora*) of the whole Institution, apparently the same year as that in which her now widowed cousin Tommasina entered the Augustinian Convent of Santa Maria delle Grazie. During the six years in which she held this office, she had much administrative business and responsibility weighing upon her. Large sums of money passed through her hands, and she always managed to spend and to account for them with the greatest care and success. Indeed "her accounts were never found wrong by a single *danaro* (farthing)." [2]

VII. Catherine and the Plague. The Outbreak of 1493.

It must have been after she had thus shown a rare devotedness and talent in an ordinary Nurse's work, and had next, as Matron, manifested, for some years, a remarkable administrative ability, that, in 1493, she rose, in both capacities, to the very height of heroism and efficiency.

1. *Catherine's general activity.*

Early in January of that year, quite exceptionally cold weather visited the city: the harbour was frozen over; and early in the spring the Plague broke out so fiercely, and raged so long—till the end of August—that of those who remained in the stricken city, four-fifths succumbed to the terrible disease. Most of the rich and noble, all those that did not occupy any official post, fled from the town. But Catherine

[1] *Vita*, p. 20*c*.

[2] *Ibid.* p. 21*c*. All the books and papers of the Hospital referring to these years up to her death were long ago destroyed by fire. I have, however, no doubt as to the, at least substantial, accuracy of the above account. For ten wills and assignments, drawn up, by various lawyers, in her presence, by her desire and at her dictation,—nine of them during the years of her weakness and illness,—are still extant, have been carefully copied out for me, and will be analyzed further on. They are all, except on one minor point, admirably precise, detailed, and wise.

not only remained at her post, but she it was no doubt who organized, or helped to organize, the out-of-door ambulance and semi-open-air wards which we know to have been instituted at this juncture on the largest scale. The great open space immediately at the back of and above the Hospital, where now still stretch the public gardens of the Acquasola, she managed to cover with rows of sailcloth tents, and appointed special Doctors (mostly Lombards) Nurses, and Priests and Franciscan Tertiaries, for the physical and spiritual care of their occupants. Throughout the weeks and months of the visitation she was daily in the midst, superintending, ordering, stimulating, steadying, consoling, strengthening this vast crowd of panic-stricken poor and severely strained workers.

2. *The pestiferous woman.*

And " on one occasion, she found " here, " a very devout woman, a Tertiary of St Francis, dying of " this " pestilential fever. The woman lay there in her agony, speechless for eight days. And Catherine constantly visited her, and would say to her, 'Call Jesus.' Unable to articulate, the woman would move her lips; and it was conjectured that she was calling Him as well as she could. And Catherine, when she saw the woman's mouth thus filled, as it were, with Jesus, could not restrain herself from kissing it with great and tender affection. And in this way she herself took the pestilential fever, and very nearly died of it. But, as soon as ever she had recovered, she was back again at her work, with the same great attention and diligence." [1]

How much there is in this little scene! Beautiful, utterly self-oblivious impulsiveness; a sleepless sense of the omnipresence of Christ as Love, and of this Love filling all things that aspire and thirst after it, as spontaneously as the liberal air and the overflowing mother's breast fill and feed even the but slightly aspiring or the painfully labouring lungs and the eager, helpless infant mouth; swift, tender, warm, whole-hearted affection for this outwardly poor and disfigured, but inwardly rich and beautiful fellow-creature and twin-vessel of election; an underlying virile elasticity of perseverance and strenuous, cheerful, methodical laboriousness; all these things are clearly there.

Only when everything had again returned to its normal

[1] *Vita*, p. 21*b*.

condition did she once more restrict herself to the administrative work of the Hospital.[1]

VIII. Catherine and Ettore Vernazza, 1493–1495.

It must have been during this epidemic of 1493 that Catherine first got to know, or at least first to work with, a man hardly less remarkable than herself.

1. *Ettore's family, marriage, and philanthropic work.*

The Genoese notary Ettore Vernazza, Catherine's junior by some twenty-three years, (as in the cases of his still greater

[1] The above paragraph is based, with Vallebona, *op. cit.* pp. 67–72, upon the assumption that Catherine took the kind of share described in the labours of this time; since it is practically unthinkable that she should not have acted as is here supposed, given the combination of the following facts, which are all beyond dispute. (1) The fully reliable Giustiniani in his *Annali* describes, under the date of 1493, the incidents of the Pestilence as given above; tells us how well, nevertheless, the sick and poor were looked after by those who, from amongst the educated classes, remained amongst them; and affirms that the Borgo di San Germano, identical with the Acquasola quarter, was assigned to those stricken by the Pestilence. (2) Agostino Adorno, Giuliano's cousin, was Doge of Genoa during this year. And the friendly terms on which the cousins were at this time are proved by Giuliano's Will of the following year (October 1494). (3) Catherine had already been Matron of the Hospital for two years and more, and was to continue to be so for another three years. She certainly did not absent herself from her post at this time. And her Hospital directly abutted against the Acquasola quarter. (4) The details furnished by all the sources conjointly with regard to her six years' Headship of the Hospital are so extraordinarily scanty that we must not too much wonder at the all but complete dearth of any allusion to a work which cannot have lasted longer than as many months. (5) The *Dialogo*, p. 222*b*, says: "She would go, too," (*i. e.* besides visiting the sick and poor in their own houses,) "to the poor of San Lazzaro, in which place she would find the greatest possible calamity." This clearly refers to some special (Lazar-, Leper-) Refuge, and the term can certainly cover aid given to the pest-stricken. And we shall see that the record here is derived from the writer's father, Ettore Vernazza, the heroic lover of the pest-stricken poor.

I have, in my text, assumed that the *Vita* gives us an anecdote relative to her visiting the pestiferous sick of Acquasola. But to do this, I have had (*a*) to take "pestiferous fever" as equivalent to "Pestilence," and to assume that it was not an isolated precursory case of the coming general visitation; (*b*) to omit, in the *Vita's* text, "nell' ospedale," as an indication where the sick woman was; and "allo stesso servizio (dell' ospedale)," as descriptive of where Catherine went back to: the anecdote may well originally have been without indication of the place in which the infection came to reduce her to death's door.

contemporaries and compatriots, Columbus, Pope Julius II, and Andrea Doria, the year of his birth remains uncertain, but is probably 1470,) was a scion of the ancient house of Vernaccia, which derived its name from a wine-producing village on the Eastern Riviera. A Riccobono Vernaccia had been Chancellor of Genoa, as far back as 1345. Ettore, the first of the family to write his name Vernazza, was the son of the Notary Pietro Vernaccia and of Battistina Spinola, his wife. A sister of his, Marietta, married into the Fieschi family.[1] And if Catherine really did go among the pestiferous sick, she can hardly have failed to meet Ettore, now twenty-three years old. For his eldest daughter, the Augustinian Canoness, the Venerable Battista Vernazza, a most careful writer and one full of a life-long vivid remembrance of her father, in an account of Ettore, written by her in Genoa in 1581 (she was born in 1497, four years after the event she describes), tells of " a great compassion which he had conceived when still very young, at the time that the pestilence raged in Genoa, and when he used to go around to aid the poor, and when he found that, by means of a preparation of cassia, he could bring them back from (certain) death to life." [2]

2. *Ettore's character ; Catherine's chief biographer.*

Ettore was, and he kept and made himself, and rare graces fashioned him ever increasingly into, a man of fine and keen, deep and world-embracing mind and heart, of an overflowing, ceaseless activity, and of a will of steel. To him, the earliest and perhaps up to the end the most intimate, certainly the most perceptive, of Catherine's disciples and chroniclers, we owe the transmission of many of the reminiscences of her conversion and early strivings (no doubt primarily derived from her own self), and of probably more than half of such authentic sayings and discourses of hers,

[1] *Inaugurazione della Statua d'Ettore Vernazza* (1863), Genova, Sordo-Muti, 1867. Most of my facts concerning Ettore and his daughters are taken from this *brochure*, with its careful biographical Discourse by Avvocato Professore Giuseppe Morro (pp. 5–31), and its ample collection of admirable wills and financial decisions (pp. 61–94).

[2] Quoted *ibid.* p. 21. It is absolutely certain that these words refer to the pestilence of 1493, since the epidemic did not again visit Genoa till 1503, when Vernazza must have been over thirty years of age. And Battista's silence as to any meeting between her Father and Catherine must not be pressed, since she nowhere mentions Catherine, and yet we know for certain how close and long was the intimacy between them.

as were recorded contemporaneously with their utterance. Indeed all that remains to us of written testimony, contemporaneous in this strict sense of the word, and that is other than legal documents, can, up to 1499, be safely attributed to him. And all such constituents of the now sadly mixed up, and most varyingly valuable, materials and successive layers of the *Vita ed Opere* as can with probability be assigned to his composition, are characterized by a remarkable clearness and consistency, restraint and refinement, elasticity and freshness of spiritual apprehension and sympathy. Thus Ettore's influence back upon the formation of Catherine's literary image and of our entire, especially of our authentic, conception of her, was predominant, and her influence upon his whole life was decisive; and hence his life can be rightly taken as an indefinite extension and new application and necessary supplementation of her own life and doctrine. I shall then, for both these reasons, try and work up what we can recover concerning the successive stages of his intercourse with Catherine and of the growth of his own life up to her death, into the corresponding vicissitudes of her remaining years.

It must have been two years later (1495) that Vernazza became her disciple; and probably some two or three years still further on that Ettore began to keep (no doubt at first only quite occasional) records of her Sayings and Doings.[1]

IX. Catherine's Health breaks down, 1496; other Events of the Same Year.

The year 1496 is marked by various events external and internal.

1. *Three external changes.*

In June, or some time before, Vernazza marries the beautiful Bartolommea Ricci, of the distinguished family of that name.

[1] The words of the *Vita*, p. 105*c*, that those who wrote this Life "saw and experienced these wonderful operations for *many years*," are given in MS. "A" as "during *fifteen consecutive* years (per quindici continui anni)," p. 366. All points to her having got to know Don Marabotto later than at this time and than Vernazza, yet only the one or the other of these two men can be meant; hence Vernazza must be intended here. But I have nowhere in the *Vita* been able to trace passages that could with probability be both attributed to Vernazza and dated before the years 1498–1499.

On the 17th of June Giuliano sells his Palace in the Via St. Agnese. And, probably at Midsummer, perhaps at Michaelmas, Catherine, forced to do so by increasing physical infirmities, resigns her office of Matron.[1]

2. *End of the extraordinary Fasts.*

Catherine " was now no more able to have a care of the government of the Hospital or of her own little house " (within its precints) " owing to her great bodily weakness. She would now find it necessary, after Communion, to take some food to restore her bodily strength, and this even if it was a fast day." We thus get the beginning of a third period with regard to such fasting powers. In the first, she had done as all the world, but had been able to keep all the Church fasts and abstinences. In the second, she had, during Lent and Advent, eaten little or nothing, and had, during the remainder of the time, lived as she had done before. And now, for the rest of her life, her eating and fasting are entirely fitful and intermittent, and she has to abandon all (at least systematic) attempts to keep even the ordinary Church fasts and abstinences.

If we are determined to insist on the accuracy of the " twenty-three Lents and twenty-two Advents " of her extraordinary fasts affirmed already by MS. " A," we shall have to understand this present inability to fast as applying, till after Lent 1496, only to the times outside of Lent and Advent, since this fasting period cannot be made to begin earlier than Lent 1476. I take it that in this, as certainly in most other cases, there was, in reality, a much more gradual transition than the *Vita* accounts would lead one to expect.

3. *She continues within the Hospital precincts. Her two maid-servants.*

Catherine had ceased to be Matron, but she did not leave the ample precincts of the Hospital; indeed she continued in the separate little house, which she had, probably since 1490,

[1] The precise date of Vernazza's marriage is unknown. But since his eldest child was born on April 15, 1497, it cannot have taken place later than June 1496. The date of the sale of the Palazzo is derived from Catherine's act of consent to the sale, preserved in the Archivio di Stato; a copy lies before me. The date of her resignation is derived from the *Vita*, p. 96*b*, which says she did so " quando fu di anni circa cinquanta." This " circa " must no doubt here, as so often (as, *e. g.* on p. 97*b*, where " circa sessanta-tre " refers to November 1509, when she was sixty-two), be interpreted as " nearly fifty " : she was really forty-nine.

been occupying with Giuliano. But it will be better to describe her abode a little later on, when we can be quite sure as to its identity.

She had now, as I think had been the case since soon after she had left her Palace, two maids in her service : the widow and Franciscan Tertiary, Benedetta Lombarda, who appears, already then as an old and valued servant, in Giuliano's will of October 1494, and who never left Catherine till her death; and a younger, unmarried maid, either Mariola Bastarda or a certain Antonietta. Argentina del Sale, too, will have often, perhaps continually, been about Catherine, aiding her in various ways; but she will not as yet have been living under the same roof with her. As we shall find, this little perfervid and untrained intelligence became the instrument, or at least the occasion, of the introduction of the largest legendary incident into the ultimate *Vita* of her mistress.

X. Events of 1497.

The next year, 1497, is marked by two events, of all but contradictory import and effect.

1. *Birth of Tommasina (Battista) Vernazza.*

On April 15 Vernazza's first child, a daughter, is born; and Catherine is her Godmother and holds her at the Font. Dottore Tommaso Moro, a learned lawyer friend of Ettore, is the Godfather, and the child is given his name and is called Tommasina. What would Catherine have felt or said had she foreseen the vicissitudes—they will occupy us in due course—through which this, her fellow God-parent, was to pass, during the storms of that Religious Revolution which were to break out so soon after her death? She would, we may be sure, have at all events been glad at the action and influence of her God-daughter towards and upon her Godfather, in those sad and most difficult times.

2. *Giuliano's death.*

And Giuliano was gravely ill ever since the beginning of the year, if not before; and some time in August or September he died.[1] He had been suffering long from a

[1] The date of Tommasina's birth comes from *Ritratti ed Elogi di Liguri Illustri*, Genova, Ponthenier; the date of the beginning of Giuliano's illness from his Codicil of January 10, 1497, in which he declares him-

chronic and most painful illness; and towards the end, "he became very impatient; and Catherine, fearful lest he should lose his soul, withdrew into another chamber, and there cried aloud for his salvation unto her tender Love, ever repeating with tears and sighs these words alone: 'O Love, I demand this soul of Thee; I beg Thee, give it me, for indeed Thou canst do so.' And having persevered thus for about half-an-hour with many a plaint, she was given at last an interior assurance of having been heard. And returning to her husband, she found him all changed and peaceful in his ways, and giving clear indications, both by words and signs, that he was fully resigned to the will of God." And "some time after his death she said to a spiritual son of hers," no doubt Vernazza: "'My son, Messer Giuliano has gone; and you know well that he was of a somewhat wayward nature, whence I suffered much mental pain. But my tender Love, before that he passed from this Life, certified me of his salvation.' And Catherine, having spoken these words, showed signs of regret at having uttered them; and he was discreet and did not answer this remark of hers, but turned the conversation to other topics." [1] At all events this conversation is thoroughly authentic, and Catherine's reserve, and her regret at having somewhat broken through her usual restraint, are profoundly characteristic: the contributors to and redactors of her Life have been increasingly blind, or

self as "languishing" and "infirm in body"; and the approximate date of his death from two entries in the Cartulary of the Bank of St. George, as to investments made by Catherine (copies in *Documenti su S. Caterina da Genova*, University Library, Genoa, B. VII, 31), of which the first, on July 14, 1497, gives her name as "Catterinetta, filia Jacobi di Fiesco et uxor Juliani Adorni"; and the second, on October 6, 1497, describes her as "uxor et heres testamentaria quondam fratris Juliani Adorni."

[1] *Vita*, pp. 122*b*, *c*, 123*a*. I have preserved the descriptive account of Catherine's prayer and of its effect, although it may possibly be but a later dramatized interpretation of the undoubtedly authentic report of her declaration made to Vernazza.—The immediate cause of Giuliano's pain and impatience is given by *Vita*, p. 122*b*, as "una gran passione d'urina"; Vallebona, p. 73, declares the malady to have been a "cestite cronica" (tape-worm).—I have omitted a short dialogue which is given, after her remark to Vernazza, as having occurred between her friends and herself, concerning her liberation from much oppression, and her own indifference to all except the will of God, because her answer is given in *oratio obliqua*, and is quite colourless and general; the passage is doubtless of no historical value: there never lived a less conventional, vapidly moralizing soul than hers.

even opposed, to all such beautifully spontaneous and human little shynesses and regrets for momentary indiscretions.

3. *Giuliano's Will.*

Giuliano had, by his Will of the 20th October, 1494, ordered his body to be buried in the Hospital Church; and this was now carried out by Catherine. A vault of some dimensions must have been made or bought, since later both she herself and Argentina del Sale declared their wish to be buried in Giuliano's " monument." Perhaps the wish of the latter was carried out.

But Giuliano had left two far more important and difficult matters to the management of Catherine,—matters which, indeed, were respectively full of pain and of anxiety for her,—Thobia, and his share in the Island of Scios. As to Thobia, he had left £500 to the Protectors of the Hospital, among which were reckoned £200 which he had already paid them through his late mother, Thobia Adorna, for the keep of this daughter of his, and had warmly recommended her to their kind care; and had arranged, in case they refused this responsibility, that Thobia (who must by now have been quite twenty-six years of age) should be regularly paid the interest on this money. He also left to Catherine, for payment to " a certain person in Religion,"—possibly a member of a Third Order, and whose identity is carefully concealed, but who cannot fail to be Thobia's mother—" £150, in repayment of the same sum, borrowed from her by himself and the said Catherine,"—money which this poor mother will have spent on the child's keep, up to the time when Giuliano told his story to Catherine.

As to his two *carati* (shares) in the lands of the Island of Scios, farmed by the Genoese Merchant Company " Maona," he desires that, if sold, his cousins Agostino and Giovanni Adorno shall be able to buy these *carati* for a lower price than would be required of any other purchaser. There are also elaborate conditions and alternatives attached to a legacy of £2,000 to his unmarried nephew Giovanni Adorno, with a view to his marrying and having legitimate children: an anxiety which of itself would show how sincere had been Giuliano's own conversion, and which was evidently not far-fetched, since in this very Will he leaves £125 to a natural sister of his, Catherine, daughter of his father Jacobo, for the boarding (no doubt during the latter years of her life) of his late mother, Thobia Adorna.

Giuliano had also left Catherine herself £1,000,—a return of her marriage dowry, and £100 from himself; and in addition "all garments, trinkets, gold, silver, cash, furniture, and articles of vertu, which might be found either in his dwelling-place or elsewhere." And he does so because he "knows and recognizes that the said Catherine, his beloved wife and heiress, has ever behaved herself well and laudably towards himself," and "wants to provide the means for her continuing to lead, after his death, her quiet, peaceful, and spiritual mode of life." And he adds the condition that, "if the said Catherine were to proceed to a second marriage (a thing which he does not think she will ever do), then he deprives her of all the legacies and rights and duties of heirship mentioned in this Will, and confers them upon the honourable Office of the Misericordia of Genoa,"—a society with and for which, as we have seen, Catherine had worked so much and so well.

Altogether Giuliano had left by this Will about £6,000 for Catherine to allot and appropriate; and quite £4,000 of this sum-total demanded careful and even anxious consideration, whilst £650 of it could not but provoke painful memories and make a call upon all her generosity. And by his Codicil of January 1497, he had given her still greater latitude of action, by declaring that, as regarded his legacy to the Hospital, Catherine should have full power and leave to abrogate or to modify it, according to her will and pleasure.[1] Thus these documents constitute an impressive proof of Giuliano's full trust in the wisdom, balance of mind and magnanimity of his wife, now herself already so broken in health.

4. *Catherine's execution of Giuliano's Will.*

It is nine months after Giuliano's death, on May 19, 1498, that we can watch and see how Catherine has been attempting to execute her trust, and how her nature has responded to these various difficult calls upon it, and to the claims of her own family. She first of all then, orders her body to be buried in the same grave with her husband, in the Hospital Church; and that only the Friars and Clergy of the Hospital shall be present at the funeral; and leaves £10 for her obsequies and £50 for Masses for herself. She next leaves to the Priest Blasio Cicero four shares of the Bank of St. George (about £200), of which he is to pay £150 to a certain

[1] I work from careful copies specially made for me direct from the originals, by Dre. Augusto Ferretto, of the Archivio di Stato in Genoa.

female Religious, in satisfaction for a certain debt. And she abrogates Giuliano's legacy to the Hospital, and, in its place, herself leaves it four shares of St. George's (at the time about £200, but always tending to increase in value), in liquidation of the £300 that remained unpaid from among the £500 of that legacy. She next leaves to Benedetta Lombarda one share of Saint George's, in addition to the similar share left her by Giuliano; and to " Antonietta, dwelling with Testatrix, £25, in case she shall live with her up to her death." As to the two *carati*, she leaves them to Giovanni Adorno, in lieu of the money bequeathed to him by Giuliano. As to her own relations, she leaves two shares of St. George's apiece to her two nieces Maria and Battista, the daughters of her eldest brother Jacobo, for their marriage portions; and, if they all die before marriage, then all this money is to go to their father. She leaves £10 to her Augustinian Canoness sister Limbania; and institutes her three brothers Jacobo, Giovanni and Lorenzo, and their heirs, her residuary legatees.

Here four things are noticeable. Catherine has herself undertaken the expenses of Thobia's keep; the apparent lessening on her part of the sum originally apportioned for the purpose by Giuliano is doubtless only apparent, and must proceed from the same cause which has produced a similar apparent diminution in the amount of Giuliano's legacy to his nephew from £2,000 to £1,500. In the next place, this is the only one out of the couple's four Wills in which the second maid is not Mariola Bastarda, but a certain Antonietta. Catherine feels uncertain as to whether Antonietta will persevere in her service to the end; and we shall find that she has again disappeared in Catherine's next will of 1506, and that Mariola has again taken up her old place. We shall find that a story, of which the authenticity and significance are most difficult to fix, attaches without doubt to one or the other of these maids. In the third place, Catherine does not sell the two *carati*, but leaves them, in lieu of the money bequeathed to him, to Giovanni Adorno; no doubt from the feeling that thus, at her death, this her share in the government and exploitation of the Greek island would be in the hands of a man in the prime of life, who could help to check malpractices. And lastly, she shows a generous forgiveness of Giuliano, a delicate magnanimity towards Thobia and Thobia's mother, and a thoughtful affection for all her own near and grown-up relations, by ordering her body to be buried in the same grave with Giuliano; by herself undertaking the charges of Thobia's keep, and appointing a priest by name for handing over Giuliano's legacy to the still unnamed mother of Thobia; and by remembering her sister, although she had long been provided for in her Convent, her three brothers, who were no doubt indefinitely richer than herself, and especially her two marriageable nieces. Altogether, of the £2,304 definitely accounted for in the Will, she leaves £60 for her own funeral and for Masses for herself; £400 for Thobia and her mother; £210 to her own relations; £125 to servants; and £1,500 to her husband's nephew. There is no trace here ofany in difference to the natural ties of kindred, or of an abstraction of mind rendering her incapable of a careful consideration and firm decision in matters of business: a point which we shall find to be of much importance, later on.

5. *Ettore's "Mandiletto"-work.*

In this year, too, if not already in the previous one, Vernazza founded the institution of the "Mandiletto." Still a young man—for he was now at most but twenty-eight—Ettore had been noticing, in his work among the poor, how much misery of all kinds obtained in commercial, money-making, hazard-loving Genoa, amongst persons who, even though ill, refused to take refuge in the hospitals; and who, however poor at present, had known better, even brilliant days, and were too proud to beg, or even to accept alms from any one who could recognize them. And hence he now organized a system for discovering and visiting such persons in their own homes, and for minimizing their pain in accepting help, by arranging that the members of this little fraternity should never visit such houses, except with some kind of little veil or handkerchief (*fazzoletto, mandiletto*) applied to their faces.[1]

Catherine, who had helped the Uffizio della Misericordia so much, and who herself so greatly disliked being noticed or even simply seen whenever she was doing or suffering anything at all out of the common, had no doubt, at least in a general way, inspired this beautifully delicate means of preserving and sparing the bashfulness of the giver and the dignity of the recipient. Throughout the remaining years of her life she must have cared to hear Vernazza's report as to the progress of this work.

[1] *Inaugurazione*, pp. 12, 13.

XI. Beginning of her Third, Last Period; End of the Extraordinary Fasts; First Relations with Don Marabotto.

But it is in the next year, 1499, that we reach the actual beginning of the third and last period of Catherine's Convert life.

1. *End of the Fasts; transfer of the "carati."*

Some of the events of this year are again predominantly external, or but continuations or consequences of previous inclinations of her will. It must have been at the end of the Lent of this spring-time that all extraordinary fasting-power, of a kind that could be foreseen and that more or less synchronized with the ecclesiastical season, left her for good and all. And she had gone on feeling strongly her share of responsibility for the government of that far-off island. Hence she betook herself, on September 18 of this year, with the Notary Battista Strata, who has drawn up nine out of the fourteen Legal Acts of Giuliano and herself, to the great palace of the Cardinal Giuliano della Rovere, who, four years later, became Pope Julius II. This palace stood by the (now destroyed) Church of San Tommaso, and was at this time the residence of Giovanni Adorno. And there, in the great Loggia looking south, Catherine dictated the substance of an Act of Cession then and there to her husband's nephew of those two *carati*, which weighed so heavily on her mind. Perhaps Giovanni was in poor health, and Catherine was too eager to eschew her responsibility in the matter to be willing to wait any longer.[1]

2. *Beginning of Catherine's relations with Don Marabotto.*

The chief event, however, from the point of view of her inner life, and which gives us a second close and most important eye-witness for her last period, was the beginning of her spiritual relations with Don Marabotto.[2] "At the end

[1] I work again from a copy made by Dre. Ferretto from the original in the Archivio di Stato, Genoa.

[2] Marabotto's help in business matters cannot, on any large scale, have begun till considerably later than his spiritual help. For whereas her Codicil of 1503 nowhere mentions Marabotto, her Will of 1506 leaves him, as we shall see, a little legacy; her Will of 1509 protects him against all harassing inquisition into the details of his administration of her affairs; and her Codicil of 1510 mentions only him and Don Carenzio. And it is incredible that business help should have been given through-

of the twenty-five years during which she had persevered in the way of God without the means of any creature," say the *Vita*, "the Lord gave her a priest, to take care both of her soul and of her body; a spiritual man and one of holy life, to whom God gave light and grace to understand His operations within her. He had been appointed Rector of the Hospital; and hence was in a position to hear her Confession, say Mass for her, and give her Holy Communion according to her convenience."[1] Now the rare and profound isolation and independence of her middle period render this turning to and finding of human help specially significant; the numerous sayings addressed to her Confessor to be found throughout the *Vita* were all, with the sole exception of those contained in the Conversion-scene, spoken to Marabotto and transmitted by him to us;[2] and probably at least half of the narrative of her Life and well-nigh all her Passion are due to Don Marabotto's pen. It is then important, and it is possible to get a fairly clear idea as to the sort of man he was.

3. *Don Marabotto's family and character; Catherine's attitude towards him.*

Don Cattaneo came from a stock even more ancient and distinguished than that of Vernazza. A Marabotto had had a lawsuit with the Bishop of Genoa in 1128; Roggiero Marabotto had lent money to the King of Sardinia in 1164; Martino Marabotto had been Ambassador to Rome, Florence, and Lucca in 1256; Pelagio of that name had been Notary to the Mint in 1435; Giorgio, a Doctor of Medicine in 1424; Ambrosio, Lieutenant-Governor of Corsica in 1459. And the

out four years, and should have failed to gain any recognition in a document which commemorates so many lesser services. Marabotto was Rector in 1504 (I owe this date to the kindness of the Rev. Padre Vincenzo Celesia, author of the MS. *Storia dell' Ospedale di Pammatone in Genova*, 1897); he was no more Rector in September 1509, but Don Jacobo Carenzio then held this post (Catherine's Codicil of that date). Indeed already in March 1509 Marabotto seems not to have been Rector (Catherine's Will of that date mentions him repeatedly, but nowhere as Rector). I take the Offices of *Rettore* (Master), and of *Rettora* (Matron), to have never been exercised simultaneously: but that, at any one time, there was always only a Rettore or a Rettora presiding over the whole Hospital. The Office of Rettora was abolished altogether in 1730 (*Storia dell' Ospedale*, p. 1135).

[1] *Vita*, p. 117*b*.

[2] The Appendix will show that the "Religioso," the "dolce figliuolo," of pp. 94, 95, and the "Religioso, figliuolo," of pp. 98, 99, must be Ettore Vernazza, and not Cattaneo Marabotto.

family, like the Fieschi, had always been Guelph: Federico Marabotto had armed nine galleys against the Ghibellines and had had a narrow escape from the latter, during a dark night of 1330; and Antonio and Domenico were known Guelph leaders in 1450 and 1452. Indeed the latter was Procurator to the Fieschi family in 1443, and thus anticipated, by sixty years and on a larger scale, Don Cattaneo's management of Catherine Fiesca's modest affairs.[1]

Don Cattaneo himself we find ever gentle, patient, devoted and full of unquestioning reverence towards Catherine; most valuably accurate and detailed in his reproduction of things, in proportion to their tangibleness; naïf and without humour, thoroughly matter of fact, readily identifying the physical with the spiritual, and thus often, unconsciously, all but succeeding in depriving Catherine's spirit, for us who have so largely to see her with his eyes, of much of its specially characteristic transcendence and of its equally characteristic ethical and spiritual immanence. Such a mind would appear better fitted to follow,—at a respectful distance,—than to lead such a spirit as Catherine's; and, indeed, to be more apt to help her as a man of business than as a man of God. As a matter of fact, however, he was quite evidently of very great help and consolation, even in purely spiritual matters, to Catherine, during these last eleven years of her life. Not as though there were any instances of his initiating, stimulating, or modifying any of her ideals or doctrines: she entirely remains, in purely spiritual matters, her own old self, and continues to grow completely along the lines of her previous development. And again he did attend, with an all but unbroken assiduity, to matters not directly belonging to his province *qua* priest,—to her much-tried, ever-shifting bodily health, and, probably some three or four years later on, to her financial affairs, which latter were still of some variety and complication, owing to her generous anxiety to do much for others, with but little of her own. But between these two opposite extremes of possible help or influence lay another middle level, in which his aid was considerable. For "whenever God worked anything within her, which impressioned her much either in soul or body, she would confer about it all with her Confessor; and he, with the grace and light of God, understood well-nigh all, and would

[1] I take all these facts from F. Federici's careful MS. work, *Famiglie Nobili di Genova, sub verbo* Marabotto.

give her answers which seemed to show that he himself felt the very thing that she was feeling herself." "And she would say, that even simply to have him by, gave her great comfort, because they understood each other, even by just looking each other in the face without speaking." [1] Marabotto's Direction consists, then, in giving her the human support of human understanding and sympathy, and, no doubt, in reminding her, in times of darkness, of the lights and truths received and communicated by her in times of consolation. Never does Marabotto see, or think he sees, as far or as clearly as she sees, when she sees at all; and it is the light derived by him from herself at one time which he administers to her soul at another.

4. *Catherine's first Confession to Don Cattaneo.*

The general tone and character of her first Confession to him are described to us, no doubt from his own contemporary record. "She said: 'Father, I know not where I am, either as to my soul or as to my body. I should like to confess, but I cannot perceive any offence committed by me.'" "And as to the sins which she mentioned," adds Marabotto, "she was not allowed to see them as so many sins, thought or said or done by herself. But her state of soul was like unto that of a small boy, who would have committed some slight offence in simple ignorance; and who, if some one told him, You have done evil, would at these words suddenly change colour and blush, and yet not because he has now an experimental knowledge of evil." "And many a time she would say to her Confessor: 'I do not want to neglect Confession, and yet I do not know to whom to give the blame of my sins; I want to accuse myself, and cannot manage it.' And yet, with all this, she made all the acts appropriate to Confession." [2]

We shall see, indeed, how keen, right up to the end, was her sense of her frailty and of her general and natural inclination to evil. And her teaching as to numerous positive and active imperfections remaining in the soul, in every soul, up

[1] *Vita*, p. 118, *a*, *b*. The first of these two passages is followed, in the same section, by two other slightly different accounts. The third of these is no doubt authentic, but refers to a still later period: it shall be given in its proper place. These two authentic accounts are (as is often the case in the *Vita*) joined together by a vague and yet absolute, unauthentic account, which declares that she told him all things (apparently on all occasions): a statement untrue of any time in her life.

[2] *Vita*, pp. 117*c*, 118*a*.

to the very end, is so clear and constant, and so admittedly derived from her own experience, that we can explain the above only by the supplementary part of her doctrine (also derived from her own experience), which insists that some greatly advanced souls do not, at the time of committing them, as yet see these their imperfections, and that, by the time they have so far further advanced as to see these imperfections, they are no more inclined to commit them. In this way, then, there would be no fully formal sin or deliberate imperfection to confess.

XII. Her Conversations with her Disciples; "Caterina Serafina." Don Marabotto and the Possessed Maid.

1. *Pure Love and Heaven.*

It is probably during the next two years of her life that occurred the beautiful scene and conversation,—so typical of her relations with her disciples during this first part of her last period (1499 to 1501), which we can think of as her spiritual Indian summer, her Aftermath. The scene has been recorded for us by her chief interlocutor, Vernazza. Probably Bartolommea, Ettore's wife, was present, and possibly also Don Marabotto. "This blessed soul," he writes, "all surrounded though she was by the deep and peaceful ocean of her Love, God, desired nevertheless to express in words, to her spiritual children, the sentiments that were within her. And many a time she would say to them: 'O would that I could tell what my heart feels!' And her children would say: 'O Mother, tell us something of it.' And she would answer: 'I cannot find words appropriate to so great a love. But this I can say with truth, that if of what my heart feels but one drop were to fall into Hell, Hell itself would altogether turn into Eternal Life.'"[1] "And one of these her spiritual children, an interior soul (*un Religioso*),"—Vernazza, present on this occasion,—"dismayed at what she was saying, replied: 'Mother, I do not understand this; if it were possible, I would gladly understand it better.' But Catherine answered: 'My son, I find it impossible to put it other-

[1] *Vita*, p. 94*c*. The three lines which follow in the printed *Vita* are wanting in MS. "A" of 1547, p. 235, and are a disfiguring gloss of R 2.

wise.' Then he, eager to understand further, said : 'Mother supposing we gave your word some interpretation, and that this corresponded to what is in your mind, would you tell us if it was so ?' 'Willingly, dear son,' rejoined Catherine, with evident pleasure."

"And the disciple continued : 'The matter might perhaps stand in this wise.' And he then explained how that the love which she was feeling united her, by participation, with the goodness of God, so that she no more distinguished herself from God. Now Hell stands for the very opposite, since all the spirits therein are in rebellion against God. If then it were possible for them to receive even a little drop of such union, it would deprive them of all rebellion against God, and would so unite them with Love, with God Himself, as to make them be in Life Eternal. For Hell is everywhere where there is such rebellion; and Life Eternal, wheresoever there is such union. And the Mother, hearing this, appeared to be in a state of interior jubilation; whence with beaming face she answered : 'O dear son, truly the matter stands as you have said; and hearing you speak, I feel it really is so. But my mind and tongue are so immersed in this Love, that I cannot myself either say or think these or other reasons.' And the Disciple then said : 'O Mother, could you not ask your Love, God, for some of these little drops of union for your sons ?' She answered, and with increased joyousness : 'I see this tender Love to be so full of condescension to these my sons, that for them I can ask nothing of It, and can only present them before His sight.'"[1]

I sincerely know not where to look for a doctrine of grander depth and breadth, of more vibrating aliveness; for one more directly the result of life, or leading more directly to it, than are those few half-utterances and delicately strong indications of an overflowing interior plenitude and radiant, all-conquering peace.

And even one such scene is sufficient to make us feel that the following passage of the *Dialogo* is, in its substance and tone, profoundly true to facts : "This soul remained henceforth" (in this third period) "many a time in company with its many spiritual friends, discoursing of the Divine Love, in such wise that they felt as though in Paradise, both

[1] *Vita*, pp. 94, 95.

collectively, and each one in his own particular way. How delightful were these colloquies! He who spoke and he who listened, each one fed on spiritual food of a delicious kind; and because the time flew so swiftly, they never could attain satiety, but, all on fire within them, they would remain there, unable at last to speak, unable to depart, as though in ecstasy."[1]

2. "*Caterina Serafina.*"

Five times the *Vita* compares her countenance, which, when she was deeply moved, had a flushed, luminous and transparent appearance, to that of an Angel or Cherub or Seraph;[2] and it even gives a story, which purports to explain how she came to be called the latter. And though this anecdote may be little more than a literary dramatization of this popular appellation of Catherine; and although, even if the scene be historical, Catherine has no kind of active share in bringing it about; yet the passage is, in any case, of some real interest, since it testifies to and typifies Catherine's abundance of moral and mental sanity and strong, serene restorative influence over unbalanced or tempted souls, and this at a time when she herself had already been in delicate health for about five years.

The story is interesting also in that it shows how strikingly like the superficial psycho-physical symptoms of persons described as possessed by an evil spirit were, and were thought to be, to those of ecstasy, hence to Catherine's own. Thus when an attack seized this "spiritual daughter of Catherine,—a woman of large mind (*alto intelletto*), who lived and died in virginity, and under the same roof with Catherine" (no doubt Catherine's second, unmarried, servant Mariola Bastarda is meant, and each must have had experience of the other's powers and wants from or before 1490 till 1497, and again from 1500 onwards),—"she would become greatly agitated and be thrown to the ground. The evil spirit would enter into her mind, and would not allow her to think of divine things. And she would thus be as one beside herself, all submerged in that malign and diabolic will."—And similarly we are told that Catherine would "throw herself to the ground, altogether beside herself," "immersed in a sea,"—in this case, "of the deepest

[1] *Vita*, p. 97*b*; 250, *a*, *b*.

[2] Angel, 50*b*; Cherub, 16*a*, 97*b*; Seraph, 130*b*.

peace"; and "she would writhe as though she were a serpent."[1]

Yet this superficial likeness between these two states,—a likeness apparent already in the similar double series of phenomena described in St. Paul's Epistles and in the Acts of the Apostles,—serves, here also, but to bring out in fuller relief the profound underlying spiritual and moral difference between the two conditions of soul. For it is precisely in Catherine's company that, when insufferable to her own self, the afflicted Mariola would recover her peace and self-possession, so that "even a silent look up to Catherine's face would help to bring relief."[2]

It is in 1500, soon after Mariola's return to her mistress (I take the maid's state of health to have occasioned her absence from Catherine for two years or so), that this spiritual daughter is represented as declaring in the first stage of one of these attacks,—or rather "the unclean spirit" possessing her is said to have exclaimed to Catherine: "We are both of us thy slaves, because of that pure love which thou possessest in thy heart"; and "full of rage at having made this admission, he threw himself on the ground, and writhed with the feet." And then when,—all this is supposed to take place in the presence of both Catherine and Don Marabotto,—the possessed one has stood up, the Confessor forces the spirit step by step to speak out and to declare successively that Catherine is "Caterina," "Adorna or Fiesca," and "Caterina Serafina," the latter being uttered amidst great torment.[3]

[1] *Vita*, pp. 47*b*, 50*a*, 72*b*. [2] *Ibid.* p. 115*b*.

[3] *Ibid.* p. 115*b*. There are three passages in the *Vita* referring to cases of possession. (*a*) Page 39*b* makes Catherine, in finishing up a discourse as to Evil being essentially but a Privation of Love, refer to a "Religioso" and to a "Spiritato," and how the latter, "costretto" by the former to tell him what he was, "answered with great force: 'I am that unhappy wretch bereft of love.' And he (the evil spirit) said so with a voice so piteous and penetrating, that it moved me (Catherine) through and through with compassion." The Possessed One is here a man. In MS. "A" (p. 92) the story is still quite loosely co-ordinated with her speech: it was originally no doubt an independent anecdote; and was, possibly after a good many intermediary literary fixations, introduced into this place and connection by R 1 or R 2. (*b*) Page 115*a*, *b*, gives the story reproduced in the text above. The Possessed One is here a woman; and here the entire passage formally claims directly to reproduce an actual scene from Catherine's life. (*c*) Page 162*a* gives an anecdote of a "figliuola spirituale" of Catherine, who had "il demonio adosso";

XIII. CATHERINE'S SYMPATHY WITH ANIMAL- AND PLANT-LIFE: HER LOVE OF THE OPEN AIR. HER DEEP SELF-KNOWLEDGE AS TO THE HEALTHINESS OR MORBIDNESS OF HER PSYCHO-PHYSICAL STATES.

1. *Increase of suffering and of range of sympathy.*

It is indeed in this last period of her life that we can most clearly see a deeply attractive mixture of personal suffering and of tender sympathy with even the humblest of all things that live. And this is doubtless not simply due to the much fuller evidence possessed by us for these last years, but is quite as much owing to the actual increase of these twin things within herself. " She was most compassionate towards all creatures; so that, if an animal were killed or a tree cut down, she could hardly bear to see them lose that being which God had given them."[1] And a beautiful communion of spirit

and tells how, at the time of her mistress's death, the " spirito " within her, " costretto," declared that he had seen Catherine unite herself with God,—and all this with " tormento," so that " pareva a sè intollerabile." This passage clearly refers to the same person as that of passage *b*.

As to the historicity of the event described in the text, we must distinguish between the general fact of Catherine's moral and psychic ascendency over Mariola, a fact as entirely beyond dispute as it is valuable and characteristic; and the occurrence of the scene as given above. As to the latter, the question of its value is of course distinct from that of its occurrence. Its supposed evidential worth is *nil*, since Mariola had been intimate with and devoted to Catherine for probably a good ten years at least. But the scene may nevertheless have actually occurred. It is true that the partly parallel case of the " Spiritato " shows how easily such a dramatization of doctrine or transference of experience can occur. And Denys the Areopagite and Jacopone da Todi are full of this comparison of the soul arrived at a state of union to an Angel, Cherub or Seraph; and these writers have greatly influenced not only Catherine's authentic teaching, but also the successive amplifications and modifications of her life and sayings. And again we shall prove that certain legendary matters were inserted in the *Vita* at a late date—between 1545 and 1551. But these passages all claim to be based upon evidence supplied by Argentina del Sale; and they were evidently not accepted by Marabotto (1582); the literary form of these legends differs much from that of our passage; and if the former are still absent from MSS. " A " and " B," the latter is already present in both. And we have such entirely first-hand proof for the curiously naïf, formal, exteriorizing character of Marabotto's mind, as to leave it always possible that he did bring about a little scene of the sort here described. If so, Marabotto's rôle in it will have been prompted, in part, by a wish still further to increase Catherine's hold upon Mariola's mind.

[1] *Vita*, p. 112*a*.

can now be traced even between plant-life and herself; and an innocent self-diversion from a too exciting concentration, and help towards a patient keeping or a bracing reconquering of calmness, is now found by her, Franciscan-like, in the open air and amidst the restful flowers and trees. Thus " at times she would seem to have her mind in a mill; and as if this mill were indeed grinding her, soul and body "; and then " she would walk up and down in the garden, and would address the plants and trees and say: 'Are not you also creatures created by my God? Are not you, too, obedient to Him?' "—even though, I think she meant to say, your life moves on so instinctive, calm, and freely expansive in the large, liberal air, as I feel it to do, by its very contrast to my own eager, crowded life, struggling in vain for a sustained perfection of equipoise and for an even momentary adequacy of self-expression. " And doing thus, she would gradually be comforted." [1]

Indeed she would, in still intenser moods, use plants and other creatures of God in a more violent fashion. But this is now no more done as of old, for direct purposes of mortification; but, at one time, from an unreflective transport of delight, delight which itself seems ever to impel noble natures to seek to mix some suffering with it; and, at another time, for the purpose of producing strong physical impressions, counter-stimulations and escapes from a too great intensity of interior feeling. " She would at times, when in the garden, seize hold of the thorn-covered twigs of the rose-bushes, with both her hands; and would not feel any pain whilst thus doing it in a transport of mind. She would also bite her hands and burn them, and this in order to divert, if possible, her interior oppression." [2]

2. *She alone keeps the sense of the truly spiritual, in the midst of her psycho-physical states.*

Indeed nothing is more characteristic of her psychic state,

[1] *Vita*, p. 72*b*.

[2] *Ibid.* p. 113*b*. I take these two motives alone to have operated throughout such actions of hers during this last period. The additional motive attributed to her (*ibid.* pp. 129*c*, 130*a*, and 134*a*), where she is represented as applying a lighted candle or live coal to her bare arm, for the purpose of testing whether her interior spiritual fire or this exterior material one is the greater, is entirely unlike Catherine's spirit. It belongs to the demonstrably legendary and disfiguring interpretations which shall be studied further on. The sentence on p. 134*a*, in which she herself is made to declare this motive, is most certainly a worthless gloss.

during these years, than the ever-increasing intensity, shiftingness and close interrelation between the physical and mental. But we shall find that, whereas those who surround her, Confessor, Doctors, Disciples, Attendants, all, in various degrees and ways, increasingly insist upon and persist in finding direct proofs of the supernatural in the purely physical phenomena of her state even when taken separately, and indeed more and more in exact proportion to their non-spiritual character: Catherine herself, although no doubt not above the medical or psychical knowledge of her time, remains admirably centred in the truly spiritual, and continually awake to the necessity of interior spiritual selection amongst and assimilation and transformation of all such psycho-physical impressions and conditions. Even in the midst of the extreme weaknesses of her last illness we shall see her only quite exceptionally, and ever for but a few instants, without this consciousness of the deep yet delicate difference in ethical value and helpfulness between the various psycho-physical things experienced by herself, and of the requirements, duties and perceptions of her own spirit with regard to them.

And this attitude is all the more remarkable because, to the outer difficulty arising from the persistent, far more immediate, and apparently more directly religious, view of all her little world about her, came two peculiarities working in the same direction from within her own self. There was the old constitutional keenness and concentration of her highly nervous physical and psychical temperament, and the rarely high pitch and swift pace of her whole inner life, which must, at all times, have rendered suspense of judgment and detachment with regard to her own sensations and quasi-physical impressions specially difficult. And there was now the new intensity and closeness of interaction between soul and body, which must have made such lofty detachment from all but the spiritual realities a matter of the rarest grace and of the most heroic self-conquest.

3. *Catherine's health does not break up completely till* 1507. The *Vita*, indeed, as we now have it, tells us that "about nine years before her death," hence in 1501, "an infirmity came upon her, which neither her attendants nor the doctors knew how to identify"; and that "there was confusion, not on her own part, but on the part of those who served her."[1] But

[1] *Vita*, p. 127*a*.

this whole Chapter XLVII (pp. 127–132) of the present *Vita*, which opens out thus, is wanting in MSS. "A" and "B"; and is composed of documents which appear, in a fuller and more primitive form and in their right chronological place, in the next three chapters (pp. 132–160), chapters without doubt predominantly due to Marabotto; and of the documents making up the present Chapter XXXVIII (pp. 98, 99), which are earlier again, in both contents and composition, and are very certainly the work of Vernazza. And this means that, though the present Chapter XLVII claims to give a general account of her condition during 1501–1510, it does not, as a matter of fact, give us anything but details belonging without doubt to 1507–1510.

The manner in which this late compiler insists upon the directly spiritual, indeed supernatural, character of even the clearly secondary and physical phenomena of her state, make it highly probable that, having once exaggerated the quality, he readily snatched at any indications (possibly a slip of the pen in some MS., writing 1501 instead of 1507; we have a similar slip in MS. "A," which on p. 193 twice writes 1506 for 1509), which favoured an early date for the beginning of her last illness. Certainly the legal documents at our disposal show her to us still variously interested and active, right up to 1507.

It will, then, be better first to describe this activity up to 1507, and to take even the general questions concerning her illness in connection with her last four years, 1507–1510.

XIV. Catherine's Social Joys and Sorrows, 1501–1507.

1. *Birth of Ettore's last two daughters.*

It will have been during these years 1501 to 1507, unless indeed already between 1497 and 1501, that Vernazza's second and third daughters were born; and if Catherine had stood Godmother to his eldest child, Tommasina, it is inconceivable that she should not have cared for Tommasina's sisters, Catetta and Ginevrina. Certainly their father, Catherine's closest friend and disciple, gave detailed attention, right up to the end of his strenuous life, to all three children; and made most thoughtful particular provision, in his still extant remarkable Will of 1517, for the youngest, Ginevrina, who at that time was the only one not yet settled in life.[1] Thus Vernazza knew how to combine all this detailed thought for his own children with the spacious public spirit of which his Dispositions are a still extant, most impressive monument; and Catherine, who was his deepest inspirer, clearly led the way here, right up to the last four years of her life. For we have already seen how she managed to conjoin, in a fashion similar to Ettore's, a universal love for Love Transcendent, with a particularism of attachment to individual souls, in which that Love is immanent.

2. *Deaths of Limbania, Jacobo, and Giovanni.*

And if she had joy over souls coming into the world, she had sorrow over souls leaving it. For in the single year 1502 she lost her only sister, Limbania, and her two elder brothers Jacobo and Giovanni. It is true that the *Vita* says: "There died several of her brothers and sisters; but, owing to the great union which she had with the tender will of God, she felt no pain, as though they had not been of her own blood."[2] But then we have already often found how subject to caution and rebate are all such general, absolute statements; this passage in particular is, by its vagueness and ambiguity (she had but one sister of her own), stamped as late and more or less secondary; and we shall trace, later on, a similar even more extensive *a priori* modification of her authentic image in the *Dialogo*. Certainly her Wills show no kind of indifference to her own relations. In that of 1498 she specially and carefully remembered these very three relations; and in proportion as these two brothers' children grow up and at all require her help, Catherine specially refers to and plans for them,—so for Jacobo's eldest daughter Maria, in view of getting her married (Wills of 1498, 1503, 1506, 1509); and for Giovanni's three sons (Wills of 1503, 1506, 1509). Jacobo's second daughter seems also to have died at this time, as she no more appears after the Will of 1498. We shall see how exactly the same affectionate interest is shown by her towards her still remaining brother and his two sons.[3]

[1] It is remarkable how tough-lived has been the legend which makes Vernazza have an only child. Not only Father Sticker (*Acta Sanctorum*, September, Vol. V, pp. 123–195) has it in 1752, but even Vallebona, in his *Perla dei Fieschi*, still repeats it in 1887. And yet the *Inaugurazione* pamphlet had appeared in Genoa in 1867, giving on pp. 13, 14, 72, 73 the fullest proofs as to the reality of these two other children.

[2] *Vita*, p. 123*b*.

[3] I get the date of 1502 for those three deaths from Angelo L. Giovo's

3. *The Triptych "Maestà."*

And she evidently still went on increasing the number of the objects of her interest and affection, and the degree of her attachment to such objects as she already loved. For in her Codicil of the next year, January 1503, she gives a careful description of a picture now belonging to herself, "a 'Majesty,' representing the Virgin Mary with Saint Joseph, and the Lord Jesus at their feet, with her" (Fieschi-Adorni) "coat-of-arms painted within and without." The picture evidently represented the Adoration of the Infant Jesus, and was painted on wood,—a triptych: with Catherine's arms painted both inside and outside the two wings. She again describes it thus fully in her Wills of 1506 and 1509, leaving it, on all those occasions to a certain Christofero de Clavaro (Christofer of Chiavari?). It is then quite clear both that this picture had been specially painted by some one for Catherine, and that Catherine, for some reason or reasons, greatly treasured it. Who then was the painter and what was the reason? I think both are not difficult to find.

We have seen how Catherine's much-loved cousin, the widowed Tommasina Fiescha, had in 1497 moved into the Monastero Nuovo in the Aquasola quarter,—close to Catherine's abode; so that the cousins will have met constantly from that time forward. We have also seen that this distinguished artist painted many a "Pietà" (the dead Christ on His Mother's lap, possibly with Angels on each side), and executed a piece of needlework again representative of a group,—this time God the Father with many Angels above, and Christ below. Indeed Federico Alizeri has succeeded in rediscovering one of her works, a representation of Christ crowned with thorns and surrounded by the Instruments and Mysteries of His Passion, painted in fine outline upon sheepskin mounted on a wood-panel.[1] And we have seen how much Catherine had, as a child, been affected by a "Pietà," and shall find her, even after this date, still affected by a religious picture. There can then be no reasonable doubt that Suor Tommasina was

MS. *Vita* of the Saint in the *Biblioteca della Missione Urbana* (Part I, ch. iii). All three names are prominent in the Will of 1498; in the Codicil of 1503, Jacobo and Giovanni are both styled "the late," and her brother Lorenzo has become the sole residuary legatee. Limbania appears nowhere after the Will of 1498.

[1] *Atti della Società Ligure di Storia Patria,* Genova, 1868, p. 411 (with plate. The article is dated 1871.

the painter and giver of this picture,—again a group, a "Maestà," instead of the usual "Pietà."

And the facts of Catherine caring to possess, to preserve, and to transmit something thus specially appropriated to herself, with her family arms upon a religious picture, are all deeply significant touches, and quite unlike what all the secondary, and even some of the primary, parts of the *Vita* would lead one to expect.

4. *Increasing care for Thobia.*

And this same Codicil shows us how her care, and no doubt her genuine affection, for Thobia was growing. For she now leaves her the income on two shares of the Bank of St. George (no doubt only a slight gift, about £2 10*s*. a year; but Catherine possesses but very little that she is free to leave as she likes, the claims upon her are very many, and the young woman is already well provided for, considering her social station), her better silk gown, a skirt, and various veils. The poor girl died in 1504 or 1505, for in Catherine's Will of 1506 she appears as "the late Thobia." She must have been about thirty years old at the time.

5. *Argentina del Sale; story of Marco del Sale's death.*

But in lieu of poor Thobia, Catherine was now given by Providence a new lowly object of affection and interest. For it was doubtless in the late spring of 1505 that occurred the incident, of which we have the beautifully simple and naïf record in Chapter XLVI of the *Vita*; a record certainly based upon information supplied by Argentina, but which I take to be the literary work of Vernazza, and to be more or less contemporary with the events described. A humble young friend or acquaintance of Catherine's, who had perhaps already been her occasional little day-servant, one Argentina de Ripalta, had now been away from her and married, for a year, to a poor navvy working in the Molo (Quay) quarter of the town; and this her husband, Marco del Sale, was now dangerously ill, indeed he was dying of a cancer in the face. And, having tried every kind of remedy, and seeing himself incurable, and being thus in great and hopeless pain, Marco had lost all patience and was as one beside himself. And then Argentina bethought herself of Catherine, and came to the Hospital, and begged her to come and see her husband, and pray to God for him.

And Catherine was at once at Argentina's disposal, and straightway went off with her. And having come into Marco's room, she greatly comforted him with her few but homely and fervent words. Then starting off again in company with Argentina, Catherine entered, near to the house and still close to the sea, into the little Church of Santa Maria delle Grazie la Vecchia,—so called to distinguish it from the more recent Chapel of the Augustinianesses, which bore the same general title,—and there, kneeling in a corner, Catherine prayed for Marco. The little seamen's Church is still in use, with its many mementoes of four centuries and more of ships foundered and of ships safely come to port. And having here finished her prayer, Catherine returned with Argentina to the Hospital. There Argentina left her, and returned to Marco, and found him so changed that from a Devil he seemed turned into an Angel. And with joyous tender feeling he asked: "O Argentina, come, tell me who is that holy soul that you brought me?" But Argentina answered: "Why, that is Madonna Caterinetta Adorna, a woman of most perfect life." And the sick man replied: "I beg of thee, by the love of God, to take care to bring her here a second time to me."

And so the next day Argentina returned to the Hospital and told all to Catherine. And Catherine again promptly came back with Argentina. But when Catherine had entered the room and approached the bed, Marco threw his arms round her, and wept for a long space of time. And then, still weeping, but with great relief, he said to her: "Madonna, the reason why I wished you to come is, first to thank you for the kindness you have shown me; and next to ask a favour of you, which I beg you not to refuse me. For when you had left this room, Our Lord Jesus Christ came to me visibly and in the form in which He appeared to the Magdalen in the garden, and gave me His most holy blessing, and pardoned me all my sins, and told me that I should prepare for death, because that I shall go to Him on Ascension-Day. Hence I pray you, most tender Mother, deign to accept Argentina as your spiritual daughter, and to keep her with you constantly. And thou, Argentina, I pray thee, be content with this plan." They both gladly declared themselves ready and content.

When Catherine had gone away, Marco sent for a certain Augustinian Friar of the Monastery of the Consolation, and carefully confessed his sins and received Holy Communion; and then ordered all his worldly affairs with a notary and with his relations. And he did all this in spite of them all who thought that his intense pain had driven him off his head, and who kept saying: "Take comfort, Marco, soon you will be well again; there is no occasion as yet for you to attend to these things."

And the Eve of the Ascension having come round, he again sent for the same Confessor, and again confessed and communicated, and got him this time to add Extreme Unction and the Recommendation of the Dying, and all this with great composure and devotion. But as the night came on, he said to the Friar: "Return to your Monastery; and when the time comes, I will give you notice." And then, alone with Argentina, he took his crucifix in his hand, and turning towards his wife he said: "Argentina, see, I leave thee Him for thy husband; prepare thyself to suffer, for I declare to thee that suffering is in store for thee." This did not fail to come about, for she suffered later on, both mentally and physically. And for the rest of the night he continued to comfort her, and to encourage her to give herself to God and to accept suffering as the ladder for mounting up to heaven. Then when the dawn had come he said: "Argentina, abide with God; the hour has come." And having finished these words, he expired; and his spirit straightway went to the window of the cell of his Confessor, and tapping against the pane said: "Ecce homo." But the Friar hearing this, at once knew that Marco had passed to his Lord.

And as soon as Marco's body had been buried, Catherine took Argentina to live with her as her spiritual daughter, and thus kept her promise. And since she loved this daughter much, she was wont to take her with her when she went out. And hence one day, when once more passing by the little Church on the little square by the Quay, she and her young daughter again went in and prayed. And on coming out, Catherine said to Argentina: "This is the place, where grace was gained in prayer for thy husband." [1]

[1] *Vita*, pp. 124*b*–126. I get Argentina's maiden name from a Will of hers of the year 1522, of which a copy exists in the MS. volume *Documenti relativi a S. Caterina da Genova*, in the Genoa University Library, B. VII, 31. I have taken Argentina to have previously known, perhaps even to have served, Catherine, because of her surprise at Marco's ignorance as to the identity of his visitor; and I have treated such possible service as but slight, because in Giuliano's Will of 1494 and in Catherine's Will and Codicil of 1498 and 1503, legacies are left to the two maids Benedetta and Mariola, but not a word appears as yet as to Argentina. The date as to the year I derive from the following facts;—(1) Catherine,

6. *Catherine's social interests in* 1506.

And in the following year, 1506, we still find Catherine full of interest and activity of the most varied kind. On March the 13th and 16th Catherine was again busy for the Hospital, by receiving the Foundlings and the various articles and monies anonymously deposited there for their keep. And these can hardly have been altogether exceptional acts, even for this period of her life.[1] And on the 21st of May she made her third Will, which is interesting for various reasons. For it is in this document that we first hear of the deaths of her two elder brothers and of Thobia, and (by implication) of that of her sister Limbania and of her second niece Battista. And we can once more trace here the continuity of her interests and attachments. Her elder niece Maria is again provided with a marriage dowry; her brother Lorenzo remains (now sole) residuary legatee; Thobia's mother gets her legacy compounded for an immediate settlement and payment; the maids Benedetta and Mariola have their legacies somewhat increased; the "Maestà" is again carefully described and allotted; and she again orders her body to be buried alongside of that of her husband.[2] Indeed fresh interests appear here. For the three sons of her second brother and the eldest son of her third brother are now grown up; and so she makes these four nephews her residuary legatees, should her brother Lorenzo die before herself. Don Marabotto has now been her Confessor and Chaplain for seven, and her Almoner for three years; and so she leaves him the income of eight shares of St. George's for his lifetime, which, at 4 per cent. would make

as soon as Marco is buried, carries out her promise to him, and receives Argentina into her house: so the *Vita*, pp. 126*c*, 125*c*. (2) Whereas in the Codicil of 1503 there is still no trace of Argentina, in the Will of 1506 she appears, and receives legacies of personal linen, etc. These gifts are somewhat increased in the Will of 1509. Argentina has evidently not been long in Catherine's service at the time of the drawing up of the Will of 1506. (3) The Protonotary Angelo L. Giovo (MS. *Vita* of the Saint of the *Biblioteca della Missione Urbana*, Part I, ch. iii) puts down the date of Marco's death as 1495. Although this is evidently wrong, I think it wise to keep at least one of his numbers, which I do by fixing upon 1505.

[1] *Documenti su S. Caterina da Genova*, University of Genoa Library, gives a note by Angelo L. Giovo, based on the Book of the Acts of the Protectors of the Hospital: "1506, Marzo, 16mo. Si vede che detta Catarinetta Adorna haveva cura dell' Hospitale, ricevendo li figli esposti e li pegni per essi."

[2] From Dre. Ferretto's copy of the original in the Archivio di Stato.

£16 a year,—the capital to go, at Marabotto's death, to her heirs. And Argentina del Sale has been with her for just about a year; and so she leaves her various articles of personal linen and bedding.[1]

But, above all, the place of this Will's redaction is new amongst the memorials of her life, and directly indicative of a still further enlargement of her influence and interests. For if of the fourteen legal documents drawn up for, and in the presence of, Giuliano or herself, eleven were composed in the small house within the great Hospital of the Pammatone, and only two others,—the Marriage-Settlement, and the Deed of Transfer in favour of Giovanni Adorno,—had hitherto been written elsewhere, this Will was executed in the Refuge for Incurables, in the Portorio quarter, in the evening of the day mentioned, in the presence of three weavers and one dyer,—two trades strongly represented in this poor and populous quarter. Now the choice of this place is deeply suggestive, because it became the chief care and final home of Ettore Vernazza's later years. Indeed it is certain that, on the death of his wife, Vernazza came and lived in the midst of these poor Incurables; and that this residence here of Catherine's closest friend did not begin later than three years from this date—hence still during Catherine's lifetime, in 1509. His far-reaching Wills of 1512 and 1517 are both dated from this Refuge, of which he was, by then, manager and chief supporter; and it is there that he died his heroic death in 1524. Hence it is certain that now already Vernazza must have been deeply interested in this fine, but at that time still languishing, work (its fixed income did not as yet amount to fully £400 a year), and he must often have been there; possibly he had even already a room of his own in the house.

There can, in any case, be no doubt, that in the choice of this place for the drawing-up of this Will, we have an indication,

[1] The clause in this Will which says, " And Testatrix, knowing that the said Giuliano her husband, left to a certain female Religious £150 : Therefore she herewith annuls the said legacy, in virtue of the power given her for this purpose," reads, at first sight, like a harsh, unjust act. But it follows upon a similar annulment of the legacy to the Hospital; and we may be quite sure that Catherine, who had now loved and served this Institution for thirty-three years, would not treat it unjustly. And in the Will of 1509 Catherine explains that the former legacy has been annulled, " in consideration of the satisfaction or settlement (*solutio*) already effected by Testatrix herself with regard to the said legacy."

all the more interesting because entirely incidental, of the wide and ever-widening range, and of the entirely solid, indeed heroic character of Catherine's interest and influence. It also shows us that she was still able to get about, although this Refuge, now the Spedale dei Chronici, is, no doubt, not far away from her Pammatone home. If she could still go there, she no doubt still could and did go to her cousin Suor Tommasina's Convent, which was certainly no further off. And I surmise that many a spiritual colloquy will have taken place, with Catherine as chief interlocutor, and Suor Tommasina and Ettore Vernazza as chief questioners and listeners, in the parlour of San Domenico and in that of the Refuge respectively.

CHAPTER V

CATHERINE'S LAST FOUR YEARS, 1506 TO 1510—SKETCH OF HER CHARACTER, DOCTRINE, AND SPIRIT

I. CATHERINE'S EXTERNAL INTERESTS AND ACTIVITIES UP TO MAY 1510. OCCASIONAL SLIGHT DEVIATIONS FROM HER OLD BALANCE. IMMENSELY CLOSE INTERCONNECTION OF HER WHOLE MENTAL AND PSYCHO-PHYSICAL NATURE. IMPRESSIONS AS CONNECTED WITH THE FIVE SENSES.

1. *Indications of external interests.*

Even during the next four years, up to May 1510, we still find various most authentic and clear indications of external interests and activities in Catherine's life. Thus, on the 21st June 1507, the Protectors of the Hospital address a letter to Don Giacobo Carenzio (who had, as they tell him, been elected Master—*Rettore*—already fifteen months previously), urging him to come and take up his post; and Catherine, who, as we shall see, was later on variously helped by this Priest, and who cared so much for the Hospital, cannot have remained indifferent to that first election and to this present reminder.

Again on the 6th December 1507, the Protectors, Lorenzo Spinola, Manfredo Fornari, and Emmanuele Fiesco, met in Catherine's room, and decided, no doubt with her advice and co-operation, to allow another widow-lady and devotee of the Hospital, Brigidina, wife of the late Giacomo Castagneto, to settle within its precincts.[1] Then on 27th November 1508 she makes a Codicil, leaving an additional £25 to Mariola, and a further article of dress to Argentina; and declaring that she is " entirely content " with Don Marabotto's administration of her monies and charities. Don Cattaneo has then now become her Almoner, and her charitable activity continues large. The document is drawn up by Ettore Vernazza,

[1] *Documenti :* extracts by Giovo from " Acts of the Protectors."

an unimpeachable witness to Marabotto's rectitude and exactness.[1]

Indeed as late down as 18th March 1509 her long Will of that date shows an admirable persistence of her old attachment for and interest in her surviving brother, niece (the provision for Maria's possible marriage is particularly careful and detailed), and nephews (the youngest of the latter, Giovanni, is omitted, no doubt because he had now become a Cardinal, with a corresponding income); in Don Marabotto, who retains the same little pension; in her three maids Benedetta, Mariola, and Argentina, all of whose legacies get somewhat increased; and in the fortunes of the Hospital and of Thobia's mother (she repeats her account of what she has already done for them).[2]

2. *Occasional imperfection of judgment.*

Yet now at last we can find symptoms of the final break-up of her health, and of an occasional slight or momentary deviation from, or diminution of, her old completeness of balance in both judgment, taste, and feeling,—although even now this occurs only in matters of relatively secondary importance, and but heightens the impressiveness of the still unbroken front which she maintains, in all her fully deliberate acts, with regard to all essential matters. Indeed, it is not difficult to feel, even where one cannot directly trace, in all such acts and matters, a still further deepening of the heroic watchfulness and childlike spontaneity, and of the humility and tender *naïveté* and creatureliness, of her general tone and attitude.

3. *Close-knittedness of her psycho-physical organism: her spiritual utilization of this.*

But before recounting the few instances in which we can trace an indication of partly physical depression, or of some lessening of mental alertness or volitional power in secondary matters, or of slight passing unwilled *maladif* impressions, let us attempt a somewhat methodic description of the extreme sensitiveness and immensely close interconnection of her whole psycho-physical nature, and of the general modifications, both in quality and in quantity, which these impressions were wont to go through; and all this, just now,

[1] From Dott. Ferretto's careful copy of the original in the Archivio di Stato, Genoa.

[2] *Ibid.*

on occasion of incidents closely similar to those already experienced in her past life.

It would indeed be altogether mistaken to class all this sensitiveness as necessarily but a form of illness; for the great majority, and all the most characteristic, of her apparently physical pains and troubles, are but varieties and heightenings of the always unusually swift and profound impressionableness of her whole psycho-physical organism. With the sole exception of that attack of pestilential fever (probably in the year 1493), I can nowhere, right up to three days before her death, find any trace in her life of illnesses or disturbances of any but a psycho-physical, nerve-functional type.

Indeed her psychic self is throughout so impressionable, and the mind is, ever since her Conversion, so active, dominant, and absorbed in the actual and attempted apprehension of the great realities which, though invisible, require for their vivid apprehension an imaginative pictorial embodiment: that we shall have, in a later chapter, to ask ourselves the question whether it was not the mind, or the imagination at the mind's bidding, which thus affected the psycho-physical life, rather than the psycho-physical life which, primarily independent of the former, offered itself as but so much raw, still unrelated material, to the fashioning, transforming mind. Especially will it be necessary to consider carefully the influence upon her mind, and upon the chronicler's accounts of her state, which may have been exercised by the writings of the Areopagite and of Jacopone. It will then become clear that these authors have undoubtedly contributed to the form in which these truths and realities were, if not actually apprehended by Catherine, at least described by her disciples.

Yet even this point remains, in Catherine's case, (and indeed in that of all the great Saints,) of no real spiritual or moral importance, since all these great and generous souls persist in ever using these psycho-physical things, whether they be projections or "givennesses," as but so many instruments and materials for the apprehension, illustration, acquisition, and purification of spiritual truth and of the spirit's own fulness and depth. And Catherine's persistence in this attitude of utilization and transcendence of what the natural man so continuously tends to make his direct aim and final limit continues practically unbroken to the end. I will group these psychic impressions according to the five senses.

4. *Impressions connected with the sense of touch.*

The earliest, and up to the end the most marked and general, of all such unusual impressions appears to have been one connected with the sense of touch,—that feeling of mostly interior, but later on also of exterior, warmth, indeed often of intense heat and burning, which comes to her, the first as though sunshine were bathing her within or without, the second sometimes as though a great fire were enveloping her, and sometimes as though a living flame were piercing her within.

Already in 1473, on the occasion of her Conversion, we find unmistakable indications of such sensations; they are, however, of a predominantly pleasurable kind. And I take it that during her great lonely middle-period they will, in so much as present, have been of a similar nature. But later on from after 1499 onwards, these sensations and attacks become increasingly painful,[1] and are specially described, and variously alluded to, under the terms of *operation*, *assault*, *siege*. When specially keen and concentrated, and accompanied by some piercing psycho-spiritual perception, they appear under the terms of *arrow*, *wound*; and the perception itself bears then the name of *ray* or *spark* (of divine love).[2]

Now we lookers-on can, of course, with more or less ease, mentally separate, in a general way, the latter, the spiritual apprehension, creation, and content, from the former, the psycho-physical occasion, material, and form; although it is certainly difficult, and probably impossible, to decide, at least in any one case, how far it is her mental activity that occasions her psycho-physical condition, or how far it is the latter which occasions the former. But what actually and demonstrably happened in Catherine's case, was something incomparably beyond the range to which such psycho-physical considerations apply. For to her, psychically, a keenly sentient; rationally, a deeply thinking, feeling, and willing creature,—these experi-

[1] In the printed *Vita* a passage occurs on p. 10*b*, describing the interior heat which accompanied her great fasts (1476–1499). But the passage is wanting in the MSS., and is no doubt only a gloss to explain how, at those times, she came to drink water mixed with vinegar.

[2] "Operazione": *Vita*, pp. 106*c*, 117*b*, 121*b*, 143*b*, 148*b*, 149*c*. "Assalto": pp. 138*b*, *c* (3); 139*a*; 143, *b*, *c* (3); 144*a* (2); 148*a*. "Assedio": p. 118*b*. "Saetta": pp. 141*a*, 145*a*. "Ferita": p. 141*a*, *c* (2). "Raggio": pp. 133*b*, 157*c*. "Scintilla": pp. 132*a*, 148*b*. The "ferita" occurs already (as a "dolce ferita") in the account of her Conversion, pp. 4, 5; and "saetta," "ferita," "raggio," and "scintilla" appear very often in her own sayings.

ences, howsoever classable, were most real, and, in course of time, more and more penetrating and painful; and they were, to her own consciousness, entirely prior to any interpretation or utilization of them. Hence, for the present at all events, we had better take these states as they presented themselves to her immediate and ordinary consciousness. And this very same immensely sentient soul was so firmly centred, deep down below and beyond the psycho-physical, in the Moral and Spiritual, that these experiences were welcomed and actively used but as so many means and materials for ethical purification and character-building, and for the analogical apprehension and illustration of spiritual truths.

Thus it is that these sensations of burning which, during her years of health, were themselves so pleasurable and peaceful, helped, as we shall find when we come to consider her doctrine, to suggest and illustrate for her the joys and health-giving influence of the presence of God, both here and in Paradise, and of the soul's apprehension of God, as light for the understanding and warmth for the affections and the will. And when, with her failing health, these sensations turned into painful, in part seemingly physical attacks,—attacks which, however, left the mind in an increased and ever-increasing peace and contentment,—they again helped her to gain and develop her doctrine concerning Purgatory.

In both cases her teaching gained thus a vividness of quasi-directly sensible experience, of something in a manner actually seen and felt, since it was built up out of suggestions derived from direct sensations and psycho-physical states. And yet in both cases not all such sensations, of themselves quite valueless and uninstructive from an ethical and religious point of view, could have helped towards anything of spiritual significance, had they not been sifted, taken up, organized and transformed in and into a large and deep spiritual experience and personality. There is absolutely nothing automatic or necessary in the crowning, ethically significant stages of this whole process, however rapid and instinctive and effortless, and simply of a piece with the psycho-physical occasions, these utilizations and grace-impelled and grace-informed creations may appear. We shall, in proof of this, soon see how physical and literal and spiritually insignificant remained, during the last four months of her life, the apprehensions of her disciples as to these heats and piercing sensations: these good, indeed devoted, people seem incapable of measuring spiritual love by anything higher than thermometer-readings or other physical tangibilities. And we shall also have to record one or two momentary instances when this heat-feeling and apprehension clearly assumed a *maladif* character in Catherine herself.

5. *Impressions connected with taste and smell.*

The unusual sense-perceptions which were the next to be aroused were apparently those of taste and smell: although the one certain indication I can find of such an unusual psycho-physical taste-and-smell impression, of a pleasurable and not clearly *maladif* character, is not earlier than 1499.[1] It came to her in connection with the one great devotion of her whole convert life,—the Holy Eucharist. "Having on one occasion received Holy Communion, so much odour and sweetness came to her, that she seemed to be in Paradise. Whence, feeling this, she straightway turned towards her Love and said: 'O Love, dost Thou perhaps intend to draw me to Thyself with these savours? I want them not, since I want nothing but Thee alone, and all of Thee.'"[2] Here, then, she turns away from and transcends, precisely as St. John of the Cross was soon to insist so strongly that we should do, the sensible and immediate, and reaches on to the spiritual, ultimate, and personal. And similarly some such psycho-physical experience seems pre-supposed in her declaration: "If a Consecrated Host and unconsecrated ones were to be given to me, I should distinguish the former from the latter as I do wine from water."[3] Yet her biographer can truthfully insist upon love being the original cause of such recognition: "She said this, because the Consecrated Host sent forth a certain ray of love which pierced her heart." And she herself gives a still more spiritual parallel instance and explanation of such recognition: "If I were to be shown the Court of Heaven, with all its members robed in one and the same manner, in suchwise that there would, so far, be no

[1] The passage in *Vita*, p. 10*b*, which declares that she "felt" (tasted) something sweet within her, upon drinking that salt and sour water during her long fasts, is wanting in the MSS., and is itself an interesting attempt to materialize her saying, on p. 11*b*, as to the "other thing" (*i.e.* the love of God), that she was "feeling" (tasting) within herself.

[2] *Vita*, p. 8*a*.

[3] *Ibid.* p. 9*b*. The present conclusion of the sentence, and all the parallels throughout the rest of the page, show plainly that the sentence originally read as I have given it.

perceptible difference between God and the Angels: the love which I have in my heart would still recognize God, as readily as the dog recognizes his master." This love indeed would move out to Him even more swiftly and easily, because "love, which is God Himself, finds in an instant, without any means, its own end and ultimate repose." [1]

Clearly *maladif* over-sensitiveness and shiftingness of the senses of taste and scent will appear presently, during the last months of her life.

6. *Hearing and sight.*

The most important and mental of the senses, hearing and sight, appear, on the contrary, with little or nothing particularly unusual about them, throughout her life.

For as to her sense of hearing, the inner voices already described as heard by her at different times, cannot fairly be classed under this or any other sense-perception, healthy or otherwise; since they appear to have been most vivid and clear thoughts presented to her mind, with in each case the consciousness that they were the suggestions of Mind,—of a Spirit other than her own. They appear to have always been described by herself as "words spoken to the mind," "words as it were heard." [2] Traces of any *maladif* affection of this sense will be difficult or impossible to find, even during her last illness.

And as to sight, always so closely akin to mental processes, anything at all really exceptional cannot, I think, be found in her life so far at all. For her evidently great impressionableness to certain religious pictures,—so as a child, in regard to the "Pietà," and now again apparently with the "Maestà,"—and to certain sights of nature, cannot fairly be considered abnormal. And as to Visions, the only one recorded so far, that of the Bleeding Christ, was primarily a mentally mediated experience: "the Lord showed Himself to her in the spirit," says the account, no doubt in full accordance with her own analysis of such experiences.[3] Some few disturbances of this sense will, however, appear during the course of her last illness.

[1] *Vita*, p. 9*b* [2] *Ibid.* p. 16*b*. [3] *Ibid.* p. 5*b*.

II. More or Less *Maladif* Experiences and Actions.

The amplest proof of the deep and delicate impressionableness of her nature is probably, however, to be found in that profound melancholy, that positive disgust with everything within her and without, and that strong desire for death which we found to have possessed her during the three months previous to her Conversion in March 1473. For we should note that that melancholy did not directly spring from spiritual motives or considerations : it was previous to all definite sorrow for sin and to all full and willed sense of things religious and eternal. Indeed, with the appearance of the religious standards and certitudes, that crushing universal feeling of melancholy and of positive disgust breaks up, and yields to contrasted joys and sorrows, and to a buoyant energy in the very midst and through the very means of suffering and of sacrifice. Thus the dawn of her spiritual re-birth was indeed dark and oppressive; but this oppression did not directly proceed from any clear consciousness of the Perfect and Eternal which arose within her only as part and parcel of this explicit Conversion. The oppression simply indicated, of itself, a nature so sensitive and claimful, as to require, in order to achieve any degree of contentment, a spiritual, regenerative, re-interpretative power capable of responding to and matching the deepest realities of life. That nature was thus full of the need of such realities and of such contact with them, but was without the power of producing, or of adequately responding to, such realities,—or indeed of imaginatively forecasting them. And similarly in 1507, the dawn of her painful, joyful-sorrowful birthday to eternity was again dark and oppressive and productive of an intense desire for death, a desire which had, apparently, been entirely absent from her soul ever since 1473. Here again this oppression was not directly religious or moral, but, taken in itself, was simply psycho-physical. Indeed this oppression marks the beginning of the special limitations, difficulties, and slightly deflecting influences now introduced into her life by henceforth steadily increasing positive illness. I propose, then, to begin with this opening depression of hers, and next to go through the main incidents of her remaining life, as far as possible, in strictly chronological order. I will group all this around six main facts and dates.

1. *Desire for death*, 1507.

"In the year 1507 she on one occasion was present at the recitation of the Offices for the Dead. And a desire to die came upon her. And she said: 'O Love, I desire nothing but Thee, and Thee in Thine own manner: but, if it pleases Thee, allow me at least to go and see others die and be buried, in order that I may see in others that great good, which it does not please Thee should as yet be in myself.' And her Love consented to this; and consequently, for a certain space of time, she went to see die and be buried all those who died in the Hospital. And as, later on, her union with this her tender Love increased, her desire for death disappeared little by little." [1]

She is, then, still active, and moves about in the spacious Hospital and in the adjoining Church. And this desire, as it gradually disappeared, will, doubtless, not have left mere blanks in her consciousness, or have reduced the sum-total of her feelings; but, with that diminution, some of her old tenderness for and interest in others will have reappeared. And again we see how no one set of feelings, one "psychosis," ever simply repeats itself, in even one and the same soul: for Catherine's positive disgust with all things, which prepared and accompanied her desire for death in 1473, is absent from the otherwise similar desire of 1507. In both cases there is the same sheer "givenness" and isolation of the feeling. *Then*, she did not desire death to escape temptation or sin; *now*, she does not desire it, directly and within her emotional nature, in order to get to God: in each case the feeling stands simply by itself, and is not immediately connected with religion at all. And finally, this incident, and its later equivalent repetitions in November 1509 and September 1510, prove once again on what a veritable bed of Procrustes those determined *a-priorists*, the Redactors of the *Vita*, have

[1] *Vita*, p. 98, *a*, *b*. This is the first of three incidents, given in chronological order, all referring to her desire for death, which make up Chapter XXXVIII of the printed *Vita*. The last two are, beyond all doubt, conversations with Vernazza; and this first incident is also probably transmitted to us by him.—I have in my translation left out the numerous glosses by which the various Redactors have desperately attempted to eviscerate this story, attempts based on the double conviction, that Catherine was already absolutely perfect, and that "every desire is imperfect" (p. 100*a*). These changes will be studied later on.

placed, pulled about and mutilated, as far as in them lay, the immensely spontaneous and rich personality of Catherine, in their determination to find her ever all-perfect, and perfect after their own fixed pattern. For it proves to demonstration, either that Catherine continued liable to human imperfections, or that not all desires are imperfect. And both these things are true, beyond the possibility of doubt.

2. *The scent-impression from Don Cattaneo's hand.*

And next we get an instance of clearly abnormal sense-perception, which is deeply interesting because of the vivid, first-hand form in which the fact has come down to us, and still more on account of its impressive illustration of the two possible mental attitudes towards such matters. It will have occurred in 1508; and Don Marabotto is, in any case, the other interlocutor in the scene, and its chronicler. And if there is undoubtedly a somewhat ludicrous *naïveté* about his attitude at the time of the occurrence, there is also a striking simplicity and self-oblivion in the perfectly objective manner in which he chronicles the scene in all its bearings, and Catherine's marked superiority to himself. It is this complete directness and simplicity of motive which, on the side of character, will have bound these otherwise strangely diverse souls together; and which rendered Don Marabotto, even simply as a character, not unworthy of his close intimacy with Catherine.

The abnormality here concerns the sense of smell alone; the impression here lasts a considerable time: and now she acquiesces in it, but only for the purpose of moving through it, as a mere means. "Having been infirm for many days, Catherine one day took the hand of her Confessor and smelt it: and its odour penetrated right to her heart," so that "for many days this perfume restored and nourished her, body and soul." Don Marabotto then asks her what kind of thing this odour is that she is smelling. And she tells him that it is an odour so penetrating and sweet, as to seem capable of bringing the dead to life; that God had sent it to her, to strengthen her soul and body, now that these were so much oppressed; and hence "since God grants me this odour, I am determined to derive strength from it, as long as He shall please that I shall do so." But Marabotto, "thinking that he must surely be able to perceive what was being transmitted by himself, went smelling his own hand, but to no effect." And Catherine gently rebuked his action by declaring: "The things which depend entirely upon God's own free gift, He does not give to those that seek them. Indeed He gives such things at all, only in cases of great necessity, and as an occasion of great spiritual profit." [1]

The impression and consolation are here still connected with the Holy Eucharist : for the hand which she smells is no doubt the right one,—the hand which was wont daily to consecrate in her presence and daily to communicate her. The declaration as to the odour's power to raise the dead to life has occurred already in connection with the Holy Eucharist, and will have been in part suggested to her by such Johannine passages as " I am the . . . Life," " I am the Living Bread," " he that eateth this Bread shall live," shall be made to live, " for ever." And although the odour is here the prominent impression, and "savours" are wanting, yet "sweetness" still occurs, probably as a sort of sensation of tasting.—Marabotto's mind has in it, on this occasion, two plausible assumptions, each strengthening the other ; and Catherine controverts both. He evidently thinks : " Catherine's states are all most valuable, hence real, hence objective : if then she says she smells this or that, others will be able to do so too." And : "What a man transmits, that he can himself experience : hence, on this ground also, I should be able to smell this perfume."—And Catherine's mind evidently also contains two very different convictions : the first, that experiences, even when thus but semi-spiritual, are, for all their reality, not directly transferable from soul to soul; and the second, that all such sensible and semi-sensible experiences, whether normal or exceptional, are all but means at the disposal of the free-willing spirit, means which become limits and obstacles as soon as they are treated as ends.

Thus if this experience points to a certain abnormality of condition in the peripheral, psycho-physical regions of the soul, Catherine's attitude towards it, and towards the whole question occasioned by it, has got a massive depth of sanity about it, perhaps unattainable by, certainly untested in, the always and simply, even peripherally, healthy soul.

3. *Shifting of her burial-place.*

And in her Will of March 1509 we find traces of a

[1] *Vita*, pp. 118, *b*, *c*, 119*b*, 119*a*. This vivid and simple dialogue is followed (p. 119*b*) by a clearly secondary parallel discourse of Catherine. Only the descriptive end of this latter paragraph is no doubt authentic, and has been incorporated in the above translation.

certain weakening of her former ample business capacity, and of her vigilance, perseverance, and balance, in spite of friendly pressure or criticism, with regard to matters of practical import. For, as to her general incapacity for business, the Will contains a clause exempting Marabotto from all future challenge of his administration of her monies, up to the date of the making of this Will. And this clause finds its explanation in the admission of the *Vita*, with regard to her life during these last years, that, owing to the mysterious and shifting nature of her infirmity, "there was confusion in governing her," "confusion not on her own part, but on that of those who served her," [1] words which will grow still clearer in our account of her last four months. For this state of her health must have rendered the administration of her affairs by another both necessary and difficult. And as to the diminution of her vigilance and perseverance in matters of not directly spiritual or moral import, we have here, for the first time, a departure from her resolution, emphatically expressed in the Wills and Codicil of 1498, 1503, 1506, of being buried beside her husband. She now orders herself to be buried in the Church of San Nicolò in Boschetto, and that so much is to be spent on the funeral as shall seem fit to Don Marabotto.

Three points should here be borne in mind. For one thing, Catherine had a long-standing affection for that beautifully situated Pilgrimage-Church, partly no doubt from associations dating back to her summer *villegiatura* days at the neighbouring Prà, and partly, probably, from memories connected with her sister Limbania, since, as we have already seen, Limbania's Convent of Santa Maria delle Grazie was the joint foundation of the two Genoese Monasteries of San Teodoro fuore le Mura and of San Nicolò in Boschetto. Limbania had died in that Convent in 1502, and Catherine had, in her Codicil of 1503, left a small sum for mortuary Masses for herself to the Monastery of San Nicolò.

But, next, it was doubtless the growing conviction as to her sanctity amongst her immediate friends, and their desire to keep her grave and remains, as an eventual place and object of veneration, distinct from any others, perhaps specially from those of her husband, whose defective reputation might otherwise damage or delay the growth of such a cultus of his wife, which was the determining cause of this change in the place

[1] *Vita*, p. 127*a*.

of sepulture. These friends were able to prevail, no doubt because her interest and determination in such matters had become weakened by ill-health of now thirteen years' duration. And they will have fixed upon this place some four English miles away, partly because it happened to be one she loved, but also because thus no question of separating her remains from those of Giuliano would formally arise. Her later Codicil will prove the presence of both these motives, and Catherine's unconsciousness as to the situation, and the vagueness of her acquiescence.

And finally, we must note that, if this action of her *entourage* offends our present-day tastes and susceptibilities, it was yet thoroughly in accordance with a quite hoary tradition and feeling in such matters, and was in no sense an idea special to, or originated by, this group of persons; and again, that the four Protectors of the Hospital (the trustees and executors of the Will), her sole surviving brother Lorenzo (the residuary legatee), and above all her closest, great-souled friend Vernazza (one of the six witnesses), are all parties to the pious stratagem, and share its responsibility with Marabotto.

4. *The "scintilla"-experience; spiritual refreshment derived from a picture.*

We have next an important group of experiences and convictions in November 1509. "On the 11th November 1509, there came upon her an insupportable fire of infinite love; and she declared that there had been shown to her one single spark (scintilla) of Pure Love, and that this had been but for a short moment; and that, had it lasted even a little longer, she would have expired because of its great force. She could hardly eat, nor speak so as to be heard, in consequence of this penetrating wound of love that she had received in her heart." [1]

Few events of her life have left such profound traces, so

[1] I translate the above from the oldest account of the event, given by MS. "A," p. 193, at the opening of its Chapter XXIX (the number is accidentally omitted), which is headed: "How in the year 1506, on the 11th of November, there came upon her so great a burning in the heart, that she wondered at her not expiring." This 1506, repeated in the opening line of the chapter itself, is an undoubted slip; for she is said to be 63 years old (and she was in her 63rd year in 1509), and the place occupied by the corresponding paragraph in the printed *Vita*, p. 133*b* (within a year of her death, p. 132*b*, and some time before December 1509, p. 138*b*), again clearly marks the date as 1509).

many echoes and waves and wavelets as it were, throughout both her authentic sayings and the various secondary and tertiary imitations, recastings, and expansions of her original account as has this scintilla-experience. I will here translate the nine varying impressions and exclamations which, proceeding from different minds and different dates, have all but one, been worked up by the *Vita* into a single paragraph, which, by its very multitude of flickerings as to meaning and of experimentations as to form, gives us a striking picture of the deep and many-sided influence of this single event, so short in its clock-time duration. "This creature, all lost in her own self, found her true self in one instant in God." "Although she reputed herself to be very poor, yet she remained rich in the divine love." "She, knowing the grace and operation to be all from God, remained lost in herself, and living only in God." "She gave her free-will to God, and God then restored it to her." "She gave her free-will to God, and God thereupon worked with its means." "O the great wonder, to see a man established in the midst of so many miseries, and yet God having so great a care of him! All tongues are incapable of expressing it, all intellects of understanding it." "That man becomes foolish in the eyes of the world, to whom Thou, O Lord God, dost manifest even but the slightest spark of Thine unspeakable Love." "Thou, O God, desirest to exalt man, and to make him as though another God, by means of love." Of later date or type: "In God she saw all the operations, by means of which He had caused her to merit (in the past)." And of still later, clearly secondary, character: "God showed her in one instant the succession of His (future) operation, as though she would have to die of a great martyrdom." [1]

And this great experience of hers led on to a scene which, whilst emphasizing the psycho-physical effect, occasion or concomitant of such spiritual experiences, also gives us the strong instance of her impressionableness to pictures in particular. "Finding herself in such ardour, she felt herself compelled to turn to a figure of the Woman of Samaria at the well with

[1] *Vita*, p. 132*a*, *b*. The first eight sentences have been in part fused by R 1 into fewer larger periods. The last sentence is wanting in MSS. "A" and "B"; although clearly formed upon the model and with the material of the previous sentences, it appears in the printed *Vita* as referring to an "altra vista" (see p. 133*b*).

her Lord; and in her extreme distress Catherine addressed Him thus: 'O Lord, I pray Thee, give me a little drop of this water, which of old Thou didst give to the Samaritan woman, since I can no more bear so great a fire.' And suddenly, in that instant, there was given her a little drop of that divine water; and by it she was refreshed within and without, and she had rest for some appreciable time." [1] But, above all, this experience and its precursor were, if not the actual beginning, at least the culminating point in the experiences or projections which led to or articulated her doctrine on Purgatory. In a later chapter I hope to trace the connection between those experiences and this doctrine. Here we must add two other vivid interior experiences and convictions of hers which are placed by the *Vita*, no doubt rightly, in direct succession to, and in more or less connection with, the great "scintilla"-operation, although neither of them appears amongst the images and conceptions which make up the *Trattato del Purgatorio*.

"One day" (she recounted this herself) "she appeared to herself to abide suspended in mid-air. And the spiritual part wanted to attach itself to heaven; but her other part wished to attach itself to earth: yet neither the one nor the other managed to become possessed of its object, and simply abode thus in mid-air, without achieving its desire. And after abiding thus for a long time, the part which was drawing her to heaven seemed to her to be gaining the upper hand (over the other part), and, little by little, the spiritual part forcibly drew her upwards, so that at every moment she saw herself moving further and further away from earth. And although this at first seemed to be a strange thing to the part that was being drawn, and this part was ill content to be thus forced; yet when it had been so far removed, as no more to be able to see the earth, then it began to lose its earthly instinct and affection, and to perceive and to relish the things which were relished by the spiritual part. And this spiritual part never ceased from drawing it heavenward. And so at last these two parts came to a common accord." [2] And again on

[1] *Vita*, p. 135*a*. I have, in Catherine's speech, omitted a final clause, "which burns me entirely within and without," because it is not necessary to the sense, and violates the rhythm, which is ever present in all Catherine's authentic sayings.

[2] *Ibid.* pp. 135*c*, 136*a*. I have omitted two glosses introduced by "cioè," "that is"; and three short amplifications, which introduce a direct

another occasion: "The soul is so desirous of departing from the body to unite itself with God, that its body appears to it a veritable Purgatory, which keeps it distant from its true object." [1]

This group of experiences straightway enforces some important spiritual laws. For one thing, this scintilla-experience, since her Conversion the deepest of her life, is clearly also the richest and most complex,—witness the numerous, mutually supplementary or critical, attempts at analysis furnished by even her immediate companions. And this experience is only simple in the sense in which white light, which combines all the prismatic colours, or a living healthy human body, composed of numberless constituents, is simple.

And next, nothing indicates that this experience was of a character essentially different from that of her older contemplations; and everything appears to show that it was, substantially, a grace addressed to, and an act performed by, her spiritual nature,—her intelligence and free will, God's Spirit stimulating and sustaining hers in a quite exceptional degree, and hence less than ever weakening or supplanting this her spirit's action. It was as much a gift of herself by herself to God, as if it had not been a pure grace from Him; and yet her very power and wish and determination to give herself, were rendered possible and became actual through that pure prevenient, accompanying and subsequent gift of God.

Again, it is certain that either there was no clear mental scheme, reasoning, or picture during the experience, or that, if there was, it consisted of a spatial simultaneity rather than of a temporal succession, and that it showed her, if her own soul at all, then that soul in its most universally human, typical aspects and relations. In no case was there anything historical or prophetical, strictly biographical about it.

And then we have, even though she could give no kind of definite account of it, the most solid reasons for accepting this experience as genuine, wholesome, and valuable. For she evidently fully believed in it herself; and we shall see how clearly and readily she continued, even after this experience, to distinguish between wholesome and mental, and *maladif* and simply psychic, states of abstraction. Again it

conflict between the two parts. There is, within this particular picture and scene, no direct conflict, but, at first, a complete contrariety of aim.

[1] *Vita*, p. 136*c*. This is one out of four or five parallel sayings which are accumulated here. They shall be examined later on.

became the occasion and material of most deep and fruitful spiritual doctrine; whereas nothing is more empty and unsuggestive than are the bare, brute "facts" of all merely nervous or hysterical hallucinations. It also demonstrably strengthened her will for the last deep sufferings and sacrifices yet to be gone through, and no doubt added a fresh stimulus to her already profound influence over Vernazza, and pricked him onwards on his career of the most solid, heroic philanthropy and self-sacrifice. And yet we can see that her psycho-physical organism is now functionally weak and ill. For great physical exhaustion now follows upon an experience substantially the same as those which used to strengthen her so markedly even in physical respects.

As to the scene with the picture, we again get a case not unlike the odour of Marabotto's hand, in so much as here too the experience hovers between the mental and physical, and there is a sensible impression as from a physical substance with reference to a Person,—this taste of a "divine water" moving here on to Christ, to God, the Living Water, as that smell of sweetness moves on to the "Living Bread," Christ, and God. It is, unfortunately, impossible to identify that picture, which may well have been a fresco-painting in some building or passage of the Hospital, since destroyed, or on some extant wall, whitewashed since those days. The vivid picturings of the soul in mid-air, and of the soul in the purgatory of its body, will be considered in connection with her psycho-physical states and her doctrine.

But before leaving this November experience, we must give two significant conversations held by her with Vernazza at the time, and which have been no doubt handed down to us by himself. "One day, speaking of this" (the scintilla-) "event with a spiritual person (*Religioso*), she called it 'a giddiness' (*vertigine*). But that person said to her: 'Mother, I beg of you that you will yourself select a person who may happen to suit your mind (*soddisfaccia alla mente vestra*), and will narrate to this person the graces which God has granted to you, so that, when you come to die, these graces may not remain hidden and unknown, and an opportunity for God's praise and glory may not thus be lost.' And she then answered that she was entirely willing (*ben contenta*), if this be pleasing to her tender Love; and that, in that case, she would not choose another person than himself, although she was convinced that it was impossible to describe even a small fragment of such interior experiences as occurred between God and her soul; and that as to exterior things, few or none had taken place in her case." Here again we have evidence as to her habit of making light of and transcending all psycho-physical phenomena, however striking and mysterious; and we get a positive authorization conferred by herself upon Vernazza, such as is claimed by no other contributor to the *Vita*.

And "speaking with him some days later, she said: 'Son, I have had a certain prick of conscience, of which I will tell you. The other day, when you told me that I might possibly remain dead some day during one of those giddinesses, there seemed to arise in me, at that moment, a feeling of joy, a profound aspiration which said: "O, if that hour would but come!" And then this feeling suddenly ceased. Now I declare to you, that I do not wish that in this matter there should be any glimpse (scintilla) of a desire of my own for earth or heaven, or for any other created thing; but that I wish to leave all things to the disposition of God.' Then this person answered, that there was no occasion for her to have a prick of conscience, because, although joy had awaked in her mind, and a sudden exclamation had occurred there, at the mention of the word 'death,' yet that nothing of this had proceeded from the will, nor had it been endorsed by the reason; but that it had proceeded solely from the instinct of the pleasure-loving soul (*anima*), which ever, according to its nature, tends to such an end. And how the proof that this was a correct account, lay in this, that her prick of conscience had not really penetrated to the depths of her heart, but had remained on the surface, at the same slight depth at which the movement of joy had remained. And she confessed that the matter really stood thus, and remained satisfied." [1]

Here three points are of interest. I take her impulse of deep longing to die in one of those trances, to have arisen, not simply from joy at the thought of dying, but from joy at the prospect of dying of joy,—of dying with the joy fixed in

[1] *Vita*, pp. 98*c*, 99*a*; 99*b*, *c*. I have, in the first conversation, omitted the introductory attribution of her use of the word "giddiness" to humility; and, in the second, suppressed the conclusion which repeatedly declares that never again did any such desire arise within her. For both clauses have got a vague and secondary form, and the second is in direct contradiction with the facts.

that moment in the soul for ever. For heaven itself appears here not as a synonym for God, but as a creature, as the summing up of infinite and endless consolation of all right kinds, spiritual and psycho-physical. And it is this that makes her scruple thoroughly understandable, and but one more instance of her virile fight with all direct attachment to the consequences and concomitants of devotedness.—And next we should note her deep trust in the spiritual experience and wisdom of Vernazza, the layman and lawyer, some twenty-five years her junior; and her asking his advice on a matter which we would readily suppose her to reserve for Don Marabotto, who by now had been her Confessor and Spiritual Adviser for many years.—And lastly, the depth and delicacy of Vernazza's analysis are most striking, with their clear perception of the various levels and degrees of true selfhood and volition within the human soul: she had really had neither a full will, nor a deliberate wish, nor indeed any penetrating, spontaneous reproach of conscience; she had, in fact, been suffering from a scruple, and he was required, and was able, to make her see that this had been the case.

5. *Catherine's sense of intense cold, and her attitude towards Don Marabotto.*

And in December 1509 and January 1510 we come across a group of experiences and actions, in some respects different from, and supplementary of, the set just concluded. For "in the month of December she suffered from great cold,"—I take this cold to have been, at least partially, special to her state, and not to have proceeded primarily from the winter temperature,—"but she paid no attention to it." "And behold one night there came so great an attack (*assalto*) upon her, that she could not conceal it. There was a great heaving of the body, much bile was evacuated, and the nose bled. And she then sent for her Confessor, and said to him: 'Father, it seems to me that I must die, because of the many weakenings of various sorts (*accidenti*) that have happened to me.'" "And this attack (*assalto*) lasted for about three hours," "her body trembling like a leaf." "And then her body became quiet again, but was now so broken and weak that it was necessary to give her minced chicken to revive her; and a good many days had to pass before she returned to her (latter-day) vigour." [1]

[1] *Vita*, 138*c*.

And "on the 10th of January 1510, she appeared determined to see her Confessor no more, either as to help and comfort for her soul or as to her bodily health. It seemed to her that he was too indulgent to herself, in her sayings and doings. But the fact was, that he saw it to be necessary that she should do all that her instinct prompted her to say or do; and it would indeed have been well-nigh impossible to force her to act against these interior movements of hers. Yet since she was herself in cause, she did not acknowledge such necessities (*ordinazioni*); rather these actions of hers appeared to her but as so many disordered doings, and she went forcing herself to try and not give trouble to those who were good enough to put up with her (*chi la comportava*).—And when night came, she locked herself up alone into a separate room, refusing food or conversation or comfort from any one. But after a while she had to come out, with a view to rendering a certain service, and her Confessor managed to slip into the room unobserved and to hide himself there. And she, having returned and locked herself in, and thinking herself quite alone, said with a sobbing voice to her Lord: 'O Lord, what wouldest Thou have me do further in this world? I neither see nor hear, nor eat nor sleep; I do not know what I do or what I say. I feel as though I were a dead thing. There is no creature that understands me; I find myself lonely, unknown, poor, naked, strange, and different from the rest of the world; and hence I know not any more how to live with (my fellow-) creatures upon earth.' These and such-like words she spoke so piteously, that her Confessor could bear it no longer; and he discovered himself, and came up to and spoke to her. And God gave him grace, so that she remained comforted in mind and body by his words, and was in fair health for a good many days after." [1]

Nevertheless "her Confessor, since his continual intercourse and close familiarity with Catherine gave occasion to murmurs on the part of some who did not fully understand his special work and its necessity, left her and was absent for three days" (probably shortly after the scene just related), "for the pur-

[1] *Vita*, pp. 139*b*, 140*b*, *c*. I have omitted the evidently derivative, transcendentally reflective, second of the three paragraphs in which this story now appears; the explanatory glosses of the same tone as that paragraph; a redundant sentence in Catherine's speech; and the evidently late and schematic designation of "assalto" for the entire incident, which is, surely, nothing of the sort.

pose of testing that work of his, and seeing whether it was indeed all from God, and thus to escape all scruple in the matter. But when, three days later, he returned to her house, and had learnt and considered the various accidents and incidents which had occurred meanwhile, he was so entirely satisfied with the evidence afforded by experiment, that he lost all scruple in the matter, and indeed regretted having made the trial, because of the great distress which she had suffered from it." It will have been on this occasion that she said to him: "I seem to see that God has given to you this one care of myself, and hence that you should not attend to anything else. For now I can no longer support alone so many exterior and interior oppressions (*assedi*). When you leave me, I go lamenting about the house, saying that you are cruel and do not understand my extreme necessity; for if you did, you would pay greater attention to it." [1]

And it will have been later on again, in February and March, that she intimated, during two of her violent attacks (on the first occasion by signs, on the second by words), her impression that she would succumb, and her wish to receive Extreme Unction. But Don Marabotto correctly judged that she would safely get through these seizures, and the anointing was put off for the present.[2]

This group is again interesting. For it gives us evidence as to how dependent this character and career of the rarest loneliness and independence had now become upon human help and sympathy; and lets us see how illness had now introduced an excessive suddenness, absoluteness, and shiftingness into her feelings and minor actions, and an occasional slight querulousness into her remarks. It shows us her old social, altruistic instincts and standard still at work within her; for she still suffers from the consciousness, whenever she is thrown back upon herself, of being different from other people; she still longs to attend to the wants of others, regrets the trouble she gives them, and feels grateful for the services they render; and she still busies herself, in the reduced measure now

[1] *Vita*, pp. 120*b*; 119*c*, 120*a*. The sequence and date assumed above I think to be, all things considered, the most likely among the possible alternatives. As to her remarks to Marabotto, they appear in the *Vita* before his three days' absence. But the interior evidence seems strongly in favour of my inversion of that (evidently, in any case, very loose and quite unemphasized) order.

[2] *Ibid.* pp. 141*c*, 143*c*.

possible to her, with services of her own to others,—a "certain service," which she had to render, had sufficed to break through her self-imposed seclusion. It lets us see how watchful against and suspicious of self, and of what could flatter and indulge it, she still remained; and how independent her judgment continued, even with regard to her Confessor. And this her judgment we shall have good reason to hold to have been remarkably well-grounded, in so far as this, that had only Marabotto possessed a deeper insight into her psycho-physical state and less of a determination to treat all her states and impulses as equally solid and spiritual, or at least as equally to be yielded to, he could have helped her more; and she would then, thus helped, have been able, even now, fully to resist or to give way, in proportion to the healthiness or the morbidness of the attack. And finally we see how truly serviceable and necessary, and indeed repeatedly right where her own estimate was wrong, was the help and sympathy and judgment of her Confessor; and how difficult, entirely unselfish, and devoted was his action and attitude. It is interesting to note that Catherine was probably always right in her instinct as to matters directly affecting herself, where the will came in, or could be made to come in; and that she was wrong only in such a point of mere physical fact and determinism as whether or not, and how long, her physical strength would hold out.

6. *Events from January to May* 1510.

I will here try to put together, in their actual succession from January to May 1510, the chief psycho-physical phenomena and their parallel utilizations, together with such mental and spiritual experiences and actions as seem to have been only quite indirectly, or not all, occasioned by her state of health. In a later chapter I propose to study all this health matter in some detail. Here I would simply warn the reader against treating, with certainly most of her chroniclers, these psycho-physical phenomena as separately and directly spiritual or miraculous or ethically significant. Found alone, they would now, on the contrary, directly suggest simply nervous disorder of some kind or other, a thing which, in itself, is always an evil. Their interest and spiritual importance arises for us entirely from their predominantly mental qualities; from their appearance in a person of such powerful mind and large and efficient character; and from their splendidly ethico-religious utilization by that same person.

On one day " she had an impression (' wound,' *ferita*) which was so great, that she lost her speech and sight, and abode in this manner some three hours. She made signs with her hands, of feeling as it were red-hot pincers attacking her heart and other interior parts. But for all this, she did not lose her full consciousness (*intelletto*)." This was the second occasion on which she indicated her wish to be anointed.[1] On another day " it was impossible to keep her in bed : she seemed like a creature placed in a great flame of fire, and it was impossible to touch her skin, because of the acute pain which she felt from any such touch." [2]

A little later on " she abode in so great a peace and interior contentment that she was " in all respects " considerably relieved and reinvigorated (*ristorata*). But she did not long remain in this condition. For very soon she was in a state of interior nudity and aridity, and she prayed : ' Never hitherto, O my Lord, have I asked Thee for anything for myself : now I pray Thee with all my might, that Thou mayest not will to separate me from Thee. Thou well knowest, O Lord, that I could not bear this.' And to her disciples she said, in connection with this desolation : ' If a man were to take a soul from Paradise, how do you think such a soul would feel? You might give it all the pleasures in the world, and as much more as you can imagine : and yet all would be but Hell, because of the memory of that divine union ' (formerly possessed, and now lost)." [3]

Again a little later on "she had another attack (*assalto*), when all her body trembled, especially her right shoulder. It was impossible to move her from her bed; she did not eat, drank next to nothing, and did not sleep." [4] On another day,

[1] *Vita*, p. 141*c*.

[2] *Ibid.* 142*a*. MSS. " A " and " B " open out their chapter on her last illness with the statement that it was (only) four months before her death that she took to her bed. I take it that from the end of January 1510 onwards, she was often in bed, yet still sometimes out of it; but that from mid-May to the end she no more left it.

[3] *Ibid.* p. 142*b*, *c*. I have, in her prayer, omitted the first seven words of the present text : " (Già sono trentacinque anni in circa, che) giammai, Signor mio . . ." For she would hardly inform God of the approximate number of years of her convert life; the double " già " points to a gloss; and such a gloss would almost irresistibly find its way into this place, so as to mitigate the absoluteness of the statement.

[4] *Ibid.* p. 143*b*. I have omitted the words : " which (the right shoulder) appeared as though severed from the body; and similarly one rib seemed severed from the others . . ." They have precisely the same " colour,"

" she had another attack,"—this was the occasion of her third indication of a wish to receive Extreme Unction,—" a spasm in the throat and mouth, so that she could not speak, nor open her eyes, nor keep her breath except with extreme difficulty." " They applied cupping-glasses, with a view to aiding her to find her breath and to regain speech, yet these helped but little." [1] For another day we are told that " in her flesh were certain concavities, as though it were dough, and the thumb had been pressed into it. And she called out in a loud voice, because of the great pain." [2]

On another day " her pains made her call out as loudly as she could, and she dragged herself about on her bed. And those that stood by were dumfounded, at seeing a body, which appeared to be healthy, in such a tormented state. And then she would laugh, speak as one in health, and say to the others, not to be sorrowful on her account, since she was very contented. And this " set of attacks " lasted four days; she then had a little rest; and, after this, those attacks returned as before." [3]

This group is in so far particularly difficult, as we have to try to decide whether, and if so how far, these pains of hers were primarily psychical, and, in some way and degree, originally, and by force of long habits of concentrated religious thinking and picturing, suggested, or at least stimulated, by the mind itself; or whether these pains were primarily physical, although evidently only functional and preponderantly nervous. For on the answer to that question depends, if

and no doubt proceed from the same contributor, as the longer passage relative to her supposed stigmatization, absent from all the MSS., but given in the printed *Vita* on the authority of Argentina.

[1] *Vita*, pp. 143*c*, 71*c*. The second passage, though occurring in an early chapter of the *Vita*, undoubtedly belongs to these final months and fits well into this particular day.

[2] *Ibid*. p. 144*a*. I have accepted this passage, because of its great vividness. But pp. 139*b*–145*b* of the printed *Vita* do not exist in the MSS.

[3] *Ibid*. p. 145*b*. On pp. 145*c*, 146*a*, she is said to have, during this time, seen many visions of Angels, to have laughed in their company, and to have herself recounted this after these occurrences. She is similarly declared to have seen Evil Spirits (*i Demoni*), but only with slight fear. And these passages occur also in the MSS.—But they stand so entirely outside of any context or attribution to any definite days; such general assertions prove, throughout the *Vita*, to be so little trustworthy; and they are such vague and colourless doubles of similar, but definitely dated and characterized, reports to be accepted in their place a little lower down, that I cannot but reject them here.

not our selection from amongst, at least our interpretation of, the largely contradictory, successively "doctored," and more or less violently schematized evidence, of which the above passages give the most characteristic and primitive parts. If it was the mind itself which, unconsciously to its owner, suggested these pains, then we can and must accept, as quite contemporary and indeed fully exact, those passages which make her peace and even sensible consolation arise during the same moments as, and in exact proportion to, the presence of the pains. If, on the other hand, the pains arose independently of the subconscious mind, and were merely mastered by the conscious intelligence and will, then it seems reasonable to assume that we have here, as is certainly the case in other matters and places in the *Vita*, an ideal foreshortening, juxtaposition, and unification of what, in the actual experience, occurred more lengthily and successively.

It is certainly remarkable in this connection, that, whereas we have had a clearly marked case of mental, spiritual desolation, outside of one of these attacks, it is at least very difficult to find anything certainly of the kind during one of them; indeed the juxtaposition of, not simply profound spiritual peace, but of sensible, also psychic or quasi-psychic, consolation with those pains, is so constant and apparently spontaneous, that secondary, or at least schematic and *a priori*, reporting seems to have been at work rather in the passages which affirm the excessiveness of those pains, than in those which insist that those pains were, so to speak, *not* pains. All her own authentic sayings leave the impression of immense psycho-spiritual sensitiveness, of much actual mental and emotional suffering as well as joy, but not, I think, of purely physical suffering. "I find so much contentment on the part of my spirit and so much peace in my mind, that tongue could not tell nor reason comprehend it; but on the part of my humanity" (her psycho-physical organism) "all my pains are, so to say, not pains," she says, shortly after a particularly violent attack, with four "accidents." And a contributor declares that the joy and the torment ever arose together. It is true that another passage says that, during such attacks, "her disciples, seeing her suffer so much, desired that she should expire, so as no more to have to see her in such great and continuous torment"; but then this desire of theirs was evidently rather a sympathetic feeling than a deliberate judgment, for, once she has got over the attack, all this desire of theirs disappears as rapidly as it had come.[1]

III. Catherine's History from May to September 9, 1510.

1. *Catherine and the Physicians.*

It is at the end of the preceding months that we are told how " the Physician " (possibly the Hospital House-Surgeon) " attempted to administer medicine to her. But it gave rise to such repeated 'accidents' (vomitings), that she all but died of it, and remained very weak." [2]

" And four months before she died," hence in mid-May, " many physicians were called together. And they saw and examined the patient, but failed to find any trace of bodily infirmity, in spite of the care and attention bestowed by them on the case. And she declared her conviction that her infirmity was not of a kind requiring physicians or bodily physic. But on the physicians persevering and ordering her, she obediently took all that they prescribed, although with great difficulty and to her hurt. Until at last those same physicians concluded that there was no remedy within the art of medicine applicable to the case, and that the infirmity was supernatural." [3]

" But now there supervened, on his return from England, an excellent Genoese physician, Maestro Giovan Battista Boerio, who, for many years, had been in the service of the English King, Henry VII. And Boerio visited Catherine, and warned her to beware of giving scandal by refusing medical treatment. And she, in return, assured him that it grieved her much if she scandalized any one; and that she was prepared to use any remedy for her ailment, if such could be found." And indeed " joy arose within her, at the hope of being cured by him. But in the following night much " psycho-physical " pain and trouble came upon her," and " she then reproved her natural self (*umanità*), saying: 'Thou sufferest this, because thou didst rejoice without (just) cause.' " Yet after about three weeks' trial of every kind of remedy, a trial which left her as it found her, Boerio abandoned the task, but " henceforward held

[1] *Vita*, pp. 144*b*; 145*c*. [2] *Ibid.* p. 145*c*.
[3] *Ibid.* p. 146*b*.

Catherine in esteem and reverence, calling her 'Mother,' and often visiting her." [1]

Here we have an interesting group of facts. For one thing, we know how King Henry "had for years been visited by regular fits of the gout; his strength visibly wasted away, and every spring the most serious apprehensions were entertained of his life." "He had also pains in the chest and difficulty of respiration." And, "in the spring of 1509 the King sank under the violence of the disease." [2] And thus Boerio will, a year after the death of his royal master, have been called in to the sick-bed of the Viceroy's daughter, not simply as a court physician, or as a generally skilful doctor, but as a man known to have had long experience of a case which prima facie was not at all unlike Catherine's.

Then it is impossible not to feel throughout these and other passages of the *Vita* which are concerned with physicians, a curious combination of contradictory feelings. There is reproof of the doctors' presumption in venturing to begin by treating her illness as though it were a simply natural one; and there is the proud pleasure at thus getting, through the breakdown of this their presumptuous undertaking, professional testimony to the supernatural character of her infirmity. And the two motives lead to the self-contradictory over-emphasizing both of the Physicians' moral worth and finality of testimony at the end of each experience, and of their rationalistic rashness in being willing to try again, a rashness assumed to be apparent to every one but themselves before each new attempt. For they must be represented as worthy and skilful men; else what value has their testimony? And their action must be intrinsically foolish from the outset; else what becomes of the transparently and separately supernatural character of her illness? [3]

[1] *Vita*, pp. 146*c*–147*c*.

[2] Lingard's *History of England*, ed. 1855, Vol. IV, p. 166; James Gairdner, *Henry VII*, London, 1889, p. 208.

[3] The five passages of the *Vita* concerning Physicians (pp. 71*c*, 72*a*; 145*c*, 146*b*; 146*c*–147*c*; 158*c*, 159*a*) all bear very clear marks of successive additions, glosses, and recastings,—always in the direction indicated above.

The entire Boerio-episode (pp. 146*c*–147*c*) is wanting in all the MSS. It is, however, most plainly authentic. I believe both the episode and a further passage concerning Boerio to have been furnished by Boerio's son, a Secular Priest, who died a septuagenarian in 1561; his monument still exists in the Church of the Santa Annunciata, at Sturla, near Genoa. See the *Biografia Medica Ligure*, by Dottore G. B. Pescetto, Genova, 1846, Vol. I, p. 104.—There are some suspicious symptoms connected with that

And then we can still see fairly clearly that Catherine does not share the views of practically all her attendants, and of certainly all the later contributors to and revisers of the *Vita*. For even now the book still leaves intact the passages which show her as hoping to be cured by Boerio, and as then condemning herself for having rejoiced without cause,—evidently, without supernatural justification; as prepared to believe that the physicians might be able to find an appropriate remedy, and as willingly trying the remedies they actually offer her; and as indeed declaring her doubt whether any physic would do her any good, yet nowhere announcing a conviction as to the directly and separately supernatural character of her illness. "Her attendants," says the obviously most authentic continuation of the passage concerning the cupping-glasses given further back, "let these attacks come and go, with as little damage as possible. Her body had to be and was sustained without the aid of medicine, and solely by means of great care and great vigilance." [1]

2. *Catherine and Don Carenzio, Argentina, and Ettore Vernazza.*

It will have been the end of June, or the beginning of July, when these medical experiments ceased. But before them (on March 11 and twice in April), and again three times during them (in May and June), monies were paid, in Catherine's name, by Don Giacomo Carenzio, now resident as Rettore in the Hospital, in the matter of the granting of Indulgences to the Church attached to the Hospital. And although this affair, occurring thus so late on in her illness, in which we have already found her not always to have dominated the plans of her attendants, cannot well be pressed as necessarily characteristic of her, yet I take it to be quite likely that she still took some active part in the matter.[2]

Catherine certainly still attended to business, even two months later; for, on August 3, Vernazza drew up a Codicil

first consultation of Physicians: Boerio's interviews read as though they had not been quite recently preceded by such an activity—and it is possible that we have here an account produced by a retrogressive doubling of the undoubtedly authentic consultation of the 10th of September, to be described presently. Still, there is nothing intrinsically improbable in the account itself. I have, then, allowed both consultations to stand.

[1] *Vita*, p. 72*a*.

[2] Copies of these six entries in the *Manuale Cartualrii* of the Hospital exist attached to the MS. *Vita* in the *Biblioteca della Missione Urbana*.

in her presence " in the bedroom of Argentina del Sale," says the document itself. Since the Inventory, still extant, of the things found in Catherine's rooms at the time of her death gives a list of the bedclothes of only two beds, and these two beds are then both in the same room, and the one bed is Catherine's, and the other is that of the *famiglia* (the servant) Argentina : it is clear that, for at least the last six weeks of her life, Catherine had only one person sleeping in her little house with her, and that this person was the navvy Marco's little widow. I take it, with Vallebona, that the room was really Catherine's ordinary bedroom ; but that, as Argentina now slept there as regularly as her mistress herself, Catherine preferred, whether from humility or affection (the latter motive seems the more probable), to think of the room as belonging to Argentina.[1]

For some reason unknown to us, Vernazza, Catherine's closest friend, must have left Genoa soon after drawing up this Codicil. For he did not draw up or witness her final Codicil of September 12, although, when in Genoa at all, he now lived close by, and although this final Codicil but gave effect to the plan regarding her sepulture which underlay the change introduced into the Will of March 1509, a Will which had been witnessed by himself. And, as we shall see, he was absent, indeed far away (*lontano*), from her death-bed, some six weeks after the date at which we have now arrived. I think we can only explain this departure by assuming that already now, before his inspirer's death, his zeal and activity had expanded beyond the limits of the Genoese Republic ; and that, dying as she already was, and devoted to her as he ever remained, he nevertheless (since there was now so little that he could hope to do for her own person, and there was so much to do elsewhere in the way of developing and applying her spirit and teachings) now rode off to Venice or to Rome, as we know him to have done, so often and for so long, during the fourteen remaining years of his life. And we have in this a fact peculiarly characteristic of these two expansive souls,—of the influence of the one, the frail woman, dying in her little sick-room, and of the execution of her world-embracing aspirations by the other, the strong man, battling, often at the risk of his very life, for the

[1] From the copy of the original Codicil in the Archivio di Stato, made for me by Dre. Ferretto. The Inventory exists attached to the MS. *Vita* just mentioned.

poor and oppressed, outside, on the great trysting-field of men's passions and requirements.

3. *Psycho-physical condition and its utilization, August 10 to 27.*

But Catherine, lying in her sick-room, suffered on August 10 from one of her great burnings. "And next day, whilst her body was still in pain and trouble, God drew her mind upwards to Himself. And she fixed her eyes on the ceiling, and remained thus almost immovable for an hour, and spoke not but laughed joyously. And when she had returned to her more ordinary consciousness, she said this one thing only: 'O Lord, do with me whatsoever Thou wilt.'"[1]

On August 15, she, "when about to communicate, addressed many beautiful words to the Blessed Sacrament, so that every one present was moved to tears."[2] During the following day and night she suffered so greatly, that "all considered she would certainly die. She asked,"—this was the third or even fourth time,—"for Extreme Unction, and" this time "it was given her, and she received it with great devotion."

[1] *Vita*, p. 148*b*. It is remarkable that, since January 10, this is the first date given by the *Vita;* that a series of dated days then extends onwards to August 28 (pp. 148*a*–152*a*); that then a gap occurs, filled in with a general but authentic account (pp. 152*b*–153*c*), evidently by another hand, the same writer who gave us the (also dateless) account from mid-January to mid-May (pp. 141*b*–145*b*); and that the dated chronicle is finally carried on from September 2 to the end, September 15 (pp. 153*c*-161*a*). If I am right as to the oneness of authorship as regards these two undated parts, then they are either not by Vernazza; or if they are, then Vernazza must have been about Catherine till September 2.

Now the *Vita*, p. 120*b*, tells us how Marabotto on one occasion left her "for three days," at a time when she was already suffering much from "accidenti." It is evident, that this absence fits in admirably with the gap already mentioned. Hence these dateless accounts can hardly be by Marabotto; and indeed their whole tone and point of view are unlike his. They might be by Carenzio: we shall see how strikingly objective and precise are the oldest constituents of the report as to the last three days of her life, during which, or at least at the end of which, Marabotto was as certainly absent as was Vernazza. There is, however, I think, some difference of tone between this latter report, and those dateless passages; whereas those passages are strikingly similar, in form and tone, to the oldest constituents of the *Trattato*, which are undoubtedly the literary work of Vernazza.

The probabilities then are, that these dateless accounts are by Vernazza; and that he left Genoa on September 1 or 2.

[2] *Vita*, p. 148*c*. "Disse molte belle parole al santo sacramento [e ai circonstanti, con tanto fervore e pietà,] che ognuno ne piangeva per divozione." I have omitted the bracketed words, as a disfiguring gloss.

"On the day following," the 17th, "she was in a state of jubilation of heart (*giubilo di cuore*), which manifested itself exteriorly in merry laughter. And, having been asked as to the cause, she said that she had seen various most beautiful, merry, and joyous countenances, so that she had been unable to refrain from laughing. And this impression continued throughout several days, during which she appeared to be improved in health."[1] But on August 22 or 23, "she again had a day of much heat and trouble. She remained maimed (paralyzed) in her right hand and in one finger of the left hand. And then she remained as though dead for about sixteen hours."[2]

In the night of the 23rd or 24th (Feast of St. Bartholomew) she had "a great attack in mind and body; and being unable to speak, she made the sign of the Cross upon her heart. And, later on, she was understood to have been molested by a diabolical temptation."[3]

On the 25th "she was in great sickness. And she caused her windows to be opened, so as to be able to see the sky. And, as the night came on, she had many candles lit; and she chanted, as well as she could, the 'Veni, Creator Spiritus.' And when she had finished she fixed her eyes upon the sky, and remained thus an hour and a half, making many gestures with her hands and eyes. And when she had resumed her ordinary consciousness (*quando fù ritornata in sè*), she said repeatedly: 'Let us go'; and then added: 'No more earth, no more earth.' And her body remained greatly shaken from this contemplation (*vista*)." And on August 27 "she saw herself as though bereft of her body and of its animating soul, and her spirit alone in God above. And after this she addressed those present and said: 'Let only those come in who may be necessary.'"[4]

[1] *Vita*, p. 149*b*. I have neglected the numerous glosses to this account, and have read "several" instead of "seven" days, since she was again in great distress on August 22, or 23 at latest (*ibid.* p. 149*c*).

[2] *Ibid.* p. 149*c*. I have here omitted an evidently later insertion and transition between that highly localized paralysis and the death-like sickness of the whole of her; and have made the latter come on after the former, for how otherwise could any one know about that paralysis?

[3] *Ibid.* p. 150*b*. This fact and passage have occasioned an interesting succession of obvious accretions and restatements.

[4] *Ibid.* p. 151*a*, *b*. I have in the text followed the MSS. as against the printed *Vita*, and have omitted a long clause, which attempts to find the explanation of these words of hers in a subsequent permanent change of attitude towards all those from whom she asked or received a service.

This particular group is specially interesting. For it shows us Catherine's love of the large and expansive, of the spiritually simple and interior, and of the supernatural and transcendent in her look-out into the open; in her vivid apprehension of her spirit bereft of all things except the Supreme Spirit, that spirit's native element and home; and in her gaze into the starlit Italian August sky above. And it gives us indications, elsewhere so rare in her life, of her attachment to the visible, audible, tangible vehicles and expressions of religion, as so many helps and occasions of its immanence in our minds and hearts, in her signing her heart with the sign of the Cross, her having the candles lit, and her chanting a definite traditional Church hymn, and in her fourth demand of Extreme Unction and devout reception of it. It is also noticeable how vivid and yet how undefined are her impressions of those countenances, since neither she herself anywhere, nor even her chroniclers in this place, explicitly identify them with Angels; and how still more general and indefinite remains the "diabolic temptation," since in this case, only when it was over, was she "understood" to have been thus tempted. Indeed any directly diabolical temptation would be profoundly uncharacteristic of her special call and way: all through the records of her life and teaching it is the selfish, claimful Self that she fears "more than a demon," "worse than the devil"; she is, in a very true sense, too busy watching, fighting, ignoring, supplanting Self, and ever putting, keeping, and replacing God, Love, in Self's stead, to give or find occasion for what, in this her immensely strenuous inner life, would have been a remoter conflict.

4. *Persistent self-knowledge and excessive impressionableness.* The *Vita* next gives us five most vivid but undated paragraphs as to her health. I will take them together with such other dated occurrences as will bring us down to September 10.

There is first a characteristic general fact, and a probably often repeated remark of Catherine's. "At times she would have no pulse, and at other times she would have a good one; often she would seem to sleep; and from this state she would awake, at one time completely herself again, and at other times so limp, oppressed, and shattered as to be unable to move. And those that attended on her did not know how to distinguish one state from the other. And hence, on coming to, she would sometimes say, 'Why did you let me remain in this quietude, from which I have almost died?'"[1] Thus Catherine's attendants are helplessly at sea concerning her psycho-physical condition, and they identify, and directly supernaturalize, each and all of her successive and simultaneous states. But Catherine herself remains clearly conscious of different levels and values in these states: of normal, grace-impelled, freely-willed, strength-bringing contemplations and quietudes; and of sickly, weakening, more or less hysterical, lassitudes and failures. And she is thus aware of the deep difference between the two sets of states, that are externally so similar, at the very time of experiencing the one or the other of them; and is conscious, at the same time, both of being unable, by her own unaided will, to give effect, from within, to this her own knowledge, and of being able and willing, indeed anxious, to follow the lead and the pressure of wisely discriminating will-acts, proceeding from without, and, as it were, meeting her own wishes half-way, and thus turning them into effective willings. She herself has still the knowledge, but, now she is ill, she has no more the power. They have the power, but not the knowledge. And she knows all this, through God's illumination working in and upon her own long and rich experiences, sound good sense, severe self-detachment, close self-observation, and incorruptible veracity of mind; and she knows it in spite of, and in direct opposition to, the far more flattering misconceptions, and entirely well-meant and sincere opinions (representative of the traditional and contemporary consensus of view on these obscure matters) of the servants, lawyers, physicians, relatives, and priests about her. The incident is closely parallel to her scruple as to Marabotto's spoiling her; and one more similar detail will be mentioned later on.

But next, we get now abundant evidence that she was ill indeed. There is the rapidly shifting fancifulness of the senses of taste and smell, together with an ever-increasing difficulty of swallowing. "She would, at times, be so thirsty as to feel capable of drinking all the water of the sea, and yet she could not, as a matter of fact, manage to swallow even one little drop of water." "Seeing on one occasion a melon, and conceiving a great desire to eat it, she had it given to her. But hardly had she a piece of it in her mouth, but she rejected it with great disgust." "She often bathed her mouth

[1] *Vita*, p. 153*b*.

with water, and then suddenly she would reject it." "To-day the smell of wine would please her, and she would bathe her hands and face in it, with great relish; and to-morrow she would dislike it so much, as to be unable any longer to see or smell it in her room."[1] And, in strict conformity with this detail, I find an entry in the Hospital account-book for this time of money disbursed to the account of Catherine, for a cask of wine for her use.[2]

Yet her biographers are evidently only stating the simple truth when they declare that she continued to receive Holy Communion with ease and safety; for not only are there three quite unsuspicious passages, descriptive of her receptions of It, under most difficult circumstances; but we find, on counting up the incidental and bare mentions of her Communions, that, during the fourteen days from September 2 to 15, her death-day, she communicated ten times, and one or two further Communions may have been accidentally omitted.

There is, again, an occasional abnormal sensitiveness to colours, and their mental connotations, at least in connection with red. "On September 2, a Physician, a friend of hers,"—no doubt Maestro Boerio,—"came to visit her, robed in his Doctor's 'scarlet,'" as was no doubt the custom when visiting patients of quality. "And she bore this sight for a little, so as not to hurt his feelings. But when she could bear it no longer, she said to him: 'Sir, I can no further bear the sight of this gown of yours, because of what it represents (suggests) to me.' The Physician departed at once and returned clad in another," a black "gown." The Chronicler, probably Boerio's priest-son, is no doubt substantially right in interpreting this as meaning that the scarlet suggested to her a seraph aflame with divine love. Yet I find, from the inventory of her final possessions, that she possessed, and doubtless used, among her bedclothes a vermilion silk coverlet and a vermilion blanket,—an undoubted indication of her love for this colour.[3] These two vicissitudes of her colour-affection no doubt mutually supplement and explain each other: when not over-impressionable and not already stimulated to the full of her

[1] *Vita*, pp. 150*a*, 154*b*, 127*c*, 153*c*.

[2] A copy of this entry exists, in the Priest Giovo's handwriting, in the collection of Documents prefixed to the MS. *Vita* of St. Catherine, in the *Biblioteca della Missione Urbana*, Genoa.

[3] *Vita*, p. 154*b*, and the Inventory among the documents in the *Vita* volume of the *Biblioteca della Missione*.

capacity, this colour would suggest her central doctrine and experience, and would be pleasurable; when over-impressionable and already stimulated as much as, then and there, she could bear and utilize, the colour would but strain and disturb her.

And, finally, there are sensations and impressions of extreme heat and cold, and excessive sensibility or insensibility in tactual matters. "At one time she was cold; and at another, burning hot." "On one day," early in September, "she suffered great cold in her right arm, followed by acute pain"; and on September 7, "her body felt all on fire; and, since it seemed to her as though the whole world were aflame, she asked whether this were the case, and had her windows opened, so as to be reassured as to the real facts."[1]

"At times she would be sensitive to such a degree, that it was impossible to touch her sheets or a hair of her head; she would, if this were done, cry out as though she had been grievously wounded."[2] The temporary paralysis and anaesthetic conditions have been already described.

5. *Three spiritually significant events, September* 4–9.

We can next consider together three spiritually significant incidents which occurred during these penultimate days of hers.

"On September 4 she lay there in her bed, in great pain, her arms stretched out in suchwise that she appeared like a body nailed to a cross; as she was within, so did she appear without." Here, then, she finds a certain attraction and help in an external, quasi-ritual attitude and act; for this attitude, however spontaneous and but subconscious, was doubtless not simply accidental or the mere result of pain. It is, with the Pietà-picture of her childhood and the Conversion-vision of the Bleeding Christ, one of the only three direct references to the Passion which I can find throughout her whole life and teaching. This little act gave occasion to the "Spiritual Stigmata"-legend, which is inserted here, in two paragraphs, by the *Vita*, on the alleged, and I think actual, authority of

[1] *Vita*, pp. 153*a*, 155*a*; 157*c*, 158*a*. For this 7th September three heat-and-light impressions are given: (1) "A ray of divine love"; (2) "a vision of fiery stairs"; and (3) this apprehension of the whole world on fire. Perhaps the first also is authentic; the last is certainly so. The middle one seems to be secondary, and to have slipped in to form a transition and link between the other two accounts.

[2] *Ibid*. p. 153*a*.

the credulous and long-lived Argentina. The legend is wanting in all the MSS.; its late genesis and growth is clearly traceable.[1]

"On September 5, some time after her Communion, she suddenly had a sight (*vista*) of herself, as dead and lying in a truckle-bed, with many Religious, robed in black, around her. And she rejoiced greatly at this sight. But afterwards, having a prick of conscience because of this rejoicing, she confessed it to her Confessor."[2] Here we have once more a particular desire within Catherine's soul, and a scruple consequent upon it; and all this but ten days before her death.

And on the 9th, after Communion, there was "suddenly shown her a sight of her (spiritual) miseries; and this gave great annoyance (*noia*) to her mind. And, as soon as she was able to tell (confess) them, she did so; and the sight then departed from her."[3] Here, then, we have clear

[1] *Vita*, p. 155*b*, *c*. A third paragraph, pp. 155*c*, 156*a* (equally wanting in all the MSS. and claiming to be based on the authority of Argentina), follows here, and tells how the latter saw one of her mistress's arms grow over half a palm in additional length, during the following night; and again how Catherine had told her, Argentina, that she, Catherine, "would before her death bear the stigmata and mysteries of the Passion in her own person." These "facts" are thoroughly characteristic of the source from which they are no doubt derived.—A fourth paragraph, p. 156*b*, *c*, has also been omitted by me, although it occurs also in the MSS. It contains a long prayer put into Catherine's mouth, and modelled on our Lord's High Priestly Prayer in John xvii, 1–13. It is far too long, elaborate, and uncharacteristic to be authentic.

[2] *Ibid*. p. 156*c*.

[3] *Ibid*. p. 158*b*. I have here omitted, after "miseries," the clause "through which she had passed." For during her middle period she seems indeed not to have seen her faults till after she herself had got beyond them: yet that particular dispensation was then vouchsafed her because of the excessive pain which the sight of still present imperfections would have caused her; and it is that peculiarity which explains the extreme rarity or absence of Confession during that time. But now we have both the pain and the Confession: and I cannot find any instances, as in this case, of (evidently keen) annoyance, or of Confession, with respect to past and overcome imperfections.—I have also omitted a sentence after "departed from her": "not that they were matters of any importance, but every slightest defect was intolerable to her." For this is to judge the Saint by another standard than that of her own conscience, and to make her sanctity consist of scrupulosity.—And I have dropped a further notice for the same day,—a "vista" vouchsafed to her of "a pure and perfect mind, into which only the memory of divine things can still enter," with her corresponding laugh and exclamation: "O, to find oneself in this degree (of perfection) at the time of death!" For, beautiful as it is, this clause but reproduces, in the softened form of a general and joyous

testimony to imperfections perceived by herself as still within her, and to her Confession of them as such; things characteristic of her third as against her second period, but which most of the contributors to the *Vita* try hard to obscure even here.

IV. The Last Six Days of Catherine's Life, September 10–15.

And now the events of real significance which occurred during the last six days of her life can be grouped under six heads.

1. *A great consultation of Physicians, September* 10.

On the 10th there occurred a second, and last, great consultation of Physicians. The number is this time given—they were ten: "of whom several are still alive," writes the final Redactor of the printed *Vita* of 1551. And, in this case, they did not prescribe any remedies; but "examining her and inspecting everything with great diligence, they finally concluded that such a case was (must be) a supernatural and divine thing, since neither the pulse, nor any of the secretions, nor any other symptom, showed any trace of any infirmity. They were astounded, and departed recommending themselves to her prayers." "When she was not oppressed or tormented by her attacks (*accidenti*), she seemed well; when she was being stifled by them (*suffocata*), she seemed dead: and again, suddenly, the opposite condition would be seen. And hence it was most clearly understood, that all this operation was produced (*ordinata*) by the divine goodness itself." [1]

Here we have a clear exposition of the two sets of phenomena which specially impressed her *entourage*, and of the reasoning by which these appearances were turned into direct proofs of the Metaphysical, indeed of the Supernatural. There are three assumptions at work here. What exceeds the knowledge of the Physicians of any one period, can be safely held to exceed not only human knowledge throughout all coming ages, but the powers of nature itself. All purely natural illness is either simply physical or simply

aspiration, what the previous anecdote had given as a particular and depressing consciousness. And the previous anecdote was evidently offensive to both Redactors.

[1] *Vita*, pp. 158*c*, 159*a*, *b*.

mental, and always shows traces of a simply physical or of a simply mental kind. And all purely natural illness is either slow in its transitions, or, at least, not sudden in its transitions back and up to apparent health. And these assumptions must have lain in those minds as part and parcel of their hereditary furniture, in so far as they did not energize and aspire, and did not, by moving out and up into the regions of Action and of the Spiritual, of the Dynamic and of Love, transcend all that is mechanically transmissible, and, with it, all that was bound to change and be proved inadequate in the knowledge of their time. It was their very religion which, with its strong predisposition and determination to find immediate, independent, tangible, medically certified proofs for an exceptional, indeed exclusive action of God, kept these Physicians thus, even religiously, tied down in and by the Contingent and Transitory. And it was her very religion which, by its grandly ethico-spiritual Transcendence, kept Catherine above and outside the very possibility of growing obsolete or old. We now see, with even painful clearness, how inadequate, indeed how directly suggestive of the contrary, were those Physicians' and Redactors' treasured proofs. For neither the absence of all symptoms of physical or of clearly mental disease, nor the presence of an astounding frequency, abruptness, and completeness of change in the psycho-physical actions and functions of the living person, nor, above all, the conjunction of these two peculiarities are for us now, taken by themselves, anything but indications of nervous, hysterical derangement. It is in spite of these things, or at least only on occasion of them, that Catherine is great. Indeed one fails to see how, in any case, such purely psycho-physical phenomenal data could, of themselves and directly, ever compel any such metaphysical and spiritual conclusions. And, be it noted, only in proportion as men abandon such impossible enterprises, do they become sufficiently detached from these phenomena to be able accurately to gauge their nature. These attendants who build so much on these phenomena do not see them as they are; Catherine, who builds nothing on them, and who simply uses them as fresh means and occasions of ethico-spiritual growth, sees them, to an astonishing extent, as they really are.

2. *The final Codicil, September* 12.

On the 12th, " she communicated as usual, but tasted no other food, and after this she remained a very long time without speaking. And after they had been bathing her mouth for some time, she exclaimed, 'I am suffocating' (*io affogo*). She said this because a little drop of water had trickled into her throat, and she could not gulp it down." And in the evening the Notary Saccheri drew up in her presence, with her nephew Francesco Fiesco and the maid Argentina del Sale as two of the seven witnesses, a last Codicil, in which she, "although languishing in body, yet possessed of her faculties (*in sua sana memoria esistente*), ordained that her body should be buried in such a place and Church as should be ordained by Don Jacobo Carenzio, the present Rector of the Hospital, and Don Cattaneo Marabotto." And "at ten o'clock at night she complained of a very great heat (fire), and then ejected from the mouth much black blood. And black spots appeared all over her body, with very severe suffering. And her sight became so weak that she could barely distinguish one person from the other." [1]

Here at last we can plainly see the object which had moved her friends, eighteen months before, to get her to fix upon San Nicolò in Boschetto as her burial-place. They now, when she is at the point of death, and in the last moment of fairly lucid mind, get her finally to declare,—not that she is to be buried in the Hospital Church apart from her husband, though this is what they themselves intend to do, but simply that her grave is to be wheresoever Dons Marabotto and Carenzio shall decide. It is interesting to note to how late a date her friends thought it wise to postpone such a move, and in how indirect and roundabout a fashion they had to attain their end. Yet it is again plain that the whole scheme was willed and executed by her family and friends unanimously; for, if Vernazza had been a witness to the previous Will, so was Francesco Fiesco now a witness to this Codicil.—We should also note that, if the difficulty in swallowing of the early day is still entirely in keeping with her lifelong psycho-physical peculiarities, the attack at night is the first in her life when the blood lost is described as of bad quality

[1] *Vita*, p. 159*c*. The Codicil I give from Dre. Ferretto's copy of the original in the Archivio di Stato, Genoa. I have, in the *Vita* passage, omitted a sentence which now stands between the drop-of-water incident, and that of the attack at night, which declares: "All this day she remained without speaking, without ever opening her eyes or eating or drinking"; for it would be difficult, if we retain it, to find room for the drawing up of the Codicil, which certainly took place before the attack.

and where spots appear on her person, indeed where any symptom of definite illness is recorded. But now at last it is evident that downright physical mischief is at work.

3. *Symptoms of organic lesion and delirium, September* 13. Before dawn "on the 13th, she evacuated much blood of a bad quality and great heat, so that she remained even weaker than before. Nevertheless she again communicated at her usual hour." And later on "she fixed her gaze immovably upon the ceiling, and made many gestures with her mouth and hands. The bystanders asked her what it was that she was seeing, and she said: 'Drive away that beast that wants to eat . . . ,' and the remainder of the words could not be made out."[1]

Here two points are of pathetic interest. This great heat of her blood was considered, no doubt from the first by at least some of her attendants, and then later on more and more by the Redactors, as so directly marvellous, spiritually significant, and confirmatory of sayings of her own as to her interior ardours, that three various though parallel anecdotes and proofs as to the intensity of its heat are solemnly printed here by the *Vita*, only the first of which appears in the MSS. Purely secondary, physical matters are thus, with a short-sighted good faith and admiration, eagerly utilized to naturalize and obscure a soaringly spiritual personality. Truly, she was not simply mistaken as to her isolation: she too had the privilege to share some of the piercing loneliness of Christ.

And next, we have here her last coherent utterance; and the care and fearless honesty with which it has been chronicled and printed as such—and as the concluding words of a chapter (Chapter L), up to at least the fourth edition, Venice 1601—are truly admirable. The words, "that wants to eat," appear in MSS. "A" and "B," and are, I think, authentic. They may mean that the beast was looking about for some unspecified food, or that it was wanting to devour her (the former is, I think, the more likely meaning, for there is no indication of fright, and *devorare* would, in the latter case, be the more natural word). We have, in any case, a quasi-physical, distinctly *maladif* impression; one which, as regards at least its apparently sensible embodiment, was the simple projection of her own mind. And indeed there is nothing to

[1] *Vita*, p. 160*a*.

show that she had any consciousness of any spiritual significance about it. It has got all the opaque, uninteresting character of mere, given, unrelated, and unsuggestive fact, which all such purely nervous projections always have; and stands thus in complete and instructive contrast to her finely suggestive and transparent, spiritually significant *Viste*, which contributed so largely to the volitional stimulation and moral and religious witness and truth of her life.

4. *Catherine's death, dawn of September* 15, 1510.

During the early night hours of "the 14th, she again lost much blood, and she weakened much in her speech. Yet she once more, and it was the last time, communicated as usual. And throughout this day she lay there, with her pulse so slight as to be unfindable." And "many devoted friends were present."

And as the subsequent night ceased to be Saturday and became Sunday, the 15th, "she was asked whether she wished to communicate. But she then pointed with her right index-finger towards the sky." And her friends understood that she wished to indicate by this that she had to go and communicate in heaven. "And at this moment, this blessed soul gently expired, in great peace and tranquillity, and flew to her tender and much desired Love." [1]

Here three points are of interest. Catherine undoubtedly died at, or shortly before, dawn on the 15th September, as is clearly required by the older account on page 160*c* of the *Vita*. Yet a second account, sufficiently early to appear in all the MSS., is given on page 161*c*, according to which she died on the 14th. The reason of this latter pragmatic "correction" is obvious: the 15th is but the Octave of the Nativity of the Blessed Virgin, the 14th is the Feast of the Exaltation of the Cross. The temptation to find a final, strikingly appropriate synchronism, when, to do so, her death need only be pushed back some six hours at most, was too great to be resisted to the end; and an untrained, enthusiastic, imaginative mind like Argentina's would, probably from the very first, have almost unconsciously helped to establish, or perhaps she single-handedly fixed, this date.

And next, the "many friends" present will no doubt have included her sole surviving brother Lorenzo and his son Francesco, who, only three days before, had witnessed her

[1] *Vita*, pp. 160*c*, 161*a*.

Codicil; one or other of the four "Protectors" of the Hospital; Don Carenzio, the Rector; and Argentina del Sale. But Vernazza, as we already know, was far away; and, as we shall find in a moment, Mariola, and, above all, Marabotto, though both in Genoa, were both absent from her death-bed. Now it is certain that the absence of Marabotto cannot have been accidental, for death had evidently been recognized by all to be imminent, ever since the 12th at least; and he himself would certainly not have put anything in the world before attending Catherine at the moment of her death. Nor, as we shall find, was he ill just now. Yet we must, I think, suppose him to have been (at least off and on) about her person, during the 12th, up to the drawing up of the Codicil, which directly concerns himself together with Carenzio. His own name appears second, no doubt because, as the document itself mentions, Carenzio and not he is now Rector of the Hospital in which the document is being drawn up. Marabotto will have withdrawn after the attack on that night which left Catherine hardly capable of any further distinguishing one person from another; and he will have retired because Carenzio, from some little jealousy or feeling of punctilio, cared to claim the right, as Rector, alone to attend her at the last; or for some other slight reason such as this. In any case, there is here one more indication of a certain friction and rivalry amongst her attendants and chroniclers, which, however painful, will help us in our study of the peculiarities of her biography. There is, however, nothing to show that Marabotto's final withdrawal took place at the instigation, or even with the knowledge, of Catherine; and the cause of that withdrawal can certainly not have been a grave one.

And finally, there appeared eventually, at earliest in the fifth edition, 1615, but possibly not till the sixth, in 1645, or even later, a gloss which effectually prevents her "unedifying" remark of the 13th from being her last utterance. After the words, "and at this moment, this blessed soul," there then appears the clause: "saying: 'Into Thy hands, O Lord, I commend my spirit.'" The passage occurs in the late and entirely secondary MS. "F," which contains also other demonstrably legendary "embellishments."

5. *Intimations of her death vouchsafed to friends.*

The *Vita* gives an account of seven intimations or apparitions, vouchsafed at the moment of her death to as many chosen friends and disciples,—so many communications of her passage and instant complete union with God. Although no names are given, it is easy to identify the first six persons as Argentina del Sale, " a spiritual daughter of hers, present at her death " ; Mariola Bastarda, " another spiritual daughter of hers, who had an evil spirit upon her (*il demonio adosso*) " ; Maestro Boerio, "a physician, her devotee" ; Ettore Vernazza, " a very spiritual man and her devotee " ; Tommasa Fiesca, " a holy Religious woman, most devoted to her " ; and Benedetta Lombarda, " another Religious woman, who had been a member of her household (*sua famigliare*)." The seventh and last, " a nun " (*una monaca*), is so little characterized, as to be incapable of certain identification : possibly Battista Vernazza is meant, who, though but thirteen years old, was already an Augustinian Novice.[1]

The order in which the first six names appear is evidently determined partly by the degree of physical proximity to Catherine—Argentina by her bedside, comes before Boerio in another house in Genoa, and Boerio comes before Vernazza, since the latter is far away (*lontano*) ; partly by sex—Boerio and Vernazza, though simple laymen, appear before the three Religious women ; and partly by the abnormal spiritual condition, and consequent increase in the value of the testimony, of the souls concerned—Mariola the Possessed comes first among all those not actually present at the death. Even this order, and still more the form of all these little notices, show plainly that the stress is laid, not so much on the intimation of the death, as on that of the immediate entrance into glory. Note that there is no reference anywhere to Don Carenzio, certainly as much present at the death as Argentina ; nor, within this particular list, to Don Marabotto, as certainly absent as Ettore Vernazza.

It is disappointing to find that, whereas such intimations, or at least communications as to death at the moment of its occurrence, belong to the best authenticated of the more mysterious human experiences, and although we would expect to find some such unmistakably vivid and first-hand accounts at this point in the life of one so spiritually great and so deeply loved as was Catherine, the accounts are all, with the possible exception of that concerning Boerio, very general and colourless. As to Boerio we are told : " A

[1] *Vita*, pp. 161*c*–163*a*.

Physician, her devotee, was asleep, but awoke at the moment of her passing, and heard a voice which said to him: 'Abide with God; I am now going to Paradise.' And he called his wife and said to her: 'Madonna Caterina has died at this moment'; and this turned out to have been the case."[1]

Two insipid, vague, and gossipy fragments concerning Don Marabotto strive to make up for his absence from the list of the seven recipients of synchronizing intimations. "Her Confessor during that night (14th to 15th) and throughout the following day (15th), had no notice whatever concerning her." This is told as if it had been something spiritually remarkable, whereas it was evidently but strangely unkind on the part of the other friends of Catherine. "The next day (16th) he attempted to say a Mass for the Dead for the soul of Catherine." He evidently had been told on the evening of the 15th, or quite early on the 16th, for there is here no claim to any supernatural intimation. "And he found himself unable to pray for her in particular. And again on the following day, whilst saying a Mass in honour of several Martyrs, his mind was suddenly, from the Introit onwards, fixed upon Catherine's spiritual martyrdom, so that his abundant weeping made it difficult for him to finish his Mass."[2] There is, as so often with Marabotto, something slightly comical, and yet respectable, because thoroughly genuine, loyal, and truthful, about this his eager desire to experience something unusual, the careful registration of something quite commonplace, and the wistful attempt to make it out extraordinary after all.

6. *Alleged miraculous condition of Catherine's skin and heart.*

There remain two more medical details, which are, however, of some significance in connection with the spirit of her *entourage.*

Her skin is declared to have been, after death, of a yellow colour throughout. Indeed in various places of the *Vita* yellow or red colour is noted in connection with her person, but generally as localized about the region of the heart. But the accounts vary, indeed contradict each other, so much, that I shrink from finally adopting any one account.[3]

[1] *Vita*, p. 162*b*.

[2] *Ibid.* pp. 163*b*–164*a*.

[3] *Ibid.* p. 153*a* (end of August or beginning of September 1510), "through the intense heat of this fire of love she became yellow all over, like the colour of saffron"; p. 161*b*, "(after death) that yellow colour was

The action of her heart was often laborious or even acutely painful: "At the last, owing to the great fire of pure and penetrating love, that burnt within her heart, the skin over it became so tender as to be unable to be touched. It seemed as though she had a wound right through her heart. And she often held her hand over it; and it would pant like a pair of bellows, on one day more than on another." [1] And how often had not Catherine spoken of the wondrous things, the spiritual joys and sufferings, that she felt within her heart! And so some of her materializing biographers, probably some of her attendants before them, doubt not that "if only her (physical) heart had been examined after death, some marvellous sign would have been found upon it." [2] We even find a report that "this holy soul, several months before her death, left an order that, after her death, her body should be opened and her heart examined, because they would find it all consumed (burnt up) by love. Nevertheless her friends did not dare to do so." [3] This sheer legend will have been due to Argentina, and will have become articulate long after the first deposition of Catherine's remains. There is certainly no other, indeed no kind of authentic, evidence of any such wish or hesitation on the part of any one at the time. It is sad to note how rapidly and easily, all but inevitably, the vivid, spiritual ideas and experiences of Catherine were thus materialized and spoilt.

spread over her whole body, which at first had only been around the region of the heart"; p. 164*c* (on opening her coffin in the autumn of 1511), "the skin which corresponded to the heart was still red in sign of the ardent love which she had harboured in it, the rest of the body was yellow."

[1] *Vita*, pp. 17*c*, 18*a*, (97*c*).

[2] *Ibid.* p. 129*b*, (165*c*). In both places there is an explicit reference to Saint Ignatius (of Antioch), "whose heart, when examined after his martyrdom, was found to have written upon it, in letters of gold, the sweet name of Jesus." Perhaps also two lines of Jacopone da Todi had some influence here. In *Loda* LXXXVIII, v. 11, he says of the perfected soul: "The heart annihilates itself, undone (melted down) as though it were wax, and finds itself, after this act, bearing the figure (the seal-impression) of Christ Himself."

[3] *Ibid.* p. 165*c*

V. Sketch of Catherine's Spiritual Character and Significance.

Before proceeding further to what is really still a necessary part and elucidation of Catherine's spiritual character and special significance,—her doctrine and the posthumous effect, extension, and application of her life and teaching upon and by means of her greatest disciples,—it may be well to pause a little, and to try to give, as far as the largely fragmentary and vague evidence permits, a short and vivid picture and summary, in part retrospective and in part prospective, of the special type, meaning and importance of Catherine's personality and spiritual attitude, and of the interrelation of the two. In so doing I propose to move, as far as possible, from the psycho-physical and temperamental peculiarities and determinisms of her case, up to the spiritual characteristics and ethical self-determinations; and to try to note everywhere what she was not as definitely as what she was. For only thus shall we have some adequate apprehension of the "beggarly elements" which she found, and of the spiritual organism and centre of far-reaching influence which she left. And only thus too will it be possible to see at all clearly the cost, the limitations, and the special functions, temporary and permanent, of her particular kind of soul and sanctity.

1. *Her special temperament.*

It is clear then, first, that in her we have to do with a highly nervous, delicately poised, immensely sensitive and impressionable pyscho-physical organism and temperament. It was a temperament which, had it been unmatched by a mind and will at least its equals; had these latter not found, or been found by, a definite, rich, and supernaturally powerful, historical, and institutional religion; and had not the mind and will, with this religious help, been kept in constant operation upon it, would have spelt, if not moral ruin, at least lifelong ineffectualness. Yet, as a matter of fact, not only did this temperament not dominate her, with the apparently rare and incomplete exceptions of some but semi-voluntary, short impressions and acts during the last months of her life; but it became one of the chief instruments and materials of her life's work and worth. Only together with such a mind and will, is such a temperament not a grave drawback; and even with them it is an obvious danger, and requires their constant careful checking and active shaping.

And this temperament involved an unusually large subconscious life. All souls have some amount of this life, but many have it but slight and shallow: she had it of a quite extraordinary degree and depth. A coral reef, growing up from, and just peering above, a hundred fathom-deep ocean, would be an appropriate picture of the large predominance of subconsciousness in this spacious soul. And even this circumstance alone would cause her spiritual lights and fully conscious experiences to come abruptly, and in the form of quasi-physical seizures and surprises. Continuous, and possibly long, incubations of ideas and feelings would thus be taking place in the subconscious region, and these feelings and ideas would then, when fully ripe, or on some slight stimulation from the conscious region or directly from the outer world, make sudden irruptions into that full consciousness. Nor would such natural suddenness of full consciousness really militate against the claim to supernaturalness of the ideas and feelings thus revealed. For they would still be most rightly conceived as the work of God's Spirit in and through the action of her own spirit: not their causation and their source, but simply the suddenness of their revelation and the channel of their outlet would lose in supernaturalness.

And hers was a soul with habitually large fields of consciousness. Apparently from her conversion onwards, and certainly during the last fourteen years of her life, the moments or days of narrow fields were, till quite the last weeks or even days, comparatively rare; and their narrowness was evidently always felt as most painful and oppressive. And the interior occupation was so intense; the several fields succeeded each other with such an apparent automatism and quality of even physical seizure; and they were either so entrancing by their largeness or so depressing by their narrowness: that to souls not in tune with hers, she must, in the former moods, have appeared as egoistic, as (in a sense) too much of a man, as one absorbed in great but purely general, super-personal ideas which were making her forget both her own and her fellow-creature's minor wants; and, in the latter moods, as downrightly egotistic, as (in a way) too much of a woman, as one engrossed in her own purely individual, small and fanciful troubles and trials. Yet the "Egoism" is not dominant during her middle period, since it is certain that her charitable and administrative activities, and close affective interest in the daily, physical and emotional lot and demands of the poor and lowly, were most real and considerable. And, in her third period, it was this very "Egoism" which, as we shall see, was the form and means of the interior apprehension and exterior elaboration of her most original and suggestive doctrines, and became the occasion for her stimulation of other intensely active souls on to great nation-wide enterprises of the most practical, permanent, and heroic kind. And the "Egotistic" moods are unapparent before the last two years or less of her life; and they then are clearly but the occasional, involuntary suspensions or partial yieldings of her normally iron will,—rare checks and intermittences, which, with little or no preventible faultiness on her own part, give us pathetically vivid glimpses of what that normal life of hers cost her to achieve and to maintain, and of what she would have been, if bereft of God's generosity ever awakening, deepening, and operating through her own.

All this sensitiveness, subconsciousness, spaciousness, variety, and suddenness of apprehension and feeling; all this largely chaotic, mutually conflicting, raw material of her spiritual life, even if it had existed alongside of but feeble and inert powers of organization and transformation, would not have failed to produce considerable suffering; although, in such a case, that suffering would have remained largely inarticulate, and would have left the soul checked and counterchecked by various tyrannous passions and fancies. The soul would thus have been less efficient and persuasive than the least subconscious and sensitive specimens of average and "common-sense" humanity. But, in her case, all this unusually turbulent raw material was in unusually close contiguity to powers of mind and of will of a rare breadth and strength. And this very closeness of apposition and width of contrast, and this great strength of mind and will, made all that disordered multiplicity, distraction, and dispersion of her clamorous, many-headed, many-hearted nature, a tyranny impossible and unnecessary to bear. And yet to achieve the actual escape from such a tyranny, the mastering of such a rabble, and the harmonization of such a chaos, meant a constant and immense effort, a practically unbroken grace-getting and self-giving, an ever-growing heroism and indeed sanctity, and, with and through all these things, a corresponding expansion and virile joy. It can thus be said, in all simple truth, that she became a saint because she had to; that she became it, to prevent herself going to pieces: she literally had to save, and actually did save, the fruitful life of reason and of love, by ceaselessly fighting her immensely sensitive, absolute, and claimful self.

2. *Catherine and Marriage.*

Catherine's mind was without humour or wit; and this was, of course, a serious drawback. And her temperament was of so excessive a mentality as to amount to something more or less abnormal. For not only is there no trace about her, at any time, of moral vulgarity of any kind, or of any tendency to it; and this is, of course, a grand strength; but she seems at all times to have been greatly lacking in that quite innocent and normal sensuousness, which appears to form a necessary element of the complete human personality. It is true that in the anecdotes of her impulsive and yet reverent affection for the pestiferous woman and the cancerous workman, with the finely self-oblivious sympathy which moves her to kiss the mouth of the first, and long to remain with her arms around the neck of the other, there is the beautiful tenderness and daring of a great positive purity, of the purity of flame and not of snow. And her love of her servants, Argentina in particular, and of poor Thobia, is exquisitely true and constant. Yet even all this can hardly be classed with the element referred to, with that love of children and of women as the bearers of them, that instinct of union with all that is pure and fruitful in the normal life of sex, such as is so beautifully present throughout St. Luke's Gospel, but which is, at least relatively, absent from St. John's.

Possibly her unhappy and childless marriage determined the non-development or the mortification of any tendencies to such a temper. But the absence referred to was more probably caused by her congenital psychical temperament and state themselves; and, if so, it would point to her as a person hardly intended for marriage, and as one who, through no fault of her own, could not satisfy the less purely mental of the perfectly licit requirements which make up the many-levelled wants of a normal, or at least ordinary, man's and husband's nature. Pompilia's dying words, in Browning's "Ring and the Book," would, probably at any time after her premature involuntary marriage, have found an appropriate place upon Catherine's lips, had she ever thought it loyal or kind to utter them: "'In heaven there is neither marriage nor giving in marriage.' How like Jesus Christ to say that!"

Yet it is at least as difficult to think of her as really intended for the cloister. That early wish of hers to join a religious community, sincere and keen as it no doubt was at the time, evidently faded away completely, probably already before her conversion thirteen years later, and certainly before her widowhood. Perhaps she would have been best suited, throughout her adult years, to the life of an unmarried woman living in the world,—to the kind of life which she actually led during her widowhood, with such changes in it as her earlier, robuster health would have involved for those earlier years. She would thus, throughout her life, have divided her energies, in various degrees and combinations, between attention to the multiform, practical, physico-emotional wants of the poor; the give and take of stimulation and enlightenment to and from some few large-hearted, heroically operative friends; and, as source and centre of all such actual achievements and of indefinitely greater possibilities, indeed as a life already largely eternal and creative,—contemplative prayer of various degrees and kinds. But such a life, if it would have left out much disappointment and suffering, and not for herself alone, yet would also have been without the special occasions and incentives to her sudden conversion and long patience and detailed magnanimity. Her life, in appearing on the surface as less of a failure, would at bottom have been less of a spiritual success.

Indeed the failures and fragmentarinesses of her life, even if and where more than merely apparent to us or even to herself, helped and still help to give a poignant forcefulness to her example and teaching. There is nothing pre- or post-arranged, nothing artificial or stagey, nothing, in the deliberate occupations of her convert life, that is simple brooding about this woman: when she thinks or prays, she does so; when she acts, she acts; when she suffers, she suffers; and there is an end of it. The infinitely winning qualities of a simple veracity; of a successive livingness, because ever operative occupation with the actual real moment, and not with the after-shadow of the past nor with the fore-shadow of the future; and, through all this, of a healthy creatureliness are thus spread over all she does,—over her virtues, which are never reflected as such within her own pure mind, and over her very weaknesses and failings which, summed up in their source, her false self, are ever being acknowledged, feared, and fought, with a heroism not less massive because its methods are so wisely indirect.

3. *Catherine and Friendship and the Poor.*

It is plain that Catherine's temperament was naturally a profoundly sad one, although her acutest attacks of melancholy were generally succeeded by some unusually great expansion, illumination or consolidation of soul. She had, to adopt a term of recent psychology, a very low "difference-threshold": easily and swiftly would her consciousness be affected by every kind of irritant: even a slight stimulation would at once produce pain, anxiety, or oppression of mind or soul. She was thus evidently made for a few lifelong friends, for such as would deserve the privilege of giving much sympathy and patience, and of getting back helps and stimulations indefinitely greater both in quality and kind; and was not fitted for many acquaintances of the ordinary kind, with their hurry of disjointed, hand-to-mouth, half-awake thinking, feeling, and doing.

And it is very noticeable that her friendships and attachments of all kinds were of a steadiness and perseverance to which there are no real exceptions. To Giuliano, markedly inferior in nature though he evidently was to her, and positively unfaithful during the early years of their long, ill-assorted marriage, she remained faithful even during those first years which she herself never ceased to condemn as her pre-conversion period; she behaved with true magnanimity towards himself and Thobia and Thobia's mother; and she even evinced a certain affective attachment to him and to his memory. And it would hardly be fair to quote the change in the dispositions as to her place of burial in proof of a change in her dispositions towards him. She whose affectionate interest in Thobia is shown, by irrefragable documentary proof, to have persevered, indeed increased, to the end of the poor young woman's life, will not have changed in her feelings towards her own dead husband. Towards her brothers and sister, her nephews and nieces, her numerous Wills and Codicils show that she entertained a constant and operative affection.

These same documents prove that her affection and gratitude towards Don Marabotto were equally sincere and provident. It is true that she twice broke off relations with him, although only for a day and three days respectively; and, at the last, this devoted friend of the last eleven years of her life was no more about her. Yet we have remarked that those two former absences were but caused by reasonable fears of getting spoilt by him; and that the final absence was no doubt in no way her doing. And perhaps the most impressive of all her attachments were that to the Hospital, as representative of the sick poor whom she had served, so actively and at such cost to self, for twenty-five years and more,—all her legal dispositions and her very domicile for the last thirty years of her life proclaim the permanent prominence of this interest; and her affection towards her servants, since nothing could be more considerate, thoughtful, equable, and persevering than her care and love for Benedetta, Mariola, and Argentina. Here again I cannot find any certain exceptions: for we know nothing of the history of the servant Antoinetta except that, even on the one occasion of her mention, it appeared already doubtful whether the girl herself would care to remain with her mistress to the end.

There is but one apparent, and indeed a startling, exception to this unbroken continuity of affection. Ettore Vernazza, certainly the greatest and closest, the most docile and the most influential, of her disciples, he to whom we owe the transmission of the larger and the most precious part of her teaching and spirit, and who, as will be seen, became, after her death even more than before it, and more and more right up to his own heroic end, the living reproduction and extension of the very deepest and greatest experiences and influences of her life: Vernazza appears nowhere in her Wills, except as, on one occasion, the actual drawer of the document, and, on another, as a witness. And he was far away, and clearly not accidentally, at the time of her death. I take it to be quite certain that we have here not an exception, at the point of her fullest sympathy, to that gratitude and permanence of feeling which obtained demonstrably in the other, lesser cases; but that this silence and this departure are to be explained, the former entirely, and the latter in part, by the special character as much of Ettore as of Catherine, and by the special form which their friendship assumed in consequence. I shall return to this point in my chapter on Vernazza.

4. *Her Absorptions and Ecstatic States.*

Catherine's states of absorption in prayer, such as we find ever since her conversion, were transparently real and sincere, and were so swift and spontaneous as to appear quasi-involuntary. They were evidently, together with, and largely on occasion of, her reception of the Holy Eucharist, the chief means and the ordinary form of the accessions of strength and growth to her spiritual life.

Possibly throughout the four years of the first period of her convert life, certainly and increasingly throughout the twenty-two years of the second, middle period, these absorptions occurred frequently, indeed daily; they were long, and lasted up to six hours at a stretch; and they were apparently timed by herself, and never rendered her incapable of hearing or attending to any call to acts of duty or of charity, and of breaking off then and there. And throughout these years she seems to have known but one kind of absorption, this primarily spiritual one, which appears to have been a particularly deep Prayer of Quiet; and she appears to have always been, if exercised, yet also profoundly sustained and strengthened, by it, even physically, for the large activity and numerous trials and sufferings awaiting her on her return to her ordinary life. And these were the years during which she lived with no mediate guidance.

During the last eleven, perhaps even thirteen years of her life, first one, and then, considerably later, a second change occurs in these respects. First these profound, healthy, and fruitful absorptions, and the power to occasion or effect, to bear or endorse them, diminish greatly, though apparently gradually, in length, regularity, and efficiency; indeed they do so almost as markedly as does the capacity for external work, their former complement and correlative. The spiritual life now breaks up into a greater variety of shorter and more fitful incidents and manifestations. The sympathy of friends, the sustaining counsel of priests, and the communication on her part of many spiritual thoughts and experiences take, in large part, the place of those long spells of the Prayer of Quiet or of Union, and still more of that external activity which are both now becoming more and more impossible to her. And next,—though not, as far as our evidence goes, before the last six months or so of her life,—there arises a second series of absorptions, externally closely similar, yet internally profoundly different. These latter absorptions are primarily psychical and involuntary, indeed psychopathic. And she herself shows and declares her knowledge of this their pathological character, her ability to distinguish them from their healthy rivals, her inability to throw them off unaided; her wish that others should rouse her from them, and her power to accept and second such initiation coming to her from a will-centre other than her own.

Now her attendants and biographers, possibly all of them and even during her lifetime, considered and called those healthy absorptions " ecstasies "; and though we have clear evidence of her ever having shrunk from so naming them herself, and though, here as everywhere, she habitually turned away from considering the form and psycho-physical concomitants of her spiritual experiences, and concentrated her attention on their content and ethico-religious truth and power, there seems to be no special reason for quarrelling with their application of this term. Yet it is of great importance to observe that none of her teaching can with propriety be called directly Pneumatic. For I can find nothing that even purports to have been spoken in a state of trance, nor anything authentic that claims to convey, during her time of ordinary consciousness, anything learnt during those states of absorption other than what, in a lesser degree, is probably experienced, during at least some rare moments, by all souls that have attained to the so-called Prayer of Quiet. It is quite clear, I think, that in all these authentic passages the states of absorption are treated substantially as times when the conscious region of her soul, a region always relatively shallow, sinks down into the ever-present deep regions of subconsciousness; and hence as experiences which can only be described indirectly,—in their effects, as traced by and in the conscious soul, after its rising up again, from this immersion in subconsciousness, to its more ordinary condition of so-called " full consciousness," *i. e.* as full a consciousness as is normal, for this particular soul, in the majority of moments as are not devoted to physical sleep.

But if apparently none of Catherine's contemplations are derived directly from things learnt during these times of absorption; those contemplations are, none the less, all indirectly influenced, in the most powerful and multiform manner, by these absorptions. For these absorptions constituted the moments of the soul's feeding and harmonization, and they enriched and concentrated it, for the service of its fellows, and for other occasions of further self-enlargement. And these absorptions, with their combination of experienced fruitfulness and undeniable obscurity, for the very soul that has passed through them, when this soul has returned to ordinary consciousness, give to all, even to the most lucid of her sayings, a beautiful margin of mist and mystery, a never-ceasing sense of the incomprehensibility, and yet of the soul's capacity for an intellectual adumbration, of the realities and truths in which our whole spiritual life is rooted,—realities and truths which she is thus, without even a touch of inconsistency, ever struggling to apprehend and to communicate a little less inadequately than before.

5. *Catherine's teaching.*

Catherine's teaching, as we have it, is, at first sight, strangely abstract and impersonal. God nowhere appears in it, at least in so many words, either as Father, or as Friend, or as Bridegroom of the soul. This comes no doubt, in part, from the circumstance that she had never known the joys of maternity, and had never, for one moment, experienced the soul-entrancing power of full conjugal union. It comes, perhaps, even more, from her somewhat abnormal temperament, the (in some respects) exclusive mentality which we have already noted. But it certainly springs at its deepest from one of the central requirements and experiences of her spiritual life; and must be interpreted by the place and the function which this apparently abstract teaching occupies within this large experimental life of hers which stimulates, utilizes, and transcends it all. For here again we are brought back to her rare thirst, her imperious need, for unification; to the fact that she was a living, closely knit, ever-increasing spiritual organism, if there ever was one.

This unification tended, in its reasoned, theoretic presentation, even to overshoot the mark: for it would be impossible to press those of her sayings in which her true self appears as literally God, or her state of quiet as a complete motionlessness or even immovability. Yet in practice this unification ever remained admirably balanced and fruitful, since, in and for her actual life, it was being ever conceived and applied as but a whole-hearted, constantly renewed, continuously necessary, costing and yet enriching, endeavour to harmonize and integrate the ever-increasing elements and explications of her nature and experience. And even on the two points mentioned, her theory gives an admirably vivid presentment of the prima facie impression produced by its deepest experiences upon every devoted soul.

And on other points her theory is, even as such, admirably

sober, closely knit, and stimulating. For, as to the cause of Evil, she ever restricts herself to finding it in her own nature, and to fighting it there: hence the personality of Evil, though nowhere denied, yet rarely if ever concerns her, and never does so directly in her strenuous and practical life. Yet, on the other hand, this fight takes, with her, the form not primarily of a conflict with this or that particular fault, these several conflicts then summing themselves up into a more or less interconnected warfare; but it makes straight for the very root-centre of all the particular faults, and, by constantly checking and starving that, suppresses these. And hence the Positive, Radical character of Evil is, in practice, continuously emphasized by her.

Yet this root-centre of Evil within her was most certainly not conceived by her as a merely general and abstract false self or self-seeking. Her biographers, mostly over-anxious to prove the innocence of her nature, even at the expense of the heroism of her life and of the reasonableness and truthfulness of her statements, are no doubt responsible for the constant air of would-be devout and amiable (!) exaggeration which she wears on all this self-fighting side of her. Yet we have, I think, but to take the simplest and most authentic of the rival accounts,—those which give us the smallest quantity of self-denunciation, and we can understand the quality of this self-blame, and can fix its special, entirely concrete and pressing, occasion and object. For considering the immense claimfulness, the cruel jealousy, the tyrannous fancifulness, the brooding inventiveness, the at last incurable absoluteness of the weak and bad side and tendency of a temperament and natural character such as hers, had it been allowed to have its way, there is, I think, nothing really excessive or morbid, nothing that is not most healthy and humble, and hence sensible and admirably self-cognitive and truthful, about this heroic strenuousness, this ever-watchful, courageous fear of self, and those declarations of hers that this false self was as bad as any devil. To such a temperament and *attrait* as hers only one master could be deliberately taken, or could be long borne, as centre of the soul: God *or* Self;—not two: God *and* Self. And hence all practice or even tolerance of, as it were, separate compartments of the soul; all "a little of this, and not too much of that" spirit; all "making the best of both worlds" temper; all treatment of religion as a means to other ends, or as so much uninterpreted inheritance and dead furniture or fixed and frozen possession of the mind, or as a respectable concomitant and condiment or tolerable parasite to other interests: all such things must have been more really impossible to her than would have been the lapse into self-sufficiency and self-idolatry, and the attempt to find happiness in such a downward unification.

And the one true divine root-centre of her individual soul is ever, at the same time, experienced and conceived as present, in various degrees and ways, simply everywhere, and in everything. All the world of spirits is thus linked together; and a certain slightest remnant of a union exists even between Heaven and Hell, between the lost and the saved. For there is no absolute or really infinite Evil existent anywhere; whilst everywhere there are some traces of and communications from the Absolute Good, the Source and Creator of the substantial being of all things that are. And to possess even God, and all of God, herself alone exclusively, would have been to her, we can say it boldly, a truly intolerable state, if this state were conceived as accompanied by any consciousness of the existence of other rational creatures entirely excluded from any and every degree or kind of such possession. It is, on the contrary, the apprehension of how she, as but one of the countless creatures of God, is allowed to share in the effluence of the one Light and Life and Love, an effluence which, identical in essential character everywhere, is not entirely absent anywhere: it is the abounding consciousness of this universal bond and brotherhood, this complete freedom from all sectarian exclusiveness and from all exhaustive appropriation of God, the Sun of the Universe, by any or all of the just or unjust, upon all of whom He shines: it is all this that constitutes her element of unity, saneness, and breadth, the one half of her faith and the greater part of her spiritual joy.

And the other half of her faith constitutes her element of difference, multiplicity and depth, and is itself made up of two distinct convictions. No two creatures have been created by God with the same capacities; and, although they are each called by Him to possess Him to the full of their respective capability, they will necessarily, even if they all be fully faithful to their call, possess Him in indefinitely and innumerably various degrees and ways. And, so far, there is still nothing but joy in her soul. Indeed we can say that the previous element of unity and breadth calls for this second element of diversity and depth; and that only in and with the other can each element attain to its own full development and significance, and thus the two together can constitute a living whole.

But the second conviction as to difference is a sombre and saddening one. For she holds further that the diversity is not only one of degrees of goodness and a universal fulness of variously sized living vessels of life and joy; but that there is also a diversity in the degree of self-making or self-marring on the part of the free-willing, self-determining creatures of God. Here too she still, it is true, finds the omnipresent divine Goodness at work, and in a double fashion and degree. The self-marring of some, probably, in her view, of most souls, gets slowly and blissfully albeit painfully unmade by the voluntary acceptance, on the part of these souls, of the suffering rightly attaching, in a quite determinist manner, to all direct, deliberate, and detached pleasure-seeking of the false self. And this is Purgatory, which is essentially the same whether thus willed and suffered in this world or in the next. And the self-marring of other, probably the minority of, sinful souls, though no longer capable of any essential unmaking, is yet in so far overruled by the divine Goodness (which, here as everywhere, is greater than the creature's badness), that even here there ever remains a certain residue of moral goodness, and that a certain mitigation of the suffering which necessarily accompanies the remaining and indeed preponderant evil is mercifully effected by God. And this is Hell, which is essentially the same, whether thus, as to its pain, not willed but suffered here or hereafter. Thus she neither holds an *Apocatastasis*, a Final Restitution of all things,—what might be called a Universal Purgatory, nor a Gradual Mitigation of the sufferings of the lost; but the eventual complete purgation and restitution applies only to some, though probably to most, souls, and the mitigation of this suffering, in the case of the lost, is not gradual but instantaneous.

Here again, then, we find her thirst for unification strikingly at work. For she discovers one single divine Goodness as active and efficient throughout the universe; and she everywhere finds spiritual pain to consist in the discordance felt by the rational creature between its actual contingent condition and its own indestructible ideal, and such pain to be everywhere automatically consequent upon deliberate acts of self-will. Hence the suffering is nowhere separately willed or separately sent by God; and, in all cases of restoration, the suffering, in proportion as it is freely willed by the sufferer, is ever medicinal and curative and never vindictive. It is these considerations which make her able to endure this sombre side of reality.

Now it is all this second set of beliefs, all this faith in diversity, multiplicity, and depth, which prevents any touch of real Pantheism or Indifferentism from defacing the breadth of her outlook, and effectually neutralizes any tendency to a sheer Optimism or Monism. She loves God's Light and Love so much, that she is indefatigable in seeking, and constantly happy in finding, and incapable of not loving, even the merest glimpses of it, everywhere. And yet, precisely on that same account, everywhere the central passion of her soul is given to fostering the further growth of this Light and Love, to already loving it even more as it will or may be than as it already is, and thus deeply loving it already, in order that it may be still more lovable by and by. And thus the universality, and what we may call the particularity, of God's self-communication and of the creature's response, are equally preserved, and in suchwise that each safeguards, supplements, and stimulates the other. And thus her grace-stimulated craving, both for indefinite expansion and breadth and for indefinite concentration and depth, is met and nourished by this width and distance, this clarity and dimness of outlook on to the rich and awe-inspiring greatness of God and of His world of souls.

And union with this one Centre is, for all rational free-willing creatures, to be achieved, at any one and at every moment, by the whole-hearted willing and doing, by the full endorsing, of some one thing,—some one unique state and duty offered to the soul in that one unique moment. Thus life gets apparently broken up into so many successive steps and degrees of work, each to be attended to as though it were the first and last; and as so much special material and occasion for the practice of unification, ostensibly in the matter supplied and for the moment which supplies it, but really in the soul to which it is offered and for the totality of its life. Her soul is, even if taken at any one moment, and still more, of course, if considered in its successive history, overflowing with various acts, with (as it were) so many numberless waves and wavelets, currents and cross-currents of volition; and the warp and woof of her life's weaving is really close-knit with numberless threads of single willings, preceded and succeeded by single perceptions, conceptions, and feelings of the soul. Yet the very fulness of this flow and the closeness of this weaving, their great and ever-increasing orderliness and spontaneity, such as we can and must conceive them to have been present during the majority of the moments of her convert and waking life, tended, during such times, to obliterate any clear consciousness of their different constituents, and to produce the impression of one single state, even one single act. And this very action, even inasmuch as thus felt to be simple and one, is furthermore experienced psychically as a surprise and seizure from without, rather than as a self-determination from within. And this psychic peculiarity is taken by her as but the occasion and emotional, quasi-sensible picturing of the ever-present and ever-growing experience and conviction that all right human action, the very self-donation of the creature, is the Creator's best gift, and that the very act of her own mind and heart, in all its complete inalienableness and spontaneity, is yet, in the last resort, but an illumination and stimulation coming from beyond the reaches of her own mind and will, from the mind and will of God. And thus Ethics are englobed by Religion, Having by Doing, and Doing by Being: yet not so that, in her fullest life, any of the higher things suppress the lower, but so that each stimulates the very things that it transcends.

6. *Catherine's literary obligations. Her corrections of the Neo-Platonist positions.*

We shall trace further on how largely and spontaneously she has, from out of the many different possible types and forms of spirituality, chosen out, assimilated and further explicated certain Platonic and especially certain Neo-Platonic conceptions. We shall be unable to suggest any likely intermediary, or to assume with certainty a direct derivation, for these conceptions from Plato, or indeed from Plotinus or Proclus; and shall nevertheless be obliged to postulate some now untraceable communication, on some most important points, between Plato and herself. Besides this, she derives one Platonic conception from the Book of Wisdom and a corresponding passage in St. Paul; and a certain general Platonic tone and imagery from the Johannine Gospel and First Epistle. Her Neo-Platonism, on the contrary, she derives, massively and all but pure, through two of the Pseudo-Dionysian books and her dearly loved Franciscan Mystic

Poet, Jacopone da Todi. It is indeed to the Pauline, Johannine, Dionysian, and Jacopone writings that she owes, with the exception of a certain group of Platonic conceptions, practically all that she did not directly derive from her own psychical and spiritual experiences.

Now her assimilation of this particular strain of doctrine has remained but partial and theoretical with respect to those parts of Dionysian Neo-Platonism which were not borne out by the facts of her own Christian experience; but it has extended even to her emotional attitude and practice, in cases where the doctrine was borne out by these facts.

Thus we shall find that she often speaks theoretically of Evil as simply negative, as the varyingly great absence of Good. Yet, in practice and in her autobiographical picturings, she fights her bad self, to the very last, as a truly positive force. The force of God is everywhere conceived as indefinitely greater, as, indeed, alone infinite; yet the force of Evil is practically experienced and pictured as real and positive also, in its kind and degree.

Again, she often speaks as though her spiritual life had, at some one particular moment, simply arrived at its final culmination, and had attained God and perfection with complete finality,—such, at least, as this particular soul of hers can achieve. Yet, very shortly after, we find her unmistakably in renewed movement and conflict, and observe her mind to be now fully aware of that past "perfection" having been but imperfect, because that act or state is now seen from a height higher than that former level: hence that "perfection" was perfect, at most, in relation to its helps and opportunities in and for its own special movement.

Again, it is at times as though she conceived her body to be a sheer clog and prison-house to the soul, and as though the soul's weakness and sinfulness were essentially due to its union with the flesh. But here especially her later commentators have amplified and systematized her teaching almost beyond recognition; the authentic sayings of this kind, though too strong to be pressed, are few, and belong exclusively to the last stages of her illness; and, above all, these declarations are checked and entirely eclipsed by her normal and constant view as to the specific nature of Moral Evil. For this Evil consists, for her, essentially in the self-idolatry, the claimful self-centredness of the natural man, ever tending, in a thousand mostly roundabout ways, to make means and ends, centre and circumference, Sun and Planet change places, and to put some more or less subtle wilfulness and pleasure-seeking in the place of Duty, Happiness, and God. Few, even amongst the Saints, can have realized and exemplified more profoundly the indelible difference between pleasure and happiness, between the false and the true self; and few have more keenly, patiently felt and taught that the soul's true life is, even eventually, not a keeping or a getting what the lower instincts crave: but that, on the contrary, a whole world of pleasures which, however base and short and misery-productive, can be intensely and irreplaceably pleasurable while they last, has successively to be sacrificed, for good and all; and that what is retained has gradually to proceed from other motives, to be grouped around other centres, and be ever only a part and a servant, and never a master or the whole. The gulf between every kind of Auto-centricism and the Theo-centric life, between mere Eudaemonism and Religion, could not be found anywhere more constant or profound.

Again, it is at times as though the absence or suppression of even the noblest of human fellow-feelings and of particular, parental and friendly, attachments, and not their purification and deepening, multiplication and harmonization, were the end and aim of perfection. But little or nothing of this belongs, I think, to any deliberate and enduring theory of hers, still less to her full and normal practice; and the impression of such inhumanity is, in so far as it is derived from authentic documents, entirely caused by and restricted to her early convert reaction, and her late over-strained or worn-out psycho-physical condition.

Again, it is sometimes as though she believed indeed in an energizing and progress of the soul, yet held this progress to be, after conversion, an absolutely unbroken, equable, necessary and automatic increase in perfection; and that such a soul's last state is, necessarily and in all respects, better than were its previous stages.—The Redactors of her life most undoubtedly think this. Because, for instance, she was Matron from 1490 to 1496, and could no more fill the post from 1496 to 1510:—therefore "not to give part of her activity to such external work was more perfect than to give it," is the argument that underlies their scheme for these two periods.—Yet I can find nothing in her teaching to show that she held any such view. She was, indeed, ever too much absorbed, by the experiences and duties of her successive moments, to find even the leisure of mind requisite for the manufacture of so doctrinaire a system. And indeed there is nothing in the conception of sanctity, or in that of a gradual and general increase in generosity and purity of the saintly soul's dispositions and intentions, which requires us to hold that such a soul's last state and efficiency is, in every respect, better than the first. For the range and volume of the efficiency, wisdom, balance, appropriateness of even our goodness is not determined by our will and the graces given to our will alone. Physical and psychical health and strength, illness and weakness; helps and hindrances from friends and foes; the changing influences and limitations of growing age; and the ever-shifting combinations of all these and of similar things,—things and combinations which are all but indirectly attainable by our wills in any way: all this is ever as truly at work upon us as our wills and God's spiritual graces are in operation directly within ourselves. And if Catherine's richness, breadth and balance of soul are, considering her special and successive health and circumstances, remarkable up to the very end, and probably actually grew to some extent with the growing obstacles, yet those qualities hardly grew or could grow *pari passu* with these obstacles. The manifold efficiency and the unity in multiplicity were distinctly greater before 1496 than after. And thus the Saints too join their lowlier brethren in paying the pathetic debt of our common mortality. They too can be called upon to survive the culmination of their many-sided power, and to retain perpetual youth only as regards their intention and the central ideas and the spiritual substance of their soul.

Once more she seems as though, to make up for this apparent suppression of the element of time, unduly to press the category of space, at least in her contemplations. We shall see how often in these contemplations God Himself, and the soul, or at least its various states, appear as places; so that the whole spiritual life and world come thus to look rather like an atomic co-ordination, a projection on to space and a static mechanism, than an interpenetrative subordination, a production in time or at least in duration, and a dynamic organism.—Yet it will be found that all this imagery is consciously, though no doubt quite naturally, used only *as* imagery, and that it is thus used both because it was spontaneously presented to her mind by her psychic peculiarities and because it readily adapted itself as a vehicle to express one of the deepest experiences and convictions of her spirit.

For her psychic peculiarities involved, on the one hand, a curiously rapid and complete change and difference of states of consciousness, and, on the other hand, a remarkable absence (or at least dimness) of consciousness as to this transition itself, which, however abrupt, was of course as truly a part of her inner life as were the several completed states and outlooks. Now the apparently static element and harmony in any one of these states could, of course, be at all clearly presented in no other form than that of a spatial image; whereas the changing element in all these states seems to have accumulated chiefly in the subconscious region, to have at last suddenly burst into the conscious sphere, and to have there effected the change too rapidly to permit of, or at least to require, the presentation of this element as such, a presentation which could only have taken the form of a consciousness of time or of duration. From all this it follows that, to her immediate psychic consciousness, each of her successive experiences presented itself as ever one spatial picture, as one "place."

And the imagery, thus quasi-automatically presented to her, could not fail to be gladly used and emphasized by her to express the deepest experiences of her spiritual life. For it was the element of simultaneity, of organic interpenetration, of the God-like *Totum Simul*, which chiefly impressed her in these deepest moments. And hence the soul is conceived by her as, in its essence, eternal rather than as immortal—as, in its highest reaches and moments, outside of time and not as simply wholly within it; and as, on such occasions, vividly though indirectly conscious of the fact. Heaven itself is thought of not as eventually succeeding, with its own endless succession, to the finite succession of these our fleeting earthly days; but as already forming the usually obscure, yet ever immensely operative, background, groundwork, measure and centre of our being, now and here as truly as there and then. And hence again, Heaven, Purgatory, and Hell are for her three distinct states of the soul, already effected in their essence here below, and experienced as what they are, in part and occasionally here, and fully and continuously hereafter. Thus the fundamental cleavage in the soul's life is not between things successive,—between the Now and the Then, and at the point of death; but between things simultaneous, between the This and the That, and at the point of sin and of self-seeking.

And finally, she seems at times to speak Greek-wise, as though the soul's life consisted essentially, or even exclusively, in an intellection, a static contemplation. Yet we have already seen how robust and constant is her ethical dualism, how essentially, here below at least, happiness consists for her in a right affection and attachment, in the continuous detaching of the true self from the false self, and the attaching of the true self unto God. And we should note how that intellection itself is conceived as ever accompanied by a keen sense of its inferiority to the Reality apprehended, and as both the result and the condition and the means of love and of an increase of love. And again we should note that this sense of inferiority does not succeed the intellection, as the result of any reasoning on the disparity between the finite and Infinite, but accompanies that intellection itself, and corresponds to the surplusage of her feelings over her mental seeings, and of her experience over her knowledge. And we should add the fact that, in the most emphatic of her sayings, she makes the essence of Heaven to consist in the union of the finite with the Infinite Will; and that this doctrine alone would seem readily to harmonize with her favourite teaching as to Heaven beginning here below.

7. *Her attitude towards Historical and Institutional Religion.*

If the Platonic and Neo-Platonic elements appear, at first sight, as massive and even excessive constituents of Catherine's doctrine, Historical and Institutional Christianity seems, on a cursory survey, to contribute strangely little even to her practice. Not one of her ordinary contemplations is directly occupied with any scene from Our Lord's life. The picture of the "Pietà," so impressive to her in her nursery-days; the great Conversion-Vision of the Bleeding Christ; and the slighter cases of the signing of herself with the sign of the Cross and of her lying with outstretched arms, which occurred during the last stage of her illness, are the sole indications of any immediate occupation with the Passion; whilst the two cases of the Triptych "Maestà" and the painting representative of Our Lord at the well, (cases which indicate an attraction to the Infancy and to at least one incident of the Public Life,) complete the list of all direct attention to any incidents of Our Lord's earthly existence. As to occupation with or invocation of the Saints, inclusive of the Blessed Virgin, I can find but one instance, the invocation of St. Benedict, two days before her Conversion. We have seen, as to Sacramental Confession, how little there can have been of it, throughout the long middle period of her Convert Life; and how she was, during this time, simply without any priestly guidance. And she never was a Tertiary, nor did she belong to any Confraternity, nor did she attempt to gain Indulgences, nor did she practise popular devotions, such as the Rosary or Scapular.

Nor could these facts be quite fairly met, except to a certain relatively small extent with regard to Confession, by insistence upon the changing character of the Church's discipline, if we thus mean to assert that she did not, in these matters, act exceptionally with regard to the practice and theory of fervent souls of her own time. For, on all the points mentioned, the ordinary fervent practice was already, and had been for centuries, different; and, in the matter of priestly guidance, her chroniclers have not failed to transmit to us the wonders and murmurs of more than one contemporary.

Yet here again the prima facie impression is but very incompletely borne out by a closer study.

For first, none of these historical and institutional elements are ever formally excluded, or attacked, or slighted. Indeed, in the matter of Indulgences, we have seen how she arranged or allowed that monies of her own should be spent in procuring certain facilities for gaining them by others.

And next, special practices, more than equivalent in their irksomeness, are throughout made to take the place of ordinary practices, in so far and for so long as these latter are abstained from. An unusually severe ascetical penitential time, and then the rarest watchfulness and continuous self-renouncement, take thus, for a considerable period, the place of the sacramental forms of Penance.

And thirdly, if there is an unusual rarity in Confession there is an almost as rare frequency of Communion; and authentic anecdotes show us how she scandalized some good souls as truly by this frequency as by that rarity. Indeed throughout her convert life, an ardent devotion to the Holy Eucharist forms the very centre of her daily life; during probably thirty-five years she only quite exceptionally misses daily Communion; and she has the deepest attraction to the Mass, and a holy envy of priests for their close relation to the

Blessed Sacrament. And though there are no contemplations of hers directly occupied with the Holy Eucharist, yet we shall find this experience and doctrine to have profoundly shaped and coloured teachings and apprehensions which, at first sight, are quite disconnected with It. We can already see how all-inclusive a symbol and stimulation of her other special attractions and conceptions this central devotion could not fail to be. She found here the Infinite first condescending to the finite; so that the finite may then rise towards the Infinite; the soul's life, a hunger and a satisfaction of that hunger, through the taste of feeling rather than through the sight of reason; God giving Himself through such apparently slight vehicles, in such short moments, and under such bewilderingly humble veils; and our poor *a priori* notions and *a posteriori* analyses thus proved inadequate to the living soul and the living God.—Extreme Unction also was highly esteemed: she spontaneously demanded it some four times and finally received it with great fervour. Church hymns too—witness the "Veni, Creator," chanted on her death-bed—and liturgical lights are spontaneously used.

And lastly, her practice in the matter of Confession and of priestly advice became, during her last thirteen years, identical in frequency with that of her devout contemporaries; and thus her life ended with the practice, on all the chief points, of the average, ordinary devotional acts and habits of her time. And this final practice of the ordinary means, together with her lifelong dislike of singularity and of notice; her humble misgivings in the midst of her most peaceful originalities, and the utter absence of any tendency to think her way, inasmuch as it was at all singular, the only way or even the best way, except just now and here for her own self alone; her complete freedom from the spirit of comparing self with others, of dividing off the sheep from the goats, or of having some short, sure, and universal means or test for holiness: all this shows us plainly how Catholic and unsectarian, how truly free, not only from slavish fear and pusillanimous conformity, but also from all enthralment to merely subjective fancies, from all solipsism or conceit was her strong soul.

8. *Three stages of the Spiritual Life; Catherine represents the third.*

It has been well said that there are three stages of the spiritual life, and three corresponding classes of souls.

There are the souls that are characterized, even to the end of their earthly lives, by that, more or less complete, naturalistic Individualism, with which we all in various degrees begin. Catherine's own time and country were full of such thoroughly Individualistic, unmoral or even anti-moral men, who, however gifted and cultivated as artists, scholars, philosophers, and statesmen, must yet be counted as essentially childish and as clever animals rather than as spiritual men. And she herself had, during the five years which had preceded her conversion, tended, on the surface of her being, towards something of this kind.

Next come the souls that have recognized and have accepted Duty and Obligation, that are now striving to serve God as God, and that are attempting, with a preponderant sincerity, to live the common and universal life of the Spirit. These of necessity tend to suspect, or even to suppress and sacrifice, whatever appears to be peculiar to themselves, as so much individualistic subjectivity and insidious high treason to the objective law of Him who made their souls, and who now bids them save those souls at any cost. The large majority of the souls that were striving to serve God in Catherine's times belonged, as souls belong in these our days, and will necessarily and rightly belong up to the end, to this second, universalistic, uniformative type and class. And Catherine herself evidently belonged prominently to this type and class, during her first four convert years.

And there are, finally, an ever relatively small number of souls that are called, and a still smaller number that attain, to a state in which the Universality, Obligation, Uniformity, and Objectivity, of the second stage and class, take the form of a Spiritual Individuality, Liberty, Variety, and Subjectivity: Personality in the fullest sense of the term has now appeared. And this fullest Spiritual Personality is the profoundest opposite and foe of its naturalistic counterfeit, of those spontaneous animal liberalisms which reigned, all but unrecognized as such because all but uncontrasted by the true ideal and test of life, prior to that prostration before absolute obligation, that poignant sense of weakness and impurity, and that gain of strength and purity from beyond its furthest reaches, experienced by the soul at its conversion.

Yet that merely subjective, liberalistic Individualism of the first stage can only be kept out, even at the third stage, by retaining within the soul all the essential characteristics of the second stage,—by a continuous passing and re-passing under the Caudine Forks of the willed defeat of wayward, self-pleasing wilfulness, and of the deliberate acceptance of an objective system of ideas and experiences as interiorly binding upon the self. For if the second stage excludes the first, the third stage does not exclude the second. Yet now all this, in these rare souls, leads up to and produces a living reality bafflingly simple in its paradoxical, mysterious richness. For now the universality, obligation, and objectivity of the Law become and appear greater, not less, because incarnated in an eminently unique and unreproduceable, in a fully personal form. And at this stage only do we find a full persuasiveness.

Catherine attained unmistakably, after her four years of special penitence, to this rare third stage. For not only is she essentially as individual and unique as if she were not universal and uniform; and essentially as universal and uniform as if she were not individual: but she is indefinitely more truly original and subjective, because of her voluntary boundness and objectivity. Indeed she is solidly and really free and personal, because the continuous renunciation and expulsion of all naturalistic individuality remains, to the very end, one of the essential functions of her soul.

From all this it is clear how easy it would be to misread the lesson of her manifold life, and to turn such examples as hers from a help into a hindrance. For her melancholy temperament, her peculiar psychic health, her final external inefficiency: all this is too striking not to tempt the admiration, perhaps even the hopeless and ruinous imitation, of such crude and inexperienced souls as know not how to distinguish between the merely given materials and untransferable determinisms of each separate soul's psychical and temperamental native outfit, and the free, grace-inspired and grace-aided use made by each soul of these, its more or less unique, occasions and materials. Those materials were, of themselves, of no moral worth, and lent themselves only in part with any ease to the upbuilding and realization of her spirit's ideal. And it is only this, her wise and heroic use of her materials,—though this also, of course, is not directly transferable,—that represents the spiritually valuable constituent of the life.

Similarly with the form, and the psychic occasions or accompaniments of her very prayer and spiritual absorptions, and with some of the constituents of her doctrine, if taken as speculative and analytic and final, rather than as psychological and descriptive and preliminary. These things again could easily be misused. For the former are largely quite special and, in themselves, morally indifferent peculiarities, transformed and utilized by quite special graces and lifelong spiritual heroisms. And the latter, we shall find, were never intended to be systematic, complete or ultimate; and indeed they owe their true force and value to their being the occasional, spontaneous and immediate expressions and adumbrations of an experience indefinitely richer and more ultimate than themselves.

And finally, it would of course be absurd to take the limitations of her activity and interests, even if we were to restrict ourselves to those common to all the stages of her life, as necessarily admirable, or as universally inevitable. For there is, in the very nature of things, no equation between her one soul, however rich and stimulating, or even all the souls of her class and school, or of her age or country, on the one hand, and the totality of religious experience, and its means and incorporations, on the other hand, even if, by totality, we but mean that part of it already achieved and accepted by grace-impelled mankind.

9. *The lessons of Catherine's life.*

And yet Catherine's life and teaching will be found full of suggestion and stimulation, if they are taken in their interpenetration, and if due regard is paid to their fragmentary registration, to the necessary distinction between what, amongst all these facts, was mere means, occasion, and temporal setting, and what amongst them was aim and end, utilization and abiding import, and to the fact that all this experience is but one out of the indefinitely many applications, extensions, and mutually corrective and supplementary exemplifications of the spirit and life of Christ, as it lives itself out throughout the temperaments, races and ages of mankind. Above all it can teach us, I think, with a rare completeness, where inlies the secret of a persuasive holiness. For Catherine lets us see, with unusual clearness, how this winningness lies in the pathetically dramatic spectacle and appeal presented by a life engaged in an ever-increasing ethical and spiritual energizing,—whether in a slow shifting and pushing of its actual centre, down and in from the circumference of the soul to its true centre, and from this true centre enlarging and reorganizing its whole ever-expanding being again and again; or in an apparently sudden finding itself placed, and loyally placing itself, in this true centre, and then from there prosecuting and maintaining the organization and transformation of its varyingly peripheral life, a life treated at one time as central and complete. And this persuasiveness can here be discovered to be greater or less in proportion to the thoroughness and continuousness of this centralization and purification; to the degree in which this issues in a new, spontaneously acting ethico-spiritual personality; and to the closeness and costingness of the connection between those means and this result. Such a soul will be persuasive because of its ever seeking and finding a purifying intermediacy, a river of death, to all its merely naturalistic self-seeking.

And it is this nobly ascetic requirement and search and end which no doubt explain what, at first sight, is strange, both in its presence and in its attractiveness, in her own case and more or less in that of all the mature and complete Saints,—I mean, the large predominance of an apparently Pantheistic element in her life, the strong emphasis laid upon an apparent Thing-Conception of God and of the human spirit.

It was clearly not alone because of the Neo-Platonist element and influence of the books she chiefly used that she, in true Greek fashion, finds and allows so large a place for conceptions of things, for images derived from the natural elements, and for mental abstractions, in her religious experiences and teachings: God appearing in them predominantly as Sun, Light, Fire, Air, Ocean; Beauty, Truth, Love, Goodness. For, after all, other elements could be found in these very books, and other writings were known to her besides these books: hence this her preference for just these elements still demands an explanation.

Nor was it ultimately because, nervously high-pitched and strained as she was by nature, she even physically craved and required an immense expansion for this her excessive natural concentration. She thus evidently longed first to move through, and to bathe and rest and spread out her psychic self, in an ample region, in an enduring state of quasi-unconsciousness, in an (as it were) innocently animal or even simply vegetative objectivity, indeed in an apparent bare element and mere Thing, before, thus rested, braced, and as it were now healthily reconcentrated, she more directly met the Infinite Concentration and Determination, the Personal Spirit, God. For, after all, hers was so heroic a spirit, and so self-distrustful, indeed self-suspecting, a heart, that a mere psychic affinity or requirement would have failed so permanently and deliberately to captivate her mind.

Nor, finally, was it ultimately because her domestic sorrows or inexperiences, or even her very psychic peculiarities and apparent lack of all even innocent sensuousness, left the images of Bride and Bridegroom, of Parent and Child, perhaps even of Friend, respectively painful, empty, or pale to her consciousness. For, even so, she could and did care, with a beautiful affectiveness of her own, for her brothers and sister, for Vernazza, her "spiritual son," and for many a humble toiler or domestic. And indeed her whole tendency is ultimately to find God's special home, the only one of His dwelling-places which we men really know, in the human heart of hearts.

The ultimate and determining reason was no doubt her deep spiritual experience and conviction (as vivid as ever was the psychic tendency which gave it form and additional emotional edge and momentum) that she must continuously first quench and drown her feverish immediacy, her clamorous, claimful false self, and must lose herself, as a merely natural Individual, in the river and ocean of the Thing, of Law, of that apparently ruthless Determinism which fronts life everywhere, before she could find herself again as a Person, in union with and in presence of an infinite Spirit and Personality.

Thus Greek Fate is here retained, but it is transformed through being transplaced. For Fate has here ceased to be ultimate and above the very gods, the poor gods who were so predominantly the mere projections of man's Individualism: Fate is here intermediate and a way to God—the great God, the source and ideal of all Personality. And indeed this Fate is not, ultimately, simply separate from God; it is indeed omnipresent, but everywhere only as the preliminary and subaltern, expression, for us men, of the Divine Freedom that lies hidden and operating behind it. And we men attain to some of this Freedom only by the inclusion within our spiritual life of that Fate-passage and of our actual constant passing through it, on and on.

10. *Three points where Catherine is comparatively original; and a fourth point where she is practically unique.*

In the general tendency and form of her inner life and conviction Catherine has, of course, substantially nothing but what she shares with all the Mystics, in proportion as these retain Law, Ethics, and Personality; and she has much that forms part of the convictions of all Christians, indeed of all Theists. Yet in the degree and precise manner of her elaboration and application of those things, and again in the circumstances of their documentary transmission, Catherine will, I think, be found in three points comparatively original, and in a fourth point practically unique.

First she has, as we have seen, not only a strikingly persistent attitude of transcendence and detachment with regard to her psycho-physical state in general (this is indeed an attitude common to all ethically sound and fruitful Mystics: witness in particular St. John of the Cross); but she has also a most remarkable faculty and activity of discrimination between her own healthy and morbid states. Even this latter power she probably shares, in various degrees, with all such ethical-minded Mystics as nevertheless suffered from a partially *maladif* psycho-physical condition: witness especially St. Teresa.—Yet contemporary documentary evidence, for not only such actual variations between healthy and unhealthy states, but also for the Mystic's knowledge of and witness to the existence of both and to the difference between the two, is necessarily rare. I know of no evidence more vivid and final, although of much that is larger in amount, than the evidence furnished by Catherine's *Vita*.

And next she has both a constant, deep sense that religion never consists simply in ends but in means as well, and never ceases to use and practise the latter; and a concomitant keen apprehension of the difference between means and ends, and ever illustrates this sense of difference by the striking variety and liberty of the practical attitude which she is successively moved to take, and actually does take, towards this or that of the Institutional helps of the Church. Here again she but exemplifies a principle which underlies the practice of all the Saints, in proportion to their maturity and full normality. And indeed our Lord Himself, the Model and the King of Saints, when asked which was the greatest of the Commandments, did not answer that He could not and would not tell, since to distinguish at all between greater and lesser Commandments would be liberalism; but, on the contrary, fully endorsed and canonized such a distinction and discrimination, by actually pointing out two Commandments as the greatest, and by declaring that from them depended all the law and the prophets. Hence to organize, and more and more to find and give their right, relative place and influence to all the different things practised and believed, is as important as is the corresponding practice and acceptance of all these different things. Yet, here again, full evidence both for such fidelity and docility and for such variety and liberty of soul, with regard to the means of religion, is rare: the records of the modern Saints mostly give us but the docility; those of the Fathers of the desert generally give us but the liberty: Catherine's *Vita* gives us both.

And thirdly, she is, amongst formally canonized Saints, a rare example of a contemplative and mystic who, from first to last, leads at the same time the common life of marriage and of widowhood in the world. Here again any misapprehension of the importance or significance of this fact would readily lead to folly. For it is undeniable that it has been the monastic life which, in however great variations of degree, form and lasting success, has furnished Christendom at large with an impersonation of self-renunciation sufficiently isolated, massive and continuous to be deeply impressive upon the sluggish spiritual apprehension of the average man. And indeed self-renunciation is so universally necessary and so universally difficult; upon its presence and activity religion, and all and every kind of rational human life depend so largely; without its tonic presence they are so necessarily but a dilettantism, a delusion or an hypocrisy: that to body it forth for all men must ever remain an honour and a duty specially incumbent upon some kind of Monasticism. For it is but right, and indeed alone respectful, to the Spirit of God, so manifold and mysterious in its gifts and inspirations, that every degree and kind of healthy and heroic self-renunciation should be practised and embodied; and that special honour should attach to its most massive manifestations.

Yet our general knowledge of poor, rarely balanced human nature and our detailed historical experience respectively anticipate and demonstrate how easy it is, on this point also, to confound the means with the end, and a part with the whole. And by such confusion either self-renunciation, that very salt of all truly human existence, gets actually stapled up in one corner of the wide world and of multiform life; or this apparent stapling becomes but a pedantic pretence and would-be monopoly, the salt meanwhile losing all its savour. And these two abuses and errors easily coalesce and reinforce each other. The fact is that the total work and duty of collective humanity,—the production of a maximum of true recollection, rest and detachment, effected in and through a maximum of right dispersion, action, and attachment; above all a maximum of ethico-spiritual transformation of the world and, in and through such work, of each single worker,—is too high for any single soul, or even class or vocation, to hope to exhaust. Only by all and each joining hands and supplementing each other can all these numberless degrees and kinds of call and goodness, together, slowly, throughout the ages, get nearer and nearer to that inexhaustible ideal which lies so deep and ineradicable within the heart of each and all. And thus will the two fundamental movements of the soul, as it were its expiration and its inspiration, the going out to gather and the coming home to garner, be kept up, in various degrees, by every human soul, and each soul and vocation will as keenly feel the need of supplementation, as it will apprehend the beauty and importance of the special contribution it is called to make to the whole, a whole here, as everywhere, greater than any of its parts, although requiring them each and all.—Now Catherine suggests and illustrates such a doctrine with rare impressiveness: for the pure and efficient love of God and man, the one end and measure for us all, ever consciously dominates all and every means within her admirably balanced and unified mind; and the renunciative element is under mostly quite ordinary exterior forms, as complete and constant as it could be found anywhere.

And lastly, her doctrine contains one conviction, or group of convictions, as original as, in such matters, one can expect to find. We get here the soul's voluntary plunge into Purgatory, its seeking and finding relief, from the now painful pleasure of sin, in the now joy-producing pain of purification; and the soul's discovery and acquisition, if and when in predominantly good dispositions, of its ever-fuller peace and bliss, because its ever-increasing harmonization, in freely willing the suffering intrinsically consequent upon its own past evil pleasures and the resulting present imperfections of its will. And this cycle of facts and laws here springs from, and begins with, the soul's life Here and Now, and is held to extend (on the ever-present assumption of the substantial persistence of the spirit's fundamental spiritual properties and laws) to the soul's life Then and There. Thus these two lives differ with her rather in extent and intensity than in kind. I think that, taken just thus, and with this degree of explicitness, this group of convictions is practically unique. We shall study and illustrate this particular cycle of doctrine in full detail. But it is indeed time now to move on to a more systematic and general account of her teaching.

CHAPTER VI

CATHERINE'S DOCTRINE

THE attentive reader will no doubt have perceived how great have been the difficulties at every step taken, in the previous chapters, towards a critically clear and solid account of Catherine's life. He will, then, be quite prepared again to find difficulties, though largely of another order, in the task that now lies before us,—the attempt at a clear and authentic reproduction of her teaching.

1. *Four difficulties in the utilization of the sources.*

The sources are, it is true, at first sight, fairly abundant,—altogether about one hundred of the two hundred and eighty pages of the *Vita ed Opere.* But four peculiarities render their utilization a matter of much labour and caution.

For one thing, they certainly include no piece written by herself, and probably none written down before 1497. Catherine's memory can no doubt be trusted, and with it much of the oldest version of those great turning-points of her inner life which occurred long before that date, and which she thus, later on, communicated to her closest friends. Yet hers was a mind so constantly absorbed in present experiences and in self-renewal as to be all but incapable of dwelling, in any detail, upon her past experiences or judgments.

And next, within and for this her "doctrinal," her "widowed" and "suffering" period, we are perplexed by the total absence of logical or indeed of any other order in the presentation of these discourses and contemplations. We have either to do without any order at all, or to construct one for ourselves,—which latter course of itself already means a reconstruction of the book.

But far more delicate is the task presented by the third peculiarity,—the fact, demonstrated both by the internal evidence and analysis and by the external evidence of the MSS., of the bewildering variety of forms and connections in which one and the same doctrine, sometimes an obviously unique saying, will appear. Six, ten, even twelve or more variants are the rule, not the exception. And I am specially thinking, under this heading, of *contemporary variations*—that is, variations of form that can reasonably be attributed either to her own initiative at work under differences of mood and of starting-point; or to the variety of the minds who apprehended and registered this teaching at the time of its delivery; or to both influences simultaneously. In the first case we get, say, her doctrine as to man's weakness and sinfulness, in two moments of depression and consolation respectively, registered by one and the same disciple,—say, by Vernazza or by Marabotto. In the second case we get some such two sayings as rendered the one by Vernazza and the other by Marabotto severally. And in the third case we get both the depressed and the joyful original sayings, as they have passed through the minds of both Vernazza and Marabotto.

And lastly, we get another class, *redactional variations*; and these it is often as difficult as it is always necessary to detect. I mean the parallel passages, evolved in course of time by her attendants or constructed by successive redactors, more or less on the model of, but also with more or less of departure from, her own authentic sayings: blurred, partly inaccurate echoes, as it were, of her own living voice. These will generally have grown up but semi-consciously, or at least have arisen from simple motives of her glorification or of literary filling-in or rounding-off. For we must not forget the forty years which passed between her death and the *Vita*.

I am thinking here too of the *theological limitations and corrections*, introduced into the older text in the form of definite counter statements, which we shall find to be especially visible in the *Trattato*; and of the, doubtless preponderatingly unconscious, modifications of an analogous kind which determined the composition of the *Dialogo*, and are traceable throughout that whole long work. For here again we have to remember how, between her living teachings, so ardent and familiar, so entirely from within and unoccupied with the world without, which reached up to 1510, and even the earliest MS. redaction of the contemporary jotting down of those sayings which we still possess,—that of 1547,—runs the great upheaval of the Protestant Reformation, beginning with Luther's Theses of 1517. Catherine's own fellow God-parent to Vernazza's eldest daughter, the Doctor of Laws Tommaso Moro, had meanwhile become a Calvinist (1537), and then had returned to the Catholic Obedience in 1539, first under this his God-daughter's influence. No wonder that what, under the magic suasion of her living personality, in times as yet free from the controversial and polemical tone and temper, and through and for her friends already won to and comprehensive of her teachings, had been certainly registered, and perhaps for a while transmitted, in its own pristine, winningly daring and unguarded, form, would, with her old friends dead and a new generation grown up and engrossed in attack and defence of various points of the Catholic position, be felt to require tempering and safeguarding, rewriting and controversial utilization. Hence we get three successive steps. The theological counter-statements in the *Trattato*, probably introduced between 1524 and 1530. The controversial point and utilization attempted in the very title of the *Vita* which promises, " una utile e cattolica dimostrazione e declarazione del Purgatorio," and in the Preface, which declares the book to contain things " specially necessary in these our turbulent times," touches which go back probably to 1536, perhaps even to 1524–1530. And the composition of the entire *Dialogo*, hardly begun before 1546.[1]

It is interesting to note how neither for the approbation of the first edition in 1551 (by the Dominican Fra Geronimo of Genoa), nor during the examination by the Congregation of Rites and the final approbation by Pope Innocent XI, 1677–1683, was any additional correction required or (as far as I know) even suggested. The latter point is particularly striking; for we have thus the very Pope who, in 1687, condemned Molinos' teaching, solemnly approving Catherine's doctrine four years before, after a seven years' examination.

2. *Catholic principles concerning the teaching of Canonized Saints.*

Now it is a well-known principle of Catholic theology, propounded with classic clearness and finality by Pope Benedict XIV, in his standard work *On the Beatification and Canonization of the Servants of God*, that such an approbation of their sayings or writings binds neither the Church nor her individual members to more than the two points, which are alone necessary with respect to the possibility and advisability of the future Beatification and Canonization of the author of the sayings or writings in question. The Church and her

[1] These and similar matters will be found carefully studied in the Appendix.

individual members are thus bound only to hold the perfect orthodoxy and Catholic piety of such a saintly writer's intentions, and again the (at least interpretative) orthodoxy of these his writings, and their spiritual usefulness for some class or classes of souls. But every kind and degree of respectful but deliberate criticism and of dissent is allowed, if only based upon solid reasons and combined with a full acceptance of those two points.

And indeed it is plain that heroism in action and suffering is one thing, and philosophical genius, training and balance is another; and even, again, that deep and delicate experiences on the one hand, and the power of their at all adequate analysis and psychological description, are two things and not one. Still, it is also evident that in proportion as a Saint's doctrine is, professedly or at all events actually, based upon or occasioned by his own experience will it rightly demand a double measure of respectful study. For, in such a case, we can be sure not only of the saintly intentions of the teacher, but also of his doctrines being an attempt, however partially successful, at expressing certain first-hand, unusually deep and vivid experiences of the religious life, experiences which, taken in their substance and totality, constitute the very essence of his sanctity.

Now this is manifestly the case with Catherine. And hence she furnishes us with those very conditions of fruitful discussion, so difficult to get in religious matters. On the one hand, her undoubted sanctity and the personal experimental basis of her doctrine gain for her our willingness, indeed determination, first of all patiently to study and assimilate and sympathetically to reconstruct her special spiritual world from her own inner starting- and growing-point, and all this, at this first stage, without any question as to the completeness or final truth and value of the intellectual analyses and syntheses of these experiences elaborated by herself. And, on the other hand, we find ourselves driven, at our second stage, to examine the literary sources and philosophical and theological implications of this her teaching—if pressed; and to make various respectful, but firm and free distinctions and reservations, with regard to these sources and affinities. For here, in these her analyses and syntheses, a special quality of her own temperament is ever at work, and causes her to express, as best she can, a concentration of a whole host of the strongest feelings concerning just the one point of that one moment's experience, with a momentary complete exclusion of all the rest. Here, again, her dependence, for her categories of thought and general language, imagery and scheme of doctrine, upon Fra Jacopone da Todi and upon the Pseudo-Dionysian writings is readily traceable,—the latter, compositions which we have only now succeeded in tracing, with final completeness and precision, to their predominantly Neo-Platonist source. And here we cannot but carefully consider the impressive series of Church pronouncements which have occurred since Catherine spoke and her devotees wrote. All these matters shall be carefully studied in the second volume.

3. *The fortunate circumstances of Catherine's teaching.*

It was a rare combination of numerous special circumstances,—several of them unique,—which rendered possible the retention and indeed solemn approbation of the difficult and daring doctrine and language not rarely to be met with in the *Vita* (in contradistinction to the so-called *Opere*).

For one thing, the originator, the subject-matter and form, above all the school of her doctrine, all combined to secure it the largest possible amount of liberty and sympathetic interpretation. The originator, the soul from whom the doctrine had proceeded, had not herself written down one word of it; but she had spoken it all, warm from the very heart which loved and lived it: the cold and chilling process of deliberate composition had but little part in the whole matter, and that part was not hers. The subject-matter was not primarily dogmatic, and not at all political or legal; it dealt not with theological systems or visible institutions, but with the experiences of single souls: and at all times a great latitude has been allowed in such subject-matter, when proceeding, as here, from some saintly soul as the direct expression of its own experience. The form was not systematic, and aimed at no completeness; all was incidentally addressed to a few devoted disciples, in short monologues or homely conversations. The title *Trattato*, given later on to the collection of her detached thoughts on Purgatory, is thoroughly misleading; her whole spirit and form were precisely not that of the treatise. And the school to which she so obviously belonged was probably her chief protection. Indeed, the doctrinally difficult passages are, in a true sense, the least personal of her sayings: we shall find all their doctrinal presuppositions,—as to the immobility, indefectibility, deification of the soul; the possession by the soul of God without means or measure; and the like,—to go back to the writings which, purporting to be by the Areopagite Dionysius, the Convert of St. Paul, but composed in reality between A.D. 490 and 520, so profoundly influenced all mystical thinking and expression for one thousand years and more of the Church's life.

And again, the period during which the corpus of Catherine's doctrine was in process of formation was specially favourable to such large toleration. For if she died in 1510, ten years before the outbreak of the Protestant Reformation, with its inevitable reaction, her chief chronicler, the saintly philanthropist Vernazza, did not die, a true martyr to that boundless love of souls which he had derived from his great-souled friend, till 1524; and her Confessor Marabotto did not depart till 1528. Thus her doctrine would remain substantially untouched and treasured up till some twenty years after her death, and thirteen years after the great upheaval.

We have already noted that (somewhere about 1528, and on to 1551) her teaching *did* meet with some opposition. It will be interesting to study (in the Appendix) how the objection arose and was met. Here it must suffice to point out that, whereas Catherine's Purgatorial doctrine is free from any final difficulty on the score of orthodoxy, it is just that doctrine which was hedged in and glossed before all the rest; and that whereas other parts of her teaching, in the form given in the *Vita*, are full of such difficulty, they remain strangely unmodified to this very day. It will appear that the *Dialogo* was in part composed to perform an office towards those doctrinal chapters of the *Vita*, similar to that performed by the glosses in and towards the text of the *Trattato*. Hence the glosses of the *Trattato* will have, in the following collection of sayings, to be removed from my text, and the statements of the *Dialogo* will have to be ignored in my text. These glosses or re-statements shall be considered later on, whenever these additions or substitutions are of sufficient interest.

4. *The theological order of presentation adopted.*

Then again, it is far from easy to settle upon the right order and method of presentation. The more closely we study the chapters in question the more do we find that the strange discomfort and disgust, engendered by any lengthy reading of them, proceeds from the curiously infelicitous manner of their composition. These chapters, in so much as they supply genuine materials, consist of a large number of detached, usually short sayings, of every kind of tone and mood, occasion and mental and emotional context and connotation, and yet all concerning but a few great central realities and truths. These sayings in themselves do not at all represent links in a chain of reasoning; they are numberless variations on some few fundamental experiences of the soul. Hence they require to be given in loose co-ordination, or in free grouping around some great central truth; somewhat like what is done, with such marked felicity, for Our Lord's own sayings, which also are occasional and freely various, by the oldest of our Gospels, St. Mark. "And," "and again," can be used to join these recurrent similitudes, aspirations, emotional reflections; not "because" nor "therefore," still less "firstly," "secondly," "thirdly," as the Redactors have been so fond of doing. Hence the reader in the *Vita* feels himself in a constant state of abortive motion, and is ever being promised a precision which usually ends in vagueness.

Let us then group these parallel sayings around some few great central truths or dispositions. But what is the order of these great centres to be? Here again a difficulty occurs, and this time from the very nature of the doctrine concerned. For the special characteristic of her teaching, a teaching so largely derived both from her own intensely unitive character and (through the Dionysian writings, Proclus and Plotinus) from Plato himself, is precisely an infinitely close-woven organization, in which part vibrates in sympathy with part, in which each point carries with it the whole, and in which each one idea and feeling passes, as it were, right through, and colours and is coloured by all the rest. It would be almost as satisfactory to turn the impassioned discourse of Diotima in the Symposium into a series of numbered propositions, as here to try and detach any one feeling or idea from out of the living network of its fellows, in and through which it is, and gets and gives, its special self.

The historical order (*i. e.* the order in which, successively, each doctrine grew up and dominated her thinking) is, alas! as we have seen, out of the question.—The psychological order (*i. e.* the order in which the doctrines, such as we have them, would reproduce themselves within her own mind during that last period of her life, 1496–1510) would doubtless throw most light upon the special characteristics of her spirituality, and upon the hidden springs of her doctrine. But it is far too difficult, and must remain too largely hypothetical, to be even distantly aimed at here and now : some such attempt will be made in a later chapter, with the help of the materials first collected and grouped here in a more conventional way.—The theological order (*i. e.* the order in which these doctrines would appear if made to find their places in an ordinary manual of scholastic theology) is the one that I shall here endeavour to follow as far as possible. For thus I can start with a scheme so thoroughly familiar as nowhere itself to require any explanation; and I can thus help to bring out, from the first, the characteristic peculiarities of the mystical position generally, and of her own variety of it in particular.

I will then take here, successively, her teachings as to God in Himself, and Creation; Sin, Redemption, and Sanctification; and the Last Things. But I do so quite loosely, for I shall try nowhere to break off any bridge that she herself has thrown across from one subject to the other, and shall be satisfied if I can succeed in grouping her doctrine even approximately within those three divisions, according to the predominance of this or that point of her teaching. And, for this, I shall not shrink from a repeated utilization of one and the same text, when (as happens so often) it looks in many directions, and becomes fully clear only in juxtaposition with various parts of her teaching.

5. *Literary sources of Catherine's teaching.*

We have evidence, as regards literary influences, that Catherine fed her mind on three books or sets of books: the Bible, the Pseudo-Dionysian Treatises, and the *Lode* of Jacopone da Todi.

The allusions to passages of Scripture are continual, but mostly of a swiftly passing, combinatory, allegorizing kind. Direct quotations and attempts at penetrating the objective sense of particular passages are rare, for most of the direct quotations are clearly due to her historians, not to herself; yet they exist and put her direct study of Scripture beyond all doubt. Her favourite Bible books were evidently Isaiah and the Psalms, and the Pauline and Johannine writings. Some touches (remarkably few for a mystic) are derived from the Canticle of Canticles, and many less obvious ones from the Synoptic Gospels; but there are no certain traces, I think, of any other Old Testament books, nor, in the Pauline group, of any passage from the Pastoral Epistles.

The evidence for her direct knowledge and use of Dionysius is, it is true, but circumstantial. But the following three facts seem, conjoined as they are in her case, sufficient to prove this knowledge. (i) We have already seen how her cousin and close spiritual friend, Suor Tommasa, wrote a devotional treatise on Denys the Areopagite, presumably before Catherine's death, since Tommasa was sixty-two years of age in that year 1510; it would be strange indeed if Catherine did not, even if but from this quarter, get to know some of the Dionysian writings, perhaps even whilst they could still only be read in MS. form. (ii) Marsilio Ficino published in Florence, in 1492, his Latin translation of the *Mystical Theology* and of the *Divine Names,* with a copious commentary; and the book, dedicated to Giovanni de' Medici, Archbishop of Florence and future Pope Leo X, found its way at once to all the larger centres of life, learning and devotion in Italy. Thus Catherine lived still eighteen years after the publication of this, the first printed, edition of any part of Denys (original or translation); even if she did not know these writings before, it seems again very unlikely that she would not get to know them now. (iii) There are, it is true, no direct quotations from Denys, nor does his name appear in the *Vita ed Opere,* except in that account of Suor Tommasa. But numerous sayings of Catherine bear, as we shall see later on, so striking a resemblance to passages in those two books of Denys, that it is difficult to explain them by merely mediate infiltration; and that those sayings ultimately, as to their literary occasion, go back to the Areopagite, is incontestable. I quote Denys from the usually careful translation of the Rev. John Parker : *The Works of Dionysius the Areopagite,* Pt. I, London, Oxford, 1897, with certain corrections of my own.

The proofs for her knowledge and love of Jacopone da Todi's Italian " Praises " is, on the other hand, direct and explicit. The *Vita,* p. 37, makes her say : " Listen to what Fra Jacopone says in one of his *Lode,* beginning : ' O amor di povertade,' " and then gives her word-for-word commentary on verse 23 of this his *Loda* LVIII. Words from this same verse are again quoted by her on p. 62; the opening line of this *Loda* is put into her mouth on p. 83; and another verse, the sixth, is quoted by her, as by the Blessed Jacopone, on p. 92. I have been able to find many other sayings of hers which are hardly less directly suggested by the great Umbrian than these. Here, again, she probably knew the *Lode* in MS. form before they appeared in print in 1490; but will in any case have known them in this their printed form. I have carefully studied in this, the first printed edition (Florence: Bonaccorsi), all the *Lode* bearing upon subjects and doctrines dear to Catherine. They are twenty in all, from among the hundred and two numbers of that collection.[1]

9. *The Psycho-physical Occasions or Reflexes of her Doctrine. Her special reaction under and use of her literary sources shall be examined in a later chapter.*

The psycho-physical occasions or reflexes of her various teachings, as far as the interconnection can be traced with probability, shall also be studied in the second volume. But already here I would have the reader clearly to understand, that nowhere are such psycho-physical conditions and experiences to be considered the *causes* of her doctrine, as though the lower produced the higher, and as though the spiritual were the automatic resultant and necessary precipitate of certain accidental, involuntary conditions in time and space. For everywhere such conditions can only, at best, be accepted as the occasions or materials, for the development or illustration of some spiritual doctrine, or, contrariwise, as the psychic effects and embodiments of some vividly realized invisible truth or law; whilst this spiritual teaching itself is derived from far other and deeper causes,—the interaction of her own experience and free spiritual powers and of God's grace, and the conflict of these with her own passions, the whole helped or hindered by the world without.

I. God as Creative Love. The Creature's True and False Self; True and False Love.

1. *Creation, an overflow of Goodness.*

First, then, we will take the sayings about Creation, and the original, substantially indelible character of all created beings. "I saw a sight which satisfied me much. I was shown the Living Fountain of Goodness, which was (as yet) all within Itself alone, without any kind of participation. And next I saw that It began to participate with the creature, and made that very beautiful company of Angels, in order that this company might enjoy His ineffable glory, without asking

[1] *Lode* III, XIII, XXXIII, XXXV, XLV, LVIII (*a*) and (*b*), LXXIII, LXXV (*a*) and (*b*), LXXVII, LXXIX, LXXXI, LXXXIII, LXXXV, LXXXVIII, LXXXIX, LXXXX, LXXXXVII, LXXXXIX.

any other return from the Angels than that they should recognize themselves to be creatures created by His supreme goodness. . . . And hence, when they were clothed in sin by their pride and disobedience, God suddenly subtracted from them the participation of His goodness. . . . Yet He did not subtract it all, for in that case they would have remained still more malign than they (actually) are, and they would have had Hell infinite in pain, as they now have it in time." . . . "When we ourselves shall depart from this life,—supposing we are in mortal sin,—then God would subtract from us His goodness and would leave us in our own selves, yet not altogether, since He wills that in every place there should be found His goodness accompanied by His justice. And if any creature could be found that did not participate in His goodness, that creature would be as malignant as God is good."[1]

2. *Natural conformity between God and all rational creatures.*

From her sayings as to Creation and Pure Love, Creation's cause, we come to those as to the Natural Conformity between God and Rational Creatures; His constant care for the human soul; and the consequent law of imitative love incumbent upon us. "I see God to have so great a conformity with the rational creature, that if the Devil himself could but rid himself of those garments of sin, in that instant God would unite Himself to him, and would make him into that which he, the Devil, attempted to achieve by his own power. So too with regard to man: lift off sin from his shoulders, and then allow the good God to act,—God who seems to have nothing else to do than to unite Himself to us."—"It appears to me, indeed, that God has no other business than myself."—"If man could but see the care which God takes of the soul, he would be struck with stupor within himself."—"I see that God stands all ready to give us all the aids necessary for our salvation, and that He attends to our actions solely for our good. And, on the contrary, I see man occupied with things that are opposed to his true self and of no value. And at the time of death God will say to him: 'What was there that I could do for thee, O man, that I did not do?' And man himself will then see this clearly."—"When God created man,

[1] *Vita*, pp. 32*c*, 33*a*, *b*. I must refer the reader, once for all, to the Appendix, for the explanation of the methods used in the selection and the emendation of the texts presented in this chapter.

He did not put Himself in motion for any other reason than His pure love alone. And hence, in the same way as Love Itself, for the welfare of the loved soul, does not fail in the accomplishment of anything, whatever may be the advantage or disadvantage that may accrue from thence to the Lover, so also must the love of the loved soul return to the Lover, with those same forms and modes with which it came from Him. And then such love as this, which has no regard for aught but love itself, cannot be in fear of anything." [1]

3. *Relations between Love, God; love of our true self; and false self-love.*

We can take next her teachings as to the relations between the love of God, love of our true self, and false self-love. "The love of God is our true self-love, the love characteristic of and directed to our true selves, since these selves of ours were created by and for Love Itself. The love, on the other hand, of every other thing deserves to be called self-hatred, since it deprives us of our true self-love, which is God. Hence 'Him love, Who loveth thee,' that is, Love, God; and 'him leave who doth not love thee,' that is, all other things, from God downwards." [2]

"God so loves the soul, and is so ready to give it His graces, that, when He is impeded by some sin, then men say: 'Thou hast offended God,' that is, thou hast driven away God from thee, Who, with so much love, was desiring to do thee good. And men say this, although it is really man who then suffers the damage and who offends his own true self. But because God loves us more than we love our own selves, and gives more care to our true utility than we do ourselves, therefore does He get designated as the one who is offended. And, indeed, if God could be the recipient of suffering, it would be when, by sin, He is driven away by and from us." "This corrupt expression: 'Thou hast offended God.'" "Thou couldst discover, (O soul,) that God is continually willing whatsoever our true selves are wishing; He is ever aiming at nothing but at our own true spiritual advantage." [3]

Hence happiness and joy, different from all mere pleasure, ever accompany this reconquest of our true self-love and this our re-donation of it to its true source. "Man was created for the end of possessing happiness. And having deviated from this his end, he has formed for himself a false, selfish

[1] *Vita*, pp. 29*c*; 91*c*; 30*b*; 55*c*, 56*a*; 61*a*. [2] *Ibid.* p. 76*c*.
[3] *Ibid.* pp. 101*b*; 101*a*; 79*c*.

self, which in all things struggles against the soul's true happiness." "This divine love is our proper and true love." "Man can truly know, by continual experience, that the love of God is our repose, our joy, and our life; and that (false) self-love is but constant weariness, sadness, and a (living) death of our true selves, both in this world and in the next." "All sufferings, displeasures, and pains are caused by attachment to the false self. And although adversities many a time seem to us to be unreasonable, because of certain considerations which we believe to be true and indeed quite evident; yet the fact remains that it is our own imperfection which is preventing us from seeing the truth, and this it is which causes us to feel pains, suffering, and displeasure." "O Love! if others feel an obligation to observe Thy commandments, I, on my part, freely will to have them all ten, because they are all delightful and full of love. . . . This is a point which is understandable only to him who himself experiences it; for in truth the divine precepts, although they are contrary to our sensuality, are nevertheless according to our own spirit which, of its very nature, is ever longing to be free from all bodily sensations, so as to be able to unite itself to God through love."[1]

4. *The true self instinctively hungers after God.*

The sayings as to the close correspondence between the true self and God lead us on easily to those about the true self's instinctive recognition of God, and its hunger for the possession, for the *interiorization* of God. "If I were to see the whole court of heaven all robed in one and the same manner, so that there would be no apparent difference between God and the Angels; even then the love which I have in my heart would recognize God, in the same manner as does a dog his master. Love knows how, without means, to discover its End and ultimate Repose." "If a consecrated Host were to be given me together with other non-consecrated ones I would, I think, distinguish It by the taste, as wine from water."—"When she saw the Sacrament upon the Altar in the hand of the priest, she would exclaim within herself (as it were, addressing the priest): 'O swiftly, swiftly speed It to the heart, since It is the heart's own food.'"[2]

5. *Superiority of interior graces over exterior manifestations. No good within herself apart from divine grace.*

Catherine's hunger for the interiorization of all the external

[1] *Vita*, pp. 36*b*; 80*c*, 81*a*; 74*b*. [2] *Ibid.* pp. 9*b*; *ibid.*; 8*c*.

helps of religion, even, indeed specially, of the Holy Eucharist Itself, leads us on to her statements as to the superiority of interior graces and dispositions over all exterior manifestations and sensible consolations, and as to the nature of acts produced by the false self or apart from the grace of God. "If we would esteem the operations of God" as they truly deserve, "we should attend more to things interior than to exterior ones. . . . The true light makes me see and understand that we must not look to what proceedeth from God to aid us in some special necessity and for His glory, but that we must look solely to the pure love with which He performs His work with regard to us. When the soul perceives how direct and pure are the operations of love, and that this love is not intent upon any benefit that we could confer upon It, then indeed the soul also desires, in its turn, to love with a pure love, and from the motive of the divine love alone." [1]

"This not-eating of mine is an operation of God, independent of my will, hence I can in nowise glory in it; nor should we marvel at it, for to Him such an operation is as nothing."—And to her Confessor Don Marabotto she says reprovingly, when he too wanted to smell the strange, strengthening odour which she smelt on his hand: "Such things as God alone can give" (*i. e.* states and conditions in the production of which the soul does not co-operate) "He does not give to him who seeks them; indeed, He gives them only on occasion of great need, and in order that we may draw great spiritual profit from them." [2]

"If I do anything that is evil, I do it myself alone, nor can I attribute the blame to the Devil or to any other creature but only to my own self-will, sensuality, and other such malign movements. And if all the Angels were to declare that there was any good in me, I would refuse to believe them, because I clearly recognize how that all good is in God alone, and that in me, without divine grace, there is nothing but deficiency."—"I would not that, to my separate self, even one single meritorious act should ever be attributed, even though I could at the same time be certified of no more falling from henceforward and of being saved; because such an attribution would be to me as though a Hell." "Rather would I remain in danger of eternal damnation than

[1] *Vita*, p. 11*c*. [2] *Ibid*. p. 11*b*.

be saved by, and see, such an act of the separate self." "The one sole thing in myself in which I glory is that I see in myself nothing in which I can glory."

"Yet it is necessary that we should labour and exercise ourselves, since divine grace does not give life nor render pleasing unto God except that which the soul has worked; and without work on our part grace refuses to save."—"We must never wish anything other than what happens from moment to moment, all the while, however, exercising ourselves in goodness. And to refuse to exercise oneself in goodness, and to insist upon simply awaiting what God might send, would be simply to tempt God."[1]

6. *God is Pure Love, Grace, Peace, and the Soul's True Self.*

The passages concerning the close relations between man's pure love and instinct for God, and Pure Love, God Himself, easily lead us on to those in which Pure Love, Peace, Grace, the True Self, indeed the Essence of all things are positively identified with God. "Hearing herself called" to any office of her state or of charity, "she would," even though apparently absorbed in ecstatic prayer, "arise at once, and go without any contention of mind. And she acted thus, because she fled all self-seeking as though it were the devil. And she felt at such times as though she could best express her feelings by means of the glorious Apostle's words: 'Who then shall separate me from the love of *God?*' and the remainder of the great passage. And she would say: 'I seem to see how that immovable mind of St. Paul extended much further than he was able to express in words; since Pure Love is God Himself; who then shall be able to separate Him from Himself?'" Elsewhere and on other occasions we find her declaring: "Love is God Himself"; "Pure Love is no other than God"; "the Divine love is the very God, infused by His own immense Goodness into our hearts."[2]

She also declares that: "Grace is God"; that "Peace is God,"—"wouldest thou that I show thee what thing God is? Peace,—that peace which no man finds, who departs from Him." And further still: "The proper centre of every one is God Himself"; "my *Me* is God, nor do I recognize any other *Me*, except my God Himself"; "my Being is God, not by simple participation but by a true transformation of my Being." "God is my Being, my *Me*, my Strength, my Beati-

[1] *Vita*, pp. 22*b*; 25*c*; 26*b*.—105*c*.—25*c*, 26*a*, 80*b*.
[2] *Ibid.* pp. 15*c*, 16*a*.—9*b*; 53*b*; 67*c*.

tude, my Good, my Delight." Indeed "the glorious God is the whole essence of things both visible and invisible."[1]

All these startling statements are but so many expressions of one of the most characteristic moods and attitudes of her mind and heart. For in her vehemence of love and thirst for unification she would exclaim: "I will have nothing to do with a love that would be *for* God or *in* God; this is a love which pure love cannot bear: since pure love is (simply) God Himself"; "I cannot abide to see that word *for*, and that word *in*, since they denote to my mind a something that can stand between God and myself."[2]

All this doctrine would be summed up by her in certain favourite expressions. "She was wont often to pronounce these words: 'Sweetness of God, Fulness of God, Goodness of God, Purity of God'"; and at a later time "she had continually on her lips the term '(clear) Fulness'" (Self-adequation, *nettezza*).[3]

II. Sin, Purification, Illumination.

1. *The soul's continuous imperfection. Self-love and Pure Love, their contradictory characters. Every man capable of Pure Love.*

Catherine's extreme sensitiveness is no doubt a chief cause of the peculiar form in which she experiences her sinfulness and faults and their actually slow purification, as expressed

[1] *Vita*, pp. 26*b*; 50*b*.—36*b*; 36*c*.—36*b*.

[2] *Ibid*. p. 48*b*.

[3] *Ibid*. pp. 23*c*; 27*a*. The fact of "Nettezza" remaining at last her only term for the perfection of God shows plainly how comprehensive, definite, and characteristic must have been the meaning she attached to the word. The history of this conception no doubt begins with Plato's "the Same"; and this, through Plotinus and Victorinus Afer's Latin translation of him, reappears as "the Idipsum, the Self-Same," as one of the names of God in St. Augustine; a term which in Dionysius (largely based as he is upon Plotinus's disciple Proclus) occurs continually, and can there be still everywhere translated as "Identity" or "Self-Identity" (so also Parker). But with Catherine the idea seems to have been approximated more to that of Purity, although I take it that, with her, "Purità" means the absence of all excess (of anything foreign to the true nature of God's or the soul's essence); and "Nettezza," the absence of all defect, in the shape of any failure fully to actualize all the possibilities of this same true nature. I have had to resign myself, as the least inadequate suggestions of the rich meaning of "Nettezza" and "Netto," to alternating between the sadly general terms "fulness" and "full," and the pedantic-sounding "self-adequation," with here and there "clear fulness."

in those of her sayings which refer to the growth of love and to the continuous imperfections of the soul. "From the time when I began to love Him, that love has never failed me"; "indeed it has continually grown unto its consummation in the depths of my heart." This growth takes place only step by step; and is in reality never complete, and never without certain imperfections. "The creature is incapable of knowing anything but what God gives it from day to day. If it could know (beforehand) the successive degrees that God intends to give it, it would never be quieted." "When from time to time I would advert to the matter, it seemed to me that my love was complete; but later, as time went on and as my sight grew clearer, I became aware that I had had many imperfections. . . . I did not recognize them at first, because God-Love was determined to achieve the whole only little by little, for the sake of preserving my physical life, and so as to keep my behaviour tolerable for those with whom I lived. For otherwise, with such other insight, so many excessive acts would ensue, as to make one insupportable to oneself and to others." "Every day I feel that the motes are being removed, which this Pure Love casts out (*cava fuori*). Man cannot see these imperfections; indeed, since, if he saw these motes, he could not bear the sight, God ever lets him see the work he has achieved, as though no imperfections remained in it. But all the time God does not cease from continuing to remove them." "From time to time, I feel that many instincts are being consumed within me, which before had appeared to be good and perfect; but when once they have been consumed, I understand that they were bad and imperfect. . . . These things are clearly visible in the mirror of truth, that is of Pure Love, where everything is seen crooked which before appeared straight." [1]

And yet the slowness of this purification is, in the last resort, caused, if not by the incomplete purity of her love, at least by the deep-rootedness and evasive character of the wrong self-love that has to be extirpated. "This our self-will is so subtle and so deeply rooted within our own selves, and defends itself with so many reasons, that, when we cannot manage to carry it out in one way, we carry it out in another. We do our own wills under many covers (pretexts),—of charity, of necessity, of justice, of perfection." But pure love

[1] *Vita*, pp. 15*b*, 22*c*; 23*b*; 49*a*; 69*a*.

sees through all these covers: "I saw this love to have so open and so pure an eye, its sight to be so subtle and its seeing so far-reaching, that I stood astounded." "True love wills to stand naked, without any kind of cover, in heaven and on earth, since it has not anything shameful to conceal." And "this naked love ever sees the truth; whilst self-love can neither see it nor believe in it." "Pure love loves God without any *for* (any further motive)." [1]

And man, every man, is capable of this pure love and of the truth which such love sees: "I see every one to be capable of my tender Love." "Truth being, by its very nature, communicable to all, cannot be the exclusive property of any one." [2]

2. *Exactingness of Pure Love.*

The next group of sayings deals with the purity of Love, and the severity with which this purity progressively eliminates all selfish motives and attachments, whilst itself becoming increasingly its own exceeding great beatitude. "Pure Love loves God without why or wherefore (*perchè*)." "Since Love took over the care of everything, I have not taken care of anything, nor have I been able to work with my intellect, memory and will, any more than if I had never had them. Indeed every day I feel myself more occupied in Him, and with greater fire." "I had given the keys of the house to Love, with ample permission to do all that was necessary, and determined to have no consideration for soul or body, but to see that, of all that the law of pure love required, there should not be wanting the slightest particle (*minimo chè*). And I stood so occupied in contemplating this work of Love, that if He had cast me, body and soul, into hell, hell itself would have appeared to me all love and consolation." [3]

Yet the corresponding, increasing constraint of the false self is most real. "I find myself every day more restricted, as if a man were (first) confined within the walls of a city, then in a house with an ample garden, then in a house without a garden, then in a hall, then in a room, then in an ante-room, then in the cellar of the house with but little light, then in a prison without any light at all; and then his hands were tied and his feet were in the stocks, and then his eyes were bandaged, and then he would not be given anything to eat, and then no one would be able to speak to him; and then, to

[1] *Vita*, pp. 31*c*, 32*a*.—66*a*, 66*b*, 87*c*, 107*a*.
[2] *Ibid.* pp. 75*b*, 66*b*.
[3] *Ibid.* pp. 87*c*, 106*a*, 106*c*.

crown all, every hope were taken from him of issuing thence as long as life lasted. Nor would any other comfort remain to such an one, than the knowledge that it was God who was doing all this, through love with great mercy; an insight which would give him great contentment. And yet this contentment does not diminish the pain or the oppression." [1]

3. *Blinding effect of all self-seeking. The gradual transformation of the soul.*

There is next a group of sayings as to the immense, blinding and staining effect of even slight self-seekings, and as to how God gradually transforms the soul. "God and Sin, however slight, cannot live peaceably side by side (*stare insieme*). Since some little thing that you may have in your eye does not let you see the sun, we can make a comparison between God and the sun, and then between intellectual vision and that of the bodily eye." "After considering things as they truly are, I find myself constrained to live without self." "Since the time when God has given the light to the soul, it can no more desire to operate by means of that part of itself which is ever staining all things and rendering turbid the clear water of God's grace. The soul then offers and remits itself entirely to Him, so that it can no more operate except to the degree and in the manner willed by tender Love Himself; and henceforth it does not produce works except such as are pure, full and sincere; and these are the works that please God-Love." [2]

"I will not name myself either for good or for evil, lest this my (selfish) part should esteem itself to be something." "Being determined to join myself unto God, I am in every manner bound to be the enemy of His enemies; and since I find nothing that is more His enemy than is self in me, I am constrained to hate this part of me more than any other thing; indeed, because of the contrariety that subsists between it and the spirit, I am determined to separate it from all the goods of this world and of the next, and to esteem it no more than if it were not." [3]

"When she saw others bewailing their evil inclinations, and forcing themselves greatly to resist them, and yet the more they struggled to produce a remedy for their defects, the more did they commit them, she would say to them: 'You have subjects for lamentation (*tu hai li guai*) and bewail

[1] *Vita*, p. 114*a*. [2] *Ibid.* 28*c*, 29*a*, 29*b*. [3] *Ibid.* pp. 42*b*, 43*c*.

them, and I too would be having and bewailing them; you do evil and bewail it, and I should be doing and be bewailing it as you do, if God Almighty were not holding me. You cannot defend yourself, nor can I defend myself. Hence it is necessary that we renounce the care of ourselves unto Him, Who can defend this our true self; and He will then do that which we cannot do." [1]

"As to the annihilating of man, which has to be made in God, she spoke thus: 'Take a bread, and eat it. When you have eaten it, its substance goes to nourish the body, and the rest is eliminated, because nature cannot use it at all, and indeed, if nature were to retain it, the body would die. Now, if that bread were to say to you: "Why dost thou remove me from my being? if I could, I would defend myself to conserve myself, an action natural to every creature": you would answer: "Bread, thy being was ordained for a support for my body, a body which is of more worth than thou; and hence thou oughtest to be more contented with thine end than with thy being. Live for thine end, and thou wilt not care about thy being, but thou wilt exclaim (to the body): 'Swiftly, swiftly draw me forth from my being, and put me within the operation of that end of mine, for which I was created.' . . . The soul, by the operation of God, eliminates from the body all the superfluities and evil habits acquired by sin, and retains within itself the purified body, which body thenceforth performs its operations by means of these purified senses. . . . And, when the soul has consumed all the evil inclinations of the body, God consumes all the imperfections of the soul." [2]

In each particular instance, the process was wont to be as follows: "When her selfish part saw itself tracked down by Love, Catherine would turn to Him and say: 'Even though it pain sense, content Thy will: despoil me of this spoil and clothe me with Love full, pure and sincere.'" [3]

4. *Suddenness and gratuitousness of God's light; the obstacles to its operation.*

We get next a set of apparently contrary sayings, concerning the suddenness of God's illumination; how the degree of this light cannot be determined by man; and what are, nevertheless, the conditions under which it will not act. In some cases, "the soul is made to know in an instant, by means of a new light above itself, all that God desires it to know,

[1] *Vita*, p. 42*a*. [2] *Ibid.* pp. 83*c*, 84*a*, 86*b*, 87*a*.
[3] *Ibid.* p. 108*b*.

and this with so much certainty that it would be impossible to make the soul believe otherwise. Nor is more shown it than is necessary for leading it to greater perfection." "This light is not sought by man, but God gives it unto man when He chooses; neither does the man himself know how he knows the thing that he is made to know. And if perchance man were determined to seek to know a little further than he has been made to know, he would achieve nothing, but would remain like unto a stone, without any capacity." [1]

And she would pray: "Be Thou my understanding; (thus) shall I know that which it may please Thee that I should know. Nor will I henceforth weary myself with seeking; but I will abide in peace with Thine understanding, which shall wholly occupy my mind." "If a man would see properly in spiritual matters, let him pluck out the eyes of his own presumption." "He who gazes too much upon the sun's orb, makes himself blind; even thus, I think, does pride blind many, who want to know too much." "When God finds a soul that does not move, He operates within it in His own manner, and puts His hand to greater things. He takes from this soul the key of His treasures which He had given to it, so that it might be able to enjoy them; and gives to this same soul the care of His presence, which entirely absorbs it." [2]

5. *God's way of winning souls and raising them towards pure love. The fruits of full trust.*

The next group can be made up of passages descriptive of the dealings adopted by God with a view to first winning souls as He finds them, and then raising them above mercenary hope or slavish fear; and of the childlike fearlessness inspired by perfect trust in God. As to the winning them, she says: "The selfishness of man is so contrary to God and rebellious against Him, that God Himself cannot induce the soul to do His will, except by certain stratagems (*lusinghe*): promising it things greater than those left, and giving it, even in this life, a certain consoling relish (*gusto*). And this He does, because He perceives the soul to love things visible so much, that it would never leave one, unless it saw four." [3]

And, as to God's raising of the soul, she propounds the deep doctrine, which only apparently contradicts the divine method just enunciated, as to the necessary dimness of the soul's light with regard to the intrinsic consequences of its

[1] *Vita*, pp. 81*b*. [2] *Ibid.* pp. 81*c*; 82*a*; 103*b*. [3] *Ibid.* p. 31*b*.

own acts, a dimness necessary, because alone truly purificatory, for the time that runs between its conversion, when, since it is still weak, it requires to see, and its condition of relative purity, when, since it is now strong, it can safely be again allowed to see. "If a man were to see that which, in return for his good deeds, he will have in the life to come, he would cease to occupy himself with anything but heavenly things. But God, desiring that faith should have its merit, and that man should not do good from the motive of selfishness, gives him that knowledge little by little, though always sufficiently for the degree of faith of which the man is then capable. And God ends by leading him to so great a light as to things that are above, that faith seems to have no further place.—On the other hand, if man knew that which hereafter he will have to suffer if he die in the miserable state of sin, I feel sure that, for fear of it, he would let himself be killed rather than commit one single sin. But God, unwilling as He is that man should avoid doing evil from the motive of fear, does not allow him to see so terrifying a spectacle, although He shows it in part to such souls as are so clothed and occupied by His pure love that fear can no more enter in." [1]

And as to the full trust of pure love, we have the following: "God let her hear interiorly: 'I do not want thee henceforward to turn thine eyes except towards Love; and here I would have thee stay and not to move, whatever happens to thee or to others, within or without'; 'he who trusts in Me, should not doubt about himself.'" [2]

And this Love gives of itself so fully to those that give themselves fully to It, that when asked by such souls to impetrate some grace for them she would say: "I see this tender Love to be so courteously attentive to these my spiritual children, that I cannot ask of It anything for them, but can only present them before His face." In other cases, as in those of beginnners when sick and dying, she would be "drawn to pray for" a soul, and would "impetrate" some special "grace for it." "Lord, give me this soul," she would at times pray aloud, "I beg Thee to give it me, for indeed Thou canst do so." And "when she was drawn to pray for something, she would be told in her mind: 'Command, for love is free to do so.'" [3]

[1] *Vita*, p. 54*b*, *c*. [2] *Ibid.* pp. 52*c*, 53*a*.
[3] *Ibid.* pp. 95*c*, 125*a*; 122 *c*; 76*a*.

III. The Three Categories and the Two Ways.

The next set of sayings so eminently constitutes the aggregation, if not the system, of categories under and with which Catherine habitually sees her types and pictures, and thinks and feels her experiences of divine things, that it will require careful discrimination and grouping.

1. *The Three Categories: "In," Concentration; "Out," Liberation; "Over," Elevation.*

There is, first, the great category of *in, within, down into;* that is, recollection, concentration. "The love which I have within my heart." "Since I began to love It, never again has that Love diminished; indeed It has ever grown to Its own fulness, within my innermost heart." Hence she would say to those who dwelt in admiration of her psycho-physical peculiarities: "If you but had experience (*sapeste*) of another thing which I feel within me!" And again, "If we would esteem (aright) the operations of God, we must attend more to interior than to exterior things." And, with regard to the Holy Eucharist, she would whisper, when seeing at Mass the Priest about to communicate: "O swiftly, swiftly speed It down to the heart, since it is the heart's own food"; and she would declare, with regard to her own Communion: "In the same instant in which I had It in my mouth, I felt It in my heart."[1]

There is, next, the category of *out, outside, outwards;* that is, liberation, ecstasy. "The soul which came out from God pure and full has a natural instinct to return to God as full and pure (as it came)." "The soul finds itself bound to a body entirely contrary to its own nature, and hence expects with desire its separation from the body." "God grants the grace, to some persons, of making their bodies into a Purgatory (already) in this world." "When God has led the soul on to its last stage (*passo*), the soul is so full of desire to depart from the body to unite itself with God, that its body appears to it a Purgatory, keeping it far apart from its (true) object." "The prison, in which I seem to be, is the world; the chain is the body"; "to noble (*gentili*) souls, death is the end of an obscure prison; to the remainder, it is a trouble,—to such, that is, as have fixed all their care upon what is but so much dung (*fango*)." And,

[1] *Vita*, pp. 9*b*, 15*b*; 11*b*, 8*c*; 155*a*.

whilst strenuously mortifying the body, she would answer its resistances, as though so many audible complainings, and say: "If the body is dying, well, let it die; if the body cannot bear the load, well, leave the body in the lurch (O soul)." [1]

And all this imprisonment is felt as equivalent to being outside of the soul's true home. "I seem to myself to be in this world like those who are out of their home, and who have left all their friends and relations, and who find themselves in a foreign land; and who, having accomplished the business on which they came, stand ready to depart and to return home,—home, where they ever are with heart and mind, having indeed so ardent a love of their country (*patria*), that one day spent in getting there would appear to them to last a year." [2]

And this feeling of outsideness, seen here with regard to the relations of the soul to the body and to the world, we find again with regard to sanctity and the soul. In this latter case also the greater is felt to be (as it were) entrapped, and contained only very partially within the lesser; and as though this greater could and did exist, in its full reality, only outside of the lesser. "I can no more say 'blessed' to any saint, taken in himself, because I feel it to be an inappropriate (*deforme*) word"; "I see how all the sanctity which the saints have, is outside of them and all in God." Indeed she sums this up in the saying: "I see that anything perfect is entirely outside of the creature; and that a thing is entirely imperfect, when the creature can at all contain it." Hence "the Blessed possess (*hanno*) blessedness, and yet they do not possess it. For they possess it, only in so far as they are annihilated in their own selves and are clothed with God; and they do not possess it, in so far as they remain (*si trovano*) in their particular (*proprio*) being, so as to be able to say: '*I* am blessed.'" [3]

There is, in the third place, the category of *over, above, upwards*; that is elevation, sublimation. We will begin with cases where it is conjoined with the previous categories, and will move on into more and more pure aboveness. "I am so placed and submerged in His immense love, that I seem as though in the sea entirely under water, and could on no side touch, see, or feel anything but water." And "if the sea were the food of love, there would exist no man nor woman that

[1] *Vita*, pp. 136*b*, 183*c*; 19*b*, 107*b*. [2] *Ibid*. p. 113*c*.
[3] *Ibid*. pp. 24*b*, 23*b*, 24*b*.

would not go and drown himself (*affogasse*) in it; and he who was dwelling far from this sea, would engage in nothing else but in walking to get to it and to immerse himself within it." [1] The soul here feels the water on every side of it, yet evidently chiefly above it, for it has had to plunge in, to get *under* the water.

"Listen to what Fra Jacopone says in one of his Lauds, which begins, 'O Love of Poverty.' He says: 'That which appears to thee (to be), is not; so high above is that which *is*. (True) elevation (*superbia*) is in heaven; earthy lowness (*umiltà*) leads to the soul's own destruction.' He says then: 'That which appears to thee,' that is, all things visible, 'are not,' and have not true being in them: 'so high' and great 'is He who *is*,' that is, God, in whom is all true being. 'Elevation is in heaven,' that is, true loftiness and greatness is in heaven and not on earth; 'earthy lowness leads to the soul's own destruction,' that is, affection placed in these created things, which are low and vile, since they have not in them true being, produces this result."—"I feel," she says in explanation of what and how she knows, "a first thing above the intellect; and above this thing I feel another one and a greater; and above this other one, another, still more great; and so up and up does one thing go above the other, each thing ever greater (than its predecessors), that I conclude it to be impossible to express even a spark (scintilla) as to It" (the highest and greatest of the whole series, God). Here it is interesting still to trace the influence of the same passage of Jacopone (again referred to in this place by the *Vita*), and to see why she introduced "greatness" alongside of "loftiness" into her previous paraphrase.[2]

Now this vivid impression of a strong upward movement, combined with the feeling of being in and under something, gives the following image, used by her during her last illness: "I can no longer manage to live on in this life, because I feel as though I were in it like cork under water." And this "above," unlike to "outside," is accompanied by the image, not of clothing but of nakedness; the clothes are left below. "This vehement love said to her, on one occasion: 'What art thou thinking of doing? I want thee all for myself. I want to strip thee naked, naked. The higher up thou shalt go, however great a perfection thou mayest have, the higher will

[1] *Vita*, pp. 59*c*, 76*c*, 77*a*. [2] *Ibid*. p. 37*a*.

I ever stand above thee, to ruin all thy perfections ' "—this, of course, inasmuch as she is still imperfect and falls short of the higher and higher perfections to which her soul is being led.[1]

And as to man's faculties, she says: " As the intellect reaches higher (*supera*) than speech, so does love reach higher than intellect." And again, as a universal law: " When pure love speaks, it ever speaks above nature; and all the things which it does and thinks and feels are always above nature." [2]

2. *The Two Ways : the Negative Way, God's Transcendence ; the Positive Way, God's Immanence.*

Now these three categories of within and inward, outside and outward, above and upward position and movement, can lead, and do actually lead in Catherine's case, to two separate lines of thought and feeling. And these lines are each too much a necessary logical conclusion from the constant working of these categories, and they are each again far too much, and even apart from these categories, expressive of two rival but complementary experiences, for either of them to be able to suppress or even modify the other. Each has its turn in the rich, free play of Catherine's life. I will take the negative line first, and then the positive, so as to finish up with affirmation, which will thus, as in her actual experience and practice, be all the deeper and more substantial, because it has passed, and is ever repassing, through a process of limitation and purification.

First, then, if grace and God are only within, *and* only without, *and* only above, she will and does experience contradiction and paradox in all attempts at explaining reality; she will thus find things to be obscure instead of clear; and she will end by affirming the unutterableness, the unthinkableness of God, indeed of all reality. " I see without eyes, I understand without understanding, I feel without feeling, and I taste without taste." " When the creature is purified, it sees the True; and such a sight is not a sight." " The sight of how it is God " who sends the soul its purifying trials " gives the soul a great contentment; and yet this contentment does not diminish the pain." Still, " pure love cannot suffer; nor can it understand what is meant by pain or torment." " The sun, which at first seemed so clear to me, now seems obscure; what used to seem sweet to me, now

[1] *Vita*, pp. 94*a*; 109*b*.

[2] *Ibid*. pp. 87*c*, 53*b*.

seems bitter: because all beauties and all sweetness that have an admixture of the creature are corrupt and spoilt." "As to Love, only this can we understand about It, that It is incomprehensible to the mind." "So long as a person can still talk of things divine, and can relish, understand, remember and desire them, he has not yet come to port." For indeed "all that can be said about God is not God, but only certain smallest fragments which fall from (His) table." [1]

And yet those experiences of God's presence as, apparently, in a special manner within us, and without us, and above us, also lead, by means of another connection of ideas, to another, to a positive result. For those experiences can lead us to dwell, not upon the difference of the "places," but upon the apparent fact that He is in a "place" of some sort, in space somewhere, the exact point of which is still to find; and, by thus bringing home to the mind this underlying paradox of the whole position, they can help to make the soul shrink away from this false clarity, and to fall back upon the deep, dim, true view of God as existing, for our apprehension, in certain states of soul alone, states which have all along been symbolized for us by these different "places" and "positions." And thus what before was a paradox and mystery *qua* space, because at the same time within and without, and because not found by the soul "within" unless through getting "without" itself, becomes now a paradox and mystery *qua* state, because the soul at one and the same time attains to its own happiness and loses it, indeed attains happiness only through deliberately sacrificing it. And we thus come to the great central secret of all life and love, revealed to us in its fulness in the divine paradox of our Lord's life and teaching.

God, then, first seems to be in a place, indeed to be a place. "I see all good to be in one only place, that is God." "The spirit can find no place except God, for its repose." [2]

If God be in a place, we cannot well conceive of Him as other than outside of and above the soul, which itself, even God being in a place, will be in a place also. "God has created the soul pure and full, with a certain God-ward instinct which brings happiness in its train (*istinto beatifico*)." And "the nearer the soul approaches" (is joined, *si accosta*) "to God, the more does the instinct attain to its perfection." Here the instinct within pushes the soul "onwards, outwards, up-

[1] *Vita*, pp. 23*c*, 24*a*, 23*c*, 22*c*, 61*c*; 77*b*.
[2] *Ibid*. pp. 34*c*; 175*c*.

wards." And the nearer the soul gets to God in front, outside and above of it, the happier it becomes: because, the more it satisfies this its instinct, the less it suffers from the distance from God, and the more does it enjoy His proximity.[1]

This approach is next conceived of as increasingly conveying a knowledge to the soul of God's desire for union with it; but such an approach can only be effected by means of much fight against and through the intervening ranks of the common enemies of the two friends; and, as we have already seen, chief amongst these enemies is the soul's false self. "The nearer man approaches to (*si accosta*) God, the more he knows that God desires to unite Himself with us." "Being determined to approach God, I am constrained to be the enemy of His enemies." [2]

And then, that "place" in which God was pictured as being, is found to be a state, a disposition of the soul. Now as long as the dominant tendency was to think God with clearness, and hence to picture Him as in space, that same tendency would, naturally enough, represent this place He was in as outside and above the soul. For if He is in space, He is pictured as extended, and hence as stretching further than, and outside of, the soul, which itself also is conceived as spatially extended; and if He is in a particular part of space, that part can only, for a geocentric apprehension of the world, be thought of as the upper part of space. But in proportion as the picture of physical extension and position gives way to its prompting cause, and the latter is expressed, as far as possible, unpictorially and less clearly, but more simply as what it is, viz. a spiritual intention and disposition, she is still driven indeed, in order to retain some clearness of speech, to continue to speak as of a place and of a spatial movement, but she has now no longer three categories but only one, viz. *within* and *inwards*. For a physical quantity can be and move in different places and directions in space; but a spiritual quality can only be experienced within the substance of the spirit. "God created the soul pure and full, with a certain beatific instinct of Himself" (*i. e.* of His actual presence). And hence, "in proportion as it (again) approaches to the conditions of its original creation, this beatific instinct ever increasingly discovers itself and grows stronger and stronger." [3]

[1] *Vita*, pp. 171*c*, 172*a*. [2] *Ibid.* pp. 30*a*, 29*c*; 43*c*.
[3] *Ibid.* pp. 171*c*, 172*a*.

And God being thus not without, nor indeed in space at all, she can love Him everywhere: indeed the *what* she is now constitutes the *where* she is; in a camp she can love God as dearly as in a convent, and heaven itself is already within her soul, so that only a change in the soul's dispositions could constitute hell for that soul, even in hell itself. "O Love," she exclaims, after the scene with the Friar, who had attempted to prove to her that his state of life rendered him more free and apt to love God, "who then shall impede me from loving Thee? Even if I were in the midst of a camp of soldiers, I could not be impeded from loving Thee." She had, during the interview, explained her meaning: "If I believed that your religious habit would give me but one additional glimpse" (spark, scintilla) "of love, I would without doubt take it from you by force, were I not allowed to have it otherwise. That you may be meriting more than myself, I readily concede, I am not seeking after that; let those things be yours. But that I cannot love Him as much as you can do, you will never succeed in making me even understand." "I stood so occupied in seeing the work of Love (within my soul), that if it had thrown me with soul and body into hell, hell itself would have appeared to me to be nothing but love and consolation." And, on another occasion, she says to her disciples: "If, of that which this heart of mine is feeling, one drop were to fall into hell, hell itself would become all life eternal"; and she accepts with jubilation this interpretation of her words, on the part of one of them (no doubt Vernazza): "Hell exists in every place where there is rebellion against Love, God; but Life Eternal, in every place where there is union with that same Love, God." [1]

And she now cannot but pray to possess all this love,—love being now pictured as a food, as a light, or as water, bringing life to the soul. "O tender Love, if I thought that but one glimpse of Thee were to be wanting to me, truly and indeed I could not live." "Love, I want Thee, the whole of Thee." "Never can love grow quiet, until it has arrived at its ultimate perfection." And, in gaining all God, she gains all other things besides: "O my God, all mine, everything is mine; because all that belongs to God seems all to belong to me." [2]

But if she loves all God, she can, on the other hand, love

[1] *Vita*, pp. 52*a*; 51*b*; 106*c*.—94*c*; 95*b*.
[2] *Ibid.* pp. 23*a*; 24*a*.

only Him : how, then, is she to manage to love her neighbour? "Thou commandest me to love my neighbour," she complains to her Love, "and yet I cannot love anything but Thee, nor can I admit anything else and mix it up with Thee. How, then, shall I act?" And she received the interior answer: "He who loves me, loves all that I love."[1]

But soon her love, as generous as it is strong, becomes uneasy as to its usual consequences,—the consolations, purely spiritual or predominantly psychical or even more or less physical, which come in its train. And even though she is made to understand that at least the first are necessarily bound up with love, in exact proportion to its generosity, she is determined, to the last, to love for love itself, and not for love's consequences, battling thus to keep her spirituality free from the slightest, subtlest self-seeking. "This soul said to its Love: 'Can it really be, O tender Love, that Thou art destined never to be loved without consolation or the hope of some advantage in heaven or on earth" accruing to Thy lover? "And she received the answer, that such an union could not exist without a great peace and contentment of the soul." And yet she continues to affirm: "Conscience, in its purity, cannot bear anything but God alone; of all the rest, it cannot suffer the least trifle."[2]

And she practises and illustrates this doctrine in detail. "One day, after Communion, God gave her so great a consolation that she remained in ecstasy. When she had returned to her usual state, she prayed: 'O Love, I do not wish to follow Thee for the sake of these delights, but solely from the motive of true love.'" On another similar occasion she prays: "I do not want that which proceedeth from Thee; I want Thyself alone, O tender Love." And again, "on one occasion, after Communion, there came to her so much odour and so much sweetness that she seemed to herself to be in Paradise. But instantly she turned towards her Lord and said: 'O Love, art Thou perhaps intending to draw me to Thee by means of these sensible consolations (*sapori*)? I want them not; I want nothing except Thee alone.'"[3]

[1] *Vita*, p. 60*c*. [2] *Ibid.* pp. 76*b*; 27*a*. [3] *Ibid.* pp. 8*a*; 15*b*.—8*c*.

IV. The Other Worlds.

We have now gone through Catherine's contemplations and conceptions as regards the soul's relations with its true Life and Love, here and now, on this side the veil. We have, in conclusion, to try and reproduce and illustrate her teaching as to these relations on the other side of death.

1. *No absolute break in the spirit's life at the body's death.*

Now here especially is it necessary ever to bear in mind her own presupposition, which runs throughout and sustains all her doctrine. For she is sure, beyond ever even raising a question concerning the point, that her soul and God, her two great realities and experiences, remain substantially the same behind the veil as before it, and hence that the most fundamental and universal of the soul's experiences *here* can safely be trusted to obtain *there* also. Hence, too, only such points in the Beyond are dwelt on as she can thus experimentally forecast; but these few points are, on the other hand, developed with an extraordinary vividness and fearless, rich variety of illustration. And it is abundantly clear that this assumption of the essential unity and continuity of the soul's life here and hereafter, is itself already a doctrine, and a most important one. We will then take it as such, and begin with it as the first of her teachings as to the Beyond.

" This holy soul," says the highly authoritative prologue to the *Trattato,* in close conformity with her constant assumptions and declarations, " finding herself, whilst still in the flesh, placed in the Purgatory of God's burning love,—a love which consumed (burnt, *abbrucciava*) and purified her from whatever she had to purify, in order that, on passing out of this life, she might enter at once into the immediate presence (*cospetto*) of her tender Love, God: understood, by means of this furnace of love, how the souls of the faithful abide in the place of Purgatory, to purge themselves of every stain of sin that, in this life, had been left unpurged. And as she, placed in the loving Purgatory of the divine fire, abode united to the divine Love, and content with all that It wrought within her, so she understood it to be with the souls in Purgatory." [1]

2. *Hell.*

The details of her doctrine as to the Beyond we can group

[1] *Vita* (*Trattato*), p. 169*b*. See also *Vita*, Preface, p. viii*b*; and p. 144*b*.

under three heads: the unique, momentary experience and solitary, instantaneous act of the soul, at its passing hence and beginning its purgation there; the particular dispositions, joys and sufferings of the soul during the process of purification as well as the cause and manner of the cessation of that process; and (generally treated by her as a simple contrast to this her direct and favourite purgatorial contemplation) the particular dispositions, sufferings, and alleviations of lost souls. Since her teachings on the last-named subject are more of an incidental character, I shall take them first, and make them serve, as they do with her, as a foil to her doctrine of the Intermediate State: whilst her conception of Heaven, already indicated throughout her descriptions of Pure Love, is too much of a universal implication, and too little a special department of her teaching, to be capable of presentation here.

As to the cause of Hell, she says: "It is the will's opposition to the Will of God which causes guilt; and as long as this evil will continues, so long does the guilt continue. For those, then, who have departed this life with an evil will there is no remission of the guilt, neither can there be, because there can be no more change of will." "In passing out of this life, the soul is established for good or evil, according to its deliberate purpose at the time; as it is written, 'where I shall find thee,' that is, at the hour of death, with a will either determined to sin, or sorry for sin and penitent, 'there will I judge thee.'" Or, in a more characteristic form: "There is no doubt that our spirit was created to love and enjoy: and it is this that it goes seeking in all things. But it never finds satiety in things of time; and yet it goes on hoping, on and on, to be at last able to find it. And this experience it is that helps me to understand what kind of a thing is Hell. For I see that man, by love, makes himself one single thing with God, and finds there every good; and, on the other hand, that when he is bereft of love, he remains full of as many woes as are the blessings he would have been capable of, had he not been so mad." [1]

And yet, and this is her own beautiful contribution to the traditional doctrine on this terrible and mysterious subject, neither are the sufferings of the lost infinite in amount, nor is their will entirely malign. And both these alleviations

[1] *Vita*, pp. 172*c*; 38*b*, *c*; 39*a*.

evidently exist from the first: I can find no trace anywhere in her teaching of a gradual mitigation of either the punishment or the guilt. Indeed, although she always teaches the mitigation of the suffering, it is only occasionally that she teaches the persistence of some moral good. Thus her ordinary teaching is: "Those who are found, at the moment of death, with a will determined to sin, have with them an infinite degree of guilt, and the punishment is without end"; "the sweet goodness of God sheds the rays of His mercy even into Hell: since He might most justly have given to the souls there a far greater punishment than He has." "At death God exercises His justice, yet not without mercy; since even in Hell the soul does not suffer as much as it deserves." But occasionally she goes further afield, and insists on the presence there, not only of some mercy in the punishment, but also of some good in the will. "When we shall have departed from this life in a state of sin, God will withdraw from us His goodness, and will leave us to ourselves, and yet not altogether: since He wills that in every place His goodness shall be found and not His justice alone. And if a creature could be found that did not, to some degree, participate in the divine goodness, that creature would be, one might say, as malignant as God is good." [1] There can be no doubt, as we shall see further on, that this latter is her full doctrine and is alone entirely consistent with her general principles.

Certain details of her Hell doctrine which appear in immediate contrast to, or in harmony with, some special points of her Purgatorial teaching, had better appear in connection with the latter.

3. *Purgatory; the initial experience and act.*

Let us now take, in all but complete contrast to this doctrine as to Hell, what she has to say about Purgatory. And here we have first to deal with the initial experience and act, both of them unique and momentary, of the soul destined for Purgatory. As to that experience, only one description has been preserved for us. "Once, and once only, do the souls (that are still liable to, and capable of, purgation) perceive the cause of (their) Purgatory that they bear within themselves,—namely in passing out of this life: then, but never again after that: otherwise self would come in (*vi saria una proprietà*)." [2]

[1] *Vita*, pp. 173*a*.—173*b*.—33*b*.
[2] *Ibid.* (*Trattato*), pp. 170*b* (169*c*).

And this unique and momentary experience is straightway followed by as unique and momentary an act, free and full, on the part of the experiencing soul. Catherine has described this act in every kind of mood, and from the various points of view, already drawn out by us, of her doctrine, so that we have here again a most impressive and vivid summing-up and pictorial representation of all her central teaching.

"The soul thus seeing" (its own imperfection) and, "that it cannot, because of the impediment" (of this imperfection) "attain (*accostarsi*) to its end, which is God; and that the impediment cannot be removed (*levato*) from it, except by means of Purgatory, swiftly and of its own accord (*volontieri*) casts itself into it."[1] Here we have the continuation of the outward movement: the soul is here absolutely impeded in that, now immensely swift, movement, and is brought to a dead stop, as though by something hard on the soul's own surface, which acts as a barrier between itself and God; it is offered the chance of escaping from this intolerable suffering into the lesser one of dissolving this hard obstacle in the ocean of the purifying fire: and straightway plunges into the latter.

"If the soul could find another Purgatory above the actual one, it would, so as more rapidly to remove from itself so important (*tanto*) an impediment, instantly cast itself into it, because of the impetuosity of that love which exists between God and the soul and tends to conform the soul to God."[2] Here we have an extension of the same picturing, interesting because the addition of an upwards to the outwards introduces a conflict between the image (which evidently, for the soul's plunge, requires Purgatory to lie beneath the soul), and the doctrine (which, taking Purgatory as the means between earth and heaven, cannot, if any spatial picturing be retained at all, but place Heaven at the top of the picture, and Purgatory higher up than the soul which is coming thither from earth). The deep plunge has become a high jump.

"I see the divine essence to be of such purity, that the soul which should have within it the least mote (*minimo chè*) of imperfection, would rather cast itself into a thousand hells, than find itself with that imperfection in the presence of God."[3] Here the sense of touch, of hardness, of a barrier which is checking motion, has given way to the sense of sight, of stain, of a painful contrast to an all-pure Presence; and the whole

[1] *Vita* (*T.*), p. 175*b*. [2] *Ibid.* (*T.*), p. 177*b*.
[3] *Ibid.* (*T.*), p. 176*a*; *Vita* proper, p. 78*c*.

picture is now devoid of motion. We thus have a transition to the immanental picturing, with its inward movement or look.

"The soul which, when separated from the body, does not find itself in that cleanness (*nettezza*) in which it was created, seeing in itself the stain, and that this stain cannot be purged out except by means of Purgatory, swiftly and of its own accord casts itself in; and if it did not find this ordination apt to purge that stain, in that very moment there would be spontaneously generated (*si generebbe*) within itself a Hell worse than Purgatory." [1] Here we have again reached her immanental conception, where the soul's concern is with conditions within itself, and where its joys and sorrows are within. Its trouble is, in this case, the sense of contrast, between its own original, still potential, indeed still actual though now only far down, hidden and buried, true self, and its active, obvious, superficial, false self. In so far as there is any movement before the plunge, it is an inward, introspective one; the soul as a whole is, for that previous moment, not conceived as in motion, but a movement of her self-observing part or power takes place within her from the surface to the centre; and only then, after her rapid journey from this her surface-being to those her fundamental ineradicable requirements, and after the consequent intolerably painful contrast and conflict within herself, does she cast herself, with swift whole-heartedness, with all she is and has, into the purifying place and state.

And, in full harmony with this immanental conception, the greater suffering which would arise did she abide with this sight of herself and yet without any moral change is described as springing up spontaneously within herself. "The soul, seeing Purgatory to have been ordained for the very purpose of purging away its stains, casts itself in, and seems to find a great compassion (on the part of God) in being allowed (able) to do so." This appears to be only a variety of the immanental view just given.[2]

4. *Purgatory: the subsequent process.*

We have finally to give her doctrine as to the particular dispositions, joys, and sufferings of the soul during the process of its purgation, and as to the cause and manner of the cessation of that process.

[1] *Vita* (*T.*), p. 175*a* (see p. 169*b*). [2] *Ibid.* (*T.*), p. 176*a*.

As to the dispositions, they are generally the same as those which impelled the soul to put itself in this place or condition. Only whereas then, during that initial moment, they took the form of a single act, an initiation of a new condition, now they assume the shape of a continuous state. Then the will freely tied itself; now it gladly though painfully abides by its decision and its consequences. Then the will found the relief and distraction of full, epoch-making action; now it has but to will and work out the consequences involved in that generous, all-inclusive self-determination. The range and nature of this, its continuous, action will thus be largely the very reverse of those of that momentary act. "The souls that are in Purgatory are incapable of choosing otherwise than to be in that place, nor can they any more turn their regard (*si voltare*) towards themselves, and say: 'I have committed such and such sins, for which I deserve to tarry here'; nor can they say, 'Would that I had not done them, that now I might go to Paradise'; nor yet say, '*That* soul is going out before me'; nor, 'I shall go out before *him*.' They are so completely satisfied that He should be doing all that pleases Him, and in the way it pleases Him, that they are incapable of thinking of themselves." Indeed they are unable even to see themselves, at least directly, for "these souls do not see anything, even themselves in themselves or by means of themselves, but they (only) see themselves in God." Indeed we have already seen that to do, or to be able to do, otherwise, would now "let self come in (*sarebbe una proprieta*)." [1]

And the joys and sufferings, and the original, earthly cause of the latter, are described as follows. "The souls in Purgatory have their (active) will conformed in all things to the will of God; and hence they remain there, content as far as regards their will." "As far as their will is concerned, these souls cannot find the pain to be pain, so completely are they satisfied with the ordinance of God, so entirely is their (active) will one with it in pure charity. On the other hand, they suffer a torment so extreme, that no tongue could describe it, no intellect could form the least idea of it, if God had not made it known by special grace." And indeed she says: "I shall cease to marvel at finding that Purgatory is" in its way as "horrible as Hell. For the one is made for punishing, the other for purging: hence both are made for sin,

[1] *Vita* (*T.*), pp. 169*c*, 170*a*.—182*b*.

sin which itself is so horrible and which requires that its punishment and purgation should be conformable to its own horribleness." For in Purgatory too there still exist certain remains of imperfect, sinful habits in the will. "The souls in Purgatory think much more of the opposition which they discover in themselves to the will of God," than they do of their pain. And yet, being here with their actual will fully at one with God's purifying action (an action directed against these remains of passive opposition), "I do not believe it would be possible to find any joy comparable to that of a soul in Purgatory, except the joy of the Blessed in Paradise." [1]

Now the sufferings of the soul are represented either as found by it, under the form of an obstacle to itself, whilst in motion to attain to God, a motion which in some passages is outward, in others inward; or as coming to it, whilst spatially at rest. Only in the latter case is there a further attempt at pictorially elucidating the nature of the obstacle and the cessation of the suffering. It is fairly clear that it is the latter set of passages which most fully suits her general teaching and even imagery. For, as to the imagery: after that one movement in which the soul determines its own place, we want it to abide there, without any further motion. And, as to doctrine: more and more as the soul's history is unfolded, should God's action within it appear as dominating and informing the soul's action towards God, and should change of disposition supplant change of place.

First, then, let us take the clearer but less final conception, and see the soul in movement, in a struggle for outward motion. "Because the souls that are in Purgatory have an impediment between God and themselves, and because the instinct which draws the soul on to its ultimate end is unable as yet to attain to its fulfilment (*perfezione*), an extreme fire springs up from thence (within them), a fire similar to that of Hell." We have here an application and continuation of the transcendental imagery, so that the impediment is outside or on the surface of the soul, and God is outside and above this again: but the whole picture here, at least as regards the fire, is obscure and tentative.[2]

Or the soul is still conceived as in movement, but the motion is downwards from its own surface to its own centre, a centre where resides its Peace, God Himself. "When a

[1] *Vita* (*T.*), pp. 173*c*, 174*a*; 171*b*.—64*b*; 177*b*.—170*c*.
[2] *Ibid.* (*T.*), p. 172*b*.

soul approaches more and more to that state of original purity and innocence in which it had been created, the instinct of God, bringing happiness in its train (*istinto beatifico*), reveals itself and increases on and on, with such an impetuousness of fire that any obstacle seems intolerable." [1] Here we have the immanental picturing, the soul moving down, under the influence of its instinct for God, to ever fuller masses of this instinct present within the soul's own centre. But the extreme abstractness and confusion of the language, which mixes up motion, different depths of the soul, and various dispositions of spirit, and which represents the soul as capable of approaching a state which has ceased to exist, cast doubts on the authenticity of this passage. In both these sets where the soul is in motion, we hear only of an impediment in general and without further description; and, in both cases, the fire springs up because of this impediment, whereas, as we shall see, in the self-consistent form of her teaching the Fire, God, is always present: the impediment simply renders this Fire painful, and that is all.

And next we can take the soul as spatially stationary, and as in process of qualitative change. Here we get clear and detailed pictures, both of what is given to the soul and of what is taken away from it. The images of the positive gain constitute the beautiful sixth chapter of the *Trattato*. But its present elaborate text requires to be broken up into three or four variants of one and the same simile, which are probably all authentic. I give them separately.

"If in the whole world there existed but one loaf of bread to satisfy the hunger of every creature: in such a case, if the creature had not that one bread, it could not satisfy its hunger, and hence it would remain in intolerable pain." [2] Note how, so far, the nature of the possession of the bread is not specified, it is simply "had"; and how the pain seems to remain stationary.

"Man having by nature an instinct to eat: if he does not eat, his hunger increases continually, since his instinct to eat never fails him." [3] Here all is clearer: man now takes the place of the creature in general; the possession is specified as an eating; the pain is a hunger; and this hunger is an ever-increasing one.

"If in all the world there were but one loaf of bread, and if

[1] *Vita* (*T.*), p. 172*a*. [2] *Ibid.* (*T.*), p. 174*b*. [3] *Ibid.*

only through seeing it could the creature be satisfied: the nearer that creature were to approach it (without seeing it and yet knowing that only the said bread could satisfy it), the more ardently would its natural desire for the bread be aroused within it (*si accenderebbe*),—that bread in which all its contentment is centred (*consiste*)." [1] Here the image for the nature of the appropriation has been shifted from the least noble of the senses, taste and touch, to the noblest, sight: there is still a longing, but it is a longing to see, to exercise and satiate fully the intellectual faculties. And yet the satiety is evidently conceived not as extending to these faculties alone, but as including the whole soul and spirit, since bread would otherwise cease to be the symbol here, and would have been replaced by light. Note too the subtle complication introduced by the presentation, in addition to the idea of an increase of hunger owing to lapse of time, of the suggestion that the increase is caused by a change in the spatial relations between the hungering creature and its food, and by an ever-increasing approach of that creature to this food.

"And if the soul were certain of never seeing the bread, at that moment it would have within it a perfect Hell, and become like the damned, who are cut off from all hope of ever seeing God, the true Bread. The souls in Purgatory, on the other hand, hope to see that Bread, and to satiate themselves to the full therewith; whence they suffer hunger as great as will be the degree to which they will (eventually) satiate themselves with the true Bread, God, our Love." [2] Here it is noticeable how the specific troubles of Hell and Purgatory are directly described, whereas the corresponding joys of Heaven are only incidentally indicated; and how the full sight is not preceded by a partial sight, but simply by a longing for this full sight, so that, if we were to press the application of this image, the soul in Purgatory would not see God at all. And yet, as we have seen above, souls there see, though not their particular sins, yet their general sinful habits; for what are the "impediment," the "imperfection," the "stain," which they go on feeling and seeing, but these habits? And they see themselves, though not in themselves, yet in God. But, if so, do they not see God?

The answer will doubtless be that, just as they do not see their sins any more in their specific particularity, but only

[1] *Vita (T.)*, p. 174*b*. [2] *Ibid.*

feel in themselves a dull, dead remainder of opposition and imperfection, so also they do not, after the initial moment of action and till quite the end of their suffering, see God clearly, —as clearly as they do when the process is at an end. During one instant at death they had seen (as in a picture) their sins and God, each in their own utterly contrasted concrete particularity; and this had been the specific cause of their piercing pain and swift plunge. And then came the period of comparative dimness and dulness, a sort of general sub-consciousness, when their habits of sin, and God, were felt rather than seen, the former as it were in front of the latter, but both more vaguely, and yet (and this was the unspeakable alleviation) now in a state of change and transformation. For the former, the blots and blurs, and the sense of contrariety are fading gradually out of the outlook and consciousness; and the latter, the light and life, the joy and harmony of the soul, and God, are looming clearer, nearer, and larger, on and on. And even this initial feeling, this general perception, this semi-sight and growing sight of God, is blissful beyond expression; for "every little glimpse that can be gained of God exceeds every pain and every joy that man can conceive without it."[1]

The imagery illustrative of what is taken from the soul, and how it is taken, is twofold, and follows in the one case a more transcendental, in the other case a more immanental, conception, although in each case God is represented as in motion, and the soul as abiding in the same place and simply changing its qualitative condition under the influence of that increasing approach of God and penetration by Him.

The illustration for the more transcendental view is taken from the sun's light and fire's heat and a covering. It is, as a matter of fact, made up of three sayings: one more vague and subtle, and two more clear and vivid, sayings. "The joy of a soul in Purgatory goes on increasing day by day, owing to the inflowing of God into the soul, an inflowing which increases in proportion as it consumes the impediment to its own inflowing."—God's action upon the imperfect soul is as the sun's action upon "a covered object. The object cannot respond to the rays of the sun which beat upon it (*reverberazione del sole*), not because the sun ceases to shine,—for it shines without intermission,—but because the covering inter-

[1] *Vita* (*T.*,) p. 182*b*.

venes (*opposizione*). Let the covering be consumed away, and again the object will be exposed to the sun and will answer to the rays in proportion as the work of destruction advances."—Now " Sin is the covering of the soul; and in Purgatory this covering is gradually consumed by the fire; and the more it is consumed, the more does the soul correspond and discover itself to the divine ray. And thus the one (the ray) increases, and the other (the sin) decreases, till the time (necessary for the completion of the process) is over." [1]

It is clear that we have here three parallel passages, each with its own characteristic image, all illustrative of an identical doctrine: namely, the persistent sameness of God's action, viewed in itself, and of the soul's reaction, in its essential, central laws, needs, and aspirations; and the accidental, superficial, intrinsically abnormal, inhibitory modification effected by sin in that action of God and in the corresponding reaction of the soul.—The first, dimmer and deeper saying speaks of an inflowing of God, with her usual combination of fire-and-water images. We seem here again to have the ocean of the divine fire, Itself pressing in upon the soul within It, yet here with pain and oppression, in so far as the soul resists or is unassimilated to It; and with peace and sustaining power, in so far as the soul opens out to, and is or becomes similar to, It. We hear only of an " impediment " in general, perhaps because the influx which beats against it is imaged as taking place from every side at once.—The second saying, the most vivid of the three, speaks of sunlight, and of how, whilst this sunlight itself remains one and the same, its effect differs upon one and the same object, according as that object is covered or uncovered. Here we get a " covering," since the shining is naturally imaged as coming from one side, from above, only. But here also it is the same sun which, at one time, does not profit, and, at another time, gives a renewed life to one and the same object; and it is clear, that either Catherine here abstracts altogether from the question as to what consumes the covering, or that she assumes that this consumption is effected by the sun itself.—The third saying is the least simple, and is indeed somewhat suspicious in its actual form. Yet here again we have certainly only one agent, in this case fire, which again, as in the case of the influx and of the sunlight, remains identical in itself, but

[1] *Vita* (*T.*), p. 170*c*.

varies in its effects, according as it does or does not meet with an obstacle. The ray here is a ray primarily of heat and not of light, but which is felt by the soul at first as painful, destructive flame, and at last as peaceful, life-giving warmth.

Now, amongst these three parallel sayings, it is that concerning the inflowing, which leads us gently on to the more immanental imagery—that of fire and dross. And this image is again given us in a number of closely parallel variants which now constitute one formally consecutive paragraph,—the third of Chapter X of the *Trattato*. "Gold, when once it has been (fully) purified, can be no further consumed by the action of fire, however great it be; since fire does not, strictly speaking, consume gold, but only the dross which the gold may chance to contain. So also with regard to the soul. God holds it so long in the furnace, until every imperfection is consumed away. And when it is (thus) purified, it becomes impassible; so that if, thus purified, it were to be kept in the fire, it would feel no pain; rather would such a fire be to it a fire of Divine Love, burning on without opposition, like the fire of life eternal." [1] Here the imperfection lies no more, as a covering, on the surface, nor does the purifying light or fire simply destroy that covering and then affect the bare surface; but the imperfection is mixed up with the soul, throughout the soul's entire depth, and the purification reaches correspondingly throughout the soul's entire substance. Yet, as with the covering and the covered object, so here with the dross and the impure gold, sin is conceived of as a substance alien to that of the soul. And, so far, God appears distinct from the fire: He applies it, as does the goldsmith his fire to the gold. But already there is an indication of some mysterious relation between the fire of Purgatory and that of Heaven. For if the very point of the description seems, at first sight, to be the miraculous character of the reward attached, more or less arbitrarily, to the soul's perfect purification, a character indicated by the fact that now not even fire can further hurt the soul, yet it remains certain that, the more perfect the soul, the more must it perceive and experience all things according to their real and intrinsic nature.

Another conclusion to the same simile is: "Even so does the divine fire act upon the soul: it consumes in the soul

[1] *Vita* (*T.*), p. 178*b*.

every imperfection. And, when the soul is thus purified, it abides all in God, without any foreign substance (*alcuna cosa*) within itself." [1] Here God and the fire are clearly one and the same. And the soul does not leave the fire, nor is any question raised as to what would happen were it to be put back into it; but the soul remains where it was, in the Fire, and the Fire remains what it was, God. Only the foreign substance has been burnt out of the soul, and hence the same Fire that pained it then, delights it now. Here too, however, God and the soul are two different substances; and indeed this Fire-and-Gold simile, strictly speaking, excludes any identification of them.

"The soul, when purified, abides entirely in God; its being is God." [2] Here we have the teaching as to the identity of her true self with God, which we have already found further back. But the soul's purification and union with God which there we found illustrated by the simile, so appropriate to this teaching, of the absorption of food into the living body, we find indicated here by the much less apt comparison of the transformation of gold by fire. For in this latter case, the gold remains a substance distinct from the fire, whereas the doctrine requires a simile such as a great pure fire expelling all impurity from a small, impure fire, and then itself continuing to live on, with this small fire absorbed into itself. But we shall see later on, why, besides the intrinsic difficulty of finding an at all appropriate simile for so metaphysical a doctrine, the imagery always becomes so ambiguous at this point. We shall show that a confluence of antagonistic doctrines, and some consequent hesitation in the very teaching itself, contribute to keep the images in this uncertain state. However, the possibly glossorial importation of this most authentic teaching of hers into this place and simile only helps to confirm the identity of the Fire with God, and the non-moving of the soul, throughout this group of texts. For the gold abides in the fire, as the soul abides in God; and the identification which is thus established of the painful with the joyous fire, and of both with God, is what will have suggested the introduction in this place of the further identification of the soul with God. And it is the continued abiding of the identical soul, a soul which has not moved spatially but has changed qualitatively, in the identical fire, God, which

[1] *Vita* (*T.*), p. 178*b*. [2] *Ibid.*

has helped to suggest the insertion in this place of the doctrine that the soul, in its true essence, is identical with God. God, in this final identification, would be the gold, the pure gold of the soul; and this pure gold itself would generate a fire for the consumption of all impurity, in proportion as such impurity gained ground within it. And, in proportion as this consumption takes place, does the fire sink, and leave nothing but the pure gold, the fire's cause, essence, and end. In any case, we have here one more most authentic and emphatic enforcement of the teaching that the place of Purgatory is really a state; that its painfulness is intrinsic; and that it is caused by the partial discord between spirit and Spirit, and is ended by the final complete concord between both.

CHAPTER VII

CATHERINE'S REMAINS AND CULTUS; THE FATE OF HER TWO PRIEST FRIENDS AND OF HER DOMESTICS; AND THE REMAINING HISTORY OF ETTORE VERNAZZA

INTRODUCTORY.

I NOW propose to attempt, in these last two biographical chapters, to give, first, an account of the fate of Catherine's remains and possessions; and, next, of the vicissitudes in the lives of her companions and immediate disciples. I shall thus range from the day of her death on Sunday, September 15, 1510, up to 1551, the year of the publication of the *Vita e Dottrina;* indeed, in the instance of one particular disciple, up to 1587. And I shall do so, partly as a further contribution to the knowledge of her own character and even of her doctrine, this finest expression of what she spiritually was, and of her influence upon her immediate little world; and partly in preparation for the study of the influence of this *entourage* back upon the apprehension and presentation of her figure, upon the growth of her "Legend," and upon the contemporary and gradual, simultaneous and successive, upbuilding of that complex structure, her "Life." This latter inquiry is probably too technical to interest the majority of readers, and will be found relegated to the Appendix at the end of this volume.

I shall group all the facts, alluded to above, under five heads: her burial, and the events immediately surrounding it; the different removals of the remains, and the chief stages of her Official Cultus; the fate of her two priest friends and advisers, and of her domestics; the remaining history of her closest friend Ettore Vernazza; and finally the long career, rich in autobiographical annotations, of Ettore's daughter, Catherine's God-child, Tommasina (Battista) Vernazza. We shall thus first finish up what is predominantly the story of things, and of the more external, even although the most splendid and authoritative, appreciation and authentication of her holiness; and shall only then go back to what is (almost exclusively) an interior history of souls, and one which will materially contribute to our apprehension of Catherine's special character and influence and to a vivid perception of the advantages, strength, limits, and difficulties of that particular kind of religion and of its attestation and transmission. Ettore's and Battista's stories, however, are so full that I must give three entire sections to Ettore, and one whole chapter to Battista.

I. The Burial and the Events immediately surrounding it. September 15 to December 10, 1510.

1. *The Burial, September* 16.

We have seen how, in the evening of Thursday, September 12, the already dying Catherine had, in a Codicil, declared that she desired to be buried wheresoever the priests Jacobo Carenzio and Cattaneo Marabotto should decide. She died in the early morning of Sunday, the 15th; and already on the next day, with the rapidity which, in such matters, continues characteristic of southern countries, the burial took place.

First, Dons Jacobo Carenzio and Cattaneo Marabotto declared, in a written document, that "knowing the late Donna Caterinetta to have ordained that her body should be buried in such a place as they themselves might ordain: they, in consequence, willed and ordained that her said body be buried in the Church of the Hospital."[1] And next, the funeral took place with a certain amount of pomp: for authentic copies are still extant of the expenses incurred,—among other things for wax candles, including three white-wax flambeaux, amounting in all to over one hundred pounds weight of wax.[2] The evidently highly emaciated, and hence naturally flexible, body had been enclosed in a "fine coffin of wood," and was now, at this first deposition, put in "a resting-place (*deposito*) against one of the walls" of the Church. There can be no doubt that this first resting-place was not the monument of her husband Giuliano, although the latter was

[1] A copy of this document exists prefixed to the MS. *Vita* of the *Biblioteca della Missione Urbana*.

[2] Copy in the same volume.

still visible and readily accessible for a considerable time after,—certainly up to 1522, and probably down to 1537.[1]

2. *Catherine's possessions at the time of her death.*

And next, on Tuesday the 17th, an Inventory was drawn up of the things possessed by Catherine at the moment of her death, for the use of the Hospital "Protectors," the Trustees and Executors of her Will. An authentic copy of it is still extant, and furnishes first-hand evidence for the presence, up to the very last, and amongst the tangible objects and small possessions in daily use, of memorials and expressions of the three great stages of her life, and of the (in part successive and past, in part simultaneous and still present) layers, or as it were concentric rings, of her character. We thus get a vivid presentation of that variety in unity and unity in variety, which is of the very essence of the fully living soul; and we also see how incapable of being otherwise than caricatured, if expressed in but a few hyperbolic words,

[1] *Vita*, p. 164*b*. This first coffin is still extant: it stands now, empty in a glass case, in the smaller of the two rooms shown in the Hospital as her last dwelling-place. Twice over the *Vita* talks of a "deposito," although directly only in connection with its opening "about eighteen months later," *i.e.* not before March 1512. Now Argentina del Sale declares, in a Will of the year 1522 (a copy, in Giovo's handwriting, exists in the volume of the *Biblioteca della Missione*), that she desires to be buried "in the Church of the Annunciata, in the monument of the late Giuliano Adorno." Thus Giuliano's grave was still generally known and fully accessible twelve years after Catherine's death; and it was a "monumento," not a "deposito." I have been completely baffled in all my attempts to trace the eventual fate of that monument, or even its precise site, or the precise date of its disappearance. I can but offer two alternative conjectures. (1) It stood in the choir-end of the Church. If so, it will have been covered up, promiscuously with many another vault and mortuary slab, when, in 1537, this end was cut off, for the purpose of widening the bastion which still runs behind it and above it, outside. (2) The "monument" was a slab on the floor of the nave or of some side-chapel. The present flooring of all the former, and of a large part of the Chapels, is relatively new; and it is (all but certainly) superimposed upon the old flooring or at least upon the old sepulchral slabs, since not one inscription remains visible in the nave. And if Giuliano's "monument" lay there, it will still be extant, hidden away under the present flooring.—In either case it remains remarkable that the slight trouble was not taken to shift nave-wards, or to raise to the newer nave- or chapel-flooring, the "monument" of Catherine's own husband. There are certainly monuments still visible in the Church older than 1497. It is impossible to resist the conclusion that some occasion was gladly seized for *not* moving or raising this monument, and for thus letting the saintly wife appear entirely alone in the Hospital Church, unattended by any memorial of her very imperfect husband.

was even her spirit of poverty and of mortification, in this her last stage, which, in some sense and degree, still retained and summed up, and in other ways added a special touch of a large freedom to, all the various previous stages of her life.

The list gives the things according to the rooms in which they stood, beginning with her own death-room, and, here, with her own bed. In this "*the* room" (*camera*) there are "a down coverlet," and "two large mattresses"; "three" (other) "coverlets, one of vermilion silk" and "two of" some simpler "white" material; "two blankets, one vermilion, the other white"; "five-and-a-half pairs of sheets"; and "a pillow": all this for Catherine's bed. And these clothes, together with those of the bed of the "famiglia" (the maid Argentina), constitute, together with the two bedsteads, absolutely all the chattels present in this "bedroom" (*camera*).

"In the" adjoining "room with the blue wall-hangings and the" intervening "curtain," there were: "three stuff gowns, one black and the other Franciscan-colour," *i.e.* grey; "two silk gowns"; "two jackets, one" of which was again "of grey stuff, without a lining"; seven other garments, "one being of black silk"; a very small amount of body-linen; "three table-cloths and twenty-one towels"; "two silver cups and saucers" and "six silver spoons"; "eight pewter candlesticks"; "one casserole"; "four wooden basins"; "a kettle"; and a few other poor odds-and-ends, for kitchen and sick-room use; and a three-legged table and one or two other articles of simple furniture.

And finally "a closet" (*recamera*) is mentioned, with a press in it.

It is noticeable that here, again, no printed book or manuscript of any kind is mentioned: but it is clear that she herself had, some time after her Will of March 18, 1509, given away her dearly prized "Maestà"-triptych to Christoforo di Chiavaro, for this picture nowhere occurs in this list; and something of the same kind may have occurred with one or two books.

But if we group these things somewhat differently, we at once get a vivid conception of the precise, and hence complex, sense in which she can be said to have died very poor; and we get clear indications of the three stages of her life. For the silver service is a survival from her pre-conversion, worldly-wealthy days; the pewter candlesticks, and the rough, sparse furniture, belong to her directly penitential first-conversion period and mood; and the soft, warm, gay-coloured coverlets and apparel of rich material are no doubt predominantly characteristic of her last years when, largely under Don Marabotto's wise advice, she allowed herself a greater freedom in matters of external mortification, and readily accepted bodily attentions and comforts, reserving now the fulness of her attention to matters of interior disposition and purification. She thus attained, by means of and after all those previous forms of mortification, to a perfected, evangelical liberty, in which the death to self was, if somewhat different, yet even more penetrative than before.

In the evening of this day, the Protectors of the Hospital formally renew their acceptance of the office of Trustees and Executors, imposed on them by Catherine's Will of March 18 of the previous year.[1]

3. *Distribution of Catherine's chattels.*

And thirdly, there are the various sellings, re-sellings, and distributions of her humble little collection of things, which take place with the slow multiplicity of steps, dear to all corporations. Workmen get paid, on November 22, for carrying her property on to the market-place, for the sale. On the same day Argentina receives " such things left to her in Catherine's Will as Catherine had not herself already given to her maid." And, on December 10, the remainder of that property, which had evidently been bought in by the Hospital on that November day, is finally re-valued, bought, and divided up by and between the Protectors, who take most of the large furniture; Marabotto, who buys ten things (a pair of fire-irons, a wardrobe, and a gilt article amongst them); her brother Lorenzo, who acquires four things (amongst them " a woman's work-box?—*capsetina a domina* "); and the Rector, Don Carenzio, who becomes possessed of the down coverlet and of a piece of vermilion cloth.[2]

Here the absence of all buying by or for Vernazza or a representative of his is noticeable. He was evidently still far away, busy in putting his and his dead Saint-friend's large ideas into practice; and his three daughters, the eldest of

[1] The Inventory and this Acceptance both exist, in copy, in the MS. *Vita* of the *Biblioteca della Missione*. I owe a careful copy of the former to the kindness of Don Giacomo C. Grasso, the Librarian.

[2] From the documents in the MS. *Vita* of the *Biblioteca della Missione*.

whom was but thirteen, were being brought up in two Convents.

The fate of Catherine's little house is too closely bound up with that of one of her friends for its history to be easily severable from his. It stands over to the third section.

II. The Different Removals of the Remains, and the Chief Stages of her Official Cultus.

1. *Opening of the "Deposito." Successive "translations."* Catherine's remains were left "for about eighteen months" in their first resting-place (*deposito*), by one of the walls of the "Hospital Church." But then "it was found that the spot was damp, owing to a conduit of water running under the wall. And the resting-place was broken up, and the coffin was opened: and the holy body was found entire from head to foot, without any kind of lesion." "And so great a concourse of people took place, to see the body, that the remains were left exposed indeed for eight days; but, owing to a part of them having been abstracted," apparently at the opening of the coffin, "they were exhibited shut off (from the crowd) in a side-chapel, where they could be seen but not touched." "And after this, the remains were deposited high up, in a sepulchre of marble, in the Church of the Hospital."[1]

The interest of this removal consists in three sets of facts, the last set being of capital importance among the determining causes of her cultus and eventual canonization. For one thing, we still have the accounts of the expenses incurred in connection with it, the Hospital repaying, to two ladies (one of them Donna Franchetta, the wife of Giuliano's cousin Agostino Adorno) and to Don Marabotto, the sums expended by them upon this translation and sepulchre: Marabotto's expenses being in part for "causing the stone for the sepulchre to be brought." These accounts are put down in the Hospital Cartulary under July 10, nearly twenty-two months after the first deposition; but the expenses may well have been incurred by those three friends, three or four months before. We thus find two ladies (a relative and a friend), and Don

[1] *Vita*, pp. 164*b*, *c*, 165*c*. Great and repeated stress is laid here, with unattractively realistic proofs and details, upon the damage done by the damp to the coffin and grave-clothes, and upon the contrasting spotlessness of the body.

Marabotto, to the fore; but no mention of Carenzio, although the latter was at the time, as we shall see, still Rector of the Hospital and living in Catherine's little house there.

And secondly, it is on this occasion that mention is made of the picture which I have more or less identified with the portrait reproduced in this volume. There are two highly ambiguous entries concerning it. "To account of the Sepulture of the late Donna Caterinetta Adorna, for divers expenses incurred by Don Cattaneo Marabotto: to wit, for a picture, and for causing the stone for the sepulture to be brought, £7 10s."; and "the Maintenance Committee (*fabrica*) of the Hospital, for a picture erected in the Church of the Hospital, above the Altar: to the credit of Don Cattaneo Marabotto, £9 7s."[1] Now I take it that only one interpretation is at all a probable one, viz. that both these entries, in the comfortably slipshod way in which most of these accounts were kept, refer somehow to one and the same picture; and that this picture was a portrait of Catherine. For it is certain that the second account refers in some way to Catherine and to this first transference of her remains; it is highly unlikely that two pictures of herself would be produced and paid for, on one and the same occasion; and it is most improbable that Marabotto would care, on occasion of all this popular enthusiasm for his deceased friend and penitent, to spend money on a picture representative of some figure other than her own.

The reader will note that the portrait which I thus connect with this picture has not, as yet, got any nimbus, an absence hardly possible in any much later picture.[2] And I take it that the picture was placed above an altar, possibly even *the* Altar (the High Altar) of the Church, not only because *that* was the most honorific place, but also a little because the sepulchre had been placed too high up for the relatively small picture to be sufficiently visible if attached to the monument itself.

And thirdly, we have here, in this week-long public veneration of the remains, and in this erection of her picture over one of the Church Altars, the first unmistakable beginnings of a popular cultus. For the evidences and expressions of devotion to her, which I have recorded at the time of her

[1] MS. *Vita* of the *Biblioteca della Missione*.

[2] Even the little engraving of the title-page of the first edition of the *Vita* (1551), which shows Catherine kneeling before a crucifix, represents her, not indeed with a nimbus, but with a diadem upon her head.

death, were all restricted to the circle of her personal friends, and her first deposition remained, apparently, free from any popular concourse or commotion. The series of cures attributed to her intercession does not begin till this opening of the *deposito*. Certainly the first, and possibly the first four, of these cases, as given by Padre Maineri (1737), occurred in connection with this first opening.[1] And it is certain that, if the (greater or lesser) incorruption of the body was possibly nothing even physically so very remarkable, given all the circumstances;[2] and if this fact left the question of her sanctity intrinsically entirely where it found the matter: yet the incorruption it was that gave the first, and, as it turned out, an abiding impulse to the popular devotion. Indeed, as we shall see later on, it is highly improbable that, but for this condition of the body, a cultus would ever have arisen sufficiently popular and permanent to lead on to her Beatification and Canonization. But as things now stood, the movement had been set going, and it continued on and on.

The remaining translations were: a second one, into "an honourable sepulchre lower down," still before 1551, and already mentioned in the first edition of the *Vita* of that year; a third, in 1593, when the remains were placed in their present position, but in a marble monument, up in the choir, above the Church entrance; and a fourth and fifth, in 1642 and 1694, when the body was placed, for the first and second time, in shrines having glass sides, so that the relics could be seen: that of 1694 is the one in which the remains still repose. And in 1709, Cardinal Lorenzo Fiesco being Archbishop of Genoa, the body was reclothed, on June 13, by ladies, amongst whom was a Maria B. Fiesca.[3] We thus see how unbroken was, in this case, the authentication of the remains, and how fresh remained, most naturally, the interest taken in their cultus by Catherine's most powerful family.

2. *Motives operating for Catherine's Canonization.*

It is indeed clear that Catherine's greatness,—what made

[1] Reprinted in *Vita*, p. 282*b*.

[2] A little Prayer-book marker picture, which will, I think, have been first engraved in 1737, when the body was, as indeed it is to this hour, considered quite incorrupt, already gives the large paper rose which has lain ever since in the place of the mouth and nose, which have perished long ago. But I have been unable to test the claim to incorruption further back than this.

[3] *Vita*, pp. 165*c*, 27*b*, 277*a*. In this last passage Maria Fiesca makes a declaration as to the partial fleshiness and elasticity of the body, *e.g.* of the right shoulder; and as to its extraordinary weight.

her a large, rich mind and saintly spirit,—is one thing; and that Catherine's popularity,—what occasioned the official recognition of that greatness,—is another thing. Her mind and teaching, her character and special grace and *attrait*, were of rare width and penetration; in part, they were strikingly original through just this their depth of psychological and spiritual self-consistency and closeness of touch with the soul's actual life. And these points had profoundly impressed a very small group of friends. And again, her work among the poor and sick had been long, varied, and utterly devoted. And here she had been widely appreciated. Yet these, the two lives which, between them, constituted all her sanctity and significance, had, the former nothing, and the latter but little and only mediately, to do with the forces which led on eventually to her formal canonization.

The motives for putting Rome in motion for this her canonization were, no doubt, predominantly three. There was the popular devotion, which apparently was first aroused, and was then instantly turned into a downright cultus, by the discovery, in May or June 1512, of the incorruption of her remains; and which from thenceforward continued and grew, in connection with these relics and with the physical cures and ameliorations attributed to the touch of the dead body, or of its integuments, or even of the oil of the lamp which evidently soon (presumably on occasion of that first outburst of devotion) was kept lit before Catherine's resting-place.[1] There was next the gratitude of the Hospital authorities to Catherine for her life-work amongst them; and their most natural and laudable wish to utilize her sanctity and its recognition for the benefit of the ever-continuous and pressing necessities of their vast institution and its Church. And finally, there was the feeling of clanship and the active interest taken in the matter by the (all but regal) family of the Fieschi, backed, as they were, by the Republic of Genoa and various other sovereign bodies and persons.

The combination of these three things proved sufficiently powerful to take the place of certain ordinary incentives which were wanting, and even to overcome certain unusual difficulties which were undoubtedly present, in the case. Certain incentives were lacking. For there was, in this

[1] All three classes of cases are represented in Padre Maineri's account, reproduced in the *Vita*, p. 282*b*, *c*.

instance, no Religious Order to put forward and to work, with all the continuous, unresting, unhasting momentum of an institution, for a saintly subject of its own, a subject whose glorification would bring honour and profit to the body from which she sprang, and an accession of popularity to the special object and work of that Order. And certain obstacles were present. For few characters, interior ideals and explicit teachings, could be found more *sui generis*, more profoundly, even daringly original and all re-constitutive, and less immediately understandable and copyable, than are these of Catherine. But the enthusiasm and self-interest of the populace, of a charitable institution, and of a powerful family, replaced what was thus lacking and overcame what was thus operative; and the directly visible and universally understandable part of her life and example was allowed to outweigh any objection that could be urged on the ground of the less obvious and more difficult, far more original and profound, sides of her special personality and piety.

And a matter which further helped on the canonization was that when Pope Urban VIII, in 1625, published his Bull forbidding thenceforth, under grave penalties, that any one, "even though he have died with the reputation of extraordinary Christian perfection, be called 'Blessed' or 'Saint,' until he has first been declared to be such, and to merit religious worship, by the Holy Roman See"; and ordaining that the same rule should be practised concerning persons already deceased, who were currently recognized as saints: he excepted, with regard to this second class, those who, "during an immemorial course of time" previous to the publication of this Bull, "had been venerated as saints by the people, without opposition or complaint on the part of the Church authorities." For this "time immemorial" was considered by theologians to amount, as a minimum, to a hundred years. And since religious worship had begun to be paid to her certainly not later than 1512, and the title "Beata" had already then been publicly given to her, Catherine continued, even after Pope Urban's Bull, to be invoked and venerated as "Blessed," with the knowledge, though without any positive and express approbation, of the Roman Church.[1]

[1] Maineri, in *Vita*, p. 278, *b*, *c*. The first edition of the *Vita* calls her "Beata" on its title-page. MS. "A," of 1547, 1548, has simply "Madonna Catherineta Adorna" on the Franciscan copyist's own title, and "Beata" on the title copied by him from the MS. used by him.

3. *Canonization*, 1737.

But the devotees of Catherine, naturally enough, were not content with less than a formal approbation, and, as usual, the obtaining of the latter was a very long and elaborate affair. At the beginning of 1630 a petition was sent in to Cardinal Cesarini in Rome; who, after much examination, gave his opinion on May 24, 1636. There the matter again rested for twenty-four years.—But in 1670 the very active and able Florentine, Cardinal Azzolini, (the same whose interesting correspondence with that undisciplined and wayward, but thoroughly sincere and much-maligned woman, Queen Christina of Sweden, has been recently published,) became the "Ponente," the Advocate, for the cause.[1] The Cardinal wrote in 1672 to Archbishop Spinola of Genoa for his opinion; and the latter, after much further examination, declared that the cultus of Catherine, having existed for over a century before Pope Urban's Bull, she ought, in accordance with the tenor of that Bull, to be maintained in possession of that same cultus. The Congregation of Rites approved of this sentence on March 30, 1675, and Clement X, the now eighty-five years old Altieri Pope, gave it his assent. Thus Catherine had a full official recognition as "Beata."

Next came the examination of her doctrine and "writings," from 1676 onwards, culminating in their approbation, for purposes of Canonization, by Pope Innocent XI (Odescalchi) in 1683. It is this investigation which, with some of the discussions concerning her virtues, adds considerably to our materials and means for judging of her teaching. I have already touched on these discussions; and they will occupy us again in the second volume.

And then, in 1682, Cardinal Azzolini, supported by King Louis XIV of France and the King of Spain, again presses Rome,—this time with a view to reaching Canonization. And on Cardinal Azzolini dying, Cardinal Imperiali became second "Ponente" of the cause. In 1690 the City of Genoa obtained leave from the Congregation of Rites for the recitation of the Office and for the Celebration of the Mass of the Common of Widows, in honour of Blessed Catherine; in 1733

[1] There is evidence that the many-sided Queen took an interest in Catherine, in the Oratorian G. Parpera's very careful *Beata Caterina di Genova Illustrata*, Genova, 1682. But the Index of her Latin (and Italian) MSS. in the Vatican Library contains no indication of any MS. "Life" or "Doctrine" possessed by Christina.

an Office and a Mass proper to herself were approved; and in 1734 her eulogy was inserted in the Roman Martyrology, under date of March 22 (her conversion-day): " At Genoa, the Blessed Catherine, widow, distinguished by her contempt of the world and love of God."

But meanwhile the long process as to the heroic degree of her virtues had issued in the Report of the Commission in 1716; and in the affirmative decree of the Congregation of Rites, confirmed by Clement XII (Corsini) in 1733.

And, before the conclusion of this investigation of her virtues, the examination of the miracles ascribed to her intercession had been begun in Genoa in 1730, by a deputation consisting of the Archbishop De-Franchi and two Bishops, sitting in the Archiepiscopal Palace; and six miracles were, in 1736, approved as valid, from amongst the numerous cases alleged to have occurred in 1730. And then three from amongst these six miracles were finally approved by Rome, on April 5, 1737, as efficient towards Canonization.

And at last, on April 30 of the same year, Feast of St. Catherine of Siena, Pope Clement, " in order that the faithful of Christ may, in Blessed Catherine, have a perfect example of all the virtues, and especially of the love of God and of their neighbour; and that a new honour and ornament may shine forth for the Republic of Genoa; orders the present Decree for the Canonization of the said Blessed Catherine,—a Canonization which has still to be carried out,—to be expedited and published."—And on May 18 following, on the Feast of the Holy Trinity, the same Pope performed, in the Basilica of St. John Lateran, the function of the Canonization of Blessed Catherine, together with that of three other Beati: the two Frenchmen, Vincent de Paul, Founder of the Congregation of the Mission (the Lazarists) (1576–1660), and Jean François Regis, a Jesuit Mission-Preacher in the Huguenot parts of France (1597–1640); and the Italian Giuliana Falconieri, Foundress of the Third Order of Servites (1270–1341).[1]

It was now, on this canonization-day, over two hundred and sixteen years since Catherine Fiesca Adorna, that keen and ardent spirit, had flown to God, her Love. We must return to those earlier times.

[1] The main facts and dates of these paragraphs devoted to the various Processes are derived from Padre Maineri's very clear account, first published in 1737, and reprinted at the end of the *Vita*, pp. 278–282.

III. The Fate of Catherine's Priest Friends.

Introductory.

In thus reverting to the period which immediately succeeded Catherine's death, and to the predominantly obscure and humble persons who had directly known her well, we bid adieu, indeed, to things massive, fixed, and final: yet we exchange the description of what, after all, was but an authoritative declaration of accomplished facts, for the study of that alone directly soul-stirring thing, the picture and drama of living, energizing human souls; of how these souls were being influenced by a greater one than themselves; and again of how these, thus influenced, lesser minds and hearts transmitted, developed, and coloured the tradition of the life to which they owed so much.

Now the effect, or at least the record of the effect, of the conception of Catherine formed by her two Priest friends and by her domestics back upon her transmitted image and upon the growth of her Legend, is, apart from the indications in the *Vita* already given or still to be considered, upon the whole, but slight. Still, as we shall eventually find, the few facts as to the subsequent lives of these persons, which shall now be given, are of very distinct use in appraising their respective shares in the gradual constitution of the *Vita e Dottrina*.

1. *Don Carenzio*, 1510–1513.

I take Don Jacopo Carenzio first, since he was the Priest in actual attendance upon Catherine at the last, and because he now, no doubt immediately after the funeral or at latest on the day of the removal of her chattels to the market-place, became possessed, as we shall see, of Catherine's little house. He was thus the one who alone could continue and augment a cultus as strictly local as even Argentina's had been, during those weeks, perhaps months, of sole night-charge of her dying mistress in these very rooms.

The identification of the building is complete. For as far back as October 6, 1497, not long after Giuliano's death,—he was still alive on July 14,—the Protectors of the Hospital referred to their "grant to Catherine, during her lifetime, of the enjoyment and use of a house with a greenhouse, forming part of the Hospital." And in this greenhouse she, on the evening of Sunday, March 18, 1509, had, in the presence of Vernazza and four other witnesses, dictated her Fourth Will to Battista Strata. It was, then, of a size sufficient to render it worth mentioning, and it was evidently closed in. Now there is a legal instrument, dated Saturday, August 30, 1511, drawn up at a meeting held by the four "Protectors," "in the chief (sitting-) room of the Residence of the Rector, in which the late Donna Caterinetta was wont to live." And in this they declare that, "seeing that the Reverend Don Jacopo Carenzio, the Rector, is about to go to his home at Diano, for the purpose of carrying out a matter of the greatest importance to himself, and is shortly to return from thence, and that he wishes to persevere throughout his life in the said office of Rector; and since they desire that he should willingly hasten his return, and should be able to persevere with full confidence, and should not, as long as he lives, be moved from this room together with the whole building contiguous with it, to the room which, with its appurtenant building, is at present in the course of erection as the official residence of the Rector; they have altogether conceded to the above-named Reverend Jacopo, Rector, present and accepting, the said room together with the whole building belonging to this room, for him to hold and inhabit throughout his life, together with the greenhouse." [1]

Here three points are of interest. Don Carenzio is, then, a native of the little Diano Castello on the Western Riviera hillside, some fifty English miles from Genoa and some twenty short of San Remo; and must have belonged to some humble family in that insignificant little place. His origin is thus in marked contrast to Marabotto's, and still more to Vernazza's. And next, it is clear that the house and greenhouse inhabited and used by Don Carenzio till his death are identical with those tenanted by Catherine, ever since at least the death of Giuliano. And thirdly, it is equally clear that this house was in no part identical with the two rooms still shown as the Saint's. For these latter are high up from the ground; do not now form, and probably never formed, part of a disconnected house; and they no doubt stand on another site. The little house will have been demolished at latest in 1780, when the present great quadrangle was built.[2]

Now here, in these rooms full of the memory of Catherine,

[1] Copy in the MS. *Vita* in the *Biblioteca della Missione*.

[2] So Padre Celesia, *op. cit.* p. 1121.

Don Carenzio will, not unreasonably, have hoped to live during many years. For it is not likely that he was older than, or indeed as old as, Don Marabotto, since he was now occupying that same office of Rector which Marabotto had held some six years previously. And yet Marabotto did not die till eighteen years later, whereas Carenzio's death came soon. For his funeral took place on January 7, 1513, for which day there is an entry in the Hospital Cartulary for the cost of twenty-three pounds-weight of wax candles,—less than one-fourth the amount used at Catherine's obsequies; and for that of the Priest's vestments in which the body was robed and buried.[1]

It seems unlikely that Carenzio was not buried in the Hospital Church, seeing that he died whilst, apparently, still *ex-officio* Rector of the Hospital. But, if he was interred there, his monument, like that of Giuliano, was cut off and buried away in and with the Church end in 1537, or was covered up in some restoration; for there is no trace of it either in the Church itself or in any book treating of the sepulchral monuments of Genoa.

It is remarkable also that, though he had been the one priest present at Catherine's death, and had tenanted Catherine's own rooms throughout the two years and two or three months since her death, and had, alongside of Marabotto, been appointed by Catherine herself as the person to determine the place of her sepulture: his name nowhere occurs in connection with the plan for the opening of her *deposito* some eighteen months after her death; nor with the execution of that plan; nor with any of the consequent initiations of a public cultus. It is impossible to doubt that we have here some little counter jealousy and return exclusion, a sort of answer by Marabotto to his, Marabotto's, own enforced absence from the death-chamber and his twenty-four hours' ignorance of his Penitent's death, which we had to note in its proper place. Poor little human frailties which may have appeared less petty and more completely excusable at close quarters than they look at this distance of time! I take it that, if there was a deliberate exclusion of Carenzio, the ceremony of opening the resting-place will have been timed to tally with some absence of the Rector,—say, on another visit to his native Diano.

[1] Copy in the MS. *Vita* in the *Biblioteca della Missione.*

2. *Don Marabotto*, 1510–1528.

As to Don Cattaneo Marabotto, I have not been able to discover much. We have already seen how he bought ten of Catherine's chattels on December 10, after her death. On July 7, 1511, he pays over to Catherine's old servant, the maid Maria (Mariola Bastarda), her late mistress's little legacy, in a form to be described presently.

But the most important facts concerning him—apart from his share in the *Vita*, which shall be considered at length hereafter—are the following three. There is, first, the fact (already dwelt upon) that he, and apparently he alone, initiated, or at least led and directed, the plan of opening the *deposito*, exposing the body, giving it a marble sarcophagus, and erecting a picture over an altar in the Church to Catherine. And next, that "still in 1523 Argentina del Sale was his servant,"—she had evidently then, on Catherine's death in 1510, become his attendant.[1] And thirdly, that he did not die till 1528.[2]

There seems to be but little doubt that he was, at least slightly, Catherine's junior. Yet already on his first intercourse with her, he, the Rector of the Hospital, must have been a fully mature man. I suppose him to have been born somewhere about 1450; in which case he will have been about seventy-eight at the time of his death.

In any case, he lived long enough to see and hear much of

[1] From twenty-two conclusions concerning Catherine and her circle, constituting one of the papers in the volume, *Documenti*, etc., of the University Library. They were evidently written after 1675 and before 1737 (Catherine is "Beata" throughout), but are, wherever I have been able to test them, as a rule completely right, and never entirely wrong. It is certainly somewhat strange that Argentina should, as is there stated, have "continued in the said Hospital, and was living in it still in 1523," and should have "similarly continued to be the servant of the Priest Cattaneo (Marabotto)." Still, she may have slept at the Hospital and worked at Marabotto's. I had thought of concluding from this that Marabotto had been given Catherine's house in the Hospital, after Don Carenzio's death there. But the apparently complete absence of any mention of Marabotto in the Hospital books, after July 1512, makes me shrink from doing so.

[2] I am proud of this important discovery, since even Giovo had to leave a blank for this date in his Chapter IV of Part I of his MS. *Vita*, in the *Biblioteca della Missione*, written in 1675. I found the date amongst some notes and copies, in a sprawly handwriting, not Giovo's, but the same which copied out the entry as to Carenzio's funeral expenses. It is true that in Marabotto's case this writer gives no proof or document; yet there is no reason for distrusting his assertion.

a kind to console and strengthen his devotion to Catherine and his faith in the self-rejuvenating powers of the Church, and much of a nature to dismay and alarm the gentle, peaceable old man. For there were the opening of the coffin; the incorruption; the popular concourse and enthusiasm; the graces and the cures of May to July 1512. And there were Luther's ninety-five Theses nailed to the University Church of Wittenberg, on the Eve of All-Saints, 1517; and Pope Leo X's condemnation of forty of them in 1520, and amongst them three Theses which concerned the doctrine of Purgatory, one of which must have seemed strangely like one of Catherine's own contentions. And there were the books of Henry VIII of England and of Erasmus against Luther, in 1522, 1524, and in Italy the foundation of the Capuchin Order in 1527; there were, too, the Peasants' War and Luther's marriage in Germany in 1525, and, in 1527, the sacking of Rome by the Imperial troops. And through all this world-wide, epoch-making turmoil and conflict we think of him, probably not simply from our lack of documents, as leading a quiet, obscure, somewhat narrow existence; yet one redeemed from real insignificance by his silent watchfulness and action, and still more by his writing, in honour of his large-souled Penitent, ever so sincerely felt by him as indefinitely greater than himself.

I do not know where he was buried. It was not, however, in the Hospital Church; for in that case there would have been some entry in the books of the expenses incurred in connection with his funeral.

IV. The Fate of Catherine's Three Maid-Servants.

As to Catherine's three maid-servants the facts that can still be traced are as follow.

1. *Benedetta.*

The widow and Franciscan Tertiary Benedetta Lombarda, although her name had continued to appear in the documents from Giuliano's Will in 1496 down to Catherine's last will of March 1509, disappears after this latter date entirely from sight. Since both Mariola and Argentina reappear in the Hospital books, (although Mariola had, like Benedetta, ceased to serve Catherine at the last,) it looks as though Benedetta had died between the Will of March 1509 and

Catherine's death in September 1510. Yet it is possible that Catherine herself handed over to Benedetta her little share in the former's money and chattels; and that Benedetta is no more mentioned after her mistress's death because, unlike Mariola and Argentina, she did not continue to live in and belong to the Hospital, whose accounts alone are our extant sources of information for the other two servants.

2. *Mariola.*

But as to Mariola and Argentina, and their lives after 1510, we do know something. Mariola (Maria) Bastarda had, on leaving Catherine's service,(probably only some weeks, but possibly some months before her mistress's death,) become one of the servants, or under-nurses (*filia*), of the Hospital; and, on July 7 of the following year (1511) she was clothed a Novice in the Convent of Bridgettines in Genoa, with the money left to her in Catherine's Will.[1]

The latter fact is interesting as showing how purposely vague and ambiguous, and how little capable of being pressed, are at least some of the statements of the *Vita*, if taken as they stand and prior to any distinction of documents and of their varying degrees of trustworthiness. For there we read, after the scene where the evil spirit within the maid declares Catherine's true surname to be " Serafina ": " this possessed person (*spiritata*) was endowed with a lofty intelligence, and lived to the end in virginity." Who would readily guess that we have here to do with little Mariola? The passage is, I think, in part modelled upon Acts xxi, 9: " And he " (Philip the Evangelist, one of the seven Deacons) " had four daughters virgins, who did prophesy." Even so then did Catherine, the teacher, have " a spiritual daughter," a virgin, who " prophesied," divined and announced, the true character of her mistress.—" We believe," continues the *Vita*, " that the Lord had given her this spirit to keep her humble. She finished her life in a holy manner." Who would guess that this meant profession as a Nun? The point is, I take it, kept vague in part to make the insertion of the words which

[1] Copy from Hospital Cartulary in MS. *Vita* of the *Biblioteca della Missione Urbana*: " 1511, 7 Julii: Hereditas quondam Caterinetae Adurnae, pro Maria, olim famula ipsius et filia Hospitalis, pro legato facto dictae Mariae per dictam q(uondam) Caterinetam, £50.—Mariae praedictae pro D. P. Cattaneo Marabotto, qui habuit curam guarnimentorum ipsius Mariae, dedicatae in Monasterio Sanctae Brigidae, £50."—I take these two successive entries to refer to two successive stages of the same transaction, and to but one and the same sum.

follow possible. "Nor did the evil spirit ever depart from her, till well-nigh the very end, when she was about to die." It is evident that this cannot be pressed: and that either the attacks continued to the end, but were rare and slight; or that they were serious and frequent, but ceased a considerable time before her death. For, though we do not know when she died, we have no right to assume, in evidently still so young a person, that death came soon.

3. *Argentina.*

And Argentina appears in several documents. So in an entry of the Hospital Cartulary for November 22, 1510, as to the value of the things then handed over to her in accordance with Catherine's Will. So again in three legal documents drawn up for her and in her presence,—a Will of October 1514, a Codicil of some later (unspecified) date, and a second Will of January 15, 1522. In the Codicil she doubles the little sum she had left to the Hospital in 1514; and in the last document she declares her wish to be buried "in the Church of the Annunciata, in the monument (vault) of the late Giuliano Adorno, or in such other as may seem good to . . ."; and leaves moneys "for Masses to be said for her soul, by two of the Brethren of the Monastery of San Nicolò in Boschetto."[1]

This group of papers is interesting. For we see from it how even an obscure little serving-woman was wont, in Italy, the classic country of Law and Lawyers, and during these claimful, pushing times, to have Wills and Codicils drawn up for her. We perceive, too, how proud and fond Argentina remained of her former avocation of servant to Giuliano, since only he and not his Saint-wife lay in that vault; and how, nevertheless, an uncertainty possesses her mind as to whether this can or will be carried out—no doubt owing to the fact that the vault had not received the remains of his wife, and had not indeed probably been opened again at all since his death, twenty-five years before. And we can note how Argentina, together with, and no doubt at least in part because of, her late mistress, has an affection for the Monastery and Pilgrimage Church of San Nicolò, on that wooded hill, so near to Catherine's former villa.

And Argentina appears finally in that list of conclusions (already referred to in Marabotto's case) as continuing to live

[1] From the documents given in the MS. *Vita* of the *Biblioteca della Missione Urbana.*

in the Hospital; and as still living in it in 1523; and, similarly, as continuing in the capacity of servant to Don Marabotto. I have already pointed out the difficulties inherent in this statement, but believe it to be correct. Yet it would be of considerable importance if we could reach lower down, and could fix the exact death-date of poor Marco del Sale's ardent-minded, imaginative little widow. Since she was doubtless considerably, I think quite twenty years, younger than Marabotto, and since even the latter lived on, we know, till 1528, six years after this Will, there was nothing, in the matter of actual age, to prevent her living on up to 1550 or beyond. And circumstances connected with the growth of Catherine's legend seem to point, as we shall find, to Argentina having died in any case after Marabotto, and probably not before 1547. Similarly, Catherine herself did not die till twenty-six years after her first Will (1484–1510).

V. The Two Vernazzas: their Debt to Catherine, and Catherine's Debt to them.

We now move on from these four figures which, seen against the living background of those strenuous times, appear indeed small and contracted; and which, in relation to Catherine, appear rather as a mere memory and mechanical continuation of her limitations, and specially of the phenomenal accidents and relative monotony of her sick-room period, than as a rich and vigorous, because truly personal, expansion and re-application of her many-sided action, breadth and warmth, and human practicality, during the times of her fullest self-expression. Such a new facing of the new problems, with a strength both old and new, enkindled indeed at her light and warmth, and yet developed also from the vigorously fresh centres of other deep hearts and virile minds and wills, we must now attempt to picture, in the case of the two greatest of Catherine's disciples, Ettore Vernazza and his eldest daughter Battista. And yet if, in the former four cases, while the results of this influence appeared few and insignificant, the actual fact and source of this influence were plain beyond all cavil: in these latter two instances we have, indeed, a rich crop of thoughts and acts, of wisdom and of heroism, but then it is mostly impossible to sort out what is here the direct and unmistakable outcome of Catherine's influence.

The great, open, spiritual and even temporal, battlefield, if not of Europe at least of Italy; the abuses and tyrannies, but also the necessity and the power for good, of governments; and the strenuous, tragic, and transformatory conflicts of single wills within their own soul's world, and again with other wills, both single and combined : all this lies spread out here like a map before us, seen from the bracing heights of time. There is nothing here, at least in the Ettore's case, that the most intolerantly robust, or even the most hysterically would-be strong, mind could suspect of sickliness. And yet, if undoubtedly much of all this fruitful virility in Catherine's closest friend, and in Catherine's God-daughter, proceeds from Catherine herself, it nevertheless springs up and grows within them, not as an avowed, nor probably, for the most part, even as conscious, imitation or reminiscence.

Thus here again we get an impressive instance of one profound sense in which the grain of wheat of any great and wholesome influence must die. For only if and when broken up, selected from, and assimilated to and within, another mind's and heart's life and system, can that older living organism, which yet was, in the first instance, so moving just because of its unique organization round a centre possible only to that one other soul, truly and permanently develop and enrich a living centre not its own. And so in this case too : Catherine's influence is all the more real in Ettore and Battista, because the latter are in no sense simple copies of the former. She has lived on in them, at the cost of becoming in part ignored, in part absorbed, by them : and continues to influence them through certain elements of her life that have been assimilated, and through the reinterpreted image of that life's historic reality, an image which is ever re-inviting them to do and to be, *mutatis mutandis*, what she herself had done and been.

But, indeed, (even apart from all direct influence exercised by Catherine's personality upon them, or by them upon Catherine's legend,) these two lives are interesting as further authentic illustrations of Catherine's school and spirit, and, indeed, of the mystical element of religion in general.

I shall first take the father, devoting three sections to him.

VI. Ettore Vernazza's Life, from 1509 to 1512.

Introductory.

We possess, if few, yet quite first-rate materials for the reconstruction of the remaining part of Vernazza's life. For there are his own testamentary provisions as to the disposition of his property, (as elaborate and vividly characteristic as Mr. Cecil Rhodes's,) drawn up in 1512 and 1517, and occupying twelve closely-printed octavo pages; and there is a long, homely, and admirably realistic description of his life and character, written by Battista, not, it is true, till 1581, when she was eighty-four years of age, and nearly sixty years after her father's death, but which is, there is no reason to doubt, perfectly truthful, generally accurate, and all the more moving, in that the living man and his large-hearted heroism were thus continuing to touch and inspire his daughter, at the very moment of her writing, with a finely restrained emotion, of deeds and personalities witnessed, by her own eyes and spirit, over half a century before. I shall take the several documents, not each as they stand but piecemeal, according to the dates of the events recorded or of the legal act performed.

1. *Ettore's married life; and thought of the monastic state.*

"My Father and Mother," writes Battista, "lived together" from 1496 to 1509 "in the greatest peace, since they wished each other every kind of good; so that I do not remember ever having heard one word of dissension pass between them. —And although my Mother was a beautiful and attractive young woman, and was loved by persons deserving of esteem, yet she would stay at home, alone, with her children. And my Father acted similarly, except when he was obliged to go out on some business. Otherwise I do not remember having ever noticed either of them going out to some late party (*veglià*), as is the custom in Genoa."—And she tells how "he was so abstemious" in the matter of food, "that he was wont strictly to limit the amount of bread that he ate. But my Mother, noticing this, had the breads baked very substantial."

"And when my Mother died" in the spring of 1509, "my Father thought of becoming a Lateran (Augustinian) Canon. But, on asking the advice of Padre Riccordo da Lucca," (I take it, himself a Lateran Canon,) "who was just then preaching in Genoa with very great fervour, the latter did not encourage him to carry out his intention, observing, as he did, my Father's inclination for founding works of charity." And her father proved docile. Indeed she says of him generally that "he greatly mortified his self-will, and for this reason had put himself under obedience to a priest, who had the reputation of being exceptionally devoted (*molto buono*), and obeyed him as though he had been the very voice of God." "And my Father then gave up his own house, and went to live in rooms which had been got ready for him in the Hospital for Incurables, of which he was one of the Managers and indeed one of the first *Builders*. And here he always lived, when he was in Genoa; here he died; and this institution he made his heir." [1]

Here it is interesting to note the similarities and differences between this union, so happy and thus blessed with three children, and Catherine's marriage, so unhappy and childless; between his thought of a religious vocation after his marriage was over, and Catherine's before hers was begun; and between his fifteen years of residence in the midst of the incurable poor at the *Chronici*, and Catherine's similar, though earlier and longer, life surrounded by the sick poor at the *Pammatone*. There is some likeness, too, in the matter of corporal mortification; although, with Vernazza, it is less acute, but is apparently kept up throughout his life, whilst with Catherine the active bodily mortifications are very prominent whilst they last, but are kept up thus for but a few years. As to obedience, we have here, for Vernazza, a more authoritative account than are any of the general statements on the same point with regard to Catherine; but in Catherine's case many concrete instances give us a definite idea as to the character and limits of this docility, whereas all such instances are, in Vernazza's case, restricted to the above incident alone. Yet this one example of his obedience shows how largely conceived, how simply divinatory and stimulative of his own deepest (although as yet but half-born) ideals, how ancillary to his own grace-impelled self-determination, and hence how truly liberating, were this direction and docility. The Venerable Cardinal de Berulle's determination of Descartes

[1] My quotations from this letter are all taken from Giuseppe Morro's careful address on Vernazza published in *Inaugurazione della Statua d'Ettore Vernazza*, Genova, 1867, pp. 5–31. It stands *in extenso* in the fine edition of his daughter's works: *Opere Spirituale della Ven. Madre Donna Battista Vernazza*, 6 vols., Genoa, 1755; Vol. VI, Letter XXV.

to a philosophical career, and St. Philip Neri deciding Cardinal Baronius to write his entirely open-minded, indeed severe, *Ecclesiastical Annals*, would doubtless be true parallels to this particular relationship.

2. *Ettore's great Will of* 1512.

We have already seen that Ettore was away from Genoa from about September 10, 1510, onwards, and that he was far away at the time of Catherine's death. He may well have been away most of the year 1511, nor is there indeed any indication that he was in Genoa at the opening of Catherine's *deposito* in May to July 1512. But he was certainly there in October 1512, for on the 16th of that month he drew up a munificent and far-sighted deed of gift, of one hundred shares of the Bank of St. George, to various charitable and public purposes.

Vernazza had already previously provided for his three daughters; and now orders that the interest of these other shares (a capital amounting, at the time, to the value of some £10,400) should, for the first nine years, be used by the "Protectors" of the Incurables for the benefit of that Institution, which thus occupies the first place in his solicitudes.

And then these shares should be allowed to multiply, by means of their accumulated interests and of the reinvestments of the latter, till they had reached the number of five hundred shares; and then, if and when an epidemic arose and the citizens fled from the city, the income of these shares for three years should be given to the Board of Health, for the use of those suffering from the epidemic. And when the shares had become two thousand, a commodious Lazaretto-house should be bought or built, with the income of not more than ten years. And after this, when the shares had become six thousand, one half or more of their interest should go towards the keep and nursing of the patients in this Lazaretto.

After these three stages devoted to the victims of the Plague, he determines the point at which the interest of the moneys shall be applied successively to providing marriage portions for honest poor girls of Genoa and of his home villages of Vernazza, Arvenza, and Cogoleto, preference being always given to the large clan of Vernazzi; to providing means for honest poor girls desiring to enter Convents that keep their Rule (*monasteria observantiae*), up to £100 each, with a similar preference as in the previous case.

And then he attends to the poor in general. To providing extra pay for the Notaries and Clerks of the "Uffizio della Misericordia," "on condition that they devote all their time to the interests of the poor exclusively; and that they make diligent inquiry as to the means of the poor and their several characters, and find out whether they are in real want or not, and draw up a book in which all the poor, individuals and families, shall be inscribed clearly and by name,—in each case with a note indicating whether they belong to the first, second, or third degree of necessitousness." To paying two Physicians and two Surgeons, for otherwise entirely gratuitous service of the sick poor alone, and doubling this pay during the prevalence of an epidemic, "but strictly enforcing the loss, in salary, of double the amount of any moneys they can be proved to have accepted from their patients." All this, together with these four Doctors' names, to be annually proclaimed in the streets by the town-crier. To paying a Dispenser and instituting a Dispensary, exclusively for the sick poor and entirely gratuitous, up to £2,000 a year for the latter. To appointing two Advocates and two Solicitors, for the exclusive and gratuitous service of the poor, in any and all cases of law-suits and molestations. The same proclamation as with the Doctors, to be made in this matter also. And to maintaining foundling boys and girls of Genoa, under provisions which are carefully laid down.

And then he turns to the three Institutions and their like with which he, as notary, as father and as philanthropist, has been specially identified. He fixes the point when two lectures in Philosophy or Theology, one by a Dominican and another by a Franciscan, are to be instituted, for every working day, in the Chapel of the Notaries of Genoa; when one free meal a month is to be provided for eight monastic and charitable institutions, amongst which are the Franciscans of the SS. Annunziata, the Benedictines of San Nicolò in Boschetto, the Canonesses of S. Maria delle Grazie, and the Hospital for Incurables,—"but the expenses are not to exceed £600 a year" (about six guineas each meal)—"nor is money to be given, but the eatables themselves are to be bought for, and given to, the institutions"; and when a Superintendent (*Sindaco*) of the Incurables is to be appointed, with £100 pay a year.

And then he comes back to the poor in general; and thinks also, (somewhat like unto his and Catherine's ideal,

St. Paul as "a citizen of no mean city,") of the external appearance and utility of his native town of Genoa. The point is fixed when they are to "pay for the poor their hardest imposts, especially those on food"; and when they are to "repair, decorate, and enlarge the Cathedral Church of San Lorenzo," and to "build a harbour-mole, improve the harbour, and attend to the decoration and look of the town (*ornamentis civitatis*), according to their discretion."

And he then finishes up with a characteristic reversion to efficacious solicitude for his clan, by marriage benefits for his young kinswomen in the future and by thought for his ancestors and predecessors in the past; and with a no less characteristic divinatory greatness of mind, by the creation of a kind of People's College or Working-man's University, which appears here curiously wedged in between the thoughts for his clan in the future and in the past. For he determines the points when the Protectors shall again provide for marrying honest poor girls of his three home villages, and for comforts for the prisoners at Christmas and Easter; when they are to "buy a large and well-situated house, and therein organize a public course of studies, with four Doctors of Law, four very learned Physicians, and two Masters of Grammar and Rhetoric, who shall, all ten, be each bound to deliver one lecture on every working day, and to devote all the rest of their time to the interests of the poor"; and when finally they are to provide for "Masses for his ancestors and predecessors,"—Masses for himself and immediate belongings having been already, no doubt, provided for in his previous Will, since we find such provisions repeated in his last Will, to be given later on.[1]

We thus get here a persistent preoccupation with the most manifold interests of the poor; a shrewd knowledge of men, and careful provisions calculated to rouse their indolence and to check their self-seeking; an utterly unsentimental, realistic, Charity-Organization sort of spirit shown in the insistence upon a careful and complete knowledge of the real degree and kind of want, and of the precise means appropriate for helping the various kinds of poor; a high estimate of knowledge, which he desires to offer to all, according to their various capacities and needs; and lastly, an entire freedom from pietism, for he thinks of, and provides for, harbour-works and the beautifying of the town. There is a large, open-air,

[1] The document is given in full, and carefully analyzed, in *Inaugurazione*, etc., pp. 61–70.

operative, sanely optimistic and statesmanlike spirit about it all.

And if all this is in full keeping with, and but expands and supplements, the tenacious realism of a born organizer and administrator: the soaring idealism and universalism of his saint-friend Catherine's stimulation, and his and her joint experiences and interests, are also directly suggested to us. For there is the special stress laid on the plague-stricken, whom they had tended together in 1493; the interest in physicians and in drugs for the poor, an interest in which she must have preceded him by twenty years or more; and the repeated preoccupation with the marrying of poor young women, and, next after it, with the convent-dowries of girls in socially similar circumstances, in each case especially of kinswomen of his own. This preoccupation was no doubt occasioned chiefly by the thought of his own most happy marriage and of his own children, the two elder now already well settled as Nuns, but the third still possibly to be married; yet we are also vividly reminded of Catherine's own repeated occupation with the marrying of relatives of her own, and Limbania's and her own early entrance, and wish to enter, into the Religious state. And then his benefactions include Catherine's Hospital Church, her favourite Boschetto Church, and that Convent of the Grazie, the scene of her own conversion and the home of her sister Limbania, as well as of his daughters Battista and Daniela. But indeed the whole character of the outlook, in its successive absorption in, each time, just *one* particular task; in its occupation with succour in proportion to the divinely ordained and ready-found bonds and ties of nature, bonds and ties so dear to the omnipresent God; and in its, nevertheless, in nowise restricting itself to this interest, but moving on and on, distance appearing beyond distance, with love and welcome for all the heroisms and helplessnesses: is all marked with Catherine's imperial spirit of boundless self-donation.

VII. Ettore in Rome and Naples; his Second Will; his Work in the Genoese Prisons.

1. *Ettore in Rome.*

And perhaps already in 1513, but, if so, not before March of that year (the date of Pope Leo's accession), Vernazza was in Rome,—hardly, I think, for the first time. And Battista again tells us, in her long letter of 1581, how that " the incurables in Rome "—which was then, at the beginning of Giovanni de' Medici's (Leo X's) reign, the brilliant centre of the Renaissance at its zenith—" were left to lie in baskets, moaning " for alms, " in the Churches. It was piteous to see them thus forsaken and badly cared for."

Now there is good reason to think that Vernazza had known the Pope when, as Cardinal de' Medici, he had, in 1500, stayed for some time in Genoa, in the house of his married sister, Donna Maddalena Cibò. And so Vernazza now presented himself before the Pope, " and said to him : ' You, Holiness, have a fine work in hand, in patronizing the Arts and Letters : but you cannot leave this Rome of yours saddened by so piteous a spectacle.' " And the Pope thanked him, and begged him to accept the charge of founding and undertaking the government of the Arch-Hospital. And the two " Cardinals, Caraffa," the vigorous and devoted, but harshly austere Neapolitan, who was, later on, joint-founder of the Theatines and then Pope Paul IV, " and Sauli," the Genoese, " helped him in his work. Indeed the latter said to him : ' If you require money, come to me.' "

And this Roman work of Vernazza straightway put forth two offshoots, far away. For " Caraffa founded in Venice a hospital on the model of the one in Rome." And " there happened to be in Rome " at this time " a certain Bartholommeo Stella, a rich and very generous (*molto galante*) young man. And Vernazza saw him and gained such an influence with him as to end by sending him to Brescia, to promote there also these fruits of Christian faith."

And in Rome itself " Leo X gave Vernazza practical proofs of his gratitude, and set him forth on his return journey with demonstrations of great honour (*magnifiche demonstrazioni*). And the Arch-Hospital having been thus set going and Vernazza being back in Genoa, Leo X addressed a Brief to him, informing him that his Hospital in Rome was in a state of confusion (*andava sossopra*) ; ' I think ' (adds Battista) ' because its Governors wanted each to be above the other.' And he returned to Rome, and quieted all controversy." [1] I take this second Roman journey to have been not before 1515 ; but it may have occurred any time before 1522, the year of Pope Leo's death.

[1] Battista's letter, as quoted in *Inaugurazione*, p. 16.

This group of facts shows Vernazza's directness and independence of observation, his initiative and energy, and his courage and respectful liberty of speech, qualities which are all reminiscent of Catherine's scene with the Friar; the rapidity with which a necessary work, which has been delayed for centuries, and which has required the whole-hearted vigour of a rare personality to call it into being, grows and multiplies, when once it is in existence; and the manner in which the petty, sterilizing ambitions of men can be efficiently checked only by a combination of strength of will, administrative ability, gentle tact and complete disinterestedness,—a combination which again reminds one of Catherine, the successful Rettora.

2. *Ettore in Naples.*

It will have been after this second visit to Rome that Vernazza first went to Naples. And there again "he formed a Hospital," in this case "at the risk of his life; for some evil-wishers there wanted to kill him, being unable to bear the idea that a 'foreigner' should have anything to do with the affairs of the city (*ordinasse quella città*). Once the 'Ave Maria' had sounded, he did not again issue from his lodging during that day. And yet" even among such untoward circumstances, "he managed not to leave Naples before having, with God's help, achieved his object,—of providing his much-loved poor with such an institution ready to their hand."

It was in Naples, too, evidently at the beginning of this very visit, that another generous idea and institution of his first occurred to him, or at least was first put into execution. The whole occurrence reveals a curious mixture of the most divers qualities and, indeed, requires in part to be excused, on the ground of numerous external difficulties which stood in the way of an excellent work, and of the finessing methods evidently deemed, even by good people, to be quite allowable for attaining a good end, in this age of violence, suspicion and intrigue. "A certain Religious, Padre Callisto of Piacenza, was preaching at that time in Naples. Vernazza went to him and said: 'Father, these Neapolitans are a haughty people, and refuse to bend so low as to found hospitals. But during last night the thought came to me that if a person refuses to mount ten steps—it is still possible to get him to go up fifteen; and when such a person had done the latter, he would find that he had unconsciously mounted the ten as well. Now I cannot discover a more humiliating act than the accompanying of those who have been condemned to death, on their way to execution; and in this city they are led to the gallows with their minds in a state of desperation and without any one to comfort them. Well, then, do this. Preach to the people and tell them that the very first men of Naples have been to see you, with a view to founding a society for escorting these unhappy persons; and say to them: ' Let him who cares to enter this society, come to me, to be inscribed on the rolls in a secrecy so complete that even a husband shall be unable to tell his wife.' " And Padre Callisto, after hearing these words, did, devoted man that he was, his very best, and with such good effect that many went to have themselves inscribed. " But many of those Neapolitan nobles reproved him, saying: ' Perchance you think yourself still in your Lombardy! We are nobles, and we refuse to form an escort for these culprits.' And he would answer: ' If your Lordship does not care to go, do not go. It was the very first men of Naples who sought me out, for the purpose of instituting this society.' And thus it was actually founded, and indeed became very numerous and much honoured; and those unhappy men received much comfort. And later on, this same society proceeded to found the Hospital." [1]

There is one repulsive feature in this story. For if the declaration that the very first men of the city had visited the preacher was a statement that damaged no one; which but anticipated what actually occurred soon after; and was the means for the effecting of two works, profoundly useful to all concerned in them and which could not, otherwise, at that time and place, have been carried out at all: yet it was a clear untruth. But all the rest, how admirable it is! Moral, and indeed physical courage; cool-headed, humorous, manly because unflinching, and yet quite uncynical and hopeful, knowledge of the petty perversities of the human heart; and entirely devoted, slow excogitation, concentration of will, and toughly resisting perseverance in a work of the purest philanthropy: all this and much else is visibly present.

3. *Ettore's Will of* 1517.

It may well have been after his return from this journey that Vernazza drew up the Will which we still possess, dated 7th November 1517, and which is interesting in several respects.[2] For one thing, he orders his body to be buried in

[1] *Inaugurazione*, pp. 17, 18.
[2] Printed in *Inaugurazione*, pp. 71–73.

the Church of the SS. Annunziata,—the Hospital Church, and leaves a legacy for Masses "to the Friars of the Annunziata of Genoa." [1] And he leaves a similar bequest to the Benedictines of San Nicolò in Boschetto. It is clear that he wanted to be buried in the same Hospital Church as Catherine, and had a devotion similar to hers for the Pilgrimage Church upon the hill.

Secondly, there are careful records and provisions concerning his three children. As to his two eldest, Tommasa (Battista) and Catetta (Daniela), he simply looks back and "declares that he gave to his two daughters that are in the Monastery of Santa Maria delle Grazie, to them or to the said Monastery, three thousand Genoese pounds from his own property, and two hundred pounds in addition,—(the latter) spent upon their rooms, habits, and other requisites." And that "these sums are to be counted as taking the place of dowries which would have accrued to them" (in case of marriage). But as to the youngest, Ginevrina, he looks both back and forwards. "The same Testator is well aware that he placed the said Ginevrina in the Monastery of Saint Andrew,[2] that she might grow up with good morals and in the fear of God, since Testator was unable to keep her by him, having very often been obliged, for the transaction of business in favour of the poor and for other charitable works, to proceed to Rome and other places; and that there existed written directions (of his) in the hands of the Nuns, as to Ginevrina being free, in due time and at the proper age, to choose either to serve God (in Religion), or to marry according to the social rank of the Testator." And he confirms a legacy of £500, already promised by him to Ginevrina "as appears from a certain document signed by the Abbess of the said Monastery of Saint Andrew": this money being no doubt in addition to another sum already paid by him to the

[1] The present, second and much larger and detached SS. Annunziata, on the square of that name, was not built (for the Capuchins) till 1587. In Giuliano's and Catherine's Wills of 1494, 1498, and 1506, the Hospital Church occurs indifferently as "Church of the Annunciation of the Order of Friars Minor of the Observance" with and without the addition of "adjoining the Hospital," or "adjoining the Hospital of Pammatone."

[2] This was a Cistercian Convent, founded in the twelfth century, outside one of the Genoese gates. Only its Chapel survived the destruction of the Convent at the time of the Revolutionary secularization. And even this Chapel was in January 1903 in process of demolition, to make room for the new Via Venti Settembre.

Convent; and the whole is evidently intended to pay for Ginevrina's keep, if necessary for life, in case she neither entered Religion nor married. " In case of her becoming a Nun and making her Profession in the said Monastery, he leaves her £100, for the adapting and furnishing of one room for her use; nor can these £100 be spent otherwise." And if she chooses to wed, the Protectors of the Incurables, his Executors and Heirs, " are to marry her to some young man of good reputation and behaviour, apt at managing his own affairs and at earning money,—all this as perfectly as possible, according to the judgment of the said Protectors." If she thus marries with their consent, she is to have £3,000 for her dowry; but if she marries without it, she is to have only £1,500.

Here we note Ettore's high esteem for business capabilities: they are to be required of his possible son-in-law, as one of the conditions for gaining the full dowry; and the curiously unmodern certainty with which he assumes that his still quite young daughter will desire, should she become a Nun, to do so at Sant' Andrea, and, should she neither wed nor enter Religion, is sure to care to live on for life in this one convent. As a matter of fact Ginevrina, who was evidently very happy at Sant' Andrea, took the veil there, still during her father's lifetime, hence within seven years of this date, as Sister Maria Archangela.[1]

And thirdly, we get the striking provision that " any member of the Society of Priests and Laymen " who administer the Hospital for Incurables, " shall have the use of the furniture of the Testator (there remaining), on condition that such member live in this Hospital or in that of the Pammatone (hard by), and not otherwise." He thus comes back here, once again, to one of the deepest convictions of his life: that only by actually living amongst and with the poor, poor yourself; only by doing the work which the right hand finds to do, with such might and thoroughness that both hands, indeed the whole man, body and soul, are drawn into, and are, as it were, coloured by it: that only by such fraternal-paternal sympathetic identification with its object can such service really rise above the dreary perfunctoriness and the ghastly optimism of mere officialism, and have the fruitfulness begotten only by life directly touching life. And here

[1] The three daughters' names in Religion all occur in a document of the Bank of St. George printed in *Inaugurazione*, p. 79.

Catherine's spirit and example, her long life in the very midst of the great Hospital close at hand, are once more fully apparent.

4. *Ettore in the Genoese prisons.*

And, about this time, Vernazza introduced into Genoa the practice and Society which he had first founded in Naples. It was carried out, here also, in the profoundest secrecy. His "Company of St. John the Baptist Beheaded" consisted of himself and three companions: Salvago, Lomellino, and Grimaldo. The Lomellini now owned Giuliano's former Palace in the Via S. Agnese, and the Grimaldi were one of the great Guelph families of Genoa. These four "took a house with a garden, in an out-of-the-way position; and there they started their association. And ever after, when the members met, they always prayed for these their four founders; and always, my Father being dead, began with his name: 'Dominus Hector de Vernatia requiescat in pace.'" "I once," adds Battista, "asked the priest who was their Confessor: 'What matters do they discuss, when they are thus assembled?' But he answered: 'I may not tell'; and put on a particular expression and said: 'The Hospital for Incurables has only ten thousand lire, and it spends twenty-six thousand. And the *Giuseppine* and the *Convertite*' (two other favourite good works of Vernazza) 'have also to be provided for!'"[1] Evidently the subject-matter of all this elaborate secrecy consisted in plans and means for aiding the condemned (often enough innocent or but politically guilty persons) and benefiting the poor; and the privacy was an imperious necessity in those harsh, turbulent and suspicious times. It was Vernazza's own Roman patron and collaborator, the Neapolitan Cardinal Caraffa, who later on, as Pope, imprisoned for two years (1557–1559), in the Castle of St. Angelo, the great and saintly Cardinal Morone, on ungrounded suspicion of heresy; and it was his other patron and most intimate fellow-worker, the Genoese Cardinal Sauli, who, later on, was himself tortured and put to death, the victim of political hatred and suspicion, in his own native city.

And now, (conversely from 1461, when a Fregoso Doge had driven out an Adorno,) an Adorno Doge had just driven out and exiled a Fregoso, and had executed Paolo da Novi. And Vernazza "knew well a close friend of this Doge Adorno,

[1] *Inaugurazione*, p. 18, quoting Battista's letter of 1581.

one who indeed had helped him to his dignity. And yet afterwards they became mortal enemies, and the Doge condemned his former close friend to death. Now this man having been," continues Battista, " attended by some one all night, who tried to comfort him and bring him to patience, the poor prisoner somehow derived no consolation from his attendant's endeavours, but went on repeating: 'When I remember all that I have done for him . . . !' And it was impossible to quiet him. Then he who was spending the wakeful night with him, having noted that all his words had been hitherto of no avail, inspired by God, took another way and said: 'Indeed and indeed you are right,' and made himself infirm with the infirm, and echoed all that the prisoner said, making it appear as though he himself, in a similar case, would be likely to act identically. And then, and only then, the condemned man began to feel relief, and started the telling of his own trouble. And when his companion had agreed to all his points, and at last noticed that the prisoner had thoroughly ventilated all his grievance, he said: 'Indeed, my dear brother, you do not merit this death; but reflect whether, before these occurrences, you did not perform some action which merited it.' Then the latter reconsidered his case, and said at last: 'Yes,—I killed a man.' And his companion replied: 'Behold, my brother, the true cause of your death'; and added other most appropriate words with such good effect that the man became profoundly contrite and died in the very best dispositions of soul." "Now I think," comments Battista, "that the companion was a member of the Society of St. John Baptist, and was, indeed, my Father himself; since my Father told me the story too much in vivid detail (*troppo per sottile*) for him to have been only a reporter. I believe that, to this hour, this society is carrying on the same kind of work." [1]

Here again we have the same irrepressible, humorously resourceful, tenderly shrewd and world-experienced service of God, in and through His image, in any and every fellow-man; the same breadth in thoroughness: the same universality working itself out, and achieving its substance and self-consciousness, in the particular, as we saw at work in Naples. And this activity, all but its humour, recalls the soaring, world-embracing spirit of Catherine absorbed in self-identification

[1] *Inaugurazione*, pp. 19, 20.

with the pestiferous woman's dying aspirations and with the cancer-disfigured navvy's preoccupations for his little wife.

VIII. Ettore again in Naples; his Death in Genoa; Peculiarities of his Posthumous Fame.

1. *Naples and the Signora Lunga.*

It must have been before this prison experience, for Ottaviano Fregoso was still Doge, that Vernazza was again in Naples, and that a thoroughly characteristic, romantic little episode occurred, which not all her seventy-one years of convent life, and the sixty years that had elapsed since its happening, prevent Battista from recounting with a delightfully entire sympathy.

Here in Naples, then, " he joined hands with a certain rich lady, called the Signora Lunga, for the purpose of procuring as many things as possible " for the institutions which he himself had founded or occasioned. This lady, a Spaniard, had been the wife (she was now the widow) of Giovanni Lungo or Longo, President of the Sacred Council.[1] " They went together from house to house, begging for mattresses " for the Hospital. " And this lady now withdrew from the world at large, and lived in that Hospital, and governed and ruled it; and combined with this the execution of other works of mercy. And she had so great a devotion for my Father, that she was wont to say to him: 'If you were to tell me to cut and wound my own person, indeed I would straightway do it.' But on Fregoso writing and pressing him to return to Genoa, Vernazza wrote back, that if he, the Doge, promised to be favourable to him, and to help him in a good work which he had in his mind, he, Vernazza, would come at once. And the Doge wrote back that he would do all that Vernazza wished. And then, one morning early " (no doubt at dawn), " not wishing that the Signora Lunga should see him depart, he got into the saddle. And she, by good chance, saw him, and asked him: 'Where are you going?' And he struck his spurs into his mule: 'To Genoa,' he cried; and flew away; and never saw the Signora Lunga any more." [2]

Something fresh and bracing breathes and beats here still.

[1] I derive this particular from Professore G. Morro's *Inaugurazione*, p. 20.

[2] *Inaugurazione*, p. 20.

We have here the same man who, devoted in every good and filial way to Catherine, had yet left her, no doubt then also on an errand of large-hearted mercy, even in those last days of her life; who now, once again, breaks suddenly away; and who does so again at the call of souls entirely without conventional claims upon him, and who are quite unable to repay him with anything that merely drifting nature ever can hold dear. But here the relation is evidently not that of a man towards a woman much older than himself, and of the spiritual discipleship of a relatively inexperienced soul towards one already far advanced in sanctity: it is clearly one of at least parity of age,—perhaps, indeed, the woman was the younger of the two,—and of largely equal companionship, which would presumably, unchecked, have easily led on to an entirely honourable and happy marriage. And thus, once again, his devotedness had to live and thrive on concrete, untransferable renouncements and sacrifices claimed by his true self in that unique moment and situation: and this too although he will have been at least tempted wistfully to try to delude himself with the monstrous superstition of an automatic sanctity, a merely theoretic and yet somehow real heroism.

2. *The Plague and Ettore's death in Genoa, June* 1524.

"And, arrived in Genoa," Vernazza "revealed the secret of his heart to the Doge, and his Lordship gave him seven thousand lire and the Privilege,"—the latter being necessary, "since no one cared to have the Lazaretto" (for this was Vernazza's project) "in proximity to their villas," and hence the Government had to insist upon its foundation upon the least inconvenient of the various possible sites. And Vernazza in consequence "began to construct a great building for the poor victims of the Plague, and presented it with an endowment of one hundred shares of St. George's, leaving them to multiply, so that at his death they had increased by eleven shares; and now" (in 1581) "they have reached a great number of thousands of pounds." And after continuing with an account of his further Bank dispositions, and of his early attempts to help the poor (already given by us), Battista finishes up this part of her account by declaring: "he was wont to go about saying, with conviction and great confidence, that he hoped all things from God; and that, whenever he put his hand to anything, God put the yeast into that paste." [1]

[1] *Inaugurazione*, p. 21.

And her mention of the Lazaretto then leads her on to the final, still vivid and yet self-restrained, account of her father's death. " The Plague being very severe (*calda*) in Genoa,"—it was past mid-June 1524,—" he came to visit me, and said to me: 'What do you think I had better do? I am determined in no manner to forsake the poor. Do you think I had better go about on horseback or on foot? In which way do you think I would be safest from infection?' 'Oh, Father,' I said, 'here we are coming to the Feast of the Baptist, and are at the highest of the heat; and you are determined to go amongst them?' And he: 'And is it my fate, to hear such things from you? How truly happy should I be, if I were to die for the poor!' Then I, seeing so much fortitude in that holy soul, said to him: 'Father, go.' But he was not content with looking after the Lazaretto: I think that he scoured the country far and wide. And hence he caught the infection. And on the" (Eve of) "the Feast of the Nativity of St. John Baptist," June 23, " he confessed and communicated. And in three days he quietly fell asleep in the Lord." [1]

Surely rarely has so noble a finish been so nobly told! And two things in particular are deserving of special notice. First, there is here again that characteristic combination of quiet reflective common-sense and self-oblivious devotedness. Who could anticipate that the man who so carefully weighed the respective risks of different methods of visiting the sick, would, at the same time, be full of a glad willingness, indeed desire, to die for them? Yet not only does this rich soul exhibit such a living paradox, with an apparent ease and spontaneity, but it is this very extraordinary variety in unity that is an operative cause and element both of the greatness of the act and of its appealingness.

And secondly, it is, I think, not far-fetched to find in this heroic death-ride, if not a direct or even a conscious effect, yet at all events an impressive illustration of, and practical parallel to, Catherine's teaching as to Heaven being already

[1] *Inaugurazione*, pp. 21, 22. Battista's account would lead one to place that last Communion on the Feast itself; but the various inscriptions erected by the most careful Committee of 1867, show that it occurred really on the Eve. See *Inaugurazione*, pp. 37, 39, 40. One more instance of a slight displacement of date effected by a (no doubt unconscious) desire to find a full synchronism between the Feast of the Baptist and the final Communion of one so devoted to that Saint. The Committee evidently shrank from interpreting her " three days after": it may evidently mean either the 26th or the 27th.

present everywhere where pure love energizes, and to her picture of the soul's glad Purgatorial plunge. We know that it was Vernazza himself who, say in 1497, drew forth from her that teaching; and we shall find that it was predominantly he who so carefully registered for us in writing those numerous, vivid picturings of the soul's joyously voluntary self-dedication to suffering and apparent death. And whether at the moment fully conscious of this or not, his act of some twenty years later illustrates and embodies that teaching; and that teaching again universalizes and brings home to us this action. High on horseback he goes forth, the strong, sound-bodied, whole-hearted man, deliberately sure of finding and of bringing Heaven, wheresoever pure love may be wanted and may joyously appear: joyously fruitful, amidst the very ghastliness of death. And he is rapidly brought low, first on to his bed of sickness, and in a few days into the grave. Indeed he himself had, by his own act, gladly accepted, we may say willed, all this: he himself had cast himself down and away into that deep common fosse, amongst the many thousands of his ever-obscure and now disfigured friends and fellow-dead.

3. *His posthumous fame; its unlikeness to Catherine's celebrity.*

For so it was indeed. Instead of burial in the Pammatone Church, under the same roof with his saintly inspirer, the poor pestilential body was buried away, amongst the whole army of others who, like himself, had died of the Plague, without a stone or token of any kind, to mark where this simple hero lay. Nor was it till 1633, over a century later, that a statue was erected to him at his Lazaretto. For the bust in the rooms of his "Compagnia del Mandiletto" is hardly older; and the hideous gaunt plaster statue in the Albergo dei Poveri is no doubt much younger still.

Only in 1867, on June 23, the anniversary of the day on which he prepared himself to die, was a memorial erected to him which is truly worthy of the man. Santo Varni's more than life-size marble statue, which represents Vernazza seated, a strongly built man still in his years of vigour, with a head and countenance striking because of their lofty brow, powerful chin, spiritual, mobile lips, large, keen, far-outward-looking eyes; and with thoroughly individual, operative yet sensitive hands, the left extended open, as though to give and ever again to give, and the right reposing upon the case containing the Chart of the Hospital's foundation: stands, a striking symbol, in the vestibule of the Hospital for Incurables which he founded, where for fifteen years he lived, and where he died.[1] One would be glad to think that the likeness of this admirable work of art reposed upon grounds more direct than one or other of the very late and unworthy representations that preceded it; the authentic portrait of his daughter Battista,[2] who may, after all, have been unlike him in looks; and the sympathetic imagination of a great artist. It was Vernazza himself who prevented any contemporary representation of his own features. For Battista tells us, in her letter of 1581, "he also mortified himself in any inclination to honour. Thus, as is well known, when the Lazaretto had been erected, and he was asked to have his portrait painted to be placed there, he answered: 'I do not want smoke,' and refused to act as he was bidden." [3]

Now here we cannot but find a contrast between Catherine and Ettore; yet it only concerns their posthumous earthly fate and fame. A picture of Catherine was, no doubt, no more painted in her lifetime with her knowledge than was a portrait of Ettore. Yet we know that, in her case, a picture was painted, if not secretly during her lifetime, in any case by some eye-witness, and not more than eighteen months after her death; and a popular religious Cultus to her sprang up and grew, on occasion of that early opening of her coffin. But Ettore has to wait over a century for his first artistic embodiment, and of religious Cultus there was never any question.[4] Whence this difference? Have we any kind of reason for suspecting Ettore's heroism, indeed sanctity of life and death? Was he indeed clearly much the lesser in the Kingdom of God than was his friend?

The question, it will be noted, does not imply any criticism of the Church's wise requirement of a previous Cultus, as one

[1] As to the older monuments, see *Inaugurazione*, p. 5. An excellent photograph of Varni's statue forms the title-picture to this publication.

[2] An engraving of this (now lost) portrait exists in *Ritratti ed Elogii di Liguri Illustri*, Genova, Ponthonier, and appears reproduced here as the Frontispiece to Vol. II.

[3] *Inaugurazione*, p. 26.

[4] Even such a rhetorical apostrophe as occurs in the peroration of Dottore Morro's speech (*Inaugurazione*, p. 30): "Thou worthy of incense and of altars, as was that Catherine Fieschi, whose friend and confidant and spiritual son thou wast, and who was God-mother to thy own first-born," stands, I think, alone.

of the conditions for the introduction of any and every Process; still less is there any disposition to call in question the choice of Catherine for saintly honours, a choice which this whole book would hope to demonstrate as particularly courageous, wise and indeed providential. The point raised concerns simply the psychology of popular devotion, and the human reason why, given that one was certainly a Saint and the other was presumably another one, there is this marked contrast in the posthumous history of these two lives.

Now if the question be taken thus, the answer can hardly be doubtful. Certainly not because of her profoundly original doctrine, by which Catherine is speculatively more interesting and humanly more complete than Vernazza, was Catherine prized and preferred to Vernazza by the crowd. Nor did they single her out precisely because of her works and long life of mercy, for Vernazza's labours of this kind no doubt exceeded Catherine's, both in their variety and in their visible extension. But it was the psycho-physical peculiarities of the life of Catherine, and the more or less complete incorruption of the body: these two things, neither of which has any necessary connection with that faithful and heroic use of free-will and that spirit and grace of God in which the whole substance of sanctity consists, which, each leading on and back to and strengthening the impression and tradition of the other, determined the outbreak and onflow of popular devotion in the one case, and the absence of which prevented the growth of any such cultus in the other. And thus we have here one more instance of the pathetic irony of fate, or rather one of those many mysterious operations of the divine will which, under the ebb and flow of influences that seem merely human and deteriorative, works in history for the slow upward-raising of our poor kind.

When the well-known ecstatic Augustinian Nun, Anne Catharine Emmerich, died at Dülmen, in Westphalia, on February 6, 1824, her remains also were not long allowed to rest undisturbed in the grave. Already in mid-March the poetess Luise Hensel, who had much loved and venerated her, caused the grave to be opened quite privately, in hopes of finding the body still incorrupt, and of once more being able to gaze on that striking countenance. And a few days later, on March 21 and 22, the grave and coffin were again, this time officially, opened. In both cases the body was found still incorrupt, and two pale red spots appeared on the cheeks.

But when, on October 6, 1858, the grave was opened a third and last time, nothing was found of the coffin but one nail, and the body was now represented only by so many separate bones.[1] Now when, some twenty years ago, I visited Dülmen in the company of a distinguished Münster Priest, the latter told me, as we stood together by the grave-side, that this discovery had greatly checked the survivals or beginnings of any such local and popular cultus as had been expected and hoped for by Anne Catharine's, mostly distant or foreign, admirers.

Similar cases it would be easy to multiply; and they all point to the great advantage, probably to the actually determining incentive, which accrued to the Cultus of Catherine, in that her body continued more or less incorrupt, and thus added a sensible marvel after death to the sensible marvels of her fasts and ecstasies during life. Whereas Catharine Emmerich's analogous psycho-physical condition during life was not thus reinforced by an unusual physical condition after death. And Ettore, again, had evidently nothing physically, or even psycho-physically, abnormal about him, either in life or in death.

[1] Schmöger: *Leben der gottseligen Anna Katharina Emmerich*, Freiburg, 1867, 1870, Vol. II, pp. 892, 898, 900.

CHAPTER VIII

BATTISTA VERNAZZA'S LIFE

INTRODUCTORY.

WE have, in the characters described in the previous chapter, dwelt upon figures remarkably unlike Catherine, on her psycho-physical side. Yet it would be only too easy for us now-a-days, by dwelling too much upon the foregoing contrast, to grow actually unfair to Catherine's kind of temperament and health, and to her mode of apprehending truth and of attaining sanctity. We might thus come to overlook or to under-estimate the important fact that certain psycho-physical, neural peculiarities or states most certainly constitute the general antecedents, concomitants or consequences (probably, indeed, one of the necessary though secondary conditions), not indeed of sanctity, but of at least some forms of the contemplative gift, habit, and attainment. We might, too, forget that neither this contemplative gift itself, nor even those neural peculiarities, are at all incompatible with great practical shrewdness and an unusually large external activity; indeed that such rare and costly contemplative picturings and symbolizations of the Unseen are, when true and deep, means and helps for the contemplative, in his own life and often still more in his influence upon others, towards a great recollection and concentration, which would not only turn the soul away from the dispersion and feverishness that sets in towards the close of external action, but would also bring it back renewed to such outward-moving, joyful-humble creativeness, as wholesome recollection itself requires. For without such contact with the material and the opposition of external action, recollection grows gradually empty; and without recollection, external action rapidly becomes soul-dispersive. Hence it is plain, that the true significance and living system of any such deep soul may be on too large a scale not to require, for its due exhibition, that we survey it in connection with some other supplementary life,—like unto some Gobelin design or cloth-pattern, so large as to require two contiguous walls or two human figures to show its totality by means of their combination.

Now Vernazza the father, who throughout his life possessed the most robust and normal health, can fairly be taken as Catherine's supplementary figure, for the years when ill-health was limiting her normal range of energies, on their operatively outgoing, philanthropic side; and is thus a living protest against isolating Saints' lives from their complementary extensions and effects. But Battista, his daughter, gives us, in her own person and up to the end of her life, an example of the combination and stimulating interaction of the Contemplative and the Practical, the Transcendent and the Immanental, the heroically normal and Universal and the tenderly Personal, indeed the more or less psycho-physically peculiar. Catherine was the greater, more original, and more winning Contemplative, and Ettore was more massively Practical than was Battista. Yet Battista possessed both gifts, from early times up to the end, apparently unclouded and unbroken by any kind of incapacitation.

I. Battista's Life, from April 1497 to June 1510.

We have already seen how Ettore's eldest child was born on April 15, 1497, and was held at the font by Catherine, receiving, however, the name of Tommasa, after the God-father, the celebrated Doctor of Law, Tommaso Moro. Giuliano was still alive, but already gravely ill. Nothing could well prove more clearly Vernazza's closeness of friendship for the Adorna and for Moro than his making them thus his first-born's God-parents. And Moro's subsequent history makes this, his intimate collocation and spiritual affinity with Catherine a matter suggestive of much reflection.

With her beautiful young mother still alive and living at home with her, Tommasa, a child of precocious intelligence, took to writing verse of various kinds, as early as at ten years of age. Vallebona quotes, from Semeria's *Secoli Cristiani della Liguria*, ten short lines written by her at that age, and which he apparently holds to have been addressed to her God-mother. They are, however, too vague and hyperbolical for one to be sure as to whom they are dedicated; her own mother or the Blessed Virgin would, I think, fit the case respectively as well as, or better than, Catherine. The "short days" prophesied for herself by the little girl, were destined to amount to ninety years! [1]

On her mother dying, some time in 1508 or 1509,—Bartolommea can hardly have been more than thirty-two years of age, and Ettore some six years older,—Vernazza decided, as we know, against continuing an establishment of his own and keeping his three daughters with him. It is certain from his Wills that he had no near female relative whom he could have asked to come and help, or to take, the children; and clear that he was determined not to marry again, so as to remain completely free for his philanthropic work. And hence he was driven to the alternative of boarding the girls in the two convents that we know.

And already on June 24, 1510, on the feast of her father's favourite Saint and prison-work Patron, Tommasa received the habit of an Augustinian Canoness of the Lateran, and changed her name to Battista. Catherine had still not quite twelve weeks to live, and may well have been deeply interested in her God-daughter's taking of the veil in that very Convent and at the very age where and when she herself had, half-a-century before, desired to receive it.[2] We cannot but feel that the Superiors were wise who, at that earlier date, had found thirteen too young an age for even an Italian, so early physically mature, and a Catherine, so little suited for marriage, to take even this first and revocable step in the Religious life; and we would doubtless have experienced some uneasiness at the time when Tommasa was somehow

[1] Vallebona, *op. cit.* p. 83: "Santissima mia Diva, | questo mio cor ricevi: | che quando al sole apriva | le luci a giorni brevi, | infin d'allor fei voto, | con animo devoto, | non mai, madre adorata, | esser da Te sviata." "My most holy Protectress" and "adored Mother" may apply to Catherine. But I have had to punctuate so as to make "che" = "perchè," as in Jacopone throughout: so that we now have not a declaration of time, as to when she, the Protectress, accepted Tommasa's heart (which might well have been at Baptism); but a prayer that this Mother may accept her heart, in view of the fact that she, Tommasa, had, from her first opening of her eyes to life (surely, on coming to some degree of reason), vowed never to be parted from this Mother. And thus the application to Catherine remains possible but becomes uncertain.

[2] I feel obliged to put the matter in this hypothetical form because of the several undeniable indications of Catherine's loss of interest in many, perhaps most, events and occurrences, since, at latest, the beginning of 1509.

allowed to take this identical step at the very same age. Yet we have, as we shall see, full and absolutely conclusive, because first-hand, evidence, that every one concerned in the case acted with true insight. Rarely indeed can a woman have been more emphatically in her right place, than Battista during her seventy-seven years at Santa Maria delle Grazie. And this complete and comfortable appropriateness of vocation no doubt helped her large, balanced, virile mind to feel, with the Church, that such a vocation is but one amongst the numberless forms of even heroic devotedness, a devotedness of which the essence is interior and is capable of being exercised, and which requires to be represented in every honest circumstance and calling of God's great, many-coloured world.

Of Catetta's further history, beyond her reception of the veil in the same Convent, under the name of Daniela, some time before November 1517, and of Ginevrina's later lot, beyond her becoming a Cistercian Nun, under the name of Maria Archangela, at Sant' Andrea, some time between 1517 and 1524, I have been unable to discover anything. But as to Battista, I wish to dwell upon three characteristic episodes of her long life; they all three throw much light both upon Catherine and (still more) upon the whole question of Mysticism.

II. Battista and her God-father, Tommaso Moro

The first episode illustrates the rigoristic side of the pre-Reformation Catholic temper and teaching, and the terrible complications, perplexities and pitfalls of those strenuous, confusing times. For we must now move on fifteen further years from that interview with her father, a few days before his death, in June 1524, to reach this event, the first fresh one in Battista's life of which we have a record.

1. *The early stages of Lutheranism and Calvinism.*

The Religious Revolution had now well nigh reached its culmination. Battista's father had only lived to see what may rightly be termed the first step in the Teutonic stage and element of the movement, a stage which, in spite of its political and social, indeed religious, violences and fanaticisms,—and even these came mostly after Vernazza's death,—retained, if in large part illogically yet with great practical advantage, a considerable portion of the old Catholic convictions and spiritual attitude. Luther had indeed, as we saw, published his Theses in 1517, and Pope Leo X had condemned nearly one-half of them in 1520 in his Bull of Excommunication. And Melanchthon, the mild and deeply learned, had also broken with the Old Church, and had begun, in 1521, the publication of his *Loci*. But an earnest Catholic (in this case a Teutonic) Reformer had become Pope, in the person of Adrian Dedel of Utrecht (Hadrian VI), in 1522, 1523. And in the very year of Ettore's heroic death, Erasmus, proving, under the stress of the times, substantially true to the Old Faith, was writing against Luther; whilst in Italy, Vernazza's old patron, Cardinal Caraffa, was helping to found the Theatine Order.

But within the next fifteen years matters move on and further. For first the Teutonic stage of the Revolution takes its second step, and hardens, and formally and permanently organizes itself; whilst its socially anarchical effects reach their zenith. For there are the Peasants' War and Luther's marriage in 1525; and the capture and the sack of Rome by the Imperial (largely Lutheran) troops in 1527; and the Revolutionists' assumption of the name of "Protestants," at the Diet of Speyer, in 1529. And, on the Roman Church's part, the Capuchins are founded in 1525, and the Barnabites in 1530. And this whole Teutonic stage of the Revolution can be taken as closed, for the time, by the terrible Saturnalia of the Anabaptists at Münster, 1533–1535; the executions of the Catholic Humanists, Bishop Fisher and Chancellor More, in England, 1535; and Erasmus's death in 1536.

And the second element and stage, the Romanic Revolution, was now fully and independently at work, with its indefinitely greater coldness and logical completeness, and its systematic antagonism to the Old Faith. And if the Saxon Mystical-minded Peasant-monk, Luther, stood at the head and in the centre of the first movement, the Picardese bourgeois lawyer and Humanist, Calvin, stands now at the head of this second movement. Born in 1509, he flees, now an avowed Protestant, in 1535 to Basle; and in the spring of 1536 publishes his *Institutio Religionis Christianae,* which was destined to remain his chief work.

Now it was in the summer of that year that Calvin went to stay at the Court of Renée de Valois, daughter of the French King Louis XII, and Duchess of Ferrara, who had already been gained over to the cause of the Lutheran

Reformers; and who was now influenced, by her grim, relentless guest, to move still further away from the Old Church. And though the Roman Inquisition succeeded in forcing Calvin to leave Italy, after not many weeks' stay: yet the cases of Vittoria Colonna, Bernardino Occhino, and of our Tommaso Moro, show us all plainly, though each differently, how complex and difficult, how obscure and full of pitfalls, was the situation for even permanently loyal and indeed saintly, and still more for simply earnest and eager, souls. For Vittoria Colonna, that truly saint-like daughter of the Church, not only stays, during the following year, with the Duchess Renée at Ferrara, and indeed stands God-mother to her daughter Eleonora (born June 19, 1537), the child that, later on, became the friend of the poet Tasso: but Vittoria is the close friend and confidante of that most zealous preacher, that restless, ardent, absolute-minded Bernardino Occhino, who, born in Siena in 1487, had joined the Franciscan Reform, the later Capuchins, in 1534, and indeed, in 1539, became their General. It is to Vittoria indeed that, on his deciding not to obey the summons to Rome, there to defend himself against the (no doubt, in part, unfair) attacks upon his teaching, he, in the night of August 22, 1542, before his flight and abandonment of his Order and of the Church, writes his still extant sad and saddening letter of self-exculpation.[1] But this latter catastrophe was not to take place till three years after the date at which I would now linger.

2. *Moro becomes a Calvinist: probable causes of this step.* It must, I think, have been through some influence emanating from the not very far away Ferrara, that the Genoese Tommaso Moro was, just about this time, carried away into Calvinism. We must not forget that, deplorable as was such an aberration, there were two excuses for him, which would apply no doubt, in varying degrees, to many others even of those who were, at this time, permanently lost to the Church.

For one thing the views held, and allowably held, during two or three generations, on points of Grace and Free-will, of Predestination and the corruption of the natural man, by even those whom the Church eventually raised to her Altars, were, as a matter of fact, less removed from the Protestant Reformers' positions, than were probably any views (with the exception

[1] See the admirably vivid account of, and wisely-balanced judgment concerning, these events, in the Catholic Alfred von Reumont's little book *Vittoria Colonna*, Freiburg, 1881, pp. 117–152; 194–215.

of the extreme Jansenist position) which have prevailed in the Catholic Church since the Protestant Reformation. St. Catherine, Moro's fellow God-parent, had expressed herself, in certain moods, in so rigoristic a sense on these deep matters, as to invite the comment of the Bollandist Sticker that these passages are *caute legenda*.[1] Yet Catherine, in speaking thus, simply resembled probably all her really earnest contemporaries—witness the great Paris Chancellor Jean Gerson, some time before, and the devoted Cardinals Contarini and Morone and Vittoria Colonna, a little after Catherine's own zenith.[2]

Again, the practical, moral abuses were most real and often very pressing; and whilst the numerous attempts at Reform extending now over a century (the Council of Constance had assembled in 1414) had emphasized this fact, they had also plainly shown, by their practical abortiveness, how very difficult the attainment of such a universally desired Reform persisted in appearing, if there was to be no final breach with Rome.

And the fullest consequences of such a breach could not be present to the experience, or even to the imagination, of the first who made it, as they are to us, or even as they were after the second step of the Romanic Revolution had been taken by Lelio Socino, the Sienese and his nephew Fausto Socino, the founders of Socinianism, who died respectively in 1562 and 1604,—the former shortly after Occhino had died, in 1560, miserably alone and out of the Catholic Roman Church.

3. *Battista's letter to Moro, September* 1537; *its effect.*

Now it was on September 10, 1537, that his Augustinian God-daughter wrote, to her now Calvinist God-father, a letter which occupies five pages of print in the fifth, a handsome octavo, edition of her works published in Genoa in 1755 Though the earliest of all her extant, or at least of her printed, letters, it is evidently an answer to a communication of his, in which he had urged certain objections against the Roman Church. And that communication must have been provoked by a first letter from herself—a letter which, though probably less theologically interesting and learned, will have been more uniformly touching than the one preserved. Yet if that first note had clearly succeeded in getting him to state his case,

[1] *Acta Sanctorum*, Vol. VI, pp. 192–196.

[2] For Gerson's "Rigorism," see J. B. Schwab's admirable monograph, *Johannes Gerson*, Regensburg, 1858; and for Contarini's, Morone's, and the Colonna's views, see Reumont's *Vittoria Colonna*.

this second letter also, we shall see, completely attained its still more important object.

Moro had insisted that the Roman Church followed merely human inventions in the matter of (1) Fasting; (2) Confession; (3) the Real Presence; (4) Public Prayer and Psalmody; (5) Vows; and (6) Extreme Unction.—The order is curious, but is evidently not hers but his. Extreme Unction stands in the obvious position—at the end. The vows of Religion immediately precede it, probably because, at this time, they typified something not only irrevocable but sepulchral to this ardent Calvinist. Public Prayer and Psalmody would naturally precede these vows, as an appropriate link between the life of the cloister, so largely given to the Divine Office, and the Real Presence, its celebration being and requiring the most marked of all the exhibitions of Public Prayer. Confession would stand before the Real Presence, as being actually practised before the reception of Communion. And Fasting, finally, would precede Confession, and would, most characteristically, head the whole list, because the completest and most universally binding of all Fasts is that which is antecedent to Holy Communion; and because, in beginning thus, Moro can start his attack on the Church by the criticism of something that is obviously and avowedly external.

The tone of Battista's answer is interesting throughout, for a double reason. There is in it a successful, very difficult combination of filial respect and of lofty reproof; and there runs through all the argumentation a sort of legal hard-headedness, entirely in its place on the lips of the lawyer s daughter in dealing with her lawyer correspondent. I give her answers to his second and fifth objections, since the former is interesting as touching on the point of the obligation and frequency of Sacramental Confession, which has occupied us much in her God-mother's life; and the latter gives a vivid insight into Battista's own deeply genuine and happy vocation.

As to Confession, she writes: "You hold one opinion, and the Church holds another; and to this Church it has not appeared good to constrain us to confess ourselves in public, nor always to manifest our whole interior to any and every man who may reprehend us. In this latter case we should have been left without any protection. You grudge obeying her once a year; how then would you carry out the other plan? Certainly the said Church would have but little authority if she could not lay down ordinances, according to her own judgment, concerning the mode (of administration and reception) of the Sacraments already ordained by Christ."

As to Vows, she finishes up by declaring: "According to my humble judgment, that thing cannot be called slavery which a soul elects for itself, by an act of free choice alone, and with a supreme desire. And in this matter you really can trust me, since here I am, living under the very test of experience, and yet I have no consciousness of being bound to any obligation: so little indeed that, if I had full licence from God to do all those things of which I have deprived myself by my vows, I would do neither more nor less than what I now am actually doing; indeed no taste for anything beyond these latter things arises within me. How then do you come to give the name of servitude to that which gets embraced thus with supreme delight? Perchance you will say 'not every one is thus disposed.' My dear Sir: he who does not find this inclination within him, let him not execute it. Neither Christ nor His Church constrain any one in this matter." [1]

The effect of this homely and sensible, straightforward and firm, first-hand witness to a strong soul's full daily life of faith and self-expansion in and for Christ in His extension, the Old Church, was evidently decisive, perhaps immediate. It is at least certain that Tommaso Moro came back to the Roman obedience; that he became and died a Priest and Religious; and that his return is universally attributed to the instrumentality of this letter.[2]

III. Battista's *Colloquies*, November 1554 to Ascension-Day 1555.

Yet her letters form but a small part of the literary output of this many-sided woman. Her printed writings fill six stout volumes, in all some 2,400 octavo pages, and fall into four chief divisions. The independent verses consist only of four "Canticles of Divine Love," twelve "Spiritual Canticles," and five "Sonnets." Yet even the second division, which alone fills quite five out of the six volumes, and consists of Spiritual Discourses or Dissertations, contains much verse, since the Discourse (which invariably takes its title and starting-point

[1] *Opere*, Vol. VI, p. 192.

[2] See the Preface to the *Opere*, Vol. I, p. 10.

from some, originally or interpretatively, Mystical Biblical text) usually finishes up with a chapter of eight verses, in which she sums up metrically the doctrine which she has just expounded in finely balanced and stately prose. Mostly proceeding from some Pauline, or, more often still, some Joannine text, these writings evince throughout a fine Christian-Platonist breadth of outlook and concentration and expansion of devotional feeling, and have much of that unfading freshness which appertains to the universal experiences of religion, wherever these are experienced deeply and anew and are communicated largely in the form and tone of their actual experimentation. These Discourses would also, of course, furnish all but endless parallels and illustrations to Catherine's teachings.

Yet it is the last two divisions of Battista's writings which are the most entirely characteristic and suggestive—her *Colloquies* and her *Letters*. As to the seventy-five pages of letters, I have already given extracts from two, of the years 1581 and 1539, and shall presently give portions of two others, of the years 1575 and 1576. But in this section I want to translate and comment upon a considerable portion of her *Colloquies*, so interesting for various reasons, all directly connected with the subject of this book. These contemporary annotations occupy only eleven pages of print, but they constitute, I think, one of the most instructive first-hand documents of mystical and religious psychology in existence, and have nowhere, as yet, received any of the comparative and analytic study they so richly deserve.

It is but right to remember throughout, that even all her other writings (including the Discourses which are so general and, in a manner, quite public in their tone) were, with the sole exception of her Sonnets, none of them printed with her knowledge and consent. A certain Secular Priest, Gaspare Scotto, did indeed print some at least of the Discourses, without her knowledge, during her long lifetime; but the *Colloquies* were certainly never meant for any eyes other than her own, and were doubtless not printed, or indeed known, until after her death. I suppose them to have first appeared in the collected edition of her works, published in 1602, fifteen years after her demise.

Now these *Colloquies* belong to three periods. The first set is timed vaguely *una volta;* and the third is also but approximately fixed; but the second, by far the longest and most important series, is, at its main turning-points, dated with absolute precision. And since its authenticity, the identity of the chronicler with the experiencing person, and the complete contemporaneousness of the record, are all beyond cavil or question (the majority of the entries were evidently put down by her on the very day, often probably within the hour, of the cessation of the experience thus chronicled)—the document can serve as a simply first-hand illustration of, and commentary on, the analogous experiences of Battista's God-mother, experiences which, in the latter case, were nowhere recorded by their subject, nor indeed by others till probably, in some cases, a considerable time after their occurrence. And if here again there can be no difficulty, for any sincere and consistent believer, in holding that we have to do with enlightenments of the mind and stimulations of the affections and will, proceeding as truly from God as they led back to Him: we cannot but, here again, find plentiful indications of the antecedent material, and of the co-operation, response, and special colour furnished throughout by the human subject's special sex and age, race and period, temperament, training, and reading. Not all the latter conditions put together would explain even half of the total experience; yet had these conditions been different, the total experience would have differed, not indeed in its fundamental contents, yet in its special forms and applications. As matters stand, these latter are often strikingly like those manifested in the teaching of Catherine, Battista's fellow-Genoese. I will now take the nine most interesting days of this series,[1] stopping after certain of them to point out parallels and peculiarities.

1. *Experience of November* 17, 1554.

"On (Saturday) November 17, 1554" (Battista was now fifty-seven and a half years old), "having, before Holy Communion, a great desire to die to all things, I prayed with all my heart that God, in the most perfect manner possible, would slay me and unite me with Himself. And in so doing I renounced into His hands all myself and everything existing under heaven, whilst electing God anew as my only Love, my only Solace, my only Comfort, and my All. And I refused to accept every consolation arising from such interiorness, however holy the latter might be, except inasmuch as the consolation arises whilst the interior is distinctly occupied

[1] *Opere*, ed. Genoa, 1755, Vol. V, pp. 218–227.

with God, and does not turn its gaze upon itself or upon any (other) belovèd object. Even if I could enjoy all this, quite justly, till the day of judgment, I renounce it all. Nothing pleases me, except my God. And if I were assured, which God forbid, of going (to abide) under Lucifer, still would I will, neither more nor less than my God alone. And it would be grievous to me to embrace, even for one single hour, anything else but Him.—After this Communion I remained with a most intense impression of renouncing, with regard to all things and to all moments, all myself and every other thing that is lower than Thee; and with a determination to keep Forty Days of silence, depriving myself during them, as far as my own will and inclination went, even of such reasoning as turned on religious subjects.—And acting thus, by means of Thy grace alone, I arrived, in my inner heart, at having no other actions left, except those of adoring Thee and praying for all men. Whence it happened that I experienced the most quiet and consoling week that, possibly, I have ever had, up to this hour, in all my life."

It is clear that even the first part of this week's experience was not written down later than at the end of that week; indeed it reads more as if written down on at least two, and perhaps three, occasions. We have here many close parallels to Catherine: to her exclamation of "God is my Being . . . my Delight"; to the Divine Voice heard by her, "I do not wish thee henceforth to turn thine eyes to right or left"; to the question asked, and the interior answer heard, by her, as to "love and union not being able to exist without a great contentment of soul"; to her assertions that "the attribution to her own separate self of even one single meritorious act, would be to her as though a Hell," and that "she would rather remain in eternal condemnation than be saved by such an act of the separate self"; to her Love saying within her, "that He wanted her to keep the Forty Days in His Company in the Desert"; and to her declaration that she could not pray for Vernazza and his fellow-disciples separately, but could only "present them" collectively "in His presence." And in Battista's phrase of "going under Lucifer," we have again, if we take it together with the renunciation of "all things lower than God," an illustration of those sayings of Catherine which I have grouped under the special category of "up" and "above." [1]

[1] See here, pp. 265, 266; 272; 280; 264, 265; 135; 160, 274–276.

And note, in Battista's record, how the contradiction, which appears between her affirmation of having love for God alone, and the admission that she loved herself and other things (since she is determined not to let her mental gaze rest upon these latter beloved objects), is more apparent than real. For the former love is the direct and central object of her fully deliberate and free endeavours; the latter is instinctive, continuous, inevitable, but, inasmuch as it now still remains actively willed at all, it is but the consequential and peripheral object of that willing. As in all deep religion there is here an heroic willing at work to effect a genuine displacement of the centre and object of interest; the system from being instinctively man-centred, becomes a freely willed God-centredness.

2. *Experience of November* 25, 1554.

"On Sunday" (November 25), "the Feast of St. Catherine" (Virgin Martyr of Alexandria) "was being celebrated. And I communicated with new emotion. And when I received the Host, I willed Thee, my God, alone; renouncing all the rest into Thy hands: I but desired to die and unite myself with Thee. And I felt within me those colloquies of Thine own extreme love; and Thou didst say unto me, O my Joy, 'The thing that thou seekest is (already) produced eternally in My Divine Mind. Thou desirest to feed on mutability, and I desire to feed thee on eternity.' And I do not remember in what connection Thou didst say, 'Ego ero merces tua magna nimis' (Gen. xv, 1)."

Here, on her God-mother's Saint's day, we find that act of pure love at the moment of Holy Communion so dear to Catherine also; and we get here, as in the previous group (but here, even on occasion of the Holy Eucharist), prayer and aspiration directed to God pure and simple, or to God conceived as Love and Joy, precisely as in the Fiesca's ordinary practice.[1] And the inner voice, if it says deeply mystical things, also directly quotes Scripture in Latin, whilst the scrupulous care of Battista, in registering her oblivion of the precise context in which this quotation appeared, is interestingly characteristic of her nature and experience.

3. *Experience of December* (9?), 1554.

"On Sunday" (December 9?) "I communicated; and I experienced within myself the most tender colloquies of Thy

[1] See here, pp. 116; 117, 266.

Majesty, which said to me, 'The time will come when thou must be so occupied with Me—with My Divinity, My Infinity, My Glory—that, even if thou shouldst so wish, thou wouldest be unable to break off this preoccupation. I have elected thee from amongst thousands. I want to make thee My very Self.' . . . Then Thou saidst unto me, 'I do not want thee to merit, but to return the love which I ever bear thee.'"[1]

Here we have parallels to Catherine's practice and declarations in Battista's ever-growing occupation with God; in her, at first sight, strongly pantheistic, because apparently substantial, identification of her true self with God; and in her doctrine that God desires not that we should merit, but that we should, by purely loving, make Him a return of His own pure love. And, as but an apparent contrast, note how here it is God Who chooses out Battista's soul from amongst thousands; whilst, with Catherine, we have herself instinctively choosing out God, even were He, *per impossibile*, like to one of the whole Court of Heaven (the angels, "whose number is thousands of thousands," Apoc. v, 11). For the difference consists, at bottom, only in the fact that each dwells, in these special instances, upon the other half of the complete mystic circle of the divine and human intercourse. The same complete scheme is, in reality, experienced and proclaimed both by the widow and the nun,—indeed God's prevenient election of the soul, and His special attention to it, is even more strongly emphasized by the older woman: "It appears to me, indeed, that God has no other business than myself."[2]

Remark, too, how here again an unmistakable text of Scripture appears as part of the words heard by Battista. But since it is a composite quotation—"I have elected thee," coming from Isa. xliii, 10; xliv, 1; xlviii, 10; and "elected among thousands," coming from Cant. v, 10, where the elect is (as with Catherine) the Bridegroom, and not (as with Battista) the Bride,—therefore, no doubt, it does not appear in Latin or with any reference.

4. *Experience of December* 16, 1554.

"The following Sunday" (December 16) "I communicated with a greater desire for Union than usual, and with a

[1] The last clause here is very obscure in the original: "non voglio meritare te, ma rimeritare lo amore che ti porto"; but I take the above translation to render correctly the substantial meaning.

[2] See here, pp. 265; 262, 263, 261.

more detailed sight concerning it. And after this communion I prayed in such a state of Union,—without any means either of thoughts or of anything else that could be made to intervene, remaining naked in Thy bosom as I have been from eternity. And whilst praying thus, I felt that certain words were being spoken within me, the gist of which (*la sentenza*) seems to me to have been, that my prayer did not reach to the reality of Union itself. So that there then came to my mind that which Paul says, Rom. viii (26), that 'we do not know how to pray *sicut oportet*.' And Thou saidst to me that, above all understanding of mine, Thou wouldest produce the effect; indeed the thing is already effected continuously in Thy divine mind. And Thou saidst to me, my only Love, that Thou didst will to make me Thyself; and that Thou wast all mine, with all that Thou hadst and with all Paradise; and that I was all Thine. That I should leave all, or rather the nothing; and that (then) Thou wouldst give me the all. And that Thou hadst given me this name—at which words I heard within me 'dedi te in lucem gentium'—not without good reason. And it seemed then, as though I had an inclination for nothing except the purest Union, without any means, in accordance with that detailed sight which Thou hadst given me. So then I said to Thee: 'These other things, give them to whom Thou wilt; give me but this most pure Union with Thee, free from every means.' "

Here we again have numerous parallels. Battista's state of Union, without any means that could be made to intervene, compares readily with Catherine's declaration: "I cannot abide to see that word 'for' (God) and 'in' (God), since they denote to my mind something that can stand between God and myself." Battista's description, "remaining naked in Thy bosom, as I have been from eternity," resembles Catherine's sayings: "True love wills to stand naked. This naked love sees the truth"; "the soul in that state of cleanness in which it was created"; "the angels and man, when disobedient, were clothed in sin"; and the words heard by her: "I want thee naked, naked." The answer granted to Battista, that "possessing her Lord, her only Love, she possessed at the same time all Paradise," recalls Catherine's declaration that "if of what her heart felt but one drop were to fall into Hell, Hell itself would become Eternal Life." And Battista's prayer, "these other things, give them to whom Thou wilt; give me but this most pure Union with Thee," is substantially like

Catherine's answer to the Friar, " that you should merit more than myself—I leave that in your hands; but that I cannot love Him as much as you, is a thing that you will never by any means get me to understand." [1]

And we get here two further interesting particularities as to such " locutions." In this case Battista only " feels," at the time of their occurrence, that certain words are being spoken within her (once before she has used that remarkably general term, instead of the more obvious and specific "hear"); and she possesses, on coming (evidently soon after) to write them down, a but approximate remembrance of them, and a certainty as to their substance alone. And then we find here the interesting case of two different simultaneous locutions: one voice referring to the name which our Lord had given her, and another, at this point, quoting the text, " dedi te in lucem gentium." The text, in this full form, occurs in Isaiah xlix, 6, and is there spoken by God to His servant Israel, v. 3; but part of it, expanded to " a light to the revelation of the Gentiles," is, in Luke ii, 32, quoted by Simeon of Christ. We thus, in this place, get three different, yet simultaneous, levels of consciousness within Battista's soul: her own (more or less ordinary) consciousness and " voice " recognized by her own self, as such; another, deeper, extraordinary consciousness and "voice" proceeding, according to her apprehension, from our Lord's presence and action within her; and finally a third, deepest consciousness and " voice " taken, I presume, to be directly communicated by God Himself. It is to be noted that, though interior " locutions " seem to have been fairly frequent with Catherine, there is no case on record in her life of more than two levels of consciousness, two " voices," at one and the same moment, her own and Love's.

5. *Experience of December* 23, 24, 1554.

" The following night " (December 23 to 24), " I woke up and found impressed upon my mind (the words): ' comedite bonum,' Isaiah lv (2). And this impression remained with me (throughout the day),—an impression of eating God, and of inviting all others to the same Divine food.—In the evening,—it was the Vigil of the Nativity,—I had a sight of how, God Himself having taken our nature, and having done so as the Infinite one, the very greatest virtue must be diffused through-

[1] See here, pp. 266, 268; 285; 261; 275, 159, 141.

out this same (human) nature: a truth which he knew who says: 'Plena est omnis terra gloria eius,' Isaiah vi (3). If by one man sin entered into all, by a God-man how much good has not entered into us all? Romans v, 15–19. If God has made Himself Flesh, what virtue is there which He has denied to this same flesh?—And in the night of the Nativity, after Matins, I had a sight of that extreme, eternal and incomprehensible Love, which, unable to abide within Itself, had become ecstatic into the thing It loved, and had indeed, by means of Its Almighty power, become that very thing. Whence it is that, seeing Thy Majesty gone forth out of Thyself and become me, I was determined, in virtue of that self-same love, to go forth from myself and, in every manner, make myself into Thy very Self. And Thou, my God, didst say that Thou hadst descended to the same degree as that to which Thou wantedst man to ascend."

Here Battista's "impression of eating God, and of inviting all others to the same Divine food" is substantially identical with Catherine's doctrine as to the "One Bread, God," and "all creatures hungering for this One Bread." Battista's sight of "God being diffused throughout human nature," is analogous to Catherine's teaching as to no creature existing that does not, in some measure, participate in His goodness,—although, with characteristic difference, Battista dwells on the ennoblement of that nature through the Incarnation of God, and Catherine insists upon the nobility contemporaneous with, and intrinsic to, Man's original Creation. And Battista's determination to go forth from herself is identical, in substance, with all the sayings of Catherine which I have grouped under the "outside" "outwards" category.[1]

And note how, in this group, Battista mentally sees, instead of interiorly hearing, the truth of the Incarnation of the Infinite, and of the consequent ennobling of our whole nature; how this sight then suggests to her mind a definite text (recognized by herself as such), and then an amplification of another text (not perhaps identified by her as such at all): and how the transition from that sight to these texts is so smooth and rapid that it is practically impossible to mark off precisely where she held the simply given experience to end, and her own action and comment to begin. The fact of the matter no doubt is that, in both cases, though very possibly in different

[1] See here, pp. 260, 261, 273, 274.

degrees, there was divine and human action indistinguishably co-operant throughout.

And mark again how her "vista"—"of that extreme, eternal, and incomprehensible Love which had become 'ecstatic' into the Thing it loves"; her consequent determination to "go forth from herself," and the voice which told her that He wanted her "to ascend in the same degree as He had descended": all goes back, for its literary suggestion, to the Dionysian "Divine Names": "Divine Love is ecstatic, not permitting any to be lovers of themselves but of those beloved. The very Author of all things, through an overflow of His loving goodness, becomes 'out of Himself,' and is led down from the eminence above all, to being in all." "He is at once moving and conducting Power to Himself, as it were a sort of everlasting circle." "Let us restore all loves back to the one and enfolded Love and Father of them all."[1] Not the less truly did Battista's mental lights and voluntary determinations come from God, because they consisted, for the most part, in a vivid realization and acceptation, in and for her particular case, on this Christmas night in 1554, of spiritual facts and truths which had been slowly and successively revealed, experienced, and formulated as far back as the Hebrew Prophets and the Greek Plato, and above all by our Lord, and in St. Paul's writings and the Gospel of St. John. These truths were none the less hers, because they had been successively experienced and proclaimed, so long ago by others; and their suggestion and realization to and in her, were as truly the work of God in her own case as they were in that of those others.

6. *Experience of December 27, 1554.*

"This morning" (December 27), "which is the Feast of the Evangelist John, when I awoke, I suddenly heard the words being spoken within my mind: 'To-day I am determined to divide thy soul from thy spirit'—and later on, when the Host was being elevated at Mass and I was praying about this matter, I had a sight or Thou didst say unto me—I cannot remember precisely which it was,—enough, it appeared to me that as, when the soul is divided from the body, the soul, in so far as immortal, flies to its destined place, and the entire body remains dead: so also, when the almighty hand of God makes a similar division of the soul from the spirit, the former,

[1] Ch. iv, §§ xiii, xiv, xvi (Parker, pp. 48–40).

the animal part (of man), remains dead, but the spirit, (truly) free (at last), flies to its natural place, which is God, the Living Fountain."

Here we are at once reminded of Catherine's experience of "Love once speaking within her mind"; of her sayings which dwell on the separation of the soul from the body, and on the flight of the spirit to its natural place, God; and of her sight of "the living Fountain" of Goodness.[1] But Battista's psychology is entirely clear and self-consistent, as to the precise extension of, and the precise distinction between, the terms "spirito" and "anima"; whereas, in the authentic sayings of Catherine, "anima" is used sometimes as inclusive of, and sometimes in contradistinction to, "spirito." We shall see how it is only the later systematizing *Dialogo*-writer who brings perfect consistency, and a scheme identical with Battista's, into Catherine's terminology. Yet in Catherine's image of the assimilation of bread by man, in illustration of the assimilation of man's nature by God, we find Battista's two stages of the divisional process. For there the body is first purified up to the actual level of the soul, and then the soul itself is purified perfectly, its animal part being eliminated or dominated by the spiritual part.[2]

It is interesting, too, to note how Battista cannot decide here whether this interpretation of the short sentence she had heard was mentally seen or interiorly heard by her; indeed, she is sure only that, whilst she was praying to understand the meaning of that sentence, the meaning thus sought appeared to her, by some means or other, to be so and so. It is then abundantly clear from this, that the difference between an interior sight and an interior voice, and again between either of these and the admittedly normal workings of her own mind, was, at times, so delicate, as either not to be clear to her own consciousness, even at the very time of the experience; or, at least, to fade away from her memory before she came to chronicle the experience.

7. *Experience of January* 6, 1555.

"On the Feast of the Epiphany" (January 6, 1555), "before Communion, I felt ineffable and most tender colloquies, and greatly I rejoiced because of them. For I had caused Masses to be said and prayers to be prayed, by various persons during many days, with the intention that, if these colloquies were

[1] See here, pp. 138; 277; 260.
[2] See here, p. 270.

not from Thee, I might no more experience them; but that, if they were Thine, they might be produced within me more clearly and more efficaciously. And seeing that I now felt them more than usual, and in a more admirable manner, I had and have a firm hope that they were Thine. Whence it happened that (having, on that same blessed day, to go up to receive Thee in the Sacrament), I felt Thy Majesty more than once calling me within me, 'Come, since I want to devour thee entirely.' . . . It seems to me that 'entirely' was one of the words, but I have no firm remembrance of this. But I know well that Thou saidst several times, 'Come, since I want to devour thee.' . . . To me it seemed that I merited rather to go under Lucifer, than into the Infinite Light (*Luce*)."

We get here a number of interesting parallels and contrasts to Catherine's teaching and practice. God's devouring of the soul; God pictured as Light; souls conceived as higher up or lower down in space, according to their degree of goodness or of badness; even the pleasure in a play upon words: all this finds its close counterpart in Catherine.[1] But far more important is the difference in the subject-matter of their scruples and in their respective attitudes towards psychically unusual experiences. In Catherine's case there is no record of anxieties concerning other things than her degree of detachment and her administrative responsibilities; indeed her whole practice and teaching, continuously bent as they were upon the ethico-spiritual truth and upon the practical application of her unusual experiences, make it morally certain that her anxieties never turned upon these forms and means themselves. She was, as it were, too much occupied with the content of the cup, ever to be actively perplexed as to the cup itself. Battista, on the contrary, seems to have been quite free from scruples of Catherine's melancholic type; but did not, evidently, always soar as highly as her God-mother above all anxious occupation with the form of her experiences. And, indeed, if, in this instance, it was evidently the form of her experiences which perplexed her, it was also the renewed and heightened experience of this peculiar form which reassured her.—Yet the very fact of such a perplexity, and again the moderation with which, even at the end of it all, she but "hopes that it all comes from God," shows a healthy reluct ance to trust too readily or too much to such tests and indica-

[1] See here, pp. 270; 290; 275, 270.

tions. It would probably not be unfair to put her attitude towards such things midway between Don Marabotto's readiness of belief and Catherine's soaring ethico-spiritual transcendence.

It is noticeable too that, if the inner voice is more distinct than before, Battista's anxious care for accuracy is also, if possible, more on the alert than ever: witness her remarks as to the word "all."

8. *Experience of the Second Sunday in Lent*, 1555.

"On the second Sunday (in Lent), having communicated, I felt Thine ineffable reasonings; but, since I did not write them down at once, I do not any more venture to write them down, having in great part lost the memory of them. But this I remember, that the words were like those which the Bridegroom says to the Bride in the Canticle (of Canticles)."

Here the difference between this form of apprehension and that of ordinary vivid thinking is so faintly distinct, that she can only declare that she "felt" (without deciding between hearing, seeing, or any other of the more definite senses) "reasonings" (without being sure of their "explicitation" in words or images); and she herself recognized at the time, and later on remembers that contemporary recognition of, their likeness to the texts of the Canticle of Canticles. It is evidently the profound reluctance, cultivated by her for half a century or more, to treat the deepest acts of the soul as other than directly and exclusively the acts of God in that soul, which makes her not see and admit here the large co-operation of her own mind.

Remark also a characteristic difference from Catherine, in that the latter's teaching is, we have already seen, entirely free from any influences characteristic of the Song of Songs.

9. *Experience of Ascension Day*, 1555.

"On the Lord's Ascension Day Thou didst say to me, O my Love, that, up to this point, I had walked by Faith, but that now Thou wast determined to give me direct assurance (*certezza*); and that there was no occasion for me to go on writing down Thy words, since I should read them in my own experience. And on my asking what Thou wouldst operate within me, Thou didst affirm to me that I should ever possess Thee in my heart."—"Another time I felt that I was being told: 'I generate My Son, having an infinite Cognition of Myself; similarly I generate thee, by infusing into thee that same cognition. But (this) My Cognition is without measure;

and thine shall be according to that measure which I shall, by My goodness, be impelled to give thee, in suchwise that of this cognition and of thine intellect there shall be effected one identical thing; so that I shall place My Word, My Concept, which I possess within Myself, in thee, according to the capacity for it which I shall deign to give thee; and so that, again, thy spirit shall be a son within My Son, or rather one only son with Him: and thus will I have generated thee.' Hence, O Lord, according to this Thy showing, those are generated by Thee, who, united by grace to Thy Majesty, repose in Thy Paternal Bosom, together with Thine only Begotten. But He is by nature one sole substance with Thee—He whom Thou art ever ineffably generating; and we are united with Thee, through reposing in Thy bosom by simple grace and by a singular privilege of Thy love; and in so far as we thus abide there in Thee, Thou generatest us in more and more light and ardour. Hence then Thou generatest him who abides in Thee."

We have here, in the last locution of this series, the most complicated and seemingly original of them all. Yet here also we can still find parallels to Catherine: in the addressing of God as "my Love"; in the fact that the locution proceeds from, and its interpretation is submitted, not to our Lord, but to God, to Him who indeed generates His Son without measure and directly, yet all other souls also, though in measure and by and through His Son; and in the declaration that now she should have a kind of direct assurance in lieu of Faith.[1]

And here especially we can trace the large Neo-Platonist (Dionysian) element in Battista's Mysticism. There is the first, perfect circle, God's perfect cognition of Himself, a cognition which produces a fresh (though co-eternal) centre of cognition, which latter in return perfectly cognizes Him who perfectly cognized it. And then there is a derivative imperfect circle—since that perfect cognizedness and cognizing, which is God's Son, can only be imperfectly imparted to the souls of creatures: yet again we have a circle, for the very thing which is cognized by God is, in this instance also, the same which cognizes Him. And lastly, this distance between the perfect and imperfect circles is, as far as possible, overcome by an attempted and momentary identification of the perfectly

[1] See here, pp. 138, 139; 265, 260; 272.

cognized and cognizing circle, Christ, with the perfectly cognized but imperfectly cognizing one, every human soul in its potentiality and divinely intended end.

And this large Platonist scheme of a progression of Ideas appears here coloured and Christianized, by means of four texts of the Latin Vulgate : Ps. cix, 3, " in the brightness (splendours) of the saints, from the womb, before the day star (Lucifer) I begot thee "; John i, 18, " the only-begotten Son, who is in the bosom of the Father "; xiii, 23, " there was leaning on Jesus' bosom one of His disciples whom Jesus loved "; and Luke xvi, 23, " the rich man beheld Abraham from afar, and Lazarus in his bosom." The first two passages give her the eternal and continuous generation and abiding of the Son by and in the Father; and the last two suggest a similar abiding and (interpretatively) generation, together with that Son, of the faithful soul, in and by God, continuously and for ever.

Note, too, the double meaning, so characteristic of mystical utterances, contained in the sentence, " I generate My Son, having an infinite Cognition of Myself '; which indicates both the mode of generation (" by means of an infinite cognition "), and the nature of the generated one (" who has an infinite cognition "). And by this literary device, the intense close-knitness of the perfect circle is strikingly adumbrated.

And remark how Battista finishes up this soaring flight by an interpretation of a perfect sobriety. Indeed it is this moderation and good sense along with so immense an Idealism and intense Interiority which, together, constitute her noblest characteristic and should make us overlook the comparative absence of spontaneous charm and tender freshness, which cannot but strike us if we allow ourselves to contrast the piety of Battista with that of Catherine.

IV. Some further Letters of Battista, 1575 to 1581.

Before the experiences and confidences of an almost painful privacy and emotional intensity, which require, in part, a considerable amount of patient interpretation from us, if they are to move and touch us, we found and dwelt upon a moral attitude and a document full of immediately understandable heroism and virile common-sense : the scene with her father before his death-ride, and the letter to Dottore Moro. And, somewhat similarly, three further documents succeed to these intermediate confidences, documents full of love and esteem for the externally ordinary vocation of the vast majority of us all, of a large undaunted outlook, and of a shrewd and persevering public spirit. The apparent mental contraction and subjectivity we have just passed through with her is but the recollective movement, the, as it were, drawing itself together for the spring of action on the part of an already large and expansive soul, and leads on and out to fresh and still larger horizons, and, indeed, effects them.

1. *Letter to Donna Anguisola*, 1575.

We have first a letter of June 10, 1575 (Battista was now seventy-eight years of age, and had been a Religious for sixty-five years) addressed to a widowed noblewoman with young children—the Illustrious Lady Andronica Anguisola.[1] The reader will note the transition, evidently quite natural and spontaneous in the writer, from a soaring Mysticism, full of Pauline, Johannine, and Dionysian forms, and of deep, personally experimental content, to the most practical and shrewd, wisely unflinching, homely heroism. There are few documents, I think, which show with an equal impressiveness how startlingly direct and immediate can be and is the application of such, apparently, purely transcendental, serene contemplations and affections to the struggling, clamorous world of our human passions, circumstances, difficulties, and duties: and how only that transcendence and this immanence taken and working thus together, give to the soul a height without inflation, and a concrete particularity without pettiness. I shall break up the long letter into three sections, omitting only two, relatively commonplace, passages in the middle and at the end; and shall again point out certain parallels and peculiarities at the end of each section.

(1) *Opening of the letter.*

"Most Honoured Madam in the Crucified,

"'I have come to place (cast) fire upon the earth; and what will I but that it be enkindled' (Luke xii, 49). By these most divine words we can understand, in part, to what a supreme degree such a most happy fire is of importance, since the Eternal Word came down from Heaven to kindle it in His so dearly-loved rational earth. And this great effect could not but follow, since the Paternal goodness willed to communicate to our misery the ardour which He possesses

[1] *Opere*, ed. 1755, Vol. VI, pp. 247, 248.

eternally in His Heart. And what else is this communication to us of His infinite love than the planting within our minds of His own intrinsic, incomprehensible delights? His Majesty, in His infinite courtesy, takes His delights in abiding with the children of men (Prov. viii, 31). But He desires that these delights should proceed from both sides, so that, as He takes these delights in us, by His own intrinsic natural goodness, He similarly wills that we, by means of that same goodness which is poured into us by that fire which Christ places upon our earth,—as Paul demonstrates when he says (Rom. v, 5), 'The charity of God is poured forth in our hearts by the Holy Ghost who is given to us,'—He wills, I say, that, set in motion by the immense potency of this infused fire, we should place, in return, all our delights in His Majesty; and then, to speak according to our human fashion, His unmeasured love attains to its intent. In this correspondence lie hidden away delights beyond all comprehension, considering that it is His own goodness that comes down (into us), as He demonstrates when he says, 'We will come to him, and will make our abode with him' (John xiv, 23); and that He raises us up beyond all measure in suchwise that, of the Increate Heart and of the created one, there is made, by the operation of Him who says, 'The Father who is in Me, worketh' (John x, 38; v, 17), a single most secret and inestimable union."

Here, again, we find close parallels to Catherine in "His own intrinsic incomprehensible delights," "His infinite courtesy," "the immense virtue of this infused fire," and "to speak according to our human fashion." And the whole general conception of a mutual and corresponding action and circle between God and the soul, the whole movement beginning in and by God, and leading back and ending in Him, is here, once more, the common property of Battista and her God-mother.[1] Yet "The Crucified," with which the whole letter opens, and "His Heart," the "Increate Heart," applied directly to God Himself, are expressions we should seek in vain in Catherine. The historical Christ, and a most legitimate anthropomorphism, find here a place, indeed a prominence, which they have not there. And note the sobriety with which Battista insists on the analogical character of all this speculation, for she "speaks" only "according to our human fashion"; and the allegorizing involved in the "His dearly-loved rational

[1] See here, pp. 263, 266, 280; 272, 275; 292; 277, 262.

earth," the earth that souls dwell on having here become simply identical with those souls themselves. And especially remark the mystically characteristic doubleness of meaning, and the conception of the substantiality of the divine indwelling, involved in the phrase, " His own intrinsic, incomprehensible delights." For this phrase means both " the delight which, for our minds, is intrinsically bound up with the thought of God," and the " delight which He himself takes in His indwelling whilst abiding within us " ; and the latter idea involves a belief in the soul's delight in Him being but a sympathetic echo and answer to His delight in this His own indwelling, a delight thus actually in operation within the human soul.

Mark, too, how her opening her letter with a formally announced text is but an instance of her life-long literary form of composition—the homily; how saturated is the whole with (evidently first-hand) scriptural meditation; and how wise and like her own father is her treatment of this soul, so near to delusion in the very intemperance of her search after perfection. A warning note of a claim about to be made upon her correspondent's effective self-immolation has been struck, from the first, by the words, " the Crucified " ; and yet this note is first followed by a paragraph sufficiently soaring to satisfy even the most lofty moods of the Signora Andronica.

(2) *Central part of the letter.*

" I have taken up my pen from a desire that you may be wholly and entirely devoted to the Lord, with a whole-hearted abandonment. I do not mean that you should abandon the care of your children : on the contrary, I wish that you may give the greatest care to them, both within and without. For the within, by desiring heart-wholly that they may be joined (cleave) to God, with all they are; and for the without, by helping them studiously to avoid everything that leads to sin." She then gives the examples of SS. Felicitas and Monica, and of St. Louis of France, and proceeds : " Now note, dear Madam, how great is the fruit of good government on the part of parents. Indeed, according to the little light which God designs to give me, this alone appears to me necessary—that your Ladyship should observe the counsel of St. Paul, where he says (Eph. iv, 1) ' that we should walk worthily in the vocation in which we are called.' Now *you* are called to the government of your children. Hence I pray you to study how to act, that you may be able to render a good account of it to God. You will remember how our Christ, on the point of going to His death, renders an account to His eternal Father concerning those whom His Father had given into His charge, saying, 'of them whom Thou hast given Me (in charge), I have not lost one' (John xviii, 9).

"Consider, my very dear Friend, how that our great God, being infinitely perfect, or, in better terms, perfection itself, we cannot either add to or detract from His glory even the slightest point, as the Prophet saw who said (Ps. ci, 13), 'Thou, O Lord, art ever the same' (endurest for ever), 'unchangeable and invariable.' All that we can do for Him, is to come in aid to His dear images, to His beloved children, as the Lord shows in Matt. xxv, 40, 'that which ye shall do unto one of these My least, ye shall have done it unto Me.'—I know well that you desire to withdraw yourself from all the cares of the world, in order to be able to occupy yourself entirely with God. But do you not know that 'Charity seeketh not the things that are her own' (1 Cor. xiii, 5), that is, her own utility? That desire which your Ladyship has for herself, let her have it equally for her children. Are we not obliged to love our neighbours as ourselves? (Matt. xix, 19). And hence, how much more our children! That step in perfection, of entirely abandoning all things, your Ladyship cannot take, without great damage to your neighbour,—damage, I mean, to souls. Remember how full of perils is the period of youth; I beg of you, with all possible insistence, for God's sake, to have a greater care of these young souls than of yourself, since the necessity is greater."

Here, again, there are parallels to the God-mother: in the love of that intensely unifying term, "si accostino," "cleave to," "be joined to," of St. Paul, so dear to Catherine also; in the love of all souls, as God's dear images, but specially of those bound to us by blood, so marked in Catherine's testamentary dispositions, as distinct from the descriptions, possibly even from the surface-appearances, of her last nine years; and in the greater care to be given to others than to our own selves, when their necessity is greater than ours, so heroically practised by Catherine in the case of the Plague.[1] The chief difference, here again, is the prominence given by Battista to the Historic Christ, by her quotation of the words of St. Matthew,—words which, though so obviously applicable to

[1] See here, pp. 284; 166–174; 143–145.

Catherine's work and duties, nowhere occur throughout Catherine's own contemplations or discourses.—Note again the ambiguity of the "within and without" in connection with the care to be bestowed, since the words are intended to cover respectively both Donna Anguisola's intention and exterior action, and her children's interior dispositions and visible acts.

(3) *Conclusion of the letter.*

"But pray indeed to His Majesty that He may give you grace so great as to enable you to abandon all things interiorly. Here is the point in which all perfection consists. And I will pray to him for this, in union with yourself. I most certainly desire, for my part, that your generous heart may have no other delight but God. And do you convert that human consolation which men are wont to take in their children, into a great desire that they may cleave to God; that they may not offend Him, and that they may bear His Majesty in their hearts. And when those things have been actually effected, do you then take the greatest delight in them, whilst mortifying that merely human pleasure which men take in the mutable prosperity of their children, in the most pleasing consolation which arises from their company, and in such-like things. And, from such a course of action, various advantages will follow. First, you will, I think, be thus doing what is most pleasing to God; next, you will be most useful to your neighbour; and lastly, your Ladyship will have carried off a great victory over your own self."

Here we can trace two close parallels to special points of Catherine's practice and teaching. In the doctrine that the point of all perfection consists in the interior abandonment of all things, we get but a restatement of Catherine's teaching as to God's love being practicable everywhere; and in the advice to practise interior mortification in the matter of resting in the consolation of her children's company, we have not only a parallel to Catherine's early and transitory convert practice, but also an application to human intercourse of Catherine's, and indeed also Battista's, continuous and ever-growing practice of detachment from sensible consolations in the soul's intercourse with God.[1]

We can hardly doubt that this letter was as effectual in

[1] See here, pp. 140, 141; 131, 116.

keeping Donna Anguisola within the limits of family duties, as the letter of forty-six years before had been in bringing back Dottore Moro to the world-wide spiritual family of the Ancient Church.

2. *Letter to Padre Collino*, 1576.

And we have next a letter, written in 1576, when she was seventy-nine, to that Father Serafino Collino at Cremona, to whom, five years later, she was to write the truly classical account of her father, which has been the main source of our study of that heroic figure.

And indeed already in this letter she preludes, as it were, to that outburst of filial praise, by first dwelling here upon the effects of her father's life as they were maturing visibly around her. "A very spiritual, wise, and noble person," writes Battista, "has been visiting me; and in the course of talk she asked me, 'Well, and what did you think of the great miracles that God has been working during these times of acute conflict, in this our city—miracles such as no one ever heard of throughout the course of ancient Roman history or in connection with any other warfare? And I, knowing well that this person has three Doctors of Theology living continuously in her house, guessed that these men must have carefully scrutinized and examined the whole matter. So I simply asked, 'What miracles do you mean?' And she answered me, 'The city has been for so long a time in arms, a prey to the good and to the wicked, to the wise and to the mad, and has been affording the greatest possible opportunity for acts contrary to justice. And yet, throughout the city within the walls, no one has ever been offended,—no man, in his person; no woman, in her honour; and no man or woman, in their possessions.'"

And then Battista comments on her visitor's declaration. "As to their persons, all men went about in the city with swords drawn and erect, and spoke injurious words to those of the opposite party. And it really seems as though their hands were tied, for they used their tongues indeed but not their hands; not one drop of blood has been spilt. Within the city two homicides were, no doubt, committed during this time, because of a difference on a point of honour; but none on account of party spirit. Similarly outside of Genoa the son of Signor Antonio d'Oria was killed—not by the opposite party, but by another nobleman like himself,—they had come to words. As to female honour, the women went and came to visit each other, and frequented Mass, whether they belonged to one party or to the other; and the greater number of gentlewomen went out of Genoa, accompanied by their daughters, passing through the very midst of the city, and going down the wharf to get on board their boats; and yet never was any discourtesy shown to any one of them. Similarly, with regard to possessions: quantities of these were sent out of Genoa; great masses of them were deposited in the Monasteries—and yet never even a trifle was ever taken. On this latter point we of this Convent can bear direct witness. For although so much property and money was brought to the Monastery delle Grazie, that it became difficult to move about the house because of the quantity of cases and stray boxes deposited there, nevertheless not even to the poor carriers who brought them was the slightest violence done, although they had to pass through all those drawn and raised swords; nor was a single word said to us Nuns, who appeared in the gateway to receive the goods."[1]

Now the well-informed lawyer, Professore Morro, thinks that all this was the direct result of Ettore Vernazza's far-sighted and devoted philanthropy. And he is no doubt right. For we still possess the entries, in the Cartulary of St. George, of the great works carried out by that powerful Banking Body, in conformity with and by means of Ettore's directions and moneys, amongst Genoa's teeming poor and sick and ignorant, in the years 1531 and 1553.[2] Indeed even the printed documents bring the administration of this great, ever-growing fund down to the year 1708.

And the points that here concern the character of Battista are this her omnipresent and yet bashful pride in her large-hearted father; her virile joy in the public good; her immensely sane and direct tastes as to the city's improvement; and her glad finding of a miracle in things thus readily verifiable, universal, interior, and yet profoundly operative in the visible work-a-day life of man. There is something strikingly modern in this severely social, and already more or less statistical, way of testing improvement, an improvement which is found here, not in any vaguely assumed increase of impulsive or perfunctory almsgiving in the one class, or of dependence and passivity in the other, but in the closely scrutinized proofs of a remarkable growth in general self-respect, self-mainten-

[1] *Inaugurazione*, pp. 26, 27.
[2] *Ibid.* pp. 74, 75, 77, 78. *Ibid.* p. 94.

ance, public spirit and sense of social interdependence, on the part of all parties and classes.

And in the daughter's judgment concerning all this it is again easy to trace a likeness to her father, with his careful regulations for a great Register of the Poor, and his provisions for harbour-works and the embellishment of the city. But Catherine's spirit is also present, with its emphatic insistence upon God's love as practicable everywhere, and upon truth as, of its very nature, public-spirited and meant for all.[1]

3. *Second letter to Padre Collino*, 1581.

And five years later still (she was now eighty-four) Battista writes her long account of her father's life, which we studied in connection with him, but which would well deserve a detailed analysis from the standpoint of the daughter's dispositions, so keen and large, so tender, true and immensely operative, long after most men have died, or are living on in a selfish second childhood.

V. Battista's Death, 1587.

And then at last, six years afterwards, at four o'clock in the afternoon of May 9, 1587, Pope Sixtus V being Pope and Mary Stuart having but six months still to live, Battista died in her Convent, fully three generations old. During her last years she had been allowed to communicate daily, and had thus, at the end, added one more trait of resemblance to her God-mother, who, as we know, had, for some thirty-five years of her life, found her greatest strength and consolation in this the simplest, most central and deepest of all the Christian devotions and means of Grace.[2]

One hundred and forty years had now passed since the

[1] Here, pp. 319, 320; 140, 141, 268.

[2] Date of death: *Ritratti ed Elogii di Liguri Illustri*, Genova, Ponthenier (Elogio della Ven. Battista Vernazza). Communion: *Opere della Ven. B. Vernazza*, ed. cit., Vol. I, p. 21. The portrait-frontispiece of the second volume of this work is a faithful facsimile of the portrait (a lithograph by F. Scotto) published among the *Ritratti*, between 1823 and 1830. The original picture, which will have hung in the convent of S. Marie delle Grazie, I have not been able to trace. The portrait now in possession of the Nuns of the convent of S. Maria in Passione, the successors of those Canonesses, is a quite conventional, inauthentic likeness.

birth of Catherine, and seventy-seven since her death. It is indeed time that we should, having accumulated so much material, proceed in the next volume to an examination and exposition of the underlying spiritual facts and laws specially brought home to us by the group of lives we have been studying, and of which the central figure was that, for us, largely elusive but immensely suggestive, many-sided and yet rarely beautiful, soul and influence, which the Church venerates as St. Catherine of Genoa.

CONCLUSION

WHEREIN LIES THE SECRET OF SPIRITUAL PERSUASIVENESS

But let us first conclude this volume by attempting an answer, however preliminary and general, to the definite question with which it opened out.

I. The Question.

We asked there, how any deeper, will-moving intercommunication can even be possible amongst men? For the mere possession of, and appeal to, the elementary forms of abstract thinking, which seem to be our only certain common material, instrument and measure of persuasion, appear never, of themselves, to move the will, or indeed the feelings; whereas all that is endowed with such directly will-moving power appears, not only as specifically concrete and as hopelessly boxed up within the four corners of our mutually exclusive individualities, but also as vitiated, even for each several owner, by an essentially fitful and fanciful subjectivity.

II. The Answer.

Now I think that even the survey of the three great lives, and of those four minor ones, which has been just attempted, forcibly suggests, both positively and negatively, at least the general outlines of the true answer to this pressing question.

1. Only a life sufficiently large and alive to take up and retain, within its own experimental range, at least some of the poignant question and conflict, as well as of the peace-bringing solution and calm : hence a life dramatic with a humble and homely heroism which, in rightful contact with and in rightful renunciation of the Particular and Fleeting, ever seeks and finds the Omnipresent and Eternal; and which again deepens and incarnates (for its own experience and apprehension and for the stimulation of other souls) this Transcendence in its own thus gradually purified Particular : only such a life can be largely persuasive, at least for us Westerns and in our times.

We would thus have an attempt, ever renewed, ever widening, ever deepening, at the formation of, as it were, a concrete, living, breathing image of the Abiding and the One; of Law, Love, and Duty; of God : an image formed out of the seemingly shifting, shrinking flux, and the apparently shapeless mass of our actual, bewildering human manyfold; our flesh and sweat, and tears and blood, our joy and laughter, our passions and petty revolts, our weariness and isolations. Attend primarily to minimizing or eliminating all such friction and pain; to being clear, materially simple and static, a fixed Thing, rather than vivid, formally unified, and dynamic, a growing Personality; or again, let the friction be so great, or the courage and fidelity so small, as to lead to the break-up of all genuine recollection and harmonization; and, in the former case, such a character or outlook may be considered "safe" or "correct" or "sensible"; and, in the latter, the character and outlook will not be consolidated at all, or will be breaking up : but in neither case will the life be persuasive. For to be truly winning, the soul's life must become and must keep itself full and true.

2. Now it is simply false that man can, even for his own self alone, hold spiritual reality, even from the first, in a simply passive, purely dependent, entirely automatic and painless fashion; or that he can, even at the last, possess it in a full, continuous and effortless harmony and simultaneousness.

God no doubt holds all Truth and Reality as one great Here and Now, or rather He possesses them entirely outside of space and time; nor can we attribute to Him directly any interior conflict, effort, or suffering. And, again, we ourselves too possess within our minds an element and an apprehension of the Abiding and the Simultaneous; and their rudiments operate within us, if all-diffusively yet most powerfully, from the very first. Indeed the continuous increase in definiteness and influence of that element and of its apprehension here, and the indefinite expansion and continuously conscious possession of this same element hereafter, are respectively the highest aim and fullest achievement of our spiritual life. And finally, the further the soul advances, the more it sees and realizes the profound truth, that all it does and is, is somehow given to it; and hence that, inasmuch as it is permanent at all, it is grounded upon, environed, supported, penetrated and nourished by Him who is its origin and its end. Here all the soul's actions tend to coalesce to simply being, and this being, in so far as there and then acceptable to the conscience, comes more and more to be felt and considered as the simple effect of the one direct action of God alone.

And yet as to God, some kind and degree of Incarnational doctrine is necessary, and is indeed (in varyingly perfect or imperfect forms) the common property of all higher religion; and Christians have learnt to think the profound thought, of God Himself being in a mysterious closeness to even our most secret perplexities and inarticulate pain.—And by ourselves, poor weaklings, that vast, continuous Simultaneity and Harmony of God can only be more and more nearly approached, if, upon our mostly shadowy, and (when at all clear) our short-lived consciousness of an inchoate simultaneity and harmony of our own, we work an orderly successiveness, and attempt a Melody; an humble, creaturely imitation of the Eternal, Spaceless Creator, under the deliberately accepted conditions and doubly refracting media of time and space. Real temptation, true piercing conflict, heavy darkness, and bewildering perplexity; the constant encountering (as a necessary condition and occasion of all growth) of numberless and multiform remoter risks of failing and of falling: all this forms an essential part of this painful-joyous probation and virile, because necessarily costing and largely gradual, self-constitution of man's free-willing spirit.

And the place and function, in all this spiritual growth-in-conflict, of Science, both in its most determinist and apparently most anti-spiritual mood, and in its subtler though no less destructive-seeming attitudes, will turn out, we shall find,—now that our generation is getting to know Science's special scope and implications,—to be of simply irreplaceable value and potency.

And though, in the other life, our earthly pain and temptation are to be no more, we may be sure that, even there, the essential characteristics of our nature will not be reversed. Hence we may be able, later on in this book, to hazard some not all-ungrounded conjecture as to the possible substitute and form in Heaven for what is essentially noble and creaturely in our sufferings and self-renunciations here on earth.

And lastly, though God's action in all things in general, and in our individual soul in particular, be more and more recognized as all-pervasive in proportion as the soul advances: yet this action will have to be conceived as operating in and through and with our own; as in each case finding in one sense, its very matter, in another, its very form, in our own free-willings. For Spirit and spirit, God and the creature, are not two material bodies, of which one can only be where the other is not: but, on the contrary, as regards our own spirit, God's Spirit ever works in closest penetration and stimulation of our own; just as, in return, we cannot find God's Spirit simply separate from our own spirit within ourselves. Our spirit clothes and expresses His; His Spirit first creates and then sustains and stimulates our own. The two, as regards the inner life of the human soul, rise and sink together. But more as to this too hereafter.

3. We shall indeed, throughout the next volume, have ample opportunities for noting how numerous, definite, far-reaching and at all times operative, even though still but partially unfolded, are the evidences for, and the consequences and applications of, such a fundamental conception, as they are furnished and required by all deeper human life; hence, above all, by Religion; and in Religion, again, specially by its ever largely elusive, yet ever profoundly important, constituent, the Mystical Element.

APPENDIX TO PART II

CHRONOLOGICAL ACCOUNT AND CRITICAL ANALYSIS OF THE MATERIALS FOR THE RE-CONSTITUTION OF SAINT CATHERINE'S LIFE AND TEACHING.

INTRODUCTION.

THE following laborious study of the growth and upbuilding of the Life and Legend of St. Catherine is a study worth the making. For this study will bring out fully the test and reasons which have guided the process of documentary selection and estimation adopted throughout the second part of this book, indicating thus the precise degree of reliability pertaining to my narrative. But especially will it furnish a detailed, and peculiarly instructive, example of what, with numberless differences in degree, kind, and importance, can be traced throughout the history of the transmission of the image and influence of great religious personalities and teachers. These continuously recurring phenomena can be taken as, together, constituting the general forms and laws which regulate the growth of all religious devotional biography.

I.

These general laws appear to be as follow.

1. *Three Laws.*

There is the law of *contemporary, simultaneous, spontaneous variation of apprehension.* Vernazza and Marabotto, writing down, at the time of their occurrence or communication, certain facts and sayings with an equal self-oblivion, sincerity, and truthfulness, give us apprehensions which, in great part objectively valuable, are, nevertheless, more or less differing pictures of one and the same fact or saying, or different selections from amongst the moods and manifestations of one living personality observed by them.—There is the law of *posterior, successive, reflective variation of elaboration.* The Dominican Censor and Battista Vernazza, re-thinking Catherine and her teaching, in other times and away from her direct influence, necessarily see her differently again: they are, as it were, spiritual grandchildren, who rather themselves absorb her and re-state her to their generation than they are themselves absorbed by her.—And there is the law of *conservation, juxtaposition,* and *identification.* First the Redactor of the Book of 1528–1530, and lastly the Redactor of that of 1551—probably, both times, Battista—with, in between, in 1547, the Redactor who attempted a quadripartite re-schematizing of the *Life*—could not but try and soften the variations produced by the two other laws.

2. *The third law tends to confuse the operation of the other two.*

And note how it is precisely this third law and stage which largely tends to make the effects of the two other laws into causes of vagueness, confusion, and scepticism. For instead of conceiving the unity and identity of the subject-matter (a deep spiritual personality) as essentially inexhaustible, and as requiring, for its least inadequate apprehension, precisely both those simultaneous and spontaneous, and those successive and reflective experiences and reproductions of it, as furnished by the two other laws, this stage tends to confuse the identity of the apprehended subject-matter with a sameness in the apprehension of it; and, whilst thus robbing that subject-matter of its richness and movement, to introduce an element of arrangement and timidity into the originally quite *naïf,* and hence directly impressive evidences of the observers. Yet the instinct and object of this third law is as legitimate and elementary as are those of the other two, since a real unity and utilization of all the preceding variety is as necessary as the variety to be thus integrated, and since the other two laws show a similar variety of actuation throughout religious literature.

3. *Examples.*

We find (to move in Church History back from St. Catherine) these three tendencies at work in the constitution of the Life and Legend of St. Francis of Assisi, A.D. 1181 (?) –1226, traced for us now, with so much sympathy and acumen, by M. Paul Sabatier and the Bollandists. We get them again in the case of St. Thomas of Canterbury, A.D. 1118–1171, especially in that of his Death and Miracles, so carefully studied in Dr. Edwin Abbot's remarkable book (1898). And, once more, in those Merovingian Saints, the great Martin of Tours in their midst, at the end of the fourth century, whose Lives have been so interestingly described by Bernouilli (1900).

If we take the Bible, we find (on moving here in a contrary direction) these laws again at work in the elucidation and elaboration of the great figure of Moses and of his world-historic life-work. For if here we get but little that can claim to be by his pen, or even, as literature, to be contemporaneous with him (since the earliest Corpus of Laws, the Book of the Covenant, reaches probably only in its substance back to him), yet here, too, the earliest consecutive descriptions of his life, by the Jahvist and Elohist writers, give us two different, though probably more or less simultaneous, largely *naïve*, accounts and impressions of his life and work. And these simultaneous variations are followed, later on, by the successive, increasingly reflective variations and developments of Deuteronomy and of the Priestly Code. And lastly, these documents get constituted (in probably two great stages), by Redactional work, into the great composite History and Legislation of our present last four Books of Moses.—So again with David. We have the David of some few of the Psalms; the David of the Books of Samuel, in a double series of most vivid and spontaneous, more or less simultaneous but somewhat differing, accounts; the David of the greater part of the Psalter, the result of a long process of devout successive reflection and re-interpretation; and the David of the Books of Chronicles, where pragmatic systematization reaches its height.—And so too with the Maccabean Heroes, whose history appears, apprehended with varying degrees of contemporary, simultaneous, spontaneous vividness, and of subsequent, successive, reflective pragmatism, in the documents and redactional settings of the First and Second Books of Maccabees.—And the growth indicated in these three cases covered respectively some eight hundred, seven hundred, and one hundred years.

But it is, of course, in the New Testament that the interest and importance of these laws reaches its height. If here we once more move backwards the case of St. Paul (martyred

A.D. 64) furnishes us with parallel contemporary accounts of the spontaneous type, in his own Epistles and in the six "We"-passages by the eye-witness St. Luke in the Acts of the Apostles; whilst the remaining account in the Acts is doubtless by a later, more reflective and pragmatic, writer.—And in the apprehension and interpretation of Our Lord's inexhaustible life, character, teaching, and work, we find very plainly the three tendencies and stages. We get the contemporary, simultaneous, spontaneous stage, in the cases of the Aramaic annotations of the Apostle Levi-Matthew, which we still possess, translated and incorporated both in the larger and later book, our canonical Greek St. Matthew, and in the corresponding parts of our St. Luke; and in the reminiscences of another eye-witness, presumably St. Peter, given us by a disciple in what is still the substance of our Canonical St. Mark. We get the posterior, successive, increasingly reflective or contemplative stage, chiefly in the two great types furnished, first by the Pauline, and then by the Johannine writings. And we get the juxtaposing, unifying, largely identifying stage and law operating above all in the, partly successive, Canonization of the New Testament *Corpus*. And these three stages can be taken as having their downward limits in about A.D. 30, 100, 200; so that here we cover a period of some hundred and seventy years.

4. *Three different attitudes possible.*

And, in all these and countless other cases, we can take up three different attitudes: the impoverishing, sectarian "purity" attitude; the destructive, sceptical, "identity" attitude; or the fruitful, truly Catholic "approximation" and "development" attitude. The first attitude assumes (ever in part unconsciously) the possibility and necessity of a purely objective apprehension of Personality, of such a Personality being a static entity, both in itself and in its effects upon, and its apprehendedness by, other souls, and of the earliest among the observations concerning such a Personality ever giving us such a purely objective, exhaustive picture and experience, or at least the nearest approach (in all respects) to such an exhaustive objectivity. The second attitude would so understand the admitted identity of the Personality observed as practically to identify also the simultaneous and successive observers and observations, and to eliminate all variety and growth in that spirit's own inner life and in its apprehension by other minds Only the third attitude would, by recognizing both the constant, necessary presence of a subjective element in all these simultaneous and successive apprehensions, and the indefinite richness and many-sided apprehensibleness of all great spiritual Personalities, welcome and draw out all the difference in unity of these many "reactions," as so many means, for a growing soul, towards a growing knowledge of that life and character, whose very greatness is, in part, measurable by the depth, variety, and persistence of these several effects, pictures, and embodiments of itself in different races, times, and souls.

Let us, then, betake ourselves to a systematic examination of one example of these world-wide three laws: the trouble taken will be well spent.

II.

Had I found room to print my notes in justification of the text adopted by me, the reader would have gained some idea of the exceeding complexity of the materials furnished by the printed *Vita e Dottrina*. Indeed the original Preface to that book (1551) finds it necessary to conclude with the words "we therefore" (because of the book's utility, indeed necessity, "in these turbulent times") "beg the devout reader not to be disturbed" (*stomacharsi* now changed to *meravigliarsi*) "if he finds here matters which appear to be out of their proper order" (*non ben ordinate*), "and which are sometimes repeated; since attention has been given, neither to much precision" (*distinzione*), "nor to the order of events, nor to elegance of form, but only to that truth and simplicity with which its facts and discourses were gathered by devout spiritual persons" ("her Confessor and a Spiritual Son of hers") "from the very lips of that Seraphic Woman." Both the praise and the blame of this pregnant sentence will appear to be most fully deserved.

In our Second Part we have, in imitation of all experience in life itself, been thrown *in medias res*, and have thus gained some general idea and curiosity as to the sources of our knowledge; in this Appendix we will now, without repeating details already given, take this evidence, as much as possible, in its chronological order. And at each stage I shall attempt so to analyze the evidence of that stage, as to be able to use it as a check and test of the evidence of the next stage.—We shall, however, have to bear in mind that this method has necessarily, at each earlier stage, somewhat to beg the question;

for, in order to make its meaning everywhere sufficiently clear, it has from the first to assume a confidence of tone, which can be justified only by the whole argument, and which therefore has its logical place only at the very end.

This Appendix shall consist of two Divisions, of seven stages and eight sections respectively. The first Division gives the dated Documents, or such as can readily be restricted to within certain years; and the second Division analyses the remaining, undated Corpus and attempts to fix its origin and value.

First Division: Account and Analysis of the Documents previous, and immediately subsequent, to the "Vita e Dottrina" with the "Dicchiarazione."

I. First Stage, 1456 to September 12, 1510, all Legal.

The documents of the first stage are all legal papers, and entirely contemporary and authentic. They have to furnish the skeleton which receives its clothing of flesh from the other documents. I shall here describe only those not described in Part II, and shall refer back to that Part for those already described there.

1. *Deed of* 1456.

There is, first, a deed of August 27, 1456. From amongst the shares belonging to Pomera (formerly) wife to (the late) Bartolommeo de Auria (Doria), but now (Sister) Isabella, in the convent of St. David; at the instance of Andrea de Auria, her only son, her heir, and of Francesca, the mother of Catherine, daughter of Jacobo de Fiesco: two shares of the Bank of St. George (£200) are set apart, for the benefit of the said Catherine, for her marriage, if she marries according to her Mother's advice.[1] Note how early (Catherine is not yet nine years old) her mother, Francischetta (so a note to the copy of this document, no doubt correctly, calls her, and sus-

[1] "A(nno) 1456, 27 Augti, ex Locis Pomerae uxoris Bartolomaei de Auria et a de modo Isabellae dedicatae in monasterio S. David, ad instantiam Andreae Auria, unici ejus filii ex heredis, et Franciscae matris Catherinetae filiae Jacobi de Flisco, Loci duo in ratione dictae Catherinetae per ejus maritare et (si) dictae Franciscae fecerit consilio." From parchment-bound small folio vol.: *Documenti su S. Catherina da Genova MSS.*, in R. University Library, Genoa.

pects Pomera to have been her sister), is thinking of Catherine's marriage; and how, although Catherine's father is still alive, nothing is said as to his consent, perhaps simply because, this money coming from a maternal aunt and cousin, only the mother's wishes are considered to be important here.

2. *Catherine's Marriage Settlement, January* 1463.

There is, next, Catherine's marriage settlement, made " at Genoa, in the quarter of St. Laurence, to wit in the sitting-room (*caminata*) of the residence of Francisca, formerly wife to the late Don Jacobo de Fiescho," " with the public street in front, the house of Urbano de Negro at its right, and that of Sebastiano de Negro at its left and back "; " in the evening of Thursday, January 13, 1463 "; between Giuliano Adorno, son of the late Don Jacobo, on the one hand, and Francisca, mother of Caterinetta and Jacobo and Giovanni de Fiesco, brothers of the same." Giuliano thereby pledges himself to give Catherine on their marriage, £1,000, and he " mortgages to her," up to this amount, " a certain house of his own, situate in Genoa in the quarter of St. Agnes, with the public street in front, the house of Baldassare Adorno at the right hand " (it belonged before this to Don Georgio Adorno), " and on the other hand the public street." And Francesca, Jacobo, and Giovanni promise to pay Giuliano, in bare money and in wedding outfit for Catherine, £400 on completion of the marriage, and another £400 in the course of the following two years; and they mortgage to him, up to this amount, the house in which the settlement is being made. Giuliano is to be free to live with his wife and her family in this same house, for these first two years after his marriage, without any payment.

At this date, then, Giuliano is already fatherless, and Catherine's brother Lorenzo is still too young to have any legal voice in the matter. Although Catherine is, after the first two years, not guaranteed anything beyond £1,000 capital, or say £40 a year income, her outfit is a handsome one.

3. *Catherine's first Will, June* 1484.

Then there is Catherine's first Will, June 23, 1484, after twenty-one years of marriage. She is " lying," although "fully herself in mind, intellect, and memory," yet "languid in body and weighted down by bodily infirmity, in the room, her residence, in the women's quarters of the Hospital of the Pammatone," which " she has inhabited for a considerable time (*jamdiu*)." "And knowing herself to be without children, and without hope of future offspring," she leaves the life-interest in her marriage-dowry of £1,000 to her husband, Giuliano; bids him divide up, at his death, the bulk of this capital between the Hospital and her eldest brother Jacobo (£300 to each), and her two younger brothers Giovanni and Lorenzo (£150 to each); and orders her body to be buried in the Hospital Church.[1]

Ten years, then, after her Conversion, Catherine had already been living for a considerable time within the Hospital. They do not as yet occupy a separate building, or even a set of rooms within the Hospital; and, though both live within it, they evidently occupy separate rooms in different parts of the great complex of buildings; for the room here mentioned is simply Catherine's (*camera residentiae testatricis*, where *residentiae* must be a descriptive and not a partitive genitive), and forms part and parcel of the women's wards (*in domibus mulierum*). Her absence of hope as to offspring evidently arises primarily from the life of continence she is leading. Yet this latter determination is clearly not caused by any specific knowledge of her husband's past infidelity: for Thobia must have been now some ten years old, yet there is no kind of mention of her; whilst, later on, Catherine never fails to remember her, with one exception to be presently explained. There is no mention of nephews and nieces, doubtless because her brothers were, as yet, either unmarried or childless, or, at least, daughterless. She is fairly well off, for (besides this possession of £1,000) she gets her room and board free, and Giuliano has still some property of his own more considerable than hers. And the share left by her to relations is large—£600—as over against £300 to a public charity (the Hospital), and £100, presumably, for the funeral, minor charities, and Masses. If she says nothing, as yet, as to burial in the same grave with her husband, this is doubtless because she herself appears now to be the one likely to die first.

4. *Giuliano's Will, October* 1494.

There is, fourthly, the first and last Will, October 20, 1494, of "the Reverend Sir, Brother Giuliano Adorno, professing the Third Order of St. Francis, under the care of the Friars Minor Observants," already described on pages 151, 152. The will

[1] From Dre. Ferretto's copy of the original in the Archivio di Stato, Genoa.

is drawn up in the "sitting-room" (*caminata*) of the "habitation" of the Testator. Now the Notary, Battista Strata, in a foot-note to a first draft of an (unfinished) Will of Catherine, writes: "On the day on which I drew up Don Giuliano's"; which words (owing to a multiplicity of converging indications) can only refer to this Will of October 2, 1494. And in this draft Catherine leaves legacies to the servants Benedetta (Lombarda) and Mariola Bastarda, as "abiding with, and dwelling in the house with, Testatrix." It is clear then that, by now, Catherine and Giuliano are living under the same roof, in a distinct house within the Hospital precincts, with two personal attendants for their common use. They will have moved, out of their separate single rooms, into this house, upon Catherine becoming Matron, in 1490. In this draft there appear also, for the first time, her brother Jacobo's two daughters (£100 each); and her sister, the Augustinianess Limbania (£10).

5. *Four minor documents*, 1496–1497.

There are, next, certain minor documents of 1496–1497, which modify points of previous Wills and clear up details of her life. Thus, on June 17, 1496, Catherine signs a deed of consent to the sale of the Palace in the S. Agnese (Adorni) quarter.—On January 10, 1496, Giuliano, "sane in mind although languid in body," orders, in a Codicil, that Catherine shall carry out, according to the directions of a certain Friar Minor, a vow made by himself to St. Anthony of Padua; notes that the Palace has been sold; and declares that she is to be free to annul, amend or diminish, according to her own judgment, his legacy of £500 to the Hospital.[1] And, in the Cartulary of the Bank of St. George, Catherine's name appears as an Investor: on July 14, 1497, as "wife of Giuliano Adorno"; but on October 6 as "wife and testamentary heiress of the late Giuliano Adorno."[2] These entries were considered on page 149 note. On the second occasion she orders that the Bank shall, after her death, annually pay over the interest of the fourteen shares (£1,400), now bought by her, to the Hospital of the Pammatone, in return for "the enjoyment and usufruct of a house and a greenhouse (*viridario*) of (within) the said Hospital," which had been conceded to

[1] The originals of both deeds are in the Archivio di Stato, Genoa, Atti del Not. Battista Strata, folie 39, parte II, and 96 (parte III).

[2] Copies of these two entries, in the MS. volume "Documenti . . . Caterina da Genova," University Library, Genoa, B VII 31.

her for her lifetime. The sum (about £56 a year) thus ceded by her is a handsome one, as she had, by now, well earned the use of this house by her constant labours for the Hospital, including her matronship from 1490 to 1496. I take it that she was again thinking of Thobia; so that this relatively large sum would cover at least part of the Hospital's expenses incurred for this poor girl.

6. *Catherine's second Will, May* 1498.

This has been studied on pages 152–154.

7. *Deed of Cession, September* 18, 1499; *and Codicil of January* 1503.

These have been studied on pages 155, and 168, 169.

8. *Third Will, May* 21, 1506; *and Codicil of November* 1508.

These have been described on pages 172–174; and 175, 176.

9. *Fourth and last Will, March* 18, 1509; *and two last Codicils, August* 3 *and September* 12, 1510.

These have been described on pages 185–187; 202, 203; and 212–214, respectively

We have thus described all the fifteen documents which alone still bear dates within the range of Catherine's lifetime, and whose contemporaneousness is above all challenge. They all have the pedantic, at first sight unmoving, indeed repulsive, form of legal documents. Yet the substance of quite ten of them undoubtedly proceeds from Catherine; and they all give us a most precious, precise certainty with regard to many cardinal points of locality, date, sequence, and self-determination in her life. True, neither the day, nor even the month, of her Birth or Baptism; nor the year of her Conversion; nor the date of the beginning of her Daily Communions; nor the facts as to the rarity or frequency of her Confessions; nor the day or month of Giuliano's death, have been recoverable by any contemporary attestations. But on other points we thus possess a series of absolutely reliable documents, ranging from 1456 to 1510, whose testimony nothing can be allowed to shake.

II. Second Stage: Five further Official and Legal Documents, 1511–1526; and Four Mortuary Dates, 1524–1587.

And this first stage of the evidence is followed by a second, as dry and legal, and as absolutely reliable, as the other; yet which still does not refer to any chronicle or notes of her life, (as either already extant or as in process of registration or redaction), but only to the fate of her remains and to certain turning-points in the lives of her disciples and eye-witnesses. I note here only those documents which fix for us the dates of the beginning of her Cultus, and which give us the latest contemporary proof for those persons being still alive.

1. We get thus the Hospital Account for the Moneys spent on the Religious Clothing of the Maid-Servant Mariola Bastarda, July 7, 1511; the entry in the Hospital Cartulary of the expenses incurred for the transport of stone and for a picture, in connection with the first opening of Catherine's Deposito, July 10, 1512; the account, in the same book, concerning the funeral of Don Jacobo Carenzio, who had died occupying Catherine's little house within the Hospital precincts, on January 7, 1513; a Will of the little widow-attendant Argentina del Sale, of January 15, 1522; and the Will of Don Cattaneo Marabotto, still "in good bodily and mental health," May 11, 1526,—a document drawn up in his dwelling-place, the house belonging to his friends, the Salvagii.[1]

2. And to this group we can add four further dates, the first and last two of which are completely certain. Ettore Vernazza died on June 26 or 27, 1524; the year is fixed by the great plague epidemic which carried him off, and the month and day, by his daughter's letter. Cattaneo Marabotto died, there is no reason to doubt, in 1528. Catherine's Dominican cousin and close friend, Suor Tommasa Fiescha, died, eighty-six years of age, in 1534. And Battista Vernazza died, aged ninety, on May 9, 1587.[2]

Hence, up to eighteen years after her death, the two closest of Catherine's confidants were alive; whilst one who had known her, and had been thirteen at the time of Catherine's death, was still alive seventy-seven years after that event.

[1] The first four documents exist, copied, in the *Vita* of the *Biblioteca della Missione Urbana*; the last is in the Archivio di Stato, and has been copied out plain for me by Dre. Ferretto.

[2] Ettore Vernazza: *Inaugurazione*, pp. 21, 22; 39, 40. Cattaneo Marabotto: Don Giovo's declaration among the "Conclusions" (in his own handwriting) attached to the MS. *Vita* of St. Catherine in the *Biblioteca della Missione Urbana*, Genoa. Tommasa Fiescha: Fed. Alizieri, in *Atti della Società di Storia Patria*, Vol. VIII, Genoa, 1868, p. 408. Battista Vernazza, *Opere Spirituali della Ven. B. Vernazza*, Genoa, ed. 1775, Vol. I, Preface.

III. Third Stage: Bishop Giustiniano's Account of Catherine's Life, Remains, and Biography, 1537.

Our third stage is in strikingly manifold contrast to the other two. It is represented by but one single, largely vague and rhetorical, but human and directly psychological, document; and is the first that tells us of a Life.

1. *The text.*

Monsignore Agostino Giustiniano, Bishop of Nibio, published his *Castigatissimi Annali . . . della Republica di Genova,* in Genoa, in 1537. There, on p. 223, he tells us that he was born (of socially distinguished parents) in that city in 1470. And under the date of 1510 (p. 266) he writes: "And in the month of September, it pleased God to draw to Himself Madonna Catarinetta Adorna, who was daughter of Giacobo di Flisco, Vice-Roy of Naples for King René, and wife to Giuliano Adorno, with whom she lived many years in marital chastity. And her life, after the Divine goodness had touched her heart in the years of her youth, was all charity, love, meekness, benignity, patience, incredible abstinence, and a mirror of every virtue, so that she can be compared to St. Catherine of Siena. And all the city has participated in, and has perceived, the odour of the virtues of this holy matron, who, when rapt in the spirit, spoke, amongst other matters, of the state of the souls that are in Purgatory, things excellent and rare and worthy of being attended to by such persons as have a taste for the religious and spiritual life. Her body is deposited in the Oratory of the larger Hospital, and offers a spectacle no less admirable than venerable, appearing (*come che sia*) all entire with its flesh, so that it looks alive,—as though she had been placed there to-day; and yet full twenty-five years have passed since she began to lie there dead. The great consciousness of God, the special virtues, the saintly deeds, accompanied by an immense love, which were manifested by this venerable matron, would furnish matter well worthy of being recorded here. Yet we shall pass them over, for the sake of brevity; especially since a book worthy of respect (*un digno libro*) has been composed, concerning these things exclusively, by persons worthy of confidence (*digne di fede*)."

2. *Its testimony.*

Now this is a statement which we have every reason to trust. For Bishop Giustiniano, himself a native of Genoa, forty years of age at the time of Catherine's death, was a man of education, of solid character, and of social position; who, throughout his long book, is uniformly truthful and generally accurate; and who had here no conceivable reason for inventing or seriously misstating the few facts alleged by him. These facts, as regards the matter in hand, are three: that she spoke of various (evidently various spiritual) matters, and, amongst these, of the state of the souls in Purgatory; that a Book was extant at the end of 1535, which concerned itself exclusively with Catherine; and that persons worthy of trust had produced this Book.

(1) Giustiniano knows of no writings of hers: she had not written, but had only "spoken excellent and rare things," and she had done so "when rapt in the spirit." The exaggeration here (for when in ecstasy she spoke nothing, or but a few broken words at most) is interesting, since it probably grew up as an explanation of, and consolation for, her not having herself written anything; since during the ecstasy she would be capable of anything but speech, and out of the ecstasy she would not remember the sights and sounds perceived during the trance. And yet, thus, what had to be written down by others, whilst she was in ecstasy, would be more precious, because more immediately "inspired," than what she herself could have thought, remembered, and written down, in her ordinary psycho-physical condition.

(2) The Book, in existence at the end of 1535, not only contained sayings concerning the state of the souls in Purgatory, but must have contained these sayings already collected together in a separate chapter or division. For her sayings concerning this matter by no means form the larger, or the most immediately striking, part of her authentic teaching, taken as a whole; and only if already collected into a more or less separate *corpus* would they have been singled out in this manner.—But, if this reasoning is sound and proves the existence of the *Trattato*, already more or less separate as at present, similar reasoning will prove the non-existence of the *Dialogo*. For the *Trattato*, even in its present length, fills but fifteen large-print octavo pages; while the *Dialogo* fills ninety. It is practically inconceivable that the latter document, which can never have existed otherwise than more or less separately, should have been overlooked here, where another, so much shorter, and at first sight less authoritative, a piece is dwelt on with emphasis.

(3) More than one hand had participated in the production of the Book. It is characteristic of the rhetorically loose phraseology of the times that the word "composto" is so used as to leave it quite uncertain whether several original contributors of materials and but one Redactor who constituted these materials into a Book are meant, or whether a succession of Redactors is already implied.

3. *Surviving eye-witnesses.*

Certainly by this time the three chief eye-witnesses of her later earthly existence, Carenzio, Vernazza, and Marabotto were all dead, respectively twenty-two, eleven, and seven years. Tommasa Fiesca had died in the previous year. Only Mariola Bastarda and Argentina del Sale, her old maid-servants, were probably still alive, from among the circle of Catherine's constant companions; and Battista Vernazza, who was but thirteen when her Godmother died, had still fifty-two years to live. Yet we have to come still later down amongst extant documents before we can get any further evidence, whether external or internal, as to which of these persons, or who else (probably or certainly) wrote down the original contemporary notes; and as to who constituted these notes (on one or on successive occasions) into this "Giustiniano-book," as I shall call the manuscript "Vita e Dottrina," extant in 1535.

IV. Fourth Stage: The Two Oldest Extant Manuscripts of the "Vita e Dottrina" with the "Dicchiarazione."

The fourth stage of evidence is, as to its contents, the most important of all: but it is, as we shall see, twelve years younger: it belongs to the years 1547, 1548. It consists of two Manuscripts, the duodecimo-volume B. I. 29 of the University Library; and the square octavo-volume of the Archives of the Cathedral Chapter, both in Genoa. Here, at last, we are face to face with an actual *Life* of our Saint. I have carefully collated them both upon the ninth Genoese Edition of the *Vita ed Opere*, Genova, Sordi Muti: the first MS., throughout, and the second one, sufficiently to make sure of its entire dependence upon the first. I have named them MS. A and MS. B respectively.

I. Manuscript A.

1. *Its date and scribe.*

Manuscript A is very interesting. It opens out as follows: "Jesus. Here beginneth the book in which is contained the admirable life and holy conversation of Madonna Catherinetta Adorna. . . . This book was begun and written at the request of her Magnificent Ladyship, the Lady Orientina, Consort to the most magnificent and generous, illustrious Lord Adam Centurione, when she was being vexed by a grave and well-nigh incurable infirmity, during now already thirteen months, by a Religious of the Observance . . . on the 7th of October of the year fifteen hundred and forty-seven."—And Catherine's *Life* concludes with the words: "*Laus Deo semper.* This book was written at the request of the Consort, of happy memory, of the . . . . Lord Adam Centurione, who lay vexed by a most grave infirmity, during now two years. Many a time she would sit and find consolation, in her most painful torments, by reading of the burnings (*incendii*) which were suffered, for so long a time, by this holy woman. . . . At the thirteenth hour of the fourth of February God took her to Himself. She, a few days before she passed away, begged me with tears, in the presence of the Magnificent Lady, the Lady Ginetta, her most beloved daughter, to finish that which I had undertaken to produce for her own self. And so it will be of use to the latter, and will help her to bear her pains and travails, which may the Lord alleviate, by giving her good patience."—After this follow thirty pages, containing an Italian version of St. Bernard's Sermon on the death of his brother Gerard (Chapter XXVI of his *Sermons on the Canticle of Canticles*). And the whole concludes with the words: "Finished in the year Fifteen hundred and forty-eight, on the thirteenth of February."

We have here, then, very precise dates: this *Life* was written between October 7, 1547, and February 4–13, 1548, by a Franciscan Observant, first for the wife, and then for the daughter, of a Doge of Genoa.

2. *Comparison with the Printed "Life."*

Now the whole forty-two chapters of this *Life*, together with the Sermon, are engrossed throughout, in a careful and upright uncial script. On close comparison with the Printed *Life* the differences turn out to consist, either of vocabulary and dialect, of a simply formal kind; or of additions and variations in the subject-matter, of an exceedingly trite and would-be edifying character; or of a very few additional passages of genuine importance; or of divisions, transpositions, and *lacunae*—the latter mostly of a significant and primitive kind; or, finally, of one highly interesting change, effected in his own copy, by the copyist himself.

(i) *Vocabulary.*

The Observant's vocabulary is a curious mixture of downright (late) Latin, old French, and modern Italian. So "pagura" (*paura*); "in si" (*se*, Fr. *soi*); "despecto" (*dispetto*); "alchuna," "anchora" (*alcuna, ancora*); "lingeriare" (*ligare*, Fr. *lier*); "summissa" (*sommessa*, Fr. *soumise*); "una fiata" (*una volta*, Fr. *une fois*); "dido" (*digito*, o. Fr. *doight*).[1] Some of these and such-like forms no doubt stood in his Prototype. Thus, whilst he simply copies, he writes—"pecto" and "licet"; when he makes up sentences of his own, he writes "petto" and "abenchè." And his single Chapter XIII has, on two pages, "per il che"; but, on its last two pages, it has the elsewhere universal "perochè" (*perchè*).—Yet his language is, upon the whole, so uniform, whilst his sources (as we shall see) are so varied; and again his uniform language is in such marked contrast to Giustiniano's educated Genoese Italian of 1535, and to that of the Printed *Vita* of 1551: that much of it, even where he is copying the substance of his Prototype, must be his own.

(ii) *Worthless additions and variations, of two kinds.*

The additions and variations are mostly of two kinds. They are either of a directly edifying character. So the three pages descriptive of the devotion of the crowd, on occasion of the opening of the coffin, in the spring of 1512; the very general statement as to the miracles that occurred on that occasion; and, further back, the expansion (by this Franciscan scribe) of Catherine's comments on (the Franciscan) Jacopone da Todi's "la superbia in cielo c'è."[2] And in one place, to produce edification by a sense of contrast, he adopts a touch of (doubtless legendary) gossip against Giuliano, for the heading of his Chapter XXIV runs: "How she comported herself towards her husband, who was very contrary to her temperament; and concerning her indefatigable patience in bearing with him—and even with the beatings

[1] MS. A, pp. 3; 367; 368–398; 399.
[2] *Ibid.* pp. 361–363; 364; 87, 88.

which he gave her";[1]—where the end marked off by me is no doubt the Observant's own addition,—possibly, as we shall see, on the authority of Argentina del Sale.—Or these additions are introduced to minimize or ward off scandal. So when, after expanding the parallel between the conversions of St. Paul and Catherine, he adds: "'For He spoke, and they were (re-)made' (Ps. xxxii, 9). But we must not curiously seek for the reason of this action"; and then proves his point by three further Biblical texts. So too when, after giving an abbreviated account of the contrast between Thomassina's and Catherine's rate of spiritual advancement, he again adds some Bible text and some moralizing of his own. And so again where, after reproducing the passage as to her being linked to God with a thread of gold, he expatiates, once more in Scriptural words, on the presence of filial fear and the absence of all servile fear within her. And so where, after following his Prototype (as still preserved in the Printed *Life*), and declaring his belief that it is reasonable and licit to believe her soul to have entered Heaven immediately after death, he continues: "Hence he who does believe this, does not lose in merit" (*non demerita;* an obvious *litotes* for "merits"), and he who believes it not, does not offend." In all these cases the Biblical texts appear in the Vulgate Latin.[2]

There can be no doubt that it is this slight recasting of the language, and this insertion of trite and timid moralizing of his own, which, together with the careful engrossing of his copy throughout, and its occasional pretty decoration and illumination, permitted the Observant to talk (although, even thus, in a manner most misleading for our present habits of language) of having "written this Book."

(iii) *Two genuine dates and accounts.*

Yet, even amongst the passages which appear in his MS. as additional to the later texts, are two evidently genuine and suggestive dates and accounts. There is a description of Catherine's great attack of "fire at her heart," more full and primitive, and more definitely dated than any one of its many variants and echoes to be found in the Printed *Life:* the slip in the date (he writes November 11, 1506, when his own age-indications, and the position of the anecdote, clearly require 1509) will have had something to do with the strangely

[1] MS. A, p. 160.

[2] *Ibid.* pp. 134; 168; 198–200; 329; in contrast respectively with pp. 62; 124; 76; 161 of the Printed *Life*.

uncertain position of this episode in the Printed *Life*.[1]—And further back, in opening out the beautiful story of Marco and Argentina, he writes: "There being in the quarter of the Quay (*contrada del Molo*) one Marco del Sale, suffering from a cancer in the nose, who, fourteen months before his infirmity, had taken to wife a virtuous young woman named Argentina, spiritual daughter of Madonna Catherinetta, as is said above."[2] This very precise distance of time, between that humble wedding and the poor navvy's illness, will have been derived by the Observant from Argentina herself, probably still living at the time of his writing, even now hardly sixty years old.—Hence his long-winded addition, as to the mediation of the "spiritual daughter" (certainly Argentina), in the matter of our knowledge of Catherine's prayer for the dying Giuliano,[3] may also have been derived from that gossipy little woman.

(iv) *Divisions and transpositions.*

As to the divisions and transpositions, the chief of these consist in the first six chapters of the Printed *Vita* appearing here broken up into (the first) ten chapters; in the MS. Chapters XI and XVI being gradually caught up by the Printed series,—indeed the MS. Chapter XVI corresponds to Chapters XVI to XVIII of the published book; in the Chapters XVII to XIX of the MS. corresponding to Chapters XX and XXI of the Print; and Chapters XX, XXI, and XXII of the MS., corresponding respectively to Chapters XXIV, XXV, and XXVII of the Print. Then for three Chapters follows considerable variation: the MS. Chapters XXIII, XXIV, and XXV hold the positions respectively of the Printed Chapters XXXVII, XLV and XLVI there. And then again there is likeness for three Chapters—MS. Chapters XXVI to XXVIII corresponding to Printed Chapters XXVIII and XXIX there. And once more three MS. Chapters (XXIX to XXXI), quite different in sequence to anything there, are followed by two Chapters (XXXII and XXXIII) corresponding to the Printed Chapters XXIX and XXX. Four more MS. Chapters (XXXIV to XXXVII), without any match, as to order, in the Printed book, are followed by two Chapters

[1] MS. A, p. 193, which appears, in a somewhat modified form, in the Pr. L., p. 97*c*; and, with further transformations, on pp. 139*a*; 139*c*; 140*a*; 140*b* of the same.

[2] *Ibid.* p. 169, compared with Pr. L., p. 124*c*.

[3] *Ibid.* p. 163, compared with Pr. L., p. 122*c*.

(XXXVIII and XXXIX), corresponding, respectively, to the beginning and end of Chapter XXXI there; and by Chapter XL, identical with the opening of Chapter XL and with Chapter XLI there. And, above all, Chapter XLI here, corresponds to the *Dicchiarazione* (*Trattato*) there; and is followed here by a final Chapter (XLII), made up of a bewilderingly different succession of paragraphs,—paragraphs which, in the Printed *Life*, stand in Chapters XLIX; XVII; and XLVIII to LII. And, whereas the first forty Chapters of this MS. average six or seven pages in length, Chapters XLI and XLII are respectively forty-five and forty-eight pages long.

(v) *Lacunae.*

These transpositions would alone suffice to show how complicated is the textual history of the *Vita*: we may have to consider some of them later on. But it is the *lacunae* which are especially interesting. One of these is quite certainly right, as against the printed text. Paragraphs 23 to 25 of Chapter L of the Print are wanting here. Those pages give an entirely fantastic, and formally vague, account of a supposed interior stigmatization of Catherine, and of a preposterous elongation of one of her arms,—both "facts" based explicitly upon the authority of Argentina.[1] And the circumstance of the scribe being a disciple of the stigmatized St. Francis, and the probability that Argentina was still accessible, conjoin to render the absence of these paragraphs from this MS. simply decisive against their historical character. —The longest of all the omissions, that of the *Dialogo*, must, even more, be explained on the ground of its non-existence at this time, or, at least, of its not being known to the Scribe, or again, of its having as yet no kind of authority. For not only does he make no use of, or allusion to this, very long, and (were it primitive) simply supreme document, but, as we shall find, quite a number of his facts contradict the *Dialogo's* version of them; and we shall soon see that, had he known and esteemed the document, he would not have allowed such a defiance of it to remain without correction.

Over against these two non-appearances of spurious or secondary matter, we have to set three omissions of highly valuable material. The two interconnected, obviously entirely historical, paragraphs concerning Maestro Boerio,—his attempt

[1] Pr. L., pp. 155*b*–156*a*.

to cure Catherine, and the excessive impression made upon her by his scarlet robes,[1]—are both wanting here. But we shall see that they were probably not incorporated in any *Vita*, till the preparation of the Printed *Life* of 1551.—Matters stand differently with respect to the third omission,—the beautifully vivid, inimitably daring and characteristic, Chapter XIX, containing Catherine's dialogue with the Friar, who, according to the well-informed Parpera, was a Franciscan Observant.[2] It is impossible to hold that this, most historical and well-preserved, story did not stand in the Observant's Prototype, or that it was otherwise unknown to him; its omission is doubtless deliberate and "prudential."—An interesting instance of demonstrable omission on his part, is indeed furnished also by his version of the beautiful story of Suor Tommasa's life: his abbreviation of it is so obvious and yet so unintelligent, that only a reference to the full account, which lay certainly before him and is still preserved in the Printed *Life*, makes any satisfactory sense of what he has retained.[3]

3. *Modification from a tripartite scheme to a quatripartite one.*

But the most interesting of all the differences between this MS. A of 1547 and the Printed *Life* of 1551 is another group of omissions, connected, as these are, with the one single modification introduced into his own text by the Scribe himself. The whole of the matter corresponding to the Printed *Life's* Chapter XLIV (all but the first seven lines) and that corresponding to the first three paragraphs of its Chapter XLIX, which treat consecutively, and with an inimitable vividness and a daring, unreflective truthfulness, of her most unusual self-revelations to her Confessor Don Marabotto,[4] is omitted—possibly, again, in part at least, from fear of scandal; but more probably because, even at this time, this (the most private and consecutive) contribution to the *Life*, still existed separately, perhaps from all, and presumably from most, copies of the *Vita* then in circulation. And such a copy will have been the Observant's Prototype.—Only when he had finished copying out his manuscript, will he have discovered that, if

[1] Pr. L., pp. 146*c*–147*c*; 154*b*.

[2] Pr. L., pp. 51*a*–53*b*.

[3] MS. A, p. 168, compared with Pr. L., pp. 123*b*–124*b*.

[4] Pr. L., pp. 116*c*–121*b*; 139*a*–140*c*. Retained lines: MS. p. 40 = Pr. L., p. 116*c*.

he would take any, even though silent, account of that contribution, which, by now, will have become known to him, he must, at all costs, break up and seriously modify one of his chapters. We have already studied the treble, most solemn affirmation, by Catherine and her Confessor themselves, in that Printed Chapter XLIV, as to her twenty-five years of spiritual loneliness and guidance by God alone; [1] and we have seen that (since we cannot place her Conversion before 1474, nor the beginning of her later practice of Confession after 1499) we are forced (if we take her words in their obvious sense, as applying to Confession as well as to Direction, and assume her First Convert-Period, the penitential time, to have been accompanied throughout by repeated Confessions) to make this first Period very short.

Now the volume of 1547, 1548, consists throughout of paper, all but the first three leaves and the tenth leaf, which are of parchment. The first leaf remains blank; the second contains the Observant's Preface on its obverse; the third holds, on its two sides, the first two pages of the *Vita*. That Preface was certainly written before all the rest, or at least certainly during the lifetime of Donna Orientina Centurione, *i.e.* before February 4, 1548; nor does anything in those first two (parchment and paper) pages of text suggest that they are an insertion subsequent to the following (paper) pages. At first, then, the copy will have consisted of three parchment leaves, and then of nothing but paper leaves; and the Observant will have made the last of these parchment leaves the sole and opening parchment leaf of the text of the Book.

But matters stand differently with the tenth leaf, pp. 19, 20 of the MS., which begins with the words "bisogna, sono apparecchiata a confessar"—"(if) necessary, I am prepared to confess my sins in public" (Catherine's words, on occasion of her Conversion); and ends with "(abru) savano insino al core. Poi fu tirata al Petto"—" Love, with those penetrating rays of its own, which burnt her, even to the heart. She was then drawn to the Breast" (narrative words which, in the scheme of her *Life* that follows upon the Conversion-story, mark the transition from one of this scheme's stages to another).

Now here we have clear indications that these two parchment pages hold a modified text. For that last parchment-

[1] Pr. L., p. 119*c*.

leaf word " Petto " is picked up, on the paper continuation, by " Pecto," the ordinary form of the Observant's Prototype : see his page 81. And the whole book (all but this parchment leaf and its highly restricted effects), still attributes *four years* to her First Convert-Period, her Penitential, Purgative Stage.

Indeed, this solitary parchment leaf itself still allows us to trace, (as though the leaf were a Palimpsest,) both this, the original, length of that Period, and the fact of that Period having then been the first of three, and not, as now, of four such periods.—For this leaf, in finishing up the manuscript's fourth chapter, the history of her Conversion,[1]—declares that " this sight (of her sins) and this contrition (for them) lasted *fourteen months*, during which she went on confession herself, continually increasing her self-accusation (*aggravando la colpa*); after the passing of which months, all sadness was lifted from her, nor did she have any memory of her sins,—as though she had cast them into the depths of the sea." And then, in the opening of the fifth chapter,[2] the scheme and conspectus of her Convert Life runs as follows. She is first "drawn to the feet of Christ" and abides there "*one year* until she had satisfied her conscience by Contrition, Confession, and Satisfaction."—" She next felt herself drawn, with St. John, to repose on the Breast of her Loving Lord. . . . *The sight of the sins committed by her against God would come to her*, so that she would be, as it were, wild (*arrabbiava*) with grief, and would lick the ground with her tongue; and in this wise she appeared to derive relief for her tempestuous feelings (*affannato cuore*). And she abode thus for *three years*, during which she was, as it were, wild with grief and love, with those penetrating rays of its own, which burned her to the very heart.[3] She was then drawn to the Breast "—which last parchment-leaf word is taken up by the next, ordinary paper-leaf: "Breast; and here she was shown the Heart of Christ. . . And she abode *many years* with this impression of His burning Heart.—And then she was drawn (still) further up, that is, to the Mouth; and there she was found worthy of being kissed by the true Solomon. . . . And she no more (directly) recognized her human acts, whether they had been done well or evilly; but she saw all in God." [4]

[1] MS. ch. iv = Pr. L., ch. ii, pp. 4*a*–5*c*.
[2] MS. ch. v = Pr. L., ch. ii, pp. 5*c*–6*c*.
[3] I purposely leave this sentence in its tell-tale clumsiness of form.
[4] This corresponds, as to its substance, to Pr. L., pp. 5*c*–6*c*.

We see here how the original four years of her First Period, which are still retained elsewhere by the Printed *Vita*,[1] have been broken up by the scribe of this Manuscript into two shorter (first and second) Periods, of fourteen months (one year), and three years respectively; how the copyist, both in his first apportionment of length to his new First Period, " fourteen months," and in his second assignment, now of one year (since he has to divide up the original Four years so as to get them again by addition, " *one* year " and " *three* years "), leaves us two curious echoes of the " Four " of his Prototype; how his amended description of his new second Period is still largely the old Penitential description, for she still sees her sins (a sight which is here an anachronism), and she is still prostrate on the ground (a prostration which exactly suits the Feet, but in no way the Breast of Christ); how the Observant has been half-hearted and clumsy, for he has now left two successive Breast-Periods, hardly differentiated from each other; and how he was able to shift (though not to change) the original single Breast-Period (now his second Breast-Period), because of its conveniently vague time-note of " many years." All this laborious, yet timid, incomplete and ineffectual change, thus forced upon an evidently long-established, toughly resisting composition, can only have taken place under some severe pressure of evidence; and the root-causes of the change are somehow connected with the question as to the duration, in her life, of the perception and Confession of her sins. For the Confession of her sins, which (in the old scheme) extended over four years, is now restricted to fourteen months or one year; and if contemplative and restful love are now anticipated (from the original second Period) in the new second Period of three years, yet an intense sight of her particular sins, piercing contrition for them, and a complete prostration on the ground, are all indeed retained, from the original Feet-Period, for this new second Period, but Confession has disappeared from these three years.

Now we have precisely such absolutely constraining evidence in Marabotto's treble chronicle of Catherine's own words, with regard to the twenty-five years during which she was led by God's spirit alone. It is clear then that the most important of Marabotto's notes did not exist incorporated with, or at least had not originally formed part of, and did not dominate,

[1] Pr. L., p. 14*c*.

the scheme of the *Vita* which the Observant had before him; and that, upon his later knowledge of, or pondering over them, he understood Catherine's words to have applied, not simply to Direction but to (at least at all habitual) Confession as well.

2. Manuscript B.

1. *Its very primitive heading.*

Manuscript B starts indeed with a heading demonstrably older than that of MS. A. For its "De la Mirabile Conversione et Vita de la q(uondam) donna Catherinetta Adorna" is more primitive, because of its "the late," which indicates a time of writing not yet far removed from the date of her death; its "Donna," less honorific than the "Madonna" of the other MSS.; and, above all, its giving "Conversione" before "Vita," instead of "Conversatione" after "Vita," since thus we are assured of "Conversione" being no slip of the pen for "Conversatione,"—Conversion coming necessarily before, and holy Conversation coming after, in consequence of, an admirable life.—And this title will originally have headed a booklet containing simply the story of her Conversion and early Convert life, say up to the end of Chapter VI of the Printed *Vita*, p. 17*b*; or, since even the "et Vita" of this title reads like a later addition, only up to the end of the present printed Chapter II, p. 6*c*. I think there is no doubt that we have here the original heading of a tract put together on occasion of the first public Cultus, in the summer of 1512.

2. *Body of MS. B. dependent upon MS. A.*

But the body of MS. B is demonstrably later than, indeed dependent upon, MS. A; for here the scribe silently adopts the modification, effected by the writer of MS. A in his own text, with regard to doubling the Breast-Period; and yet, even here, we have still the Observant's "Petto" for the first period, and the "Pecto" of the Observant's Prototype for the second period.[1] "Come" now appears throughout, in lieu of MS. A's "Como." And Giuliano's name is omitted (all but once, in Catherine's mouth) in the Husband-Chapter.[2]

3. *Order, division, numeration of the Chapters.*

The order, division, and numeration of the Chapters is identical with those of MS. A, all but that Chapter XXXIX of MS. A (equivalent to the unimportant pp. 82*b*–83*a* of

[1] MS. B. fol. 2*r* et *v*. [2] *Ibid*. fol. 19*r* et *v*.

Chapter XXXI in the Printed *Life*) which is here omitted. No Chapter numbered XXXIX appears here, but, after a small break behind Chapter XXXVIII, the *Trattato* follows, as Chapter XL.

4. *Laceration at end of Manuscript.*

And this Chapter XL is abruptly broken off in the midst of a penultimate paragraph: " et per gratia li sono monstrati et " are the last words. The authentication of the MS., appended immediately after this rough ending, shows this laceration to be at least as old as 1672. Nor is it a case of some complete set or sets of leaves being lost, since one leaf has had to be torn off, from the still remaining other half-sheet.[1] The last part, no doubt, contained the end of the *Trattato* and the Passion-Chapter; and will, like its Prototype, MS. A, have been without a trace of the *Dialogo*. Indeed I suspect that it was the latter circumstance which, when once this elaborate composition had come to be prized, gave rise to the, surely deliberate, destruction of the evidence for its absence here. MS. A will, in that case, have been saved from a similar fate, by its special appropriation to a powerful family; by its superior, uncial kind of script; and, above all, by its important contemporary date and dedication at the end.

V. Fifth Stage: Manuscript C.

Our next, deeply interesting stage, is represented by one single MS. in the University Library, Genoa,—catalogued as B. VII 17. It is a careful copy, made throughout by the Protonotary Angelo Luigi Giovo, and subscribed by himself on April 20, 1671, of, as he there says, "Another ancient MS. received from the Signora ——, Matron of the Great Hospital, who declared that she had herself received it from the Nuns of the Madonna delle Grazie; and which is believed, with great probability, to be the MS. copied by Ettore Vernazza and sent to the Venerable Donna Battista, his daughter. The book, in view of the antiquity of the paper, of the character of the binding of the copy, and of the other peculiarities, has been judged by experts to belong to the above-mentioned Period." The reader will soon see why I place (not necessarily the execution, but the text of) the MS.

[1] MS. B: the break, on fol. 30*r*; the abrupt ending on bottom of fol. 33*v*.

thus copied by Giovo, before the printing of the *Vita* in 1551, and will thus be helped to a decision as to the "greatly probable" attribution to Ettore Vernazza.

1. *Differences in text of MS. C from MSS. A and B.*

Giovo's Copy (my MS. C) follows, up to the end of its Chapter XLI (the *Trattato*), the division, number, and sequence of the chapters, and the peculiarities of the text, of MS. A, with an all but unbroken closeness: even the slip, of 1506 (for 1509), in the date of the great attack of "fire at heart," reappears here as it stands there (fol. 33*v* of MS. C, compared with p. 193 of MS. A). But the "Petto" and "Pecto," of respectively the first and second Breast-Periods in MSS. A and B, read here, in both cases, as simply "Petto" (MS. C, fol. 3).—There is but one at all remarkable addition in this, the *Vita*-part of the MS. In the account of the refusal to accept Catherine on the part of the Nuns of the very Convent where, as we shall see, the Prototype copied by Giovo was no doubt written, there occur the new words: "Although her Confessor was instant with them (to take her), knowing her, as he did, better than the Nuns knew her" (MS. C, fol. 1*v*). —And, in concluding further on (on its fol. 71*v* *seq.*) with the Passion-Chapter, as this stands in MS. A (Chapter XLII), a Chapter which here (for a reason to be given in a minute) is not numbered, the MS. still follows closely (although now with a few generally unimportant additions, omissions, and transpositions of paragraphs), the matter, order, and literary form of MS. A.—Only one, formally slight, but materially significant, difference exists here between Giovo's text and the Printed *Life*. The Printed *Life*, p. 142*b*, reads: "After this, she felt a hard nail at heart"; to this MS. C adds (fol. 72*r*) "so that she seemed nailed to the Cross." Neither set of words occurs in MSS. A and B. MS. C here gives us something unlike Catherine's, but very like Battista's, special spirit.

2. *The great addition: the "Dialogo," Part First.*

(1) *The "Dialogo" originally no longer.*

But it is in the pages intermediate between the *Trattato* and the Passion (foll. 53*v* to 71*v*), that lies the interest of this MS. For here we get, for the first time, the *Dialogo*, although, as yet, only its eventual First Part (pp. 185–225 in the Printed *Life*). Chapter XLI (the *Trattato*) has just finished, by only six lines short of its printed form, with the words "because that occupation with Himself which God gives to the soul, slight though it be, keeps the soul so occupied, that it exceeds everything, nor can the soul esteem anything else." And immediately next there come (53*v*) the title-words: "Here follows a certain beautiful Allegory (*Figura*) which this holy soul institutes (*fà*) concerning the Soul and the Body."—The eventual division into (17) chapters is still absent, and the work seems, at this time, to have been planned to be no longer than it is here. For it concludes with the emphatic climax: "Now the Spirit, having come to hold this creature in this manner, declared: 'I am determined henceforth no more to call her a human creature, because I see her (to be) all in God, without any (mere) humanity.'" For these words simply re-cast the last words of the scheme of her entire life, given by the *Vita*: "She said: 'I live no more, but Christ lives in me.' Hence she could no more recognize the quality of her human acts, in themselves—whether they were good or evil; but she saw all in God" (Pr. L., p. 6*c*).

(2) *The "Dialogo's" two stages, each comprising two steps, and their suggestions in the "Vita."*

Now the *Dialogo*, as here given, consists of two chief stages, and each stage contains two steps.

Chapters I to VI give the first stage—the history of a soul in a state of moral and spiritual decline and contraction: all this, in the form of a Dialogue between the Soul, the Body, and Self-Love.—Throughout this first stage Self-Love holds dominion. But, during the first step, the Soul (although it already distinguishes, with regard to what it intends to practise, between simply avoiding grave sin and striving after perfection) still continues fairly determined not to commit sin, and still leads the Body. During the second step, on the contrary, even this simple avoidance of grave sin has ceased, for now the Body leads the Soul. Thus first the Soul, and then the Body, each leads the other during one step, for "one week."—These two steps or weeks stand for the two lustres of Catherine's pre-Conversion-Period, for the lukewarm, and then the positively dissipated, lustre respectively. Chapters I to III give the first week, equivalent to the first five years of her married life, 1463 to 1468; and Chapters IV to VI give the second week, and correspond to the second five years, 1468 to 1473.[1]

[1] Hence *Dialogo* (Pr. L.), pp. 185*c*–190*c* is an expansion of the *Vita*-proper (Pr. L.), p. 31; and *Dialogo*, pp. 191*a*–198*a* is an expansion of *Vita*-proper, p. 33.

Chapters VII to XXI describe the second stage, that of Conversion and Transformation, which (notwithstanding its appearance of instantaneous and complete attainment of its end) is here presented as, in reality, by far the longer and the more difficult, although the alone fruitful and happy one. Chapters VII to XIII describe the first step. Chapters VII to IX give us the Soul's longing for Light; the spark of Pure Love shown to it, on its conversion-day; and a long address by the Soul to the Body and Self-Love, and the answers of these two.[1] In this address the Soul for the first time speaks of "*the Spirit.*"[2] Chapter X makes the Soul for the first time address "*the Lord,*" "O Signore," on the one hand: and her "*Humanity,*" "O Umanità," on the other.[3] In Chapters XI and XII the Soul stands alone, face to face with the Lord, who appears to it in two successive visions,—first as Christ alive and walking along all stained with blood from head to foot; and, on a later occasion, as Christ evidently motionless and presumably dead, with His five fountain-wounds, which are sending drops of burning blood towards mankind. And these two visions, so carefully kept apart, doubtless typify the two periods of Catherine's Convert life,—the two steps of her second stage: the moving, scourged and cross-bearing Christ stands for the active penance of the first four years or fourteen months; and the motionless, crucified Christ stands for the passive purification of the rest of her life.[4] Chapter XIII has no dialogue, but describes her active penances and good works, and mentions the Soul, Humanity, and the Spirit.[5]

And then, up to the end, in Chapters XIV to XXI, which give us the second step, the dialogue reappears, but now no more between the three *Dramatis Personae* (Soul, Body, and Self-Love) of the pre-Conversion-Period; but between the two interlocutors of the post-conversion time (the Spirit and Humanity).[6] And there is here but one sporadic mention, an invocation, of "the Lord" (p. 214*c*).

Thus only after its Conversion does the Soul itself become

[1] Hence *Dialogo* (Pr. L.), pp. 198*b*–206*b* corresponds to *Vita*-proper, pp. 4*a*–5*a*.

[2] P. 205*c*.

[3] Pp. 206*c*, 207*b*.

[4] *Dialogo*, pp. 207*c*–212*a* is thus equivalent to *Vita*-proper, p. 5*b*.

[5] *Dialogo*, pp. 212*b*–212*c* is hence equivalent to *Vita*-proper, pp. 12*b*–13*c*.

[6] *Dialogo*, pp. 213*c*–225*c* thus corresponds to *Vita*-proper, pp. 9*b*, 15*b*; 13*c*, 14*a*; 20*a*, 21*a*; 123*b*; 13*b*; 96*b*–97*a*.

aware of, or does it name, either the Spirit or its "Humanity"; and only after the two successive Christ-Visions do these two new experiences and conceptions entirely replace the three old ones of Soul, Body, and Self-Love. In a word, we have here, carefully carried through, the scheme, so clearly enunciated by Battista Vernazza in 1554, of the two successive divisions effected by God in Man, during the process of Man's purification: first, the separation (division) of the Soul from the Body; and then the separation (division) of the Spirit from the Soul.[1] And, in strict accordance with this scheme, the Soul here becomes conscious of being, in its upper reaches, Spirit, only on the day that it has broken away from the domination of the downward-tending Body, and of Self-Love. And once the Soul has thus affirmed the Spirit and denied the Body, the "Body" and the "Soul" cease to be directly mentioned; the one term "Humanity" now takes the Soul's and the Body's place. For now the Soul, in so far as it has still not completely identified itself with the Spirit, does not any more attach itself directly to the Body and the Body's pleasures,—to, as it were, the upper fringe of the Body,—but to the sensible-spiritual consolations which are the necessary concomitants and consequences of the Soul's affirmation and acceptance of the Spirit,—hence, as it were, to the lower fringe of the Spirit. "I would have thee know," the Spirit now says to Catherine, "that I fear much more an attachment to the spiritual than to the bodily taste and feeling. Man goes his way 'feeding' his spiritual sensuality upon the things which proceed from God, and yet these things are a very poison for the Pure Love of God."[2]

3. *The "Dialogo" intensifies or softens certain narratives and sayings given by the "Vita."*

Now these interesting forty pages of the first *Dialogo* derive (with the sole exception of three little touches) their entire historical materials from the *Vita e Dottrina*, and, indeed, from but those parts of this *corpus* which already appear in MSS. A and B, and in the previous pages of MS. C itself. But all these materials have been re-thought, re-pictured, re-arranged throughout, by a new, powerful, and experienced mind, a mind dominated by certain very definite, schematic conceptions as to the constitution of the human personality, the nature of holiness, and the laws of its growth,

[1] See here, pp. 353, 354.

[2] *Dialogo*, pp. 215*c*, 216*a*.

and which is determined to find or form concrete examples of these conceptions, in and from the life of Catherine.

(1) *Cases of intensifying.*

There are, first, five cases of the intensifying of authentic *Vita*-accounts, intensifications necessary, or at least ancillary, to the scheme underlying the whole *Dialogo*-composition.

As to the pre-conversion sinfulness, during her second "week," Catherine's soul is made to say: "In a short time I was enveloped in sin; and, abiding in that snare, I lost the grace (of God) and remained blind and heavy, and from spiritual I became all earthly."[1] Yet there is no evidence that Catherine, even at that time, ever committed grave sin; nor does there exist an authentic saying of hers which, however intense its expressions of contrition, conveys an impression really equivalent to this passage.—As to the form of her contrition, "so greatly was this soul alienated (from her own self) and submerged in the sight of the offence of God, that she no longer seemed a rational creature, but a terrified animal."[2] Yet the earlier accounts, which certainly do not minimize here, keep well within the limits of normal, though intense, human feeling and expression of feeling.—As to the forcible means taken by her to overcome her fastidiousness in the matter of cleanliness and in the sense of taste, "she would put the impurities into her mouth, as though they had been precious pearls."[3] Yet the original versions, drastic enough in all conscience, nowhere imply that there was any such relish, even of a merely apparent kind.—As to her post-conversion poverty, the Spirit says to her: "Thou shalt work to provide for thy living," and the narrative declares: "The Spirit made her so poor, that she would have been unable to live, had not God provided for her by the means of alms."[4] Yet we know from her wills that (though the Hospital authorities gave her free lodging, and perhaps, at first, free board as well) she retained, up to the last, an appreciable little income, and herself conferred many an alms out of these her own means.

Nevertheless, in each of these cases, the *Dialogo* exaggeration is suggested by some phrase or word in the *Vita* which has been taken up into the new context and medium of this other mind, and has come to mean something curiously (though often in form but slightly) different from

[1] *Dialogo*, p. 197*a*. [2] *Ibid.* p. 209*b*.
[3] *Ibid.* p. 223*c*. [4] *Ibid.* p. 221*c*.

that older account.—Thus, in this fourth instance, the *Vita*-accounts had said : " nel *principio* di sua conversione, molto si *esercitò*." " Viveva ancora molto *sottomessa ad ogni creatura*." " Quantunque ella fosse in tutto dedicata ed occupata negli *esercizii* di esso Spedale, nondimeno mai volle godere ne usare una minima cosa di quello per *viver suo ;* ma, per quel poco che abbisognava, si serviva della *povera* sostanza sua : onde ben si scorgeva che il suo dolce Amore era quello il quale operava in lei ogni cosa per vera unione." " Si *esercitò* nelle opere pie, cercando i *poveri*, essendo condotta delle Donne della Misericordia, e le davano danari ed altre *provvisioni*." [1] The *Dialogo*-writer has worked all this up as follows : " Io (lo Spirito) ti avviso *primieramente* voler io che tu pruovi che cosa sia esser ubbidiente, acciò tu divenghi umile e *soggetta ad ogni creatura ;* ed acciochè ti possi *esercitare*, lavorerai per provedere al *viver tuo*." " Primieramente la fece tanto *povera*, che non avrebbe potuto vivere, se Dio non l'avvesse *provveduta* per via di limosine. Poi quando le Signore della Misericordia l'addimandavano per andare a'poveri . . . ella sempre con loro andava." [2] I have italicized the words taken over by the *Dialogo*. Thus her own poor substance (*i. e.* her own modest income), and the money given to her by the *Misericordia*-ladies for distribution among the poor, becomes a substance, alms and money, given to herself as to a poor person.

The fifth case concerns the affections. In the *Vita*-proper nothing is more characteristic of Catherine, up to the spring of 1509, than her swift and deep affective sympathy, and the fearless forms of its manifestation. True, Catherine " would " (certainly up to 1490, perhaps more or less up to 1496) " abide at times," up to six hours on end, " as though dead." But, " on hearing herself called, she would suddenly arise and betake herself, in answer, to whatever was required of her, however small a service this might be." And indeed " she served the sick with most fervent affection " : thus she attended throughout a week upon a poor pestiferous woman ; and at the end, " unable further to contain herself, kissed " the dying woman " upon the mouth with great affection of heart, and so caught the pestilential fever, and well-nigh died of it." [3] —Then, too, there is the *Vita's* quite general, indeterminate remark, " she (Catherine) felt no pain at the deaths of her

[1] *Dialogo*, pp. 20*a*, 13*c*, 21*a*, 20*a*. [2] *Ibid.* pp. 220*c*, 222*c*.
[3] *Ibid.* p. 21*b*.

(two elder) brothers and of her sisters" (the latter should be "sister," unless, perhaps, a sister-in-law is included) in 1502.[1] But her extant wills have shown us how actively thoughtful she remained, even in 1506 and 1509, for her brother, nephews and nieces, and humble retainers; and the deeply affectionate scenes with Marco and Argentina occurred between 1503 and 1506. Marco, the poor navvy, was dying "of a cancer in the face," and Catherine, at Argentina's asking, "as though with prompt obedience, betook herself to him"; and he "threw his arms round Catherine's neck, and, pressing her with sobs, seemed unable to have done with weeping.[2] And then, still weeping, with great tenderness he besought Catherine to adopt his wife as her spiritual daughter," and Catherine did so, and "loved this spiritual daughter much." [3]—Only in the very late actions, the change as to her burial-place (Will of March 1509), and the exclusion of all her attendants on January 10, and of most of them on and after August 27, 1510,[4] are there indications of any absence or renunciation of tender and spontaneous human affection.

But here again the *Dialogo* both closely presses and profoundly changes the original accounts. For here the Spirit declares to her: "in these exercises" of work among the poor, "I shall keep thee . . . as though thou wast dead. I will not allow thee to make friends with any one, nor that thou shouldst have any particular affection for any relative; but I want thee to love all men, and this without affection, both poor and rich, both friends and relatives. I do not want thee, in thine interior, to know one person from the other, nor would I have thee go to any one from motives of friendship; it will suffice to go when thou art called." And thus "she went, when the *Misericordia*-ladies asked her to go into dwellings that would have frightened away all ordinary mortals. But she, on the contrary, deliberately touched these sick (*voleva toccarli*), for the purpose of giving them some refreshment to soul and body." [5]—Note how skilfully the call, and the going at the call, the affection and its spontaneous manifestations in the original accounts, have been altered and

[1] *Dialogo*, p. 123*b*.

[2] From MS. A, p. 174: "Li buttò le braccie al collo, e, stringendola con singulti, non si poteva saziar di piangere." The Printed *Vita*, p. 125*b*, has only: "La abbracciò piangendo, per lungo spazio di tempo."

[3] See here, pp. 169–171.

[4] See here, pp. 185, 186; 194; 205.

[5] *Ibid.* pp. 221, 222*a*.

crossed by the *Dialogo's* re-statement.—Here again we are strongly reminded of Battista, in her letter to the Signora Andronica in 1575, encouraging her to "abandon all things," her children included, "interiorly," and "to mortify the most pleasing consolation which arises from the children's company." Indeed, already in 1554, Battista has, in one of her own *Colloquies*, refused to accept every avoidable consolation arising from her pure election by God.[1] Only by such a reference of these *Dialogo*-passages to Battista, the many-sided, the ever-affectionate daughter and public-spirited woman, can we come to see them in a wider context; indeed only thus can they cease to be profoundly repulsive.

(2) *Cases of softening.*

There are two instances of the softening of (doubtless authentic) doctrinal sayings given by the *Vita*-proper. Her evidently impulsive exclamation: "I would not have grace or mercy, but justice and vengeance exercised against the malefactor,"—has here become: "She did not attach any importance to her sins, on the ground of the punishment awaiting them, but solely because they had been enacted against the infinite goodness of God."—And her bold declaration: "If any creature could be found which did not participate in the divine goodness, that creature would be as malignant as God is good," here reads: "The soul bereft of the Divine love becomes *well-nigh* as malignant as the Divine love is good and delightful. I say 'well-nigh,' for God shows it a little mercy."[2] The proclamation of some moral good even in lost souls, is thus weakened to an admission of some consolation in the latter.

4. *Re-statement of the Conversion-experiences of March 1474.*

But it is in the matters of Catherine's Conversion in the Convent-Chapel, on March 22, 1474, and of the Vision of the Bleeding Christ in the Palazzo Adorno, soon after, that the *Dialogo's* transformation of the *Vita*-accounts reaches its highest interest. I give it here as the chief of many such re-statements which I have carefully analyzed.

[1] See here, pp. 363; 346, 347. [2] *Ibid.* pp. 56*b*, 203*a*; 33*b*, 202*b*.

Vita-proper, pp. 4*a*–5*b*

Subitocchè se gli fù inginocchiata innanzi, receve una ferita al cuore d'immenso amore di Dio, con una vista così chiara delle sue miserie e diffetti, e della bontà di Dio che ne fù per cascare in terra. Onde . . . restò quasi fuòr di sè: e perciò internamente gridava con ardente amore: "Non più mondo, non più peccati." Ed in quel punto. . . . . . . Per la viva fiamma d'infocato amore il dolce Iddio impresse in quell' anima . . . tutta la perfezione. . . .

Vedeva ancora le offese che gli aveva fatte; e perciò gridava: "O amore mai più, mai più, peccati." Se le accese poi un odio di sè medesima, che non si poteva sopportare, e diceva: "O amore, se bisogna, sono apparecchiata di confessare i miei peccati in pubblico."

Ma volendo il Signore accendere intrinsecamente più l'amor suo in quest' anima, ed insieme il dolore dei suoi peccati, se le mostrò in ispirito colla Croce in spalla, piovendo tutto sangue, per modo che la casa le pareva tutta piena di rivoli di quel sangue, il quale vedeva essere tutto sparso per amore: il che le accese nel cuore tanto fuoco, che ne

Vita (*Dialogo*), pp. 199*c*, 200*c*, 202*c*, 208*c*, 209*a*, *b*. 209*c*, 210*a*, 211*a*, *b*.

Quando Iddio vuole purgare un anima . . . le manda il suo divino lume, facendola vedere una scintilla di quel puro amore con quale ci ama . . . essendo noi nemici per molte offese che gli abbiamo fatte. . . . E le fà vedere quel affocato amore. . . . Tutto questo fù dimostrato da Dio in un instante, coll' operazione sua purissima. . . . Questo raggio d'amore fù quello che ferì quell' anima in un istante . . . che la fece restare in quel punto quasi fuori di sè. . . .

Le fù ancora mostrato . . . quanti erano tutti i suoi diffetti . . . in modo che sommerse sè stessa con tal dispregio che avrebbe detto i suoi peccati pubbliccamente per tutta la cità, nè altro poteva dire se non: "O Signore mai piu mondo, nè peccati."

Stando l'anima in questa quasi disperazione di sè medesima . . . vedendosi un carico da disperato alle spalle, . . . era come una cosa insensata ed attonita fuori di sè. . . . Essendo un giorno in casa, le apparve in vista interiore il Signor Nostro Gesù Christo, tutto insanguinato da capo a' piedi, in modo che pareva che da quel corpo

usciva fuor di sè, e pareva una cosa insensata per tanto amore e dolore che ne sentiva.	piovesse sangue per tutta la terra dove andava; e le fù detta in occulto questa parola. "vedi tu questo sangue? tutto è sparso per amor tuo, e per soddisfazione de'tuoi peccati." In queste parole le fù data una gran ferita d'amore verso esso Signor nostro Gesù Christo, con una confidenza tale, che disparve quella prima vista tanto disperata e si rallegrò un poco in esso Signore. . . .
Questa vista le fù tanto penetrativa che	Le fù mostrata un altra vista maggior di quella, e tanto più grande che con lingua non si potrebbe dire . . . le fu infuso un raggio d'amore nel cuore. . . . Gridava e sospirava molto più e senza comparazione che della prima vista, la quale fù dell' esser maligno di sè stessa.
le pareva sempre vedere (e cogli occhi corporali)	Questo raggio d'amore le fù lasciato impresso con quelle cinque fontane di Christo, le quali mandavano goccie d'affuoccato sangue di acceso amore verso dell' uomo.
il suo Amore tutto insanguinato e confitto in Croce.	

Hence *D.* gives but one exclamation as to "world" and "sins," and constructs this out of the two (mutually differing) exclamations of the same kind given by *V.*, the second of which now stands in *V.* after the Bleeding-Christ episode. Whilst spacing all out, *D.* keeps to the order and context of *V.'s* paragraphs. And *D.* utilizes the curious, silent change from the moving Christ to the affixed Christ in *V.'s* account of the single vision in the Palace, so as to constitute two perfectly distinct visions. The Cross of both these doublets of *V.*, (the "Croce" which, in the first part of *V.'s* single account, is "in spalla," on His shoulder; and the Cross which, in the second part of the same account, He is nailed to,) has, in *D.*, disappeared from both separate visions. And yet the Cross hovers about the first vision, here transformed into a "carico alle spalle," a load upon Catherine's shoulders,—an oppression on her mind; and is presupposed in the second vision, since those "five fountains sending forth burning blood" are, of course, the wounds of Christ, whilst He hangs affixed to the Cross as described in *V.'s* second part. And the "Signore piovendo tutto sangue," and the "rivoli di sangue, sparso per amore, il che accese nel cuore tanto fuoco," of *V.*, have, in *D.*, become "quelle cinque fontane di Christo, le quali mandavano goccie d'affuocato sangue e di acceso amore."—This fountain-imagery is derived from numerous authentic sayings and "viste" of Catherine as to the "living Fount (*fonte*) of the divine goodness," or "of infinite love," and "the clear waters coming from the divine fount." The very word "fountain" (*fontana*) occurs in one of *V.'s* descriptive passages; and the idea appears in Catherine's address to Our Lord at the well (*pozzo*) of Samaria, and in her thereupon receiving refreshment of soul, by the gift of "a little drop (*gocciola*)" of that divine water.[1] And the fountains are here made to proceed from a ray of love; and this again comes from numerous authentic sayings of hers: in one case the "raggio d'amore" appears split up into several rays: "raggi . . . affocati di divino amore."[2]

5. *Three new authentic details.*

And yet these remarkable forty pages furnish us with three fresh statements or implications of detail, respectively too precise, vivid and verisimilar and too little obvious, to be easily attributable to any but a new and authentic source of information. There is the vividly precise information that, during Catherine's actively penitential period, "the love of God, wishing that she should lose all relish in what she ate, made her always carry some epatic aloes and pounded agaric about with her; and whenever she suspected that one kind of her food was about to give her more pleasure than another, she would furtively put a little of that most bitter compound upon it, before eating it." There is the formal declaration that "she also went to the poor of San Lazaro." And there is the statement, already noticed, that, after her conversion, she had "to work to provide for her living," and "that she would

[1] *Vita*, pp. 32*c*, 26*c*, 58*a*, 48*a*, 135*a*. [2] *Ibid.* pp. 76*a*, 157*c*; 103*b*.

have been unable to live, unless God had provided for her by way of alms." [1]

Now the first statement should be compared with Battista Vernazza's similarly precise, pharmaceutical detail as to the cassia used by her father in doctoring the poor in 1493, recorded by Battista, nearly ninety years later, in 1581: [2] Battista would, then, have been quite capable of remembering and recording that aloes-and-agaric detail some seventy years after the event. As to the second statement, I have already given the various solid reasons which point to Catherine's co-operation with Battista's father in his work amongst the Pestiferous, as far back as the year 1493.[3] And as to the third statement (in apparently direct conflict with the declaration in the *Vita*-proper, that, although entirely devoted to the service of the Hospital, she never would enjoy or use the slightest thing belonging to it for her own living [4]) the Wills prove to us that, however exaggerated be the language of *D.*, it, and not *V.*, is here substantially in the right. For, though she could have afforded to live in modest style, on her own little income, she did, as a matter of fact, hold her little house rent-free from the Hospital, in return for her services to it. Here also Battista would have known the precise facts from her father, who had himself drawn up or witnessed three documents referring to these matters.

6. *Battista Vernazza, the author of this first " Dialogo."*

The reader will by now be concluding with me, that all these peculiarities of the *Dialogo* point to one person as its author : Battista Vernazza. And all its other circumstances and characteristics make for the same conclusion.

(1) *Particular circumstances.*

There is the place. For the original of MS. C., in which appear the first traces, (this whole first part,) of *D.*, came from Battista's own Convent; and thus a document which, in its later narrative part, contained, as we shall find, so much primary matter due to Vernazza the father, and so much secondary composition and arrangement due to Vernazza the daughter; and which, in its dialogue part, gave much original literary work due to a Vernazza : would easily (no doubt soon after Battista's death), come to be considered as the work and the copying of Ettore Vernazza alone. And there is the date. For if this first part was written in 1548,

[1] *Vita*, pp. 212*c*, 213*a*; 222*b*; 220*c*, 221*c*. [2] See here, p. 146.
[3] See here, pp. 145, 146. [4] *Vita*, p. 21*a*.

1549, Battista would have been fifty or fifty-two years old. And we have already considered writings of hers, written, with equal subtlety of psychological distinctions and even greater vigour of style, in 1554, 1555, and even in 1575, at seventy-eight and eighty-four years of age.[1]

There is, too, the form, so curiously schematic and abstract, and, in part, far-fetched, yet based upon a minute, most ingenious use of scriptural texts. Thus those two "weeks," (symbolsfor thetwo, respectivelylukewarm and sinful, lustres,) are no doubt suggested by the "seventy weeks" which "the man Gabriel" declares to Daniel "shall be shortened upon the Jewish people, that transgression may be finished, and everlasting justice may be brought and vision may be fulfilled";[2] and by Jacob's twice seven years of servitude under Laban, and by Laban's words "make up the week of days of this match."[3] We thus get Catherine s two weeks (of years) of servitude to sin, and her two successive "matches" or alliances, entered into between her soul and body under the influence of self-love. We found a similar minute ingenuity in Battista's use of Scripture in 1554.[4]

And there is a complex, abstract, astonishingly self-consistent psychology running through the whole, and one simply identical with the psychology treated by Battista as more or less a point of revelation to herself in 1554. And, partly as effect or as cause of that psychology, the *Dialogo* has a painfully great, at times downrightly repulsive, insistence upon detachment from emotional feeling, both in intercourse with fellow-creatures, and in spiritual commerce with God, which is simply identical, in its parallelism, range, depth, and doctrinal setting, with the position which Battista takes up in her *Colloquii* of 1554.[5]

Again we get here a prominent and persistent occupation with the historic Christ and His passion, that are as unlike Catherine's as they are identical with Battista's spiritual trend. For, during her Conversion-Vision, Catherine here sees that "burning love which Our Lord Jesus Christ manifested when upon earth, from His Incarnation up to His Ascension"; and this corresponds precisely with Battista's sight (*vista*), in

[1] See here, pp. 344–358; 359–364.
[2] Dan. ix, 24.
[3] Gen. xxix, 20; xxx, 27.
[4] See here, pp. 351, 355.
[5] Compare, as to human intercourse, *Dialogo*, p. 221*b*, with Battista's advice, given here, p. 363; and, as to spiritual consolations, *Dialogo* pp. 215*c*, 216*a*, with Battista's *Colloquies*, here, pp. 346, 347.

1554, of " the Infinite Love manifested unto men, in and by the life of Christ, at the Nativity and at the Ascension." And the Christ-Vision here becomes two separate apparitions; that of the Crucified Christ is declared " greater than " that of the Walking Christ; and there is an insistence upon " those five Fountains," an image derived indeed from Catherine's "living fountain of Goodness, which participated with the creature," but which, in Catherine, is conceived in connection with God and metaphysically, and here is transferred to the historic and crucified Christ, in close keeping with Battista's whole emphatic Christo-centrism.[1]

And, finally, we find here certain daring anthropomorphisms without any full parallel in Catherine's sayings, but entirely matched by expressions of Battista. God is here not as, in Catherine's manner, Himself an irradiating Love, but is " ever standing with burning rays of love in His hand, to inflame and penetrate the hearts of men," a combination of the Thing-imagery dear to Catherine (for Love is here still a luminous, burning substance), and of the human, Personal picturing prominent with Battista (for God here has a hand, in which He holds that substance). This latter picturing (probably in 1550) is not unlike the more spiritual anthropomorphism of " the Increate Heart " of God, used by Battista in 1575, a passage already exceeded here, in the *Dialogo*, by the words, " God showed her the love with which He had suffered "—words which, if pressed, would introduce suffering into the divine nature Itself.[2]

(2) *General considerations.*

All these cumulative reasons of detail will be indefinitely fortified by what I shall have to say as to the character of the subsequent parts of the *Dialogo*, and in proof that these parts and the first instalment are by one and the same author. But, meanwhile, we can press this further general consideration, that only a person with considerable traditional authority in matters concerning Catherine, and yet a person, not a direct eye-witness or full contemporary, hence an individual without any additional information, and unhampered by the (otherwise necessary) regard for the sensitiveness of

[1] Catherine, Pr. *Vita*, p. 290*c*; Battista, in one of the *Colloquii* given in the *Opere*, *loc. cit.*, but not otherwise reproduced here; Catherine, Pr. *Vita*, pp. 209*c*, 211*c*, 211*b*, 32; Battista, here, pp. 359, 360.

[2] Catherine, Pr. *Vita*, p. 97*b*; Battista, Pr. *Vita*, p. 201*b*; here, p. 360; and *Dialogo*, p. 211*a*.

still living contributors to the original biography, can possibly have written such a document. For this production, when it first appears complete, in the first Printed *Vita* of 1551, will there occupy quite one-third of the whole book; and yet, whilst incorporating practically all, and only all, the material of those other two-thirds (the *Trattato* alone excepted), it gives to everything a fresh grouping and setting, colour and atmosphere, drift and character. Only a remarkable, powerful mind; a writer skilled in mystical subjects; one with leisure for such a careful composition; one, too, sufficiently in sympathy with Catherine to be attracted to, and helped through, the difficult task; a person living now, thirty-eight years after Catherine's death, in an environment of a kind to preserve her memory green: all these conditions must, more or less, have met and been realized in the writer of this curious, forcible book.—And Battista, the God-daughter of the heroine of the work, and the eldest, devoted daughter of the chief contributor to the already extant biography; a Contemplative with a deep interest in, and much practical experience of, the kind of spirituality to be portrayed and the sort of literature required; a Nun, during thirty-eight years, in the very Convent where Catherine's sister (one of its foundresses) had lived and died, and where Catherine herself had desired to live and where her Conversion had taken place; a woman who was but thirteen at the time when Catherine died, after nine years of much suffering and seclusion, and who, even now but fifty-one years of age, had outlived all the close friends and original chief biographers of Catherine by thirty-five, twenty-four, and twenty years: Battista, and Battista alone, united in her own person all these necessary conditions. And it will have been the sensitively original and strongly synthetic cast of Battista's mind which made the strangely fragmentary, repetitive, contradictory, static, and yet abrupt and unharmonized multiplicity of the *Vita* both irritating as it stood, and yet (with its considerable elements of unmistakably first-hand portraiture of a rarely large and lofty mind and character) profoundly stimulative to a re-thinking, re-feeling, re-stating of the whole,—at least, up to the zenith of that Soul's perfection.

But our next stage will make all this clearer still.

VI. Sixth Stage: First Printed Edition of the "Vita-Dottrina-Dicchiarazione," 1551; Examination of all it possesses in addition to MSS. A, B, and C, apart from the "Dialogo."

At last we reach the publication of the *Life*, in Genoa, in 1551.[1] A printing-press had not been established in Genoa till 1536 (by Bellone); hence the *Life* appeared only fifteen years after the earliest date possible for its publication,—other cities not being, as yet, sufficiently interested in Catherine to think of such an undertaking.—Only further on shall I attempt some analysis, estimation, and attribution of that *corpus* of earlier and earliest constituents of the Book, which, although frequently referred to at our last two stages, had there to remain unanalyzed. In these remaining two stages I intend to treat only, first of the Introductory parts of the Book, special to its printed form, and then of the Second "Chapter" of the *Dialogo* (its present Second and Third Parts).

Here then we have to deal with the matter which, amongst our extant documents, appears for the first time in the Printed *Vita* of 1551, and first with that part of it which is there devoted to the publication of the Book. This part of the matter consists, in the order of its place in the Book, of the Title with its Picture; the Approbation; the Preface; and the Subscription.

1. *Title-page.*

The Title-page has: "Book of the Admirable Life and Holy Doctrine of the Blessed Catarinetta of Genoa, in which is contained a Useful and Catholic Demonstration and Declaration of Purgatory." And underneath appears a picture of Our Lord Crucified, and Blessed Catherine on her knees before Him, and crowned with a Diadem; with the text: "I confess to Thee, Father, Lord of Heaven and Earth, that Thou hast hid these things from the wise and prudent and hast revealed them unto little ones" (Matt. xi).

Note here, in the Title, the correct and most attractive

[1] I have not succeeded in finding a copy of this rare book: the six chief libraries of Genoa; the Ambrosian Library, Milan; and the Vatican and Angelica Libraries, Rome, are certainly without it. My general description, and my special reproduction of one passage, of it are taken from a series of very careful accounts of the successive early editions of the book, preserved among the Documents relative to the Process of Catherine's Beatification of 1630–1675, in the Archiepiscopal Archives, Genoa.

baptismal form of her Christian name, Catarinetta, which appears here for the last time, either in the Title, the Heading, or the Subscription of her *Life* [2] and the disappearance, which is final, of her family name Adorna, which had figured in the titles of all the MSS. Thus " La miranda vita e sancta conversation di Madonna Catherinetta Adorna," the older heading of MS. A, which will have been that of the Giustiniano book (a heading which itself had succeeded to " De la Miranda Conversione di quondam Donna Catherinetta Adorna " of the booklet of 1512, still preserved in MS. B), has here become " La vita mirabile e dottrina santa de la Beata Catarinetta da Genoa."—And note how, for the first time, mention is made in the title of what has hitherto been but a long Chapter of the *Vita ;* and how what in the MSS. had, in that Chapter's heading, claimed but to be a matter of devotional experience (" How, by comparison of the divine fire, which she felt in her heart and which purified her soul, she saw interiorly and understood how the Souls abide in Purgatory "), has here been given, some thirty years after the Papal condemnation of Luther's theses on Purgatory, a controversial point,—it is now " a Useful and Catholic Demonstration and Declaration of Purgatory." We have here an attitude of mind inevitably different from Catherine's pure positiveness.—And remark, too, the continued non-indication of the *Dialogo,* although this is now present, like the " Dimostrazione," as a distinct document in the Book : the Dialogue is evidently still too new to be able to modify the old title-page, and to appear there alongside of a composition which, though but one-sixth of its own length, is now some thirty and more years old.

In the Picture Catherine wears a diadem, a compromise between an indication of her noble birth and a hint of the nimbus which they shrink from giving to her unequivocally. And she is kneeling before the Christ Crucified,—evidently an attitude chosen as specially typical of her whole life and doctrine, because of the passages in the *Vita :* " She ever seemed to see her Love affixed to the Cross " ; " she was next drawn to the side of the Crucified " ; " she appeared in very truth as a body affixed to a Cross," with the dependent account of her "interior stigmatization,"—"she received a new wound at her heart, so that she might feel within herself the wound in the side of her tender Love" ; and the amplifications of some of these passages in the *Dialogo.*[1] Yet only the

[1] *Vita,* pp. 5*b*, 6*b*, 155*b*–156*a*; 211*b*, 264*b*.

first three passages occur in the MSS.; and the first two are carefully restricted there to her first Conversion-Period (of four years at most), whilst the third passage refers to a (quite unusual) bodily posture, assumed by her on one single occasion during her last illness, an attitude which remained uninterpreted by herself. The fact is that the precise contrary of what this picture suggests is one of the chief characteristics of Catherine, for she is habitually absorbed in contemplations remarkably lacking in historical imagery and setting. And the *Dialogo* parallels and variants which, as we have seen, so largely increase this historical element, and especially this occupation with Christ Crucified, are characteristic, not of Catherine but of Battista. The picture is, no doubt, the consequence of this increasing emphasis laid, in her successive *Vitae,* upon a side of religion all but entirely absent from the middle and last periods of Catherine's actual life; and fully expresses Battista's feeling, who, just as she addressed her whole long letter of 1575 to Donna Anguisola, "in the Crucified," will have seen to it that the whole book concerning her own God-mother was placed at the feet of the Crucifix.

2. *The Approbation.*

The Latin Approbation runs: "I, Fra Geronimo of Genoa of the Order of Preachers, Apostolic Inquisitor into Heretical Pravity throughout the whole Dominion of Genoa, assent to this Book being committed to print, for the consolation and instruction of spiritual persons. Witness this my autograph." The points of interest in connection with this Approbation will appear, as we proceed, to consist in the reasons why such theological "corrections" as were actually introduced into the doctrinal parts of the *Vitae* had all been made long before this date, probably none of them later than 1530; and why they were, throughout, practically restricted to her very sober and correct Purgatorial teaching, and left her other, far more daring, sayings more or less untouched. I can find no traces of any theological changes introduced, for this edition of 1551, into the *Vita-Dicchiarazione* sections; but we shall see how three points and tendencies of the *Vita*-proper have been indirectly criticised and "corrected" by means of their restatement in the *Dialogo,* which was certainly finished, and possibly begun, with a view to its appearance in the company of the *Vita* and the *Dicchiarazione.*

3. *The Preface.*

The Preface consists of seven full and balanced, dignified

and self-restrained, thoroughly well-informed and yet, in part, deliberately obscure and illusive, sentences. It still excludes the idea of any literary authorship on the part of Catherine: "Madonna Caterinetta, of whose admirable Conversion, Life, and Doctrine, together with her many privileges and particular graces, we shall write. . . . Here, in her Life and Holy Doctrine is to be found. . . ." Not Catherine writes, but "we," *i. e.* the final Redactor, or all the Contributors together with him; and not her Writings are to be found here, but her "Doctrine" only. Indeed, it all "has been collected with truth and simplicity by two devout spiritual persons, from the very lips of the Seraphic Woman herself." More would quite evidently have been claimed, if more had been true.

And it contains two or three evident additions to its original text, made for this publication in view of the entire *Dialogo's* first appearance here; additions which contain an expression which may well have occasioned or helped on the legend of "Catherine, an Author," a legend which was sure to spring up at the first opportunity and provocation. The fifth sentence reads at present as follows: "Sono in questo libro [dignissimi suoi trattati dell' amor di Dio e dell' amor proprio] una bellisima e chiarissima dimostrazione del Purgatorio, e in che modo vi stiano dentro le anime contentissime, [e un bel dialogo dell' Anima con il Corpo e Amor proprio, dal quale ne seguita un amoroso colloquio dell' Anima con il suo Signore] ed altre dignissime cose da sapere, veramente tutte di eccellentissima speculazione ed utilità [e massime in questi turbolenti tempi necessarie]." [1]

Now even the last set of bracketed words seems an addition, and points to the existence of the body of this Preface at a period prior to "questi turbolenti tempi," times that I take to be 1536–1537, when Battista's God-father Moro lapsed into Calvinism. Ever since 1520, when Luther's Purgatory doctrines were condemned, these writings would have been held, if not "necessary," at least "of most excellent utility."—There is, any way, no doubt as to the two previous sets being insertions. For note, if they be retained, the slovenly repetition, by the first set, of "dignissimi" in the midst of a most finished composition; the extraordinary use of the word "Trattati," to signify either Chapter XXV (which

[1] *Vita*, pp. vii*c*, viii*a*; viii*b*.

bears the title "Dell' Amor Proprio e del Divino Amore," and is a collection of sayings pronounced on at least three different occasions), or Chapters XXV and XXVI,—in either case, Chapters which are no more significant or authentic than any other of the doctrinal chapters. And remark, in the second set, the curiously mild praise for the *Dialogo* contained in the one positive "un bel," wedged in between the two superlatives lavished on the "Dimostrazione" and the two superlatives given to the remaining doctrinal parts of the Book. The object of that first "Trattati" insertion is evidently to pick out some one or other of the already ancient Chapters of the *Vita,* which have some special likeness to the subject-matter and title of the *Dialogo,* so as to prevent the latter from looking too suspiciously different from the rest of the doctrine traditionally ascribed to Catherine.

I take this Preface to have existed, without these additions, in the "worthy book" described by Giustiniano in 1536. But as that careful writer insists upon the precise length of time, because it had been considerable, during which Catherine's body had lain incorrupt, and says nothing about the antiquity of the book, a point he would hardly have failed to urge had he been able to do so, I hesitate to push this Book, and this its Preface, further back than 1530, a very probable date for the first (at least complete) fusion of Vernazza's and Marabotto's separate contributions, since these two chief disciples would then have been dead six and two years respectively, and the culmination of Protestant "turbulence" in Calvin's open revolt and Moro's defection would not be taking place for another five and six years respectively.—Catherine indeed appears here no more as the "quondam Donna Catarinetta" of MS. B, but still as "Madonna Catherinetta, figliuola di M. Giacomo della nobilissima casa Fiesca, maritata a M. Giuliano Adorno," a designation distinctly earlier than the "Beata Catarinetta di Genoa" of the Title. And the Book, its substance, is declared to have been "collected by two spiritual persons (*Religiosi*), her devotees, from the very lips of the Seraphic Woman herself." This passage, it is true, now reads "Raccolto dai divoti religiosi (suo Confessore e un figliuolo suo spirituale)." But, where the Preface is above the suspicion of having been touched up, a "cioè" introduces such a bracket; the rhythm of this sentence, in the midst of this otherwise exquisite Preface, is woefully imperfect; and the evidently deliberate ambiguity of "divoti religiosi" is rendered all but nugatory by the considerable clearness of the bracketed information. The clause will originally have read, " Da due religiosi sui divoti," for this obviates all three objections. But, in this deliberately mysterious form, it must have been written when both were dead, and yet when the death of the last was still recent; and this again brings us to a date soon after Marabotto's death in 1528.

Who wrote this Preface? Much in it points to Battista. So the use of " cioè," so characteristic of her *Colloquies* and *Letters* and also of the *Dialogo;* and the phrase " divote persone," recurring in the *Dialogo;* [1] and the doctrinal tone of " l'amoroso Signor Nostro, sitibondo della salute delle sue razionali creature," " il suo consolatorio spirito," " la perfetta e consummata unione possibile ai viatori," and " quasi non più fide, mà già certezza," all closely like passages in her *Colloquies* and in her Letter to Donna Anguisola. The mysteriousness and equality of designation, applied to both Ettore and Don Cattaneo, would come with a special naturalness from Battista, spontaneously anxious to place her heroic father's sanctity and intimacy with Catherine on a level with those of Catherine's priest-friend and Confessor Marabotto. And, if written in 1530, Battista would at the time have been a formed writer,—a woman of thirty-three years of age.—There are, no doubt, certain differences. The *Dialogo* nowhere has such an " ancorchè . . . niente (non) dimeno " clause. " Un Serafino," " essa Serafica Donna " of this Preface, are, in strictness, unmatched in Battista's, otherwise even intenser, writings. " La perfetta e consummata unione possibile ai viatori " is a more ordinary and technical phrase than I can find elsewhere in Battista's writings. Above all, the general style and rhythm is here, somehow, a little different from that of those other writings.—Still, these differences are explicable by the writer of the Preface finding himself largely bound by the existing *Vita*-materials, and by their very niceties of expression. The Author of the Preface is certainly identical with the Redactor of the first (tripartite) *Vita e Dottrina;* and this Redactor, we shall find, must be Battista. The insertions in the Preface, containing the praise of the *Dialogo,* are certainly the work of another hand.—Upon the whole, then, we can safely attribute the Preface, in its original form, to Battista Vernazza.

[1] *Colloquies, Opere,* Vol. V, p. 219. *Letters, ibid.* Vol. VI, p. 24. *Dialogo,* pp. 187*b*, 215*b*, 220*c*, 223*b*, 237*c*, 247*b*, 248*c*, 273*b*. *Dialogo,* p. 266*b*.

4. *The Subscription.*

The subscription to the *Vita*-proper, in this first Edition, runs: "Here ends the life of the noble Matron, Catarinetta Adorna"; which thus still retains (like the Preface, but against the Title) the warmly human and precise, domestic and familiar designation of the first heading of MS. A.

VII. Seventh Stage: The Second "Chapter" of the "Dialogo," which appears for the First Time in the Printed "Vita," 1551.

1. *Three remarks concerning the two Parts of this "Chapter."*

(1) The additions to the *Dialogo* which appear here for the first time, and which amount to its present Parts Second and Third, are given in this First Edition as one single, the Second, "Chapter," following upon the older part here designated "Chapter First." In the Fourth Edition, 1601, this division of the *Dialogo* is formally announced on the Title-page: "With a Dialogue, divided into two Chapters, between the Soul, the Body, and Self Love; and (the Soul and) the Lord." I do not know precisely when those two "Chapters" were replaced by the present Three Parts, and when these Parts were divided up into the present Chapters; it was, in any case, after the sixth edition (1645).

(2) These last two Parts seem to have been written, from the first, with a view to eventual division into two. For though the whole of this Second Chapter is not much longer than the First Chapter (forty-seven and a half pages, against forty), it yet divides up very well at about half-way, since the first half here ends with a piece of moralizing narrative, applied to the whole earthly existence: "The more valiant a man is at the beginning, the greater martyrdom should he expect at the end . . . nor does God cease to make provision . . . up to that Man's death."[1]

(3) This whole "Chapter" Second is by the same author as "Chapter" First; in this Second, even more than in that First "Chapter," there are no historical materials other than those still present, more or less untouched, in the *Vita*-proper; and yet these materials have again been modified, in their sequence

[1] *Vita*: Chapter Second, pp. 226*a*–275*a*. Part Second, pp. 226*a*–245*c*; Part Third, pp. 246*a*–275*a*. The moralizing narrative; last sentence p. 245*c*.

and setting, their tone and pitch, their drift and meaning, and all this throughout by the same powerful and experienced, often deep and touching, but also, in great part, painfully abstract and straining, absolute-minded and excessive writer.

2. *General indications of identity of authorship for "Chapters" First and Second.*

(1) " Chapter " First had, we know, concluded with a paraphrase of the last stage in the scheme of Catherine's spiritual growth as given in the *Vita*-proper, and had thus reached the *ne plus ultra* of perfection for any creature, either here or in the world to come. " And now the Spirit said : ' I am determined no further to call her a human creature, since I now see her (to be) all in God, without any Humanity ' " : a statement which may well (like the corresponding Spiritual-Kiss stage in the *Vita's* scheme) [1] have been intended, at the time of its composition, both to describe directly her great middle years, 1474–1499, and to sum up generally her later life, 1499–1510.—But no such hyperbolic language, when thus applied to man as we know him, or as we can even conceive him here below, can, of course, be kept up. And thus here in the *Dialogo* (as previously in the corresponding place in the *Vita*-proper), what had originally been the conclusion of a self-contained account of her Conversion, became, owing to the desire of utilizing much extant material which directly described her years of physical break-up, but one chapter in the story of her total life. Hence, we now find, both in the *Vita*-proper and the *Dialogo*, an instructive anti-climax, in an attempted description (the *Dialogo* gives this in its " Chapter " Second) of her successive states from 1497 to her death in 1510, states and changes which, were we to take the concluding words of the *Vita*-scheme and of the *Dialogo's* " Chapter " First at all strictly, would, in great part, be impossible.

(2) In the *Dialogo's* First "Chapter" we found a remarkably free, deliberately pragmatic handling of the *Vita*-materials, in the making two different visions on two separate occasions (the Vision of the blood-stained Moving Christ, and the Vision of the blood-pouring Fixed Christ) out of the one, curiously composite, Moving-Fixed Christ-Vision of the *Vita ;* and this doubling introduced, into that First Part, a special kind of obscurity, a sort of eddying, circular, repetitive movement and practical fixedness. Similarly we find here, in the Second

[1] *Dialogo*, p. 225*c*, paraphrase of *Vita*, p. 6*c*.

"Chapter," the one description of her resumption of Confession, given by the *Vita*-proper, is made into two accounts, accounts still further separated from each other here than the two visions were separated from each other there. For the first ten and a half Chapters, pages 226*b* to 242*b*, give us her history from 1497 to 1501. And, amongst these, Chapters First to Third cover the years 1497 to 1499; and at the end of Chapter Third, page 232*b*, we get an account of how "she began to confess her sins" (necessarily, at this period, to Marabotto) "with such Contrition, that it appeared a marvellous thing"—a description which has been taken from the story of her First Conversion-Period, but which is made to do duty here, at the date of her beginning to confess, in a very different manner, to Don Marabotto, twenty-five years after those Conversion-Confessions. Yet only at the beginning of the second half of Chapter Tenth (p. 242*c*) do we hear, (wedged in between two passages, pp. 242*b*, 243*b*, which are re-castings of descriptions of a scene which occurred on January 10, 1510, *Vita*, pp. 139*a*–140*c*) of God giving her the help of a "Religioso," "suo Confessore," *i. e.* Marabotto (p. 242*c*). This is followed, not two pages later on (p. 244*b*), by a description of the experience of the "Scintilla" on August 11, 1510 (*Vita*, p. 148*b*), and by an allusion to her death on September 15, 1510 (p. 245*c*).—This doubling was no doubt effected for the purpose of introducing as much variety as possible into what is, anyhow, a monotonous narrative; of being thus able to produce a more ordinary and "correct" account of her dispositions and acts, on occasion of the resumption of her Confessions in 1499, than could be given by the direct utilization of Marabotto's description of them; and of thus, by these two narratives in lieu of that single one, giving greater place and prominence to the practice of Confession than this practice actually occupied in her real life.

3. *Closer examination of the earlier portion of "Chapter" Second.*

A closer examination of the whole Second "Chapter" of the *Dialogo* fully substantiates this conclusion, and brings out other interesting points. Let us take the eleven Chapters of the present Part Second.

(1) The first two Chapters describe her condition when "the Soul could no more correspond to the sensations of the Body,—the Body remained, as it were, without its

natural being, and dwelt confused and stunned, without knowing where it was or what it should do or say" (pp. 226*c*, 227*a*). And then the Soul begins to address "the Lord" (p. 229*a*). And on p. 230*b* we hear, for the first time, of its "sweet and cruel Purgatory." And Chapter Third tells of the Soul's painful prison-life, and of vomitings, emaciation, and occasional inability to move (pp. 230*b*–232*a*).—Now Purgatory, prison-house and these psycho-physical conditions do not appear, in the *Vita*-proper, till "nine years before her death," and, indeed, in great part only within the last year of her life.[1] Indeed it is only the characteristic intensity with which the *Dialogo* here describes the fresh access of Contrition, and the resumption of frequent Confession for evidently new offences (a description entirely inappropriate to this late stage of her life), that makes it difficult to realize that these three Chapters are dealing with 1497 to 1499. And the exaggeration here exactly corresponds to the exaggeration, in Part ("Chapter") First, of her earlier sinfulness, and her first Conversion and Contrition.

(2) Chapter Fourth then gives a short description of another "ray of love"; and then apostrophizes, in seven "oh" and "che" sentences, such a state of soul (pp. 232*c*–233*c*). Chapter Fifth contains one question and answer exchanged between the Soul and the Lord, and then three narrative-exclamatory paragraphs (pp. 233*c*–235*a*). Chapter Sixth gives two explanations by the Lord of the Soul's sufferings, interrupted by the Soul's thanks and acceptance (pp. 235*b*–237*a*). And then Chapter Seventh describes a lull in the Soul's battles and trials (pp. 237*a*–238*a*). And this lull is followed, in Chapter Eighth, by a declaration from the Lord that she has now been led up to the door of Love but has not yet entered in (pp. 238*a*–239*a*); and, in Chapter Ninth, by a dialogue (for the first time in the entire work) between the Spirit and the Soul, the former being now determined to separate itself from the latter; and, at the end of this same Chapter, by a description of this, now more or less achieved, separation (pp. 239*a*–241*a*; 241*b*).—These conflicts and dialogues between the Spirit and the Soul are closely like the conflicts and dialogues between the Spirit and "Humanity"

[1] "Nine years before her death," *Vita*, p. 127*a*; "one year before she passed away," p. 132*b*; Purgatory, pp. 128*c*, 129*a*; 136*c*, 144*b*; "Prison of the Body," p. 137*a*; emaciation, pp. 144*a*, 160*b*; vomitings, pp. 127*c*, 138*c*, 10*a*, *b*; inability to move, pp. 128*a*, 137*b*.

in Part First.[1] Yet there, the historical materials are derived chiefly from the *Vita*-proper, pp. 20*a*–21*b*, 96*b*–97*c* (which give an account of her work from 1473 to 1497); whilst here they come exclusively from pp. 133*b*–138*b* of the *Vita*-proper (which tell her experiences from November 11 to the end of December 1509).

(3) And the last two Chapters, Tenth and Eleventh, are particularly difficult and self-destructive, obscure and disappointing. The Tenth (to be fully analyzed presently), is difficult, because it starts with fragments of *Vita*-information which, in the *Vita*, rightly refer, in large part, to the beginning of the last ten years of her life, and even to 1499 in particular,—hence to a period long anterior to all that has been described in the *Dialogo* ever since Chapter Third of this Part. And these fragments are here made to lead up to a re-statement of the scene of January 10, 1510, when she shut herself off from every one, but when Marabotto managed to overhear her soliloquy (pp. 241*c*–244*a* compared with pp. 139*b*, 113*c*.) And the Eleventh Chapter is obscure and disappointing, because, after giving the "scintilla"-incident of August 11, 1510, and a final short dialogue between the "Lord" and her "Humanity" (again a combination of *Dramatis Personae* which has occurred nowhere else), it finishes, not with any description or even affirmation of her earthly end, but simply with an account as to the necessity of Purgation, and, in particular, with the words "a martyrdom which never ceases until death" (pp. 244*a*–245*c*).

4. *Closer examination of later portion of "Chapter" Second.*

Part Third, on the contrary, is peculiar in this, that its Dialogue passes exclusively between but two interlocutors, the Soul and the Lord: it thus brings back the whole composition to its opening form of strict duologue,—although there the speakers had been the (unpurified) Soul and the Body. The present thirteen Chapters constitute, in substance, a single, all but unbroken, disquisition on God's love for the Soul, and on the Soul's growth in the love of God; although the form alternates between Chapters of questions and answers, and Chapters of rapturous descriptions and apostrophizings of Love.

(1) Chapters First and Second consist of such questions and answers, and conclude with an, abruptly introduced, account

[1] *Vita*, pp. 227*a*–241*b*; 213*c*–225*c*.

of her former spiritual conversations with her friends, which (though based upon the beautiful document in the *Vita*-proper, pp. 94*b*–95*c*, and upon the fragment there, p. 97*b*, and though the narrative here has a certain noble warmth of its own) is given here merely as a something to be transcended, and which, by now, had been actually left far behind. Thus, as in Parts First and Second the *Dialogo* had given a characteristically rigoristic, indeed exaggerating, account of her Conversation and her later Purification respectively, so here again this curious book is more severe than are the authentic accounts on which it otherwise relies.

(2) Chapter Third gives a question and answer as to the comprehensibility of this love. The answer incorporates Catherine's description of her soul as, so to speak, under water in an ocean of peace; and interestingly turns the " scintilla," the "spark of love," into a "stilla," a "drop," suggested, no doubt, by the " goccia," " the drop of love," which figured so prominently in Catherine's great conversation with her spiritual children.[1]—Chapters Fourth to Sixth open out with a page where the Lord declares how the pure and love-absorbed Soul alone holds Love (p. 253); and consist, for the rest, of exclamatory descriptions of this love, the soul proffering first ten " O Amore " apostrophes (pp.253*c*–258*b*), then one " O Amore puro " address (pp. 259*c*, 260*a*). And the tenth of those apostrophes introduces a characteristic sentence from the *Vita*-proper: " the Soul,—if bereft of charity,—when it is separated from the Body, would, rather than present itself thus before that (Divine) cleanness and simplicity, cast itself into Hell." [2]—And Chapter Seventh then makes the Lord ask the Soul to tell him some of the words which it addresses to Love; the Soul does so, and the Lord approves of them (pp. 260*b*–261*b*).

(3) And then Chapter Eighth begins a narrative piece (pp. 261*c*–263*c*); but which, after a transitional, exclamatory paragraph (p. 263*c*), arrives at three short questions and answers. The first two questions and answers are by the

[1] The " scintilla," " stilla," and " immersion in the sweetness of Love " : *Dialogo*, p. 252*a*, *b*, *c*. In the *Vita*-proper " scintilla " is but once (and in a doubtful passage) so used, p. 148*b*; in the other passages " non una minima scintilla " means there " not a glimpse " of this or that, pp. 5*c*, 62*a*. " Stilla " of Blessedness, p. 119*c*; " goccia " of Love, pp. 94*b*–95*c*; " gocciola " of spiritual water (refreshment), p. 135*b*. " Ocean " and immersion therein, pp. 59*b*, 60*b*.

[2] *Vita*, pp. 78*c*, 79*a*.

Soul and the Lord respectively; the third question and answer are respectively by the Lord and the Soul (pp. 264*a*, *b*). We shall presently see that, in this set of short sentences, we have reached the culmination of the whole *Dialogo*, and that, in astonishingly explicit daring, they exceed any and all of Catherine's authentic sayings.

(4) Chapter Ninth then gives a narrative description of the apparently empty and abandoned condition of the advanced Soul, and, for this purpose, carefully utilizes (whilst completely altering the meaning and context of) Marabotto's description of Catherine's first Confession to him. And in its last paragraph it again (but here with less change) incorporates other passages of that descriptive Chapter.[1] Then comes Chapter Tenth, with a short question and answer between the Lord and the Soul, the latter partly in verse (p. 267*a*). And this is followed by two descriptive paragraphs, how that this soul " seemed to mount above Paradise itself "; " this heart is transformed into a tabernacle of God "; and " such souls, were they but known, would be adored upon earth " (pp. 267*b*, *c*; 268*a*).

(5) This description is followed by a long rapturous suspension of the dialogue form, since here the Writer himself addresses successively, in three " O " paragraphs, the " soul, heart, and mind "; " Love "; and " the Spirit naked and invisible." And, after a little exclamation as to the inadequacy of all words (this also is introduced by an "O"), he similarly invokes (in three other " O " paragraphs), " my tender Lord "; the " infinite Good "; and " the Lord " (pp. 268*b*–269*c*).—The present, most unskilful, division makes Chapter Eleventh begin with these last three of the seven " O's." And after the seventh " O " paragraph and a descriptive passage, still addressed to " the Lord," composed of five " Thou " sentences, follows another short interruption,—apologizing for the delay in the narrative and the inadequacy of the words used. And then two " Oimè," and one " O terra, terra " paragraph finish up the Writer's exclamations, and bring us back to the interrupted dialogue-form (pp. 269*c*–271*b*). Here again a violent division has been effected in the text by Chapter Twelfth being made to exclude the first, but to include the second " Oimè " (p. 271*a*). And this Chapter, after finishing the " Terra-terra " paragraph, and, with it, the whole digres-

[1] Thus *Vita* (*Dialogo*), p. 266*a* = *Vita* (proper), p. 117*b*, *c*; and *Vita* (*Dialogo*), p. 266*c* = *Vita* (proper), pp. 120*b*, 117*b*.

sion, re-opens the dialogue with a curious, serpentine, all but unbroken series of seven questions of the Soul and answers of the Lord, in which each successive question picks up the previous answer and point reached, and tries to reach a deeper one. " What is Thine Operation within man? A Moving of the heart of man. And this Movement? A Grace. And this Grace? A Ray of Love. And this Ray of Love? An Arrow. And this Arrow? A Glimpse (Scintilla) of love. And this Glimpse? An Inspiration." And at this point, description is declared to be unable to proceed further (pp. 271*b*–272*c*).

(6) And then Chapter Thirteenth finishes up the whole by two questions and descriptive answers. The first question and answer passes between the Writer's own mind and his heart, and thus again constitutes a break in the dialogue; and the second question and answer occurs between the Lord and the Soul. The first answer dwells upon personal experience, as the sole means of some real apprehension of Love; and the second answer concludes the whole book with a majestic paraphase of Catherine's doctrine as to the immanental, inevitable, self-determined, and self-endorsed character of the Soul's joys and sufferings, here and hereafter, on Earth, in Purgatory, indeed in Hell itself (pp. 273*a*–275*a*). Such passages as these make up for much of the often painfully intense, abstract, schematic, rigoristic, and too exclusively transcendental character of this remarkable book, and explain its fascination for a mind of such rare experience and breadth as was that of Friedrich Schlegel. I shall presently group together the finest sayings peculiar to the ork.

VIII. Seventh Stage continued: Minute Analysis of one Passage from the Second "Chapter."

But I must still give for this last " Chapter," as I did for the First " Chapter," a synoptic demonstration, by means of one example among many, of the strange manner in which the *Dialogo*-writer combines the most detailed dependence on the materials of the *Vita*-proper with the most sovereign independence concerning the chronology, context, and drift of those same materials.—And again I choose an originally unique occurrence and description, so as to eliminate all possibility of an explanation by an original multiplicity of facts and accounts.

Catherine as "Garzonzello" or "Figliuolino."

Dialogo (*Vita*), p. 266*a*, *b*, *c*.

Il corpo, essendo costretto seguire l'anima, resta per quel tempo quasi senz' anima, senza umano conforto,

. . . e non si sà nè si può aiutare.

Però è di bisogno che dagli altri sia aiutato, ovvero occultamente da Dio gli sia provveduto, altrimenti restarebbe quella creatura abbandonata

come un figliuolino, il quale, non avendo i suoi bisogni, altro riparo non hà se non di piangere tanto che gli sieno dati.

Non è dunque maraviglia, se a simili creature Iddio provvede di particolari persone che le aiutino, e per mezzo loro sia alle necessità dell' anima e del' corpo sovvenuto, altrimenti non potriano vivere.

Vita-proper, pp.—

117*b*. Non potendosi sopportare, per non aver più operazione nè sentimenti dell' anima, col corpo tutto debole. . . .

117*c*. "Io non sò dove mi sia."

127*a*. Quali la servivano restavano stupefatti, non sapendo che farle.

120*a*. . . . provveduto tal bisogno, a lui non restava di essa provisione memoria alcuna.

121*a*. Perseverò molti anni con bisogno che il Confessore le stasse d' appresso, per sostentare l'umanità.

117*c*. Dei peccati che diceva non le erano lasciato vedere come peccati che avesse . . . fatti, ma come d'un garzonzello, il quale da giovinetto fà qualche cosa di cui è ignorante, il quale, essendogli detto "tu hai fatto male" per questa parola muta subito di colore e diventa rosso, ma non già perche conosce il male.

119*c*. "Non posso più sopportare tanti assedi esteriori ed interiori; per questo mi hà Iddio provveduto del vostro mezzo . . . quando da mè siete partito, vò lamentandomi per la casa.

Vedi come il nostro Signor Gesù Christo lasciò *a* San Giovanni [al]la sua diletta Madre in particolar cura; e così fece ai suoi discepoli e fà sempre all' altre sue divote persone; di modo che l'uno soccorre l'altro, così all'anima come al corpo, con quella unione divina.

E perchè in generale le persone non conoscono queste operazioni, nè hanno insieme quella unione, perciò a simili cure bisognano particolari persone, colle quali Iddio operi colla sua grazia e lume.

Chi vide queste creature e non le intende, gli sono più presto d' ammirazione che di edificazione, dunque non giudicare, se non vuoi errare . . . resta l'umanita senza vigore ed abandonata quasi come morta.

120*a*. era di bosogno che il Confessore non si partisse da lei. . . . Dio, sempre glieli dava . . . tutti i sussidi all anima e al corpo . . . per mezzo di lui, al quale in quell' instante provedeva di lume e di parole convenienti alla di lei necessità.

121*b*. Questa tutto divina . . . operazione. Il Confessore era legato col vincolo del divino amore.

117*b*. Dio gli diede lume e grazia di consoscere quell' operazione.

120*b*. E perchè quella continua conversazione e stretta famigliarità facevano alcuni mormorare, non intendendo l'opera e la necessità. . . .

117*b*. . . . col corpo tutto senza vigore, quasi derelitto in se medesimo.

The *Dialogo*-writer having, as we saw, combined, for the purpose of describing Catherine's latter-day habits, *V.'s* account of her unusually peaceful dispositions of soul, obtaining in 1499, with *V.'s* account of her Penance and Confessions in 1473: now utilizes here Marabotto's account of her Confessions to him from 1499 onwards (an account which the writer had rejected there), for an entirely different purpose and context than those developed by the Confessor himself. For, in the *Vita*-proper account, it is in connection with the Confession of her sins that we get the highly original and curious "garzonzello" parallel; and Catherine's lamentations do not there occur in any relation to this parallel, but they arise only when Marabotto is not at hand to comfort her.

In the *Dialogo*-version it is simply in relation to this requirement of his presence and to its postponement, that Catherine behaves like a " figliuolino," and cries till she gets what she wants. And yet there is not the slightest doubt that it is really the " Garzonzello " Confession-passage which (left unutilized by the writer in his account of the Contrition and Confessions of her last period, *Dialogo*, pp. 231*c*–232*b*, no doubt because of the difficulty and apparent temerity of the facts and doctrines implied), has here been used after all, but with all its originality and daring carefully eliminated from it. For nowhere else, in the *Vita*-proper, does a " Garzonzello "-passage or language, or anything like them, occur; nowhere else again, in the *Dialogo* does a " figliuolino "-passage or wording, or anything really resembling them, appear; and these two, respectively unique and very peculiar, passages, both occur at one and the same stage of her life, and in connection with one and the same couple of persons.

IX. Seventh Stage concluded: Character and Authorship of this Second " Chapter."

Let us take these two points simultaneously, and move, from the more formal and literary qualities, through indications of the more or less external life-circumstances of the author, on to the writer's special views and aims in psychology and spirituality.

1. *The writer's power.*

The following passages, all more or less peculiar to the *Dialogo*, suffice, I think, to prove his power.

At the beginning of these, her last nine years, the Lord explains to Catherine the means by which Love may be known: " My love can be better known by means of interior experience than in any other way; if man is to acquire it, Love must snatch man from man himself, since it is man himself who is his own chief impediment,"[1]—a passage that recalls Thackeray's *Arthur Pendennis, his Friends and his Greatest Enemy*—namely, his own self.

These years are, a little later, described in language no doubt suggested, probably through some Patristic passage, by Plato, the harmonious. " This soul now abode like a musical

[1] *Dialogo*, p. 234*b*.

instrument which, as long as it remains furnished with chords, gives forth sweet sounds; but which, bereft of them, is silent. Thus she too, in the past, by means of the sentiments of soul and body, was wont to render so sweet a harmony, that every one who heard it rejoiced in it; but now, alienated from those sentiments, as it were without " psychic " chords, she remained entirely bare and mute."[1]

And we are told of "words which the heart alone speaks to the soul alone"[2]—a passage which recalls Pascal's saying, "The heart has reasons which Reason does not know."

Amongst the rapturous addresses we find, "O Spirit naked and invisible! No man can hold thee (here below), because of thy very nakedness! Thy dwelling-place is in Heaven, even whilst, joined to the body, thou happenest still to tarry upon earth! Thou dost not know thine own self, nor art thou known by others in this world. All thy friends and (true) relatives are in Heaven, recognized by thee alone, through an interior instinct infused by the Spirit of God."[3] An apostrophe which, in part, strongly recalls Henry Vaughan's poem, "They are all gone into a world of light, and I alone am lingering here."

The final address in this series of apostrophes to Love, God, contains the sentences: "O Lord, how great is Thy loving care, both by day and by night, for man who knows not even his own self, and far less Thee, O Lord. Thou art that great and high God, of whom we cannot speak or think, because of the ineffable super-eminence of Thy Greatness, Power, Wisdom, and Goodness infinite. Thou labourest in man and for man with Thy Love, and in return Thou willest that the whole man should act for Love, and this because, without Love, nothing good can be produced. Thou workest solely for man's true utility; and Thou willest that man should operate solely for Thine honour, and not for his own (separate) utility."[4] A passage strongly coloured by Dionysian ideas.

And yet the writer continues to think and to write, but says: "These words of mine are like ink: for ink is black and of an evil odour; and yet, by its means, many ideas are apprehended, which otherwise would be ignored altogether."[5] Here we have an image, based as it is upon a vivid sensible perception of a chemical compound, which reminds one of the

[1] *Dialogo*, p. 241*b*. [2] *Ibid.* p. 260*b*. [3] *Vita*, p. 268*c*.
[4] *Ibid.* p. 269*c*. [5] *Ibid.* p. 270*b*.

epatic-agaric passage in " Chapter " First of the *Dialogo*, and of the reference to cassia in Battista's letter of 1581.[1]

And the whole Book finishes up with two impressive passages. The First, as to the means of knowing Love, is as Pauline as is most of the remaining doctrine of the *Dialogo* : " Not by means of external signs, nor even by martyrdoms, can this love be comprehended. Only he who actually experiences it can understand something of it." [2] And the second concludes all with a forcible and comprehensive paraphrase of Catherine's central doctrine,—as to the Soul's condition and action, revealed at the moment of death : " Every man bears within his own self the sentence of his own judgment, pronounced indeed by God, yet each man himself ratifies it, in and for his own case and self. There is no place totally bereft of God's mercy. The very souls in Hell itself would suffer a greater Hell outside of it than they do within it."[3]—We have had repeated proofs of how great were Battista's gifts and experience in such-like eloquent writing, from the earlier *Dialogo*-Chapter, and from her *Colloquies* and *Letters*.

2. *Indications of special knowledge.*

I am compelled to pass over the emotional rhythm, and the mystical ambiguity and paradox, that appear, in identical forms, in Battista's avowed writings and here. But we must briefly dwell upon some special sources of interest in Catherine, and of certain knowledge of a peculiar kind, traceable in the writer of this second " Chapter " ; both sets of passages clearly point to Battista as their author.

(1) There is the deeply-felt description of Catherine's conversation with her disciples : " This soul would many times abide with her spiritual friends, discoursing of the Divine Love, in suchwise that it appeared to them all as though they were in Paradise. And indeed, what delightful colloquies took place ! Both he who spoke and he who listened, one and all would get nourished by spiritual food, of a sweet and delectable kind. And, because the time sped so quickly, they could not attain to satiety ; but they would abide so enkindled and inflamed, that they knew not what more to say. And yet they could not depart, and would seem as though in an ecstasy. Oh ! what loving repasts, what delightful food, what sweet viands, what a gracious union, what a divine companion-

[1] *Dialogo*, p. 212*c*; and here, p. 146. [2] *Ibid*. p. 273*a*.
[3] *Ibid*. p. 275*a*.

ship!" [1]—Now it is true that the writer has here certainly utilized four pregnantly descriptive lines in the *Vita*-proper, and the fine account there, undoubtedly by Ettore Vernazza, as regards these conversations.[2] Yet one readily feels, at the moved and moving tone of the re-telling here, that the writer was specially impelled to dwell with a tender, living sympathy upon those meetings of forty years ago. Now Battista must, of course, again and again, have heard from her Father's own lips, during those fourteen years that he lived on after Catherine's great soul had gone to God, of these unforgettable talks, in which he himself had played so large a part, as questioner, interpreter, and chronicler.

(2) And the other set of passages points, even more definitely, to the same daughter and father. Catherine's "humanity," being threatened by the Spirit with various future sufferings, asks to be told the precise offence, charge (*la causa*), which will bring so great a martyrdom with it, without hope of any help. But "she was answered that this grace," of knowing exactly what and why she should suffer, "would be accorded to her in due time, as happens with men condemned to death, who, by hearing read aloud to them the precise sentence pronounced upon their specific misdeeds, support with a greater peace of mind their ignominious death."—And: "Since I am forsaken on all sides," Catherine says to God, "give me at least, O Lord, some person who may be able to understand and comfort me, amidst the torments that I see coming upon me—as men are wont to do for those who are condemned to death, so that the latter may not despair."—And the natural man in such advanced souls is described as suspended in mid-air, "like unto one who is hanged, and who touches not the ground with his feet, but abides in the air, attached to the cord which has caused his death." [3] Ettore's life-long, detailed interest in, and experience of, prisoners and condemned men, whom he, the Founder of the Society of the Beheading of St. John the Baptist, so loved to attend and help throughout their last night and at the scaffold, speak here through the devoted daughter who, countless times, must have listened to

[1] *Dialogo*, p. 250*b*.

[2] *Vita*, p. 97*b*: "This creature would appear with a countenance like unto a Cherub; she gave great consolation to every one who gazed upon her, and those who visited her knew not how to depart from her." And pp. 94*b*–95*c*. See here, pp. 159–161.

[3] *Ibid.* pp. 231*a*; 242*b*; 248*c*; 249*a*.

that father's prison-experiences, which we found her describing, still most vividly, in 1581, thirty years after the publication of these *Dialogo*-passages.[1]

3. *Schematic, intensely abstract psychology.*

At this spiritual stage " there was, as it were, a chain. God, Spirit, draws to Himself the Spirit of man, and there this Spirit abides completely occupied. The Soul, which cannot abide without the Spirit, follows the Spirit, and is there kept occupied. And the Body, which is subject to the Soul, thus prevented from possessing its natural sensations and its natural sustenance, remains, as it were, forsaken and outside of its natural being."—" God at times allowed the Spirit to correspond with the Soul, and the Soul with the Body. . . . But when God withdrew that Spirit into Himself, all the rest (the Soul) followed after it; and hence the Body remained like dead." The two dividings, first of the Soul from the Body, and then of the Soul from the Spirit, so much emphasized in those other documents,[2] is thus carried through in this " Chapter " also.

4. *Rigorism.*

We find here the same exaggeration as to Catherine's faults and contrition, and the same rigoristic doctrine as in " Chapter " First, although, here also, counterbalanced by a noble tenderness of heart. Thus her but semi-conscious attachment to, and self-attribution of, spiritual consolations, is here magnified into a grave sin. " How can I act, so as to make satisfaction for this sin, which is so great and so subtle? " her soul asks God, concerning but semi-conscious attachment to spiritual consolations. And of her social affections, as manifested in her great colloquies with her friends, Catherine now says, " All other loves " than the direct love of God " now appear to me as worse than sheer self-loves."—" She began to confess her sins with so great a contrition that it appeared a wonderful thing," we are told of Catherine, in 1499–1510; yet we know, from the unimpeachable testimony of Don Marabotto himself, that " the wonderful thing" about these latter Confessions was precisely the absence of that former keen sense of, and sorrow for, specific sins.[3]

5. *Pronounced Christo-centrism and daring Anthropomorphism.*

We get, again, the predominance of the Personal concep-

[1] See here, pp. 327–329. [2] See here, pp. 353, 354.
[3] *Dialogo*, pp. 242*b*; 221*b*; 232*b*; *Vita*-proper, 117*c*, 118*a*.

tions and imagery over those of Thing or Law, and the same greater attention to the historical element of religion, which characterize Battista's writings and "Chapter First" of the *Dialogo*, as against Catherine's authentic sayings.

Catherine's energetic repudiation of "the corrupt expression, 'You have offended God,'" is replaced by God saying to Catherine, "Know that I cannot be offended by man, except when he raises an obstacle to the work which I have ordained for his good." [1] Catherine has angrily declared that the term could never be correctly used; the *Dialogo* explains how special and metaphorical is its correct use.

The Lord declares here: "I descend with a fine thread of gold, which is My secret love, and to this thread is bound a hook, which seizes the heart of men. I hold this thread in My hand and ever draw it towards Myself." The hook and hand are additions to Catherine's own declaration, "She seemed to herself to have in her heart a continous ray of Love . . . a thread of gold, as to which she had no fear that it would ever break." [2]—We get here the Wedding-feast imagery that is entirely wanting in Catherine's authentic sayings. "There is no shorter way to salvation than (the owning of) this delightful wedding-garment of charity" [3] A garment, generally in a bad sense, is quite Catherinian; a wedding-garment is exclusively Battistan.—And the parallel between St. John's care of the Blessed Virgin, and Marabotto's attendance upon Catherine,[4] is quite foreign to Catherine's mind.

And the whole *Dialogo* culminates in a double, daring yet graduated, anthropomorphic picturing of the deification of the perfect soul, interestingly different from Catherine's favourite Ocean and Fire similes, and from her description of the Soul as respectively submerged in, and transformed by, this infinite and all-penetrating living Ocean-Fire, God. The Soul asks what is the name which the Lord gives to perfect souls; and the Lord answers (in Latin, as ever with Battista) with the text of Ps. lxxxi, 6: "I have said, ye are Gods, and all of you sons of the Most High"; a text which still leaves us with separate human personalities face to face with the distinct Spirit-Person, God. And then, to the Lord's question, as to what the Soul declares its heart to be, the Soul answers (this climax has been carefully led up to all

[1] *Vita*-proper, pp. 101*b*; *Dialogo*, 247*b*.
[2] *Dialogo*, p. 248*c*; *Vita*-proper, 76*a*.
[3] *Dialogo*, p. 259*c*. [4] *Ibid*. 266*b*.

along): "I say that it is my God, wounded by love,—in Whom I live joyful and contented."—For, as in Battista's own *Colloquy* of December 10, 1554, we get three simultaneous "voices" at different depths of her consciousness, so here, in this composition of 1550, Catherine hears simultaneously within herself three voices—of the Lord, of her own soul, and of her own heart. And Catherine can here declare that now her heart is God, and God wounded by Love; for Battista can write in 1576 that, in the perfect state, "of the Increate Heart and of the created heart there is made a single, most secret and inestimable union,"[1] and that Increate Heart appears here as wounded, because God is ever, in Battista's mind, explicitly identified with Christ, and Christ's Passion is ever in her thoughts. Catherine identifies her true self with God, and God with Love; and conceives her own heart as filled with love and inflamed and pierced by it; but nowhere figures God with a Heart, or that Heart as wounded, for she has little or nothing of Battista's anthropomorphic tendency in regard to God, or of her historical picturings with regard to Christ.

The entire *Dialogo* then is the work of Battista Vernazza; and we have to eliminate it, all but completely, from the means and materials directly available for the constitution of Catherine's life and doctrine. The next Division will now attempt to deal finally with the chief of these means—the *Dimostrazione* (*Trattato*) and the *Vita*-proper.

SECOND DIVISION: ANALYSIS, ASSIGNATION, AND APPRAISEMENT OF THE "VITA-DOTTRINA-DICCHIARAZIONE" CORPUS, IN EIGHT SECTIONS.

We now find ourselves in face of the most difficult, and the alone directly important, *corpus* of documents concerning Catherine's inner life: the *Vita e Dottrina*, together with the *Dicchiarazione* or *Trattato*. It will be best to begin with this *Trattato*, and only after a careful study of this little book, which, as we know, contains the most original and valuable part of Catherine's teaching, to finish up with an examination of the, now separate, Life and (other) Doctrine.

[1] *Dialogo*, p. 264*b*; and here, pp. 349–351, 360.

I. The "Dicchiarazione": the Two Stages of its Existence.

1. *The "Dicchiarazione," from the first a booklet by itself.*

All the Manuscripts give the *Dicchiarazione* (*Trattato*) substantially as we have it at present, although always as but a Chapter of the *Vita e Dottrina*, and not, as yet, itself divided up in any way. Even the last Editions of the Printed *Vita* still retain a reference to this old arrangement: "The soul purifies itself, as do the souls in Purgatory, according to the process described in the Chapter appropriated to this matter." [1]

Yet the very length of this "Chapter," then as now, and the solemn introductory paragraph, both point to its having, at first, formed a booklet by itself. Thus the longest of the other doctrinal Chapters of MS. A (Chapters XV, XVI, XX, and XL) are respectively 29, 22, 19, and 17½ pages long; whilst the *Trattato*-Chapter XLII runs to 46 pages. Only the Narrative-Chapter XLI, the Passion, is of an exactly equal length; but we shall find that this Chapter also existed, originally, in part at least, as a separate document. And the introduction to Chapter XLII is unparalleled by anything in such a position. "This holy Soul, whilst yet in the flesh, finding herself placed in the purgatory of God's burning love, which consumed and purified her from whatever she had to purify, in order that, in passing out of this life, she might enter at once into the immediate presence of her tender Love,—God: understood, by means of this fire of love, how the souls of the faithful abide in the place of Purgatory to purge away every stain of sin which, in this life, they had not yet purged." I have here omitted (after "understood") "in her soul," as marring the rhythm; and (before "stain of sin") "rust and," since the whole group of words appears in MS. A as "ogni rubigine di macchia di peccato," requiring the suppression of at least one of the first two nouns: we shall find that "rubigine" is secondary.

I have also omitted, from what I hold was the first form of this Introduction, the present second sentence and comparison: "And as she, placed in the loving purgatory of the divine fire, abode united to this Divine Love, and content with all

[1] *Vita*, p. 144*c*.

that He wrought within her: so she understood the state of the Souls that are in Purgatory." For all the circumstances and dispositions of this contentment have already been anticipated in the "How the Souls abide in Purgatory" of the first sentence.—We can still show, I think, when and why this second sentence was added. Let us get at the reason slowly.

2. *Three differences between the first seven and the last ten Chapters.*

The first seven of the present seventeen Chapters of the *Dicchiarazione* (*Dic.*) are indeed like, but also unlike, the last ten Chapters, in three important matters.[1]

(1) All the seventeen Chapters are full of ideas, even of special words and peculiar groups of words, appearing also in various places of the *Vita*-proper. Yet the last ten Chapters alone have, in addition, four complete paragraphs standing, as such, in the *Vita*-proper. The two paragraphs of Chapter Eight, and the first paragraph of Chapter Nine, of the *Dicchiarazione* ("Più ancora dico che io veggio"—"se fosse possibile," *Vita*, pp. 175*c*–176*c*), are identical with paragraphs four and five of Chapter Thirty of the *Vita*-proper ("E perciò diceva: io veggio"—"se fosse possibile," *Vita*, pp. 78*c*, 79*a*).

Dic.'s text still keeps two primitive readings: "Gate" of Paradise, in a first saying, unassimilated to the plural "arms" of God in the second saying; against *V.'s* assimilation, "gates" and "arms." Again "stain" and "stains," alongside of "imperfection"; against *V.'s* treble "imperfection." But in all else *V.* is clearly the older text: thus "His company" (against "His glory"); "un minimo chè" (against "un minimo brusculo"); "appear before God" (against "find himself in the presence of the Divine Majesty"); "purge" (against "lift away"); and other points.

But if this general priority of the *V.*-text be admitted, then this part of *Dic.* must have been constituted at a time when these parts of *V.'s* text were already so definitely fixed in themselves, and so firmly worked into their present contexts, that the Redactor of this part of *Dic.* dared not take them simply away from their old home, and did not modify them so as to conform with the glosses traceable in the earlier Chapters of *Dic.* (note here, in Ch. VIII, the absence of the "rubigine" present in the earlier Chapters). And this means that this part of *Dic.* was constituted when this part of *V.* was no more

[1] First seven Chapters: *Vita*, pp. 169*b*–75*c*. Last ten Chapters: *Ibid.* pp. 175*c*–184*c*.

new, and *Dic.'s* own earlier chapters had been fixed for some time.

(2) All the *Dicchiarazione* Chapters are based on the assumption of a true analogy, indeed a continuity, between the soul's purgation, Here and There. But only the last ten Chapters give passages (three whole Chapters) treating exclusively of this-world sufferings, and an address to souls which, in this world, run the risk not simply of Purgatory but of Hell hereafter.

Thus Chapter Eleven (*Vita*, pp. 178*b*–179*a*) is now indeed superscribed, " Of the desire of the souls in Purgatory to be quite free from the stains of their sins " ; and contains the clause " non che possa guardare il Purgatorio siccome un Purgatorio " (179*a*). But all the chapter-headings are recent, and the heading here is quite inaccurate, for throughout the account (with the probable exception of the clause quoted, which is a gloss) the soul is simply in this world, as on pp. 23*b*, 49*b*, 61*b*, 106*a*, 114*c* of the *Vita*, which readily calls such this-world sufferings a " Purgatory," 128*b*, 136*c*, 137*a*. Here, however, much of the form (*e. g.* " to contaminate," " to occasion "), and some of the doctrine (the resurrection effected by Baptism) is alien to Catherine's habits. The Chapter is, then, made up, about equally, of genuine sayings referring exclusively to this-world purgations, and of redactional amplifications of a systematizing and sacramental kind.

Chapter Twelve (*Vita*, p. 179*b*, *c*) is now superscribed, " How suffering conjoins itself with joy in Purgatory," and concludes with " Thus the souls in Purgatory experience. . . ." Yet here too the body of the text nowhere directly refers to, or consciously implies, the other-world Purgatory ; for its last clause, " ma questa contentezza non toglie scintilla di pena," requires to be freed from the gloss, " alle Anime che sono in Purgatorio," which now stands between " contentezza " and " non."

Chapter Seventeen (*Vita*, pp. 182*c*–184*c*) now indeed opens with an explicit reference by Catherine of "this purgative form which I feel it in my mind, especially since the last two years " to the souls in " the true Purgatory " ; but this reference and the five last words of this long Chapter, " e il Purgatorio lo purifica," are clear glosses, since Catherine is here exclusively occupied with the purgative character of her this-world sufferings, and not with any likeness of them to the other-world Purgatory. And indeed, since considerations about the other-world Purgatory first occur, in any certainly authentic *Vita*-passages, only after the great " ray "-experience of November 11, 1509 (the experience stands on p. 133*b*, where the MSS. give the date; the considerations appear only on pp. 136*b*–137*a*, 144*b*, 146*b*), the " last two years " here must mean that already three years or so before her death she had come to dwell much on the purifying function of her sufferings. Only during the last ten months does she seem to have dwelt upon these sufferings as illustrating the purgations of the other life.

And finally, Chapter Fifteen (*Vita*, p. 181*b*, *c*) is headed now: " Reproofs addressed by the souls in Purgatory to worldly persons." But the text still begins with " a desire comes over me (Catherine) to cry out so as to strike fear into every man on earth," and deals throughout with her this-life fears for such persons, not with respect to Purgatory, but with regard to Hell.

(3) Even the first seven *Dicchiarazione* Chapters we shall find to contain short theological glosses. But only in the last ten Chapters can we find extensive passages incompatible with Catherine's authentic teaching, or at least quite unlike her undoubted utterances.

Chapter Thirteen (*Vita*, p. 180*a*, *b*) is now entitled: " How the souls in Purgatory are no longer in a state to merit; and how they regard the charity exercised in the world for them." Yet this very *Dicchiarazione's* utterly authentic opening sayings (*Vita*, pp. 169*c*, 170*a*, *b*) eliminate clearly the second question: such souls do not and cannot regard such charity at all. And though Catherine (who put the question of merit, even as to the soul's this-world action, so emphatically behind that of love) [1] never considers merit in connection with Purgatory, yet she conceives the souls in Purgatory as purifying themselves of certain passive habitual defects, by one initial free election of the condition of suffering, and by then continually willing the painful condition,—volitional acts and dispositions which are usually held to imply merit.

The first paragraph then opens with: " If the souls in Purgatory could purge themselves with contrition, in one instant they would pay all their debt." Yet there is no such dilemma in Catherine's authentic thought as "instant purgation through contrition, of a necessarily perfect kind," or " no purgation through such contrition "; for throughout the first seven

[1] See here, pp. 140, 141.

Chapters purgation takes place through love and general contrition, in a thorough but gradual, seemingly slow, manner, and this not because God prevents the soul's self-purification by what would be the normal means, but, contrariwise, because He does not interfere with the intrinsic, normally necessary inter-connection of sin and suffering, sorrow, self-renunciation, love and joy.

The second paragraph runs: "Of the payment not one penny is remitted to those souls. . . ." This imagery of the payment of something so external to the payer as is money, in view of so external a change as is getting out of prison, can hardly be Catherine's, at least not as the deliberate expression of her purgatorial conception. The last paragraph reads: "They are henceforth incapable of seeing except [so much as] God will[s] . . . they can no more turn [with any attachment] to see the alms given for their intention by those that are living upon earth [except within the (general) apprehension of that all-just balance of the divine will], leaving God to do as He pleases in all things [God, who pays Himself as it pleases His infinite goodness]. And if they could turn to see those alms [outside of the divine will], this would be an act of self-love (*proprietà*) . . ." (180*b*). We have here a substantially authentic saying, but the bracketed words are certain glosses, introducing the utterly un-Catherinian ideas and images of the souls being allowed to see what is being done for them, of God's balance, and of His paying Himself.

Chapter Fifteen's last paragraph (*Vita*, p. 181*c*), which warns the soul that " the (kind of) Confession and Contrition necessary for such a Plenary Indulgence (as shall instantly purify it from all sin) is a thing most difficult to gain," is also quite unlike Catherine's preoccupations, tone, and teaching.

3. *Remaining passages of the last ten Chapters not accounted for by the three peculiarities just detailed.*

The three last paragraphs of Chapter Nine (*Vita*, pp. 176*c*–177*b*) and the very similar short Chapter Fourteen (*ibid.* pp. 180*c*, 181*a*) are more painfully composite and more repeatedly worked over than, I think, even the most tormented passages of the first seven Chapters.

We thus are left with but four paragraphs, the last two of Chapter Ten (*Vita*, pp. 178*a*, *b*), and the two of Chapter Sixteen (pp. 181*c*–182*b*). These two sets form two couples of illustrative descriptions of the Purgatorial process; and, in each set, the first paragraph is easier to read but is less authentic than the second, very composite, much-glossed paragraph. The second paragraph of the first set reads : " L'oro quando è purificato [per sino a ventiquattro caratti] non si consuma poi più, per fuoco che tu gli possi dare ; perchè non si può consumare se non la sua imperfezione. Cosi | fâ il divin fuoco | dell' anima : Dio la tiene tanto al fuoco, che le consuma ogni imperfezione [e la conduce alla perfezione di ventiquattro caratti, ognuna però in suo grado]. E quando è purificata, resta tutta | in Dio[senz' alcuna cosa] | in sè stessa ; ed il suo essere è Dio | [il quale quando ha condotta a sè] l'anima cosi purificata [allora l'anima] resta impassibile [perche più non le resta da consumare] e se pure, così purificata, fosse tenuta al fuoco, non le saria penoso, anzi le saria fuoco di divino amore, come vita eterna, senza contrarietà." The bracketed words are all more or less certain glosses. But there is here, besides, a conflation (indicated by vertical lines) of two applications of the gold-dross-fire simile : " Così dell' anima : Dio la tiene . . . imperfezione. E quando è purificata, resta tutta in Dio ; e se pure, così purificata, fosse tenuta . . ." ; and " così fà il divin fuoco dell' anima, che le consuma ogni imperfezione ; e quando è purificata resta in sè stessa, ed il suo essere è Dio." Both applications are probably authentic ; the latter is too daringly simple and too delicately consistent with Catherine's surest purgatorial conceptions not to be genuine.

The second paragraph of the second set contains the important passage : " Perchè sono in grazia l'intendono e capiscono | Dio | così come sono, secondo la loro capacità ; [e perciò a quel] le dà un gran contento, il quale non manca mai ; anzi lo và loro accrescendo tanto, quanto più si approssimano a Dio." This seems a conflation of two authentic sentences : " Perchè—grazia, l'intendono e capiscono così come sono—capacità ; " and " perchè—grazia, Dio le dà un gran contento—a Dio." And the paragraph concludes with : " Ognì poca vista che si possa avere di Dio, eccede ogni [pena ed ogni] gaudio che l'uomo può capire, [e benchè la eccede, non leva loro però una scintilla di gaudio o di pena] ; " where the brackets indicate glosses, since the sight of God is directly always a source of joy.

4. *" Dic." 1 and " Dic." 2 referred to, respectively, by the first and second sentences of the Dicchiarazione's present Introduction.*

Now the result reached by our analysis of the *Dicchiarazione's* last ten Chapters, viz. that this group (with the possible exception of the two sets of similes in Chapters Ten and Sixteen and much of Chapter Seventeen), was constituted under different, later circumstances than was that of the first seven Chapters, is borne out, indeed required, by the present Narrative-paragraph which introduces all the seventeen Chapters. For the two sentences of this paragraph are similar in form but different in matter. In the first sentence the soul is " placed in Purgatory " in order that, " passing from this life, it may be presented in the sight of its tender Love, God "; Purgatory is " a place "; and the souls are in that place " to purge away every stain of sin." And this corresponds exactly to Chapters Four, Six, and Seven which deal respectively with the diverse souls that " have passed from this life " (p. 172*c*); with the sight or non-sight of " God, our Love " possessed by them (p. 174*c*); and with God and Hell as " places," and of the soul's purgatorial plunge " so as to join God " (p. 175*c*). In the second sentence, the soul, " placed in the loving Purgatory of the divine fire, stands united to the divine Love and content with all that It operates within her," and Purgatory is not called a " place." And this corresponds precisely with Chapter Twelve (p. 179*b*), " as though a man stood in a great fire . . . the love of God gives him a contentment . . ."

The second sentence, a pale, at first sight redundant, double of the first, will, then, have been added to the first sentence, when the second set of chapters was added to the first set.

II. The earlier " Dicchiarazione," and its Theological Glosses.

I will here analyse such paragraphs of these first seven chapters, as most fully illustrate the astonishing complexity of the whole, and as, between them, furnish all the theological " corrections " to be found in this earliest *Dicchiarazione*.

1. *The two Sayings-paragraphs of Chapter First* (" *Vita*," pp. 169*c*, 170*a*, *c*.).

I print these sayings (here now broken up) in parallel columns and in the order of their present position. Columns first and third (numbered together as I) will turn out to contain original sayings, and column second (numbered II) will appear as but a Redactor's restatement, which (a sort of link between the two sets) first paraphrases the set that has just preceded, and then restates the set that will immediately follow. The arabic numbers indicate the several sayings, in their original and secondary forms (the numbers of the latter being bracketed) : thus II (1), (2), (3), stands for the secondary versions of I 1, 2, 3, respectively. I double-bracket the additions (theological glosses) of the Printed text, and I single-bracket two MS. clauses which are clearly a gloss.

I 1

Le Anime che sono nel Purgatorio *non possono avere* altra elezione che di essere in esso luogo; [e questo è per *ordinazione di Dio,* il quale ha fatto questo giustamente;] *nè* si *possono* più voltare verso *sè stesse,* nè dire: " io ho fatto tali peccati, per i quali merito di *star qui* "; nè possono dire " non vorrei averli fatti, perchè *anderei* ora *in Paradiso* "; nè dire ancora " *quello* ne esce più presto di mè," ovvero " *io* nè usciro più presto di *lui.*"

II (1)

Non possono avere alcuna memoria *propria* neppure d' *altri,* nè in *bene* nè in *male* [[dacui ricevano maggior afflizione del suo ordinario]]; ma hanno tanto contento di essere nell' *ordinazione di Dio,* e che adoperi tutto quello che gli piace e come gli piace, che di *sè medesime* non ne possono pensare [[con maggiore lor pena.]]

(2) e solamente *veggiono* l'operazione della divina bontà, la quale ha tanta misericordia dell' uomo per condurlo a sè, che di pena o di bene che possa accadere in *proprietà,* non se ne può vedere.

I

2. La causa del Purgatorio che hanno in loro, *veggiono* una sol volta nel passare di questa vita, e poi mai più, imperocchè vi saria una *proprietà.*

(3) e se'l potessero vedere, non sarebbero in *carità pura.* Non *possono* vedere che siano in quelle pene per i loro peccati, e *non possono* aver quella vista nella mente : imperocchè vi sarebbe una *imperfezione attiva*

(4) la quale non può essere in esso luogo, perchè non vi si può attualmente peccare.

3. Essendo dunque in carità, e da quella *non potendo* più deviare con *attual diffetto,* non possono più volere se non il puro volere della *pura carità.*

[4. ed essendo in quel fuoco del Purgatorio, sono nell' ordinazione divina (la quale è carità pura), e non possono più in alcuna cosa da quella deviare, perchè sono privati così di attualmente peccare come sono di attualmente meritare.]

Here the middle sayings are sufficiently recent to have in II (1) imitated the secondary " ordinazione di Dio " clause present in I 1. And the two theological " corrections," still absent from MSS. A and B, both appear among these middle sayings; they attempt to explain the non-attention of the souls to all particular things, as a non-remembrance of such things as would add to their distress.

2. *The first two paragraphs of Chapter Second* (pp. 170*c*–171*b*).

Originally single sentences have here been repeatedly broken up and scattered about amongst other similarly broken-up passages : we can still trace the motive for this procedure. I first print them as they stand, double-bracketing, at the end, the interestingly obvious theological " correction " which immediately follows a most authentic, directly contrary, statement.

" Non credo che si possa trovare contentezza da comparare a

quella di un' anima del Purgatorio, eccetto quella de' Santi di Paradiso: ed ogni giorno questa contentezza cresce per l'influsso di Dio in esse anime, il quale va crescendo, siccome si và consumando l'impedimento dell' influsso. La ruggine del peccato è l'impedimento, e il fuoco và consumando la ruggine: e così l'anima sempre più si và discuoprendo al divino influsso. Siccome una cosa coperta non può corrispondere alla riverberazione del sole, non per diffetto del sole, che di continuo luce, ma per l'opposizione della copertura: così sè si consumerà la copertura, si discoprirà la cosa al sole, e tanto piu corrisponderà alla riverberazione, quanto la copertura più si andrà consumando.

"Così la ruggine (cioè il peccato) è la copertura dell' anima, e nel Purgatorio si và consumando per il fuoco: e quanto più si consuma, tanto sempre più corrisponde al vero sole Iddio: però tanto cresce la contentezza, quanto manca la ruggine e si discopre al divin raggio: e così l'uno cresce e l'altro manca, finchè sia finito il tempo. [[Non manca però la pena, ma solo il tempo di stare in essa pena.]]"

Here the last (double-bracketed) sentence is a deliberate theological correction, for it formally contradicts the precise point and necessary consequences of the whole preceding, most authentic, specially characteristic doctrine.—In that preceding part three parallel illustrative similes (between the intact general statement and the equally untouched general conclusion) have been broken up, and dovetailed into each other, in a most bewildering manner; and this from a (possibly but semi-conscious) desire to obscure a characteristic feature of her teaching. I shall now give these five sentences in English, and will disentangle the three middle ones from each other.—The general statement: "I do not think that a contentment could be found comparable to that of a soul in Purgatory, except that of the Saints in Paradise; and every day this contentment is on the increase"—The three images descriptive of the cause and mode of this increase, arranged according to the increasing materiality of their picturings. (1) "The influx of God into the soul goes increasing, in proportion as it consumes the impediment to that influx, and as the soul opens itself out more and more to the influx." (2) "As an object, if covered up, cannot correspond to the beating of the sun upon it, not through any defect in the sun, which indeed shines on continuously, but because of the opposition of the covering, (so that) if this covering be consumed, the object will open itself out to the sun: even so does the soul in Purgatory more and more correspond with the true sun, God, when its covering, sin, gets consumed." (3) "Rust is an impediment to fire, and fire goes consuming rust more and more: so does the rust, that is the sin, of the souls in Purgatory, get consumed by the fire; and their contentment grows in proportion as the rust diminishes and as the soul uncovers itself to the divine ray (of fire)."—The conclusion, which perhaps applies grammatically only to the last image, but which, as to the sense, most certainly refers to all three pictures. "And thus does the one (the influx, sun-light, fire-ray) increase, and the other (the impediment, covering, rust) decrease, until the time (necessary for the whole process) be accomplished."—The three images are in no case supplementary, but each is complete and parallel to the other two. As the fire which meets with the obstacle of the rust is the same fire as that which removes the rust, so is it in all three cases: in each case God, and His direct presence and action, are the "influx," "sun-light," "fire-ray"; in each case a sinful, morally imperfect, habit of the soul is the "impediment," "covering," "rust"; and in each case the suffering as well as the joy, and the changing relations between the two, proceed exclusively from the differing relations of but two forces: the soul and God. It is only the peculiar, Redactional dovetailing of the fragments of these three parallel similes which now conveys the impression that the divine sun-light and fire-ray reaches the uncovered soul in proportion as the soul's covering and rust is destroyed by material fire; and to convey this very impression, was, no doubt, the motive of this dovetailing. The authentic passage on p. 178*b*, tells how the same divine fire which, at first, pains because it has still to purify the soul, increasingly fills the soul with joy in proportion as it can penetrate the soul unopposed: a doctrine also explicitly taught by Catherine, in her dialogue with Vernazza as to the effect of a drop of Love were it to fall into Hell (pp. 94*c*, 95*b*).

3. *Third paragraph of Chapter Third.*

The much-tormented Chapter Third has, at the opening of its third paragraph (p. 172*b*), an interesting theological "correction." The complete passage now reads: "E perchè le anime che sono nel Purgatorio [[sono senza colpa di peccato perciò non]] hanno impedimento tra Dio e loro, [[salvo che quella pena, la quale le ha ritardate, che]] l'istinto non ha potuto avere la sua perfezione : e vedendo per certezza quanto importi ogni minimo impedimento, ed essere per necessità di giustizia ritardato esso instinto : di quì nasce un estremo fuoco." The bracketed words are two interdependent glosses. For though in some other, possibly authentic, passages the souls in Purgatory " non hanno colpa di peccato," this most certainly applies only to mortal sin or a still active, formal affirmation of venial sin ; since the very *raison d'être* of Purgatory is " the rust of sin," pp. 169*b*, 170*c*, 171*b*, 173*c*, 181*a* ; " the stain of sin," pp. 169*b*, 171*c*, 176*b* ; " a mote of imperfection," p. 176*a* ; " a stain of imperfection," p. 176*b* ; " a passive defect," p. 170*b* ; " opposition to the will of God," p. 177*b* ; an " impediment of sin," 177*b*. And the *Vita*-proper says quite plainly : " Both Purgatory and Hell are made for Sin : Hell to punish and Purgatory to purge it " (p. 64*b*).—And this gloss is in strict conformity with the glosses which affirm static suffering : in both cases all change is excluded from the soul in Purgatory, since this Purgatory is neither intrinsically necessary nor amelioratively operative within the soul.

4. *First paragraph of Chapter Fourth.*

Chapter Fourth is comparatively easy, but probably largely secondary, because uncharacteristic of her teaching. Yet it contains a " correction " deserving of notice I give the two sentences which prove both points. " Quei dell' Inferno . . . hanno seco la colpa infinitamente, e la pena [non però tanta, quanta meritano ; ma pur quella] che hanno è senza fine. Ma quei del Purgatorio hanno solamente la pena, perciocchè la colpa fù cancellata nel punto della morte . . . e così essa pena è finita, e và sempre mancando [[quanto al tempo, come s'è detto]] " (p. 173*a*).—The double-bracketed passage, directly referring to the gloss on p. 171*b*, is, like the latter, a theological " correction." But also the single-bracketed words are a gloss, since they disturb both grammar and rhythm of the passage, and introduce a point foreign to the argument which is being conducted in this place.—Indeed, even the remaining parts of these sentences are misleading, since Catherine held no such simple and absolute distinction as infinite guilt in the one case, and apparently no moral imperfection in the other. For of the lost she says : " If any creature could be found which did in nowise participate in the divine goodness, that creature would be as malignant as God is good " (p. 33*b*) ; and as to the souls in Purgatory, they are imperfect in precise proportion as they do and can suffer.

5. *First two sentences of Chapter Fifth.*

Here we find the strongest instance of the strange clumsiness characteristic of the theological " corrections." I give the sentences as they now stand, simply numbering the sentences thus amalgamated, and bracketing at once the undoubted glosses.

(1) " Le Anime del Purgatorio hanno in tutto conforme la loro volontà a quella di Dio ; e però corrisponde loro colla sua bontà, e restano contente quanto alla volontà, e purificate d'ogni lor peccato quanto alla colpa. [[Restando così quelle Anime purificate, come quando Dio le creò]]

(2) " e per essere passate di questa vita malcontente e confessate di tutti i loro peccati commessi. . . . [Iddio subito perdona loro la colpa e] non resta se non la ruggine del peccato, del quale poi si purificano nel fuoco, mediante la pena ; [e così]

(3) " purificate d'ogni colpa, unite a Dio per volontà [[veggiono chiaramente Dio, secondo il grado che fà lor conoscere, e]] veggiono [ancora] quanto importi la fruizione di Dio, e che l'anime sono state create a questo fine." (Pp. 173*c*, 174*a*.)

According to Catherine's unvarying authentic teaching, souls go to Purgatory precisely because they are *not* already " pure as when God created them," and they there do *not* " clearly see God." Indeed, the second sentence here distinctly states, that still " there remains " in them " the rust of sin," from which they " there " purify themselves. And the two " veggiono " conclusions of the third sentence contradict each other : for if they see clearly how much the fruition of God matters to them, then they do not as yet possess that full fruition, *i. e.* they do not as yet clearly see God.

These glosses are made entirely intolerable by a third Redactional sentence here, which announces " an example," or figure, of the doctrine here conveyed, and then proceeds to do so in the beautiful Chapter Sixth. For Chapter Sixth gives us the simile of the One Bread, "the bare sight of which would satiate all creatures " ; and the division of all souls into those in Purgatory, which " have the hope of seeing the Bread " ; those in Hell, which " are bereft of all hope of ever being able to see the Bread " ; and, by implication, those in Heaven, that see and satiate themselves with the Bread.

And "the nearer a man were to get to the Bread, without being able to see it, the more would the natural desire for this Bread be enkindled"; "not having it, he would abide in intolerable pain" (p. 174*b*, *c*).

III. Five Conclusions concerning the History of the "Dicchiarazione."

1. The authentic sayings, collected throughout the Seventeen Chapters, all belong, at earliest, to the last nine, and indeed probably to the last two or three, years of Catherine's life. —At the latter date Vernazza had been her close friend for twelve, and Marabotto, her Confessor for eight years. To one or the other, or to both, we undoubtedly owe the first writing down of this, originally small, nucleus of authentic sayings,—probably in (many cases) on the very day when Catherine uttered one or several of these thoughts.—The One-Bread-Simile Chapter, and one or two other passages, contain slightly varying doublets of the same saying, the registration of one of which may well be by Vernazza, and the registration of the other by Marabotto, each of these two auditors getting, perhaps, addressed by Catherine in a slightly different form, or himself looking out for that part or context of a saying which specially appealed to him, or slightly, and probably quite unconsciously, giving to the identical declaration a somewhat differing characteristic "colour" of his own. Vernazza is, however, doubtless the first chronicler of the majority of these sayings, in 1508–1510.

2. These sayings must have been collected together in a first shorter *Dicchiarazione* (equivalent to the greater part of the present first seven chapters and possibly one or two other passages), not long after her death, probably simultaneously with, but separately from, a short "Conversione" account. The first public Cultus in May–July, 1512, giving rise as it did to a painter's picture of her, cannot have failed to suscitate some such manuscript booklets. This short *Dicchiarazione* will already have had the first sentence of the present introduction prefixed to it, and this sentence, so like and yet somewhat unlike Battista's writings (Battista who was as yet only fifteen), will have been written by Ettore. These Chapters already, I think, contained the "colpa di peccato" and other technically theological passages, probably

introduced by Marabotto; but the Chapters will as yet have been free from the theological "corrections," which still come away too easily from the rest of the text (in contradistinction to the difficulty in the analysis of its other, much more resistent components) not to be considerably younger than these latter.

3. The "corrections" insist upon three doctrines, in each case in demonstrable contradiction with Catherine's authentic teaching: the complete absence of all guilt, sin, imperfection, even though merely passive and habitual, in the soul, even in its first moment in Purgatory; the simply vindictive, not curative, hence static, nature of the suffering throughout the soul's prison time, right up to this time's sudden cessation; and this soul's clear vision of God from first to last. Thus no increase or extension of purity, no work of love, is effected in or by the soul during, or by means of, its Purgatory.—Now Pope Leo the Tenth, in his Bull *Exsurge Domine* of May 16, 1520, against Luther, reprobated four propositions concerning Purgatory; and the second part of the second of these propositions declares: "It is not proved, by any reasons or by any texts of Scripture, that the souls in Purgatory are out of a state capable of merit or of an increase of Charity."[1] The Censure of this doctrine must have seemed to menace Catherine's teaching on this same point. For she nowhere indeed declares these souls to be capable of meriting, nor does she teach that there is any increase in the intensity of their love; yet (by the one free act of self-determination to Purgatory, and by the gradual extension of this determination of active love throughout all the regions and degrees of the passive will and habitual dispositions of the soul) her teaching must, to an at all nervous theologian, have seemed, at the time, to come perilously near to the admission, respectively, of merit and of an increase of love in the Beyond. And the degree in which the fight with nascent Protestantism was raging precisely around such Purgatorial questions, and the solemnity of the Pope's condemnation, at this early stage of Catherine's Cultus and reputation, must have combined to render the introduction of these disfiguring glosses an apparent necessity.—I take them to have been introduced soon after Vernazza's death in 1524, hence some twelve years after the

[1] Denzinger, *Enchiridion Definitionum*, ed. 1888, p. 178, No. 38: "Animae in Purgatorio non sunt securae de earum salute saltem omnes; nec probatum est, ullis aut rationibus aut Scripturis, ipsas esse extra statum merendi aut augendae charitatis."

constitution of these seven Chapters; presumably by the Inquisitor to the Republic of Genoa for the time being.

4. The addition of the last ten Chapters to the first seven Chapters, and of the second sentence to the Introduction, will have occurred some time after the constitution of the *Vita*-proper, say, in 1531 or 1532; but, in any case, was not due to Vernazza or Marabotto. And the glosses will have been introduced into these ten Chapters quasi-automatically, and simply as a consequence to the very deliberate "corrections" of those previous seven Chapters; for now Catherine's reputation had had another twelve years in which to grow, and the Bull had been studied for another twelve years.—But no such glosses were introduced into the *Vita*-proper, either as to this, or indeed, perhaps, any other point. For this *Vita* treated only quite incidentally of the other-world Purgatory; and this, in those times specially delicate, subject-matter had received every precautionary attention in the *Dicchiarazione* professedly devoted to it. And other, intrinsically more important points, even though treated here with great boldness, were felt to remain as open as before.

But we must now get on to this *Vita*-proper.

IV. The "Vita"-proper, its Divisions and Parts, and Chief Secondary and Authentic Constituents.

1. *The three great divisions, and their clearly secondary parts.* The *Vita*-proper, as we now have it in print, falls into three great Divisions, of respectively two, four, and two parts each. The first and last Divisions hold by far the greater amount of the primary material; whereas the middle Division only gives us here and there chapters or paragraphs of admirable freshness and beauty.

The eight opening Narrative Chapters, pp. 1*b* to 21*b*, and the next nine Chapters of Discourses, pp. 21*b* to 50*c*, form the two parts of the first Division, each part being more or less complete and homogeneous within itself; and yet they are together in marked contrast to most of the materials of the following Division. It is within the limits of this first Division, and probably even of its first part, that must subsist the materials, predominantly derived from Ettore Vernazza, of that first "Conversione"-booklet of 1512.

The second Division opens out with the most important Narrative Chapter Nineteenth, pp. 51*a*–53*c*; but the remaining seven Chapters of this its first part (pp. 53*c*–70*a*) contain very little which is not findable elsewhere in a more primary form. Then follow, as a second part, seven Chapters of a bewildering variety of form: three are largely Narrative and important (Chapters XXVII to XXIX, pp. 70*b*–77*b*); the next (Chapter XXX, pp. 77*b*–79*a*) gives Discourses, only in part authentic; the next again (Chapter XXXI, pp. 79*b*–83*c*) is chiefly Narrative and important; Chapter XXXII, pp. 83*c*–88*b*, is now one long Discourse which incorporates some short but important authentic sayings; and Chapters XXXIII to XXXV (pp. 88*c*–96*b*) are, the first, a Narrative; the last two, Discourses; and, in all three cases, preponderatingly secondary and negligible. Then a third part consists of a largely Narrative Chapter of delightful authenticity and freshness (Chapter XXXVI, pp. 94*b*–96*b*); a tryingly composite but valuable Narrative Chapter (Chapter XXXVII, pp. 96*b*–97*c*); and an important Narrative Chapter with dates (Chapter XXXVIII, pp. 98*a*–100*a*). And, as a fourth part, we get a group of three Chapters, of which the first and last contain highly original matter (Chapters XXXIX–XLI, pp. 100*a*–103*b*, 106*a*–111*b*), but of which the middle one (Chapter XL, pp. 103*c*–105*c*) can safely be neglected. Ettore's chroniclings are again strongly represented in this Division.

And the last Division consists, in its first part, of five important Narrative Chapters (Chapters XLII–XLVI, pp. 111*c*–126*c*), clearly by various hands, and of markedly manifold tone and emotional pitch. And the second part consists of the six Chapters concerning her Passion, Death, and Cultus (Chapters XLVII–LII, pp. 127*a*–166*a*), of which we can safely neglect Chapter XLVII, pp. 127*a*–131*c* (wanting in the MSS., and a mere collection of passages still present, in a more primitive form and connection, in other parts of the *Vita*); and pp. 161*c*–166*a* (which treat of events subsequent to Catherine's death). This last Division gives the most important of the communications which can with certainty be attributed to Marabotto. And as Division First's first part, Catherine's Conversion, will have existed very early in a separate form, and its second part will have, if added later, been thus added very soon; so this Third Division's second part, Catherine's Passion, will early have existed separately; and to this will have been prefixed, still in early times, the Narrative Chapters XLII, XLIII, XLV, and XLVI of the first part, all dealing with matters occurring from 1496 onwards.

2. *Five main additions of the Printed Vita as against the extant MSS.*

We have now reduced the bulk of the *Vita*-proper by 34½ pages, but the remaining 132 pages are capable of further reduction. For the Printed *Vita*, as compared with the MSS., contains, besides the already rejected Chapter XLVII, five main additions.

The first addition (in the order of the Printed *Vita*) is the beautifully vivid and daring, certainly historical scene between Catherine and the Friar (Chapter XIX, pp. 51*a*–53*b*), a record doubtless due to Ettore Vernazza, and which will have been omitted by the Franciscan Scribe of MS. A from scruples with regard to the doctrine implied.

The second is Chapter XLIV, omitted from p. 117*b* to p. 121*b*,—Catherine's declarations as to her lonely middle period and the account of her Confessions to Don Marabotto, undoubtedly here recorded by this Priest; matter again which the Franciscan Friar might well consider dangerously daring, but which, we have seen, had not yet been incorporated with the Franciscan's Prototype, perhaps indeed not with any copy of the then extant *Vita*.

The third is the fourth paragraph of Chapter XLVIII, p. 133*b*, giving a new and beautiful description of the "Scintilla" experienced by Catherine on November 11, 1509. It is of late composition, and Battista Vernazza is no doubt its author.

The fourth consists of three new paragraphs to Chapter XLIX, descriptive of Maestro Boerio's three-weeks' attempt to cure her, sometime in May–July 1510 (pp. 146*c*–147*c*), and of evidently the same Physician's visit in his scarlet robes on September 2 (p. 154*b*). Both passages, of transparent authenticity and still but little enlarged, will have been contributed by this Physician's Priest-son Giovanni Boerio, who, dying in his seventies, in 1561,[1] must himself have been twenty at the time of his Father's attendance, and may well have had his Father's contemporary notes before him when composing these interestingly vivid contributions.

[1] His Epitaph, in the Church of the Annunciation, at Sturla, just outside Genoa, is given in full in Pescetto's *Biografia Medica Ligura*, Genova, 1846, p. 104.

And the fifth brings three new paragraphs for the events of September 4, 1510 (Chapter L, pp. 155*b*–156*a*), already referred to here, on pp. 209, 210.

The MSS. read: "On the following day [4th September], being in great pain and torment, she extended her arms in suchwise as to appear in truth a body fixed to a cross; so that, according as she was in her interior, so also did she show in her exterior, and she said—" [1] Hereupon follows a long prayer so obviously modelled throughout upon Our Lord's High-Priestly prayer (John xvii, 1–26), and so elaborately reflective, that it cannot but most distantly represent anything spoken now by her who had been so interjectional in her remarks ever since August 16 (pp. 149*b*–155*b*).—Now the Printed *Vita* introduces between ". . . exterior," and "and she said," the following account: "Whence it appears to me, we should indeed believe that the spiritual stigmata were impressed in that body which was so afflicted and excruciated by her Love; and although they did not appear exteriorly, they nevertheless could easily be recognized through the Passion which she felt; and that she suffered in her body that pain which her Love had suffered on the Cross: as we read of the Apostle (Gal. vi [17]) who bore the stigmata of Our Lord Jesus Christ, not indeed exteriorly but interiorly, through the great love and desire which he felt within himself for his Lord."

"In proof that this holy woman bore the stigmata interiorly, a large silver cup was ordered to be brought in, which had a very high-standing saucer"; the cup was "full of cold water, for refreshing her hands, in the palms of which, because of the great fire that burned within her, she felt intolerable pain. And on putting her hands into it, the water became so boiling that the cup and the very saucer were greatly heated. She also sustained great heat and much pain at her feet, and hence she kept them uncovered; and at her head she similarly suffered great heat with many pains."

Argentina is then quoted as having seen how "one of" Catherine's "arms lengthened itself out by more than half a palm beyond its usual length; yet she never said one word as to whence such great pains proceeded. It is true that, on one occasion, before her last infirmity, she predicted that she would have to suffer a great malady, which would not be natural but

[1] MS. A, p. 348 = Pr. L., 155*b*, 156*b*.

different from other infirmities, and that she would die of it; and that, before her death, she would have within herself (*in sè*) the Stigmata and the Mysteries of the Passion: and this the aforesaid Argentina revealed later on to many persons."

"Now this Beata being thus, with her arms extended, in pains so great that she could not move. . . ." And then follows the "said" with the long prayer, as given in the MSS.[1] Stigmatization is thus attributed, but in two degrees and of two kinds. "Spiritual Stigmata," like St. Paul, who had them "through the great love and desire which he felt within himself for his Lord": this is the conception of the writer of the first paragraph, doubtless Battista Vernazza. "Stigmata impressed within her body," intense interior physical pain, proved to be such by the intense interior physical heat, and this heat proved by the insides of Catherine's hands causing cold water to boil: this was no doubt Argentina's view—at least as time went on. And note the interesting combination of both views effected by the Redactor in the clauses "the spiritual stigmata were impressed in her body," "through the Passion which she felt," and "she bore the stigmata interiorly."

V. Age and Authorship of the Literature Retained.

The next points to consider, in detail, are the authorship and antiquity of the literature retained by us.

1. *Indications concerning Ettore Vernazza.*

The indications to be found within the *Vita* begin at pp. 98*c*, 99*a*, where, after six lines concerning "several ecstasies" which occurred in one particular year and which Catherine herself had called "giddiness" (*vertigine*), we are told: "One day that she was talking with a Religious, that Religious said to her: 'Mother, I beg you, for the glory and honour of God, to elect some person who would satisfy your mind, and to narrate to this person the graces which God has granted to you, so that, when you die, these graces may not remain . . . unknown, and the praise and glory due for them to God may not be wanting.' And then this Soul answered that she was quite willing (*ben contenta*), if this were pleasing

[1] Pr. *Vita*, pp. 155*b*, *c*, 156*a*.

to her tender Love; and that, in that case, she would elect no other person than himself." "And then, speaking on another occasion with the said Religious, she began to narrate to him her Conversion. And she acted similarly later on, as well as she could, with regard to many other things, which have been faithfully collected and put into the present book" (*Vita*, pp. 98*c*, 99*a*). The Preface, we know, mentions "two Religious, her devotees, her Confessor and a Spiritual son of hers, by whom the (matter of the) book has been collected from the very lips of the Seraphic Woman herself" (*Vita*, p. viii*c*): and we know, beyond all cavil, that these two men were Cattaneo Marabotto, the Priest, and Ettore Vernazza, the Lawyer. The passage just given, *Vita*, pp. 98*c*, 99*a*, unmistakably refers to one of these two; and the address of "Mother," and the answer of "Son," which occurs here immediately after the words translated (p. 99*b*), fit only Vernazza.

Now the opening words of the first two, closely interconnected, paragraphs of that Chapter XXXVIII (*Vita*, p. 98*a*, *b*) are: "In the year 1507"; the first words of the next two paragraphs, which also belong together, are: "It happened in a certain year." The subjects and sequences of those two sets correspond pretty closely; and the second set is in simple juxtaposition to the first set. Yet the sets differ: the first contains a definite date but no allusion to any interlocutor, and Catherine moves about and overcomes her scruples by intercourse with God alone; the second is without a date but refers repeatedly to a witness, and Catherine is physically quiescent and solicits spiritual help from a disciple. Each set is, in its own way, equally vivid and peculiar: they can hardly be doublet narratives of the same event.—The second set, then, gives a later stage of her health and dispositions; and the "ecstasies," "giddinesses," which left her "half dead," must refer to the "assault" of November 11, 1509, which left many other, similarly deep, impressions and definite records. The penultimate paragraph of the Printed *Vita* (p. 165*c*) reads in the MSS.: "Now those who saw and observed these wonderful operations *during fifteen years;*" and this (since Marabotto did not become Catherine's Confessor nor presumably know her, at least intimately, till 1499) must refer specially to Vernazza. Thus 1495 marks the beginning of Vernazza's intimacy with Catherine; in 1497 he could ask Catherine to stand Godmother to his first child; and the *Vita* gives, pp. 122*c*, 123*a*, "what she said after her husband's death," hence in the autumn of 1497, "to a spiritual son of hers," who is certainly Vernazza, "concerning the character of Messer Giuliano."—The conversation of November 1509 is, then, not the starting-point of Vernazza's observations, or even of his registrations, but only the date from when Catherine began deliberately to tell him about her past history.—All this gives us the following canon: whatever in the *Vita* is attributable to Vernazza can, if its subject-matter is posterior to 1495, have been observed and written down by him, then and there, as it occurred; if its subject-matter is prior to 1495, then we have what, at best, is derived from Catherine's memory and communication to him. And there exists no earlier trained and reliable witness of Catherine's spiritual dispositions and sayings than Vernazza from this date onwards.

Two beautiful scenes and declarations have undoubtedly been directly witnessed and contemporaneously chronicled by Vernazza,—the conversation about Love and Hell, with Ettore as the chief interlocutor after Catherine herself (*Vita*, pp. 94*b*–95*c*), between July 1495 and 1502; and the Scene with the Friar, which it is best to put back to the end of 1495 or the beginning of 1496, since it is more natural to take her words, "if the world or a husband," as referring to a still living husband.—We can also, I think, attribute to the same intermediary the authentic central part of the analogous discourse as to "that corrupt expression: you have offended God," Chapter XXXIX, pp. 100*c*–101*b*.—And it is Ettore again through whom, doubtless, we derive all but everything that is authentic in the *Dicchiarazione*, as we have already found.

Vernazza's contributions to the second category, *i. e.* reminiscences of Catherine brought to paper by him, are also very important and more numerous; but they are, I think, generally worked up with parallel accounts due to Marabotto, as we shall presently note.

2. *Indications of Marabotto.*

The *locus classicus* concerning Don Cattaneo appears in the *Vita* in Chapter XLIV, p. 117*b*, of which long and most important Chapter (pp. 116*c*–121*b*) only the first seven lines occur in the MSS. The passage (omitting a highly glossed bracketed clause and a parallel, secondary half-sentence) runs: "After this, ( ), the Lord gave her a Priest (*Prete*) to have a care of her soul and body. [ ] He was elected Rector of the Hospital in which she abode, and he was wont to hear her

Confessions, to say Mass for her, and to give her Communion, as often as she liked. This Priest (*Sacerdote*), at the request of various spiritual persons devoted to this Beata, has written a considerable part (*buona parte*) of this work, having many times tempted her on and incited her to tell him of the singular graces which God had given her and had effected within her [; especially since (*massime che*) this Religious, owing to long experience and intercourse, knew and understood particularly well (*molto bene*) the sequence of her life]."

This introductory authentication is followed by the highly reliable and important matters described in my Chapter IV,—her manner of Confession; the incident of the perfume from Marabotto's hand; her solemn declaration as to her twenty-five years of complete interior loneliness with God; and the murmurs of some of her friends as to the closeness of their intimacy, and his consequent absence from her for three days. All this (pp. 117*b*–121*b*) was certainly written down by Marabotto himself, at the time, in substantially its present form.

Although this whole series now opens out with " la prima volta che si volle confessare a questo Religioso " (p. 117*c*), the words " a questo Religioso " are doubtless an addition of the Redactor. For everywhere else Marabotto is always " il Confessore " or " suo Confessore," whilst " un Religioso " is reserved for Vernazza: and wherever she uses any specific appellation to the Confessore,—a thing which is quite exceptional,—she says " Padre "; whilst where she does so to the Religioso, she says "Figliuolo."[1] And, wherever the Confessore addresses her, there is never any specific address; whereas the Religioso constantly addresses her as " Madre."[2]

As to " Confessore," we get one mentioned as Confessor to the Convent of S. Maria delle Grazie in 1460, p. 2*b*; the same or another Confessor of the same Convent in 1473, p. 4*a*, *c*, is called " buon Religioso." Both these men, or this one man, heard Catherine's Confessions at those dates. But, a most important point: all the other Confessore-passages throughout the book refer to after 1499, and to Marabotto alone. For this is a list of them all. On p. 7*c*: here she is " so gravely ill, as to be unable to eat," a thing belonging to the times after 1499. (In events of an obviously earlier date, —her fervent Communions,—pp. 8*a*, *c*, we get not "Confessore"

[1] *Padre*: pp. 117*b*, 118*b*; *Figliuolo*, pp. 99*b*; 94*b*, *c*, 95*a*, *b*; 122*c*.
[2] *Madre*, pp. 98*c*; 94*b*, *c*, 95*a*, *b* (twice).

but simply "Sacerdote.") On p. 10*c*: here "to test her, he commanded her to eat;" but the results of the eating are described on pp. 117*b*, 119*c*. On page 108*b*: but here her fasting is liable to damage her health, which points to after 1501. On p. 113*b*: but here the Confessore remains her sole aid, as in the accounts referring to Marabotto in January 1510 and shortly before, pp. 120*a*, 121*b*; 120*b*, 139*a–c*. On p. 115*b*: but here the possessed "spiritual daughter" is certainly Mariola Bastarda, who did not live with Catherine till after Giuliano's death in 1497. On pp. 117*b*–121*b*: the Confessore is throughout avowedly Marabotto, and a treble indication here forces us to date his Confessorship from not before 1499. The remaining "Confessore"-references,—pp. 130*a*, 138*c*, 139*a*, *b*, *c*; 140*b*, *c*; 143*c*, 156*c*, 157*b*,—are all explicitly subsequent to 1501 and pertinent to Marabotto alone.

Now there is no good reason for doubting Marabotto's original, and still largely unmodified, authorship of all the above passages in which he himself occurs. Only as to the scene with the possessed Mariola, Chapter XLIII, pp. 115*a–c*, have I long hesitated to attribute something so insignificant in substance, and yet so pompous in form, to Marabotto, either as action or as composition. Yet I have ended, for the reasons given on page 162, by thinking that, after all, this scene does go back, more or less, to him.

3. *References to other witnesses.*

There are but few other references to witnesses in the *Vita*. On p. 124*a*, in the account of Suor Tommasa Fiesca, there are "the Nuns of her first and second Monastery"—San Silvestro and the Monastero Nuovo,—and "secular persons, her familiar and devoted friends." I take this admirably vivid and *naïf* account, pp. 123*b*–124*b* (which exists in the MSS. without this sentence and Tommasa's death-date, 1534), to rest upon Suor Tommasa's own reminiscences of her heaven-storming cousin, but to be the composition of Battista Vernazza.—And on p. 158*c* "several of the ten Physicians," who assembled by Catherine's bedside on September 10, 1510, "are still alive in this year (1551)," but the very vague account of their examination is no doubt due to a non-medical pen.

VI. Analysis of the Conversion-Narratives.

Let us now take the first of the four Narrative Passages in which the largest or clearest conflations of original documents and of subsequent glosses are traceable : the Conversion-Scene and subsequent Apparition, March 1473; the "Scintilla"-Experience, November 11, 1509; the Temptation of August 23, 1510; and her Death on September 14, 1510. Roman and Arabic numerals indicate the probable provenances from different contributors, and from different narratives of each contributor, respectively; square brackets indicate glosses; and E, C, and B stand respectively for the handiwork of Ettore Vernazza, of Cattaneo Marabotto, and of Battista Vernazza.

The Two Conversion-Scenes, pp. 4*a*–5*c*.

(*a*) *In the Chapel.*

I. 1. Il giorno dopo la Festa di San Benedetto [ad istanza di sua sorella monaca] andò Caterina [per confessarsi d'] al Confessore di esso Monistero, benche non fosse disposta a confessarsi : ma la sorella le disse, "almanco vattegli a raccommandare, perchè è buon religioso"; ed, in verità era un uomo santo. 2. Subitochè se gli fù inginocchiata innanzi, ricevè una ferita al cuore d'immenso amore di Dio, con una vista così chiara delle sue miserie e diffetti e della bonta di Dio, che nè fù quasi per cascare in terra.

II. 1. Onde per quei sentimenti d'immenso amore e delle offese fatte al suo dolce Iddio, fù talmente tirata [per affetto purgato] fuor delle miserie del mondo, che restò quasi fuor di sè; I. 3. e [perciò] internamente gridava con ardente amore : "non più mondo, non più peccati." Ed in quel punto, se ella avesse avuto mille mondi, tutti gli avrebbe gettati via.

III. Per la viva fiamma del infocato amore che essa sentiva, il dolce Iddio impresse in quell' anima, e le infuse, in un subito, tutta la perfezione per grazia : onde la purgò di tutti gli affetti terreni, la illuminò col suo divin lume, facendola vedere coll' occhio interiore la sua dolce bontà, e finalmente in tutto la unì, mutò e trasformò in sè, per vera unione di buona volontà, accendendola da ogni parte col suo vivo amore.

[Stando la Santa per quella dolce ferita quasi alienata da' sensi innanzi al confessore e senza poter parlare.]

I. 4. Nè avvedendosi il Confessore del fatto, per caso fù chiamato e levasi. Dappoichè assai presto fù retornato, non potendo ella appena parlare per l'intrinseco dolore ed immenso amore, allo meglio che potè gli disse : " Padre, se vi piacesse, lascerei volontieri questa Confessione per un' altra volta " : e così fù fatto. 5. Si parti dunque Caterina e retornata a casa [si sentì così accesa e ferita di tanto amor di Dio, a lei interiormente mostrato colla vista delle sue miserie, che pareva fuors di sè] ed entrata in una camera la piu segreta che potè, ivi molto pianse [e sospirò con gran fuoco].

[In quel punto fù istrutta intrinsecamente dell' orazione, ma la sua lingua] I. 6, non poteva dir altro salvo questo : " O Amore, può essere che mi abbi chiamata [con tanto amore] e fattomi conoscere in un punto quello che colla lingua non posso esprimere? II. 2. Le sue parole in tutti quei giorni altro non erano che sospiri, e così grandi che era cosa mirabile : ed aveva una si estrema contrizione [di cuore] per le offese fatte a tanta bontà, che se non fosse stata miracolosamente sostenuta, sarebbe spirata e crepatole il cuore.

(*b*) *In the Palace.*

I. 7. (?) [Ma volendo] il Signore [accendere più intrinsecamente l'amor suo in quest' anima ed insieme il dolore dei suoi peccati,] se le mostrò in ispirito colla Croce in spalla, piovendo tutto sangue, [per modo che la casa le pareva tutta piena di rivoli di quel sangue,] il quale vedea essere tutto sparso per amore : il che le accese nel cuore tanto fuoco, che nè usciva fuor di sè [e pareva una cosa insensata per lo tanto amore e dolore che ne sentiva.]

II. 3. (?) [Questa vista le fu tanto penetrativa, che] le pareva sempre vedere (e cogli occhi corporali) il suo Amore tutto insanguinato e confitto in Croce ; e perciò gridava : " O Amore, mai più, mai più peccati." I. 8 (?) Se le accese poi un odio di sè medesima, che non si poteva sopportare, e diceva : " O Amore, se bisogna, sono apparechiata di confessare i miei peccati in pubblico."

I. 9. Dopo questo fece la sua [generale] Confessione con tanta contrizione e tali stimoli, che le passavano l'anima [. E benchè] Iddio [in quel punto che le diede la dolce ed amorosa ferita, le avesse perdonato tutti i suoi peccati, abbruciandoli col fuoco del suo immenso amore ; nondimeno volendo soddisfare alla giustizia, la fece passare per la via della soddisfazione] disponendo che questa contrizione [lume e conversione] durasse [ro] circa quatt*ro* [dici] *anni*, in capo a quali [, poichè ella ebbe soddisfatto, le fù levata della mente la predetta vista in forma tale che] mai più non vide neppure una minima scintilla dei suoi peccati, come se tutti fossero stati gettati nel profondo del mare.

There is a striking parallelism of sights, sayings, and their sequences, between the dated events in the Convent-Chapel, and the undated ones in the Palace, divided off by the passage II 2, with its vague "all these days." Both sets have a "Vista," —partly of "offese fatte"; have next "and hence she cried 'no more sin'"; and the first concludes with a wish, expressed to the Confessor, to put off her Confession, and the second with an exclamation, addressed to God, of her readiness for even a public Confession.—This Christ-Vision, or any other Passion-scene, is nowhere implied or referred to in all her recorded post-Conversion sayings and doings; the legendary instinct, we know, developed, from this single adult occupation with the Passion, the "interior stigmatization" story; and in the Palace Narrative itself there has been, in any case, *some* uncertainty, shifting, or doubling of the tradition as to that figured vision,—for the actual vision cannot have represented Christ both as walking and carrying His Cross, *and* as motionless and hanging upon it. Are the two sets, then, but two variant records of one sole event, and is the second but the result of an early determination to find more of an historical, pictorial element in Catherine's spiritual experiences than had actually been present in it?

Yet strong reasons operate on the other side. We have one, and only one, absolutely certain detail from her childhood, the presence, in her bedroom, of a Pietà (*Vita*, pp. 1*c*, 2*a*); yet nowhere, in her subsequent actions and sayings, is there the slightest allusion to this picture-scene which had so deeply moved her childhood.—And the most vivid and characteristic details of the two Conversion-experiences are delicately different in each set.

The first set, (*a*), consists of three documents. Document I 1, 2; 3; 4–6 continues the story of Catherine's relations with the "monistero" of the Madonna delle Grazie, and of her prayer on the eve of St. Benedict's day, told on pp. 2*b*–3*c*; is most vivid, precise, and homely; and is doubtless the work of E. Document II 1, 2 is a colourless parallel to I 2, 6; yet in I 2 she sees her own miseries, in II 1 she is drawn out of the miseries of the world: II is thus probably an ancient doublet, and, if so, then part of some annotations by C.

And document III is obviously from yet another, later, hand, —that which produced the originally tripartite scheme of Catherine's Convert life (pp. 5*c*–6*c*), for the three " la " (her, Catherine) after " onde " of III require but three stages of perfecting; whilst now the printed text attempts (by italicizing " unì " and " transformò ") to produce four stages, in keeping with the following, now quadripartite scheme.

The second set, (*b*), begins as though nothing had yet happened or as if, at least, the past event had been but a step towards something greater. Yet precisely such series of apparent anti-climaxes occur demonstrably elsewhere in her life.—The account of II 3 (?) is irreconcilably different from that of I 7 (?): for there Christ is moving, carrying His Cross and raining blood upon objects not Himself, here He is motionless, probably dead, affixed to the Cross, and His blood has merely stained His own body; there she sees " in the spirit," here " with bodily eyes "; there, for some minutes, here continuously; there, followed by speechless ecstasy, here, by penitential exclamations. And this II 3 (?) is not a later stage of the vision given in I 7 (?), as though, dissolving-view-like, the Moving Christ had shaded off into a Fixed Christ, (although Catherine's Viste give us such changes, *e. g.* that of the Divine Fountain's successive self-communications, *Vita*, pp. 32*c*, 33*a*). For the very Redactor treats the second " Vista " as simply identical with the first; and Battista, we saw, so entirely realizes the contradiction between the two accounts, as to make two quite distinct events out of them (*Dialogo*, pp. 209*b*, 211*a*, *b*).—This second account can hardly be a gloss, for Battista already found and respected it when at work on the Giustiniani-book of 1529 or 1530, and was thus powerfully influenced by it when composing her *Dialogo* in about 1547. Indeed, this II 3 (?) has been the starting-point of all the stigmatization-glosses elsewhere, and can hardly be a gloss itself.—If all this be so, then either Catherine herself told the Christ-Vision to one disciple in two different ways; or told it to two companions, to each in a different way; or told the story so vaguely, or with such rich vividness and ambiguity, as to be differently understood by these two different hearers. Only one of the two latter alternatives would cover the facts, since no one writer could remain unaware of the contradiction between these two accounts. Hence we here require two writers, both considerably prior to Battista and much respected by her; only E and G answer to these tests; and, in that case, the Living Christ, seen in the Spirit, comes to us through E, and the Dead Christ, seen with the bodily eyes, reaches us through C.—And then comes I 8, of clearly first-hand authority, and belonging, I think, to E's account.

I 9, concluding the *Vita's* Conversion-story, must evidently contain some words, originally belonging to document I, concerning her Confession, since I has already twice (I 4, I 8) referred to such a coming Confession. And such words are here: "Dopo questo—l'anima"; "Iddio disponendo-circa quattro *anni*" (this is the original text here); and a vivid description of her suddenly ceasing to see her particular sins.

VII. The Sayings-Passages: Three Tests for Discriminating Authentic from Secondary Sayings.

As to the Sayings, it is obviously more difficult to decide as to their provenance, authenticity, and date of enunciation and literary fixation. Yet three tests have proved solidly helpful towards gaining a respectably large collection of texts which can, with high historical probability or even certainty, be reasoned from as truly Catherine's, even in their form.

1. *Rhythm.*

There is the test of rhythm and rhyme, since the *Vita* describes her "wont" of "making rhymed sayings in her joy," and gives irrefragable proofs of her deep love of Jacopone's poetry.[1] The still obviously rhymed or rhythmical sayings all answer to the other tests of genuineness; and many sayings now turned, by successive Redactors, into more or less sheer prose, can still be restored to their original poetic form. All these rhythmic, rhymed sayings have an utterly *naïf*, expansive tone, markedly different from the high-pitched redactional rhetoric in which they are now embedded, or again from Battista's far more literary poetry: hence they cannot spring from this strong and busy intellect.—Thus she hears her Love say: "Chi di Mè | si fida, || di sè | non dubita"; possibly simply quoting, she says to her soul, "ama chi t'ama, | e chi non t'ama lascia"; and she sums up her life's ideal as, "s'io mangio o bevo, | s'io [ ] taccio o parlo, | dormo o veglio; | s'io son in chiesa, in casa, in piazza: | s'io son inferma | o sana: |

[1] *Vita*, pp. 50*b*, 37*a*–38*a*; 61*c*, 62*a*; 83*a*; 92*a*.

s'io muojo o non muojo : || ogni ora di vita mia, | tutto voglio che sia, | Dio e prossimo : || non vorrei potere ne volere, | fare, parlare nè pensare | eccetto tutto Dio.||[1]—And there are her repetitive utterances, beginning with " non più mondo, non più peccati," on March 22, 1473, and finishing with " andiàmo, non più terra, non più terra," of August 25, 1510.[2]

2. *Simplicity.*

The second test requires the sayings to be short and simple, and to be followed, in the present text, by carefully clausulated doublets, or to be themselves now glossed and expanded. Such sayings occur specially in Chapters I to VIII; XVIII and XIX; XXVII to XXIX; XXXVI to XXXVIII; XLIV to XLVI; and in Chapter L. All these Chapters are largely narrative; can in great part be traced to Vernazza or Marabotto; and yield sayings readily attributable to her first Conversion-Period (which she doubtless recounted to those Friends), or to 1495–1510, the years of her intercourse with those intimates.

3. *Originality.*

And the third test consists of a daring originality, which, often softened and counteracted by the successive Redactors, precludes all idea that sayings expressive of it may proceed from any one of less authority than herself. These sayings again are all short; they too occur, all but exclusively, in the Chapters indicated and in the *Dicchiarazione ;* they are all referable to the years 1495–1510, and to the registration first of Vernazza, and, later on, of Marabotto.

Very few of the sayings grouped together by me in my Chapter VI but satisfy at least two of these three tests.

VIII. Conclusion. At least Six Stages in the up-building of the Complete Book of 1551. The Slight Changes introduced since then. First claims to Authorship for Catherine.

1. *The Stages.*

It would appear, then, from the preceding analyses, that the successive stages in the composition and redaction of the *Vita-Dicchiarazione* complex of documents cannot have been fewer than the following :—

[1] *Vita*, pp. 53*a*, 76*c*, 73*a*. [2] *Vita*, pp. 4*b*, 151*b*.

(i) Description and Registration, (1) first by Vernazza (1495–1510), (2) then also by Marabotto (1499–1510), more or less on the day of their occurrence and utterance, of Catherine's actions, psycho-physical condition, and sayings expressive of her present spiritual experiences; and of her deliberate reminiscences concerning her past, especially her early Convert life. And similar contemporary Annotations, of much lesser volume, by (3) Suor Tommasa Fiesca, (4) Maestro Boerio, and (5) Don Giacomo Carenzio—the latter two, only since May 1510.

(ii) Redaction, probably in connection with the first public Cultus in the summer or autumn of 1512, of (1) a short *Conversione*-booklet, by Vernazza, perhaps already with slight contributions by Marabotto; (2) a short *Dicchiarazione*-booklet, also by Vernazza, probably as yet without the theological "corrections"; and (3) a short Passion-account, by Marabotto, with additions by Carenzio and, in substance, contributions by Argentina.

(iii) Redaction, after the death of the last of the two chief friends (Marabotto, in 1528), by Battista Vernazza, in 1529 or 1530, of a tripartite *Vita,* made up chiefly of II (1) and II (3), and a longer *Dicchiarazione,* now with the theological glosses, —these latter presumably from the pen of Fra Gaspar Toleto, O.P., the Inquisitor for the Republic of Genoa, or his successor, Fra Geronimo da Genova.

(iv) Partial change of the tripartite scheme of the *Vita-Dottrina* to a quadripartite one, early in 1548.

(v) Composition by Battista Vernazza of (1) the *Dialogo,* "Chapter" I alone, 1549; and then (2) of "Chapter" II (the present Parts II and III), in 1550.

(vi) Final Redaction of the text of the Printed *Vita-Dicchiarazione-Dialogo,* by means of all the preceding Documents, of which I (4) and possibly the Confession-descriptions of I (2) are now incorporated in the complete *Vita* for the first time; and, with the help of gossipy reminiscences of Argentina, possibly only now reduced to writing—in 1550, 1551. This final Redactor would again be Battista Vernazza.

2. *The Changes.*

Now from 1551 onwards this whole *corpus* has remained stationary, with the exception of purely formal modifications, such as one synonym for another; of, since 1737, her designation, on the title-page and in some other places as "Santa

Caterina da Genova," and, throughout the text, as "Caterina" (only the Ancient Preface still retains the strictly correct "Caterinetta," *Vita*, p. viii); and of two other, more important changes.

The first important change is the insertion (later than the fourth edition, Venice, 1601) at her death-moment,—between "e in quel punto" (after raising her forefinger heavenwards) "quest' anima beata" and "con una gran pace . . . spirò,"—of the words: "dicendo: In manus tuas commendo spiritum meum." This, intrinsically appropriate, last saying prevented henceforth her final, directly recorded, words from being something so little beautiful or characteristic as the "cacciate via questa bestia" with which all the MSS., and all the editions till at least 1601, had the fine courage to conclude the series of her sayings.

And the second change is a modification in the titles of the Book and of its several parts, of significance as indicating the growth of the legend attributing literary composition to her. The First Printed Edition (1551) has: "Book of the admirable Life and holy Doctrine of the Blessed Caterinetta of Genoa, in which is contained a useful and Catholic Demonstration and Declaration" (Elucidation) "of Purgatory"; and in the body of the Book this "Demonstrazione" appears as *Trattato del Purgatorio*, after the *Vita*-proper. But though the complete *Dialogo* appears here, behind the *Trattato* and divided into two "Chapters," no mention is made of it on the title-page.—The Second Edition, Florence, 1568, adds to the title: "with a Dialogue between the Soul and the Body, composed by the same," thus attributing, apparently, full literary authorship by Catherine to precisely that document with which she has least of all to do.—The Fourth Edition, Venice, 1601, simply adds, after "Dialogue," "divided into two Chapters"; and the Fifth, 1615, modifies this to "three Chapters, between the Soul, (and) the Body; Humanity, (and) Self-love; the Spirit and the Lord God, composed by the Beata herself."

The first French translation, Paris, 1598, puts the *Dialogue* before the *Treatise*, and still attributes Catherine's direct authorship to the *Dialogue* alone. But the first Latin translation, Freiburg im Breisgau, 1626, has "Life and Doctrine of Blessed Catherine Adorna . . . (and) the two excellent Treatises of the same: 1. Dialogue between the Soul and the Body; 2. Concerning Purgatory." Here both works are attributed to her, in exactly the same degree; but that degree is not clearly specified.[1]

I do not know how soon after the Sixth Edition, Naples, 1645, which is still without it, the quite unambiguous title of the Thirteenth Edition, Genoa, of about 1880: "Vita ed Opere di S. Caterina da Genova," was adopted, nor how soon the present Second Title-page to the *Trattato* and *Dialogo*—"Works of St. Catherine"—was inserted. Yet even here the old correct name for the whole Book still appears as the heading on p. 1: *Vita e Dottrina*, although now, owing to that Second Title-page, "Doctrine" only covers the Doctrinal Chapters of the *Vita*-proper.

Thus not till 1568 was anything claimed as a composition of Catherine's pen, and then only the *Dialogue;* and not till 1626 was the *Treatise* put into the same category as the *Dialogue*. Pope Clement XII, in his Bull of Canonization in 1737, declares the *Dialogue* to be her composition, whilst nothing is said concerning the *Treatise*, although the Bull itself most wisely follows the account of the *Vita*-proper, and softens down or ignores the different version of the *Dialogue*, in the two crucial cases of Catherine's Vision of the Bleeding Christ and of the degree of her poverty.[2]

[1] I derive all these titles from the Documents in the Curia Arcivescovile of Genoa already referred to. The Editions 1568, 1601, I have examined in the Ambrosian Library, Milan.

[2] The Bull is given in full by Fr. Sticker: *Acta Sanctorum*, Sept., Vol. V, ed. 1866, pp. 181 F–188 A. See there, p. 183 B, E. In the former passage the two descriptions are rightly attributed to the same event; and the contradiction between them is ably eliminated by the Bull's words: "She seemed to herself to behold the image of the suffering Saviour" (instead of *Vita*, p. 5*b*, "affixed to the Cross"); and, in the latter passage, the description of her poverty is kept free from the extravagances of the *Dialogo*, pp. 220*c*, 221*c*.

END OF VOL. I

VOLUME SECOND

CRITICAL STUDIES

PART III
CRITICAL

THE MYSTICAL ELEMENT OF RELIGION

CHAPTER IX

PSYCHO-PHYSICAL AND TEMPERAMENTAL QUESTIONS

INTRODUCTORY.

1. *Plan of Part Three.*

The picture of Catherine's life and teaching which was attempted in the previous volume will, I hope, have been sufficiently vivid to stimulate in the reader a desire to try and go deeper, and to get as near as may be to the driving forces, the metaphysical depths of her life. And yet it is obvious that, if we would understand something of these, we must proceed slowly and thoroughly, and must begin with comparatively superficial questions. Or rather, we must begin by studying her temperamental and psycho-physical endowment and condition, and then the literary influences that stimulated and helped to mould these things, as though all this were *not* secondary and but the material and occasion of the forces and self-determinations to be considered later on.

2. *Defects of ancient psycho-physical theory.*

Now as to those temperamental and neural matters, to which this chapter shall be devoted, the reader will, no doubt long ago, have discovered that it is precisely here that not a little of the *Vita e Dottrina* is faded and withered beyond recall, or has even become positively repulsive to us. The constant assumption, and frequent explicit insistence, on the part of more or less all the contributors, upon the immediate and separate significance, indeed the directly miraculous character, of certain psycho-physical states—states which, taken thus separately, would now be inevitably classed as most explicable neural abnormalities,—all this atmosphere of nervous high-pitch and tremulousness has now become a matter demanding a difficult historical imagination and magnanimity, if we would be just to those who held such views, and would thus benefit to the full from these past positions and misconceptions.

Thus when we read the views of perhaps all her educated attendants: "this condition, in which her body remained alive without food or medicine, was a supernatural thing"; "her state was clearly understood to be supernatural when, in so short a time, so great a change was seen"; and "she became yellow all over,—a manifest sign that her humanity was being entirely consumed in the fire of divine love": [1] we feel indeed that we can no more follow. And when we read, as part of one of the late additions, the worthless legends gathered from, or occasioned by, the uneducated Argentina: "in proof that she bore the stigmata within her,—on putting her hands in a cup of cold water, the latter became so boiling hot that it greatly heated the very saucer beneath it": [2] we are necessarily disgusted. And when, worst of all, she is made, by a demonstrable, probable double misinterpretation of an externally similar action, to burn her bare arm with a live charcoal or lighted candle, with intent to see which fire, this external one or that interior one of the divine love, were the greater: [3] we can, even if we have the good fortune of being able, by means of the critical analysis of the sources, to put this absurd story to the discredit of her eulogists, but feel the pathos of such well-meant perversity, which took so sure a way for rendering ridiculous one who, take her all in all, is so truly great.[4]

3. *Slow growth of Neurology.*

We should, of course, be very patient in such matters: for psycho-physical knowledge was, as yet, in its very infancy, witness the all-important fact that the nerves were, in our modern sense of the term, still as unknown as they were to the whole of Græco-Roman antiquity, with which "neuron" and "nervus" ever meant "muscle" or "ligament" and, deriva-

[1] *Vita*, pp. 143*b*; 149*b*, 159*b*; 153*a*. [2] *Ibid.* p. 153*c*.

[3] *Ibid.* pp. 129*c*, 134*a*.

[4] I have already traced the steps in the growth of this legend. It is no doubt this element in the biography which irritated John Wesley, the man of absolute judgments; although he himself, with shrewd good sense, indicates its possible secondary origin. "I am sure this was a fool of a Saint; that is, if it was not the folly of her historian, who has aggrandized her into a mere idiot" (*Journal*, ed. P. L. Parker, London, 1903).

tively, " energy," but never consciously what they now mean in the strict medical sense. Thus the *Vita* (1551) writes: " There remained no member or muscle (*nervo*) of her body that was not tormented by fire within it "; " one rib was separated from the others, with great pains in the ligaments (*nervi*) and bones "; and " all her body was excruciated and her muscles (*nervi*) were tormented": [1] where, in the first and last case, visible muscular convulsive movements are clearly meant. St. Teresa, in her own *Life* (1561 or 1562), writes: " Nervous pains, according to the physicians, are intolerable; and all my nerves were shrunk "; and " if the rapture lasts, all the nerves are made to feel it." [2] Even Fénelon (died 1715) can still write of the human body: " The bones sustain the flesh which envelops them; the nerves " (ligaments, minor muscles) " which are stretched along them, constitute all their strength; and the muscles, by inflation and elongation at the points where the nerves are intertwined with them, produce the most precise and regular movements." [3] Here the soul acts directly upon the muscles, and, through these and their dependent ligaments, upon the bones and the flesh.

4. *Permanent values of the ancient theory.*

And yet that old position with regard to the rarer psycho-physical states has a right to our respectful and sympathetic study.

For one thing, we are now coming again to recognize, more and more, how real and remarkable are certain psycho-physical states and facts, whether simply morbid or fruitfully utilized states, so long derided, by the bulk of Scientists, as mere childish legend or deliberate imposture; and to see how natural, indeed inevitable it was, that these, at that time quite inexplicable, things should have been attributed to a direct and discontinuous kind of Divine intervention. We, on our part, have then to guard against the Philistinism both of the Rationalists and of the older Supernaturalists, and will neither measure our assent to facts by our ability to explain them, nor postulate the unmediated action of God wherever our powers of explanation fail us. On this point we have admirable models of sympathetic docility towards facts, in the works of Prof. Pierre Janet, in his medico-psychological

[1] *Vita*, pp. 127*c*, 143*b*, 144*b*.
[2] *Life*, tr. by D. Lewis, London, ed. 1888, pp. 27, 420.
[3] *Existence de Dieu*, I, 1, 31: *Œuvres*, ed. Versailles, 1820, Vol. I, p. 51.

investigations of present-day morbid cases; of Hermann Gunkel and Heinrich Weinel, in their examination of mostly healthy psycho-physical phenomena in early Christian times and writings; and of William James, in his study of instances of various kinds, both past and present.[1]

And next, these (at first sight physical) phenomena are turning out, more and more, to be the direct or indirect consequence of the action of mind: no doubt, in the first instance, of the human mind, but still of mind, both free-willing and automatically operative. And at the same time this action is, more and more, seen to be limited and variously occasioned by the physical organism, and to be accompanied or followed, in a determinist fashion, by certain changes in that organism. Yet if we have now immeasurably more knowledge than men had, even fifty years ago, of this latter ceaselessly active, limiting, occasioning influence of the body upon the mind, we have also immeasurably more precise and numerous facts and knowledge in testimony of the all but boundless effect of mind over body. Here, again, Prof. Janet's writings, those of Alfred Binet, and the Dominican Père Coconnier's very sensible book register a mass of material, although of the morbid type.[2]

And further, such remarkable peripheral states and phenomena are getting again to be rightly looked for in at least some types of unusual spiritual insight and power (although such states are found to be indicative, in exact proportion to the spiritual greatness of their subject, of a substantially different mental and moral condition of soul). Witness again the Unitarian Prof. James's *Varieties*, and the Church-Historical works of the Broad Lutheran German scholars Weinel, Bernouilli, and Duhm.[3]

And lastly, the very closeness with which modern experimental and analytical psychology is exploring the phenomena

[1] Pierre Janet, *Automatisme Psychologique*, ed. 1903; *Etat Mental des Hystériques*, 2 vols., 1892, 1893. Hermann Gunkel, *Die Wirkungen des heiligen Geistes*, Göttingen, 1899. Heinrich Weinel, *Die Wirkungen des Geistes und der Geister*, Freiburg, 1899. William James, *The Varieties of Religious Experience*, London, 1902.

[2] Pierre Janet, *op. cit.* Alfred Binet, *Les Altérations de la Personnalité*, Paris, 1902. M. Th. Coconnier, *L'Hypnotisme Franc*, Paris, 1897.

[3] W. James, *op. cit.*, especially pp. 1–25. H. Weinel, *op. cit.*, especially pp. 128–137; 161–208. Bernouilli, *Die Heiligen der Merowinger*, Tübingen, 1900, pp. 2–6. B. Duhm, *Das Geheimniss in der Religion*, Tübingen, 1896.

of our consciousness is once more bringing into ever-clearer relief the irrepressible metaphysical apprehensions and affirmations involved and implied by the experience of every human mind, from its first dim apprehension in infancy of a "something," as yet undifferentiated by it into subjective and objective, up to its mature and reflective affirmation of the trans-subjective validity of its "positions," or at least of its negations—pure scepticism turning out to be practically impossible. Here we have, with respect to that apprehension, such admirable workers as Henri Bergson in France, and Professors Henry Jones and James Ward in England; and, for this affirmation, such striking thinkers as the French Maurice Blondel, and the Germans Johannes Volkelt and Hugo Münsterberg. And Mgr. Mercier of Louvain, now Cardinal Mercier, has contributed some valuable criticism of certain points in these positions.[1]

5. *Difficulties of this inquiry.*

Now here I am met at once by two special difficulties, the one personal to myself and to Catherine, and the other one of method. For, with regard to those three first sets of recent explorations of a psycho-physical kind, I am no physician at all, and not primarily a psychologist. And again, in Catherine's instance, the evidence as to her psycho-physical states is not, as with St. Teresa and some few other cases, furnished by writings from the pen of the very person who experienced them, and it is at all copious and precise only for the period when she was admittedly ill and physically incapacitated.—And yet these last thirteen years of her life occupy a most prominent place in her biography; it is during, and on occasion of, those psycho-physical states, and largely with the materials furnished by them, that, precisely in those years, she built up her noblest legacy, her great Purgatorial teaching; the illness was (quite evidently) of a predominantly psychical type, and concerns more the psychologist than the physician, being closely connected with her particular temperament and type of spirituality, a temperament and type to be found again and again among the Saints. All this

[1] H. Bergson, *Essai sur les Données Immédiates de la Conscience*, ed. 1898. H. Jones, *The Philosophy of Lotze*, 1895. J. Ward, *Naturalism and Agnosticism*, 2 vols., 1899. M. Blondel, *l'Action*, 1893. J. Volkelt, *Kant's Erkenntnisstheorie*, 1879; *Erfahrung und Denken*, 1886. H. Münsterberg, *Psychology and Life*, 1899. D. Mercier, *Critériologie Générale*, ed. 1900.

and more makes it simply impossible for me to shrink from some study of the matter, and permits me to hope for some success in attempting, slowly and cautiously, to arrive at certain general conclusions of a spiritually important kind.

But then there is also the difficulty of method. For if we begin the study of these psycho-physical peculiarities and states by judging them from the temperamental and psychological standpoint, we can hardly escape from treating them, at least for the moment, as self-explanatory, and hence from using these our preliminary conclusions about such neural phenonema as the measure, type, and explanation of and for all such other facts and apprehensions as our further study of the religious mind and experience may bring before us. In this wise, these our psychological conclusions would furnish not only a negative test and positive material, but also the exclusive standard for all further study. And such a procedure, until and unless it were justified in its method, would evidently be nothing but a surreptitious begging of the question.—Yet to begin with the fullest analysis of the elementary and normal phenomena of consciousness and of its implications and inviolable prerequisites, would too readily land us in metaphysics which have themselves to operate in and with those immediate and continuous experiences; and hence these latter experiences, whether normal and healthy, or, as here, unusual and in part *maladif*, must be carefully studied first. We have, however, to guard most cautiously against our allowing this, our preliminary, analysis and description of psycho-physical states from imperceptibly blocking the way to, or occupying the ground of, our ultimate analysis and metaphysical synthesis and explanation. Only this latter will be able, by a final outward movement from within, to show the true place and worth of the more or less phenomenal series, passed by us in review on our previous inward movement from without.

6. *Threefold division.*

I propose, then, in this chapter, to take, as separately as is compatible with such a method, the temperamental, psycho-physical side of Catherine's life. I shall first take those last thirteen years of admitted illness, as those which are alone at all fully known to us by contemporary evidence.—I shall then make a jump back to her first period,—to the first sixteen years up to her marriage, with the next ten years of relaxation, and the following four years of her conversion and active penitence. I take these next, because, of these thirty years, we have her own late memories, as registered for us by her disciples, at the time of her narration of the facts concerned.—And only then, with these materials and instruments thus gathered from after and before, shall I try to master the (for us very obscure) middle period, and to arrive at some estimate of her temperamental peripheral condition during these twenty years of her fullest expansion.—I shall conclude the chapter by taking Catherine in her general, lifelong temperament, and by comparing and contrasting this type and modality of spiritual character and apprehension with the other rival forms of, and approaches to, religious truth and goodness as these are furnished for us by history.

The ultimate metaphysical questions and valuation are reserved for the penultimate chapter of my book.

I. Catherine's Third Period, 1497 to 1510.

1. *Increasing illness of Catherine's last years.*

Beginning with her third and last period (1497–1510), there can be no doubt that throughout it she was ill and increasingly so. Her closest friends and observers attest it. It is presumably Ettore Vernazza who tells us, for 1497, " when she was about fifty years of age, she ceased to be able to attend either to the Hospital or to her own house, owing to her great bodily weakness. Even on Fast-days she was obliged, after Holy Communion, to take some food to sustain her strength." Probably Marabotto it is who tells us that, in 1499, " after twenty-five years she could no further bear her spiritual loneliness, either because of old age or because of her great bodily weakness." We hear from a later Redactor that, " about nine years before her death (*i. e.* about 1501), there came to her an infirmity." And then, especially from November 1509, May 1510, and August 1510 onwards, she is declared and described as more and more ill.[1] Indeed she herself, both by her acts and by her words, emphatically admits her incapacitation. For it is clearly ill-health which drives her to abandon the Matronship and even all minor continuous work for the Hospital. In her Wills we find indeed that, as late as

[1] *Vita*, pp. 96*c*; 117*b*; 127*a*; 97*c*, 133*b* (dated November 11, 1509, in MSS.); 146*b*; 148*a*,

May 21, 1506, she was able to get to the neighbouring Hospital for Incurables; and that even on November 27, 1508, she was "healthy in mind and body." But her Codicil of January 5, 1503, was drawn up in the presence of nine witnesses at midnight,—a sure sign of some acute ill-health. Indeed already on July 23, 1484, she is lying "infirm in bed, in her room in the Women's quarter of the Hospital, oppressed with bodily infirmity."[1]

2. *Abnormal sensations, impressions and moods.*

Her attendants are all puzzled by the multitude and intensity, the mobility and the self-contradictory character of the psycho-physical manifestations. Perhaps already before 1497 "she would press thorny rose-twigs in both her hands, and this without any pain"; and so late as about three weeks before her death "she remained paralyzed (*manca*,)" and no doubt anaesthetic "in one (the right) hand and in one finger of the other hand."—Probably again before 1497 "her body could not," at times, "be moved from the sitting posture without the application of force." In February or March 1510 "she could not move out of her bed"; in August "on some occasions she could not move the lips or the tongue, or the arms or legs, unless helped to do so,—especially on the left side,—and this would, at times, last three or four hours."—In December 1509 "she suffered from great cold," as part of her peculiar condition; on September 4, 1510, "she suffered from great cold in the right arm."[2]

On other occasions she is, on the contrary, intensely hyperaesthetic. Some time in February or March 1510, "for a day and a night, her flesh could not be touched, because of the great pain that such touching caused her." At the end of August "she was so sensitive, that it was impossible to touch her very bedclothes or the bedstead, or a single hair on her head, because in such case she would cry out as though she had been grievously wounded."—These states seem to have

[1] From my authenticated copies of the original wills in the Archivio di Stato, Genoa.

[2] *Vita*, pp. 113*b*, 149*c*; 143*b*, 152*c*; 138*b*, 155*a*. Note the parallels in St. Teresa's *Life*, written by herself, tr. D. Lewis, ed. 1888. P. 234: "When these (spiritual) impetuosities are not very violent, the soul seeks relief through certain penances; the painfulness of which, and even the shedding of blood, are no more felt than if the body were dead." P. 30: "I was unable to move either arm or foot, or hand or head, unless others moved me. I could move, however, I think, one finger of my right hand." P. 31: "I was paralytic, though getting better, for about three years."

been usually accompanied by sensations of great heat: for on the former occasion "she seemed like a creature placed in a great flame of fire"; whilst on the latter "she had her tongue and lips so inflamed, that they seemed as though actual fire."

And movement appears to have been more often increased than diminished. In the last case indeed "she did not move nor speak nor see; but, when thus immovable, she suffered more than when she could cry out and turn about in her bed." But in the former instance "she could not be kept in bed"; and in April 1510 "she cried aloud, and could not keep herself from moving about, on her bed, on hands and feet."—There are curious localizations of apparently automatic movements. During an attack somewhere in March 1510 "her flesh was all in a tremble, particularly the right shoulder"; on later occasions "an arm, a leg, a hand would tremble, and she would seem to have a spasm within her, with all-but-unbroken acute pains in the flanks, the shoulders, the abdomen, the feet and the brain." On an earlier occasion "her body writhed in great distress." On another day "she seemed all on fire and lost her power of speech, and made signs with her head and hands." On one day in February or March 1510 "she lost both speech and sight, though not her intelligence"; and on September 12 "her sight was so weak, that she could hardly any further distinguish or recognize her attendants." —The heat is liable to be curiously localized. Early in September 1510 "she had a great heat situated in and on her left ear, which lasted for three hours; the ear was red and felt very hot to the touch of others."

Various kinds of haemorrhage are not uncommon. On the last-mentioned occasion bloody urine is passed; bleeding of the nose, with loss of bile, occurs in December 1509; very black blood is lost by the mouth, whilst black spots appear all over her person, on September 12, 1510; and more blood is evacuated on the following day. In February or March 1510 "there were in her flesh certain places which had become concave, like as paste looks where a finger has been put into it." At the end of August 1510 "her skin became saffron-yellow all over."

Troubles of breathing and of heart-action are frequently acute. Somewhere about March 1510 "she had such a spasm in her throat and mouth as to be unable, for about an hour, to speak or to open her eyes, and that she could hardly regain her breath." "Cupping-glasses were applied to her side, to ease her heart, and lung-action, but with little effect." On one occasion "she made signs indicative of feeling as though burning pincers were seizing her heart"; and on a day soon after "she felt like a hard nail at her heart."[1]

Disturbances of the power of swallowing and of nutrition are often grave and sudden, and in curious contradiction to her abnormally acute and shifting longing for and revulsion from certain specific kinds of food. On August 22, 1510, "she was so thirsty that she felt as though she could drink up the very ocean"; "yet she could not," in fact, "manage to swallow even one little drop of water." On September 10 "her attendants continuously gave her drinking water; but she would straightway return it from her mouth." And on September 12, "whilst her mouth was being bathed, she exclaimed, 'I am suffocating,'—and this because a drop of water had trickled down her throat—a drop which she was unable to gulp down." And on a day in August "she saw a melon and had a great desire to eat it; but hardly did she have some of it in her mouth, when she rejected it with intense disgust." So too with odours. A little later, "on one day the smell of wine would please her, and she would bathe her hands and face in it with great relish; and next day she would so much dislike it, that she could not bear to see or smell it in her room."—And so too with colours. On September 2 "a physician-friend came to visit her in his scarlet robes; and she bore the sight a little, so as not to pain him." But she then declared that she could no longer bear it; and he went, and returned to her in his ordinary black

[1] Hyper-aesthesia and sensation of heat: *Vita*, pp. 142*a*, 153*a*. Increase of movement: *ibid.* and pp. 145*b*, 143*a*, 153*c*, 141*a*. Loss of speech and sight: pp. 141*b*, 141*c*, 159*c*. Localization of heat: p. 157*b*. Haemorrhages: 138*c*, 159*c*, 160*a*. Concavities and jaundice: pp. 144*a*, 153*a*. Spasms: pp. 143*c*, 71*c*, 141*c*, 142*b*. Cf. St. Teresa, *loc. cit.* p. 30: "As to touching me, that was impossible, for I was so bruised that I could not endure it. They used to move me in a sheet, one holding one end, and another the other." P. 31: "I began to crawl on my hands and feet." P. 263: "I felt myself on fire: this inward fire and despair . . ." P. 17: "The fainting fits began to be more frequent; and my heart was so seriously affected, that those who saw it were alarmed." P. 27: "It seemed to me as if my heart had been seized by sharp teeth." P. 235: "I saw, in the Angel's hand, a long spear of gold, and at the iron's point there seemed to be a little fire. He appeared to me to be thrusting it at times into my heart, and to pierce my very entrails. . . . The pain is not bodily, but spiritual."

habit. And yet we have seen, from the Inventory of her effects, that she loved to have vermilion colour upon her bed and person.[1]

And her emotional moods are analogously intense and rapidly shifting. In the spring of 1510 "she cried aloud because of the great pain: this attack lasted a day and a night"; in the night of August 10 "she tossed about with many exclamations"; and at the beginning of September "she cried out with a loud voice." At other times, she laughs for joy. So at the end of April "she would laugh without speaking"; on August 11 "she fixed her eyes steadily on the ceiling; and for about an hour she abode all but immovable, and spoke not, but kept laughing in a very joyous fashion"; on August 17 great interior jubilation "expressed itself in merry laughter"; and on the evening of September 7 "her joy appeared exteriorly in laughter which lasted, with but small interruptions, for some two hours."—And her entire apparent condition would shift from one such extreme to the other with extraordinary swiftness. In the autumn of 1509 "she many times remained as though dead; and at other times she would appear as healthy,—as though she had never anything the matter with her." Already in December 1509 she herself, after much vomiting and loss of blood, had sent for her Confessor and had declared that "she felt as though she must die in consequence of these many accidents." Yet even on September 10, 1510, "when she was not being oppressed and tormented by her accidents (attacks), she seemed to be in good health; but when she was being suffocated by them, she seemed as one dead."[2]

[1] Swallow: *Vita*, pp. 149*c*, 150*a*; 159*b*; 159*c*; 150*a*. Odours and colours: 153*c*, 154*b*. Cf. St. Teresa, *loc. cit.* p. 27: "I could eat nothing whatever, only drink. I had a great loathing for food." P. 43: "I have been suffering for twenty years from sickness every morning." P. 30: "There was a choking in my throat. . . . I could not swallow even a drop of water." P. 263: "A sense of oppression, of stifling."

[2] Exclamations: *Vita*, pp. 144*a*, 148*b*, 155*a*. Laughter: *ibid.* 145*c*, 148*b*, 149*b*, 157*c*. Sudden changes of condition: 135*b*, 138*c*, 159*b*. Cf. St. Teresa, *loc. cit.* pp. 28, 29: "That very night," Feast of the Assumption, 1537, "my sickness became so acute that, for about four days, I remained insensible. For a day and a half the grave was open, waiting for my body. But it pleased Our Lord I should come to myself. I wished to go to confession at once. Though my sufferings were unendurable, and my perceptions dull, yet my confession was, I believe, complete. I communicated with many tears."

II. Conclusions concerning Catherine's Psycho-physical Condition during this last Period.

1. *Her illness not primarily physical. Her self-diagnosis.*

Now we saw, at the beginning of this chapter, how readily her attendants concluded, from all these extreme, multiple, swift-changing and self-contradictory states, to their directly and separately supernatural origin.—And indeed the diagnosis and treatment of her case showed clearly that it was not primarily physical. So in the case, probably in November 1509, of the cupping-glasses, when "she got medically treated for a bodily infirmity, whilst her real trouble was fire of the spirit"; so with a medicine given to her by the resident Hospital physician, some time in April 1510, "from taking which she nearly died"; so with Giovanni Boerio's three-weeks' treatment of her, in May 1510, a treatment which led to no other results than momentary additional distress; and so with the declaration of the ten Physicians who, even on September 10, four days before her death, "could find no trace of disease in her pulse, secretions, or any other symptom," and who consequently abstained from prescribing anything. And hence, more or less throughout her last nine years, "there was confusion in the management of her, not on her own part, but on that of those who served her."[1]

For—and these two further points are of primary importance—the tending of her, as distinct from physic, was throughout held by herself to be of great importance; and yet this care was declared by her to be often useless or harmful, owing to the powers of discrimination possessed by her attendants being as much below their good-will, as her own knowledge as to the differences between her healthy and *maladif* states exceeded her power of herself acting upon this knowledge against these sickly conditions. "She would often appear to be asleep; and would awake from such a state, at one time, quite refreshed, and, at another time, so limp and broken down as to be unable to move. Those that served her knew not how to distinguish one state from the other;

[1] *Vita*, pp. 71*c*; 145*c*; 147*b*; 159*c*, 159*a*; 127*a*. Cf. St. Teresa, *loc. cit.* p. 23: "I was in my sister's house, for the purpose of undergoing medical treatment—they took the utmost care of my comfort." P. 27: "In two months, so strong were the medicines, my life was nearly worn out." "The physicians gave me up: they said I was consumptive."

and on recovering from an attack of the latter sort, she would say to them : ' Why did you let me continue in that state of quiet, from which I have all but died ? ' " So, on September 5, " she cried aloud on waking from a state of quiet, which had appeared to be (healthy) quietude, but had not been so." And indeed, already on January 10 previous, she had shut herself off from her Confessor, " because it seemed to her that he bore with her too much in her sayings and doings."

Yet, at least after this time, Marabotto does oppose her sometimes. Thus on two, somewhat later, occasions she respectively makes signs, and asks, that Extreme Unction be given her; but only some four months later did she actually receive it. In these cases, then, she either had not, even at bottom, a correct physical self-knowledge; or her requests had been prompted, at the time, by her secondary, *maladif* consciousness alone.—When first visited by Boerio, she takes pleasure in the thought of getting possibly cured by him; but " in the following night, when great pain came upon her, she reproved herself, saying, ' You are suffering this, because you allowed yourself to rejoice without cause.' " But this declaration distinctly falls short of any necessary implication of a directly supernatural origin of her malady, as the *Vita* here will have it, and but refers, either to the continuance of earthly existence not deserving such joy, or to her persistent fundamental consciousness that the phenomena were partly the fruitful, profitable occasions, and partly the price paid, for the mind's close intercourse with things divine.

Indeed her (otherwise unbroken) attitude is one, both of quiet conviction that physic cannot help her, and of gentle readiness to let the physicians try whatever they may think worth the trying : so with the cupping-glasses, and the various examinations and physickings. Especially is this disposition clear in her short dialogue with Boerio, where, in answer to his assertion that she ought to beware of giving scandal to all the world by saying that her infirmity had no need of remedies, and that she ought to look upon such an attitude as " a kind of hypocrisy," she declares : " I am sorry if any one is scandalized because of me; and I am ready to use any remedy for my infirmity, supposing that it can be found." [1]

[1] Self-knowledge as to " quietudes " : *Vita*, pp. 153*b*, 157*a*. Marabotto's attitude : 139*b*; 141*c*, 143*c*, 149*a*. Relations with Boerio : 147*c*, 147*b*. Cf. St. Teresa, *loc. cit*. p. 86 : " My health has been much better since I have ceased to look after my ease and comforts."

2. *Her preoccupation with the spiritual suggestions afforded by the phenomena.*

It would, indeed, be a grave misreading of her whole character and habits of mind to think of her as at all engrossed in her psycho-physical states as such, and as having ever formally considered and decided that they must either come directly from God or be amenable to medicine. On the contrary, she is too habitually absorbed in the consideration and contemplation of certain great spiritual doctrines and realities, to have the leisure or inclination for any such questions.—Indeed it is this very absorption in those spiritual realities which has ended by suggesting, with an extraordinary readiness, frequency and vividness, through her mind to her senses, and by these back to her mind, certain psycho-physical images and illustrations for those very doctrines, until her whole psycho-physical organism has been, all but entirely, modified and moulded into an apt instrument and manifestation for and of that world unseen.

Thus, after her greatest psycho-physical and spiritual experience in November 1509, she declares to Vernazza, when he urges her to let him write down the graces she has received from God, that "it would, strictly speaking, be impossible to narrate those interior things; whilst, of exterior ones, few or none have happened to me." And she never entirely loses her mental consciousness in any state not recognized by herself as *maladif*. So, on a day of great psycho-physical trouble in February or March 1510, "they thought she must expire; but, though she lost both sight and speech, she never lost her intelligence." And even on September 11 and 12, amidst foodlessness and suffocations, her intelligence still persists.—In the March previous "her mind appeared to grow daily in contentment." Some days later, her attendants "saw how, after an hour of spasm and breathlessness, and then a great restriction of all her being, she returned to her normal condition, and addressed many beautiful words to them." And later on, "her attendants were amazed at seeing a body, which seemed to be healthy, in such a tormented condition." But "soon after she laughed and spoke as one in health, and told them not to distress themselves about her, since she was very contented; but that they should see to it that they did much good, since the way of God is very narrow."[1]

[1] Remark to Vernazza: *Vita*, pp. 98*c*, 99*a*. Persistence of intelligence: 141*c*; 159*b*, *c*; 143*a*; 143*c*; 145*b*. Cf. St. Teresa, *loc. cit.* p. 408: "She"

3. *Interaction and mutual suggestion of her spiritual and physical states.*

As to the extraordinary closeness and readiness for mutual response between her sensible impressions and her thoughts and emotions—her sensations turning, all but automatically, into religious emotions, and her thoughts and feelings translating themselves into appropriate psycho-physical states—we have a mass of interesting evidence.

Thus when, about the end of November 1509, in response to her seeing, on some wall of the Hospital, a picture of Our Lord at the Well of Samaria, and to her asking Him for one drop of that Divine water, " instantly a drop was given to her which refreshed her within and without." The spiritual idea and emotion is here accompanied and further stimulated by the keenest psycho-physical impression of drinking. And such an impression can even become painful through its excessive suggestiveness. Thus she herself explains to Maestro Boerio, on September 2, 1510, that she cannot long bear the sight of his scarlet robe " because of what it suggests (represents) to my memory,"—no doubt the fire of divine love. Three days later, on the contrary, " she mentally saw herself lying upon a bier, surrounded by many Religious robed in black," and greatly rejoiced at the sight. Here the very impression of black, the colour of death, will have conveyed, during this special mood of hers, a downright psycho-physical pleasure, somewhat as Boerio's reappearance, on the former occasion, in a black gown, had been a sensible relief to her.

So also with scents. When, certainly after 1499, " she perceived, on the (right) hand of her Confessor, an odour which penetrated her very heart," and " which abode with her and restored both mind and body for many days," we have again a primarily mental act and state which she herself knows well to be untransferable, even to Don Marabotto himself. Here the association of ideas was, no doubt, the right hand of the Priest and her daily reception, by means of it, of the Holy Eucharist. For the latter, " the Bread from heaven, having

(Teresa herself) " never saw anything with her bodily eyes, nor heard anything with her bodily ears." P. 189 : " The words of the divine locutions are very distinctly formed; but by the bodily ear they are not heard." P. 191 : " In ecstasy, the memory can hardly do anything at all, and the imagination is, as it were, suspended." P. 142 : " You see and feel yourself carried away, you know not whither." P. 187 ; " I fell into a trance; I was carried out of myself. It was most plain."

within it all manner of delight," is already connected in her mind with an impression of sweet odour. "One day, on receiving Communion, so much odour and sweetness came to her, that she seemed to herself to be in Paradise." Probably the love for, and then the disgust at, the smell of wine, was also connected with her Eucharistic experiences. Certainly "one day, having received Holy Communion, she was granted so great a consolation as to fall into an ecstasy, so that when the Priest wanted to give her to drink from the Chalice (with unconsecrated wine) she had to be brought back by force to her ordinary consciousness." Vivid memories of both sets of psycho-physical impressions are, I think, at work when she says: "If a consecrated Host were to be given to me amongst unconsecrated ones, I should be able to distinguish it by the very taste, as I do wine from water." And as the sight of red rapidly became painful from the very excess of its mental suggestiveness, so will the smell of wine have been both specially dear and specially painful to her.[1]

Indeed her psycho-physical troubles possess, for the most part, a still traceable, most delicate selectiveness as to date, range, form, combination, and other peculiarities. Thus some of the most acute attacks coincide, in their date of occurrence and general character, as the biographers point out, with special saint's and holy days: so in the night leading into St. Lawrence's day, August 9 and 10, 1510; so on the Vigil of St. Bartholomew's day, August 24; and so in the night previous to and on the Feast (August 28) of St. Augustine, special Patron of her only sister's Order and of the Convent in which her own Conversion had taken place thirty-seven years before. Yet we have also seen how that these synchronisms did not rise to the heights which were soon desired by her biographers, for we know that she died, not (as they would

[1] Picture: *Vita*, p. 135*a*. Red and black robes: 154*b*, 156*c*. Suggestions of odour: 118*c*, 119*a*; 9*c*, 8*a*, 9*b*. Cf. St. Teresa, *loc. cit.* pp. 57, 58: "One day, I saw a picture of Christ most grievously wounded: the very sight of it moved me." P. 247: "I used to pray much to Our Lord for that living water of which He spoke to the Samaritan woman: I had always a picture of it with this inscription: 'Domine, da mihi aquam.'" P. 231: "Once when I was holding in my hand the cross of my rosary, He took it from me into His own hand. He returned it; but it was then four large stones incomparably more precious than diamonds: the five wounds were delineated on them with the most admirable art. He said to me that for the future that cross would appear so to me always, and so it did. The precious stones were seen, however, only by myself."

have it) on the Feast of the Exaltation of the Cross, September 14, but early on the day following.

Thus too as to her incapacity to swallow and retain food, we find that, up to the end, with the rarest exceptions of a directly physical kind, she retained the most complete facility in receiving Holy Communion: so on September 2, 1510, when "all ordinary food was returned, but the Holy Eucharist she retained without any difficulty"; and so too on September 4, when, after "lying for close upon twelve hours with closed eyes, speechless and all but immovable," Marabotto himself feared to communicate her, but "she made a sign to him, with a joyous countenance, to have no fear, and she communicated with ease, and soon after began to speak, owing to the vigour given to her by the Sacrament." Yet here too the abnormality is not complete: some ordinary food is retained, now and then; so, minced chicken, specially mentioned for December 1509, and on September 3, 1510.

As to her heat-attacks and the corresponding extreme—the sense of intense cold,—it is clear how close is their connection with her profound concentration upon the conception of God as Love, and upon the image of Love as fire. It is these sudden and intense psycho-physical, spiritually suggestive because spiritually suggested, heat-attacks which are, I think, always meant by the terms "assault" (*assalto*), "stroke" (*ferita*), and "arrow" (*saetta*): terms which already indicate the mental quality of these attacks. And these heats are mostly localized in a doctrinally suggestive manner: they centre in and around the heart, or on the tongue and lips, or they envelop the whole person "as though it were placed in a great flame of fire," or "in a glowing furnace." Indeed these heats are often so described, by her attendants or herself, as to imply their predominantly psycho-physical nature: "it was necessary, with a view to prolonging her life, to use many means for lightening the strain of that interior fire upon her mind"; and "I feel," she says herself, on occasion of such an attack, "so great a contentment on the part of the spirit, as to be unutterable; whilst, on the part of my humanity, all the pains are, so to say, no pains."

As to her boundless thirst, her inability to drink, and her sense of strangulation, their doctrinal suggestions are largely clear. Thus when "she was so thirsty as to feel able to drink up all the waters of the sea," and when she calls out "I am suffocating" (drowning, *io affogo*), we are at once reminded of her great saying : " If the sea were all so much love, there would not live man or woman who would not go to drown himself in it (*si affogasse*)." And when, at the end of August 1510, unable to drink, she herself declares "all the water that is on earth could not give me the least refreshment," there is, perhaps, an implied contrast to that " little drop of divine water " which had so much refreshed her a year before.

And finally, the various paralyses and death-like swoons seem, at least in part, to follow from, and to represent, the death of the spirit to the life of the senses, and to mirror the intensity with which perfection has been conceived and practised as " Love going forth out of self, and abiding all in God and separated from man." Thus when, on August 22, 1510, " she had a day of great heat, and abode paralyzed in one hand and in one finger of the other hand for about sixteen hours, and she was so greatly occupied (absorbed), that she neither spoke, nor opened her eyes, nor could take any food."[1]

4. *Only two cases of spiritually unsuggestive impressions.* It is indeed profoundly instructive to note how that, in exact proportion as a human-mental mediation and suggestion of a religious kind is directly traceable or at least probable in any or all of these things, is that thing also worthy of being considered as having ultimately the Divine Spirit Itself for its first cause as well as last end ; and that, in exact proportion as this kind of human mediation and suggestion is impossible or unlikely, the thing turns out to be unworthy of being attributed, in any special sense, to the spirit of God Himself.

Of such spiritually opaque, religiously unused and apparently unuseable, hysteriform impressions, I can, even during the last days of these nine years of admitted infirmity, find but two clear instances,—instances which, by their very

[1] Synchronisms : *Vita*, pp. 148*b*; 150*b*; 152*a*, 160*c*, 161*b*. Communion and ordinary food : 154*a*, 154*c*, 138*c*; 154*c*. Heats : " Assalto," *e.g.* 138*b*, *c*; 143*a*, *c*; " ferita " and " saetta," *e.g.* 141*a*, *c*; 145*a*. Their localization : 135*a*, 141*c*; 153*a*; 142*a*, 158*a*. Their psycho-physical character : 135*b*, 144*b*. Thirst and its suggestion : 149*c*, 159*c*; 76*c*; 152*b*, 135*a*. Paralyses : 134*b*; 149*c*. Cf. St. Teresa, *op. cit.* p. 28 : her death-swoon occurs on evening of the Assumption. P. 235 : Heat, piercing of the heart as by a spear, and a spiritual (not bodily) pain, are all united in the experience of the heart-piercing Angel. P. 423 : " Another prayer very common is a certain kind of wounding; for it really seems to the soul as if an arrow were thrust through the heart or through itself. The suffering is not one of sense, nor is the wound physical; it is in the interior of the soul."

unlikeness to the mass of her spiritually transparent, readily used impressions, strongly confirm our high estimate of the all but totality of her psycho-physical states, as experienced and understood and used by herself. On September 7, 1510, after having seen and wisely utilized the spiritually suggestive image of " a great ladder of fire," she ends by having so vivid an hallucination of the whole world being on fire " that she asked whether it were not so, and caused her windows to be opened that the facts might be ascertained; and " she abode the whole night, possessed by that imagination," as the *Vita* itself calls this impression. At night, on September 11, she complained of a very great heat, and cast forth from her mouth very black blood; and black spots came out all over her body. And on the 13th, " she was seen with her eyes fixed upon the ceiling, and with much movement of the lips and hands; and she answered her attendants' queries as to what she was seeing with 'Drive away that beast . . . .' the remaining words being inaudible." [1]

Here we have, I think, the only two merely factual, unsuggestive, and hence simply delusive, impressions really experienced by herself and recorded in the *Vita*, a book whose very eagerness to discover things of this kind and readiness to take them as directly supernatural is a guarantee that no other marked instances of the kind have been omitted or suppressed. And these two impressions both take place within a week of her death, and respectively four days before, and two days after, the first clear case of organic disease or lesion to be found anywhere in the life.

[1] *Vita*, pp. 158*a*; 160*a*. Cf. St. Teresa, *op. cit.* p. 41 : " We saw something like a great toad crawling towards us . . . The impression it made on me was such, that I think it must have had a meaning." Contrast with this naïvely sensible sight and the absence of all interior assurance, such a spiritual vision as " Christ stood before me, stern and grave. I saw Him with the eyes of the soul. The impression remained with me that the vision was from God, and not an imagination " (pp. 40, 41). Another quasi-sensible sight, with no interior assurance, or question as to its provenance and value, is given on pp. 248, 249 : " Once Satan, in an abominable shape, appeared on my left hand. I looked at his mouth in particular, because he spoke, and it was horrible. A huge flame seemed to issue out of his body, perfectly bright without any shadow." Another such impression is recorded on p. 252 : " I thought the evil spirits would have suffocated me one night . . . I saw a great troop of them rush away as if tumbling over a precipice."

III. Catherine's Psycho-physical Condition, its Likeness and Unlikeness to Hysteria.

Only by a quite unfair magnifying or multiplying of the two incidents just described could we come to hold, with Mr. Baring-Gould, that Catherine was simply a sufferer from hysteria, and that the Roman Church did well to canonize her on the ground of her having, in spite of this malady, managed to achieve much useful work amongst the sick and poor.[1] Here we shall do well to consider three groups of facts.

1. *Misapprehensions as to hysteria.*

The first group gives the reasons why we should try and get rid of the terror and horror still so often felt in connection with the very name of this malady. This now quite demonstrably excessive, indeed largely mythical, connotation of the term springs from four causes.

First, the very name still tends to suggest, as the causes or conditions of the malady, things fit only for discussion in medical reviews. But then, ever since 1855, all limitation to, or special connection with, anything peculiarly female, or indeed generally sexual, has been increasingly shown to be false, until now no serious authority on the matter can be found to espouse the old view. The malady is now well known to attack men as well as women, and to have no special relation to things of sex at all.[2]

Next, probably as a consequence from the initial error, this disorder was supposed to come predominantly from, or to lead to, moral impurity, or at least to be ordinarily accompanied by strong erotic propensions. But here the now carefully observed facts are imperatively hostile : of the 120 living cases most carefully studied by Prof. Janet, only four showed the predominance of any such tendencies, a proportion undoubtedly not above the percentage to be found amongst non-hysterical persons.[3]

And again, the term was long synonymous with untruthfulness and deceit. But here again Prof. Janet shows how unfounded is this prejudice, since it but springs from the mis-

[1] *Lives of the Saints*, ed. 1898, Vol. X, September 15.

[2] Pierre Janet, *Etat Mental des Hystériques*, 2 vols., Paris, 1892, 1894 : Vol. II, pp. 260, 261 ; 280 ; Vol. I, pp. 225, 63.

[3] *Ibid.* Vol. I, pp. 63, 225, 226.

placed promptitude with which the earlier observers refused to believe what they had not as yet sufficiently examined and could not at all explain, and from the malady being itself equivalent to a more or less extensive breaking-up of the normal inter-connection between the several, successive or simultaneous states, and, as it were, layers of the one personality. He is convinced that real untruthfulness is no commoner among such patients than it is among healthy persons.[1]

And, finally, it is no doubt felt that, apart from all such specifically moral suspicions, the malady involves all kinds of fancies and inaccuracies of feeling and of perception, and that it frequently passes into downright insanity. And this is no doubt the one objection which does retain some of its old cogency. Still, it is well to note that, as has now been fully established, the elements of the human mind are and remain the same throughout the whole range of its conditions, from the sanest to the maddest, whilst only their proportion and admixture, and the presence or absence and the kind of synthesis necessary to hold them together differentiate these various states of mind. In true insanity there is no such synthesis; in hysteria the synthesis, however slight and peculiar, is always still traceable throughout the widespread disgregation of the elements and states.[2] And it is this very persistence of the fundamental unity, together with the strikingly different combination and considerable disgregation of its elements, that makes the study of hysteria so fruitful for the knowledge of the fully healthy mind and of its unity; whilst the continuance of all the elements of the normal intelligence, even in insanity, readily explains why it is apparently so easy to see insanity everywhere, and to treat genius and sanctity as but so much degeneracy.

2. *Hysteriform phenomena observable in Catherine's case.*

The second group of facts consists in the phenomena which, in Catherine's case, are like or identical to what is observable in cases of hysteria.

There is, perhaps above all else, the anaesthetic condition, which was presumably co-extensive with her paralytic states. "Anaesthesia," says Prof. Janet, "can be considered as the type of the other symptoms of hysteria; it exists in the great majority of cases, it is thoroughly characteristic of the malady.

[1] Pierre Janet, *Etat Mental*, Vol. I, pp. 226, 227.

[2] *Ibid.* Vol. II, pp. 253, 257.

In its most frequent localization (semi-anaesthesia) it affects one of the lateral halves of the body, and this half is usually the left side." Or, " a finger or hand will be affected." Such " insensibility can be very frequent and very profound " ; but " it disappears suddenly " and even " varies from one moment to another." [1]

Then there is the corresponding counter-phenomenon of hyper-aesthesia. "The slightest contact provokes great pains, exclamations, and spasms. The painful zones have their seat mostly on the abdomen or on the hips." And " sensation in these states is not painful in itself, by its own intensity, but by its quality, its characteristics; it has become the signal, by association of ideas, for the production of a set of extremely painful phenomena." So, with the colour-sense : "one patient adores the colour red, and sees in its dullest shade ' sparkling rays which penetrate to her very heart and warm her through and through.' " But " another one finds this ' a repulsive colour and one capable of producing nausea.' " And similarly with the senses of taste and odour.[2]

Then, too, the inability to stand or walk, with the conservation, at times, of the power to crawl; the acceptance, followed by the rejection, of food, because of certain spasms in the throat or stomach, and the curious, mentally explicable, exceptions to this incapacity; the sense, even at other times, of strangulation; heart palpitations, fever heats, strange haemorrhages from the stomach or even from the lung; red patches on the skin and emotional jaundice all over it, and one or two other peculiarities.[3]

Then, as to a particular kind of quietude, from which Catherine warns her attendants to rouse her, we find a patient who " ceases her reading, without showing any sign of doing so. She gets taken to be profoundly attentive; it is, however, but one of her attacks of ' fixity.' And she has promptly to be shaken out of this state, or, in a few minutes, there will be no getting her out of it."

As to Catherine's consciousness of possessing an extraordinary fineness of discrimination between sensibly identical

[1] Pierre Janet, *Etat Mental*, Vol. I, pp. 7, 8, 11, 12, 57, 21.
[2] *Ibid.* Vol. II, pp. 82, 91; 70, 71.
[3] *Ibid.* Vol. II. Troubles of movement, pp. 105, 106; of nutrition, pp. 285, 70, 71; strangulation, heart palpitation, fever heats, p. 282; haemorrhages and red patches, p. 283; jaundice (*ictère emotionnel*), p. 287; and note the " ischurie," p. 283, top, compared with *Vita*, p. 12*a*.

objects, we see that "if one points out, to some of these patients, an imaginary portrait upon a plain white card, and mixes this card with other similar ones, they will almost always find again the portrait on the same card." And similarly as to her attaching a particular quasi-sensible perception to Marabotto's hand alone, we find that, if M. Janet touches Léonie's hand, he having suggested a nosegay to her, she will henceforth, when he touches the hand, see that nosegay; whereas, if another person touches that same hand, Léonie will see nothing special.

As to Catherine's feelings of criminality and of being already dead, M. Janet quotes M., who says, "I am like a criminal about to be punished"; and R., who declares, "It seems to me that I am dead." As to the hallucination of a Beast, Marcelle suffers from the same impression.[1]

And,—perhaps the most important of all these surface-resemblances,—there is Catherine's apparent freedom from all emotion at the deaths of her brothers and sister, and her extraordinary dependence upon, and claimfulness towards, her Confessor alone. "These patients rapidly lose the social feelings: Berthe, who for some time preserved some affection for her brother, ends by losing all interest in him; Marcelle, at the very beginning of her illness, separates herself from every one." "It is always their own personality which dominates their thoughts." Yet these patients have "an extraordinary attachment to their physician. For him they are resolved to do all things. In return, they are extremely exacting,—he is to occupy himself entirely with each one alone. Only a very superficial observer would ascribe this feeling to a vulgar source."[2]

3. *Catherine's personality not disintegrated.*

But a third group of facts clearly differentiates Catherine's case, even in these years of avowed ill-health, from such patients; and these facts become clearer and more numerous in precise proportion as we move away from peripheral, psycho-physical phenomena and mechanisms, and dwell upon her practically unbroken mental and moral characteristics, and upon the use and meaning, the place and context of these things within her ample life.

For as to her relations with her attendants, even now it is still she who leads, who suggests, who influences; a strong

[1] Pierre Janet, *Etat Mental*, Vol. I, p. 140; Vol. II, pp. 14, 72, 165.
[2] *Ibid.* Vol. I, pp. 218, 219; 158, 159.

and self-consistent will shows itself still, under all this shifting psycho-physical surface. Thus Don Marabotto now administers, it is true, all her money and charitable affairs for her. But it is she who insists, alone and unaided, upon the true spiritual function of that impression of odour on his hand.—Vernazza, no doubt, has now to help her in the fight against subtle scruples, on occasion of her deepest depressions. But her far more frequent times of light and joy are in nowise occasions of a simply subjective self-engrossment or of a purely psycho-physical interest, for her mind is absorbed if in but a few, yet in inexhaustibly fruitful and universally applicable ideas and experiences of a spiritual kind, such as helped to urge this friend on to his world-renewing impulses and determinations.—Her closest relations and friends, one must admit, succeed by their action, taken eighteen months and then again two days before her death, in getting her to desist from ordering her burial by the side of her husband. But we have seen, in the one case, how indirectly, and, in the other case, how suddenly and even then quite informally, they had to gain their point.—Her attendants in general, and Marabotto in particular, certainly paid her an engrossed attention, and the all but endlessness of her superficial fancies and requirements have been chronicled by them with a naïve and wearisome fulness. But then she herself is well aware that, had they but the requisite knowledge as to how and when to apply them, some sturdy opposition and a greater roughness of handling would, on their part, be of the greatest use to her, in this her psychical infirmity; indeed her shutting herself away from Marabotto, as late as January 1510, is directly caused by her sense and fear of being spoilt by him.

It is true again that, already in 1502, we hear, in a probably exaggerated but still possibly semi-authentic account, of her indifference of feeling with regard to the deaths of two brothers and of her only sister; and that, from January 1510 onwards, she gradually excludes all her attendants from her sick-room, with, eventually, the sole exceptions of Marabotto or Carenzio and Argentina. But her Wills show conclusively how persistent were her detailed interest in, and dispositions for, the requirements of her surviving brother, nephews, and nieces; of poor Thobia and the girl's hidden mother; of her priest-attendants, and of each and all of her humblest domestics; of the natives in the far-away Greek Island of

Scios; and, above all, of the Hospital and its great work which she had ever loved so well.

We have indeed found two cases, both from within the last week of her life, of mentally opaque and spiritually unsuggestive and unutilized impressions which are truly analogous to those characteristic of hysteria. But we have also seen how forcibly these two solitary cases bring out, by contrast, the spiritual transparency and fruitfulness of her usual, finely reflective picturings of these last years. For here it is her own deliberate and spiritual mind which joyously greets, and straightway utilizes and transcends, the psycho-physical occurrences; and it does so, not because these occurrences are, or are taken to be, the causes or requisites or objects of her faith and spiritual insight, but because, on the contrary, they meet and clothe an already exuberant faith and insight—spiritual certainties derived from quite another source.

And finally, if the monotony and superficial pettiness of the sick-room can easily pall upon us, especially when presented with the credulities and hectic exaggerations which disfigure so much of the *Vita's* description of it; we must, in justice, as I have attempted to do in my seventh and eighth chapters, count in, as part of her biography, her deep affection for and persistent influence with Ettore and Battista Vernazza, and the exemplification of her doctrine by these virile souls, makers of history in the wide, varied world of men.[1]

In a word, it is plain at once that, given the necessarily limited number of ways in which the psycho-physical organism reacts under mental stimulations, certain neural phenomena may, in any two cases, be, in themselves, perfectly similar, although their respective mental causes or occasions may be as different, each from the other, as the Moonlight Sonata of Beethoven, or the working out of the Law of Gravitation by Newton, or the elaboration of the implications of the Categorical Imperative by Kant, are different from the sudden jumping of a live mouse in the face of an hysterically-disposed young woman, or as the various causes of tears and laughter throughout the whole world.

[1] The biographical chapters of Volume I give all the facts and references alluded to in this paragraph. It would be easy to find parallels for most of these peripheral disturbances and great central normalities in St. Teresa's life.

IV. First Period of Catherine's Life, 1447 to 1477, in its Three Stages.

If we next go back to the first period of her life, in its three stages of the sixteen years of her girlhood, 1447–1463, the first ten years of her married life, 1463–1473, and the four years of her Conversion and active Penitence, 1473–1477, we shall find, I think, in the matter of temperament and psycho-physical conditions, little or nothing but a rare degree of spiritual sensitiveness, and an extraordinary close-knittedness of body and mind.

1. *From her childhood to her conversion.*

Thus, already in her early childhood, that picture of the Pietà seems to have suggested religious ideas and feelings with the suddenness and emotional solidity of a physical seizure—an impression still undimmed when she herself recounted it, some fifty years later, to her two intimates.—It is true that during those first, deeply unhappy ten years of marriage, we cannot readily find more than indications of a most profound and brooding melancholy, the apparent result of but two factors,—a naturally sad disposition and acutely painful domestic circumstances. Yet it is clear, from the sequel, that more and other things lay behind. It is indeed evident that she possessed a congenitally melancholy temperament; that nothing but the rarest combination of conditions could have brought out, into something like elastic play and varied exercise, her great but few and naturally excessive qualities of mind and heart; that these conditions were not only absent, but were replaced by circumstances of the most painful kind; and that she will hardly, at this time, have had even a moment's clear consciousness of any other sources than just those conditions for her deep, keen, and ever-increasing dissatisfaction with all things, her own self included: all peace and joy, the very capacity for either seemed gone, and gone for ever. But it is only the third stage, with its sudden-seeming conversion on March 20, 1473, and the then following four years of strenuously active self-immolation and dedication to the humblest service of others, which lets us see deep into those previous years of sullen gloom and apparently hopeless drift and dreary wastage.

The two stages really belong to one another, and the depth of the former gloom and dreariness stood in direct proportion and relation to the capacities of that nature and to the height of their satisfaction in the later light and vigour brought to and assimilated by them. It was the sense, at that previous time still inarticulate, but none the less mightily operative, of the insufficiency of all things merely contingent, of all things taken as such and inevitably found to be such, that had been adding, and was now discovered to have added, a quite determining weight and poignancy to the natural pressure of her temperament and external lot. And this temperament and lot, which had not alone produced that sadness, could still less of themselves remove it, whatever might be its cause. Her sense of emptiness and impotence could indeed add to her sense of fulness and of power, once these latter had come; but of themselves the former could no more give her the latter, than hunger, which indeed makes bread to taste delicious, can give us real bread and, with it, that delight.

And it was such real bread of life and real power which now came to her. For if the tests of reality in such things are their persistence and large and rich spiritual applicability and fruitfulness, then something profoundly real and important took place in the soul of that sad and weary woman of six-and-twenty, within that Convent-chapel, at that Annunciation-tide. Her four years of heroic persistence; her unbroken Hospital service of a quarter of a century; her lofty magnanimity towards her husband, Thobia and Thobia's mother; her profound influence upon Vernazza, in urging him on to his splendid labours throughout Italy, and to his grand death in plague-stricken Genoa; her daringly original, yet immensely persuasive, doctrine,—nearly all this dates back, completely for her consciousness and very largely in reality, to those few moments on that memorable day.

2. *Her conversion not sudden nor visionary.*

But two points, concerning the manner and form of this experience, are, though of but secondary spiritual interest, far more difficult to decide. There is, for one thing, the indubitable impression, for her own mind and for ours, of complete suddenness and newness in her change. Was this suddenness and newness merely apparent, or real as well? And should this suddenness, if real, be taken as in itself and directly supernatural?

Now it is certain that Catherine, up to ten years before,

had been full of definitely religious acts and dispositions. Had she not, already at thirteen, wanted to be a Nun, and, at eight or so, been deeply moved by a picture of the dead Christ in His Mother's lap? Hence, ideas and feelings of self-dedication and of the Christ-God's hatred of sin and love for her had, in earlier and during longer times than those of her comparative carelessness, soaked into and formed her mental and emotional bent, and will have in so far shaped her will, as to make the later determination along those earlier lines of its operation, comparatively easy, even after those years of relaxation and deviation. Yet it is clear that there was not here, as indeed there is nowhere, any mere repetition of the past. New combinations and an indefinitely deeper apprehension of the great religious ideas and facts of God's holiness and man's weakness, of the necessity for the soul to reach its own true depth or to suffer fruitlessly, and of God having Himself to meet and feed this movement and hunger which He has Himself implanted; new combinations and depths of emotion, and an indefinite expansion and heroic determination of the will: were all certainly here, and were new as compared with even the most religious moments in the past.

As to the suddenness, we cannot but take it as, in large part, simply apparent,—a dim apprehension of what then became clear having been previously quite oppressively with her. And, in any case, this suddenness seems to belong rather to the temperamental peculiarities and necessary forms of her particular experiences than to the essence and content of her spiritual life. For, whatever she thinks, feels, says or does throughout her life, she does and experiences with actual suddenness, or at least with a sense of suddenness; and there is clearly no more necessary connection between such suddenness and grace and true self-renouncement, than there is between gradualness and mere nature; both suddenness and gradualness being but simple modes, more or less fixed for each individual, yet differing from each to each, modes in which God's grace and man's will interact and manifest themselves in different souls.[1]

And then there is the question as to whether or not this

[1] Prof. W. James has got some very sensible considerations on the pace of a conversion (as distinct from its spiritual significance, depth, persistence, and fruitfulness) being primarily a matter of temperament: *Varieties of Religious Experience*, 1902, pp. 227–240.

conversion-experience took the form of a vision. We have seen, in the Appendix, how considerable are the difficulties which beset the account of the Bleeding Christ Vision in the Palace; and how the story of the previous visionless experience in the Chapel is free from all such objections. But, even supposing the two accounts to be equally reliable, it is the first, the visionless experience, which was demonstrably the more important and the more abidingly operative of the two. More important, for it is during those visionless moments that her conversion is first effected; and more abiding, for, according to all the ancient accounts, the impression of the Bleeding Christ Vision disappeared utterly at the end of at longest four years, whereas the memory of the visionless conversion moments remained with her, as an operative force, up to the very last. Witness the free self-casting of the soul into painful-joyous Purgation, into Love, into God (without any picturing of the historic Christ), which forms one of the two constituents of her great latter-day teaching; and how entirely free from directly historic elements all her recorded visions of the middle period turn out to be.[1]

3. *Peculiarities of her active penitence.*

As to the four years of Active Penitence, we must beware of losing the sense of the dependence, the simple, spontaneous instrumentality, in which the negative and restrictive side of her action stood towards the positive and expansive one. An immense affirmation, an anticipating, creative buoyancy and resourcefulness, had come full flood into her life; and had shifted her centre of deliberate interest and willing away from the disordered, pleasure-seeking, sore and sulky lesser self in

[1] By the term "visionless," I do not mean to affirm anything as to the presence or absence of ideas or mental images during the times so described, but to register the simple fact, that, for her own memory after the event, she was, at the time, without any one persistent, external-seeming image.—Note how St. Ignatius Loyola in his *Testament*, ed. London, 1900, pp. 91, 92, considered the profoundest spiritual experience of his life to have been one unaccompanied or expressed by any vision: "On his way" to a Church near Manresa, "he sat down facing the stream, which was running deep. While he was sitting there, the eyes of his mind were opened," not so as to see any kind of vision, but "so as to understand and comprehend spiritual things . . . with such clearness that for him all these things were made new. If all the enlightenment and help he had received from God in the whole course of his life . . . were gathered together in one heap, these all would appear less than he had been given at this one time."

which her true personality had for so long been enmeshed. Thus all this strenuous work of transforming and raising her lower levels of inclinations and of habit to the likeness and heights of her now deliberate loftiest standard was not taking place for the sake of something which actually was, or which even seemed to be, less than what she had possessed or had, even dimly, sought before, nor with a view to her true self's contraction. But, on the contrary, the work was for the end of that indefinite More, of that great pushing upwards of her soul's centre and widening out of its circumference, which she could herself confirm and increase only by such ever-renewed warfare against what she now recognized as her false and crippling self.

And it is noticeable how soon and how largely, even still within this stage, her attitude became "passive." She pretty early came to do these numerous definite acts of penance without any deliberate selection or full attention to them. As in her third period her absorption in large spiritual ideas spontaneously suggests certain corresponding psycho-physical phenomena, which then, in return, stimulate anew the apprehensions of the mind; so here, towards the end of the first period, penitential love ends by quite spontaneously suggesting divers external acts of penitence, which readily become so much fresh stimulation for love.

I take this time to have been as yet free from visions or ecstasies—at least of the later lengthy and specific type. For the Bleeding Christ experience, even if fully historical, occurred within the first conversion-days, and only its vivid memory prolonged itself throughout those penitential years; whilst all such other visions, as have been handed down to us, do not treat of conversion and penance, at least in any active and personal sense. And only towards the end of these years do the psycho-physical phenomena as to the abstention from food begin to show themselves. The consideration of both the Visions and the Fasts had, then, better be reserved for the great central period.

V. The Second, Great Middle Period of Catherine's Life, 1477 to 1499.

It is most natural yet very regrettable that we should know so little as to Catherine's spiritual life, or even as to her psycho-physical condition, during these central twenty-two years of her life. It is natural, for she had, at this time, neither Physician nor Confessor busy with her, and the very richness and balanced fulness of this epoch of her life may well have helped to produce but little that could have been specially seized and registered by either. Yet it is regrettable, since here we have what, at least for us human observers, constitutes the culmination and the true measure of her life, the first period looking but like the preparation, and the third period, like the price paid for such a rich expansion.—Yet we know something about three matters of considerable psycho-physical and temperamental interest, which are specially characteristic of this time: her attitude towards food; her ecstasies and visions; and certain peculiarities in her conception and practice of the spiritual warfare.

1. *Her extraordinary fasts.*

As to food, it is clear that, however much we may be able or bound to deduct from the accounts, there remains a solid nucleus of remarkable fact. During some twenty years she evidently went, for a fairly equal number of days,—some thirty in Advent and some forty in Lent, seventy in all annually,—with all but no food; and was, during these fasts, at least as vigorous and active as when her nutrition was normal. For it is not fairly possible to make these great fasts end much before 1496, when she ceased to be Matron of the Hospital; and they cannot have begun much after 1475 or 1476: so that practically the whole of her devoted service and administration in and of that great institution fell within these years, of which well-nigh one-fifth was covered by these all but total abstentions from food. Yet here again we are compelled to take these things, not separately, and as directly supernatural, but in connection with everything else; and to consider the resultant whole as the effect and evidence of a strong mind and will operating upon and through an immensely responsive psycho-physical organism.

For here again we easily find a significant system and delicate selectiveness both in the constant approximate synchronisms—these incapacities occurring about Advent and Lent; and in the foods exempted—since there is no difficulty in connection with the daily Holy Eucharist, with the unconsecrated wine given to her, as to all Communicants in that age at Genoa, immediately after Communion, or with water when seasoned penitentially with salt or vinegar. And if the actual heightening of nervous energy and balance, recorded as having generally accompanied these two fasts, is indeed a striking testimony to the extraordinary powers of her mind and will, we must not forget that these fruitful fasts were accompanied, and no doubt rendered possible, by the second great psychical peculiarity of these middle years, her ecstasies.

2. *Her ecstasies and visions.*

It is indeed remarkable how these two conditions and functions, her fasts and her ecstasies of a definite, lengthy and strength-bringing kind, arise, persist and then fade out of her life together. And since, in ecstasy, the respiration, the circulation, and the other physical functions are all slackened and simplified; the mind is occupied with fewer, simpler, larger ideas, harmonious amongst themselves; and the emotions and the will are, for the time, saved the conflict and confusion, the stress and strain, of the fully waking moments; and considering that Catherine was peculiarly sensitive to all this flux and friction, and that she was now often in a more or less ecstatic trance from two up to eight hours: it follows that the amount of food required to heal the breach made by life's wear and tear would, by these ecstasies, be considerably reduced. And indeed it will have been these contemplative absorptions which directly mediated for her those accessions of vigour: and that they did so, in such a soul and for the uses to which she put this strength, is their fullest justification as thoroughly wholesome, at least in their ultimate outcome, in and for this particular life.

And the visions recorded have these two characteristics, that they all deal with metaphysical realities and relations—God as source and end of all things, as Light and food of the soul, and similar conceptions, and never directly with historical persons, scenes, or institutions; and that, whereas the non-ecstatic picturings of her last period are grandly original, and demonstrably based upon her own spiritual experience, these second-period ecstatic visions are readily traceable to New Testament, Neo-Platonist, and Franciscan precursors, and have little more originality than this special selection from amongst other possible literary sources.

3. *Special character of her spiritual warfare.*

Catherine's ecstasies lead us easily on to the special method of her spiritual warfare, which can, I think, be summed up in three maxims: "One thing, and only one at a time"; "Ever fight self, and you need not trouble about any other foe"; and "Fight self by an heroic indirectness and by love, for love,—through a continuous self-donation to Pure Love alone."

Studying here these great convictions simply in their temperamental occasions, colouring, and limitations, we can readily discover how the "one thing at a time" maxim springs from the same disposition as that which found such refreshment in ecstasy. For here too, partly from a congenital incapacity to take things lightly, partly from an equally characteristic sensitiveness to the conflict and confusion incident to the introduction of any fresh multiplicity into the consciousness, she requires, even in her non-ecstatic moments, to have her attention specially concentrated upon one all-important idea, one point in the field of consciousness. And, by a faithful wholeness of attention to the successive spiritually significant circumstances and obligations, interior impressions and lights, which her praying, thinking, suffering, actively bring round to her notice, she manages, by such single steps, gradually to go a very long way, and, by such severe successiveness, to build up a rich simultaneity. For each of these faithfully accepted and fully willed and utilized acts and states, received into her one ever-growing and deepening personality, leave memories and stimulations behind them, and mingle, as subconscious elements, with the conscious acts which follow later on.

4. *Two remarkable consequences of this kind of warfare.*

There were two specially remarkable consequences of this constant watchful fixation of the one spiritually significant point in each congeries of circumstances, and of the manner in which (partly perhaps as the occasion, but probably in great part as the effect of this attention) one interior condition of apparent fixity would suddenly shift to another condition of a different kind but of a similar apparent stability. There was the manner in which, during these years, she appears to have escaped the committing of any at all definite offences against the better and best lights of that particular moment; and there was the way in which she would realize the faultiness and subtle self-seeking of any one state, only at the moment of its disappearing to make room for another.

I take the accounts of both these remarkable peculiarities to be substantially accurate, since, if the first condition had not obtained, we should have found her practising more or less frequent Confession, as we find her doing in the first and third, but not in this period; and if the second condition had not existed, we should have had, for this period also, some such vivid account of painful scruples arising from the impression of actually present unfaithfulnesses, such as has been preserved for her last years. And indeed, as soon as we have vividly conceived a state in which a soul (by a wise utilization of the quite exceptional successiveness and simplification to which it has been, in great part, driven by its temperamental requirements, and by a constant heroic watchfulness) has managed to exclude from its life, during a long series of years, all fully deliberate resistances to, or lapses from, its contemporaneous better insight: one sees at once that a consciousness of faultiness could come to her only at those moments when, one state and level giving place to another, she could, for the moment, see the former habits and their implicit defects in the clear light of their contrast to her new, deeper insights and dispositions.

Now it is evident that here again we have in part (in the curious quasi-fixity of each state, and then the sudden replacement of it by another) something which, taken alone, is simply psychically peculiar and spiritually indifferent. The persistent sense of gradual or of rapid change in the midst of a certain continuity and indeed abidingness, characteristic of the average moments of the average soul, is, taken in itself, more true to life and to the normal reaction of the human mind, and not less capable of spiritual utilization, than is Catherine's peculiarity. Her heroic utilization of her special psychic life for purposes of self-fighting, and the degree in which, as we shall find in a later chapter, she succeeded in moulding this life into a shape representative of certain great spiritual truths: these things it is which constitute here the spiritually significant element.

And her second peculiarity of religious practice was her great simplification and intensification of the spiritual combat. Simplification: for she does not fight directly either the Devil or the World; she directly fights the "Flesh" alone, and recognizes but one immediate opponent, her own lower self. Hence the references to the world are always simply as to an extension or indefinite repetition of that same self, or of similar lower selves; and those to the devil are, except where she declares her own lower self "a very devil," extraordinarily rare, and, in their authentic forms, never directly and formally connected with her own spiritual interests and struggles. And Intensification : for she conceives this lower self, against which all her fighting is turned, as capable of any enormity, as actually cloaking itself successively in every kind of disguise, and as more or less vitiating even the most spiritual-seeming of her states and acts.

And here again we can, I think, clearly trace the influence of her special temperament and psycho-physical functioning, yet in a direction opposite to that in which we would naturally expect it. For it is not so much that this temperament led her to exaggerate the badness of her false self, or to elaborate a myth concerning its (all but completely separate) existence, as that, owing in large part to that temperament and functioning, her false self *was* both unusually distinct from her true self and particularly clamorous and claimful. It would indeed be well for hagiography if, in all cases, at least an attempt were made to discover and present the precise and particular good and bad selves, worked for and fought by the particular saint : for it is just this double particularization of the common warfare in every individual soul that gives the poignant interest and instructiveness, and a bracing sense of reality to these lonely yet typical, unique yet universal struggles, defeats, and victories.

And in Catherine's case her special temperament; her particular attitude during the ten years' laxity, and again during the last years' times of obscurity and scruple; even some of her sayings probably still belonging to this middle period; but above all the precise point and edge of her counter-ideal and *attrait:* all indicate clearly enough what was her congenital defect. A great self-engrossment of a downrightly selfish kind; a grouping of all things round such a self-adoring *Ego ;* a noiseless but determined elimination from her life and memory of all that would not or could not, then and there, be drawn and woven into the organism and functioning of this immensely self-seeking, infinitely woundable and wounded, endlessly self-doctoring " I " and " Me " : a self intensely, although not sexually, jealous, envious and exacting, incapable of easy accommodation, of pleasure in half successes, of humour and brightness, of joyous " once-born " creatureliness : all this was certainly to be found, in strong tendency at least, in the untrained parts and periods of her character and life.

And then the same peculiarity and sensitiveness of her

psycho-physical organism which, in her last period, ended by mirroring her mental spiritual apprehensions and picturings in her very body, and which, even at this time, has been traced by us in the curious long fixities and rapid changes of her fields of consciousness, clearly operates also and already here, in separating off this false self from the good one and in heightening the apprehension of that false self to almost a perception in space, or to an all but physical sensation.

We thus get something of which the interesting cases of "doubleness of personality," so much studied of late years, are, as it were, purely psychical, definitely *maladif* caricatures; the great difference consisting in Catherine herself possessing, at all times, the consciousness and memory of both sides, of both "selves," and of each as both actual and potential, within the range of her one great personality. Indeed it is this very multiplicity thus englobed and utilized by that higher unity, which gives depth to her sanity and sanctity.[1]

5. *Precise object and end of her striving.*

And all this is confirmed and completed, as already hinted, by the precise object of her ideal, the particular means and special end of the struggle. Here, at the very culmination of her inner life and aim, we find the deepest traces of her temperamental requirements; and here, in what she seeks, there is again an immense concentration and a significant choice. The distinctions between obligation and supererogation, between merit and grace, are not utilized but transcended; the conception of God having anger as well as love arouses as keen a sense of intolerableness as that of God's envy aroused in Plato, and God appears to her as, in Himself, continuously loving.

This love of God, again, is seen to be present everywhere, and, of Itself, everywhere to effect happiness. The dispositions of souls are indeed held to vary within each soul and between soul and soul, and to determine the differences in their reception, and consequently in the effect upon them, of God's one universal love: but the soul's reward and punishment are not something distinct from its state, they are but that very state prolonged and articulated, since man can indeed go against his deepest requirements but can never

[1] I would draw the reader's attention to the very interesting parallels to many of the above-mentioned peculiarities furnished both by St. Teresa in her *Life, passim,* and by Battista Vernazza in the Autobiographical statements which I have given here in Chapter VIII.

finally suppress them. Heaven, Purgatory, Hell are thus not places as well as states, nor do they begin only in the beyond : they are states alone, and begin already here. And Grace and Love, and Love and Christ, and Christ and Spirit, and hence Grace and Love and Christ and Spirit are, at bottom, one, and this One is God. Hence God, loving Himself in and through us, is alone our full true self. Here, in this constant stretching out and forward of her whole being into and towards the ocean of light and love, of God the All in All, it is not hard to recognize a soul which finds happiness only when looking out and away from self, and turning, in more or less ecstatic contemplation and action, towards that Infinite Country, that great Over-Againstness, God.

And, in her sensitive shrinking from the idea of an angry God, we find the instinctive reaction of a nature too naturally prone itself to angry claimfulness, and which had been too much driven out of its self-occupation by the painful sense of interior self-division consequent upon that jealousy, not to find it intolerable to get out of that little Scylla of her own hungry self only to fall into a great Charybdis, an apparent mere enlargement and canonization of that same self, in the angry God Himself.

And if her second peculiarity, the concentration of the fight upon an unusually isolated and intense false self, had introduced an element of at least relative Rigorism and contraction into her spirituality, this third peculiarity brings a compensating movement of quasi-Pantheism, of immense expansion. Here the crushed plant expands in boundless air, light and warmth; the parched seaweed floats and unfolds itself in an immense ocean of pure waters—the soul, as it were, breathes and bathes in God's peace and love. And it is evident that the great super-sensible realities and relations adumbrated by such figures, did not, with her, lead to mere dry or vague apprehensions. Even in this period, although here with a peaceful, bracing orderliness and harmony, the reality thus long and closely dwelt on and lived with was, as it were, physically seen and felt in these its images by a ready response of her immensely docile psycho-physical organism.

6. *Catherine possessed two out of the three conditions apparently necessary for stigmatization.*

And in this connection we should note how largely reasonable was the expectation of some of her disciples of finding some permanent physical effects upon her body; and yet why she not only had not the stigmata of the Passion, but why she could not have them. For, of the three apparently necessary conditions for such stigmatization, she had indeed two—a long and intense absorption in religious ideas, and a specially sensitive psycho-physical temperament and organization of the ecstatic type; but the third condition, the concentration of that absorption upon Our Lord's Passion and wounds, was wholly wanting—at least after those four actively penitential and during those twenty-two ecstatic years. We can, however, say most truly that although, since at all events 1477, her visions and contemplations were all concerning purely metaphysical, eternal realities, or certain ceaselessly repeated experiences of the human soul, or laws and types derived from the greatest of Christian institutions, her daily solace, the Holy Eucharist: yet that these verities ended by producing definite images in her senses, and certain observable though passing impressions upon her body, so that we can here talk of sensible shadows or "stigmata" of things purely spiritual and eternal.

And if, in the cases of some ecstatic saints, mental pathologists of a more or less materialistic type have, at times, shown excessive suspicion as to some of the causes and effects of these saints' devotion to Our Lord's Humanity under the imagery and categories of the Canticle of Canticles—all such suspicions, fair or unfair, have absolutely no foothold in Catherine's life, since not only is there here no devotion to God or to Our Lord as Bridegroom of the Bridal soul: there is no direct contemplative occupation with the historic Christ and no figuring of Him or of God under human attributes or relations at all. I think that her temperament and health had something to do with her habitual dwelling upon Thing-symbols of God: Ocean—Air—Fire—picturings which, conceived with her psycho-physical vividness, must, in their expanse, have rested and purified her in a way that historical contingencies and details would not have done. The doctrinal and metaphysical side of the matter will be considered later on.

VI. Three Rules which seem to Govern the Relations between Psycho-physical Peculiarities and Sanctity in General.

If we next inquire how matters stand historically with regard to the relations between ecstatic states and psycho-physical peculiarities on the one hand, and sanctity in general on the other hand, we shall find, I think, that the following three rules or laws really cover, in a necessarily general, somewhat schematic way, all the chief points, at all certain or practically important, in this complex and delicate matter.

1. *Intense spiritual energizing is accompanied by autosuggestion and mono-ideism.*

It is clear, for one thing, that as simply all and every mental, emotional, and volitional energizing is necessarily and always accompanied by corresponding nerve-states, and that if we had not some neural sensitiveness and neural adaptability, we could not—whilst living our earthly life—think, or feel, or will in regard to anything whatsoever: a certain special degree of at least potential psycho-physical sensitiveness and adaptability must be taken to be, not the productive cause, but a necessary condition for the exercise, of any considerable range and depth of mind and will, and hence of sanctity in general; and that the actual aiming at, and gradual achievement of, sanctity in these, thus merely possible cases, spiritualizes and further defines this sensitiveness, as the instrument, material, and expression of the soul's work.[1] And this work of the heroic soul will necessarily consist, in great part, in attending to, calling up, and, as far as may be, both fixing and ever renovating certain few great dominant ideas, and in attempting by every means to saturate the imagination with images and figures, historical and symbolic, as so many incarnations of these great verities.

We get thus what, taken simply phenomenally and without as yet any inquiry as to an ultimate reality pressing in upon the soul,—a divine stimulation underlying all its sincere and fruitful action,—is a spiritual mono-ideism and auto-suggestion, of a more or less general kind. But, at this stage, these activities and their psycho-physical concomitants and results will, though different in kind, be no more abnormal than is the mono-ideism and auto-suggestion of the mathematician, the tactician, and the constructive statesman. Newton, Napoleon, and Richelieu: they were all dominated by some great central idea, and they all for long years dwelt upon it and worked for it within themselves, till it became alive and

[1] The omnipresence of neural conditions and consequences for all and every mental and volitional activity has been admirably brought out by Prof. W. James, in his *Varieties of Religious Experience*, 1902, Vol. I, pp. 1–25.

aflame in their imaginations and their outward-moving wills, before, yet as the means of, its taking external and visible shape. And, in all the cases that we can test in detail, the psycho-physical accompaniments of all this profound mental-volitional energy were most marked. In the cases of Newton and Napoleon, for instance, a classification of their energizings solely according to their neural accompaniments would force us to class these great discoverers and organizers amongst psycho-physical eccentrics. Yet the truth and value of their work and character has, of course, to be measured, not by this its neural fringe and cost, but by its central spiritual truth and fruitfulness.

2. *Such mechanisms specially marked in Philosophers, Musicians, Poets, and Mystical Religionists.*

The mystical and contemplative element in the religious life, and the group of saints amongst whom this element is predominant, no doubt give us a still larger amount of what, again taking the matter phenomenally and not ultimately, is once more mono-ideism and auto-suggestion, and entails a correspondingly larger amount of psycho-physical impressionableness and reaction utilized by the mind. But here also, from the simplest forms of the "prayer of quiet" to absorptions of an approximately ecstatic type, we have something which, though different in kind and value, is yet no more abnormal than are the highest flights and absorptions of the Philosopher, the Musician, and the Poet. And yet, in such cases as Kant and Beethoven, a classifier of humanity according to its psycho-physical phenomena alone would put these great discoverers and creators, without hesitation, amongst hopeless and useless hypochondriacs. Yet here again the truth of their ideas and the work of their lives have to be measured by quite other things than by this their neural concomitance and cost.

3. *Ecstatics possess a peculiar psycho-physical organization.*

The downright ecstatics and hearers of voices and seers of visions have all, wherever we are able to trace their temperamental and neural constitution and history, possessed and developed a definitely peculiar psycho-physical organization. We have traced it in Catherine and indicated it in St. Teresa. We find it again in St. Maria Magdalena dei Pazzi and in St. Marguerite Marie Alacocque, in modern times, and in St. Catherine of Siena and St. Francis of Assisi in mediaeval times. For early Christian times we are too ignorant as regards the psycho-physical organization of St. Ignatius of Antioch, Hermas, and St. Cyprian, to be able to establish a connection between their temperamental endowments and their hearing of voices and seeing of visions—in the last two cases we get much that looks like more or less of a mere conventional literary device.[1]

We are, however, in a fair position for judging, in the typical and thoroughly original case of St. Paul. In 2 Cor. xiii, 7, 8, after speaking of the abundant revelations accorded to him, he adds that " lest I be lifted up, a thorn " (literally, a stake) " in the flesh was given to me, an Angel of Satan to buffet me." And though " I thrice besought the Lord that it might depart from me, the Lord answered me, ' My grace is sufficient for thee; for grace is perfected in infirmity.' " And he was consequently determined " rather " to " glory in his infirmities, so that the power of Christ may dwell within " him. And in Gal. iv, 14, 15, written about the same time, he reminds his readers how he had " preached to them through the infirmity of the flesh," commending them because they " did not despise nor loathe their temptation in his flesh " (this is no doubt the correct reading), " but had received him as an Angel of God, as Christ Jesus."

Now the most ancient interpretation of this " thorn " or " stake " is some kind of bodily complaint,—violent headache or earache is mentioned by Tertullian de Pudicitia, 13, and by St. Jerome, Comm. in Gal. *loc. cit.* Indeed St. Paul's own description of his " bodily presence " as " weak," and his " spoken word " as " contemptible " (2 Cor. x, 10), points this way. It seems plain that it cannot have been carnal temptations (only in the sixth century did this interpretation become firmly established), for he could not have gloried in these, nor could they, hidden as they would be within his heart, have exposed him to the contempt of others. Indeed he expressly excludes such troubles from his life, where, in advising those who were thus oppressed to marry, he gives the preference to the single life, and declares, " I would that all men were even as I myself " (1 Cor. vii, 7).

The attacks of this trouble were evidently acutely painful: note the metaphor of a stake driven into the live flesh and the Angel of Satan who buffeted him. (And compare St.

[1] H. Weinel's *Die Wirkungen des Geistes und der Geister im nachapostolischen Zeitalter, bis auf Irenäus*, 1899, contains an admirably careful investigation of these things.

Teresa's account: "An Angel of God appeared to me to be thrusting at times a long spear into my heart and to pierce my very entrails"; "the pain was so great that it made me moan"; "it really seems to the soul as if an arrow were thrust through the heart or through itself; the suffering is not one of sense, neither is the wound physical"; and how, on another occasion, she heard Our Lord answer her: "Serve thou Me, and meddle not with this.")[1]

These attacks would come suddenly, even in the course of his public ministry, rendering him, in so far, an object of derision and of loathing. (Compare here St. Teresa's declaration: "During the rapture, the body is very often perfectly powerless; it continues in the position it was in when the rapture came upon it: if sitting, sitting; if the hands were open, or if they were shut, they will remain open or shut"; "if the body" was "standing or kneeling, it remains so.")[2]

Yet these attacks were evidently somehow connected, both in fact and in his consciousness, with his Visions; and they were recurrent. The vision of the Third Heaven and his apparently first attack seem to have been practically coincident,—about A.D. 44. We find a second attack hanging about him for some time, on his first preaching in Galatia, about A.D. 51 or 52 (see 1 Thess. ii, 18; 1 Cor. ii, 3). And a third attack appears to have come in A.D. 57 or 58, when the Second Epistle to the Corinthians and that to the Galatians were written; note the words (2 Cor. i, 9), "Yea" (in addition to his share in the public persecution), "we ourselves have had the answer of death within ourselves, that we should not trust in ourselves, but in God which raiseth the dead." (And compare here St. Teresa: in July 1547 "for about four days I remained insensible. They must have regarded me as dead more than once. For a day and a half the grave was open in my monastery, waiting for my body. But it pleased Our Lord I should come to myself.")[3] Dr. Lightfoot gives as a parallel the epileptiform seizures of King Alfred, which, sudden, acutely painful, at times death-like, and protracted, tended to render the royal power despicable in the eyes of the world.[4] Yet, except for the difference of sex and of

[1] *Life*, written by herself, ed. cit. pp. 235, 423; 136.

[2] *Ibid.* pp. 149, 420.

[3] *Ibid.* pp. xxii, 28.

[4] It is to Dr. Lightfoot's fine Excursus in *St. Paul's Epistle to the Galatians*, ed. 1881, pp. 186–191, that I owe all the Pauline texts and most of the considerations reproduced above.

relative privacy, St. Teresa's states, which I have given here, are more closely similar, in so much as they are intimately connected with religious visions and voices.

And, amongst Old Testament figures, we can find a similar connection, on a still larger scale, in the case of Ezekiel, the most definitely ecstatic, though (upon the whole) the least original, of the literary Prophets. For, as to the visionary element, we have his own records of three visions of the glory of Jahve; of five other ecstasies, three of which are accompanied by remarkable telepathic, second-sight activities; and of twelve symbolic (better: representative) prophetic actions, which are now all rightly coming to be considered as having been externally carried out by him.[1] And we get psycho-physical states, as marked as in any other ecstatic saint. For we hear how Jahve on one occasion says to him: "But thou, son of man, lay thyself on thy left side" (*i. e.* according to Jewish orientation, towards the North) "and I shall lay the guilt of the house of Israel" (the Northern Kingdom) "upon thee; the number of days that thou shalt lie upon it, shalt thou bear their guilt. But I appoint unto thee the years of their guilt, as a (corresponding) number of days, (namely) one hundred and fifty days. . . . And, when thou hast done with them, thou shalt lay thyself on thy right side" (*i. e.* towards the South), "and thou shalt bear the guilt of the house of Judah" (the Southern Kingdom); "one day for each year shall I appoint unto thee. And behold I shall lay cords upon thee, that thou shalt be unable to turn from one side to the other, till thou hast ended the days of thy boundness" (iv, 4–8). Krätzschmar, no doubt rightly, finds here a case of hemiplegia and anaesthesia, functional cataleptic paralysis lasting during five months on the left side, and then shifting for about six weeks to the right side. And the *alalia* (speechlessness), which no doubt accompanied this state, is referred to on three other occasions: xxiv, 27; xxix, 31; xxxiii, 22. And note how Jahve's address to Ezekiel, "son of man," which occurs in this book over ninety times, and but once in the whole of the rest of the Old Testament (Dan. viii,

[1] Visions of Jahve's glory: i, 1–28; iii, 22–27; xl, 1; xliv, 4. The five other Ecstasies and Visions: viii, 1 foll.; xi, 1 foll.; xxiv, 1 foll.; xxxiii, 22; xxxvii, 1 foll. Second Sight: viii, 16; xi, 13; xxiv, 1. Representative Actions: iv, 1–3, 7; iv, 4–6, 8; iv, 10; ix, 11–15; xii, 1–16; xii, 17–20; xxi, 11, 12; xxi, 23–32; xxiv, 1-14; xxiv, 15–27; xxxiii, 22; xxxvii, 15–28.

17), evidently stands here for the sense of his creaturely nothingness, so characteristic of the true ecstatic.[1]

Now, at this last stage, the analogy of the other non-religious activities of the healthy mind and of their psycho-physical conditions and effects forsakes us; but not the principle which has guided us all along. For here, as from the very first, some such conditions and effects are inevitable; and the simple fact of this occurrence, apart from the question of their particular character, is something thoroughly normal. And here again, and more than ever, the emphasis and decisions have to lie with, and to depend upon, the mental and volitional work and the spiritual truth and reality achieved in and for the recipient, and, through him, in and for others.

Even at the earlier stages, to cling to the form, as distinct from the content and end, of these things was to be thoroughly unfair to this their content and end, within the spacious economy of the spirit's life; at this stage such clinging becomes destructive of all true religion. For if the mere psycho-physical forms and phenomena of ecstasy, of vision, of hearing of voices is, in proportion to their psycho-physical intensity and seeming automatism and quasi-physical objectivity, to be taken as necessarily a means and mark of sanctity or of insight, or, at least, as something presumably sent direct by God or else as diabolical, something necessarily super- or preter-natural: then the lunatic asylums contain more miracles, saints, and sages, or their direct, strangely similar antipodes, than all the most fervent or perverted churches, monasteries, and families upon God's earth. For in asylums we find ecstasies, visions, voices, all more, not less marked, all more, not less irresistibly objective-seeing to the recipient, than anything to be found outside.

Yet apply impartially to both sets the test, not of form, but of content, of spiritual fruitfulness and of many-sided applicability—and this surface-similarity yields at once to a fundamental difference. Indeed all the great mystics, and this in precise proportion to their greatness, have ever taught

[1] The above translation and interpretation is based upon Krätzschmar's admirably psychological commentary, *Das Buch Ezechiel*, Göttingen, 1900, pp. v, vi; 45, 49. But I think he is wrong in taking that six months' abnormal condition to have given rise, in Ezekiel's mind, to a belief in a previous divine order and to an interpretation of this order. All the strictly analogical cases of religious ecstasy, not hysteria, point to a strong mental impression, such as that order and belief having preceded and occasioned the peculiar psycho-physical state.

that, the mystical capacities and habits being but means and not ends, only such ecstasies are valuable as leave the soul, and the very body as its instrument, strengthened and improved; and that visions and voices are to be accepted by the mind only in proportion as they convey some spiritual truth of importance to it or to others, and as they actually help it to become more humble, true, and loving.

And there can be no doubt that these things worked thus with such great ecstatic mystics as Ezekiel, the man of the great prophetic schemes and the permanently fruitful picturing of the Good Shepherd; as St. Paul, the greatest missionary and organizer ever given to the Christian Church; as St. Francis of Assisi, the salt and leaven and light of the Church and of society, in his day and more or less ever since; as St. Catherine of Siena, the free-spoken, docile reinspirer of the Papacy; as Jeanne d'Arc, the maiden deliverer of a Nation; as St. Teresa, reformer of a great Order. All these, and countless others, would, quite evidently, have achieved less, not more, of interior light and of far-reaching helpfulness of a kind readily recognized by all specifically religious souls, had they been without the rest, the bracing, the experience furnished to them by their ecstasies and allied states and apprehensions.

VII. Perennial Freshness of the Great Mystics' Main Spiritual Test, in Contradistinction to their Secondary, Psychological Contention. Two Special Difficulties.

1. *A false and a true test of mystical experience.*

Now it is deeply interesting to note how entirely unweakened, indeed how impressively strengthened, by the intervening severe test of whole centuries of further experience and of thought, has remained the main and direct, the spiritual test of the great Mystics, in contradistinction to their secondary psychological contention with respect to such experiences. The secondary, psychological contention is well reproduced by St. Teresa where she says: "When I speak, I go on with my understanding arranging what I am saying; but, if I am spoken to by others, I do nothing else but listen without any labour." In the former case, "the soul," if it be in good faith, "cannot possibly fail to see clearly that itself arranges the words and utters them to itself. How then can the understanding have time enough to arrange these locutions? They require time." [1] Now this particular argument for their supernaturalness derived from the psychological form—from the suddenness, clearness, and apparent automatism of these locutions—has ceased to carry weight, owing to our present, curiously recent, knowledge concerning the subconscious region of the mind, and the occasionally sudden irruption of that region's contents into the field of that same mind's ordinary, full consciousness. In the Ven. Battista Vernazza's case we have a particularly clear instance of such a long accumulation,—by means of much, in great part full, attention to certain spiritual ideas, words, and images,—in the subconscious regions of a particularly strong and deeply sincere and saintly mind; and the sudden irruption from those regions of certain clear and apparently quite spontaneous words and images into the field of her mind's full consciousness.[2]

But the reference to the great Mystics' chief and direct test, upon which they dwell with an assurance and self-consistency far surpassing that which accompanies their psychological argument,—the spiritual content and effects of such experiences,—this, retains all its cogency. St. Teresa tells us: "When Our Lord speaks, it is both word and work: His words are deeds." "I found myself, through these words alone, tranquil and strong, courageous and confident, at rest and enlightened: I felt I could maintain against all the world that my prayer was the work of God." "I could not believe that Satan, if he wished to deceive me, could have recourse to means so adverse to his purpose as this, of rooting out my faults, and implanting virtues and spiritual strength: for I saw clearly that I had become another person, by means of these visions." "So efficacious was the vision, and such was the nature of the words spoken to me, that I could not possibly doubt that they came from Him." "I was in a trance; and the effects of it were such, that I could have no doubt it came from God." On another occasion she writes less positively even of the great test: "She never undertook anything merely because it came to her in prayer. For all that her Confessors told her that these things came from

[1] *Op. cit.* pp. 190*c*; 192*c*, 193*a*.

[2] See Prof. W. James's admirable account of these irruptions in his *Varieties of Religious Experience*, 1902, pp. 231–237.

God, she never so thoroughly believed them that she could swear to it herself, though it did seem to her that they were spiritually safe, because of the effects thereof."[1] This doctrine is still the last word of wisdom in these matters.

2. *First special difficulty in testing ecstasies.*

Yet it is only at this last stage that two special difficulties occur, the one philosophical, the other moral. The philosophical difficulty is as follows. As long as the earlier stages are in progress, it is not difficult to understand that the soul may be gradually building up for herself a world of spiritual apprehensions, and a corresponding spiritual and moral character, by a process which, looked at merely phenomenally and separately, appears as a simple case of mono-ideism and auto-suggestion, but which can and should be conceived, when studied in its ultimate cause and end, as due to the pressure and influence of God's spirit working in and through the spirit of man,—the Creator causing His own little human creature freely to create for itself some copy of and approach to its own eternally subsisting, substantial Cause and Crown. There the operation of such an underlying Supreme Cause, and a consequent relation between the world thus conceived and built up by the human soul and the real world of the Divine Spirit, appears possible, because the things which the soul is thus made to suggest to itself are ideas, and because even these ideas are clearly recognized by the soul as only instruments and approaches to the realities for which they stand. But here, in this last stage, we get the suggestion, not of ideas, but of psycho-physical impressions, and these impressions are, apparently, not taken as but distantly illustrative, but as somehow one with the spiritual realities for which they stand. Is not, *e. g.*, Catherine's joy at this stage centred precisely in the downright feeling, smelling, seeing, of ocean waters, penetrating odours, all-enveloping light; and in the identification of those waters, odours, lights, with God Himself, so that God becomes at last an object of direct, passive, sensible perception? Have we not then here at last reached pure delusion?

Not so, in proportion as the mystic is great and spiritual, and as he here still clings to the principles common to all true religion. For, in proportion as he is and does this, will he find and regard the mind as deeper and more operative

[1] *Life*, written by Herself, pp. 190*b*; 196*b*; 224*c*; 295*c*; 413*b*.

than sense, and God's Spirit as penetrating and transcending both the one and the other. And hence he will (at least implicitly) regard those psycho-physical impressions as but sense-like and really mental; and he will consider this mental impression and projection as indeed produced by the presence and action of the Spirit within his mind or of the pressure of spiritual realities upon it, but will hold that this whole mental process, with these its spatial- and temporal-seeming embodiments, these sights and sounds, has only a relation and analogical likeness to, and is not and cannot be identical with, those realities of an intrinsically super-spatial, super-temporal order.—And thus here as everywhere, although here necessarily more than ever, we find again the conception of the Transcendent yet also Immanent Spirit, effecting in the human spirit the ever-increasing apprehension of Himself, accompanied in this spirit by an ever-keener sense of His incomprehensibility for all but Himself. And here again the truth, and more especially the divine origin of these apprehensions, is tested and guaranteed on and on by the consequent deepening of that spiritual and ethical fruitfulness and death to self, which are the common aspirations of every deepest moment and every sincerest movement within the universal heart of man.

Thus, as regards the mentality of these experiences, Catherine constantly speaks of seeing " as though with the eyes of the body." And St. Teresa tells us of her visions with " the eyes of the soul " ; of how at first she " did not know that it was possible to see anything otherwise than with the eyes of the body " ; of how, in reality " she never," in her true visions and locutions, " saw anything with her bodily eyes, nor heard anything with her bodily ears " ; and of how indeed she later on, on one occasion, " saw nothing with the eyes of the body, nothing with the eyes of the soul,"—she " simply felt Christ close by her,"—evidently again with the soul. Thus, too, Catherine tells us, that " as the intellect exceeds language, so does love exceed intellection " ; and how vividly she feels that " all that can be said of God," compared to the great Reality, " is but tiny crumbs from the great Master's table." [1]

And, as to the inadequacy of these impressions, the classical authority on such things, St. John of the Cross, declares : " He that will rely on the letter of the divine locutions or on the intelligible form of the vision, will of necessity fall into

[1] *Vita*, passim; *Life*, ed. cit. pp. 40, 41; 408; 206. *Vita*, pp. 87*c*, 77*b*.

delusion; for he does not yield to the Spirit in detachment from sense." "He who shall give attention to these motes of the Spirit alone will, in the end, have no spirituality at all." "All visions, revelations, and heavenly feelings, and whatever is greater than these, are not worth the least act of humility, bearing the fruits of that charity which neither values nor seeks itself, which thinketh well not of self but of all others." Indeed "virtue does not consist in these apprehensions. Let men then cease to regard, and labour to forget them, that they may be free." For "spiritual supernatural knowledge is of two kinds, one distinct and special," which comprises "visions, revelations, locutions, and spiritual impressions"; "the other confused, obscure, and general," which "has but one form, that of contemplation which is the work of faith. The soul is to be led into this, by directing it thereto through all the rest, beginning with the first, and detaching it from them."

Hence "many souls, to whom visions have never come, are incomparably more advanced in the way of perfection than others to whom many have been given"; and "they who are already perfect, receive these visitations of the Spirit of God in peace; ecstasies cease, for they were only graces to prepare them for this greater grace." Hence, too, "one desire only doth God allow and suffer in His Presence: that of perfectly observing His law and of carrying the Cross of Christ. In the Ark of the Covenant there was but the Book of the Law, the Rod of Aaron, and the Pot of Manna. Even so that soul, which has no other aim than the perfect observance of the Law of God and the carrying of the Cross of Christ, will be a true Ark containing the true Manna, which is God." And this perfected soul's intellectual apprehensions will, in their very mixture of light and conscious obscurity, more and more approach and forestall the eternal condition of the beatified soul. "One of the greatest favours, bestowed transiently on the soul in this life, is to enable it to see so distinctly and to feel so profoundly, that it cannot comprehend Him at all. These souls are herein, in some degree, like the Saints in Heaven, where they who know Him most perfectly perceive most clearly that He is infinitely incomprehensible; for those who have the less clear vision do not perceive so distinctly as the others how greatly He transcends their vision." [1]

[1] *Ascent of Mount Carmel*, ed. cit. pp. 159, 163; 264, 265, 102, 195; *Spiritual Canticle*, ed. cit. p. 238; *Ascent*, pp. 26, 27; *Canticle*, pp. 206, 207.

3. *Second special difficulty in testing ecstasies.*

The second special difficulty is this. Have not at least some of the saints of this definitely ecstatic type shown more psycho-physical abnormality than spiritually fruitful origination or utilization of such things, so that their whole life seems penetrated by a fantastic spirit? And have not many others, who, at their best, may not have been amenable to this charge, ended with shattered nerve- and will-power, with an organism apparently incapable of any further growth or use, even if we restrict our survey exclusively to strength-bringing ecstasy and to a contemplative prayer of some traceable significance?

(1) As a good instance of the apparent predominance of psycho-physical and even spiritual strangeness, we can take the Venerable Sister Lukardis, Cistercian Nun of Ober-Weimar, born probably in 1276. Her life is published from a unique Latin MS. by the Bollandists (*Analecta*, Vol. XVIII, pp. 305–367, Bruxelles, 1899), and presents us with a mediaevally naïve and strangely unanalytic, yet extraordinarily vivid picture of things actually seen by the writer. "Although," say the most competent editors, "we know not the name nor profession of the Author, whether he belonged to the Friars or to the Monks,[1] it is certain that he was a contemporary of Lukardis, that he knew her intimately, and that he learnt many details from her fellow-nuns. And though we shall be slow to agree with him when he ascribes all the strange things which she experienced in her soul and body to divine influence, yet we should beware of considering him to be in bad faith. For, though he erred perchance in ascribing to a divine operation things which are simply the work of nature, such a vice is common amongst those who transmit such things."[2] I take the chief points in the order of their narration by the *Vita*.

"Soon after Lukardis had, at twelve years of age, taken the Cistercian habit, her mother died," over twelve English miles away, at Erfurt, yet Lukardis "saw the scene" in such detail "in the spirit," that, when her sister came to tell her, she, Lukardis, "anticipated her with an account of the day, the place and hour of the death, of the clothes then being worn by their mother, of the precise position of the bed and of the hospital, and of the persons present at the time."

[1] Two Confessors of hers are mentioned by her, *Vita*, p. 352; Fathers Henry of Mühlhausen, and Eberhard of the Friars Preachers.

[2] *Analecta, loc. cit.* p. 310.

She soon suffered from " stone " in the bladder; " quartan, tertian, and continuous fevers," and from fainting fits; also from contraction of the muscles (*nervi*) of the hands, so that the latter were all but useless and could not even hold the staff on which she had to lean in walking, till they had been "tightly wrapped round in certain clothes." Yet "she would, at times, strike her hands so vehemently against each other, that they resounded as though they had been wooden boards." " When lying in bed she would sometimes, as it were, plant her feet beneath her, hang her head down " backwards, " and raise her abdomen and chest, making thus, as it were, a highly curved arch of her person." Indeed sometimes " she would for a long while stand upon her head and shoulders, with her feet up in air, but with her garments adhering to her limbs, as though they had been sewn on to them." " Often, too, by day or night, she was wont to run with a most impetuous course;—she understood that, by this her course, she was compensating Christ for His earthly course of thirty-three years."[1]

" On one occasion she had a vision of Christ, in which He said to her: 'Join thy hands to My hands, and thy feet to My feet, and thy breast to My breast, and thus shall I be aided by thee to suffer less.' And instantly she felt a most keen pain of wounds," in all three regions, " although wounds did not as yet appear to sight." But " as she bore the memory of the hammering of the nails into Christ upon the Cross within her heart, so did she exercise herself in outward deed. For she was frequently wont, with the middle finger of one hand, impetuously to wound the other in the place appropriate to the stigmata; then to withdraw her finger to the distance of a cubit, and straightway again impetuously to wound herself. Those middle fingers felt hard like metal. And about the sixth and ninth hour she would impetuously wound herself with her finger in the breast, at the appropriate place for the wound."—After about two years " Christ appeared to her in the night of Blessed Gregory, Pope " (St. Gregory VII, May 26?), " pressed her right hand firmly in His, and declared, ' I desire thee to suffer with Me.' On her consenting, a wound instantly appeared in her right hand; about ten days later a wound in the left hand; and thus successively the five wounds were found in her body." " The wounds of the scourging

[1] *Analecta*, pp. 311–313.

were also found upon her, of a finger's length, and having a certain hard skin around them." [1]

"At whiles she would lie like one dead throughout the day; yet her countenance was very attractive, owing to a wondrous flushed look. And even if a needle was pressed into her flesh, she felt no pain."—"On one occasion she was carried upon her couch by two sisters into the Lady Chapel, to the very spot where her body now reposes. After having been left there alone for about an hour, the Blessed Virgin appeared to her, with her beloved Infant, Jesus, in her arms, and suckling Him. And Lukardis, contrary to the law of her strength"—she had, by now, been long confined to a reclining posture—"arose from her couch and began to stand upright. And at this juncture one of the Sisters opened the Chapel door a little, and, on looking in, marvelled at Lukardis being able to stand, but withdrew and forbade the other Sisters from approaching thither, since she feared that, if they saw her standing thus, they might declare her to be quite able, if she but chose, to arise and stand at any time. Upon the Blessed Virgin twice insisting upon being asked for some special favour, and Lukardis declaring, 'I desire that thou slake my thirst with that same milk with which I now see thee suckling thy beloved Son,' the Blessed Virgin came up to her, and gave her to drink of her milk." And when later on Lukardis was fetched by the Sisters, she was "found reclining on her couch. And for three days and nights she took neither food nor drink, and could not see the light of day. And as a precaution, since her death was feared, Extreme Unction was administered to her. And, later on, the Sister who had seen her standing in the Chapel, gradually drew the whole story from her." [2]

"After she had lain, very weak, and, as it were, in a state of contracture, for eleven years, it happened that, about the ninth hour of one Good Friday, the natural bodily heat and colour forsook her; she seemed nowise to breathe; her wounds bled more than usual; she appeared to be dead. And her fellow-Sisters wept greatly. Yet about Vesper-time she opened her eyes and began to move; and her companions were wondrously consoled. And then in the Easter night, about the hour of Christ's Resurrection, as, with the other sick Sisters, she lay in her bed placed so as to be able to hear the Divine

[1] *Analecta*, pp. 314, 315. [2] *Vita, loc. cit.* pp. 317, 319.

Office, she felt all her limbs to be as it were suffused with a most refreshing dew. And straightway she saw stretched down to her from Heaven a hand, as it were of the Blessed Virgin, which stroked her wounds and all the painful places, the ligaments and joints of her members, gently and compassionately. After which she straightway felt how that all her members, which before had for so long been severely contracted, and how the knots, formed by the ligaments (*nervi*), were being efficaciously resolved and equally distended, so that she considered herself freed from her hard bondage. She arose unaided from her couch, proceeded to the near-by entrance to the Choir, and prostrated herself there, in fervent orison, with her arms outstretched in cross-form, for a very long hour. And then, commanded by the Abbess to rise, she readily arose without help, stood with pleasure, and walked whithersoever she would." "At all times she ever suffered more from the cold than any of her companions." [1]

"As, during those eleven years that she lay like one paralyzed, she was wont, on every Friday, to lie with her arms expanded as though on the Cross, and her feet one on the top of the other; so, after the Lord had so wonderfully raised her on that Paschal day, she, on every Friday and every Lenten day, would stand erect with her arms outstretched, crosswise, and, without any support, on one foot only, with the other foot planted upon its fellow, from the hour of noon to that of Vespers."—"Whilst she was still uncured, and required some delicate refection which the Convent could not afford, there came to her," one day, "the most loving Infant, bearing in His Hand the leg of a chicken, newly roasted, and begging her to eat it for His sake." She did so, and was wonderfully strengthened. Apparently late on in her life "they procured, with much labour and diligence, all kinds of drinkables from different and even from distant places for her. But she, having tasted any one of them, would straightway shake her head, close her lips, and then declare that she could not drink it up." "However delicious in itself, it seemed to be so much gall and wormwood when applied to her mouth." [2]

And if we look, not at seemingly childish fantasticalness in certain mystical lives, but at the later state of shattered health and apparently weakened nerve- and will-power which appears

[1] *Vita*, pp. 319, 320. [2] *Ibid.*, *loc. cit.* pp. 327, 334, 352.

so frequently to be the price paid for the definitely ecstatic type of religion, even where it has been spiritually fruitful, our anxiety is readily renewed. Look at the nine, possibly thirteen, last years of Catherine's, or at the last period of St. Margaret Mary's life; note the similar cases of SS. Maria Magdalena de Pazzi and Juliana Falconieri. And we have a figure of all but pure suffering and passivity in St. Lidwina of Schiedam (1380–1433), over which M. Huysmans has managed to be so thoroughly morbid.

(2) And if such lives strike us as too exceptional to be taken, with whatever deductions, as a case in point, we can find a thoroughly fair instance in the life of Father Isaac Hecker. Here we have a man of extraordinary breadth, solidity, and activity of mind and character, and whose mysticism is of the most sober and harmonious kind. Yet his close companion and most faithful chronicler, Father Walter Elliott, tells us: "From severe colds, acute headaches, and weakness of the digestive organs, Father Hecker was at all times a frequent sufferer. But, towards the end of the year 1871, his headaches became much more painful, his appetite forsook him, and sleeplessness and excitability of the nervous system were added to his other ailments. Remedies of every kind were tried, but without permanent relief. By the summer of 1872 he was wholly incapacitated." "The physical sufferings of those last sixteen" (out of the sixty-nine) "years of his life were never such as to impair his mental soundness . . . though his organs of speech were sometimes too slow for his thoughts." His digestion and nervous system had been impaired by excessive abstinence in early manhood, and by excessive work in later life, "till at last the body struck work altogether. During the sixteen years of his illness every symptom of bodily illness was aggravated by the least attention to community affairs or business matters, and also by interior trials," although he still managed, by heroic efforts, at times directly to serve his congregation and to write some remarkable papers. Yet this state continued, practically unbroken, up to the end, on December 22, 1888.[1] And although the various proximate causes, indicated by Father Elliott, had no doubt been operative here, there can, in view of the numerous similar cases, be no question that the most fundamental of the reasons of this general condition of health was his strongly

[1] *The Life of Father Hecker*, by the Rev. Walter Elliott, New York, 1894, pp. 371, 372, 418.

mystical type and habit of mind and his corresponding psycho-physical organization.

(3) In view of those fantasticalnesses and of these exhaustions, we cannot but ask whether these things are not a terrible price to pay for such states? whether such states should not be disallowed by all solid morality, and should not prompt men of sense to try and stamp them out? And, above all, we seem placed once more, with added anxiety, before the question whether what is liable to end in such sad general incapacitation was not, from the first, directly productive of, and indeed simply produced by, some merely subjective, simply psycho-physical abnormality and morbidness?

(4) Three points here call for consideration. Let us, for one thing, never forget that physical health is not the true end of human life, but only one of its most important means and conditions. The ideal man is not, primarily and directly, a physical machine, perfect as such in its development and function, to which would be tacked on, as a sort of concomitant or means, the mental, moral, and spiritual life and character. But the ideal man is precisely this latter life and character, with the psycho-physical organism sustained and developed in such, and only such, a degree, direction, and combination, as may make it the best possible substratum, stimulus, instrument, material, and expression for and of that spiritual personality.[1] Hence, the true question here is not whether such a type of life as we are considering exacts a serious physical tribute or not, but whether the specifically human effects and fruits of that life are worth that cost.

No one denies that mining, or warfare, or hospital work, both spiritual and medical, involve grave risks to life, nor that the preparation of many chemicals is directly and inevitably injurious to health. Yet no one thinks of abolishing such occupations or of blaming those who follow them, and rightly so; for instant death may and should be risked, the slow but certain undermining of the physical health may be laudably embarked on, if only the mind and character are not damaged, and if the end to be attained is found

[1] Robert Browning, in *Rabbi Ben Ezra*, viii; Matthew Arnold, in *Culture and Anarchy*, 21; Prof. James Seth, in *A Study of Ethical Principles*, 1894, pp. 260–262; and Prof. Percy Gardner, in *Oxford at the Cross Roads*, 1903, pp. 12–14, have all admirably insisted upon this most important point.

to be necessary or seriously helpful, and unattainable by other means.

The simple fact, then, of frequent and subsequent, or even of universal and concomitant ill-health in such mystical cases, or even the proof of this ill-health being a direct consequence or necessary condition of that mystical life, can but push back the debate, and simply raises the question as to the serious value of that habit and activity. Only a decision adverse to that serious value would constitute those facts into a condemnation of that activity itself.

And, next, it must be plain to any one endowed with an appreciable dose of the mystical sense, and with a sufficiently large knowledge of human nature and of religious apprehension in the past and present,—that, if it is doubtless possible quite erroneously to treat all men as having a considerable element of mysticism in them, and hence to strain and spoil souls belonging to one of the other types : it is equally possible to starve those that possess this element in an operative degree. Atrophy is as truly a malady as plethora.

And here the question is an individual one : would that particular temperament and psycho-physical organism congenial to Sister Lukardis, to Catherine Fiesca Adorna, to Marguerite Marie Alacocque, and to Isaac Hecker, have—taking the whole existence and output together—produced more useful work, and have apprehended and presented more of abiding truth, had their ecstatic states or tendencies been, if possible, absent or suppressed? Does not this type of apprehension, this, as it were, incubation, harmonization, and vivifying of their otherwise painfully fragmentary and heavy impressions, stand out,—in their central, creative periods,—as the one thoroughly appropriate means and form of their true self-development and self-expression, and of such an apprehension and showing forth of spiritual truth as to them,—to them and not to you and me,—was possible? And if we are bound to admit that, even in such cases, ecstasy appears, psycho-physically, as a kind of second state, and that these personalities find or regain their fullest joy and deepest strength only in and from such a state; yet we know too that such ecstasy is not, as in the trances of hysteria and of other functional disorders, simply discontinuous from the ordinary, primary state of such souls; and that,—again contrary to those *maladif* trances,—whenever the ecstasy answers to the tests insisted upon by the great mystics, viz. a true and valuable ethico-spiritual content and effect, it also, in the long run, leaves the very body strengthened and improved.

And if, after this, their productive period, some of these persons end by losing their psycho-physical health, it is far from unreasonable to suppose that the actual alternative to those ecstasies and this break-up, would, *for them*, have been a lifelong dreary languor and melancholy self-absorption, somewhat after the pattern of Catherine's last ten pre-conversion years. Thus for her, and doubtless for most of the spiritually considerable ecstatics, life was, taken all in all, indefinitely happier, richer, and more fruitful in religious truth and holiness, with the help of those ecstatic states, than it would have been if these states had been absent or could have been suppressed.

And thirdly, here again, even from the point of view of psycho-physical health and its protection, it is precisely the actual practice and, as interpreted by it, the deepest sayings of the standard Christian mystics which are being most powerfully confirmed,—although necessarily by largely new reasons and with important modifications in the analysis and application of their doctrine,—by all that we have gained, during the last forty years, in definite knowledge of the psycho-physical regions and functions of human nature, and, during two centuries and more, in enlargement and precision of our religious-historical outlook.

If we consider the specific health-dangers of this way, we shall find, I think, that their roots are ever two. These dangers, and with them the probability of delusion or at least of spiritual barrenness, always become actual, and often acute, the minute that we allow ourselves to attach a primary and independent importance to the psycho-physical form and means of these things, as against their spiritual-ethical content, suggestions, and end; or that we take the whole man, or at least the whole of the religious man, to consist of the specifically mystical habits and life alone. Now the first of these dangers has been ceaselessly exposed and fought by all the great ethical and Christian mystics of the past, *e.g.* St. John of the Cross and St. Teresa; and the latter has been ever enforced by the actual practice, as social religionists, of these same mystics, even if and when some of their sayings, or the logical drift of their speculative system, left insufficient room or no intrinsic necessity and function for such things.

(5) And everything that has happened and is happening in the world of psychological and philosophical research, in the world of historico-critical investigation into the past history and modalities of religion, and in the world of our own present religious experience and requirements, has but brought to light fresh facts, forces, and connections, in proof both of the right and irreplaceableness of the Mystical element in life and religion, and of the reality and constant presence of these its two dangers. For, as to these dangers, we now know, with extraordinary clearness and certainty, how necessary, constant and far-reaching is, on its phenomenal surface, the auto-suggestive, mono-ideistic power and mechanism of the mind; yet how easily, in some states, too much can be made of such vivid apprehensions and quasi-sensible imagings of invisible reality,—things admirable as means, ruinous as ends. And we also know, with an astonishing universality of application, how great a multiplicity in unity is necessarily presented by every concrete object and by every mental act and emotional state of every sane human being throughout every moment of his waking life; and how this unity is actually constituted and measured by the multiplicity of the materials and by the degree of their harmonization.—Hence, not the absence of the Mystical element, but the presence both of it and of the other constituents of religion, will turn out to be the safeguard of our deepest life and of its sanity, a sanity which demands a balanced fulness of the soul's three fundamental pairs of activities: sensible perception and picturing memory; reflection, speculative and analytic; and emotion and volition, all issuing in interior and exterior acts, and these latter, again, providing so much fresh material and occasions for renewed action and for a growing unification in an increasing variety, on and on.

The metaphysical and faith questions, necessarily raised by the phenomenal facts and mechanisms here considered, but which cannot be answered at this level, will be discussed in a later chapter. Here we can but once more point out, in conclusion, that no amount of admitted or demonstrated auto-suggestion or mono-ideism in the phenomenal reaches and mechanism of the mind decides, of itself, anything whatsoever about, and still less against, the objective truth and spiritual value of the ultimate causes, dominant ideas, and final results of the process; nor as to whether and how far the whole great movement is, at bottom, occasioned and directed by the

Supreme Spirit, God, working, in and through man, towards man's apprehension and manifestation of Himself.[1]

[1] I owe much clearness of conception as to the function of auto-suggestion and mono-ideism to the very remarkable paper of Prof. Emile Boutroux, " La Psychologie du Mysticisme," in the *Bulletin de l'Institut Psychologique International*, Paris, 1902, pp. 9–26: Engl. tr. in the *International Journal of Ethics*, Philadelphia, Jan. 1908. There are also many most useful facts and reflections in Prof. Henri Joly's *Psychology of the Saints*, Engl. tr., 1898, pp. 64–117.

CHAPTER X

THE MAIN LITERARY SOURCES OF CATHERINE'S CONCEPTIONS

INTRODUCTORY.

1. *The main literary sources of Catherine's teaching are four.* The main literary sources of Catherine's conceptions can be grouped under four heads: the New Testament, Pauline and Johannine writings; the Christian Neo-Platonist, Areopagite books; and the Franciscan, Jacopone da Todi's teachings. And here, as in all cases of such partial dependence, we have to distinguish between the apparently accidental occasions (her seemingly fortuitous acquaintance with these particular writings), and the certainly necessary causes (the intrinsic requirements of her own mind and soul, and its special reactions under, and transformations of, these materials and stimulations). And during this latter process this mind's original trend itself undergoes, in its turn, not only much development, but even some modification. She would no doubt owe her close knowledge of the first two sets of writings to the Augustinian Canonesses, (her sister Limbania amongst them,) and to their Augustinian-Pauline tradition; her acquaintance with the third set, to her Dominican cousin; and her intimacy with the fourth, to the Franciscans of the Hospital. Yet only her own spiritual affinity for similar religious states and ideals, and her already at least partial experience of them, could ever have made these writings to her what they actually became: direct stimulations, indeed considerable elements and often curiously vivid expressions, of her own immediate interior life.

2. *Plan of the following study of these sources.* I shall, in this chapter, first try to draw out those characteristics of each group, which were either specially accepted or transformed, neglected or supplanted by her, and carefully to note the particular nature of these her reactions and refashion-

ings. And I shall end up by a short account of what she and all four sets have got in common, and of what she has brought, as a gift of her own, to that common stock which had given her so much. And since her distinct and direct use of the Pauline and Johannine writings is quite certain, whereas all her knowledge of Neo-Platonism seems to have been mediated by pseudo-Dionysius alone, and all her Franciscanism appears, as far as literary sources go, to take its rise from Jacopone, I shall give four divisions to her chief literary sources, and a fifth section to the stream common to them all.[1]

I. The Pauline Writings: The Two Sources of their Pre-conversion Assumptions; Catherine's Preponderant Attitude towards each Position.

It is well that the chronological order requires us to begin with St. Paul, for he is probably, if not the most extensive, yet the most intense of all these influences upon Catherine's mind. I here take the points of his experience and teaching which thus concern us in the probable order of their development in the Apostle's own consciousness,—his pre-conversion assumptions and positions, first, and the convictions gained at and after his conversion or clarified last;[2] and under each heading I shall group together, once for all, the chief reactions of Catherine's religious consciousness.

Now those Pauline pre-conversion assumptions and positions come from two chief sources—Palestinian, Rabbinical Judaism (for he was the disciple of the Pharisee, Gamaliel, at Jerusalem), and a Hellenistic religiousness closely akin to, though not derived from, Philo (for he had been born in the intensely Hellenistic Cilician city Tarsus, at that time a most important seat of Greek learning in general and of the Stoic philosophy in particular). And we shall find that Catherine

[1] In Chapter XII, § iv, I shall show reason for strongly suspecting that Catherine possessed some knowledge, probably derived from an intermediate Christian source, of certain passages in Plato's Dialogues. But the influence of these passages can, in any case, only be traced in her Purgatorial doctrine, and had better be discussed together with this doctrine itself.

[2] My chief obligations are here to Prof. H. J. Holtzmann's *Lehrbuch der Neutestamentlichen Theologie*, 1897, Vol. II, pp. 1–225: "Der Paulinismus"; but I have also learnt from Estius and Dr. Lightfoot, and from my own direct studies in St. Paul, Philo, and Plato.

appropriates especially this, his Hellenistic element; indeed, that at times she sympathizes rather with the still more intensely Hellenistic attitude exemplified by Philo, than with the limitations introduced by St. Paul.

1. *St. Paul's Anthropology in general.*

If we take the Pauline Anthropology first, we at once come upon a profoundly dualistic attitude.

(1) There is, in general, "the outer" and "the inner" man, 2 Cor. iv, 16; and the latter is not the exclusive privilege of the redeemed,—the contrast is that between the merely natural individual and the moral personality. And this contrast, foreign to the ancient Hebrews, is first worked out, with clear consciousness, by Plato, who, *e. g.*, in his *Banquet*, causes one of the characters to say: "Socrates has thrown this Silenus-like form around himself externally, as in the case of those Silenus-statues which enclose a statuette of Apollo; but, when he is opened, how full is he found to be of temperance within"; and who treats this contrast as typical of the dualism inherent to all human life here on earth.[1]—This contrast exists throughout Catherine's teaching as regards the thing itself, although her terms are different. She has, for reasons which will appear presently, no one constant term for "the inner man," but "the outer man" is continuously styled "la umanità."

(2) The "outer man" consists for St. Paul of the body's earthly material, "the flesh"; and of the animating principle of the flesh, "the psyche," which is inseparably connected with that flesh, and which dies for good and all at the death of the latter; whereas the form of "the body" is capable of resuscitation, and is then filled out by a finer material, "glory."[2]—Here Catherine has no precise or constant word for the "psyche"; her "umanità" generally stands for the "psyche" *plus* body and flesh, all in one; and her "anima" practically always means part or the whole of "the inner man," and mostly stands for "mind." And there is no occasion for her to reflect upon any distinction between the form and the matter of the body, since she nowhere directly busies herself with the resurrection.

The "inner man" consists for St. Paul in the Mind, the Heart, and the Conscience. The Mind (*noûs*), corresponding roughly to our theoretical and practical Reason, has a certain tendency towards God: "The invisible things of God are

[1] *Symposium*, 216*e*. [2] 1 Cor. xv, 35–53.

seen by the mind in the works of creation," Rom. i, 20; and there is "a law of the mind" which is fought by "the law of sin," Rom. vii, 23; and this, although there is also a "mind of the flesh," Col. ii, 18; "a reprobate mind," Rom. i, 28; and a "renovation of the mind," Rom. xii, 2.—Catherine clings throughout most closely to the Pauline use of the term, as far as that use is favourable: note how she perceives invisible things "colla mente mia."

The Heart is even more accessible to the divine influence,—at least, it is to it that God gives "the first fruits of the Spirit" and "the Spirit of His Son, crying Abba, Father," Gal. iv, 6; 2 Cor. i, 22. As an organ of immediate perception it is so parallel to the Mind, that we can hear of "eyes of the heart"; yet it is also the seat of feeling, of will, and of moral consciousness, Eph. i, 18; 2 Cor. ii, 4; 1 Cor. iv, 5; Rom. ii, 15. It can stand for the inner life generally; or, like the Mind, it can become darkened and impenitent; whilst again, over the heart God's love is poured out, God's peace keeps guard, and we believe with the heart, 1 Cor. xiv, 25; Rom. i, 21; ii, 5; v, 5; Phil. iv, 7; Rom. x, 9.—All this again, as far as it is favourable, is closely followed by Catherine; indeed the persistence with which she comes back to certain effects wrought upon her heart by the Spirit, Christ,—effects which some of her followers readily interpreted as so many physical miracles,—was no doubt occasioned or stimulated by 2 Cor. iii, 3, "Be ye an epistle of Christ, written by the Spirit of the living God . . . upon the fleshly tables of the heart."

And Conscience, "Syneidēsis"—that late Greek word introduced by St. Paul as a technical term into the Christian vocabulary—includes our "conscience," but is as comprehensive as our "consciousness."—Catherine practically never uses the term: no doubt because, in the narrower of the two senses which had become the ordinary one, it was too predominantly ethical to satisfy her overwhelmingly religious preoccupations.

(3) Now, with regard to this whole dualism of the "outer" and the "inner man," its application to the resurrection of the body in St. Paul and in St. Catherine shall occupy us in connection with her Eschatology; here I would but indicate the two Pauline moods or attitudes towards the earthly body, and Catherine's continuous reproduction of but one of these. For his magnificent conception of the Christian society, in which each person, by a different specific gift and duty,

co-operates towards the production of an organic whole, a whole which in return develops and dignifies those its constituents, is worked out by means of the image of the human earthly body, in which each member is a necessary part and constituent of the complete organism, which is greater than, and which gives full dignity to, each and all these its factors (1 Cor. xii). And he thus, in his most deliberate and systematic mood, shows very clearly how deeply he has realized the dignity of the human body, as the instrument both for the development of the soul itself and for the work of that soul in and upon the visible world.

But in his other mood, which remains secondary and sporadic throughout his writings, his attitude is acutely dualistic. His one direct expression of it occurs in 2 Cor. v, 1–4: "For we know that, if our earthly house of this tent be dissolved, we have a building of God, a house not made with hands, eternal in the heavens. For in this also we groan, desiring to be clothed upon with our habitation that is from heaven. We who are in this tabernacle do groan, being burthened." Now this passage is undoubtedly modelled by St. Paul upon the Book of Wisdom, ix, 15: "For the corruptible body is a load upon the soul, and the earthly habitation presseth down the mind that museth upon many things." And this latter saying again is as certainly formed upon Plato (*Phaedo*, 81 *c*): "It behoves us to think of the body as oppressive and heavy and earthlike and visible. And hence the soul, being of such a nature as we have seen, when possessing such a body, is both burthened and dragged down again into the visible world." [1] And it is this conception of the Hellenic Athenian Plato (about 380 B.C.) which, passing through the Hellenistic Alexandrian Jewish Wisdom-writer (80 B.C. ?) and then through the Hellenistically tinctured ex-Rabbi, Paul of Tarsus (52 A.D.), still powerfully, indeed all but continuously, influences the mind of the Genoese Christian Catherine, especially during the years from A.D. 1496 to 1510.

Catherine's still more pessimistic figure of the body as a prison-house and furnace of purification for the soul, is no doubt the resultant of suggestions received, probably in part through intermediary literature, from the following three

[1] E. Grafe, "Verhältniss der paulinischen Schriften zur Sapientia Salomonis," in *Theol. Abhandlungen Carl von Weizsäcker Gewidmet*, 1892, pp. 274–276.

passages :—(1) Plato, in his *Cratylus* (400 B.C.), makes Socrates say : " Some declare that the body (*sōma*) is the grave (*sēma*) of the soul, as she finds herself at present. The Orphite poets seem to have invented the appellation : they held that the soul is thus paying the penalty of sin, and that the body is an enclosure which may be likened to a prison, in which the soul is enclosed until the penalty is paid." (2) St. Matt. v, 25, 26, gives Our Lord's words : " Be thou reconciled with thine adversary whilst he is still with thee on the way . . . lest the Judge hand thee over to the prison-warder, and thou be cast into prison. . . . Thou shalt not go forth thence, until thou hast paid the uttermost farthing." And (3) St. Paul declares, 1 Cor. iii, 15 : " Every man's work shall be tested by fire. If any man's work shall be burned, he shall suffer loss : but he himself shall be saved ; yet so as through fire." These three passages combined will readily suggest, to a soul thirsting for purification and possessed of an extremely sensitive psycho-physical organization with its attendant liability to fever heats, the picture of the body as a flame-full prison-house,—a purgatory of the soul.

2. *St. Paul's conception of " Spirit."*

A very difficult complication and varying element is introduced into St. Paul's Anthropology by the term into which he has poured all that is most original, deepest, most deliberate and abiding in his teaching,—the Spirit, " Pneuma." For somewhat as he uses the term " Sarx," the flesh, both in its loose popular signification of " mankind in general " ; and in a precise, technical sense of " the matter which composes the earthly body " ; so also he has, occasionally, a loose popular use of the term " spirit," when it figures as but a fourth parallel to " mind," " heart," and " conscience " ; and, usually, a very strict and technical use of it, when it designates the Spirit, God Himself.

(1) Now it is precisely in the latter case that his doctrine attains its fullest depth and its greatest difficulty. For here the Spirit, the Pneuma, is, strictly speaking, only one—the Spirit of God, God Himself, in His action either outside or inside the human mind, Noûs. And in such passages of St. Paul, where man seems to possess a distinct pneuma of his own, by far the greater number only apparently contradict this doctrine. For in some, so in 1 Cor. ii, the context is dominated by a comparison between the divine and the human consciousness, so that, in v. 11, man's Noûs is

designated Pneuma, and in v. 16, and Rom. xi, 34, the Lord's Pneuma is called His Noûs. And the " spirit of the world " contrasted here, in v. 11, with the " Spirit of God," is a still further deliberate laxity of expression, similar to that of Satan as " the God of this world," 2 Cor. iv, 4. In other passages,—so Rom. viii, 16; i, 9; viii, 10, and even in 1 Cor. v, 5 (the " spirit " of the incestuous Corinthian which is to be saved),—we seem to have " spirit " either as the mind in so far as the object of the Spirit's communications, or as the mind transformed by the Spirit's influence. And if we can hear of a " defilement of the spirit," 2 Cor. vii, 1, we are also told that we can forget the fact of the body being the temple of the holy Spirit, 1 Cor. vi, 19; and that this temple's profanation " grieves the holy Spirit," Eph. iv, 30. Very few, sporadic, and short passages remain in which " the spirit of man " cannot clearly be shown to have a deliberately derivative sense.

Catherine, in this great matter, completely follows St. Paul. For she too has loosely-knit moods and passages, in which " spirito " appears as a natural endowment of her own, parallel to, or identical with, the " mente." But when speaking strictly, and in her intense moods, she means by " spirito," the Spirit, Christ, Love, God, a Power which, though in its nature profoundly distinct and different from her entire self-seeking self, can and does come to dwell within, and to supplant, this self. Indeed her highly characteristic saying, " my Me is God," with her own explanations of it, expresses, if pressed, even more than this. In these moods, the term " mente " is usually absent, just as in St. Paul.

Now in his formally doctrinal *Loci*, St. Paul defines the Divine Pneuma and the human Sarx, not merely as ontologically contrary substances, but as keenly conflicting, ethically contradictory principles. An anti-spiritual power, lust, possesses the flesh and the whole outer man, whilst, in an indefinitely higher degree and manner, the Spirit, which finds an echo in the mind, the inner man, is a spontaneous, counter-working force; and these two energies fight out the battle in man, and for his complete domination, Rom. vi, 12–14; vii, 22, 23; viii, 4–13. And this dualistic conception is in close affinity to all that was noblest in the Hellenistic world of St. Paul's own day; but is in marked contrast to the pre-exilic, specifically Jewish Old Testament view, where we have but the contrast between the visible and transitory, and the

Invisible and Eternal; and the consciousness of the weakness and fallibility of " flesh and blood." And this latter is the temper of mind that dominates the Synoptic Gospels : " The spirit indeed is willing, but the flesh is weak " ; and " Father, forgive them, for they know not what they do," are here the divinely serene and infinitely fruitful leading notes.—And Catherine, on this point, is habitually on the Synoptist side : man is, for her, far more weak and ignorant than forcibly and deliberately wicked. Yet her detailed intensity towards the successive cloaks of self-love is still, as it were, a shadow and echo of the fierce, and far more massive, flesh-and-spirit struggle in St. Paul.

3. *The Angry and the Loving God.*

And, as against the intense wickedness of man, we find in St. Paul an emphatic insistence—although this is directly derived from the Old Testament and Rabbinical tradition—upon the anger and indignation of God, Rom. ii, 8, and frequently.—Here Catherine is in explicit contrast with him, in so far as the anger would be held to stand for an emotion not proceeding from love and not ameliorative in its aim and operation. This attitude sprang no doubt, in part, from the strong influence upon her of the Dionysian teaching concerning the negative character of evil; possibly still more from her continuous pondering of the text, " Like as a father pitieth his children, so the Lord pitieth them that fear Him. For He knoweth our frame; He remembereth that we are dust," Ps. ciii, 13, 14,—where she dwells upon the fact that we are all His children rather than upon the fact that we do not all fear Him; but certainly, most of all, from her habitual dwelling upon the other side of St. Paul's teaching, that concerning the Love of God.

Now the depth and glow of Paul's faith and love go clearly back to his conversion, an event which colours and influences all his feeling and teaching for some thirty-four years, up to the end. And similarly Catherine's conversion-experience has been found by us to determine the sequence and all the chief points of her Purgatorial teaching, some thirty-seven years after that supreme event.

Already Philo had, under Platonic influence, believed in an Ideal Man, a Heavenly Man; had identified him with the Logos, the Word or Wisdom of God; and had held him to be in some way ethereal and luminous,—never arriving at either a definitely personal or a simply impersonal conception of this at one time intermediate Being, at another time this supreme attribute of God. St. Paul, under the profound impression of the Historic Christ and the great experience on the road to Damascus, perceives the Risen, Heavenly Jesus as possessed of a luminous, ethereal body, a body of "glory," Acts xxii, 11. And this Christ is, for St. Paul, identical with "the Spirit": "the Lord is the Spirit," 2 Cor. iii, 17; and "to be in Christ" and "Christ is in us" are parallel terms to those of "to be in the Spirit" and "the Spirit is within us" respectively. In all four cases we get Christ or the Spirit conceived as an element, as it were an ocean of ethereal light, in which souls are plunged and which penetrates them. In Catherine we have, at her conversion, this same perception and conception of Spirit as an ethereal light, and of Christ as Spirit; and up to the end she more and more appears to herself to bathe, to be submerged in, an ocean of light, which, at the same time, fills her within and penetrates her through and through.

But again, and specially since his conversion, St. Paul thinks of God as loving, as Love, and this conception henceforth largely supplants the Old Testament conception of the angry God. This loving God is chiefly manifested through the loving Christ: indeed the love of Christ and the love of God are the same thing. And this Christ-Love dwells within us.[1] And Catherine, since her mind has perceived Love to be the central character of God, and has adopted fire as love's fullest image, cannot but hold,—God and Love and Christ and Spirit being all one and the same thing,—that Christ-Spirit-Fire is in her and she in It. The yellow light-image, which all but alone typifies God's friendliness in the Bible, is thus turned into a red fire-image. And yet this latter in so far retains with Catherine something of its older connotation of anger, that the Fire and Heat appear in her teaching more as symbols of the suffering caused by the opposition of man's at least partial impurity to the Spirit, Christ, Love, God, and of the pain attendant upon that Spirit's action, even where it can still purify; whereas the Light and Illumination mostly express the peaceful penetration of man's spirit by God's Spirit, and the blissful gain accruing from such penetration.

[1] "The love of Christ," Rom. viii, 35, is identical with "the love of God which is in Christ Jesus," Rom. viii, 39. "The Spirit of God dwelleth in you," Rom. viii, 9; 1 Cor. iii, 16. "I live, not I: but Christ liveth in me," Gal. ii, 20.

4. *The Risen Christ and the Heavenly Adam.*

St. Paul dwells continuously upon the post-earthly, the Risen Christ, and upon Him in His identity with the pre-earthly, the Heavenly Man: so that the historical Jesus tends to become, all but for the final acts in the Supper-room and upon the Cross, a transitory episode;—a super-earthly biography all but supplants the earthly one, since His death and resurrection and their immediate contexts are all but the only two events dwelt upon, and form but the two constituents of one inseparable whole.—Here Catherine is deeply Pauline in her striking non-occupation with the details of the earthly life (the scene with the Woman at the Well being the single exception), and in her continuous insistence upon Christ as the life-giving Spirit. Indeed, even the death is strangely absent. There is but the one doubtful contrary instance, in any case a quite early and sporadic one, of the Vision of the Bleeding Christ. The fact is that, in her teaching, the self-donation of God in general, in His mysterious love for each individual soul, and of Christ in particular, in His Eucharistic presence as our daily food, take all their special depth of tenderness from her vivid realization of the whole teaching, temper, life, and death of Jesus Christ; and that teaching derives its profundity of feeling only from all this latter complexus of facts and convictions.

5. *Reconciliation, Justification, Sanctification.*

(1) St. Paul has two lines of thought concerning Reconciliation. In the objective, juridical, more Judaic conception, the attention is concentrated on the one moment of Christ's death, and the consequences appear as though instantaneous and automatic; in the other, the subjective, ethical, more Hellenistic conception, the attention is spread over the whole action of the Christ's incarnational self-humiliation, and the consequences are realized only if and when we strive to imitate Him,—they are a voluntary and continuous process. Catherine's fundamental conversion-experience and all her later teachings attach her Reconciliation to the entire act of ceaseless Divine "ecstasy," self-humiliation, and redemptive immanence in Man, of which the whole earthly life and death of Christ are the centre and culmination; but though the human soul's corresponding action is conceived as continuous, once it has begun, she loves to dwell upon this whole action as itself the gift of God and the consequence of His prevenient act.

(2) As to Justification, we have again, in St. Paul, a pre-

ponderatingly Jewish juridical conception of adoption, in which a purely vicarious justice and imputed righteousness seem to be taught; and an ethical conception of immanent justice, based on his own experience and expressed by means of Hellenistic forms, according to which " the love of God hath been shed abroad in our hearts," Rom. v, 5. And he often insists strenuously upon excluding every human merit from the moment and act of justification, insisting upon its being a " free gift " of God.—Catherine absorbs herself in the second, ethical conception, and certainly understands this love of God as primarily God's, the Spirit's, Christ's love, as Love Itself poured out in our hearts; and she often breaks out into angry protests against the very suggestion of any act, or part of an act, dear to God, proceeding from her natural or separate self, indeed, if we press her expressions, from herself at all.

(3) As to Sanctification, St. Paul has three couples of contrasted conceptions. The first couple conceives the Spirit, either Old Testament-wise, as manifesting and accrediting Itself in extraordinary, sudden, sporadic, miraculous gifts and doings—*e. g.* in ecstatic speaking with tongues; or,—and this is the more frequent and the decisive conception,—as an abiding, equable penetration and spiritual reformation of its recipient. Here the faithful " live and walk in the spirit," are " driven by the spirit," " serve God in the spirit," are " temples of the Spirit," Gal. v, 25; Rom. viii, 14; vii, 6; 1 Cor. vi, 19: the Spirit has become the creative source of a supernatural character-building.[1]—Here Catherine, in contrast to most of her friends, who are wedded to the first view, is strongly attached to the second view, perhaps the deepest of St. Paul's conceptions.

The second couple conceives Sanctification either juridically and moves dramatically from act to act,—the Sacrifice on the Cross and the Resurrection of the Son of God, the sentence of Justification and the Adoption as sons of God; or ethically, and presupposes everywhere continuous processes,—beginning with the reception of the Spirit, and ending with " the Lord is the Spirit."—Here Catherine has curiously little of the dramatic and prominently personal conception: only in the imperfect soul's acutely painful moment, of standing before and seeing God immediately after death, do we get one link in this chain, in a somewhat modified form. For the rest,

[1] H. J. Holtzmann, *op. cit.* Vol. II, p. 145.

the ethical and continuous conception is present practically throughout her teaching, but in a curious, apparently paradoxical form, to be noticed in a minute.

And the third couple either treats Sanctification as, at each moment of its actual presence, practically infallible and complete: "We who died to sin, how shall we any longer live therein?" "Freed from sin, ye became servants of righteousness"; "now we are discharged from the law, having died, to that wherein we were beholden; so that we serve in newness of spirit"; "they that are after the flesh, do mind the things of the flesh; but they that are after the Spirit, the things of the Spirit," Rom. vi, 2, 18; vii, 6; viii, 5. Or it considers Sanctification as only approximately complete, so long as man has to live here below, not only in the Spirit, Rom. viii, 9, but also in the flesh, Gal. ii, 20. The faithful have indeed crucified the flesh once for all, Gal. v, 24: yet they have continually to mortify their members anew, Col. iii, 5, and by the Spirit to destroy the works of the flesh, Rom. viii, 13. The "fear of the Lord," "of God," does not cease to be a motive for the sanctified, 2 Cor. v, 11; vii, 1. To "walk in the Spirit," "in the light," has to be insisted on (1 Thess. v, 4–8; Rom. xiii, 11–14), as long as the eternal day has not yet arisen for us. And even in Romans, chapter vi, we find admonitions, vv. 12, 13, 19, which, if we press the other conception, are quite superfluous.[1]

And here Catherine, in her intense sympathy with each of these contrasted conceptions, offers us a combination of both in a state of unstable equilibrium and delicate tension. I take it that it is not her immensely impulsive and impatient temperament, nor survivals of the Old Testament idea as to instantaneousness being the special characteristic of divine action, but her deep and noble sense of the givenness and pure grace of religion, and of God's omnipotence being, if possible, exceeded only by His overflowing, self-communicative love, which chiefly determine her curious presentation and emotional experience of spiritual growth and life as a movement composed of sudden shiftings upwards, with long apparently complete pauses in between. For here this form (of so many instants, of which each is complete in itself) stands for her as the least inadequate symbol, as a kind of shattered mirror, not of time at all, but of eternity; whilst the succession and difference between these instants indicates a growth in

[1] Holtzmann, *op. cit.* Vol. II, pp. 151, 152.

the apprehending soul, which has, in reality, been proceeding also in between these instants and not only during them. And this remarkable scheme presents her conviction that, in principle, the work of the all-powerful, all-loving Spirit cannot, of itself, be other than final and complete, and yet that, as a matter of fact, it never is so, in weak, self-deceptive, and variously resisting man, but ever turns out to require a fresh and deeper application. And this succession of sudden jerks onwards and upwards, after long, apparently complete pauses between them, gives to her fundamentally ethical and continuous conception something of the look of the forensic, dramatic series, with its separate acts,—a series which would otherwise be all but unrepresented in her picture of the soul's life on this side of death and of its life (immediately after its vivid sight of God and itself, and its act of free-election) in the Beyond.

6. *Pauline Social Ethics.*

As to Social Ethics, St. Paul's worldward movement is strongly represented in Catherine's teaching. Her great sayings as to God being servable not only in the married state, but in a camp of (mercenary) soldiers; and as to her determination violently to appropriate the monk's cowl, should this his state be necessary to the attainment of the highest love of God, are full of the tone of Rom. xiv, 14, 20, "nothing is unclean of itself: save that to him who accounteth anything to be unclean, to him it is unclean,"—"all things are clean"; and of 1 Cor. x, 26, 28, "the earth is the Lord's, and the fulness thereof." And her sense of her soul's positive relation to nature, *e. g.* trees, was no doubt in part awakened by that striking passage, Rom. viii, 19, "the expectation of the creation waiteth the revealing of the sons of God; for the creation was subjected to vanity, not of its own will."

On the other hand, it would be impossible confidently to identify her own attitude concerning marriage with that of St. Paul, since, as we know, her peculiar health and her unhappiness with Giuliano make it impossible to speak here with any certainty of the mature woman's deliberate judgment concerning continence and marriage. Yet her impulsive protestation, in the scene with the monk, against any idea of being debarred by her state from as perfect a love of God as his,—whilst, of course, not in contradiction with the Pauline and generally Catholic positions in the matter, seems to imply an emotional attitude somewhat different from that of some of the Apostle's sayings. Indeed, in her whole general and unconscious position as to how a woman should hold herself in religious things it is interesting to note the absence of all influence from those Pauline sayings which, herein like Philo (and indeed the whole ancient world) treat man alone as " the (direct) image and glory (reflex) of God," and the woman as but " the glory (reflex) of the man," 1 Cor. xi, 7. Everywhere she appears full, on the contrary, of St. Paul's other (more characteristic and deliberate) strain, according to which, as there is " neither Jew nor Gentile, bond nor free " before God, so " neither is the woman without the man, nor the man without the woman, in the Lord," 1 Cor. xi, 11.—And in social matters generally, Catherine's convert life and practice shows, in the active mortifications of its first penitential part, in her persistent great aloofness from all things of sense as regards her own gratification, and in the ecstasies and love of solitude which marked the zenith of her power, a close sympathy with, and no doubt in part a direct imitation of, St. Paul's Arabian retirement, chastisement of his body, and lonely concentration upon rapt communion with God. Yet she as strongly exemplifies St. Paul's other, the outward movement, the love-impelled, whole-hearted service of the poorest, world-forgotten, sick and sorrowing brethren. And the whole resultant rhythmic life has got such fine spontaneity, emotional and efficacious fulness, and expansive joy about it, as to suggest at once those unfading teachings of St. Paul which had so largely occasioned it,—those hymns in praise of that love " which minds not high things but condescends to things that are lowly," Rom. xii, 16; " becomes all things to all men," 1 Cor. ix, 22; " rejoices with them that rejoice, and weeps with them that weep," Rom. xii, 15; and which, as the twin love of God and man, is not only the chief member of the central ethical triad, but, already here below, itself becomes the subject which exercises the other two virtues, for it is " love " that " believeth all things, hopeth all things," even before that eternity in which love alone will never vanish away, *ibid.* xiii, 7, 8. Here Catherine with Paul triumphs completely over time: their actions and teaching are as completely fresh now, after well-nigh nineteen and four centuries, as when they first experienced, willed, and uttered them.

7. *Sacramental teachings.*

In Sacramental matters it is interesting to note St. Paul's

close correlation of Baptism and the Holy Eucharist: "All (our fathers) were baptized unto Moses in the cloud and in the sea; and did all eat the same spiritual meat; and did all drink the same spiritual drink," 1 Cor. x, 3; "in one Spirit were we all baptized into one body, . . . and were all made to drink of one Spirit," Christ, His blood, *ibid.* xii, 13. And Catherine is influenced by these passages, when she represents the soul as hungering for, and drowning itself in, the ocean of spiritual sustenance which is Love, Christ, God: but she attaches the similes, which are distributed by St. Paul among the two Rites, to the Holy Eucharist alone. Baptism had been a grown man's deliberate act in Paul's case,—an act immediately subsequent to, and directly expressive of, his conversion, the culminating experience of his life; and, as a great Church organizer, he could not but dwell with an equal insistence upon the two chief Sacraments.

Catherine had received baptism as an unconscious infant, and the event lay far back in that pre-conversion time, which was all but completely ousted from her memory by the great experience of some twenty-five years later. And in the latter experience it was (more or less from the first and soon all but exclusively) the sense of a divine encirclement and sustenance, of an addition of love, rather than a consciousness of the subtraction of sins or of a divine purification, that possessed her. In her late, though profoundly characteristic Purgatorial teaching, the soul again plunges into an ocean; but now, since the soul is rather defiled than hungry, and wills rather to be purified than to be fed, this plunge is indeed a kind of Baptism by Immersion. Yet we have no more the symbol of water, for the long state and effects to which that swift act leads, but we have, instead, fire and light, and, in one place, once again bread and the hunger for bread. And this is no doubt because, in these Purgatorial picturings, it is her conversion-experience of love under the symbols of light and of fire, and her forty years of daily hungering for the Holy Eucharist and Love Incarnate, which furnish the emotional colours and the intellectual outlines.

8. *Eschatological matters.*

In Eschatological matters the main points of contact and of contrast appear to be four; and three of the differences are occasioned by St. Paul's preoccupation with Christ's Second Coming, with the Resurrection of the body, and with the General Judgment, mostly as three events in close temporal correlation, and likely to occur soon; whilst Catherine abstracts entirely from all three.

(1) Thus St. Paul is naturally busy with the question as to the Time when he shall be with Christ. In 1 Thess. iv, 15, he speaks of "we that are alive, that are left for the coming of the Lord," *i. e.* he expects this event during his own lifetime; whilst in Phil. i, 23, he "desires to depart and be with Christ," *i. e.* he has ceased confidently to expect this coming before his own death. But Catherine dwells exclusively, with this latter conception, upon the moment of death, as that when the soul shall see, and be finally confirmed in its union with, Love, Christ, God; for into her earthly lifetime Love, Christ, God, can and do come, but invisibly, and she may still lose full union with them for ever.

(2) As to the Place, it is notoriously obscure whether St. Paul thinks of it, as do the Old Testament and the Apocalypse, as the renovated earth, or as the sky, or as the intervening space. The risen faithful who "shall be caught up in the clouds to meet the Lord," 1 Thess. iv, 17, seem clearly to be meeting Him, in mid-air, as He descends upon earth; and "Jerusalem above," Gal. iv, 26, may well, as in Apoc. iii, 12; xxi, 2, be conceived as destined to come down upon earth. But Catherine, though she constantly talks of Heaven, Purgatory, Hell, as "places," makes it plain that such "places" are for her but vivid symbols for states of soul. God Himself repeatedly appears in her sayings as "the soul's place"; and it is this "place," the soul's true spiritual birthplace and home which, ever identical and bliss-conferring in itself, is variously experienced by the soul, in exact accordance with its dispositions,—as that profoundly painful, or that joyfully distressing, or that supremely blissful "place" which respectively we call Hell, and Purgatory, and Heaven.

(3) As to the Body, we have already noted St. Paul's doctrine intermediate between the Palestinian and Alexandrian Jewish teaching, that it will rise indeed, but composed henceforth of "glory" and no more of "flesh." It is this his requirement of a body, however spiritual, which underlies his anxiety to be "found clothed, not naked," at and after death, 2 Cor. v, 3. Indeed, in this whole passage, v, 1–4, "our earthly house of this habitation," and "a building of God not made with hands," no doubt mean, respectively, the present body of flesh and the future body of glory; just as the various, highly complex, conceptions of "clothed," "unclothed," "clothed upon,"

refer to the different conditions of the soul with a body of flesh, without a body at all, and with a body of glory.—Now this passage, owing to its extreme complication and abstruseness of doctrine, has come down to us in texts and versions of every conceivable form; and this uncertainty has helped Catherine towards her very free utilization of it. For she not only, as ever, simply ignores all questions of a risen body, and transfers the concept of a luminous ethereal substance from the body to the soul itself, and refers the "nakedness," "unclothing," "clothing," and "clothing upon" to conditions obtaining, not between the soul and the body, but between the soul and God; but she also, in most cases, takes the nakedness as the desirable state, since typical of the soul's faithful self-exposure to the all-purifying rays of God's light and fire, and interprets the "unclothing" as the penitential stripping from off itself of those pretences and corrupt incrustations which prevent God's blissful action upon it.

(4) And, finally, as to the Judgment, we have in St. Paul a double current,—the inherited Judaistic conception of a forensic retribution; Christ, the divine Judge, externally applying such and such statutory rewards and punishments to such and such good and evil deeds,—so in Rom. ii, 6–10; and the experimental conception, helped on to articulation by Hellenistic influences, of the bodily resurrection and man's whole final destiny as the necessary resultant and manifestation of an internal process, the presence of the Spirit and of the power of God,—so in the later parts of Romans, in Gal. vi, 8, and in 1 Cor. vi, 14; 2 Cor. xiii, 4.—Among Catherine's sayings also we find some passages—but these the less characteristic and mostly of doubtful authenticity,—where reward and punishment, indeed the three "places" themselves, appear as so many separate institutions of God, which get externally applied to certain good and evil deeds. But these are completely overshadowed in number, sure authenticity, emotional intensity, and organic connection with her other teachings, by sayings of the second type, where the soul's fate is but the necessary consequence of its own deliberate choice and gradually formed dispositions, the result, inseparable since the first from its self-identification with this or that of the various possible will-attitudes towards God.

(5) We can then sum up the main points of contact and of difference between Paul and Catherine, by saying that, in both cases, everything leads up to, or looks back upon, a great

culminating, directly personal experience of shortest clock-time duration, whence all their doctrine, wherever emphatic, is but an attempt to articulate and universalize this original experience; and that if in Paul there remains more of explicit occupation with the last great events of the earthly life of Jesus, yet in both there is the same insistence upon the life-giving Spirit, the eternal Christ, manifesting His inexhaustible power in the transformation of souls, on and on, here and now, into the likeness of Himself.

II. The Johannine Writings.

On moving now from the Pauline to the Johannine writings, we shall find that Catherine's obligations to these latter are but rarely as deep, yet that they cover a wider reach of ideas and images. I take this fresh source of influence under the double heading of the general relations of the Johannine teaching to other, previous or contemporary, conceptions; and of this same teaching considered in itself.[1]

1. *Johannine teaching contrasted with other systems.*

(1) As to the general relations towards other positions, we get here, towards Judaism and Paganism, an emphatic insistence upon the novelty and independence of Christianity as regards not only Paganism, but even the previous Judaism, "The law was given by Moses; grace and truth came by Jesus Christ," i, 17; and upon the Logos, Christ, as "the Light that enlighteneth every man that cometh into the world," "unto his own," *i. e.* men in general; for this Light "was in the world, and the world was made by Him," i, 9–11. There is thus a divinely-implanted, innate tendency towards this light, extant in man prior to the explicit act of faith, and operative outside of the Christian body: "Every one that is of the truth heareth my voice," xviii, 37: "he that doeth the truth cometh to the light," iii, 21: "begotten," as he is, not of man but "of God," i, 13; 1 John iii, 9. And thus Samaritans, Greeks, and Heathens act and speak in the best dispositions, iv, 42; xii, 20–24; x, 16; whilst such terms and sayings as "the Saviour of the World," "God so loved the world," iv, 42,

[1] My chief obligations are here again to Dr. H. J. Holtzmann's *Neutestamentliche Theologie*, 1897, Vol. II, pp. 354–390; 394–396; 399–401; 426–430; 447–466; 466–521.

iii, 16, are the most universalistic declarations to be found in the New Testament.—And this current dominates the whole of Catherine's temper and teaching: this certainty as to the innate affinity of every human soul to the Light, Love, Christ, God, gives a tone of exultation to the musings of this otherwise melancholy woman. Whereas the Johannine passages of a contrasting exclusiveness and even fierceness of tone, such as "all that came before Me are thieves and robbers," x, 8; "ye are from your father the devil," viii, 44; "ye shall die in your sin," viii, 21; "your sin remaineth," ix, 41, are without any parallel among Catherine's sayings. Indeed it is plain that Catherine, whilst as sure as the Evangelist that all man's goodness comes from God, nowhere, except in her own case, finds man's evil to be diabolic in character.

(2) With regard to Paulinism, the Johannine writings give us a continuation and extension of the representation of the soul's mystical union with Christ, as a local abiding in the element Christ. Indeed it is in these writings that we find the terms "to abide in" the light, 1 John ii, 10, in God, 1 John iv, 13, in Christ, 1 John ii, 6, 24, 27, iii, 6, 24, and in His love, John xv, 9, 1 John iv, 16; the corresponding expressions, "God abideth in us," 1 John iv, 12, 16, "Christ abideth in us," 1 John iii, 24, and "love abideth in us," 1 John iv, 16; the two immanences coupled together, where the communicant "abideth in Me and I in him," vi, 56, and where the members of His mystical body are bidden to "abide in Me and I in you," xv, 4; and the supreme pattern of all these interpenetrations, "I am in the Father, and the Father in Me," xiv, 10.—And it is from here that Catherine primarily gets the literary suggestions for her images of the soul plunged into, and filled by, an ocean of Light, Love, Christ, God; and again from here, more than from St. Paul, she gets her favourite term μένειν (It. *restare*), around which are grouped, in her mind, most of the quietistic-sounding elements of her teaching.

(3) As to the points of contact between the Johannine teaching and Alexandrianism, we find that three are vividly renewed by Catherine.

Philo had taught: "God ceases not from acting: as to burn is the property of fire, so to act is the property of God," *Legg. Alleg.* I, 3. And in John we find: "God is a Spirit," and "My Father worketh even until now, and I work," iv, 24; v, 17. And God as pure Spiritual Energy, as the *Actus*

Purus, is a truth and experience that penetrates the whole life of Catherine.

The work of Christ is not dwelt on in its earthly beginnings; but it is traced up and back, in the form of a spiritual "Genesis," to His life and work as the Logos in Heaven, where He abides "in the bosom of the Father," and whence He learns what He "hath declared" to us, i, 18; just as, in his turn, the disciple whom Jesus loved "was reclining" at the Last Supper "on the bosom of Jesus," and later on "beareth witness concerning the things" which he had learnt there, xiii, 23; xxi, 24. So also Catherine transcends the early earthly life of Christ altogether, and habitually dwells upon Him as the Light and as Love, as God in His own Self-Manifestation; and upon the ever-abiding sustenance afforded by this Light and Life and Love to the faithful soul reclining and resting upon it.

And the contrast between the Spiritual and the Material, the Abiding and the Transitory, is symbolized throughout John, in exact accord with Philo, under the spatial categories of upper and lower, and of extension: "Ye are from beneath, I am from above," viii, 23; "He that cometh from heaven, is above all," iii, 31; and "in my Father's house," that upper world, "there are many mansions," abiding-places, xiv, 2. Hence all things divine here below have descended from above: regeneration, iii, 3; the Spirit, i, 32; Angels, i, 51; the Son of God Himself, iii, 13: and they mount once more up above, so especially Christ Himself, iii, 13; vi, 62. And the things of that upper world are the true things: "the true light," "the true adorers," "the true vine," "the true bread from Heaven," i, 9; iv, 23; xv, 1; vi, 32: all this in contrast to the shadowy semi-realities of the lower world.—Catherine is here in fullest accord with the spatial imagery generally; she even talks of God Himself, not only as in a place, but as Himself a place, as the soul's "loco." But she has, for reasons explained elsewhere, generally to abandon the upper-and-lower category when picturing the soul's self-dedication to purification, since, for this act, she mostly figures a downward plunge into suffering; and she gives us a number of striking sayings, in which she explicitly re-translates all this quantitative spatial imagery into its underlying meaning of qualitative spiritual states.

(4) As to the Johannine approximations and antagonisms to Gnosticism, Catherine's position is as follows. In the Synoptic

accounts, Our Lord makes the acquisition of eternal life depend upon the keeping of the two great commandments of the love of God and of one's neighbour, Luke x, 26–28, and parallels. In John Our Lord says : " this is life eternal, that they should know Thee the only true God, and Him Whom Thou didst send, even Jesus Christ," xvii, 3. To "know," *γινώσκειν*, occurs twenty-five times in 1 John alone. Here the final object of every soul is to believe and to know : " they received and knew of a truth . . . and believed," xvii, 8 ; " we have believed and know," vi, 69 ; or "we know and have believed," 1 John iv, 16. And Catherine also lays much stress upon faith ending, even here below, in a certain vivid knowledge; but this knowledge is, with her, less doctrinally articulated, no doubt in part because there was no Gnosticism fronting her, to force on such articulation.

And the Johannine writings compare this higher mental knowledge to the lower, sensible perception : " He that cometh from heaven," witnesseth to what he hath "seen and heard," iii, 32 ; " if He shall be manifested, we shall see Him even as He is," 1 John iii, 2. And they have three special terms, in common with Gnosticism, for the object of such knowledge : Life, Light, and Fulness (*Plerōma*),—the latter, as a technical term, appearing in the New Testament only in John i, 16, and in the Epistles to the Colossians and Ephesians. Catherine, also, is ever experiencing and conceiving the mental apprehensions of faith, as so many quasi-sensible, ocular, perceptions; and Life and Light are constantly mentioned, and Fulness is, at least, implied in the psycho-physical concomitants or consequences of her thinkings.

On the other hand, she does not follow John in the intensely dualistic elements of his teaching,—the sort of determinist, all but innate, distinction between "the darkness," " the men who loved the darkness rather than the light," and the Light itself and those who loved it, i, 4, 5 ; iii, 19,—children of God and children of the devil—the latter all but incapable of being saved, viii, 38–47 ; x, 26 ; xi, 52 ; xiv, 17. Rather is she like him in his all but complete silence as to " the anger of God," —a term which he uses once only, iii, 36, as against the twenty-two instances of it in St. Paul.

And she is full to overflowing of the great central, profoundly un- and anti-Gnostic, sensitively Christian teachings of St. John : as to the Light, the only-begotten Son, having been given by God, because God so loved the world; as to

Jesus having loved his own even to the end; as to the object of Christ's manifestation of His Father's name to men, being that God's love for Christ, and indeed Christ Himself, might be within them; and as to how, if they love Him, they will keep His commandments,—His commandment to love each other as He has loved them, iii, 21; iii, 16; xiii, 1; xvii, 26; xiv, 15; xv, 17. In this last great declaration especially do we find the very epitome of Catherine's life and spirit, of her who can never think of Him as Light and Knowledge only, but ever insists on His being Fire and Love as well; and who has but one commandment, that of Love-impelled, Love-seeking loving.

(5) And lastly, in relation to organized, Ecclesiastical Christianity, the Johannine writings dwell, as regards the more general principles, on points which, where positive, are simply pre-supposed by Catherine; and, where negative, find no echo within her.

The Johannine writings insist continually upon the unity and inter-communion of the faithful: "They shall become one fold, one shepherd"; Christ's death was in order "that He might gather the scattered children of God into one"; He prays to the Father that believers "may be one, as we are one"; and He leaves as His legacy His seamless robe, x, 16; xi, 52; xvii, 21; xix, 24. And these same writings have a painfully absolute condemnation for all outside of this visible fold: "The whole world lies in evil"; its "Prince is the Devil"; "the blood of Jesus cleanseth us from all sin," within the community alone; false prophets, those who have gone forth from the community, are not to be prayed for, are not even to be saluted, 1 John v, 19; John xii, 31; John i, 7; v, 16; 2 John, 10. For the great and necessary fight with Gnosticism has already begun in these writings.

But Catherine dies before the unity of Christendom is again in jeopardy through the Protestant Reformation, and she never dwells—this is doubtless a limit—upon the Christian community, as such. And her enthusiastic sympathy with the spiritual teachings of Jacopone da Todi, who, some two centuries before, had, as one of the prophetic opposition, vehemently attacked the intensely theocratic policy of Pope Boniface VIII, and had suffered a long imprisonment at his hands; her tender care for the schismatic population of the far-away Greek island of Chios; and her intimacy with Dre. Tommaso Moro, who, later on, became for a while a

Calvinist; all indicate how free from all suspiciousness towards individual Catholics, or of fierceness against other religious bodies and persons, was her deeply filial attachment to the Church.

In the Synoptists Our Lord declares, as to the exorcist who worked cures in His name, although not a follower of His, that " he that is not against us, is for us," and refuses to accede to His disciples' proposal to interfere with his activity, Mark ix, 38–41; and He points, as to the means of inheriting eternal life, to the keeping of the two great commandments, as these are already formulated in the Old Testament, and insists that this neighbour, whom here we are bidden to love, is any and every man, Luke x, 25–37. The Johannine writings insist strongly upon the strict necessity of full, explicit adhesion: the commandment of love which Our Lord gives is here " My commandment," " a new commandment," one held "from the beginning "—in the Christian community; and the command to " love one another " is here addressed to the brethren in their relations to their fellow-believers only, xiii, 34; xiii, 35; xv, 12, 17. Catherine's feeling, in this matter, is clearly with the Synoptists.

2. *Johannine teaching considered in itself.*

If we next take the Johannine teachings in themselves, we shall find the following interesting points of contact or contrast to exist between John and Catherine.

(1) In matters of Theology proper, she is completely penetrated by the great doctrine, more explicit in St. John even than in St. Paul, that "God is Love," 1 John iv, 8; and by the conceptions of God and of Christ " working always " as Life, Light, and Love.—But whereas, in the first Epistle of John, God Himself is " eternal life " and " light," v, 20; i, 5; and, in the Gospel, it is Christ Who, in the first instance, appears as Life and as Light, xi, 25; viii, 12: Catherine nowhere distinguishes at all between Christ and God. And similarly, whereas in St. John " God doth not give " unto Christ " the Spirit by measure "; and Christ promises to the disciples " another Paraclete," *i. e.* the Holy Spirit, iii, 34; xiv, 16; and indeed the Son and the Spirit appear, throughout, as distinct from one another as do the Son and the Father: in Catherine we get, practically everywhere, an exclusive concentration upon the fact, so often implied or declared by St. Paul, of Love, Christ, being Himself Spirit.

(2) The Johannine Soteriology has, I think, influenced

Catherine as follows. Christ's redemptive work appears, in the more original current of that teaching, under the symbols of the Word, Light, Bread, as the self-revelation of God. For in proportion that this Logos-Light and Bread enlightens and nourishes, does He drive away darkness and weakness, and, with them, sin, and this previously to any historic acts of His earthly life. And, in this connection, there is but little stress laid upon penance and the forgiveness of sins as compared with the Synoptic accounts, and the term of turning back, *στρέφειν*, is absent here.—But that same redemptive work appears, in the more Pauline of the two Johannine currents, as the direct result of so many vicarious, atoning deeds, the historic Passion and Death of Our Lord. Here there is indeed sin, a " sin of the world," and specially for this sin is Christ the propitiation : " God so loved the world, as to give His only-begotten Son "—Him " the Lamb of God, that taketh away the sins of the world," i, 29; 1 John ii, 2; John ii, 16; i, 29, 36.

Catherine, with the probably incomplete exception of her Conversion and Penance-period, concentrates her attention, with a striking degree of exclusiveness, upon the former group of conceptions. With her too the God-Christ is—all but solely—conceived as Light which, in so far as it is not hindered, operates the healing and the growth of souls. And in her great picture of all souls inevitably hungering for the sight of the One Bread, God, she has operated a fusion between two of the Johannine images, the Light which is seen and the Bread which is eaten : here the bare sight (in reality, a satiating sight) of the Bread suffices. If, for the self-manifesting God-Christ, she has, besides the Johaninne Light-image, a Fire-symbol, which has its literary antecedents rather in the Old Testament than in the New, this comes from the fact that she is largely occupied with the pain of the impressions and processes undergone by already God-loving yet still imperfectly pure souls, and that fierce fire is as appropriate a symbol for such pain as is peaceful light for joy.

Now this painfulness is, in Catherine's teaching, the direct result of whatever may be incomplete and piecemeal in the soul's state and process of purification. And this her conception, of Perfect Love being mostly attained only through a series of apparently sudden shifts, each seemingly final, is no doubt in part moulded upon the practically identical Johannine teaching as to Faith.

True, we have already seen that her conception of the nature of God's action upon the soul, and of the soul's reaction under this His touch, is more akin to the rich Synoptic idea of a disposition and determination of the soul's whole being, (a cordial trust at least as much as an intellectual apprehension and clear assent), than to the Johannine view, which lays a predominant stress upon mental apprehension and assent. And again, she nowhere presents anything analogous to the Johannine, already scholastic, formulations of the object of this Faith and Trust,—all of them explicitly concerned with the nature of Christ.

But, everywhere in the Johannine writings, the living Person and Spirit aimed at by these definitions is considered as experienced by the soul in a succession of ever-deepening intuitions and acts of Faith. Already at the Jordan, Andrew and Nathaniel have declared Jesus to be the Christ, the Son of God, i, 41, 49; yet they, His disciples, are said to have believed in Him at Cana, in consequence of His miracle there, ii, 11. Already at Capernaum Peter asserts for the twelve, "We have believed and know that Thou art the Holy One of God," vi, 69; yet still, at the Last Supper, Christ exhorts them to believe in Him, xiv, 10, 11, and predicts future events to them, in order that, when these predictions come true, their faith may still further increase, xiii, 19; xiv, 29. And, as far on as after the Resurrection we hear that the Beloved Disciple "saw" (the empty tomb) "and believed," xx, 8, 29. We thus get in John precisely the same logically paradoxical, but psychologically and spiritually most accurate and profound, combination of an apparent completeness of Faith at each point of special illumination, with a sudden re-beginning and impulsive upward shifting of the soul's Light and Believing, which is so characteristic of Catherine's experience and teaching as to the successive levels of the soul's Fire, Light and Love. And the opposite movement—of the fading away of the Light and the Faith—can be traced in John, as the corresponding doctrine of the going out of the Fire, Light and Love within the Soul can be found in Catherine.

Again, both John and Catherine are penetrated with the sense that this Faith and Love is somehow waked up in souls by a true touch of God, a touch to which they spontaneously respond, because they already possess a substantial affinity to Him. "His," the Good Shepherd's, "sheep hear His voice," x, 16; they hear it, because they are already His : the Light solicits and is accepted by the soul, because the soul itself is light-like and light-requiring, and because it proceeds originally from this very Light which would now reinforce the soul's own deepest requirements. This great truth appears also in those profound Johannine passages: "No man can come to Me, unless the Father which sent Me draw him"; and "I manifested Thy name unto the men whom Thou gavest Me out of the world," vi, 44; xvii, 6.

And this attractive force is also a faculty of Christ: "I will draw all men unto Myself," xii, 32. And note how Catherine, ever completely identifying God, Christ, Light, Love, and, where these work in imperfectly pure souls, Fire, is stimulated by the last-quoted text to extend God's, Christ's, Love's drawing, attraction, to all men; to limit only, in various degrees, these various men's response to it; and to realize so intensely that a generous yielding to this our ineradicable deepest *attrait* is our fullest joy, and the resisting it is our one final misery, as to picture the soul, penitent for this its mad resistance, plunging itself, now eagerly responsive to that intense attraction, into God and a growing conformity with Him.

(3) As to points concerning the Sacraments where Catherine is influenced by John, we find that here again Baptismal conceptions are passed over by her. She does not allude to the water in the discourse to Nicodemus, iii, 5, although she is full of other ideas suggested there; but she dwells upon the water in the address to the Woman at the Well, iv, 10–15, that "living water," which is, for her, the spirit's spiritual sustenance, Love, Christ, God, and insensibly glides over into the images and experiences attaching, for her, to the Holy Eucharist.

But, as to this the greatest of the Sacraments and the all-absorbing devotion of her life, her symbols and concepts are all suggested by the Fourth Gospel, in contrast to the Synoptists and St. Paul. For the Holy Eucharist is, with her, ever detached from any direct memory of the Last Supper, Passion, and Death, the original, historical, unique occasions which still form its setting in the pre-Johannine writings, although those greatest proofs of a divinely boundless self-immolation undoubtedly give to her devotion to the Blessed Sacrament its beautiful enthusiasm and tenderness. The Holy Eucharist ever appears with her, as with St. John, attached to the scene of the multiplication of the breads,—a feast of joy and of life, with Christ at the zenith of His earthly hope and power. For not " a shewing of the death " in " the eating of this bread," 1 Cor. xi, 26, is dwelt on by John; but we have : " I am the living Bread . . . if any man eat of this bread, he shall live for ever," John vi, 51.

And Catherine follows John in thinking predominantly of the single soul, when dwelling upon the Holy Eucharist. For if John presents a great open-air Love-Feast in lieu of Paul's Upper Chamber and Supper with the twelve, he, as over against Paul's profoundly social standpoint, has, throughout this his Eucharistic chapter, but three indications of the plural as against some fourteen singulars.

And, finally, John's change from the future tense, with its reference to a coming historic institution, " the meat which . . . the Son of Man shall give unto you," vi, 27, to the present tense, with its declaration of an eternal fact and relation, " I am " (now and always) " the living bread which came down out of heaven," vi, 51, will have helped Catherine towards the conception of the eternal Christ-God offering Himself as their ceaseless spiritual food to His creatures, possessed as they are by an indestructible spiritual hunger for Himself. For if the Eucharistic food, Bread, Body, has already been declared by St. Paul to be " spiritual," 2 Cor. iii, 17, in St. John also it has to be spiritual, for it is here " the true bread from heaven " and " the bread of life "; and Christ declares here " it is the Spirit that quickeneth, the flesh (alone) profiteth nothing," vi, 32, 63. Hence Catherine is, again through the Holy Eucharist and St. John, brought back to her favourite Pauline conception of the Lord as Himself " Spirit," " the Life-giving Spirit," 2 Cor. iii, 17; 1 Cor. xv, 45.

(4) And if we conclude with the Johannine Eschatology, we shall find that Catherine has penetrated deep into the following conceptions, which undoubtedly, even in their union, present us with a less rich outlook than that furnished by the Synoptists, but which may be said to constitute the central spirit of Our Lord's teaching.

Like John, who has but two mentions of " the Kingdom of God," iii, 3, 5, and who elsewhere ever speaks of " Life," Catherine has nowhere " the Kingdom," but everywhere " Life." Like him she conceives the process of Conversion as a " making alive " of the moribund, darkened, cold soul, by the Light, Love, Christ, God, v, 21–29, when He, Who is Himself " the Life," xi, 25, and " the Spirit," iv, 24, speaks to the soul " words " that are " spirit and life," vi, 63; for then the soul that gives ear to His words "hath eternal life," v, 24.

Again Catherine, for the most part, appropriates and develops that one out of the two Johannine currents of doctrine concerning the Judgment, which treats the latter as already determined and forestalled by Man's present personal attitude towards the Light. The judgment is thus simply a discrimination, according to the original meaning of the noun κρίσις—like when God in the beginning "divided the light from the darkness," Gen. i, 5; a discrimination substantially effected already here and now, "he that believeth on Him, is not judged; he that believeth not hath been judged already," iii, 18. But the other current of doctrine, so prominent in the Synoptists is not absent from St. John,—the teaching as to a later, external and visible, forensic judgment. And Catherine has a similar intermixture of two currents, yet with a strong predominance of the immanental, present conception of the matter.

And even for that one volitional act in the beyond, which, according to her doctrine, has a certain constitutive importance for the whole eternity of all still partially impure souls—for that voluntary plunge—we can find an analogue in the Johannine writings, although here there is no reference to the after life. For throughout the greater part of his teaching—from iii, 15, 16, apparently up to the end of the Gospel,—the possession of spiritual Life is consequent upon the soul's own acts of Faith, and not, as one would expect from his other, more characteristic teaching, upon its Regeneration from above, iii, 3. And the result of such acts of Faith is a "Metabasis," a "passing over from death to life," v, 24; 1 John iii, 14. Catherine will have conceived such an act of Faith as predominantly an act of Love, and the act as itself already that Metabasis; and will, most characteristically, have quickened the movement, and have altered its direction from the horizontal to the vertical, so that the "passing, going over," becomes a "plunge down into" Life. For indeed the Fire she plunges into is, in her doctrine, Life Itself; since it is Light, Love, Christ, and God.

Catherine, once more, is John's most faithful disciple, where he declares that Life to stream out immediately from the life-giving object of Faith into the life-seeking subject of that Faith, from the believed God into the believing soul: "I am the Bread of Life: he that cometh to Me shall not hunger";

"he that abideth in Me, and I in him, the same beareth much fruit"; vi, 35; xv, 5.

And finally, she follows John closely where he insists upon Simultaneity and Eternity as contrasted with Succession and Immortality, so as even to abstract from the bodily resurrection. He who "hath passed out of death into life" (already) "possesses eternal life"; "whosoever liveth and believeth on Me, shall never die" (at any time); "this," already and of itself, "is life eternal, that they should know Thee, the only true God, and Him Whom Thou didst send, even Jesus Christ;" and the soul's abiding in such an experience is Christ's own joy, transplanted into it, and a joy which is full, v, 24; xi, 26; xvii, 3; xv, 11. And there is here such an insistence upon an unbroken spiritual life, in spite of and right through physical death, that, to Martha's declaration that her brother will arise at the last day, xi, 24, Jesus answers, "I am the Resurrection and the Life: he that believeth on Me, though he die" the bodily death, "shall live" on in his soul; indeed "every man who liveth" the life of the body, "and who believeth in Me, shall never die" (at any time) in his soul, xi, 25, 26. John's other line of thought, in which the bodily resurrection is prominent, remains without any definite or systematic response in Catherine's teaching.

(5) We can then summarize the influence exercised by John upon Catherine by saying that he encouraged her to conceive religion as an experience of eternity; as a true, living knowledge of things spiritual; indeed as a direct touch of man's soul by God Himself, culminating in man's certainty that God is Love.

III. The Areopagite Writings.

Catherine's close relations to the Areopagite, the Pseudo-Dionysius, are of peculiar interest, in their manifold agreement, difference, or non-responsiveness; and this although the ideas thus assimilated are mostly of lesser depth and importance than those derived from the New Testament writings just considered. They can be grouped conveniently under the subject-matters of God's creative, providential, and restorative, outgoing, His action upon souls and all things extant, and of the reasons for the different results of this action; of certain symbols used to characterize that essential action of

God upon His creatures; of the states and energizings of the soul, in so far as it is responsive to that action; of certain terms concerning these reactions of the soul; and of the final result of the whole process. I shall try and get back, in most cases, to the Areopagite's Neo-Platonist sources, the dry, intensely scholastic Proclus, and that great soul, the prince of the non-Christian Mystics, Plotinus.[1]

1. *God's general action.*

As to God's action, we have in Dionysius the Circle with the three stages of its movement,—a conception so dear to Catherine. "Theologians call Him the Esteemed and the Loved, and again Love and Loving-kindness, as being a Power at once propulsive and leading up" and back "to Himself; a loving movement self-moved, which pre-exists in the Good, and bubbles forth from the Good to things existing, and which again returns to the Good—as it were a sort of everlasting circle whirling round, because of the Good, from the Good, in the Good, and to the Good,—ever advancing and remaining and returning in the same and throughout the same." This is "the power of the divine similitude" present throughout creation, "which turns all created things to their cause."[2] The doctrine is derived from Proclus: "Everything caused both abides in its cause and proceeds from it and returns to it"; and "everything that proceeds from something returns, by a natural instinct, to that from which it proceeds."[3] And Plotinus had led the way: "there" in the super-sensible world, experienced in moments of ecstasy, "in touch and union with the One, the soul begets Beauty, Justice and Virtue: and that place and life is, for it, its principle and end: principle, since it springs from thence; end, because the Good is there, and because, once arrived there, the soul becomes what it was at first."[4]

[1] I am much indebted to the thorough and convincing monograph of the Catholic Priest and Professor Dr. Hugo Koch, *Pseudo-Dionysius Areopagita in seinen Beziehungen zum Neo-Platonismus und Mysterienwesen*, Mainz, 1900, for a fuller understanding of the relations between Dionysius, Proclus, and Plotinus. I have also found much help in H. F. Müller's admirable German translation of Plotinus, a translation greatly superior to Thomas Taylor's English or to Bouillet's French translation. And I have greatly benefited by the admirable study of Plotinus in Dr. Edward Caird's *Evolution of Theology in the Greek Philosophers*, 1904, Vol. II, pp. 210–346.

[2] *The Divine Names*, iii, 1; ix, 4: English translation by Parker, 1897, pp. 49, 50; 106.

[3] *Institutio Theologica*, c. 35; c. 31.

[4] *Enneads*, vi, ch. ix, 9.

And Dionysius has the doctrine, so dear to Catherine, that " the Source of Good is indeed present to all, but all are not," by their intention, " present to It; yet, by our aptitude for Divine union, we all," in a sense, " are present to It." " It shines, on Its own part, equally upon all things capable of participation in It." [1] Already Plotinus had finely said: " The One is not far away from any one, and yet is liable to be far away from one and all, since, present though It be, It is " efficaciously " present only to such as are capable of receiving It, and are so disposed as to adapt themselves to It and, as it were, to seize and touch It by their likeness to It, . . . when, in a word, the soul is in the state in which it was when it came from It." [2]

We have again in Dionysius the combination, so characteristic of Catherine, of a tender respect for the substance of human nature, as good and ever respected by God, and of a keen sense of the pathetic weakness of man's sense-clogged spirit here below. " Providence, as befits its goodness, provides for each being suitably: for to destroy nature is not a function of Providence." " All those who cavil at the Divine Justice, unconsciously commit a manifest injustice. For they say that immortality ought to be in mortals, and perfection in the imperfect . . . and perfect power in the weak, and that the temporal should be eternal . . . in a word, they assign the properties of one thing to another." [3]

2. *Symbols of God's action.*

(1) As to the symbols of God's action, we have first the Chain or Rope, Catherine's " fune," that " rope of His pure Love," of which " an end was thrown to her from heaven." [4] This symbol was no doubt suggested by Dionysius: " Let us then elevate our very selves by our prayers to the higher ascent of the Divine . . . rays; as though a luminous chain (rope, σειρά) were suspended from the celestial heights and reached down hither, and we, by ever stretching out to it up and up . . . were thus carried upwards." [5] And this passage again goes back to Proclus, who describes the " chain (rope) of love " as " having its entirely simple and hidden highest point fixed amongst the very first ranks of the Gods"; its middle effluence

[1] *Divine Names*, iii, 1; ix, 4: Parker, pp. 27, 104.
[2] *Enneads*, vi, ch. ix, 4.
[3] *Divine Names*, viii, 7: Parker, pp. 98, 99.
[4] *Vita*, pp. 47*c*, 48*a*.
[5] *Divine Names*, iii, 1: Parker, pp. 27, 28.

"amongst the Gods higher than the (sensible) world"; and its third, lowest, part, as "divided multiformly throughout the (sensible) world." "The divine Love implants one common bond (chain) and one indissoluble friendship in and between each soul (that participates in its power), and between all and the Beautiful Itself."[1] And this simile of a chain from heaven, which in Dionysius is luminous, and in Catherine and Proclus is loving, goes back, across Plato (*Theaetetus* 153*c* and *Republic*, X, 61*b*, 99*c*) to Homer, where it again is luminous (golden). For, in the *Iliad*, viii, 17–20, Zeus says to the Gods in Olympus, "So as to see all things, do you, O Gods and Goddesses all, hang a golden chain from heaven, and do you all seize hold of it"—so as thus to descend to earth.

(2) We have next the symbol of the Sun and its purifying, healing Light, under which God and His action are rapturously proclaimed by Dionysius. "Even as our sun, by its very being, enlightens all things able to partake of its light in their various degrees, so also the Good, by its very existence, sends unto all things that be, the rays of its entire goodness, according to their capacity for them. By means of these rays they are purified from all corruption and death . . . and are separated from instability." "The Divine Goodness, this our great sun, enlightens . . . nourishes, perfects, renews." Even the pure can thus be made purer still. "He, the Good, is called spiritual light . . . he cleanses the mental vision of the very angels: they taste, as it were, the light."[2] All this imagery goes back, in the first instance, to Proclus. For Proclus puts in parallel "sun" and "God," and "to be enlightened" and "to be deified"; makes all purifying forces to coalesce in the activity of the Sun-God, Apollo Katharsios, the Purifier, who "everywhere unifies multiplicity . . . purifying the entire heaven and all living things throughout the world"; and describes how "from above, from his superheavenly post, Apollo scatters the arrows of Zeus,—his rays upon all the world."[3] The Sun's rays, here as powerful as the bolts of Zeus, thus begin to play the part still assigned to them in Catherine's imagery of the "Saëtte" and "Radii" of the divine Light and Love. And the substance of the whole symbol goes back, through fine sayings of Plotinus and through Philo, to Plato, who calls the Sun "the offspring

[1] *In Platonis Alcibiadem*, ii, 78 *seq.*
[2] *Divine Names*, iv, 1; iv, 5: Parker, pp. 32, 33; 38.
[3] *In Parmenidem*, iv, 34. *In Cratylum*, pp. 103; 107.

of the Good and analogous to it," and who (doubtless rightly) takes Homer's "golden chain" to be nothing but the Sun-rays,—thus identifying the two symbols.[1]

(3) Fire, as a symbol for God and His action, is thus praised by Dionysius: "The sacred theologians often describe the super-essential Essence in terms of Fire . . . For sensible fire is, so to say, present in all things, and pervades them all without mingling with them, and is received by all things; . . . it is intolerable yet invisible; it masters all things by its own might, and yet it but brings the things in which it resides to (the development of) their own energy; it has a transforming power; it communicates itself to all who approach it in any degree; . . . it has the power of dividing (what it seizes); it bears upwards; it is penetrating; . . . it increases its own self in a hidden manner; it suddenly shines forth."[2]—All these qualities, and the delicate transitions from fire to light and from light back to fire, and from heat immanent to heat applied from without, we can find again, vividly assimilated and experienced, in Catherine's teaching and emotional life. But the Sun-light predominates in Dionysius, the Fire-heat in Catherine; and whereas the former explicitly attaches purification only to the Sun-light, the latter connects the cleansing chiefly with Fire-heat, no doubt because the Greek man is busy chiefly with the intellectually cognitive, and the Italian woman with the morally ameliorative, activities and interests of the mind and soul.

3. *The soul's reaction.*

(1) As to the soul's reaction under God's action, and its return to Him, we first get, in Dionysius, the insistence upon Mystical Quietude and Silence, which, according to him, are strictly necessary, since only like can know and become one with like, and God is "Peace and Repose" and, "as compared with every known progression, Immobility," and "the one all-perfect source and cause of the Peace of all"; and He is Silence, "the Angels are, as it were, the heralds of the Divine Silence,"—teaching not unlike that of St. Ignatius of Antioch, "Jesus Christ . . . the Word which proceeds from Silence."[3] Hence "in proportion as we ascend to the higher designations of God, do our expressions become more and more circumscribed"; and at last "we shall find, not a little speaking,

[1] *Republic*, VI, 508*c*. *Theaetetus*, 153*c*.

[2] *Heavenly Hierarchy*, xv, 2: Parker, pp. 56, 57.

[3] *Divine Names*, xi, 1; iv, 2: Parker, pp. 113, 34. *Ad Magnesios*, viii, 2.

but a complete absence of speech and of conception." [1] As Proclus has it : " Let this Fountain of Godhead be honoured on our part by silence and by the union which is above silence." [2] And Plotinus says : " This," the Divine, " Light comes not from anywhere nor disappears any whither, but simply shines or shines not : hence we must not pursue after it, but must abide in quietness till it appears." And when it does appear, " the contemplative, as one rapt and divinely inspired, abides here with quietude in a motionless condition, . . . being entirely stable, and becoming, as it were, stability itself." [3]—All this still finds its echo in Catherine.—But the treble (cognitive) movement of the Angelic and human mind,—the circular, the straight-line, and the spiral,—which Dionysius, in direct imitation of Proclus, carefully develops throughout three sections, is quite absent from Catherine's mind.[4]

(2) We next get, in Dionysius, the following teachings as to Mystical Vision and Union. " The Unity-above-Mind is placed above the minds; and the Good-above-word is unutterable by word." " There is, further, the most divine knowledge of Almighty God, which is known through not knowing . . . when the mind, having stood apart from all existing things, and having then also dismissed itself, has been made one with the super-luminous rays." " We must contemplate things divine by our whole selves standing out of our whole selves, and becoming wholly of God." "By the resistless and absolute ecstasy, in all purity, from out of thyself and all things, thou wilt be carried on high, to the super-essential ray of the divine darkness." " It is during the cessation of every mental energizing, that such a union of the deified minds and of the super-divine light takes place." [5] And the original cause and final effect of such a going forth from self, are indicated in words which were worked out in a vivid fulness by Catherine's whole convert life : " Divine Love is ecstatic, not permitting any lovers to belong to themselves, but only to those beloved by them. And this love, the

[1] *Mystic Theology*, iii : Parker, p. 135.

[2] *Platonic Theology*, III, p. 132.

[3] *Enneads*, v, ch. v, 8; vi, ch. ix, 11.

[4] *Divine Names*, iv, 8–10 : Parker, pp. 42–45. *In Parmenidem*, vi, 52 (see Koch, p. 152).

[5] *Divine Names*, i, 1; vii, 3; vii, 1; *Mystic Theology*, 1; *Divine Names*, vii, 3 : Parker, pp. 2; 91, 92; 87; 130; 91, 92.

superior beings show by being full of forethought for their inferiors; those equal in rank, by their mutual coherence; and the inferior by a looking back and up to the superior ones." [1]

Dionysius here everywhere follows Proclus. Yet the noblest Neo-Platonist sayings are again furnished by Plotinus: "We are not cut off or severed from the Light, but we breathe and consist in It, since It ever enlightens and bears us, as long as It is what It is." In the moments of Union, "we are able to see both Him and ourself,—ourself in dazzling splendour, full of spiritual light, or rather one with the pure Light Itself . . . our life's flame is then enkindled." "There the soul rests, after it has fled up, away from evil, to the place which is free from evils . . . and the true life is there." "Arrived there, the soul becomes that which she was at first." [2] And if Plotinus has thus already got the symbolism of place, he is as fully aware as Catherine herself that, for purposes of vivid presentation, he is spatializing spiritual, that is, unextended, qualitative states and realities. "Things incorporeal do not get excluded by bodies; they are severed only by otherness and difference: hence, when such otherness is absent, they, not differing, are near each other." And already, as with Catherine, there is the apparent finality, and yet also the renewed search for more. "The seer and the seen have become one, as though it were a case not of vision but of union." "When he shall have crossed over as the image to its Archetype, then he will have reached his journey's end." And yet this "ecstasy, simplification, and donation of one's self," this "quiet," is still also "a striving after contact," "a musing to achieve union." [3]

4. *Terminology of the soul's reaction.*

(1) Certain terms and conceptions in connection with the soul's return to God, which are specially dear to Catherine, already appear, fully developed, in Dionysius, Proclus, and Plotinus; in part, even in Plato. Her "suddenly" (*subito*) appears but rarely in Dionysius, *e. g.* in *Heavenly Hierarchy* xv, 2; but it is carefully explained by him in his Third Epistle, specially devoted to the subject.[4] It is common in Plotinus: "Suddenly the soul saw, without seeing how it saw"; "suddenly thou shalt receive light," "suddenly shining."[5] And

[1] *Divine Names*, iv, 13: Parker, p. 48.
[2] *Enneads*, vi, ch. ix, 9.
[3] *Ibid.* vi, ch. ix, 8; ch. vi, 11.
[4] Parker, p. 142.
[5] *Enneads*, vi, ch. vii, 36; v, ch. iii, 17; v, ch. v, 7.

in Plato we find: "He who has learnt to see the Beautiful in due order and succession, when he comes towards the end, will suddenly perceive a Nature of wondrous beauty—Beauty alone, absolute, separate, simple and everlasting": a passage which derives its imagery from the Epopteia of the Eleusynian Mysteries,—the sudden appearance, the curtain being withdrawn, upon the stage whereon the Heathen Mystery-play was being performed, under a peculiar fairy-illumination, of the figures of Demeter, Kore, and Iacchus, as the culmination of a long succession of purifications and initiations.[1]

Catherine's "wound," or "wounding stroke," (*ferita*), is, in part, the necessary consequence of the "arrow" conception already considered; in part, the echo of that group of terms which, in Dionysius and Proclus even more than in Plotinus, express the painfully sudden and overwhelming, free-grace character of God's action upon the soul,—especially of ἐπιβολή, "immissio," a "coming-upon," a "hitting," a very common word in the Areopagite; μετοχή, "communication," and παραδοχή, "reception," being the corresponding terms for God's and the soul's share in this encounter respectively. Thus: "Unions, whether we call them immissions or receptions from God."[2]

"Presence," "presenza," παρανσιά, is another favourite term, as with Catherine so also with Dionysius and Proclus. Thus the Areopagite: "The presence of the spiritual light causes recollection and unity in those that are being enlightened with it," "His wholly inconceivable presence."[3] And Proclus: "Every perfect spiritual contact and communion is owing to the presence of God."[4] And the conception of a sudden presence goes back, among the Neo-Platonists, to Plato and the Greek Mysteries, in which the God was held suddenly to arrive and to take part in the sacred dance. Such rings of sacred dancers, "choirs," are still characteristic of Dionysius—*e.g. Heavenly Hierarchy*, vii, 4—but they are quite wanting in Catherine.—But "contact," "touch" ἐπαφή,—said of God's direct action upon the soul,—a conception so intensely active in Catherine's mind and life, is again a favourite term with Dionysius and Proclus. The former declares this "touch" to

[1] *Symposium*, 210 E. See the admirable elucidations in Rhode's *Psyche*, ed. 1898, Vol. I, p. 298; Vol. II, pp. 279; 283, 284.

[2] *Divine Names*, i, 5: Parker, p. 8.

[3] *Divine Names*, iv, 6; *Mystic Theology*, i, iii: Parker, pp. 39, 132.

[4] *In Alcibiadem*, ii, 302.

be neither "sensible" nor "intelligible," and that "we are brought into contact with things unutterable"; the latter talks of "perfect spiritual contact."[1]

The symbols of "Nakedness" and "Garments," as indicative respectively of the soul's purity and impurity or self-delusion, are, though most prominent in Catherine, rare in Dionysius. But his declaration: "The nakedness of the (Angels') feet indicates purification from the addition of all things external, and assimilation to the divine simplicity" exactly expresses her idea.[2] And Proclus has it more fully: The soul, on descending into the body, forsakes unity, "and around her, from all sides, there grow multiform kinds of existence and manifold garments"; "love of honour is the last garment of souls"; and "when," in mounting up, "we lay aside our passions and garments which, in coming down, we had put on, we must also strip off that last garment, in order that, having become (entirely) naked, we may establish ourselves before God, having made ourselves like to the divine life."[3]

(2) Again, as to Triads, it is interesting to note that Catherine has nothing about the three stages or ways of the inner life, —purgative, illuminative, unitive,—of which Dionysius is full, and which are already indicated in Proclus; for we can find but two in her life, the purgative and unitive, and in her teaching these two alone appear, mostly in close combination, sometimes in strong contrast. Nor has she anything about the three degrees or kinds of prayer,—Meditation, Contemplation, Union,—as indicated in Dionysius: "It behoves us, by our prayers, to be lifted into proximity with the Divine Trinity; and then, by still further approaching it, to be initiated . . .; and (lastly) to make ourselves one with it"; and as taught by Proclus: "Knowledge leads, then follows proximity, and then union."[4] With her we only get Contemplation and Union.—Nor do we get in her anything about thrice three choirs of Angels, or three orders of Christian Ministrants, or three classes of Christian people, or thrice three groups of Sacraments and Sacramental acts. For she is too intensely bent upon immediate intercourse with God, and too much absorbed in the sense of profound unity and again of innumerable

[1] *Mystic Theology*, iv, v; *Divine Names*, i, 1: Parker, pp. 136, 137; 1; *In Alcibiadem*, ii, 302.

[2] *Heavenly Hierarchy*, ch. xv, s. 3: Parker, p. 60.

[3] *In Alcibiadem*, iii, 75.

[4] *Divine Names*, iii, 1: Parker, pp. 27, 28. *In Parmenidem*, iv, 68.

multiplicity, to be attracted by Dionysius's Neo-Platonist ladder of carefully graduated intermediaries, or by his continuous interest in triads of every kind. Catherine thus follows the current in Dionysius which insists upon direct contact between the soul and the transcendent God, and ignores the other, which bridges over the abyss between the two by carefully graduated intermediaries: these intermediaries having become, with her, successive stages of purification and of ever more penetrating union of the one soul with the one God.

5. *Deification, especially through the Eucharist.*

As to the end of the whole process, we find that Deification, so frequently implied or suggested by Catherine, is formally taught by Dionysius: "A union of the deified minds" (ἐκθεουμένων); the heavenly and the earthly Hierachy have the power and task "to communicate to their subjects, according to the dignity of each, the sacred deification" (ἐκθέωσις); "we are led up, by means of the multiform of sensible symbols, to the uniform Deification."[1] "The One is the very God," says Proclus, "but the Mind (the Noûs) is the divinest of beings, and the soul is divine, and the body is godlike. . . . And every body that is God-like is so through the soul having become divine; and every soul that is divine, is so through the Mind being very divine; and every Mind that is thus very divine, is so through participation in the Divine One."[2] There are preformations of this doctrine in Plotinus and echoes of it throughout Catherine's sayings.

And the Areopagite's teaching that the chief means and the culmination of this deification are found and reached in the reception of the Holy Eucharist will no doubt also have stimulated Catherine's mind: "The Communicant is led to the summit of deiformation, as far as this is possible for him."[3] And her soul responds completely to the beautiful Dionysian-Proclian teaching concerning God's presence in all things, as the cause of the profound sympathy which binds them all together. "They say," declares Dionysius, "that He is in minds . . . and in bodies, and in heaven and in earth; (indeed that He is) sun, fire, water, spirit . . . all things existing, and yet again not one of all things existing." "The

1 *Divine Names*, i, 5; *Ecclesiastical Hierarchy*, i, 2; *Divine Names*, ix, 5; Parker, pp. 8, 69, 104.
2 *Institutio Theologica*, c. 129.
3 *Ecclesiastical Hierarchy*, iii, 3, 7; Parker, p. 97.

distribution of boundless power passes from Almighty God to all things, and no single being but has intellectual, or rational, or sensible, or vital, or essential power." "The gifts of the unfailing Power pass on to men and (lesser) living creatures, to plants, and to the entire nature of the Universe."[1] This latter passage was suggested by Proclus: "One would say that, through participation in the One, all things are deified, each according to its rank, inclusive of the very lowest of beings." "The image of the One and the inter-communion existing through it,—this it is that produces the extant sympathy" which permeates all things.[2]—But Catherine has nowhere the term "echo," which is so dear to Dionysius: "His all-surpassing power holds together and preserves even the remotest of its echoes"; "the sun and plants are or hold most distant echoes of the Good and of Life"; indeed even the licentious man still possesses, in his very passion, "as it were a faint echo of Union and of Friendship."[3]

6. *Dionysius and Catherine; three agreements and differences.*

I conclude with three important points of difference and similarity between Catherine and Dionysius.

(1) Catherine abstains from the use of those repulsive, impossibly hyperbolic epithets such as "the Super-Good," "the Above-Mind," which Dionysius is never weary of applying to God, and is content with ever feeling and declaring how high above the very best conception which she can form of mind and of goodness He undoubtedly is; thus wisely moderated, I take it, by her constant experience and faith as to God's immediate presence within the human soul, which soul cannot, consequently, be presented as entirely remote from the nature of God.

(2) Catherine transforms over-intense and impoverishing insistence upon the pure Oneness of God, such as we find it even in Dionysius and still more in Proclus, into a, sometimes equally over-intense, conception as to the oneness of our union with Him, leaving Him to be still conceived as an overflowing richness of all kinds.

(3) And Catherine keeps, in an interesting manner, the Hellenic, and specifically Platonic, formulation for the deepest of her experiences and teachings, since her standing designation

[1] *Divine Names*, i, 6; viii, 3; 5: Parker, pp. 10, 95, 96.
[2] *In Parmenidem*, iv, 34; v.
[3] *Divine Names*, viii, 2; iv, 4; iv, 20; Parker, pp. 95, 84, 57.

of God and of Our Lord is never personal, "My Lover" or "My Friend"; but, as it were, elemental, "Love" or "My Love." Her keen self-purifying instinct and reverence for God will have spontaneously inclined her thus to consider Him first as an Ocean of Being in which to quench and drown her small, clamorous individuality, and this as a necessary step towards reconstituting that true personality, which, itself spirit, would be penetrated and sustained by the Spirit, Christ, God. And then the Pauline-Johannine picturings of God as a quasi-place and extended substance ("from Him and in Him and to Him," "in the Spirit," "in Christ," "God is Charity and he that abideth in Charity, abideth in Him") will have strongly confirmed this trend. Yet Dionysius too must have greatly helped on this movement of her mind. For in Dionysius the standing appellations for God are, in true Neo-Platonist fashion, derived from extended or diffusive material substances or conditions, Light, Fire, Fountain, Ocean; and from that pervasive emotion, Love, strictly speaking Desire, Eros.

Now this, for our modern and Christian feeling, curiously impersonal, general and abstract method goes back, through Proclus and Plotinus, to Plato, who, above all in his *Symposium*, is dominated by the two tendencies and requirements, of identifying the First and Perfect with the most General and the most Abstract; and of making the very pre-requisites and instruments of the search for It,—even the earthly Eros, still so far from the Heavenly Eros and from the Christian Agapē,—into occasions, effects or instalments of and for the great Reality sought by them. And since it is thus the love, the desire, the eros, of things beautiful, and true, and good,—a love first sensible, then intellectual, and at last spiritual, which makes us seek and find It, the Beauty, Truth, and Goodness which is First Cause and Final End of the whole series, this Cause and End will be considered not as a Lover but as Love Itself. It is plain, I think, that it is specially this second motive, this requirement of a pervading organization and circle of and within the life of spirits and of the Spirit, which has also determined Catherine to retain Plato's terminology.

IV. Jacopone da Todi's "Lode."

In the case of Jacopone, the suddenly wife-bereft and converted lawyer, an ardent poet doubled by a soaring, daring mystic, with an astonishing richness of simultaneous symbols and conceptions and rapidity of successive complements and contrasts, it will really be simplest if I take the chief touches which have characteristically stimulated Catherine or have left her unaffected, in the order and grouping in which they appear in his chief "Lode," as these latter are given in the first printed edition, probably the very one used by Catherine.[1]

1. *Lode XIII, XXIII, XXXV, XLV.*

In Loda XIII "the vicious soul is likened unto Hell," vv. 1–7; and "the soul that yesterday was Hell, to-day has turned into Heaven," v. 8. We thus get here, precisely as in Catherine, the spaceless conditions of the soul and their modifications treated under the symbols of places and of the spatial change from one place to the other.

In Loda XXIII we first have five successive purifications and purities of Love, "carnal, counterfeit, self-seeking, natural, spiritual, transformed," vv. 1–6; and then the symbols of spatial location and movement reappear, "if height does not abase itself, it cannot participate with, nor communicate itself to, the lowest grade"; all which is frequent with Catherine. But she nowhere echoes the teaching reproduced here, v. 10, as to the Divine Trinity being figured in man's three faculties of soul.

Loda XXXV gives us a sort of Christian Stoicism very dear to Catherine: "Thou, my soul, hast been created in great elevation; thy nature is grounded in great nobility (*gentilezza*)," v. 7; "thou hast not thy life in created things; it is necessary for thee to breathe in other countries, to mount up to God, thine inheritance, Who (alone) can satisfy thy poverty," v. 10; "great is the honour which thou doest to God, when thou abidest (*stare*) in Him, in thy (true) nobility," v. 11.

[1] *Laude de lo contemplativo et extatico B. F. Jacopone de lo Ordine de lo Seraphico S. Francesco.* . . . In Firenze, per Ser Francesco Bonaccorsi, MCCCCLXXXX. Only the sheets are numbered; and two Lode have, by mistake, been both numbered LVIII: I have indicated them by LVIII*a* and LVIII*b* respectively. I have much felt the absence of any monograph on the sources and characters of Jacopone's doctrine.

Loda XLV gives "the Five Modes in which God appears in the Soul"—"the state of fear"; curative, "healing-love"; "the way of love"; "the paternal mode"; "the mode of espousals." Catherine leaves the last two, anthropomorphic and familial, conceptions quite unused, and passes in her life, at one bound, from the first to the third mode.

2. *Lode LVIIIa, LVIIIb.*

The fine Loda LVIII*a*, "Of Holy Poverty, Mistress of all Things," has evidently suggested much to Catherine. "Waters, rivers, lakes, and ocean, fish within them and their swimming; airs, winds, birds, and all their flying: all these turn to jewels for me," v. 10. How readily the sense of water, and of rapid movement within it, passes here into that of air, and of swift locomotion within *it!* And both these movements are felt to represent, in vivid fashion, certain very different experiences of the soul.—"Moon, Sun, Sky, and Stars,—even these are *not* amongst my treasures: above the very sky those things abide, which are the object of my song," v. 11. The positive, "analogic" method has here turned suddenly into the negative, "apophatic" one; and yet, even here, we still have the spatial symbolism, for the best is the highest up,—indeed it is this very symbolism which is made to add point to the negative declaration, a declaration which nevertheless clearly implies the mere symbolism of that spatialization. All this is fully absorbed by Catherine.—"Since God has my will, . . . my wings have such feathers that from earth to heaven there is no distance for me," v. 12. Here we see how Plato filters through, complete, to Jacopone; but only in his central idea to Catherine. For the *Phaedrus*, 246*b*, *c*, teaches: "The perfect soul then, having become winged, soars upwards, and is the ruler of the universe; whilst the imperfect soul sheds her feathers and is borne downwards, till it settles on the solid ground." Catherine never mentions wings nor feathers, but often dwells upon flying.

The great Loda LVIII*b*, "Of Holy Poverty and its Treble Heaven," (one passage of which is formally quoted and carefully expounded by Catherine), is a combination of Platonism, Paulinism, and Franciscanism, and has specially influenced her through its Platonist element. Verses 1–9 contain a fine apostrophe to Poverty. "O Love of Poverty, Reign of tranquillity! Poverty, high Wisdom! to be subject to nothing; through despising to possess all things created!" v. 1: all this is echoed by Catherine. But the ex-lawyer's declaration that such a soul " has neither judge nor notary," v. 3, did certainly not determine her literally, for we have had before us some fifteen cases in which she had recourse to lawyers. " God makes not His abode in a narrow heart; thou art, oh man, precisely as great as thine affection may be. The spirit of poverty possesses so ample a bosom, that Deity Itself takes up its dwelling there," v. 8. Catherine's deepest self seems to breathe from out of this profound saying.

Verses 10 to 30 describe the three heavens of successive self-despoilments. The firmamental heaven, which typifies the four-fold renouncement,—of honour, riches, science, reputation of sanctity, has left no echo in Catherine. The stellar heaven is " composed of solidified clear waters (*aque solidate*) " ; here " the four winds " cease " that move the sea,—that perturb the mind : fear and hope, grief and joy," 11–14. Here Plato again touches Catherine through Jacopone. For the *Symposium*, 197*a*, declares : " Love it is that produces peace among men and calm on the sea, a cessation of the winds, and repose and sleep even in trouble " ; and Jacopone identifies the middle " crystalline " heaven, (" the waters above " of Genesis, chap. i,) with Plato's " sea " ; takes Plato's (four) winds as the soul's chief passions ; and considers Plato's " peace " and " windlessness " as equivalent to the " much silence," which, says the Apocalypse, " arose in heaven," viii, 1, interpreted here as " in mid-heaven." " Not to fear Hell, nor to hope for Heaven, to rejoice in no good, to grieve over no adversity," v. 16, is a formulation unlike Catherine, although single sayings of hers stand for sentiments analogous to the first and last.—" If the virtues are naked, and the vices are not garmented,—mortal wounds get given to the soul," v. 19, has a symbolism exactly opposite to Catherine's, who, we know, loves to glorify " nakedness " as the soul's purity.— " The highest heaven " is " beyond even the imagings of the mortified fancy " ; " of every good it has despoiled thee, and has expropriated thee from all virtue : lay up as a treasure this thy gain,—the sense of thine own vileness." " O purified Love ! it alone lives in the truth ! " These verses, 20–22, have left a deep impress upon Catherine, although she wisely does not press that " expropriation from virtue," which goes back at least to Plotinus, for whom the true Ecstatic is " beyond the choir of the virtues." [1]

[1] *Enneads*, vi, ch. ix, 11.

"That which appears to thee (as extant), is not truly existent: so high (above) is that which truly is. True elevation of soul (*la superbia*) dwells in heaven above, and baseness of mind (*humilitade*) leads to damnation," v. 24, is a saying to which we still have Catherine's detailed commentary. In its markedly Platonic distinction between an upper true and a lower seeming world, and in its characteristically mystical love of paradox and a play upon words, it is more curious than abidingly important; but in its deeply Christian consciousness of "pride" and "humility," in their ordinary ethical sense, being respectively the subtlest vice and the noblest virtue, it rises sheer above all Platonist and Neo-Platonist apprehension.

"Love abides in prison, in that darksome light! All light there is darkness, and all darkness there is as the day," vv. 26, 27. Here Catherine no doubt found aids towards her prison-conception,—of the loving soul imprisoned in the earthly body, and of the imperfect, yet loving, disembodied souls imprisoned in Purgatory; and towards articulating her strong sense of the change in the meaning and value of the same symbols, as the soul grows in depth and experience. But her symbolization of God, and of our apprehension of Him as Light and Fire, is too solidly established in her mind, to allow her to emphasize the darkness-symbol with any reference to Him.

"There where Christ is enclosed (in the soul), all the old is changed by Him,—the one is transformed into the Other, in a marvellous union. To live as I and yet not I; and my very being to be not mine: this is so great a cross-purpose (*traversio*), that I know not how to define it," vv. 28–30. This vivid description, based of course upon St. Paul, of the apparent shifting of the very centre of the soul's personality, has left clear echoes in Catherine's sayings; but the explicit reference to Christ is here as characteristically Franciscan as it is unlike Catherine's special habits.—And the great poem ends with a *refrain* of its opening apostrophe.

3. *Lode LXXIV, LXXIX, LXXXI, LXXXIII.*

In the dramatically vivid Dialogue between the Old and the Young Friar "Concerning the divers manners of contemplating the Cross," Loda LXXIV, the elder says to the younger man: "And I find the Cross full of arrows, which issue from its side: they get fixed in my heart. The Archer has aimed them at me; He causes me to be pierced," v. 6. The Cross is here a bow; and yet the arrows evidently issue not from it, but, as so many rays, from the Sun, the Light-Christ, Who is laid upon it,—from the heart of the Crucified. Catherine maintains the rays and arrows, and the Sun and Fire from which they issue; but the Cross and the Crucified, presupposed here throughout, appear not, even to this extent, in her post-conversion picturings.—" You abide by the warmth, but I abide within the fire; to you it is delight, but I am burning through and through, I cannot find a place of refuge in this furnace," v. 13. All this has been echoed throughout by Catherine.

Loda LXXIX, " Of the Divine Love and its Praises," has evidently much influenced her. " O joyous wound, delightful wound, gladsome wound, for him who is wounded by Thee, O Love!" " O Love, divine Fire! Love full of laughter and playfulness!" " O Love, sweet and suave; O Love, Thou art the key of heaven! Ship that Thou art, bring me to port and calm the tempest," vv. 3, 6, 16. All this we have found reproduced in her similes and experiences. " Love, bounteous in spending Thyself; Love with wide-spread tables!" " Love, Thou art the One that loves, and the Means wherewith the heart loves Thee!" vv. 24, 26. These verses give us the wide, wide world outlook, the connection between Love and the Holy Eucharist, and the identity of the Subject, Means, and Object of Love, which are all so much dwelt upon by Catherine.

Loda LXXXI is interesting by the way in which, although treating of " the love of Christ upon the Cross," it everywhere apostrophizes Love and not the Lover, and treats the former, again like Catherine, as a kind of boundless living substance; indeed v. 17 must have helped to suggest one of her favourite conceptions: " O great Love, greater than the great sea! Oh! the man who is drowned within it, under it, and with it all around him, whilst he knows not where he is!"

Loda LXXXIII has two touches dear to Catherine. " O Love, whose name is ' I love '—the plural is never found," v. 5, —a saying which evidently is directed, not against a social conception of religion, but against a denial of the Divine Love being Source as well as Object of our love; and " I did not love Thee with any gain to myself, until I loved Thee for Thine own sake," v. 15,—a declaration of wondrous depth and simplicity.

4. *Lode LXXXVIII, LXXXIX, LXXXX, LXXXXVIII, LXXXXIX.*

The great Loda LXXXVIII, " How the soul complains to God concerning the excessive ardours of the love infused into it," contains numerous touches which have been interestingly responded to or ignored by Catherine. " All my will is on fire with Love, is united, transformed (into It); who can bear such Love? Nor fire nor sword can part the loving soul and her Love; a thing so united cannot be divided; neither suffering nor death can henceforth mount up to that height where the soul abides in ecstasy," vv. 5, 6: a combination of St. Paul and Plotinus, quite after Catherine's heart. But " the light of the sun appears to me obscure, now that I see that resplendent Countenance," v. 7, has an anthropomorphic touch to which she does not respond; and " I have given all my heart, that it may possess that Lover who renews me so,—O Beauty ancient and ever new! " v. 10, has the personal designation " Lover," which, again, is alien to her vocabulary.

" Seeing such Beauty, I have been drawn out of myself . . . and the heart now gets undone, melted as though it were wax, and finds itself again, with the likeness of Christ upon it," v. 11, must have stimulated, by its first part, some of her own experiences, and will, by its second part, taken literally, have helped on the fantastic expectations of her attendants. " Love rises to such ardour, that the heart seems to be transfixed as with a knife," v. 14, no doubt both expressed an experience of Jacopone and helped to constitute the form of a similar experience on the part of Catherine. " As iron, which is all on fire, as dawn, made resplendent by the sun, lose their own form (nature) and exist in another, so is it with the pure mind, when clothed by Thee, O Love," v. 21, contains ideas, (all but the symbol of clothing), very dear to Catherine. But the astonishingly daring words: " Since my soul has been transformed into Truth, into Thee, O Christ alone, into Thee Who art tender Loving,—not to myself but to Thee can be imputed what I do. Hence, if I please Thee not, Thou dost not please Thine Own Self, O Love! " v. 22, remain unechoed by her, no doubt because her states shift from one to another, and she wisely abstains from pushing the articulation of any one of them to its own separate logical limit.

" Thou wast born into the world by love and not by flesh, O Love become Man (*humanato Amore*)," v. 27, is like her in its interesting persistence in the "Love" (not "Lover") designation, but is unlike her in its definite reference to the historic Incarnation. "Love, O Love, Jesus, I have reached the haven," v. 32, is closely like her, all but the explicit mention of the historic name; and "Love, O Love, Thou art the full-orbed circle," "Thou art both warp and woof," beginning and end, material and transforming agency, v. 33, is Catherine's central idea, expressed in a form much calculated to impress it upon her.

The daring and profound Loda LXXXIX, "How the soul, by holy self-annihilation and love, reaches an unknowable and indescribable state," contains again numerous touches which have been assimilated by Catherine. So with: "Drawn forth, out of her natural state, into that unmeasurable condition whither love goes to drown itself, the soul, having plunged into the abyss of this ocean, henceforth cannot find, on any side, any means of issuing forth from it," vv. 12, 13. So also with: "Since thou dost no longer love thyself, but alone that Goodness . . . it has become necessary for thee again to love thyself, but with His Love,—into so great an unity hast thou been drawn by Him," vv. 52–54. So too with: "All Faith ceases for the soul to whom it has been given to see; and all Hope, since it now actually holds what it used to seek," v. 70, although this is more absolute than are her similar utterances. —But especially are the startling words interesting: "In this transformation, thou drinkest Another, and that Other drinketh thee (*tu bevi e sei bevuto, in transformazione*)," v. 98, which, in their second part, are identical with R. Browning's "My end, to slake Thy thirst":[1] for they will have helped to support or to encourage Catherine's corresponding inversion—the teaching of an eating, an assimilation, not of God by man, but of man by God. Both sets of images go back, of course, to the Eucharistic reception by the soul of the God-man Christ, under the forms of Bread eaten and of Wine drunk.

The striking Loda LXXXX, "How the soul arrives at a treble state of annihilation," has doubtless suggested much to Catherine. "He who has become the very Cause of all things" (*chi è cosa d'ogni cosa*) "can never more desire anything," v. 4, is, it is true, more daring, because more quietly explicit, than any saying of hers. But v. 13 has been echoed by her throughout: "The heavens have grown stagnant; their

[1] *Rabbi Ben Ezra*, XXXI.

silence constrains me to cry aloud : 'O profound Ocean, the very depth of Thine Abyss has constrained me to attempt and drown myself within it,'"—where note the interestingly antique presupposition of the music of the spheres, which has now stopped, and of the watery constitution of the crystalline heaven, which allows of stagnation; and the rapidity of the change in the impressions,—from immobility to silence, and from air to water. Indeed that Ocean is one as much of air as of water, and as little the one as the other; and its attractive force is still that innate affinity between the river-soul and its living Source and Home, the Ocean God, which we have so constantly found in Plotinus, Proclus, and Dionysius. "The land of promise is, for such a soul, no longer one of promise only: for the perfect soul already reigns within that land. Men can thus transform themselves, in any and every place," v. 18, has, in its touching and lofty Stoic-Christian teaching, found the noblest response and re-utterance in and by Catherine's words and life.

Loda LXXXXVIII, "Of the Incarnation of the Divine Word," full though it is of beautiful Franciscanism, has left her uninfluenced. But the fine Loda LXXXXIX, "How true Love is not idle," contains touches which have sunk deep into her mind. "Splendour that givest to all the world its light, O Love Jesus . . . heaven and earth are by Thee; Thine action resplends in all things and all things turn to Thee. Only the sinner despises Thy Love and severs himself from Thee, his Creator," v. 6, is, in its substance, taken over by her. "O ye cold sinners!" v. 12, is her favourite epithet. And vv. 13, 14, with their rapid ringing of the changes on the different sense-perceptions, will, by their shifting vividness, have helped on a similar iridescence in her own imagery: "O Odour, that transcendest every sweetness! O living river of Delight . . . that causest the very dead to return to their vigour! In heaven Thy lovers possess Thine immense Sweetness, tasting there those savoury morsels."

And finally Loda LXXXVII, "Of true and false discretion," which, in vv. 12–20, consists of a dialogue between "the Flesh" and "the Reason," will have helped to suggest the slight beginnings of this form of apprehension to Catherine which we have found amongst her authentic sayings and experiences, and which were, later on, developed on so large a scale, by Battista Vernazza, throughout her long *Dialogo della Beata Caterina*.

5. Jacopone it is, then, who furnished Catherine with much help towards that rare combination of deep feeling with severely abstract thinking which, if at times it somewhat strains and wearies us moderns who would ever end with the concrete, gives a nobly virile, bracing note to even the most effective of her sayings.

V. Points common to all Five Minds; and Catherine's Main Difference from her Four Predecessors.

If we now consider for a moment the general points common to the four writers just considered and to Catherine, we readily note that all five are profoundly reflective and interpretative in their attitude towards the given contingencies of traditional religion; that they all tend to find the Then and There of History still at work, in various degrees, Here and Now, throughout Time and Space, and in the last resort, above and behind both these categories, in a spaceless, timeless Present. And if only three, Paul, Jacopone, and Catherine, bear marks, throughout all they think and feel and do and are, of the cataclysmic conversion-crisis through which they had passed,—the temporally intermediate two, John and Dionysius, have also got, but in a more indirect form, much of a similar Dualism. All five are, in these and other respects, indefinitely closer to each other than any one of them is to the still richer, more complete, and more entirely balanced though less articulated, Synoptic teaching, which enfolds all that is abiding in those other five, whilst they, even if united, do not approximately exhaust the substance of that teaching.

And if we would briefly define the main point on which Catherine holds views additional to, or other than, those other four, we must point to her Purgatorial teaching, which has received but little or no direct suggestion from any one of them, and which, whatever may have been its literary precursors and occasions, gives, perhaps more than anything else, a peculiarly human and personal, original and yet still modern, touch to what would otherwise be, to our feeling, too abstract and antique a spiritual physiognomy.

CHAPTER XI

CATHERINE'S LESS ULTIMATE THIS-WORLD DOCTRINES

INTRODUCTORY: CATHERINE'S LESS ULTIMATE POSITIONS, CONCERNING OUR LIFE HERE, ARE FOUR.

WE have now attempted, (by means of a doubtless more or less artificial distinction between things that, in real life, constitute parts of one whole in a state of hardly separable interpenetration,) a presentation of Catherine's special, mental and psycho-physical, character and temperament, and of the principal literary stimulations and materials which acted upon, and in return were refashioned by, that character; and we have also given, in sufficient detail, the resultant doctrines and world-view acquired and developed by that deep soul and noble mind. The most important and difficult part of our task remains, however, still to be accomplished,—the attempt to get an (at least approximate) estimate of the abiding meaning, place, and worth of this whole, highly synthesized position, for and within the religious life generally and our present-day requirements in particular. For the general outline of the Introduction, (intended there more as an instrument of research and classification for the literature and history then about to be examined, than as this history's final religious appraisement,) cannot dispense us from now attempting something more precise and ultimate.—I propose, then, to give the next four chapters to an examination of Catherine's principal positions and practices, the first two, respectively, to "the less ultimate This-World Doctrines"; and "the Other-World Doctrines," or "the Eschatology"; and the last two to "the Ultimate Implications and Problems" underlying both. The last chapter shall then sum up the whole book, and consider the abiding place and function of Mysticism, in its contrast to, and supplementation of, Asceticism, Institutionalism, and the Scientific Habit and Activity of the Mind.

Now I think the less ultimate spiritual positions, as far as they concern our life here below, which are specially represented, or at least forcibly suggested by, Catherine, can reasonably be accounted as four: Interpretative Religion; a strongly Dualistic attitude towards the body; Quietude and Passivity; and Pure Love. I shall devote a section to each position.

I. Interpretative Religion.

1. *Difficulties of the Subjective element of Religion.*

Now, by Interpretative Religion, I do not mean to imply that there is anywhere, in *rerum natura*, such a thing as a religion which is not interpretative, which does not consist as truly of a reaction on the part of the believing soul to certain stimulations of and within it, as of these latter stimulations and actions. As every (even but semi-conscious) act and state of the human mind, ever embraces both such action of the object and such reaction of the subject,—a relatively crude fact of sensation or of feeling borne in upon it, and an interpretation, an incorporation of this fact by, and into, the living tissue and organism of this mind: so is it also, necessarily and above all, with the deepest and most richly complex of all human acts and states,—the specifically religious ones. But if this interpretative activity of the mind was present from the very dawn of human reason, and exists in each individual in the precise proportion as mind can be predicated as operative within him at all: this mental activity is yet the last element in the compound process and result which is, or can be, perceived as such by the mind itself. The process is too near to the observer, even when he is once awake to its existence; he is too much occupied with the materials brought before his mind and with moulding and sorting them out; and this moulding and sorting activity is itself too rapid and too deeply independent of those materials as to its form, and too closely dependent upon them as to its content, for the observation by the mind of this same mind's contributions towards its own affirmations of reality and of the nature of this reality, not ever to appear late in the history of the human race or in the life of any human individual, or not to be, even when it appears difficult, a fitful and an imperfect mental exercise.

And when the discovery of this constant contribution of the mind to its own affirmations of reality is first made, it can hardly fail, for the time being, to occasion misgivings and anxieties of a more or less sceptical kind. Is not the whole of what I have hitherto taken to be a solid world of sense outside me, and the whole of the world of necessary truth and of obligatory goodness within me,—is it not, perhaps, all a merely individual creation of my single mind—a mind cut off from all effective intercourse with reality,—my neighbour's mind included? For all having, so far, been held to be objective, the mind readily flies to the other extreme, and suspects all to be subjective. Or if all my apprehensions and certainties are the resultants from the interaction between impressions received by my senses and mind and reactions and elaborations on the part of this mind with regard to those impressions, how can I be sure of apprehending rightly, unless I can divide each constituent off from the other? And yet, how can I effect such a continuous discounting of my mind's action by means of my own mind itself?

And this objection is felt most keenly in religion, when the religious soul first wakes up to the fact that itself, of necessity and continuously, contributes, by its own action, to the constitution of those affirmations and certainties, which, until then, seemed, without a doubt, to be directly borne in upon a purely receptive, automatically registering mind, from that extra-, super-human world which it thus affirmed. Here also, all having for so long been assumed to be purely objective, the temptation now arises to consider it all as purely subjective. Or again, if we insist upon holding that, here too, there are both objective and subjective elements, we readily experience keen distress at our inability clearly to divide off the objective, which is surely the reality, from the subjective, which can hardly fail to be its travesty.

And finally, this doubt and trouble would seem to find specially ready material in the mystical element and form of religion. For here, as we have already seen, psycho-physical and auto-suggestive phenomena and mechanisms abound; here especially does the mind cling to an immediate access to Reality; and here the ordinary checks and complements afforded by the Historical and Institutional, the Analytically Rational, and the Volitional, Practical elements of Religion are at a minimum. Little but the Emotional and the Speculatively Rational elements seems to remain; and these, more than any others, appear incapable of admitting that they are anything other than the pure and direct effects and expressions of spiritual Reality.

What, then, shall we think of all this?

2. *Answers to the above difficulties.*

We evidently must, in the first instance, guard against any attempt at doing a doctrinaire violence to the undeniable facts of our consciousness or of its docile analysis, by explaining all our knowledge, or only even all our knowledge of any single thing, as either of purely subjective or of purely objective provenance; for everywhere and always these two elements co-exist in all human apprehension, reason, feeling, will, and faith. We find, throughout, an organization, an indissoluble organism, of subjective and objective, hence a unity in diversity, which is indeed so great that (for our own experience and with respect to our own minds at all events), the Subjective does not and cannot exist without the Objective, nor the Objective without the Subjective.

In the next place, we must beware against exalting the Objective against the Subjective, or the Subjective against the Objective, as if Life, Reality, and Truth consisted in the one rather than the other. Because the subjective element is, on the first showing, a work of our own minds, it does not follow (as we shall see more clearly when studying the ultimate problems) that its operations are bereft of correspondence with reality, or, at least, that they are further from reality than are our sense-perceptions. For just as the degree of worth represented by these sense-perceptions can range from the crudest delusion to a stimulation of primary importance and exquisite precision, so also our mental and emotional reaction and penetration represent almost any and every degree of accuracy and value.

And, above all, as already implied, the true priority and superiority lies, not with one of these constituents against the other, but with the total subjective-objective interaction and resultant, which is superior, and indeed gives their place and worth to, those ever interdependent parts.

Now, in the general human experience, the Objective element is constituted, in the first instance and for clear and ready analysis, by the sense-stimulations; and, after some mental response to and elaboration of these, by the larger psychic moods; and later still, by the examples of great spiritual attitudes and of great personalities offered by other souls to the soul that keeps itself open to such impressions. And though the sense of Reality (as contrasted with Appearance), of the Abiding and Infinite (as different from the Passing and the Finite), are doubtless awakened, however faintly and inarticulately, in the human soul from the first, as the background and presupposition of the foreground and the middle-distances of its total world of perceptions and aspirations: yet all these middle-distances, as well as that great background and groundwork, would remain unawakened but for those humble little sense-perceptions on the one hand, and intercourse with human fellow-creatures on the other. And in such intercourse with the minds and souls, or with the literary remains and other monuments of souls, either still living here or gone hence some two thousand years or more, a mass of mental and moral impressions and stimulations, which, in those souls, were largely their own elaborations, offer themselves to any one human mind, or to the minds of a whole generation or country, with the apparent homogeneity of a purely objective, as it were a sense-impression.

Especially in Religion the Historical and Institutional (as Religion's manifestation in space and time), come down to us thus from the past and surround us in the present, and either press in upon us with a painful weight, or support us with a comforting solidity, thus giving them many of the qualities of things physically seen and touched, say, a mystery play or a vast cathedral. And, on the other hand, the Rational, (whether Analytic or Synthetic,) and the Emotional and Volitional Elements, whenever they are at all preponderant or relatively independent of the other, more objective ones, are liable, in Religion, to look quite exceptionally subjective,—and this in the unfavourable sense of the word, as though either superfluous and fantastic, or as dangerous and destructive.—And yet both that look of the objective elements being, in Religion, more self-sufficing than they appear to be in the ordinary psychic, or the artistic, or social, or scientific life; and that impression conveyed by the subjective elements in Religion, as being there less necessary or more dangerous than elsewhere, are doubtless deceptive. These impressions are simply caused by two very certain facts. Religion is the deepest and most inclusive of all the soul's energizings and experiences, and hence all its constituents reveal a difference, at least in amount and degree, when compared with the corresponding constituents of the more superficial and more partial activities of the soul; and Religion, just because of this, requires the fullest action and co-operation, the most perfect unity, in and through diversity, of all the soul's powers, and all mere non-use of any of these forces, even any restriction to the use of but one or two, is here, more readily and extensively than elsewhere, detrimental both to the non-exercised and to the exercised forces, and, above all, is impoverishing to the soul itself and to its religion.

Hence, here as elsewhere, but more than anywhere, our ideal standard will be the greatest possible development of, and inter-stimulation between, each and all of the religious elements, with the greatest possible unity in the resulting organism. And yet,—in view of the very greatness of the result aimed at, and of the fact that its even approximate attainment can, even for any one age of the world, be reasonably expected only from the co-operation of the differently endowed and attracted races and nations, social and moral grades, sexes, ages and individuals that make up mankind,—we shall not only be very tolerant of, we shall positively encourage, largely one-sided developments, provided that each keeps some touch with the elements which itself knows not how to develop in abundance, and that it considers its own self, and works out its own special gift and *attrait*, as but one out of many variously gifted and apportioned fellow-servants in the Kingdom, —as only one of the countless, mutually complementary, individually ever imperfect, part-expressions of the manifold greatness, of the rich unity of spiritual humanity as willed by God, and of God Himself.

3. *Partial developments of the full Gospel Ideal.*

Now in the New Testament we have a most instructive, at first sight puzzling phenomenon, illustrative of the positions just taken up. For here it is clear that, with regard to the distinction between richly many-sided but as yet unarticulated religion, and comparatively one-sided and limited but profoundly developed religion, we have two considerably contrasted types of spiritual tone and teaching. We get the predominantly "Objective" strand of life and doctrine, in the pre-Pauline parts and in their non-Pauline echoes, *i. e.* in the substance of the Synoptic tradition, and in the Epistles of St. James and of St. Peter; and we find the predominantly "Subjective" strain in the "Pauline" parts, St. Paul's Epistles and the Johannine Gospel and Letters.—And it has become more and more clear that it is the pre-Pauline parts which give us the most immediately and literally faithful, and especially the most complete and many-sided, picture of Our Lord's precise words and actions; whereas the Pauline parts give us rather what some of these great creative forces were and became for the first generations of Christians and for the most penetrating of Christ's early disciples and lovers. And yet it is the latter documents which, at first sight, appear to be the deeper, the wider, and the more profoundly spiritual; whereas the former look more superficial, more temporal and local, and more simply popular and material.

And yet,—though this first impression has been held to be finally true by large masses of Christians; although the Greek Fathers predominantly, and, in the West, the great soul of an Augustine, and the powerful but one-sided personalities of a Luther and a Calvin have, in various degrees and ways, helped to articulate and all but finally fix it for the general Christian consciousness: this view is yielding, somewhat slowly but none the less surely, to the sense that it is the Synoptic, the pre-Pauline tradition which contains the fuller arsenal of the spiritual forces which have transfigured and which still inspire the world of souls. This, of course, does not mean that the Pauline-Johannine developments were not necessary, or are not abiding elements towards the understanding of the Christian spirit.

And, to come to the true answer to our objection, such a judgment does not mean that the reflective penetration and reapplication of the original more spontaneous message was, from the very nature of the case, inferior to the first less articulated announcement of the Good Tidings. But it merely signifies that this necessary process of reflection could only be applied to parts of the original, immensely rich and varied, because utterly living, divinely spiritual, whole; and that, thus, the special balance and tension which characterized the original, complete spirit and temper, could, however profoundly, be reproduced only in part. For the time being this later penetration and resetting of some elements from among the whole of Our Lord's divinely rich and simple life and teaching, necessarily and rightly, yet none the less most really, ignored, or put for the time into some other context, certain other sides and aspects of that primitive treasure of inexhaustible experience. Only the full, equable, and simultaneous unfolding of all the petals could have realized the promise and content of the bud; whereas the bud, holding enfolded within itself such various elements and combinations of truth, could not expand its petals otherwise than successively, hence, at any one moment only somewhat onesidedly and partially. Each and all of these unfoldings bring some further insight into, and articulation of, the original spiritual organism; and that they are not more, but less, than the totality of that primitive experience and revelation, does not prove that such reflective work is wrong or even simply dispensable,—for, on the contrary, in some degree or form it was and ever is necessary to the soul's apprehension of that life and truth,—but simply implies the immensity of the spiritual light and impulsion given by Our Lord, and the relative smallness of even the greatest of His followers.

Thus only if it could be shown that those parts of the New Testament which doubtless give us the nearest approach to the actual words and deeds of Our Lord require us to conceive them as having been without the reflective and emotional element; or again that, in the case of the more derivative parts of the New Testament, it is their reflectiveness, and not their relative incompleteness and onesidedness, that cause them to be more readily englobed in the former world, than that former world in the latter: could the facts here found be used as an argument against the importance and strict necessity for religion of the reflective and emotional, the "Subjective" elements, alongside of the "Objective," the Historical and Institutional ones.

It is a most legitimate ground for consolation to a Catholic when he finds the necessities of life and those of learned research both driving us more and more to this conclusion; for it is not deniable that Catholicism has ever refused to do more than include the Pauline and Johannine theologies amongst its earliest and most normative stimulations and expressions; and that it has ever retained, far more than Protestantism, the sense, which (upon the whole) is most unbrokenly preserved by the Synoptists, of, if I may so phrase it, the Christianity of certain true elements in the pre- and extra-Christian religions. For it is in the Synoptists that we get the clear presentation of Our Lord's attitude towards the Jewish Church of His time, as one, even at its keenest, analogous to that of Savonarola, and not to that of a Luther, still less of a Calvin, towards the Christian Church of their day.—Indeed in these documents all idea of limiting Christianity to what He brought of new, appears as foreign to His mind as it ever has been to that of the Catholic Church. Here we get the most spontaneous and many-sided expression of that divinely human, widely traditional and social, all-welcoming and all-transforming spirit, which embraces both grace *and* nature, eternity *and* time, soul *and* body, attachment *and* detachment. The Pauline strain stands for the stress necessary to the full spiritualization of all those occasions and materials, as against all, mere unregenerate or static, retention of the simple rudiments or empty names of those things; and predominantly insists upon grace, *not* nature; eternity, *not* time; soul, *not* body; the cross and death here, the Crown and Life hereafter. No wonder it is this latter strain that gets repeated, with varying truth and success, in times of acute transition, and by characters more antithetic than synthetic, more great at developing a part of the truth than the whole.

Thinkers, of such wide historical outlook and unimpeachable detachment from immediate controversial interest as Prof. Wilhelm Dilthey and Dr. Edward Caird, have brought out, with admirable force, this greater fulness of content offered by the Synoptists, and how the Pauline-Johannine writings give us the first and most important of those concentrations upon, and in part philosophic and mystical reinterpretations of, certain constituents of the original happenings, actions and message, as apprehended and transmitted by the first eye-witnesses and believers.[1]—Here I would but try and drive home the apparently vague, but in reality ever pressing and concrete, lesson afforded by the clear and dominant fact of these two groups within the New Testament itself:—of how no mere accumulation of external happenings, or of external testimony as to their having happened,—no amount of history or of institutionalism, taken as sheer, purely positive givennesses,—can anywhere be found, or can anywhere suffice for the human mind and conscience, in the apprehension and embodiment of the truth. For although, in Our Lord's most literally transmitted sayings and doings, this continuous and inalienable element of the apprehending, organizing, vitalizing mind

[1] E. Caird, "St. Paul and the Idea of Evolution," *Hibbert Journal*, Vol. II, 1904, pp. 1–19. W. Dilthey has shown this by implication, in his studies of Erasmus, Luther, and Zwingli: *Archiv für Geschichte der Philosophie*, Vol. V, 1892, especially, pp. 381–385.

and heart,—on His part above all, but also on the part of His several hearers and chroniclers,—can mostly still be traced and must everywhere be assumed: yet it is in the Pauline-Johannine literature that the ever important, the rightly and fruitfully "subjective," the speculative and emotional, the mystical and the volitional strain can best be studied, both as to its necessity and as to its special character and dangers, because here it is developed to the relative exclusion of the other factors of complete religion.

4. *The exclusive emotionalism of Dionysius and Jacopone.*

Now if even in St. Paul and St. John there is a strong predominance of these reflective-emotional elements, in Dionysius and Jacopone they threaten to become exclusive of everything else. Especially is this the case with the Pseudo-Areopagite, steeped as he is in reflection upon reflections and in emotion upon emotions, often of the most subtle kind: a Christian echo, with curiously slight modifications, of Neo-Platonism in its last stage,—hence, unfortunately, of the over-systematic and largely artificial Proclus, instead of the predominantly experimental and often truly sublime Plotinus. And even Jacopone, although he has distinctly more of the historic element, is still predominantly reflective-emotional, and presents us with many a hardly modified Platonic or Stoic doctrine, derived no doubt from late Graeco-Roman writers and their mediaeval Christian echoes.

5. *Catherine's interpretation of the Gospel Ideal.*

Catherine herself, although delightfully free from the long scale of mediations between the soul and God which forms one of the predominant doctrines of the Areopagite, continues and emphasizes most of what is common, and much of what is special to, all and each of these four writers; she is a reflective saint, if ever there was one. And of her too we shall have to say that she is great by what she possesses, and not by what she is without: great because of her noble embodiment of the reflective and emotional, the mystical and volitional elements of Christianity and Religion generally. Religion is here, at first sight at least, all but entirely a thought and an emotion; yet all this thought and emotion is directed to, and occasioned by, an abiding Reality which originates, sustains, regulates, and fulfils it. And although this Reality is in large part conceived, in Greek and specially in Neo-Platonist fashion, rather under its timeless and spaceless, or at least under its cosmic aspect, rather as Law and Substance, than as Personality and Spirit: yet, already because of the strong influence upon her of the noblest Platonic doctrine, it is loved as overflowing Love and Goodness, as cause and end of all lesser love and goodness; and the real, though but rarely articulated, acceptance and influence of History and Institutions, above all the enthusiastic devotion to the Holy Eucharist with all its great implications, gives to the whole a profoundly Christian tone and temper.

True, the Church at large, indeed the single soul (if we would take such a soul as our standard of completeness) requires a larger proportion of those crisp, definite outlines, of those factual, historical, and institutional elements; a very little less than what remains in Catherine of these elements, and her religion would be a simple, even though deep religiosity, a general aspiration, not a definite finding, an explicit religion. Yet it remains certain, although ever readily forgotten by religious souls, especially by theological apologists, that without some degree and kind of those outgoing, apprehending, interpreting activities, no religion is possible. Only the question as to what these activities should be, and what is their true place and function within the whole religious life, remains an open one. And this question we can study with profit in connection with such a life and teaching as Catherine's, which brings out, with a spontaneous, childlike profundity and daring, the elemental religious passion, the spiritual hunger and thirst of man when he is once fully awake; the depths within him anticipating the heights above him; the affinity to and contact with the Infinite implied and required by that nobly incurable restlessness of his heart, which finds its rest in Him alone Who made it.

II. Dualistic Attitude towards the Body.

And if Catherine is profoundly reflective, that reflection is, in its general drift, deeply dualistic,—at least in the matter of body and spirit. Their difference and incompatibility; the spirit's fleeing of the body; the spirit's getting outside of it,—by ecstasy, for a little while, even in this earthly life, and by this earthly body's death, for good and all; the body a prison-house, a true purgatory to the soul: all this hangs well together, and is largely, in its very form, of ultimately Neo-Platonist or Platonic origin.

1. *New Testament valuations of the body.*

Now here is one of the promised instances of a double type—if not of doctrine, yet at least of emotional valuation in the New Testament.

(1) In the Synoptist documents, (with the but apparent, or at least solitary, exceptions, of Jesus' Fasting in the Desert and of His commendation of those who have made themselves eunuchs for the Kingdom of Heaven,)[1] we find no direct or acute antagonism to the body, even to the average earthly human body, in the teaching and practice of Our Lord. The Second Coming and its proximity do indeed, here also, dwarf all earthly concerns, in so far as earthly.[2] This background to the teaching and its tradition was, in course of time, in part abstracted from, in part restated.—The entrance into life is through the narrow gate and the steep way; only if a man turn, can he enter into the Kingdom of God; only if he lose his soul, can he find it:[3] this great teaching and example, as to life and joy being ever reached through death to self and by the whole-hearted turning of the soul from its false self to its true source, God: remains, in the very form of its promulgation as given by the Synoptists, the fundamental test and standard of all truly spiritual life and progress. But as to the body in particular, Jesus here knows indeed that "the flesh is weak," and that we musy pray for strength against its weakness:[4] but He nowhere declares it evil—an inevitable prison-house or a natural antagonist to the spirit. The beautiful balance of an unbroken, unstrained nature, and a corresponding doctrine as full of sober earnestness as it is free from all concentrated or systematic dualism, are here everywhere apparent.

(2) It is St. Paul, the man of the strongest bodily passions and temptations, he who became suddenly free from them by the all-transforming lightning-flash of his conversion, who, on and on, remained vividly conscious of what he had been and, but for that grace, still would be, and of what, through that grace, he had become. The deepest shadows are thus ever

[1] Mark i, 13, and parallels; Matt. xix, 10–12.

[2] Mark vi, 8; Matt. x, 26–38; viii, 19–22; xiii, 30–32; xxvi, 42, and parallels.

[3] Matt. vii, 13, 14; xviii, 1–5; xvi, 24–28.

[4] Mark xiv, 38, and parallels.

kept in closest contrast to the highest lights; and the line of demarcation between them runs here along the division between body and soul. "O wretched man that I am! who shall deliver me out of the body of this death?" "In my flesh dwelleth no good thing": [1] are sayings which are both keener in their tone and more limited in their range than are Our Lord's. And we have seen how, in one of his most depressed moods, he transiently adopts and carries on a specifically Platonist attitude towards the body's relation to the soul, as he finds it in that beautiful, profoundly Hellenistic treatise, the Book of Wisdom.[2] This attitude evidently represents, in his strenuous and deeply Christian character, only a passing feeling; for, if we pressed it home, we could hardly reconcile it with his doctrine as to the reality and nature of the body's resurrection. It is indeed clear how the Platonist, and especially the Neo-Platonist, mode of conceiving that relation excludes any and every kind of body from the soul's final stage of purification and happiness; and how the Synoptic, and indeed the generally Christian conception of it, necessarily eliminates that keen and abiding dualism characteristic of the late Greek attitude.

2. *Platonic, Synoptic, and Pauline elements in Catherine's view.*

Now in Catherine we generally find an interesting combination of the Platonic form with the Synoptic substance and spirit: and this can, of course, be achieved only because that abiding form itself is made to signify a changed set and connection of ideas.

(1) We have seen how she dwells much, Plotinus-like, upon the soul's stripping itself of all its numerous garments, and exposing itself naked to the rays of God's healing light. Yet in the original Platonic scheme these garments are put on by the soul in its descent from spirit into matter, and are stripped off again in its ascent back out of matter into spirit; in both cases, they stand for the body and its effects. In Catherine, even more than in Plotinus, the garments stand for various evil self-attachments and self-delusions of the soul; and against these evils and dangers the Synoptists furnish endless warnings. And yet she insists upon purity, clear separation, complete abstraction of the soul, in such terms as still to show plainly enough the originally Neo-

[1] Rom. vii, 24, 18.
[2] 2 Cor. v, 1–4 = Wisd. of Sol. ix, 15.

Platonist provenance of much of her form; for in the Neo-Platonists we get, even more markedly than here, a like insistence upon the natural dissimilarity of the body and the soul, and a cognate longing to get away from it in ecstasy and death. But whilst in the Neo-Platonists there is, at the bottom of all this, a predominant belief that the senses are the primary source and occasion of all sin, so that sin is essentially the contamination of spirit by matter: in Catherine, (although she shares to the full Plotinus's thirst for ecstasy, as the escape from division and trouble into unity and peace,) impurity stands primarily for self-complacency,—belief in, and love of, our imaginary independence of even God Himself; and purity means, in the first instance, the loving Him and His whole system of souls and of life, and one's own self only in and as part of that system.

It is very instructive to note, in this connection, how, after her four years of directly penitential and ascetical practice, (an activity which, even then, extended quite as much to matters of decentralization of the self as of bodily mortification,) her warfare is, in the first instance, all but exclusively directed against the successive refuges and ambushes of self-complacency and self-centredness. Thus there is significance in the secondary place occupied, (even in the *Vita*, and doubtless still more in her own mind,) by the question of continence; indeed her great declaration to the Friar indicates plainly her profound concentration upon the continuous practice of, and growth in, Love Divine, and her comparative indifference to the question of the systematic renunciation of anything but sin and selfish attachments and self-centrednesses of any kind. Her conception of sinners as "cold," even more than as dark or stained; of God as Fire, even more than as Light; and of purity as indefinitely increasable, since Love can grow on and on: all similarly point to this finely positive, flame-, not snow-conception, in which purity has ceased to be primarily, as with the Greeks, a simple absence of soiledness, even if it be moral soiledness, and has become, as with the Synoptic teaching, something primarily positive, love itself.

In her occasionally intense insistence upon herself as being all evil, a very Devil, and in some of her picturings of her interior combat, we get, on the other hand, echoes, not of Plato, nor again of the Synoptist teaching, but of St. Paul's "in my flesh there dwelleth no good thing," and of his combat between flesh and spirit.—Yet the evil which she is thus conscious of, is not sensual nor even sensible evil and temptation, but consists in her unbounded natural claimfulness and intense inclination to sensitive self-absorption.—And this gives, indeed, to these feminine echoes of St. Paul a certain thin shrillness which the original tones have not got, standing there for the massive experiences of a man violently solicitated by both sense and spirit. But it leaves her free to note, as regards the flesh, the whole bodily organism, (and this in beautiful sympathy with Our Lord's own genially fervent, homely heroic spirit,) not its wickedness, but its weakness, its short-livedness, and its appeal for merciful allowance to God, " Who knows that we are dust." Instead of a direct and pointed dualism of two distinct substances informed by all but incurably antagonistic principles, we thus get a direct conflict between two dispositions of the soul, and a but imperfect correspondence between the body and that soul.

(2) There is, indeed, no doubt that the very ancient association of the ideas of Fire and of spiritual Purification goes back, in the first instance, to the conception of the soul being necessarily stained by the very fact of its connection with the body, and of those stains being finally removed by the body's death and cremation. We find this severely self-consistent view scattered up and down Hellenic religion and literature.[1] And even in Catherine the fire, a sense of fever-heat, still seizes the body, and this body wastes away, and leaves the soul more and more pure, during those last years of illness.—Yet the striking identity, between that old cluster of ideas and her own forms of thought, brings out, all the more clearly, the immense road traversed by spirituality between the substance of those ideas and the essence of this thought. For in her teaching, which is but symbolized or at most occasioned by those physico-psychical fever-heats, the Fire is, at bottom, so spiritual and so directly busy with the soul alone, that it is ever identical with itself in Heaven, Hell, Purgatory, and on earth, and stands for God Himself; and that its effects are not the destruction of a foreign substance, but the bringing back, wherever and as far as possible, of the fire-like soul's disposition and equality to full harmony with its Fire-source and Parent, God Himself.

[1] See Erwin Rohde's *Psyche*, ed. 1898, Vol. II, p. 101, n. 2.

(3) Only the Prison-house simile for the body, as essentially an earthly purgatory for the soul, must be admitted, I think, to remain a primarily Platonic, not fully Christianizable conception; just as the absence of all reference by her to the resurrection of the body will have been, in part, occasioned by the strong element of Platonism in her general selection and combination of ideas. Yet it would obviously be unfair to press these two points too much, since, as to the resurrection, her long illness and evidently constant physical discomfort must, even of themselves, have disinclined her to all picturing of an abiding, even though highly spiritualized, bodily organization; and as to the likeness of her body to a prison and purgatory of the soul, we are expressly told that it began only with the specially suffering last part of her life.

3. *Dualism pragmatic, not final. Its limits.*

Now, for this whole matter of the right conception as to the relations of body and soul, it is clear that any more than partial and increasingly superable antagonism between body and spirit cannot be accepted.

(1) A final Dualism is unsound in Psychology, since all the first materials, stimulations, and instruments for even our most abstract thinking are supplied to us by our sense-perceptions, hence also through the body. It is narrow in Cosmology, for we do not want to isolate man in this great universe of visible things; and his link with animal- and plant-life, and even with the mineral creation is, increasingly as we descend in the scale of beings, his body. It is ruinous for Ethics, because purity, in such a physical-spiritual being as is man, consists precisely in spiritual standards and laws extending to and transforming his merely physical inclinations. It is directly contradictory of the central truth and temper of Christianity, since these require a full acceptance of the substantial goodness and the thorough sanctifiableness of man's body; of God's condescension to man's whole physico-spiritual organism; and of the persistence or reanimation of all that is essential to man's true personality across and after death. And it is, at bottom, profoundly un-Catholic; the whole Sacramental system, the entire deep and noble conception of the normal relations between the Invisible and the Visible being throughout of the Incarnational type,—an action of the one in the other, which develops the agent and subject at the same time that it spiritualizes the patient, the object, is in direct conflict

with it. Neo-Platonism came more and more to treat the body and the entire visible creation as an intrinsic obstacle to spirit, to be eliminated by the latter as completely as possible; at least this very prominent strain within it was undoubtedly pushed on to this extreme by the Gnostic sects. But Christianity has ever to come back to its central pre-supposition —the substantial goodness and spiritual utility and transfigurableness of body and matter; and to its final end,—the actual transformation of them by the spirit into ever more adequate instruments, materials, and expressions of abiding ethical and religious values and realities.

(2) The fact is that here, as practically at every chief turning-point in ethical and religious philosophy, the movement of the specifically Christian life and conviction is not a circle round a single centre,—detachment; but an ellipse round two centres,—detachment and attachment. And precisely in this difficult, but immensely fruitful, oscillation and rhythm between, as it were, the two poles of the spiritual life; in this fleeing and seeking, in the recollection back and away from the visible (so as to allay the dust and fever of growing distraction, and to reharmonize the soul and its new gains according to the intrinsic requirements and ideals of the spirit), and in the subsequent, renewed immersion in the visible (in view both of gaining fresh concrete stimulation and content for the spiritual life, and of gradually shaping and permeating the visible according to and with spiritual ends and forces): in this combination, and not in either of these two movements taken alone, consists the completeness and culmination of Christianity.[1]

(3) It no doubt looks, at first sight, as though the Church, by her canonization of the Monastic Ideal, gave us, for the ultimate pattern and measure of all Christian perfection, as pure and simple a flight of the soul from the body and the world, as (short of insanity or suicide) can be made in this life. But here we have to remember three things.

In the first place, the Church not only forbids all attacks upon the legitimacy, indeed sanctity, of marriage, or upon its necessity, indeed duty, for mankind at large; but St. Augustine and St. Thomas only articulate her ordinary, strenuously anti-

[1] I owe much help towards acquiring this very important conception, and all the above similes, to Prof. Ernst Troeltsch's admirable exposition in his "Grundprobleme der Ethik," *Zeitschrift f. Theologie und Kirche*, 1902, pp. 163–178.

Manichean teaching, in declaring that man was originally created by God, in body and in soul, not for celibacy but for marriage; and that only owing to the accidental event of the Fall and of its effects,—the introduction of disorder and excess into human nature, but not any corruption of its substance and foundations,—does any inferiority,—the dispositions, motives, and circumstances being equal,—attach to marriage as compared with virginity.[1] Hence, still, the absolute ideal would be that man could and did use marriage as all other legitimate functions and things of sense, as a necessary, and ever more and more perfected, means and expression of truly human spirituality, a spirituality which ever requires some non-spiritual material in which to work, and by working in which the soul itself, not only spiritualizes it, but increasingly develops its own self.

And secondly, detachment, unification, spiritual recollection is the more difficult, and the less obviously necessary, of the two movements, and yet is precisely the one which (by coming upon the extant or inchoate attachments, and by suppressing or purifying them according as they are bad or good) first stamps any and every life as definitely religious at all. No wonder, then, that it is this sacred detachment and love of the Cross that we notice, first of all, in the life and doctrine of Our Lord and of all His followers, indeed in all truly religious souls throughout the world; and that the Church should by her teaching and selection of striking examples, ever preach and uphold this most necessary test and ingredient, this very salt of all virile and fruitful spirituality.

But, in the third place, a man need only directly attack the family, society, the state; or art, literature, science,—as intrinsically evil or even as, in practice, true hindrances to moral and religious perfection,—and the Church,—both the learning and experimenting, and the official and formulating Church,—will at once disavow him: so strong is, at bottom, the instinct that attachment and variety of interests,—variety both in kind and in degree—that materials, occasions, and objects for spirituality to leaven and to raise, and to work on in order to be itself deepened and developed,—are as truly essential to the spiritual life as are detachment, and unity, and transcendence of ultimate motive and aim; these latter furnishing to the soul the power gradually to penetrate

[1] *St. Augustine*, ed. Ben., Vol. X, 590*b*, 613*a*, 1973*c*, etc. St. Thomas, *Summa Theol.*, suppl., qu. 62, art. 2.

all that material, and, in and through this labour, more and more to articulate its own spiritual character.

(4) No man can become, or is proclaimed to have become, a Christian saint, who has not thus achieved a profound spiritualization and unification of a more or less recalcitrant material and multiplicity. In some cases, it is the unity and detachment that greatly predominate over the multiplicity and attachment,—as, say, in the Fathers of the Desert. In other cases, it is the variety and attachment that strikes us first of all,—as, for instance, in Sir Thomas More and Edmund Campion. And, in a third set of cases, it is the depth of the unity and detachment, in the breadth of the variety and attachment, which is the dominant characteristic, so with St. Paul and St. Augustine. Catherine herself belongs, for her great middle period, rather to the third group than to either of the other two; only during her penitential period and her last long illness does she clearly belong to the group of intensely detached and unified saints.—It is evidently impossible in such a matter to do more than insist upon the necessity of both movements; upon the immensely fruitful friction and tension which their well-ordered alternation introduces into the soul's inner life; and upon the full ideal and ultimate measure for the complete and perfected man, humanity at large, being a maximum of multiplicity and attachment permeated and purified by a maximum of unity and detachment. The life which can englobe and organize both these movements, with their manifold interaction, will have a multitude of warm attachments, without fever or distraction, and a great unity of pure detachment, without coldness or emptiness: it will have the, winning because rich, simplicity and wondrous combination of apparent inevitableness and of seeming paradox furnished by all true life, hence exhibited in its greatest fulness by the religious life which, at its deepest, is deeper than any other kind of life.

III. Quietude and Passivity. Points in this tendency to be considered here.

We have inevitably somewhat anticipated another matter, in which Catherine shows all the true Mystic's affinities: the craving for simplification and permanence of the soul's states, —her practice and teaching as to Quietude and Passivity.

Pushed fully home, this tendency involves four closely related, increasingly profound, convictions and experiences. Utter unification of the soul's functions, indeed utter unity of its substance: *i. e.* the soul does one single thing, and seems to do it by one single act; itself is simply one, and expresses itself by one sole act. Passivity of the soul: *i. e.* the soul does not apparently act at all, it simply *is* and receives—it is now nothing but one pure immense recipiency. Immediacy of contact between the soul and God: *i. e.* there seems to be nothing separating, or indeed in any way between, the soul and God. And, finally, an apparent coalescence of the soul and God: *i. e.* the soul *is* God, and God *is* the soul.—Only the first two points, and then the closely related question of Pure Love, shall occupy us here; the last two points must stand over for our penultimate chapter.

1. *Distinction between experiences, their expression, and their analysis.*

We have already studied the psycho-physical occasions, concomitants, and embodiments of Catherine's keen desire for, and profound experience of, spiritual unification and passivity; and we can have no kind of doubt as to the factual reality and the practical fruitfulness of the state so vividly described by her. Here we have only to inquire into the accuracy of the analysis and terminology effected and employed by her, in so far as they seem to claim more than simply to describe the soul's own feeling and impression as to these states thus experienced by itself. We have then to consider the nature and truth of what can roughly be styled Quietism and Passivity.

Now here especially will it be necessary for us carefully to distinguish between the direct experiences, impressions, and instinctive requirements of the soul,—here all souls, in precise proportion to their depth and delicacy of holiness and of self-knowledge are our masters, and furnish us with our only materials and tests; and, on the other hand, the implications and analysis of these states, as, in the first instance, psychological, and then as requiring elucidation with regard to their ontological cause and reality by means of a religious philosophy,—here, psychology, and religious philosophy, especially also the discriminations and decisions of theologians and Church authorities as expressive of these ultimate questions, will be our guides.[1]

[1] My chief authorities throughout this section have been Bossuet's *Instruction sur les Etats d'Oraison* of 1687, with the important documents

(1) If we start from the history of the nomenclature which, (though present only partially in Catherine's sayings, for she nowhere uses the term "passivity"), runs, with however varying a completeness, right through the Christian Mystics more or less from the first, we shall find that it consists, roughly, of three stages, and, throughout, of two currents. There is the Pre-Pauline and Pre-Philonian stage; the stage of Paul, Philo, and John, through Clement and Origen, on to Gregory of Nyssa and St. Augustine; and the stage from the Pseudo-Dionysius onward, down to Nicolas of Coes inclusive, and which, to this hour, still largely influences us all.—And there are the two currents. The one tends so to emphasize the sense and reality of the soul's simple receptivity, and of what the soul receives at such, apparently, purely receptive times, as to ignore, or even practically deny, the undeniable fact that this very receptivity is, inevitably, an act of its own. Its decisive terms are Passivity, Fixedness, Oneness. The other current realizes that Grace does not destroy, violate, or supplant Nature, either entirely or in part, but that it awakens, purifies, and completes it, so that every divine influx is also ever a stimulation of all the good and true energy already, even though latently, present in the soul. And its characteristic terms are "Action" (as distinguished from "Activity"), Growth, Harmony.

(2) And we should note with care that these two currents are not simply Heathen and Christian respectively. For if that great, indeed all but central, term and conception of "Action" has been wisely generalized by most Christian Mystics, as the truly Christian substitute for the strongly Neo-Platonist term "Passivity": that term and conception of "Action" was first fixed and elucidated by Aristotle, who, as Mr. Schiller well puts it, "has packed into his technical term 'Energeia,' and especially into the combination 'Unmoving Energy,' all that was most distinctive, most original,

prefixed and appended to it (*Œuvres de Bossuet*, ed. Versailles, 1817, Vol. XXVII); Fénelon's chief apologetic works, especially his *Instruction Pastorale*, his *Lettres en Réponse à Divers Ecrits ou Mémoires*, his *Lettre sur l'Etat Passif*, and his two Latin Letters to Pope Clement XI (*Œuvres de Fénelon*, ed. Versailles, 1820, Vols. IV, VI, VIII, and IX); and Abbé Gosselin's admirably clear, impartial, cautious, and authoritative *Analyse de la Controverse du Quiétisme*. I have studied these works, and the condemned propositions of the Beghards, of Molinos, and of Fénelon, very carefully, and believe myself to have, in my text, taken up a position identical with M. Gosselin's.

most fundamental, and most profound in his philosophy"; [1] whilst the second term, "Passivity," goes on figuring in Christian Mystics and Mystical Theologies—(in spite of its demonstrably dangerous suggestions and frequently scandalous history)—because the religious, especially the Christian, consciousness requires a term for the expression of one element of all its deepest experiences, that character of "givenness" and of grace, of merciful anticipation by God, which marks all such states, in exact proportion to their depth and to the soul's awakeness.

(3) Now Aristotle's conception of God's Unmoving Energy, is taken over by St. Thomas in the form of God being One Actus Purus,—sheer Energy, His very peace and stillness coming from the brimming fulness of His infinite life. And even finite spirit, whilst fully retaining, indeed deepening, its own character, can and does penetrate finite spirit through and through,—the law of Physics, which does not admit more than one body in any one place, having here no kind of application,—so that the Infinite Spirit is at once conceived unspiritually, if He is conceived as supplanting, and not as penetrating, stimulating, and transforming the finite spirits whom He made into an increasing likeness to Him, their Maker. And hence according to the unanimous teaching of the most experienced and explicit of the specifically Theistic and Christian Mystics, the appearance, the soul's own impression, of a cessation of life and energy of the soul in periods of special union with God or of great advance in spirituality, is an appearance only. Indeed this, at such times strong, impression of rest springs most certainly from an unusually large amount of actualized energy, an energy which is now penetrating, and finding expression by, every pore and fibre of the soul. The whole moral and spiritual creature expands and rests, yes; but this very rest is produced by Action "unperceived because so fleet," so near, so all fulfilling; or rather by a tissue of single acts, mental, emotional, volitional, so finely interwoven, so exceptionally stimulative and expressive of the soul's deepest aspirations, that these acts are not perceived as so many single acts, indeed that their very collective presence is apt to remain unnoticed by the soul itself.

(4) Close parallels to such a state are abundant in all

[1] F. C. S. Schiller, Essay "Activity and Substance," pp. 204–227,—an admirably thorough piece of work, in *Humanism*, 1903. See his p. 208.

phases and directions of the soul's life. The happiest and most fruitful moments for our aesthetic sense, those in which our mind expands most and grows most, hence is most active in aesthetic " action " (though not " activity ") are those in which we are unforcedly and massively absorbed in drinking in, with quiet intentness, the contrasts and harmonies, the grand unity in variety, the very presence and spirit of an alpine upland, or of a river's flowing, or of the ocean's outspread, or of the Parthenon sculptures or of Rafael's madonnas. At such moments we altogether cease to be directly conscious of ourselves, of time or of the body's whereabouts; and when we return to our ordinary psychical and mental condition, we do so with an undeniable sense of added strength and youthfulness,—somewhat as though our face, old and haggard, were, after gazing in utter self-oblivion upon some resplendent youthfulness, to feel, beyond all doubt, all its many wrinkles to have gone. And so too with the mind's absorption in some great poem or philosophy or character.—In all these cases, the mind or soul energizes and develops, in precise proportion as it is so absorbed in the contemplation of these various over-againstnesses, these " countries " of the spirit, as to cease to notice its own overflowing action. It is only when the mind but partially attends that a part of it remains at leisure to note the attention of the other part; when the mind is fully engrossed, and hence most keenly active, there is no part of it sufficiently disengaged to note the fact of the engrossment and action of, now, the whole mind. And, with the direct consciousness of our mind's action, we lose, for the time being, all clear consciousness of the mind's very existence. And let it be carefully noted, this absence of the direct consciousness of the self is as truly characteristic of the deepest, most creative, moments of full external action: the degree of mind and will-force operating in Nelson at Trafalgar and in Napoleon at Waterloo, or again in St. Ignatius of Antioch in the Amphitheatre, and in Savonarola at the stake, was evidently in the precisely contrary ratio to their direct consciousness of it or of themselves at all.

(5) Now if such " Passivity," or Action, is in reality the condition in which the soul attains to its fullest energizing, we can argue back, from this universal principle, to the nature of the various stages and kinds of the Prayer and States of Quiet. In each case, that is, we shall combat the still very common conception that,—though orthodoxy, it is admitted,

requires *some* human action to remain throughout,—such Prayer and States consist (not only as to the immediate feeling of their subjects, but in reality and in their ultimate analysis) in an ever-increasing preponderance of divine action within the soul, and an ever-decreasing remnant of acts of the soul itself. For such a view assumes that God supplants man, and that, so to speak, His Hand appears unclothed alongside of the tissue woven by man's own mind; whereas God everywhere but stimulates and supports man whom He has made, and His Hand moves ever underneath and behind the tissue,—a tissue which, at best, can become as it were a glove, and suggest the latent hand. The Divine Action will thus stimulate and inform the human action somewhat like the force that drives the blood within the stag's young antlers, or like the energy that pushes the tender sap-full fern-buds up through the hard, heavy ground.

Thus a special intensity of divine help and presence, and an unusual degree of holiness and of union, have nothing to do with the fewness of the soul's own acts at such times, but with their quality,—with the preponderance amongst them of divinely informed acts as against merely natural, or wrongly self-seeking, or downrightly sinful acts. And since it is certain that living simplicity is but the harmony and unification, the synthesis, of an organism, and hence is great in precise proportion to the greater perfection of that synthesis, it follows that the living, utterly one-seeming Action or State will, at such times, contain a maximum number of interpenetrating acts and energies, all worked up into this harmonious whole.

2. *Four causes of inadequate analysis.*

It is plain, I think, that one thoroughly normal, one accidental, and two mischievous, causes have all conspired to arrest or to deflect the analysis of most of the Mystics themselves concerning Simplicity.

For one thing, the soul, as has just been shown, at such moments of harmonious concentration and of willing and thinking in union with God's Light and Will, necessarily ceases, more or less, to be conscious of its own operations, and, in looking back, braced and rested as it now is, it cannot but think that it either did not act at all, or that its action was reduced to a minimum. For how otherwise could it now feel so rested, when, after its ordinary activity, it feels so tired and dissatisfied? and how otherwise could it be so unable to give any clear account of what happened in those minutes of union? Yet it is, on the contrary, the very fulness of the action which has rested, by expanding, the soul; and which has made the soul, returned to its ordinary distractedness, incapable of clearly explaining that, now past, concentration.

The accidental cause has been the fairly frequent, though not necessary, connection of the more pronounced instances of such habits of mind with more or less of the psycho-physical phenomena of ecstasy, in the technical sense of the word. For, in such trances, the breathing and circulation are retarded, and the operation of the senses is in part suspended. And it was easy to reason, from such visible, literal simplification of the physical life, to a similar modification of the soul's action at such times; and, from the assumed desirableness of that psycho-physical condition, to the advantage of the supposed corresponding state of the soul itself. Any tendency to an extreme dualism, as to the relations between body and soul, would thus directly help on an inclination to downright Quietism.—Here it is, on the contrary, certain that only in so far as those psycho-physical simplifications are the results of, or conditions for, a deepening multiplicity in unity, a fuller synthetic action of the soul, or, at least, of a fuller penetration by the soul of even one limited experience or idea—an operation which entails not less, but more, energizing of the soul,—are such psycho-physical simplifications of any spiritual advantage or significance. And in such cases they could not be indications of the cessation or diminution of the deepest and most docile energizing of the soul.

And the mischievous causes were a mistake in Psychology and a mistake in Theology. For, as to Psychology, not only was simplicity assumed, (through a mistaken acceptance of the soul's own feeling, as furnishing the ultimate analysis of its state,) to consist, at any one moment, of an act materially and literally one, instead of a great organism of various simultaneous energizings; but this one act was often held to require no kind of repetition. Since the act was one as against any simultaneous multiplicity, so was it one as against any successive multiplicity, even if this latter were taken as a repetition differentiated by number alone. And yet here again energizing *is* energizing; and though the soul's acts overlap and interpenetrate each other, and though when, by their number and harmony, they completely fill and pacify the soul, many of them are simultaneously or successively present to the soul in their effects alone: it is nevertheless the renewal, however peaceful and unperceived, of these acts, which keeps the state of soul in existence. For these acts are not simply unowned acts that happen to be present within the soul; they are the soul's own acts, whether, in addition, the soul is directly conscious of them or not.

And, theologically, the idea was often at work that it was more worthy of God to operate alone and, as it were, *in vacuo*; and more creaturely of man to make, or try to make, such a void for Him. Yet this is in direct conflict with the fundamental Christian doctrine, of the Condescension, the Incarnation of God to and in human nature, and of the persistence, and elevation of this humanity, even in the case of Christ Himself. God's action does not keep outside of, nor does it replace, man's action; but it is,—Our Lord Himself has told us,—that of yeast working in meal, which manifests its hidden power in proportion to the mass of meal which it penetrates and transforms.

3. *Four Quietistic aberrations.*

Now it is certain that the error of Quietism has, in no doubt many cases, not remained confined to such mistakes in psychological analysis and theological doctrine, but that these have joined hands with, and have furnished a defence to, sloth and love of dreamy ease, or to some impatience of the necessary details of life, or to fanatical attachment to some one mood and form of experience; and that they have, thus reinforced, ravaged not a few wills and souls.

Four chief Quietistic aberrations can be studied in history.

(1) The neglect or even contempt of vocal prayer, and of the historical and institutional elements of religion, at least in the case of more advanced souls, is one of these abuses.—Now it is true, and Catherine has been a striking instance, that the proportion of all these different elements towards one another vary, and should vary, considerably between soul and soul, according to the *attrait* and degree of advance of each; that the soul's most solid advance is in the direction of an ever-deepened spiritual devotedness, and not in that of a multiplication of particular devotions; that the use of even the more central of those elements and means may, for souls called to the prayer of Quiet, become remarkably elastic and largely unmethodized; and that, for such souls (and, in various degrees and ways, sooner or later, for perhaps most other souls), a prayer of peacefully humble expectation and of all

but inarticulate, practically indescribable, brooding of love, and of dim, expansive trust and conformity is possible, sometimes alone possible, and is proved right and useful, if it leaves them strengthened to act and to suffer, to help and to devote themselves to their fellows, to Christ, and to God.

But it remains equally true, even for these as for all other souls, that the historical and institutional elements must ever remain represented, and sufficiently represented; indeed the persistence in these elements of religion will be one of the chief means for avoiding delusion. We have St. Teresa's experience and teaching here, as a truly classical instance. And if the prayer of Quiet will give a special colour, depth, and unity to those more contingent-seeming practices, these practices will, in return, give a particular definiteness, content, and creaturely quality to that prayer. And thus too the universally and profoundly important union and interchange with souls of other, equally legitimate, kinds and degrees of spirituality will be kept up. Only the sum-total of all these souls, only the complete invisible Church, is the full Bride of Christ; and though the souls composing her may and should each contribute a varying predominance of different elements, no soul should be entirely without a certain amount of each of these constituents.

(2) Another abuse is the neglect, contempt, or misapplied fear of not directly religious occupations and labours which, however otherwise appropriate or even necessary to this soul's growth and destination, tend to disturb its quiet and to absorb a part of its time and attention. Here it is doubtless true that the other elements of religion are also all more or less apprehensive and jealous with regard to actual, or even only possible, non-religious rival interests. And it is certain that they are all right in so far as that a certain interior leisureliness and recollection, a certain ultimate preference for the spiritualizing religious force of the soul as against the materials, non-religious and other, which that force is to penetrate, are necessary to the soul that would advance.

But the fear that characterizes the Historical and Institutional elements is rather a fear, respectively, of error and of disobedience and singularity, whereas on the part of the Mystical element it is a fear of distraction and absorption away from the *Unum Necessarium* of the soul. Perhaps even among the Canonized Mystics there is none that has more impressively warned us, both by word and example, against this insidious danger, than the distinguished Platonist scholar and deep spiritual writer, Père Jean Nicolas Grou, who, right through the long mystical period of his life, alternated his prayer of Quiet with extensive and vigorous critical work on the Graeco-Latin classics, and whose practice only wants further expansion and application, (according to the largely increased or changed conditions of such not directly religious work,) in order to bear much fruit, not only for criticism and science, but, (by the return-effect of such occupations upon the soul's general temper and particular devotional habits,) for spirituality itself. But we must return to this point more fully in our last chapter.

(3) The third abuse is the neglect or contempt of morality, especially on its social, visible, and physical sides. Particular Mystics, and even whole Mystical schools and movements, have undoubtedly in some instances, and have, possibly, in many more cases, been maligned on this point, since even such a spotless life as Fénelon's, and that of such a profoundly well-intentioned woman as Madame Guyon, did not, for a time, escape the most unjust suspicions. It is also true that, as a man advances in spirituality, he lays increasing stress upon the intention and general attitude of the agent, and increasingly requires to be judged by the same interior standard, if he is to be rightly understood at all. God may and does, to humble and purify him, allow painful temptations and trials from within to combine, apparently, against him, with persecutions and much isolation from without. And the difference rather than the similarity, between Religion and Morality,—the sense of pure grace, of free pardon, of the strange profound "givenness" of even our fullest willings and of our most emphatically personal achievements,—can and should grow in him more and more.

And yet it is clear that there must have been some fire to account for all that smoke of accusation; that the material and the effect outwards, the *body* of an action, do matter, as well as does that action's *spirit;* that this body does not only act thus outwards, but also inwards, back upon the spirit of the act and of the agent; and that temptations and trials are purifying, not by their simple presence but in proportion as they are resisted, or, if they have been yielded to, in proportion as such defeats are sincerely deplored and renounced. Thus everywhere the full development of any one part of life, and the true unity of the whole, have to be achieved through the gradual assimilation of at first largely recalcitrant other elements, and within an ever-abiding multiplicity—a maximum number of parts and functions interacting within one great organism. And hence not the outrage, neglect, or supersession of morality, but, on the contrary, its deeper development, by more precise differentiation from, and more organic integration into, religion proper, must, here again and here above all, be the final aim. Once more again it is the Incarnational type which is the only fully true, the only genuinely Christian one.

(4) And, finally, there are certain hardly classifiable fanaticisms, which are nevertheless a strictly logical consequence from a wrongly understood Quiet and Passivity,—from Quietism in its unfavourable, condemned sense. I am thinking of such a case as that of Margarethe Peters, a young Quietist, who caused herself to be crucified by her girl-companions, at Wildenspuch, near Schaffhausen, in 1823,—in order to carry out, in full literalness and separateness, the utmost and most painful passivity and dependence and resistless self-donation, in direct imitation of the culminating act of Christ's life on earth and of His truest followers.[1] Here, in the deliberate suicide of this undoubtedly noble Lutheran girl, we get an act which but brings out the strength and weakness of Quietism wherever found. For the greatest constituents of the Christian spirit are undoubtedly there: free self-sacrifice, impelled by love of God, of Christ, and of all men, and by hatred of self.—Yet, because they here suppress other, equally necessary, constituents, and are out of their proper context and bereft of their proper checks, they but render possible and actual a deed of piteous self-delusion. How terrible is false simplification, the short cut taken by pure logic, operating without a sufficient induction from facts, and within an ardent self-immolating temperament!

4. *Rome's condemnation of Quietism.*

All this is abundantly sufficient to explain and justify Rome's condemnation of Quietism. The term "Quietists" appears, I think, for the first time,—at least in an invidious sense,—in the Letter which Cardinal Caraccioli, Archbishop

[1] See Heinrich Heppe, *Geschichte der Quietistischen Mystik*, Berlin, 1875, p. 521. The obviously strong partisan bias of the author against Rome,—of which more lower down,—does not destroy the great value of the large collection of now, in many cases, most rare and inaccessible documents given, often *in extenso*, in this interesting book.

of Naples, addressed to Pope Innocent XI (Odescalchi) on June 30, 1682, and in which he graphically describes the abuses which, (under pretext or through the misapplication of spiritual Quiet and Passivity,) had now appeared in his Diocese: souls apparently incapable of using their beads or making the sign of the Cross; or which will neither say a vocal prayer nor go to Confession; or which, when in this prayer of Quiet, even when at Holy Communion, will strive to drive away any image, even of Our Lord Himself, that may present itself to their imagination; or which tear down a Crucifix, as a hindrance to union with God; or which look upon all the thoughts that come to them in the quietude of prayer, as so many rays and effluences from God Himself, exempting them henceforth from every law.[1]

Yet it is important to bear well in mind, the special circumstances, the admitted limits, and the probable signification of Rome's condemnations.

(1) As to the circumstances of the time, it appears certain that it was the ready circulation of the doctrines of the Spanish priest, Miguel de Molinos in the *Guida Spirituale*, 1675, and the abuses of the kind we have just now detailed, and that sprang from this circulation, which formed the primary reason and motive for the otherwise excessively severe treatment of a man and a book, which had both received the very highest and the most deliberate ecclesiastical approbations. That these two circumstances were the determining causes of at least the severity of his condemnation is well brought out by the circumstance that, during his two years' trial (1685–1687), not only the short *Guida* but his whole obtainable correspondence (some twenty thousand letters) were examined, and that it is at least as much on such occasional manuscript material, and on Molinos's own oral admissions, —in prison and doubtless, in part at least, under torture,— that the condemnation was based, containing, as it does, certain revoltingly immoral propositions and confessions, admittedly absent from his published writings.

But if at least some shadow of doubt rests upon the moral character of Molinos, not a shadow of such suspicion or of doubt concerning his perfectly Catholic intentions can, in justice, be allowed to rest upon his chief follower and the most distinguished apologist for his doctrine, the saintly Oratorian

[1] Heppe, *op. cit.* pp. 130–133.

and Bishop, the much-tried Cardinal Petrucci; any more than Fénelon's moral and spiritual character, or deeply Catholic spirit and intentions, can, (in spite of the painfully fierce and unjust attack upon both by Bossuet in his formally classic invective, *Relation sur le Quiétisme*,) for one moment be called in question.[1] Other admittedly deeply spiritual and entirely well-intentioned Catholics, whose writings were also condemned during this time when devotional expressions having an at all quietistic tinge or drift were very severely judged, are Mère Marie de l'Incarnation (Marie Guyard), a French Ursuline Religious, who died in Canada in 1672, and the process of whose Beatification has been introduced; the saintly French layman, Jean de Bernières-Louvigny, much admired by Fénelon, who died in 1659; the very interior, though at times somewhat fantastic, Secular Priest, Henri Marie Boudon, who died in 1702; and the very austere but highly experienced ascetical writer, the Jesuit Père Joseph Surin, whom Bossuet had formally approved, and who died in 1668.[2] But Madame Guyon herself, that much-tried and vehemently opposed woman, was held, by many an undoubtedly Catholic-minded, experienced and close observer, to be (in spite of the largely misleading and indeed incorrect character of many of her analyses and expressions) a truly saintly, entirely filial Catholic.[3]

(2) As to the limits of these condemnations, we must remember that only two of them,—those of Molinos and of Fénelon,—claim to be directly doctrinal at all; and that Fénelon was never really compromised in the question of Quietism proper, but was condemned on questions of Pure Love alone. Bossuet himself was far less sound as against the central Quietist doctrine of the One Act, which, unless formally revoked, lasts on throughout life, and hence need never be repeated; Fénelon's early criticism of the Molinos propositions remains one of the clearest extant refutations of that error. Again in the matter of the Passivity of advanced souls, Bossuet was distinctly less normal and sober than Fénelon: for whilst

[1] There is a good article on Petrucci in the Catholic Freiburg *Kirchen-lexikon*, 2nd ed., 1895; and Heppe, in his *Geschichte*, pp. 135–144, gives extracts from his chief book. Bossuet's attack, *Œuvres*, ed. 1817, Vol. XXIX.

[2] Reusch, *Der Index der verbotenen Bücher*, 1885, Vol. II, pp. 611; 622, 623; 625.

[3] Gosselin's *Analyse, Œuvres de Fénelon*, ed. cit. Vol. IV, pp. xci–xcv.

Fénelon taught that in no state does the soul lose all capacity, although the facility may greatly vary, to produce distinct acts of the virtues or vocal prayers and other partially external exercises, Bossuet taught that, in some cases, all capacity of this kind is abolished.[1] "I take," says Fénelon, "the terms 'Passive' and 'Passivity' as they actually appear everywhere in the language of the (sound) Mystics, as something opposed to the terms 'active' and 'activity': 'Passivity,' taken in the sense of an entire inaction of the will, would be a heresy." And he then opposes "Passivity," not to "Action," but to that "Activity," which is a merely natural, restless, and hurried excitation.[2]

(3) And as to the abiding significance of the whole anti-quietist decisions and measures, we shall do well to consider the following large facts. From St. Paul and St. John to Clement of Alexandria and Origen; from these to Dionysius the Areopagite; from the Areopagite to St. Bernard of Clairvaux and then the Franciscan and Dominican Mystics; from these, again, on to the great Renaissance and Counter-Reformation saints and writers of this type,—the German Cardinal Nicolas of Coes and the Italian St. Catherine of Genoa, the Spaniards St. Teresa and St. John of the Cross, and the French Saint Francis de Sales and Saint Jane Frances de Chantal, we get a particular type of religious experience and doctrine, which but unfolds and concentrates, with an unusual articulation, breadth, and depth, what is to be found, on some sides of their spiritual character and teaching, among Saints and religious souls of the more mixed type, such as St. Augustine, St. Anselm, St. Thomas of Aquin, and St. Ignatius Loyola. And this mixed type, bearing within it a considerable amount of that mystical quiet and emotional-speculative element, is again but a deepening, a purification and a realization of one of the profoundest affinities and constituents of every human heart and will.

Hence, even in the thickest of the quietist controversy, when that mystical element must have seemed, to many, to be discredited once for all, those best acquainted with the rich history of the Church, and with the manifold requirements of the abiding religious consciousness, could not and did not doubt that all that was good, deep, and true in that element

[1] Fénelon, *Explication . . . des Propositions de Molinos* (*Œuvres*, Vol. IV, pp. 25–86). Gosselin, *Analyse* (*ibid.* pp. ccxvi–ccxxiii).
[2] *Œuvres de Fénelon*, Vol. VIII, pp. 6, 7.

would continue to be upheld by, and represented in, the Church.—And it is not difficult to point to the more or less Mystical souls furnished by the Monks, the Friars; the Clerks-Regular, specially the Jesuits; the Secular Clergy; and the Laity, down to the present day. Such writers and Saints as the Père de Caussade (*d.* about 1770) on the one hand, and Père Jean N. Grou (*d.* 1803) and the Curé d'Ars (*d.* 1859) on the other hand, carry on the two streams of the predominantly mystical and of the mixed type,—streams so clearly observable before 1687 and 1699. Quietism, the doctrine of the One Act; Passivity in a literal sense, as the absence or imperfection of the power and use of initiative on the soul's part in any and every state: these doctrines were finally condemned, and most rightly and necessarily condemned; the Prayer of Quiet, and various states and degrees of an ever-increasing predominance of Action over Activity,—an Action which is all the more the soul's very own, because the more occasioned, directed, and informed by God's action and stimulation,—these, and the other chief lines of the ancient experience and practice, remain as true, correct, and necessary as ever.

5. *Rome's alleged change of front.*

And yet it is undeniable that the Roman events between 1675 and 1688 do seem, at first sight, to justify the strongly Protestant Dr. Heppe's contention that those twelve years,—not to speak of the later troubles of Madame Guyon and of Fénelon,—witnessed a complete *volte face*, a formal self-stultification, of the Roman teaching and authority, on these difficult but immediately important matters.

(1) Let us put aside the many passages in Molinos's *Guida* which were but (more or less) literal reproductions of the teachings of such solemnly approved authorities as Saints Teresa, Peter of Alcantara, John of the Cross, Francis de Sales and Jane Frances de Chantal,—passages which, of course, remained uncondemned even in Molinos's pages, but which it would often be difficult to distinguish from the parts of his book that were censured. Yet there still remain such facts as the following.

Juan Falconi's *Alfabeto* and *Lettera* were at their Fifth Italian edition, 1680, and all five editions had been approved by the Master of the Apostolic Palace; but only in 1688 were these writings forbidden. Yet the *Lettera* contains, with unsurpassed directness and clearness, the central doctrine of

Quietism: an exhortation to the production of one single lively Act of Faith, which will then continue uninterruptedly through the whole earthly life into eternity, and which, consequently, is not to be repeated.[1]

Molinos's *Guida* and *Breve Trattato* appeared in Rome, respectively in 1675 and 1681, with the approbations of five theologians, four of whom were Consultors of the Holy Office,—the Archbishop of Reggio; the Minister-General of the Franciscans; the late General of the Carmelites; Father Martin Esparza, the same Jesuit Theologian-Professor of the Roman College who, some years before, had been one of those who had examined and approved St. Catherine's *Vita ed Opere;* and the actual General of the Carmelites.[2]

Even after these two writings of Molinos had been criticised by the Jesuits Bell Huomo and Segneri and the Clerk Regular Regio, (Segneri enjoying a deservedly immense reputation, and showing in this affair much moderation and a strong sense of the legitimate claims of Mysticism,) the Inquisition examined these criticisms, and forbade, not the incriminated writings of Molinos and Petrucci, but the critique of Bell Huomo *donec corrigatur,* and those of Regio and of Segneri (in his *Lettera* of 1681) absolutely. Segneri's subsequent *Concordia* almost cost him his life, so strong was the popular veneration of Molinos.

Molinos indeed was the guest of Pope Innocent XI himself, and the friend and confidant, amongst countless other spiritually-minded souls, of various Cardinals, especially of the deeply devout Petrucci, Bishop of Jesi, who was raised to the Cardinalate eighteen months after the beginning of Molinos's trial. The imprisonment of Molinos began in May 1685, but the trial did not end till August 1687, when (after nineteen " Principal Errors of the New Contemplation " had been censured by the Holy Office in February 1687) sixty-eight propositions, out of the two hundred and sixty-three which had been urged against him, were solemnly condemned: of these the clearly and directly immoral ones being admittedly not derived from any printed book, or indeed any ever published letter of Molinos.[3]

[1] Heppe, *op. cit.* p. 62. Reusch, *op. cit.* Vol. II, pp. 619, 620.

[2] I write with these approbations before me, as reprinted in the *Recueil de Diverses Pièces concernant le Quiétisme*, Amsterdam, 1688.

[3] *Œuvres de Bossuet*, ed. 1817, Vol. XXVII, pp. 497–502. Heppe, *op. cit.* pp. 27g n.; 273–281. Denzinger, *Encheiridion*, ed. 1888, pp. 266–274.

(2) To estimate Rome's attitude (as far as it concerns the ultimate truth and completeness of these doctrines, taken in their most characteristic and explicit forms) fairly, we shall have to put aside all questions as to the motives that impelled, and the methods that were employed, by either side against the other. Molinos may have been even worse than the condemned propositions represent, and yet Petrucci would remain a saintly soul; and we certainly are driven to ask with Leibniz: " Si Molinos a caché du venin sous ce miel, est-il juste que Petrucci et autres personnes de mérite en soient responsables? "[1] But neither the wickedness of the one nor the sanctity of the other would make the doctrines propounded by them, objectively, any less solid or more spiritual than they are in themselves. The acutely anti-Roman Anglican Bishop Burnet may not have invented or exaggerated when he wrote from Rome, during those critical years, that one of the chief motives which actuated the opponents of the Quietists was the fact that, though the latter " were observed to become more strict in their lives, more retired and serious in their mental devotions, yet . . . they were not so assiduous at Mass, nor so earnest to procure Masses to be said for their friends: nor . . . so frequently either at Confession or in processions ": and so " the trade of those that live by these things was sensibly sunk."[2] And the cruel injustice of many details and processes of the movement against the Quietists,—a movement which soon had much of the character of a popular scare and panic, in reaction against a previous, in part, heedless enthusiasm,—are beyond dispute or justification. Yet mercenary and ruthless as part of the motives and much of the action of the anti-quietists doubtlessly were, the question as to the worth and wisdom of Quietism, (taken objectively, and not as an excusable counter-excess but as a true synthesis of the spiritual life,) remains precisely where it was before.

(3) Now I think that two peculiarities, most difficult to notice at the time, seriously differentiate the Molinist movement from the great current of fully Catholic Mysticism, even in those points and elements where the two are materially alike or even identical; and yet that these peculiarities are but the caricature (through further emphasis and systematization) of certain elements present, in a more latent and sporadic

[1] Reusch, *op. cit.* Vol. II, p. 618 *n.* 1.

[2] See Heppe, p. 264, n.

manner, in the formulae and philosophic assumptions or explanations of the older Mysticism,—elements which had been borrowed too largely from an, at bottom, profoundly anti-Incarnational philosophy, not to be of far less value and of much greater danger than the profoundly true experiences, nobly spiritual maxims, and exquisite psychological descriptions which that predominantly Neo-Platonist framework handed on.

The first peculiarity is that the older Mystics, especially those of the type of St. Catherine of Genoa and St. John of the Cross, but even also those of the more " mixed " type of Mysticism, such as St. Teresa, had indeed quite freely used terms which are vividly true as descriptions of the prima facie aspect and emotional impression of certain states and experiences of the soul : " empty," " fixed," " motionless," " the reason and the will have ceased to act," " doing nothing," " incapable of doing anything," " moved by irresistible grace," " but one act," " one single desire " : these and equivalent expressions occur again and again. But these sayings do not here lead up to such a deliberate and exclusive rule as is that given by Falconi, and repeated by Molinos in his *Guida*, Nos. 103–106.[1]

This doctrine of the One Act, in this its negative form,—for it is not to be repeated,—and in its application to the whole waking and sleeping life, is first an exclusive concentration upon, and then a wholesale extension of, one out of the several trends of the older teaching, a doctrine which, compared with that teaching in its completeness, is thin and doctrinaire, and as untrue to the full psychological explanation and working requirements of the soul as it is readily abusable in practice and contrary to the Incarnational type of religion. It is impossible not to feel that the manifold great ocean-waters of life, that the diversely blowing winds of God's Spirit are here, somehow, expected to flow and breathe in a little short-cut, single channel, through a tiny pipe; one more infallible recipe or prescription is here offered to us, hardly more adequate than the many similar " sure " roads to salvation, declared by this or that body of devout religionists to attach to the practice or possession of this or that particular prayer or particular religious object.

And the second difference is that the older Catholic Mystics

[1] *Recueil de Diverses Pièces*, pp. 61, 62.

leave less the impression that the external side of religion, its *body*, is of little or no importance, and indeed very readily an obstacle to its interior side, its *soul*. And this, again, for the simple reason that their teaching is, in general, less systematic and pointed, more incidental, and careless of much self-consistency.

(4) Yet these two differences have largely sprung from the simple pressing and further extension of precisely the least satisfactory, the explanatory and systematic side,—the form as against the content,—of the older Mystics. For once the more specifically Neo-Platonist constituent, in those Mystics' explanation and systematization, was isolated from the elements of other *provenance* which there had kept it in check, and now became, as it were, hypostasized and self-sufficient, this constituent could not but reveal, more clearly than before, its inadequacy as a form for the intensely organic and "incarnational" spiritual realities and processes which it attempted to show forth. That Neo-Platonist constituent, always present in those ancient Mystics, had ever tended to conceive the soul's unity, at any one moment, as a something outside of all multiplicity whatsoever. Hence this character of the simultaneous unity had only to be extended to the successive unity,—and the literally One Act, as in the present so throughout the future, became a necessary postulate.

And that same constituent had, even in those great teachers of profound maxims, exquisite religious psychology, and noblest living, tended, (however efficaciously checked by all this their Christian experience and by certain specifically Platonist and Aristotelian elements of their philosophy,) towards depreciating the necessity, importance, indeed even the preponderant utility, of the External, Contingent, Historical and Institutional, and of the interchange, the inter-stimulation between these sides and expressions of religion and its internal centre and spirit.

Perhaps, amongst all the great ecclesiastically authorized Mystics of that past, the then most recent of them all, St. John of the Cross, comes, by his (theoretically continuous though in his practice by no means exclusive) insistence upon the abstractive and universal, the obscure and invisible, the self-despoiling and simplifying element and movement, nearest to an exclusion of the other element and movement. Indeed the Quietists' generally strong insistence upon the necessity of a Director and upon Frequent Communion gives their teaching, when taken in its completeness, a prima facie greater Institutionalism than is offered by the spiritual theory of the great Spaniard. Yet if, even in him, one misses, in his theoretical system, a sufficiently organic necessity for the outgoing movement, a movement begun by God Himself, and which cannot but be of fundamental importance and influence for believers in the Incarnation, there is as complete an absence of the doctrinaire One-Act recipe for perfection as in the most Historical and Institutional of Christian teachers. But more about this hereafter.

6. *Four needs recognized by Quietism.*

Quietism, then, has undoubtedly isolated and further exaggerated certain explanatory elements of the older Mysticism which, even there, were largely a weakness and not a strength; has thus underrated and starved the Particular, Visible, Historical, Institutional constituents of Religion; and has, indeed, misunderstood the nature of true Unity everywhere. Yet the very eagerness with which it was welcomed at the time,—in France and Italy especially,—and this, not only as a fashion by the *Quidnuncs*, but as so much spiritual food and life by many a deeply religious soul; and the difficulty, and not infrequent ruthlessness of its suppression, indicate plainly enough that, with all its faults and dangers, it was divining and attempting to supply certain profound and abiding needs of the soul. I take these needs to be the following four.

(1) Man has an ineradicable, and, when rightly assuaged, profoundly fruitful thirst for Unity,—for Unification, Synthesis, Harmonization; for a living System, an Organization both within and without himself, in which each constituent gains its full expansion and significance through being, and more and more becoming, just *that* part and function of a great, dynamic whole; a sense of the essential and ultimate organic connection of all things, in so far as, in any degree or form, they are fair and true and good. And this sense and inevitable requirement alone explain the surprise and pain caused, at first, to us all, by the actual condition of mutual aloofness and hostility, characteristic of most of the constituents of the world within us, as of the world around us, towards their fellow-constituents. A truly atomistic world,—even an atomistic conception of the world,—of life, as a collection of things one alongside of another, on and on, is utterly repulsive to any deeply religious spirit whose self-

knowledge is at all equal to its aspirations.—No wonder, then, if the Quietists, haunted by the false alternative of one such impenetrable atom-act or of an indefinite number of them, chose the One Act, and not a multitude of them.

(2) Man has a deep-seated necessity to purify himself by detachment, not only from things that are illicit but even from those that are essential and towards which he is bound to practise a deep and warm attachment. There is no shadow of theoretical or ultimate contradiction here: to love one's country deeply, yet not to be a *Chauvinist;* to love one's wife tenderly, yet not to be uxorious; to care profoundly for one's children, yet to train, rebuke, and ever brace them, when necessary, up to suffering and even death itself: these things so little exclude each the other, that each attachment can only rightly grow in and through the corresponding detachment. The imperfection in all these cases, and in all the analogous, specifically religious ones, lies not in the objects to be loved, nor in these objects being many and of various degrees and kinds of lovableness, nor in the right (both effective and affective, appropriately varied) love of them: but simply in our actual manner of loving them.—No wonder then that Quietism, face to face with the false alternative of either Attachment or Detachment, chose Detachment, (the salt and the leaven of life) and not attachment (life's meat and meal).

(3) Man has a profound, though ever largely latent, capacity and need for admiration, trust, faith; and does not by any means improve solely by direct efforts at self-improvement, and by explicit examinations of his efforts and failures; but, (a little from the first, and very soon as much, and later on far more,) he progresses by means of a happy absorption in anything clean and fruitful that can and does lift him out of and above his smaller self altogether.—And such an absorption will necessarily be unaccompanied, at the time, by any direct consciousness on the part of the mind as to this its absorption. And, religiously, such quiet concentrations will, in so far as they are at all analyzable after the event, consist in a quite inarticulate, and yet profound and spiritually renovating, sense of God; and they will have to be tested, not by their describable content, but by their ethical and religious effects. "Psychology and religion," says that great psychological authority, Prof. William James, "both admit that there are forces, seemingly outside of the conscious individual, that bring

redemption to his life." "A man's conscious wit and will, so far as they strain after the ideal, are aiming at something only dimly and inaccurately imagined, whilst the deeper forces of organic ripening within him tend towards a rearrangement that is pretty surely definite, and definitely different from what he consciously conceives and determines. It may consequently be actually interfered with by efforts of too direct and energetic a kind on our part."[1]—No wonder then that Quietism, finding this element of quiet incubation much ignored and starved in the lives of most religious souls, flew to the other extreme, of making this inarticulateness and wise indirectness of striving into the one test and measure of the perfection of all the constituents of the religious life, instead of insisting upon various degrees and combination of full and direct consciousness and articulation, and of much dimness and indirect alertness, as each requiring the other, and as both required by the complete and normal life of the soul.

(4) And Man has a deep-seated sense of shame, in precise proportion as he becomes spiritually awake, about appropriating to himself his virtues and spiritual insight, even in so much as he perceives and admits his possession of them. Not all his consciousness and conviction of the reality of his own efforts and initiative, can or does prevent a growing sense that this very giving of his is (in a true sense) God's gift,—that his very seeking of God ever implies that he had, in some degree, already found God,—that God had already sought him out, in order that he might seek and find God.—No wonder then that, once more shrinking from a Unity constituted in a Multiplicity, Quietism should, (with the apparently sole choice before it, of God Himself operating literally all, or of man subtracting something from that exclusive action and honour of God,) have chosen God alone and entire, rather than, as it were, a fragmentary, limited, baffled influence and efficiency of the Almighty within His Own creature. Yet here again the greater does not supplant, but informs, the lesser; and the Incarnational action of God is, in this supreme question also, the central truth and secret of Christianity.

7. *Multiplicity and unity, in different proportions, needful for all spiritual life.*

We find, then, that it is essential for even the most advanced souls, that they should keep and increase the sense and the

[1] *Varieties of Religious Experience*, 1902, pp. 209, 211.

practice of a right multiplicity, as ever a constituent and essential condition of every concrete, living unity; of a right attachment, as ever the necessary material and content for a fruitful and enriching detachment; of a right consciousness and articulation of images, thoughts, feelings, volitions, and external acts, as ever stimulations, restful alternations, and food for a wise and strengthening prayer or states of Quiet and inarticulation; and of a right personal initiative and responsibility, as the most precious means and element for the operations of God.

We find, too, that it is equally important, for even the most imperfect souls, to be helped towards some, (though but ever semi-conscious and intermittent,) sense of the unity which alone can give much worth or meaning to their multiplicity; of the detachment which alone can purify and spiritualize their attachments; of the self-oblivion, in rapt and peaceful admiration, which alone can save even their right self-watchings and self-improvements from still further centring them in themselves; and of the true self-abandonment to pure grace and the breathing of God's Spirit, which alone can give a touch of winning freedom and of joyful spaciousness to all the prudence and right fear and conscious responsibility which, left alone, will hip, darken and weigh down the religious soul.

And thus we shall find that there is no degree of perfection for any one set of souls which is not, in some form and amount, prefigured and required by all other souls of good-will; and again, that there is no one constituent, to which any one soul is specially drawn, which does not require the supplementation and corrective of some other constituents, more fully represented in other souls of possibly lower sanctity.

Thus each soul and grade requires all the others; and thus the measure of a soul's greatness is not its possessing things which cannot, in any degree or way, be found in, or expected of, all human souls, in proportion as they are fully and characteristically human, but, on the contrary, its being full of a spirit and a force which, in different degrees and forms, are the very salt and yeast, the very light and life, of all men in every place and time.

The following weighty declaration, long ascribed to St. Thomas Aquinas, fully covers, I think, the doctrine and ideal aimed at throughout this section: "Already in this life we ought continuously to enjoy God, as a thing most fully our own, in all our works. . . . Great is the blindness and exceeding the folly of many souls that are ever seeking God, continuously sighing after God, and frequently desiring God: whilst, all the time, they are themselves the tabernacles of the living God . . . since their soul is the seat of God, in which He continuously reposes. Now who but a fool deliberately seeks a tool which he possesses under lock and key? or who can use and profit by an instrument which he is seeking? or who can draw comfort from food for which he hungers, but which he does not relish at leisure? Like unto all this is the life of many a just soul, which ever seeks God and never tarries to enjoy Him; and all the works of such an one are, on this account, less perfect."[1]

IV. Pure Love, or Disinterested Religion: its Distinction from Quietism.

The problem of Pure Love, of Disinterested Religion, can hardly, in practice, be distinguished from that of Quiet and Passivity, if only because Quietists, (those who have considered perfection to diminish more and more the number of the soul's acts, or at least to eliminate more and more the need of distinctness or difference between them,) have, quite inevitably, ever given a special prominence to the question as to what should be the character of those few acts, of that one unbroken act. For once allow this their main question we should all have to answer in the Quietist's way,—viz. that this single act must, for a perfect soul, be the most perfect of the acts possible to man, and hence must be an act of Pure Love.—Yet it is well to realize clearly that, if Quietism necessitates an even excessive and unreal doctrine of Pure Love, a moderate and solid Pure-Love teaching has no kind of necessary connection with Quietism. For even though my interior life be necessarily one continuous stream and tissue of acts, countless in their number, variety, and degrees of interpenetration, it in nowise follows that acts of Pure Love are not the best, or are impossible; nor that, in proportion as Pure Love informs the soul's multiform acts, such acts must lose in depth and delicacy of variety and articu-

[1] *De Beatitudine*, c. 3, 3.

lation. Indeed here, with regard to the very culmination of the interior life, we shall again find and must again test the two conceptions: the finally abstractive and materially simplifying one, which must ever have any one real thing outside of another; and the incarnational and synthetic one, which finds spiritual realities and forces working the one inside and through the other. And the latter view will appear the true one.

1. *New Testament teaching as to Pure Love.*

Now we must first try and get some clear ideas as to how this difficult matter stands in the New Testament,—in the Synoptic tradition and in the Pauline-Johannine teaching respectively. Here again it is the former which, (though on its surface it appears as the more ordinary and the more locally coloured teaching,) is the richer, in its grandly elastic and manifold simplicity; and it is the latter which has most profoundly penetrated and articulated the ultimate meaning and genius of a part of Our Lord's doctrine, yet at the cost of a certain narrowing of the variety and breadth of that outlook. In both cases I shall move, from the easier and more popular teaching, to the deepest and most original enunciations and explanations.[1]

(1) The Synoptic teaching starts throughout from the ordinary post-exilic Jewish feeling and teaching, which indeed recognizes the ceremonial obligations and the more tangible amongst the ethical demands as standing under the categorical inperative of the Legal "Thou Shalt," but places the large territory of the finer moral precepts outside of the Law. So with the "Zedakah," the "Justice" of almsdeeds, and with the "Gemiluth Chasadim," the "works of mercy," such as visiting the sick, burying the dead, and rejoicing with the joyful and sorrowing with the sorrowful. Thus Rabbi Simon the Just tells us: "The world rests on three things: on the Law (*Thorah*), on Worship (*Abodah*), and on Works of Mercy (*Gemiluth Chasadim*)"; and Rabbi Eleazar declared the "Gemiluth Chasadim" to be above the "Zedakah."[2] And it is especially in view of these works of supererogation that rewards, and indeed a strict scale of rewards, are conceived.

[1] I have been much helped in my own direct studies of the sources by W. Bousset's *Die Religion des Judenthums im Neutestamentlichen Zeitalter*, 1903; by H. J. Holtzmann's *Neutestamentliche Theologie*, 1897; and A. Jülicher's *Gleichnissreden Jesu*, Theil 2, 1899.

[2] Bousset, pp. 395, 396.

Thus already in the Book of Tobit, (written somewhere between 175 and 25 B.C.,) we have Tobit instructing his son Tobias that "Prayer is good with Fasting and Alms, more than to buy up treasures of gold. For Alms delivereth from death . . . they that practise Mercy and Justice shall live long."[1] And one of the sayings of the Jewish Fathers declares: "So much trouble, so much reward."[2]

Now this whole scheme and its spirit seems, at first sight, to be taken over quite unchanged by Our Lord. The very Beatitudes end with: "Rejoice . . . because your reward is great in heaven." And, in the following Sermon, his hearers are bidden to beware of doing their "Zedakah,"—the "Justice" of Prayer, Fasting, Almsdeeds in order to be seen by men; since, in that case, "ye shall not have reward from your Father Who is in heaven." And this is driven home in detail: these three kinds of Justice are to be done "in secret," and "thy Father will repay thee." Even Prayer itself thus appears as a meritorious good work, one of the means to "treasure up treasures in heaven." Similarly, the rich man is bid "Go sell whatsoever thou hast and give to the poor; and thou shalt have a treasure in heaven." Even "he that shall give you a cup of cold water in My name, shall not lose his reward." Indeed we have the general principle, "the labourer is worthy of his hire."[3]

And yet we can follow the delicate indications of the presence, and the transitions to the expression, of the deeper apprehension and truth. For, on the part of God, the reward appears, in the first instance, as in intrinsic relation to the deed. The reward is the deed's congenital equivalent: "Blessed are the merciful, for they shall obtain mercy"; "if ye forgive men their trespasses, your heavenly Father will also forgive you"; and "everyone who shall confess Me before men, him will I also confess before My Father Who is in heaven."[4] Or the reward appears as a just inversion of the ordinary results of the action thus rewarded: "Blessed are the meek: for they shall inherit the earth"; take the highest seat at a banquet, and you will be forced down to the lowest, take the lowest, and you will be moved up to the highest; and, generally, "he that findeth his life, shall lose it; and

[1] Ch. xii, 8, 9; see too ch. ii, 2, 7.
[2] Pirke Aboth, v, 23.
[3] Matt. v, 12; vi, 4, 6, 18, 20; Mark x, 21; ix, 41; Luke x, 7.
[4] Matt. v, 7; vi, 14; x, 32.

he that loseth his life for My sake shall find it."[1] Or the reward appears as an effect organically connected with the deed, as its cause or condition: "Blessed are the pure of heart: for they shall see God."[2] And then the reward comes to vary, although the deed remains quantitatively identical, solely because of that deed's qualitative difference, *i.e.* according to the variation in its motive: "He that receiveth a prophet in the name of a prophet shall receive a prophet's reward; and he that receiveth a righteous man in the name of a righteous man shall receive a righteous man's reward."[3] And then the reward moves up and up and becomes a grace, through being so far in excess of the work done: "Every one who hath left houses . . . or father . . . or children, or lands for My name's sake, shall receive" manifold, indeed "a hundred-fold"—"a full . . . and overflowing measure shall they pour into your lap"; and "whosoever shall humble himself, shall be exalted,"—not simply back to his original level, but into the Kingdom of Heaven. So, too, "Thou hast been faithful over a few things, I will set thee over many things"; indeed this faithful servant's master "shall place him over all his possessions;" or rather, "blessed are those servants whom the Lord, when He cometh, shall find watching: verily I say unto you, that he shall gird himself . . . and shall come and serve them."[4]

This immense disproportion between the work and its reward, and the consequent grace-character of the latter, is driven home with a purposely paradoxical, provocative pointedness, in the two Parables of the Wedding Garment and of the Equal Payment of the Unequal Labourers, both of which are in St. Matthew alone. The former concerns the soul's call to the kingdom, and that soul's response. The King here, after having formally invited a certain select number of previously warned relatives and nobles, who all, as such, had a *claim* upon him (Matt. xxii, 3), sends out invitations with absolute indiscrimination,—to men with no claims or with less than none; to "bad" as well as "good." And it is the King, again, who gratuitously supplies them each with the appropriate white wedding-feast garment. He has thus a double right to expect all his guests to be thus clothed,

[1] Matt. v, 5; Luke xiv, 8–11; Matt. x, 39.

[2] Matt. v, 8.

[3] Matt. x, 41.

[4] Matt. xix, 29; Mark x, 23; Luke vi, 38; Matt. xxiii, 12; xxv, 21; xxiv, 47; Luke xii, 37.

and to punish instantly, not the mere negligence, but the active rejection implied on the part of the man clothed in his ordinary clothing (vv. 11, 12). Both call and investiture have been here throughout pure graces, which rendered possible, and which invited but did not force, an acceptance.[1]

The second Parable describes the "Householder" who hired labourers for his vineyard at the first, third, sixth, ninth, and even eleventh hour,—each and all of them for a penny a day; who actually pays out to them, at the end of the day, this one identical pay; and who, to the labourer of the first shift who complains, "These last have spent but one hour, and thou hast made them equal unto us, which have borne the burden and heat of the day," declares, "Friend, I do thee no wrong: didst thou not agree with me for a penny? Take up that which is thine, and go thy way: it is my will to give unto this last even as unto thee. Is it not lawful for me to do what I will with mine own? or is thine eye evil (art thou envious) because I am good" (because I choose to be bountiful)? (Matt. xx, 1–15). Here again the overflowing generosity of God's grace is brought home to us, as operating according to other standards than those of ordinary daily life: nor is this operation unjust, for the Householder paid their due to the first set of workers, whilst rewarding, far above their worth, those poor labourers of the last hour. But, as Jülicher well points out, "we should not pedantically insist upon finding here a doctrine of the strict equality of souls in the Beyond—a doctrine contradicted by other declarations of Jesus. Only the *claim* of single groups of souls to preferential treatment is combated here . . . : a certain fundamental religious disposition is to be awakened." And, as Bugge rightly notes, "the great supreme conception which lies at the bottom of the parable has, parablewise, remained here unnamed: Paul has found the expressive term for it,—'Grace.'"[2]

And we get corresponding, increasingly spiritual interpretations with regard to man's action and man's merit. First, all ostentation in the doing of the deed cancels all reward in the Beyond; so, in the case of each of the three branches of "Justice."[3] And then the worker is to be satisfied, day by

[1] Interesting reasons and parallels for holding the Wedding Garment to have been the gift of the King, in Bugge's *Die Haupt-Parabeln Jesu*, 1900, pp. 316, 317.

[2] Jülicher, *op. cit.* p. 467. Bugge, *op. cit.* p. 277.

[3] Matt. vi, 1, 2, 5, 16.

day, with that day's pay and sustenance: "Give us this day our daily bread," every soul is to pray; the divine Householder will say, "Didst thou not agree with me for a penny? Take up that which is thine and go thy way." And even "when ye shall have done all the things that are commanded you, say, 'We are unprofitable servants, we have done that which it was our duty to do.'" They are invited to look away from self, to "seek ye first His Kingdom and His righteousness," and then "all these things," their very necessaries for earthly life, "shall be added unto you." Indeed it is the boundlessly generous self-communicativeness of God Himself which is to be His disciples' deliberate ideal, "be ye perfect, as your heavenly Father is perfect"; and the production of this likeness within themselves is to be the ultimate end and crown of their most heroic, most costly acts: "love your enemies, and pray for them that persecute you: that you may be sons of your Father which is in Heaven: for He maketh His sun to rise on the evil and the good, and sendeth rain upon the just and the unjust." And the more there is of such self-oblivious love, the more will even the gravest sins be entirely blotted out, and the more rapid will be the full sanctification of the soul, as Our Lord solemnly declares concerning the sinful woman in St. Luke, "her sins, which are many, are forgiven; because she loved much."[1]

In all this matter it is St. Luke's Gospel which is specially interesting as showing, so to speak, side by side, an increased Rabbinical-like preciseness of balance between work and reward, and yet the adoption, doubtlessly under Pauline influence, of St. Paul's central term in lieu of the old Jewish terminology. For, in one of its curious so-called "Ebionite" passages, this Gospel works up the Parable of the Talents, with its only approximate relation between the deeds and their rewards (Matt. xxv, 14–30), into the Parable of the Pounds (Luke xix, 12–27), with its mathematically symmetrical interdependence between the quantities of the merit and those of this merit's reward: the man who makes ten

[1] Matt. vi, 11; xx, 14; Luke xvii, 10; Matt. vi, 33; v, 48, 44, 45; Luke vii, 47. It seems plain that the Parable of the Two Debtors, which appears in this last passage, declares how pardon awakens love; and that the sinful woman's act and Our Lord's direct comment on it, which are now made to serve as that Parable's frame, demonstrate how love produces pardon. In my text I have been busy only with the second of these twin truths.

pounds is placed over ten cities, and he who makes five, over five. And, on the other hand, in a Lukan equivalent for part of the Sermon on the Mount, St. Matthew's "reward" is replaced by "grace": "If ye do good to them that do good to you, what thank (χάρις) have you? . . . and if ye lend to them of whom ye hope to receive, what thank have you?"[1]

(2) St. Paul indeed it is who, in the specially characteristic portions of his teaching, unfolds, by means of a partly original terminology, the deepest motives and implications of Our Lord's own divinely deep sayings and doings, and never wearies of insisting upon the Grace-character of the soul's call and salvation,—the Free Mercy, the Pure Love which God shows to us, and the sheer dependence and complete self-donation, the pure love which we owe to Him, and which, at the soul's best, it can and does give Him.

It is true that in the contrasting, the traditional layer of his teaching, we find the old Jewish terminology still intact: "God will render unto every man according to his works"; "we must all be made manifest before the Judgment-seat of Christ; that each one may receive . . . according to what he hath done, whether it be good or bad."[2] Indeed it is precisely in St. Paul's pages that we find the two most difficult and, at first sight, least spiritual sayings concerning this matter to be discovered in the whole New Testament: "If in this life only we have hoped in Christ, we are of all men most pitiable." And: "If the dead are not raised . . . let us eat and drink, for to-morrow we die."[3] But these two passages must doubtless be taken partly as arguments adapted to the dispositions of his hearers,—the "Let us eat and drink" conclusion is given in the words of a current Heathen Greek proverb,—and, still more, as expressions not so much of a formal doctrine as of a mood, of one out of the many intense, mutually supplementary and corrective moods of that rich nature.

According to his own deepest, most deliberate, and most systematic teaching, it is the life of Christ, the living Christ, energizing even now within the faithful soul, that constitutes both the primary source and the ultimate motive of Christian sanctity. "I have been crucified with Christ; yet I live; and yet no longer I, but Christ liveth in me." And through this divine-human life within us "we faint not; but though our outward man is decaying, yet our inward man is renewed day by

[1] Luke vi, 33, 34. [2] Rom. ii, 6; 2 Cor. v, 10.
[3] 1 Cor. xv, 19, 32.

day." Indeed the Lord Himself said to him: "My grace is sufficient for thee; for My power is made perfect in weakness"; and hence he, Paul, could declare: "Gladly therefore will I glory in my weaknesses, that the strength of Christ may rest upon me." And thus, with Christ living within him, he can exclaim: "If God is for us, who is against us? . . . Who shall separate us from the love of Christ? shall tribulation, or anguish, . . . or the sword? . . . In all these things we are more than conquerors, through Him that loved us. For I am persuaded that neither death, nor life . . . nor things present nor things to come . . . shall be able to separate us from the love of God." "Whether we live therefore, or die, we are the Lord's." [1] We thus get here a reinsistence upon, and a further deepening of, perhaps the profoundest utterance of the whole Old Testament: "What have I in Heaven besides Thee? and besides Thee I seek nothing upon earth. Even though my flesh and my heart faint, Thou art my rock and my portion for ever." [2]

And then that deathless hymn to Pure Love, the thirteenth chapter of the First Epistle to the Corinthians, not only culminates with the proclamation that, of all man can hope and wish and will and do, of all his doings and his graces, "but now abideth Faith, Hope, Love, (Charity) these three: and the greatest of these is Love (Charity)." But the Love that has this primacy is Pure Love, for "it seeketh not its own." And though of this Love alone it is said that "it never passeth away," ever persists in the Beyond: yet even here already it can and does get exercised,—and this, not only without any suppression of parallel acts of the other virtues, but with these other virtues and their specific motives now taken over and deepened, each in its special characteristic, by the supreme virtue and motive of Pure Love: "Love beareth all things, believeth all things, hopeth all things." [3] Thus Faith, Hope, Patience, and all the other virtues, they all remain, but it is Love that is now the ultimate motive of all their specific motives. These, his culminating teachings, indicate clearly enough that virtue's rewards are regarded by him, ultimately and substantially, as "the wages of going on and not to die"; or rather that they are, in their essence, manifestations of that Eternal Life which is already energizing within souls that earnestly seek God, even here and now.

1 Gal. ii, 20; 2 Cor. iv, 16; xii, 9; Rom. viii, 31, 35, 37–39; xiv, 8.
2 Ps. lxxiii (lxxii), v, 25. I follow Duhm's restoration of the text.
3 1 Cor. xiii, 13; 8, 7.

This Life, then, however great may be its further expansion and the soul's consciousness of possessing it, already holds within itself sufficient, indeed abundant motives, (in the fulfilment of its own deepest nature and of its now awakened requirements of harmony, strength, and peace through self-donation,) for giving itself ever more and more to God.

(3) And with regard to the Johannine teaching, it will be enough for us to refer back to the texts discussed in the preceding chapter, and to note how large and specially characteristic is here the current which insists upon the reward being already, at least inchoatively, enclosed in the deed itself, and upon this deed being the result and expression of Eternal Life operating within the faithful soul, even already, Here and Now. Only the declaration that "perfect love casteth out fear," that it does not tolerate fear alongside of itself, 1 John iv, 18, appears to be contrary to the Pauline doctrine that Perfect Love, "Love" itself "beareth all things, believeth, hopeth, endureth all things," 1 Cor. xiii. 7. Love then can animate other virtues: why not then a holy fear? But this Johannine saying seems in fact modelled upon St. Paul's quotation and use of a passage from the Septuagint: "Cast out the bondwoman (the slave-servant) and her son, for the son of the bondwoman shall not be heir together with the son of the free," Gal. iv, 30; and hence this saying will not exclude "children of the free-woman,"—a holy fear as well as faith, hope, patience,—but only "children of the slave-woman," superstition, presumption, weakmindedness, and slavish fear.

2. *The "Pure Love" controversy.*

In turning now to the controversy as to Pure Love (1694–1699) and its assured results, we shall have again to distinguish carefully between the lives and intentions of the writers who were censured, and the doctrines, analytic or systematic, taught or implied by them, which were condemned. This distinction is easier in this case than in that of Quietism, for the chief writer concerned here is Fénelon, as to whose pure and spiritual character and deeply Catholic intentions there never has been any serious doubt.

But in this instance we have to make a further distinction —viz. between the objective drift of at least part of his *Explication des Maximes des Saints sur la Vie Intérieure*, published in 1697, and especially the twenty-three propositions extracted from it which were condemned by Pope Innocent

XII in 1699; and the teaching which he increasingly clarified and improved in his numerous apologetic writings against Bossuet and other opponents in this memorable controversy—especially in his Latin writings, intended for transmission to the Pope, and written as late as 1710 and 1712.[1] It is certain that Bishops and theologians who opposed his *Maximes* were found warmly endorsing such pieces as his wonderfully clear and sober *Première Réponse aux Difficultés de M. l'Evêque de Chartres.* It is these pieces, comprising also his remarkably rich *Instruction Pastorale,* his admirably penetrating *Lettre sur l'Oraison Passive* and *Lettre sur la Charité,* and his extraordinarily compact and balanced Second Epistle to Pope Clement XI, 1712 (where all the censured ambiguities and expressions are carefully avoided), which alone among Fénelon's writings shall be accepted in what follows.[2] Indeed even the earlier of these writings fail in but one thing—in justifying the actual text of the condemned book, as distinguished from the intentions of its writer. Bishop Hedley sums up the real position with the treble authority of a spiritually trained Monk, of a practised theological writer, and of a Catholic Bishop of long experience: "The doctrine intended by Fénelon, in his *Maximes des Saints,* and as explained by him during his controversy with Bossuet, has never been censured, although the opposite party laboured hard for its condemnation. Fifteen years after the condemnation of his book, we find him re-stating to Pope Clement XI (who, as Cardinal, had drawn up the Brief of his condemnations), in careful scholastic language the doctrine intended by himself, but which he himself had mis-stated in his popular treatise. As there were errors, the other side, whatever the crudity or novelty of some of its contentions, whatever its motives or methods—and some of them were far from creditable—was sure in the end to succeed. And it is well that it should have succeeded as far as it did succeed."[3]

In any case, we shall have to beware of considering Bossuet's contentions as to the specific character of Charity, Love, and as to the possibility, for man here below, of single acts of pure love, to be representative of the ordinary Catholic teaching

[1] *Œuvres,* ed. Versailles, 1820, Vols. IV to IX.

[2] *Réponse : Œuvres,* Vol. IV, pp. 119–132; *Instruction : ibid.* pp. 181–308; *Lettre sur l'Oraison,* Vol. VIII, pp. 3–82; *Lettre sur la Charité,* Vol. IX, pp. 3–36; *Epistola II, ibid.* pp. 617–677.

[3] *The Spiritual Letters of Fénelon,* London, 1892, Vol. I, pp. xi, xii.

either before or since the condemnation. On both these fundamental points Fénelon's positions are demonstrably, and indeed have been generally admitted to be, a mere re-statement of that teaching, as is shown, for instance, in the Jesuit Father Deharbe's solid and sober, thoroughly traditional and highly authorized essay: *Die vollkommene Liebe Gottes . . . dargestellt nach der Lehre des h. Thomas von Aquin*, Regensburg, 1856. It is this most useful treatise and the admirable *Analyse Raisonnée de la Controverse du Quiétisme* of the Abbé Gosselin,[1] (which has already much helped me in the preceding section,) that have been my chief aids in my careful study, back through Bossuet and Fénelon, to St. Thomas and his chief commentators, Sylvius, who died in 1649, and Cardinal Cajetan, who died in 1534, and to the other chief authorities beyond them.—I group the main points, which alone need concern us here, under three heads: the specific Nature of Pure Love; single Acts of Pure Love; a State of Pure Love.

(1) Now as to the specific Nature of Charity, or Pure, Perfect Love, St. Thomas tells us: "One Kind of Love is perfect, the other kind is imperfect. Perfect Love is that wherewith a man is loved for his own sake: as, for instance, when some one wishes well to another person, for that other person's sake, in the manner in which a man loves his friend. Imperfect love is the love wherewith a man loves something, not for its own sake, but in order that this good thing may accrue to himself,—in the manner in which a man loves a thing that he covets. Now the former kind of love pertains to Charity, which clings to God for His own sake, whereas it is Hope that pertains to the second kind of love, since he who hopes aims at obtaining something for himself."[2] And Cardinal Cajetan explains that this wishing well to God, "this good that we can will God to have, is double. The good that is in Him, that (strictly speaking) is God Himself,—we can, by Love, will Him to have it, when we find our delight in God being what He is. And the good that is but referred to God,—His honour and Kingdom and the Obedience we owe him,—this we can will, not only by finding our pleasure in it, but by labouring at its maintenance and increase with all our might."[3]

And, says St. Thomas, such Perfect Love alone is Love in

[1] *Œuvres de Fénelon*, ed. 1820, Vol. IV, pp. lxxix–ccxxxiv.
[2] *Summa Theologica*, II, ii, qu. 17, art. 8, in corp.
[3] Comment in II, ii, qu. 23, art. 1.

its strict sense and " the most excellent of all the virtues " : for " ever that which exists for its own sake is greater than that which exists in view of something else. Now Faith and Hope attain indeed to God, yet as the source from which there accrue to us the knowledge of the Truth and the acquisition of the Good ; whilst Love attains to God Himself, with a view to abide in Him, and not that some advantage may accrue to us from Him." And perhaps still more clearly : " When a man loves something so as to covet it, he apprehends it as something pertaining to his own well-being. The lover here stands towards the object beloved, as towards something which is his property." [1] And note how, although he teaches that whereas " the beatitude of man, as regards its cause and its object, is something increate," *i. e.* God Himself, " the essence of the beatitude itself is something created," for " men are rendered blessed by participation, and this participation in beatitude is something created " : yet he is careful to explain some of his more incidental passages, in which he speaks of this essence of beatitude as itself man's end, by the *ex professo* declaration : " God " alone " is man's ultimate end, and beatitude is only as it were an end before the very end, an end in immediate proximity to the ultimate end." [2]

(2) And next, as to the possibility, actual occurrence and desirableness of single Acts of such Pure Love, even here below : all this is assumed as a matter of course throughout St. Thomas's *ex professo* teaching on the matter. For throughout the passages concerning the Nature of Pure Love he is not exclusively, indeed not even primarily, busy with man's acts in the future life, but with the respective characteristics of man's various acts as executed and as analyzable, more or less perfectly, already here below. And nowhere does he warn us against concluding, from his reiterated insistence upon the essential characteristics of Pure Love, that such love cannot, as a matter of fact, be practised, at least in single acts, here below at all. Hence it is clear that, according to him, the soul as it advances in perfection will—alongside of acts of supernatural Faith, Hope, Fear, etc. (and the production of such acts will never cease), produce more and more acts of Pure Love : not necessarily more, as compared

[1] *Summa*, II, ii, qu. 23, art. 6, concl., et in corp.; I, ii, qu. 28, art. 1, in corp., et ad 2. See also II, ii, qu. 17, art. 6, in corp.; qu. 28, art. 1 ad 3; I, ii, qu. 28, art. 1, in corp., et ad 2.

[2] In Libr. sent. IV, dist. 49, art. 2.

with the other kinds of contemporary acts, but certainly more as compared with its former acts of the same character.

But there is a further, profoundly and delicately experienced doctrine. Not only can Pure Love be exercised in single and simple acts, alongside of single and simple acts of other kinds of virtues, supernatural or otherwise: but Pure Love can itself come to command or to inform acts which in themselves bear, and will now bear in increased degree, the characteristics of the other kinds of acts. St. Thomas tells us, with admirable clearness: "An act can be derived from Charity in one of two ways. In the first way, the act is elicited by Charity itself, and such a virtuous act requires no other virtue beside Charity,—as in the case of loving the Good, rejoicing in it, and mourning over its opposite. In the second way, an act proceeds from Charity in the sense of being commanded by it: and in this manner,—since Charity" has the full range of and "commands all the virtues, as ordering them (each and all) to their (ultimate) end,—an act can proceed from Charity whilst nevertheless belonging to any other special virtue." And he assures us that: "The merit of eternal life," "the fountain-head of meriting," "pertains primarily to, consists in Charity, and pertains to and consists in other kinds of supernatural acts in only a secondary manner,—that is, only in so far as these acts are commanded or informed by Charity" or Pure Love.[1]

Let us take some instances of such two-fold manifestations of identical motives and virtues, according as these motives and virtues operate in simple co-ordination, or within a compound and organic system. In the scholar's life, Greek and Latin and Hebrew may be acquired, each simply for its own sake and each alongside of the other; or they can be acquired, from the immediate motive indeed of knowing each in its own specific nature as thoroughly as possible, yet with the ultimate, ever more and more conscious and all-penetrating, motive of thus acquiring means and materials for the science of language, or for the study of philosophy, or for research into early phases of the Jewish-Christian religion. In the family life, a man, woman, or child can live for himself or herself, and then for his or her other immediate relatives, each taken as separate alongside of the other, or he or she may get more and more dominated by the conception and claims of the family as an organic whole, and may end by working

[1] *Summa Theol.*, III, qu. 85, art. 2 ad 1; I, ii, qu. 114, art. 4, in corp. In Libr. sent. III, dist. 30, art. 5.

largely, even with respect to himself, as but for so many constituents of that larger organism in which alone each part can attain its fullest significance. And especially a young mother can live for her own health and joys, and then, alongside of these, for those of her child, or she can get to the point of sustaining her own physical health and her mental hopes and will to live as so many means and conditions for feeding and fostering the claimful body and soul of her child.

So again, in the creatively artistic life, we can have a Dante writing prose and poetry and painting a picture, and a Rafael painting pictures and writing sonnets; or we can have Wagner bringing all his activities of scholar, poet, painter, musician, stage-manager,—each retaining, and indeed indefinitely increasing, its specific character and capabilities,—to contribute, by endless mutual stimulation and interaction, to something other and greater than any one of them individually or even than the simple addition of them all,—to a great Music-Drama and multiform yet intensely unified image of life itself. And an organist can draw out, as he plays, the *Vox Humana* stop, and then another and another limitedly efficacious organ-stop, whilst each new-comer takes the place of its predecessor or a place beside it; or he can draw out the *Grand Jeu* stop, which sets all the other stops to work in endless interaction, with itself permeating and organizing the whole. We thus, in these and countless other cases, and in every variety of degree within each case, get two kinds of variety, what we may call the simple and the compound diversification. And everywhere we can find that the richest variety not only can coexist with, but that it requires and is required by, indeed that it is a necessary constituent and occasion of, the deepest and most delicate unity.[1]

(3) And finally, as to a State of Pure Love. Only here do we reach the class of questions to which the condemnations of Fénelon really apply.

We shall do well to begin by bearing in mind the very ancient, practically unbroken, very orthodox Christian discrimination of faithful souls,—sometimes into the two classes of Mercenaries (or Slaves) and Friends or Children, the latter

[1] Some of the finest descriptions of these profoundly organized states common, in some degrees and forms, to all mankind, are to be found in the tenth and eleventh books of St. Augustine's *Confessions*, A.D. 397, and in Henri Bergson's *Essai sur les Données Immédiates de la Conscience*, 1898.

of whom the great Clement of Alexandria, who died about A.D. 215, called " Gnostics," " Gnosis " being his term for perfection (this scheme is the one to which Catherine's life and teaching conform); or into the three classes of Servants (Slaves); Mercenaries; and Friends (or Children), as is already worked out with full explicitness by Saints Basil, Gregory of Nazianzum, and Gregory of Nyssa, who died in the years 379, 389, and 395 (?) respectively. Now Clement places the Mercenary on the left of the Sanctuary, but the " Gnostic " on the right; and, whilst declaring that the former " are those who, by means of renouncing things perishable, hope to receive the goods of incorruption in exchange," he demands of the "Gnostic" that "he approach the saving word neither from the fear of punishment, nor from the motive of reward, but simply because He is good."[1] And St. Basil, echoed in this by his two contemporaries, teaches that, " We obey God and avoid vices, from the fear of punishment, and in that case we take on the resemblance of Slaves. Or we keep the precepts, because of the utility that we derive from the recompense, thus resembling Mercenaries. Or finally, from love of Him who has given us the law, we obey with joy at having been judged worthy of serving so great and good a God, and thus we imitate the affection of Children towards their parents."[2] And, in the case of all these Fathers, it is clear that, not only single acts, but whole states of soul and life are meant.

But the increased fineness in the analysis of interior experiences and dispositions has since then required, and the Church formulations have most wisely demanded, that these three classes be not so sharply distinguished as to make any one soul seem exclusively and unchangeably to pertain to any one of them; and, still more, that these three divisions be taken to represent, even where and whilst they are most completely realized, only the predominant character of the majority of the acts constituting the respective state of soul. For it is clear that not only is there, and can there be, no such thing, on earth at least, as a state composed of one unrepeated act; but there is no such thing as a condition of soul made up solely of acts of " simple " Pure Love, or even of supernatural acts of all sorts commanded throughout by Charity, or indeed solely of supernatural acts, both simple and commanded. The " One-act " state is a chimera; the state of "simple" acts

[1] *Stromata*, Book IV, ch. vi, 30, 1; ch. iv, 15, 6.
[2] Proemium in *Reg. Fus. Tract*, n. 3, Vol. II, pp. 329, 330.

of Pure Love alone would, if possible, involve the neglect of numberless other virtues and duties; and the last two states are indeed highly desirable, but it would be fanaticism to think we could completely attain to them here below.

Yet there is nothing in any Church-censure to prevent, and there is much in the teaching and life of countless saints to invite, our holding the possibility, hence the working ideal and standard, for even here below, of a state in which two kinds of acts, which are still good in their degree, would be in a considerable minority: acts of merely natural, unspiritualized hope, fear, desire, etc.; and acts of supernatural hope, fear, desire, etc., in so far as not commanded by Charity. For even in this state not fully deliberate venial sins would occasionally be committed, far more would a certain number of acts of an unspiritualized, unsupernatural kind occur. And the necessary variety among the supernatural acts would in nowise be impaired,—it would indeed be greatly stimulated, by Pure Love being now, for the most part, the ultimate motive of their exercise.

Sylvius, in his highly authoritative commentary on St. Thomas, puts the matter admirably: "We may not love God in view of reward in suchwise as to make eternal life the true and ultimate end of our love, or to love God because of it, so that without the reward we would not love Him . . . We must love God with reference to the eternal reward in suchwise that we put forth indeed both love and good works in view of such beatitude,—in so far as the latter is the end proposed to these works by God Himself; yet that we subordinate this our beatitude to the love of God as the true and ultimate end," so that "if we had no beatitude to expect at all, we should nevertheless still love Him and execute good works for His own sake alone. In this manner we shall first love God above all things and for His own sake; and we shall next keep the eternal reward before us, for the sake of God and of His honour."[1] A man in these dispositions would still hope, and desire, and fear, and regret, and strive for, and aspire to conditions, things, persons both of earth and of the beyond, both for himself and for others, both for time and for eternity: but all this, for the most part, from the ultimate motive, penetrating, deepening, unifying all the other motives,—of the love of Love, Christ, Spirit, God.

[1] *Summa Theol.*, II, ii, qu. 27, art. 3.

Any hesitation to accept the reality or possibility of such a state cannot, then, be based upon such acceptance involving any kind of Quietism, but simply on the admittedly great elevation of such a condition. Yet this latter objection seems to be sufficiently met if we continuously insist that even such a state neither exempts souls from the commission of (more or less deliberate) venial sin; nor is ever entirely equable; nor is incapable of being completely lost; nor, as we have just contended, is ever without more or less numerous acts of an unsupernaturalized kind, and still less without acts of the supernatural virtues other than Love and unprompted by Love.

And all fear of fanaticism will be finally removed by a further most necessary and grandly enlarging insistence upon the Mercenaries and even the Servants having passing moments, and producing varyingly numerous single acts, of Pure Love and of the other supernatural virtues prompted by Pure Love. All souls in a state of Grace throughout God's wide wide world,—every constituent, however slight and recent, of the great soul of the Church throughout every sex, age, race, clime, and external organization, would thus have some touches, some at least incidental beginnings of Pure Love, and of the other supernatural virtues prompted by Pure Love. All souls would thus, in proportion to their degree of grace and of fidelity, have some of those touches; and the progress of all would consist in the degree to which that variety of acts would become informed and commanded by the supreme motive of all motives, Pure and Perfect Love.[1]

And with such an Ideal, required by fundamental Catholic positions, ever increasingly actuating the soul and binding it to all souls beneath, around, above it, what there is of truth in the savage attacks of Spinoza and of Kant and of such recent

[1] The obligation for all of acts of Pure Love is clearly taught by the condemnations, passed by Popes Alexander VII and Innocent XI, upon the opposite contention, in 1665 and 1679: "Homo nullo unquam vitae suae tempore tenetur elicere actum Fidei, Spei et Charitatis, ex vi praeceptorum divinorum ad eas virtutes pertinentium." Note here how "Charitas" necessarily means Pure Love, since Imperfect Love has already been mentioned in "Spes."—"Probabile est, ne singulis quidem rigorose quinquenniis per se obligare praeceptum charitatis erga Deum. Tunc solum obligat, quando tenemur justificari et non habemus aliam viam qua justificari possumus." Here Pure Love is undoubtedly meant by "Charitas," since, outside of the use of the sacraments, Pure Love alone justifies.

writers as A. E. Taylor,[1] upon the supposed hypocritical self-seeking in the practice and temper of average Christians, would lose all its force.

3. *Cognate Problems.*

Three much-discussed cognate matters require some elucidation here. They answer to the questions: Does reference to the self, as for instance in acts of gratitude and thanksgiving, prevent an act from being one of Pure Love? Is the pleasurableness, normally ever attached and subsequent to all virtuous acts, to be regarded as part of the reward from which Pure Love abstracts? And finally are, I will not say any technically ecstatic or other in part psycho-physical peculiarities and manifestations, but even active Contemplation or the simple Prayer of Quiet, necessary conditions or expressions of a state of Pure Love,—understood in the sense explained above?

(1) As to reference to the self, it is highly important to distinguish between acts of Pure Love, and attempts, by means of the maximum possible degree of abstraction, to apprehend the absolute character and being of God. For these two things have no necessary connection, and yet they have been frequently confounded. St. Teresa's noble confession of past error, and consequent doubly valuable, amended teaching is perhaps the most classical pronouncement extant upon this profoundly important point.[2] The contingent, spatial and temporal, manifestations and communications of God, above all as we have them in the life of Our Lord and in those who have come nearest to Him, but also, in their several degrees and forms, in the lives of each one of us: all these, in their sacred, awakening and healing, particularity and closeness of contact, can and should be occasions and materials for the most perfect, for the purest Love.

Indeed it is well never to forget that nothing, and least of all God, the deepest of all the realities, is known to us at all, except in and by means of its relation to our own self or to our fellow-creatures. Hence if Love were Pure only in proportion as it could be based upon our apprehension of God as independent of all relation to ourselves, Pure Love would be simply impossible for us.—But, in truth, such a conception would, in addition, be false in itself: it would imply that the

[1] *The Problem of Conduct*, 1901, p. 329, n.

[2] *Life, written by Herself*, ch. XXII, tr. by David Lewis, ed. 1888, pp. 162–174.

whole great Incarnation-fact and -doctrine,—the whole of that great root of all religion, the certainty that it is because God has first loved us that we can love Him, that He is a self-revealing God, and One whom we can know and reach because " in Him we live and move and have our being "—was taking us, not towards, but away from, our true goal. There are, surely, few sadder and, at bottom, more deeply uncreaturely, unchristian attitudes, than that which would seek or measure perfection in and by the greatest possible abstraction from all those touching contingencies which God Himself has vouchsafed to our nature,—a nature formed by Himself to require such plentiful contact with the historical and visible. —And if God's pure love for us can and does manifest itself in such contingent acts, then our love can and should become and manifest itself purer and purer by means, not only of the prayer of formless abstraction and expectation, but also by the contemplation of these contingencies and by the production of analogously contingent acts. And if so, then certainly gratitude, in so far as it truly deserves the name, can and does belong to Pure Love, for the very characteristic of such gratitude consists in a desire to give and not to receive.[1]

Not, then, the degree of disoccupation with the Contingent, even of the contingent of our own life, but the degree of freedom from self-seeking, and of the harmonization and subordination of all these contingencies in and under the supreme motive of the Pure Love and service of God in man and of man in God, is the standard and test of Christian perfection.

(2) As to the pleasureableness which, in normal psychic conditions, more or less immediately accompanies or follows the virtuous acts of the soul, the realizations of its own deeper and deepest ideals, we should note that, in its earthly degree and form, it is not included in what theologians mean by the "rewards" of virtuous action. And in this they are thoroughly self-consistent, for they adhere, I think with practical unanimity, to Catherine's doctrine that these immediate consequences of virtuous acts are not to be considered a matter of positive and, as it were, separate divine institution, —as something which, given the fundamental character of

[1] Deharbe, *op. cit.* pp. 139–179, has an admirable exposition and proof of this point, backed up by conclusive experiences and analyses of Saints and Schoolmen.

man's spiritual nature, might have been otherwise; but as what,—given the immutable nature of God and of the image of that nature in His creature, man,—follows from an intrinsic, quite spontaneous necessity.—Hence, at this point especially, would it be foolish and fanatical, because contrary to the immanental nature of things, and to the right interplay of the elemental forces of all life, to attempt the suppression even of the several actual irruptions of such pleasure, and still more of the source and recurrence of this delectation. Fortunately success is here as impossible as it would be undesirable,—as much so as, on a lower plane, would be the suppression of the pleasure concomitant with the necessary kinds and degrees of eating. Indeed, it is clear, upon reflection, that unless a man (at least implicitly) accepts and (indirectly) wills that spiritual or physical pleasure, he cannot profitably eat his food or love his God.

But from this in nowise follows what Bossuet tried so hard to prove,—that what is thus necessarily present in man, as a psychical or physical prompting and satisfaction, must also of necessity be willed by him, directly and as his determining reason and justification. In turning to eat, man cannot help feeling a psychic pleasure of an all but purely physical kind; and, if he is wise, he will make no attempt to meddle with this feeling. But he can either deliberately will, as his action's object, that pleasure which is thus inevitably incident to the act, and the more he does so, the more simply greedy and sensual he will become; or he can directly will, as his determining end, that sustenance of life and strength for his work and spiritual growth, which is the justification and ultimate reason of eating (the *rationale* of that very pleasure so wisely attached by nature, as a stimulus, to a process so necessary to the very highest objects), and the more he does so, the more manly and spiritual he will grow.

And so with every one of man's wondrously manifold and different physical, psychical, spiritual requirements and actions, within the wide range of his right nature and ideals. There is not one of them,—not the most purely physical-seeming of these acts,—which he cannot ennoble and spiritualize by, as it were, meeting it,—by willing it, more and more, because of its rational end and justification. And there is not one of them, —not an act which, judged simply by its direct subject-matter and by the soul's faculties immediately engaged, would be the most purely mental and religious of acts,—which man cannot degrade and de-spiritualize, by, as it were, following it, by willing it more and more because of its psychical attraction and pleasurable concomitance alone. For, in the former case, the act, however gross may seem its material, is made the occasion and instrument of spiritual character-building and of the constitution of liberty; in the latter case, the act, however ethereal its body, is but the occasion and means of the soul's dispersion in the mere phenomenal flux of the surface of existence, and of its subjection to the determinism which obtains here.[1]

Catherine's whole convert life is one long series of the most striking examples of an heroic delicacy in self-knowledge and self-fighting in this matter: a delicacy which, as to the degree of its possibility and desirableness in any particular soul, is, however, peculiarly dependent upon that soul's special circumstances, temperament, *attrait*, and degree of perfection reached and to be reached.

(3) And, finally, as to the relations between the Contemplative forms of Prayer, and Acts and variously complete States of Pure Love; and, again, of such Prayer and Love, and Abnormal or Miraculous conditions: it is clear that, if there is no true Contemplation without much Pure Love, there can be much Pure Love without Contemplation.

Abbé Gosselin well sums up the ordinary Catholic teaching. "Meditation consists of discursive acts which are easily distinguished from each other, both because of the kind of strain and shock with which they are produced, and because of the diversity of their objects. It is the ordinary foundation of the interior life and the ordinary prayer of beginners, whose imperfect love requires to be thus excited and sustained by distinct and reflective acts. Contemplation consists, strictly speaking, in direct 'non-reflex' acts,—acts so simple and peaceful as to have nothing salient by which the soul could distinguish one from the other. It is called by the Mystical Saints 'a simple and loving look,' as discriminating it from meditation and the latter's many methodic and discursive acts, and as limiting it to a simple and loving consideration and view of God and of divine things, certified and rendered present to the soul by faith. It is the ordinary prayer of perfect souls, or at least of those that have already made much progress in the divine love. For the more purely

[1] See Deharbe's excellent remarks, *op. cit.* pp. 109, 110, n.

a soul loves God, the less it requires to be sustained by distinct, reflective acts; reasoning becomes a fatigue and an embarrassment to it in its prayer—it longs but to love and to contemplate the object of its love."

Or as Fénelon puts it: "'Passivity,' 'Action,' is not precisely itself Pure Love, but is the mode in which Pure Love operates. . . . 'Passivity,' 'Action,' is not precisely the purity of Love, but is the effect of that purity."[1] Yet, as M. Gosselin adds, "It must be admitted that without Contemplation the soul can arrive at a very high perfection; and that the most discursive meditation, and hence still more all prayer as it becomes effective, often includes certain direct acts which form an admixture and beginning of contemplation."[2]

And as to any supposed necessary relations between the very highest contemplation and the most complete state of Pure Love on the one hand, and anything abnormal or miraculous on the other hand, Fénelon, in this point remarkably more sober than Bossuet, well sums up the most authoritative and classical Church-teaching on the matter: "'Passive' Contemplation is but Pure Contemplation: 'Active' Contemplation being one which is still mixed with hurried and discursive acts. When Contemplation has ceased to have any remnant of this hurry, of this 'activity,' it is entirely 'Passive,' that is, peaceful, in its acts." "This free and loving look of the soul means acts of the understanding,—for it is a look; and acts of the will, for the look is a loving one; and acts produced by free-will, without any strict necessity, for the look is a free look." "We should not compare Passive Contemplation," as did Bossuet, "to prophecy, or to the gift of tongues or of miracles; nor may we say that this mystical state consists principally in something wrought by God within us without our co-operation, and where, consequently, there neither is nor can be any merit. We must, on the contrary, to speak correctly, say that the substance of such Passive Prayer, taken in its specific acts, is free, meritorious, and operated within us by a grace that acts together with us" "It is the attraction to the acts which the soul now produces which, as by a secondary and counter-effect, occasions a quasi-incapacity for those acts which it does not produce. Now this attraction is not of a

[1] *Analyse, loc. cit.* pp. cxxii, cxxiii, *Lettre sur l'Oraison Passive, Œuvres,* Vol. VIII, p. 47.

[2] *Analyse,* p. cxxiii.

kind to deprive the soul of the use of its free-will: we see this from the nature of the acts which this attraction causes the soul to produce. Whence I conclude that this same attraction does not, again, deprive it of its liberty with regard to the acts which it prevents. The attraction but prevents the latter in the way it produces the other,—by an efficacious influence that involves no sheer necessity." "'Passivity,' if it comes from God, ever leaves the soul fully free for the exercise of the distinct virtues demanded by God in the Gospel; the *attrait* is truly divine only in so far as it draws the soul on to the perfect fulfilment of the evangelical counsels and promises concerning all the virtues." "The inspiration of the Passive state is but an habitual inspiration for the interior acts of evangelical piety. It renders the Passive soul neither infallible nor impeccable, nor independent of the Church even for its interior direction, nor exempt from the obligation of meriting and growing in virtue. . . . The inspiration of the passive soul differs from that of actively just souls only in being purer; that is, more exempt from all natural self-seeking, more full, more simple, more continuous, and more developed at each moment. We have, throughout, ever one and the same inspiration, which but grows in perfection and purity in proportion as the soul renounces itself more, and becomes more sensitive to the divine impressions." [1]

Thus we get an impressive, simple and yet varied, conception of spirituality, in which a real continuity, and a power and obligation of mutual understanding and aid underlies all the changes of degree and form, from first to last. For from first to last there are different degrees, but of the same supernatural grace acting in and upon the same human nature responsive in different degrees and ways. From first to last there is, necessarily and at every step, the Supernatural: at no point is there any necessary presence of, or essential connection with, the Miraculous or the Abnormal.

4. *Spinoza, Leibniz, Kant.*

Theology and Philosophy have not ceased to occupy themselves, at least indirectly, with the substance of these great questions, since they furnished the subject-matter to Bossuet and Fénelon in their memorable controversy; somewhat over-subtle although some of it was in its earlier phases, owing to Fénelon's chivalrous anxiety to defend, as far as possible, the

[1] *Lettre sur l'Oraison Passive, Œuvres*, Vol. VIII, pp. 10; 18, 11, 12; 14, 15; 74.

very expressions, often so nebulous and shifting, of his cousin, Madame Guyon.

(1) Indeed about twenty years before that controversy, Spinoza had, in his *Theologico-Political Treatise*, and then, more impressively still, in his *Ethics*, made a brilliant assault upon all, especially all religious, self-seeking. Also on this point these writings showed that strange, pathetic combination of grandly religious intuitions and instincts with a Naturalistic system which, logically, leaves no room for those deepest requirements of that great soul; and here they revealed, in addition, considerable injustice towards the, doubtless very mixed and imperfect, motives of average humanity.

True intuition speaks in his *Treatise* (published in 1670) in the words: "Since the love of God is man's supreme beatitude and the final end and scope of all human actions: it follows that only that man conforms to the divine law, who strives to love God, not from fear of punishment, nor from the love of some other thing, such as delights, fame, and so forth, but from this motive alone, that he knows God, or that he knows the knowledge and love of God, to be his supreme end." But a little further back we learn that "the more we know the things of Nature, the greater and the more perfect knowledge of God do we acquire"; a frank application of the pure Pantheism of his reasoned system.

In his *Ethics*, again, a noble intuition finds voice where he says: "Even if we did not know our Mind," our individual soul, "to be eternal, we should still put Piety and Religion and, in a word, all those virtues that are to be referred to magnanimity and generosity, first in our esteem." But he is doubtless excessive in his picturing of the downright, systematic immorality of attitude of ordinary men—the "slaves" and "mercenaries." "Unless this hope of laying aside the burdens of Piety and Religion after death and of receiving the price of their service, and this fear of being punished by dire punishments after death were in men, and if they, contrariwise, believed that their minds would perish with their bodies: they would let themselves go to their natural inclination and would decide to rule all their actions according to their lust." And he is doubtlessly, though nobly, excessive in his contrary ideal: "He who loves God cannot strive that God shall love him in return,"—an ideal which is, however, certainly in part determined by his philosophy, which knows no ultimate abiding personality or consciousness either in God or man.

Yet, once again, we have him at his inspiring best when, Catherine-like, he tells us: "The supreme Good of those who pursue virtue is common to them all, and all are equally able to rejoice in it"; and "this love towards God is incapable of being stained by the passions of envy and bitterness, but is increased in proportion as we figure to ourselves a larger number of men joined to God by the same bonds of love"; when he declares: "we do not enjoy beatitude because we master our passions; rather, contrariwise, do we master our passions because we enjoy beatitude"; and when he insists, with no doubt too indiscriminating, too Jacopone-like, a simplification, upon what, in its substance, is a profound truth: "the intellectual," the pure "love of the soul for God is the very love of God, wherewith God loves Himself."[1]

(2) It was, however, the astonishingly circumspect and many-sided Leibniz who, indefinitely smaller soul though he was, succeeded, perhaps better than any other modern philosopher, in successfully combining the divers constitutive elements of the act and state of Pure Love, when he wrote in 1714: "Since true Pure Love consists in a state of soul which makes me find pleasure in the perfections and the felicity of the object loved by me, this love cannot but give us the greatest pleasure of which we are capable, when God is that object. And, though this love be disinterested, it already constitutes, even thus simply by itself, our greatest good and deepest interest."

Or, as he wrote in 1698: "Our love of others cannot be separated from our true good, nor our love of God from our felicity. But it is equally certain that the consideration of our own particular good, as distinguished from the pleasure which we taste in seeing the felicity of another, does not enter into Pure Love." And earlier still he had defined the act of loving as "the finding one's pleasure in the felicity of another"; and had concluded thence that Love is for man essentially an enjoyment, although the specific motive of love is not the pleasure or the particular good of him who loves, but the good or the felicity of the beloved object.[2]

[1] *Tractatus Theologico-Politicus*, c. iv, opening of par. 4, ed. Van Vloten et Land, 1895, Vol. II, p. 4; *ibid.* middle of par. 3, p. 3; *Ethica*, p. v, prop. xli, *ibid.* Vol. I, p. 264; *ibid. Scholion*, p. 265; *ibid.* prop. xix, p. 251; *ibid.* prop. xx, p. 251; *ibid.* prop. xlii, p. 265; *ibid.* prop. xxxvi, p. 261.

[2] *Die Philosophischen Schriften von Leibniz*, ed. Gebhardt, Vol. VI, 1885, pp. 605, 606; and quotation in Gosselin's *Analyse, Œuvres de Fénelon*, 1820, Vol. IV, pp. clxxviii, clxxvii.

(3) Yet it is especially Kant who, with his predominant hostility to all Eudaemonism in Morality and Religion, has, more than all others, renewed the controversy as to the relations between virtue and piety on the one hand, and self-seeking motives on the other, and who is popularly credited with an entirely self-consistent antagonism to even such a wise and necessary attitude as are the amended positions of Fénelon and those of Leibniz. And yet I sincerely doubt whether (if we put aside the question as to the strictly logical consequences of his Critical Idealism, such as that Idealism appears in its greatest purity in the *Critique of Pure Reason*, 1781; and if we neglect the numerous, often grossly unjust, Spinoza-like sallies against the supposed undiluted mercenariness of ordinary piety, which abound in his *Religion within the Limits of Pure Reason*, 1793) we could readily find any explicit pronouncement hopelessly antagonistic to the Catholic Pure-Love doctrine.

Certainly the position taken up towards this point in that very pregnant and curious, largely-overlooked little treatise, *The Canon of Pure Reason*, which (evidently an earlier and complete sketch), has been inserted by him into his later, larger, but materially altered scheme of the *Critique* of 1781, (where it now forms the *Zweite Hauptstück* of the *Transcendentale Methodenlehre*, ed. Kehrbach, Reclam, pp. 603–628), appears to be substantially acceptable.[1] "Happiness consists in the satisfaction of all our inclinations, according to their various character, intensity, and duration. The law of practical action, in so far as it is derived from the motive of happiness, I call Pragmatic, a Rule of Good Sense; the same law, in so far as it has for its motive only the becoming worthy of such happiness, I call Moral, the Moral Law. Now Morality already by itself constitutes a system, but Happiness does not do so, except in so far as Happiness is distributed in exact accordance with Morality. But such a distribution is only possible in the intelligible world,"—the world beyond phenomena which can be reached by our reason alone—" and under a wise Originator and Ruler. Such an One, together with life in such a world—a world which we are obliged to consider as a future one—reason finds itself forced to assume, or else to look upon the moral laws as empty phantoms, since the necessary result of these laws,—a result which that same reason

[1] It is to Schweizer's admirable monograph, *Die Religions-Philosophie Kant's*, 1899, pp. 4–70, that I owe my clear apprehension of this very interesting doubleness in Kant's outlook.

connects with their very idea,—would have to fall away, if that assumption were to go. Hence every one looks upon the moral laws as *commandments*, a thing which they could not be, if they did not conjoin with their rule consequences of *a priori* appropriateness, and hence if they did not carry with them *promises* and *threats*. But this too they can do only if they lie within the compass of a Single Necessary Being, Itself the Supreme Good, Which alone can render possible such a unity embracing both means and end.—Happiness alone is, for our reason, far from being the Complete Good, for reason does not approve of Happiness unless it be united with the being worthy of Happiness, *i. e.* Moral Rectitude. But Morality alone, and with it the simple being worthy of happiness, is also far from the Complete Good. Even if reason, free from any consideration of any interest of its own, were to put itself in the position of a being that had to distribute all happiness to others alone, it could not judge otherwise: for, in the complete idea of practical action, both points are in essential conjunction, yet in suchwise that it is the moral disposition which, as condition, first renders possible a sharing in happiness, and not the prospect of happiness which first gives an opening to the moral disposition. For, in this latter case, the disposition would not be moral, and, consequently, would not deserve that complete happiness to which reason can assign no other limitation than such as springs from our own immoral attitude of will." [1]

In his *Foundation of the Metaphysic of Morals*, 1785, the noble apostrophe to the Good Will no doubt appears formally to proclaim as possible and desirable a complete human disposition, in which no considerations of Happiness play any part: "The good will is good, not through what it effects or produces, not through its utility for the attainment of any intention or end, but it is good through the quality of the volition alone; that is, it is good in itself. . . ." "If, with its greatest efforts, nothing were to be effected by it, and only the good will itself were to remain, this bare will would yet shine in lonely splendour as a jewel,—as something which has its full value in itself." But further on he shows us how, after all, "this good will cannot, then, be the only and the whole good, but still it is the highest good and the condition for all the rest, even for our desire of happiness." [2] Certain

[1] *Loc. cit.* pp. 611, 614, 615, 616.
[2] Kant's *Werke*, ed. Berlin Academy, Vol. IV, 1903, pp. 393, 394; 396.

exaggerations, which are next developed by him here, shall be considered in a later chapter.

5. *Four important points.*

Here I will but put together, in conclusion, four positions which I have rejoiced to find in two such utterly, indeed at times recklessly, independent writers as Professor Georg Simmel of Berlin and Professor A. E. Taylor.

(1) Dr. Simmel declares, with admirable cogency: "The concept of religion completely loses in Kant, owing to his rationalistic manner of discovering in it a mere compound of the moral interest and the striving after happiness, its most specific and deepest character. No doubt these two apprehensions are also essential to religion, but precisely the direction in which Kant conjoins them,—that duty issues in happiness, is the least characteristic of religion, and is only determined by his Moralism, which refuses to recognize the striving after happiness as a valuable motive. The opposite direction appears to me as far more decisively a part of religion and of its incomparable force: for we thus find in religion precisely that ideal power, which makes it the duty of man to win his own salvation. According to the Kantian Moralism, it is every man's private affair how he shall meet his requirement of happiness; and to turn such a private aspiration into an objective, ideal claim, would be for Kant a contradiction and abomination. In reality, however, religion itself *requires* that man should have a care for his own welfare and beatitude, and in this consists its incomparable force of attraction." [1] Let the reader note how entirely this agrees with, whilst properly safeguarding, the doctrine of Pure Love: it is the precise position of the best critics of the unamended Fénelon.

(2) Professor Taylor insists that "it is possible to desire directly and immediately pleasant experiences which are not my own. . . . Because it is *I* who in every case have the pleasure of the anticipation, it is assumed that it must be I who am to experience the realization of the anticipation." Yet "it is really no more paradoxical that I should anticipate with pleasure some event which is not to form part of my own direct sensible experience, than it is that I should find pleasure in the anticipation at twenty of myself at eighty." "The austerest saints will and can mortify themselves as a thing well-pleasing

[1] Kant, 1904, p. 131.

to God." [1] In this way the joy of each constituent of the Kingdom of God in the joys of all the rest, and in the all-pervading joy of God, is seen to be as possible as it is undoubtedly actual: the problem of the relation between pleasure and egoism is solved.

(3) And Professor Taylor again insists upon how pleasant experiences, which do not owe their pleasantness to their relation to a previous anticipation, are not, properly speaking, good or worthy. It is by "satisfactions" and not by mere "pleasures" that "even the most confirmed Hedonist must compute the goodness of a life. . . . Only when the pleasant experience includes in itself the realization of an idea is it truly good." [2] But, if so, then the experience will be good, not in proportion as it is unpleasant, as Kant was so prone to imply; nor directly in proportion as it is pleasant, although pleasantness will accompany or succeed it, of a finer quality if not of a greater intensity, according as the idea which it embodies is good: but directly in proportion to the goodness of that idea. Thus all things licit, from sense to spirit, will find their place and function in such acts, and in a life composed of such acts, spirit expressing itself in terms of sense. And the purification, continuously necessary for the ever more adequate expression of the one in and by the other, will be something different from any attempt at suppressing this means of expression. Thus here again the great Christian Incarnation-Doctrine appears as the deepest truth, and as the solution of the problem as to the relations of pleasure and duty.[3]

(4) And finally, as to the ever-present need and importance of a theory concerning these matters, Professor Taylor points out, not only that some such theory is necessary to the full human life, but that it must place an infinite ideal before us: paradox though it may sound, nothing less is truly practical, for "any end that is to be permanently felt as worth striving for, must be infinite," and therefore "in a sense infinitely remote"; and hence "if indifference to the demand for a

[1] *The Problem of Conduct*, pp. 336, 337; 329.

[2] *Ibid.* p. 327.

[3] See James Seth, *A Study of Ethical Principles*, 1894, pp. 193–236 where this position, denominated there "Eudaemonism," is contrasted with "Hedonism," uniquely or at least predominantly occupied with the act's sensational materials or concomitances, and "Rigorism," with its one-sided insistence upon the rational form and end of action.

practicable ideal be the mark of a dreamer or a fanatic, contentment with a finite and practicable ideal is no less undeniably the mark of an *esprit borné*." [1]

Here Fénelon has adequately interpreted the permanent and complete requirements of the religious life and spirit. "You tell me," he says to his adversaries, "that 'Christianity is not a school of Metaphysicians.' All Christians cannot, it is true, be Metaphysicians; but the principal Theologians have great need to be such. It was by a sublime Metaphysic that St. Augustine soared above the majority of the other Fathers, who were, for the rest, as fully versed in Scripture and Tradition. It was by his lofty Metaphysic that St. Gregory of Nazianzum has merited the distinguishing title of *Theologian*. It is by Metaphysic that St. Anselm and St. Thomas have been such great luminaries of the Church. True, the Church is not 'a school of Metaphysicians,' who dispute without docility, as did the ancient sects of philosophers. Yet she is a school in which St. Paul teaches that Charity is more perfect than Hope, and in which the holiest Doctors declare, in accordance with the principles of the Fathers, that Love is more perfect, precisely because it 'abides in God, not in view of any benefit that may accrue to us from so doing.'" "I know well," Fénelon writes to a friend, "that men misuse the doctrines of Pure Love and Resignation; I know that there are hypocrites who, under cover of such noble terms, overthrow the Gospel. Yet it is the worst of all procedures to attempt the destruction of perfect things, from a fear that men will make a wrong use of them." Notwithstanding all misuse of the doctrine—"the very perfection of Christianity is Pure Love." [2]

[1] Taylor, *op. cit.* p. 901.

[2] *Seconde Lettre à Monsieur de Paris, Œuvres*, Vol. V, pp. 268, 269. *Lettres de M. de Cambrai à un de ses Amis, ibid.*, Vol. IV, p. 168.

CHAPTER XII

THE AFTER-LIFE PROBLEMS AND DOCTRINES

MOVING on now to the questions concerning the After-Life, it will be convenient to consider them under five heads: the chief present-day positions and perplexities with regard to belief in the After-Life in General; the main implications and convictions inherent to an Eschatology such as Catherine's; and then the principal characteristics, difficulties, and helps of her tendencies and teachings concerning Hell, Purgatory, and Heaven. And throughout the Chapter we shall busy ourselves directly only with the After-Life in the sense of a heightened, or at least an equal, consciousness after death, as compared to that which existed before death: the belief in a shrunken state of survival, in non-annihilation, appearing to be as certainly the universal minimum of belief as such a minimum is not Immortality.

I. THE CHIEF PRESENT-DAY PROBLEMS, PERPLEXITIES, AND REQUIREMENTS WITH REGARD TO THE AFTER-LIFE IN GENERAL.

Now I take our chief present-day problems, perplexities, and resultant requirements with regard to the After-Life in general, to fall into three groups, according as those problems are predominantly Historical, or Philosophical, or directly Practical and Ethical.

1. *Three Historical Difficulties.*

The Historical group now brings very clearly and certainly before us the striking non-universality, the startling lateness, and the generally strange fitfulness and apparent unreasonableness characterizing the earliest stage of belief in the soul's heightened, or at least equivalent, consciousness after death.

(1) Now with respect to the Non-Universality of the doctrine, it is true that, in China, Confucianism is full of care for the dead. "Throughout the Empire, the authorities are obliged to

hold three annual sacrifices for the refreshment and rest of the souls of the dead in general." "It is hardly doubtful that the cultus of Ancestors formed the chief institution in classical Confucianism, and constituted the very centre of religion for the people. Even now ancestor-worship is the only form of religion for which rules, applicable to the various classes among the Emperor's subjects, are laid down in the Dynastic Statutes." And Professor De Groot, from whom I am quoting, gives an interesting conspectus of the numberless ways in which the religious service of the dead penetrates Chinese life.[1]—Yet we hear of Kong-Tse (Confucius) himself (551–478 B.C.), that, though he insisted upon the most scrupulous execution of the three hundred rules of the then extant temple-ceremonial, which were no doubt largely busy with the dead, and though he said that one should sacrifice to the spirits as if they were present, he designated, in several of his sayings, occupation with theological problems as useless: "as long as we do not know men, how shall we know spirits? As long as we do not understand life, how should we fathom death?" And to questions relative to the spirits and the dead, he would give evasive answers.[2] Thus the founder of the most characteristic of the Chinese religions was without any clear and consistent conviction on the point in question.

In India we find, for Brahmanic religion, certain unmistakable Immortality-Doctrines (in the sense of the survival of the soul's self-consciousness), expressed in the hymns of the *Rig-Veda*.—But already, in the philosophizings of the *Upanishads*, we get a world-soul, and this soul's exclusive permanence: "to attain to true unity, the very duality of subject and object is to disappear. The terms Atman and Brahman here express the true Being which vivifies all beings and appearances, and with which cognizing man reunites himself whilst losing his individual existence."[3]

And if we move on to Buddhism, with its hundreds of millions of adherents in Burmah, Tibet, China, and Japan, we can learn, from the classical work of Oldenberg, how interestingly deep down lies the reason for the long conflict between

[1] Chantepie de la Saussaye, *Lehrbuch der Religions-Geschichte*, ed. 1905, Vol. I, pp. 69, 73–83.

[2] Chantepie de la Saussaye, *Lehrbuch der Religions-Geschichte*, ed. 1887, Vol. I, pp. 248, 249.

[3] *Ibid.* pp. 358, 373.

scholars as to whether Nirvana is or is not to be taken for the complete extinction of the individual soul. "Everything, in the Buddhist dogmatic system, is part and parcel of a circle of Becoming and of Dissolution: all things are but a Dhamma, a Sankhara; and all Dhamma, all Sankhara are but temporary. . . . The Mutable, Conditioned is here thinkable only as conditioned by another Mutable and Conditioned. If we follow the dialectic consequence alone, there is no seeing how, according to this system, there can remain over, when a succession and mutual destruction of things conditioning and of things conditioned has run its course, anything but a pure vacuum." And we have also such a saying of the Buddha as the following. "Now if, O disciples, the Ego (*atta*) and anything appertaining to the Ego (*attaniya*) cannot be comprehended with accuracy and certainty, is not then the faith which declares: 'This is the world, and this is the Ego; this shall I become at death,—firm, constant, eternal, unchangeable,—thus shall I be there, throughout eternity,'—is not this sheer empty folly?" "How should it not, O Lord, be sheer empty folly?" answer the disciples. "One who spoke thus," is Oldenberg's weighty comment, "cannot have been far from the conviction that Nirvana is annihilation. Yet it is understandable how the very thinkers, who were capable of bearing this consequence, should have hesitated to raise it to the rank of an official dogma of the community. . . . Hence the official doctrine of the Buddhist Church attained the form, that, on the question of the real existence of the Ego, of whether or not the perfected saint lives on after death, the exalted Buddha has taught nothing. Indeed the legally obligatory doctrine of the old community required of its votaries an explicit renunciation of all knowledge concerning the existence or non-existence of completely redeemed souls."

"Buddhism," so Oldenberg sums up the matter, with, I think, the substantial adhesion of all present-day competent authorities, "teaches that there is a way out of the world of created things, out into the dark Infinite. Does this way lead to new being? or does it lead to nothingness? Buddhist belief maintains itself on the knife's edge of these alternatives. The desire of the heart, as it longs for the Eternal, is not left without something, and yet the thinking mind is not given a something that it could grasp and retain. The thought of the Infinite, the Eternal, could not be present at all, and yet vanish further away than here, where, a mere breath and on the point of sinking into sheer nothingness, it threatens to disappear altogether." [1] This vast Buddhist community, numbering, perhaps, a third of the human race, should not, then, be forgotten, when we urge the contrary instances of the religions of Assyria and Babylonia; of Egypt; of Greece and Rome; and, above all, of the Jews and Christianity.

Yet it is well to remember that such non-universality of belief is at least as real, to this very hour, for such a fundamental religious truth and practice as Monotheism and Monolatry; such purely Ethical convictions as Monogamy and the Illicitness of Slavery; such a plain dictate of the universal humanitarian ideal as the illegitimacy of the application of physical compulsion in matters of religious conviction; and such directly demonstrable psychical and natural facts as subconsciousness in the human soul, the sexual character of plants, and the earth's rotundity and rotation around the sun. In none of these cases can we claim more than that the higher, truer doctrine,—that is, the one which explains and transcends the element of truth contained in its predecessor and opposite,—is explicitly reached by a part only of humanity, and is but implied and required by other men, at their best. Yet this is clearly enough for leaving us free to decide,—reasonably conclusive evidence for their truth being forthcoming,—in favour of the views of the minority: since the assumption of an equality of spiritual and moral insight and advance throughout mankind is as little based upon fact, as would be the supposition of men's equal physical strength or height, or of any other quality or circumstance of their nature and environment.

(2) The lateness of the doctrine's appearance, precisely in the cases where there can be no doubt of its standing for a conviction of an endless persistence of a heightened consciousness after death,—that is, amongst the Greeks (and Romans) and the Jews (and Christians),—has now been well established by critical historical research.

With regard to the Greeks,[2] the matter is particularly plain,

[1] Oldenberg, *Buddha*, ed. 1897, pp. 310–328; especially 313, 314; 316, 317; 327, 328.

[2] My chief authority here has been that astonishingly living and many-sided book, Erwin Rohde's *Psyche*, ed. 1898, especially Vol. II, pp. 263–295 (Plato); Vol. I, pp. 14–90 (Homer); 91–110 (Hesiod); pp. 146–199 (the Heroes); pp. 279–319, and Vol. II, pp. 1–136 (Eleusinian Mysteries, Dionysian Religion, the Orphics). The culminating interest of this great work lies in this last treble section and in the Plato part.

since we can still trace even in Plato, (427 to 347 B.C.), who, next to Our Lord Himself and to St. Paul, is doubtless the greatest and most influential teacher of full individual Immortality that the world has seen, two periods of thought in this matter, and can show that the first was without any such certain conviction. In his *Apology of Socrates*, written soon after the execution in 399 B.C., he makes his great master, close to his end, declare that death would bring to man either a complete unconsciousness, like to a dreamless sleep, or a transition into another life,—a life here pictured like to the Homeric Hades. Both possibilities Socrates made to accept resignedly, in full reliance on the justice of the Gods, and to look no further; how should he know what is known to no man?—And this is Plato's own earlier teaching. For in the very *Republic* which, in its chronologically later constituents, (especially in Book V, 471*c*, to the end of Book VIII, Book IX, 560*d* to 588*a*, and Book X up to 608*b*), so insists upon and develops the truth and importance of Immortality in the strictest, indeed the sublimest sense: we get, in its earlier portions, (especially in Book II, 10*c*, to Book V, 460*c*), no trace of any such conviction. For, in these earlier passages, the Guardians in the Ideal State are not to consider what may come after death: the central theme is the manner in which Justice carries with it its own recompense; and the rewards, that are popularly wont to be placed before the soul, are referred to ironically,—Socrates is determined to do without such hopes. In those later portions, on the contrary, there is the greatest insistence upon the importance of caring, not for this short life alone, but for the soul's "whole time" and for what awaits it after death. And in the still later parts, (as in Books VI and VII,) the sublimest form of Immortality is presupposed as true and actual throughout. Thus in Greece it is not till about 390–380 B.C., and in Plato himself not till his middle life, that we get a quite definite and final doctrine of the Immortality of all souls, and of a blessed after-existence for every just and holy life here below.

For the survival after the body's death, indubitably attributed to the Psyche in the Homeric Poems, is conceived there, throughout, as a miserably shrunken consciousness, and one which is dependent for its continuance upon the good offices bestowed by the survivors upon the corpse and grave. And the translation of the still living Menelaus to Elysium

(Od. IV, 560–568) is probably a later insertion; belongs to a small class of exceptional cases; implies the writer's inability to conceive a heightened consciousness for the soul, after the soul's separation from the body; and is based, not upon any virtue or reward, but upon Menelaus's family-relationship to Zeus. Ganymede gets similarly translated because of his physical beauty (*Il.* XX, 232 *seq.*).

Hesiod, though later than Homer as a writer, gives us, in his account of the Five Ages of the World (*Works and Days*, ll. 109–201), some traces of an Animistic conception of a heightened life of the bodiless soul beyond the grave,—a conception which had been neglected or suppressed by Homer, but which had evidently been preserved alive in the popular religion of, at least, Central Greece. Yet Hesiod knows of such a life only for the Golden and for the Silver Ages, and for some miraculous, exceptional cases of the fourth, the Heroic Age: already in the third, the Bronze Age, and still more emphatically in his own fifth, the Iron Age, there are no such consolations: nothing but the shrunken consciousness of the Homeric after-death Psyche is, quite evidently, felt by him to be the lot of all souls in the hard, iron present.

The Cultus of the Heroes is already registered in Draco's Athenian Laws, in about 620 B.C., as a traditional custom. And these Heroes have certainly lived at one time as men upon earth, and have become heroes only after death; their souls, though severed from the body, live a heightened imperishable life, indeed one that can mightily help men here below and now,—so at Delphi and at Salamis against the Persians. Yet here again each case of such an elevation was felt to be a miracle, an exception incapable of becoming a universal law: not even the germ of a belief in the Immortality of the soul as such seems to be here.

The Cultus of the Nether-World Deities, of the Departed generally, and, as the culmination of all this movement, the Eleusinian Mysteries, must not be conceived as involving or as leading to, any belief in the ecstatic elevation of the soul, or consciousness of its God-likeness; and such unending bliss as is secured, is gained by men, not because they are virtuous and devout, but through their initiation into the Mysteries. Rohde assures us, rightly I think, that "it remains unproved that, during the classical period of Greek culture, the belief in Judges and a Judgment to be held in Hades over the deeds done by men on earth, had struck root among the people";

Professor Percy Gardner adds his great authority to the same conclusion.[1] Here again it is Plato who is the first to take up a clearly and consistently spiritual and universalistic position.

Indeed it is only in the predominantly neuropathic, indeed largely immoral and repulsive, forms of the Dionysiac sect and movement, (at work, perhaps, already in the eighth century B.C. and which leads on to the formation of the more aristocratic and priestly Orphic communities) that a demonstrable and direct belief arose in the soul's intrinsic God-likeness, or even divinity, and in its immortality, or even eternity; and that stimulations, materials, and conceptions were furnished to Greek thought, which are traceable wheresoever it henceforth inclines to belief in the soul's intrinsic Immortality.

Yet the leaven spread but slowly into philosophy. For the Ionian philosophers, and among them Heraclitus, the impressive teacher of the flux of all things, flourish from about 600 to 430 B.C.; but, *naïve* Materialists and Pantheists as they are, they frankly exclude all survival of individual consciousness after death. The Eleatic philosophers live between 550 and 450 B.C., and are all busy with *a priori* logical constructions of the physical world, conceived as sole and self-explanatory; and amongst them is Parmenides, the powerful propounder of the complete identity and immutability of all reality. Those transcendent spiritual beliefs appear first as part, indeed as the very foundation, although still rather of a mode of life than of a formal philosophy, in the teaching and community of Pythagoras, who seems to have lived about 580 to 490 B.C., and who certainly emigrated from Asia Minor to Croton in Southern Italy. The soul appears here as intrinsically immortal, indeed without beginning and without end. And then Immortality forms one (the mystical) of the two thoroughly heterogeneous elements of the, otherwise predominantly Ionic and Materialistic, philosophy of Empedocles of Agrigentum in Sicily, about 490 to 435 B.C. In both these cases the Dionysiac-Orphic provenance of the "Immortality"-doctrines is clearly apparent.

And then, among the poets who bridge over the period up to Plato, we find Pindar, who, alongside of reproductions of the ordinary, popular conceptions, gives us at times lofty,

[1] *Psyche*, Vol. I, pp. 308, 312. *New Chapters in Greek History*, 1892, pp. 333, 334.

Orphic-like teachings as to the eternity, the migration, and the eventual persistent rest and happiness of the just Soul, and as to the suffering of the unjust one; Aeschylus, who primarily dwells upon the Gods' judgment in this life, and who makes occasional allusions to the after-life which are partly still of the Homeric type; Sophocles, who indeed refers to the special privileges which, in the after-life, attend upon the souls that have here been initiated into the Eleusinian Mysteries, and who causes Oedipus to be translated, whilst still alive, to Other-World happiness, but who knows nothing of an unceasing heightened consciousness for all men after death; and Euripides, who, showing plainly the influence of the Sophists, gives expression, alongside of Pantheistic identifications of the soul and of the aether, to every kind of misgiving and doubt as to any survival after death.

And as to the appearance of the doctrine among the Jews, we again find a surprising lateness. I follow here, with but minor contributions and modifications from other writers and myself, the main conclusions of Dr. Charles's standard *Critical History of the Doctrine of a Future Life*, London, 1899, whose close knowledge of the subject is unsurpassed, and who finds as many and as early attestations as are well-nigh findable by serious workers.[1]

" The primitive beliefs of the individual Israelite regarding the future life, being derived from Ancestor-worship, were implicitly antagonistic to Yahwism, from its first proclamation by Moses. . . . This antagonism becomes explicit and results in the final triumph of Yahwism." And to the early Israelite, even under Yahwism, " the religious unit was " not the individual but " the family or tribe." Thus, even fully six centuries after Moses, " the message of the prophets of the eighth century," Amos, Hosea, Isaiah, Micah, " is still directed to the nation, and the judgments they proclaim are collective punishment for collective guilt. It is not till late in the seventh century B.C. that the problem of individual retribution really emerged, and received its first solution in the teaching of Jeremiah." And " the further development of these ideas," by the teaching of Ezekiel and of some of the Psalms and Proverbs, as regards individual responsibility and retribution in this life, and by the deep misgivings and keen questionings of Job and Ecclesiastes, as to the adequacy of

[1] See also the important study of the Abbé Touzard, *Le Développement de la Doctrine de l'Immortalité, Revue Biblique*, 1898, pp. 207–241.

this teaching, "led inevitably to the conception of a blessed life beyond the grave."

Yet throughout the Hebrew Old Testament the Eschatology of the Nation greatly predominates over that of the Individual. Indeed in pre-Exilic times "the day of Yahwe," with its national judgments, constitutes the all but exclusive subject of the prophetic teaching as to the future. Only from the Exile, (597 to 538 B.C.), onwards, does the eschatological development begin to grow in complexity, for now the individualism first preached by Jeremiah begins to maintain its claim also. But not till the close of the fourth century, or the beginning of the third century B.C., do the separate eschatologies of the individual and of the nation issue finally in their synthesis: the righteous individual will participate in the Messianic Kingdom, the righteous dead of Israel will arise to share therein,—thus in Isaiah xxvi, 1–19, a passage which it is difficult to place earlier than about 334 B.C. The resurrection is here limited to the just. In Daniel xii, 2, which is probably not earlier than 165 B.C., the resurrection is extended, not indeed to all members of Israel, but, with respective good and evil effects, to its martyrs and apostates.

And the slowness and incompleteness of the development throughout the Hebrew Old Testament is strikingly illustrated by the great paucity of texts which yield, without the application of undue pressure, any clear conviction or hope of a heightened, or even a sheer, maintenance of the soul's this-life consciousness and force after death. Besides the passages just indicated, Dr. Charles can only find Psalms xlix and lxxiii, and Job xix, 25–27, all three, according to him, later than Ezekiel, who died in 571 B.C.[1] The textually uncertain and obscure Job-passage (xix, 25, 26) must be discounted, since it evidently demands interpretation according to the plain presupposition and point of the great poem as a whole.—And the same result is reached by the numerous, entirely unambiguous, passages which maintain the negative persuasion. In the hymn put into the mouth of the sick king Hezekiah, for about 713 B.C., (a composition which seems to be very late, perhaps only of the second century B.C.), we hear: "The grave cannot praise Thee . . . they that go down into the pit cannot hope for truth. The living, the living, he shall praise Thee, as I do this day." And the Psalter contains

[1] Charles, *op. cit.* pp. 52, 53; 58; 61; 84; 124, 125; 126–132; 68–77.

numerous similar declarations. Thus vi, 5: "In death there is no remembrance of Thee: in the grave who shall give Thee thanks?" and cxv, 17: "The dead praise not the Lord, neither any that go down into silence; but *we* praise the Lord." See also Psalms xxx, 19; lxxxviii, 11.

Indeed the name for the Departed is Rephaim, "the limp, the powerless ones." Stade well says: "According to the ancient Israelitish conception the entire human being, body and soul, outlasts death, whilst losing all that makes life worth living. That which persists in Sheol for all eternity is the form of man, emptied of all content. Antique thought ignores as yet that there exists no such thing as a form without substance. The conception has as little in common with the conviction of the Immortality of the Soul, which found its chief support in Greek ideas, as with the expectation of the Resurrection, which grew out of the Jewish Messianic hope, or with the Christian anticipation of Eternal Life, which is also based upon religious motives." [1]

Yet, with respect to this objection from the lateness of the doctrine, we must not forget that fully consistent Monotheism and Monogamy are also late, but not, on that account, less true or less precious; and indeed that, as a universal rule, the human mind has acquired at all adequate convictions as to most certain and precious truths but slowly and haltingly. This process is manifest even in Astronomy, Geology, Botany, Human Anatomy. It could not fail to be, not less but more the case in a matter like this which, if it concerns us most deeply, is yet both too close to us to be readily appreciated in its true proportions, and too little a matter of mathematical demonstration or of direct experience not to take much time to develop, and not to demand an ever-renewed acquisition and purification, being, as it is, the postulate and completion of man's ethical and spiritual faiths, at their deepest and fullest.

(3) And with regard to the unsatisfactory character of some of the earliest manifestations of the belief, this point is brought home to us, with startling vividness, in the beginnings of the doctrine in ancient Greece. For Rohde's very careful and competent examination of precisely this side of the whole question shows conclusively (even though I think, with Crusius, that he has overlooked certain rudiments of analogous but

[1] B. Stade, *Biblische Theologie des Alten Testaments*, Vol. I, 1905, p. 184.

healthy experiences and beliefs in pre-Dionysiac Greece) how new and permanently effective a contribution to the full doctrine was made, for the Hellenic world and hence indirectly for all Western humanity, by the self-knowledge gained in that wildly orgiastic upheaval, those dervish-like dances and ecstatic fits during the Dionysian night-celebrations on the Thracian mountain-sides. Indeed Rohde traces how from these experiences, partly from the continuation of them, partly from the reaction against them, on the part of the intensely dualistic and ascetic teaching and training of the Orphic sect, there arose, and filtered through to Pythagoras, to Plato, and to the whole Neo-Platonist school, the clear conception and precise terminology concerning ecstatic, enthusiastic states, the divinity and eternity of the human soul, its punitive lapse into and imprisonment within the body, and its need of purification throughout the earthly life and of liberation through death from this its incurably accidental and impeding companion.—Thus we get here, concerning one of the chief sources of at least the formulation of our belief in Immortality, what looks a very nest of suspicious, repulsive circumstances:—psycho-physical phenomena, which, quite explicable to, and indeed explained by, us now as in nowise supernatural, could not fail to appear portentous to those men who first experienced them; unmoral or immoral attitudes and activities of mind and will; and demonstrable excesses of feeling and conception as regards both the static goodness, the downright divinity, eternity, and increateness of the soul, and the unmixed evil of the body with its entirely disconnected alongsideness to the soul. Does not all this spell a mass of wild hallucination, impurity, fanaticism, and superstition?

Yet here again it behoves us, if not to accept, yet also not to reject, in wholesale fashion and in haste. For the profoundly experienced Professor Pierre Janet shows [1] us, what is now assumed as an axiom, and as the ultimate justification of the present widespread interest in the study of Hysteria, that "we must admit for the moral world the great principle universally admitted for the physical world since Claude Bernard,—viz. that the laws of illness are, at bottom, the same as those of health, and that, in the former, there is but the exaggeration or the diminution of phenomena which existed already in the latter."

And if thus our recent studies of morbid mentalities have

[1] *L'Automatisme Psychologique*, ed. 1903, p. 5.

been able to throw a flood of light upon the mechanism and character of the healthy mind, a mind more difficult to analyze precisely because of the harmonious interaction of its forces, there is nothing very surprising if man, in the past, learnt to know his own fundamental nature better in and through periods of abnormal excitation than in those of normal balance. And the resultant doctrines in the case in question only required, and demand again and again, a careful pruning and harmonizing to show forth an extraordinary volume of abiding truth. The insuppressible difference between mind and matter, and the distinction between the fully recollected soul (intuitive reason), and explicit reasoning; the immeasurable superiority of mind over matter, and the superiority of that full reason over this "thin" reasoning; the certainty, involved in all our inevitable mental categories and assumptions and in all our motives for action, of this mind and intuition being more like the cause of all things than are those other inferior realities and activities; the indestructibleness of the postulates and standards of objective and infinite Beauty, Truth, Goodness, of our consciousness of being intrinsically bound to them, and of our inmost humanity and its relative greatness being measurable by just this our consciousness of this our obligation, and hence by the keenness of our sense of failure, and by our striving after purification and the realization of our immanental possibilities: all this remains deeply fruitful and true.

And those crude early experiences and analyses certainly point to what, even now, are our most solid reasons for belief in Immortality: for if man's mind and soul can thus keenly suffer from the sense of the contingency and mutability of all things directly observed by it without and within, it must itself be, at least in part or potentially, outside of this flux which it so vividly apprehends as *not* Permanence, *not* Rest, *not* true Life. Let us overlook, then, and forgive the first tumultuous, childishly rude and clumsy, mentally and emotionally hyper-aesthetic forms of apprehension of these great spiritual facts and laws, forms which are not, after all, more misleading than is the ordinary anaesthetic condition of our apprehending faculties towards these fundamental forces and testimonies of our lot and nature. Not the wholesale rejection, then, of even those crude Dionysian witnessings, still less of the already more clarified Orphic teaching, and least of all of Plato's great utilizations and spiritualizations can be required of us, but only a reinterpretation of those first impressions and of mankind's analogous experiences, and a sifting and testing of the latter by the light of all that has been deeply lived through, and seriously thought out, by spiritually awake humanity ever since.—And we should remember that the history of the doctrine among the Jews is, as has already been intimated, grandly free from any such suspicious occasions and concomitances.

2. *Two Philosophical Difficulties.*

Yet it is precisely this latter, social, body-and-soul-survival doctrine which brings the second group of objections, the philosophical difficulties, to clear articulation. For thus we are unavoidably driven to one or other of the equally difficult alternatives, of a bodiless life of the soul, and of a survival or resurrection of the body.

(1) Christianity, by its explicit teachings, and even more by its whole drift and interior affinities, requires the survival of all that is essential to the whole man, and conceives this whole as constituted, not by thought alone but also by feeling and will and the power of effectuation; so that the body, or some unpicturable equivalent to it, seems necessary to this physico-spiritual, ultimately organic conception of what man is and must continue to be, if he is to remain man at all.—And Psychology, on its part, is showing us, more and more, how astonishingly wide and deep is the dependence, at least for their actuation, of the various functions and expressions of man's character and spirit upon his bodily frame. For not only is the reasoning faculty seen, ever since Aristotle, to depend, for its material and stimulation, upon the impressions of the senses, nor can we represent it to ourselves otherwise than as seated in the brain or in some such physical organism, but the interesting Lange-James observations and theory make it likely that also the emotions,—the feelings as distinct from sensations,—ever result, as a matter of fact, from certain foregoing, physico-neural impressions and modifications, which latter follow upon this or that perception of the mind, a perception which would otherwise, as is the case in certain neural lesions and anaesthesias, remain entirely dry and unemotional.[1]—And the sense of the Infinite, which we have had such reason to take as the very centre of religion, arises ever, within man's life here below, in contrast to, and as a con-

[1] W. James, *The Principles of Psychology*, 1891, Vol. II, pp. 442–467.

comitant and supplementation of, his perception of the Finite and Contingent, and hence not without his senses being alive and active.

Now all this fits in admirably with the whole Jewish-Christian respect for, high claims upon, and constant training of the body, the senses, the emotions, and with the importance attached to the Visible and Audible,—History, Institutions, Society.—Yet our difficulties are clear. For however spiritually we may conceive a bodily survival or resurrection; however completely we may place the identity of the various stages of the body in this life, and the sameness between the body before death and after the resurrection, in the identity of its quasi-creator, the body-weaving soul, we can in nowise picture to ourselves such a new, indefinitely more spiritual, incorporation, and we bring upon ourselves acute difficulties, for both before and after this unpicturable event. Before the resurrection there would have to be unconsciousness between death and that event; but thus the future life is broken up, and for no spiritual reason. Or there would be consciousness; but then the substitute for the body, that occasions this consciousness, would, apparently, render all further revivification of the body unnecessary. And if we take the resurrection as effected, we promptly feel how mixed and clumsy, how inadequate, how less, and not more, than the best and noblest elements of our experience and aspirations even here and now, is such a, still essentially temporal and spatial, mode of existence.

I take it that, against all this, we can but continue to maintain two points. The soul's life after bodily death is not a matter of experience or of logical demonstration, but a postulate of faith and a consequence from our realization of the human spirit's worth; and hence is as little capable of being satisfactorily pictured, as are all the other great spiritual realities which can nevertheless be shown to be presupposed and implicitly affirmed by every act of faith in the final truth and abiding importance of anything whatsoever.—And again, it is not worth while to attempt to rescue, Aristotle-wise, just that single, and doubtless not the highest, function of man's spirit and character, his dialectic faculty, or even his intellectual intuitive power, for the purpose of thus escaping, or at least minimizing, the difficulties attendant upon the belief in Immortality. If we postulate, as we do, man's survival, we must postulate, without being able to fill in or to justify any details of the scheme, the survival of all that may and does constitute man's true and ultimate personality. How much or how little this may precisely mean, we evidently know but very imperfectly: but we know enough to be confident that it means more than the abstractive, increasingly dualistic school of Plato, Philo, Plotinus, Proclus would allow.

(2) But speculative reason seems also to raise a quite general objection, based upon man's littleness within the immense Universe, and upon the arbitrariness of excepting those tiny points, those centres of human consciousness, men's souls, from the flux, the ceaseless becoming and undoing, of all the other parts of that mighty whole, immortal, surely, only *as* a whole.

Here we can safely say that, at least in this precise form, the difficulty springs predominantly not from reason or experience, but from an untutored imagination. For all our knowledge of that great external world, which this objection supposes to englobe our small internal world, as a part inferior, or at most but equal, to the other parts of that whole, is dependent upon this interior world of ours; and however truly inherent in that external world we may hold that world's laws to be, those laws can, after all, be shown to be as truly the result of our own mind's spontaneous work,—an architectonic building up by this mind of the sense-impressions conveyed to it from without. And that whole Universe, in so far as it is material, cannot be compared, either in kind or in dignity, to Mind: only the indications there, parallel in this to our experiences within our own mind, of a Mind and Spirit infinitely greater and nobler than, yet with a certain affinity to, our own,—only these constitute that outer world as great as this our inner world. Indeed it is plain that Materialism is so far from constituting the solution to the problem of existence, that even Psycho-Physical Parallelism, even the attribution of any ultimate reality to Matter, are on their trial. It is anyhow already clear that, of the two, it is easier and nearer to the truth to maintain that Matter and its categories are simply modes in the manifestation of Mind to minds and in the apprehension of Mind by minds, than to declare Mind to be but a function or resultant of Matter.[1]

But if all this is so, then no simply sensible predominance of the sensible Universe, nor even any ascertainment of the

[1] See Prof. James Ward's closely knit proof in his *Naturalism and Agnosticism*, 2nd ed., 1905, and his striking address, "Mechanism and Morals," *Hibbert Journal*, October, 1905.

mere flux and interchange of and between all things material and their elements, can reasonably affect the question as to the superiority and permanence of Mind. But we shall return, in the next chapter, to the difficulties special to the Immortality of individual human spirits or personalities,—for this is, I think, the point at which the problem is still acute.

3. *Three Ethico-Practical Difficulties.*

The last group of objections is directly practical and ethical, and raises three points : the small space and influence occupied and exercised, apparently, by such a belief, in the spiritual life of even serious persons; the seemingly selfish, ungenerous type of religion and of moral tone fostered by definite belief in, or at least occupation with, the thought of an individual future life, as contrasted with the nobility of tone engendered by such denials or abstractions from all such beliefs as we find in Spinoza and Schleiermacher; and, finally, the plausibility of the teaching, on the part of some distinguished thinkers and poets, that a positive conviction of this our short earthly life being the sole span of our individual consciousness is directly productive of a certain deep tenderness, an heroic concentration of attention, and a virile truthfulness, which are unattainable, which indeed are weakened or rendered impossible by, the necessarily vague anticipation of an unending future life; a hope which, where operative at all, can but dwarf and deaden all earthly aspiration and endeavour.

(1) As to the first point, which has perhaps never been more brilliantly affirmed than by Mr. Schiller,[1] I altogether doubt whether the numerous appearances, which admittedly seem to point that way, are rightly interpreted by such a conclusion. For it is, for one thing, most certainly possible to be deeply convinced of the reality and importance of the soul's heightened after-life, and to have no kind of belief or interest in Psychical Research, at least in such Research as an intrinsically valuable aid to any specifically religious convictions. No aloofness from such attempts to find spiritual realities at the phenomenal level can, (unless it is clear that the majority of educated Western Europeans share the naïve assumptions of this position), indicate negation of, or indifference to, the belief in Immortality.—And next, it is equally certain that precisely the most fruitful form of the belief is that which conceives the After-life as already involved in this

[1] "The Desire for Immortality," in *Humanism*, 1903, pp. 228–249.

one, and which, therefore, dwells specially, not upon the posteriority in time, but upon the difference in kind of that spiritual life of the soul which, even *hic et nunc*, can be sought after and experienced, in ever imperfect degrees no doubt, yet really and more and more. Here we ever get an approach to Simultaneity and Eternity, instead of sheer succession and clock-time : and here the fundamental attitude of the believer would appear only if pressed to deny or exclude the deathlessness of the spirit and its life,—the usual latency and simple implication of the positive conviction, in nowise diminishing this conviction's reality.—And, finally, it would have to be seen whether those who are indifferent or sceptical as to Immortal or Eternal Life, are appreciably fewer and largely other than those who are careless as to the other deep implications and requirements of spiritual experience. We may well doubt whether they would turn out to be so.

(2) As to the second point, we have already found how utterly insuppressible is the pleasure, normally concomitant upon every act of noble self-conquest; and how, though we can and should perform such and all other acts, as far as possible, from the ultimate, determining motive of thereby furthering the realization of the Kingdom of God, there can be no solid truthfulness or sane nobility in insisting upon attempts at thinking away and denying the fact and utility of that concomitant pleasure. But if so, then a further, other-world extension of that realization and of this concomitant happiness, and a belief here below in such an eventual extension, cannot of themselves be ignoble or debasing. Occasions for every degree and kind of purely selfish and faultily natural acts, of acts inchoatively supernatural but still predominantly slavish, reappear here, in close parallel to the variety of disposition displayed by men towards every kind of reality and ideal, towards the Family, Science, the State, Humanity, where the same concomitances and the same high uses and mean abuses are ever possible and actual. Neither here nor there should we attempt to impoverish truth and life, in order to exclude the possibility of their abuse.—And it would, of course, be profoundly unfair to contrast such a rarely noble spirit as Spinoza among the deniers with the average mind from among the affirmers. The average or the majority of the deniers would not, I think, appear as more generous and devoted than the corresponding average or majority on the other side.

(3) And as to the supposed directly beneficial effects of a positive denial of Immortality, such as have been sung for us by George Eliot and Giovanni Pascoli, we can safely affirm that the special tendernesses and quiet heroisms, deduced by them from such a negation, are too obviously dependent upon spiritual implications and instincts, for us to be able to put them directly to the credit of that denial. Only in so far as Immortality were not a postulate intrinsically connected with belief in objective and obligatory Beauty, Truth, and Goodness,—in God as our origin and end,—could its persistent and deliberate denial not be injurious to these fundamental convictions and to the ultimate health of the soul's life : and of this intrinsic non-connection there is no sufficient evidence.—Certainly, in such a case as Spinoza's, the same strain of reasoning which makes him abandon individual Immortality ought, in logic, to prevent him, a mere hopelessly determined link in the *Natura Naturata*, from ever attaining to the free self-dedication of himself, as now a fully responsible member of the *Natura Naturans*. And if not all the grand depth of his spiritual instinct and moral nobility, and its persistence in spite of its having no logical room in the fixedly naturalistic element of his teaching, can be urged as an argument in favour of the ultimate truth and ethical helpfulness of that whole element, neither can it be urged with respect to what is presumably one part of that element, his denial of personal Immortality.

II. Catherine's General After-Life Conceptions.

Now Catherine's general After-Life Conceptions in part bring into interesting prominence, in part really meet and overcome, the perplexities and mutually destructive alternatives which we have just considered. I shall here again leave over to the next chapter the simply ultimate questions, such as that of the pure Eternity *versus* the Unendingness of the soul; but shall allow myself, as to one set of her general ideas, a little digression as to the probability of their ultimate literary suggestion by Plato.—These Platonic passages probably reached her too indirectly, and by means and in forms which I have too entirely failed to discover, for me to be able to discuss them in my chapter devoted to her assured and demonstrably direct literary sources. But these sayings of

Plato greatly help to illustrate the meaning of her doctrine. —I shall group these, her general, positions and implications under four heads, and shall consider three of these as, in substance, profoundly satisfactory, but one of them, the second, as acceptable only with many limitations, although this second has obviously much influenced the form given by her to several of those other conceptions.

1. *Forecasts of the Hereafter, based upon present experience.* First, then, we get, as the fundamental presupposition of the whole Eschatology, a grandly sane, simple, and profound doctrine formulated over and over again and applied throughout, with a splendid consistency, as the key and limit to all her anticipations and picturings. Only because of the fact, and of our conviction of the fact, of the unbroken continuity and identity of God with Himself, of the human soul with itself, and of the deepest of the relations subsisting between that God and the soul, across the chasm formed by our body's death, and only in proportion as we can and do experience and achieve, during this our earthly life, certain spiritual laws and realities of a sufficiently elemental, universal, and fruitful, more or less time- and space-less character, can we (whilst ever remembering the analogical nature of such picturings even as to the soul's life here) safely and profitably forecast certain general features of the future which is thus already so largely a present. But, given these conditions in the present, we can and should forecast the future, to the extent implied. And as Plato's great imaginative projection, his life-work, the *Republic,* achieves its original end, (of making more readily understandable, by objectivizing, on a large scale, the life of the inner city of our own soul,) in so far as he has rightly understood the human soul and has found appropriate representations of its powers, laws, and ideals in his future commonwealth, even if we cannot accept this picture for political purposes and in all its details : so is it also with Catherine's projection, which, if bolder in its subject-matter, is, most rightly, indefinitely more general in its indications than is Plato's great diagram of the soul. Man's spiritual personality, being held by her to survive death,—to retain its identity and an at least equivalent consciousness, of that identity,—the deepest experiences of that personality before the body's death are conceived as re-experienced by it, in a heightened degree and form, after death itself. Hence these great pictures, of what the soul will

experience then, would remain profoundly true of what the soul seeks and requires now, even if there were no *then* at all.

And note particularly how only with regard to one stage and condition of the spirit's future life,—that of the purification of the imperfect soul,—does she indulge in any at all direct doctrine or detailed picturing; and this, doubtless, not only because she has experienced much concerning this matter in her own life here, but also because the projection of these experiences would still give us, not the ultimate state, but more or less only a prolongation of our mixed, joy-in-suffering life upon earth. As to the two ultimate states, we get only quite incidental glimpses, although even these are strongly marked by her general position and method.

2. *Catherine's forecasts and present experience correspondingly limited.*

And next, coming to the projection itself, we naturally find it to present all the strength and limitations of her own spiritual experiences which are thus projected : her attitude towards the body and towards human fellowship, (two subjects which are shown to be closely inter-related by the continuous manner in which they stand and fall together throughout the history of philosophy and religion,) thus constitute the second general peculiarity of her Eschatology. We have already noted, in her life, her strongly ecstatic, body-ignoring, body-escaping type of religion; and how, even in her case, it tended to starve the corporate, institutional conceptions and affections. Here, in the projection, we find both the cause and the effect again, and on a larger scale. Her continuous psycho-physical discomforts and keen thirst for a unity and simplicity as rapid and complete as possible, the joy and strength derived from ecstatic habits and affinities, would all make her, without even herself being aware of it, drop all further thought as to the future fate of that oppressive " prison-house " from which her spirit had at last got free.

Now such non-occupation with the fate of the body and of her fellow-souls may appear quite appropriate in her Purgatorial Eschatology, yet we cannot but find that, even here, it already possesses grave disadvantages, and that it persists throughout all her After-life conceptions. For in all the states and stages of the soul we get a markedly unsocial, a *sola cum solo* picture. And yet there is, perhaps, no more striking difference, amongst their many affinities, between Platonism and Christianity than the intense Individualism which marks the great Greek's doctrine, and the profoundly social conception which pervades Our Lord's own teaching,—in each case as regards the next life as well as this one. Plotinus's great culminating commendation of "the flight of the alone to the Alone" continues Plato's tradition; whereas, if even St. Paul and the Joannine writings speak at times as though the individual soul attained to its full personality in and by direct intercourse with God alone, the Synoptic Gospels, and at bottom also those two great lovers of Our Lord's spirit, never cease to emphasize the social constituent of the soul's life both here and hereafter. The Kingdom of Heaven, the Soul of the Church, as truly constitutes the different personalities, their spirituality and their joy, as they constitute it,—that great Organism which, as such, is both first and last in the Divine thought and love.

Here, in the at least partial ignoring of these great social facts, we touch the main defect of most mystical outlooks; yet this defect does not arise from what they possess, but from what they lack. For solitude, and the abstractive, unifying, intuitive, emotional, mystical element is also wanted, and this element and movement Catherine exemplifies in rare perfection. Indeed, in the great classical, central period of her life she had, as we know, combined all this with much of the outward movement, society, detailed observation, attachment, the morally *en-static*, the immanental type. Unfortunately the same ill-health and ever-increasing predominance of the former element, which turned her, quite naturally, to these eschatological contemplations, and which indeed helped to give them their touching tone of first-hand experience, also tended, of necessity, to make her drop even such slight and lingering social elements as had formerly coloured her thought. It is, then, only towards the understanding and deepening of the former of these two necessary movements of religion, that these, her latter-day enlargements of some of her deepest experiences and convictions will be found true helps.

Yet if the usual *ad extra* disadvantages of such an abstractive position towards the body are thus exemplified by her, in this her unsocial, individualistic attitude, it is most interesting to note how entirely she avoids the usual *ad intra* drawbacks of this same position. For if her whole attention, and, increasingly, even her consciousness are, in true ecstatic guise, absorbed away from her fellows and concentrated exclusively upon God in herself and herself in God, yet this consciousness consists not only of *Noûs*, that dry theoretic reason which, already by Plato, but still more by Aristotle, is alone conceived as surviving the body, but contains also the upper range of *Thumos*,—all those passions of the noblest kind,—love, admiration, gratitude, utter self-donation, joy in purifying suffering and in an ever-growing self-realization as part of the great plan of God,—all the highest notes in that wondrous scale of deep feeling and of emotionally coloured willing which Plato made dependent, not for its character but for the possibility of its operation, upon the body's union with the soul.—And thus we see how, in her conception of the soul's own self within itself and of its relation to God, the Christian idea of Personality, as of a many-sided organism in which Love and Will are the very flower of the whole, has triumphed over the Platonic presentation of the Spirit, in so far as this is taken to require and achieve an ultimate sublimation free from all emotive elements. Thus in her doctrine the whole Personality survives death, although this Personality energizes only, as it were upwards, to God alone, and not also sideways and downwards, towards its fellows and the lesser children of God.

3. *Catherine's forecast influenced by Plato.*

Catherine's third peculiarity consists in a rich and profound organization of two doctrines, the one libertarian, the other determinist; and requires considerable quotation from Plato, whose teachings, bereft of all transmigration-fancies, seem clearly to reappear here, (however complex may have been the mediation,) in Catherine's great conception.

The determinist doctrine maintains that virtue and vice, in proportion as they are allowed their full development, spontaneously and necessarily attain to their own congenital consummation, a consummation which consists, respectively, in the bliss inseparable from the final and complete identity between the inevitable results upon itself of the soul's deliberate endeavours, and the indestructible requirements of this same soul's fundamental nature; and in the misery of the, now fully felt but only gradually superable, or even, in other cases, insuperable, antagonism between the inevitable consequences within its own self of the soul's more or less deliberate choosings, and those same, here also ineradicable, demands of its own truest nature.

As Marsilio Ficino says, in his *Theologia Platonica*,

published in Florence in 1482: "Virtue is reward in its first budding, reward is virtue full-grown. Vice is punishment at the moment of its birth; punishment is vice at its consummation. For, in each of these cases, one and the same thing is first the simple seed and then the full ear of corn; and one and the same thing is the full ear of corn and then the food of man. Precisely the very things then that we sow in this our (earthly) autumn, shall we reap in that (other-world) summer-day." [1] It is true that forensic terms and images are also not wanting in Catherine's sayings; but these, in part, run simply parallel to the immanental conception without modifying it; in part, they are in its service; and, in part, they are the work of the theologians' arrangements and glosses discussed in my Appendix

And the libertarian doctrine declares that it is the soul itself which, in the beyond and immediately after death, chooses the least painful, because the most expressive of her then actual desires, from among the states which the natural effects upon her own self of her own earthly choosings have left her interiorly free to choose.

Now it is in this second doctrine especially that we find so detailed an anticipation by Plato of a whole number of highly original and characteristic points and combinations of points, as to render a fortuitous concurrence between Catherine and Plato practically impossible. Yet I have sought in vain, among Catherine's authentic sayings, actions, possessions, or friends, for any trace of direct acquaintance with any of Plato's writings. But Ficino's Latin translation of Plato, published, with immense applause, in Florence in 1483, 1484, must have been known, in those intensely Platonizing times, to even non-professed Humanists in Genoa, long before Catherine's death in 1510, so that one or other of her intimates may have communicated the substance of these Platonic doctrines to her. [2] Plotinus, of whom Ficino published a Latin translation in 1492, contains but a feeble echo of Plato on this point. Proclus, directly known only very little till much after

[1] *Op. cit.* Lib. XVIII, c. x, ed. 1559, fol. 3413.

[2] Neither she nor her friends can have derived these doctrines from Ficino's *Theologia Platonica*, Florence, 1482, since precisely the points in question are quite curiously absent from, or barely recognizable in, that book. See its cc. x and xi, Book XVIII, on "the State of the Impure Soul" and "the State of the Imperfect Soul" respectively: ed. 1559, fol. 340, *v. seq.* See also foll. 318*r*, 319*v*.

Catherine's time, is in even worse case. The Areopagite, who has so continuously taken over whole passages from all three writers, although directly almost exclusively from Proclus, contains nothing more immediately to the purpose than his impressive sayings concerning Providence's continuous non-forcing of the human personality in its fundamental constitution and its free elections with their inevitable consequences; hence Catherine cannot have derived her ideas, in the crisp definiteness which they retain in her sayings, from her cousin the Dominican nun and the Areopagite. And it is certain, as we have seen, how scattered and inchoate are the hints which she may have found in St. Paul, the Joannine writings, and Jacopone da Todi. St. Augustine contains nothing that would be directly available,—an otherwise likely source considering Catherine's close connection with the Augustinian Canonesses of S. Maria delle Grazie.

In Plato, then, we get five conceptions and symbolic pictures that are practically identical with those of Catherine.

(1) First we get the conception of souls having each, in exact accordance with the respective differences of their moral and spiritual disposition and character, as these have been constituted by them here below, a "place" or environment, expressive of that character, ready for their occupation after the body's death. "The soul that is pure departs at death, herself invisible, to the invisible world,—to the divine, immortal and rational: thither arriving, she lives in bliss. But the soul that is impure at the time of her departure and is . . . engrossed by the corporeal . . . , is weighed down and drawn back again into the visible place (world)."

And this scheme, of like disposition seeking a like place, is then carried out, by the help of the theory of transmigration, as a re-incarnation of these various characters into environments, bodies, exactly corresponding to them: gluttonous souls are assigned to asses' bodies, tyrannous souls to those of wolves, and so on: in a word, "there is no difficulty in assigning to all 'a whither' (a place) answering to their general natures and propensities." [1] For this corresponds to a law which runs throughout all things,—a determinism of consequences which does not prevent the liberty of causes. "The King of the universe contrived a general plan, by which a thing of a certain nature found a seat and place of a certain

[1] *Phaedo*, 81*a*–82*a*.

kind. But the formation of this nature, he left to the wills of individuals."

Or, with the further spatial imagery of movements up, level, or down, we get: "All things that have a soul change . . . and, in changing, move according to law and the order of destiny. Lesser changes of nature move on level ground, but great crimes sink . . . into the so-called lower places . . .; and, when the soul becomes greatly different and divine, she also greatly changes her place, which is now altogether holy."[1] The original, divinely intended "places" of souls are all high and good, and similar to each other though not identical, each soul having its own special "place"; and for this congenital "place" each soul has a resistible yet ineradicable home-sickness. "The first incarnation" of human souls which "distributes each soul to a star," is ordained to be similar for all. . . . "And when they have been of necessity implanted in bodily forms, should they master their passions . . . they live in righteousness; if otherwise, in unrighteousness. And he who lived well through his allotted time shall be conveyed once more to a habitation in his kindred star, and there shall enjoy a blissful and congenial life; but failing this he shall pass into . . . such a form of (further) incarnation as fits his disposition . . . until he shall overcome, by reason, all that burthen that afterwards clung around him."[2]

If from all this we exclude the soul's existence before any beginning of its body, its transmigration into other bodies, and the self-sufficiency of reason; and if we make it all to be penetrated by God's presence, grace, and love, and by our corresponding or conflicting emotional and volitional as well as intellectual attitude: we shall get Catherine's position exactly.

(2) But again, in at least one phase of his thinking, Plato pictures the purification of the imperfect soul as effected, or at least as begun, not in a succession of "places" of an extensionally small but organic kind, bodies, but in a "place" of an extensionally larger but inorganic sort,—the shore of a lake, where the soul has to wait. "The Acherusian lake is

[1] *Laws*, X, 904*a–e*.

[2] *Timaeus*, 41*d*, *e*; 42*b*, *d*. I have, for clearness' sake, turned Plato's indirect sentences into direct ones; and have taken the *Timaeus* after the *Laws*, although it is chronologically prior to them, because the full balance of his system, (which requires the originally lofty "place" of each individual soul),—is, I think, abandoned in the *Laws*: see 904*a*.

the lake to the shores of which the many go when they are dead; and, after waiting an appointed time, which to some is longer and to others shorter, they are sent back to be born as animals." Here we evidently get a survival of the conception, predominant in Homer, of a pain-and-joyless Hades, but limited here to the middle, the imperfect class of souls, and followed, in their case, by transmigration, to which alone, apparently, purification is directly attached.

In the same Dialogue we read later on: "Those who appear to have lived neither well nor ill . . . go to the river Acheron, and are carried to the lake; and there they dwell and are purified of their evil deeds . . . and are absolved and receive the rewards of their good deeds according to their deserts." Here we have, evidently, still the same "many" and the same place, the shores of the Acherusian lake, but also an explicit affirmation of purification effected there, for this purification is now followed directly, not by reincarnation, but by the ultimate happiness in the soul's original and fundamentally congenial "place." And this scheme is far more conformable to Plato's fundamental position: for how can bodies, even lower than the human, help to purify the soul which has become impure precisely on occasion of its human body?—We can see how the Christian Purgatorial doctrine derives some of its pictures from the second of these parallel passages; yet that the "longer or shorter waiting" of the first passage also enters into that teaching,—especially in its more ordinary modern form, according to which there is, in this state, no intrinsic purification.

And lower down we find: "Those who have committed crimes which, although great, are not unpardonable,—for these it is necessary to plunge (ἐμπεσεῖν) into Tartarus, the pains of which they are compelled to undergo for a year; but at the end of the year they are borne to the Acherusian lake. But those who appear incurable by reason of the greatness of their crimes . . . such their appropriate destiny hurls (ῥίπτει) into Tartarus, whence they never come forth." Here we get a Purgatory, pictured as a watery substance in which the more gravely impure of the curable souls are immersed before arriving at the easier purification, the waiting on the dry land alongside the lake; this Purgatory is, as a "place" and, in intensity, identical with Hell; and into this place the curable souls "plunge" and the incurable ones are "hurled." Of this third passage Catherine retains the identification of the pains of Purgatory and those of Hell; the "plunge," or "hurling," of two distinct classes of souls into these pains; and the mitigation, after a time, previous to complete cessation, of the suffering in the case of the curable class. But the "plunge," with her, is common to all degrees of imperfectly pure souls; there is, for all these souls, no change of "place" during their purgation, but only a mitigation of suffering; and this mitigation is at work gradually and from the first. And the ordinary modern Purgatorial teaching is like this passage, in that it keeps the curable souls in Tartarus, say, for one year, and lets them suffer there, apparently without mitigation, throughout that time: and that, in the case of both classes of souls, it conceives the punishment as extrinsic, vindictive, and inoperative.

And a fourth *Phaedo* passage tells us: "Those who are remarkable for having led holy lives are released from this earthly prison, and go to their pure home, which is above, and dwell in the purer earth," the Isles of the Just, in Oceanus. "And those, again, amongst these who have duly purified themselves with philosophy, live henceforth altogether without the body, in mansions fairer far than these." Here we get, alongside of the two Purgatories and the one Hell, two Heavens, of which the first is but taken over from Homer and Pindar, but of which the second is Plato's own conception. Catherine, in entire accord with the ordinary teaching, has got but one "place" of each kind; and her Heaven corresponds, apart from his formal and final exclusion of every sort of body, to the second of these Platonic Heavens; whilst, here again, the all-encompassing presence of God's love for souls as of the soul's love for God, which, in her teaching, is the beginning, means, and end of the whole movement, effects an indefinite difference between the two positions.[1]

(3) Yet Plato, in his most characteristic moods, explicitly anticipates Catherine as to the intrinsic, ameliorative nature and work of Purgatory: "The proper office of punishment is twofold: he who is rightly punished ought either to become better . . . by it, or he ought to be made an example to his fellows, that they may see what he suffers and . . . become better. Those who are punished by Gods and men and improved, are those whose sins are curable . . . by pain and

[1] These four passages are all within pp. 110*b*–114*d* of the *Phaedo*.

suffering :—for there is no other way in which they can be delivered from evil, as in this world so also in the other. But the others are incurable—the time has passed at which they can receive any benefit themselves. . . . Rhadamanthus," the chief of the three nether-world judges, " looks with admiration on the soul of some just one, who has lived in holiness and truth . . . and sends him " without any intervening suffering " to the Isles of the Blessed. . . . I consider how I shall present my soul whole and undefiled before the Judge, in that day." [1] Here the last sentence is strikingly like in form as well as in spirit to many a saying of St. Paul and Catherine.

(4) But the following most original passages give us a sentiment and an image which, in their special drift, are as opposed to St. Paul, and indeed to the ordinary Christian consciousness, as they are dear to Catherine, in this matter so strongly, although probably unconsciously, Platonist, indeed Neo-Platonist, in her affinities. " In the time of Kronos, indeed down to that of Zeus, the Judgment was given on the day on which men were to die," *i. e.* immediately *before* their death; " and the consequence was, that the judgments were not well given,—the souls found their way to the wrong places. Zeus said : ' The reason is, that the judged have their clothes on, for they are alive. . . . There are many, having evil souls, who are apparelled in fair bodies or wrapt round in wealth and rank. . . . The Judges are awed by them ; and they themselves too have their clothes on when judging : their eyes and ears and their whole bodies are interposed, as a veil, before their own souls. What is to be done ? . . . Men shall be entirely stript before they are judged, for they shall be judged when dead ; the Judge too shall be naked, that is, dead : he, with his naked soul, shall pierce into the other naked soul immediately *after* each man dies . . . and is bereft of all his kith and kin, and has left behind him all his brave attire upon earth, and thus the Judgment will be just.' " [2] —If we compare this with St. Paul's precisely contrary instinct and desire to be " clothed upon " at death, " lest we be found naked," *i. e.* without the protection of any kind of body ; and then realize Catherine's intense longing for "nudità,"—to strip herself here, as far as possible, from all imperfection and self-delusion before the final stripping off of the body in death, and to appear, utterly naked, before the utterly naked eye of

[1] *Gorgias*, pp. 525*b*, *c*; 526*c*, *d*. [2] *Ibid.* p. 523*b–e*.

God, so that no "clothes" should remain requiring to be burnt away by the purifying fires,[1] the profound affinity of sentiment and imagery between Catherine and Plato—and this on a point essentially Platonic,—is very striking.

(5) But, above all, in his deep doctrine as to the soul's spontaneous choice after death of that condition, "place," which, owing to the natural effects within her of her earthly willings and self-formation, she cannot but now find the most congenial to herself, Plato appears as the ultimate source of a literary kind for Catherine's most original view, which otherwise is, I think, without predecessors. "The souls," he tells us in the *Republic,* "immediately on their arrival in the other world, were required to go to Lachesis," one of the three Fates. And "an interpreter, having taken from her lap a number of lots and plans of life, spoke as follows: 'Thus saith Lachesis, the daughter of Necessity. . . . "Your destiny shall not be allotted to you, but you shall choose it for yourselves. Let him who draws the first lot, be the first to choose a life which shall be his irrevocably. . . . The responsibility lies with the chooser, Heaven is guiltless."'" "No settled character of soul was included in the plans of life, because, with the change of life, the soul inevitably became changed itself." "It was a truly wonderful sight, to watch how each soul selected its life. . . . When all the souls had chosen their lives, Lachesis dispatched with each of them the Destiny he had selected, to guard his life and satisfy his choice."[2] And in the *Phaedrus* Plato tells us that "at the end of the first thousand years" (of the first incarnation) "the good souls and also the evil souls both come to cast lots and to choose their second life; and they may take any that they like."[3]

In both the dialogues the lots are evidently taken over from popular mythology, but are here made merely to introduce a certain orderly succession among the spontaneous choosings of the souls themselves, whilst the lap of the daughter of Necessity, spread out before all the choosers previous to their choice, and the separate, specially appropriate Destiny that accompanies each soul after its choice, indicate plainly that, although the choice itself is the free act and pure self-expression of each soul's then present disposition, yet that this disposition is the necessary result of its earthly volitions and

[1] 2 Cor. v, 2, 3.—*Vita*, pp. 109*b*, 66*a*, 171*a*.
[2] *Republic*, X, pp. 617*e*, 619*e*, 920*e*. [3] *Phaedrus*, p. 249*b*.

self-development or self-deformation, and that the choice now made becomes, in its turn, the cause of certain inevitable consequences,—of a special environment which itself is then productive of special effects upon, and of special occasions for, the final working out of this soul's character.—Plotinus retains the doctrine: "the soul chooses there" in the Other world,—"its Daemon and its kind of life."[1] But neither Proclus nor Dionysius has the doctrine, whilst Catherine, on the contrary, reproduces it with a penetrating completeness.

4. *Simplifications characteristic of Catherine's Eschatology.*

And under our last, fourth head, we can group the simplifications characteristic of Catherine's Eschatology.

(1) One simplification has, of course, for now some fifteen hundred years, been the ordinary Christian conception: I mean the elimination of the time-element between the moment of death and the beginning of the three states. Yet it is interesting to note how by far the greatest of the Latin Fathers, St. Augustine, who died in 430 A.D., still clings predominantly to the older Christian and Jewish conception of the soul abiding in a state of shrunken, joy-and-painless consciousness from the moment of the body's death up to that of the general resurrection and judgment. "After this short life, thou wilt not yet be where the saints will be," *i. e.* in Heaven. "Thou wilt not yet be there: who is ignorant of this? But thou canst straightway be where the rich man descried the ulcerous beggar to be a-resting, far away," *i. e.* in Limbo. "Placed in that rest, thou canst await the day of judgment with security, when thou shalt receive thy body also, when thou shalt be changed so as to be equal to an Angel."[2] Only with regard to Purgatory, a state held by him, in writings of his last years, 410–430 A.D., to be possible, indeed probable, does he make an exception to his general rule: for such purification would have to take place "in the interval of time between the death of the body and the last day of condemnation and reward."[3]

It is doubtless the still further fading away of the expectation, so vivid and universal in early Christian times, of the proximity of Our Lord's Second Advent, and the tacit

[1] *Enneads*, III, 4, 5.
[2] Enarr. in Ps. xxxvi, § 1, n. 10, ed. Ben., col. 375*b*. See also *Enchiridion*, CIX, *ibid.* col. 402*d*.
[3] So in the *De Civitate Dei*, Lib. XXI, c. xxvi, n. 4, *ibid.* col. 1037*d*.

prevalence of Greek affinities and conceptions concerning the bodiless soul, that helped to eliminate, at last universally, this interval of waiting, in the case of souls too good or too bad for purgation, from the general consciousness of at least Western Christendom. The gain in this was the great simplification and concentration of the immediate outlook and interest; the loss was the diminished apprehension of the essentially complex, concrete, synthetic character of man's nature, and of the necessity for our assuming that this characteristic will be somehow preserved in this nature's ultimate perfection.

(2) There is a second simplification in Catherine which, though here St. Augustine leads the way, is less common among Christians: her three other-world "places" are not, according to her ultimate thought, three distinct spatial extensions and localities, filled, respectively, with ceaselessly suffering, temporarily suffering, and ceaselessly blessed souls; but they are, (notwithstanding all the terms necessitated by such spatial picturings as "entering," "coming out," "plunging into,") so many distinct states and conditions of the soul, of a painful, mixed, or joyful character. We shall have these her ultimate ideas very fully before us presently. But here I would only remark that this her union of a picturing faculty, as vivid as the keenest sense-perception, and of a complete non-enslavement to, a vigorous utilization of, these life-like spatial projections, by a religious instinct and experience which never forgets that God and souls are spirits, to whom our ordinary categories of space and extension, time and motion, do not and cannot in strictness apply, is as rare as it is admirable; and that, though her intensely anti-corporeal and non-social attitude made such a position more immediately easy for her than it can be for those who remain keenly aware of the great truths involved in the doctrines of the Resurrection of the Body and the Communion of Saints, this her trend of thought brings into full articulation precisely the deepest of our spiritual apprehensions and requirements, whilst it is not her fault if it but further accentuates some of our intellectual perplexities.

We get much in St. Augustine, which he himself declares to have derived, in the first instance, from "the writings of the Platonists," which doubtless means above all Plotinus, (that keen spiritual thinker who can so readily be traced throughout this part of the great Convert's teaching,) as to this profound incommensurableness between spiritual presence, energizing, and affectedness on the one hand, and spatial position, extension, and movement on the other. "What place is there within me, to which my God can come? . . . I would not exist at all, unless Thou already wert within me." "Thou wast never a place, and yet we have receded from Thee; and we have drawn near to Thee, yet Thou art never a place." "Are we submerged and do we emerge? Yet it is not places into which we are plunged and out of which we rise. What can be more like to places and yet more unlike? For here the affections are in case,—the impurity of our spirit, which flows downwards, oppressed by the love of earthly cares; and the holiness of Thy Spirit, which lifts us upwards with the love of security." [1] For, as he teaches "the spiritual creature can only be changed by times,"—a succession within a duration: "by remembering what it had forgotten, or by learning what it did not know, or by willing what it did not will. The bodily creature can be changed by times and places, by spatial motion, "from earth to heaven, from heaven to earth, from east to west." "That thing is not moved through space which is not extended in space . . . the soul is not considered to move in space, unless it be held to be a body." [2]

In applying the doctrine just expressed to eschatological matters, St. Augustine concludes: "If it be asked whether the soul, when it goes forth from the body, is borne to some corporeal places, or to such as, though incorporeal, are like to bodies, or to what is more excellent than either: I readily answer that, unless it have some kind of body, it is not borne to bodily places at all, or, at least, that it is not borne to them by bodily motion. . . . But I myself do not think that it possesses any body, when it goes forth from this earthly body. . . . It gets borne, according to its deserts, to spiritual conditions, or to penal places having a similitude to bodies." [3]

The reader will readily note a curiously uncertain frame of mind in this last utterance. I take it that Plotinian influences are here being checked by the Jewish conception of certain, definitely located, provision-chambers (*promptuaria*), in which

[1] *Confess.*, Lib. I, c. 2, n. 1; X, c. 26; XIII, c. 7.

[2] *De Genesi ad litt.*, Lib. VIII, n. 39, ed. Ben. col. 387*b*; n. 43, col. 389*a*.

[3] *Ibid.* Lib. XII, n. 32, col. 507*c*. He soon after attempts to decide in favour of "incorporeal places," as the other-world destination of all classes of human souls.

all souls are placed for safe keeping, between the time of the body's death and its resurrection. So in the Fourth Book of Esra (of about 90 A.D.), "the souls of the just in their chambers said: 'How long are we to remain here?'"; and in the Apocalypse of Baruch (of about 150–250 A.D.), "at the coming of the Messiah, the provision-chambers will open, in which the" whole, precise "number of the souls of the just have been kept, and they will come forth." [1]

But it is St. Thomas Aquinas who, by the explicit and consistent adoption and classification of these *promptuaria receptacula*, reveals to us more clearly the perplexities and fancifulnesses involved in the strictly spatial conception. "Although bodies are not assigned to souls (immediately) after death, yet certain bodily places are congruously assigned to these souls in accordance with the degree of their dignity, in which places they are, as it were, locally, in the manner in which bodiless things can be in space: each soul having a higher place assigned to it, according as it approaches more or less to the first substance, God, whose seat, according to Scripture, is Heaven." "In the Scriptures God is called the Sun, since He is the principle of spiritual life, as the physical sun is of bodily life; and, according to this convention, . . . souls spiritually illuminated have a greater fitness for luminous bodies, and sin-darkened souls for dark places." "It is probable that, as to local position, Hell and the Limbo of the Fathers constitute one and the same place, or are more or less continuous." "The place of Purgatory adjoins (that of) Hell." "There are altogether five places ready to receive (*receptanda*) souls bereft of their bodies: Paradise, the Limbo of the Fathers, Purgatory, Hell, and the Limbo of Infants." [2]

No doubt all these positions became the common scholastic teaching. But then, as Cardinal Bellarmine cogently points out: "no ancient, as far as I know, has written that the Earthly Paradise was destroyed . . . and I have read a large number who affirm its existence. This is the doctrine of all the Scholastics, beginning with St. Thomas, and of the Fathers . . . St. Augustine indeed appears to rank this truth amongst the dogmas of faith." [3] We shall do well, then, not to press

[1] Esra IV, iv, 35. See also iv, 41; vii, 32, 80, 95, 101. Apocalypse of Baruch, xxx, 2.

[2] *Summa Theol.*, suppl., qu. 69, art. 1, in corp. et ad 3; art. 6, in corp.; Appendix de Purgat., art. 2, in corp.; suppl., qu. 69, art. 7 concl.

[3] *De gratia primi hominis* XIV.

these literal localization-schemes, especially since, according to St. Augustine's penetrating analysis, our spiritual experiences, already in this our earthly existence, have a distinctly non-spatial character. Catherine's position, if applied to the central life of man here, and hence presumptively hereafter, remains as true and fresh and unassailable as ever.

(3) And her last simplification consists in taking the Fire of Hell, the Fire of Purgatory, and the Fire and Light of Heaven as profoundly appropriate symbols or descriptions of the variously painful or joyous impressions produced, through the differing volitional attitudes of souls towards Him, by the one God's intrinsically identical presence in each and all. In all three cases, throughout their several grades, there are ever but two realities, the Spirit-God and the spirit-soul, in various states of inter-relation.

Here again it is Catherine's complete abstraction from the body which renders such a view easy and, in a manner, necessary for her mind. But here I would only emphasize the impressive simplicity and spirituality of view which thus, as in the material world it finds the one sun-light and the one fire-heat, which, in themselves everywhere the same, vary indefinitely in their effects, owing to the varying condition of the different bodies which meet the rays and flames; so, in the Spiritual World it discovers One supreme spiritual Energy and Influence which, whilst ever self-identical, is assimilated, deflected, or resisted by the lesser spirits, with inevitably joyous, mixed, or painful states of soul, since they can each and all resist, but cannot eradicate that Energy's impression within their deepest selves. And though, even with her, the Sun-light image remains quasi-Hellenic and Intellectual, and the Fire-heat picture is more immediately Christian and Moral: yet she also frequently takes the sunlight as the symbol of the achieved Harmony and Peace, and the Fire-heat as that of more or less persisting Conflict and Pain. She is doubtless right in keeping both symbols, and in ever thinking of each as ultimately implying the other, for God is Beauty and Truth, as well as Goodness and Love, and man is made with the indestructible aspiration after Him in His living completeness.

And here again Catherine has a complicated doctrinal history behind her.

We have already considered the numerous Scriptural passages where God and His effects upon the soul are symbolized as light and fire; and those again where joy or, contrariwise, trial and suffering are respectively pictured by the same physical properties. And Catherine takes the latter passages as directly explanatory of the first, in so far as these joys and sufferings are spiritual in their causes or effects.

Among the Greek Fathers, Clement of Alexandria tells us that "the Fire" of Purgatory,—for he has no Eternal Damnation,—"is a rational," spiritual, "fire that penetrates the soul"; and Origen teaches that "each sinner himself lights the flame of his own fire, and is not thrown into a fire that has been lit before that moment and that exists in front of him. . . . His conscience is agitated and pierced by its own pricks." Saints Gregory of Nyssa and Gregory of Nazianzum are more or less influenced by Origen on this point. And St. John Damascene, who died in about 750 A.D., says explicitly that the fire of Hell is not a material fire, that it is very different from our ordinary fire, and that men hardly know what it is.[1]

Among the Latins, St. Ambrose declares: "neither is the gnashing, a gnashing of bodily teeth; nor is the everlasting fire, a fire of bodily flames; nor is the worm, a bodily one."—St. Jerome, in one passage, counts the theory of the non-physical fire as one of Origen's errors; but elsewhere he mentions it without any unfavourable note, and even enumerates several Scripture-texts which favour it, and admits that "'the worm which dieth not and the fire which is not quenched,' is understood, by the majority of interpreters (*a plerisque*), of the conscience of sinners which tortures them."[2] —St. Augustine, in 413 A.D., declares: "In the matter of the pains of the wicked, both the unquenchable fire and the intensely living worm are interpreted differently by different commentators. Some interpreters refer both to the body, others refer both to the soul; and some take the fire literally, in application to the body, and the worm figuratively, in application to the soul, which latter opinion appears the more credible." Yet when, during the last years of his life, he came, somewhat tentatively, to hold an other-world Purgatory as well, he throughout assimilated this Purgatory's fire to the

[1] Clemens, *Stromata*, VII, 6. Origen, *De Princ.*, II, 10, 4. St. Greg. Nyss., *Orat.*, XL, 36. St. Greg. Nazianz., *Poema de Seipso*, I, 546. St. Joann. Damasc., *De Fide Orthod.*, cap. ult.

[2] St. Ambros., *In Lucam*, VII, 205. St. Hieron., Ep. 124, 7; *Apol. contra Ruf.*, II; in Isa. lxv, 24.

fire of this-world sufferings. Thus in 422 A.D.: "Souls which renounce the wood, hay, straw, built upon that foundation (1 Cor. iii, 11–15), not without pain indeed (since they loved these things with a carnal affection), but with faith in the foundation, a faith operative through love . . . arrive at salvation, through a certain fire of pain. . . . Whether men suffer these things in this life only, or such-like judgments follow even after this life—in either case, this interpretation of that text is not discordant with the truth." "'He shall be saved yet so as by fire,' because the pain, over the loss of the things he loved, burns him. It is not incredible that some such thing takes place even after this life . . . that some of the faithful are saved by a certain purgatorial fire, more quickly or more slowly, according as they have less or more loved perishable things." [1]

St. Thomas, voicing and leading Scholastic opinion, teaches that the fire of Purgatory is the same as that of Hell; and Cardinal Bellarmine, who died in 1621, tells us: "The common opinion of theologians is that the fire of Purgatory is a real and true fire, of the same kind as an earthly fire. This opinion, it is true, is not of faith, but it is very probable,"—because of the "consent of the scholastics, who cannot be despised without temerity," and also because of "the eruptions of Mount Etna." [2] Yet the Council of Florence had, in 1439, restricted itself to the quite general proposition that "if men die truly penitent, in the love of God, before they have satisfied . . . for their sins . . . their souls are purified by purgatorial pains after death"; thus very deliberately avoiding all commitment as to the nature of these pains.[3] Cardinal Gousset, who died in 1866, tells us: "The more common opinion amongst theologians makes the sufferings of Purgatory to consist in the pain of fire, or at least in a pain analogous to that of fire." [4] This latter position is practically identical with Catherine's.

As to the fire of Hell, although here especially the Scholastics, old and new, are unanimous, it is certain that there is no definition or solemn judgment of the Church declaring it

[1] *Liber de Fide* (A.D. 413), 27, 29; ed. Ben., coll. 313*b*, 314*c*. *De octo Dulcit. quaest.* (A.D. 422) 12, 13; *ibid.* coll. 219*d*, 220*a*. Repeated in *Enchiridion* (? A.D. 423), LXIX; *ibid.* col. 382*b*, *c*.

[2] *De Purgatorio*, II, 11.

[3] Denzinger, *Enchiridion*, ed. 1888, No. LXXIII.

[4] *Theol. Dogm.*, Vol. II, num. 206.

to be material. On this point again we find St. Thomas and those who follow him involved in practically endless difficulties and in, for us now, increasingly intolerable subtleties, where they try to show how a material fire can affect an immaterial spirit. Bossuet, so severely orthodox in all such matters, preaching, before the Court, about sin becoming in Hell the chastisement of the sinner, does not hesitate to finish thus: "We bear within our hearts the instrument of our punishment. 'Therefore have I brought forth a fire from the midst of thee, it hath devoured thee' (Ezek. xxviii, 18). I shall not send it against thee from afar, it will ignite in thy conscience, its flames will arise from thy midst, and it will be thy sins which will produce it." [1]—And the Abbé F. Dubois, in a careful article in the Ecclesiastical *Revue du Clergé Français* of Paris, has recently expressed the conviction that "the best minds of our time, which are above being suspected of yielding to mere passing fashions, feel the necessity of abandoning the literal interpretation, judged to be insufficient, of the ancient symbols; and of returning to a freer exegesis, of which some of the Ancients have given us the example." [2] Among these helpful "Ancients" we cannot but count Catherine, with her One God Who is the Fire of Pain and the Light of Joy to souls, according as they resist Him or will Him, either here or hereafter.

III. Catherine and Eternal Punishment

Introductory: four doctrines and difficulties to be considered.

Taking now the three great after-life conditions separately, in the order of Hell, Purgatory, and Heaven, I would first of all note that some readers may be disappointed that Catherine did not, like our own English Mystic, the entirely orthodox optimist, Mother Juliana of Norwich—her *Revelations* belong to the year 1373 A.D.—simply proclaim that, whilst the teaching and meaning of Christ and His Church would come true, all, in ways known to God alone, would yet be well.[3] In this manner, without any weakening of traditional teaching, the

[1] *Œuvres*, ed. Versailles, 1816, Vol. XI, p. 376.

[2] *Le feu du Purgatoire est-il un feu corporel? op. cit.*, 1902, pp. 263–284; 270. I owe most of my references on this point to this paper.

[3] *Sixteen Revelations of Mother Juliana of Norwich*, 1373, ed. 1902, pp. 73, 74, 78.

whole dread secret as to the future of evil-doers is left in the hands of God, and a beautifully boundless trust and hope glows throughout those contemplations.

Yet, as I hope to show as we go along, certain assumptions and conceptions, involved in the doctrine of Eternal Punishment, cannot be systematically excluded, or even simply ignored, without a grave weakening of the specifically Christian earnestness; and that, grand as is, in certain respects, the idea of the Apocatastasis, the Final Restitution of all Things and Souls—as taught by Clement and Origen—it is not, at bottom, compatible with the whole drift, philosophy, and tone, (even apart from specific sayings) of Our Lord. And this latter teaching—of the simply abiding significance and effect of our deliberate elections during this our one testing-time,—and not that of an indefinite series of chances and purifications with an ultimate disappearance of all difference between the results of the worst life and the best, answers to the deepest postulates and aspirations of the most complete and delicate ethical and spiritual sense. For minds that can discriminate between shifting fashions and solid growth in abiding truth, that will patiently seek out the deepest instinct and simplest implications underlying the popular presentations of the Doctrine of Abiding Consequences, and that take these implications as but part of a larger whole: this doctrine still, and now again, presents itself as a permanent element of the full religious consciousness.

It would certainly be unfair to press Catherine's rare and incidental sayings on Hell into a formal system. Yet those remarks are deep and suggestive, and help too much to interpret, supplement, and balance her central, Purgatorial teaching, and indeed to elucidate her general religious principles, for us to be able to pass them over. We have already sufficiently considered the question as to the nature of the Fire; and that as to Evil Spirits is reserved for the next Chapter. Here I shall consider four doctrines and difficulties, together with Catherine's attitude towards them: the soul's final fate, dependent upon the character of the will's act or active disposition at the moment of the body's death; the total moral perversion of the lost; the mitigation of their pains; and the eternity of their punishment.

1. *Eternity dependent on the earthly life's last moment.*

Now as to the soul's final fate being made dependent upon the character of that soul's particular act or disposition at the last moment previous to death, this teaching, prominent in parts of the *Trattato* and *Vita*, goes back ultimately to Ezekiel, who, as Prof. Charles interestingly shows, introduces a double individualism into the older, Social and Organic, Eschatology of the Hebrew Prophets. For Man is seen, by him, as responsible for his own acts alone, and as himself working out separately his own salvation or his own doom; and this individual man again is looked at, not in his organic unity, but as repeating himself in a succession of separate religious acts. The individual act is taken to be a true expression of the whole man at the moment of its occurrence: and hence, if this act is wicked at the moment of the advent of the Kingdom, the agent will rightfully be destroyed; but if it be righteous, he will be preserved.[1]—Now the profound truth and genuine advance thus proclaimed, who can doubt them? And yet it is clear that the doctrine here is solidly true, only if taken as the explicitation and supplement, and even in part as the corrective, of the previously predominant teaching. Take the Ezekielian doctrine as complete, even for its own time, or as final over against the later, the Gospel depth of teaching, (with its union of the social body and of individual souls, and of the soul's single acts and of the general disposition produced by and reacting upon these acts), and you get an all but solipsistic Individualism and an atomistic Psychology, and you offend Christianity and Science equally.

It is evident that Catherine, if she can fairly be taxed with what, if pressed, would, in her doctrine rather than in her life, be an excessive Individualism, is, in her general teaching and practice, admirably free from Psychological Atomism; indeed did any soul ever understand better the profound reality of habits, general dispositions, tones of mind and feeling and will, as distinct from the single acts that gradually build them up and that, in return, are encircled and coloured by them all? Her whole Purgatorial doctrine stands and falls by this distinction, and this although, with a profound self-knowledge, she does not hesitate to make the soul express, in one particular act after death,—that of the Plunge,—an even deeper level of its true attitude of will and of its moral character than is constituted by those imperfect habits of the will, habits which it will take so much suffering and acceptance of suffering gradually to rectify.

[1] *Critical History of the Doctrine of a Future Life*, 1899, pp. 63, 64.

Thus the passages in which Catherine seems to teach that God can and does, as it were, catch souls unawares, calling them away, and finally deciding their fate on occasion of any and every *de facto* volitional condition at the instant of death, however little expressive of the radical determination of that soul such an act or surface-state may be, will have, (even if they be genuine, and most of them have doubtlessly grown, perhaps have completely sprung up, under the pen of sermonizing scribes,) to be taken as hortatory, hence as partly hyperbolical. And such an admission will in nowise deny the possibility for the soul to express its deliberate and full disposition and determination in a single act or combination of acts; nor that the other-world effects will follow according to such deep, deliberate orientations of the character: it will only deny that, at any and every moment, any and every act of the soul sufficiently expresses its deliberate disposition. Certainly it is comparatively rarely that the soul exerts its full liberty, in an act of true, spiritual self-realization; and an analogous rarity cannot but be postulated by religious philosophy for contrary acts, of an approximately equal fulness of deliberation and accuracy of representation, with regard to the soul's volitional state. And yet the operative influence towards such rare, fully self-expressive acts of the right kind, and the aid towards similar, massive, and truly representative volitions of the wrong kind, afforded by even quite ordinary half-awake acts and habits of respectively good or evil quality are so undeniable, and it is so impossible to draw a general line as to where such wishes pass into full willings and deliberate states: that the prevalence of a hortatory attitude towards the whole subject is right and indeed inevitable.

2. *The reprobate will of the lost.*

As to Moral Perversion, the reprobate will of the lost, we find that Catherine approaches the question from two different, and at bottom, on this point, incompatible, systems; but some incidental and short sayings of hers give us suggestive hints towards a consistent position in this difficult matter.

Catherine has a double approach. For, consistently with the strong Neo-Platonist, Dionysian strain in her mind, she frequently teaches and implies that Evil is the absence of Good, of Love, and nothing positive at all. In this case Evil would not only be less strong than good—only Manichaeans would maintain that they were equal—but, as against the constructive force of good, it would have no kind even of destructive strength. Varying amounts, degrees, and kinds of good, but good and only good, everywhere, would render all, even transitory, pollution of the soul, and all, even passing, purification of it, so much actual impossibility and theoretical superstition. All that survived at all, could but be good; and at most some good might be added, but no evil could be removed, since none would exist.—Yet all this is, of course, strongly denied and supplanted by the, at first sight, less beautiful, but far deeper and alone fully Christian, position of her specifically Purgatorial teaching. Here Evil is something positive, an active disposition, orientation, and attachment of the will; it is not without destructive force; and its cure is a positive change in that will and its habits, and not a mere addition of good. Yet it is plain that, even exclusively within the implications of this deeper conviction, there is no necessity to postulate unmixed evil in the disposition of any soul. In some the evil would be triumphing over the good; in others good would be triumphing over evil,—each over the other, in every degree of good or of evil, up to the all but complete extinction of all inclinations to evil or to good respectively.

And Catherine has suggestive sayings. For one or two of them go, at least in their implications, beyond a declaration as to the presence of God's extrinsic mercy in Hell, a presence indicated by a mitigation of the souls' sufferings to below what these souls deserve; and even beyond the Areopagite's insistence upon the presence of some real good in these souls, since he hardly gets beyond their continuous possession of those non-moral goods, existence, intelligence, and will-power.[1] For when she says, "The ray of God's mercy shines even in Hell," she need not, indeed, mean more than that extrinsic mercy, and its effect, that mitigation. But when she declares: "if a creature could be found that did not participate in the divine Goodness,—that creature would, as it were, be as malignant as God is good," we cannot, I think, avoid applying this to the moral dispositions of such souls.[2]

Now I know that St. Thomas had already taught, in at first sight identical terms: "Evil cannot exist (quite) pure without the admixture of good, as the Supreme Good exists free from all admixture of evil. . . . Those who are detained

[1] *Divine Names*, ch. iv, secs. xxiii, xxiv: Parker, pp. 61–64.
[2] *Vita*, pp. 173*b*; 33*b*.

in Hell, are not bereft of all good" ; [1] and yet he undoubtedly maintained the complete depravation of the will's dispositions in these souls. And, again, after Catherine's first declaration there follow, (at least in the text handed down in the *Vita*,) words which explain that extrinsic mercy, not as mitigating the finite amount of suffering due to the sinner, but as turning the infinite suffering due to the sinner's infinite malice, into a finite, though indefinite amount; and hence, in the second declaration, a corresponding interior mercy may be signified—God's grace preventing the sinner from being infinitely wicked.

But Catherine, unlike St. Thomas, expressly speaks not only of Good and Evil, but of Good and Malignancy; and Malignancy undoubtedly refers to dispositions of the will. And even if the words, now found as the sequel to the first saying, be authentic, they belong to a different occasion, and cannot be allowed to force the meaning of words spoken at another time. In this latter saying the words "as it were" show plainly that she is not thinking of a possible infiniteness of human wickedness which has been changed, through God's mercy, to an actual finitude of evil; but is simply asking herself whether a man could be, not infinitely but wholly, malignant. For she answers that, were this possible, a man would "as it were" be as malignant as God is good, and thus shows that the malignancy, which she denies, would only in a sense form a counterpart to God's benevolence: since, though the man would be as entirely malignant as God is entirely good, God would still remain infinite in His goodness as against the finitude of Man's wickedness.

The difficulties of such a combination of convictions are, of course, numerous and great. Psychologically it seems hard to understand why this remnant of good disposition should be unable to germinate further and further good, so that, at last, good would leaven the whole soul. From the point of view of any Theodicy, it appears difficult to justify the unending exclusion of such a soul from growth in, and the acquirement of, a predominantly good will and the happiness that accompanies such a will. And the testimony of Our Lord Himself and of the general doctrine of the Church appear definitely opposed: for does not His solemn declaration: "Hell, where their worm dieth not" (Mark ix, 48), find

[1] *Summa Theol.*, suppl., qu. 69, art. 7 ad 9.

its authoritative interpretation in the common Church teaching as to the utterly reprobate will of the lost? And indeed Catherine herself, in her great saying that if but one little drop of Love could fall into Hell (that is, surely, if but the least beginning of a right disposition towards God could enter those souls) Hell would be turned into Heaven, seems clearly to endorse this position.

And yet, we have full experience in this life of genuinely good dispositions being present, and yet not triumphing or even spreading within the soul; of such conditions being, in various degrees, our own fault; and of such defeat bringing necessarily with it more or less of keen suffering.—There would be no injustice if, after a full, good chance and sufficient aid had been given to the soul to actualize its capabilities of spiritual self-constitution, such a soul's deliberately sporadic, culpably non-predominant, good did not, even eventually, lead to the full satisfaction of that soul's essential cravings.—The saying attributed to Our Lord, which appears in St. Mark alone, is a pure quotation from Isaiah lxvi, 24 and Ecclesiasticus vii, 17, and does not seem to require more than an abiding distress of conscience, an eternal keenness of remorse.

Again, the common Church-teaching is undoubtedly voiced by St. Thomas in the words, " Since these souls are completely averse to the final end of right reason, they must be declared to be without any good will." Yet St. Thomas himself (partly in explanation of the Areopagite's words, " the evil spirits desire the good and the best, namely, to be, to live, and to understand "), is obliged to distinguish between such souls' deliberate will and their " natural will and inclination," and to proclaim that this latter, " which is not from themselves but from the Author of nature, who put this inclination into nature . . . can indeed be good." [1] And, if we would not construct a scheme flatly contradictory of all earthly experience, we can hardly restrict the soul, even in the beyond, to entirely indeliberate, good inclinations, and to fully deliberate, bad volitions, but cannot help interposing an indefinite variety of inchoative energizings, half-wishes, and the like, and thinking of these as mixed with good and evil. Indeed this conclusion seems also required by the common teaching that the suffering there differs from soul to soul, and this because of the different degrees of the guilt: for such degrees depend

[1] Dionysius, *Divine Names*, ch. iv, sec. xxiii: Parker, p. 63. St. Thomas, *Summa Theol.*, suppl., qu. 98, art. 1, in corp.

undoubtedly even more upon the degree of deliberation and massiveness of the will than upon the degree of objective badness in the deed, and hence can hardly fail to leave variously small or large fragments of more or less good and imperfectly deliberate wishings and energizings present in the soul.

And finally Catherine's " little drop of Love " would, she says, " at once " turn Hell into Heaven, and hence cannot mean some ordinary good moral disposition or even such supernatural virtues as theological Faith and Hope, but Pure Love alone, which latter queen of all the virtues she is explicitly discussing there. Thus she in nowise requires the absence from these souls of a certain remnant of semi-deliberate virtue of a less exalted, and not necessarily regenerative kind.

3. *Mitigation of the sufferings of the lost.*

As to the Mitigation of the Suffering, it is remarkable that Catherine, who has been so bold concerning the source of the pains, and the dispositions, of the lost souls, does not more explicitly teach such an alleviation. I say "remarkable," because important Fathers and Churches, that were quite uninfected by Origenism, have held and have acted upon such a doctrine. St. Augustine, in his *Enchiridion* (423 A.D. (?)) tells us that " in so far as " the Offering of the Sacrifice of the Altar and Alms " profit " souls in the beyond, " they profit them by procuring a full remission (of the punishment), or at least that their damnation may become more tolerable." And after warning men against believing in an end to the sufferings of the lost, he adds : " But let them consider, if they like, that the sufferings of the damned are somewhat mitigated during certain intervals of time." [1]—Saints John Chrysostom and John Damascene, thoroughly orthodox Greek Fathers, and the deeply devout hymn-writer Prudentius among the Latins, teach similar doctrine; and in many ancient Latin missals, ranging from the eleventh to the fourteenth century, prayers for the Mitigation of the Sufferings of the Damned are to be found.[2]

Hence the great Jesuit Theologian Petau, though not himself sharing this view, can declare : " Concerning such a breathing-time (*respiratio*) of lost souls, nothing certain has as

[1] *Enchiridion*, CX, ed. Ben., col. 403*c*; CXII, col. 404*c*.

[2] The passages here referred to will be found carefully quoted and discussed in Petavius's great *Dogmata Theologica, De Angelis*, III, viii, 16, 17, with Zaccaria's important note (ed. Fournials, 1866, Vol. IV, pp. 119–121).

yet been decreed by the Catholic Church, so that this opinion of most holy Fathers should not temerariously be rejected as absurd, even though it be foreign to the common opinion of Catholics in our time." [1] And the Abbé Emery, that great Catholic Christian, the second founder of St. Sulpice, who died in 1811, showed, in a treatise *On the Mitigation of the Pains of the Damned,* that this view had also been held by certain Scholastic Theologians, and had been defended, without any opposition, by Mark of Ephesus, in the Sessions of the Council of Florence (1439 A.D.); and concluded that this doctrine was not contrary to the Catholic Faith and did not deserve any censure. The most learned Theologians in Rome found nothing reprehensible in this treatise, and Pope Pius VII caused his Theologian, the Barnabite General, Padre Fontana, to thank M. Emery for the copy sent by him to the Holy Father.[2]

Catherine herself cannot well have been thinking of anything but some such Mitigation when she so emphatically teaches that God's mercy extends even into Hell. Indeed, even the continuation of this great saying in the present *Vita*-text formally teaches such Mitigation, yet practically withdraws it, by making it consist in a rebate and change, from an infinitude in degree and duration into a finitude in degree though not in duration.[3] But, as we have already found, this highly schematic statement is doubtless one of the later glosses, in which case her true meaning must have been substantially that of the Fathers referred to, viz. that the suffering, taken as anyhow finite in its degree, gets mercifully mitigated for these souls.—And, if she was here also faithful to her general principles, she will have conceived the mitigation, not as simply sporadic and arbitrary, but as more or less progressive, and connected with the presence in these souls of those various degrees of semi-voluntary good inclinations and wishes, required by her other saying. Even if these wishings could slowly and slightly increase, and the sufferings could similarly decrease, this would in nowise imply or require a final full rectification of the deliberate will itself, and hence not a complete extinction of the resultant suffering. Hell would still remain essentially

[1] *Dogmata Theologica,* Vol. IV, p. 120*b*. See also the interesting note in the Benedictine Edition of *St. Augustine,* Vol. VI, col. 403.

[2] *Vie de M. Emery,* by M. Gosselin, Paris, 1862, Vol. II, pp. 322–324.

[3] *Vita* (*Trattato*), p. 173*b*.

distinct from Purgatory; for in Purgatory the deliberate, active will is good from the first, and only the various semi-volitions and old habits are imperfect, but are being gradually brought into full harmony with that will, by the now complete willing of the soul; and hence this state has an end; whereas in Hell the deliberate, active will is bad from the first, and only various partially deliberate wishes and tendencies are good, but cannot be brought to fruition in a full virtuous determination of the dominant character of the soul, and hence *this* state has no end.

4. *The Endlessness of Hell.*

And lastly, as to the Endlessness of this condition of the Lost, it is, of course, plain that Catherine held this defined doctrine; and again, that "the chief weight, in the Church-teaching as to Hell, rests upon Hell's Eternity." [1]

Here I would suggest five groups of considerations:

(1) Precisely this Eternity appears to be the feature of all others which is ever increasingly decried by contemporary philosophy and liberal theology as impossible and revolting. Thus it is frequently argued as though, not the indiscriminateness nor the materiality nor the forensic externality nor the complete fixity of the sufferings, nor again the complete malignity of the lost were incredible, and hence the unendingness of such conditions were impossible of acceptance; but, on the contrary, as though,—be the degree and nature of those sufferings conceived as ever so discriminated, spiritual, interior and relatively mobile, and as occasioned and accompanied by a disposition in which semi-voluntary good is present,—the simple assumption of anything unending or final about them, at once renders the whole doctrine impossible to believe. It is true that Tennyson and Browning take the doctrine simply in its popular Calvinistic form, and then reject it; and even John Stuart Mill and Frederick Denison Maurice hardly consider the eternity separately. But certainly that thoughtful and religious-minded writer, Mr. W. R. Greg, brings forward the eternity-doctrine as, already in itself, "a *curiosa infelicitas* which is almost stupidity on the part of the Church." [2]

(2) Yet it is plain how strongly, even in Mr. Greg's case, the supposed (local, physical, indiscriminate, etc.) nature of the state affects the writer's judgment as to the possibility of its unendingness,—as indeed is inevitable. And it is even

[1] So Atzberger, in Scheeben's *Dogmatik*, Vol. IV (1903), p. 826.
[2] *Enigmas of Life*, ed. 1892, p. 255.

clearer, I think, that precisely this eternity-doctrine stands for a truth which is but an ever-present mysterious corollary to every deeply ethical or spiritual, and, above all, every specifically Christian view of life. For every such view comes, surely, into hopeless collision with its own inalienable requirements if it *will* hold that the deepest ethical and spiritual acts and conditions are,—avowedly performed though they be in time and space—simply temporary in their inmost nature and effects; whereas every vigorously ethical religion, in so far as it has reached a definite personal-immortality doctrine at all, cannot admit that the soul's deliberate character remains without any strictly final and permanent results. The fact is that we get here to a profound ethical and spiritual postulate, which cannot be adequately set aside on the ground that it is the product of barbarous ages and vindictive minds, since this objection applies only to the physical picturings, the indiscriminateness, non-mitigation, and utter reprobation; or on the ground that a long, keen purification, hence a temporally finite suffering, would do as well, since, when all this has com pletely passed away, there would be an entire obliteration of all difference in the consequences of right and wrong; or that acts and dispositions built up in time cannot have other than finite consequences, since this is to naturalize radically the deepest things of life; or finally that " Evil," as the Areopagite would have it, " is not,"[1] since thus the very existence of the conviction as to free-will and sin becomes more inexplicable than the theoretical difficulties against Libertarianism are insoluble.—Against this deep requirement of the most alert and complete ethical and spiritual life the wave of any Apocatastasis-doctrine or -emotion will, in the long run, ever break itself in vain.

(3) The doctrine of Conditional Immortality has, I think, many undeniable advantages over every kind of Origenism. This view does not, as is often imputed to it, believe in the annihilation by Omnipotence of the naturally immortal souls of impenitent grave sinners; but simply holds that human souls begin with the capacity of acquiring, with the help of God's Spirit, a spiritual personality, built up out of the mere possibilities and partial tendencies of their highly mixed natures, which, if left uncultivated and untranscended, become definitely fixed at the first, phenomenal, merely individual

[1] *Divine Names*, ch. iv, secs. 23, 24: Parker, pp. 70, 71.

level,—so that spiritual personality alone deserves to live on and does so, whilst this animal individuality does not deserve and does not do so. The soul is thus not simply born as, but can become more and more, that " inner man " who alone persists, indeed who " is renewed day by day, even though our outward man perish."[1]

This conception thus fully retains, indeed increases, the profound ultimate difference between the results of spiritual and personal, and of animal and simply individual life respectively,—standing, as it does, at the antipodes to Origenism; it eliminates all unmoralized, unspiritualized elements from the ultimate world, without keeping souls in an apparently fruitless suffering; and it gives full emphasis to a supremely important, though continually forgotten fact,—the profoundly expensive, creative, positive process and nature of spiritual character. No wonder, then, that great thinkers and scholars, such as Goethe, Richard Rothe, Heinrich Holtzmann, and some Frenchmen and Englishmen have held this view.[2]

Yet the objections against this view, taken in its strictness, are surely conclusive. For how can an originally simply mortal substance, force, or entity become immortal, and a phenomenal nature be leavened by a spiritual principle which, *ex hypothesi*, is not present within it? And how misleadingly hyperbolical, according to this, would be the greatest spiritual exhortations, beginning with those of Our Lord Himself!

(4) And yet the conception of Conditional Immortality cannot be far from the truth, since everything, surely, points to a lowered consciousness in the souls in question, or at least to one lower than that in the ultimate state of the saved. This conception of the shrunken condition of these souls was certainly held by Catherine, even if the other, the view of a heightened, consciousness, appears in hortatory passages which just *may* be authentic; and indeed only that conception is conformable with her fundamental position that love alone is fully positive and alone gives vital strength, and that all fully deliberate love is absent from the lost souls. And if we

[1] 2 Cor. iv, 16.

[2] See H. J. Holtzmann, Richard Rothe's *Speculatives System*, 1899, pp. 110, 111; 123, 124;—Georg Class, *Phänomenologie und Ontologie des Menschlichen Geistes*, 1896, pp. 220, 221;—and that strange mixture of stimulating thought, deep earnestness, and fantastic prejudice, Edward White's *Life of Christ*, ed. 1876.

consider how predominantly hortatory in tone and object the ordinary teaching on this point cannot fail to be; and, on the other hand, how close to Manichaeism, any serious equating of the force and intensity of life and consciousness between the Saved and the Lost would be, we can hardly fail to find ourselves free, indeed compelled, to hold a lesser consciousness for the Lost than for the Saved. Whilst the joyful life of the Saved would range, in harmonious intensity, beyond all that we can experience here, the painful consciousness of the Lost would be, in various degrees, indefinitely less. The Saved would thus not be only *other* than the Lost, they would actually be *more*: for God is Life supreme, and, where there is more affinity with God, there is more life, and more consciousness.

(5) But, if the view just stated is the more likely one, then we cannot soften the sufferings of those souls, by giving them a sense of Eternity, of one unending momentary Now, instead of our earthly sense of Succession, as Cardinal Newman and Father Tyrrell have attempted to do, in a very instructive and obviously orthodox manner.[1] I shall presently argue strongly in favour of some consciousness of Eternity being traceable in our best moments here, and of this consciousness being doubtless more extended in the future blessed life. But here I have only to consider whether for one who, like Catherine, follows the analogy of earthly experience, the Lost should be considered nearer to, or further from, such a *Totum-Simul* consciousness than we possess now, here below, at our best? And to this the answer must, surely, be that they are further away from it. Yet God in His Mercy may allow this greater successiveness, if unaccompanied by any keen memory or prevision, to help in effecting that mitigation of the suffering which we have already allowed.

IV. Catherine and Purgatory.

1. *Introductory.*

(1) *Changed feeling concerning Purgatory.*

In the matter of a Purgatory, a very striking return of religious feeling towards its normal equilibrium has been occurring in the most unexpected, entirely unprejudiced

[1] *Grammar of Assent*, 1870 p. 417. *Hard Sayings*, 1898, p. 113.

quarters, within the last century and a half. In Germany we have Lessing, who, in the wake of Leibniz, encourages the acceptance of "that middle state which the greater part of our fellow-Christians have adopted": Schleiermacher, who calls the overpassing of a middle state by a violent leap at death "a magical proceeding"; David F. Strauss, who entirely agrees; Carl von Hase, who, in his very Manual of Anti-Roman Polemics admits that "most men when they die are probably too good for Hell, but they are certainly too bad for Heaven"; the delicately thoughtful philosopher Fechner who, in the most sober-minded of his religious works, insists upon our "conceiving the life beyond according to the analogy of this-life conditions," and refers wistfully to "the belief which is found amongst all peoples and is quite shrunken only among Protestants—that the living can still do something to aid the dead"; and Prof. Anrich, probably the greatest contemporary authority on the Hellenic elements incorporated in Christian doctrine, declares, all definite Protestant though he is, that "legitimate religious postulates underlie the doctrine of Purgatory."[1] And in England that sensitively religious Unitarian, W. R. Greg, tells us "Purgatory, ranging from a single day to a century of ages, offers that borderland of discriminating retribution for which justice and humanity cry out"; and the Positivist, John Stuart Mill, declares at the end of his life: "All the probabilities in case of a future life are that such as we have been made or have made ourselves before the change, such we shall enter into the life hereafter. . . . To imagine that a miracle will be wrought at death . . . making perfect every one whom it is His will to include among His elect . . . is utterly opposed to every presumption that can be adduced from the light of nature."[2]

(2) *Causes of the previous prejudice.*

Indeed the general principle of ameliorative suffering is so

[1] G. E. Lessing, "Leibniz von den Ewigen Strafen," in Lessing's *Sämmtliche Werke*, ed. Lachmann-Muncker, 1895, Vol. XI, p. 486. D. F. Strauss, *Die christliche Glaubenslehre*, 1841, Vol. II, pp. 684, 685. Carl von Hase, *Handbuch der protestantischen Polemik*, ed. 1864, p. 422. G. T. Fechner, *Die drei Gründe und Motive des Glaubens*, 1863, pp. 146, 147, 177. G. Anrich, "Clemens und Origenes, als Begründer der Lehre vom Fegfeuer," in *Theologische Abhandlungen für H. J. Holtzmann*, 1902, p. 120.

[2] W. R. Greg, *Enigmas of Life*, ed. 1892, pp. 256, 257, 259. J. S. Mill, *Three Essays on Religion*, ed. 1874, p. 211.

obviously true and inexhaustibly profound that only many, long-lived abuses in the practice, and a frequent obscuration in the teaching, of the doctrine, can explain and excuse the sad neglect, indeed discredit, into which the very principle and root-doctrine has fallen among well-nigh one-half of Western Christendom. As to the deplorably widespread existence, at the time of the Protestant Reformation, of both these causes, which largely occasioned or strengthened each other, we have the unimpeachable authority of the Council of Trent itself: for it orders the Bishops "not to permit that uncertain doctrines, or such as labour under the presumption of falsity, be propagated and taught," and "to prohibit, as so many scandals and stones of stumbling for the faithful, whatever belongs to a certain curiosity or superstition or savours of filthy lucre."[1] The cautious admissions of the strictly Catholic scholar-theologian, Dr. N. Paulus, and the precise documentary additions and corrections to Paulus furnished, directly from the contemporary documents, by the fair-minded Protestant worker at Reformation History, Prof. T. Brieger, now furnish us, conjointly, with the most vivid and detailed picture of the sad subtleties and abuses which gave occasion to that Decree.[2]

(3) *Catherine's purgatorial conceptions avoid those causes. Her conceptions harbour two currents of thought.*

It is surely not a small recommendation of Catherine's mode of conceiving Purgatory, that it cuts, as we shall see, at the very root of those abuses. Yet we must first face certain opposite dangers and ambiguities which are closely intertwined with the group of terms and images taken over, for the purpose of describing an immanental Purgation, by her and her great Alexandrian Christian predecessors, from the Greek Heathen world. And only after the delimitation of the defect in the suggestions which still so readily operate from out of these originally Hellenic ideas, can we consider the difficulties and imperfections peculiar to the other, in modern times the predominant, element in the complete teaching as to the Middle State, an element mostly of Jewish and Roman provenance, and aiming at an extrinsically punitive conception. Both currents can be properly elucidated only if we first take them historically.

[1] Sess. XXV, Decret. de Purgatorio, med.

[2] N. Paulus, *Johann Tetzel*, 1899. Brieger's review, *Theologische Literatur-Zeitung*, 1900, coll. 117, 118.

1. *Jewish prayers for the dead.*

It is admitted on all hands that, in the practical form of Prayers for the Dead, the general doctrine of a Middle State can be traced back, in Judaism, up to the important passage in the Second Book of Maccabees, c. xii, vv. 43–45, where Judas Maccabaeus sends about two thousand drachms of silver to Jerusalem, in order that a Sin-Offering may be offered up for the Jews fallen in battle against Gorgias, upon whose bodies heathen amulets had been found. "He did excellently in this . . . it is a holy and devout thought. Hence he instituted the Sin-Offering for the dead, that they might be loosed from their sins." That battle occurred in 166 B.C., and this book appears to have been written in 124 B.C., in Egypt, by a Jew of the school of the Pharisees.

Now it is difficult not to recognize, in the doctrinal comment upon the facts here given, rather as yet the opinions of a Judaeo-Alexandrian circle, which was small even at the time of the composition of the comment, than the general opinion of Judaism at the date of Judas's act. For if this act had been prompted by a clear and generally accepted conviction as to the resurrection, and the efficacy of prayers for the dead, the writer would have had no occasion or inclination to make an induction of his own as to the meaning and worth of that act; and we should find some indications of such a doctrine and practice in the voluminous works of Philo and Josephus, some century and a half later on. But all such indications are wanting in these writers.

And in the New Testament there is, with regard to helping the dead, only that curious passage: "If the dead are not raised at all, why then are they baptized for them?"[1] where St. Paul refers, without either acceptance or blame, to a contemporary custom among Christian Proselytes from Paganism, who offered up that bath of initiation for the benefit of the souls of deceased relatives who had died without any such purification. Perhaps not till Rabbi Akiba's time, about 130 A.D., had prayers for the dead become part of the regular Synagogue ritual. By 200 A.D. Tertullian speaks of the practice as of an established usage among the Christian communities: "we make oblations for the Dead, on their anniversary, every year"; although "if you ask where is the law concerning this custom in Scripture, you cannot read of

[1] 1 Cor. xv, 29.

any such there. Tradition will appear before you as its initiator, custom as its confirmer, and faith as its observer." [1]

It is interesting to note how considerably subsequent to the practice is, in this instance also, its clear doctrinal justification. Indeed the Jews are, to this hour, extraordinarily deficient in explicit, harmonious conceptions on the matter. Certainly throughout Prof. W. Bacher's five volumes of Sayings of the Jewish Rabbis from 30 B.C. to 400 A.D., I can only find the following saying, by Jochanan the Amoraean, who died 279 A.D.: "There are three books before God, in which men are inscribed according to their merit and their guilt: that of the perfectly devout, that of the perfect evil-doers, and that of the middle, the uncertain souls. The devout and the evil-doers receive their sentence on New Year's day . . . the first, unto life; the second, unto death. As to middle souls, their sentence remains in suspense till the day of Atonement: if by then they have done penance, they get written down alongside of the devout; if not, they are written down alongside of the evil-doers." [2]

2. *Alexandrine Fathers on Purgatory.*

Yet it is the Platonizing Alexandrian Fathers Clement and Origen (they died, respectively, in about 215 A.D. and in 254 A.D.), who are the first, and to this hour the most important, Christian spokesmen for a state of true intrinsic purgation. We have already deliberately rejected their Universalism; but this error in no way weakens the profound truth of their teaching as to the immanental, necessary interconnection between suffering and morally imperfect habits, and as to the ameliorative effects of suffering where, as in Purgatory, it is willed by a right moral determination. Thus Clement: "As children at the hands of their teacher or father, so also are we punished by Providence. God does not avenge Himself, for vengeance is to repay evil by evil, but His punishment aims at our good." "Although a punishment, it is an emendation of the soul." "The training which men call punishments." [3] And Origen: "The fury of God's vengeance profits unto the purification of souls; the punishment is unto purgation."

[1] *De Corona*, III, IV. See M. Salomon Reinach's interesting paper, "l'Origine des Prières pour les Morts," in *Cultes, Mythes, et Religions*, 1905, pp. 316–331.

[2] W. Bacher, *Die Agada der palästinenischen Amoräer*, Vol. I, 1892, p. 331.

[3] *Strom.*, VII, 26 (Migne, *Ser. Graec*, Vol. IX, col. 541); I, 26 (*ibid.* Vol. VIII, col. 916); VII, 26 (*ibid.* Vol. IX, col. 540).

"These souls receive, in the prison, not the retribution of their folly, but a benefaction in the purification from the evils contracted in that folly,—a purification effected by means of salutary troubles."[1]

Now Clement is fully aware of the chief source for his formulation of these deeply spiritual and Christian instincts and convictions. "Plato speaks well when he teaches that 'men who are punished, experience in truth a benefit: for those who get justly punished, profit through their souls becoming better.'"[2] But Plato, in contradistinction from Clement, holds that this applies only to such imperfect souls as "have sinned curable sins"; he has a Hell as well as a Purgatory: yet his Purgatory, as Clement's, truly purges: the souls are there because they are partially impure, and they cease to be there when they are completely purified.

And Plato, in his turn, makes no secret as to whence he got his suggestions and raw materials, *viz.* the Orphic priesthood and its literature, which, ever since the sixth century B.C., had been succeeding to and supplanting the previous Orgiastic Dionysianism.[3] Plato gives us vivid pictures of their doings in Athens, at the time of his writing, in about 380 B.C. "Mendicant prophets go to rich men's doors, and persuade these men that they have a power committed to them of making an atonement for their sins, or for those of their fathers, by sacrifices and incantations . . . and they persuade whole cities that expiations and purifications of sin may be made by sacrifices and amusements which fill a vacant hour, and are equally at the service of the living and the dead."[4]—Yet from these men, thus scorned as well-nigh sheer impostors, Plato takes over certain conceptions and formulations which contribute one of the profoundest, still unexhausted elements to his teaching,—although this element is, at bottom, in conflict with that beautiful but inadequate, quite anti-Orphic, conception of his—the purely negative character of Evil. For the Orphic literary remains, fragmentary and late though they be, plainly teach that moral or ritual transgressions are a defilement of the soul, an infliction of positive stains upon it; that these single offences and "spots" produce a generally

[1] *De Princ.*, II, 10, 6. *De Orat.*, XXIX, p. 263.

[2] *Paedag.*, I, 8, p. 51; and Plato, *Gorgias*, p. 477*a*.

[3] I owe here almost everything to the truly classical account in Rohde's *Psyche*, ed. 1898, Vol. II, pp. 1–136.

[4] *Republic*, II, p. 364*b*, *c*, *e*.

sinful and "spotted" condition; and that this condition is amenable to and requires purification by suffering,—water, or more frequently fire, which wash or burn out these stains of sin. So Plutarch (who died about 120 A.D.) still declares that the souls in Hades have stains of different colours according to the different passions; and the object of the purificatory punishment is "that, these stains having been worn away, the soul may become altogether resplendent." And Virgil, when he declares "the guilt which infects the soul is washed out or burnt out . . . until a long time-span has effaced the clotted stain, and leaves the heavenly conscience pure": is utilizing an Orphic-Pythagorean Hades-book.[1]

This conception of positive stains is carefully taken over by the Alexandrian Fathers: Clement speaks of "removing, by continuous prayer, the stains (κηλίδας) contracted through former sins," and declares that "the Gnostic," the perfect Christian, "fears not death, having purified himself from all the spots (σπίλους) on his soul." And Origen describes "the pure soul that is not weighed down by leaden weights of wickedness," where the spots have turned to leaden pellets such as were fastened to fishing-nets. Hence, says Clement, "post-baptismal sins have to be purified out" of the soul; and, says Origen, "these rivers of fire are declared to be of God, who causes the evil that is mixed up with the whole soul to disappear from out of it."[2]

In Pseudo-Dionysius the non-Orphic, purely negative, view prevails: "Evil is neither in demons nor in us as an existent evil, but as a failure and dearth in the perfection of our own proper goods." And St. Thomas similarly declares that "different souls have correspondingly different stains, like shadows differ in accordance with the difference of the bodies which interpose themselves between the light."[3]

But Catherine, in this inconsistent with her own general Privation-doctrine, again conceives the stain, the "macchia del peccato," as Cardinal Manning has acutely observed, not simply as a deprivation of the light of glory, but "as the cause, not the effect, of God's not shining into the soul": it includes

[1] I take these passages from Anrich's *Clemens und Origenes*, *op. cit.* p. 102, n. 5.

[2] Clemens, *Strom.*, V, 3, p. 236. Origen, *Contra Cels.*, VII, 13. Clemens, *Strom.*, IV, 24. Origen, *Contra Cels.*, IV, 13.

[3] Dionysius, *Divine Names*, ch. iv, sec. 24: Parker, p. 64. St. Thomas, *Summa Theol.*, I, ii, qu. 86, art. 1 ad 3 et concl.

in it the idea of an imperfection, weakness with regard to virtue, bad (secondary) dispositions, and unheavenly tastes.[1]

3. *The true and the false in the Orphic conception.*

Now precisely in this profoundly true conception of Positive Stain there lurk certain dangers, which all proceed from the original Orphic diagnosis concerning the source of these stains, and these dangers will have to be carefully guarded against.

(1) The conviction as to the purificatory power of fire was no doubt, originally, the direct consequence from the Orphic belief as to the intrinsically staining and imprisoning effect of the body upon the soul. "The soul, as the Orphics say, is enclosed in the body, in punishment for the punishable acts"; "liberations" from the body, and "purifications" of the living and the dead, ever, with them, proceed together. And hence to burn the dead body was considered to purify the soul that had been stained by that prison-house: the slain Clytemnestra, says Euripides, "is purified, as to her body, by fire," for, as the Scholiast explains, "fire purifies all things, and burnt bodies are considered holy."[2] And such an intensely anti-body attitude we find, not only fully developed later on into a deliberate anti-Incarnational doctrine, among the Gnostics, but, as we have already seen, slighter traces of this same tone may be found in the (doubtless Alexandrian) Book of Wisdom, and in one, not formally doctrinal passage, a momentary echo of it, in St. Paul himself. And Catherine's attitude is generally, and often strongly, in this direction.

(2) A careful distinction is evidently necessary here. The doctrine that sin defiles,—affects the quality of the soul's moral and spiritual dispositions, and that this defilement and perversion, ever occasioned by the search after facile pleasure or the flight from fruitful pain, can normally be removed, and corrected only by a long discipline of fully accepted, gradually restorative pain, either here, or hereafter, or both: are profound anticipations, and have been most rightly made integral parts, of the Christian life and conception. The doctrine that the body is essentially a mere accident or superaddition or necessary defilement to the soul, is profoundly untrue, in its exaggeration and one-sidedness: for if the body is the occasion of the least spiritual of our sins, it can and should become the

[1] *Treatise on Purgatory*, by St. Catherine of Genoa, ed. 1880, p. 31.

[2] Plato, *Cratylus*, p. 400c. *Republic*, II, p. 364e. Euripides, *Orestes*, XXX, *seq.*, with Schol. Rohde, *op. cit.*, Vol. II, p. 101, n. 2.

chief servant of the spirit; the slow and difficult training of this servant is one of the most important means of development for the soul itself; and many faults and vices are not occasioned by the body at all, whilst none are directly and necessarily caused by it. Without the body, we should not have impurity, but neither should we have specifically human purity of soul; and without it, given the persistence and activity of the soul, there could be as great, perhaps greater, pride and *solipsism*, the most anti-Christian of all the vices. Hence if, in Our Lord's teaching, we find no trace of a Gnostic desire for purification from all things bodily as essentially soul-staining, we do find a profound insistence upon purity of heart, and upon the soul's real, active "turning," conversion, (an interior change from an un- or anti-moral attitude to an ethical and spiritual dependence upon God), as a *sine qua non* condition for entrance into the Kingdom of Heaven. And the Joannine teachings re-affirm this great truth for us as a *Metabasis*, a moving from Death over to Life.

4. *Catherine's conceptions as to the character of the stains and of their purgation.*

And this idea, as to intrinsic purgation through suffering of impurities contracted by the soul, can be kept thoroughly Christian, if we ever insist, with Catherine in her most emphatic and deepest teachings, that Purgation can and should be effected in this life, hence in the body,—in and through all the right uses of the body, as well as in and through all the legitimate and will-strengthening abstentions from such uses; that the subject-matter of such purgation are the habits and inclinations contrary to our best spiritual lights, and which we have largely ourselves built up by our variously perverse or slothful acts, but which in no case are directly caused by the body, and in many cases are not even occasioned by it; and, finally, that holiness consists primarily, not in the absence of faults, but in the presence of spiritual force, in Love creative, Love triumphant,—the soul becoming flame rather than snow, and dwelling upon what to do, give and be, rather than upon what to shun.—Catherine's predominant, ultimate tone possesses this profound positiveness, and corrects all but entirely whatever, if taken alone, would appear to render the soul's substantial purity impossible in this life; to constitute the body a direct and necessary cause of impurity to the soul; and to find the ideal of perfection in the negative condition of being free from stain.

In her greatest sayings, and in her actual life, Purity is found to be Love, and this Love is exercised, not only in the inward, home-coming, recollective movement,—in the purifying of the soul's dispositions, but also in the outgoing, world-visiting, dispersive movement,—in action towards fellow-souls.

5. *Judaeo-Roman conception of Purgatory.*

And this social side and movement brings us to the second element and current in the complete doctrine of a Middle State,—a constituent which possesses affinities and advantages, and produces excesses and abuses, directly contrary to those proper to the element of an intrinsic purgation.

(1) Here we get early Christian utilizations, for purposes of a doctrine concerning the Intermediate State, of sayings and images which dwell directly only upon certain extrinsic consequences of evil-doing, or which, again, describe a future historical and social event,—the Last Day. For already Origen interprets, in his beautiful *Treatise on Prayer*, XXIX, 16, Our Lord's words as to the debtor: "And thou be cast into prison . . . thou shalt by no means come out thence, till thou hast paid the last farthing," Matt. v, 25, 26, as applying to Purgatory. And in his *Contra Celsum*, VII, 13, he already takes, as the Biblical *locus classicus* for a Purgatory, St. Paul's words as to how men build, upon the one foundation Christ, either gold, silver, gems, or wood, hay, stubble; and how fire will test each man's work; and, if the work remain, he shall receive a reward, but if it be burnt, he shall suffer loss and yet he himself shall be saved yet so as by fire, 1 Cor. iii, 10–15. It appears certain, however, that St. Paul is, in this passage, thinking directly of the Last Day, the End of the World, with its accompaniment of physical fire, and as to how far the various human beings, then on earth, will be able to endure the dread stress and testing of that crisis; and he holds that some will be fit to bear it and some will not.

Such a destruction of the world by fire appears elsewhere in Palestinian Jewish literature,—in the Book of Enoch and the Testament of Levi; and in the New Testament, in 2 Peter iii, 12: "The heavens being on fire shall be dissolved, and the elements shall melt with fervent heat." Josephus, *Antiquities*, XI, ii, 3, teaches a destruction by fire and another by water. And the Stoics, to whom also Clement and Origen appeal, had gradually modified their first doctrine of a simply cosmological Ekpyrōsis, a renovation of the physical universe by fire, into a moral purification of the earth, occasioned by, and applied to, the sinfulness of man. Thus Seneca has the double, water-and-fire, instrument: "At that time the tide" of the sea "will be borne along free from all measure, for the same reason which will cause the future conflagration. Both occur when it seems fit to God to initiate a better order of things and to have done with the old. . . . The judgment of mankind being concluded, the primitive order of things will be recalled, and to the earth will be re-given man innocent of crimes."[1]

(2) It is interesting to note how—largely under the influence of the forensic temper and growth of the Canonical Penitential system, and of its successive relaxations in the form of substituted lighter good works, Indulgences,—the Latin half of Christendom, ever more social and immediately practical than the Greek portion, came, in general, more and more to dwell upon two ideas suggested to their minds by those two, Gospel and Pauline, passages. The one idea was that souls which, whilst fundamentally well-disposed, are not fit for Heaven at the body's death, can receive instant purification by the momentary fire of the Particular Judgment; and the other held that, thus already entirely purified and interiorly fit for Heaven, they are but detained (in what we ought, properly, to term a *Satisfactorium*), to suffer the now completely non-ameliorative, simply vindictive, infliction of punishment,—a punishment still, in strict justice, due to them for past sins, of which the guilt and the deteriorating effects upon their own souls have been fully remitted and cured.

In this way it was felt that the complete unchangeableness of the condition of every kind of soul after death, or at least after the Particular Judgment (a Judgment held practically to synchronize with death), was assured. And indeed how could there be any interior growth in Purgatory, seeing that there is no meriting there? Again it was thought that thus the vision of God at the moment of Judgment was given an operative value for the spiritual amelioration of souls which, already in substantially good dispositions, could hardly be held to pass through so profound an experience without intrinsic improvement, as the other view seemed to hold.—And, above all, this form of the doctrine was found greatly to favour the multiplication among the people of prayers, Masses and good-works for the dead; since the *modus operandi* of

[1] *Natur. quaest.* III, 28, 7; 30, 7, 8.

such acts seemed thus to become entirely clear, simple, immediate, and, as it were, measurable and mechanical. For these souls in their "Satisfactorium," being, from its very beginning, already completely purged and fit for Heaven,—God is, as it were, free to relax at any instant, in favour of sufficiently fervent or numerous intercessions, the exigencies of his entirely extrinsic justice.

(3) The position of a purely extrinsic punishment is emphasized, with even unusual vehemence, in the theological glosses inserted, in about 1512 to 1529, in Catherine's *Dicchiarazione*. Yet it is probably the very influential Jesuit theologian Francesco Suarez, who died in 1617, who has done most towards formulating and theologically popularizing this view. All the guilt of sin, he teaches, is remitted (in these Middle souls) at the first moment of the soul's separation from the body, by means of a single act of contrition, whereby the will is wholly converted to God, and turned away from every venial sin. "And in this way sin may be remitted, as to its guilt, in Purgatory, because the soul's purification dates from this moment";—in strictness, from before the first moment of what should be here termed the "Satisfactorium." As to bad habits and vicious inclinations, "we ought not to imagine that the soul is detained for these": but "they are either taken away at the moment of death, or expelled by an infusion of the contrary virtues when the soul enters into glory."[1] This highly artificial, inorganic view is adopted, amongst other of our contemporary theologians, by Atzberger, the continuator of Scheeben.[2]

6. *The Judaeo-Roman conception must be taken in synthesis with the Alexandrine.*

Now it is plain that the long-enduring Penitential system of the Latin Church, and the doctrine and practice of Indulgences stand for certain important truths liable to being insufficiently emphasized by the Greek teachings concerning an intrinsically ameliorative *Purgatorium*, and that there can be no question of simply eliminating these truths. But neither are they capable of simple co-ordination with, still less of super-ordination to, those most profound and spiritually central immanental positions. As between the primarily forensic and governmental, and the directly ethical and spiritual, it will be the former that will have to be conceived

[1] Disp. XI, Sec. iv, art. 2, §§ 13, 10; Disp. XLVII, Sec. i, art. 6.
[2] Scheeben's *Dogmatik*, Vol. IV, 1903, pp. 856 (No. 93), 723.

and practised as, somehow, an expression and amplification of, and a practical corrective and means to, the latter.[1]

(1) The ordinary, indeed the strictly obligatory, Church teaching clearly marks the suggested relation as the right one, at three, simply cardinal points. We are bound, by the Confession of Faith of Michael Palaeologus, 1267 A.D., and by the Decree of the Council of Florence, 1429 A.D., to hold that these Middle souls "are purged after death by purgatorial or cathartic pains"; and by that of Trent "that there is a Purgatory."[2] Yet we have here a true *lucus a non lucendo,* if this place or state does not involve purgation: for no theologian dares explicitly to transfer and restrict the name "Purgatory" to the instant of the soul's Particular Judgment; even Suarez, as we have seen, has to extend the name somehow.

Next we are bound, by the same three great Decrees, to hold indeed that "the Masses, Prayers, Alms, and other pious offices of the Faithful Living are profitable towards the relief of these pains," yet this by mode of "suffrage," since, as the severely orthodox Jesuit, Father H. Hurter, explains in his standard *Theologiae Dogmaticae Compendium,* "the fruit of this impetration and satisfaction is not infallible, for it depends upon the merciful acceptance of God."[3] Hence in no case can we, short of superstition, conceive such good works as operating automatically: so that the *a priori* simplest view concerning the mode of operation of these prayers is declared to be mistaken. We can and ought, then, to choose among the conceptions, not in proportion to their mechanical simplicity, but according to their spiritual richness and to their analogy with our deepest this-life experiences.

And we are all bound, by the Decree of Trent and the Condemnation of Baius, 1567 A.D., to hold that Contrition springing from Perfect Love reconciles man with God, even before Confession, and this also outside of cases of necessity or of martyrdom.[4] Indeed, it is the common doctrine that one single act of Pure Love abolishes, not only Hell, but Purgatory, so that, if the soul were to die whilst that act was in operation,

[1] See Abbé Boudhinon's careful article, "Sur l'Histoire des Indulgences," *Revue d'Histoire et de Littérature Religieuses,* 1898, pp. 435–455, for a vivid illustration of the necessity of explaining the details of this doctrine and practice by history of the most patient kind.

[2] Denzinger, *Enchiridion,* ed. 1888, Nos. 387, 588, 859.

[3] Denzinger, *ibid.*, Hurter, *op. cit.* ed. 1893, Vol. III, p. 591.

[4] Denzinger, *ibid.*, ed. 1888, Nos. 778, 951.

it would forthwith be in Heaven. If then, in case of perfect purity, the soul is at once in heaven, the soul cannot be quite pure and yet continue in Purgatory.

(2) It is thus plain that, as regards Sin in its relation to the Sinner, there are, in strictness, ever three points to consider: the guilty act, the reflex effect of the act upon the disposition of the agent, and the punishment; for all theologians admit that the more or less bad disposition, contracted through the sinful act, remains in the soul, except in the case of Perfect Contrition, after the guilt of the act has been remitted. But whilst the holders of an Extrinsic, Vindictive Purgatory, work for a punishment as independent as possible of these moral effects of sin still present in the pardoned soul, the advocates of an Intrinsic, Ameliorative Purgatory find the punishment to centre in the pain and difficulty attendant upon "getting slowly back to fully virtuous dispositions, through retracing the steps we have taken in departing from it."[1] And the system of Indulgences appears, in this latter view, to find its chief justification in that it keeps up a link with the past Penitential system of the Church; that it vividly recalls and applies the profound truth of the interaction, for good even more than for evil, between all human souls, alive and dead; and that it insists upon the readily forgotten truth of even the forgiven sinner, the man with the good determination, having ordinarily still much to do and to suffer before he is quit of the effects of his sin.

(3) And the difficulties and motives special to those who supplant the Intrinsic, Ameliorating Purgatory by an Extrinsic, Vindicative *Satisfactorium*, can indeed be met by those who would preserve that beautifully dynamic, ethical, and spiritual conception. For we can hold that the fundamental condition,—the particular determination of the active will,—remains quite unchanged, from Death to Heaven, in these souls; that this determination of the active will requires more or less of time and suffering fully to permeate and assimilate to itself all the semi-voluntary wishes and habits of the soul; and that this permeation takes place among conditions in which the soul's acts are too little resisted and too certain of success to be constituted meritorious. We can take Catherine's beautiful Plunge-conception as indicating the kind of operation effected in and by the soul, at and through the momentary vision of God. And we can feel convinced that it is ever, in

[1] Cardinal Manning in *Treatise*, ed. cit. p. 31.

the long run, profoundly dangerous to try to clarify and simplify doctrines beyond or against the scope and direction of the analogies of Nature and of Grace, which are ever so dynamic and organic in type: for the poor and simple, as truly as the rich and learned, ever require, not to be merely taken and left as they are, but to be raised and trained to the most adequate conceptions possible to each.—It is, in any case, very certain that the marked and widespread movement of return to belief in a Middle State is distinctly towards a truly Purgative Purgatory, although few of these sincere truth-seekers are aware, as is Dr. Anrich, that they are groping after a doctrine all but quite explained away by a large body of late Scholastic and Neo-Scholastic theologians.[1]

(4) Yet it is very satisfactory to note how numerous, and especially how important are, after all is said, the theologians who have continued to walk, in this matter, in the footsteps of the great Alexandrines. St. Gregory of Nyssa teaches a healing of the soul in the beyond and a purification by fire.[2] St. Augustine says that "fire burns up the work of him who thinketh of the things of this world, since possessions, that are loved, do not perish without pain on the part of their possessor. It is not incredible that something of this sort takes place after this life."[3]

St. Thomas declares most plainly: "Venial guilt, in a soul which dies in a state of grace, is remitted after this life by the purging fire, because that pain, which is in some manner accepted by the will, has, in virtue of grace, the power of expiating all such guilt as can co-exist with a state of grace." "After this life . . . there can be merit with respect to some accidental reward, so long as a man remains in some manner in a state of probation: and hence there can be meritorious acts in Purgatory, with respect to the remission of venial sin."[4]—Dante (*d.* 1321) also appears, as Father Faber finely notes, to hold such a voluntary, immanental Purgatory, where the poet sees an Angel impelling, across the sea at dawn, a bark filled with souls bent for Purgatory: for the boat is described as driving towards the shore so lightly as to draw no wake upon the water.[5]

[1] *Op. cit.* pp. 119, 120: "The Purgatory of the Catholic Church, in strictness, bears its name without warrant."
[2] *Cat.*, cc. viii, 35.
[3] *De octo Dulcitii quaest.* 12, 13.
[4] *Summa Theol.*, app., qu. 2, art. 4, in corp. et ad 4.
[5] *Divina Commedia*, Purg. II, 40–42. See Faber, *All for Jesus*, ed. 1889, p. 361.

Cardinal Bellarmine, perhaps the greatest of all anti-Protestant theologians (*d.* 1621) teaches that " venial sin is remitted in Purgatory *quoad culpam,*" and that " this guilt, as St. Thomas rightly insists, is remitted in Purgatory by an act of love and patient endurance." [1] St. Francis of Sales, that high ascetical authority (*d.* 1622), declares : " By Purgatory we understand a place where souls undergo purgation, for a while, from the stains and imperfections which they have carried away with them from this mortal life." [2]

And recently and in England we have had Father Faber, Cardinal Manning, and Cardinal Newman, although differing from each other on many other points, fully united in holding and propagating this finely life-like, purgative conception of Purgatory.[3]

7. *A final difficulty.*

One final point concerning a Middle State. In the Synoptic tradition there is a recurrent insistence upon the forgiveness of particular sins, at particular moments, by particular human and divine acts of contrition and pardon. In the Purgatorial teaching the stress lies upon entire states and habits, stains and perversities of soul, and upon God's general grace working, in and through immanently necessary, freely accepted sufferings, on to a slow purification of the complete personality. As Origen says : " The soul's single acts, good or bad, go by; but, according to their quality, they give form and figure to the mind of the agent, and leave it either good or bad, and destined for pains or for rewards." [4]

The antagonism here is but apparent. For the fact that a certain condition of soul precedes, and that another condition succeeds, each act of the same soul, in proportion as this act is full and deliberate, does not prevent the corresponding, complementary fact that such acts take the preceding condition as their occasion, and make the succeeding condition into a further expression of themselves. Single acts which fully express the character, whether good or bad, are doubtless rarer than is mostly thought. Yet Catherine, in union with the Gospels and the Church, is deeply convinced

[1] *De Purgatorio*, Lib. I, c. iv, 6; c. xiv, 22.

[2] *Les Controverses*, Pt. III, ch. ii, art. 1 (end); *Œuvres*, Annecy, 1892 *seq.*, Vol. I, p. 365.

[3] Faber's *All for Jesus*, 1853, ch. ix, sec. 4; Cardinal Manning's Appendix (B) to Engl. tr. of St. Catherine's *Treatise on Purgatory*, 1858; Cardinal Newman's *Dream of Gerontius*, 1865.

[4] *In Rom.*, Tom. i, p. 477.

of the power of one single act of Pure Love to abolish, not of course the effects outward, but the reflex spiritual consequences upon the soul itself, of sinful acts or states.

Catherine's picture again, of the deliberate Plunge into Purgatory, gives us a similar heroic act which, summing up the whole soul's active volitions, initiates and encloses the whole subsequent purification, but which itself involves a prevenient act of Divine Love and mercy, to which this act of human love is but the return and response. Indeed, as we know, this plunge-conception was but the direct projection, on to the other-world-picture, of her own personal experience at her conversion, when a short span of clock-time held acts of love received and acts of love returned, which transformed all her previous condition, and initiated a whole series of states ever more expressive of her truest self.—Act and state and state and act, each presupposes and requires the other: and both are present in the Synoptic pictures, and both are operative in the Purgatorial teaching; although in the former the accounts are so brief as to make states and acts alike look as though one single act; and, in the latter, the descriptions are so large as to make the single acts almost disappear behind the states.

V. Catherine and Heaven—Three Perplexities to be considered.

We have found a truly Purgational Middle state, with its sense of succession, its mixture of joy and suffering, and its growth and fruitfulness, to be profoundly consonant with all our deepest spiritual experiences and requirements. But what about Heaven, which we must, apparently, hold to consist of a sense of simultaneity, a condition of mere reproductiveness and utterly uneventful finality, and a state of unmixed, unchanging joy?—Here again, even if in a lesser degree, certain experiences of the human soul can help us to a few general positions of great spiritual fruitfulness, which can reasonably claim an analogical applicability to the Beyond, and which, thus taken as our ultimate ideals, cannot fail to stimulate the growth of our personality, and, with it, of further insight into these great realities. I shall here consider three main questions, which will roughly correspond to the three perplexities just indicated.

1. *Time and Heaven.*

Our first question, then, is as to the probable character of man's happiest ultimate consciousness,—whether it is one of succession or of simultaneity: in other words, whether, besides the disappearance of the category of space (a point already discussed), there is likely to be the lapse of the category of time also.—And let it be noted that the retention of the latter sense for Hell, and even for Purgatory, does not prejudge the question as to its presence or absence in Heaven, since those two states are admittedly non-normative, whereas the latter represents the very ideal and measure of man's full destination and perfection.

(1) Now it is still usual, amongst those who abandon the ultimacy of the space-category, simultaneously to drop, as necessarily concomitant, the time-category also. Tennyson, among the poets, does so, in his beautiful "Crossing the Bar": "From out our bourne of Time and Place, the flood may bear me far"; and Prof. H. J. Holtzmann, among speculative theologians, in criticising Rothe's conception of man as a quite ultimately spatial-temporal being, treats these two questions as standing and falling together.[1]—Yet a careful study of Kant's critique of the two categories of Space and Time suffices to convince us of the indefinitely richer content, and more ultimate reality, of the latter. Indeed, I shall attempt to show more fully in the next chapter, with the aid of M. Henri Bergson, that mathematical, uniform clock-time is indeed an artificial compound, which is made up of our profound experience of a duration in which the constituents (sensations, imaginations, thoughts, feelings, willings) of the succession ever, in varying degrees, overlap, interpenetrate, and modify each other, and the quite automatic and necessary simplification and misrepresentation of this experience by its imaginary projection on to space,—its restatement, by our picturing faculty, as a perfectly equable succession of mutally exclusive moments. It is in that interpenetrative duration, not in this atomistic clock-time, that our deeper human experiences take place.

(2) But that sense of duration, is it indeed our deepest apprehension? Dr. Holtzmann points out finely how that we are well aware, in our profoundest experiences, of "that permanently incomprehensible fact,—the existence of, as it

1 *Richard Rothe's Spekulatives System*, 1899, pp. 123, 124.

were, a prism, through which the unitary ray of light, which fills our consciousness with a real content, is spread out into a colour-spectrum, so that what, in itself, exists in pure unitedness" and simultaneity, "becomes intelligible to us only as a juxtaposition in space and a succession in time. Beyond the prism, there are no such two things." And he shows how keenly conscious we are, at times, of that deepest mode of apprehension and of being which is a Simultaneity, an eternal Here and Now; and how ruinous to our spiritual life would be a full triumph of the category of time.[1]

But it is St. Augustine who has, so far, found the noblest expression for the deepest human experiences in this whole matter of Duration and Simultaneity, as against mere Clock-Time, although, here as with regard to Space, he is deeply indebted to Plotinus. "In thee, O my soul, I measure time,—I measure the impression which passing events make upon thee, who remainest when those events have passed: this present impression then, and not those events which had to pass in order to produce it, do I measure, when I measure time." "The three times," tenses, "past, present, and future . . . are certain three affections in the soul, I find them there and nowhere else. There is the present memory of past events, the present perception of present ones, and the present expectation of future ones." God possesses "the splendour of ever-tarrying Eternity," which is "incomparable with never-tarrying times," since in it "nothing passes, but the content of everything abides simply present." And in the next life "perhaps our own thoughts also will not be flowing, going from one thing to another, but we shall see all we know simultaneously, in one intuition." St. Thomas indeed is more positive: "All things will," in Heaven, "be seen simultaneously and not successively."[2]

(3) If then, even here below, we can so clearly demonstrate the conventionality of mere Clock-Time, and can even conceive a perfect Simultaneity as the sole form of the consciousness of God, we cannot well avoid holding that, in the other life, the clock-time convention will completely cease, and that, though the sense of Duration is not likely completely to disappear (since, in this life at least, this sense is certainly not

[1] *Richard Rothe's Spekulatives System*, 1899, pp. 69; 74, 75.

[2] St. Augustine, *Confessions*, Lib. XI, ch. xxvii, 3; ch. xx; ch. xi. *De Trinit.*, Lib. XV, ch. 16, ed. Ben., col. 1492 D.—St. Thomas, *Summa Theol.*, I, qu. 12, art. 10, in corp.

merely phenomenal for man, and its entire absence would apparently make man into God), the category of Simultaneity will, as a sort of strong background-consciousness, englobe and profoundly unify the sense of Duration. And, the more God-like the soul, the more would this sense of Simultaneity predominate over the sense of Duration.

2. *The Ultimate Good, concrete, not abstract.*

Our second question concerns the kind and degree of variety in unity which we should conceive to characterize the life of God, and of the soul in its God-likeness. Is this type and measure of all life to be conceived as a maximum of abstraction or as a maximum of concretion; as pure thought alone, or as also emotion and will; as solitary and self-centred, or as social and outgoing; and as simply reproductive, or also as operative?

(1) Now it is certain that nothing is easier, and nothing has been more common, than to take the limitations of our earthly conditions, and especially those attendant upon the strictly contemplative, and, still more, those connected with the technically ecstatic states, as so many advantages, or even as furnishing a complete scheme of the soul's ultimate life.

As we have already repeatedly seen in less final matters, so here once more, at the end, we can trace the sad impoverishment to the spiritual outlook produced by the esteem in which the antique world generally held the psycho-physical peculiarities of trances, as directly valuable or even as prophetic of the soul's ultimate condition; the contraposition and exaltation, already on the part of Plato and Aristotle, of a supposed non-actively contemplative, above a supposed non-contemplatively active life; the largely excessive, not fully Christianizable, doctrines of the Neo-Platonists as to the Negative, Abstractive way, when taken as self-sufficient, and as to Quiet, Passivity, and Emptiness of Soul, when understood literally; and the conception, rarely far away from the ancient thinkers, of the soul as a substance which, full-grown, fixed and stainless at the first, requires but to be kept free from stain up to the end.

And yet the diminution of vitality in the trance, and even the inattention to more than one thing at a time in Contemplation, are, in themselves, defects, at best the price paid for certain gains; the active and the contemplative life are, ultimately, but two mutually complementary sides of life, so that no life ever quite succeeds in eliminating either element, and life, *caeteris paribus*, is complete and perfect, in proportion as it embraces both elements, each at its fullest, and the two in a perfect interaction; the Negative, Abstractive way peremptorily requires also the other, the Affirmative, Concrete way; the Quiet, Passivity, Emptiness are really, when wholesome, an incubation for, or a rest from, Action, indeed they are themselves a profound action and peace, and the soul is primarily a Force and an Energy, and Holiness is a growth of that Energy in Love, in full Being, and in creative, spiritual Personality.

(2) Now on this whole matter the European Christian Mystics, strongly influenced by, yet also largely developing, certain doctrines of the Greeks, have, I think, made two most profound contributions to the truths of the spirit, and have seriously fallen short of reality in three respects.

The first contribution can, indeed, be credited to Aristotle, whose luminous formulations concerning Energeia, Action (as excluding Motion, or Activity), we have already referred to. Here to *be* is to *act*, and Energeia, a being's perfect functioning and fullest self-expression in action, is not some kind of movement or process; but, on the contrary, all movement and process is only an imperfect kind of Energeia. Man, in his life here, only catches brief glimpses of such an Action; but God is not so hampered,—He is ever completely all that He can be, His Action is kept up inexhaustibly and ever generates supreme bliss; it is an unchanging, unmoving Energeia.[1] —And St. Thomas echoes this great doctrine, for all the Christian schoolmen: " A thing is declared to be perfect, in proportion as it is in act,"—as all its potentialities are expressed in action; and hence " the First Principle must be supremely in act," " God's Actuality is identical with His Potentiality," " God is Pure Action (*Actus Purus*)." [2]—Yet it is doubtless the Christian Mystics who have most fully experienced, and emotionally vivified, this great truth, and who cease not, in all their more characteristic teachings, from insisting upon the ever-increasing acquisition of " Action," the fully fruitful, peaceful functioning of the whole soul, at the expense of " activity," the restless, sterile distraction and

[1] I am here but giving an abstract of Mr. F. C. S. Schiller's admirable essay, " Activity and Substance," pp. 204–227 of his *Humanism*, 1903, where all the Aristotelian passages are carefully quoted and discussed. He is surely right in translating ἠρεμία by " constancy," not by " rest."

[2] *Summa Theol.*, I, qu. 4, art. 1, concl. qu. 25, art. 1 ad 2 et concl.

internecine conflict of its powers. And Heaven, for them, ever consists in an unbroken Action, devoid of all "activity," rendering the soul, in its degree, like to that Purest Action, God, who, Himself "Life," is, as our Lord declared, "not the God of the dead, but of the living."[1]

And the second contribution can, in part, be traced back to Plato, who does not weary, in the great middle period of his writings, from insisting upon the greatness of the nobler passions, and who already apprehends a Heavenly Eros which in part conflicts with, in part transcends, the Earthly one. But here especially it is Christianity, and in particular Christian Mysticism, which have fully experienced and proclaimed that "God" is "Love," and that the greatest of all the soul's acts and virtues is Charity, Pure Love. And hence the Pure Act of God, and the Action of the God-like soul, are conceived not, Aristotle-like, as acts of pure intelligence alone, but as tinged through and through with a noble emotion.

(3) But in three matters the Mystics, as such and as a whole, have, here especially under the predominant influence of Greek thought, remained inadequate to the great spiritual realities, as most fully revealed to us by Christianity. The three points are so closely interconnected that it will be best first to illustrate, and then to criticise them, together.

(i) Aristotle here introduces the mischief. For it is he who in his great, simply immeasurably influential, theological tractate, Chapters VI to X of the Twelfth Book of his *Metaphysic*, has presented to us God as "the one first unmoved Mover" of the Universe, but Who moves it as desired by it, not as desiring it, as outside of it, not as also inside it. God here is sheer Pure Thought, Noēsis, for "contemplation is the most joyful and the best" of actions. And "Thought" here "thinks the divinest and worthiest, without change," hence "It thinks Itself, and the Thinking is a Thinking of Thought."[2] We have here, as Dr. Caird strikingly puts it, a God necessarily shut up within Himself, "of purer eyes than to behold, not only iniquity but even contingency and finitude, and His whole activity is one act of pure self-contemplation." "The ideal activity which connects God with the world, appears thus as in the world and not in God."[3]

[1] Matt. xxii, 32. [2] *Metaphysic*, xii, 1072*b*, 1074*b*.

[3] E. Caird, *Evolution of Theology in the Greek Philosophers*, 1904, Vol. II, pp. 12, 16. See here, too, the fine discussion of the other, rightly immanental as well as transcendental, teaching of Aristotle, pp. 15, 21.

(ii) Now we have already allowed that the Mystics avoid Aristotle's elimination of emotion from man's deepest action, and of emotion's equivalent from the life of God. But they are, for the most part, much influenced in their speculations by this intensely Greek, aristocratic, intellectualist conception, in the three points of a disdain of the Contingent and Historical; of a superiority to volitional, productive energizing; and of a presentation of God as unsocial, and as occupied directly with Himself alone. We have already studied numerous examples of the first two, deeply un-Christian, errors as they have more or less influenced Christian Mysticism; the third mistake, of a purely Transcendental, Deistic God, is indeed never consistently maintained by any Christian, and Catherine, in particular, is ever dominated by the contrary great doctrine, adumbrated by Plato and fully revealed by Our Lord, of the impulse to give Itself intrinsic to Goodness, so that God, as Supreme Goodness, becomes the Supreme Self-giver, and thus the direct example and motive for our own self-donation to Him. Yet even so deeply religious a non-Christian as Plotinus, and such speculative thinkers as Eriugena and Eckhart (who certainly intended to remain Christians) continue all three mistakes, and especially insist upon a Supreme Being, Whose true centre, His Godhead, is out of all relation to anything but Himself. And even the orthodox Scholastics, and St. Thomas himself, attempt at times to combine, with the noblest Platonic and the deepest Christian teachings, certain elements, which, in strictness, have no place in an Incarnational Religion.

(iii) For, at times, the fullest, deepest Action is still not conceived, even by St. Thomas, as a Harmony, an Organization of all Man's essential powers, the more the better. "In the active life, which is occupied with many things, there is less of beatitude than in the contemplative life, which is busy with one thing alone,—the contemplation of Truth"; "beatitude must consist essentially in the action of the intellect; and only accidentally in the action of the will."[1] God is still primarily intelligence: "God's intelligence is His substance"; whereas "volition must be in God, since there is intelligence in Him," and "Love must of necessity be declared to be in God, since there is volition in Him."[2] God is still, in a certain sense, shut up in Himself: "As He understands things other than

[1] *Summa Theol.*, I, ii, qu. 3, art. 2 ad 4; art. 4, concl.

[2] *Ibid.*, I, qu. 14, art. 4, in corp.; qu. 19, art. 1, concl.; qu. 20, art. 1, concl.

Himself, by understanding His own essence, so He wills things other than Himself, by willing His own goodness." "God enjoys not anything beside Himself, but enjoys Himself alone."[1] —And we get, in correspondence to this absorption of God in Himself, an absorption of man in God, of so direct and exclusive a kind, as, if pressed, to eliminate all serious, permanent value, for our soul, in God's actual creation of our fellow-creatures. "He who knoweth Thee and creatures, is not, on this account, happier than if he knows them not; but he is happy because of Thee alone." And "the perfection of Love is essential to beatitude, with respect to the Love of God, not with respect to the Love of one's neighbour. If there were but one soul alone to enjoy God, it would be blessèd, even though it were without a single fellow-creature whom it could love."[2]

(iv) And yet St. Thomas's own deeply Christian sense, explicit sayings of Our Lord or of St. Paul, and even, in part, certain of the fuller apprehensions of the Greeks, can make the great Dominican again uncertain, or can bring him to entirely satisfactory declarations, on each of these points. For we get the declaration that direct knowledge of individual things, and quasi-creative operativeness are essential to all true perfection. "To understand something merely in general and not in particular, is to know it imperfectly"; Our Lord Himself has taught us that "the very hairs of your head are all numbered"; hence God must "know all other individual things with a distinct and proper knowledge."—And "a thing is most perfect, when it can make another like unto itself. But by tending to its own perfection, each thing tends to become more and more like God. Hence everything tends to be like God, in so far as it tends to be the cause of other things."[3]—We get a full insistence, with St. Paul (in 1 Cor. xiii), upon our love of God, an act of the will, as nobler than our cognition of Him; and with Plato and St. John, upon God's forthgoing Love for His creatures, as the very crown and measure of His perfection. "Everything in nature has, as regards its own good, a certain inclination to diffuse itself amongst others, as far as possible. And this applies, in a supreme degree, to the Divine Goodness, from which all perfection is derived."

[1] *Summa Theol.*, I, qu. 9, art. 2, 3; qu. 14, art. 2 ad 2; I, ii, qu. 3, art. 2 ad 4.

[2] *Ibid.*, I, qu. 12, art. 8 ad 4; I, ii, qu. 4, art. 8 ad 3.

[3] *Ibid.*, I, qu. 14, art. 8, in corp.; art. 11, contra et concl.; art 8, concl.—*Contra Gent.*, Lib. III, c. xxi, in fine.

"Love, Joy, Delight can be predicated of God"; Love which, of its very essence, "causes the lover to bear himself to the beloved as to his own self": so that we must say with Dionysius that "He, the very Cause of all things, becomes ecstatic, moves out of Himself, by the abundance of His loving goodness, in the providence exercised by Him towards all things extant."[1]

(v) And we get in St. Thomas, when he is too much dominated by the abstractive trend, a most interesting, because logically necessitated and quite unconscious, collision with certain sayings of Our Lord. For he then explains Matt. xviii, 10, "their," the children's, "Angels see without ceasing the face of their Father who is in Heaven" as teaching that "the action (*operatio*), by which Angels are conjoined to the increate Good, is, in them, unique and sempiternal"; whereas his commentators are driven to admit that the text, contrariwise, implies that these Angels have two simultaneous "operations," and that their succouring action in nowise disturbs their intellectual contemplation. Hence, even if we press Matt. xxii, 30, that we "shall be as the Angels of God," we still have an organism of peaceful Action, composed of intellectual, affective, volitional, productive acts operating between the soul and God, and the soul and other souls, each constituent and object working and attained in and through all the others.

(vi) Indeed all Our Lord's Synoptic teachings, as to man's ultimate standard and destiny, belong to this God-in-man and man-in-God type of doctrine: for there the two great commandments are strictly inseparable; God's interest in the world is direct and detailed,—it is part of His supreme greatness that He cares for every sparrow that falls to the ground; and man, in the Kingdom of God, will sit down at a banquet, the unmistakable type of social joys.—And even the Apocalypse, which has, upon the whole, helped on so much the conception of an exclusive, unproductive entrancement of each soul singly in God alone, shows the deepest emotion when picturing all the souls, from countless tribes and nations, standing before the throne,—an emotion which can, surely, not be taken as foreign to those souls themselves.[2]

[1] *Summa Theol.*, II, ii, qu. 3, art. 4, 4; I, qu. 19, art. 2, in corp.; qu. 20, art. 1 ad 1; ad 3; art. 2 ad 1.

[2] Mark xii, 28–34 and parallels; Matt. x, 29; Luke xii, 6; Matt. xxv, 10; Mark xiv, 25 and parallels, and elsewhere; Apoc. vii, 9.

But, indeed, Our Lord's whole life and message become unintelligible, and the Church loses its deepest roots, unless the Kingdom of God is, for us human souls, as truly a part of our ultimate destiny as is God Himself, that God who fully reveals to us His own deepest nature as the Good Shepherd, the lover of each single sheep and of the flock as a whole.[1]

(4) We shall, then, do well to hold that the soul's ultimate beatitude will consist in its own greatest possible self-realization in its God-likeness,—an Action free from all Activity, but full of a knowing, feeling, willing, receiving, giving, effectuating, all which will energize between God and the soul, and the soul and other souls,—each force and element functioning in its proper place, but each stimulated to its fullest expansion, and hence to its deepest delight, by the corresponding vitalization of the other powers and ends, and of other similar centres of rich action.

3. *The pain-element of Bliss.*

And our third, last question is whether our deepest this-life apprehensions and experiences give us any reason for holding that a certain equivalent for what is noblest in devoted suffering, heroic self-oblivion, patient persistence in lonely willing, will be present in the life of the Blessed. It would certainly be a gain could we discover such an equivalent, for a pure glut of happiness, an unbroken state of sheer enjoyment, can as little be made attractive to our most spiritual requirements, as the ideal of an action containing an element of, or equivalent for, devoted and fruitful effort and renunciation can lose its perennial fascination for what is most Christian within us.

(1) It is not difficult, I take it, to find such an element, which we cannot think away from any future condition of the soul without making that soul into God Himself. The ultimate cause of this element shall be considered, as Personality, in our next chapter: here I can but indicate this element at work in our relations to our fellow-men and to God.—Already St. Thomas, throughout one current of his teaching, is full of the dignity of right individuality. "The Multitude and Diversity of natures in the Universe proceed directly from the intention of God, who brought them into being, in order to communicate His goodness to them, and to have It represented by them. And since It could not be sufficiently represented

[1] Matt. xviii, 12–14; Luke xv, 1–10; John x, 11–16 (Ezekiel xxxiv, 12–19).

by one creature alone, He produced many and diverse ones, so that what is wanting to the one towards this office, should be supplied by the other." [1] Hence the multiplication of the Angels, who differ specifically each from all the rest, adds more of nobility and perfection to the Universe, than does the multiplication of men, who differ only individually.[2] And Cardinal Nicolas of Coes writes, in 1457 A.D., "Every man is, as it were, a separate species, because of his perfectibility." [3] As Prof. Josiah Royce tells us in 1901, "What is real, is not only a content of experience and the embodiment of a type; but an individual content of experience, and the unique embodiment of a type." [4]

(2) Now in the future beatitude, where the full development of this uniqueness in personality cannot, as so often here, be stunted or misapplied, all this will evidently reach its zenith. But, if so, then it follows that, although one of the two greatest of the joys of those souls will be their love and understanding of each other,—this love and trust, given as it will be to the other souls, in their full, unique personality, will, of necessity, exceed the comprehension of the giving personalities. Hence there will still be an equivalent for that trust and venture, that creative faith in the love and devotion given by us to our fellows, and found by us in them, which are, here below, the noblest concomitants and conditions of the pain and the cost and the joy in every virile love and self-dedication.—There is then an element of truth in Lessing's words of 1773: "The human soul is incapable of even one unmixed emotion,—one that, down to its minutest constituent, would be nothing but pleasurable or nothing but painful: let alone of a condition in which it would experience nothing but such unmixed emotions."—For, as Prof. Troeltsch says finely in 1903, "Everything historical retains, in spite of all its relation to absolute values, something of irrationality,"—of impenetrableness to finite minds, "and of individuality. Indeed just this mixture is the special characteristic of the lot and dignity of man; nor is a Beyond for him conceivable in which it would altogether cease. Doubt and unrest can indeed give way to clear sight and certitude: yet this very clarity and assurance

[1] *Summa Theol.*, I, qu. 47, art. 1, in corp.

[2] *Ibid.*, I, qu. 50, art. 4 ad 3; ad 2; in corp. *Contra Gent.*, Lib. II, c. xciii.

[3] *Excitationum*, Lib. VIII, 604.

[4] *The World and the Individual*, Vol. II, p. 430.

will, in each human soul, still bear a certain individual character," fully comprehensible to the other souls by love and trust alone.[1]

(3) And this same element we find, of course, in a still greater degree,—although, as I shall argue later on, our experimental knowledge of God is greater than is our knowledge of our fellow-creatures,—in the relations between our love of God and our knowledge of Him. St. Thomas tells us most solidly: "Individual Being applies to God, in so far as it implies Incommunicableness." Indeed, "*Person* signifies the most perfect thing in nature,"—"the subsistence of an individual in a rational nature." "And since the dignity of the divine nature exceeds every other dignity, this name of Person is applicable, in a supreme degree, to God." And again: "God, as infinite, cannot be held infinitely by anything finite"; and hence "only in the sense in which comprehension is opposed to a seeking after Him, is God comprehended, *i.e.* possessed, by the Blessed." And hence the texts: "I press on, if so be that I may apprehend that for which also I was apprehended" (Phil. iii, 12); "then shall I know even as also I have been known" (1 Cor. xiii, 12); and "we shall see Him as He is" (1 John iii, 2): all refer to such a possession of God. In the last text "the adverb 'as' only signifies 'we shall see His essence' and not 'we shall have as perfect a mode of vision as God has a mode of being.'"[2]—Here again, then, we find that souls loving God in His Infinite Individuality, will necessarily love Him beyond their intellectual comprehension of Him; the element of devoted trust, of free self-donation to One fully known only through and in such an act, will thus remain to man for ever. St. John of the Cross proclaimed this great truth: "One of the greatest favours of God, bestowed transiently upon the soul in this life, is its ability to see so distinctly, and to feel so profoundly, that . . . it cannot comprehend Him at all. These souls are herein, in some degree, like to the souls in heaven, where they who know Him most perfectly perceive most clearly that He is infinitely incomprehensible; for those that have the less clear vision, do not perceive so distinctly as the others how greatly He transcends their

[1] G. E. Lessing: *Leibniz von den Ewigen Strafen*, *Werke*, ed. Lachmann-Muncker, Vol. XI, 1895, p. 482. E. Troeltsch, *Theologische Rundschau*, 1893, p. 72.

[2] *Summa Theol.*, I, art. 7, in corp.; art. 6 ad 1.

vision." [1] With this teaching, so consonant with Catherine's experimental method, and her continuous trust in the persistence of the deepest relations of the soul to God, of the self-identical soul to the unchanging God, we can conclude this study of her Eschatology.

[1] " A Spiritual Canticle," stanza vii, 10, in *Works*, transl. by D. Lewis, ed. 1891, pp. 206, 207.

CHAPTER XIII

THE FIRST THREE ULTIMATE QUESTIONS. THE RELATIONS BETWEEN MORALITY, MYSTICISM, PHILOSOPHY, AND RELIGION. MYSTICISM AND THE LIMITS OF HUMAN EXPERIENCE AND KNOWLEDGE. MYSTICISM AND THE NATURE OF EVIL.

I TAKE the ultimate questions involved in the religious positions which are taken up by Catherine, and indeed by the Christian Mystics generally, and which we have studied in the preceding two chapters, to be four. In the order of their increasing difficulty they are: the question as to the relations between Morality, Mysticism, Philosophy, and Religion; that as to the Limits of Human Knowledge, and as to the special character and worth of the Mystics' claim to Trans-subjective Cognition; that as to the Nature of Evil and the Goodness or Badness of Human Nature; and that as to Personality,—the character of, and the relations between, the human spirit and the Divine Spirit. The consideration of these deepest matters in the next two chapters will, I hope, in spite of its inevitable element of dimness and of repetition, do much towards binding together and clarifying the convictions which we have been slowly acquiring,—ever, in part, with a reference to these coming ultimate alternatives and choices.

I. The Relations between Morality and Mysticism, Philosophy and Religion.

Now the first of these questions has not, for most of the more strenuous of our educated contemporaries, become, so far again, a living question at all. A morally good and pure, a socially useful and active life,—all this in the sense and with the range attributed to these terms by ordinary parlance: this and this alone is, for doubtless the predominant public present-day consciousness, the true object, end, and measure of all healthy religion; whatever is alongside of, or beyond, or other than, or anything but a direct and exclusive incentive to this, is so much superstition and fanaticism. According to this view, at least one-half of Catherine's activity at all times, and well-nigh the whole of it during her last period, would be practically worthless. Thus only certain elements of such a life would be retained even for and in religion, and even these would be bereft of all that has hitherto been held to be their specifically religious sense and setting.

1. *Kant's non-mystical religion.*

It is doubtless Kant who, among the philosophers, has been the most consistent and influential in inculcating such non-Mystical Religion. "Religion," he says in 1793, "is, on its subjective side, the cognition of all our duties as so many Divine Commandments." "The delusion that we can effect something, in view of our justification before God, by means of acts of religious worship, is religious superstition; and the delusion that we can effect something by attempts at a supposed intercourse with God, is religious fanaticism. . . . Such a feeling of the immediate presence of the Supreme Being, and such a discrimination between this feeling and every other, even moral, feeling, would imply a capacity for an intuition, which is without any corresponding organ in human nature. . . . If then a Church doctrine is to abolish or to prevent all religious delusion, it must,—over and above its statutory teachings, with which it cannot, for the present, entirely dispense,—contain within itself a principle which shall enable it to bring about the religion of a pure life, as the true end of the whole movement, and then to dispense with those temporary doctrines." [1]

It is deeply instructive to note how thoroughly this, at first sight, solid and triumphant view, has not only continued to be refuted by the actual practice and experience of specifically religious souls, but how explicitly it is being discredited by precisely the more delicately perceptive, the more truly detached and comprehensive, students and philosophers of religion of the present day,—heirs, let us not forget in justice to Kant, of the intervening profound development of the historical sense, and of the history and psychology of religion.—Thus that most vigorous, independent thinker, Prof. Simmel of Berlin, writes in 1904: "Kant has, I think, simply

[1] *Religion innerhalb der Grenzen der blossen Vernunft*, Werke, ed. Hartenstein, 1868, Vol. VI, pp. 252, 274.

passed by the essentials of religion,—that is to say, of that reality which historically bears the name of religion. Only the reflection, that the harmony of complete happiness with complete morality is producible by a Divine Being alone, is here supposed to lead us to believe in such a Being. There is here a complete absence of that direct laying hold of the Divine by our souls, because of our intrinsic needs, which characterizes all genuine piety. And the religious sense is not recognized as an organism with a unity of its own, as a growth springing from its own root. The entirely specific character of religion, which is resolvable neither into morality nor into a thirst after happiness: the direct self-surrender of the soul to a higher reality, the giving and taking, the unification and differentiation,—that quite organic unity of the religious experience, which we can but most imperfectly indicate by a multiplicity of some such, simultaneously valid, antitheses: this, there is no evidence to show, was ever really known to Kant. What was religion for Augustine and Francis of Assisi, he was unable to reproduce in himself; indeed religion, of this type, he readily rejects as fanaticism. Here lay the limit both of his own nature and of his own times." [1]

The rich mind of Prof. Troeltsch is, perhaps, more entirely just: "As Kant's theory of knowledge is throughout dependent upon the state of contemporary psychology, so also is his theory of religious knowledge dependent upon the psychology of religion predominant in his day. Locke, Leibniz, Pascal had already recognized the essentially practical character of all religion; and since their psychology was unable to conceive the 'practical' otherwise than as the moral, it had looked upon Religion as Morality furnished forth with its metaphysical concomitants. And as soon as this psychology had become the very backbone of his conception of Religion, Morality gained an entirely one-sided predominance over Kant's mind,—considerably, indeed, beyond his own personal feelings and perceptions." For he remains deeply penetrated by "the conceptions of Regeneration and Redemption; the idea of divine Grace and Wisdom, which accepts the totality of a soul's good disposition in lieu of that soul's ever defective single good works; the belief in a Providence which strengthens the Good throughout the world against Evil; adoring awe in face of the majesty of the

[1] *Kant*, 1904, pp. 129–132.

Supersensible"; and "all these" conceptions "are no more simply moral, they are specifically religious thoughts."[1]

Such a fuller conception of religion is admirably insisted on by that penetrating philosopher and historian of philosophy, Prof. Windelband: "Actual Religion, in its complete reality, belongs to all the spheres of life, and yet transcends them all, as something new and *sui generis*. It is first an interior life—an apprehending, cognizing, feeling, willing, accomplishing. But this accomplishing leads it on to being also an exterior life; an acting out, according to their various standards, of such feeling and willing; and an outward expression of that inner life in general, in ritual acts and divine worship. Yet this worship takes it beyond the little circle of the individual, and constitutes the corporate acts of a community, a social, external organization with visible institutions. And yet Religion ever claims to be more than the whole series of such empirical facts and doings, it ever transcends mere earthly experience, and is an intercourse with the inmost nature and foundation of all reality; it is a life in and with God, a metaphysical life. All these elements belong to the complete concept of actual religion."[2] I would add, that they each stimulate the other, the external, *e. g.* being not only the expression of the awakened internal, but also the occasion of that awakening.

And the great Dutch scholar, Prof. C. P. Tiele, unexcelled in the knowledge of the actual course taken by the great religions of the world, declares: "All progress, not only in Morality, but also in Science, Philosophy, Art, necessarily exerts an influence upon that of Religion. But . . . Religion is not, on that account, identical with Ethics any more than with Philosophy or Art. All these manifestations of the human spirit respond to certain needs of man; but none of them, not even Morality, is capable of supplying the want which Religion alone can satisfy. . . . Religion differs from the other manifestations of the human mind" in this, that whereas "in the domain of Art, the feelings and the imagination predominate; in that of Philosophy, abstract thought is paramount"; and "the main object of Science is to know accurately, whilst Ethics are chiefly concerned with the emotions and with the fruit they

[1] *Das Historische in Kant's Religions-philosophie, Kant-Studien*, 1904, pp. 43, 44.

[2] "Das Heilige," in *Präludien*, 1903, pp. 356, 357.

yield: in Religion all these factors operate alike, and if their equilibrium be disturbed, a morbid religious condition is the result." [1]

2. *Ritschlian modification of Kant's view.*

It is deeply interesting to note the particular manner in which Kant's impoverishment of the concept of religion has been in part retained, in part modified, by the Ritschlian school,—I am thinking especially of that vigorous writer, Prof. Wilhelm Hermann.

(1) If in Kant we get the belief in God derived from reflection upon Goodness and Happiness, and as the only possible means of their ultimate coalescence: in Hermann we still get the Categorical Imperative, but the thirst for Happiness has been replaced by the historic figure of Jesus Christ. "Two forces of different kinds," he says, "ever produce the certainty of Faith: the impression of an Historic Figure which approaches us in Time; and the Moral Law which, when we have heard it, we can understand in its Eternal Truth. Faith arises, when a man recognizes, in the appearance of Jesus, that symbol of his own existence which gives him the courage to recognize in the Eternal, which claims him in the Moral Imperative, the source of true life for his own self." [2]—And these two sole co-efficients of all entirely living religion are made to exclude, as we have already seen, especially all Mysticism from the life of Faith. "True, outside of Christianity, Mysticism will everywhere arise, as the very flower of the religious development. But a Christian is bound to declare the mystical experience of God to be a delusion. Once he has experienced his elevation, by Christ alone, above his own previous nature, he cannot believe that another man can attain the same result, simply by means of recollection within his own self. . . . We are Christians precisely because we have struck, in the person of Jesus, upon a fact which is incomparably richer in content than the feelings that arise within ourselves." "Only because Christ is present for us can we possess God with complete clearness and certainty." And, with Luther,—who remained, however, thoroughly faithful to the Primitive and Mediæval high esteem for the Mystical element of religion;—"right prayer is a work of faith, and only a Christian can perform it."

[1] *Elements of the Science of Religion*, 1897, Vol. I, pp. 274, 275; Vol. II, p. 23.

[2] *Der Verkehr des Christen mit Gott*, ed. 1892, p. 281.

And, more moderately: "We have no desire to penetrate through Christ on to God: for we consider that in God Himself we still find nothing but Christ." [1]

(2) Now it is surely plain that we have here a most understandable, indeed respectable, reaction against all empty, sentimental Subjectivism, and a virile affirmation of the essential importance of the Concrete and Historical. And, in particular, the insistence upon the supreme value and irreplaceable character and function of Christ is profoundly true. —Yet three counter-considerations have ever to be borne in mind. (i) It remains certain that we do not know, or experience anything, to which we can attribute any fuller reality, which is either purely objective or purely subjective; and that there exists no process of knowing or experiencing such a reality which would exclude either the objective or the subjective factor. "Whatever claims to be fully real," either as apprehending subject or as apprehended object, "must be an individual . . . an organic whole, which has its principle of unity in itself." The truly real, then, is a thing that has an inside; and the sharp antithesis drawn, although in contrary directions, by Aristotle and by Kant, between the Phenomenal and the Intelligible worlds, does not exist in the reality either of our apprehending selves, or of our apprehended fellow-men, or God.[2]—But Hermann is so haunted by the bogey-fear of the subjective resonance within us being necessarily useless towards, indeed obstructive of, the right apprehension of the object thus responded to, that he is driven to follow the will-o'-the-wisp ideal of a pure, entirely exclusive objectivity.

(ii) Bent on this will-o'-the-wisp quest of an exclusive objectivity, he has to define all Mysticism in terms of Exclusive Mysticism, and then to reject such an aberration. "Wherever the influence of God upon the soul is sought and found solely in an interior experience of the individual soul, in an excitation of the feelings which is supposed directly to reveal the true nature of this experience, *viz.* in a state of possession by God, and this without anything exterior being apprehended and held fast with a clear consciousness, without the positive content of some mental contemplation setting

[1] *Der Verkehr des Christen mit Gott*, ed. 1892, pp. 27, 28; 230, 231; 262; 23.

[2] E. Caird, *Development of Theology in the Greek Philosophers*, Vol. I, pp. 367, 362. The whole chapter, "Does the Primacy belong to Reason or to Will?" pp. 350–382, is admirable in its richness and balance.

thoughts in motion and raising the spiritual level of the soul's life; *there* is Mystical Piety."[1]

Now it is, of course, true that false Mysticism does attempt such an impossible feat as the thing at which Hermann is thus aiming. But, even here, the facts and problems are again misstated. Just now the object presented was everything, and the apprehending subject was nothing. Here, on the contrary, the apprehension by the subject is pressed to the degree of requiring the soul to remain throughout reflexly aware of its own processes.

Already in 1798 Kant had, in full acceptance of the great distinction worked out by Leibniz in the years 1701–1709, but not published till 1765, declared: "We can be mediately conscious of an apprehension as to which we have no direct consciousness"; and "the field of our obscure apprehensions,—that is, apprehensions and impressions of which we are not directly conscious, although we can conclude without doubt that we have them,—is immeasurable, whereas clear apprehensions constitute but a very few points within the complete extent of our mental life."[2] This great fact psychologists can now describe with greater knowledge and precision: yet the observations and analyses of Pierre Janet, William James, James Ward and others, concerning Subconsciousness, have but confirmed and deepened the Leibnizian-Kantian apprehensions. Without much dim apprehension, no clear perception; nothing is more certain than this.

And it is certain, also, that this absence of reflex consciousness, of perceiving that we are apprehending, applies not only to impressions of sensible objects, or to apprehensions of realities inferior in richness, in interiority, to our own nature, but also, indeed especially, to apprehensions of realities superior, in dignity and profundity of organization, to our own constitution. When engrossed in a great landscape of Turner, the Parthenon sculptures, a sonata of Beethoven, Dante's *Paradiso;* or when lost in the contemplation of the seemingly endless spaces of the heavens, or of the apparently boundless times of geology; or when absorbed in the mysterious greatness of Mind, so incommensurable with

[1] *Verkehr des Christen mit Gott*, pp. 15, 16.

[2] I. Kant, "Anthropologie," in *Werke*, ed. Berlin Academy, Vol. VII, 1907, pp. 135, 136. G. W. Leibniz, "Nouveaux Essais sur l'Entendement," in *Die philosophischen Schriften von G. W. L.*," ed. Gerhardt, Vol. V, 1882, pp. 8, 10; 45, 69, 100, 121, 122.

matter, and of Personality, so truly presupposed in all these appreciations yet so transcendent of even their collectivity—we are as little occupied with the facts of our engrossment, our self-oblivion, our absorption, or with the aim and use of such immensely beneficial self-oblivion, as we are, in our ordinary, loosely-knit states, occupied with the impression which, nevertheless, is being produced upon our senses and mind by some small insect or slight ray of light to which we are not giving our attention, or which may be incapable of impressing us sufficiently to be thus attended to and clearly perceived.[1] And, as in the case of these under-impressions, so in that of those over-impressions, we can often judge, as to their actual occurrence and fruitfulness, only from their after-effects, although this indirect proof will, in each case, be of quite peculiar cogency.—All this leaves ample room for that prayer of simple quiet, so largely practised by the Saints, and indeed for all such states of recollection which, though the soul, on coming from them, cannot discover definite ideas or picturings to have been contained in them, leave the soul braced to love, work, and suffer for God and man, beyond its previous level. Prof. William James is too deeply versed a Psychologist not fully to understand the complete normality of such conditions, and the entire satisfactoriness of such tests [2]

(iii) And finally, it is indeed true that God reveals Himself to us, at all fully, in Human History alone, and within this history, more fully still, in the lives and experiences of the Saints of all the stages of religion, and, in a supreme and normative manner, in the life and teaching of Jesus Christ; that we have thus a true immanence of the Divine in the Human; and that it is folly to attempt the finding or the making of any shorter way to God than that of the closest contact with His own condescensions. Yet such a wisely Historical and fully Christian attitude would be imperilled, not secured, by such an excessive Christocentrism, indeed such *Panchristism*, as that of Prof. Hermann.

We shall indeed beware of all indifferentist levelling-down of the various religions of the world. For, as Prof. Robertson Smith, who knew so well the chief great religions, most wisely said, " To say that God speaks to all men alike,

[1] All this first clearly formulated by Leibniz, *op. cit.* pp. 121, 122.

[2] See his *Varieties of Religious Experience*, 1902, pp. 209–211; 242, 243; and elsewhere.

and gives the same communication directly to all without the use of a revealing agency, reduces religion to Pure Mysticism. In point of fact it is not true of any man that what he believes and knows of God, has come to him directly through the voice of nature and conscience." And he adds : " History has not taught us anything in true religion to add to the New Testament. Jesus Christ still stands as high above us as He did above His disciples, the perfect Master, the supreme head of the fellowship of all true religion." [1]

Yet we must equally guard against making even Our Lord into so exclusive a centre and home of all that is divine, as to cause Him to come into an entirely God-forsaken, completely God-forgetting world, a world which did not and could not, in any degree or manner whatsoever, rightly know, love, or serve God at all; and against so conceiving the religion, taught and practised by Him, as to deprive it of all affinity with, or room for, such admittedly universal forces and resultants of the human soul and the religious sense as are dim apprehension, formless recollection, pictureless emotion, and the sense of the Hiddenness and Transcendence of the very God, Who is also Immanent and Self-Revealing, in various degrees and ways, in every place and time. Indeed, these two forces : the diffused Religiosity and more or less inchoate religion, readily discoverable, by a generous docility, more or less throughout the world of human souls, and the concentrated spirituality and concrete, thoroughly characteristic Religion, which has its culmination, after its ample preludings in the Hebrew Prophets, in the Divine-Human figure and spirit of Jesus Christ : are interdependent, in somewhat the way in which vague, widely spread Subconsciousness requires, and is required by, definite, narrowly localized Consciousness in each human mind. Precisely because there have been and are previous and simultaneous lesser communications of, and correspondences with, the one " Light that enlighteneth every man that cometh into the world " ; because men can and do believe according to various, relatively preliminary, degrees and ways, in God and a Providence, in Sin and Contrition, without a knowledge of the Historic Christ (although never without the stimulation of some, often world-forgotten, historic personality, and ever with some real, though unconscious approximation to His type of life and teaching), therefore can

[1] *The Prophets of Israel*, 1882, pp. 11, 12; 10, 11.

Christ be the very centre, and sole supreme manifestation and measure of all this light. Not only can Christ remain supreme, even though Moses and Elijah, Amos and Isaiah, Jeremiah and Ezekiel; and indeed, in their own other degrees and ways, Plato and Plotinus, Epictetus and Marcus Aurelius, Gautama Buddha and Rabbi Akiba be all revered as God-loved and God-loving, as, in various amounts, truly, spiritually great: but only thus can His central importance be fully realized.

There is certainly much in Our Lord's own attitude, as we have already found, to demand such a view; and Clement of Alexandria, Origen and St. Justin Martyr have emphasized it continually. And there is no necessary Naturalism here—for the position is entirely compatible with the profoundest belief in the great truth that it is Grace which everywhere produces the various degrees of God-pleasing religion to be found scattered throughout the world. Father Tyrrell has admirably said: "God's salutary workings in man's heart have always been directed, however remotely, to the life of Grace and Glory; of 'the Order of mere nature,' and its exigencies, we have no experimental knowledge. . . . In the present order, Theism is but embryonic Christianity, and Christianity is but developed Theism: 'purely natural' religion is what might have been, but never was." [1]

(3) Now this must suffice as a sketch of the relations between (Historical) Religion and Mysticism, and will have shown why I cannot but regret that so accomplished a scholar as Prof. Morris Jastrow should class all and every Mysticism, whether Pure or Mixed, as so far forth a religious malady; why I rejoice that so admirably circumspect an investigator as Prof. C. P. Tiele should, (in the form of a strenuous insistence upon the apprehension, indeed the ontological action of, the Infinite, by and within the human spirit, as the very soul and mainspring of Religion), so admirably reinforce the fundamental importance of the Mystical apprehensions; why I most warmly endorse Prof. Rauwenhoff's presentment of Mysticism as, with Intellectualism and Moralism, one of the three psychological forms of religion, which are each legitimate and necessary, and which each require the check of the other two, if they are not to degenerate each into some corruption special to the exclusive develop-

[1] *Lex Orandi*, 1903, pp. xxix, xxxi.

ment of that particular form; and why I cordially applaud the unequalled analysis and description by Prof. Eucken of the manner in which "Universal Religion" is at work, as an often obscure yet (in the long run) most powerful leaven, throughout all specifically human life,—Sciences, Art, Philosophy, and Ethics, calling for, and alone satisfied with, the answering force and articulation of "Characteristic Religion," each requiring and required by the other, each already containing the other in embryo, and both ever operating together, in proportion as Man and Religion attain to their fullness.[1]

3. *Hermann's impossible simplification concerning philosophy.* But what shall we say as to the relations between Religion and Philosophy? Here again Hermann is the vigorous champion of a very prevalent and plausible simplification. "There exists no Theory of Knowledge for such things as we hold to be real in the strength of faith. In such religious affirmations, the believer demolishes every bridge between his conviction and that which Science can recognize as real." Indeed Hermann's attitude is here throughout identical with that of his master, Albrecht Ritschl: Metaphysics of any and every kind appear everywhere, to both writers, as essentially unnecessary, unreal, misleading, as so much inflation and delusion of soul.—Yet this again is quite demonstrably excessive, and can indeed be explained only as an all but inevitable recoil from the contrary metaphysical excesses of the Hegelian school.

(1) Since the culmination of that reaction, "it has," as Prof. H. J. Holtzmann, himself so profoundly historical and so free from all extreme metaphysical bent, tells us, "become quite impossible any further to deny the metaphysical factors which had a share in constituting such types of New Testament doctrine as the Pauline and Johannine. Indeed, not even if we were to reduce the New Testament to the Synoptic Gospels and the Acts on the one hand, and to the Pastoral Epistles, the Epistle of James and the Apocalypse on the other hand, would the elements which spring from speculative sources be entirely eliminated. And since, again, the Old Testament religion, in its last stage, assimilated similarly

[1] M. Jastrow, *The Study of Religion*, 1901, pp. 279–286. C. P. Tiele, *Elements of the Science of Religion*, 1897, Vol. II, pp. 227–234; L. W. E. Rauwenhoff, *Religions-philosophie*, Germ. tr., ed. 1894, pp. 109–124. R. Eucken, *Der Wahrheitsgehalt der Religion*, 1901, pp. 59–238; 303–399. There are important points in pp. 425–438, which I do not accept.

metaphysical materials from the East and from the West; since Mohammedanism, in its Persian and Indian branches, did the same with regard to the older civilized religions of Middle and Eastern Asia; since also these latter religions received a speculative articulation in even the most ancient times, so that they are both Philosophy and Religion simultaneously: we are forced to ask ourselves, whether so frequent a concomitant of religion is satisfactorily explicable as a mere symptom of falsification or decay." And whilst answering that the primary organ for religion is Feeling and Conscience, he points out how large an amount of Speculation was, nevertheless, required and exercised by a St. Augustine, even after his unforgettable experiences of the sufferings attendant upon Sin, and of their cure by Grace alone.[1]

(2) The fact is that, if man cannot apprehend the objects,—the historic and other facts,—of Religion, without certain subjective organs, dispositions, and effects, any more than can all these subjective capacities, without those objects, produce religious convictions and acts, or be waked up into becoming efficient forces: neither can man thus experience and effect the deepest foundations and developments of his own true personality in and through contact with the divine Spirit, without being more or less stimulated into some kind of, at least rudimentary, Philosophy as to these his profoundest experiences of reality, and as to their rights and duties towards the rest of what he is and knows.

(3) Indeed his very Religion is already, in itself, the profoundest Metaphysical Affirmation. As the deeply historical-minded Prof. Tiele admits: "Every man in his sound senses, who does not lead the life of a half-dormant animal, philosophizes in his own way"; and "religious doctrine rests on a metaphysical foundation; unless convinced of the reality of a supersensual world, it builds upon sand."[2] Or as Prof. Eucken, the most eloquent champion of this central characteristic of all vital religion, exclaims: "If we never, as a matter of fact, get beyond merely subjective psychological processes, and we can nowhere trace within us the action of cosmic forces; if we in no case experience through them an enlargement, elevation, and transformation of our nature: then not all the endeavours of its well-meaning friends can preserve religion from sinking to the level of a mere illusion. Without a

[1] *Rothe's Spekulatives System*, 1899, pp. 25, 26.
[2] *Elements of the Science of Religion*, 1897, Vol. II, pp. 61, 62.

universal and real principle, without hyper-empirical processes, there can be no permanence for religion." [1]

(4) Some kind of philosophy, then, will inevitably accompany, follow, and stimulate religion, were it only as the, necessarily ever inadequate, attempt at giving a fitting expression to the essentially metaphysical character of belief in a supersensible world, in God, in man's spiritual capacities and in God's redemption of man. Not because the patient analysis of the completer human personalities, (as these are to be found throughout the length and breadth of history,) requires the elimination of a wholesome Mysticism and a sober Metaphysic from among the elements and effects of the fullest Manhood and Religion; but because of the ever serious difficulties and the liability to grave abuses attendant upon both these forces, the inevitably excessive reactions against these abuses, and the recurrent necessity of remodelling much of the theory and practice of both, in accordance with the growth of our knowledge of the human mind, (a necessity which, at first sight, seems to stultify all the hyper-empirical claims of both these forces): only because of this have many men of sense and goodness come to speak as though religion, even at its fullest, could and should get on without either, contenting itself to be a somewhat sentimental, Immanental Ethics.

(5) Yet, against such misgivings, perhaps the most immediately impressive counter-argument is the procession, so largely made up of men and of movements not usually reckoned as exclusively or directly religious, whose very greatness,—one which humanity will not let die,—is closely interwoven with Mystical and Metaphysical affirmations. There are, among philosophers, a Spinoza and a Leibniz, a Fichte, Hegel, Schopenhauer, a Trendelenburg and a Lotze, with the later stages of a John Mill, a Littré, and a Herbert Spencer; among poets, a Pindar and Aeschylus, a Lucretius and Vergil, a Lessing and a Goethe, a Wordsworth and a Browning; among historians, a Thucydides and a Tacitus, a St. Simon and de Tocqueville, a Carlyle, a Jacob Grimm, a Droysen and a Ranke; among scientists, a Copernicus and a Kepler, a Newton, a Lyell, indeed, largely still, also a Darwin; and among men of action, a Moltke and a Gordon, a Burke and a von Stein. Shear any of these men of their Mystical and

[1] *Der Kampf um einen geistigen Lebensinhalt,* 1896, p. 309.

Metaphysical elements, and you will have shorn Samson of his locks.

And if we can frame a contrary list of men of force and distinction, who have represented an un- or even an anti-Mystical and anti-Metaphysical type : Caesar and Hannibal, Napoleon and Bismarck, Voltaire and Laplace, Hume and Bentham, Huxley and Mommsen, we must ever remember the complex truth as to the Polarity of Life,—the strict necessity of the movement towards an intensely close contact with empirical reality, as well as of the movement back to recollection; the frequent sickliness of the recollective movement, as found in the average practice of life, which cannot but produce a reaction and contrary excess; and hence the legitimacy of what this second type has got of positiveness and of corrective criticism. Yet here too the greatness will consist directly in what these men are and have, not in what they are not; and wherever this their brutal-seeming sense of the apparent brutalities of life is combined with an apprehension of a higher world and of a deeper reality, *there* something fuller and more true has been attained than is reached by such strong but incomplete humanity alone.

4. *Religion and Morality, their kinship and difference.*

And, finally, as to Religion and Morality, we should note how that the men, who deny all essential connection between Religion and Mysticism and Religion and Philosophy, ever, when they do retain Religion at all, tend to identify it with Morality, if not as to the motives, yet as to the contents of the two forces. And yet it is not difficult to show that, if the relation between Religion and Morality is closer than that between Religion and Philosophy, though not as intimate as is that between Historical-Institutional Religion and Mysticism : Religion and Morality are nevertheless not identical.

(1) This non-identity is indicated by the broad historical fact that, though the development of Religion tells upon that of Morality, and *vice versa* : yet that the rate of development of these two forces is practically never the same, even in one and the same soul, still less in any one country or race. In each case we get various inequalities between the two developments, which would be impossible, were the two forces different only in name.

We reach again the same conclusion, if we note, what Dr. Edward Caird has so well pointed out, " the imperfection of the subjective religion of the prophets and psalmists of

Israel,"—who nevertheless already possessed a very advanced type of profoundly ethical religion,—" shown by its inability to overcome the legal and ceremonial system of worship to which it was opposed"; as, "in like manner, Protestantism . . . has never been able decisively to conquer the system of Rome."[1] For this, as indeed the failure of Buddhism to absorb and supersede Hindooism, evidently implies that Religion cannot find its full development and equilibrium in an exclusive concentration upon Morality Proper, as alone essential; and hence that complete Religion embraces other things besides Morality.

Once more we find non-identity between the very Ethics directly postulated by Religion at its deepest, and the Ethics immediately required by the Family, Society, the State, Art, Science, and Philosophy. As Prof. Troeltsch admirably puts it, "the special characteristic of our modern consciousness resides in the insistence both upon the Religious, the That-world Ends, *and* upon the Cultural, This-world Ends, which latter are taken as Ends-in-themselves: it is precisely in this combination that this consciousness finds its richness, power, and freedom, but also its painful interior tension and its difficult problems." "As in Christian Ethics we must recognize the predominance of an Objective Religious End,—for here certain relations of the soul to God are the chief commandments and the supreme good,—so in the Cultural Ends we should frankly recognize objective Moral Ends of an Immanental kind." And in seeking after the right relations between the two, we shall have to conclude that "Ethics, for us, are not, at first, a unity but a multiplicity: man grows up amongst a number of moral ends, the unification of which is his life's task and problem, and not its starting-point." And this multiplicity "is" more precisely "a polarity in human nature, for it contains two poles—that of Religious and that of Humane Ethics, neither of which can be ignored without moral damage, but which, nevertheless, cannot be brought under a common formula." "We can but keep a sufficient space open for the action of both forms, so that from their interaction there may ever result, with the least possible difficulty, the deepening of the Humane Ends by the Christian Ethics, and the humanizing of the Christian End by the Humane Ethics, so that life may become a service of God

[1] *The Evolution of Religion*, 1893, Vol. II, p. 313.

within the Cultural Ends, and that the service of God may transfigure the world." [1]

We can perceive the difference between the two forces most clearly in Our Lord's life and teaching—say, the Sermon on the Mount; in the intolerableness of every exegesis which attempts to reduce the ultimate meaning and worth of this world-renewing religious document to what it has of literal applicability in the field of morality proper. Schopenhauer expressed a profound intuition in the words: "It would be a most unworthy manner of speech to declare the sublime Founder of the Christian Religion, whose life is proposed to us as the model of all virtue, to have been the most reasonable of men, and that his maxims contained but the best instruction towards an entirely reasonable life." [2]

(2) The fact is that Religion ever insists, even where it but seems to be teaching certain moral rules and motives as appropriate to this visible world of ours, upon presenting them in the setting of a fuller, deeper world than that immediately required as the field of action and as the justification of ordinary morality. Thus whilst, in Morality Proper, the concepts of Responsibility, Prudence, Merit, Reward, Irretrievableness, are necessarily primary; in Religious Ethics the ideas of Trust, Grace, Heroism, Love, Free Pardon, Spiritual Renovation are, as necessarily, supreme. And hence it is not accidental, although of course not necessary, that we often find men with a keen religious sense but with a defective moral practice or even conception, and men with a strong moral sense and a want of religious perception; that Mystics, with their keen sense for one element of religion, so often seem, and sometimes are, careless of morality proper; and that, in such recent cases (deeply instructive in their very aberrations) as that of Nietzsche, we get a fierce anti-Moralism combined with a thirst for a higher and deeper world than this visible one, which not all its fantastic form, nor even all Nietzsche's later rant against concrete religion, can prevent from being essentially religious.[3]

(3) We have then, here, the deepest instance of the law and

[1] "Grund-probleme der Ethik," in *Zeitschrift für Theologie und Kirche*, 1902, pp. 164; 166, 167; 172.

[2] *Die Welt als Wille und Vorstellung*, I, Anhang, p. 653.

[3] A. E. Taylor's *The Problem of Conduct*, 1901, contains, pp. 469–487, a very vigorous and suggestive study of the similarities and differences between Morality and Religion, marred though it is by paradox and impatience.

necessity which we have, so often, found at the shallower levels of the spirit's life. For here, once more, there is one apprehension, force, life,—This-world Morality,—which requires penetration and development, in nowise destruction, by another, a deeper power, That-world Ethics and Religion. Let the one weaken or blunt the edge and impact of the other, and it has, at the same time, weakened itself. For here again we have, not a Thing which simply exists, by persistence in its dull unpenetratingness and dead impenetrability, but a Life, growing by the incorporation and organization, within its ampler range, of lesser lives, each with its own legitimate autonomy.

II. Mysticism and the Limits of Human Knowledge and Experience.

But have not even the most sober-minded of the Partial Mystics greatly exceeded the limits of human knowledge, more or less continuously, throughout their conclusions? Is Kant completely in the wrong? And are not the Positivists right in restricting all certain cognition to the experiences of the senses and to the Mathematico-Physical Sciences built upon those experiences? And, again, is there such a thing at all as specifically Mystical Experience or Knowledge? And, if so, what is its worth?—I must keep the elaboration of the (ultimately connected) question, as to the nature of the realities experienced or known—as to the human spirit and the Divine Spirit, and their inter-relations, hence as to Pantheism and Personality—for the next chapter, and can here but prepare the ground for it, by the elucidation of certain important points in general Epistemology, and of the more obvious characteristics of Mystical apprehension.

1. *Positivist Epistemology an error.*

As regards general Epistemology, we may well take up the following positions.

(1) We cannot but reject, with Prof. Volkelt, as a mere vulgar error, the Positivist limitation of trans-subjectively valid knowledge to direct sense-perception and to the laws of the so-called Empirical Sciences. For, as he shows conclusively, the only fact which is absolutely indubitable, is that of the bare occurrence of our (possibly utterly misleading) sensations and impressions. Some of these are, it is true,

accompanied by a certain pressure upon our minds to credit them with trans-subjective validity; and the fact of this (possibly quite misleading) pressure is itself part of our undeniable experience. Yet we can, if we will, treat this pressure also as no more than a meaningless occurrence, and not as evidencing the trans-subjective reality which it seems to indicate. No man, it is true, has ever succeeded in consistently carrying out such a refusal of assent,—since no scepticism is so thorough but that it derives its very power, against the trans-subjective validity of some of the impressions furnished with trans-subjective pressure, from an utterly inconsistent acceptance, as trans-subjectively valid, of other impressions furnished with a precisely similar trans-subjective intimation. Yet the fact remains that, in all such cases of trans-subjective pressure, the mind has "an immediate experience of which the content is precisely this, that we are justified in proceeding with these concepts into what is absolutely beyond the possibility of being experienced by us." "Positivistic Cognition," to which no man, Positivist included, can systematically restrict himself, "abides absolutely within the immediately experienced. Logical Cognition," which every man practises surreptitiously if not avowedly, "exceeds experience at every step, and conceptually determines what is absolutely incapable of being experienced, yet the justification for this kind of cognition is, here also, an immediately experienced certitude." [1]

We have, "then, immediately experienced presentations which of themselves already constitute a knowledge,—our first knowledge, and the only one possessed of absolute indubitableness." And some of these presentations "are accompanied by a kind of immediate certainty or revelation that, in some way, they reach right into the Thing-in-Itself, that they directly express something objectively valid, present in that Thing-in-Itself"; and "this pressure ever involves, should the contradictory of what it enunciates be admitted as objectively existent, the self-destruction of objective reality."—"And this pressure can, in any one case, be resisted by the mind; an act of endorsement, of a kind of faith, is necessary on the part of the mind : for these presentations, furnished with such pressure, do not transform themselves into the Things-in-Themselves directly,—we do not come to see objective reality simply face to face." [2] And we find thus that "*in principle* the

[1] J. Volkelt, *Immanuel Kant's Erkenntnisstheorie*, 1879, pp. 258, 259.
[2] *Ibid.* pp. 206, 208, 209.

entire range of reality, right down to its last depths, lies open to cognition, proceeding according to the principle of the necessities of thought. For he who recognizes this principle, thereby admits that the necessities of thought have trans-subjective significance, so that, if any affirmation concerning the ultimate reasons and depths of Reality can be shown to be necessary in thought, this affirmation possesses as rightful a claim to trans-subjective validity, as any determination, necessary in thought, which concern only such parts of the Thing-in-Itself as are the nearest neighbours to our sense-impressions concerning it. Everywhere our principle leaves us only the question whether thought, as a matter of fact, does or does not react, under the given problems, with the said logical constraint and pressure." [1]

(2) We can next insist upon how we have thus already found that the acquisition of even so rudimentary an outline of Reality, as to be ever in part presupposed in the attacks of the most radical sceptics, necessarily involves a certain emotive disposition and volitional action. And, over and above this partially withholdable assent, such quite elementary thinking will also ever require the concomitant energizing of the picturing faculty. And again, the more interior and spiritual are this thinking's subject-matters, the more will it be permeated by, and be inseparable from, deep feeling. It is then all man's faculties conjoined, it is the whole man, who normally thus gives, without reflecting on it, his all, to gain even this elementary nucleus of certainty as to Reality. "Even receptivity," as Prof. Ward well says, "is activity"; for even where non-voluntary, it is never indifferent. "Not mere receptivity, but conative or selective activity, is the essence of subjective reality." Or, with Prof. Volkelt: "Purely isolated thought,"—which, in actual life ever more or less of a fiction, is not rarely set up by individuals as an ideal,—"is, however intensified and interiorized, something ever only formal, something, in the final resort, insignificant and shadowy."—And, concurrently with the recognition of this fact, man will come to find that "the ultimate Substance or Power of and in the world,"—that objective reality which is the essential counterpart to his own subjective reality,—"is something possessed of a true, deep content and of a positive aim, and alive according to the analogy of a willing individual

[1] J. Volkelt, *Immanuel Kant's Erkenntnisstheorie*, 1879, p. 244.

The world would thus be a Logical Process only in the sense that this concrete fundamental Power is bound by the ideal necessity of its own nature." [1]

(3) And again, I would note with Volkelt how Kant, owing to his notoriously intense natural tendency to universal Dualism, never admits, even as a point for preliminary settlement, the possibility that our subjective conceptions of Objective Reality may have some true relation to that Reality. His professed ignorance as to the nature of that Reality changes instantaneously, quite unbeknown to himself, into an absolute unvarying, negative knowledge concerning that Reality,—he simply *knows* that it is *utterly heterogeneous* to our conception of it. Thus he finds the view that "God has implanted into the human mind certain categories and concepts of a kind spontaneously to harmonize with things," to be "the most preposterous solution that we could possibly choose." [2] Thus the epistemological difference between Presentation and Thing-in-Itself becomes a metaphysical exclusion of each by the other. And yet we know of no fact, whether of experience or of thought, to prevent something which is *my* presentation existing also, in so far as it is the content of that presentation, outside of this presentment. Indeed Psychology and Epistemology have, driven by every reason and stopped by none, more and more denied and refuted this excessive, indeed gratuitous, Dualism.

As Prof. Henry Jones well puts it: "The hypothesis that knowledge consists of two elements which are so radically different as to be capable of description only by defining each negatively in terms of the other, the pure manifold or differences of sense, and a purely universal or relative thought," breaks down under the fact that "pure thought and the manifold of sense pass into each other, the one proving meaningless and the other helpless in its isolation." These elements "are only aspects of one fact, co-relates mutually penetrating each other, distinguishable in thought, but not separable as existences." Hence we must not "make logical remnants do the work of an intelligence which is never purely formal, upon a material which is

[1] James Ward, "Present Problems of Psychology," in (American) *Philosophical Review*, 1904, p. 607. J. Volkelt, *Kant's Erkenntnisstheorie*, p. 241.

[2] In a letter of 1772, *Briefe*, ed. Berlin Academy, Vol. I, 1900, p. 126.

nowhere a pure manifold": for "the difference between the primary data of thought on the one hand, and the highest kinds of systematized knowledge on the other, is no difference . . . between a mere particular and a mere universal, or a mere content and a mere form; but it is a difference in comprehensiveness of articulation." However primary may be the distinction of subjective and objective, "we are not entitled to forget the unity of the reality in which the distinction takes place." If we begin with the purely subjective, we must doubtless end there; but then, in spite of certain, never self-consistent, philosophical hypotheses, "the purely subjective is as completely beyond our reach as the purely objective." [1]

Prof. Ward indeed pushes the matter, I think rightly, even a step further. He points out how readily, owing to the ambiguous term "consciousness," "we confound experience with knowledge"; but holds that experience is the wider term. "Knowledge must fall within experience, and experience extend beyond knowledge. Thus I am not left to infer my own being from my knowing. . . . Objective reality is immediately 'given,' or immediately 'there,' not inferred." But the subjective reality is not immediately given, immediately there. "There is no such parallelism between the two. . . . The subjective factor in experience is not *datum* but *recipiens*: it is not 'there' but 'here'; a 'here' relative to that 'there.'" [2] Nothing of this, I think, really conflicts with the positions we have adopted from Volkelt, since "experience" is evidently used here in a sense inclusive of the presentations, the trans-subjective pressure and the endorsement of the latter's estimations,—the three elements which, according also to Volkelt, form an organism which even the most daring subjectivism can never consistently reject. At most, the term "experience" is more extended in Prof. Ward, since it includes all three elements, than in Prof. Volkelt, who restricts it to the two first.

(4) And further, we must take care to find room for the only unforced explanation of the wondrous fact that "although," as Dr. Volkelt strikingly says, "the various schools of philosophy"—this is largely true of those of theology also,—are "in part essentially determined by historical

[1] H. Jones, *A Critical Account of the Philosophy of Lotze*, 1895, pp. 102–104; 106, 107; 108, 111.

[2] *The Present Problems*, pp. 606, 607.

currents, forces which follow other standards than those of logical necessity" : yet "these points of view and modes of thought, thus determined by" apparently non-logical "history, subserve nevertheless logical necessity, indeed represent its" slow, intermittent, yet real "progressive realization." The explanation is that "the forces of history are, unbeknown to themselves, planned, in their depths, for agreement with the necessities and ends of thought and of truth." "And thus the different spheres" and levels "of spiritual life and endeavour appear as originally intended for each other, so that each sphere, whilst consciously striving only after its own particular laws and standards, in reality furthers the objects of the rest." For "only the operative presence of such an original, teleological inter-relation can explain how historic forces, by their influence upon, and determination of, philosophical thinking, can, instead of staining and spoiling it by the introduction of religious, artistic, political, and other motives, actually advance it most essentially." [1]—Here then we get a still further enlargement of the already wide range of interaction, within the human mind, between forces which, at first sight, appear simply external to, indeed destructive of, each other; and a corresponding increase in the indications of the immense breadth, depth, and closeness of inter-penetration characterizing the operative ground-plan, the pre-existing Harmony and Teleology of the fundamental forces of Reality. Thus once more man's spirit appears as possessed of a large interiority; and as met, supported and penetrated, by a Spirit stupendously rich in spiritual energy.

(5) And finally, let us never forget that "the only experience immediately accessible to us" men, "is our own; this, in spite of its complexity, is the first we know." [2] And this means that we have direct experience and anything like adequate knowledge, (because knowledge from within,) not of things, but of mind and will, of spiritual life struggling within an animal life; and that in face, say, of plant-life, and still more of a pebble or of a star, we have a difficulty as to an at all appropriate and penetrative apprehension, which, if opposite to, is also in a sense greater than, the difficulty inherent to our apprehension of God Himself. For towards this latter apprehension we have got the convergent testimony

[1] J. Volkelt, *Erfahrung und Denken*, 1886, p. 485.

[2] James Ward, "On the Definition of Psychology," in *Journal of Psychology*, Vol. I, 1904, p. 25.

of certain great, never quite obliterable facts without us and within ourselves.

There is the upward trend, the ever-increased complexity of organization, the growing depth and interiority in the animate world,—Plant-Life itself being already, very probably, possessed of a vague consciousness, and Man, at the other end of the scale, summing up the tendency of the whole series in a deep self-consciousness which, at the same time, makes him alone keenly aware of the great difference, in the midst of the true kinship, between himself and the humbler members of that one world. For Natural Selection can but describe the results and explain part of the method of this upward trend, but cannot penetrate to its ultimate cause and end.

There is, again, the great, deep fact of the mutually necessary, mutually stimulating presence and interaction, within our own mental and spiritual life, of sense-impressions, imaginative picturings, rational categories, emotional activities, and volitional acts; and, again, of subject and object; and, once more, of general, philosophic Thought and the contingencies of History. For the immanental inter-adaptation and Teleology, that mysteriously link together all these, profoundly disparate-seeming, realms and forces is far too deep-down, it too much surprises, and exacts too much of us, it too much reveals itself, precisely at the end of much labour of our own and in our truest and most balanced moods, as the mostly unarticulated presupposition and explanation of both the great cost and the rich fruitfulness of every approximately complete actuation of all our faculties, each with and in the others, and in and with their appropriate objects, to be permanently ruled out of court as mere sentimentalism or baseless apologetic.

And there is the deepest fact of all, the one which precisely constitutes the specific characteristic of all true humanity, the sense of mental oppression, of intolerable imprisonment inflicted by the very idea of the merely contingent, the simply phenomenal and Finite, and the accompanying noble restlessness and ready dwarfing of all man's best achievements by the agent's own Ideal of Perfection. For this latter sense is, precisely in the greater souls, so spontaneous and so keen, so immensely operative in never leaving our, otherwise indolent and readily self-delusive, self-complacent race fully and long satisfied with anything that passes entirely away, or that is admittedly merely a subjective fancy, even though this fancy be shared by every member of the human race: and this sense operates so explosively within Sceptics as well as Dogmatists, within would-be Agnostic Scientists as well as in the most Intellectualist Theologians; it so humbles, startles, and alone so braces, sweetens, widens, indeed constitutes our humanity: as to be unforcedly explicable only by admitting that man's spirit's experience is not shut up within man's own clear analysis or picturing of it; that it is indefinitely wider, and somehow, in its deepest reaches, is directly touched, affected, in part determined, by the Infinite Spirit Itself. "Man never knows how anthropomorphic he is," says Goethe. Yes, but it was a man, Goethe, it is at bottom all men, in proportion as they are fully, sensitively such, who have somehow discovered this truth; who suffer from its continuous evidences, as spontaneously as from the toothache or from insomnia; and whose deepest moments give them a vivid sense of how immensely the Spirit, thus directly experienced by their spirit, transcends, and yet also is required by and is immanent in, their keen sense of the Finitude and Contingency present throughout the world of sense-perception and of clear intellectual formulation.

(6) With Plato and Plotinus, Clement of Alexandria and St. Augustine, St. Bernard, Cardinal Nicolas of Coes and Leibniz in the past; with Cardinal Newman, Professors Maurice Blondel and Henri Bergson, Siegwart, Eucken, Troeltsch and Tiele, Igino Petrone and Edward Caird, in the present; with the explicit assent of practically all the great Mystics of all ages and countries, and the implicit instinct, and at least partial, practical admission, of all sane and developed human souls; we will then have to postulate here, not merely an intellectual reasoning upon finite data, which would somehow result in so operative a sense of the Infinite; nor even simply a mental category of Infinitude which, evoked in man by and together with the apprehension of things finite, would, somehow, have so massive, so explosive an effect against our finding satisfaction in the other categories, categories which, after all, would not be more subjective, than itself: but the ontological presence of, and the operative penetration by the Infinite Spirit, within the human spirit. This Spirit's presence would produce, on occasion of man's apprehension or volition of things contingent and finite, the keen sense of disappointment, of contrast with the Simultaneous,

Abiding, and Infinite.—And let the reader note that this is not Ontologism, for we here neither deduce our other ideas from the idea of God, nor do we argue from ideas and their clarity, but from living forces and their operativeness.

We thus get man's spirit placed within a world of varying degrees of depth and interiority, the different levels and kinds of which are necessary, as so many materials, stimulants, obstacles, and objects, for the development of that spirit's various capacities, which themselves again interact the one upon the other, and react upon and within that world. For if man's experience of God is not a mere discursively reasoned conclusion from the data of sense, yet man's spirit experiences the Divine Spirit and the spirits of his fellow-men on occasion of, and as a kind of contrast, background, and support to, the actuation of his senses, imagination, reason, feeling, and volition, and, at least at first and in the long run, not otherwise.

2. *No distinct faculty of Mystical apprehension.*

Is there, then, strictly speaking, such a thing as a specifically distinct, self-sufficing, purely Mystical mode of apprehending Reality? I take it, *distinctly not;* and that all the errors of the Exclusive Mystic proceed precisely from the contention that Mysticism does constitute such an entirely separate, completely self-supported kind of human experience. —This denial does not, of course, mean that soul does not differ quite indefinitely from soul, in the amount and kind of the recollective, intuitive, deeply emotive element possessed and exercised by it concurrently or alternately with other elements,—the sense of the Infinite within and without the Finite springing up in the soul on occasion of its contact with the Contingent; nor, again, that these more or less congenital differences and vocations amongst souls cannot and are not still further developed by grace and heroism into types of religious apprehension and life, so strikingly divergent, as, at first sight, to seem hardly even supplementary the one to the other. But it means that, in even the most purely contingent-seeming soul, and in its apparently but Institutional and Historical assents and acts, there ever is, there never can fail to be, *some*, however implicit, however slight, however intermittent, sense and experience of the Infinite, evidenced by at least some dissatisfaction with the Finite, except as this Finitude is an occasion for growth in, and a part-expression of, that Infinite, our true home. And, again, it means, that even the most exclusively mystical-seeming soul ever depends, for the fulness and healthiness of even the most purely mystical of its acts and states, as really upon its past and present contacts with the Contingent, Temporal, and Spatial, and with social facts and elements, as upon its movement of concentration, and the sense and experience, evoked on occasion of those contacts or of their memories, of the Infinite within and around those finitudes and itself.

Only thus does Mysticism attain to its true, full dignity, which consists precisely in being, not everything in any one soul, but something in every soul of man; and in presenting, at its fullest, the amplest development, among certain special natures with the help of certain special graces and heroisms, of what, in some degree and form, is present in every truly human soul, and in such a soul's every, at all genuine and complete, grace-stimulated religious act and state. And only thus does it, as Partial Mysticism, retain all the strength and escape the weaknesses and dangers of would-be Pure Mysticism, as regards the mode and character of Religious Experience, Knowledge, and Life.

3. *The first four pairs of weaknesses and strengths special to the Mystics.*

I take the Mystic's weaknesses and strengths to go together in pairs, and that there are seven such pairs. Only the first four shall be considered here; the fifth and the last two couples are reserved respectively for the following, and for the last section, of this chapter.

(1) The Mystic finds his joy in the recollective movement and movements of the soul; and hence ever tends, *qua* Mystic, to ignore and neglect, or to over-minimize, the absolutely necessary contact of the mind and will with the things of sense. He will often write as though, could he but completely shut off his mind from all sense-perceptions,—even of grand scenery, or noble works of art, or scenes of human devotedness, suffering, and peace,—it would be proportionately fuller of God.—Yet this drift is ever more or less contradicted by his practice, often at the very moment of such argument: for no religious writers are more prolific in vivid imagery derived from noble sensible objects and scenes than are the Mystics, —whose characteristic mood is an intuition, a resting in a kind of vision of things invisible.—And this contradiction is satisfactory, since it is quite certain that if the mind, heart, and will could be completely absorbed, (from the first or for

any length of time,) in the flight from the sensible, it would become as dangerously empty and languid concerning things invisible themselves as, with nothing but an outgoing occupation with the sensible, it would become distracted and feverish. It is this aversion from Outgoing and from the world of sense, of the contemporaneous contingencies environing the soul, that gives to Mysticism, as such, its shadowy character, its floating above, rather than penetrating into, reality,—in contradiction, where this tendency becomes too exclusive, to the Incarnational philosophy and practice of Christianity, and indeed of every complete and sound psychology.

And yet the Incoming, what the deep religious thinker Kierkegaard has so profoundly analyzed in his doctrine of "Repetition,"[1]—recollection and peaceful browsing among the materials brought in by the soul's Outgoing,—is most essential. Indeed it is the more difficult, and, though never alone sufficient, yet ever the more centrally religious, of the two movements necessary for the acquisition of spiritual experience and life.

(2) Again, the Mystic finds his full delight in all that approximates most nearly to Simultaneity, and Eternity; and consequently turns away, *qua* Mystic, from the Successive and Temporal presented by History.—Yet here also there are two movements, both necessary for man. He will, by the one, once more in fullest sympathy with the grand Christian love of lowliness, strive hard to get into close, and ever closer, touch with the successivenesses of History, especially those of Our Lord's earthly life and of His closest followers. Without this touch he will become empty, inflated, as St. Teresa found to be the case with herself, when following the false principle of deliberate and systematic abstraction from Christ's temporal words and acts: for man's soul, though it does not energize in mere Clock-Time, cannot grow if we attempt to eliminate Duration, that interpenetrative, overlapping kind of Succession, which is already, as it were, halfway to the Simultaneity of God. It is this aversion from Clock-Time Succession and even from Duration which gives to Mysticism, as such, its remarkable preference for Spatial images, and its strong bent towards concepts of a Static and Determinist type, profoundly antagonistic though these are

[1] There is a good description of this doctrine in H. Höffding's *Sören Kierkegaard*, Stuttgart, 1896, pp. 100–104.

to the Dynamic and Libertarian character which ever marks the occasions and conditions for the acquiring of religious experience.

And yet, here again, the Mystic is clinging, even one-sidedly, to the more central, more specifically religious, of the two movements. For it is certain that God is indeed Simultaneous and Eternal; that it is right thus to try and apprehend, what appears to us stretched out successively in time, as simultaneously present in the one great Now of God; and that our deepest experiences testify to History itself being ever more than mere process, and to have within it a certain contribution from, a certain approximation to and expression of, Eternity.

(3) And again, the Mystic finds his joy in the sense of a Pure Reception of the Purely Objective; that God should do all and should receive the credit of all, is here a primary requirement.—And yet all penetrating Psychology, Epistemology, and Ethics find this very receptivity, however seemingly only such, to be, where healthy and fruitful, ever an action, a conation of the soul,—an energizing and volition which, as we have seen, are present in its very cognition of anything affirmed by it as trans-subjective, from a grain of sand up to the great God Himself. This antipathy to even a relative, God-willed independence and power of self-excitation, gives Mysticism, as such, its constant bent towards Quietism; and hence, with regard to the means and nature of knowledge, its tendency to speak of such a purely spiritual effect as Grace, and such purely spiritual beings as the Soul and God, as though they were literally sensible objects sensibly impressing themselves upon the Mystic's purely passive senses. This tendency reinforces the Mystic's thirst for pictorial, simultaneous presentation and intuition of the verities apprehended by him, but is in curious contradiction to his even excessive conceptions concerning the utter separateness and difference from all things material of all such spiritual realities.—And yet, here too, it is doubtless deeply important ever to remember, and to act in accordance with, the great truth that God Himself is apprehended by us only if there be action of our own, and that, from elementary moral dispositions right up to consummate sanctity, the whole man has ever to act and will more and more manysidedly, fully, and persistently.

But the corresponding, indeed the anterior and more

centrally religious, truth here is, that all this range of our activity could never begin, and, if it could, would lose itself *in vacuo*, unless there already were Reality around it and within it, as the stimulus and object for all this energizing,—a Reality which, as Prof. Ward has told us with respect to Epistemology, must, for a certain dim but most true experience of ours, be simply given, not sought and found. And indeed the operations of Grace are ever more or less penetrating and soliciting, though nowhere forcing, the free assent of the natural soul : we should be unable to seek God unless He had already found us and had thus, deep down within ourselves, caused us to seek and find Him. And hence thus again the most indispensable, the truest form of experience underlies reasoning, and is a kind of not directly analyzable, but indirectly most operative, intuition or instinct of the soul.

(4) And yet the Mystic, in one of his moods (the corresponding, contradictory mood of a Pantheistic identification of his true self with God shall be considered in our next chapter), finds his joy in so exalting the difference of nature between himself and God, and the incomprehensibility of God for every finite intelligence, as,—were we to press his words,—to cut away all ground for any experience or knowledge sufficient to justify him in even a guess as to what God is like or is not like, and for any attempt at intercourse with, and at becoming like unto, One who is so utterly unlike himself.

4. *Criticism of the fourth pair, mystical "Agnosticism."*

Now this acutely paradoxical position, of an entire certainty as to God's complete difference from ourselves, has been maintained and articulated, with a consistency and vividness beyond that of any Mystic known to me, by that most stimulating, profound, tragically non-mystical, religious ascetic and thinker, the Lutheran Dane, Sören Kierkegaard (1813–1855). His early friend, but philosophical opponent, Prof. Höffding, describes him as insisting that "the suffering incident to the religious life is necessarily involved in the very nature of the religious relation. For the relation of the soul to God is a relation to a Being utterly different from man, a Being which cannot confront man as his Superlative and Ideal, and which nevertheless is to rule within him." "What wonder, then," as Kierkegaard says, "if the Jew held that the vision of God meant death, and if the Heathen believed that to enter upon relations with God was the beginning of insanity?" For the man who lives for God "is a fish out of water."[1]—We have here what, if an error, is yet possible only to profoundly religious souls; indeed it would be easy to point out very similar passages in St. Catherine and St. John of the Cross. Yet Höffding is clearly in the right in maintaining that "Qualitative or Absolute difference abolishes all possibility of any positive relation. . . . If religious zeal, in its eagerness to push the Object of religion to the highest height, establishes a yawning abyss between this Object and the life whose ideal It is still to remain,—such zeal contradicts itself. For a God who is not Ideal and Exemplar, is no God."[2]

Berkeley raised similar objections against analogous positions of the Pseudo-Dionysius, in his Alciphron in 1732.[3] Indeed the Belgian Jesuit, Balthazar Corderius, has a very satisfactory note on this matter in his edition, in 1634, of the Areopagite,[4] in which he shows how all the negative propositions of Mystical Theology, *e. g.* "God is not Being, not Life," presuppose a certain affirmative position, *e. g.* "God is Being and Life, in a manner infinitely more sublime and perfect than we are able to comprehend"; and gives reasons and authorities, from St. Jerome to St. Thomas inclusive, for holding that some kind and degree of direct confused knowledge (I should prefer, with modern writers, to call it experience) of God's existence and nature is possessed by the human soul, independently of its reasoning from the data of sense.

St. Thomas's admissions are especially striking, as he usually elaborates a position which ignores, and would logically exclude, such "confused knowledge." In his *Exposition and Questions on the Book of Boetius on the Trinity*, after arguments to show that we know indeed *that* God is, but not *what* He is,—at most only what He is not, he says: "We should recognize, however, that it is impossible, with regard to anything, to know whether it exists, unless, in some way or other, we know *what* it is, either with a perfect or with a confused knowledge. . . . Hence also with regard to God,—we could not know whether He exists, unless we somehow knew *what* He is, even though in a confused manner." And this

[1] Höffding's *Kierkegaard*, pp. 119, 120.
[2] *Ibid*. p. 123.
[3] See *Works*, ed. London, 1898, Vol. II, pp. 299–306.
[4] *Quaestio Mystica*, at the end of the notes to Chapter V of Dionysius's *Mystical Theology*, ed. Migne, 1889, Vol. I, pp. 1050–1058.

knowledge of *what* He is, is interestingly, because unconsciously, admitted in one of the passages directed to proving that we can but know *that* He is. "In our earthly state we cannot attain to a knowledge of Himself beyond the fact that He exists. And yet, among those who know *that* He is, the one knows this more perfectly than the other." [1] For it is plain that, even if the knowledge of the existence of something were possible without any knowledge of that thing's nature, no difference or increase in such knowledge of the thing's bare existence would be possible. The different degrees in the knowledge, which is here declared to be one concerning the bare existence of God, can, as a matter of fact, exist only in knowledge concerning His nature. I shall have to return to this great question further on.

Here I would only point out how well Battista Vernazza has, in her *Dialogo*, realized the importance of a modification in such acutely dualistic statements as those occasionally met with in the *Vita*. For, in the *Dialogo*, the utter qualitative difference between God and the Soul, and the Soul and the Body, which find so striking an utterance in one of Catherine's moods, is ever carefully limited to the soul's sinful acts and habits, and to the body's unspiritualized condition; so that the soul, when generous and faithful to God's grace, can and does grow less and less unlike God, and the body can, in its turn, become more and more an instrument and expression of the soul. A pity only that Battista has continued Catherine's occasional over-emphasis in the parallel matter of the knowledge of God: since, even in the *Dialogo*, we get statements which, if pressed, would imply that even the crudest, indeed the most immoral conception of God is, objectively, no farther removed from the reality than is the most spiritual idea that man can attain of Him.

It would indeed be well if the Christian Mystics who, since about 500 A.D., are more and more dependent for their formulations upon the Areopagite, had followed, in this matter, not his more usual and more paradoxical, but his exceptional, thoroughly sober vein of teaching,—that contained in the third chapter of his *Mystical Theology*, where he finds degrees of worth and approximation among the affirmative attributions, and degrees of unfitness and distance among the negative ones. "Are not life and goodness more

[1] *In Librum Boetii de Trinitate*, in D. Thomae Aquinatis *Opera*, ed. altera Veneta, Vol. VIII, 1776, pp. 341*b*, 342*a*; 291*a*.

cognate to Him than air and stone? And is He not further removed from debauchery and wrath, than from ineffableness and incomprehensibility"?[1] But such a scale of approximations would be utterly impossible did we not somehow, at least dimly, experience or know *what* He is.

We shall then have to amend the Mystic's apparent Agnosticism on three points. We shall have to drop any hard and fast distinction between knowledge of God's Existence and knowledge of His Nature, since both necessarily more or less stand and fall together. We shall have to replace the terms as to our utter ignorance as to what He is, by terms expressive of an experience which, if not directly and independently clear and analyzable to the reflex, critical reason, can yet be shown to be profoundly real and indefinitely potent in the life of man's whole rational and volitional being. It is this dim, deep experience which ever causes our reflex knowledge of God to appear no knowledge at all. And we shall reject any absolute qualitative difference between the soul's deepest possibilities and ideals, and God; and shall, in its stead, maintain an absolute difference between God, and all our downward inclinations, acts, and habits, and an indefinite difference, in worth and dignity, between God and the very best that, with His help, we can aim at and become. With regard to every truly existent subject-matter, we can trace the indefinitely wider range and the more delicate penetration possessed by our dim yet true direct contact and experience, as contrasted with our reflex analysis concerning all such contacts and experiences; and this surplusage is at its highest in connection with God, Who is not simply a Thing alongside of other things, but the Spirit, our spirit's Origin, Sustainer, and End, "in whom we live and move and have our being."

III. Mysticism and the Question of Evil.

Introductory: Exclusive and Inclusive Mysticism in Relation to Optimism.

The four couples of weaknesses and corresponding strong points characteristic of Mysticism that we have just considered, and the fact that, in each case, they ever spring respectively

[1] *Mystical Theology*, Dr. Parker, pp. 135, 136. I have somewhat modified Parker's rendering.

from an attempt to make Mysticism be the all of religion, and from a readiness to keep it as but one of the elements more or less present in, and necessary for, every degree and form of the full life of the human soul: make one wish for two English terms, as useful as are the German names "Mystik" and "Mystizismus," for briefly indicating respectively "the legitimate share of Feeling in the constitution of the religious life, and the one-sidedness of a religion in which the Understanding and the Will," and indeed also the Memory and the Senses, with their respective variously external occasions, vehicles, and objects, "do not come to their rights," as Prof. Rauwenhoff well defines the matter.[1] I somehow shrink from the term "Mysticality" for his "Mystizismus"; and must rest content with the three terms—of "Mysticism," as covering both the right and the wrong use of feeling in religion; and of "True" or "Inclusive Mysticism," and of "Pseudo-" or "Exclusive Mysticism," as denoting respectively the legitimate, and the (quantitatively or qualitatively) mistaken, share of emotion in the religious life.

Now the four matters, which we have just considered, have allowed us to reach an answer not all unlike that of Nicolas of Coes, Leibniz, and Hegel,—one which, if it remained alone or quite final, would, in face of the fulness of real life, strike us all, nowadays, as somewhat superficial, because too Optimistic and Panlogistic in its trend. The fifth set of difficulties and problems now to be faced will seem almost to justify Schopenhauer at his gloomiest. Yet we must bear in mind that our direct business here is not with the problem of Evil in general, but only with the special helps and hindrances, afforded by inclusive and by Exclusive Mysticism respectively, towards apprehending the true nature of Evil and turning even it into an occasion for a deeper good. In this case the special helps and hindrances fall under three heads.

1. *Mysticism too optimistic. Evil positive, but not supreme.*

(1) First of all, I would strongly insist upon the following great fact to which human life and history bear witness, if we but take and test these latter on a large scale and with a patient persistency. It is, that not the smoother, easier times and circumstances in the lives of individuals and of peoples, but, on the contrary, the harder and hardest trials of every

[1] *Religions-philosophie*, German tr. ed. 1894, p. 116. His scheme finds three psychological forms and constituents in all religion, Intellectualism, Mysticism, Moralism, each with its own advantages and dangers.

conceivable kind, and the unshrinking, full acceptance of these, as part of the price of conscience and of its growing light, have ever been the occasions of the deepest trust in and love of God to which man has attained. In Jewish History, the Exile called forth a Jeremiah and Ezekiel, and the profound ideal of the Suffering Servant; the persecution of Antiochus Epiphanes raised up a Judas Maccabaeus; and the troubles under the Emperor Hadrian, a Rabbi Akiba. And in Christian History, the persecutions from Nero to Robespierre have each occasioned the formation of heroic lovers of Love Crucified. And such great figures do not simply manage to live, apart from all the turmoil, in some Mystic upper region of their own; but they face and plunge into the very heart of the strife, and get and give spiritual strength on occasion of this closest contact with loneliness, outrage, pain, and death. And this fact can be traced throughout history.

Not as though suffering automatically deepens and widens man into a true spiritual personality,—of itself it does not even tend to this; nor as though there were not souls grown hard or low, or frivolous or bitter, under suffering,—to leave madness and suicide unconsidered,—souls in which it would be difficult to find any avoidable grave fault. But that, wherever there is the fullest, deepest, interiority of human character and influence, *there* can ever be found profound trials and sufferings which have been thus utilized and transfigured. It is doubtless Our Lord's uniquely full and clear proclamation of this mysterious efficacity of all suffering nobly borne; above all it is the supreme exemplification and fecundity of this deepest law of life, afforded and imparted by His own self-immolation, that has given its special power to Christianity, and, in so doing, has, more profoundly than ever before or elsewhere, brought home to us a certain Teleology here also,—the deepest ever discovered to man. For though we fail in our attempts at explaining how or why, with an All-knowing, All-powerful, and All-loving God, there can be Evil at all, we can but recognize the law, which is ever being brought home to us, of a mysterious capacity for purification and development of man's spiritual character, on occasion and with the help of trouble, pain, and death itself.

(2) Now all this, we must admit, is practised and noted directly and in detail, only by the Ascetical and the Outward-going elements in Religion; whereas Mysticism, as such, is optimistic, not only as is Christianity, with respect to the end,

but, in practice, with regard to the actual state of things already encircling it as well. For so careful a selection and so rigorous an abstraction is practised by Mysticism, as such, towards the welter of contingencies around it, that the rough shocks, the bitter tonics, the expansive birth-pangs of the spirit's deeper life, in and by means of the flux of time and sense, of the conflict with hostile fellow-creatures, and of the claimfulness of the lower self, are known by it only in their result, not in their process, or rather only as this process ebbs and fades away, in such recollective moments, into the distance.

No wonder, then, that Mysticism, as such, has ever tended to deny all positive character to Evil. We have already found how strongly this is the case with the prince of Mystic philosophers, Plotinus. But even St. Augustine, with his massive experience, and (in his other mood) even excessive realization, of the destructive force of Evil and of the corrupt inclinations of man's heart, has one whole large current of teaching expressive of the purely negative character of Evil. The two currents, the hot and concrete, and the cold and abstract one, appear alternately in the very *Confessions*, of 397 A.D. There, ten years after his conversion, he can write : " All things that are corrupted, are deprived of good. But, if they are deprived of all good, they will cease to exist. . . . In so far, then, as they exist, they are good. . . . Evil is no substance." Notwithstanding such Neo-Platonist interpretations, he had found Evil a terribly powerful force ; the directly autobiographical chapters of this same great book proclaim this truth with unsurpassable vividness,—he is here fully Christian.[1] And in his unfinished work against the Pelagianizing Monk Julianus, in 429 A.D., he even declares—characteristically, whilst discussing the Origin of Sin : " Such and so great was Adam's sin, that it was able to turn (human) nature itself into this evil." Indeed, already in 418, he had maintained that " this wound " (of Original Sin) " forces all that is born of that human race to be under the Devil, so that the latter, so to speak, plucks the fruit from the fruit-tree of his own planting." [2]

[1] *Confessions :* " Evil, Negative," VII, 12, etc. " Evil, Positive," VI, 15; VIII, 5, 11, etc.

[2] *Opus Imperfectum*, III, 56, ed. Ben., Vol. X, col. 1750*b*. *De Nuptiis et Concupiscentia*, I, 23, *ibid*. col. 625*a*.—M. L. Grandgeorge, in his memoir *St. Augustin et le Neo-Platonisme*, 1896, gives an interesting collection of such Negative and Positive declarations, and traces the former to their precise sources in Plotinus, pp. 126, 127; 130, 131.

Pseudo-Dionysius, writing about 500 A.D., has evidently no such massive personal experience to oppose to the Neo-Platonic influence, an influence which, in the writings of Proclus (who died 485 A.D.), is now at its height. "Evil," he says, "is neither in Demons nor in us, as an existent (positive) evil, but (only) as a failure and dearth of the perfection of our own proper goods." [1] He says this and more of the same kind, but nothing as to the dread power of Evil. St. Thomas Aquinas (who died in 1271 A.D.) is, as we know, largely under the influence of the Negative conception : thus " the stain of sin is not something positive, existent in the soul. . . . It is like a shadow, which is the privation of light." [2]

Catherine, though otherwise much influenced by the Negative conception, as *e.g.* in her definition of a soul possessed by the Evil Spirit as one suffering from a " privation of love," finds the stain of sin, doubtless from her own experience, to be something distinctly positive, with considerable power of resistance and propagation.[3]—Mother Juliana of Norwich had, in 1373, also formulated both conceptions. " I saw not Sin, for I believe it hath no manner of substance, nor no part of being " : Neo-Platonist theory. " Sin is so vile and so mickle for to hate, that it may be likened to no pain. . . . All is good but Sin, and naught is evil but Sin " : Christian experience.[4]

Eckhart had, still further back (he died in 1327 A.D.), insisted much that " Evil is nothing but privation, or falling away from Being ; not an effect, but a defect " : [5] yet he also finds much work to do in combating this somehow very powerful " defect."—Not till we get to Spinoza (who died in 1677) do we get the Negative conception pushed home to its only logical conclusion : " By Reality and Perfection, I mean the same thing. . . . All knowledge of Evil is inadequate knowledge. . . . If the human mind had nothing but adequate ideas, it would not form any notion of Evil." [6]

(3) As regards the Christian Mystics, their negative conception of evil, all but completely restricted as it was to cosmolo-

[1] *Divine Names*, ch. iv, sec. xxiv.

[2] *Summa Theol.*, I, ii, qu. 86, art. 1 ad 3.

[3] *Vita*, pp. 39*b*, 116*b*.

[4] *Sixteen Revelations*, ed. 1902, pp. 69, 70.

[5] Meister Ekhart's " Lateinische Schriften," published by Denifle, *Archiv f. Litteratur u. Kirchengeschichte des M. A.*, 1886, p. 662.

[6] *Ethica*, II, def. vi; IV, prop. lxiv et coroll.; ed. Van Vloten et Land. 1895, Vol. I, pp. 73, 225.

gical theory, did those Mystics themselves little or no harm; since their tone of feeling and their volitional life, indeed a large part of their very speculation, were determined, not by such Neo-Platonist theories, but by the concrete experiences of Sin, Conscience, and Grace, and by the great Christian historical manifestation of the powers of all three.—It is clear too that our modern alternative: "positive-negative," is not simply identical with the scholastic alternative: "substantial-accidental," which latter alternative is sometimes predominant in the minds of these ancient theorizers; and that, once the question was formulated in the latter way, they were profoundly right in refusing to hypostatize Evil, in denying that there exists any distinct thing or being wholly bad.—Yet it is equally clear how very Greek and how little Christian is such a preoccupation (in face of the question of the nature of Evil) with the concepts of Substance and Accident, rather than with that of Will; and how strangely insufficient, in view of the tragic conflicts and ruins of real life, is all even sporadic, denial, of a certain obstructive and destructive efficacy in the bad will, and of a mysterious, direct perversity and formal, intentional malignity in that will at its worst.

(4) On these two points it is undeniable that Kant (with all his self-contradictions, insufficiencies, and positive errors on other important matters) has adequately formulated the practical dispositions and teachings of the fully awakened Christian consciousness, and hence, pre-eminently, of the great Saints in the past, although, in the matter of the perverse will, the Partial Mystics have, even in their theory, (though usually only as part of the doctrine of Original Sin,) largely forestalled his analysis. "Nowhere in this our world, nowhere even outside it, is anything thinkable as good without any reservation, but the good will alone." "That a corrupt inclination to evil is rooted in man, does not require any formal proof, in view of the clamorous examples furnished to all men by the experience of human behaviour. If you would have such cases from the so-called state of nature, where some philosophers have looked for the chief home of man's natural goodness, you need only compare, with such an hypothesis, the unprovoked cruelties enacted in Tofoa, New Zealand . . . and the ceaseless scenes of murder in the North-Western American deserts, where no human being derives the slightest advantage from them,—and you

will quickly have more than sufficient evidence before you to induce the abandonment of such a view. But if you consider that human nature is better studied in a state of civilization, since there its gifts have a better chance of development,—you will have to listen to a long melancholy string of accusations : of secret falseness, even among friends; of an inclination to hate him to whom we owe much; of a cordiality which yet leaves the observation true that 'there is something in the misfortune of even our best friend which does not altogether displease us' : so that you will quickly have enough of the vices of culture, the most offensive of all, and will prefer to turn away your look from human nature altogether, lest you fall yourself into another vice,—that of hatred of mankind." [1]

It is sad to think how completely this virile, poignant sense of the dread realities of human life again disappeared from the teachings of such post-Kantians as Hegel and Schleiermacher,—in other important respects so much more satisfactory than Kant. As Mr. Tennant has well said, in a stimulating book which, on this point at least, voices the unsophisticated, fully awakened conscience and Christian sense with refreshing directness, "for Jesus Christ and for the Christian consciousness, sin means something infinitely deeper and more real than what it can have meant for Spinoza or the followers of Hegel." [2] Here again we have now in Prof. Eucken, a philosopher who, free from ultimate Pessimism, lets us hear once more those tones which are alone adequate to the painful reality. "In great things and in small, there exists an evil disposition beyond all simple selfishness: hatred and envy, even where the hater's self-interest is not touched; an antipathy to things great and divine; a pleasure found in the disfigurement or destruction of the Good. . . . Indeed the mysterious fact of Evil, as a positive opposition to Good, has never ceased to occupy the deepest minds. . . . The concept of moral guilt cannot be got rid of, try as we may." [3]

(5) And yet even with regard to this matter, Mysticism re-

[1] *Grundlegung zur Metaphysik der Sitten*, 1785, *Werke*, ed. Berlin Academy, Vol. IV, 1903, p. 393. *Religion innerhalb der Grenzen der reinen Vernunft*, 1793, *Werke*, ed. Hartenstein, Vol. VI, 1868, pp. 127, 128.

[2] *The Origin and Propagation of Sin*, 1902, p. 125.

[3] *Wahrheits-gehalt der Religion*, 1901, pp. 271, 272.

presents a profound compensating truth and movement, which we cannot, without grave detriment, lose out of the complete religious life. For in life at large, and in human life and history in particular, it would be sheer perversity to deny that there is much immediate, delightful, noble Beauty, Truth, and Goodness; and these also have a right to the soul's careful, ruminating attention. And it is the Mystical element that furnishes this rumination.—Again, " it is part of the essential character of human consciousness, as a Synthesis and an organizing Unity, that, as long as the life of that consciousness lasts at all, not only contrast and tension, but also concentration and equilibrium must manifest themselves. Taking life's standard from life itself, we cannot admit its decisive constituent to lie in tension alone." [1] And it is the Mystical mood that helps to establish this equilibrium.—And finally, deep peace, an overflowing possession and attainment, and a noble joy, are immensely, irreplaceably powerful towards growth in personality and spiritual fruitfulness. Nothing, then, would be more shortsighted than to try and keep the soul from a deep, ample, recollective movement, from feeding upon and relishing, from as it were stretching itself out and bathing in, spiritual air and sunshine, in a rapt admiration, in a deep experience of the greatness, the beauty, the truth, and the goodness of the World, of Life, of God.

2. *Mysticism and the Origin of Evil.*

The second hindrance and help, afforded respectively by Exclusive and by Inclusive Mysticism in the matter of Evil, concerns the question of its Origin.

(1) Now it appears strange at first sight that, instead of first directly realizing and picturing the undeniable, profoundly important facts of man's interior conflict, his continuous lapses from his own deepest standard, and his need of a help not his own to become what he cannot but wish to be, and of leaving the theory as to how man came by this condition to the second place; the Mystics should so largely—witness Catherine—directly express only this theory, and should face what is happening *hic et nunc* all but exclusively under the picture of the prehistoric beginnings of these happenings, in the state of innocence and the lapse of the first man. For men of other religious modalities have held this doctrine as firmly as the Mystics, yet have mostly dwelt directly upon the central core

[1] Prof. Höffding, in his *Sören Kierkegaard*, pp. 130, 131.

of goodness and the weakness and sinfulness to be found in man; whilst the Mystics had even less scruple than other kinds of devout souls in embodying experimental truths in concepts and symbols other than the common ones.

(2) I think that, here again, it was the Neo-Platonist literary influence, so strong also on other points with the Mystics of the past, and a psychological trend characteristic of the Mystical habit of mind, which conjoined thus to concentrate the Mystic's attention upon the doctrines of Original Justice and of a First Lapse, and to give to these doctrines the peculiar form and tone taken on by them here. We have noted, for instance, in the case of Catherine herself, how powerfully her thought and feeling, as to the first human soul's first lapse into sin, is influenced by the idea of each human soul's lapse into a body; and we have found this latter idea to be, notwithstanding its echoes in the Deutero-Canonical Book of Wisdom and in one non-doctrinal passage in St. Paul, not Christian but Neo-Platonist. Yet it is this strongly anti-body idea that could not fail to attract Mysticism, as such.—And the conception as to the plenary righteousness of that first soul before its lapse, which she gets from Christian theology, is similarly influenced, in her theorized emotion and thought, by the Neo-Platonist idea of every soul having already existed, perfectly spotless, previous to its incarnation: a view which could not but immensely attract such a high-strung temperament, with its immense requirement of something fixed and picturable on which to rest. Thus here the ideal for each soul's future would have been already real in each soul's past. In this past the soul would have been, as it were, a mirror of a particular fixed size and fixed intensity of lustre; its business here below consists in removing the impurities adhering to this mirror's surface, and in guarding it against fresh stains.

(3) Now it is well known how it was St. Augustine, that mighty and daring, yet at times ponderous, intellect, who, (so long a mental captive of the Manichees and then so profoundly influenced by Plotinus,) was impelled, by the experiences of his own disordered earlier life and by his ardent African nature, to formulate by far the most explicit and influential of the doctrines upon these difficult matters. And if, with the aid of the Abbé Turmel's admirable articles on the subject, we can, with a fairly open mind, study his successive, profoundly varying, speculations and conclusions concerning the Nature and

Origin of Sin,[1] we shall not fail to be deeply impressed with the largely impassable maze of opposite extremes, contradictions and difficulties of every kind, in which that adventurous mind involved itself.—And to these difficulties immanent to the doctrine,—at least, in the form it takes in St. Augustine's hands,—has, of course, to be added the serious moral danger that would at once result, were we, by too emphatic or literal an insistence upon the true guiltiness of Original sin, to weaken the chief axiom of all true morality—that the concurrence of the personality, in a freely-willed assent, is necessarily involved in the idea of sin and guilt.—And now the ever-accumulating number and weight of even the most certain facts and most moderate inductions of Anthropology and Ethnology are abolishing all evidential grounds for holding a primitive high level of human knowledge and innocence, and a single sudden plunge into a fallen estate, as above, apparently against, all our physiological, psychological, historical evidences and analogies, (which all point to a gradual rise from lowly beginnings,) and are reducing such a conception to a pure postulate of Theology.

Yet Anthropology and Ethnology leave in undisturbed possession the great truths of Faith that " man's condition denotes a fall from the Divine intention, a parody of God's purpose in human history," and that "sin is exceedingly sinful for us in whom it is a deliberate grieving of the Holy Spirit " ; and they actually reinforce the profound verities that " the realization of our better self is a stupendously difficult task," and as to " Man's crying need of grace, and his capacity for a gospel of Redemption." [2] But they point, with a force great in proportion to the highly various, cumulatively operative, immensely interpretative character of the evidence,—to the conclusion that " Sin," as the Anglican Archdeacon Wilson strikingly puts it, "is . . . the survival or misuse of habits and tendencies that were incidental to an earlier stage of development. . . . Their sinfulness would thus lie in their anachronism, in their resistance to the . . . Divine force that makes for moral development and righteousness." Certainly

[1] " Le Dogme du Pêché Originel dans S. Augustin," *Revue d'Histoire et de Littérature Religieuses*, 1901, 1902. See too F. R. Tennant, *The Sources of the Doctrine of the Fall and Original Sin*, 1903, which, however, descends only to St. Ambrose inclusively.

[2] So F. R. Tennant, *The Origin and Propagation of Sin*, 1902, pp. 131, 110.

"the human infant" appears to careful observers, as Mr. Tennant notes, "as simply a non-moral animal," with corresponding impulses and propensities. According to this view "morality consists in the formation of the non-moral material of nature into character . . ."; so that "if goodness consists essentially in man's steady moralization of the raw material of morality, its opposite, sin, cannot consist in the material awaiting moralization, but in the will's failure to completely moralize it." "Evil" would thus be "not the result of a transition from the good, but good and evil would" both alike "be voluntary developments from what is ethically neutral."[1] Dr. Wilson finds, accordingly, that "this conflict of freedom and conscience is precisely what is related as 'the Fall' *sub specie historiae.*" Scripture "tells of the fall of a creature from unconscious innocence to conscious guilt. But this fall from innocence" would thus be, "in another sense, a rise to a higher grade of being."[2]

(4) It is, in any case, highly satisfactory for a Catholic to remember that the acute form, given to the doctrine of Original Sin by St. Augustine, has never been finally accepted by the Catholic Roman Church; indeed, that the Tridentine Definition expressly declares that Concupiscence does not, in strictness, possess the nature of Sin, but arises naturally, on the withdrawal of the *donum superadditum*,—so that Mr. Tennant can admit, in strictest accuracy, that "in this respect, the Roman theology is more philosophical than that of the Symbols of Protestant Christendom."[3] It is true that the insistence upon "Original Sin" possessing somehow "the true and proper nature of Sin" remains a grave difficulty, even in this Tridentine formulation of the doctrine; whilst the objections, already referred to as accumulating against the theory in general, retain some of their cogency against other parts of this decree.—Yet we have here an impressive proclamation of the profoundest truths: the spiritual greatness of God's plan for us, the substantial goodness of the material still ready to our hand for the execution of that plan, and His necessary help ever ready from the first; the reality of our lapse, away from all these, into sin, and of the effects of such lapse upon the soul; the abiding conflict between sense and spirit, the old man and the new, within each one of us;

[1] F. R. Tennant, *The Origin and Propagation of Sin*, 1902, pp. 82, 95; 107, 108; 115.

[2] *Ibid.* p. 83.

[3] *Ibid.* p. 153.

and the close solidarity of our poor, upward-aspiring, downward-plunging race, in evil as well as in good.

(5) And as to the Christian Mystics, their one particular danger here,—that of a Static Conception of man's spirit as somehow constituted, from the first, a substance of a definite, final size and dignity, which but demands the removal of disfiguring impurities, is largely eliminated, even in theory, and all but completely overcome in practice, by the doctrine and the practice of Pure Love. For in "Charity" we get a directly dynamic, expansive conception and experience: man's spirit is, at first, potential rather than actual, and has to be conquered and brought, as it were, to such and such a size and close-knitness of organization, by much fight with, and by the slow transformation of, the animal and selfish nature. Thus Pure Love, Charity, Agape, has to fight it out, inch by inch, with another, still positive force, impure love, concupiscence, Eros, in all the latter's multiform disguises. Here Purity has become something intensely positive and of boundless capacities for growth; as St. Thomas says, "Pure Love has no limit to its increase, for it is a certain participation in the Infinite Love, which is the Holy Spirit." [1]—In this utterly real, deeply Christian way do these Mystics overcome Neo-Platonist static abstractions, and simultaneously regain, in their practical theory and emotional perception, the great truth of the deep, subtle force of Evil, against which Pure Love has to stand, in virile guard, as long as earth's vigil lasts. And the longest and most difficult of these conflicts is found, —here again in utterly Christian fashion,—not in the sensual tendencies proceeding from the body, but in the self-adoration, the solipsism of the spirit. We have found this in Catherine: at her best she ever has something of the large Stoic joy at being but a citizen in a divine Cosmopolis; yet but Love and Humility, those profoundest of the Christian affections, have indefinitely deepened the truth of the outlook, and the range of the work to be done, in and for herself and others.

(6) Yet even apart from Pure Love, Mysticism can accurately be said to apprehend an important truth when, along its static line of thought and feeling, it sees each soul as, from the first, a substance of a particular, final size. For each soul is doubtless intended, from the first, to express a particular thought and wish of God, to form one, never simply replaceable

[1] *Summa Theol.*, II, ii, qu. 24, art. 7, in corp.

member in His Kingdom, to attain to a unique kind and degree of personality: and though it can refuse to endorse and carry out this plan, the plan remains within it, in the form of never entirely suppressible longings. The Mystic, then, sees much here also.

3. *The warfare against Evil. Pseudo-Mysticism.*

The third of the relations between Mysticism and the conception and experience of Evil requires a further elucidation of an important distinction, which we have already found at work all along, more or less consciously, between the higher and the lower Mysticism, and their respective, profoundly divergent, tempers, objects, and range.

(1) Prof. Münsterberg discriminates between these two Mysticisms with a brilliant excessiveness, and ends by reserving the word " Mysticism " for the rejected kind alone. " As soon as we speak of psychical objects,—of ideas, feelings, and volitions,—as subject-matters of our direct consciousness and experience, we have put before ourselves an artificial product, a transformation, to which the categories of real life no longer apply." In this artificial product causal connections have taken the place of final ends. But " History, Practical Life, . . . Morality, Religion have nothing to do with these psychological constructions; the categories of Psychology," treated by Münsterberg himself as a Natural, Determinist Science, " must not intrude into their teleological domains. But if," on the other hand, " the categories belonging to Reality," which is Spiritual and Libertarian, " are forced on to the psychological system, a system which was framed " by our mind " in the interest of causal explanation, we get a cheap mixture, which satisfies neither the one aim nor the other. Just this is the effect of Mysticism. It is the personal, emotional view applied, not to the world of Reality, where it fits, but to the Physical and Psychological worlds, which are constructed by the human logical will, with a view to gaining an impersonal, unemotional causal system. . . . The ideals of Ethics and Religion . . . have now been projected into the atomistic structure " (of the Causal System), " and have thus become dependent upon this system's nature; they find their right of existence limited to the regions where ignorance of Nature leaves blanks in the Causal System, and have to tremble at every advance which Science makes." It is to this projection alone that Münsterberg would apply the term " Mysticism," which thus becomes exclusively " the doctrine that the pro-

cesses in the world of physical and psychical objects are not always subject to natural laws, but are influenced, at times, in a manner fundamentally inexplicable from the standpoint of the causal conception of Nature. . . . Yet, the special interest of the Mystic stands and falls here with his conviction that, in these extra-causal combinations," thus operative right within and at the level of this causal system, " we have a " direct, demonstrable " manifestation of a positive system of quite another kind, a System of Values, a system dominated, not by Mechanism, but by Significance." [1]

(2) Now we have been given here a doubtless excessively antithetic and dualistic picture of what, in actual life, is a close-knit variety in unity,—that interaction between, and anticipation of the whole in, the parts, and that indication of the later stages in the earlier,—which is so strikingly operative in the order and organization of the various constituents and stages of the processes and growth of the human mind and character, and which appears again in the Reality apprehended, reproduced, and enriched by man's powers.

Even in the humblest of our Sense-perceptions, there is already a mind perceiving and a Mind perceived; and, in the most abstract and artificial of our intellectual constructions, there is not only a logical requirement, but also, underlying this requirement as this cause's deepest cause, an ever-growing if unarticulated experience and sense that only by the closest contact with the most impersonal-seeming, impersonally conceived forces of life and nature, and by the deepest recollection within its own interior world of mind and will, can man's soul adequately develop and keep alive, within itself, a solid degree and consciousness of Spirit, Free-will, Personality, Eternity, and God. Thus, in proportion as he comes more deeply to advance in the true occasions of his spirit's growth, does man still further emphasize and differentiate these two levels : the shallower, spatial-temporal, mathematico-physical, quantitative and determinist aspect of reality and level of apprehension; and the deeper, alone at all adequate, experience of all the fuller degrees of Reality and effectuations of the spirit's life, with their overlapping, interpenetrating Succession, (their Duration), and their Libertarianism, Interiority, and Sense of the Infinite. He thus emphasizes both levels, because the determinist level is found to be, though never the source or

[1] *Psychology and Life*, 1899, pp. 267, 268. *Grundzüge der Psychologie*, Vol. I, 1900, pp. 170, 171.

direct cause, yet ever a necessary awakener and purifier of the Libertarian level.

Strictly within the temporal-spatial, quantitative method and level, indeed, we can nowhere find Teleology; but if we look back upon these quantitative superficialities from the qualitative, durational and personal, spiritual level and standpoint, (which alone constitute our direct experience,) we find that the quantitative, causal level and method is everywhere inadequate to exhaust or rightly to picture Reality, in exact proportion to this reality's degree of fulness and of worth. From the simplest Vegetable-Cell up to Orchids and Insectivorous Plants; from these on to Protozoans and up, through Insects, Reptiles, and Birds, to the most intelligent of Domestic Animals; from these on to Man, the Savage, and up to the most cultured or saintly of human personalities: we have everywhere, and increasingly, an inside, an organism, a subject as well as an object,—a series which is, probably from the first, endowed with some kind of dim consciousness, and which increasingly possessed of a more and more definite consciousness, culminates in the full self-consciousness of the most fully human man. And everywhere here, though in indefinitely increasing measure, it is the individualizing and historical, the organic and soul-conceptions and experiences which constitute the most characteristic and important truths and reality about and in these beings. For the higher up we get in this scale of Reality, the more does the Interior determine and express itself in the Exterior, and the more does not only kind differ from kind of being, but even the single individual from the other individuals within each several kind. And yet nowhere, not even in free-willing, most individualized, personal Man do we find the quantitative, determinist envelope simply torn asunder and revealing the qualitative, libertarian spirit perfectly naked and directly testable by chronometer, measuring-rod, or crucible. The spirit is thus ever like unto a gloved hand, which, let it move ever so spontaneously, will ever, in the first instance, present the five senses with a glove which, to their exclusive tests, appears as but dead and motionless leather.

(3) Now we have already in Chapter IX studied the contrasting attitudes of Catherine and her attendants towards one class of such effects,—those attributed to the Divine Spirit,—and hence, in principle, towards this whole question. Yet it is in the matter of phenomena, taken to be directly Diabolic

or Preternatural, that a Pseudo-Mysticism has been specially fruitful in strangely materialistic fantasies. As late as 1774 the *Institutiones Theologiae Mysticae* of Dom Schram, O.S.B., a book which even yet enjoys considerable authority, still solemnly described, as so many facts, cases of Diabolical *Incubi* and *Succubae*. Even in 1836–1842 the layman Joseph Görres could still devote a full half of his widely influential *Mystik* to "Diabolical Mysticism,"—witchcraft, etc.; a large space to "Natural Mysticism,"—divination, lycanthropy, vampires, etc.; and a considerable part of the "Divine Mysticism," to various directly miraculous phenomenalisms. The Abbé Ribet could still, in his *La Mystique Divine, distinguée de ses Contrefaçons Diaboliques*, of 1895, give us a similarly uncritical mixture and transposition of tests and levels. But the terrible ravages of the belief in witchcraft in the later Middle Ages, and, only a few years back, the humiliating fraud and craze concerning "Diana Vaughan," are alone abundantly sufficient to warn believers in the positive character of Evil away from all, solidly avoidable, approaches to such dangerous forms of this belief.[1]

(4) Yet the higher and highest Mystical attitude has never ceased to find its fullest, most penetrating expression in the life and teaching of devoted children of the Roman Church,—several of whom have been proclaimed Doctors and Models by that Church herself. And by a conjunction of four characteristics these great normative lives and teachers still point the way, out of and beyond all false or sickly Mysticism, on to the wholesome and the true.

(i) There is, first, the grand trust in and love of God's beautiful, wide world, and in and of the manifold truth and goodness present throughout life,—realities which we have already found rightly to be dwelt on, in certain recollective movements and moments, to the momentary exclusion of their positively operative, yet ever weaker, opposites. "Well I wote," says Mother Juliana, "that heaven and earth, and all that is made, is great, large, fair and good"; "the full-head of joy is to behold God in all," and "truly to enjoy in Our Lord, is a full

[1] Mr. W. R. Inge, in his useful *Christian Mysticism*, 1899, has some sharp expressions of disgust against these long-lived survivals within the Catholic Church. And though his own tone towards Rome in general belongs also, surely, to a more or less barbaric past, he has done good service in drawing forcible attention to the matter.

lovely thanking in His sight."[1] This completely un-Manichaean attitude,—so Christian when held as the ultimate among the divers, sad and joyful, strenuous and contemplative moods of the soul,—is as strongly present in Clement of Alexandria, in the Sts. Catherine of Siena and of Genoa, in St. John of the Cross, and indeed in the recollective moments of all the great Mystics.

(ii) There is, next, a strong insistence upon the soul having to transcend all particular lights and impressions, in precise proportion to their apparently extraordinary character, if it would become strong and truly spiritual. "He that will rely on the letter of the divine locution, or on the intellectual form of the vision, will necessarily fall into delusion. 'The letter killeth, the spirit quickeneth'; we must therefore reject the literal sense, and abide in the obscurity of faith." "One desire only doth God allow in His presence, that of perfectly observing His law and carrying the Cross of Christ. . . . That soul, which has no other aim, will be a true ark containing the true Manna, which is God." "One act of the will, wrought in charity, is more precious in the eyes of God, than that which all the visions and revelations of heaven might effect." "Let men cease to regard these supernatural apprehensions . . . that they may be free."[2] Here the essence of the doctrine lies in the importance attached to this transcendence, and not in the particular views of the Saint concerning the character of this or that miraculous-seeming phenomenon to be transcended.

(iii) And this essential doctrine retains all its cogency, even though we hold the strict necessity of a contrary, alternating movement of definite occupation with the Concrete, Contingent, Historical, Institutional, in thought and action. For this occupation will be with the normal, typical means, duties, and facts of human and religious life; and, whilst fully conscious of the Supernatural working in and with these seemingly but natural materials, will, with St. Augustine, pray God to "grant men to perceive in little things the common-seeming indications of things both small and great," and, with him, will see a greater miracle in the yearly transformation of the vine's watery sap into wine, and in the germination of any single seed, than even in that of Cana.[3]

[1] *Sixteen Revelations*, ed. 1902, pp. 23, 84, 101.

[2] *Ascent of Mount Carmel*, tr. Lewis, 1891, pp. 159; 26, 27; 195, 265.

[3] *Confessions*, Bk. XI, ch. xxiii, 1. Tract in Johann. Ev., VIII, 1; XXIV, 1: ed. Ben., Vol. III, 2, coll. 1770 *b*, 1958 *d*.

(iv) And then there is, upon the whole, a tendency to concentrate, at these recollective stages, the soul's attention upon Christ and God alone. "I believe I understand," says Mother Juliana, "the ministration of holy Angels, as Clerks tell; but it was not shewed to me. For Himself is nearest and meekest, highest and lowest, and doeth all. God alone took our nature, and none but He; Christ alone worked our salvation, and none but He." [1] And thus we get a wholesome check upon the Neo-Platonist countless mediations, of which the reflex is still to be found in the Areopagite. God indeed is alone held, with all Catholic theologians, to be capable of penetrating to the soul's centre, and the fight against Evil is simplified to a watch and war against Self, in the form of an ever-increasing engrossment in the thought of God, and in the interests of His Kingdom. "Only a soul in union with God," says St. John of the Cross, "is capable of this profound loving knowledge: for this knowledge is itself that union. . . . The Devil has no power to simulate anything so great." "Self-love," says Père Grou, "is the sole source of all the illusions of the spiritual life. . . . Jesus Christ on one occasion said to St. Catherine of Siena: 'My daughter, think of Me, and I will think of thee': a short epitome of all perfection. 'Wheresoever thou findest self,' says the *Imitation*, 'drop that self': the soul's degree of fidelity to this precept is the true measure of its advancement." [2] The highly authorized *Manuel de Théologie Mystique* of the Abbé Lejeune, 1897, gives but one-sixth of its three-hundred pages to the discussion of all quasi-miraculous phenomena, puts them all apart from the substance of Contemplation and of the Mystical Life, and dwells much upon the manifold dangers of such, never essential, things. The French Oratorian, Abbé L. Laberthonnière, represents, in the *Annales de Philosophie Chrétienne*, a spirituality as full of a delicate Mysticism as it is free from any attachment to extraordinary phenomena. The same can be said of the Rev. George Tyrrell's *Hard Sayings* and *External Religion*. And the Abbé Sandreau has furnished us with two books of the most solid tradition and discrimination in all these matters.[3]

[1] *Sixteen Revelations*, ed. cit. p. 210.

[2] J. N. Grou, *Méditations sur l'Amour de Dieu*, Nouvelle ed. Perisse, pp. 268, 271.

[3] L. Laberthonnière, *Annales de Philosophie Chrétienne*, 1905, 1906. G. Tyrrell, *Hard Sayings*, 1898; *External Religion*, 1902. A. Sandreau, *La Vie d'Union à Dieu*, 1900; *L'Etat Mystique*, 1903.

(5) And we should, in justice, remember that the Phenomenalist Mysticism, objected to by Prof. Münsterberg and so sternly transcended by St. John of the Cross, is precisely what is still hankered after, and treated as of spiritual worth, by present-day Spiritualism. Indeed, even Prof. James's in many respects valuable *Varieties of Religious Experience* is seriously damaged by a cognate tendency to treat Religion, or at least Mysticism, as an abnormal faculty for perceiving phenomena inexplicable by physical and psychical science.

(6) And finally, with respect to the personality of Evil, we must not forget that "there are drawings to evil as to good, which are not mere self-temptations, . . . but which derive from other wills than our own; strictly, it is only persons that can tempt us." [1]

[1] M. D. Petre, *The Soul's Orbit*, 1904, p. 113.

CHAPTER XIV

THE TWO FINAL PROBLEMS: MYSTICISM AND PANTHEISM, THE IMMANENCE OF GOD, AND SPIRITUAL PERSONALITY, HUMAN AND DIVINE

INTRODUCTORY.

Impossibility of completely abstracting from the theoretical form in the study of the experimental matter.

We now come to the last two of our final difficulties and problems—the supposed or real relations between Inclusive or Exclusive Mysticism and Pantheism; and the question concerning the Immanence of God and Spiritual Personality, Human and Divine.

(1) A preliminary difficulty in this, our deepest, task arises from the fact that, whereas the evidences of a predominantly individual, personal, directly experimental kind, furnished by every at all deeply religious soul, have hitherto been all but completely overlooked by trained historical investigators, in favour of the study of the theological concepts and formulations accepted and transmitted by such souls, now the opposite extreme is tending to predominate, as in Prof. William James's *Varieties of Religious Experience*, 1902, or in Prof. Weinel's interesting study, *The Effects of the Spirit and of the Spirits in the Sub-Apostolic Age*, 1899. For here, as Prof. Bousset points out in connection with the latter book, we get an all but complete overlooking of the fact that, even in the most individual experience, there is always some intellectual framework or conception, some more or less traditional form, which had previously found lodgment in, and had been more or less accepted by, that soul; so that, though the experience itself, where at all deep, is never the mere precipitate of a conventionally accepted traditional intellectual form, it is nevertheless, even when more or less in conflict with this form, never completely independent of it.[1]

[1] *Göttinger Gelehrte Anzeigen*, 1901, p. 757.

—Yet though we cannot discriminate in full detail, we can show certain peculiarities in the traditional Jewish, Mohammedan, Christian Mysticism to be not intrinsic to the Mystical apprehensions as such, but to come from the then prevalent philosophies which deflected those apprehensions in those particular ways.

(2) In view then of this inevitable interrelation between the experimental, personal matter and the theoretical, traditional form, I shall first consider the Aristotelian and Neo-Platonist conceptions concerning the relations between the General and the Particular, between God and Individual Things, as being the two, partly rival yet largely similar, systems that, between them, have most profoundly influenced the intellectual starting-point, analysis, and formulation of those experiences; and shall try to show the special attraction and danger of these conceptions for the mystically religious temperament. I shall next discuss the conceptions as to the relations between God and the individual personality,—the Noûs, the Spirit, and the Soul,—which, still largely Aristotelian and Neo-Platonist, have even more profoundly commended themselves to those Mystics, since these conceptions so largely met some of those Mystics' requirements, and indeed remain still, in part, the best analysis procurable. I shall, thirdly, face the question as to any intrinsic tendency to Pantheism in Mysticism as such, and as to the significance and the possible utility of any such tendency, keeping all fuller description of the right check upon it for my last chapter. And finally, I shall consider what degree and form of the Divine Immanence in the human soul, of direct Experience or Knowledge of God on the part of man, and of "Personality" in God, appear to result from the most careful analysis of the deepest religious consciousness, and from the requirements of the Sciences and of Life.

I. Relations between the General and the Particular, God and Individual Things, according to Aristotle, the Neo-Platonists, and the Medieval Strict Realists.

1. *Aristotle, Plato, Plotinus, Proclus.*

(1) With regard to the relations between the General and Particular, we should note Aristotle's final perplexities and contradictions, arising from his failure to harmonize or to

transcend, by means of a new and self-consistent conception, the two currents, the Platonic and the specifically Aristotelian, which make up his thought. For, with him as with Plato, all Knowledge has to do with Reality: hence Reality alone, in the highest, primary sense of the word, can form the highest, primary object of Knowledge; Knowledge will be busy, primarily, with the Essence, the Substance of things. But with him, as against Plato, every substance is unique, whence it would follow that all knowledge refers, at bottom, to the Individual,—individual beings would form, not only the starting-point, but also the content and object of knowledge. —Yet this is what Aristotle, once more at one with Plato, stoutly denies: Science, even where it penetrates most deeply into the Particular, is never directed to individual things as such, but always to General Concepts; and this, not because of our human incapacity completely to know the Individual, as such, but because the General, in spite of the Particular being better known to us, is more primitive and more knowable, as alone possessing that Immutability which must characterize all objects of true knowledge.[1] The true Essence of things consists only in what is thought in their Concept, which concept is always some Universal; yet this Universal exists only in Individual Beings, which are thus declared true Substances: here are two contentions, the possibility of whose co-existence he fails to explain. Indeed at one time it is the Form, at another it is the Individual Being, composed of Form and Matter, which appears as real; and Matter, again, appears both as the Indefinite General and as the Cause of Individual Particularity.[2]

(2) Now Plato had indeed insisted upon ascending to even greater abstraction, unity, and generality, as the sure process for attaining to the truth of things; and had retained what is, for us, a strangely unpersonal, abstract element, precisely in his highest concept, since God here is hardly personal, but the Idea of Good, a Substance distinct from all other things, yet not, on this account, an Individual. Yet Plato's profoundly aesthetic, social, ethical, above all religious, consciousness forced him to the inconsistency of proclaiming that, as the Sun is higher than the light and the eye, so the Good is higher than (mere) Being and Knowledge; and this Supreme Idea of the Good gives to things their Being, and to the under-

[1] Zeller, *Philosophie der Griechen*, II, 2, ed. 1879, pp. 309, 312.

[2] *Ibid.* p. 348.

standing its power of Cognition, and is the Cause of all Rightness and Beauty, the Source of all Reality and Reason, and hence, not only a final, but also an efficient Cause,—indeed *the* Cause, pure and simple.[1] In the *Philebus* he tells us explicitly that the Good and the Divine Reason are identical; and in the *Timaeus* the Demiurge, the World-Former, looks indeed to the Image of the World, in order to copy it: yet the Demiurge is also himself this image which he copies.[2] We thus still have a supreme Multiplicity in Unity as the characteristic of the deepest Reality; and its chief attribute, Goodness, is not the most abstract and aloof, but the most rich in qualities and the most boundlessly self-communicative: "He was good, so he desired that all things should be as like unto himself as possible."[3] And Aristotle, (although he places God altogether outside the visible world, and attributes to Him there one sole action, the thinking of his own thought, and one quasi-emotion, intellectual joy at this thinking,) still maintains, in this shrunken form, the identity of the Good and of the Supreme Reason, Noûs, and a certain Multiplicity in Unity, and a true self-consciousness, within Him.

(3) It is Plotinus who is the first expressly to put the Godhead,—in strict obedience to the Abstractive scheme,—beyond all Multiplicity, hence above the highest Reason itself, for reason ever contains at least the duality of Subject thinking and of Object thought; above Being, for all being has ever a multitude of determinations; and above every part and the totality of All Things, for it is the cause of them all. The Cause is here ever outside the effect, the Unity outside the Multiplicity, what is thought outside of what thinks. The First is thus purely transcendent,—with one characteristic exception: although above Being, Energy, Thought, and Thinking, Beauty, Virtue, Life, It is still the Good; and because of this, though utterly self-sufficing and without action of any kind, It, "as it were," overflows, and this overflow produces a Second.[4] And only this Second is here the Noûs, possessed of what Aristotle attributes to the First: it is no sheer

[1] Republic, VI, 508*e*; VII, 517*b*; and Zeller, *ibid*. II, 1, ed. 1889, pp. 707–710.

[2] *Philebus*, 22*c*; *Timaeus*, 28*a*, *c*; 92*c* (with the reading ὅδε ὁ κόσμος . . . εἰκὼν τοῦ ποιητοῦ).

[3] *Timaeus*, 29*e*.

[4] *Enneads*, I, vii, 1, 61*d*; I, viii, 2, 72*e*; VI, viii, 16, end. See, for all this, Zeller, *Philosophie der Griechen*, III, ii, ed. 1881, pp. 476–480; 483; 510–414.

Unity, " all things are together there, yet are they there discriminated " : it is contemplative Thinking of itself; it is pure and perfect Action.[1]

(4) And Proclus who, through the Pseudo-Dionysius, is the chief mediator between Plato and Plotinus on the one hand, and the Medieval Mystics and Scholastics on the other, is, with his immense thirst for Unity, necessarily absorbed by the question as to the Law according to which all things are conjoined to a whole. And this Law is for him the process of the Many out of the One, and their inclination back to the One; for this process and inclination determine the connection of all things, and the precise place occupied by each thing in that connection. All things move in the circle of procession from their cause, and of return to it; the simplest beings are the most perfect; the most complex are the most imperfect.[2]

2. *The Anti-Proclian current, in the Areopagite's view.*

Now in the Pseudo-Dionysius we find an interesting oscillation between genuine Neo-Platonism, which finds Beings perfect in proportion to the fewness and universality of their attributes, although, with it, he inconsistently holds Goodness, —the deepest but not the most general attribute,—to be the most perfect of all; and Aristotelianism at its richest, when it finds Beings perfect according to the multiplicity and depth of their attributes. Dionysius himself becomes aware of the dead-lock thence ensuing. " The Divine name of the Good is extended to things being and to things not being,"—a statement forced upon him by his keeping, with Plato and Plotinus, Goodness as the supreme attribute, and yet driving home, more completely than they, their first principle that Generality and Perfection rise and sink together. " The Name of Being is extended to all things being " and stretches further than Life. " The name of Life is extended to all things living " and stretches further than Wisdom. " The Name of Wisdom is extended," only, " to all the intellectual, and rational, and sensible."

But if so, " for what reason do we affirm " (as he has been doing in the previous sections), " that Life," the less extended, " is superior to (mere) Being," the more extended? " and that Wisdom," though less extended, " is superior to mere Life," the more extended? And he answers in favour of

[1] *Enneads*, VIII, ix, 350*b*; VI, 2317, 610*d*; III, ix, 3, 358*a*, *b*.
[2] Zeller, *op. cit.* III, ii, pp. 787–789.

depth and richness of attributes. "If any one assumed the intellectual to be without being or life, the objection might hold good. But if the Divine Minds," the Angels, "both are above all other beings, and live above all other living creatures, and think and know above sensible perception and reasoning, and aspire beyond all other existent and aspiring beings, to . . . the Beautiful and Good: then they encircle the Good more closely." For "the things that participate more in the one and boundless-giving God, are more . . . divine, than those that come behind them in gifts." [1] And with abiding truth he says: "Those who place attributes on That which is above every attribute, should derive the affirmation from what is more cognate to It; but those who abstract, with regard to That which is above every abstraction, should derive the negation from what is further removed from It. Are not, *e. g.* Life and Goodness more cognate to It than air and stone? And is It not further removed from debauch and anger than from ineffableness and incomprehensibility?" [2]

But more usually Dionysius shows little or no preference for any particular attribution or denegation; all are taken to fall short so infinitely as to eliminate any question as to degrees of failure. "The Deity-Above-All . . . is neither Soul nor Mind, neither One nor Oneness, neither Deity nor Goodness." [3] God is thus purely transcendent.

3. *Continuators of the Proclian current.*

The influence of the Areopagite was notoriously immense throughout the Middle Ages,—indeed unchecked,—along its Proclian, Emanational, Ultra-Unitive current,—among the Pantheists from the Christian, Mohammedan and Jewish camps.

(1) Thus Scotus Eriugena (who died in about 877 A.D.) insists: "In strict parlance, the Divine Nature Itself exists alone in all things, and nothing exists which is not that Nature. The Lord and the Creature are one and the same thing." "It is its own Self that the Holy Trinity loves, sees, moves within us." One of his fundamental ideas is the equivalence of the degrees of abstraction and those of existence; he simply hypostatizes the logical table.[4] Eriugena was condemned.

[1] *Divine Names*, ch. v, sec. 1: tr. Parker, pp. 73–75.
[2] *Mystical Theology*, ch. iii: Parker, pp. 135, 136.
[3] *Ibid.*, ch. iv, sec. 2: Parker, pp. 136, 137.
[4] *De Divisione Naturae*, III, 17; I, 78. Ueberweg-Heinze, *Grundriss der Geschichte der Philosophie*, Vol. II, ed. 1898, p. 159.

(2) But the Pseudo-Aristotelian, really Proclian, *Liber de Causis*, written by a Mohammedan in about 850 A.D., became, from its translation into Latin in about 1180 A.D. onwards, an authority among the orthodox Scholastics. It takes, as "an example of the (*true*) doctrine as to Causes, Being, Living-Being, and Man. Here it is necessary that the thing Being should exist first of all, and next Living-Being, and last Man. Living-Being is the proximate, Being is the remote cause of Man; hence Being is in a higher degree the cause of Man than is Living-Being, since Being is the cause of Living-Being, which latter again is the cause of Man." . . . "Being, (of the kind) which is before Eternity, is the first cause. . . . Being is more general than Eternity. . . . Being of the kind which is with and after Eternity, is the first of created things . . . It is above Sense, and Soul, and Intelligence." [1]

(3) The Mohammedan Avicenna, who died in 1037 A.D., is mostly Aristotelian in philosophy and Orthodox in religious intention, and, translated into Latin, was much used by St. Thomas. Yet he has lapses into pure Pantheism, such as: "The true Being that belongs to God, is not His only, but is the Being of all things, and comes forth abundantly from His Being. That which all things desire is Being: Being is Goodness; the perfection of Being is the perfection of Goodness." [2]

(4) And the Spanish Jew, Ibn Gebirol (Avicebron), who died about 1070 A.D., is predominantly Proclian, but with a form of Pantheism which, in parts, strikingly foreshadows Spinoza. His masterly *Fons Vitae*, as translated into Latin, exercised a profound influence upon Duns Scotus. "Below the first Maker there is nothing but what is both matter and form." "All things are resolvable into Matter and Form. If all things were resolvable into a single root," (that is, into Form alone,) there would be no difference between that one root and the one Maker." There exists a universal Matter and a universal Form. The first, or universal Matter, is a substance existing by itself, which sustains diversity, and is one in number: it is capable of receiving all the different kinds of forms. The universal Form is a substance which constitutes the essence of all the different kinds of forms. . . . By means of the knowledge of this universal Form, the

[1] Secs. 2, 4, ed. Bardenhewer, 1882, pp. 163–166.

[2] Commentarius, in *Aristolelis Metaphysica*, Tract. VIII, cap. 6, quoted by Denifle, *Archiv f. Litteratur-u-Kirchengeschichte*, 1886, p. 520.

knowledge of every (less general) form is acquired,—is deduced from it and resolved into it." "Being falls under four categories, answering to: whether it is, what it is, what is its quality, and why it is: but, of these, the first in order of dignity is the category which inquires whether it is at all."[1] We thus get again the degree of worth strictly identical with the degree of generality.

4. *Inconsistencies of Aquinas and Scotus.*

(1) St. Thomas, the chief of the orthodox Scholastics, has embodied the entire Dionysian writings in his own works, but labours assiduously—and successfully, as far as his own statements are concerned—to guard against the Pantheistic tendencies special to strict Realism. Yet it is clear, from his frequent warnings and difficult distinctions regarding the double sense of the proposition, "God is sheer Being," and from the ease with which we find Eckhart, an entirely consistent Realist, lapse into the Pantheistic sense, how immanent is the danger to any severe form of the system.[2] And he fails to give us a thoroughly understandable and consistent account as to the relations between the General and the Particular, between Form and Matter, and between these two pairs of conceptions. Thus "Materia signata," matter, as bearing certain dimensions, "is the principle of individuation":[3] yet this *quantum* is already an individually determined quantity, and *this* determination remains unexplained. And certain forms exist separately, without matter, in which case each single form is a separate species; as with the Angels and, pre-eminently, with God.—Yet, as already Duns Scotus insisted, Aquinas' general principle seems to require the non-existence of pure forms as distinct beings, and the partial materiality of all individual beings.[4]

(2) And Duns Scotus teaches, in explicit return to Avicebron, that every created substance consists of matter as well as of form, and that there is but one, First Matter, which is identical in every particular and derivative kind of matter. The world appears to him as a gigantic tree, whose root is this indeterminate matter; whose branches are the transitory substances;

[1] Ibn Gebirol, *Fons Vitae*, ed. Bäumker, 1895: IV, 6, pp. 225, 224; V, 22, p. 298; II, 20, pp. 60–61; V, 24, p. 301.

[2] *De Ente et Essentia*, c. vi. *Summa Theol.*, I, qu. 3, art. 4 ad 1; and elsewhere.

[3] *De Ente et Essentia*, c. ii.

[4] See Ueberweg-Heinze, *op. cit.* pp. 280, 281.

whose leaves the changeable accidents; whose flowers, the rational souls; whose fruit are the Angels: and which God has planted and which He tends. Here again the order of Efficacity,—with the tell-tale exception of God,—is identical with that of Generality.[1]

5. *Eckhart's Pantheistic trend.*

But it is Eckhart who consistently develops the Pantheistic trend of a rigorous Intellectualism. The very competent and strongly Thomistic Father Denifle shows how Eckhart strictly followed the general scholastic doctrine, as enunciated by Avicenna: "In every creature its Being is one thing, and is from another, its Essence is another thing, and is not from another"; whereas in God, Being and Essence are identical. And Denifle adds: "Eckhart will have been unable to answer for himself the question as to what, in strictness, the 'Esse' is, in distinction from the 'Essentia'; indeed no one could have told him, with precision. . . . Eckhart leaves intact the distinction between the Essence of God and that of the creature; but, doubtless in part because of this, he feels himself free,—in starting from an ambiguous text of Boetius,—to break down the careful discriminations established by St. Thomas, in view of this same text, between Universal Being, Common to all things extant, and Divine Being, reserved by Aquinas for God alone."[2] "What things are nearer to each other, than anything that *is* and Being? There is nothing between them." "Very Being," the Being of God, "is the actualizing Form of every form, everywhere." "In one word," adds Denifle, "the Being of God constitutes the formal Being of all things."[3] The degrees of Generality and Abstract Thinkableness are again also the degrees of Reality and Worth: "the Eternal Word assumed to Itself, not this or that human being, but a human nature which existed bare, unparticularized." "Being and Knowableness are identical."

When speaking systematically Eckhart is strictly Plotinian: "God and Godhead are as distinct as earth is from heaven." "The Godhead has left all things to God: It owns nought, wills nought, requires nought, effects nought, produces nought." "Thou shalt love the Godhead as It truly is: a non-God,

[1] *De rerum Principio*, qu. viii. Ueberweg-Heinze, *op. cit.* pp. 295, 296.

[2] H. S. Denifle, *Meister Eckhart's Lateinische Schriften*, *loc. cit.* pp. 489, 490; 540, n. 6.

[3] *Ibid.* p. 519.

non-Spirit, non-Person . . . a sheer, pure, clear One, severed from all duality : let us sink down into that One, throughout eternity, from Nothing unto Nothing, so help us God." "The Godhead Itself remains unknown to Itself." "It is God who energizes and speaks one single thing,—His Son, the Holy Ghost, and all creatures. . . . Where God speaks it, there it is all God; here, where man understands it, it is God and creature." [1] No wonder that the following are among the propositions condemned by Pope John XXII in 1329 : "God produces me as His own Being, a Being identical, not merely similar"; and, "I speak as falsely when I call God (the Godhead) good, as if I call white, black." [2]

6. *The logical goal of strict Realism.*

This series of facts, which could be indefinitely extended, well illustrates the persistence of "the fundamental doctrine common to all forms of Realism,—of the species as an entity in the individuals, common to all and *identical* in each, an entity to which individual differences adhere as accidents," as Prof. Pringle Pattison accurately defines the matter. "Yet when existence is in question, it is the individual, not the universal, that is real; and the real individual is not a compound of species and accidents, but is individual to the inmost fibre of his being." Not as though Nominalism were in the right. For "each finite individual has its" special "place in the one real universe, with all the parts of which it is inseparably connected. But the universe is itself an individual or real whole, containing all its parts within itself, and not a universal of the logical order, containing its exemplifications under it." [3] And, above all, minds, spirits, persons,—however truly they may approximate more and more to certain great types of rationality, virtue, and religion, which types are thus increasingly expressive of God's self-revealing purpose and nature,—are ever, not merely numerically different, as between one individual and the other, but, both in its potentialities and especially in its spiritual actualization, no one soul can or does take the place of any other.

And if we ask what there is in any strict Realism to attract the Mystical sense, we shall find it, I think, in the insistence of such Realism upon Unity, Universality, and Stability.

[1] *Meister Eckhart*, ed. Pfeiffer, 1857, pp. 158, 1; 99, 8; 180, 15; 532, 30; 320, 27; 288, 26; 207, 27.

[2] Denzinger, *Enchiridion Symbolorum*, ed. 1888, Nos. 437, 455.

[3] *Hegelianism and Personality*, ed. 1893, pp. 230, 231, and note.

Yet in so far as Mysticism, in such a case Exclusive Mysticism, tends to oust the Outgoing movement of the soul, it empties these forms of their Multiple, Individual, and Energizing content. Inclusive Mysticism may be truly said alone to attain to the true Mystic's desires; for only by the interaction of both movements, and of all the powers of the soul, will the said soul escape the ever-increasing poverty of content characteristic of the strict Realist's pyramid of conceptions; a poverty undoubtedly antagonistic tothe secret aspiration of Mysticism, which is essentially an apprehension, admiration, and love of the infinite depths and riches of Reality—of this Reality no doubt present everywhere, yet in indefinitely various, and mutually complementary and stimulative forms and degrees. And the readiness with which Mysticism expressed itself in the Nominalist Categories,—distinctly less adequate to a healthy, Partial Mysticism than the more moderate forms of Realism,—shows how little intrinsic was the link which seemed to bind it to a Realism of the most rigorous kind.

II. Relations between God and the Human Soul.

In taking next the question as to the relations between God and the Human Soul, we shall find our difficulties increased, because, here especially, the Philosophers and even the Biblical Writers have, with regard to religious experience, used expressions and furnished stimulations of a generally complex and unclarified, intermittent, and unharmonized kind; and especially because certain specifically religious experiences and requirements have operated here with a unique intensity, at one time in a Pantheistic, at another in a more or less Deistic, direction. The reader will specially note the points in the following doctrines which helped on the conception that a certain centre or highest part of the soul is God, or a part of God, Himself.

1. *Plato and Aristotle. "The Noûs."*

(1) Plato teaches the pre-existence and the post-existence (immortality) of the soul, as two interdependent truths. In his earlier stage, *e. g.* the *Phaedrus*, he so little discriminates, in his argument for immortality, between the individual soul and the World-Soul, as to argue that "the Self-Moving" Soul generally "is the beginning of motion, and this motion,"

(specially here in connection with the human soul,) "can neither be destroyed nor begotten, since, in that case, the heavens and all generation would collapse." Yet individual souls are not, according to him, emanations of the World-Soul; but, as the particular ideas stand beside the Supreme Idea, so do the particular souls stand beside the Soul of the Whole, in a distinct peculiarity of their own.[1]—And again, since the soul has lapsed from a purer, its appropriate, life into the body, and has thus no original, intrinsic relation to this body, the activity of the senses, indeed in strictness even that of the emotions, cannot form part of its essential nature. Only the highest part of the soul, the Reason, *Noûs*, which, as "sun-like, God-like," can apprehend the sun, God, is one and simple, as are all the ideas, immortal; whereas the soul's lower part consists of two elements,—the nobler, the irascible, and the ignobler, the concupiscible passions. But how the unity of the soul's life can co-exist with this psychical tritomy, is a question no doubt never formulated even to himself by Plato: we certainly have only three beings bound together, not one being active in different directions.[2]

(2) Aristotle, if more sober in his general doctrine, brings some special obscurities and contradictions. For whilst the pre-existence of the soul, taken as a whole, is formally denied, and indeed its very origin is linked to that of the body, its rational part, the Noûs, comes into the physical organism from outside of the matter altogether, and an impersonal pre-existence is distinctly predicated of it,—in strict conformity with his doctrine that the Supreme Noûs does not directly act upon, or produce things in, the world.[3]

2. *St. Paul. The "Spirit."*

But it is St. Paul who, in his Mystical outbursts and in the systematic parts of his doctrine, as against the simply hortatory level of his teaching, gives us the earliest, one of the deepest, and to this hour by far the most influential, among the at all detailed experiences and schemes, accepted by and operative among Christians, as to the relations of the human soul to God. And here again, and with characteristic intensity,

[1] *Phaedrus*, 245*d*; Zeller, *op. cit.* II, 1, ed. 1889, p. 830.

[2] *Ibid.* pp. 843, 844; 849, 850.

[3] Pre-existence of the Noûs: *Gen. Anim.*, II, 3, 736*b*; *de Anima*, III, 5, 430*a*; Zeller, *op. cit.* II, 2, ed. 1879, pp. 593, 595. The Supreme Noûs, purely transcendent: *Metaph.*, XII, 7–10. But see Dr. Edward Caird's admirable pp. 1–30, Vol. II, of his *Evolution of Theology in the Greek Philosophers*, 1904.

certain overlapping double meanings and conceptions, and some vivid descriptions of experiences readily suggestive of the divinity of the soul's highest part, repeatedly appear.

(1) In the systematic passages we not only find the terms *Psyche*, "Soul," for the vital force of the body; and *Noûs*, ("Mind,") "Heart," and "Conscience," for various aspects and functions of man's rational and volitional nature: but a special insistence upon *Pneuma*, "Spirit," mostly in a quite special sense of the word. Thus in 1 Cor. ii, 14, 15, we get an absolute contrast between the psychic or sarkic, the simply natural man, and the Pneumatic, the Spiritual one, all capacity for understanding the Spirit of God being denied to the former. The Spiritual thus appears as itself already the Divine, and the Spirit as the exclusive, characteristic property of God, something which is foreign to man, apart from his Christian renovation and elevation to a higher form of existence. Only with the entrance of faith and its consequences into the mind and will of man, does this transcendent Spirit become an immanent principle: "through His Spirit that dwelleth in you."[1] —Hence, in the more systematic Pauline Anthropology, *Pneuma* cannot be taken as belonging to man's original endowment. Certainly in 1 Cor. ii, 11, the term "the spirit of a man" appears simply because the whole passage is dominated by a comparison between the Divine and the human consciousness, which allows simultaneously of the use of the conversely incorrect term, "the mind of God,"—here, v. 16, and in Rom. xi, 34. And the term "the spirit of the world," 1 Cor. ii. 12, is used in contrast with "the Spirit of God," and as loosely as the term "the God of this world," is applied, in 2 Cor. iv, 4, to Satan.—Only some four passages are difficult to interpret thus: *e.g.* "All defilement of flesh and spirit" (2 Cor. vii, 1); for how can God, Spirit, be defiled? Yet we can "forget that our body is a temple of the Holy Spirit," 1 Cor. vi, 19; and its defilement can "grieve the Holy Spirit" (Eph. iv, 30).[2]

And note how parallel to his conception of this immanence of the transcendent Spirit is St. Paul's conception, based upon his personal, mystical experience, of the indwelling of Christ in the regenerate human soul. Saul had indeed been

[1] Rom. viii, 11. See too Rom. viii, 9, 14; 1 Cor. iii, 16; vi, 11; vii, 40; xii, 3.

[2] H. J. Holtzmann, *Lehrbuch der N. T. Theology*, 1897, Vol. II, pp. 9–12; 15–18.

won to Jesus Christ, not by the history of Jesus' earthly life, but by the direct manifestation of the heavenly Spirit-Christ, on the way to Damascus : whence he teaches that only those who know Him as Spirit, can truly " be in Christ,"—an expression formed on the model of " to be in the Spirit," as in Mark xii, 36, and Apoc. i, 10.

(2) And then these terms take on, in specifically Pauline Mystical passages, a suggestion of a local extension and environment, and express, like the corresponding formulae "in God," "in the Spirit," the conception of an abiding within as it were an element,—that of the exalted Christ and His Divine glory. Or Christ is within us, as the Spirit also is said to be, so that the regenerate personality, by its closeness of intercourse with the personality of Christ, can become one single Spirit with Him, 1 Cor. vi, 17. " As the air is the element in which man moves, and yet again the element of life which is present within the man: so the Pneuma-Christ is for St. Paul both the Ocean of the Divine Being, into which the Christian, since his reception of the Spirit, is plunged," and in which he disports himself, " and a stream which, derived from that Ocean, is specially introduced within his individual life."[1] Catherine's profound indebtedness to this Mystical Pauline doctrine has already been studied; here we are but considering this doctrine in so far as suggestive, to the Mystics, of the identity between the true self and God,—an identity readily reached, if we press such passages as " Christ, our life "; " to live is Christ "; " I live, not I, but Christ liveth in me."[2]

3. *Plotinus.*

Some two centuries later, Plotinus brings his profound influence to bear in the direction of such identification. For as the First, the One, which, as we saw, possesses, for him, no Self-consciousness, Life, or Being, produces the Second, the Noûs, which, possessed of all these attributes, exercises them directly in self-contemplation alone; and yet this Second is so closely like that First as to be " light from light ": so does the Second produce the Third, the Human Psyche, which, though " a thing by itself," is a " god-like (divine) thing," since it possesses " a more divine part, the part which is neighbour to what is above, the Noûs, with which and from

[1] H. J. Holtzmann, *op. cit.* Vol. II, pp. 79, 80. Johannes Weiss, *Die Nachfolge Christi*, 1895, p. 95.

[2] Col. iii, 4; Phil. i, 21; Gal. ii, 20.

which Noûs the Psyche exists."—The Psyche is " an image of the Noûs " : " as outward speech expresses inward thought, so is the Psyche a concept of the Noûs,—a certain energy of the Noûs, as the Noûs itself is an energy of the First Cause." " As with fire, where we distinguish the heat that abides within the fire and the heat that is emitted by it . . . so must we conceive the Psyche not as wholly flowing forth from, but as in part abiding in, in part proceeding from the Noûs." [1]

And towards the end of the great Ninth Book of the Sixth Ennead, he tells how in Ecstasy " the soul sees the Source of Life . . . the Ground of Goodness, the Root of the Soul. . . . For we are not cut off from or outside of It . . . but we breathe and consist in It : since It does not give and then retire, but ever lifts and bears us, so long as It is what It is." " We must stand alone in It and must become It alone, after stripping off all the rest that hangs about us. . . . There we can behold both Him and our own selves,—ourselves, full of intellectual light, or rather as Pure Light Itself, having become God, or rather as being simply He . . . abiding altogether unmoved, having become as it were Stability Itself." " When man has moved out of himself away to God, like the image to its Prototype, he has reached his journey's end." " And this is the life of the Gods and of divine and blessed man . . . a flight of the alone to the Alone." [2]

4. *Eckhart's position. Ruysbroek.*

(1) Eckhart gives us both Plotinian positions—the God-likeness and the downright Divinity of the soul. " The Spark (*das Fünkelein*) of the Soul . . . is a light impressed upon its uppermost part, and an image of the Divine Nature, which is ever at war with all that is not divine. It is not one of the several powers of the soul. . . . Its name is Synteresis,"—*i.e.* conscience. " The nine powers of the soul are all servants of that man of the soul, and help him on to the soul's Source." [3]—But in one of the condemned propositions he says : " There is something in the soul which is Increate and Uncreatable ; if the whole soul were such, it would be (entirely) Increate and Uncreatable. And this is the Intellect,"—standing here exactly for Plotinus's Noûs.[4]

(2) Ruysbroek (who died in 1381) combines a considerable

[1] *Enneads*, V, book 1, cc. 3 and 6.
[2] *Ibid.* VI, book 9, 9 and 11.
[3] *Eckhart*, ed. Pfeiffer, pp. 113, 33 ; 469, 40, 36.
[4] Denzinger, *op. cit.* No. 454.

fundamental sobriety with much of St. Paul's daring and many echoes of Plotinus. "The unity of our spirit with God is of two kinds,—essential and actual. According to its essence, our spirit receives, in its innermost highest part, the visit of Christ, without means and without intermission; for the life which we are in God, in our Eternal Image, and that which we have and are in ourselves, according to the essence of our being . . . are without distinction.—But this essential unity of our spirit with God has no consistency in itself, but abides in God and flows out from and depends on Him." The actual unity of our spirit with God, caused by Grace, confers upon us not His Image, but His Likeness, "and though we cannot lose the Image of God, nor our natural unity with Him,—if we lose His Likeness, His Grace, Christ, who, in this case, comes to us with mediations and intermissions, we shall be damned." [1]

5. *St. Teresa's mediating view.*

St. Teresa's teachings contain interesting faint echoes of the old perplexities and daring doctrines concerning the nature of the Spirit; but articulate a strikingly persistent conviction that the soul holds God Himself as distinct from His graces, possessing thus some direct experience of this His presence. "I cannot understand what the mind is, nor how it differs from the soul or the spirit either: all three seem to me to be but one, though the soul sometimes leaps forth out of itself, like a fire which has become a flame: the flame ascends high above the fire, but it is still the same flame of the same fire." "Something subtle and swift seems to issue from the soul, to ascend to its highest part and to go whither Our Lord will . . . it seems a flight. This little bird of the spirit seems to have escaped out of the prison of the body." Indeed "the soul is then not in itself . . . it seems to me to have its dwelling higher than even the highest part of itself." [2]—"In the beginning I did not know that God is present in all things. . . . Unlearned men used to tell me that He was present only by His grace. I could not believe that . . . A most learned Dominican told me He was present Himself . . . this was a great comfort to me." "To look upon Our Lord as being in the innermost parts of the soul . . . is a much more profitable method, than that of looking upon Him as external to

[1] *Vier Schriften von Johannes Ruysbroek*, ed. Ullmann, 1848, pp. 106, 107.

[2] *Life, written by Herself*, tr. D. Lewis, ed. 1888, pp. 124, 421, 146.

us." "The living God was in my soul." And even, "hitherto" up to 1555, "my life was my own; my life, since then, is the life which God lived in me."[1]

6. *Immanence, not Pantheism.*

St. Teresa's teaching as to God's own presence in the soul points plainly, I think, to the truth insisted on by the Catholic theologian Schwab, in his admirable monograph on Gerson. "Neither speculation nor feeling are satisfied with a Pure Transcendence of God; and hence the whole effort of true Mysticism is directed, whilst not abolishing His Transcendence, to embrace and experience God, His living presence, in the innermost soul,—that is, to insist, in some way or other, upon the Immanence of God. Reject all such endeavours as Pantheistic, insist sharply upon the specific eternal difference between God and the Creature: and the Speculative, Mystical depths fade away, with all their fascination."[2] Not in finding Pantheism already here, with the imminent risk of falling into a cold Deism, but in a rigorous insistence, with all the great Inclusive Mystics, upon the spiritual and moral effects, as the tests of the reality and worth of such experiences, and, with the Ascetical and Historical souls, upon also the other movement—an outgoing in some kind of contact with, and labour at, the contingencies and particularities of life and mind—will the true safeguard for this element of the soul's life be found.[3]

III. Mysticism and Pantheism: their Differences and Points of Likeness.

But does not Mysticism, not only find God in the soul, but the soul to be God? Is it not, as such, already Pantheism? Or, if not, what is their difference?

1. *Plotinus and Spinoza compared.*

Now Dr. Edward Caird, in his fine book, *The Evolution of Theology in the Greek Philosophers*, 1904, tells us that "Mysticism is religion in its most concentrated and exclusive form; it is that attitude of mind in which all other relations

[1] *Life, written by Herself*, tr. D. Lewis, ed. 1888, pp. 355, 130, 430; 174.

[2] J. B. Schwab, *Johannes Gerson*, 1858, pp. 361, 362.

[3] I can find but one, secondary Ecclesiastical Censure of the doctrine of God's substantial presence in the soul,—the censure passed by the Paris Sorbonne on Peter Lombard. The same Sorbonne repeatedly censured St. Thomas on other points.

are swallowed up in the relation of the soul to God"; and that "Plotinus is the Mystic *par excellence*." [1] And he then proceeds to contrast Plotinus, the typical Mystic, with Spinoza, the true Pantheist.

"Whether" or not "Spinoza, in his negation of the limits of the finite, still leaves it open to himself to admit a reality in finite things which is *not* negated," and "to conceive of the absolute substance as manifesting itself in attributes and modes": "it is very clear that he does so conceive it, and that, for all those finite things which he treats as negative and illusory in themselves, he finds in God a ground of reality . . . which can be as little destroyed as the divine substance itself." "God, *Deus sive Natura*, is conceived as the immanent principle of the universe, or perhaps rather the universe is conceived as immanent in God."—Thus to him "the movement by which he dissolves the finite in the infinite, and the movement by which he finds the finite again in the infinite, are equally essential. If for him the world is nothing apart from God, God is nothing apart from His realization in the world." This is true Pantheism.[2]

But in Plotinus the *via negativa* involves a negation of the finite and determinate in all its forms; hence here it is impossible to find the finite again in the infinite. The Absolute One is here not immanent but transcendent.[3] "While the lower always has need of the higher, the higher is regarded as having no need" for any purpose "of the lower"; and "the Highest has no need of anything but Itself." "Such a process cannot be reversed": "in ascending, Plotinus has drawn the ladder after him, and left himself no possibility of descending again. The movement, in which he is guided by definite and explicit thought, is always upwards; while, in describing the movement downwards, he has to take refuge in metaphors and analogies," for the purpose of indicating a purely self-occupied activity which only accidentally produces an external effect, *e.g.* "the One as it were overflows, and produces another than itself." [4] "Thus we have the strange paradox that the Being who is absolute, is yet conceived as in a sense external to the relative and finite, and that He leaves the relative and finite in a kind of unreal independence." "On the one side, we have a

[1] Vol. II, pp. 210, 211.
[2] *Ibid.* pp. 230, 231.
[3] *Ibid.* p. 231.
[4] *Ibid.* pp. 253–257. *Enneads*, V, book ii, 1.

life which is nothing apart from God, and which, nevertheless, can never be united to him, except as it loses itself altogether; and, on the other side, an Absolute, which yet is not immanent in the life it originates, but abides in transcendent isolation from it. . . . It is this contradiction which . . . makes the writings of Plotinus the supreme expression of Mysticism." [1]

Now I think, with this admirable critic, that we cannot but take Spinoza as the classical representative of that parallelistic Pantheism to which most of our contemporary systems of psycho-physical parallelism belong. As Prof. Troeltsch well puts it, " we have here a complete parallelism between every single event in the physical world, which event is already entirely explicable from its own antecedents within that physical world, and every event of a psychical kind, which, nevertheless, is itself also entirely explicable from its own psychical antecedents alone." And " this parallelism again is but two sides of the one World-Substance, Which is neither Nature nor Spirit, and Whose law is neither natural nor spiritual law, but Which is Being in general and Law in general." In this one World-Substance, with its parallel self-manifestations as extension and as thought, Spinoza finds the ultimate truth of Religion, as against the Indeterminist, Anthropomorphic elements of all the popular religions,—errors which have sprung, the Anthropomorphic from man's natural inclination to interpret Ultimate Reality, with its complete neutrality towards the distinctions of Psychical and Physical, by the Psychic side, as the one nearest to our own selves; and the Indeterminist from the attribution of that indetermination to the World-Substance which, even in Psychology, is already a simple illusion and analytical blunder.

" It is in the combination," concludes Professor Troeltsch, " of such a recognition of the strict determination of all natural causation, and of such a rejection of materialism (with its denial of the independence of the psychic world), that rests the immense power of Pantheism at the present time." [2] On the other hand, the supposed Pantheistic positions of the later Lessing, of Herder, Goethe and many another predominantly aesthetic thinker, must, although far richer and more nearly adequate conceptions of full reality, be assigned,

[1] Vol. II, pp. 232, 233.

[2] " Religions-philosophie," in *Die Philosophie im Beginn des zwanzigsten Jahrhunderts*, 1904, Vol. I, pp. 115, 117.

qua Pantheism, a secondary place, as inconsistent, because already largely Teleological, indeed Theistic Philosophies.

2. *Complete Pantheism non-religious; why approached by Mysticism.*

Now the former, the full Pantheism, must, I think, be declared, with Rauwenhoff, to be only in name a religious position at all. "In its essence it is simply a complete Monism, a recognition of the *Pan* in its unity and indivisibility, and hence a simple view of the world, not a religious conception." [1]—Yet deeply religious souls can be more or less, indeed profoundly, influenced by such a Monism, so that we can get Mystics with an outlook considerably more Spinozist than Plotinian. There can, *e.g.*, be no doubt as to both the deeply religious temper and the strongly Pantheistic conceptions of Eckhart in the Middle Ages, and of Schleiermacher in modern times; and indeed Spinoza himself is, apart from all questions as to the logical implications and results of his intellectual system, and as to the justice of his attacks upon the historical religions, a soul of massive religious intuition and aspiration.

But further: Mystically tempered souls,—and the typical and complete religious soul will ever possess a mystical element in its composition,—have three special *attraits* which necessarily bring them into an at least apparent proximity to Pantheism.

(1) For one thing Mysticism, like Pantheism, has a great, indeed (if left unchecked by the out-going-movement) an excessive, thirst for Unity, for a Unity less and less possessed of Multiplicity; and the transition from holding the Pure Transcendence of this Unity to a conviction of its Exclusive Immanence becomes easy and insignificant, in proportion to the emptiness of content increasingly characterizing this Oneness.

(2) Then again, like Pantheists, Mystics dwell much upon the strict call to abandon all self-centredness, upon the death to self, the loss of self; and in proportion as they dwell upon this self to be thus rejected, and as they enlarge the range of this petty self, do they approach each other more and more.

(3) And lastly, there is a peculiarity about the Mystical habit of mind, which inevitably approximates it to the Pantheistic mode of thought, and which, if not continuously taken by the Mystic soul itself as an inevitable, but most demonstrable, in-

[1] *Religions-philosophie*, Germ. tr., ed. 1894, p. 140.

adequacy, will react upon the substance of this soul's thought in a truly Pantheistic sense. This peculiarity results from the Mystic's ever-present double tendency of absorbing himself, away from the Successive and Temporal, in the Simultaneity and Eternity of God, conceiving thus all reality as partaking, in proportion to its depth and greater likeness to Him, in this *Totum Simul* character of its ultimate Author and End; and of clinging to such vivid picturings of this reality as are within his, this Mystic's reach. Now such a Simultaneity can be pictorially represented to the mind only by the Spatial imagery of co-existent Extensions,—say of air, water, light, or fire: and these representations, if dwelt on as at all adequate, will necessarily suggest a Determinism of a Mathematico-Physical, Extensional type, *i.e.* one, and the dominant, side of Spinozistic Pantheism.—It is here, I think, that we get the double cause for the Pantheistic-seeming trend of almost all the Mystical imagery. For even the marked Emanationism of much in Plotinus, and of still more in Proclus,—the latter still showing through many a phrase in Dionysius,—appears in their images as operating upon a fixed Extensional foundation: and indeed these very overflowings, owing to the self-centredness and emptiness of content of their Source, the One, and to their accidental yet automatic character, help still further to give to the whole outlook a strikingly materialistic, mechanical, in so far Pantheistic, character.

3. *Points on which Mysticism has usefully approximated to Pantheism.*

And yet we must not overlook the profound, irreplaceable services that are rendered by Mysticism,—provided always it remains but one of two great movements of the living soul,—even on the points in which it thus approximates to Pantheism. These services, I think, are three.

(1) The first of these services has been interestingly illustrated by Prof. A. S. Pringle Pattison, from the case of Dr. James Martineau's writings, and the largely unmediated co-existence there of two different modes of conceiving God. "The first mode represents God simply as another, higher Person; the second represents Him as the soul of souls. The former, Deistic and Hebraic, rests upon an inferential knowledge of God, derived either from the experience of His resistance to our will through the forces of Nature, or from that of His restraint upon us in the voice of Conscience,—

God, in both cases, being regarded as completely separated from the human soul, and His existence and character apprehended and demonstrated by a process of reasoning.—The second mode is distinctly and intensely Christian, and consists in the apprehension of God as the Infinite including all finite existences, as the immanent Absolute who progressively manifests His character in the Ideals of Truth, Beauty, Righteousness, and Love." And Professor Pattison points out, with Professor Upton, that it was Dr. Martineau's almost morbid dread of Pantheism which was responsible for the inadequate expression given to this Mystical, or "Speculative" element in his religious philosophy. For only if we do not resist such Mysticism, do we gain and retain a vivid experience of how "Consciousness of imperfection and the pursuit of perfection are alike possible to man only through the universal life of thought and goodness in which he shares, and which, at once an indwelling presence and an unattainable ideal, draws him on and always on." "Personality is" thus "not 'unitary' in Martineau's sense, as occupying one side of a relation, and unable to be also on the other. The very capacity of knowledge and morality implies that the person . . . is capable of regarding himself and all other beings from what Martineau well names 'the station of the Father of Spirits.'"[1]

I would, however, guard here against any exclusion of a seeking or finding of God in Nature and in Conscience: only the contrary exclusion of the finding of God within the soul, and the insistence upon a complete separation of Him from that soul, are inacceptable in the "Hebraic" mood. For a coming and a going, a movement inwards and outwards, checks and counter-checks, friction, contrast, battle and storm, are necessary conditions and ingredients of the soul's growth in its sense of appurtenance to Spirit and to Peace.

(2) A further service rendered by this Pantheistic-seeming Mysticism,—though always only so long as it remains not the only or last word of Religion,—is that it alone discovers the truly spiritual function and fruitfulness of Deterministic Science. For only if Man deeply requires a profound de-subjectivizing, a great shifting of the centre of his interest, away from the petty, claimful, animal self, with its "I against all the world," to a great kingdom of souls, in which Man

[1] "Martineau's Philosophy," *Hibbert Journal*, Vol. I, 1902, pp. 458, 457.

gains his larger, spiritual, unique personality, with its " I as part of, and for all the world," by accepting to be but one amongst thousands of similar constituents in a system expressive of the thoughts of God; and only if Mathematico-Physical Science is specially fitted to provide such a bath, and hence is so taken, with all its apparently ruinous Determinism and seeming Godlessness: is such Science really safe from apologetic emasculation; or from running, a mere unrelated dilettantism, alongside of the deepest interests of the soul; or from, in its turn, crushing or at least hampering the deepest, the spiritual life of man. Hence all the greater Partial Mystics have got a something about them which indicates that they have indeed passed through fire and water, that their poor selfishness has been purified in a bath of painfully-bracing spiritual air and light, through which they have emerged into a larger, fuller life. And Nicolas of Coes, Pascal, Malebranche are but three men out of many whose Mysticism and whose Mathematico-Physical Science thus interstimulated each other and jointly deepened their souls.

We shall find, further on, that this purificatory power of such Science has been distinctly heightened for us now. Yet, both then and now, there could and can be such purification only for those who realize and practise religion as sufficiently ultimate and wide and deep to englobe, (as one of religion's necessary stimulants), an unweakened, utterly alien-seeming Determinism in the middle regions of the soul's experience and outlook. Such an englobement can most justly be declared to be Christianity driven fully home. For thus is Man purified and saved,—if he already possesses the dominant religious motive and conviction,—by a close contact with Matter; and the Cross is plunged into the very centre of his soul's life, operating there a sure division between the perishing animal Individual and the abiding spiritual Personality: the deathless Incarnational and Redemptive religion becomes thus truly operative there.

(3) And the last service, rendered by such Mysticism, is to keep alive in the soul the profoundly important consciousness of the prerequisites, elements and affinities of a Universally Human kind, which are necessary to, and present in, all Religion, however definitely Concrete, Historical and Institutional it may have become. Such special, characteristic Revelations, Doctrines and Institutions, as we find them in

all the great Historical Religions, and in their full normative substance and form in Christianity and Catholicism, can indeed alone completely develop, preserve and spread Religion in its depth and truth; yet they ever presuppose a general, usually dim but most real, religious sense and experience, indeed a real presence and operation of the Infinite and of God in all men.

It is, then, not an indifferentist blindness to the profound differences, in their degree of truth, between the religions of the world, nor an insufficient realization of man's strict need of historical and institutional lights and aids for the development and direction of that general religious sense and experience, which make the mind revolt from sayings such as those we have already quoted from the strongly Protestant Prof. Wilhelm Hermann, and to which we can add the following. "Everywhere, outside of Christianity, Mysticism will arise, as the very flower of the religious development. But the Christian must declare such Mystical experience of God to be a delusion." For "what is truly Christian is *ipso facto* not Mystical." "We are Christians because, in the Humanity of Jesus, we have struck upon a fact which is of incomparably richer content, than are the feelings that arise within our own selves." Indeed, "I should have failed to recognize the hand of God even in what my own dead father did for me, had not, by means of my Christian education, God appeared to me, in the Historic Christ." [1]—As if it were possible to consider Plato and Plotinus, in those religious intuitions and feelings of theirs which helped to win an Augustine from crass Manichaeism to a deep Spiritualism, and which continue to breathe and burn as part-elements in countless sayings of Christian philosophers and saints, to have been simply deluded, or mere idle subjectivists! As if we could apprehend even Christ, without some most real, however dim and general, sense of religion and presence of God within us to which He could appeal! And as if Jeremiah, Ezekiel and the Maccabaean Martyrs, and many a devoted soul within Mohammedanism or in Brahmanic India, could not and did not apprehend something of God's providence in their earthly father's love towards them!

No wonder that, after all this, Hermann can,—as against Richard Rothe who, in spite of more than one fantastic if not

[1] *Der Verkehr des Christen mit Gott*, ed. 1892, pp. 27, 15, 28, 231.

fanatical aberration, had, on some of the deepest religious matters, a rarely penetrating perception,—write in a thoroughly patronizing manner concerning Catholic Mysticism. For this Mysticism necessarily appears to him not as, at its best, the most massive and profound development of one type of the ultimate religion,—a type in which one necessary element of all balanced religious life is at the fullest expansion compatible with a still sufficient amount and healthiness of the other necessary elements of such a life,—but only as "a form of religion which has brought out and rendered visible such a content of interior life as is capable of being produced within the limits of Catholic piety." [1] The true, pure Protestant possesses, according to Hermann, apparently much less, in reality much more,—the Categorical Imperative of Conscience and the Jesus of History, as the double one-and-all of his, the only spiritual religion.—Yet if Christianity is indeed the religion of the Divine Founder, Who declared that he that is not against Him is for Him; or of Paul, who could appeal to the heathen Athenians and to all men for the truth and experience that in God "we live and move and have our being"; or of the great Fourth Gospel, which tells us that Christ, the True Light, enlighteneth every man that cometh into the world, a light which to this hour cannot, for the great majority, be through historic knowledge of the Historic Christ at all; or of Clement of Alexandria and of Justin Martyr, who loved to find deep apprehensions and operations of God scattered about among the Heathen; or of Aquinas, who, in the wake of the Areopagite and others, so warmly dwells upon how Grace does not destroy, but presupposes and perfects Nature: then such an exclusive amalgam of Moralism and History, though doubtless a most honest and intelligible reaction against opposite excesses, is a sad impoverishment of Christianity, in its essential, world-wide, Catholic character.

Indeed, to be fair, there have never been wanting richer and more balanced Protestant thinkers strongly to emphasize this profound many-sidedness and universality of Christianity: so, at present, in Germany, Profs. Eucken, Troeltsch, Class, Siebeck and others; and, in England, Prof. A. S. P. Pattison and Mr. J. R. Illingworth. In all these cases there is ever a strong sympathy with Mysticism properly understood

1 *Der Verkehr des Christen mit Gott*, ed. 1892, pp. 20; 19–25.

as the surest safeguard against such distressing contractions as is this of Hermann, and that of Albrecht Ritschl before him.

4. *Christianity excludes complete and final Pantheism.* And yet, as we have repeatedly found, Christianity has, in its fundamental Revelation and Experience, ever implied and affirmed such a conception of Unity, of Self-Surrender, and of the Divine Action, as to render any Pantheistic interpretation of these things ever incomplete and transitional.

(1) The Unity here is nowhere, even ultimately, the sheer Oneness of a simply identical Substance, but a Unity deriving its very close-knitness from its perfect organization of not simply identical elements or relations.

The Self-Surrender here is not a simply final resolution, of laboriously constituted centres of human spiritual consciousness and personality, back into a morally indifferent All, but a means and passage, for the soul, from a spiritually worthless self-entrenchment within a merely psycho-physical apartness and lust to live, on to a spiritual devotedness, an incorporation, as one necessary subject, into the Kingdom of souls,—the abiding, living expression of the abiding, living God.

And, above all, God's Action is not a mechanico-physical, determinist, simultaneous Extension, nor even an automatic, accidental, unconscious Emanation, but, as already Plato divined,—an intuition lost again by Aristotle, and, in his logic, denied by Plotinus,—a voluntary outgoing and self-communication of the supreme self-conscious Spirit, God. For Plato tells us that " the reason why Nature and this Universe of things was framed by Him Who framed it, is that God is good . . . and desired that all things should be as like Himself as it was possible for them to be." [1] Yet this pregnant apprehension never attains here to its full significance, because the Divine Intelligence is conceived only as manifesting itself in relation to something given from without, —the pre-existing, chaotic Matter. And for Aristotle God does not love this Givenness; for " the first Mover moves " (all things) only " as desired " by them: He Himself desires, loves, wills nothing whatsoever, and thinks and knows nothing but His own self alone.[2] And in Plotinus this same transcendence is still further emphasized, for the Absolute One here transcends even all thought and self-consciousness.

[1] *Timaeus*, 29*e*, *seq*.
[2] *Metaph*., VII, 1072*b*; IX, 1074*b*.

(2) It is in Christianity, after noble preludings in Judaism, that we get the full deliberate proclamation, in the great Life and Teaching, of the profound fact,—the Self-Manifestation of the Loving God, the Spirit-God moving out to the spirit-man, and spirit-man only thus capable of a return movement to the Spirit-God. As Schelling said, " God can only give Himself to His creatures as He gives a self to them," and, with it, the capacity of participating in His life. We thus get a relation begun and rendered possible by God's utterly prevenient, pure, *ecstatic* love of Man, a relation which, in its essence spiritual, personal and libertarian, leaves behind it, as but vain travesties of such ultimate Realities, all Emanational or Parallelistic Pantheism, useful though these latter systems are as symbols of the Mathematico-Physical level and kind of reality and apprehension. Yet this spiritual relation is here, unlike Plotinus's more or less Emanational conception of it, not indeed simply invertible, as Spinoza would have it, (for Man is ontologically dependent upon God, whereas God is not thus dependent upon Man), but nevertheless largely one of true mutuality. And this mutuality of the relation is not simply a positive enactment of God, but is expressive, in its degree and mode, of God's intrinsic moral nature. For God is here the Source as well as the Object of all love; hence He Himself possesses the supreme equivalent for this our noblest emotion, and is moved to free acts of outgoing, in the creation and preservation, the revelation to, and the redemption of finite spirits, as so many sucessive, mutually supplementary, and increasingly fuller expressions and objects of this His nature. " God is Love "; " God so loved the world, that He gave His only-begotten Son "; " Let us love God, for God hath first loved us "; " if any man will do the will of God, he shall know of the doctrine if it be from God " : God's Infinity is here, not the negation of the relatively independent life of His creatures, but the very reason and source of their freedom.[1]

In the concluding chapter I hope to give a sketch of the actual operation of the true correctives to any excessive, Plotinian or Spinozistic, tendencies in the Mystical trend, especially when utilizing Mathematico-Physical Science at the soul's middle level; and of History at the ultimate reaches of the soul's life.

[1] See Caird, *op. cit.* II, p. 337.

IV. The Divine Immanence; Spiritual Personality

1. *Pantheism.*

As to our fourth question, the Divine Immanence and Personality, our last quotations from St. Teresa give us, I think, our true starting-point. For it is evident that, between affirming the simple Divinity of the innermost centre of the soul, and declaring that the soul ever experiences only the Grace of God, *i. e.* certain created effects, sent by Him from the far-away seat of His own full presence, there is room for a middle position which, whilst ever holding the definite creatureliness of the soul, in all its reaches, puts God Himself into the soul and the soul into God, in degrees and with results which vary indeed indefinitely according to its good-will and its call, yet which all involve and constitute a presence ever profoundly real, ever operative before and beyond all the soul's own operations. These latter operations are, indeed, even possible only through all this Divine anticipation, origination, preservation, stimulation, and, at bottom,—in so far as man is enabled and required by God to reach a certain real self-constitution,—through a mysterious Self-Limitation of God's own Action,—a Divine Self-Restraint.

There can be little doubt that such a *Panentheism* is all that many a daring, in strictness Pantheistic, saying of the Christian, perhaps also of the Jewish and Mohammedan, Mystics aimed at. Only the soul's ineradicable capacity, need and desire for its Divine Lodger and Sustainer would constitute, in this conception, the intrinsic characteristic of human nature; and it is rather the too close identification, in feeling and emotional expression, of the desire and the Desired, of the hunger and the Food, and the too exclusive realization of the deep truth that this desire and hunger do not cause, but are themselves preceded and caused by, their Object,—it is the over-vivid perception of this real dynamism, rather than any *a priori* theory of static substances and identities—which, certainly in many cases, has produced the appearance of Pantheism.

And again it is certain that we have to beware of taking the apparent irruption or ingrafting,—in the case of the operations of Grace,—of an entirely heterogeneous Force and Reality into what seems the already completely closed circle of our natural functions and aspirations, as the complete and ultimate truth of the situation. However utterly different that Force may feel to all else that we are aware of within ourselves, however entirely unmeditated may seem its manifestations: it is clear that we should be unable to recognize even this Its difference, to welcome or resist It, above all to find It a response to our deepest cravings, unless we had some natural true affinity to It, and some dim but most real experience of It from the first. Only with such a general religiosity and vague sense, from a certain contact, of the Infinite, is the recognition of definite, historical Religious Facts and Figures as true, significant, binding upon my will and conscience, explicable at all.

2. *Aquinas on our direct semi-consciousness of God's indwelling.*

St. Thomas, along one line of doctrine, has some excellent teachings about all this group of questions. For though he tells us that "the names which we give to God and creatures, are predicated of God" only "according to a certain relation of the creature to God, as its Principle and Cause, in which latter the perfections of all things pre-exist in an excellent manner": [1] yet he explicitly admits, in one place, that we necessarily have some real, immediate experience of the Nature of God, for that "it is impossible, with regard to anything, to know whether it exists,"—and he has admitted that natural reason can attain to a knowledge of God's bare existence,—"unless we somehow know what is its nature," at least "with a confused knowledge"; whence "also with regard to God, we could not know whether He exists, unless we somehow know, even though confusedly, what He is."—God, though transcendent, is also truly immanent in the human soul: "God is in all things, as the agent is present in that wherein it acts. Created Being is as true an effect of God's Being, as to burn is the true effect of fire. God is above all things,—by the excellence of His nature, and yet He is intimately present within all things, as the cause of the Being of all."—And man has a natural exigency of the face-to-face Vision of God, hence of the Order of Grace, however entirely its attainment may be beyond his natural powers: "There is in man a natural longing to know the cause, when he sees an effect: whence if the intellect of the rational

[1] *Summa Theol.*, I, qu. 13, art. 5, concl. et in corp. (See the interesting note, "The Meaning of Analogy," in Fr. Tyrrell's *Lex Orandi*, 1903, pp. 80–83.) *In Librum Boetii de Trinitate*: D. Thomae Aquinatis *Opera*, ed. Veneta Altera, 1776, p. 341*b*, 342*a*.

creature could not attain to the First Cause of things,"—here in the highest form, that of the Beatific vision of God—" the longing of its nature would remain void and vain." [1]

But it is the great Mystical Saints and writers who continuously have, in the very forefront of their consciousness and assumptions, not a simply moral and aspirational, but an Ontological and Pre-established relation between the soul and God; and not a simply discursive apprehension, but a direct though dim Experience of the Infinite and of God. And these positions really underlie even their most complete-seeming negations, as we have already seen in the case of the Areopagite.

3. *Gradual recognition of the function of subconsciousness.* Indeed, we can safely affirm that the last four centuries, and even the last four decades, have more and more confirmed the reality and indirect demonstrableness of such a presence and sense of the Infinite; ever more or less obscurely, but none the less profoundly, operative in the innermost normal consciousness of mankind: a presence and sense which, though they can be starved and verbally denied, cannot be completely suppressed; and which, though they do not, if unendorsed, constitute even the most elementary faith, far less a developed Historical or Mystical Religion, are simply necessary prerequisites to all these latter stimulations and consolidations.

(1) As we have already found, it is only since Leibniz that we know, systematically, how great is the range of every man's Obscure Presentations, his dim Experience as against his Clear or distinct Presentations, his explicit Knowledge; and how the Clear depends even more upon the Dim, than the Dim upon the Clear. And further discoveries and proofs in this direction are no older than 1888.[2]

(2) Again, it is the growing experience of the difficulties and complexities of Psychology, History, Epistemology, and of the apparent unescapableness and yet pain of man's mere anthropomorphisms, that makes the persistence of his search for, and sense of, Objective Truth and Reality, and the keen-

[1] *Summa Theol.*, I, qu. 12, art. 1, in corp.

[2] For Leibniz, see especially his *Nouveaux Essais*, written in 1701–1709, but not published till 1765: *Die Philosophischen Schriften von G. W. Leibniz*, ed. Gebhardt, Vol. V, 1882, especially pp. 45; 67; 69; 121, 122. For the date 1888, see W. James's *Varieties of Religious Experience*, 1902, p. 233.

ness of his suffering when he appears to himself as imprisoned in mere subjectivity, deeply impressive. For the more man feels, and suffers from feeling himself purely subjective, the more is it clear that he is not merely subjective: he could never be conscious of the fact, if he were. "Suppose that all your objects in life were realized . . . would this be a great joy and happiness to you?" John Stuart Mill asked himself; and "an irrepressible self-consciousness distinctly answered 'No.'"[1] Whether in bad health just then or not, Mill was here touching the very depths of the characteristically human sense. In all such cases only a certain profound apprehension of Abiding Reality, the Infinite, adequately explains the keen, operative sense of contrast and disappointment.

(3) And further, we have before us, with a fulness and delicate discrimination undreamed of in other ages, the immense variety, within a certain general psychological unity, of the great and small Historical Religions, past and present, of the world. Facing all this mass of evidence, Prof. Troeltsch can ask, more confidently than ever: "Are not our religious requirements, requirements of Something that one must have somehow first experienced in order to require It? Are they not founded upon some kind of Experience as to the Object, Which Itself first awakens the thought of an ultimate infinite meaning attaching to existence, and Which, in the conflict with selfishness, sensuality and self-will, draws the nobler part of the human will, with ever new force, to Itself?" "All deep and energetic religion is in a certain state of tension towards Culture, for the simple reason that it is seeking something else and something higher."[2] And Prof. C. P. Tiele, so massively learned in all the great religions, concludes: "'Religion,' says Feuerbach, 'proceeds from man's wishes' . . . ; according to others, it is the outcome of man's dissatisfaction with the external world. . . . But why should man torment himself with wishes which he never sees fulfilled around him, and which the rationalistic philosopher declares to be illusions? Why? surely, because he cannot help it. . . . The Infinite, very Being as opposed to continual becoming and perishing,—or call It what you will,—*that* is the Principle which gives him constant unrest, because It dwells within him." And

[1] *Autobiography*, ed. 1875, pp. 133, 134.
[2] "Die Selbständigkeit der Religion": *Zeitschrift f. Theologie u. Kirche*, 1895, pp. 404, 405.

against Prof. Max Müller,—who had, however, on this point, arrived at a position very like Tiele's own,—he impressively insists that "the origin of religion consists," not in a "perception of the Infinite," but "in the fact that Man *has* the Infinite within him."—I would only contend further that the instinct of the Infinite awakens simultaneously with our sense-perceptions and categories of thinking, and passes, together with them and with the deeper, more volitional experiences, through every degree and stage of obscurity and relative clearness. "Whatever name we give it,—instinct; innate, original, or unconscious form of thought; or form of conception,—it is the specifically human element in man." [1] But if all this be true, then the Mystics are amongst the great benefactors of our race: for it is especially this presence of the Infinite in Man, and man's universal subjection to an operative consciousness of it, which are the deepest cause and the constant object of the adoring awe of all truly spiritual Mystics, in all times and places.

[1] *Elements of the Science of Religion*, 1897, Vol. II, pp. 227–231.

CHAPTER XV

SUMMING UP OF THE WHOLE BOOK. BACK THROUGH ASCETICISM, SOCIAL RELIGION, AND THE SCIENTIFIC HABIT OF MIND, TO THE MYSTICAL ELEMENT OF RELIGION.

I NOW propose to conclude, by getting, through three successively easier matters, back to the starting-point of this whole book, and, in doing so, to sum up and delimitate, more and more clearly, the practical lessons learnt during its long course. These three last matters and points of observation shall be Asceticism, Institutionalism, and Mental Activity and Discipline, or the Scientific Habit—all three in their relation to the Mystical Element of Religion.

I. Asceticism and Mysticism.

Now in the matter of Asceticism, we can again conveniently consider three points.

1. *Ordinary Asceticism practised by Mystics.*

There is, first, the (generally severe) Asceticism which is ever connected with at least some one phase, an early one, of every genuine Mystic's history, yet which does not differ essentially from the direct training in self-conquest to which practically all pre-Protestant, and most of the old Protestant earnest Christians considered themselves obliged.

(1) Now it is deeply interesting to note how marked has been, off and on throughout the last century and now again quite recently, the renewal of comprehension and respect for the general principle of Asceticism, in quarters certainly free from all preliminary bias in favour of Medieval Christianity Schopenhauer wrote in 1843: "Not only the religions of the East but also genuine Christianity shows, throughout its systems, that fundamental characteristic of Asceticism which my philosophy elucidates. . . . Precisely in its doctrines of

renunciation, self-denial, complete chastity, in a word, of general mortification of the will, lie the deepest truth, the high value, the sublime character of Christianity. It thus belongs to the old, true, and lofty ideal of mankind, in opposition to the false, shallow, and ruinous optimism of Greek Paganism, Judaism and Islam." "Protestantism, by eliminating Asceticism and its central point, the meritoriousness of celibacy, has, by this alone, already abandoned the innermost kernel of Christianity. . . . For Christianity is the doctrine of the deep guilt of the human race . . . and of the heart's thirst after redemption from it, a redemption which can be acquired only through the abnegation of self,—that is, through a complete conversion of human nature." [1]—And the optimistically tempered American Unitarian, the deeply versed Psychologist, Prof. William James, tells us in 1902: "In its spiritual meaning, Asceticism stands for nothing less than for the essence of the twice-born philosophy." "The Metaphysical mystery, that he who feeds on death, that feeds on men, possesses life supereminently, and meets best the secret demands of the Universe, is the truth of which Asceticism has been the faithful champion. The folly of the cross, so inexplicable by the intellect, has, yet, its indestructible, vital meaning. . . . Naturalistic optimism is mere syllabub and sponge-cake in comparison." [2]

(2) Indeed, the only thing at all special to Mysticism, in its attitude towards this general principle and practice of Asceticism, is that it ever practises Asceticism as a means towards, or at least as the make-weight and safeguard of, Contemplation, which latter is as essentially Synthetic, and, in so far, peaceful and delightful, as the former is Analytic, polemical and painful; whereas non-Mystical souls will practise Asceticism directly with a view to greater aloofness from sin, and greater readiness and strength to perform the various calls of duty. And hence, if we but grant the legitimacy of the general principle of ordinary Asceticism, we shall find the Mystical form of this Asceticism to be the more easily comprehensible variety of that principle. For the Mystic's practice, as concerns this point, is more varied and inclusive than that of others, since he does not even tend to make the whole of his inner life into a system of checks and of tension.

[1] *Die Welt als Wille und Vorstellung*, ed. Griesbach, Vol. II, pp. 725, 734, 736.

[2] *The Varieties of Religious Experience*, 1902, pp. 362, 364.

The expansive, reconciling movement operates in him most strongly also, and, where of the right kind, this expansive movement helps, even more than the restrictive one, to purify humble, and deepen his heart and soul.

2. *God's Transcendence a source of suffering.*

There is, however, a second, essentially different source and kind of suffering in some sorts and degrees of Mysticism, and indeed in other *attraits* of the spiritual life, which is deeply interesting, because based upon a profound Metaphysical apprehension. Although, at bottom, the opposite extreme to Pantheism, it readily expresses itself, for reasons that will presently appear, in terms that have a curiously Pantheistic colour.

(1) St. John of the Cross writes in 1578 : " It is a principle of philosophy, that all means must . . . have a certain resemblance to the end, such as shall be sufficient for the object in view. If therefore the understanding is to be united to God, . . . it must make use of those means which can effect that union, that is, means which are most like unto God. . . . But there is no essential likeness or communion between creatures and Him, the distance between His divine nature and their nature is infinite. No creature therefore . . . nothing that the imagination may conceive or the understanding comprehend . . . in this life . . . can be a proximate means of union with God," for " it is all most unlike God, and most disproportionate to Him." " The understanding . . . must be pure and empty of all sensible objects, all clear intellectual perceptions, resting on faith : for faith is the sole proximate and proportionate means of the soul's union with God." [1]

Now it is certain, as we have already found, that the awakened human soul ever possesses a dim but real experience of the Infinite, and that, in proportion as it is called to the Mystical way, this sense will be deepened into various degrees of the Prayer of Quiet and of Union, and that here, more plainly than elsewhere, will appear the universal necessity of the soul's own response, by acts and the habit of Faith, to all and every experience which otherwise remains but so much unused material for the soul's advance. And it is equally certain that St. John of the Cross is one of the greatest of such contemplatives, and that neither his intuition

[1] *Ascent of Mount Carmel*, tr. David Lewis, ed. 1889, pp. 94, 95, 97.

and actual practice, nor even his sayings, (so long as any one saying belonging to one trend is set off against another belonging to the other trend,) contravenes the Christian and Catholic positions.—Yet it cannot be denied that, were we to press his "negative way" into becoming the only one; and especially were we to take, without discount, such a virtual repudiation, as is furnished by any insistence upon the above words, of any essential, objective difference in value between our various apprehensions of Him and approaches to Him: the whole system and *rationale* of External, Sacramental and Historical Religion, indeed of the Incarnation, in any degree and form, would have to go, as so many stumbling-blocks to the soul's advance. For the whole principle of all such Religion implies the profound importance of the Here and the Now, the Contingent and the Finite, and of the Immanence of God, in various degrees and ways, within them.

Indications of this incompatibility, as little systematically realized here as in the Areopagite, are afforded by various remarks of his, belonging in reality to another trend. Thus, immediately before his denial of any essential likeness or communion between any creature and God, he says: "It is true that all creatures bear a certain relation to God and are tokens of His Being, some more, some less, according to the greater perfection of their nature." And of Our Lord's sacred Humanity he says: "What a perfect living image was Our Saviour upon earth: yet those who had no faith, though they were constantly about Him, and saw His wonderful works, were not benefited by His presence." [1] But even here the immense importance, indeed downright necessity for Faith, of such external and historical stimuli, objects and materials,—in the latter instance all this at its very deepest,—remains unemphasized, through his engrossment in the necessity of Faith for the fructification of all these things.

In other places this Faith appears as though working so outside of all things imageable, as to have to turn rapidly away from all picturings, as, at best, only momentary starting-points for the advanced soul. "Let the faithful soul take care that, whilst contemplating an image, the senses be not absorbed in it, whether it be material or in the imagination, and whether the devotion it excites be spiritual or sensible. Let him . . . venerate the image as the Church commands

[1] *Ascent*, pp. 94; 350.

and lift up his mind at once from the material image to those whom it represents. He who shall do this, will never be deluded." [1] Here, again, along the line of argument absorbing the saint in this book, there is no fully logical ground left for the Incarnational, Historical, Sacramental scheme of the Infinite immanent in the finite, and of spirit stimulated in contact with matter, with everywhere the need of the condescensions of God and of our ascensions by means of careful attention to them.

Sören Kierkegaard, that deep solitary Dane, with so much about him like to Pascal the Frenchman, and Hurrell Froude the Englishman, and who, though Lutheran in all his bringing up, was so deeply attracted by Catholic Asceticism, has, in recent times (he died in 1855), pushed the doctrine of the qualitative, absolute difference between God and all that we ourselves can think, feel, will or be, to lengths beyond even the transcendental element,—we must admit this to be the greatly preponderant one,—in the great Spaniard's formal teaching. And it is especially in this non-Mystical Ascetic that we get an impressive picture of the peculiar kind of suffering and asceticism, which results from such a conviction to a profoundly sensitive, absorbedly religious soul; and here too we can, I think, discover the precise excess and onesidedness involved in this whole tendency. Professor Höffding, in his most interesting monograph on his friend, tells us how "for Kierkegaard, . . . the will gets monopolized by religious Ethics from the very first; there is no time for Contemplation or Mysticism." "To tear the will away," Kierkegaard himself says, "from all finite aims and conditions . . . requires a painful effort and this effort's ceaseless repetition. And if, in addition to this, the soul has, in spite of all its striving, to be as though it simply were not, it becomes clear that the religious life signifies a dedication to suffering and to self-destruction. What wonder, then, that, for the Jew, death was the price of seeing God; or that, for the Gentile, the soul's entering into closer relations with the Deity meant the beginning of madness?" For "the soul's relation to God is a relation to a Being absolutely different from Man, who cannot confront him as his Superlative or Ideal, and who, nevertheless, is to rule in his inmost soul. Hence a necessary division, ever productive of new pains, is operative within man, as long

[1] *Ascent*, p. 353.

as he perseveres in this spiritual endeavour. . . . A finite being, he is to live in the Infinite and Absolute: he is there like a fish upon dry land." [1]

Now Prof. Höffding applies a double, most cogent criticism to this position.—The one is religious, and has already been quoted. "A God Who is not Ideal and Pattern is no God. Hence the contention that the Nature of the Godhead is, of necessity, qualitatively different from that of Man, has ever occasioned ethical and religious misgivings."—And the other is psychological. "Tension can indeed be necessary for the truth and the force of life. But tension, taken by itself, cannot furnish the true measure of life. For the general nature of consciousness is a synthesis, a comprehensive unity: not only contrast, but also concentration, must make itself felt, as long as the life of consciousness endures." [2]

It is deeply interesting to note how Catherine, and at bottom St. John of the Cross and the Exclusive Mystics generally, escape, through their practice and in some of their most emphatic teachings, from Kierkegaard's excess, no doubt in part precisely because they *are* Mystics, since the exclusive Mystic's contemplative habit is, at bottom, a Synthetic one. Yet we should realize the deep truth which underlies the very exaggerations of this onesidedly Analytic and Ascetical view. For if God is the deepest ideal, the ultimate driving force and the true congenital element and environment of Man, such as Man cannot but secretly wish to will deliberately, and which, at his best, Man truly wills to hold and serve: yet God remains ever simply incompatible with that part of each man's condition and volition which does not correspond to the best and deepest which that Man himself sees or could see to be the better, *hic et nunc*; and, again, He is ever, even as compared with any man's potential best, infinitely more and nobler, and, though here not in simple contradiction, yet at a degree of perfection which enables Him, the Supreme Spirit, to penetrate, as Immanent Sustainer or Stimulator, and to confront, as Transcendent Ideal and End, the little human spirit, so great in precisely this its keen sense of experienced contrast.

Catherine exhibits well this double relation, of true contradiction, and of contrast, both based upon a certain genuine

[1] *Sören Kierkegaard*, von Harald Höffding, Germ. tr. 1896, pp. 116, 118, 120.

[2] *Ibid*. pp. 122; 130, 131.

affinity between the human soul and God. On one side of herself she is indeed a veritable fish out of water; but, on the other side of her, she is a fish happily disporting itself in its very element, in the boundless ocean of God. On the one side, snapping after air, in that seemingly over-rarified atmosphere in which the animal man, the mere selfish individual, cannot live; on the other side, expanding her soul's lungs and drinking in light, life, and love, in that same truly rich atmosphere, which, Itself Spirit, feeds and sustains her growing spiritual personality. And the *Dialogo*, in spite of its frequently painful abstractness and empty unity, has, upon the whole, a profound hold upon this great doctrine.

Yet it is in Catherine's own culminating intuition,—of the soul's free choice of Purgatory, as a joyful relief from the piercing pain of what otherwise would last for ever,—the vividly perceived contrast between God's purity and her soul's impurity, that we get, in the closest combination, indeed mutual causation, this double sense of Man's nearness to and distance from, of his likeness and unlikeness to God. For only if man is, in the deepest instincts of his soul, truly related to God, and is capable of feeling, (indeed he ever actually, though mostly dimly, experiences,) God's presence and this, man's own, in great part but potential, affinity to Him: can suffering be conceived to arise from the keen realization of the contrast between God and man's own actual condition at any one moment; and can any expectation, indeed a swift vivid instinct, arise within man's soul that the painful, directly contradictory, discrepancy can and will, gradually though never simply automatically, be removed. And though, even eventually, the creature cannot, doubtless, ever become simply God, yet it can attain, in an indefinitely higher degree, to that affinity and union of will with God, which, in its highest reaches and moments, it already now substantially possesses; and hence to that full creaturely self-constitution and joy in which, utterly trusting, giving itself to, and willing God, it will, through and in Him, form an abidingly specific, unique constituent and link of His invisible kingdom of souls, on and on.

3. *Discipline of fleeing and of facing the Multiple and Contingent.*

But there is a third attitude, peculiar (because of its preponderance) to the Mystics as such, an attitude in a manner intermediate between that of ordinary Asceticism, and that of the Suffering just described. The implications and effects of, and the correctives for, this third attitude will occupy us up to the end of this book. I refer to the careful turning-away from all Multiplicity and Contingency, from the Visible and Successive, from all that does or can distract and dissipate, which is so essential and prevailing a feature in all Mysticism, which indeed, in Exclusive Mysticism, is frankly made into the one sole movement towards, and measure of, the soul's perfection.

(1) It is true that to this tendency, when and in so far as it has come so deeply to permeate the habits of a soul as to form a kind of second nature, the name Asceticism cannot, in strictness, be any more applied; since now the pain will lie, not in this turning away from all that dust and friction, but, on the contrary, in any forcing of the soul back into that turmoil. And doubtless many, perhaps most, souls with a pronouncedly mystical *attrait*, are particularly sensitive to all, even partial and momentary, conflict. Yet we can nevertheless appropriately discuss the matter under the general heading of Asceticism, since, as a rule, much practice and sacrifice go to build up this habit; since, in every case, this Abstractive Habit shares with Ordinary Asceticism a pronounced hostility to many influences and forces ever actually operative within and around the undisciplined natural man; and since, above all, the very complements and correctives for this Abstractiveness will have to come from a further, deeper and wider Asceticism, to be described presently.

(2) As to Ordinary Asceticism and this Abstractiveness, the former fights the world and the self directly, and then only in so far as they are discovered to be positively evil or definitely to hinder positive good; it is directly attracted by the clash and friction involved in such fighting; and it has no special desire for even a transitory intense unification of the soul's life: whereas the Abstractiveness turns away from, and rises above, the world and the phenomenal self; their very existence, their contingency, the struggles alive within them, and their (as it seems) inevitably disturbing effect upon the soul,—are all felt as purely dissatisfying; and an innermost longing for a perfect and continuous unification and overflowing harmony of its inner life here possess the spirit.

(3) Now we have just seen how a movement of integration, of synthesizing all the soul's piecemeal, inter-jostling acquisitions, of restful healing of its wounds and rents, of sinking back,

(from the glare and glitter of clear, and then ever fragmentary perception, and from the hurry, strain and rapidly ensuing distraction involved in all lengthy external action), into a peaceful, dim rumination and unification, is absolutely necessary, though in very various degrees and forms, for all in any way complete and mature souls.—And we have, further back, realized that a certain, obscure but profoundly powerful, direct instinct and impression of God in the soul is doubtless at work here, and, indeed, throughout all the deeper and nobler movements of our wondrously various inner life. But what concerns us here, is the question whether the *complete* action of the soul, (if man would grow in accordance with his ineradicable nature, environment, and specific grace and call,) does not as truly involve a corresponding counter-movement to this intensely unitive and intuitive movement which, with most men, and in most moments of even the minority of men, forms but an indirectly willed condition and spontaneous background of the soul.

(4) We have been finding, further, that all the Contingencies, Multiplicities and Mediations which, one and all, tend to appear to the Mystic as so many resistances and distractions, can roughly be grouped under two ultimate heads. These intruders are fellow-souls, or groups of fellow-souls,—some social organism, the Family, Society, the State, the Church, who provoke, in numberless degrees and ways, individual affection, devotion, distraction, jealousy, as from person towards person. Or else the intruders are Things and Mechanical Laws, and these usually leave the Mystic indifferent or irritate or distract him; but they can become for him great opportunities of rest, and occasions for self-discipline.

Yet this distinction between Persons and Things, (although vital for the true apprehension of all deeper, above all of the deepest Reality, and for the delicate discrimination between what are but the means and what are the ends in a truly spiritual life,) does not prevent various gradations within, and continuous interaction between, each of these two great groups. For in proportion as, in the Personal group, the Individual appears as but parcel and expression of one of the social organisms, does the impression of determinist Law, of an impersonal Thing or blind Force, begin to mix with, and gradually to prevail over, that of Personality. And in proportion as, in the Impersonal group, Science comes to include all careful and methodical study, according to the most appropriate methods, of any and every kind of truth and reality; and as it moves away from the conceptions of purely quantitative matter, and of the merely numerically different, entirely interchangeable, physical happenings, (all so many mere automatic illustrations of mechanical Law,) on, through the lowly organisms of plant-life, and the ever higher interiority and richer consciousness of animal life, up to Man, with his ever qualitative Mind, and his ever non-interchangeable, ever "effortful," achievements and elaborations of types of beauty, truth and goodness in Human History,—does Science itself come back, in its very method and subject-matter, ever more nearly, to the great personal starting-point, standard and ultimate motive of all our specifically human activity and worth.

(5) Indeed, the two great continuous facts of man's life, first that he thinks, feels, wills, and acts, in and with the help or hindrance of that profoundly material Thing, his physical body, and on occasion of, with regard to, the materials furnished by the stimulations and impressions of his senses; and again, that these latter awaken within him those, in themselves, highly abstract and Thing-like categories of his mind which penetrate and give form to these materials; are enough to show how close is the pressure, and how continuous the effect, of Things upon the slow upbuilding of Personality.

(6) Fair approximations to these two kinds of Things, with their quite irreplaceable specific functions within the economy of the human mental life,—the intensely concrete and particular Sense-Impressions, and the intensely abstract and general Mental Categories,—reappear within the economy of Characteristic Religion, in its Sacraments and its Doctrine. And conversely, there exists, *in rerum natura,* no Science worth having which is not, ultimately, the resultant of, and which does not require and call forth, on and on, certain special qualities, and combinations of qualities, of the truly ethical, spiritual Personality. Courage, patience, perseverance, candour, simplicity, self-oblivion, continuous generosity towards others and willing correction of even one's own most cherished views,—these things and their like are not the quantitative determinations of Matter, but the qualitative characteristics of Mind.

(7) I shall now, therefore, successively take Mysticism in its attitude towards these two great groups of claimants upon

its attention, the Personal and the Impersonal, even though any strictly separate discussion of elements which, in practice, ever appear together, cannot but have some artificiality. And an apparent further complication will be caused by our having, in each case, to contrast what Mysticism would do, if it became Exclusive, with what it must be restricted to doing, if it is to remain Inclusive, *i. e.* if it is to be but one element in the constitution of that multiplicity in unity, the deep spiritual Personality. The larger Asceticism will thus turn out to be a wider and deeper means towards perfection than even genuine Mysticism itself, since this Asceticism will have to include both this Mysticism and the counter movement within the one single, disciplined and purified life of the soul.

II. Social Religion and Mysticism.

Introductory: the ruinousness of Exclusive Mysticism.

Prof. Harnack says in his *Dogmengeschichte*: "An old fairy tale tells of a man who lived in ignorance, dirt and wretchedness; and whom God invited, on a certain day, to wish whatsoever he might fancy, and it should be given him. And the man began to wish things, and ever more things, and ever higher things, and all these things were given him. At last he became presumptuous, and desired to become as the great God Himself: when lo, instantly he was sitting there again, in his dirt and misery. Now the history of Religion,—especially amongst the Greeks and Orientals,—closely resembles this fairy tale. For they began by wishing for themselves certain sensible goods, and then political, aesthetic, moral and intellectual goods: and they were given them all. And then they became Christians and desired perfect knowledge and a super-moral life: they even wished to become, already here below, as God Himself, in insight, beatitude and life. And behold, they fell, not at once indeed, but with a fall that could not be arrested, down to the lowest level, back into ignorance, dirt and barbarism. . . . Like unto their near spiritual relations, the Neo-Platonists, they were at first over-stimulated, and soon became jaded, and hence required ever stronger stimulants. And in the end, all these exquisite aspirations and enjoyments turned into their opposite extreme." [1]

[1] *Lehrbuch der Dogmengeschichte*, ed. 1888, Vol. II, pp. 413, 414; 417.

However much may want discounting or supplementing here, there is, surely, a formidable amount of truth in this picture. And, if so, is Mysticism, at least in its Dionysian type, not deeply to blame? And where is the safeguard against such terrible abuses?

Now Prof. Harnack has himself shown us elsewhere that there is a sense in which Monasticism should be considered eternal, even among and for Protestants. "Monasticism," he says plaintively, in his account of the first three centuries of Protestantism, "even as it is conceivable and necessary among Evangelical Christians, disappeared altogether. And yet every community requires persons, who live *exclusively* for its purposes; hence the Church too requires volunteers who shall renounce 'the world' and shall dedicate themselves entirely to the service of their neighbour." [1]—And again, scholars of such breadth of knowledge and independence of judgement as Professor Tiele and his school, insist strongly upon the necessity of Ecclesiastical Institutions and Doctrines. The day of belief in the normality, indeed in the possibility for mankind in general, of a would-be quite individual, entirely spiritual, quite "pure" religion, is certainly over and gone, presumably for good and all, amongst all competent workers.—Nor, once more, can the general Mystical sense of the unsatisfying character of all things finite, and of the Immanence of the Infinite in our poor lives, be, in itself, to blame: for we have found these experiences to mingle with, and to characterize, all the noblest, most fully human acts and personalities.—But, if so, what are the peculiarities in the religion of those times and races, which helped to produce the result pictured in the *Dogmengeschichte?*

Now here, to get a fairly final answer, we must throw together the question of the ordinary Christian Asceticism and that of the Abstraction peculiar to the Mystics; and we must ask whether the general emotive-volitional attitude towards Man and Life,—the theory and practice as to Transcendence and Immanence, Detachment and Attachment, which, from about 500 A.D. to, say, 1450 A.D., predominantly preceded, accompanied, and both expanded and deflected the specifically Christian and normally human experience in Eastern Christendom, were not (however natural, indeed inevitable, and in part useful for those times and races), the chief of the

[1] *Das Wesen des Christenthums*, ed. 1902, pp. 180, 181.

causes which turned so much of the good of Mysticism into downright harm. At bottom this is once more the question as to the one-sided character of Neo-Platonism,—its incapacity to find any descending movement of the Divine into Human life.

1. *True relation of the soul to its fellows. God's "jealousy."* Let us take first the relation of the single human soul to its fellow-souls.

(1) Now Kierkegaard tells us: "the Absolute is cruel, for it demands *all*, whilst the Relative ever continues to demand *some* attention from us."[1] And the Reverend George Tyrrell, in his stimulating paper, *Poet and Mystic*, shows us that, as regards the relations between man's love for man and man's love for God, there are two conceptions and answers in reply to the question as to the precise sense in which God is "a jealous God," and demands to be loved alone. In the first, easier, more popular conception, He is practically thought of as the First of Creatures, competing with the rest for Man's love, and is here placed alongside of them. Hence the inference that whatever love they win from us by reason of their inherent goodness, is taken from Him: He is not loved perfectly, till He is loved alone. But in the second, more difficult and rarer conception, God is placed, not alongside of creatures but behind them, as the light which shines through a crystal and lends it whatever lustre it may have. He is loved here, not apart from, but through and in them. Hence if only the affection be of the right kind as to mode and object, the more the better. The love of Him is the "form," the principle of order and harmony; our natural affections are the "matter" harmonized and set in order; it is the soul, they are the body, of that one Divine Love whose adequate object is God in, and not apart from, His creatures.[2] Thus we have already found that even the immensely abstractive and austere St. John of the Cross tells us: "No one desires to be loved except for his goodness; and when we love in this way, our love is pleasing unto God and in great liberty; and if there be attachment in it, there is greater attachment to God." And this doctrine he continuously, deliberately practises, half-a-century after his Profession, for he writes to his penitent, Donna Juana de Pedrazas in 1589: "All that is wanting now, is that I should forget you; but

[1] Höffding's *Kierkegaard*, p. 119.

[2] *The Faith of the Million*, 1901, Vol. II, pp. 49, 50; 52, 53.

consider how that is to be forgotten which is ever present to the soul." [1]

But Father Tyrrell rightly observes: "To square this view with the general ascetic tradition of the faithful at large is exceedingly difficult." [2] Yet I cannot help thinking that a somewhat different reconciliation, than the one attempted by him,[3] really meets all the substantial requirements of the case.

(2) I take it, then, that an all-important double law or twin fact, or rather a single law and fact whose unity is composed of two elements, is, to some extent, present throughout all characteristically human life, although its full and balanced realization, even in theory and still more in practice, is ever, necessarily, a more or less unfulfilled ideal: viz. that not only there exist certain objects, acts, and affections that are simply wrong, and others that are simply right or perfect, either for all men or for some men: but that there exist simply no acts and affections which, however right, however obligatory, however essential to the perfection of us all or of some of us, do not require, on our own part, a certain alternation of interior reserve and detachment away from, and of familiarity and attachment to, them and their objects. This general law applies as truly to Contemplation as it does to Marriage.

And next, the element of detachment which has to penetrate and purify simply all attachments,—even the attachment to detachment itself,—is the more difficult, the less obvious, the more profoundly spiritual and human element and movement, although only on condition that ever some amount of the other, of the outgoing element and movement, and of attachment, remains. For here, as everywhere, there is no good and operative yeast except with and in flour; there can be no purification and unity without a material and a multiplicity to purify and to unite.

And again, given the very limited power of attention and articulation possessed by individual man, and the importance to the human community of having impressive embodiments and examples of this, in various degrees and ways, universally ever all-but-forgotten, universally difficult, universally necessary, universally ennobling renunciation: we get the

[1] *Works*, tr. David Lewis, ed. 1889, 1891, Vol. I, p. 308; Vol. II, p. 541.
[2] *Op. cit.* p. 53.
[3] *Ibid.* pp. 55, 56.

reason and justification for the setting apart of men specially drawn and devoted to a maximum, or to the most difficult kinds, of this renunciation. As the practically universal instinct, or rudimentary capacity, for Art, Science, and Philanthropy finds its full expression in artists, scientists, philanthropists, whose specific glory and ever necessary corrective it is that they but articulate clearly, embody massively and, as it were, precipitate what is dimly and intermittingly present, as it were in solution, throughout the consciousness and requirements of Mankind; and neither the inarticulate instinct, diffused among all, would completely suffice for any one of the majority, without the full articulation by a few, nor the full articulation by this minority could thrive, even for this minority itself, were it not environed by, and did it not voice, that dumb yearning of the race at large: so, and far more, does the general religiosity and sense of the Infinite, and even its ever-present element and requirement of Transcendence and Detachment, seek and call forth some typical, wholesomely provocative incorporation,—yet, here, with an even subtler and stronger interdependence, between the general demand and the particular supply.

And note that, if the minority will thus represent a maximum of "form," with a minimum of "matter," and the majority a maximum of "matter," with a minimum of "form": yet some form as well as some matter must be held by each; and the ideal to which, by their mutual supplementations, antagonisms, and corrections, they will have more and more to approximate our corporate humanity will be a maximum of "matter," permeated and spiritualized by a maximum of "form." If it is easy for the soul to let itself be invaded and choked by the wrong kind of "matter," or even simply by an excess of the right kind, so that it will be unable to stamp the "matter" with spiritual "form"; the opposite extreme also, where the spiritual forces have not left to them a sufficiency of material to penetrate or of life-giving friction to overcome, is ever a most real abuse.

2. *Ordinary Ascesis corrected by Social Christianity.*

Now it is very certain that Ordinary Asceticism and Social Christianity are, in their conjunction, far less open to this latter danger than is the Mystical and Contemplative Detachment. For the former combination possesses the priceless conception of the soul's personality being constituted in and through the organism of the religious society,—the visible and invisible Church. This Society is no mere congeries of severally self-sufficing units, each exclusively and directly dependent upon God alone; but, as in St. Paul's grand figure of the body, an organism, giving their place and dignity to each several organ, each different, each necessary, and each influencing and influenced by all the others. We have here, as it were, a great living Cloth of Gold, with, not only the woof going from God to Man and from Man to God, but also the warp going from Man to Man,—the greatest to the least, and the least back to the greatest. And thus here the primary and full Bride of Christ never is, nor can be, any individual soul, but only this complete organism of all faithful souls throughout time and space; and the single soul is such a Bride only in so far as it forms an operative constituent of this larger whole.—And hence the soul of a Mystical habit will escape the danger of emptiness and inflation if it keeps up some,—as much indeed as it can, without permanent distraction or real violation of its special helps and call,—of that outgoing, social, co-operative action and spirit, which, in the more ordinary Christian life, has to form the all but exclusive occupation of the soul, and which here, indeed, runs the risk of degenerating into mere feverish, distracted "activity."

I take the right scheme for this complex matter to have been all but completely outlined by Plato, in the first plan of his *Republic*, and indeed to have been largely derived by Christian thinkers from this source; and the excessive and one-sided conception to have been largely determined by his later additions and changes in that great book, especially as these have been all but exclusively enforced, and still further exaggerated, by Plotinus and Proclus. As Erwin Rohde finely says of this later teaching of Plato: "It was at the zenith of his life and thinking that Plato completed his ideal picture of the State, according to the requirements of his wisdom. Over the broad foundation of a population discriminated according to classes, (a foundation which, in its totality and organization, was to embody the virtue of justice in a form visible even from afar, and which formerly had seemed to him to fulfil the whole function of the perfect State,) there now soars, pointing up into the super-mundane ether, a highest crown and pinnacle, to which all the lower serves but as a substructure to render possible this life in the highest air. A small handful of citizens, the Philosophers, form this final point of the pyramid of the State. In this

State, ordered throughout according to the ends of ethics, these Philosophers will, it is true, take part in the Government, not joyously, but for duty's sake; as soon, however, as duty permits, they will eagerly return to that super-mundane contemplation, which is the end and true content of their life's activity. Indeed, in reality, the Ideal State is now built up, step by step, for the ' one ultimate ' purpose of preparing an abode for these Contemplatives, of training them in their vocation, the highest extant, and of providing a means for the insertion of Dialectic, as a special form of life and the highest aim of human endeavour, into the general organism of the earthly, civilized life. ' The so-called virtues ' all here sink into the shade before the highest force of the soul, the mystic Contemplation of the Eternal. . . . To bring his own life to ripeness for its own redemption, *that* is now the perfect sage's true, his immediate duty. If, nevertheless, he has still to bethink himself of acting upon and of moulding the world the virtues will spontaneously present themselves to him: for he now possesses Virtue itself; it has become his essential condition." [1]

It is truly impressive to find here, in its most perfect and most influential form, that ruinously untrue doctrine of the separation of any one set of men from the mass of their fellows, and of Contemplation from interest in other souls, taking the place, (in the same great mind, in the same great book,) of the beautifully humble, rich, and true view of a constant, necessary interchange of gifts and duties between the various constituents of a highly articulated organism, a whole which is indefinitely greater than, and is alone the full means, end and measure of, all its several, even its noblest, parts.—Yet the Christian, indeed every at all specifically religious, reader, will have strongly felt that the second scheme possesses, nevertheless, at least one point of advantage over the earlier one. For it alone brings out clearly that element of Transcendence, that sense and thirst of the Infinite, which we have agreed upon as the deepest characteristic of man. And if this point be thus true and important, then another,—the making of Contemplation into a special vocation,—can hardly be altogether incorrect.

But if this is our judgment, how are we to harmonize these two points of Plato's later scheme with the general

[1] *Psyche*, ed. 1898, Vol. II, pp. 292, 293.

positions of the earlier one? Or, rather, how are we to actuate and to synthesize our complex present-day requirements and duties, Christian and yet also Modern, Transcendental and yet Immanental too? For if we have any delicately vivid sense of, and sympathy with, the original, very simple, intensely transcendental, form and emphasis of the Christian teaching, and any substantial share in the present complex sense of obligation to various laws and conceptions immanent in different this-world organizations and systems: we shall readily feel how indefinitely more difficult and deep the question has become since Plato's, and indeed since the Schoolmen's time.

3. *Preliminary Pessimism and ultimate Optimism of Christianity.*

Now I think it is Prof. Ernst Troeltsch who has most fully explicitated the precise centre of this difficulty, which, in its acuteness, is a distinctly modern one, and the direction in which alone the problem's true solution should be sought.

(1) "The chief problem of Christian Ethics," he says, "is busy," not with the relation between certain subjective means and dispositions, but "with the relation between certain objective ends, which have, in some way, to be thought together by the same mind as so many several objects, and to be brought by it and within it to the greatest possible unity. And the difficulty here lies in the fact, that the sub-lunar among these ends are none the less moral ends, bearing the full specific character of moral values,—that they are ends-in-themselves, and necessary for their own sakes, even at the cost of man's natural happiness; and yet that they operate in the visible world, and adhere to historical formations which proceed from man's natural constitution, and dominate his earthly horizon; whilst the Super-worldly End cannot share its rule with any other end. Yet the special characteristic of modern civilization resides precisely in such a simultaneous insistence upon the Inner-worldly Ends, as possessing the nature of ends-in-themselves, and upon the Religious, Super-worldly End: it is indeed from just this combination that this civilization derives its peculiar richness, power, and freedom, but also its painful, interior tension and its difficult problems."

(2) The true solution of the difficulty surely is that "Ethical life is not, in its beginnings, a unity but a multiplicity: man grows up amidst a number of moral ends, whose unification is

not his starting-point but his problem. And this multiplicity can be still further defined as the polarity of two poles, inherent in man's nature, of which the two chief types proceed respectively from the religious and from the inner-worldly self-determination of the soul,—the polarity of Religious, and that of Humane Ethics, neither of which can be dispensed with without moral damage, yet which cannot be brought completely under a common formula. On this polarity depends the richness, but also the difficulty, of our life, since the sub-lunar ends remain, to a large extent, conditioned by the necessities and pre-requisites of their own special subject-matters, and since only on condition of being thus recognized as ends in themselves, can they attain to their morally educative power." [1]

(3) Or, to put the same matter from the point of view of definitely Christian experience and conviction: "The formula, for the specific nature of Christianity, can only be a complex conception,—the special Christian form," articulation and correction, "of the fundamental thoughts concerning God, World, Man and Redemption which," with indefinite variations of fulness and worth, "are found existing together in all the religions. And the tension present in this multiplicity of elements thus brought together is of an importance equal to that of the multiplicity itself; indeed in this tension resides the main driving-force of Religion. Christianity" in particular "embraces a polarity within itself, and its formula must be dualistic; it resembles, not a circle with one centre, but an ellipse with two focuses. For Christianity is," unchangeably, "an Ethics of Redemption, with a conception of the world both optimistic and pessimistic, both transcendental and immanental, and an apprehension both of a severe antagonism and of a close interior union between the world and God. It is, in principle, a Dualism, and yet a Dualism which is ever in process of abolition by Faith and Action. It is a purely Religious Ethic, which concentrates man's soul, with abrupt exclusiveness, upon the values of the interior life; and yet, again, it is a Humane Ethic, busy with the moulding and transforming of nature, and through love bringing about an eventual reconciliation with it. At one time the one, at another time the other, of these poles is prominent: but neither of them may be completely absent, if the Christian

[1] "Grundprobleme der Ethik": *Zeitschrift für Theologie und Kirche*, 1902, pp. 164, 167.

outlook is to be maintained.—And yet the original germ of the whole vast growth and movement ever remains an intensely, abruptly Transcendent Ethic, and can never simply pass over into a purely Immanental Ethic. The Gospel ever remains, with all possible clearness and keenness, a Promise of Redemption, leading us, away from the world, from nature and from sin, from earthly sorrow and earthly error, on and on to God; and which cannot allow the last word to be spoken in this life. Great as are its incentives to Reconciliation, it is never entirely resolvable into them. And the importance of that classical beginning ever consists in continuously calling back the human heart, away from all Culture and Immanence, to that which lies above both." [1]

(4) We thus get at last a conception which really covers, I think, all the chief elements of this complex matter. But the reader will have noted that it does so by treating the whole problem as one of Spiritual Dynamics, and not of Intellectual Statics. For the conception holds and requires the existence and cultivation of three kinds of action and movement in the soul. There are, first, the various centres of human energy and duty of a primarily This-world character, each of which possesses its own kind and degree of autonomy, laws, and obligations. There is, next, the attempt at organizing an increasing interaction between, and at harmonizing, (whilst never emasculating or eliminating,) these various, severally characteristic, systems of life and production into an ever larger ultimate unity. And, lastly, there is as strong a turning away from all this occupation with the Contingent and Finite, to the sense and apprehension of the Infinite and Abiding. And this dynamic system is so rich, even in the amount of it which can claim the practice of the majority of souls, as to require definite alternations in the occupations of such souls, ranging thus, in more or less rhythmic succession, from earth to Heaven and from Heaven back again to earth.

(5) And so great and so inexhaustible is this living system, even by mankind at large, that it has to be more or less parcelled out amongst various groups of men, each group possessing its own predominant *attrait*,—either to work out one of those immanental interests, say Art, Natural Science, Politics; or to fructify one or more of these relatively inde-

[1] "Was heisst Wesen des Christenthums?" *Christliche Welt*, 1903, I, coll. 583, 584. The Abbé Loisy has also dwelt, with rare impressiveness, upon the intensely Other-Worldly character of the first Christian teaching.

pendent interests, by crossing it with one or more of the others; or to attempt to embrace the whole of these intra-mundane interests in one preliminary final system; or to turn away from this whole system and its contents to the Transcendent and Infinite; or finally to strive to combine, as far as possible, this latter Fleeing to the Infinite with all that former Seeking of the Finite.—We shall thus get specialists within one single domain; and more many-sided workers who fertilize one Science by another; and philosophers of Science or of History, or of both, who strive to reach the *rationale* of all knowledge of the Finite and Contingent; and Ascetics and Contemplatives who, respectively, call forth and dwell upon the sense and presence of the Infinite and Abiding, underlying and accompanying all the definite apprehensions of things contingent; and finally, the minds and wills that feel called to attempt as complete a development and organization as possible of all these movements.

4. *Subdivision of spiritual labour: its necessity and its dangers.*

And yet all the subdivision of labour we have just required can avoid doing harm, directly or indirectly, (by leading to Materialism, Rationalism, or Fanaticism, to one or other of the frequent but ever mischievous "Atomisms,") only on condition that it is felt and worked *as* such a subdivision. In other words, every soul must retain and cultivate some sense of, and respect for, the other chief human activities not primarily its own. For, as a matter of fact, even the least rich or developed individual requires and practises a certain amount, in an inchoate form, of each and all of these energizings; and he can, fruitfully for himself and others, exercise a maximum amount of any one of them, only if he does not altogether and deliberately neglect and exclude the others; and, above all, if, in imagination and in actual practice, he habitually turns to his fellow-men, of the other types and centres, to supplement, and to be supplemented by, them.

It will be found, I think, that the quite undeniable abuses that have been special to the Ascetic and Contemplative methods and states, have all primarily sprung from that most plausible error that, if these energizings are, in a sense, the highest in and for man, then they can, at least in man's ideal action and condition, dispense with other and lower energizings and objects altogether. Yet both for man's practice here and even for his ideal state in the hereafter, this is not so. There is no such thing,—either in human experience or in the human ideal, when both are adequately analyzed and formulated,—as discursive reasoning, without intuitive reason; or clear analysis and sense of contrast, without dim synthesis and a deep consciousness of similarity or continuity; or detachment of the will from evil, without attachment of the higher feelings to things good; or the apprehension and requirements of Multiplicity, without those of Unity; or the vivid experience of Contingency, Mutation, and the Worthlessly Subjective, without the, if obscure yet most powerful, instinct of the Infinite and Abiding, of the true Objective and Valuable Subjective. Thus, for humanity at large entirely, and for each human individual more or less, each member of these couples requires, and is occasioned by, the other, and *vice versa.*

The maxims that follow from this great fact are as plain in reason, and as immensely fruitful in practice, as they are difficult, though ever freshly interesting, to carry out, at all consistently, even in theory and still more in act. For the object of a wise living will now consist in introducing an ever greater unity into the multiplicity of our lives,—up to the point where this unity's constituents would, like the opposing metals in an electric battery, become too much alike still to produce a fruitful interaction, and where the unity would, thus and otherwise, become empty and mechanical; and an ever greater multiplicity into the unity,—up to the point where that multiplicity would, seriously and permanently, break up or weaken true recollection; and in more and more expanding this whole individual organism, by its insertion, as a constituent part, into larger groups and systems of interests. The Family, the Nation, Human Society, the Church,—these are the chief of the larger organizations into which the inchoate, largely only potential, organism of the individual man is at first simply passively born, yet which, if he would grow, (not in spite of them, a hopeless task, but by them,) he will have deliberately to endorse and will, as though they were his own creations.

5. *Mystics and Spiritual Direction.*

It is interesting to note the special characteristics attaching to the one social relation emphasized by the medieval and modern varieties of Western Catholic Mysticism; and the effect which a larger development of the other chief forces and modalities of the Catholic spiritual life necessarily has upon this relation. I am thinking of the part played by the Director, the soul's leader and adviser, in the lives of these Mystics,—a part which differs, in three respects, from that of the ordinary Confessor in the life of the more active or "mixed" type of Catholic.

(1) For one thing, there is here a striking variety and range, in the ecclesiastical and social position of the persons thus providentially given and deliberately chosen. The early German Franciscan Preacher, Berthold of Regensburg, owes his initiation into the Interior Life to his Franciscan Novice-Master, the Partial Mystic, David of Augsburg, whose writings still give forth for us their steady light and genial warmth; the French widowed noblewoman and Religious Foundress, St. Jane Frances de Chantal, is helped on her course to high contemplation by the Secular Priest and Bishop, St. Francis de Sales; the French Jesuit, Jean Nicolas Grou, is initiated, after twenty-four years' life and training in his Order, by the Visitation Nun, Sœur Pélagie, into that more Mystical spirituality, which constitutes the special characteristic of his chief spiritual books; the great Spaniard, St. Teresa herself, tells us how "a saintly nobleman . . . a married layman, who had spent nearly forty years in prayer, seems to me to have been, by the pains he took, the beginning of salvation to my soul"—"his power was great"; and the English Anchorite, Mother Juliana of Norwich, "a simple, unlettered creature," seems to have found no special leader on to her rarely deep, wide, and tender teachings, but to have been led and stimulated, beyond and after her first general Benedictine training, by God's Providence alone, working through the few and quite ordinary surroundings and influences of her Anchorage at Norwich.[1] It would be difficult to find anything to improve in this noble liberty of these great children of God; nor would a larger influence of the other modalities necessarily restrict this ample range.

(2) Again, the souls of this type seem, for the most part, to realize more fully and continuously than those of the ordinary, simply active and ascetical kind, that the "blind obedience" towards such leaders, so often praised in their disciples and

[1] *Deutsche Mystiker des Mittelalters*, ed. Pfeiffer, Vol. I, 1845, pp. xli, xlii. Any Life of St. Jane F. de Chantal. A. Cadrès, *Le P. Jean N. Grou*, 1866, pp. 13, 14. St. Teresa's *Life, written by Herself*, tr. David Lewis, ed. 1888, pp. 176, 177; 186. *Revelations of Divine Love, showed to Mother Juliana of Norwich*, ed. 1902, p. 4.

penitents, is, where wholesome and strengthening, essentially a simple, tenacious adherence, during the inevitable times of darkness and perplexity, to the encouragements given by the guide to persevere along the course and towards the truths which this soul itself saw clearly, often through the instrumentality of this leader, when it was in light and capable of a peaceful, deliberate decision. For however much the light may have been given it through this human mediation, (and the most numerous, and generally the most important, of our lights, have been acquired thus through the spoken, written, or acted instrumentality of fellow-souls,)—yet the light was seen, and had (in the first instance) to be seen, by the disciple's own spiritual eye; and it is but to help it in keeping faithful to this light (which, in the first and last instance, is God's light and its own) that the leader stands by and helps. But, given this important condition, there remains the simple, experimental fact that, not only can and do others often see our spiritual whereabouts and God's *attrait* for us more clearly than we do ourselves, but such unselfseeking transmission and such humbly simple reception of light between man and man adds a moral and spiritual security and beauty to the illumination, (all other conditions being equal and appropriate,) not to be found otherwise. It is interesting to note the courageous, balanced, and certainly quite unprejudiced, testimony borne to these important points, by so widely read, and yet upon the whole strongly Protestant, a pair of scholars, as Miss Alice Gardner and her very distinguished brother, Professor Percy Gardner.[1]

(3) And finally, the souls of this type have, (at least for the two purposes of the suscitation of actual insight, and for bearing witness to this, now past, experience during the soul's periods of gloom), often tended,—in Western Christendom and during Medieval and still more in Modern times,—to exalt the office and power of the Director, in the life of the soul of the Mystical type, very markedly beyond the functions, rights and duties of the ordinary Confessor in the spiritual life of the ordinary Catholic.

Indeed they and their interpreters have, in those times and places, often insisted upon the guarantee of safety thus afforded, and upon the necessity of such formal and systematic mediation, with an absoluteness and vehemence

[1] A. Gardner, "Confession and Direction," in *The Conflict of Duties*, 1903, pp. 223–229. P. Gardner, in *The Liberal Churchman*, 1905, p. 266.

impossible to conciliate with any full and balanced, especially with any at all orthodox, reading of Church History. For this feature is as marked in the condemned book of Molinos and of most of the other Quietists, as it is in such thoroughly approved Partial Mysticism as that of Père Lallemant and Père Grou : hence it alone cannot, surely, render a soul completely safe against excesses and delusions. And this feature was markedly in abeyance, often indeed, for aught we know, completely wanting, at least in any frequent and methodic form, in the numerous cases of the Egyptian and other Fathers of the Desert : hence it cannot be strictly essential to all genuine Contemplation in all times and places.

(4) The dominant and quite certain fact here seems to be that, in proportion as the Abstractive movement of the soul is taken as self-sufficient, and a Contemplative life is attempted as something substantially independent of any concrete, social, and devotional helps and duties, the soul gets into a state of danger, which no amount of predominance of the Director can really render safe; whereas, in proportion as the soul takes care to practise, in its own special degree and manner, the outgoing movement towards Multiplicity and Contingency, (particular attention to particular religious facts and particular service of particular persons), does such right, quite ordinary-seeming, active subordination to, and incorporation within, the great sacred organisms of the Family, Society, and the Church, or of any wise and helpful subdivision of these, furnish material, purgation and check for the other movement, and render superfluous any great or universal predominance of Direction. St. Teresa is, here also, wonderfully many-sided and balanced. Just as she comes to regret having ever turned aside from Christ's Sacred Humanity, so too she possesses, indeed she never loses, the sense of the profoundly social character of Christianity : she dies as she had lived, full of an explicit and deep love for the Kingdom of God and the Church.

6. *Mysticism predominantly Individualistic.*

Yet it is clear that the strong point of the Mystics, as such, does not lie in the direction of the great social spirituality which finds God in our neighbour and in the great human organizations, through and in which, after all, man in great part becomes and is truly man. They are, as such, Individualistic; the relation between God and the individual soul here ever tends to appear as constituted by these two forces alone. A fresh proof, if one were still wanting, that Mysticism is but one of the elements of Religion,—for Religion requires both the Social and the Individual, the Corporate and the Lonely movement and life.

It is truly inspiring to note how emphatic is the concurrence of all the deepest and most circumspect contemporary Psychology, Epistemology, Ethics, and History and Philosophy of the Sciences and of Religion, in these general conclusions, which find, within the slow and many-sided growth and upbuilding of the spiritual personality, a true and necessary place and function for all the great and permanent capabilities, aspirations and energizings of the human soul. Thus no system of religion can be complete and deeply fruitful which does not embrace, (in every possible kind of healthy development, proportion and combination), the several souls and the several types of souls who, between them, will afford a maximum of clear apprehension and precise reasoning, *and* of dim experience and intuitive reason; of particular attention to the Contingent (Historical Events and Persons, and Institutional Acts and Means) *and* of General Recollection and Contemplation and Hungering after the Infinite; and of reproductive Admiration and Loving Intellection, *and* of quasi-creative, truly productive Action upon and within Nature and other souls, attaining, by such Action, most nearly to the supreme attribute, the Pure Energizing of God.

Thus Pseudo-Dionysius and St. John of the Cross will, even in their most Negative doctrines, remain right and necessary in all stages of the Church's life,—on condition, however, of being taken as but one of two great movements, of which the other, the Positive movement, must also ever receive careful attention : since only between them is attained that all-important oscillation of the religious pendulum, that interaction between the soul's meal and the soul's yeast, that furnishing of friction for force to overcome, and of force to overcome the friction, that material for the soul to mould, and in moulding which to develop itself, that alternate expiration and inspiration, upon which the soul's mysterious death-in-life and life-in-death so continuously depends.

III. The Scientific Habit and Mysticism.

Introductory. Difficulty yet Necessity of finding a True Place and Function for Science in the Spiritual Life.

Now it is certain that such an oscillatory movement, such a give-and-take, such a larger Asceticism, built up out of the alternate engrossment in and abstraction from variously, yet in each case really, attractive levels, functions and objects of human life and experience, is still comparatively easy, as long as we restrict it to two out of the three great groups of energizings which are ever, at least potentially, present in the soul, and which ever inevitably help to make or mar, to develop or to stunt, the totality of the soul's life, and hence also of the strictly spiritual life. The Historical-Institutional, and the Mystical-Volitional groups and forces, the High-Church and the Low-Church trend, the Memory- and the Will-energies, do indeed coalesce, in times of peace, with the Reason-energy, though, even then, with some difficulty. But in times of war,—on occasion of any special or excessive action on the part of this third group, the Critical-Speculative, the Broad-Church trend, and the energizing of the Understanding,—they readily combine against every degree of the latter. It is as though the fundamental vowels A and U could not but combine to oust the fundamental vowel I; or as if the primary colours Red and Blue *must* join to crush out the primary colour Yellow.

Indeed, it is undoubtedly just this matter of the full and continuous recognition of, and allocation of a special function to, this third element within the same great spiritual organism which englobes the other two, which is now the great central difficulty and pressing problem of more or less every degree and kind of religious life. For the admission of this third element appears frequently to be ruinous to the other two; yet the other two, when kept away from it, seem to lose their vigour and persuasive power.—And yet it is, I think, exactly at this crucial point that the conception of the spiritual life as essentially a Dynamism, a slow constitution of an ever fuller, deeper, more close-knit unity in, and by means of, the soul's ineradicable trinity of forces, shows all its fruitfulness, if we but work down to a sufficiently large apprehension of the capacities and requirements of human nature, moved and aided by divine grace, and to a very precise delimitation of the special object and function of Mysticism.

1. *Science and Religion: each autonomous at its own level; and, thus, each helpful to the other.*

Erwin Rohde has well described Plato's attitude towards Science and Mysticism respectively, and towards the question of their inter-relation. "The flight from the things of this World is, for Plato, already in itself an acquisition of those of the Beyond, and an assimilation to the Divine. For this poor world, that solicits our senses, the philosopher has, at bottom, nothing but negation. Incapable as it is of furnishing a material that can be truly known, the whole domain of the Transitory and Becoming has no intrinsic significance for Science as understood by him. The perception of things which are ever merely relative, and which simultaneously manifest contradictory qualities, has its sole use in stimulating and inviting the soul to press on to the Absolute." [1]

Here we should frankly admit that the soul's hunger for the Infinite is, as the great Athenian so deeply realized, the very mainspring of Religion; and yet we must maintain that it is precisely this single bound away, instead of the ever-repeated double movement of a coming and a going, which not only helped to suppress, or at least gravely to stunt, the growth of the sciences of external observation and experiment, but (and this is the special point,—the demonstrable other side of the medal,) also, in its degree, prevented religion from attaining to its true depth, by thus cutting off, as far as Plato's conviction prevailed, the very material, stimulation, and in part the instruments, for the soul's outgoing, spiritualizing work, together with this work's profound reflex effect upon the worker, as a unique occasion for the growth and self-detachment of the soul.

Now the necessity for such a first stage and movement, which, as far as possible both immanental and phenomenalist, shall be applied and restricted to the special methods, direct objects, and precise range of each particular Science, and the importance of the safeguarding of this scientific liberty, are now clearly perceived, by the leading men of Religion, Philosophy, Psychology and Physics, in connection with the maintenance and acquisition of sincere and fruitful Science.— It is also increasingly seen that, even short of Religion, a

[1] *Psyche*, ed. 1898, Vol. II, p. 289.

second, an interpretative, an at least Philosophical stage and movement is necessary for the full explicitation of Science's own assumptions and affinities. And the keeping of these two movements clearly distinct or even strongly contrasted, is felt, by some far-sighted Theologians, to be a help towards securing, not only a candid attitude of Science towards its own subject-matters, but also a right independence of Philosophy and Theology towards the other Sciences. Thus Cardinal Newman has brought out, with startling force, the necessarily non-moral, non-religious character of Physico-Mathematical Science, taken simply within its direct subject-matter and method. "Physical science never travels beyond the examination of cause and effect. Its object is to resolve the complexity of phenomena into simple elements and principles; but when it has reached those first elements, principles and laws, its mission is at an end; it keeps within that material system with which it began, and never ventures beyond the 'flammantia moenia mundi.' The physicist as such will never ask himself by what influence, external to the universe, the universe is sustained; simply because he is a physicist. If, indeed, he be a religious man, he will, of course, have a very different view of the subject; . . . and this, not because physical science says anything different, but simply because it says nothing at all on the subject, nor can do by the very undertaking with which it set out." Or, as he elsewhere sympathetically sums up Bacon's method of proceeding: "The inquiry into physical causes passes over for the moment the existence of God. In other words, physical science is, in a certain sense, atheistic, for the very reason that it is not theology." [1]

2. *Science builds up a preliminary world that has to be corrected by Philosophy and Religion, at and for their deeper levels.*

The additional experience and analysis of the last half-century apparently forces us, however, to maintain not only that Physico-Mathematical Science, and all knowledge brought strictly to the type of that Science, does not itself pronounce on the Ultimate Questions; but that this Science, as such, actually presents us with a picture of reality which,

1 "Christianity and Physical Science" (1855), in *Idea of a University*, ed. 1873, pp. 432, 433. "University Teaching" (1852), *ibid.* p. 222. See Mr. R. E. Froude's interesting paper, "Scientific Speculation and the Unity of Truth," *Dublin Review*, Oct. 1900, pp. 353–368.

at the deeper level even of Epistemology and of the more ultimate Psychology, and still more at that of Religion, requires to be taken as more or less artificial, and as demanding, not simply completion, but, except for its own special purposes, correction as well. Thus we have seen how M. Bergson finds Clock-Time to be an artificial, compound concept, which seriously travesties Duration, the reality actually experienced by us; and Space appears as in even a worse predicament. M. Emil Boutroux in France, Dottore Igino Petrone in Italy, Profs. Eucken and Troeltsch in Germany, Profs. James Ward and Pringle Pattison in Great Britain, and Profs. William James, Hugo Münsterberg and Josiah Royce in America are, in spite of differences on other points, united in insistence upon, or have even worked out in much detail, such a distinction between the first stage and level of Determinist, Atomistic, Inorganic Nature and our concepts of it, and the second stage and level of Libertarian, Synthetic, and Organic Spiritual Reality, and our experience of it. And the penetrating labours of Profs. Windelband, Rickert, and others, towards building up a veritable *Organon* of the Historical Sciences, are bringing into the clearest relief these two several degrees of Reality and types of Knowledge, the Historical being the indefinitely deeper and more adequate, and the one which ultimately englobes the other.[1]

A profoundly significant current in modern philosophy will thus be brought, in part at least, to articulate expression and application. This current is well described by Prof. Volkelt. "German philosophy since Kant reveals, in manifold forms and under various disguises, the attempt to recognize, in Epistemology, Metaphysics, and Ethics, such kinds of Certainty, such domains of Being, such human Volitions and Values, as lie beyond reason, constitute a something that it cannot grasp, and are rooted in some other kind of foundation. In variously struggling, indeed stammering utterances, expression is given to the assurance that not everything in the world is resolvable into Logic and Thought, but that mighty resisting remainders are extant, which perhaps even constitute the most important thing in the world. . . . Such a longing after such a Reality can be

[1] W. Windelband, *Geschichte und Naturwissenschaft*, 1894. H. Rickert, *Kulturwissenschaft und Naturwissenschaft*, 1899. And, above all, H. Rickert, *Die Grenzen der Naturwissenschaftlichen Begriffsbildung*, 1902.

traced in Hamann, Jacobi, Herder, in Novalis, Friedrich Schlegel, the youthful Schleiermacher, and Jean Paul. Indeed, even in Hegel, the adorer of Reason, the movement of Negation, which is the very soul of his philosophy, is, at bottom, nothing but the Irrational," the Super-Rational, "element violently pressed into the form of Reason; and again the single Thing, the This, the Here and the Now, are felt by him as . . . a something beyond Reason. And has not the Irrational found expression in Kant, in his doctrines of the unconditional Liberty of the Will and of Radical Evil? In the later Schelling and his spiritual relatives the Irrational has found far more explicit recognition; whilst Schopenhauer brings the point to its fullest expression. Yet even Nietzsche still possesses such an element, in his doctrine of the 'Over-Man.'"[1] And in England we find this same element, in various degrees and in two chief divergent forms, in the Cambridge Platonists, Samuel Taylor Coleridge and Thomas Hill Green on the one hand; and in Bishop Butler and Cardinal Newman on the other hand.

We can thus point to much clear recognition, or at least to a considerable influence, of the profound truth that Science and Wisdom can each prosper and help and supplement the other, only if each possesses a certain real autonomy, a power fully to become and to remain itself, and, in various degrees and ways, to stimulate, check and thwart the other. And this truth ever presupposes, what human experience, in the long run, proves to be a fact,—that the different kinds, spheres, and levels of man's apprehension, and of the total reality thus apprehended by him, are already immanently planned each for the other, within a great, largely dormant system of the world. Thus Man can and should call this congenital inter-relatedness into ever more vigorous and more fruitful play; whereas, if it were not already present deep within the very nature of things, no amount of human effort or ingenuity could ever evoke or insert it. Prof. Volkelt has, as we have seen, illustrated this great fact very strikingly, with regard to the relation extant between the apparently sheer contingencies of human History and the requirements of Philosophy, of normative thought and ideal truth. Yet a similar interconnection can be traced elsewhere, between any other two or more levels and spheres of wholesome and permanent human apprehension and action, in their relation

[1] *Schopenhauer*, 1900, pp. 344, 345.

to various degrees and kinds of reality, as this environs man or inheres in him.

3. *Necessity of the "Thing-element" in Religion.*

But let us note that the recognition, of an at all emphatic, systematic kind, of such inter-relatedness is, so far, almost limited to the moods and persons preoccupied with the right claims of Science or of Philosophy upon each other or upon the remainder of Life; and is, as yet, all but wanting, when Life is approached from the side of the specifically Religious requirements and of the Spiritual consolidation of man's soul. Yet here especially, at by far the most important point of the whole matter, the unique place and significance of Science can now be very clearly grasped.

Indeed it is deeply interesting to note how largely the fundamental characteristics of Catholicism really meet, or rather how they strictly require, some such vivid conception and vigorous use of the Determinist Thing and of its level for the full constitution of our true depth, our Spiritual Personality itself. If we take, *e. g.*, the criticisms addressed, by so earnest and acute a mind as the intensely Protestant Emile Sulze, to the whole Thing-Element and -Concept, as these are at work in the Catholic practice and position, we shall find his sense of the difference between Thing and Spirit to be as enviably keen, and his idea of the end and ultimate measure of Religion to be as sound and deep, as his conception of the means towards developing Religion and the Spirit is curiously inadequate.

(1) "Personality," says Sulze, "is, for Religion and Morality, the supreme Good, of which the source is in God, and the end, the fruit, and the manifestation is in Man." [1] This I take to be profoundly true, especially if we insist upon Perfect Personality being Supreme and Perfect Spirit; and, again, upon our imperfect personality and spirit as possessed of certain profound affinities to, and as penetrable and actually moved by, that Perfect Spirit.

(2) "The value of Personality nowhere finds a full recognition in Catholicism; Catholicism indeed is Pantheism." Now this harsh judgment is based upon two sets of allegations, which, though treated by Sulze as of the same nature, are, I would submit, essentially different, and this because of their definitely different places and functions in the Catholic system.

[1] *Wie ist der Kampf um die Bedeutung . . . Jesu zu beendigen?* 1901, p. 9.

"The Impersonal Godhead, the bond which unites the three Persons, stands above the Persons. Hence those who took religion seriously had to lose themselves, pantheistically, in the abyss of the Divinity. And in Christ the Person was even looked upon as the product of two Natures, the Divine and the Human, hence of two Impersonal Forces." [1] Here two peculiarities in the early Conciliar Definitions are emphasized, which were doubtless as helpful, indeed necessary, for the apprehension of the great abiding truths thus conveyed to the Greco-Roman mind, as they are now in need of reinterpretation in the light of our greater sensitiveness to the difference, in character and in value, which obtains between the concept of Spirit and Personality and that of Substances and Things.

But Sulze continues, without any change in the kind or degree of his criticism: "Impersonal miraculous means, created by the Hierarchy, are put by it in the place of the sanctifying mutual intercourse of the children of God." "Christianity, torn away from the religious and moral life, became thus a special, technical apparatus, without any religious or spiritual worth. Ecclesiastical Christianity has become a Pantheism, Materialism, indeed Atheism." [2] We have so continuously ourselves insisted upon the profound danger, and frequently operative abuse, of any and all complete apartness between any one means, function, or *attrait* of the spiritual life and the others, that we can, without any unfairness, restrict ourselves here to the attack upon the general acceptation of Impersonal means as helps towards the constitution of Personality. Now Sulze's principle here,—that only directly personal means can help to achieve the end of Personality,—is most undoubtedly false, unless Mathematico-Physical Science is also to be ruled out of life, as necessarily destructive of, or at least as necessarily non-conductive to, Personality.

(3) Indeed Sulze himself tells us, most truly, that, "for Religion also, Science is a bath of purification"; and that "Doctrine and the Sacraments are aids, in the hands of Christ and of the Community, towards representing the riches of their interior life and offering these to believing hearts." [3] This latter pronouncement is, however, still clearly insufficient.

[1] *Wie ist der Kampf um die Bedeutung . . . Jesu zu beendigen?* 1901, p. 10.

[2] *Ibid.* pp. 10, 11.

[3] *Ibid.* pp. 26, 27.

For if there is a double truth which, at the end of well-nigh five centuries, ought to have burnt itself indelibly into the mind and conscience of us all, it is, surely, the following. On the one hand, Man, unless he develops a vigorous alternating counter-movement, ever grows like to the instruments of his labour and self-development, and hence, whilst busy with Things, (whether these be Natural Happenings and their Sciences, or Religious Institutions and Doctrines,) he inclines to become, quite unawares, limited and assimilated to them,—himself thus a Thing among Things, instead of, through such various Things, winning an ever fuller apprehension of and growth in Spiritual Personality. Yet, on the other hand, without such a movement of close contact with the Thing, (both the intensely concrete, the Here and Now Contingency, and the profoundly Abstract, the stringent Universal Law,) and without the pleasure and pain derived from the accompanying sense of contraction and of expansion, of contrast, conflict, supplementation and renovation,—there is no fullest discipline or most solid growth of the true spiritual Personality.

(4) Thus Science, as Sulze himself clearly sees, not merely aids us to represent and to communicate our personality acquired elsewhere, but the shock, friction, contrast, the slow, continuous discipline, far more, beyond doubt, than any positive content furnished by such science, can and should constitute an essential part of the soul's spiritual fertilization. And similarly, if we move on into the directly religious life, the Sacramental contacts and Doctrinal systems (the former so intensely concrete, the latter often so abstract,) are not simply means towards representing and transmitting spirituality acquired elsewhere : but they are amongst the means, and, in some form and degree, the necessary, indeed actually universal means, towards the awakening and developing and fulfilling of this our spiritual personality.

4. *Three possible relations between Thing and Thought, Determinism and Spirit.*

It remains no doubt profoundly true that, with the awakening of the Mystical sense, will come a more or less acute consciousness of an at least superficial and preliminary, difference between this sense, with its specific habits and informations, and those means and forms, in part so contingent and external, in part so intensely abstract and yet so precise. But it is equally certain that such a soul, and at such a stage, even as it continues to require, in some respects more than ever, for its general balanced development, some of the irreplaceable discipline and manly, bracing humiliation of the close external observation and severe abstract generalization of Science : so also does it continue to require, for the deepening of the spirit and for the growth of creatureliness, the contact with religious Things,—the profoundly concrete Sacraments and the intensely abstract Doctrines of the religious community.

(1) In one of Trendelenburg's most penetrating essays, he shows us how, between blind Force and conscious Thought,—if we presuppose any tendency towards unity to exist between them,—there can be but three possible relations. " Either Force stands before Thought, so that Thought is not the primitive reality, but the result and accident of blind Force; or Thought stands before Force, so that blind Force is not itself the primitive reality, but the effluence of Thought; or finally, Thought and Force are, at bottom, only one and the same thing, and differ only in our mind's conception of them." And only one of these three positions can, by any possibility, be the true one : hence their internecine conflict.[1]

(2) Now Religion, in its normal, central stream, stands most undoubtedly for Thought before Force, the second, the Theistic view. And yet it would be profoundly impoverishing for our outlook and practice, and would but prepare a dangerous reaction in ourselves or others, were we ever to ignore the immense influence, in the history, not only of philosophical speculation, but even of religious feeling and aspiration, not indeed of the first, the Materialist, view, (which owes all its strength to non-religious causes or to a rebound against religious excesses,) but of the third, the Pantheistic, Monistic, view, whose classical exponent Spinoza will probably remain unto all time.

(3) If we examine into what constitutes the religious plausibility and power of this view, we shall find, I think, that it proceeds, above all, from the fact that, only too often, the second, the Theistic view and practice, leaves almost or quite out of sight the purification and slow constitution of the Individual into a Person, by means of the Thing-element, the apparently blind Determinism of Natural Law and Natural Happenings. Yet nothing can be more certain than that we must admit and place this undeniable, increasingly obtrusive,

[1] " Ueber den letzten Unterschied der philosophischen Systeme," 1847, in *Beiträge zur Philosophie*, 1855, Vol. II, p. 10.

element and power *somewhere* in our lives: if we will not own it as a means, it will grip us as our end. The unpurified, all but merely natural, animal, lustful and selfish individual man, is far too like to the brutes and plants, indeed even to the inorganic substances that so palpably surround him, for it not to be a fantastic thought to such thinkers as Spinoza, (and indeed it would be an excessive effort to himself,) to believe that he is likely, taken simply in this condition, to outlast, and is capable of dominating, the huge framework of the visible world, into which his whole bodily and psychical mechanism is placed, and to which it is bound by a thousand ties and closest similarities: his little selfish thinkings cannot but seem mere bubbles on a boundless expanse of mere matter; all creation cannot, surely, originate in, depend from, and move up to, a Mind and Spirit in any way like unto this trivial ingenuity.

(4) It is true, of course, that Spinoza ended,—as far as the logic of his system went,—by " purifying " away not only this animal Individualism, but Spiritual Personality as well, and this because he takes Mathematico-Physical concepts to be as directly applicable and as adequate to Ultimate Reality as are the Ethico-Spiritual categories. We have then to admit that even so rich and rare, so deeply religious a spirit as Spinoza could insist upon purification by the " preliminary Pantheism," and yet could remain, in theory, the eager exponent of an ultimate Pantheism. Like the Greeks, he not only passes through a middle distance, a range of experience which appears dominated by austere Fate and blind Fortune, but finds Fate even in ultimate Reality. Whilst, however, the Greeks often thought of Fate as superior even to the Gods, Spinoza finds Ultimate Reality to be neither Nature nor Spirit, but simply Being in General, with a Law which is neither Natural nor Spiritual Law, but Law in general. This General Being and General Law then bifurcate, with the most rigorous determinism and complete impartiality, step by step, into parallel and ever co-present manifestations of Nature and of Spirit, and of their respective laws, which, though different, are also each strictly determined within their own series.[1]

(5) But Spinoza's error here undoubtedly lies in his *de facto*

[1] See the admirably lucid analysis in Prof. Troeltsch's " Religions-philosophie," in *Die Philosophie im Beginn des zwanzigsten Jahrhunderts*, 1904, Vol. I, p. 116, already referred to further back.

violent bending (in spite of this theoretical Parallelism) of all Knowledge, Reality, and Life, under the sole Mathematico-Physical categories and method; and in the insistence upon attaining to ultimate Truth by one single bound and with complete adequacy and clearness. And the greatness here consists in the keen and massive sense of three profound truths. He never forgets that Mathematico-Physical Science is rigidly determinist, and that it stands for a certain important truth and penetrates to a certain depth of reality. He never ceases to feel how impure, selfish, petty is the natural man, and how pure, disinterested, noble, can and should be the spiritual personality. And he never lets go the sense that, somehow, that science must be able to help towards this purification.

(6) Now these three truths must be preserved, whilst the Mathematico-Physical one-sidedness and the "one-step" error must be carefully eliminated. And indeed it is plain that only by such elimination can those truths operate within a fully congenial system. For only thus, with a dissimilarity between the Ultimate, Libertarian, Spiritual Reality, and the Intermediate, Determinist, Physico-Mathematical Range, can we explain and maintain the pain, not only of the selfish but also of the true self, in face the Mere Thing; and only thus is all such pain and trouble worth having, since only thus it leads to the fuller development and the solid constitution of an abiding, interior, mental and volitional Personality.

5. *Purification of the Personality by the impersonal.*

Prof. H. J. Holtzmann has got an eloquent page concerning the kind of Dualism which is more than ever desirable for souls, if they would achieve a full and virile personality in this our day. "It would appear to be the wiser course for us to recognize the incompatibility between merely natural existence and truly personal life, just as it is, in its whole acute non-reconciliation; to insert this conflict into our complete outlook on to Life in its full breadth and depth, and to find the harmonization in God the Infinite, in whom alone such parallels can meet, and not deliberately to blind our right eye or our left, in order to force that outlook into one single aspect,—a degree of unification which, when achieved in this violent manner, would mean for us, at the same time, a point of absolute inertia, of eternal stagnation." And he then shows how it is precisely the interaction within our minds, feelings, and volitions, of, on the one hand, the boundless world of nature, with its majestic impersonality, and on the other hand, the inexhaustible, indefinitely deeper realm of personal life, as it appears within the stream of human history, which is best adapted to give us some fuller glimpses of the greatness of God and of the specific character of religion.[1]

The religious imagination, mind, heart, and will,—that is to say, the complete, fully normal human being at his deepest,—has thus been more and more forced, by an increasingly articulated experience of the forces and requirements of actual life, to hold and to practise, with ever-renewed attempts at their most perfect interstimulation and mutual supplementation, a profoundly costing, yet immensely fruitful, trinity in unity of convictions on this point.

In every time, place, and race, man will continue to be or to become religious, in proportion to his efficacious faith in, and love of, the overflowing reality and worth of the great direct objects of religion,—God and the soul, and their inter-relation in and through the Kingdom of God, the Church, and its Divine-Human Head,—the whole constituting God's condescension towards and immanence in man, and man's response and orientation towards the transcendent God.

And again, in every age, place, and race, man will be or will become deeply religious, in proportion to the keenness with which he realizes the immense need of spiritual growth and purification for his, at best, but inchoate personality.

But,—and this third point we must admit, in the precise extension and application given to it here, to be characteristically modern,—man will, (if he belongs to our time and to our Western races, and is determined fully to utilize our special circumstances, lights and trials, as so many means towards his own spiritualization,) have carefully to keep in living touch with that secondary and preliminary reality, the Thing-world, the Impersonal Element, Physical Science and Determinist Law. He will have to pass and repass beneath these Caudine forks; to plunge and to replunge into and through this fiery torrent; and, almost a merely animal individual at the beginning and on this side of such docile bendings and such courageous plungings, he will, (if he combines them with, and effects them through, those two other, abiding and ultimate, directly religious convictions,) straighten himself up again to greater heights, and will come forth from the torrent each time a somewhat purer and more developed

[1] *Richard Rothe's Spekulatives System*, 1899, pp. 205, 206.

spiritual person than he was before such contraction and purgation.

6. *This position new for Science, not for Religion.*

Yet even this third point has, if we will but look to its substantial significance and religious function, been equivalently held and practised ever since the Twice-Born life, the deeper religion, has been lived at all.

(1) The Ascetic's self-thwarting, and the Mystic's self-oblivion and seeking after Pure Love, what are they but the expressions of the very same necessities and motives which we would wish to see fully operative here? For we are not, of course, here thinking of anything simply intellectual, and fit only for the educated few. Any poor laundry-girl, who carefully studies and carries out the laws of successful washing, who moves, in alternation, away from this concentration on the Thing, to recollection and increasingly affective prayer and rudimentary contemplation, and who seeks the fuller growth of her spirit and of its union with God, in this coming and going, to and from the Visible and Contingent, to and from the Spiritual and Infinite, and in what these several levels have of contrast and of conflict; or any lowly farm-labourer or blacksmith or miner, who would proceed similarly with his external determinist mechanical work, and with his deeply internal requirements and spiritual growth and consolidation: would all be carrying out precisely what is here intended.

(2) As a matter of fact, the source of such novelty, as may be found here, is not on the side of religion, but on that of science. For the conception of Nature of the ancient Greek Physicists, and indeed that of Aristotle, required to be profoundly de-humanized, de-sentimentalized: a rigorous mathematical Determinism and soulless Mechanism became the right and necessary ideal of Physical Science. But, long before the elaboration of this concept of the ruthless Thing and of its blind Force, Our Lord had, by His Life and Teaching, brought to man, with abidingly unforgettable, divine depth and vividness, the sense of Spirit and Personality, with its liberty and interiority, its far-looking wisdom and its regenerating, creative power of love. And for some thirteen centuries after this supreme spiritual revelation and discovery, that old anthropomorphic and anthropocentric conception of the Physical Universe continued, well-nigh unchanged, even among the earlier and middle schoolmen,

and was readily harmonized with that Spiritual world. Yet they were harmonized, upon the whole, by a juxtaposition which, in proportion as the conception of Nature became Determinist and Mechanical, has turned out more and more untenable; and which, like all simple juxtapositions, could not, as such, have any spiritually educative force. But Spiritual Reality has now,—for those who have become thoroughly awake to the great changes operated, for good and all, in man's conception of the Physical Universe during now three centuries,—to be found under, behind, across these Physical Phenomena and Laws, which both check and beckon on the mind and soul of man, in quest of their ultimate mainstay and motivation.

(3) And let us note how much some such discipline and asceticism is required by the whole Christian temper and tradition, and the weakening of some older forms of it.

During the first three generations Christians were profoundly sobered by the keen expectation of Our Lord's proximate Second Coming, and of the end of the entire earthly order of things, to which all their natural affections spontaneously clung; and again and again, up to well-nigh the Crusading Age, this poignant and yet exultant expectation seized upon the hearts of Christians. And then, especially from St. Augustine's teaching onwards, an all-pervading, frequently very severe, conviction as to the profound effects of Original Sin, a pessimistic turning away from the future of this sub-lunar world, as leading up to the great Apostacy, and a concentration upon Man's pre-historic beginnings, as incomparably eclipsing all that mankind would ever achieve here below, came and largely took the place, as the sobering, detaching element in Christianity, of the vivid expectation of the Parousia which had characterized the earlier Christian times.

Clearly, the Parousia and the Original Sin conception have ceased to exercise their old, poignantly detaching power upon us. Yet we much require some such special channel and instrument for the preservation and acquisition of the absolutely essential temper of Detachment and Other-Worldliness. I think that this instrument and channel of purification and detachment—if we have that thirst for the More and the Other than all things visible can give to our souls, (a thirst which the religious sense alone can supply and without which we are religiously but half-awake,)—is offered to us now by Science, in the sense and for the reasons already described.

7. *Three kinds of occupation with Science.*

Let the reader note that thus, and, I submit, thus only, we can and do enlist the religious passion itself on the side of disinterested, rightly autonomous science. For thus the harmony between the different aspects and levels of life is not, (except for our general faith in its already present latent reality, and in its capacity for ultimate full realization and manifestation,) the static starting-point or automatically persisting fact in man's life; but it is, on the contrary, his ever difficult, never completely realized goal,—a goal which can be reached only by an even greater transformation within the worker than within the materials worked upon by him,—a transformation in great part effected by the enlargement and purification, incidental to the inclusion of that large range of Determinist Thing-laws and experiences within the Spirit's Libertarian, Personal life.

It is plain that there are three kinds and degrees of occupation with Things and Science, and with their special level of truth and reality; and that in proportion as their practice within, and in aid of, the spiritual life is difficult, in the same proportion, (given the soul's adequacy to this particular amount of differentiation and pressure,)—is this practice purifying. And though but few souls will be called to any appreciable amount of activity within the third degree, all souls can be proved, I think, to require a considerable amount of the first two kinds, whilst mankind at large most undoubtedly demands careful, thorough work of all three sorts.

The first kind is that of the man with a hobby. His directly religious acts and his toilsome bread-winning will thus get relieved and alternated by, say, a little Botany or a little Numismatics, or by any other "safe" science, taken in a "safe" dose, in an easy, *dilettante* fashion, for purposes of such recreation. This kind is already in fairly general operation, and is clearly useful in its degree and way, but it has, of course, no purificatory force at all.

The second kind is that of the man whose profession is some kind of science which has, by now, achieved a more or less secure place alongside of, or even within, religious doctrines and feelings,—such as Astronomy or Greek Archaeology. Here the purification will be in proportion to the loyal thoroughness with which he fully maintains, indeed develops, the special characteristics and autonomy both of these Sciences, as the foreground, part-material and stimulation, and of Religion, as the groundwork, background and ultimate interpreter and moulder of his complete and organized life; and with which he makes each contribute to the development of the other and of the entire personality, its apprehensions and its work. This second kind is still comparatively rare, doubtless, in great part, because of the considerable cost and the lifelong practice and training involved in what readily looks like a deliberate complicating and endangering of things, otherwise, each severally, simple and safe.

And the third kind is that of him whose systematic mental activity is devoted to some science or research, which is still in process of winning full and peaceful recognition by official Theology,—say, Biological Evolution or Biblical Criticism. Here the purification will, for a soul capable of such a strain, be at its fullest, provided such a soul is deeply moved by, and keeps devotedly faithful to, the love of God, and of man, of humble labour and of self-renouncing purification, and, within this great ideal and determination, maintains and ameliorates with care the methods, categories and tests special both to these sciences and investigations, and to their ultimate interpretation and utilization in the philosophy and life of religion. For here there will, as yet, be no possibility of so shunting the scientific activity on to one side, or of limiting it to a carefully pegged-out region, as to let Religion and Science energize as forces of the same kind and same level, the same clearness and same finality; but the Science will here have to be passed through, as the surface-level, on the way to Religion as underlying all. What would otherwise readily tend to become, as it were, a mental Geography, would thus here give way to what might be pictured as a spiritual Geology.

8. *Historical Science, Religion's present, but not ultimate, problem.*

The reader will have noted that, for each of these three stages, I have taken an Historico-Cultural as well as a Mathematico-Physical Science, though I am well aware of the profound difference between them, both as to their pre-requisites and method, and their aim and depth. And, again, I know well that, for the present, the chief intellectual difficulty of Religion, or at least the main conflict or friction between the Sciences and Theology, seems to proceed, not from Physical Science but from Historical Criticism, especially as applied to the New Testament, so that, on this ground also, I ought, apparently, to keep these two types of Science separate.—Yet it is clear, I think, that, however distinct, indeed different, should be the methods of these two sorts of Science, they are in so far alike, if taken as a means of purification for the soul bent upon its own deepening, that both require a slow, orderly, disinterested procedure, capable of fruitfulness only by the recurring sacrifice of endless petty self-seekings and obstinate fancies, and this in face of that natural eagerness and absoluteness of mind which strong religious emotions will, unless they too be disciplined and purified, only tend to increase and stereotype.

The matters brought up by Historical Criticism for the study and readjustment of Theology, and for utilization by Religion, are indeed numerous and in part difficult. Yet the still more general and fundamental alternatives lie not here, but with the questions as to the nature and range of Science taken in its narrower sense,—as concerned with Quantity, Mechanism, and Determinism alone.

If Science of this Thing-type be all that, in any manner or degree, we can apprehend in conformity with reality or can live by fruitfully: then History and Religion of every kind must be capable of a strict assimilation to it, or they must go. But if such Science constitute only one kind, and, though the clearest and most easily transferable, yet the least deep, and the least adequate to the ultimate and spiritual reality, among the chief levels of apprehension and of life which can be truly experienced and fruitfully lived by man; and if the Historical and Spiritual level can be shown to find room for, indeed to require, the Natural and Mechanical level, whilst this latter, taken as ultimate, cannot accommodate, but is forced to crush or to deny, the former: then a refusal to accept more than can be expressed and analyzed by such Physico-Mathematical Science would be an uprooting and a discrowning of the fuller life, and would ignore the complete human personality, from one of whose wants the entire impulse to such Science took its rise.

As a matter of fact, we find the following three alternatives.

Level all down to Mathematico-Physical Science, and you deny the specific constituents of Spirituality, and you render impossible the growth of the Person out of, and at the expense of, the Individual. Proclaim the Person and its Religion, as though they were static substances adequately present from the first, and ignore, evade or thwart that Thing-level and method as far as ever you can, and you will, in so far, keep back the all but simply animal Individual from attaining to his full spiritual Personality. But let grace wake up, in such an Individual, the sense of the specific characteristics of Spirituality and the thirst to become a full and ever fuller Person, and this in contact and conflict with, as well as in recollective abstraction from, the apparently chance contingencies of History and Criticism, and the seemingly fatalistic mechanisms of Physics and Mathematics: and you will be able, by humility, generosity, and an ever-renewed alternation of such outgoing, dispersive efforts and of such incoming recollection and affective prayer, gradually to push out and to fill in the outlines of your better nature, and to reorganize it all according to the Spirit and to Grace, becoming thus a deep man, a true personality.

Once again: take the intermediate, the Thing-level as final, and you yourself sink down more and more into a casual Thing, a soulless Law; Materialism, or, at best, some kind of Pantheism, must become your practice and your creed.—Take the anterior, the Individual-level as final, and you will remain something all but stationary, and if not merely a Thing yet not fully a Person; and if brought face to face with many an Agnostic or Pantheist of the nobler sort, who is in process of purification from such childish self-centredness by means of the persistently frank and vivid apprehension of the Mechanical, Determinist, Thing-and-Fate level of experience and degree of truth, you will, even if you have acquired certain fragmentary convictions and practices of religion, appear strangely less, instead of more, than your adversary, to any one capable of equitably comparing that Agnostic and yourself—you who, if Faith be right, ought surely to be not less but more of a personality than that non-believing soul.

But take the last, the Spiritual, Personal level as alone ultimate, and yet as necessarily requiring, to be truly reached and maintained, that the little, selfish, predominantly animal-minded, human being should ever pass and repass from this, his Individualistic plane and attitude, through the Thing-and-Fate region, out and on to the "shining table-land, whereof our God Himself is sun and moon": and you will, in time, gain a depth and an expansion, a persuasive force, an harmoniousness and intelligibleness with which, everything else being equal, the Pantheistic or Agnostic self-renunciation cannot truly compare. For, in these circumstances, the latter type will, at best, but prophesy and prepare the consummation actually reached by the integrational, dynamic religiousness, the Individual transformed more and more into Spirit and Person, by the help of the Thing and of Determinist Law. Freedom, Interiority, Intelligence, Will, Grace, and Love, the profoundest Personality, a reality out of all proportion more worthy and more ultimate than the most utterly unbounded universe of a simply material kind could ever be, thus appear here, in full contradiction of Pantheism, as ultimate and abiding; and yet all that is great and legitimate in Pantheism has been retained, as an intermediate element and stage, of a deeply purifying kind.

9. *Return to Saints John of the Cross and Catherine of Genoa.*

And thus we come back to the old, sublime wisdom of St. John of the Cross, in all that it has of continuous thirst after the soul's purification and expansion, and of a longing to lose itself, its every pettiness and egoistic separateness, in an abstract, universal, quasi-impersonal disposition and reality, such as God here seems to require and to offer as the means to Himself. Only that now we have been furnished, by the ever-clearer self-differentiation of Mathematico-Physical Science, with a zone of pure, sheer Thing, mere soulless Law, a zone capable of absorbing all those elements from out of our thought and feeling which, if left freely to mingle with the deeper level of the growing Spiritual Personality, would give to this an unmistakably Pantheistic tinge and trend. Hence, now the soul will have, in one of its two latter movements, to give a close attention to contingent facts and happenings and to abstract laws, possessed of no direct religious significance or interpretableness which, precisely because of this, will, if practised as part of the larger whole of the purificatory, spiritual upbuilding of the soul, in no way weaken, but stimulate and furnish materials for the other movement, the one specially propounded by the great Spaniard, in which the soul turns away, from all this particularity, to a general recollection and contemplative prayer.

And we are thus, perhaps, in even closer touch with Catherine's central idea,—the soul's voluntary plunge into a painful yet joyous purgation, into a state, and as it were an element, which purges away, (since the soul itself freely accepts the process,) all that deflects, stunts, or weakens the realization of the soul's deepest longings,—the hard self-centredness, petty self-mirrorings, and jealous claimfulness, above all. For though, in Catherine's conception, this at first both painful and joyful, and then more and more, and at last entirely, joyful, ocean of light and fire is directly God and His effects upon the increasingly responsive and unresisting soul: yet the apparent Thing-quality here, the seemingly ruthless Determinism of Law, in which the little individual is lost for good and all, and which only the spiritual personality can survive, are impressively prominent throughout this great scheme. And though we cannot, of course, take the element and zone of the sheer Thing and of Determinist Law as God, or as directly expressive of His nature, yet we can and must hold it, (in what it is in itself, in what it is as a construction of our minds, and in its purificatory function and influence upon our unpurified but purifiable souls,) to come from God and to lead to Him. And thus here also we escape any touch of ultimate Pantheism, without falling into any cold Deism or shallow Optimism. For just because we retain, at the shallower level, the ruthlessly impersonal element, can we, by freely willed, repeated passing through such fatalistic-seeming law, become, from individuals, persons; from semi-things, spirits,—spirits more and more penetrated by and apprehensive of the Spirit, God, the source and sustainer of all this growth and reality.

And yet, let us remember once more, the foreground and preliminary stage to even the sublimest of such lives will never, here below at least, be abidingly transcended, or completely harmonized with the groundwork and ultimate stage, by the human personality. Indeed our whole contention has been that, with every conceivable variation of degree, of kind, and of mutual relation, these two stages, and some sort of friction between them, are necessary, throughout this life, for the full development, the self-discipline, and the adequate consolidation, at the expense of the childish, sophistic individual, of the true spiritual Personality.

IV. Final Summary and Return to the Starting-point of the Whole Inquiry: the Necessity, and yet the Almost Inevitable Mutual Hostility, of the Three Great Forces of the Soul and of the Three Corresponding Elements of Religion.

Our introductory position as to the three great forces of the soul, with the corresponding three great elements of religion, appears, then, to have stood the test of our detailed investigation. For each of these forces and corresponding elements has turned out to be necessary to religion, and yet to become destructive of itself and of religion in general where this soul-force and religious element is allowed gravely to cripple, or all but to exclude, the other forces and elements, and their vigorous and normal action and influence.

1. *Each of these three forces and elements is indeed necessary, but ruinously destructive where it more or less ousts the other two.*

(1) The psychic force or faculty by which we remember and picture things and scenes; the law of our being which requires that sense-impressions should stimulate our thinking and feeling into action, and that symbols, woven by the picturing faculty out of these impressions, should then express these our thoughts and feelings; and the need we have, for the due awakening, discipline and supplementation of every kind and degree of experience and action, that social tradition, social environment, social succession should ever be before and around and after our single lives: correspond to and demand the Institutional and Historical Element of Religion. This element is as strictly necessary as are that force and that law.

Yet if this force and need of the soul, and this religious element are allowed to emasculate the other two primary soul-forces and needs and the religious elements corresponding to them, it will inevitably degenerate into more or less of a Superstition,—an oppressive materialization and dangerous would-be absolute fixation of even quite secondary and temporary expressions and analyses of religion; a ruinous belief in the direct transferableness of religious conviction; and a predominance of political, legal, physically coercive concepts and practices with regard to those most interior, strong yet delicate, readily thwarted or weakened, springs of all moral and religious character,—spiritual sincerity and spontaneity and the liberty of the children of God. We thus get too great a preponderance of the " Objective," of Law and Thing, as against Conviction and Person; of Priest as against Prophet; of the movement from without inwards, as against the movements from within outwards.

The Spanish Inquisition we found to be probably the most striking example and warning here. Yet the Eastern Christian Churches have doubtless exhibited these symptoms, if less acutely, yet more extensively and persistently. And the Protestant Reformation-Movement, (even in the later lives of its protagonists, Luther, Zwingli, and Calvin,) much of orthodox Lutheranism and Calvinism, and some forms and phases of Anglican Highchurchism and of Scotch Presbyterianism, show various degrees and forms of a similar one-sidedness. In Judaism the excesses in the Priestly type of Old Testament religion, especially as traceable after the Exile, and their partial continuation in Rabbinism, furnish other, instructive instances of such more or less partial growth,—the Pharisees and the Jerusalem Sanhedrin being here the fullest representatives of the spirit in question. The classical Heathen Roman religion was, throughout, too Naturalistic for its, all but exclusive, externalism and legalism to be felt as seriously oppressive of any other, considerable element of that religion. And much the same could doubtless be said of Indian Brahmanism to this day. But in orthodox Mohammedanism we get the truly classical instance of such a predominance, in all its imposing strength and terrible, because all but irremediable, weakness—with its utterly unanalytic, unspeculative, unmystical, thing-like, rock-solid faith; its detailed rigidity and exhaustive fixity; its stringent unity of organization and military spirit of entirely blind obedience; its direct, quite unambiguous intolerance, and ever ready appeal to the sword, as the normal and chief instrument for the propagation of the spirit; and its entirely inadequate apprehension of man's need of purification and regeneration in all his untutored loves, fears, hopes and hates.

(2) Then there is the soul-force by which we analyze and synthesize, and the law of our being which requires us to weigh, compare, combine, transfer, or ignore the details and the evidential worth of what has been brought home to us

through the stimulation of our senses, by our picturing faculty and memory, and by means of our Social, Historical, and Institutional environment, and which orders us to harmonize all these findings into as much as may be of an intelligible whole of religion, and to integrate this religious whole within some kind of, at least rough, general conception as to our entire life's experience. And this force and law are answered by the Critical-Historical and Synthetic-Philosophical element of religion. We thus get Positive and Dogmatic Theology. And this element is as humanly inevitable and religiously necessary as is that soul-force and law.

Yet here again, if this force, law, and element are allowed superciliously to ignore, or violently to explain away, the other kinds of approaches and contributions to religious truth and experience, special to the other two soul-forces and religious elements, we shall get another destructive one-sidedness, a Rationalistic Fanaticism, only too often followed by a lengthy Agnosticism and Indifference. Whilst the Rationalist Fanaticism lasts, everything will doubtless appear clear and simple to the soul, but then this " everything " will but represent the merest skimmings upon the face of the mighty deep of living, complete religion,—a petty, artificial arrangement by the human mind of the little which, there and then, it can easily harmonize into a whole, or even simply a direct hypostatizing of the mind's own bare categories.

The worship of the Goddess of Reason at Notre-Dame of Paris we found to be here, perhaps, the most striking instance. Yet Rationalist excesses, varying from a cold Deism down to an ever short-lived formal Atheism, and the lassitude of a worldly-wise Indifferentism, are traceable within all the great religions. Thus a large proportion of the educated members of the ancient Greco-Roman world were, from the Sophists and the Second Punic War onward, stricken with such a blight. The Sadducees are typical of this tendency among the Jews for some two centuries. The tough persistence of a mostly obscure current of destructive free-thought throughout Western Europe in the Middle Ages shows well the difficulty and importance of a mental and spiritual victory over these forces of radical negation, and of not simply driving them beneath the surface of society. And the ready lapse of the most daring and intense of the Medieval, Jewish and Christian, Scholastics into a thoroughly Pantheistic Panlogism, points to the prevalence, among these circles, of a certain tyranny of the abstractive and logical faculty over the other powers and intimations of the soul.—Unitarianism again is, in its origins and older form, notwithstanding its even excessive anti-Pantheism, strongly Scholastic in its whole temper and method, and this without the important correctives and supplementations brought to that method by the largely Mystical and Immanental Angel of the Schools. The greater part of the "Aufklärung"-Movement was vitiated by an often even severer, impoverishment of the whole conception of religion. And, in our day, the Liberal movements within the various Christian bodies, and again among Brahmanic religionists in India, rarely escape altogether from ignoring or explaining away the dark and toilsome aspects of life, and the inevitable excess of all deep reality, and indeed of our very experience of it, above our clear, methodical, intellectual analysis and synthesis of it. Too often and for too long all such groups have inclined to assimilate all Experience to clear Knowledge, all clear Knowledge to Physico-Mathematical Science, all Religion to Ethics, and all Ethics to a simple belief in the ultimacy of Determinist, Atomistic Science. The situation is decidedly improving now; History and Culture are being found to have other, more ultimate categories, than are those of Mathematics and Physics, and to bring us a larger amount of reality, and Ethics and Religion are discovered to be as truly distinct as they are closely allied and necessary, each to the deepest development of the other.

(3) The faculty and action of the soul, finally, by which we have an however dim yet direct and (in its general effects) immensely potent, sense and feeling, an immediate experience of Objective Reality, of the Infinite and Abiding, of a Spirit not all unlike yet distinct from our own, Which penetrates and works within these our finite spirits and in the world at large, especially in human history; and by which we will, and give a definite result and expression to, our various memories, thinkings, feelings, and intuitions, as waked up by their various special stimulants and by the influence of each upon all the others; is met by the Mystical and the directly Operative element of Religion. And here again we have a force and law of the human spirit, and a corresponding element of religion, which can indeed be starved or driven

into a most dangerous isolation and revolt, but which are simply indestructible.

The Apocalyptic Orgies of the Münster Anabaptists we found to be perhaps the most striking illustration of the dire mischief that can spring from this third group of elemental soul-forces, when they ignore or dominate the other two. Yet some such Emotional Fanaticism can be traced, in various degrees and forms, throughout all such religious groups, schools, and individuals as seriously attempt to practise Pure Mysticism,—that is, religious Intuition and Emotion unchecked by the other two soul-forces and religious elements, or by the alternation of external action and careful contact with human Society and its needs and helps, Art and Science, and the rest.

Thus we find that, after the immense, luxuriant prevalence of an intensely intuitive, emotional, tumultuously various apprehension and manifestation of religion during the first two generations of Christians, and even after the deep, wise supplementation and spiritualization of this element by St. Paul, who in his own person so strikingly combined the Institutional, Rational and Intuitive-Emotional forces and elements, this whole force and element rapidly all but disappeared for long from Western Christian orthodoxy. And Montanism in still early times, and, during the very height of the Middle Ages, the Waldensian and Albigensian movements—all predominantly intuitive, enthusiastic, individualist—appear as so many revolutionary explosions, threatening the whole fabric of Christendom with dissolution. The "Eternal Gospel" movement of Abbot Joachim, on the other hand, gives us the intuitional-emotive element in a more purified, institutionally and rationally supplemented form.

Again we find that, for a while, in reaction from an all but hopelessly corrupt civilization, the Fathers of the Desert attained in many cases, by means of an all but Exclusive Mysticism, to a type of sanctity and to the inculcation of a lesson which the Church has gratefully recognized. We have to admit that many of the Italian, French and Spanish Quietists of the seventeenth century were no doubt excessively, or even quite unjustly, suspected or pursued, as far at least as their own personal motives and the effect of their doctrines upon their own characters were concerned : and that the general reaction against even the proved, grave excesses of some of these men and women, went often dangerously far in the contrary direction. Indeed even the fierce fanaticism of the Dutch-Westphalian Apocalyptic Intuitionists can but excuse, not justify, the policy of quite indiscriminately ruthless extermination pursued by Luther, Zwingli and Calvin, and by their official churches after their deaths, towards any and all Illuminism, however ethically pure and socially operative. The " Society of Friends " which, measured by the smallness of its numbers, has given to the world an astonishingly large band of devoted lovers of humankind, is a living witness to the possibility of such an Illuminism.

And we can note how the sane and solid, deep and delicate constituents, which had existed, mixed up with all kinds of fantastic, often hysterical and anti-moral exaltations, within most of those all but purely Intuitionist circles, gradually found their escape away into all sorts of unlikely quarters, helping to give much of their interiority and religious warmth, not only to various, now fairly sober-minded, Nonconformist Protestant bodies on the Continent, in England and America, but also to the more religious-tempered and more spiritually perceptive among modern philosophers—such as Spinoza, Kant, Fichte, Schleiermacher, Schelling and Fechner.

Within the Jewish world, we get much of this element at its noblest and at its worst, in the true and false Prophets respectively; then among the Essenes, for the times between the Maccabean resistance and the revolt of Bar Cochba; and later on in the Kabbala. The Mohammedans still furnish the example of the Sufi-movement. The Classical Heathen world produced the Neo-Platonist and the Mithraic movements; and we can still study, as a living thing, the Buddhist Mysticism of Thibet.

We have then, here too, something thoroughly elemental, which requires both persistent operative recognition and a continuous and profound purification and supplementation by becoming incorporated within a large living system of all the fundamental forces of the soul, each operating and operated upon according to the intrinsic nature and legitimate range of each.

2. *Each element double; endless combinations and conflicts.*

We have also found that these three forces and elements are each double, and that collisions, but also most fruitful interactions, can and do obtain between even these yoke-fellows: between Institutionalism and History,—the Present and the Past, a direct Sense-Impression and Picture and a Memory; between Criticism and Construction,—Analysis and acuteness of mind, and Synthesis and richness and balance of imagination, head, heart, and will; and between Mysticism and Action, as respectively Intuitive and quiescent and Volitional and effortful.

And both the three forces and elements as a whole, and the single members of each pair, can and do appear in every possible variety of combination with, and of opposition against, the others, although there is a special affinity between the Critical-Speculative- and the Intuitive-Volitional pairs (in combination against the Sense-and-Memory pair); between the Sense-and-Memory pair and the single member of Action; and between the single members of Speculation and of Intuition. Yet, ultimately, not any one pair or member can bear its fullest fruit, without the aid of all the others; and there is not one that, in actual human nature, does not tend to emasculate, or to oust as much as possible from the soul, the other pairs or single members.

3. *Our entire religious activity but one element of our complete spirit-life.*

And we have noted further, how even the fullest development in any one soul of all these three couples of specifically religious activities—even supposing that they could be developed to their fullest, without any participation in and conflict with other degrees and kinds of life and reality—do not, by any means, exhaust the range of even the simplest soul's actual energizings.

(1) For over and beyond the specifically religious life—though this, where genuine, is ever the deepest, the central life—every soul lives, and has to live, various other lives. And indeed—and this is the point which specially concerns religion—the soul cannot attain to its fullest possible spiritual development, without the vigorous specific action and differentiation of forces and functions of a not directly religious character, which will have to energize, each according to its own intrinsic nature, within the ever ampler, and ever more closely-knit, organization of the complete life of the soul.

(2) And within this complete life, the three pairs of religious forces and elements each possess their own special affinities and antipathies for certain of the forces and elements which constitute the other, less central organizations of man's marvellously rich activity. The Historical-Institutional

element of Religion has necessarily a special affinity for, and borrows much of its form from, social, legal, political history and institutions of a general kind. The Critical-Speculative element of religion is necessarily cognate to, and in a state of interchange with, the general historical criticism and philosophical insight attained during the ages and amongst the races in which any particular religion is intellectually systematized. And the Mystical-Operative element is necessarily influenced by, and largely utilizes the general emotive and volitional gifts and habits, peculiar to the various ages and peoples within which this double religious element is in operation.

(3) It is thus abundantly clear how greatly a work so manifold in its means, and so harmonious in its end, requires, if it is to come to a considerable degree of realization, that single souls, and single classes and types of souls, should have around them a large and varied Historical and Institutional, a Social life both of a specifically religious and of a general kind, and that, within this large ambit of the actualized religion of others and of the still largely potential religion of their own souls, they shall develop and be helped to realize their own deepest spiritual capacities and *attrait*. They will have to develop these special capabilities to the utmost degree compatible with some practice of the other chief elements of religion, with a continuous respect for and belief in the necessity of the other types of soul, and with a profound belief in, and love of, the full, organized community of all devoted souls, which builds up, and is built up by, all this variety in unity. The Kingdom of God, the Church, will thus be more and more found and made to be the means of an ever more distinct articulation, within an ever more fruitful interaction, of the various *attraits*, gifts, vocations, and types of souls which constitute its society. And these souls in return will, precisely by this their articulation within this ampler system, bring to this society an ever richer content of variety in harmony, of action and warfare within an ever deeper fruitfulness and peace.

4. *Two conditions of the fruitfulness of the entire process.* Yet even the simplest effort, within this innumerable sequence and simultaneity of activities, will lack the fullest truth and religious depth and fruitfulness, unless two experiences, convictions and motives are in operation throughout the whole, and penetrate its every part, as salt and yeast,

atmosphere and light penetrate, and purify and preserve our physical food and bodily senses.

The vivid, continuous sense that God, the Spirit upholding our poor little spirits, is the true originator and the true end of the whole movement, in all it may have of spiritual beauty, truth, goodness and vitality; that all the various levels and kinds of reality and action are, in whatever they have of worth, already immanently fitted to stimulate, supplement and purify each other by Him Who, an Infinite Spiritual Interiority Himself, gives thus to each one of us indefinite opportunities for actualizing our own degree and kind of spiritual possibility and ideal; and that He it is Who, however dimly yet directly, touches our souls and awakens them, in and through all those minor stimulations and apprehensions, to that noblest, incurable discontent with our own petty self and to that sense of and thirst for the Infinite and Abiding, which articulates man's deepest requirement and characteristic: this is the first experience and conviction, without which all life, and life's centre, religion, are flat and dreary, vain and philistine.

And the second conviction is the continuous sense of the ever necessary, ever fruitful, ever bliss-producing Cross of Christ—the great law and fact that only through self-renunciation and suffering can the soul win its true self, its abiding joy in union with the Source of Life, with God Who has left to us, human souls, the choice between two things alone: the noble pangs of spiritual child-birth, of painful-joyous expansion and growth; and the shameful ache of spiritual death, of dreary contraction and decay.

Now it is especially these two, ever primary and supreme, ever deepest and simplest yet most easily forgotten, bracing yet costing, supremely virile truths and experiences—facts which increasingly can and ever should waken up, and themselves be vivified by, all the other activities and gifts of God which we have studied—these two eyes of religion and twin pulse-beats of its very heart, that have been realized, with magnificent persistence and intensity, by the greatest of the Inclusive Mystics.

And amongst these Mystics, Caterinetta Fiesca Adorna, the Saint of Genoa, has appeared to us as one who, in spite of not a little obscurity and uncertainty and vagueness in the historical evidences for her life and teaching, of not a few limitations of natural character and of opportunity, and of several peculiarities which, wonderful to her *entourage*, can but perplex or repel us now, shines forth, in precisely these two central matters, with a penetrating attractiveness, rarely matched, hardly surpassed, by Saints and Heroes of far more varied, humorous, readily understandable, massive gifts and actions. And these very limits and defects of her natural character and opportunities, of her contemporary disciples and later panegyrists, and of our means for studying and ascertaining the facts and precise value of the life she lived, and of the legend which it occasioned, may, we can hope, but help to give a richer articulation and wider applicability to our study of the character and necessity, the limits, dangers and helpfulness of the Mystic Element of Religion.

INDEX

(Some corrections of mistakes in names and references, as given in the foregoing work, have been silently effected in the following Index)

I. OF SUBJECT-MATTERS

II. OF LITERARY REFERENCES

(The more general literary references given under names of authors in Part I)